THE SCOUTING NOTEBOOK 2003

Editors/The Scouting Notebook
THOM HENNINGER
JIM HENZLER
TONY NISTLER

The photographs which appear in *The Scouting Notebook 2003* were furnished individually by the following Major League Baseball teams, whose cooperation is gratefully acknowledged: Anaheim Angels, Baltimore Orioles, Boston Red Sox, Chicago White Sox/Ron Vesely, Cleveland Indians, Detroit Tigers, Kansas City Royals, Minnesota Twins, New York Yankees, Oakland Athletics, Seattle Mariners, Tampa Bay Devil Rays, Texas Rangers, Toronto Blue Jays, Arizona Diamondbacks, Atlanta Braves, Chicago Cubs, Cincinnati Reds, Colorado Rockies, Florida Marlins, Houston Astros, Los Angeles Dodgers, Milwaukee Brewers, Montreal Expos, New York Mets, Philadelphia Phillies, Pittsburgh Pirates, St. Louis Cardinals, San Diego Padres and San Francisco Giants.

ON THE COVER: Top: Jason Giambi photo by John Dunn for The Sporting News; bottom left to right: Barry Bonds by Dilip Vishwanat/The Sporting News, Sammy Sosa by Dilip Vishwanat/The Sporting News, Curt Schilling by Dilip Vishwanat/The Sporting News; spine: Jason Giambi by John Dunn for The Sporting News.

Major league statistics compiled by STATS, Inc., a News Corporation Company, 8130 Lehigh Avenue, Morton Grove, IL 60053. STATS is a trademark of Sports Team Analysis and Tracking Systems, Inc.

ISBN: 0-89204-705-4

10 9 8 7 6 5 4 3 2 1

Table of Contents

The Scouting Staff

The scouting reports on each team's ballpark, manager and significant players were written by the following people, in conjunction with our editors:

Anaheim Angels	Bill Shaikin *Los Angeles Times/* *Baseball America*
Baltimore Orioles	Rick Wilton *Sports Weekly Hot Sheet*
Boston Red Sox	Mat Olkin *Sports Weekly*
Chicago White Sox*	Phil Rogers *Chicago Tribune/* *Baseball America*
Cleveland Indians	Paul Hoynes *Cleveland Plain Dealer*
Detroit Tigers	Pat Caputo *Oakland (Mich.) Press/* *Baseball America*
Kansas City Royals*	Marc Bowman *STATS, Inc.*
Minnesota Twins	Dennis Brackin *Minneapolis* *Star Tribune*
New York Yankees	Mat Olkin *Sports Weekly*
Oakland Athletics	Lawr Michaels *www.creativesports.com*
Seattle Mariners	Mat Olkin *Sports Weekly*
Tampa Bay Devil Rays	Marc Topkin *St. Petersburg Times/* *Baseball America*
Texas Rangers*	Gerry Fraley *Dallas Morning News/* *Baseball America*
Toronto Blue Jays	Tom Maloney *STATS, Inc.*
Arizona Diamondbacks	Ed Price *East Valley Tribune* *(Mesa, Ariz)*
Atlanta Braves*	Bill Ballew *Baseball America*
Chicago Cubs	Mat Olkin *Sports Weekly*
Cincinnati Reds	Peter Pascarelli *ESPN*
Colorado Rockies*	Tracy Ringolsby *Rocky Mountain News* *(Denver)/Baseball America*
Florida Marlins*	Mike Berardino *South Florida Sun-Sentinel*
Houston Astros	Jim Carley *Sporting News*
Los Angeles Dodgers*	Don Hartack *STATS, Inc.*
Milwaukee Brewers	Mat Olkin *Sports Weekly*
Montreal Expos*	Trace Wood *www.longgandhi.com*
New York Mets*	Bill Ballew *Baseball America*
Philadelphia Phillies*	Tony Blengino *Diamond Library* *(Future Stars)*
Pittsburgh Pirates*	John Perrotto *Beaver County (Pa.) Times/* *Baseball America*
St. Louis Cardinals	Peter Pascarelli *ESPN*
San Diego Padres*	Trace Wood *www.longgandhi.com*
San Francisco Giants	Joe Roderick *Contra Costa Times*

The minor league prospect reports were written by Thom Henninger (AL), Jim Henzler (NL), Dan Ford (Cubs) and the individual team writers as noted with an asterisk (*). We'd like to thank the player-development personnel who were willing to discuss their teams' farm systems. *Baseball America's* Jim Callis also was a big help when it came to filling in blanks. The "Other Anaheim Angels," etc., were written by the STATS, Inc. publications staff. I'd also like to thank Ryan Balock, Taylor Bechtold, Norm DeNosaquo, Brian Hogan, Corey Roberts and John Strougal for their integral roles in helping to get this edition to print.

—Tony Nistler

Introduction

Welcome to the ninth edition of *The Scouting Notebook*. This is the 14th annual book of scouting reports that STATS, Inc. has created. We get several prominent baseball analysts and have them give us detailed reports on every major league player who saw significant action last season. We think you'll agree that our scouting staff features some of the top baseball minds around. Special thanks to Marc Bowman, Paul Hoynes and John Perrotto, who have contributed to all 14 books.

This is an encyclopedia of contemporary major league baseball. We tell you about the strengths and weaknesses of hundreds of players. Our analysis extends beyond major league players, too, covering each club's top minor league prospects. We study the statistics and we talk to the scouts. We look for the true ability that may have been exaggerated or obscured by the hype.

The Ballparks

We report on each club's ballpark. We detail how each stadium affects hitters, pitchers and fielders in general, as well as which players it helps and hurts the most. We also project what the park will do to rookies and other newcomers in 2003. We provide vital statistics for each park, such as its dimensions, capacity, elevation, playing surface and the amount of foul territory.

We also present our trademark park indexes. In a variety of statistical categories, we show how the home team and its opponents performed at the park and on the road. Interleague games aren't included. By comparing the overall totals at the park and on the road, we get a measure of the stadium's impact. We divide the home totals by the road totals and multiply by 100 to get the park index. An index of greater than 100 shows that the park favors a particular statistic, while an index of less than 100 means the opposite.

Most of the indexes are calculated on a per at-bat basis. Runs, hits, errors and infield errors are figured on a per-game basis. For most parks, we present data for both 2002 and the last three years overall. If the park's configuration has changed since the end of the 2000 season, we present the data for the different setups separately.

Most of the abbreviations are common, with these exceptions:

E-Infield: Infield errors.

LHB-Avg: Batting average by lefthanded hitters.

LHB-HR: Home runs by lefthanded hitters.

RHB-Avg: Batting average by righthanded hitters.

RHB-HR: Home runs by righthanded hitters.

We also list any indexes in which the park ranked in the top or bottom three in its league in 2002.

The Managers

On these pages, we analyze each manager's strengths and weaknesses, style and strategy, and outlook for 2003. We present his 2002 and career managerial record, and we also show how often he used starting pitchers on various days of rest. We compare his use and the performance of his starters to the league average.

We also provide statistical breakdowns detailing his handling of his pitching staff and his use of strategies like the sacrifice, the hit-and-run and defensive substitutions. To qualify for the rankings, a manager had to have his team for at least 100 games in 2002. Some of the terms listed in the statistics and rankings sections may be unfamiliar.

They include:

Hit & Run Success %: The percentage of hit-and-runs resulting in baserunner advancement with no double play.

Platoon Pct.: Frequency that the manager gets his hitters the platoon advantage (lefty vs. righty and vice versa). Switch-hitters always are considered to have the advantage.

Defensive Subs: The number of straight defensive substitutions with the team leading by four runs or fewer.

High-Pitch Outings: The number of times a manager's starting pitchers threw more than 120 pitches in a ballgame.

Quick/Slow Hooks: A Quick Hook occurs when a pitcher is removed after having pitched less than six innings and given up three runs or fewer. A Slow Hook occurs when a pitcher works more than nine innings, allows seven or more runs, or his total innings and runs equal 13 or more.

First-Batter Platoon Percentage: The percentage of times a manager's relievers had a platoon advantage over the first hitter they faced (lefty vs. lefty, righty vs. righty).

Mid-Inning Changes: The number of times the manager changed pitchers in the middle of an inning.

Pitchouts with a Runner Moving: The number of times the opposition was running when the manager called a pitchout.

Sacrifice Bunt Percentage: The percentage of bunts resulting in sacrifices or hits with runners on.

Starting Lineups Used: Based on batting order, 1-8 for National Leaguers, 1-9 for American Leaguers.

2+ Pitching Changes in Low-Scoring Games: The number of times a manager used at least three pitchers in a game in which his team allowed two runs or fewer.

The Players

For each major league team, we give extensive reports on 22 players. Twelve of them get a full page of scouting information, while 10 receive half-page reports. Because we like to get this book into your hands as soon as possible, players are listed with their 2002 clubs. We keep abreast of postseason transactions, and all player moves that took place through December 14, 2002 are noted. If you can't find a particular player, check the detailed index in the back.

Pages for primary players have two columns. The left column provides an in-depth report by an analyst. The right column contains statistical information:

Position: The first position shown is the player's most common position in 2002. Positions at which he played 10 or more games also are shown. For pitchers, SP stands for starting pitcher and RP for relief pitcher.

Bats and Throws: L represents for lefthanded, R stands for righthanded, and B represents both (switch-hitter).

Ht: Height.

Wt: Weight.

Opening Day Age: This is the player's age on April 1, 2003.

Born: Birthdate and birthplace.

ML Seasons: This number indicates the number of different major league seasons in which the player has appeared. For example, if a player was called up to play in September in each of the last three seasons, the number shown would be 3. This is different from major league service, which is used to determine arbitration and free-agency eligibility.

Overall Statistics: These are traditional major league statistics for the player's 2002 season and his career. The one non-traditional stat that appears here is ratio, which is the number of baserunners allowed by a pitcher per inning:((hits + walks)/IP).

Where He Hits The Ball

For every major league game in 2002, STATS reporters entered into our computers every single ball hit into play. They kept track of the type of batted balls—grounders, flyballs, popups, line drives and bunts—as well as the distance each ball traveled. Direction was tracked by dividing the field into 26 "wedges" projecting out from home plate. Distance was measured in 10-foot increments outward from home plate.

Below are the 2002 hitting diagrams for lefthanded-hitting Ryan Klesko of the San Diego Padres. The chart on the left shows where Klesko hit the ball against lefthanders, while the chart on the right shows what he did against righties.

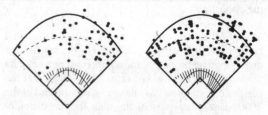

Vs. LHP   **Vs. RHP**

In the diagrams, groundballs and short line drives are shown by the lines of various lengths in the infield. The longer the line, the more groundballs and line drives were hit in that direction. As you can see from the charts on page 2, Klesko was able to pull the ball effectively and show power against lefties, but that wasn't always the case. The Atlanta product fared poorly against southpaws in his early days with the Braves, and manager Bobby Cox never gave him many at-bats against them.

Klesko's hit charts versus lefthanded pitching often looked like a spray hitter without power. After he was dealt to San Diego prior to the 2000 campaign, he played regularly against southpaws for the first time. Since then, his slugging mark against southpaws has jumped from .380 in 2000 to .409 in 2001 to a career-best .490 last summer. With his impressive bat speed, Klesko posted career-best hitting percentages versus lefties in 2002, including a .287 average and .372 on-base percentage.

A lot of experimentation went into producing the hitting diagrams. When we first started, we tried to show every single batted ball that was put into play by each player. We found that the charts became very cluttered for everyday players, so we began experimenting with trying to show only the most meaningful information. When all was said and done, here's what we ended up with:

a. Popups and bunts are excluded. We excluded popups because 95 percent of these are caught regardless of how fielders are positioned. We excluded bunts because defensing a bunt is an entirely different strategy primarily used against a select number of players or in specific situations.

b. For groundballs and short line drives, we include all batted balls.

c. For balls hit to the outfield, we excluded isolated points only if the chart contains more than 125 batted balls to the outfield. In such cases, if a player hits only one ball to a given area and had no other batted balls in the vicinity all season, we exclude it because it doesn't give a true indication of a tendency.

Other notes of interest:

The field is drawn to scale, with the outfield fence reaching 400 feet in center and 330 feet down the lines. Ballparks are configured differently, so a dot inside of the fence might have been a home run. Similarly, a dot outside the fence might actually have been in play.

Line drives under 170 feet are part of the infield. We give responsibility for short liners to the infielders.

No distinction is made between hits and outs.

How Often He Throws Strikes

Our STATS reporters also tracked every pitch thrown in a major league game in 2002. The pitching graphs show how often the hurler throws strikes in different situations. Our data shows most pitchers will toss a strike between 40 and 80 percent of the time. Therefore we've constructed the chart to represent the 40-80 percent range.

The strike count includes swinging strikes, taken strikes, foul balls and balls put in play. Though not all batted balls come on pitches thrown within the strike zone, our theory is that most are and the ones that aren't would be difficult to judge. Our charts reflect these assumptions.

The charts are broken into four categories. *All Pitches* is straightforward, as is *First Pitch*. We define *Ahead* as counts with more strikes than balls. *Behind* includes counts with more balls than strikes. The appropriate league average is shown in each chart.

Below are the 2002 league averages. The American League threw a slightly higher percentage of strikes than the American League, the first time in all 14 years we have tracked this.

Strike Percentage by League—2002		
	American	National
All Pitches	62.9%	62.8%
First Pitch	58.5%	58.4%
Ahead in the Count	60.7%	60.8%
Behind in the Count	67.5%	67.1%

2002 Situational Stats

There are eight situational breakdowns for every primary player. *Home* and *Road* show performance in his home ballpark and on the road. *First Half* and *Scnd Half* show performance before and after the 2002 All-Star break. For hitters, *LHP* and *RHP* show how the player hit against lefthanders and righthanders. For pitchers, *LHB* and *RHB* show how the opposition lefthanders and righthanders hit against the pitcher. *Sc Pos* shows batting or pitching performance with runners in scoring position. *Clutch* shows batting or pitching performance in clutch situations, defined as the seventh inning or later with the batting team ahead by one run, tied or with the tying run on base, at bat or on deck. Our definition is consistent with save situations.

2002 Rankings

This section shows how the player ranked in his league and among his teammates. Because of space considerations, we omitted some of the less interesting rankings when a player placed high in numerous categories.

We include many less traditional categories. The Definitions and Qualifications section below provides details for these statistics.

Definitions and Qualifications

The following are definitions and qualifications for the Major League Leaders and Rankings.

Definitions:

Times on Base — Hits plus walks plus hit-by-pitch.

Groundball-Flyball Ratio — Groundballs hit divided by the total of flyballs and popups hit. Bunts and line drives are excluded.

Runs/Times on Base — Runs scored divided by times on base.

Clutch — A player's batting average in the late innings of close games, defined as the seventh inning or later with the batting team ahead by one run, tied or with the tying run on base, at bat or on deck.

Bases Loaded — A player's batting average in bases-loaded situations.

GDP per GDP situation — Groundball double plays divided by groundball double-play situations, defined as a man on first base with less than two out.

Percentage of Pitches Taken — The percentage of pitches a player lets go by without swinging.

Percentage Swings Put In Play — The percentage of swings resulting in a batted ball into fair territory or a foul-ball out.

Run Support per Nine Innings — The number of runs scored for a pitcher while he was pitching, scaled to a nine-inning figure.

Baserunners per Nine Innings — The total of hits, walks and hit batsmen allowed per nine innings.

Strikeout-Walk Ratio — Strikeouts divided by walks.

Stolen-Base Percentage Allowed — Stolen bases divided by stolen-base attempts.

Save Percentage — Saves divided by save opportunities. Save opportunities include saves plus blown saves.

Blown Saves — A blown save is charged any time a pitcher enters a game in a save situation and loses the lead. A save situation is defined as any time a reliever enters the game with a lead, isn't the pitcher of record and either a) pitches at least one inning with a lead of no more than three runs; b) enters the game with the potential tying run on base, at bat or on deck; or c) pitches effectively for at least three innings.

Holds — A hold is given to a pitcher when he enters a game in a save situation and is removed before the end of the game while maintaining his team's lead. The pitcher must retire at least one batter to get a hold.

Percentage of Inherited Runners Scored — Percentage of runners already on base when a pitcher enters a game that he allows to score.

First Batter Efficiency — The batting average allowed by a reliever to the first batter he faces in a game.

Qualifications:

In order to be ranked, a player had to qualify with a minimum number of opportunities, as follows:

Batters

Batting average, slugging percentage, on-base percentage, home run frequency, groundball-flyball ratio, runs scored per time reached base and pitches seen per plate appearance — 3.1 plate appearances per team game

Percentage of pitches taken, lowest percentage of swings that missed and percentage of swings put into play — 9.26 pitches seen per team game

Percentage of extra bases taken as a runner — .09 opportunities to advance per team game

Stolen-base percentage — .12 stolen-base attempts per team game

Runners in scoring position — .62 plate appearances with runners in scoring position per team game

Clutch — .31 plate appearances in the clutch per team game

Bases loaded — .06 plate appearances with the bases loaded per team game

GDP per GDP situation — .31 plate appearances in GDP situations per team game

BA vs. LHP — .77 plate appearances against left-handers per team game

BA vs. RHP — 2.33 plate appearances against righthanders per team game

BA at home — 1.55 plate appearances at home per team game

BA on the road — 1.55 plate appearances on the road per team game

Leadoff on-base percentage — .93 plate appearances in

the No. 1 lineup spot per team game

Cleanup slugging percentage — .93 plate appearances in the No. 4 lineup spot per team game

BA on 3-1 count — .06 plate appearances with a 3-1 count per team game

BA with 2 strikes — .62 plate appearances with two strikes per team game

BA on 0-2 count — .12 plate appearances with an 0-2 count per team game

BA on 3-2 count — .12 plate appearances with a 3-2 count per team game

Pitchers

Earned run average, run support per nine innings, baserunners per nine innings, batting average allowed, slugging percentage allowed, on-base percentage allowed, home runs per nine innings, strikeouts per nine innings, strikeout-walk ratio, stolen-base percentage allowed, GDPs per nine innings, pitches thrown per batter and groundball-flyball ratio against—one inning per team game

Winning percentage — .09 decisions per team game

GDPs induced per GDP situation — .19 batters faced in GDP situations per team game

BA allowed, runners in scoring position — .77 batters faced with runners in scoring position per team game

ERA at home — .5 innings at home per team game

ERA on the road — .5 innings on the road per team game

BA vs. LHB — .77 lefthanders faced per team game

BA vs. RHB — 1.39 righthanders faced per team game

Relievers

ERA, batting average allowed, baserunners per nine innings, strikeouts per nine innings — .31 relief innings per team game

Save percentage — .12 save opportunities per team game

Percentage of inherited runners scoring — .19 inherited runners per team game

First batter efficiency — .25 games in relief per team game

Fielders

Percentage caught stealing by catchers — .43 stolen-base attempts per team game

Fielding percentage — .62 games at a position per team game (.19 chances per team game for pitchers)

Other Players

Some players didn't play enough to merit a full- or half-page essay, and aren't young enough or good enough to deserve a prospect report. But they did play in the majors last year, so we give them a brief evaluation. Following the half-page reports for each team, you'll find a page devoted to these part-timers under the heading "Other Anaheim Angels," etc. Each player gets a short summary and his 2003 Outlook is graded as follows:

A — Should be an important contributor.
B — Should play most of the season in the majors and contribute.
C — Unlikely to play much in the majors or contribute much if he does.
D — Unlikely to play in the majors.

Minor League Prospects

We present two pages of minor league prospects for each team. Prospect writers spoke directly to major league player-development personnel and also looked beyond athletic tools by analyzing statistics. Each club has seven or eight featured prospects. We try to include most of the top phenoms, but our primary emphasis is on advanced players with the best chance of contributing in the majors in 2003.

We also include an organizational overview for each team, which gives you a glimpse into the current state of each club's minor league system. In addition, we summarize a few more notable prospects per team in a section called "Others to Watch."

Where we mention that managers voted a player as the best in a specific category in his league, our source is *Baseball America*.

Major League Leaders

After the team sections, we provide a complete listing of MLB leaders for the 2002 season. The top three players in each category are shown for the American and National Leagues. You'll notice a STATS flavor to these leaders. Not only do we show the leaders for the common categories such as batting average, home runs and ERA, but you'll also find less traditional categories like steals of third and total pitches thrown.

American League Players

Edison International Field

Offense

The Angels did not adjust the field dimensions, but the production of runs, hits and home runs dropped below the league average last year after ranking well above the league average in 2001. The Angels hit better on the road, not so much a reflection of their pretty fair ballpark but of the hitter-friendly parks around the league. Still, the ball absolutely flies out of the park on warm summer afternoons, so hitters should benefit from the Angels' decision to abandon Sunday evening games in favor of 1 p.m. starts in 2003.

Defense

The infield surface presents a challenge during the dog days of summer, since you can't water the field often enough to keep groundballs from shooting off the dirt. But second baseman Adam Kennedy and shortstop David Eckstein worked overtime in practice and cut their combined number of home errors nearly in half. Visiting right fielders can be startled by the 18-foot-high wall in right field, which redirects apparent home runs back into play.

Who It Helps the Most

Center fielders can exhaust themselves between chasing down balls hit into the spacious alley in left-center and chasing down balls caroming off that huge wall in right, so line-drive hitters can benefit. The fence in right-center is closer to home plate than the one in left-center, so lefty pull-hitters pick up a few extra hits on flyballs that clank against the 18-foot wall.

Who It Hurts the Most

Darin Erstad resumed poking line drives into left field—making him the one lefty hurt by Edison, since left fielders play shallower than right fielders. He hit .258 at home, .307 on the road. He still signed a four-year contract extension.

Rookies & Newcomers

There will be few of either in 2003. Francisco Rodriguez, the Angels' wondrous phenom, proved during the playoffs that he could strike a batter out no matter how loud the crowd or how important the game.

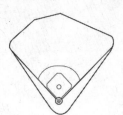

Dimensions: LF-330, LCF-387, CF-400, RCF-370, RF-330

Capacity: 45,030

Elevation: 160 feet

Surface: Grass

Foul Territory: Average

Park Factors

2002 Season

| | Home Games | | | Away Games | | | |
	Angels	Opp	Total	Angels	Opp	Total	Index
G	72	72	144	72	72	144	
Avg	.277	.242	.259	.286	.244	.266	97
AB	2467	2489	4956	2603	2353	4956	100
R	358	284	642	399	284	683	94
H	683	603	1286	745	574	1319	97
2B	142	114	256	156	98	254	101
3B	17	4	21	9	12	21	100
HR	62	67	129	73	81	154	84
BB	198	234	432	210	229	439	98
SO	352	459	811	364	434	798	102
E	40	46	86	43	62	105	82
E-Infield	33	37	70	41	48	89	79
LHB-Avg	.280	.241	.261	.295	.234	.269	97
LHB-HR	28	30	58	35	34	69	83
RHB-Avg	.274	.244	.258	.277	.251	.264	98
RHB-HR	34	37	71	38	47	85	84

2000-2002

| | Home Games | | | Away Games | | | |
	Angels	Opp	Total	Angels	Opp	Total	Index
G	216	216	432	216	216	432	
Avg	.274	.263	.268	.271	.259	.265	101
AB	7316	7595	14911	7660	7159	14819	101
R	1055	1019	2074	1066	992	2058	101
H	2003	1997	4000	2075	1855	3930	102
2B	373	391	764	438	325	763	100
3B	38	16	54	43	34	77	70
HR	255	241	496	223	256	479	103
BB	698	749	1447	691	771	1462	98
SO	1189	1271	2460	1303	1205	2508	97
E	157	137	294	142	152	294	100
E-Infield	139	108	247	127	121	248	100
LHB-Avg	.281	.256	.269	.269	.258	.264	102
LHB-HR	114	96	210	113	110	223	93
RHB-Avg	.266	.268	.267	.273	.260	.266	100
RHB-HR	141	145	286	110	146	256	111

2002 Rankings (American League)

- Lowest infield-error factor
- Third-lowest error factor

Mike Scioscia

2002 Season

After parent company Disney had boosted the player payroll to a club-record $60 million, the Angels stumbled to the worst start in franchise history at 6-14. Mike Scioscia quickly faced questions about his job security. But Anaheim then embarked on a 21-3 run and finished the regular season at 99-63, the best record in franchise history. By November, with a World Series championship on his resume, the only questions Scioscia faced were those about winning the American League Manager of the Year Award.

Offense

Scioscia and hitting coach Mickey Hatcher stressed in spring training that the Angels could not succeed without an unselfish offensive style that emphasized on-base percentage, making contact, hit-and-run plays, taking the extra base and giving up an at-bat to advance a runner via a bunt or groundball. Then Scioscia shut up, empowering team leader Darin Erstad and his teammates to enforce the philosophy and take credit for its success. The results spoke for themselves.

Pitching & Defense

In three years under Scioscia and pitching coach Bud Black, the Angels' ERA has dropped from 5.00 to 4.20 to 3.69. The Angels have nurtured top-quality starters in Jarrod Washburn and Ramon Ortiz, and Black has done wonders with a low-cost bullpen. Errors dropped for the third consecutive year as well, from 134 to 103 to 87, with Scioscia tutoring catcher Bengie Molina, who won a Gold Glove, and infield/first-base coach Alfredo Griffin working overtime to transform second baseman Adam Kennedy and shortstop David Eckstein into smooth fielders.

2003 Outlook

Scioscia was second-guessed after his first major postseason decision, leaving closer Troy Percival in the bullpen as the Angels blew a lead in the eighth inning of the playoff opener, but virtually every other call came up golden. Not every call will work out so well in 2003, and not every player will be happy, but there is no doubting the credibility and trust Scioscia earned by leading an allegedly cursed team to the promised land.

Born: 11/27/58 in Upper Darby, PA

Playing Experience: 1980-1992, LA

Managerial Experience: 3 seasons

Manager Statistics

Year	Team, Lg	W	L	Pct	GB	Finish
2002	Anaheim, AL	99	63	.611	4.0	2nd West
3 Seasons		256	230	.527	–	–

2002 Starting Pitchers by Days Rest

	<=3	4	5	6+
Angels Starts	1	79	51	23
Angels ERA	–	3.86	3.76	5.31
AL Avg Starts	1	83	44	24
AL ERA	7.15	4.59	4.27	5.03

2002 Situational Stats

	Mike Scioscia	AL Average
Hit & Run Success %	44.5	36.0
Stolen Base Success %	69.6	68.1
Platoon Pct.	63.9	58.9
Defensive Subs	16	23
High-Pitch Outings	5	6
Quick/Slow Hooks	10/10	19/14
Sacrifice Attempts	68	53

2002 Rankings (American League)

- 1st in squeeze plays (6), hit-and-run attempts (128), pinch-hitters used (141) and first-batter platoon percentage
- 2nd in stolen base attempts (168), steals of second base (102), sacrifice bunt attempts, hit-and-run success percentage and pitchouts with a runner moving (8)
- 3rd in double steals (4), sacrifice-bunt percentage (85.3%), pitchouts (33), starts on three days rest, one-batter pitcher appearances (43) and 2+ pitching changes in low-scoring games (33)

Garret Anderson

2002 Season

The national media practically affixed the adjective "overlooked" to Garret Anderson's name during the 2002 season. As the Angels ascended toward their first playoff berth in 16 years, the almost obligatory line included some variation of "the surprising Angels, led by the overlooked Garret Anderson." His statistics were a little better, though not significantly better, than the ones he posted in his previous seven seasons, but he finally was rewarded with his first All-Star selection. Anderson, the cleanup hitter on the World Series champions, finished fourth in the MVP race.

Hitting

Since 1996—the year Anderson became an everyday player—the only major leaguers with more hits are Alex Rodriguez and Derek Jeter. While many of his teammates are picky about first pitches, Anderson almost certainly will swing at a first-pitch fastball. He can be fooled by a sweeping breaking ball, but he can just as easily volley that pitch into left field. The Angels long ago accepted his reluctance to take walks, but he hits righties and lefties with equal ease, performs well in the clutch and has added the longball to his game.

Baserunning & Defense

Angels coaches consider Anderson the best left fielder in the American League. Anderson seldom dives for a ball, but he takes pride in smart positioning. His arm is average at best, but his whirl-and-throw move after fielding a ball hit down the line is so smooth that he can force a runner to hold at first on an otherwise routine double. Stolen bases aren't a big part of his game, but he will take the extra base on an unsuspecting outfielder.

2003 Outlook

Anderson now has played in at least 156 games in each of the past five seasons, with at least 183 hits each year. He has driven in 363 runs over the past three seasons. It's difficult to envision Anderson putting up numbers so spectacular that he runs away with an MVP award, but the Angels are mighty pleased with the excellent season that has become typical for him.

Position: LF/CF/DH
Bats: L **Throws:** L
Ht: 6' 3" **Wt:** 228

Opening Day Age: 30
Born: 6/30/72 in Los Angeles, CA
ML Seasons: 9

Overall Statistics

	G	AB	R	H	D	T	HR	RBI	SB	BB	SO	Avg	OBP	Slg
'02	158	638	93	195	56	3	29	123	6	30	80	.306	.332	.539
Car.	1206	4817	623	1432	300	23	164	756	60	220	649	.297	.326	.471

Where He Hits the Ball

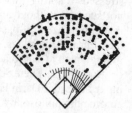

Vs. LHP   **Vs. RHP**

2002 Situational Stats

	AB	H	HR	RBI	Avg		AB	H	HR	RBI	Avg
Home	309	92	13	58	.298	LHP	208	59	11	41	.284
Road	329	103	16	65	.313	RHP	430	136	18	82	.316
First Half	350	102	15	63	.291	Sc Pos	180	57	10	96	.317
Scnd Half	288	93	14	60	.323	Clutch	95	28	2	17	.295

2002 Rankings (American League)

- 1st in doubles
- 3rd in fielding percentage in left field (.993) and fewest pitches seen per plate appearance (3.06)
- Led the Angels in at-bats, hits, doubles, total bases (344), RBI, sacrifice flies (10), intentional walks (11), games played, slugging percentage, cleanup slugging percentage (.554) and batting average on the road
- Led AL left fielders in RBI

Kevin Appier

2002 Season

The Angels accepted Kevin Appier—and the remaining $32 million of his contract—in a trade with the Mets as the price for shedding the weight of disgruntled first baseman Mo Vaughn and his *even fatter* contract. But Appier also provided quality starting pitching. In the first two months of the season, he was the Angels' top starter, giving up more than two earned runs twice in his first 10 starts. He won 14 games, a number he has exceeded just twice since 1995, and he did not miss a start.

Pitching

For the first time in a major league career that started in 1989, Appier pitched a full season but did not pitch a complete game, a development that reflected manager Mike Scioscia's conservative approach to pitch counts as well as Appier's evolution into a strictly finesse pitcher. His fastball rarely reaches 90 MPH, and he would rather have batters chase his curve, slider and splitter. When batters decline to do so, he can sneak a fastball on the inside corner to get ahead in the count. His funky delivery often gets out of whack for several innings, or several starts, at a time.

Defense

Appier did not commit an error last year, but that funky delivery also restricts his ability to cover ground on balls hit on either side of him. He has a decent pickoff move, good enough for an actual pickoff every now and then and certainly good enough to keep runners close. Of the 16 runners who tried to steal with Appier pitching and Gold Glover Bengie Molina catching, 11 were thrown out.

2003 Outlook

Appier faded by the end of last year, pitching a total of 14.2 innings in his final three regular-season starts and 21.2 innings in five postseason starts. But he still posted a winning record for the 11th time in 13 full seasons. The Angels hope he will be rejuvenated after the long season, especially with two years and $23 million left on his contract, but their strong bullpen can allow Appier to prosper as a six-inning starter.

Position: SP
Bats: R **Throws:** R
Ht: 6' 2" **Wt:** 200

Opening Day Age: 35
Born: 12/6/67 in Lancaster, CA
ML Seasons: 14
Pronunciation: APE-ee-er

Overall Statistics

	W	L	Pct.	ERA	G	GS	Sv	IP	H	BB	SO	HR	Ratio
'02	14	12	.538	3.92	32	32	0	188.1	191	64	132	23	1.35
Car.	161	127	.559	3.65	389	377	0	2479.2	2298	887	1937	211	1.28

How Often He Throws Strikes

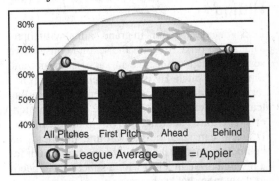

◎ = League Average   ■ = Appier

2002 Situational Stats

	W	L	ERA	Sv	IP		AB	H	HR	RBI	Avg
Home	6	8	3.76	0	107.2	LHB	376	94	11	30	.250
Road	8	4	4.13	0	80.2	RHB	339	97	12	50	.286
First Half	6	7	4.69	0	94.0	Sc Pos	138	44	5	53	.319
Scnd Half	8	5	3.15	0	94.1	Clutch	31	8	1	6	.258

2002 Rankings (American League)

- 1st in fielding percentage at pitcher (1.000) and most pitches thrown per batter (3.99)
- 2nd in runners caught stealing (13)
- 5th in lowest groundball-flyball ratio allowed (0.8)
- 6th in highest batting average allowed with runners in scoring position
- 7th in lowest stolen-base percentage allowed (45.8)
- 8th in losses
- Led the Angels in losses, games started, hits allowed, hit batsmen (7), wild pitches (7), runners caught stealing (13) and lowest stolen-base percentage allowed (45.8)

David Eckstein

2002 Season

Think about this: David Eckstein finished 11th in the American League MVP voting, tied with Nomar Garciaparra of the Boston Red Sox. Garciaparra is a superstar shortstop. Eckstein is an accidental shortstop, a player with few tools, a 5-foot-8 guy claimed on waivers in the hope he might develop into a utility infielder. However, assuming value correlates to winning, the voters cast their ballots wisely by including Eckstein, the catalyst and leadoff hitter for the World Series champions. When he scored a run, the Angels were 58-17 (.773). When he did not reach base, they were 9-19 (.321).

Hitting

Eckstein led the majors in grand slams, with three. That was a fluke. But, for the second consecutive season, he led the league in sacrifice bunts and times hit by pitch. He is an old-school leadoff hitter, taking pitches and fouling them off, providing teammates with a good look at the opposing pitcher's repertoire and tiring him out in the meantime. Eckstein can slap the ball around the field, hit behind a runner on the hit-and-run, drop a bunt for a hit, and drive in a run with a squeeze. He needs to draw more walks, however.

Baserunning & Defense

If you want flashy, don't watch Eckstein play shortstop. If you want classic, don't watch Eckstein play shortstop. His range is limited—although improving—and his throws to first base are almost painful to watch. But he gets the job done, displaying an uncanny knack for smart positioning. He stole 21 bases, though his success rate fell to 62 percent last year. He is not the fastest runner on the team, but he might be the most opportunistic.

2003 Outlook

The emergence of Adam Kennedy as a championship-caliber second baseman means that Eckstein, formerly considered a stopgap shortstop and second baseman-in-waiting, is expected to remain at short. He'll certainly remain atop the batting order, because he has mastered fundamentals and not just swinging for the fences.

Position: SS
Bats: R **Throws:** R
Ht: 5' 8" **Wt:** 170

Opening Day Age: 28
Born: 1/20/75 in Sanford, FL
ML Seasons: 2
Pronunciation: eck-STYNE

Overall Statistics

	G	AB	R	H	D	T	HR	RBI	SB	BB	SO	Avg	OBP	Slg
'02	152	608	107	178	22	6	8	63	21	45	44	.293	.363	.388
Car.	305	1190	189	344	48	8	12	104	50	88	104	.289	.359	.373

Where He Hits the Ball

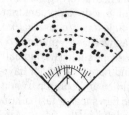
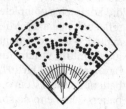

Vs. LHP   **Vs. RHP**

2002 Situational Stats

	AB	H	HR	RBI	Avg		AB	H	HR	RBI	Avg
Home	288	83	3	38	.288	LHP	172	52	4	23	.302
Road	320	95	5	25	.297	RHP	436	126	4	40	.289
First Half	303	82	4	41	.271	Sc Pos	154	44	4	57	.286
Scnd Half	305	96	4	22	.315	Clutch	86	23	1	13	.267

2002 Rankings (American League)

- 1st in sacrifice bunts (14), hit by pitch (27) and lowest percentage of swings that missed (7.5)
- 2nd in caught stealing (13) and bunts in play (35)
- 3rd in highest percentage of swings put into play (53.9)
- 4th in singles and lowest stolen-base percentage (61.8)
- Led the Angels in runs scored, singles, triples, sacrifice bunts (14), caught stealing (13), hit by pitch (27), times on base (250), plate appearances (702), bunts in play (35) and highest percentage of swings put into play (53.9)

Darin Erstad

2002 Season

Darin Erstad's statistics were not overwhelming, which left national analysts scratching their heads when the Angels signed him to a four-year, $32-million contract extension in August. But Erstad was the undisputed team leader, the one who set the example by sacrificing at-bats and statistics to advance runners and then enforcing the Angels' unselfish "small-ball" style among the rest of the hitters. He still scored 99 runs, stole 23 bases, won a Gold Glove and hit .352 in postseason play. A fracture of the hook of the hamate bone in his right hand, suffered late in the World Series, led to December surgery to remove the hook.

Hitting

Erstad rebounded from an abysmal 2001, but not as decisively as the jump in batting average (.258 to .283) would indicate. He had fewer doubles and one more home run, and his OBP actually declined, because his walks plummeted (62 to 27). But he again became a useful player against lefties. So his line-drive swing fit nicely between David Eckstein and Tim Salmon in a lineup built not on power but on making contact, hit-and-run plays and taking the extra base.

Baserunning & Defense

Erstad, the fastest player on the team, led the Angels' relentless charge on the bases. He races from first base to third as well as anyone in the league. He won his second Gold Glove, this time as a center fielder after winning one as a left fielder in 2000. His arm is not powerful, but he had 11 assists, tied for fifth in the league among all outfielders. His spectacular defensive style—diving to the ground and slamming into outfield walls—makes him susceptible to injury; he missed seven games after suffering a concussion last year.

2003 Outlook

As each year passes, Erstad's 2000 season looks more like a career year rather than a breakthrough to superstar status. He hit .355-25-100 with 240 hits that year. In his other five full seasons, he never has reached .300, or 180 hits, or 20 homers, or 85 RBI. From their No. 2 hitter the Angels will be happy with leadership, terrific defense, and the willingness and ability to advance runners.

Position: CF
Bats: L **Throws:** L
Ht: 6' 2" **Wt:** 220

Opening Day Age: 28
Born: 6/4/74 in Jamestown, ND
ML Seasons: 7
Pronunciation: ER-stad

Overall Statistics

	G	AB	R	H	D	T	HR	RBI	SB	BB	SO	Avg	OBP	Slg
'02	150	625	99	177	28	4	10	73	23	27	67	.283	.313	.389
Car.	935	3801	610	1107	202	24	96	468	134	311	555	.291	.346	.433

Where He Hits the Ball

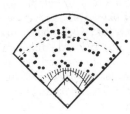 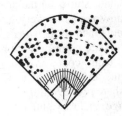

Vs. LHP   **Vs. RHP**

2002 Situational Stats

	AB	H	HR	RBI	Avg		AB	H	HR	RBI	Avg
Home	302	78	2	29	.258	LHP	193	54	2	26	.280
Road	323	99	8	44	.307	RHP	432	123	8	47	.285
First Half	332	103	6	51	.310	Sc Pos	166	43	3	61	.259
Scnd Half	293	74	4	22	.253	Clutch	89	31	2	18	.348

2002 Rankings (American League)

- 1st in fielding percentage in center field (.998)
- 2nd in assists in center field (11)
- 3rd in stolen-base percentage (88.5)
- 6th in singles and fewest pitches seen per plate appearance (3.42)
- 7th in batting average on an 0-2 count (.299) and lowest slugging percentage
- 8th in highest percentage of swings put into play (51.6) and batting average in the clutch
- 9th in at-bats, stolen bases and lowest HR frequency (62.5 ABs per HR)
- Led the Angels in stolen bases, highest groundball-flyball ratio (1.5) and stolen-base percentage (88.5)

Troy Glaus

2002 Season

As Troy Glaus muddled through the middle of the season, hitting .198 with six home runs in June and July, he kept insisting the relevant statistics were runs scored and runs batted in. By the end of the year, although his hits, doubles, home runs and walks were down from the 2001 season, he had scored 99 runs, driven in a career-high 111 and batted .293 with men in scoring position, up from .253 in 2001. He recovered his power stroke at the best of times, hitting eight home runs in September and seven in October, and winning World Series MVP honors.

Hitting

Glaus still is on the cusp of superstardom but for now remains a very good player prone to strike-outs, and to the streakiness for which power hitters are notorious. He has a terrific eye, although hitting coach Mickey Hatcher sometimes is uncomfortable that Glaus takes more than his share of called third strikes. His .230 batting average against righthanders reflects in part his tendency to pull most pitches rather than drive outside ones into right field, but he made progress toward the end of the season. If he uses the opposite-field power with which he is blessed, the Angels believe he could approach .300 with 40-50 home runs and 130-140 RBI.

Baserunning & Defense

Glaus is an asset at third base, with unexpected quickness for a 245-pound man and excellent range. He has one of the strongest infield arms in the league, although his throws on routine plays sometime sail. He has good baserunning instincts and surprisingly good speed.

2003 Outlook

With the raw power that can carry a team for a week or two and a cannon of a right arm, Glaus has the most impressive tools on the team, which sometimes breeds frustration among scouts. But he has driven in 100 runs in his second, third and fourth full major league seasons and, at 26, he still has time to emerge as a dominant player.

Position: 3B
Bats: R **Throws:** R
Ht: 6' 5" **Wt:** 245

Opening Day Age: 26
Born: 8/3/76 in Tarzana, CA
ML Seasons: 5
Pronunciation: GLOSS

Overall Statistics

	G	AB	R	H	D	T	HR	RBI	SB	BB	SO	Avg	OBP	Slg
'02	156	569	99	142	24	1	30	111	10	88	144	.250	.352	.453
Car.	678	2436	423	617	137	4	148	423	40	393	659	.253	.359	.495

Where He Hits the Ball

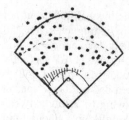

Vs. LHP   **Vs. RHP**

2002 Situational Stats

	AB	H	HR	RBI	Avg		AB	H	HR	RBI	Avg
Home	272	67	13	53	.246	LHP	161	48	10	41	.298
Road	297	75	17	58	.253	RHP	408	94	20	70	.230
First Half	306	74	15	58	.242	Sc Pos	164	48	10	85	.293
Scnd Half	263	68	15	53	.259	Clutch	91	23	7	18	.253

2002 Rankings (American League)

- 1st in batting average with the bases loaded (.600)
- 3rd in strikeouts and errors at third base (20)
- 4th in lowest batting average vs. righthanded pitchers and lowest fielding percentage at third base (.950)
- 6th in highest percentage of swings that missed (27.2)
- 7th in walks
- 8th in RBI
- Led the Angels in home runs, walks, strikeouts, pitches seen (2,664), HR frequency (19.0 ABs per HR), most pitches seen per plate appearance (3.97) and batting average with the bases loaded (.600)

Adam Kennedy

Position: 2B
Bats: L **Throws:** R
Ht: 6' 1" **Wt:** 192

Opening Day Age: 27
Born: 1/10/76 in Riverside, CA
ML Seasons: 4

2002 Season

At the start of the season, Adam Kennedy ranked as the Angel most likely to lose his job. By the end of the season, he had anchored himself at second base, ranking seventh in the league with a .312 batting average. He hit .404 in August, the highest monthly average in the league last year. He also batted .340 in postseason play, including a wondrous game in which he hit three home runs.

Hitting

In a season in which he had the fewest plate appearances of his three-year career, Kennedy set career marks in batting average, on-base percentage and slugging percentage. Manager Mike Scioscia typically benched Kennedy against lefthanders in favor of Jose Nieves or Benji Gil. But Kennedy held his own, hitting .275 against southpaws in 69 at-bats, and he ought to get a full-time job in 2003. His performance is outstanding for a No. 9 hitter, but he must draw more walks and strike out less if he wants to bat at the top of the lineup.

Baserunning & Defense

Kennedy worked overtime with infield/first-base coach Alfredo Griffin in spring training, and the results were impressive enough to turn Kennedy from a liability into an asset at second base. He made the routine plays, improved dramatically at turning the double play and displayed a flair for ranging to his right and making a strong off-balance throw to first base. He is not the fastest man on the team, but he is aggressive about turning singles into doubles.

2003 Outlook

The Angels considered Kennedy their most improved player, and fans no longer cry about the trade that sent All-Star outfielder Jim Edmonds to St. Louis for Kennedy and long-departed pitcher Kent Bottenfield. Kennedy has earned the chance to play every day this year. It still is conceivable that he could someday be traded so that the Angels could shift David Eckstein to second base and promote a shortstop prospect—either Alfredo Amezaga or Brian Specht—but not this year, and perhaps not at all if Kennedy keeps progressing.

Overall Statistics

	G	AB	R	H	D	T	HR	RBI	SB	BB	SO	Avg	OBP	Slg
'02	144	474	65	148	32	6	7	52	17	19	80	.312	.345	.449
Car.	470	1652	207	462	100	21	23	180	51	77	232	.280	.317	.407

Where He Hits the Ball

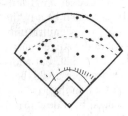

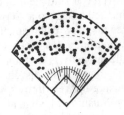

Vs. LHP   **Vs. RHP**

2002 Situational Stats

	AB	H	HR	RBI	Avg		AB	H	HR	RBI	Avg
Home	224	72	6	30	.321	LHP	69	19	3	9	.275
Road	250	76	1	22	.304	RHP	405	129	4	43	.319
First Half	248	74	2	24	.298	Sc Pos	128	35	1	41	.273
Scnd Half	226	74	5	28	.327	Clutch	95	26	1	4	.274

2002 Rankings (American League)

- 3rd in fielding percentage at second base (.983)
- 5th in errors at second base (11) and batting average with two strikes (.258)
- Led the Angels in batting average, triples, fewest GDPs per GDP situation (5.8%), batting average vs. righthanded pitchers and batting average at home

John Lackey

2002 Season

In the most significant in-season personnel move of their Championship year, the Angels promoted John Lackey from the minor leagues in June, entrusting a starting spot to a rookie and bumping Scott Schoeneweis into the bullpen. The Angels badly needed a lefthanded reliever, and Schoeneweis prospered in that role. Lackey prospered, too. He lost just four of 18 starts, won the game that clinched the Angels' first playoff berth in 16 years, and won Game 7 of the World Series, becoming the first rookie to do so in 93 years.

Pitching

By the World Series, the baseball world had discovered a statistical anomaly: Lackey held lefthanded hitters to a .208 average, 10th best in the league, but righthanders hit .317 against him, worst in the league. Lackey and the Angels insist the anomaly is nothing more than that, but additional work on his curve and slider could help ensure that. He throws his fastball in the low 90s, with natural movement enhanced by a downward delivery off his 6-foot-6 frame. The coaches marvel at his ability to throw a first-pitch strike on the corners of the plate.

Defense

Lackey fields his position well, as might be expected from a player who spent most of his youth as a first baseman. That background helps him handle with ease those plays which require him to cover first. In 34 starts between the major and minor leagues, he threw 12 wild pitches and balked four times, figures that should decline with experience.

2003 Outlook

Lackey pitched 232.1 innings last year, from the minor leagues through Game 7 of the World Series, and admitted to some fatigue at the end of the regular season. He did not pitch more than five innings in any of his final four regular-season starts, and the Angels did not start him during the American League Division Series. The Angels believe the strapping young Texan can join Jarrod Washburn at the head of their rotation for years to come.

Position: SP
Bats: R **Throws:** R
Ht: 6' 6" **Wt:** 205

Opening Day Age: 24
Born: 10/23/78 in Abilene, TX
ML Seasons: 1

Overall Statistics

	W	L	Pct.	ERA	G	GS	Sv	IP	H	BB	SO	HR	Ratio
'02	9	4	.692	3.66	18	18	0	108.1	113	33	69	10	1.35
Car.	9	4	.692	3.66	18	18	0	108.1	113	33	69	10	1.35

How Often He Throws Strikes

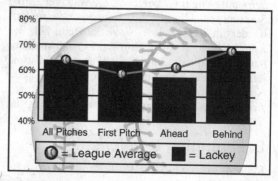

2002 Situational Stats

	W	L	ERA	Sv	IP		AB	H	HR	RBI	Avg
Home	4	1	3.52	0	46.0	LHB	197	41	1	18	.208
Road	5	3	3.75	0	62.1	RHB	227	72	9	25	.317
First Half	1	1	2.70	0	20.0	Sc Pos	90	21	1	30	.233
Scnd Half	8	3	3.87	0	88.1	Clutch	13	6	1	2	.462

2002 Rankings (American League)

- 1st in highest batting average allowed vs. righthanded batters
- 4th in balks (2)
- 5th in wins among rookies
- 10th in lowest batting average allowed vs. lefthanded batters
- Led the Angels in wild pitches (7), stolen bases allowed (12) and highest groundball-flyball ratio allowed (1.3)

Ramon Ortiz

2002 Season

The Angels already had suggested that Ramon Ortiz was too advanced to use "young pitcher" as an explanation for development that at times seemed painfully slow. In the winter visa crackdown that followed, Ortiz matured in the blink of an eye, as his Opening Day age jumped from 26 to 29. The Angels shrugged and signed him to a four-year contract, and he responded by winning 15 games, leading the team in innings pitched, ranking seventh in the league in strikeouts and holding opponents to a .230 batting average.

Pitching

Manager Mike Scioscia and pitching coach Bud Black repeatedly stressed to Ortiz that he needed to develop the mental toughness to shake off home runs. Ortiz did yield 40 homers, most in the major leagues, but the Angels noted that 32 of them were solo. In the meantime, he increased his strikeout total from 2001 while giving up fewer runs, hits and walks. He can maintain velocity on his mid-90s fastball well into a game, and his slider and changeup also serve him well.

Defense

Ortiz is below average on defense, more for an occasional lapse in concentration than for a lack of ability. He is average at best in holding runners on base. In spring training, Ortiz asked that Bengie Molina catch all of his starts, and the statistics reflect that comfort: in 163.2 innings pitching to Molina, Ortiz posted a 3.08 ERA; in 53 innings with other catchers, he posted a 5.87 ERA.

2003 Outlook

When the Angels selected their starter for Game 7 of the World Series, they bypassed Ortiz for rookie John Lackey. But Ortiz still finished the season by going 8-0 in his final 12 starts, including three postseason starts, and he recorded four of the Angels' seven complete games. He'll start the 2003 season behind Jarrod Washburn and Lackey, but Ortiz has the best pure stuff among the starters, and Anaheim believes he can mature into a 20-game winner.

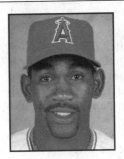

Position: SP
Bats: R **Throws:** R
Ht: 6' 0" **Wt:** 170

Opening Day Age: 30
Born: 3/23/73 in Carabobo, DR
ML Seasons: 4
Pronunciation: or-TEEZ

Overall Statistics

	W	L	Pct.	ERA	G	GS	Sv	IP	H	BB	SO	HR	Ratio
'02	15	9	.625	3.77	32	32	0	217.1	188	68	162	40	1.18
Car.	38	29	.567	4.46	91	91	0	585.2	557	224	414	90	1.33

How Often He Throws Strikes

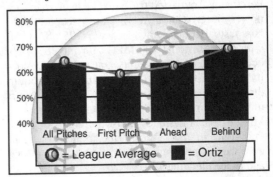

= League Average   = Ortiz

2002 Situational Stats

	W	L	ERA	Sv	IP		AB	H	HR	RBI	Avg
Home	7	4	3.62	0	102.0	LHB	404	88	22	46	.218
Road	8	5	3.90	0	115.1	RHB	412	100	18	42	.243
First Half	8	6	3.21	0	126.0	Sc Pos	167	35	5	50	.210
Scnd Half	7	3	4.53	0	91.1	Clutch	47	15	2	7	.319

2002 Rankings (American League)

- 1st in home runs allowed, balks (3) and most home runs allowed per nine innings (1.66)
- 3rd in errors at pitcher (4) and lowest fielding percentage at pitcher (.871)
- 4th in complete games (4), most run support per nine innings (6.7) and lowest batting average allowed with runners in scoring position
- 6th in runners caught stealing (9) and lowest batting average allowed (.230)
- Led the Angels in games started, complete games (4), innings pitched, batters faced (896), home runs allowed, walks allowed, strikeouts, wild pitches (7), balks (3) and pickoff throws (98)

Troy Percival

2002 Season

For Troy Percival, what started as a season in crisis ended in triumph. Bothered by a strained ribcage, he made three appearances during the Angels' 6-14 start and failed to retire seven of the 12 batters he faced. But the injury healed, and so did Anaheim. The veteran closer finished with a career-best 1.92 ERA and his second 40-save campaign. Percival added seven saves in postseason play and was on the mound for the final out of the first postseason series victory in franchise history, the ALCS and the World Series.

Pitching

Percival has outlasted the typical career span of a power closer without relying on a second pitch. His fastball consistently registers 95-98 MPH, with the occasional 100-MPH blur mixed in. He occasionally throws his curve, at a drop in velocity of some 20 MPH. He got a critical strikeout in the ALCS on a changeup he uses so rarely that it might not appear in scouting reports. Manager Mike Scioscia hesitates to use Percival for more than one inning. During the regular season, Percival entered four games in the eighth inning and twice blew the save.

Defense

Percival is so tough to hit—and so easy to run on—that most opponents will attempt to steal second. Even discounting several runners who swiped second base on what was officially credited as defensive indifference, opposing runners stole five of six bases with Percival on the mound. His wild delivery does not leave him in good position to field groundballs.

2003 Outlook

Percival broke into the major leagues in 1995 as a setup man for Lee Smith. In 1996, the Angels traded Smith and anointed Percival their closer. Francisco Rodriguez, the Anaheim phenom, broke into the majors last September and established himself as Percival's setup man last October. Percival's two-year, $16 million contract extension kicks in this year, and Rodriguez is expected to continue to set up Percival until the contract runs out or the Angels no longer are contenders, whichever comes first.

Position: RP
Bats: R **Throws:** R
Ht: 6' 3" **Wt:** 235

Opening Day Age: 33
Born: 8/9/69 in Fontana, CA
ML Seasons: 8
Pronunciation: PURR-si-vul

Overall Statistics

	W	L	Pct.	ERA	G	GS	Sv	IP	H	BB	SO	HR	Ratio
'02	4	1	.800	1.92	58	0	40	56.1	38	25	68	5	1.12
Car.	27	30	.474	2.95	475	0	250	487.2	317	211	599	49	1.08

How Often He Throws Strikes

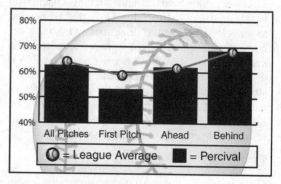

- ◉ = League Average ■ = Percival

2002 Situational Stats

	W	L	ERA	Sv	IP			AB	H	HR	RBI	Avg
Home	4	0	1.56	24	34.2		LHB	93	23	5	15	.247
Road	0	1	2.49	16	21.2		RHB	109	15	0	6	.138
First Half	3	1	2.22	21	28.1		Sc Pos	55	12	2	18	.218
Scnd Half	1	0	1.61	19	28.0		Clutch	157	29	2	18	.185

2002 Rankings (American League)

- 1st in save percentage (90.9)
- 2nd in most strikeouts per nine innings in relief (10.9)
- 3rd in saves, relief ERA (1.92) and lowest batting average allowed in relief (.188)
- 6th in save opportunities (44)
- 7th in games finished (50)
- Led the Angels in saves, games finished (50), save opportunities (44), save percentage (90.9), blown saves (4), relief ERA (1.92), lowest batting average allowed in relief (.188), most strikeouts per nine innings in relief (10.9) and fewest baserunners allowed per nine innings in relief (10.1)

Tim Salmon

2002 Season

Tim Salmon did not hit a home run in his first 68 at-bats and did not lift his batting average above .200 until May 10, forcing the Angels to fear the worst—that Salmon's injury-plagued wreck of a 2001 season marked not an aberration but a career in rapid decline. After all, he was healthy in 2002, and manager Mike Scioscia insisted Salmon's bat speed was dramatically improved. The bat finally came around, and the longest-serving member of the Angels finished a typically productive season by hitting .346 in the World Series, then hoisting the championship trophy above his head as he ran a victory lap at Edison Field.

Hitting

Salmon mixed clutch hitting with his trademark ability to get on base, driving in David Eckstein and Darin Erstad ahead of him and providing RBI opportunities for Garret Anderson and Troy Glaus behind him. Salmon hit .316 with men in scoring position, one year after hitting a paltry .171 in that situation. He remains susceptible to pitches on the inside or outside corner, taking more than his fair share of called third strikes and taking check swings that cost him strikes as well.

Baserunning & Defense

Salmon, once considered one of the elite outfielders in the league, strictly is average now. His arm remains strong and accurate, but his range is diminished and balls over his head can baffle him. Salmon started 21 games at DH and, after the Angels acquired Alex Ochoa in July, Scioscia commonly deployed Ochoa as Salmon's defensive replacement. Salmon is not slow, but he is not notably aggressive on the bases, either.

2003 Outlook

Despite having loose bodies removed from his left knee in November, Salmon figures to start in right field on Opening Day for the 11th consecutive season. The gradual transition from the outfield to DH, though, appears to have begun. He has three years and $29 million remaining on his contract, and the Angels' primary concern is keeping Salmon healthy and productive for the life of the deal. Their minor league system has yet to groom a right fielder to replace him.

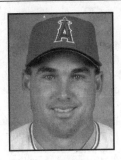

Position: RF/DH
Bats: R **Throws:** R
Ht: 6' 3" **Wt:** 225

Opening Day Age: 34
Born: 8/24/68 in Long Beach, CA
ML Seasons: 11
Pronunciation: SAM-en

Overall Statistics

G	AB	R	H	D	T	HR	RBI	SB	BB	SO	Avg	OBP	Slg
138	483	84	138	37	1	22	88	6	71	102	.286	.380	.503
1388	5009	863	1426	289	18	269	894	44	850	1182	.285	.390	.511

Where He Hits the Ball

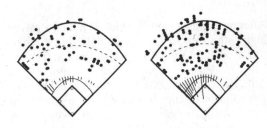

Vs. LHP   **Vs. RHP**

2002 Situational Stats

	AB	H	HR	RBI	Avg		AB	H	HR	RBI	Avg
Home	231	62	10	38	.268	LHP	137	41	5	23	.299
Road	252	76	12	50	.302	RHP	346	97	17	65	.280
First Half	298	84	14	55	.282	Sc Pos	155	49	10	72	.316
Scnd Half	185	54	8	33	.292	Clutch	82	25	5	12	.305

2002 Rankings (American League)

- 3rd in lowest batting average on an 0-2 count (.032)
- 4th in fielding percentage in right field (.986)
- 5th in on-base percentage vs. lefthanded pitchers (.411)
- Led the Angels in on-base percentage

Aaron Sele

2002 Season

When the Angels signed Aaron Sele in January 2002 to the richest contract they ever had awarded a free-agent pitcher—$24 million over three years—they did not ask for dominance. They *did* ask Sele to pitch 200 innings, win 15 or so games and work with the younger pitchers on the staff. He was enormously helpful in the latter area, but less so in the other two. For the first time in five years, he failed to pitch 200 innings or win 15 games, in large part because a rotator cuff injury sidelined him for five weeks. And, as the Angels set a franchise record for victories, Sele posted a losing record for the first time in six years.

Pitching

After an August game in which Sele tied a career high with seven walks, he complained of discomfort in his right shoulder. An examination the next day revealed the righthander had a torn rotator cuff. He also acknowledged throughout the season an inconsistency in following one good pitch with another, troubling for a pitcher whose fastball strictly is average. He allowed 13.8 baserunners per nine innings, and erratic command of his trademark curve contributed to a frightening regression in batting average allowed to opposing lefthanders.

Defense

Sele is a competent if unspectacular fielder. He throws to first base quite frequently, although those efforts do not deter the better baserunners. He picked no one off last year. Still, of the 13 runners who tried to steal with him on the mound, only six were successful.

2003 Outlook

Sele worked diligently to rehab his shoulder in the hope of returning for the playoffs. The Angels nonetheless left him off the postseason roster. He did not undergo surgery to repair the torn rotator cuff until late October, jeopardizing his chances of being ready for spring training. With another $16 million invested in Sele, Anaheim hopes that the injury accounted for his rough times last year, but if not, Mickey Callaway, Scott Schoeneweis and Chris Bootcheck all are candidates to fill out the rotation.

Position: SP
Bats: R **Throws:** R
Ht: 6' 5" **Wt:** 220

Opening Day Age: 32
Born: 6/25/70 in Golden Valley, MN
ML Seasons: 10
Pronunciation: SEE-lee

Overall Statistics

	W	L	Pct.	ERA	G	GS	Sv	IP	H	BB	SO	HR	Ratio
'02	8	9	.471	4.89	26	26	0	160.0	190	49	82	21	1.49
Car.	115	77	.599	4.39	268	267	0	1626.1	1770	597	1164	158	1.46

How Often He Throws Strikes

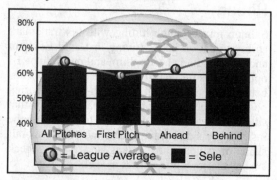

○ = League Average   ■ = Sele

2002 Situational Stats

	W	L	ERA	Sv	IP		AB	H	HR	RBI	Avg
Home	5	2	4.12	0	94.0	LHB	317	100	7	40	.315
Road	3	7	6.00	0	66.0	RHB	318	90	14	41	.283
First Half	7	5	5.03	0	105.2	Sc Pos	144	34	3	53	.236
Scnd Half	1	4	4.64	0	54.1	Clutch	17	4	0	1	.235

2002 Rankings (American League)

- 10th in lowest batting average allowed with runners in scoring position
- Led the Angels in hit batsmen (7)

Jarrod Washburn

2002 Season

Jarrod Washburn emerged as the Angels' ace last season, earning a Cy Young vote by ranking among American League leaders in victories, ERA, winning percentage and opponents' batting average. He did not lose between April 13 and July 27, a span of 17 starts that included a 12-game winning streak—the longest such streak in the league last year and a single-season franchise record. Washburn's 18 victories were the most by an Angels pitcher since 1991, when Mark Langston won 19.

Pitching

Washburn baffles and frustrates opposing hitters by throwing almost all fastballs, none overpowering. But the fastballs do not look alike, as he gets late movement and expertly varies speeds from 83-92 MPH. And, in an era where pitchers are trained to keep the ball down, Washburn retires more than a few hitters on tantalizingly high heat. He abandoned an ineffective curve in spring training, and he will not win on his slider and change, but he threw many more offspeed pitches than usual in the AL playoffs, against teams familiar with his repertoire and perhaps because of a tired arm.

Defense

Washburn picked off 12 runners in 2001, so opposing runners were duly cautious in 2002. He still picked off two runners and held the rest closely enough that catchers Bengie and Jose Molina could throw out five of 10 trying to steal. Washburn combines outstanding deception in his leg kick and an excellent slide step. He is quick off the mound and fields his position well.

2003 Outlook

The innings piled up for Washburn last season. He won once in five postseason starts, with a 5.02 ERA, but the Angels believe all will be fine after a winter of rest and conditioning workouts similar to the ones he completed prior to the 2002 campaign. Last year, Washburn started on Opening Day, in the Angels' first playoff game in 16 years and in their first-ever World Series game. He figures to start on Opening Day again, in the quest to repeat.

Position: SP
Bats: L **Throws:** L
Ht: 6' 1" **Wt:** 187

Opening Day Age: 28
Born: 8/13/74 in La Crosse, WI
ML Seasons: 5

Overall Statistics

	W	L	Pct.	ERA	G	GS	Sv	IP	H	BB	SO	HR	Ratio
'02	18	6	.750	3.15	32	32	0	206.0	183	59	139	19	1.17
Car.	46	26	.639	3.81	107	97	0	619.1	574	203	401	77	1.25

How Often He Throws Strikes

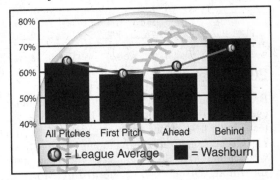

= League Average = Washburn

2002 Situational Stats

	W	L	ERA	Sv	IP		AB	H	HR	RBI	Avg
Home	5	3	3.79	0	90.1	LHB	181	36	5	15	.199
Road	13	3	2.65	0	115.2	RHB	598	147	14	50	.246
First Half	9	2	3.21	0	106.2	Sc Pos	164	38	1	38	.232
Scnd Half	9	4	3.08	0	99.1	Clutch	56	15	0	6	.268

2002 Rankings (American League)

- 1st in lowest groundball-flyball ratio allowed (0.6) and fewest GDPs induced per nine innings (0.3)
- 3rd in winning percentage, lowest ERA on the road and most pitches thrown per batter (3.95)
- 4th in lowest batting average allowed vs. lefthanded batters
- Led the Angels in ERA, wins, games started, pitches thrown (3,362), lowest slugging percentage allowed (.375), lowest on-base percentage allowed (.289), lowest ERA on the road, fewest home runs allowed per nine innings (.83) and fewest walks per nine innings (2.6)

Brendan Donnelly

Position: RP
Bats: R **Throws:** R
Ht: 6' 3" **Wt:** 205

Opening Day Age: 31
Born: 7/4/71 in
Washington, DC
ML Seasons: 1

Overall Statistics

	W	L	Pct.	ERA	G	GS	Sv	IP	H	BB	SO	HR	Ratio
'02	1	1	.500	2.17	46	0	1	49.2	32	19	54	2	1.03
Car.	1	1	.500	2.17	46	0	1	49.2	32	19	54	2	1.03

2002 Situational Stats

	W	L	ERA	Sv	IP		AB	H	HR	RBI	Avg
Home	1	0	2.42	1	26.0	LHB	66	16	2	10	.242
Road	0	1	1.90	0	23.2	RHB	108	16	0	5	.148
First Half	0	0	6.14	0	7.1	Sc Pos	47	9	0	11	.191
Scnd Half	1	1	1.49	1	42.1	Clutch	93	16	1	8	.172

2002 Season

Brendan Donnelly made his major league debut at age 30, after he had pitched for 14 minor league teams over 10 seasons and been released by six big league organizations (including Tampa Bay, who let him go to clear a minor league roster spot for future Disney movie hero Jim Morris). Donnelly enjoyed a heroic rookie season, finding himself among the AL leaders in stranding inherited runners (84 percent) and retiring the first batter faced (91 percent).

Pitching & Defense

Donnelly gets most of his outs with a lively fastball, thrown in the low 90s and with movement. After a rocky initiation, the Angels sent him back to the minor leagues and reminded him a strikeout pitcher must throw strikes. When he returned to the parent club for good in July, his first 9.2 frames included no runs, no walks, two hits and 15 strikeouts. He is adequate on defense.

2003 Outlook

While the world marveled at phenom Francisco Rodriguez, Donnelly was the Angels' best pitcher during the World Series. With Rodriguez slated for the eighth inning and closer Troy Percival for the ninth, Donnelly and Ben Weber will open the year passing the baton to Rodriguez and Percival.

Brad Fullmer

Position: DH/1B
Bats: L **Throws:** R
Ht: 6' 0" **Wt:** 220

Opening Day Age: 28
Born: 1/17/75 in
Chatsworth, CA
ML Seasons: 6

Overall Statistics

	G	AB	R	H	D	T	HR	RBI	SB	BB	SO	Avg	OBP	Slg
'02	130	429	75	124	35	6	19	59	10	32	44	.289	.357	.531
Car.	668	2325	322	655	175	13	94	374	26	163	312	.282	.335	.489

2002 Situational Stats

	AB	H	HR	RBI	Avg		AB	H	HR	RBI	Avg
Home	206	59	9	28	.286	LHP	63	14	2	7	.222
Road	223	65	10	31	.291	RHP	366	110	17	52	.301
First Half	238	64	10	30	.269	Sc Pos	106	28	2	38	.264
Scnd Half	191	60	9	29	.314	Clutch	53	12	1	6	.226

2002 Season

When the Angels acquired Brad Fullmer in a trade with Toronto in January 2002, they trumpeted him as their everyday designated hitter. But, with April marking just the second homerless month of Fullmer's career (June, 1999), Mike Scioscia benched him against lefthanders. Scioscia stuck with his platoon the rest of the way, and Fullmer finished with just 429 at-bats.

Hitting, Baserunning & Defense

Fullmer might never again match the 32 home runs he hit for the Blue Jays in 2000, but his .531 slugging percentage last season ranked second to Garret Anderson among the Angels. Fullmer remains a pull-hitter who swings very hard, but he manages to keep his strikeouts in check. He stole a career-high 10 bases in 2002, thrilling the Angels with his aggressiveness on the basepaths. He played 29 games at first base and made one error, providing an adequate option on those days when Scioscia wanted to rest Scott Spiezio.

2003 Outlook

Fullmer wants to play every day, as the Angels originally promised, and they would consider trading him. But he is not eligible for free agency, and it is difficult to argue with success. If he remains in Anaheim, he likely returns in a platoon role.

Bengie Molina \Gold Glover

Position: C
Bats: R **Throws:** R
Ht: 5'11" **Wt:** 210

Opening Day Age: 28
Born: 7/20/74 in Rio Piedras, PR
ML Seasons: 5

Overall Statistics

	G	AB	R	H	D	T	HR	RBI	SB	BB	SO	Avg	OBP	Slg
'02	122	428	34	105	18	0	5	47	0	15	34	.245	.274	.322
Car.	381	1328	132	349	54	2	26	168	1	60	124	.263	.301	.365

2002 Situational Stats

	AB	H	HR	RBI	Avg		AB	H	HR	RBI	Avg
Home	212	47	2	20	.222	LHP	125	31	1	12	.248
Road	216	58	3	27	.269	RHP	303	74	4	35	.244
First Half	270	71	1	34	.263	Sc Pos	127	29	2	41	.228
Scnd Half	158	34	4	13	.215	Clutch	76	21	1	12	.276

2002 Season

For the first time in 11 seasons, Ivan Rodriguez did not win the AL Gold Glove for catchers. Bengie Molina did, after making one error and throwing out 43 percent of opposing baserunners. He hit only one home run in the first four months of the regular season, and batted just .203 over the final two months, but he caught all 16 postseason games and posted a .286 mark in the World Series.

Hitting, Baserunning & Defense

Molina makes contact, which makes him particularly valuable in an offense in which hit-and-run plays are called for often. He struck out 34 times in 428 at-bats overall, eight times in 127 at-bats with men in scoring position. He is one of the slowest runners in the major leagues. His ability to throw is unquestioned, and his pitchers love working with him, but he has trouble blocking balls that bounce outside the strike zone.

2003 Outlook

Injuries dogged Molina throughout the minors, and hamstring strains plagued him in 2001 and 2002. Manager Mike Scioscia hopes to minimize the injury risk by limiting him to about 120 games, with Molina's younger brother Jose—a terrific defensive catcher in his own right—on hand to back up.

Alex Ochoa

Position: RF/LF
Bats: R **Throws:** R
Ht: 6' 0" **Wt:** 200

Opening Day Age: 31
Born: 3/29/72 in Miami, FL
ML Seasons: 8
Pronunciation: oh-CHO-ah

Overall Statistics

	G	AB	R	H	D	T	HR	RBI	SB	BB	SO	Avg	OBP	Slg
'02	122	280	40	73	16	0	8	31	10	42	35	.261	.361	.404
Car.	807	2143	320	597	131	19	46	261	56	203	288	.279	.344	.422

2002 Situational Stats

	AB	H	HR	RBI	Avg		AB	H	HR	RBI	Avg
Home	151	33	4	15	.219	LHP	114	31	3	14	.272
Road	129	40	4	16	.310	RHP	166	42	5	17	.253
First Half	169	43	4	15	.254	Sc Pos	84	21	0	22	.250
Scnd Half	111	30	4	16	.270	Clutch	61	10	1	6	.164

2002 Season

The Angels acquired Alex Ochoa from Milwaukee at the July 31 trading deadline. Ten days later, Tim Salmon was hit by a pitch and forced onto the disabled list. Salmon missed four weeks, and in his absence the Angels went 16-6 with Ochoa and Orlando Palmeiro sharing right field. When Salmon returned, Ochoa became his late-inning defensive replacement.

Hitting, Baserunning & Defense

Ochoa fit in nicely with an old-school Angels offense, with flashes of power but more importantly the ability to reach base, make contact and proceed swiftly around the bases. Ochoa walked more than he struck out last season, for the second time in four seasons. His speed impressed the Angels not only on the bases but on defense, and his powerful arm wowed coaches and teammates.

2003 Outlook

With his formidable tools, Ochoa ascended to the major leagues touted as a superstar in the making. But with undeveloped power, he has topped 300 at-bats once in seven major league seasons and has been traded seven times in eight years. After the Angels chose not to offer him salary arbitration, Ochoa will open 2003 in a different uniform.

Orlando Palmeiro

Position: RF/LF/CF
Bats: L **Throws:** L
Ht: 5'10" **Wt:** 182

Opening Day Age: 34
Born: 1/19/69 in
Hoboken, NJ
ML Seasons: 8
Pronunciation:
PALL-mare-oh

Overall Statistics

	G	AB	R	H	D	T	HR	RBI	SB	BB	SO	Avg	OBP	Slg
'02	110	263	35	79	12	1	0	31	7	30	22	.300	.368	.354
Car.	645	1459	204	410	69	10	3	138	29	178	132	.281	.361	.348

2002 Situational Stats

	AB	H	HR	RBI	Avg		AB	H	HR	RBI	Avg
Home	126	41	0	17	.325	LHP	34	14	0	2	.412
Road	137	38	0	14	.277	RHP	229	65	0	29	.284
First Half	120	37	0	10	.308	Sc Pos	73	24	0	31	.329
Scnd Half	143	42	0	21	.294	Clutch	47	13	0	3	.277

2002 Season

With the Angels off to the worst start in franchise history, manager Mike Scioscia posted an April 24 lineup in which Orlando Palmeiro batted third. The Angels desperately needed offense, even at the risk of what might have been perceived as a panic move. But he had three hits, the Angels won 10-6 to start a 21-3 run, and Scioscia had discovered another lineup option. Palmeiro batted third in the starting lineup 24 times during the season, and Anaheim was 19-5 in those games.

Hitting, Baserunning & Defense

Palmeiro doesn't hit for power, but he slaps the ball around the field and makes good contact— exceptional contact, really, for a bench player not afforded the chance to maintain timing with daily at-bats. He walks more than he strikes out and has done so each year since 1997. He is a good bunter. He works the count, taking and fouling off pitches. He is a competent backup at all three outfield positions with an arm best suited for left, but he is not a gifted baserunner.

2003 Outlook

While Palmeiro needs just three pinch-hits to break Winston Llenas' franchise record, Llenas' record will stand. Palmeiro filed for free agency, and the Angels didn't offer salary arbitration.

Francisco Rodriguez

Position: RP
Bats: R **Throws:** R
Ht: 6' 0" **Wt:** 175

Opening Day Age: 21
Born: 1/7/82 in Caracas, VZ
ML Seasons: 1

Overall Statistics

	W	L	Pct.	ERA	G	GS	Sv	IP	H	BB	SO	HR	Ratio
'02	0	0	–	0.00	5	0	0	5.2	3	2	13	0	0.88
Car.	0	0	–	0.00	5	0	0	5.2	3	2	13	0	0.88

2002 Situational Stats

	W	L	ERA	Sv	IP		AB	H	HR	RBI	Avg
Home	0	0	0.00	0	2.1	LHB	7	2	0	0	.286
Road	0	0	0.00	0	3.1	RHB	11	1	0	1	.091
First Half	0	0	–	0	0.0	Sc Pos	5	0	0	1	.000
Scnd Half	0	0	0.00	0	5.2	Clutch	4	2	0	1	.500

2002 Season

After three years of injury and inconsistency as a starter, never higher than Class-A level, the Angels weren't sure what to make of Francisco Rodriguez. They switched him to the bullpen, almost out of desperation, and struck gold. He roared through Double- and Triple-A and into the majors, and—after striking out 13 in 5.2 innings as a September callup—onto the playoff roster.

Pitching & Defense

Rodriguez mixes a 95-MPH fastball with an 83-MPH slider, both with wondrous movement. The fastball cuts and darts and at its best resembles the ones thrown by Mariano Rivera, while the slider leaves batters flailing helplessly as it sweeps away from the strike zone. Rodriguez has a changeup, but it clearly is his third-best pitch and one he seldom needs to use as a short reliever.

2003 Outlook

Rodriguez' postseason was so dominant that national commentators wondered why the Angels wouldn't turn the 21-year-old into a starter. The answer, of course, is that they already had tried that. Rodriguez, at first resistant to relieving, now believes his arm holds up better in shorter outings. They envision him and closer Troy Percival dominating the eighth and ninth innings, respectively.

Scott Schoeneweis

Position: RP/SP
Bats: L **Throws:** L
Ht: 6' 0" **Wt:** 185

Opening Day Age: 29
Born: 10/2/73 in Long Branch, NJ
ML Seasons: 4
Pronunciation: SHOW-en-WEISS

Overall Statistics

	W	L	Pct.	ERA	G	GS	Sv	IP	H	BB	SO	HR	Ratio
'02	9	8	.529	4.88	54	15	1	118.0	119	49	65	17	1.42
Car.	27	30	.474	5.19	144	74	1	532.2	576	207	269	63	1.47

2002 Situational Stats

	W	L	ERA	Sv	IP		AB	H	HR	RBI	Avg
Home	5	2	3.41	1	60.2	LHB	129	26	5	13	.202
Road	4	6	6.44	0	57.1	RHB	321	93	12	53	.290
First Half	7	6	5.34	0	92.2	Sc Pos	114	29	2	45	.254
Scnd Half	2	2	3.20	1	25.1	Clutch	73	18	4	9	.247

2002 Season

By the end of June, when Scott Schoeneweis was 6-6 with a 5.38 ERA, the Angels had seen enough, sending him to the bullpen and replacing him in the rotation with rookie John Lackey. Schoeneweis flourished in relief, posting a 3.25 ERA overall, and a 1.71 ERA from July 17 on (after fellow lefty pen-mate Dennis Cook was diagnosed with a torn rotator cuff).

Pitching & Defense

Schoeneweis throws a lively if not overpowering fastball and a power sinker, more than enough to befuddle lefthanded hitters. He worked diligently on a change in spring training but failed to establish it as an effective pitch during the regular season, so his arsenal was better suited for a relief role. He is an excellent fielder but lacks an effective pickoff move, and sharp runners usually can pick a spot for a stolen base.

2003 Outlook

Schoeneweis last year accepted his relief role with grace, but he considers himself too young to settle into the role of lefthanded relief specialist and would prefer to start. However, the Angels believe he has found his niche, and so long as they're willing to risk annual arbitration hearings, they control his rights for the next three seasons.

Scott Spiezio

Position: 1B/3B
Bats: B **Throws:** R
Ht: 6' 2" **Wt:** 225

Opening Day Age: 30
Born: 9/21/72 in Joliet, IL
ML Seasons: 7
Pronunciation: SPEE-zio

Overall Statistics

	G	AB	R	H	D	T	HR	RBI	SB	BB	SO	Avg	OBP	Slg
'02	153	491	80	140	34	2	12	82	6	67	52	.285	.371	.436
Car.	774	2465	333	641	147	13	75	341	22	262	344	.260	.332	.422

2002 Situational Stats

	AB	H	HR	RBI	Avg		AB	H	HR	RBI	Avg
Home	251	70	7	39	.279	LHP	152	56	6	35	.368
Road	240	70	5	43	.292	RHP	339	84	6	47	.248
First Half	244	65	4	39	.266	Sc Pos	137	46	4	68	.336
Scnd Half	247	75	8	43	.304	Clutch	81	34	4	17	.420

2002 Season

Scott Spiezio was an overnight sensation last year. With Mo Vaughn gone, the Angels planned for Spiezio to share time at first base with Shawn Wooten, but Wooten missed the first three months after suffering an injury in spring training. By the time he returned, first base belonged to Spiezio. He drove in 33 runs over the final two months of the regular season and 19 more in the playoffs, tying a postseason record.

Hitting, Baserunning & Defense

Spiezio would not fit on a team that needed a power-hitting first baseman. But he flourished within an Angels lineup that allowed him to bat seventh and play to his strengths in making contact and reaching base. He walked more than he struck out, and although his track record suggested he could not hit lefthanders, he hit .368 against them, ranking second in the league. Spiezio played Gold Glove-caliber defense at first base and filled in ably at third base and in the outfield. He is not here for his speed.

2003 Outlook

First base is his. For the first time since 1997, when the Oakland Athletics asked Spiezio whether he could play second base and he fibbed and said yes, he has an everyday job.

Ben Weber

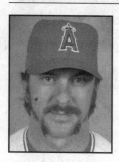

Position: RP
Bats: R **Throws:** R
Ht: 6' 4" **Wt:** 210

Opening Day Age: 33
Born: 11/17/69 in Port Arthur, TX
ML Seasons: 3
Pronunciation: WEBB-er

Overall Statistics

	W	L	Pct.	ERA	G	GS	Sv	IP	H	BB	SO	HR	Ratio
'02	7	2	.778	2.54	63	0	7	78.0	70	22	43	4	1.18
Car.	14	5	.737	3.41	138	0	7	169.0	164	59	97	8	1.32

2002 Situational Stats

	W	L	ERA	Sv	IP		AB	H	HR	RBI	Avg
Home	3	2	2.79	5	42.0	LHB	103	25	1	13	.243
Road	4	0	2.25	2	36.0	RHB	178	45	3	15	.253
First Half	4	2	3.07	1	41.0	Sc Pos	67	14	0	20	.209
Scnd Half	3	0	1.95	6	37.0	Clutch	159	42	3	19	.264

2002 Season

For the second consecutive season, the Angels found Ben Weber to be a useful and versatile reliever. He bettered his rookie season of 2001 with a 7-2 record, seven saves and a 2.54 ERA in 2002. In the absence of closer Troy Percival, Weber converted all four of his save opportunities. After a rocky start, he went 6-0 with a 1.96 ERA over his final 52 appearances.

Pitching & Defense

Weber thrives on movement—his own and that of his pitches. Hitters unfamiliar with his wild delivery, with head shaking and elbows and legs flying, can lose the ball for a split second. His fastball hits the low 90s, but he survives by keeping the ball down and inducing double plays. Despite the motion in his delivery, Weber is solid in the field and was perfect in 19 chances last year. He does not pay much attention to the running game.

2003 Outlook

This season is the final one before Weber is eligible for a hefty raise via salary arbitration. The Angels have righthanded relievers aplenty, none of whom will be arbitration-eligible next winter, so they might find room within their budget to keep Weber only if he delivers another solid campaign.

Shawn Wooten

Position: DH/1B
Bats: R **Throws:** R
Ht: 5'10" **Wt:** 225

Opening Day Age: 30
Born: 7/24/72 in Glendora, CA
ML Seasons: 3

Overall Statistics

	G	AB	R	H	D	T	HR	RBI	SB	BB	SO	Avg	OBP	Slg
'02	49	113	13	33	8	0	3	19	2	6	24	.292	.331	.442
Car.	135	343	39	107	17	1	11	52	4	11	66	.312	.337	.464

2002 Situational Stats

	AB	H	HR	RBI	Avg		AB	H	HR	RBI	Avg
Home	54	19	2	11	.352	LHP	71	20	3	14	.282
Road	59	14	1	8	.237	RHP	42	13	0	5	.310
First Half	0	0	0	0	–	Sc Pos	28	10	1	15	.357
Scnd Half	113	33	3	19	.292	Clutch	24	5	0	3	.208

2002 Season

Shawn Wooten missed the final month of the 2001 season because of wrist surgery, and he missed the first three months of 2002 because of a spring injury that required thumb surgery. Then, on rehabilitation for the thumb injury, he strained a muscle in his side. In the first game after the All-Star break, he finally made his season debut. . . and he homered. He hit .292 during the regular season and .474 in postseason play.

Hitting, Baserunning & Defense

Wooten is here to hit, period. He has impressive bat speed, he can drive a pitch against either righthanders or lefties, and he hit .357 with men in scoring position. He can play first base, and in a pinch can play third base or catch, but he is best suited to DH. He is not a factor on the bases.

2003 Outlook

Wooten figures to return as the righthanded designated hitter, but that role could expand should the Angels trade Brad Fullmer, the lefthanded half of that platoon. The Angels have searched for years for a powerful bat off the bench, however. Wooten's career pinch-hitting average is .368 (7-for-19), and that also could become his role over the next few years.

Other Anaheim Angels

Clay Bellinger (Pos: 1B, **Age**: 34, **Bats**: R)

	G	AB	R	H	D	T	HR	RBI	SB	BB	SO	Avg	OBP	Slg
'02	2	1	0	0	0	0	0	0	0	0	1	.000	.000	.000
Car.	183	311	57	60	11	3	12	35	7	22	82	.193	.257	.363

Bellinger has shown a lack of patience at nearly every level in the professional ranks. He spent most of 2002 in Triple-A, batting .256 with 87 strikeouts in 89 games. Comparably, he walked 13 times. 2003 Outlook: C

Mickey Callaway (Pos: RHP, **Age**: 27)

	W	L	Pct.	ERA	G	GS	Sv	IP	H	BB	SO	HR	Ratio
'02	2	1	.667	4.19	6	6	0	34.1	31	11	23	4	1.22
Car.	3	3	.500	5.52	13	10	0	58.2	64	27	36	8	1.55

Callaway, who was acquired from the Devil Rays in a trade last winter, spent most of 2002 in Triple-A, going 9-2 with a 1.68 ERA in 17 games. He could battle for a spot in the Angels' rotation. 2003 Outlook: C

Dennis Cook (Pos: LHP, **Age**: 40)

	W	L	Pct.	ERA	G	GS	Sv	IP	H	BB	SO	HR	Ratio
'02	1	1	.500	3.38	37	0	0	24.0	21	10	13	2	1.29
Car.	64	46	.582	3.91	665	71	9	1011.2	950	390	739	130	1.32

After posting a 2.86 ERA in 33 games, Cook missed extended time with a tear in the labrum of his pitching shoulder. Instead of surgery, he decided on rehab. He posted a 9.00 ERA after his return, underwent surgery after the season and is contemplating retirement. 2003 Outlook: C

Jeff DaVanon (Pos: CF, **Age**: 29, **Bats**: B)

	G	AB	R	H	D	T	HR	RBI	SB	BB	SO	Avg	OBP	Slg
'02	16	30	3	5	3	0	1	4	1	2	6	.167	.219	.367
Car.	63	138	14	26	5	2	7	17	2	15	42	.188	.266	.406

DaVanon has posted impressive numbers on the minor league level, batting .335 in 317 games over the past five seasons. However, he has been unable to replicate those stats in the majors. 2003 Outlook: C

Sal Fasano (Pos: C, **Age**: 31, **Bats**: R)

	G	AB	R	H	D	T	HR	RBI	SB	BB	SO	Avg	OBP	Slg
'02	2	1	0	0	0	0	0	0	0	0	1	.000	.000	.000
Car.	254	669	89	144	27	0	30	95	2	51	189	.215	.300	.390

Fasano has spent time in six different organizations since the start of the 2001 season. He was released by Anaheim in November, but should sign a minor league deal with another team before spring training. 2003 Outlook: C

Chone Figgins (Pos: 2B, **Age**: 25, **Bats**: B)

	G	AB	R	H	D	T	HR	RBI	SB	BB	SO	Avg	OBP	Slg
'02	15	12	6	2	1	0	0	1	2	0	5	.167	.167	.250
Car.	15	12	6	2	1	0	0	1	2	0	5	.167	.167	.250

Figgins enjoyed his best season as a professional last season. In 125 games in Triple-A, he set career highs with a .305 batting average, seven homers, 62 RBI, 18 triples and 39 stolen bases. 2003 Outlook: C

Benji Gil (Pos: 2B/SS, **Age**: 30, **Bats**: R)

	G	AB	R	H	D	T	HR	RBI	SB	BB	SO	Avg	OBP	Slg
'02	61	130	11	37	8	1	3	20	2	5	33	.285	.307	.431
Car.	542	1485	146	357	70	11	31	162	19	98	415	.240	.288	.365

Gil has made a habit of playing well early before tailing off after the All-Star break. He hit .324 through mid-July, but struggled thereafter, batting just .242. A similar role is expected in 2003. 2003 Outlook: B

Al Levine (Pos: RHP, **Age**: 34)

	W	L	Pct.	ERA	G	GS	Sv	IP	H	BB	SO	HR	Ratio
'02	4	4	.500	4.24	52	0	5	63.2	61	34	40	8	1.49
Car.	18	23	.439	3.91	288	7	9	423.1	431	179	212	49	1.44

After a career year in 2001, Levine's numbers slipped in 2002, mainly because of a battle with shoulder tendinitis. Still, he topped 50 appearances for the fourth straight year. 2003 Outlook: B

Mark Lukasiewicz (Pos: LHP, **Age**: 30)

	W	L	Pct.	ERA	G	GS	Sv	IP	H	BB	SO	HR	Ratio
'02	2	0	1.000	3.86	17	0	0	14.0	17	9	15	0	1.86
Car.	2	2	.500	5.20	41	0	0	36.1	38	18	40	6	1.54

The Angels have given Lukasiewicz a taste of the majors each of the last two seasons. If Anaheim is in need of a lefthander in the bullpen this spring, he has a good shot at making the team. 2003 Outlook: C

Jose Molina (Pos: C, **Age**: 27, **Bats**: R)

	G	AB	R	H	D	T	HR	RBI	SB	BB	SO	Avg	OBP	Slg
'02	29	70	5	19	3	0	0	5	0	5	15	.271	.312	.314
Car.	54	126	16	34	7	0	2	10	0	10	27	.270	.319	.373

Molina doesn't possess much power, but he has improved his consistency, batting better than .300 in the minors the last two seasons. He likely will back up his brother Bengie at catcher this year. 2003 Outlook: C

Jose Nieves (Pos: 2B/SS, **Age**: 27, **Bats**: R)

	G	AB	R	H	D	T	HR	RBI	SB	BB	SO	Avg	OBP	Slg
'02	45	97	17	28	2	0	0	6	1	2	14	.289	.303	.309
Car.	212	530	55	128	20	5	9	51	2	23	102	.242	.278	.349

Because of his inconsistency both offensively and defensively, Nieves has found it difficult to stick in the major leagues. He committed seven errors in 37 games in the field last season. 2003 Outlook: C

Lou Pote (Pos: RHP, **Age**: 31)

	W	L	Pct.	ERA	G	GS	Sv	IP	H	BB	SO	HR	Ratio
'02	0	2	.000	3.22	31	0	0	50.1	33	26	32	7	1.17
Car.	4	4	.500	3.49	127	2	6	216.2	196	87	162	23	1.31

Pote is a versatile pitcher, but has struggled with locating his fastball. The Angels talked of Pote joining the rotation and used him exclusively as a starter in Triple-A last season. 2003 Outlook: C

Julio Ramirez (**Pos**: CF, **Age**: 25, **Bats**: R)

	G	AB	R	H	D	T	HR	RBI	SB	BB	SO	Avg	OBP	Slg
'02	29	32	6	9	0	1	1	7	0	2	14	.281	.343	.438
Car.	66	90	11	15	1	1	1	10	2	5	35	.167	.219	.233

Ramirez had a chance to spend most of the 2002 season with the Angels, but missed nearly three months with a strained calf. He was released in November and re-signed in December. 2003 Outlook: C

Scot Shields (**Pos**: RHP, **Age**: 27)

	W	L	Pct.	ERA	G	GS	Sv	IP	H	BB	SO	HR	Ratio
'02	5	3	.625	2.20	29	1	0	49.0	31	21	30	4	1.06
Car.	5	3	.625	1.80	37	1	0	60.0	39	28	37	4	1.12

Shields was called up in June and spent the rest of the season on the Angels' roster. After posting a 4.09 ERA in his first six games, Shields settled down, finishing the season with a 2.20 ERA. 2003 Outlook: C

Donne Wall (**Pos**: RHP, **Age**: 35)

	W	L	Pct.	ERA	G	GS	Sv	IP	H	BB	SO	HR	Ratio
'02	0	0	–	6.43	17	0	0	21.0	17	7	13	3	1.14
Car.	31	28	.525	4.20	234	37	2	474.0	468	155	322	62	1.31

Wall battled arm tightness and struggled in 17 appearances with Anaheim last season. He was released in June before signing a minor league deal with Colorado. 2003 Outlook: C

Matt Wise (**Pos**: RHP, **Age**: 27)

	W	L	Pct.	ERA	G	GS	Sv	IP	H	BB	SO	HR	Ratio
'02	0	0	–	3.24	7	0	0	8.1	7	1	6	0	0.96
Car.	4	7	.364	4.74	26	15	0	95.0	94	32	76	18	1.33

Over his last two seasons in Triple-A, Wise has struck out 187 batters in 201.1 innings, while walking just 32. A starter nearly all of his career, Wise made seven relief appearances with Anaheim in 2002. 2003 Outlook: C

Anaheim Angels Minor League Prospects

Organization Overview:

The farm system paid off in the 2002 postseason, as Francisco Rodriguez mowed down hitters and John Lackey won Game 7 of the World Series. Winning it all tends to keep the major league incumbents in place. Still, outfielder Robb Quinlan may make the 2003 roster. Others, including Alfredo Amezaga, Nathan Haynes, Bobby Jenks and Chris Bootcheck, will be knocking on the door soon. Other key players in Anaheim's future passed through Class-A Cedar Rapids in 2002. Keep an eye on Jeff Mathis, Casey Kotchman, Dallas McPherson and hurlers Johan Santana, Joe Saunders, Steve Shell, Joe Torres and Jake Woods.

Alfredo Amezaga

Position: SS **Opening Day Age:** 25
Bats: B **Throws:** R **Born:** 1/16/78 in
Ht: 5' 10" **Wt:** 165 Obregon, Mexico

Recent Statistics

	G	AB	R	H	D	T	HR	RBI	SB	BB	SO	Avg
2002 AAA Salt Lake	128	518	77	130	25	7	6	51	23	45	100	.251
2002 AL Anaheim	12	13	3	7	2	0	0	2	1	0	1	.538

This junior college vet, drafted in 1999, is a polished defensive player. Amezaga made good contact and controlled the strike zone early in his career, and his plate discipline didn't suffer when he took up switch-hitting in 2000. But he's hit a wall offensively since reaching Triple-A Salt Lake in 2001. His plate discipline needs more work, and although he's a fairly consistent hitter from the right side, he isn't as effective making adjustments from the left side. With good hands, speed and instincts, Amezaga can keep his team in games with his defense. He needs to generate strikeout and walk totals more in line with good little-ball guys if he's going to become a productive big leaguer.

Chris Bootcheck

Position: P **Opening Day Age:** 24
Bats: R **Throws:** R **Born:** 10/24/78 in
Ht: 6' 5" **Wt:** 205 Laporte, IN

Recent Statistics

	W	L	ERA	G	GS	Sv	IP	H	R	BB	SO	HR
2001 A Rancho Cuca	8	4	3.93	15	14	0	87.0	84	45	23	86	11
2001 AA Arkansas	3	3	5.45	6	6	0	36.1	39	25	11	22	3
2002 AA Arkansas	8	7	4.81	19	19	0	116.0	130	68	35	90	11
2002 AAA Salt Lake	4	3	3.88	9	9	0	58.0	64	29	16	38	5

One of two first-round picks in 2000, Bootcheck signed too late to play until 2001. A slow start and shoulder tendinitis compromised his pro debut, but he heated up in the summer months and earned a promotion to Double-A Arkansas. In 2002 he split time between Arkansas and Triple-A Salt Lake, going 12-10 with a 4.50 ERA. He often fell victim to one bad inning, usually early in the game, but he was a better pitcher in the second half at Salt Lake. Bootcheck improved at adjusting to the high minors' better hitters, and he was more confident in a changeup that has lagged behind his impressive low-90s sinker and cut fastball. He experienced some forearm soreness in the Arizona Fall League, but he should be ready to go in the spring.

Rich Fischer

Position: P **Opening Day Age:** 22
Bats: R **Throws:** R **Born:** 10/21/80 in
Ht: 6' 3" **Wt:** 180 Fontana, CA

Recent Statistics

	W	L	ERA	G	GS	Sv	IP	H	R	BB	SO	HR
2001 A Cedar Rapds	9	7	4.20	20	20	0	130.2	131	73	33	97	8
2002 A Rancho Cuca	7	8	3.50	19	19	0	131.0	118	61	29	138	14
2002 AA Arkansas	1	3	4.23	7	7	0	44.2	40	22	10	36	4

A junior college shortstop, Fischer was moved to the mound when the Angels drafted him as a 21st-rounder in 2000. Reaching Double-A ball in his third pro season, he's advanced more rapidly than expected, in part because he's a mentally tough kid who always competes and doesn't give in to hitters. Fischer throws a 92-95 MPH fastball and a decent slider, pitches that he can throw consistently for strikes. He has a feel for the changeup, but it's not as far along. A better changeup is needed to counter lefthanded hitters. Fischer, who worked 175.2 innings in 2002, experienced some shoulder stiffness late in the year, but he is expected to be ready for spring training.

Nathan Haynes

Position: OF **Opening Day Age:** 23
Bats: L **Throws:** L **Born:** 9/7/79 in Oakland,
Ht: 5' 9" **Wt:** 170 CA

Recent Statistics

	G	AB	R	H	D	T	HR	RBI	SB	BB	SO	Avg
2001 AA Arkansas	79	316	49	98	11	5	5	23	33	32	65	.310
2002 A Rancho Cuca	11	50	6	14	0	0	0	2	6	4	8	.280
2002 AAA Salt Lake	67	283	37	80	14	6	2	12	10	12	53	.283

Drafted in 1997, Haynes maximized his above-average speed at two high Class-A stops in '99 by shortening his swing, hitting the ball on the ground more and drawing more walks. Since then, he's struggled with injuries and being effective with his little-ball skills. An assortment of injuries plagued him in 2000, including a bad right wrist, and he had minor knee surgery before the 2001 season. Last year, Haynes tore a thumb ligament early in the spring and didn't play until June. That set him back in his first exposure to Triple-A ball, and it took him time to get back on track. Defensively, Haynes combines speed and good instincts to show terrific range in center. Just 23, he still has time to fine-tune his little-ball skills and plate patience for the majors.

Bobby Jenks

Position: P
Bats: R **Throws:** R
Ht: 6' 3" **Wt:** 240

Opening Day Age: 22
Born: 3/14/81 in Mission Hills, CA

Recent Statistics

		W	L	ERA	G	GS	Sv	IP	H	R	BB	SO	HR
2001 A Cedar Rapds		3	7	5.27	21	21	0	99.0	90	74	64	98	10
2001 AA Arkansas		1	0	3.60	2	2	0	10.0	8	5	5	10	0
2002 AA Arkansas		3	6	4.66	10	10	0	58.0	49	34	44	58	2
2002 A Rancho Cuca		3	5	4.82	11	10	0	65.1	50	42	46	64	4

A 2000 pick, Jenks arrived with an explosive mid-90s fastball, hard curve and little else. Throwing strikes and developing an offspeed pitch have proved difficult. Makeup issues also have slowed his development. Jenks started last season at Double-A Arkansas, but he was suspended in May for a rules violation, and then demoted to high Class-A Rancho Cucamonga. After an inconsistent season, Jenks rebounded in the Arizona Fall League. His curve was a phenomenal strikeout pitch, because he could throw it for strikes and he threw his changeup with more confidence. If he can learn to command his fastball, which now approaches 100 MPH, Jenks will be a big league staff ace or closer.

Casey Kotchman

Position: 1B
Bats: L **Throws:** L
Ht: 6' 3" **Wt:** 210

Opening Day Age: 20
Born: 2/22/83 in St. Petersburg, FL

Recent Statistics

		G	AB	R	H	D	T	HR	RBI	SB	BB	SO	Avg
2001 R Angels		4	15	5	9	1	0	1	5	0	3	2	.600
2001 R Provo		7	22	6	11	3	0	0	7	0	2	0	.500
2002 A Cedar Rapds		81	288	42	81	30	1	5	50	2	48	37	.281

Only health issues have concerned the Angels about Kotchman, their first-round pick in 2001. He adjusted quickly to the wood bat and hit .541 in 37 Rookie-level at-bats before hyperextending his right forearm on a backswing and missing the rest of the season. Last summer he missed several weeks after jamming his left wrist during an awkward slide in early July. Otherwise, it's all good news about the sweet-swinging, lefthanded-hitting first baseman. Eventually, Kotchman should generate impressive power. Already he has a career .411 OBP because of sound plate patience that has produced more walks than strikeouts as a pro.

Jeff Mathis

Position: C
Bats: R **Throws:** R
Ht: 6' 0" **Wt:** 180

Opening Day Age: 20
Born: 3/31/83 in Marianna, FL

Recent Statistics

		G	AB	R	H	D	T	HR	RBI	SB	BB	SO	Avg
2001 R Angels		7	23	1	7	1	0	0	3	0	2	4	.304
2001 R Provo		22	77	14	23	6	3	0	18	1	11	13	.299
2002 A Cedar Rapds		128	491	75	141	41	3	10	73	7	40	75	.287

Mathis was destined for Florida State before going in the first round of the 2001 draft. He enjoyed a terrific season in the Class-A Midwest League in 2002, producing a team-record 41 doubles and 10 homers with his gap power at Cedar Rapids. Defensively, Mathis is an advanced receiver with a strong arm that ranked among the Midwest League's best at throwing out basestealers. He's also a quiet leader who works hard. He was struck in the eye by a pitch late in the year, but he'll be ready for 2003.

Robb Quinlan

Position: 1B
Bats: R **Throws:** R
Ht: 6' 1" **Wt:** 195

Opening Day Age: 26
Born: 3/17/77 in St. Paul, MN

Recent Statistics

		G	AB	R	H	D	T	HR	RBI	SB	BB	SO	Avg
2001 AA Arkansas		129	492	82	145	33	7	14	79	0	53	84	.295
2002 AAA Salt Lake		136	528	95	176	31	13	20	112	8	41	93	.333

Quinlan's never made prospect lists. Yet, he's hit every step of the way since the Angels drafted him from Minnesota in 1999. And the raw numbers have been better at each level, culminating in an MVP season in the Triple-A Pacific Coast League in 2002. He got off to a slow start at Salt Lake, but by May he was driving the ball into the gaps for doubles and triples, alternately pulling pitches and spraying them to right. His bat will decide his major league fate. He doesn't have the power to bop, but Quinlan's climb should be a reminder not to count him out of a big league role. Defensively, he's limited to first base and the corner-outfield spots. His arm is just adequate, so he may be better suited to left field. He may join the Angels as a bench player.

Others to Watch

Even with Casey Kotchman and Jeff Mathis on the Class-A Cedar Rapids roster, third baseman **Dallas McPherson** (22) led the club in walks, homers and RBI. Like Mathis, he's a disciplined worker. He generated lots of doubles, and more power is likely as he plays more. He's also a solid fielder. . . Righthander **Johan Santana** (19) has been a strikeout machine in his first two minor league seasons, averaging more than one per inning with a mid-90s fastball and slider. The sky's the limit for this teenager, who now stands 6-foot-5 and was 14-8 (4.16) at Class-A Cedar Rapids. . . Selected 12th overall in last summer's draft, southpaw **Joe Saunders** (21) showed good command in the Rookie-level Pioneer League, where he worked on a slider that was a decent complement to a 90-MPH fastball and changeup when he reached Class-A Cedar Rapids. He was dominant at times after the promotion. . . . Two promising lefties in the system, **Joe Torres** (20) and **Jake Woods** (21), also were at Cedar Rapids in 2002. Woods was 10-5 (3.05) and moved ahead of Torres developmentally. Torres still is trying to recover his velocity from an ill-advised offseason weightlifting program a year ago that left him too bulky. His curve still is his best pitch, and he was 11-8 (3.52) without having his best stuff.

Oriole Park at Camden Yards

Offense

The Baltimore front office abandoned its one-year experiment with a more pitcher-friendly ballpark and returned Oriole Park at Camden Yards to its 2000 dimensions. The results were a ballpark that saw noteworthy increases in its home-run indices in 2002. Otherwise, Camden Yards was well below average in yielding doubles, at the bottom of the American League in triples, and below league average in runs allowed. The 25-foot wall in right field provides pitchers with some help in reducing home runs hit to right-center field.

Defense

Baltimore continues to field an infield that has average range, especially up the middle, and the infield grass is kept taller to slow groundballs heading to the outfield. The low output of doubles and triples indicates that Camden Yards is an easy ballpark to play for most outfielders. The foul territory is about average for the major leagues.

Who It Helps the Most

The Orioles hit for more power at Camden Yards. Baltimore pitchers have posted a lower ERA by roughly three-quarters of a run at home in each of the past two years. Jay Gibbons found Camden Yards more to his liking, stroking 17 of his 28 home runs there. In his first season back after major elbow surgery, Scott Erickson was much more effective at home.

Who It Hurts the Most

Chris Singleton and Melvin Mora hit better on the road. Starter Sidney Ponson allowed 19 of his 26 home runs at home, and his ERA away from Camden Yards was 0.66 better than at home in 2002. Southpaw Buddy Groom posted a road ERA of more than two runs better on the road than at home.

Rookies & Newcomers

Serious arm injuries have stalled the anticipated arrival of a couple of top-flight pitching prospects, and position prospects who can help are at least a year away. The Orioles are looking at power hitters in the free-agent market, and the park should look inviting to them.

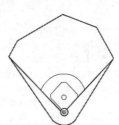

Dimensions: LF-333, LCF-364, CF-400, RCF-373, RF-318

Capacity: 48,190

Elevation: 20 feet

Surface: Grass

Foul Territory: Average

Park Factors

2002 Season

	Home Games Orioles	Opp	Total	Away Games Orioles	Opp	Total	Index
G	72	72	144	72	72	144	
Avg	.246	.260	.253	.247	.280	.263	96
AB	2406	2543	4949	2483	2461	4944	100
R	292	331	623	300	374	674	92
H	592	661	1253	614	688	1302	96
2B	111	109	220	160	129	289	76
3B	10	5	15	12	19	31	48
HR	81	101	182	66	91	157	116
BB	207	241	448	195	242	437	102
SO	425	426	851	432	448	880	97
E	42	54	96	36	38	74	130
E-Infield	33	46	79	29	32	61	130
LHB-Avg	.253	.248	.250	.261	.281	.273	92
LHB-HR	30	47	77	20	49	69	109
RHB-Avg	.243	.272	.256	.241	.279	.257	99
RHB-HR	51	54	105	46	42	88	121

2001 Season

	Home Games Orioles	Opp	Total	Away Games Orioles	Opp	Total	Index
G	71	71	142	73	73	146	
Avg	.242	.260	.252	.257	.272	.265	95
AB	2306	2505	4811	2567	2464	5031	98
R	267	351	618	349	373	722	88
H	558	652	1210	661	671	1332	93
2B	104	128	232	139	152	291	83
3B	11	10	21	10	17	27	81
HR	50	87	137	63	83	146	98
BB	217	221	438	239	233	472	97
SO	421	432	853	451	409	860	104
E	47	48	95	56	52	108	90
E-Infield	45	42	87	50	43	93	96
LHB-Avg	.213	.259	.239	.256	.283	.271	88
LHB-HR	24	40	64	23	46	69	96
RHB-Avg	.259	.262	.260	.259	.263	.260	100
RHB-HR	26	47	73	40	37	77	100

2002 Rankings (American League)

- Highest error factor
- Highest infield-error factor
- Lowest triple factor
- Lowest LHB batting-average factor
- Second-lowest batting-average factor
- Second-lowest double factor
- Third-lowest run factor

Mike Hargrove

2002 Season

The Orioles began the 2002 season playing close to .500 baseball in April and showing signs of improvement. June was the Orioles' best month, as they finished 14-13 before slipping a bit in July and August. For the second year in a row, Mike Hargrove had to endure an awful month that side-tracked the entire season. This time it was September, when Baltimore won only four games. Up until their collapse in September, the Orioles played solid baseball.

Offense

The Orioles finished ninth in the American League in homers, so Hargrove's managerial style requires stealing the extra base and employing the hit-and-run whenever he can. The Orioles finished fourth in both stolen bases and hit-and-run attempts in the AL. Still, Hargrove's team could muster only a 13th-place finish in runs scored, in part because the lineup fails to draw walks, finishing barely better than .300 in on-base percentage. Hargrove continually shuffles players in and out of the lineup looking for the right combinations. He also plays young players and gets the most out of the limited talent on his roster.

Pitching & Defense

Hargrove used the pitchout 41 times, the second-highest total in the AL, as he aggressively attempts to keep the opponents' running game in check. He prefers to leave his regulars in the game rather than substitute defensively late in contests. The improved Baltimore bullpen, which posted a 3.49 ERA last season, gave Hargrove more confidence in his pitching staff late in games. The Orioles lack a deep starting rotation, and Hargrove rarely had the luxury of leaving his starters in the game past the 100-pitch level.

2003 Outlook

If the Orioles of April-August in 2002 show up this season, Baltimore should be a .500 team. If they play like the team that finished 4-24 in September, Hargrove and the O's are in for a very long season. Baltimore's farm system isn't on the verge of producing any high-quality prospects, making the near future bleak for any hopes of significant improvement.

Born: 10/26/49 in Perryton, TX

Playing Experience: 1974-1985, Tex, SD, Cle

Managerial Experience: 12 seasons

Manager Statistics

Year	Team, Lg	W	L	Pct	GB	Finish
2002	Baltimore, AL	67	95	.414	36.5	4th East
12 Seasons		925	872	.515	–	–

2002 Starting Pitchers by Days Rest

	<=3	4	5	6+
Orioles Starts	0	72	56	23
Orioles ERA	–	4.76	4.95	5.35
AL Avg Starts	1	83	44	24
AL ERA	7.15	4.59	4.27	5.03

2002 Situational Stats

	Mike Hargrove	AL Average
Hit & Run Success %	33.3	36.0
Stolen Base Success %	69.6	68.1
Platoon Pct.	51.8	58.9
Defensive Subs	19	23
High-Pitch Outings	7	6
Quick/Slow Hooks	17/8	19/14
Sacrifice Attempts	56	53

2002 Rankings (American League)

- 2nd in pitchouts (41)
- 3rd in steals of second base (93), steals of third base (17), fewest caught stealings of third base (3), squeeze plays (5) and pitchouts with a runner moving (7)

Tony Batista

2002 Season

A more mature Tony Batista posted or tied his second-highest single-season totals in home runs, runs scored and at-bats, as he became an everyday fixture in his first full year with the Orioles. He also set career highs in walks, doubles and hit-by-pitch (11). Still, Batista continued a three-year trend of hitting well for half a season, before faltering at the plate after the All-Star break.

Hitting

Batista's wide-open stance is one of the most unorthodox in the majors, with his left foot facing toward third base and three-quarters of his body facing the pitcher before he starts his swing by striding toward the mound and assuming a more natural hitting position. While this allows Batista to see inside pitches better, his ability to reach some outside pitches, especially slow breaking balls, is restricted. Also, his long, looping swing makes him more susceptible to prolonged slumps and generates a high number of popups and flyballs. The vast majority of his power continues to come against righthanders.

Baserunning & Defense

While he's just three seasons removed from playing shortstop, Batista isn't displaying as much range at third base as he had in the past couple of seasons. His throws, especially from behind the third-base bag, can be looping and slow getting to first base. He retains the middle-infield quickness that allows him to charge bunts and slow hoppers, and he often makes the play look routine. His quick first step does not translate into stolen bases, and while he's an intelligent baserunner, he can't score from first unless it's on a triple.

2003 Outlook

Batista enters the last year of a four-year, $16 million contract he signed with the Blue Jays, and he should be motivated to post a career year that is somewhere between his 2002 campaign and his .263-41-114 season in 2000. At age 29, Batista is entering the prime of his career, especially in regards to power and his ability to garner a few extra walks.

Position: 3B
Bats: R **Throws:** R
Ht: 6' 0" **Wt:** 205

Opening Day Age: 29
Born: 12/9/73 in Puerto Plata, DR
ML Seasons: 7
Pronunciation: bah-TEESE-tah

Overall Statistics

	G	AB	R	H	D	T	HR	RBI	SB	BB	SO	Avg	OBP	Slg
'02	161	615	90	150	36	1	31	87	5	50	107	.244	.309	.457
Car.	861	3052	439	784	161	14	156	472	29	206	569	.257	.308	.472

Where He Hits the Ball

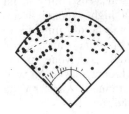
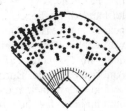

Vs. LHP   **Vs. RHP**

2002 Situational Stats

	AB	H	HR	RBI	Avg		AB	H	HR	RBI	Avg
Home	301	76	14	41	.252	LHP	158	37	3	11	.234
Road	314	74	17	46	.236	RHP	457	113	28	76	.247
First Half	316	85	19	53	.269	Sc Pos	155	35	6	56	.226
Scnd Half	299	65	12	34	.217	Clutch	100	25	2	14	.250

2002 Rankings (American League)

- 3rd in lowest groundball-flyball ratio (0.5) and lowest cleanup slugging percentage (.399)
- 4th in fielding percentage at third base (.962)
- 5th in games played
- 6th in errors at third base (16)
- 7th in pitches seen (2,723) and lowest batting average
- Led the Orioles in home runs, at-bats, runs scored, hits, singles, doubles, total bases (281), RBI, intentional walks (9), pitches seen (2,723), plate appearances (682), games played and lowest percentage of swings on the first pitch (16.8)
- Led AL third basemen in home runs

Mike Bordick

2002 Season

Mike Bordick struggled with a weakened right shoulder last spring, the result of surgery in August 2001, but he rebounded in early May to play well until he fractured his right kneecap in July. When he returned in August, Bordick struggled at the plate, but he didn't commit an error after April 10 and set the all-time record for errorless chances (542 and counting) and games (110) by a shortstop.

Hitting

Bordick's shoulder problems reduced some of the gap power in his swing, and he wasn't nearly as effective at pulling inside pitches to left field as he had been in previous seasons. His ability to hit lefthanded pitchers for a high average disappeared last season. One area he did improve in was coaxing a walk at opportune times, going deep in the count as well as anyone in the American League. Bordick continues to hit well behind the runner, move runners over with the bunt and execute the hit-and-run.

Baserunning & Defense

The knee and shoulder woes that Bordick has battled the past couple of seasons have reduced his range in the field, and his throws aren't as strong as they were just a couple of seasons ago. Bordick isn't as adept at reaching groundballs up the middle as he has been in the past. While he still can make the throw from the shortstop hole, it's his vast knowledge of the hitters that allows him to be in the right position and remain a steady fielder. On the bases, he no longer is a consistent stolen-base threat.

2003 Outlook

Bordick's conditioning is well known, but Father Time is catching up to him in the form of knee and shoulder injuries. The Orioles were open to bringing him back for one more season, but they insisted on a dramatic pay cut and the two sides could not reach an agreement. Not offered salary arbitration, Bordick can't return until May 1. While he initially indicated that he would return only to play for Baltimore, he is looking for a starting job, or possibly a reserve role on a contender.

Position: SS
Bats: R **Throws:** R
Ht: 5'11" **Wt:** 175

Opening Day Age: 37
Born: 7/21/65 in Marquette, MI
ML Seasons: 13
Pronunciation: BOR-dick

Overall Statistics

	G	AB	R	H	D	T	HR	RBI	SB	BB	SO	Avg	OBP	Slg
'02	117	367	37	85	19	3	8	36	7	35	63	.232	.302	.365
Car.	1618	5427	637	1406	239	28	86	572	93	467	740	.259	.322	.361

Where He Hits the Ball

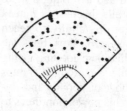
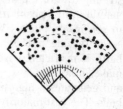

Vs. LHP   **Vs. RHP**

2002 Situational Stats

	AB	H	HR	RBI	Avg		AB	H	HR	RBI	Avg
Home	198	49	6	21	.247	LHP	110	26	3	6	.236
Road	169	36	2	15	.213	RHP	257	59	5	30	.230
First Half	244	58	3	21	.238	Sc Pos	82	19	3	28	.232
Scnd Half	123	27	5	15	.220	Clutch	59	11	0	3	.186

2002 Rankings (American League)

- 1st in fielding percentage at shortstop (.998)
- 3rd in lowest batting average on a 3-2 count (.114)
- Led the Orioles in most pitches seen per plate appearance (4.00), highest percentage of pitches taken (59.0) and batting average on an 0-2 count (.214)

Jeff Conine

2002 Season

After coming off one of the best seasons of his career, the Orioles signed Jeff Conine to a contract extension last winter as a reward. He caught fire in May, generating eight home runs before succumbing to a right hamstring injury in mid-June that plagued him for the remainder of the season. The injury reduced his power after the All-Star break and relegated him to day-to-day status for most of the second half.

Hitting

Conine has hit pitchers well from both sides of the plate, though he nicks southpaws for a slightly higher average and for much more power. He continues to be Baltimore's best hitter at going to right and right-center field, preferring to go with the pitch rather than pulling outside offerings. Conine continues to be one the American League's best at producing sacrifice flies and working the count to his benefit. His walk total declined last season, a strong indicator that he now approaches his at-bats as a run producer in the middle of the order.

Baserunning & Defense

Conine's reputation as a crafty basestealer continues late into his career, as he went the entire 2002 season without being thrown out. He rarely gets thrown out going from first to third, although he now is considered a station-to-station baserunner unless the ball is driven deep into the gap. Conine's glovework around the first-base bag is average, but he's comfortable charging bunts that are his responsibility. While he can play third and the corner-outfield spots, he's used almost exclusively now at first base. His throws across the diamond from first base are average but accurate.

2003 Outlook

The Orioles continue to look at Conine as a stabilizing influence and a middle-of-the-order hitter. He's a professional hitter who knows his limitations, but we've already seen the best he'll produce in a Baltimore uniform. He will see action mostly at first base this season, but his at-bats might be reduced slightly as the Orioles look to get the younger hitters more playing time.

Position: 1B
Bats: R **Throws:** R
Ht: 6' 1" **Wt:** 220

Opening Day Age: 36
Born: 6/27/66 in Tacoma, WA
ML Seasons: 12
Pronunciation: COH-nine

Overall Statistics

	G	AB	R	H	D	T	HR	RBI	SB	BB	SO	Avg	OBP	Slg
'02	116	451	44	123	26	4	15	63	8	25	66	.273	.307	.448
Car.	1361	4779	606	1375	255	25	161	757	35	468	861	.288	.350	.453

Where He Hits the Ball

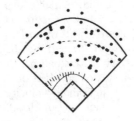
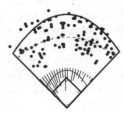

Vs. LHP   **Vs. RHP**

2002 Situational Stats

	AB	H	HR	RBI	Avg		AB	H	HR	RBI	Avg
Home	238	68	12	39	.286	LHP	113	33	6	20	.292
Road	213	55	3	24	.258	RHP	338	90	9	43	.266
First Half	256	67	10	45	.262	Sc Pos	110	27	5	47	.245
Scnd Half	195	56	5	18	.287	Clutch	82	26	2	7	.317

2002 Rankings (American League)

- 2nd in errors at first base (10)
- 4th in sacrifice flies (10)
- 7th in lowest cleanup slugging percentage (.464)
- Led the Orioles in sacrifice flies (10), batting average vs. lefthanded pitchers, cleanup slugging percentage (.464) and slugging percentage vs. lefthanded pitchers (.504)

Scott Erickson

2002 Season

Scott Erickson had Tommy John surgery in August 2000, costing him all of the 2001 season, but he was nearly ready by the start of 2002. Erickson initially strayed from using his trademark slider, but as he gained confidence and arm strength, he worked his former trademark pitch back into his repertoire. He finished with 28 starts but wasn't nearly the starter he was before the surgery. Personal problems became an issue during the second half, and the Orioles shut him down for the year at the end of August.

Pitching

Before having Tommy John surgery, Erickson relied heavily on a sharp-breaking slider and a two-seem fastball that had good sinking action on it. Last season, the sinking fastball still was effective, but a lack of arm strength strained out the pitch at times. The velocity on his fastball hasn't returned to his pre-injury levels of 90 MPH on a consistent basis. The decrease in both his velocity and pitch movement, plus a lack of command, have caused an increase in the number of home runs he allows. The high hit totals also indicate that Erickson is not all the way back yet.

Defense

Because of his lanky frame, Erickson does not get off the mound quickly, making him susceptible to slow rollers and bunts to his right. Overall, he fields his position adequately. His move to first base is deliberate, rarely catching a baserunner napping at first base. Erickson continues to struggle with a slide step, further making him easy to run on.

2003 Outlook

By the time he was shutdown last August, Erickson was pain-free and showing no ill signs from his elbow surgery. But not all of his velocity, pitch movement and command had returned to pre-surgery levels. After the season, Erickson was diagnosed with a partially torn labrum that will require rehabilitation to prepare him for 2003. No surgery is planned. If he is healthy in 2003, the Orioles would like to see him assist the young pitchers who are on the staff. How effective he'll be on the mound is very much in question.

Position: SP
Bats: R **Throws:** R
Ht: 6' 4" **Wt:** 230

Opening Day Age: 35
Born: 2/2/68 in Long Beach, CA
ML Seasons: 12

Overall Statistics

	W	L	Pct.	ERA	G	GS	Sv	IP	H	BB	SO	HR	Ratio
'02	5	12	.294	5.55	29	28	0	160.2	192	68	74	20	1.62
Car.	140	128	.522	4.51	355	350	0	2267.0	2473	813	1226	211	1.45

How Often He Throws Strikes

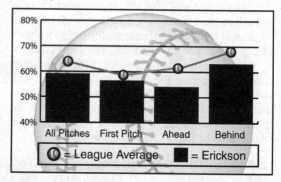

= League Average   ■ = Erickson

2002 Situational Stats

	W	L	ERA	Sv	IP		AB	H	HR	RBI	Avg
Home	4	5	4.60	0	92.0	LHB	342	104	13	54	.304
Road	1	7	6.82	0	68.2	RHB	291	88	7	45	.302
First Half	3	8	4.41	0	112.1	Sc Pos	171	52	8	79	.304
Scnd Half	2	4	8.19	0	48.1	Clutch	37	10	2	6	.270

2002 Rankings (American League)

- 4th in errors at pitcher (3) and highest batting average allowed vs. righthanded batters
- 6th in runners caught stealing (9) and lowest winning percentage
- 8th in losses and stolen bases allowed (17)
- 9th in complete games (3)
- 10th in walks allowed, GDPs induced (22) and highest ERA at home
- Led the Orioles in games started, complete games (3), hits allowed, walks allowed, hit batsmen (8), stolen bases allowed (17), runners caught stealing (9), GDPs induced (22) and highest groundball-flyball ratio allowed (2.3)

Jay Gibbons

Position: RF/1B/DH
Bats: L **Throws:** L
Ht: 6' 0" **Wt:** 200

Opening Day Age: 26
Born: 3/2/77 in
Oakland County, MI
ML Seasons: 2

2002 Season

Jay Gibbons provided the Orioles with some much-needed power in 2001, his first full season in the majors. But last season was in doubt early on after he was shut down during winter ball due to recurring pain in his right wrist. He battled the sore wrist most of the season, but was able to muster almost 500 at-bats before his campaign ended with his second surgery on his right wrist in two years.

Hitting

The lefty-swinging Gibbons struggles at times against southpaws and has yet to establish himself as a full-time hitter. His swing is quick and short, allowing him to pull inside pitches with power and not be tied up by fastballs. When his right wrist is healthy, he has the ability to take the outside pitch to the power alley in left field for a double or home run. Though he doesn't strike out at a high rate, Gibbons isn't one of the Orioles' better hit-and-run guys at this time of his career.

Baserunning & Defense

Gibbons began his career as an above-average first baseman in the Toronto system, but he has played more left field than first base since moving over to the Orioles. His range in left is limited, but he makes the plays on the balls that are hit within his reach. While his throws are accurate and improving from left, he still has a below-average corner-outfield arm. Because of his lack of foot speed, Gibbons is a station-to-station runner who struggles to score from second base unless the ball is hit into the gap. He's not a threat to steal bases.

2003 Outlook

In the minors, Gibbons was a .300-plus hitter who hit southpaws equally as well as righthanders. The Orioles expect him to start displaying those skills this year as he continues to split time between left field, first base and the designated-hitter spot. If his right wrist is healthy for the 2003 season, Gibbons should improve upon last summer's numbers.

Overall Statistics

	G	AB	R	H	D	T	HR	RBI	SB	BB	SO	Avg	OBP	Slg
'02	136	490	71	121	29	1	28	69	1	45	66	.247	.311	.482
Car.	209	715	98	174	39	1	43	105	1	62	105	.243	.307	.481

Where He Hits the Ball

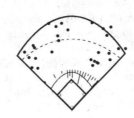 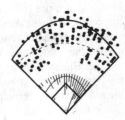

Vs. LHP   **Vs. RHP**

2002 Situational Stats

	AB	H	HR	RBI	Avg		AB	H	HR	RBI	Avg
Home	237	60	17	35	.253	LHP	98	23	2	10	.235
Road	253	61	11	34	.241	RHP	392	98	26	59	.250
First Half	263	67	14	36	.255	Sc Pos	105	28	5	42	.267
Scnd Half	227	54	14	33	.238	Clutch	74	19	4	10	.257

2002 Rankings (American League)

- 5th in highest percentage of swings on the first pitch (39.9)
- 6th in assists in right field (6)
- 9th in lowest batting average and lowest percentage of pitches taken (47.1)
- Led the Orioles in slugging percentage, HR frequency (17.5 ABs per HR) and slugging percentage vs. righthanded pitchers (.508)

Jerry Hairston Jr.

Great Range

2002 Season

Jerry Hairston rebounded somewhat from a very disappointing 2001 season, posting hitting percentages that more closely resembled his earlier campaigns. He began the season as the Orioles' leadoff hitter, but his .279 on-base percentage in the leadoff spot forced Baltimore to drop him to the bottom of the order. His 21 stolen bases led the team in 2002.

Hitting

Hairston hits the ball into the air too often, rather than on the ground where he can better utilize his natural speed. This flaw prevents him from solidifying his hold on the No. 1 spot in the lineup. He's much more productive batting ninth, where there is a lot less pressure on him. High pitches, especially fastballs, tend to give him trouble as he climbs the ladder instead of displaying plate discipline. Hairston continues to pull outside pitches too much but is showing improvement in that area. His swing remains compact, giving hope that it will level out in the future.

Baserunning & Defense

Hairston's stolen-base percentage greatly improved in 2002, as he learned to read pitchers better and not rely totally on his speed. His first step is one of the quicker ones in the majors, drawing a lot of attention from opposing pitchers. Hairston can score from second on most base hits to the outfield and goes from first to third with the best on the Orioles. At second base, his range isn't quite in the Robbie Alomar class, but he's still one of the American League's best. Hairston does a solid job of turning the double play and his footwork around second base is above average. He handles slowly hit balls in his direction without any problems.

2003 Outlook

While the Orioles need Hairston to step up as a leadoff hitter, all the evidence suggests he hits much better at the bottom of the order with less pressure. If he ever reduces the flyballs that his uppercut swing produces, Hairston will become one of the better-hitting second basemen in the AL.

Position: 2B
Bats: R **Throws:** R
Ht: 5'10" **Wt:** 175

Opening Day Age: 26
Born: 5/29/76 in Naperville, IL
ML Seasons: 5

Overall Statistics

	G	AB	R	H	D	T	HR	RBI	SB	BB	SO	Avg	OBP	Slg
'02	122	426	55	114	25	3	5	32	21	34	55	.268	.329	.376
Car.	386	1320	173	331	67	9	22	115	67	110	175	.251	.320	.365

Where He Hits the Ball

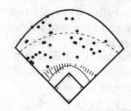 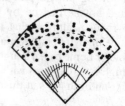

Vs. LHP   **Vs. RHP**

2002 Situational Stats

	AB	H	HR	RBI	Avg		AB	H	HR	RBI	Avg
Home	227	59	2	14	.260	LHP	118	31	1	4	.263
Road	199	55	3	18	.276	RHP	308	83	4	28	.269
First Half	175	41	1	14	.234	Sc Pos	99	26	0	26	.263
Scnd Half	251	73	4	18	.291	Clutch	81	20	1	5	.247

2002 Rankings (American League)

- 3rd in lowest percentage of swings that missed (9.4)
- 4th in bunts in play (25) and fielding percentage at second base (.982)
- Led the Orioles in sacrifice bunts (8), stolen bases, bunts in play (25), lowest percentage of swings that missed (9.4), highest percentage of swings put into play (48.4), highest percentage of extra bases taken as a runner (69.0) and batting average on the road

Jason Johnson

Position: SP
Bats: R **Throws:** R
Ht: 6' 6" **Wt:** 235

Opening Day Age: 29
Born: 10/27/73 in
Santa Barbara, CA
ML Seasons: 6

2002 Season

Jason Johnson had two trips to the disabled list, one for a fractured finger and the other for shoulder tendinitis. He never seemed to get his season on track. The Orioles planned on Johnson being the ace of the staff in 2002, a role he never assumed. One improvement that Johnson did show last season was better control. He threw strikes more often and avoided walking batters at key moments.

Pitching

Johnson's bread-and-butter pitch is a sharp-breaking curveball that is above average. He has improved his command of the pitch, and now he's able to throw it consistently when behind in the count. His four-seam fastball is improving but not yet an out pitch. Johnson's offspeed pitch is an average offering, and he lacks consistency with it. In the spring, Johnson experimented with a forkball as an alternative, but abandoned it when the injuries became a factor. Johnson does a decent job of setting up hitters, but his ability to work deep into games still is in question. His ability to keep the ball down in the strike zone has improved, and he now allows more groundballs than flyballs.

Defense

The 6-foot-6 Johnson has a deliberate move to the plate and is slow to cover bunts to either his right or left. His pickoff move and focus on baserunners have improved, and he has greatly decreased the number of stolen bases that he allows. He covers first base adequately when needed and his throws to the first-base bag are accurate.

2003 Outlook

If Johnson is completely healthy this season, the Orioles want him to surpass 200 innings and assume the role of staff ace. He mostly needs to improve his stamina, so he can pitch later into his starts. Johnson enters the last year of a two-year deal, and that should provide extra motivation. This should be the season he reaches 15 wins and establishes himself as one of the up-and-coming starters in the American League.

Overall Statistics

	W	L	Pct.	ERA	G	GS	Sv	IP	H	BB	SO	HR	Ratio
'02	5	14	.263	4.59	22	22	0	131.1	141	41	97	19	1.39
Car.	26	48	.351	5.14	117	101	0	616.1	658	262	400	95	1.49

How Often He Throws Strikes

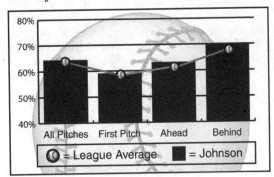

2002 Situational Stats

	W	L	ERA	Sv	IP		AB	H	HR	RBI	Avg
Home	1	8	4.50	0	62.0	LHB	249	65	7	30	.261
Road	4	6	4.67	0	69.1	RHB	262	76	12	32	.290
First Half	3	5	3.82	0	61.1	Sc Pos	120	31	4	41	.258
Scnd Half	2	9	5.27	0	70.0	Clutch	28	5	1	2	.179

2002 Rankings (American League)

- 3rd in lowest winning percentage
- 7th in losses
- Led the Orioles in losses, pickoff throws (70), highest strikeout-walk ratio (2.4), most GDPs induced per nine innings (1.3), most strikeouts per nine innings (6.6) and fewest walks per nine innings (2.8)

Jorge Julio

2002 Season

Rookie Jorge Julio began the season as a short reliever and finished 2002 with 25 saves, a dazzling 1.99 ERA and the Orioles' closer job. In between, Julio grew into a dominating stopper, allowing just one earned run and posting a 0.37 ERA in July and August. If not for the Orioles posting a 4-32 record to end the season, he would have surpassed the 30-save plateau.

Pitching

Julio throws a four-seam fastball that regularly reaches 96-98 MPH with movement. He's more effective with the pitch when he throws it up in the strike zone, tempting hitters to chase it. His slider is of the power variety, reaching the high 80s on occasion and complementing his fastball. He likes to spot the slider on the outside corner of the plate to righthanded batters. Because his changeup is very inconsistent and he struggles to locate the pitch in the strike zone, he rarely throws it except to waste a pitch. Despite his youth, Julio showed improved command and control as the season wore on.

Defense

Because he's a power pitcher, Julio helps his catchers by getting the ball to the plate quickly. Still, basestealers were a perfect 7-for-7 against him last season. His follow-through to home plate is exaggerated enough to move him out of good fielding position, although he covers first base without hesitation and bunts do not give him problems.

2003 Outlook

Unlike with Ryan Kohlmeier the year before, the Orioles know they have a bona fide closer in Julio. As long as Baltimore does not burn him out due to a lack of bullpen depth and poor starting pitching, he should thrive in this role for seasons to come. If the Orioles fare better, he could surpass the 35-save plateau this season and gain recognition as one of the best young closers in the game.

Position: RP
Bats: R **Throws:** R
Ht: 6' 1" **Wt:** 190

Opening Day Age: 24
Born: 3/3/79 in Caracas, VZ
ML Seasons: 2

Overall Statistics

	W	L	Pct.	ERA	G	GS	Sv	IP	H	BB	SO	HR	Ratio
'02	5	6	.455	1.99	67	0	25	68.0	55	27	55	5	1.21
Car.	6	7	.462	2.42	85	0	25	89.1	80	36	77	7	1.30

How Often He Throws Strikes

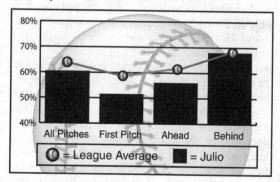

= League Average ■ = Julio

2002 Situational Stats

	W	L	ERA	Sv	IP		AB	H	HR	RBI	Avg
Home	3	3	2.08	12	34.2	LHB	127	27	2	12	.213
Road	2	3	1.89	13	33.1	RHB	131	28	3	11	.214
First Half	4	5	2.43	17	40.2	Sc Pos	74	16	2	19	.216
Scnd Half	1	1	1.32	8	27.1	Clutch	159	39	4	21	.245

2002 Rankings (American League)

- 4th in games finished (61) and relief ERA (1.99)
- 5th in relief losses (6) and lowest save percentage (80.6)
- 7th in blown saves (6)
- Led the Orioles in saves, games finished (61), wild pitches (8), save opportunities (31), save percentage (80.6), blown saves (6) and relief losses (6)

Rodrigo Lopez

2002 Season

Rodrigo Lopez replaced the disappointing Josh Towers in the starting rotation in late April, and as the saying goes, the rest is history. The surprising Lopez was inked to a one-year deal in November 2001, and this Mexican League import became the Orioles' best starting pitcher. He led all rookies in wins, strikeouts, ERA and innings pitched. Lopez also finished 12th in the American League in ERA.

Pitching

Lopez relies on his control and an ability to mix his pitches to keep hitters off stride. That's because his fastball reaches just the high 80s and he doesn't have one out pitch. He can spot his curve for strikes, mix in a decent changeup to keep hitters honest, or push them off the plate with his slider. When Lopez is on, hitters are kept off stride by his ability to keep them guessing which pitch is coming at which speed. Lopez does get in trouble occasionally when he strays from changing speeds and relies too much on his fastball-slider combination. Because of his pitching style, lefthanded hitters aren't able to sit on his average fastball, thus he usually is effective against them. Lopez pitches much better at night, when it is more difficult to judge the speed of his pitches.

Defense

Lopez does a decent job of varying his move to first base to keep runners at bay. Because he finishes in a good position at the end of his windup, he's able to efficiently field bunts and slow rollers around the mound. He covers first base when the situation arises and makes strong throws to first when needed.

2003 Outlook

The Orioles believe Lopez is a real find who will be a fixture in the rotation for seasons to come. While his 2002 effort earned him a second-place finish in the AL Rookie of the Year vote, he must continue to change speeds and maintain his control to be effective. And based on his minor league career, that is not a foregone conclusion.

Position: SP
Bats: R **Throws:** R
Ht: 6' 1" **Wt:** 180

Opening Day Age: 27
Born: 12/14/75 in Tlalnepantla, Mexico
ML Seasons: 2
Pronunciation: rod-REE-go

Baltimore

Overall Statistics

	W	L	Pct.	ERA	G	GS	Sv	IP	H	BB	SO	HR	Ratio
'02	15	9	.625	3.57	33	28	0	196.2	172	62	136	23	1.19
Car.	15	12	.556	4.15	39	34	0	221.1	212	75	153	28	1.30

How Often He Throws Strikes

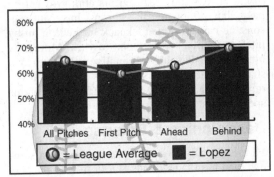

= League Average   = Lopez

2002 Situational Stats

	W	L	ERA	Sv	IP		AB	H	HR	RBI	Avg
Home	7	3	3.45	0	91.1	LHB	386	88	10	38	.228
Road	8	6	3.67	0	105.1	RHB	349	84	13	37	.241
First Half	8	3	3.04	0	106.2	Sc Pos	138	35	5	48	.254
Scnd Half	7	6	4.20	0	90.0	Clutch	34	9	0	2	.265

2002 Rankings (American League)

- 1st in ERA among rookies and wins among rookies
- 2nd in losses among rookies
- 5th in highest stolen-base percentage allowed (77.8)
- Led the Orioles in games started, innings pitched, batters faced (809), strikeouts, pitches thrown (2,982), winning percentage, lowest batting average allowed (.234), lowest slugging percentage allowed (.382), lowest on-base percentage allowed (.297), fewest pitches thrown per batter (3.69), lowest ERA at home, lowest ERA on the road, most run support per nine innings (6.2) and fewest home runs allowed per nine innings (1.05)

Melvin Mora

2002 Season

Melvin Mora put on a surprising home-run display last season for a player of his size, posting six home runs in June en route to a career-best 19 longballs. He also reached career highs in numerous other categories, with the notable exception of batting average. A tendency to swing for the fences and a lack of stamina caused his numbers to plummet after the All-Star break.

Hitting

Though he has good speed, Mora continues to swing for the fences, generating too many fly-balls. The newfound power and a slight uppercut swing have greatly reduced his ability to get on base, thus prolonging his slumps. In recent seasons, he has developed a knack for getting hit by pitches. From a contact point of view, Mora now hits righthanders about equally well, due to a sharp decline against southpaws in 2002. Mora rarely bunts and fails to take advantage of his speed to first base.

Baserunning & Defense

Mora stole only 16 bases in 26 attempts last summer, and hasn't shown the ability to read pitchers and make full use of his speed. While he is the best on the team at going from first to third, and he can score from first on a double, mental mistakes and a lack of focus get him in trouble on the bases. As an outfielder, especially in center, Mora covers more ground than the average center fielder, but not enough to make him an exceptional outfielder. His ability to play shortstop in a pinch helps the Orioles when injuries strike, but a weak and inaccurate arm makes him a liability in the middle infield.

2003 Outlook

While the power he displayed last season was both a surprise and a positive, Mora's game is speed and getting on base. The Orioles are concerned this newfound power will curtail his ability to get on base or improve his batting average. His versatility in the field will keep him in the lineup on a regular basis, but he's not a classic leadoff hitter, something the Orioles desperately need.

Position: LF/SS/CF/2B
Bats: R **Throws:** R
Ht: 5'10" **Wt:** 180

Opening Day Age: 31
Born: 2/2/72 in Agua Negra, VZ
ML Seasons: 4
Pronunciation: MORE-a

Overall Statistics

	G	AB	R	H	D	T	HR	RBI	SB	BB	SO	Avg	OBP	Slg
'02	149	557	86	130	30	4	19	64	16	70	108	.233	.338	.404
Car.	475	1438	201	358	80	9	34	160	41	150	286	.249	.334	.388

Where He Hits the Ball

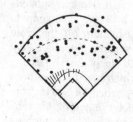

Vs. LHP   **Vs. RHP**

2002 Situational Stats

	AB	H	HR	RBI	Avg		AB	H	HR	RBI	Avg
Home	270	59	8	35	.219	LHP	146	35	4	12	.240
Road	287	71	11	29	.247	RHP	411	95	15	52	.231
First Half	306	81	11	37	.265	Sc Pos	128	29	5	49	.227
Scnd Half	251	49	8	27	.195	Clutch	89	17	2	9	.191

2002 Rankings (American League)

- 2nd in hit by pitch (20) and lowest batting average
- 3rd in lowest stolen-base percentage (61.5) and lowest batting average at home
- 4th in assists in left field (6)
- 5th in lowest batting average vs. righthanded pitchers
- 6th in caught stealing (10) and lowest batting average on a 3-2 count (.133)
- Led the Orioles in caught stealing (10), walks, hit by pitch (20), times on base (220), batting average with the bases loaded (.400) and on-base percentage for a leadoff hitter (.342)

Sidney Ponson

2002 Season

For the second time in two seasons, injuries hindered Sidney Ponson's season, generating doubts about his durability. Two years ago it was elbow tendinitis. Last season it was shoulder pain, due mainly to a slight tear in his rotator cuff that the Orioles are hoping to rehabilitate rather than surgically repair. When Ponson was healthy, as he was in June, he was very effective as a starter, but his shoulder problems led to slumps and a stint on the disabled list in August.

Pitching

When healthy, Ponson has a fastball that can reach 92-94 MPH, but that has been far too rare in recent seasons. His slider is an improving pitch and one that he has gained better command of recently. Ponson all but abandoned a forkball last season because of his history of arm problems. That's too bad because it did serve as a decent offspeed pitch. One improvement in his pitching is his ability to keep the ball down in the strike zone and generate more groundballs than flyballs, all of which helps keep the ball in the ballpark.

Defense

Because of his large frame, Ponson is somewhat slow getting off the mound. But he is flawless with the bunts and slow rollers he fields. His move to first is average, but his ability to make a quick move to the plate when he's pitching from the stretch helps keep some baserunners at bay. Ponson covers first base adequately and rarely gets caught out of position.

2003 Outlook

The torn rotator cuff and biceps tendinitis that compromised his season have to be a concern to the Orioles, especially after he suffered from elbow tendinitis the year before. They continue to harp on him about his conditioning, believing that if he came to spring training with a lot less weight it would take some of the strain off his arm. The 2003 picture is cloudy due to his injury concerns, and he can't be counted on to pitch an entire injury-free season.

Position: SP
Bats: R **Throws:** R
Ht: 6' 1" **Wt:** 225

Opening Day Age: 26
Born: 11/2/76 in Noord, Aruba
ML Seasons: 5
Pronunciation: pon-SONE

Overall Statistics

	W	L	Pct.	ERA	G	GS	Sv	IP	H	BB	SO	HR	Ratio
'02	7	9	.438	4.09	28	28	0	176.0	172	63	120	26	1.34
Car.	41	53	.436	4.74	146	135	1	881.1	940	305	553	131	1.41

How Often He Throws Strikes

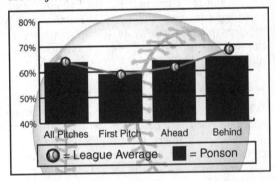

= League Average   = Ponson

2002 Situational Stats

	W	L	ERA	Sv	IP		AB	H	HR	RBI	Avg
Home	4	5	4.33	0	99.2	LHB	325	79	12	28	.243
Road	3	4	3.77	0	76.1	RHB	341	93	14	47	.273
First Half	3	4	4.14	0	108.2	Sc Pos	136	35	2	42	.257
Scnd Half	4	5	4.01	0	67.1	Clutch	54	17	3	8	.315

2002 Rankings (American League)

- 1st in fielding percentage at pitcher (1.000)
- 4th in least run support per nine innings (4.1)
- 7th in highest groundball-flyball ratio allowed (1.5), most home runs allowed per nine innings (1.33) and highest walks per nine innings (3.2)
- 9th in complete games (3)
- 10th in most GDPs induced per nine innings (0.9) and lowest strikeout-walk ratio (1.9)
- Led the Orioles in games started, complete games (3) and home runs allowed

Chris Richard

2002 Season

Chris Richard began last season on the 60-day disabled list after having surgery on his left shoulder in November 2001. While Richard worked hard on his rehab early in the season, he wasn't able to regain enough arm strength to play until July 31. Once he did return, his swing was crisp but lacked power due to his shoulder woes.

Hitting

When healthy, Richard's level swing allows him to spray the ball to all fields and go with where the pitch is located. He's never fared well against southpaws. While his at-bats with runners in scoring position were few in 2002, Richard continued to struggle in those situations. His ability to hit offspeed pitches and lay off pitches in the dirt improves as he gains valuable experience at the major league level.

Baserunning & Defense

While Richard does not have above-average speed, he does have quick feet, which allows him to get a quick jump. He struggles some going from first to third and scoring from second on anything but a gap hit. Still, he's a savvy baserunner. In the field, Richard displays solid glovework around the first-base bag and is adept at digging out throws in the dirt. His throws across the diamond have been solid, but his shoulder surgery compromised his ability to make throws in the outfield last summer. Richard uses his quick jump in the outfield to compensate for an overall lack of speed.

2003 Outlook

The weakness in his left shoulder at the end of last season is a concern. If he hasn't regained his arm strength by the time he arrives in camp, Richard may be limited to DH duties or first base. If Richard is stronger, the Orioles will look for more power from him, a commodity they also are shopping for during the offseason.

Position: DH
Bats: L **Throws:** L
Ht: 6' 2" **Wt:** 190

Opening Day Age: 28
Born: 6/7/74 in San Diego, CA
ML Seasons: 3

Overall Statistics

	G	AB	R	H	D	T	HR	RBI	SB	BB	SO	Avg	OBP	Slg
'02	50	155	15	36	11	0	4	21	0	12	30	.232	.292	.381
Car.	248	853	128	221	56	5	33	119	18	74	170	.259	.325	.453

Where He Hits the Ball

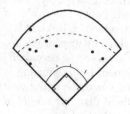 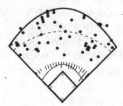

Vs. LHP　　　　**Vs. RHP**

2002 Situational Stats

	AB	H	HR	RBI	Avg		AB	H	HR	RBI	Avg
Home	75	15	2	10	.200	LHP	16	4	0	1	.250
Road	80	21	2	11	.263	RHP	139	32	4	20	.230
First Half	0	0	0	0	–	Sc Pos	40	8	0	13	.200
Scnd Half	155	36	4	21	.232	Clutch	24	6	0	1	.250

2002 Rankings (American League)

- Led the Orioles in batting average on a 3-1 count (.500)

Marty Cordova

Position: LF/DH
Bats: R **Throws:** R
Ht: 6' 0" **Wt:** 206

Opening Day Age: 33
Born: 7/10/69 in Las Vegas, NV
ML Seasons: 8
Pronunciation: core-DOE-vuh

Overall Statistics

	G	AB	R	H	D	T	HR	RBI	SB	BB	SO	Avg	OBP	Slg
'02	131	458	55	116	25	2	18	64	1	47	111	.253	.325	.434
Car.	943	3389	475	931	191	18	121	536	56	321	725	.275	.343	.449

2002 Situational Stats

	AB	H	HR	RBI	Avg		AB	H	HR	RBI	Avg
Home	216	51	11	30	.236	LHP	135	37	7	19	.274
Road	242	65	7	34	.269	RHP	323	79	11	45	.245
First Half	260	72	9	40	.277	Sc Pos	119	33	5	44	.277
Scnd Half	198	44	9	24	.222	Clutch	82	15	1	6	.183

2002 Season

Marty Cordova was signed to a three-year, $9.1 million contract last winter after posting a near career year with Cleveland in 2001. He got out of the gate quickly, fashioning a .344 average in April, but he never reached the run-producing form that Baltimore had hoped for. It was obvious early on that Cordova was pressing, as evidenced by the 111 strikeouts, which tied his career high.

Hitting, Baserunning & Defense

While Cordova makes consistent contact, he doesn't have the swing to be a major power source in the middle of the lineup. Rather, he's more of a contact hitter who hits behind the runner and produces gap hits. Breaking balls thrown low in the dirt continue to plague him. His lack of foot speed is a liability at the plate, as he grounds into plenty of double plays. On the basepaths, he no longer is opportunistic in taking the extra base. He usually handles any ball hit within his limited range in left field, but his arm is below average and he rarely registers an assist.

2003 Outlook

While the Orioles continue to look for a major run producer, it's unlikely Cordova is the answer. His inability to remain healthy for an entire season is likely to curtail his production again this season.

Sean Douglass

Position: SP
Bats: R **Throws:** R
Ht: 6' 6" **Wt:** 198

Opening Day Age: 23
Born: 4/28/79 in Lancaster, CA
ML Seasons: 2

Overall Statistics

	W	L	Pct.	ERA	G	GS	Sv	IP	H	BB	SO	HR	Ratio
'02	0	5	.000	6.08	15	8	0	53.1	58	35	44	10	1.74
Car.	2	6	.250	5.86	19	12	0	73.2	79	46	61	13	1.70

2002 Situational Stats

	W	L	ERA	Sv	IP		AB	H	HR	RBI	Avg
Home	0	2	4.97	0	25.1	LHB	104	28	8	22	.269
Road	0	3	7.07	0	28.0	RHB	101	30	2	13	.297
First Half	0	1	5.79	0	23.1	Sc Pos	58	17	5	27	.293
Scnd Half	0	4	6.30	0	30.0	Clutch	10	4	1	2	.400

2002 Season

The Orioles were hoping Sean Douglass' second trip to the majors would be more productive than his brief 2001 debut. Unfortunately, he failed to win a game in 15 appearances and eight starts, losing five times in two different stints with Baltimore. Douglass failed to deliver, like many of the Orioles' pitching prospects in recent memory.

Pitching & Defense

Douglass has to mix pitches successfully because he's yet to develop one dominating pitch. His fastball has been clocked in the low 90s, but it lacks enough movement to be an out pitch. His change-up is average because he struggles to use the same arm action as his fastball. Douglass' slider has the most promise due to its late break. His pitching motion is smooth and his mechanics fairly consistent, though his 6-foot-6 frame makes throwing from a consistent release point difficult. He's a decent athlete who gets off the mound and fields his position without any problems. His move to first base is typical of the average righthander.

2003 Outlook

The Orioles hope that Douglass can establish himself as an end-of-the-rotation starter this season. If not, he'll spend another summer shuttling between Triple-A ball and the majors.

Travis Driskill

Position: SP/RP
Bats: R **Throws:** R
Ht: 6' 0" **Wt:** 225

Opening Day Age: 31
Born: 8/1/71 in Omaha, NE
ML Seasons: 1

Overall Statistics

	W	L	Pct.	ERA	G	GS	Sv	IP	H	BB	SO	HR	Ratio
'02	8	8	.500	4.95	29	19	0	132.2	150	48	78	21	1.49
Car.	8	8	.500	4.95	29	19	0	132.2	150	48	78	21	1.49

2002 Situational Stats

	W	L	ERA	Sv	IP			AB	H	HR	RBI	Avg
Home	1	6	5.15	0	64.2	LHB		280	81	11	32	.289
Road	7	2	4.76	0	68.0	RHB		249	69	10	32	.277
First Half	6	1	4.01	0	60.2	Sc Pos		111	27	4	38	.243
Scnd Half	2	7	5.75	0	72.0	Clutch		16	5	1	2	.313

2002 Season

Journeyman Travis Driskill was signed to a minor league deal by the Orioles in November 2001, made his major league debut in late April and stuck on the roster the entire season. His best month was May, when he went 2-0 with a 3.43 ERA. Once the scouting reports on him got around, hitters started to hit him pretty hard later in the year.

Pitching & Defense

Driskill relies on a hard-breaking slider that is above average and very effective at times. He mixes in an average fastball with good control to help keep hitters off stride. The weakness in his repertoire is a lack of an offspeed pitch that would keep hitters guessing. So he doesn't have enough pitches and the ability to change speeds to be an effective starter, and his stuff isn't good enough to be a short reliever. He fields his position adequately, though bunts to his right have given him problems. Driskill's move to first base is average.

2003 Outlook

Give Driskill credit for sticking around beyond his 30th birthday before making it to the majors. But like most journeyman types, how long he remains in Baltimore depends on how well younger pitchers perform the following spring.

Geronimo Gil

Position: C
Bats: R **Throws:** R
Ht: 6' 2" **Wt:** 195

Opening Day Age: 27
Born: 8/7/75 in Oaxaca, Mexico
ML Seasons: 2
Pronunciation: heel

Overall Statistics

	G	AB	R	H	D	T	HR	RBI	SB	BB	SO	Avg	OBP	Slg
'02	125	422	33	98	19	0	12	45	2	21	88	.232	.270	.363
Car.	142	480	36	115	21	0	12	51	2	26	95	.240	.282	.358

2002 Situational Stats

	AB	H	HR	RBI	Avg		AB	H	HR	RBI	Avg
Home	193	46	5	19	.238	LHP	109	26	4	10	.239
Road	229	52	7	26	.227	RHP	313	72	8	35	.230
First Half	220	58	8	33	.264	Sc Pos	102	23	1	30	.225
Scnd Half	202	40	4	12	.198	Clutch	63	18	2	8	.286

2002 Season

When they acquired Geronimo Gil from the Dodgers in 2001, the Orioles knew that he was a solid defensive catcher. The huge question was, would he hit? The first half of the season, especially in April when he hit five home runs, Gil provided consistent contact and surprising power. But as the season rolled along, Gil wore down in his first full major league campaign, batting .185 in August and September.

Hitting, Baserunning & Defense

Gil hits righthanders and southpaws about equally well, though he generates a bit more power against lefties. Offspeed stuff gave him trouble at times when pitchers caught him sitting on the fastball too much. Gil calls a solid game behind the plate and does a good job of blocking pitches in the dirt. The one thing he needs to work on is the running game. More accurate throws to second base could reduce the number of stolen bases allowed. On the basepaths, he's a typically slow, plodding catcher.

2003 Outlook

The Orioles got more from Gil than they expected during the first half of last season. If he can improve his stamina and control the opponents' running game better, he could solidify his hold on the Orioles' catching job.

Buddy Groom

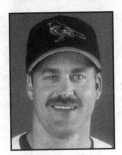

Position: RP
Bats: L **Throws:** L
Ht: 6' 2" **Wt:** 207

Opening Day Age: 37
Born: 7/10/65 in Dallas, TX
ML Seasons: 11

Overall Statistics

	W	L	Pct.	ERA	G	GS	Sv	IP	H	BB	SO	HR	Ratio
'02	3	2	.600	1.60	70	0	2	62.0	44	12	48	4	0.90
Car.	25	27	.481	4.56	619	15	25	595.2	649	218	408	55	1.46

2002 Situational Stats

	W	L	ERA	Sv	IP		AB	H	HR	RBI	Avg
Home	2	1	2.67	1	30.1	LHB	94	17	2	7	.181
Road	1	1	0.57	1	31.2	RHB	130	27	2	13	.208
First Half	2	2	1.89	1	33.1	Sc Pos	54	14	3	19	.259
Scnd Half	1	0	1.26	1	28.2	Clutch	146	28	2	14	.192

2002 Season

For the seventh straight season, Buddy Groom worked at least 70 games as a reliever. And last season was a career best for the still-improving 37-year-old lefthander. He posted a career-low 1.60 ERA and allowed only 44 hits in 62 innings of work.

Pitching & Defense

Groom relies heavily on a sharp-breaking curveball that makes lefthanded hitters' knees buckle. The cut fastball that he continues to work on has allowed him to be more effective against righthanded hitters and keeps batters from honing in on the curveball. He uses a changeup at times, but more to give the hitter something different to look at rather than as a pitch he likes to throw for strikes. His move to first base is solid, keeping most baserunners on their guard. Bunts and slow rollers hit to his left give him a bit more trouble than those hit toward third, but he isn't a liability in the field.

2003 Outlook

There isn't any reason that Groom can't continue successfully in a short-relief role. But any chances of him earning a part-time closer's role have disappeared with the development of Jorge Julio.

Willis Roberts

Position: RP
Bats: R **Throws:** R
Ht: 6' 3" **Wt:** 175

Opening Day Age: 27
Born: 6/19/75 in San Cristobal, DR
ML Seasons: 3

Overall Statistics

	W	L	Pct.	ERA	G	GS	Sv	IP	H	BB	SO	HR	Ratio
'02	5	4	.556	3.36	66	0	1	75.0	79	32	51	5	1.48
Car.	14	14	.500	4.41	113	18	7	208.1	224	87	146	20	1.49

2002 Situational Stats

	W	L	ERA	Sv	IP		AB	H	HR	RBI	Avg
Home	5	2	1.85	0	43.2	LHB	116	32	1	18	.276
Road	0	2	5.46	1	31.1	RHB	177	47	4	23	.266
First Half	5	2	1.99	1	49.2	Sc Pos	99	25	0	32	.253
Scnd Half	0	2	6.04	0	25.1	Clutch	138	36	2	20	.261

2002 Season

The Orioles looked to Willis Roberts as a potential power closer, based on his short stint in that role in 2001. But he wasn't as dominant in the spring, and the rise of Jorge Julio cast Roberts into a lesser role. Even though Roberts finished the first half of 2002 with a 1.99 ERA, the second half of the season was a disaster, especially in September when he posted a 10.80 ERA.

Pitching & Defense

Roberts throws both a two-seam and four-seam fastball, which reaches 94 MPH. He mixes in a slider to keep hitters from sitting on his fastballs, but his inconsistency in getting that pitch over the plate hurts him. Because he doesn't change speeds well, he's been relegated to the bullpen. When Roberts struggles, it's usually due to inconsistent mechanics and walking the first batter he faces. His move to first is as deliberate as his ability to field his position.

2003 Outlook

Before Roberts' collapse in September, Baltimore thought he was established as a short reliever and would provide depth in front of Jorge Julio. He enters spring training with question marks surrounding his role, and he must prove he deserves to remain in the majors.

B.J. Ryan

Position: RP
Bats: L **Throws:** L
Ht: 6' 6" **Wt:** 230

Opening Day Age: 27
Born: 12/28/75 in
Bossier City, LA
ML Seasons: 4

Overall Statistics

	W	L	Pct.	ERA	G	GS	Sv	IP	H	BB	SO	HR	Ratio
'02	2	1	.667	4.68	67	0	1	57.2	51	33	56	7	1.46
Car.	7	8	.467	4.66	184	0	3	173.2	147	107	180	20	1.46

2002 Situational Stats

	W	L	ERA	Sv	IP		AB	H	HR	RBI	Avg
Home	0	0	4.34	1	29.0	LHB	99	19	5	15	.192
Road	2	1	5.02	0	28.2	RHB	113	32	2	15	.283
First Half	1	0	7.18	0	26.1	Sc Pos	72	19	3	24	.264
Scnd Half	1	1	2.59	1	31.1	Clutch	78	19	2	10	.244

2002 Season

Rather than improving as the Orioles had hoped, B.J. Ryan merely duplicated a 2001 season that didn't answer all of the questions about his potential. He continued to be a lefty specialist only, a role that the Orioles hoped he'd expand on in 2002. Despite struggling early on, Ryan turned it around after the All-Star break, limiting opponents to a paltry .198 batting average.

Pitching & Defense

Ryan has one of the American League's more deceptive pitching motions, which allows him to hide the ball. His best pitch is a slider that is above average. His fastball routinely is clocked in the low 90s, but he can't rely on it to get hitters out on a regular basis. He continues to dominate against lefthanded batters, while righthanded hitters still give him problems. His move to first base is solid, and he fields his position adequately.

2003 Outlook

The Orioles would like to expand Ryan's role beyond that of a lefty specialist, but retiring righthanded hitters remains a struggle. So once again the Baltimore coaching staff is asking him to master a second pitch to get righthanded batters out. If last season is any indication, that isn't likely to happen.

David Segui

Position: DH
Bats: B **Throws:** L
Ht: 6' 1" **Wt:** 202

Opening Day Age: 36
Born: 7/19/66 in Kansas City, KS
ML Seasons: 13
Pronunciation: seh-GHEE

Overall Statistics

	G	AB	R	H	D	T	HR	RBI	SB	BB	SO	Avg	OBP	Slg
'02	26	95	10	25	4	0	2	16	0	11	22	.263	.336	.368
Car.	1371	4564	649	1333	271	15	133	652	16	493	627	.292	.359	.445

2002 Situational Stats

	AB	H	HR	RBI	Avg		AB	H	HR	RBI	Avg
Home	51	12	1	10	.235	LHP	26	5	0	3	.192
Road	44	13	1	6	.295	RHP	69	20	2	13	.290
First Half	95	25	2	16	.263	Sc Pos	26	9	0	14	.346
Scnd Half	0	0	0	0	–	Clutch	11	1	1	1	.091

2002 Season

A strained right Achilles' tendon early in the season and a sore left wrist in early May, which led to surgery, reduced David Segui's season to just 95 at-bats, almost all at the DH spot.

Hitting, Baserunning & Defense

When healthy, Segui sprays the ball to all parts of the ballpark and makes solid contact. Batting lefthanded, he can take an inside fastball and turn on it, pulling it down the right-field line. Or he can go with an outside breaking ball to left and left-center field. From the right side of the plate, Segui goes to right field much more often than pulling pitches to left field. Knee and Achilles injuries have reduced his mobility around first base, and he's now just an average first baseman. Bunts hit in front of him are not the routine out they used to be. Segui is now a station-to-station runner who rarely scores from second base unless it's a triple or double to the outfield wall.

2003 Outlook

While Segui has two years remaining on his contract, rumors circulated at the end of last season that injuries would cut short his career. While the Orioles would like him to return mainly as a DH, they have enough candidates for the job to replace him.

Chris Singleton

Position: CF
Bats: L **Throws:** L
Ht: 6' 2" **Wt:** 210

Opening Day Age: 30
Born: 8/15/72 in
Martinez, CA
ML Seasons: 4

Overall Statistics

	G	AB	R	H	D	T	HR	RBI	SB	BB	SO	Avg	OBP	Slg
'02	136	466	67	122	30	6	9	50	20	21	83	.262	.296	.410
Car.	556	1865	279	518	104	22	44	229	74	98	274	.278	.313	.428

2002 Situational Stats

	AB	H	HR	RBI	Avg		AB	H	HR	RBI	Avg
Home	222	56	4	22	.252	LHP	72	15	2	12	.208
Road	244	66	5	28	.270	RHP	394	107	7	38	.272
First Half	257	64	4	30	.249	Sc Pos	110	25	3	42	.227
Scnd Half	209	58	5	20	.278	Clutch	81	21	1	10	.259

2002 Season

The Orioles acquired Chris Singleton from the White Sox for prospect Willie Harris in order to solidify their defense in center field. They were pleased with the speed he brought to the lineup. But like the White Sox, they were disappointed in his lack of ability to get on base with regularity.

Hitting, Baserunning & Defense

Singleton has more of an uppercut swing than a typical top-of-the-order hitter needs, and while that produces a high amount of doubles and some home runs, it also causes problems. He hits too many flyballs, and groundballs on outside pitches come in bunches. He has improved his ability to read pitchers, making him efficient when attempting to steal. He can score from first on extra-base hits and can go from first to third on gap hits to right field. He has excellent range in the outfield and gets the most out of an average arm.

2003 Outlook

Baltimore would like to see more walks than doubles from Singleton, and if that adjustment happens, he would be moved to the leadoff spot. He's been better than the other options the Orioles have for center, but the play of Gary Matthews Jr. in 2002 has them contemplating a new 2003 address for Singleton.

John Stephens

Position: SP
Bats: R **Throws:** R
Ht: 6' 1" **Wt:** 204

Opening Day Age: 23
Born: 11/15/79 in
Sydney, Australia
ML Seasons: 1

Overall Statistics

	W	L	Pct.	ERA	G	GS	Sv	IP	H	BB	SO	HR	Ratio
'02	2	5	.286	6.09	12	11	0	65.0	68	22	56	13	1.38
Car.	2	5	.286	6.09	12	11	0	65.0	68	22	56	13	1.38

2002 Situational Stats

	W	L	ERA	Sv	IP		AB	H	HR	RBI	Avg
Home	2	2	5.25	0	36.0	LHB	123	33	6	20	.268
Road	0	3	7.14	0	29.0	RHB	128	35	7	24	.273
First Half	0	0	—	0	0.0	Sc Pos	53	17	3	29	.321
Scnd Half	2	5	6.09	0	65.0	Clutch	4	1	0	1	.250

2002 Season

The desperate Orioles recalled John Stephens in late July to fill a void in the starting rotation and he struggled mightily. He gave up a whopping 13 home runs in just 65 innings of work and looked overmatched at the major league level.

Pitching & Defense

Signed out of Australia in 1996, Stephens hasn't regained the velocity lost on his fastball from a 1998 whiplash-like injury while diving for a bunt. He's a tactician while pitching, mixing a mid-80s fastball with various types of changeups and an above-average curveball. When he's on, as he often was in the minors, he's mixing his pitches effectively, changing speeds and using his fastball to help keep hitters off the plate. When his control is off just a bit, he gets into trouble. His move to first base and his fielding ability are average.

2003 Outlook

Stephens pitched with a fractured right foot in 2002, but the severity of the injury wasn't discovered until late in the season. He'll be ready by spring training, when he'll have to show he can mix his stuff well enough to survive in the majors and be a serviceable pitcher. Improved control will be key to his second big league go-round in 2003.

Rick Bauer (**Pos**: RHP, **Age**: 26)

	W	L	Pct.	ERA	G	GS	Sv	IP	H	BB	SO	HR	Ratio
'02	6	7	.462	3.98	56	1	1	83.2	84	36	45	12	1.43
Car.	6	12	.333	4.17	62	7	1	116.2	119	45	61	19	1.41

A fastball-slider pitcher with decent movement on his fastball, Bauer didn't dominate hitters in the high minors and will have to battle to establish himself in the Baltimore pen in his second year. 2003 Outlook: B

Steve Bechler (**Pos**: RHP, **Age**: 23)

	W	L	Pct.	ERA	G	GS	Sv	IP	H	BB	SO	HR	Ratio
'02	0	0	–	13.50	3	0	0	4.2	6	4	3	3	2.14
Car.	0	0	–	13.50	3	0	0	4.2	6	4	3	3	2.14

Bechler went 8-12 with a 4.00 ERA between Double-A Bowie and Triple-A Rochester. He reached the majors for the first time in his career, allowing runs in three September appearances. 2003 Outlook: C

Larry Bigbie (**Pos**: LF, **Age**: 25, **Bats**: L)

	G	AB	R	H	D	T	HR	RBI	SB	BB	SO	Avg	OBP	Slg
'02	16	34	1	6	1	0	0	3	1	1	11	.176	.194	.206
Car.	63	165	16	36	7	0	2	14	5	18	53	.218	.293	.297

Bigbie is a natural hitter who was expected to show more pop, and a shoulder injury curtailed a hot start at Triple-A Rochester in '02. Time is running out to show some power as a corner outfielder. 2003 Outlook: C

Chris Brock (**Pos**: RHP, **Age**: 32)

	W	L	Pct.	ERA	G	GS	Sv	IP	H	BB	SO	HR	Ratio
'02	2	1	.667	4.70	22	0	0	44.0	52	14	21	6	1.50
Car.	18	17	.514	4.81	148	30	1	335.0	361	137	227	56	1.49

Brock pitched quite well in July and August, but struggled to open and close 2002. While he pitched OK overall, he made $1 million and was eligible for arbitration, so he was released. 2003 Outlook: B

Raul Casanova (**Pos**: C, **Age**: 30, **Bats**: B)

	G	AB	R	H	D	T	HR	RBI	SB	BB	SO	Avg	OBP	Slg
'02	33	88	3	16	1	0	1	8	0	10	19	.182	.270	.227
Car.	332	942	81	219	37	4	28	113	2	85	172	.232	.301	.369

Casanova began last season sharing the Brewers' catching job. But a torn ulnar collateral ligament landed him on the disabled list in May. He eventually was released by Milwaukee and then Baltimore. 2003 Outlook: C

Howie Clark (**Pos**: DH, **Age**: 29, **Bats**: L)

	G	AB	R	H	D	T	HR	RBI	SB	BB	SO	Avg	OBP	Slg
'02	14	53	3	16	5	0	0	4	0	3	6	.302	.362	.396
Car.	14	53	3	16	5	0	0	4	0	3	6	.302	.362	.396

Clark enjoyed one of his better Triple-A seasons in 2002, posting a .309 average and .369 OBP. He put up similar numbers in his major league debut in July, earning a minor league contract with Toronto. 2003 Outlook: C

Eric DuBose (**Pos**: LHP, **Age**: 26)

	W	L	Pct.	ERA	G	GS	Sv	IP	H	BB	SO	HR	Ratio
'02	0	0	–	3.00	4	0	0	6.0	7	1	4	1	1.33
Car.	0	0	–	3.00	4	0	0	6.0	7	1	4	1	1.33

DuBose has struggled to excel at the Double-A level, but he was very good in the Double-A Bowie pen in 2002. He reached Baltimore in September and pitched effectively in four games. 2003 Outlook: C

Brook Fordyce (**Pos**: C, **Age**: 32, **Bats**: R)

	G	AB	R	H	D	T	HR	RBI	SB	BB	SO	Avg	OBP	Slg
'02	56	130	7	30	8	0	1	8	1	9	19	.231	.301	.315
Car.	461	1308	130	341	85	2	33	148	6	91	217	.261	.314	.404

Fordyce peaked in 1999-2000, when he enjoyed a brief run as a starting catcher. Those days are all but over, even though the O's garnered just a .232 average and .277 OBP from their 2002 catchers. 2003 Outlook: C

Luis Garcia (**Pos**: CF, **Age**: 27, **Bats**: R)

	G	AB	R	H	D	T	HR	RBI	SB	BB	SO	Avg	OBP	Slg
'02	6	3	0	1	0	0	0	0	0	0	1	.333	.333	.333
Car.	6	3	0	1	0	0	0	0	0	0	1	.333	.333	.333

This former White Sox prospect returned to the North American game after three years away. But he didn't hit much at Triple-A Rochester and got just a brief cup-of-coffee in May. 2003 Outlook: C

Pat Hentgen (**Pos**: RHP, **Age**: 34)

	W	L	Pct.	ERA	G	GS	Sv	IP	H	BB	SO	HR	Ratio
'02	0	4	.000	7.77	4	4	0	22.0	31	10	11	6	1.86
Car.	122	95	.562	4.22	298	268	0	1834.1	1871	675	1157	228	1.39

After signing a two-year deal with the O's before the 2001 season, Hentgen underwent Tommy John surgery that August and returned late in 2002. The O's have signed him to a 2003 contract with a 2004 option. 2003 Outlook: B

Jose Leon (**Pos**: 1B/3B, **Age**: 26, **Bats**: R)

	G	AB	R	H	D	T	HR	RBI	SB	BB	SO	Avg	OBP	Slg
'02	36	89	8	22	2	0	3	10	1	3	20	.247	.280	.371
Car.	36	89	8	22	2	0	3	10	1	3	20	.247	.280	.371

There isn't much here to get excited about, but Leon did hit .290 and slug .452 in 62 at-bats against lefties. He played errorless ball at first and third, but those positions demand some pop. 2003 Outlook: C

Luis Lopez (**Pos**: SS/2B, **Age**: 32, **Bats**: B)

	G	AB	R	H	D	T	HR	RBI	SB	BB	SO	Avg	OBP	Slg
'02	58	117	11	23	6	0	2	10	1	5	21	.197	.230	.299
Car.	648	1505	164	368	77	7	21	141	10	96	317	.245	.299	.347

Lopez had been a serviceable utilityman with the Mets and Brewers, but he didn't hit much with the O's. His .152 average with runners in scoring position hurt, and he was released at season's end. 2003 Outlook: C

Fernando Lunar (Pos: C, Age: 25, Bats: R)

	G	AB	R	H	D	T	HR	RBI	SB	BB	SO	Avg	OBP	Slg
'02	2	0	0	0	0	0	0	0	0	0	0	—	—	—
Car.	97	237	13	53	8	0	0	22	0	10	51	.224	.275	.257

While Lunar made the Opening Day roster as the third catcher, he was sent to Triple-A Rochester in April. Injuries and a .193 average marred his season, but he has signed a minor league deal with Texas. 2003 Outlook: C

Calvin Maduro (Pos: RHP, Age: 28)

	W	L	Pct.	ERA	G	GS	Sv	IP	H	BB	SO	HR	Ratio
'02	2	5	.286	5.56	12	10	0	56.2	64	22	29	12	1.52
Car.	10	19	.345	5.78	68	39	0	260.0	272	118	140	43	1.50

The O's were hoping Maduro finally might come around in 2002, but elbow tendinitis sidelined him and he had surgery in June for a bone spur. He cleared waivers in October and became a free agent. 2003 Outlook: C

Luis Matos (Pos: RF, Age: 24, Bats: R)

	G	AB	R	H	D	T	HR	RBI	SB	BB	SO	Avg	OBP	Slg
'02	17	31	0	4	1	0	0	1	1	1	6	.129	.156	.161
Car.	120	311	37	66	14	3	5	30	21	24	66	.212	.276	.325

Matos broke the hamate bone in his left hand during spring training and didn't return until June. His glove is more ready for the majors than his bat. Matos posted a decent .370 OBP at Double-A Bowie. 2003 Outlook: B

Gary Matthews Jr. (Pos: RF/LF/CF, Age: 28, Bats: B)

	G	AB	R	H	D	T	HR	RBI	SB	BB	SO	Avg	OBP	Slg
'02	111	345	54	95	25	3	7	38	15	43	69	.275	.354	.426
Car.	366	944	145	225	41	7	25	103	28	127	206	.238	.329	.376

Did he turn a corner with the O's in 2002, or did he simply have a hot run? Matthews is in line to take the starting center-field job from Chris Singleton after his decent showing. 2003 Outlook: B

Ryan McGuire (Pos: 1B, Age: 31, Bats: L)

	G	AB	R	H	D	T	HR	RBI	SB	BB	SO	Avg	OBP	Slg
'02	17	26	0	2	1	0	0	2	0	2	7	.077	.143	.115
Car.	368	631	64	133	34	4	7	55	3	88	144	.211	.306	.311

McGuire got another brief chance with his fourth team in four years, but going 2-for-26 without a single hitting percentage in sight of the Mendoza line doesn't help the cause despite Triple-A success. 2003 Outlook: C

Izzy Molina (Pos: C, Age: 31, Bats: R)

	G	AB	R	H	D	T	HR	RBI	SB	BB	SO	Avg	OBP	Slg
'02	1	3	1	1	0	0	0	0	0	0	0	.333	.333	.333
Car.	69	141	8	29	5	1	3	8	0	4	20	.206	.228	.319

Molina had a career year at the plate in 2001, batting .305 at Triple-A Syracuse, but he was under the Mendoza line in Triple-A ball last year and didn't get much of a look. The O's still re-signed him. 2003 Outlook: C

Mike Moriarty (Pos: SS, Age: 29, Bats: R)

	G	AB	R	H	D	T	HR	RBI	SB	BB	SO	Avg	OBP	Slg
'02	8	16	0	3	1	0	0	3	0	0	2	.188	.188	.250
Car.	8	16	0	3	1	0	0	3	0	0	2	.188	.188	.250

Moriarty got his first cup-of-coffee in the majors early in his fifth Triple-A season in 2002, but didn't get a return call after showing less power. The Jays have signed him to a minor league deal. 2003 Outlook: C

Yorkis Perez (Pos: LHP, Age: 35)

	W	L	Pct.	ERA	G	GS	Sv	IP	H	BB	SO	HR	Ratio
'02	0	0	—	3.29	23	0	1	27.1	21	14	25	4	1.28
Car.	14	15	.483	4.44	337	0	2	282.0	251	147	259	29	1.41

Perez resurfaced in pro ball after two years away, pitched well in the minors and joined the O's in June. His walks were high, but he pitched OK before a September appendectomy and October release. 2003 Outlook: C

Brian Roberts (Pos: 2B, Age: 25, Bats: B)

	G	AB	R	H	D	T	HR	RBI	SB	BB	SO	Avg	OBP	Slg
'02	38	128	18	29	6	0	1	11	9	15	21	.227	.308	.297
Car.	113	401	60	98	18	3	3	28	21	28	57	.244	.292	.327

Roberts has posted strong OBPs in the minors, but he hasn't done the same or hit well in Baltimore. He should make the O's as a utility player, and eventually could emerge as the team's shortstop. 2003 Outlook: C

Josh Towers (Pos: RHP, Age: 26)

	W	L	Pct.	ERA	G	GS	Sv	IP	H	BB	SO	HR	Ratio
'02	0	3	.000	7.90	5	3	0	27.1	42	5	13	11	1.72
Car.	8	13	.381	5.05	29	23	0	167.2	207	21	71	32	1.36

Towers, a control specialist who was exceptional in the minors, couldn't fool big league hitters in 2002 and then went 0-9 (7.57) at Triple-A Rochester. The Jays signed him to a minor league deal. 2003 Outlook: C

Baltimore

Baltimore Orioles Minor League Prospects

Organization Overview:

While pitching prospects Sean Douglass and John Stephens got their feet wet in Baltimore in 2002, it was discouraging news that the system's two best pitching talents, lefties Eric Bedard and Rich Stahl, missed a majority of the season with injuries. Bedard will be out for all of 2003 after Tommy John surgery. The good news is, a number of others made solid steps toward Baltimore last summer, including Darnell McDonald, Tripper Johnson, Mike Fontenot, Doug Gredvig and John Maine. The new management team of Mike Flanagan and Jim Beattie faces the task of rebuilding this once-proud franchise.

Erik Bedard

Position: P
Bats: L **Throws:** L
Ht: 6' 1" **Wt:** 186

Opening Day Age: 24
Born: 3/6/79 in Navan, Canada

Recent Statistics

	W	L	ERA	G	GS	Sv	IP	H	R	BB	SO	HR
2002 AA Bowie	6	3	1.97	13	12	0	68.2	43	18	30	66	0
2002 AL Baltimore	0	0	13.50	2	0	0	0.2	1	0	1	0	0

A 1999 sixth-round pick from rural Ontario, Bedard emerged from a Connecticut community college and was a pleasant surprise in 2001, following up a solid season at Class-A Delmarva in 2000 with a 9-2 (2.15) performance at high-A Frederick. The velocity of his fastball had jumped from the high 80s to the low 90s, but more importantly, he had good movement on all of his pitches. His changeup was a bit behind his fastball and curve heading into the 2002 season, but he was outstanding early on at Double-A Bowie, blanking opponents in roughly half his starts and getting a brief callup to Baltimore before he experienced elbow pain in June. A slight ligament tear was detected, and rest and rehab over the summer didn't help, leading to Tommy John surgery in early September. He'll miss all of 2003.

Mike Fontenot

Position: 2B
Bats: L **Throws:** R
Ht: 5' 8" **Wt:** 178

Opening Day Age: 22
Born: 6/9/80 in Slidell, LA

Recent Statistics

	G	AB	R	H	D	T	HR	RBI	SB	BB	SO	Avg
2002 A Frederick	122	481	61	127	16	4	8	53	13	42	117	.264

The 19th overall pick out of Louisiana State in 2001, Fontenot didn't sign until that September and played only in some instructional league action before debuting in 2002. The layoff didn't hurt him, even at high Class-A Frederick, where he showed an aggressive bat and hit .264 in his first taste of the pro game. He's not big, but he's strong with good offensive potential and a solid all-around game. Defensively, he made a lot of throwing errors at second base, but their frequency dwindled in the second half as he settled in and adjusted to the faster game. He showed quick hands and smooth work on the double-play pivot. He'll need to control his aggressiveness and cut down his strikeouts batting near the top of the order, but the Orioles anticipate his pitch selectivity will come.

Doug Gredvig

Position: 1B
Bats: R **Throws:** R
Ht: 6' 3" **Wt:** 231

Opening Day Age: 23
Born: 8/25/79 in Roseville, CA

Recent Statistics

	G	AB	R	H	D	T	HR	RBI	SB	BB	SO	Avg
2001 A Frederick	129	484	71	123	35	2	20	62	2	37	125	.254
2002 AA Bowie	129	465	48	128	22	1	14	80	2	46	94	.275

A fifth-round pick in 2000, Gredvig gave a glimpse of his power potential by stroking 35 doubles and 20 homers at high Class-A Frederick in 2001. He showed quick hands at the plate and decent defensive skills at first base, but a key question had been his weight and conditioning. A year ago he underwent an offseason training program that dropped some baggage and toned him up. Then, in his first exposure to Double-A pitchers last summer, Gredvig made better contact, dropped his strikeout rate and walked more. He showed good discipline at the plate, and the Orioles see him as a middle-of-the-order type. His defensive game also improved in 2002. Gredvig is repeating his offseason regimen this year, and he may begin 2003 at Triple-A Ottawa.

Tripper Johnson

Position: 3B
Bats: R **Throws:** R
Ht: 6' 1" **Wt:** 195

Opening Day Age: 20
Born: 4/28/82 in Bellevue, WA

Recent Statistics

	G	AB	R	H	D	T	HR	RBI	SB	BB	SO	Avg
2001 R Bluefield	43	157	24	41	6	1	2	26	4	11	37	.261
2002 A Delmarva	136	493	73	128	32	6	11	71	19	62	88	.260

Johnson was the Orioles' first-round pick in 2000, a potential fast-track candidate at third base, but a slow start and a shoulder injury that limited him to DH duties kept him in rookie ball for all of 2001. Johnson participated in that same offseason workout program with good friend Doug Gredvig a year ago, and Johnson produced a very consistent year at Class-A Delmarva in 2002. A quiet, low-key professional about his work, Johnson experienced a surge in plate discipline as he accumulated at-bats. Johnson's defensive game was good at Delmarva, especially in light of his lost time in the field in 2001 because of injury.

Rommie Lewis

Position: P   **Opening Day Age:** 20
Bats: L **Throws:** L   **Born:** 9/2/82 in Bellevue,
Ht: 6' 6" **Wt:** 200   WA

Recent Statistics

	W	L	ERA	G	GS	Sv	IP	H	R	BB	SO	HR
2001 R Orioles	1	1	2.14	10	7	0	33.2	37	16	6	27	3
2001 A Frederick	0	1	9.00	1	0	0	4.0	8	7	1	2	1
2002 A Delmarva	1	2	2.15	53	0	25	71.0	50	19	20	77	1

A high school teammate of Tripper Johnson in suburban Seattle, Lewis was a fourth-round pick in 2001. Despite allowing more than one earned run in just one of seven Rookie-level starts after he was drafted, he went to the bullpen at Class-A Delmarva last summer. There he posted 25 saves, fanned more than a batter an inning and allowed just over one baserunner per frame. Lewis has a loose, live arm and may move into a starting rotation in 2003. The Orioles would like to see how he does. He throws an 88-91 MPH fastball, a great changeup and a good breaking ball.

Darnell McDonald

Position: OF   **Opening Day Age:** 24
Bats: R **Throws:** R   **Born:** 11/17/78 in Fort
Ht: 5' 11" **Wt:** 210   Collins, CO

Recent Statistics

	G	AB	R	H	D	T	HR	RBI	SB	BB	SO	Avg
2001 AA Bowie	30	117	16	33	7	1	3	21	3	9	28	.282
2001 AAA Rochester	104	391	37	93	19	2	2	35	13	29	75	.238
2002 AA Bowie	37	144	21	42	9	1	4	15	9	22	27	.292
2002 AAA Rochester	91	332	43	96	21	6	6	35	11	32	78	.289

The athletic McDonald was a two-sport star when the Orioles made him a first-round pick in 1997, but the Orioles believe they have worked the football out of him. He has improved steadily through five years of playing only baseball, though he still strikes out too often for the type of hitter he is. His hitting percentages climbed markedly in the high minors in 2002, a sign of a more disciplined approach at the plate and his overall conversion into a ballplayer. He has great speed and gets the ball in the outfield. Though he is better suited to a corner, he could play center field. More time in Triple-A ball is needed to make him more consistent.

Keith Reed

Position: OF   **Opening Day Age:** 24
Bats: R **Throws:** R   **Born:** 10/8/78 in
Ht: 6' 4" **Wt:** 215   Yarmouth Port, MA

Recent Statistics

	G	AB	R	H	D	T	HR	RBI	SB	BB	SO	Avg
2001 A Frederick	72	267	28	72	14	0	7	29	8	13	57	.270
2001 AA Bowie	18	67	7	17	3	0	1	8	2	6	10	.254
2001 AAA Rochester	20	74	11	23	7	1	2	11	1	5	14	.311
2002 AA Bowie	137	488	57	120	20	1	15	64	3	40	107	.246

Reed went to Providence College, where he played basketball and was recruited to play baseball. Only after a big junior year in 1999 did the baseball world take notice. Reed has five-tool talent, but he has struggled to convert those tools into productive skills. His progress was compromised in 2001 by a lingering hand injury, yet he did some of his best hitting at Triple-A Rochester late that year. But in 2002, he failed to make consistent contact at Double-A Bowie. His pitch recognition remains below average and he swings at a lot of bad offerings, but he'll drive balls into the gaps when he's on a good streak. Reed demonstrates good speed, great range and an impressive arm in the outfield.

Eddie Rogers

Position: SS   **Opening Day Age:** 24
Bats: R **Throws:** R   **Born:** 8/29/78 in San
Ht: 6' 1" **Wt:** 172   Pedro de Macoris, DR

Recent Statistics

	G	AB	R	H	D	T	HR	RBI	SB	BB	SO	Avg
2002 AA Bowie	112	422	59	110	26	2	11	57	14	16	70	.261
2002 AL Baltimore	5	3	0	0	0	0	0	0	0	0	0	.000

His five-tool potential includes what it takes defensively to play shortstop—great arm, speed and impressive range—though Rogers must fine-tune those skills and reduce his errors on routine plays. His 2002 season started slowly, when new visa regulations delayed his arrival and exposed him as three years older. That makes his budding power over the last two years less impressive, but there's still room for excitement if his bat comes around. More than anything, Rogers needs to learn better plate discipline and his walk rate must improve. If he learns to limit his swings to pitches in the strike zone, Rogers has the stroke to put up impressive numbers.

Others to Watch

Six-foot-7 righthander **Daniel Cabrera** (21) saw his velocity jump from the low 80s to 92-94 MPH in 2002, but just as critical to his solid showing in the Rookie-level Appy League was his improved command of the fastball. He fanned more than a batter an inning at Bluefield. . . Cut loose after one year of rookie ball with Oakland, lefthanded-hitting **Luis Jimenez** (21) batted .375 and slugged .597 in the Rookie-level Appy League. He's big and strong with excellent bat control. Plus, he runs well and displayed plate discipline that was impressive for someone his age. . . The O's sixth-round pick in June, righthander **John Maine** (21) debuted at short-season Aberdeen by recording his first 11 outs on strikeouts. Using a moving low-90s fastball and slider, Maine improved as he moved up to Class-A Delmarva, finishing the year with a 1.45 ERA and 60 strikeouts in 43.1 innings. . . Six-foot-7 lefthander **Rich Stahl** (21) displayed the loose delivery and mid-90s heat of a future No. 1 starter. A bone spur in his shoulder that led to surgery shut him down after just 68 innings in 2001, and another bone spur early in 2002 required another procedure. He should be ready to go in the spring, but it will take time to see if Stahl can recapture his loose action and velocity.

Fenway Park

Offense

Fenway hasn't been a good home-run park for years, but its obsolete reputation survives nonetheless. (The construction of luxury boxes in the early 1980s cut off the winds that used to help carry balls over the Green Monster.) It remains a good hitters' park overall, though, because it boosts singles and doubles. The small foul territory, good batter's eye and high left-field wall all contribute to that. Lefthanded hitters are able to take just as much advantage as righthanded ones, provided they are able to use the entire field.

Defense

Right field is more demanding here than in any other park—it requires the range of a center fielder, a strong enough arm to throw from 380 feet away and the instincts to play the tricky angle near the foul pole. A left fielder who knows how to play the wall can hold some drives off it to long singles. The park used to be known as a graveyard for southpaws, but there's little reason to believe it's still so, now that it's no longer a righthanded power hitter's paradise.

Who It Helps the Most

The Red Sox have surprisingly few players who take good advantage of Fenway, which might have something to do with their unimpressive record at home last year. Brian Daubach and Nomar Garciaparra hit for a better average there, and backup Doug Mirabelli has shown some pop at Fenway in limited time. John Burkett pitched well there last year in his first season in Boston.

Who It Hurts the Most

In his two years in the majors, Shea Hillenbrand has hit for more power with a better average on the road. Trot Nixon loses a few home runs each year. Casey Fossum had a much higher ERA at home in 2002, but wasn't hit any harder there.

Rookies & Newcomers

New second baseman Todd Walker should hit .300 and be a doubles machine based in Fenway. Middle-infield prospect Freddy Sanchez might hit .300 as a part-time player.

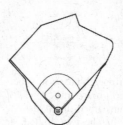

Dimensions: LF-310, LCF-379, CF-420, RCF-380, RF-302

Capacity: 33,991

Elevation: 21 feet

Surface: Grass

Foul Territory: Small

Park Factors

2002 Season

	Home Games Red Sox	Opp	Total	Away Games Red Sox	Opp	Total	Index
G	72	72	144	72	72	144	
Avg	.280	.251	.265	.287	.236	.263	101
AB	2415	2478	4893	2634	2379	5013	98
R	365	312	677	431	283	714	95
H	676	621	1297	755	562	1317	98
2B	159	145	304	163	97	260	120
3B	14	6	20	14	16	30	68
HR	71	58	129	91	76	167	79
BB	248	173	421	249	202	451	96
SO	400	544	944	420	488	908	107
E	53	54	107	38	47	85	126
E-Infield	43	44	87	32	41	73	119
LHB-Avg	.276	.230	.252	.273	.244	.259	97
LHB-HR	29	21	50	44	42	86	63
RHB-Avg	.283	.268	.276	.300	.229	.266	104
RHB-HR	42	37	79	47	34	81	95

2000-2002

	Home Games Red Sox	Opp	Total	Away Games Red Sox	Opp	Total	Index
G	216	216	432	215	215	430	
Avg	.277	.259	.268	.270	.245	.258	104
AB	7344	7593	14937	7737	7174	14911	100
R	1080	1003	2083	1144	928	2072	100
H	2034	1965	3999	2091	1758	3849	103
2B	461	410	871	433	330	763	114
3B	49	31	80	34	42	76	105
HR	217	190	407	279	223	502	81
BB	762	611	1373	746	684	1430	96
SO	1334	1666	3000	1382	1514	2896	103
E	160	147	307	130	125	255	120
E-Infield	137	121	258	106	107	213	121
LHB-Avg	.275	.253	.264	.262	.242	.252	104
LHB-HR	107	75	182	147	110	257	74
RHB-Avg	.279	.264	.271	.278	.248	.263	103
RHB-HR	110	115	225	132	113	245	88

2002 Rankings (American League)

- Second-highest double factor
- Second-highest error factor
- Third-highest infield-error factor
- Lowest LHB home-run factor
- Third-lowest triple factor

Grady Little

2002 Season

Though the Red Sox won 93 games under first-year manager Grady Little, it was hard to call the 2002 season a success. Despite getting off to a 40-17 start, suffering hardly any significant injuries and making several key pickups in midseason, the team saw its postseason hopes slip away during a slow, maddening second-half decline that included an inordinate amount of one-run losses.

Offense

Little used a set lineup, which was dictated, to a certain extent, by the talent on hand. Still, he rarely gave Shea Hillenbrand or Johnny Damon a day off, even as Hillenbrand wore down in the second half and Damon played through a knee injury. He gave Tony Clark abundant opportunity to find his stroke, but the money Clark was being paid might have required that. Strategically, he did what most managers would do with such a lineup, letting Damon run but otherwise relying on the big hitters to do what they do best.

Pitching & Defense

The one area where Little often went against the book was in gaining the platoon advantage. He was unafraid to have a righthanded pitcher walk a righthanded hitter to pitch to a lefthanded one, or to send up a righthanded pinch-hitter against a righthanded pitcher. Some managers seem to be slaves to the left-right game, but Little seems more concerned with how individual hitters match up with individual pitchers' stuff, and how well a pitcher is throwing. While he deserves some credit for Derek Lowe's success, Lowe's conversion to a starter was an experiment Little inherited rather than originated.

2003 Outlook

When Little was hired during spring training, most of the coaching staff already was in place, so it was seen as a vote of confidence when he was allowed to choose new coaches after the season. All agree that the talent is there, so it will be up to Little to get the players to play to their potential for the entire season this time around.

Born: 3/03/50 in Abilene, TX

Playing Experience: No major league playing experience

Managerial Experience: 1 season

Boston

Manager Statistics

Year	Team, Lg	W	L	Pct	GB	Finish
2002	Boston, AL	93	69	.574	10.5	2nd East
1 Season		93	69	.574	–	–

2002 Starting Pitchers by Days Rest

	<=3	4	5	6+
Red Sox Starts	1	70	57	23
Red Sox ERA	10.38	3.93	3.00	3.28
AL Avg Starts	1	83	44	24
AL ERA	7.15	4.59	4.27	5.03

2002 Situational Stats

	Grady Little	AL Average
Hit & Run Success %	31.4	36.0
Stolen Base Success %	74.1	68.1
Platoon Pct.	59.3	58.9
Defensive Subs	14	23
High-Pitch Outings	2	6
Quick/Slow Hooks	16/12	19/14
Sacrifice Attempts	35	53

2002 Rankings (American League)

- 1st in pitchouts (51) and pitchouts with a runner moving (9)
- 2nd in stolen-base percentage and saves with over 1 inning pitched (11)
- 3rd in fewest caught stealings of second base (23) and starts on three days rest

Johnny Damon

2002 Season

Coming off a disappointing 2001 season in Oakland, Johnny Damon became a free agent and signed a four-year deal with Boston. His season mirrored the team's: good overall, but somewhat disappointing in that a strong start was followed by long, gradual slide. In Damon's defense, a knee problem slowed him for much of the second half, but he never complained or took himself out of the lineup. His speed added an element historically lacking in Boston's attack, and his class and professionalism were appreciated in a clubhouse that had been strife-torn the season before.

Hitting

Damon is a terrific leadoff hitter because he not only has the requisite skills but understands how to use them. Using a short, quick stroke, he sprays hard line drives to all fields, often legging them into doubles or triples. He also hangs in well against lefthanders' breaking balls. Opposing third basemen know he's always a threat to bunt for a hit if they play him too deep. He works the count well and is excellent at protecting the plate with two strikes.

Baserunning & Defense

Damon's first-step quickness and fine straight-ahead speed make him a rangy center fielder and fearsome baserunner. With a righthander on the mound, Damon is one of the better basestealers around, though he has trouble reading southpaws' moves. His biggest weakness is a well-below average throwing arm.

2003 Outlook

One thing Damon is a virtual lock to deliver is a full season; in seven-plus years in the majors, he has yet to miss appreciable time with an injury. This year, with two healthy legs again, he has a good chance to get his average back above .300. Even if he doesn't, he'll continue to be a critical component in the Red Sox' attack.

Position: CF
Bats: L **Throws:** L
Ht: 6' 2" **Wt:** 190

Opening Day Age: 29
Born: 11/5/73 in Fort Riley, KS
ML Seasons: 8
Pronunciation: DAY-mun

Overall Statistics

	G	AB	R	H	D	T	HR	RBI	SB	BB	SO	Avg	OBP	Slg
'02	154	623	118	178	34	11	14	63	31	65	70	.286	.356	.443
Car.	1112	4324	730	1237	224	62	88	464	214	401	490	.286	.348	.428

Where He Hits the Ball

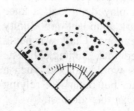 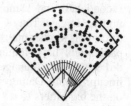

Vs. LHP **Vs. RHP**

2002 Situational Stats

	AB	H	HR	RBI	Avg		AB	H	HR	RBI	Avg
Home	289	82	5	25	.284	LHP	157	48	3	14	.306
Road	334	96	9	38	.287	RHP	466	130	11	49	.279
First Half	331	102	6	41	.308	Sc Pos	125	33	2	48	.264
Scnd Half	292	76	8	22	.260	Clutch	71	17	2	6	.239

2002 Rankings (American League)

- 1st in triples
- 2nd in fielding percentage in center field (.997)
- 3rd in fewest GDPs per GDP situation (3.7%)
- 4th in stolen bases
- 5th in runs scored, pitches seen (2,727) and stolen-base percentage (83.8)
- 6th in assists in center field (7)
- Led the Red Sox in runs scored, triples, stolen bases, caught stealing (6), times on base (249), pitches seen (2,727), plate appearances (702), stolen-base percentage (83.8), bunts in play (12), fewest GDPs per GDP situation (3.7%) and batting average with the bases loaded (.412)

Brian Daubach

2002 Season

There was very little new about Brain Daubach's 2002 season. He hit in the middle third of the order against righthanders and produced numbers that virtually matched his career norms. The only surprising thing was that he played 48 games in the outfield without embarrassing himself.

Hitting

The reason Daubach is in the majors is that he has enough power to hit in an RBI spot against righthanded pitchers. Not at all a dead-pull hitter, he has learned to use the Monster if a pitcher insists on keeping the ball away from him. He's better off sitting against most southpaws, and can be made to chase breaking balls in the dirt by lefties and righties alike. Few hitters run hot-and-cold to the extremes Daubach does. He's hit only .143 in 42 career at-bats as a pinch-hitter, striking out nearly half the time.

Baserunning & Defense

For a couple of months last year, while first base and the DH spot were occupied, Daubach was pressed into service as a left fielder. Fenway helped minimize his serious lack of range and overall inexperience, and he generally caught whatever he could get to. The only position where he could survive on a regular basis is first, where he's similarly immobile but makes the plays he has to make. He's no factor on the bases.

2003 Outlook

Daubach is up for arbitration, and there's a chance the Red Sox will non-tender him. He's useful to keep around at the right price, but his skill set is not irreplaceable. If he doesn't return, he'll likely wind up as part of another team's first-base platoon.

Position: 1B/LF/DH/RF
Bats: L **Throws:** R
Ht: 6' 1" **Wt:** 233

Opening Day Age: 31
Born: 2/11/72 in Belleville, IL
ML Seasons: 5
Pronunciation: DAW-back
Nickname: The Belleville Basher

Overall Statistics

	G	AB	R	H	D	T	HR	RBI	SB	BB	SO	Avg	OBP	Slg
'02	137	444	62	118	24	2	20	78	2	51	126	.266	.348	.464
Car.	521	1742	232	463	118	10	84	301	4	185	461	.266	.341	.490

Where He Hits the Ball

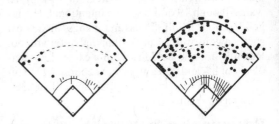

Vs. LHP   **Vs. RHP**

2002 Situational Stats

	AB	H	HR	RBI	Avg		AB	H	HR	RBI	Avg
Home	216	63	11	44	.292	LHP	62	15	3	16	.242
Road	228	55	9	34	.241	RHP	382	103	17	62	.270
First Half	219	56	12	38	.256	Sc Pos	141	42	8	61	.298
Scnd Half	225	62	8	40	.276	Clutch	49	9	1	7	.184

2002 Rankings (American League)

- 4th in lowest percentage of swings put into play (34.7)
- 8th in most pitches seen per plate appearance (4.05)
- 10th in errors at first base (5), lowest batting average in the clutch and lowest batting average on an 0-2 count (.063)
- Led the Red Sox in strikeouts and most pitches seen per plate appearance (4.05)

Boston

57

Cliff Floyd

2002 Season

Cliff Floyd got two chances to get to the postseason last year, but unfortunately for him, neither one worked out. He was dealt from Florida to Montreal at the All-Star break, but had trouble readjusting to Olympic Stadium's artificial turf, and the Expos soon fell back from the pack. Two weeks later he was sent to Boston, and this time he produced just fine, but once again his new team faded. He had a fine season overall despite his usual series of nagging injuries.

Hitting

Floyd comes out hacking and tees off against pitchers who are hasty enough to try to get ahead with a first-pitch fastball. He was a bit more patient last year, setting a career high with 76 walks, though 19 of them were intentional. He has good power to all fields and hangs in against southpaws as well as any lefthanded hitter around. Running hot-and-cold has been a career-long tendency of his and 2002 was no exception. Floyd hit .224 in July and followed that up with a .325 showing in August.

Baserunning & Defense

Though bothered by a sore left knee much of last season, Floyd still put his surprisingly good speed to use on the bases and in the field. He's an excellent percentage basestealer who's learned to pick his spots. He has good range for a corner outfielder and played the Monster adequately for a newcomer to the American League. His arm is passable for right field. He may be reaching the point in his career where a return to first base would be worth considering, in order to save wear and tear on his legs.

2003 Outlook

Floyd became a free agent over the winter, and apparently was comfortable enough in Boston to consider returning. With his injury history, he carries some risk, but his lefthanded bat would be a valuable addition to the heart of any team's order.

Position: RF/LF/DH
Bats: L **Throws:** R
Ht: 6' 4" **Wt:** 260

Opening Day Age: 30
Born: 12/5/72 in Chicago, IL
ML Seasons: 10

Overall Statistics

	G	AB	R	H	D	T	HR	RBI	SB	BB	SO	Avg	OBP	Slg
'02	146	520	86	150	43	0	28	79	15	76	106	.288	.388	.533
Car.	955	3132	510	891	225	17	132	508	115	347	627	.284	.361	.494

Where He Hits the Ball

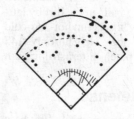 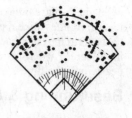

Vs. LHP   **Vs. RHP**

2002 Situational Stats

	AB	H	HR	RBI	Avg		AB	H	HR	RBI	Avg
Home	277	78	13	37	.282	LHP	154	38	10	24	.247
Road	243	72	15	42	.296	RHP	366	112	18	55	.306
First Half	296	85	18	57	.287	Sc Pos	151	40	6	51	.265
Scnd Half	224	65	10	22	.290	Clutch	76	15	2	5	.197

2002 Rankings (American League)

• Led the Red Sox in steals of third (2)

Nomar Garciaparra

Future MVP

2002 Season

After wrist surgery virtually wiped out Nomar Garciaparra's 2001 season, it was a relief to Red Sox fans to see him come back and play in a career-high 156 games in 2002. His season was unarguably terrific, but it was slightly below Garciaparra's pre-injury standards and sometimes frustrating for him.

Hitting

Garciaparra hit 13 first-pitch homers last year, the third-highest total in the majors; it's amazing that he can remain so dangerous on the first pitch even when pitchers know how aggressive he is early in the count. His strong, quick wrists allow him to adjust in mid-swing to any pitch type and location and still hit the ball hard. He has good power from straightaway center to the left-field line, although he pulled the ball more often than ever last year. This might have been more a result of the way he was being pitched than a conscious decision, though. In fact, he had shed some bulk over the winter in an effort to avoid the minor muscle pulls that had bothered him in the past.

Baserunning & Defense

Garciaparra's quickness and agility translate into superior range afield. Though he led American League shortstops with 25 errors, many were on balls other shortstops never would have reached. His arm strength allows him to make crisp throws even when on the run. He has the speed to steal bases—though he rarely is called upon to do so— and is one of the club's best baserunners.

2003 Outlook

For a star of Garciaparra's magnitude, it's understandable that every minor ache and pain is fretted over. Still, the only injury that's ever kept him out for a significant stretch was the wrist problem, which he's proven is no longer a concern. There's every reason to expect him to turn in many more terrific seasons.

Position: SS
Bats: R **Throws:** R
Ht: 6' 0" **Wt:** 190

Opening Day Age: 29
Born: 7/23/73 in Whittier, CA
ML Seasons: 7
Pronunciation: no-mar GARCIA-par-uh

Overall Statistics

	G	AB	R	H	D	T	HR	RBI	SB	BB	SO	Avg	OBP	Slg
'02	156	635	101	197	56	5	24	120	5	41	63	.310	.352	.528
Car.	772	3154	565	1033	235	34	145	564	63	232	329	.328	.375	.562

Where He Hits the Ball

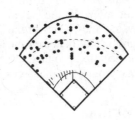 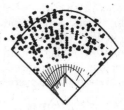

Vs. LHP   **Vs. RHP**

2002 Situational Stats

	AB	H	HR	RBI	Avg		AB	H	HR	RBI	Avg
Home	314	103	10	55	.328	LHP	118	36	3	21	.305
Road	321	94	14	65	.293	RHP	517	161	21	99	.311
First Half	327	102	11	66	.312	Sc Pos	165	54	7	90	.327
Scnd Half	308	95	13	54	.308	Clutch	84	27	4	16	.321

2002 Rankings (American League)

- 1st in doubles, errors at shortstop (25), lowest percentage of pitches taken (41.8) and lowest fielding percentage at shortstop (.965)
- 2nd in sacrifice flies (11), fewest pitches seen per plate appearance (3.06) and highest percentage of swings on the first pitch (50.4)
- 5th in hits
- 6th in total bases (335), RBI and batting average at home
- 7th in at-bats and lowest groundball-flyball ratio (0.7)
- Led the Red Sox in at-bats, hits, doubles, total bases (335), RBI, sacrifice flies (11) and games played
- Led AL shortstops in batting average

Boston

Shea Hillenbrand

2002 Season

Shea Hillenbrand broke from the gates with a red-hot April, just as he had the year before. This time, though, he avoided the deep slump that soon had followed last time around. Hillenbrand even was voted a starting spot in the All-Star Game. His power waned in the second half, but he finished with better numbers than most had expected.

Hitting

Hillenbrand made real improvement last year, hitting balls with authority more often, although it's important to keep in mind that much of the increase in his raw totals was simply the result of getting 35 percent more at-bats. A line-drive hitter who uses the whole field, he often hits the ball to the biggest part of Fenway, and thus is one of the few Red Sox who hits significantly better on the road. While he realized the need to become more patient, and even made some progress in that area, he remains quite averse to walking.

Baserunning & Defense

Fielding is another area in which Hillenbrand has made strides but still has room for improvement, having tied for the major league lead in errors by a third baseman in 2002. He has a strong enough arm and good enough reactions for the position, and he is at his best when given little time to react. When given time to set and throw, he sometimes chokes the ball. He's an average baserunner and rarely is a threat to run.

2003 Outlook

Hillenbrand took firm hold of the Red Sox' third-base job with his strong season last year. Still, it may be hard for him to take another step forward—he'll turn 28 this July, and it's hard to expect continued power growth from someone with his line-drive, spray-hitting approach. On the other hand, getting a few more days off might help him better maintain his strength.

Position: 3B
Bats: R **Throws:** R
Ht: 6' 1" **Wt:** 211

Opening Day Age: 27
Born: 7/27/75 in Mesa, AZ
ML Seasons: 2
Pronunciation: SHAY

Overall Statistics

	G	AB	R	H	D	T	HR	RBI	SB	BB	SO	Avg	OBP	Slg
'02	156	634	94	186	43	4	18	83	4	25	95	.293	.330	.459
Car.	295	1102	146	309	63	6	30	132	7	38	156	.280	.313	.430

Where He Hits the Ball

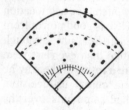 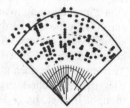

Vs. LHP   **Vs. RHP**

2002 Situational Stats

	AB	H	HR	RBI	Avg		AB	H	HR	RBI	Avg
Home	311	82	5	35	.264	LHP	119	32	1	12	.269
Road	323	104	13	48	.322	RHP	515	154	17	71	.299
First Half	339	101	13	51	.298	Sc Pos	170	48	9	72	.282
Scnd Half	295	85	5	32	.288	Clutch	80	30	4	15	.375

2002 Rankings (American League)

- 1st in errors at third base (23)
- 2nd in lowest fielding percentage at third base (.943)
- 5th in batting average in the clutch
- 6th in doubles and GDPs (18)
- 7th in hit by pitch (12)
- 8th in at-bats and singles
- 9th in batting average on the road
- 10th in hits
- Led the Red Sox in singles, hit by pitch (12), GDPs (18), games played, batting average in the clutch and batting average on a 3-1 count (.529)
- Led AL third basemen in batting average

Derek Lowe

2002 Season

Coming off a nightmare 2001 season in which he'd lost his job as the Red Sox' closer, Derek Lowe staged one of the most dramatic turn-arounds imaginable. Installed in the starting rotation, he no-hit the Devil Rays on April 27 and went on to finish second in the American League in both wins and ERA. He was as consistently effective as any starter in the game, allowing three runs or fewer in 25 of his 32 starts. Lowe capped his 2002 effort with a third-place showing in the AL Cy Young vote.

Pitching

Known for his dazzling sinker, Lowe made the adjustments necessary to succeed as a starter by refining his cutter and making better use of his curve and changeup. These changes helped him neutralize lefthanded hitters, who had given him trouble in the past. He has very good command, particularly for a pitcher whose ball has so much movement. It's harder to get the ball in the air against him than any major league pitcher, and when a batter reaches first base against him, it's often only the prelude to a double play. He maintained his stamina well, especially considering that he hadn't started regularly in five years.

Defense

Lowe does a decent job of flagging down the many comebackers he induces, but he also knows when to let his infielders handle them. Teams run on him to stay out of the double play, and his tendency to pitch at or below the knees makes it tough for his catcher to get off good throws. Opposing basestealers were successful against Lowe nearly 75 percent of the time in 2002.

2003 Outlook

The type of sustained excellence Lowe displayed last year cannot be dismissed as a mere fluke. Besides, he had been nearly as effective in relief in 1999 and 2000 before 2001's meltdown. He's now shown he can survive and thrive in a starting role, and there's no reason to think he won't continue to do just that in 2003 and beyond.

Position: SP
Bats: R **Throws:** R
Ht: 6' 6" **Wt:** 214

Opening Day Age: 29
Born: 6/1/73 in
Dearborn, MI
ML Seasons: 6

Overall Statistics

	W	L	Pct.	ERA	G	GS	Sv	IP	H	BB	SO	HR	Ratio
'02	21	8	.724	2.58	32	32	0	219.2	166	48	127	12	0.97
Car.	41	40	.506	3.31	330	54	85	704.0	643	189	497	48	1.18

How Often He Throws Strikes

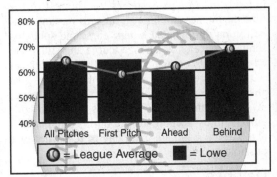

2002 Situational Stats

	W	L	ERA	Sv	IP		AB	H	HR	RBI	Avg
Home	9	4	2.10	0	107.0	LHB	407	85	6	31	.209
Road	12	4	3.04	0	112.2	RHB	380	81	6	27	.213
First Half	12	4	2.36	0	118.0	Sc Pos	141	31	3	42	.220
Scnd Half	9	4	2.83	0	101.2	Clutch	37	6	0	2	.162

2002 Rankings (American League)

- 1st in lowest slugging percentage allowed (.302), highest groundball-flyball ratio allowed (3.5), lowest ERA at home and fielding percentage at pitcher (1.000)
- 2nd in ERA, wins, lowest on-base percentage allowed (.266), most run support per nine innings (6.8) and fewest home runs allowed per nine innings (.49)
- 3rd in GDPs induced (28) and lowest batting average allowed (.211)
- Led the Red Sox in wins, games started, innings pitched, GDPs induced (28), lowest ERA at home, most run support per nine innings (6.8) and fewest home runs allowed per nine innings (.49)

Boston

Pedro Martinez

2002 Season

Coming into 2002, Pedro Martinez was a major question mark. He'd missed most of the second half of 2001 with a small tear in his rotator cuff, and had undertaken a strengthening program over the winter in hopes of avoiding surgery. Though his health was an ongoing concern and he seemed at times to be less than 100 percent, the results were there, as he stayed in the rotation all year and delivered a Cy Young-quality performance.

Pitching

Martinez still has all his weapons; the only real difference is that he no longer dials it up to the mid-90s until he really needs to. The rest of the time, he pitches at 90 MPH, runs his moving fastball in on righthanded hitters' fists, and spots his screwball-like circle change, curve and slider. He has excellent command of all his pitches and can put a hitter away with any of them. Once he gets ahead and can make the hitter expand the zone, he's nearly unhittable. The club is careful to safeguard him by keeping an eye on his pitch counts and by giving him an extra day of rest whenever possible.

Defense

Light on his feet, Martinez fields his position well and keeps runners close with a good spin move to first. He prefers to save his effort by simply looking runners back, though. He's become pretty tough to run on, and he picked off a pair of runners last season.

2003 Outlook

The anxiety about Martinez' shoulder may never abate completely, but he's shown he can pitch with it and still be dominant. He went into the off-season planning to repeat last winter's rigorous workout regimen. Though another breakdown is always a possibility, there's no reason he can't be just as dominant again this season.

Position: SP
Bats: R **Throws:** R
Ht: 5'11" **Wt:** 180

Opening Day Age: 31
Born: 10/25/71 in Manoguayabo, DR
ML Seasons: 11

Overall Statistics

	W	L	Pct.	ERA	G	GS	Sv	IP	H	BB	SO	HR	Ratio
'02	20	4	.833	2.26	30	30	0	199.1	144	40	239	13	0.92
Car.	152	63	.707	2.62	326	259	3	1892.1	1406	507	2220	142	1.01

How Often He Throws Strikes

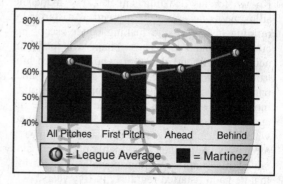

Ⓒ = League Average   ■ = Martinez

2002 Situational Stats

	W	L	ERA	Sv	IP		AB	H	HR	RBI	Avg
Home	10	2	2.71	0	89.2	LHB	428	87	7	32	.203
Road	10	2	1.89	0	109.2	RHB	298	57	6	23	.191
First Half	11	2	2.72	0	115.2	Sc Pos	153	30	0	36	.196
Scnd Half	9	2	1.61	0	83.2	Clutch	30	6	1	4	.200

2002 Rankings (American League)

- 1st in ERA, strikeouts, winning percentage, highest strikeout-walk ratio (6.0), lowest batting average allowed (.198), lowest on-base percentage allowed (.254), lowest ERA on the road, lowest batting average allowed vs. righthanded batters and most strikeouts per nine innings (10.8)
- 2nd in lowest slugging percentage allowed (.309)
- 3rd in wins, hit batsmen (15), lowest batting average allowed with runners in scoring position and fewest home runs allowed per nine innings (.59)

Trot Nixon

2002 Season

In many ways, Trot Nixon's 2002 season was like Nixon himself—unspectacular but solid all around. Though he hit for the lowest average of his four full major league seasons, he maintained his power numbers from the year before and drove in a career-high 94 runs.

Hitting

Nixon is a strong, patient hitter who has a good mix of power and on-base skills. He often batted second or third in 2001, but was dropped to the lower third of the order last year after the return of Nomar Garciaparra and the addition of Johnny Damon. He likes to look over the first pitch and isn't afraid to work deep counts. The one major weakness in his game is his inability to hit left-handers with authority. Though he made marginal improvement in that area in 2002, he still struck out in one-third of his at-bats against them. He's quite capable of hitting in an RBI slot against righthanders, though.

Baserunning & Defense

Though Nixon's natural speed is unspectacular, he makes the most of it in every way. With good reads and all-out hustle, he covers Fenway's cavernous right field very well and is capable of covering center when asked. Some right fielders merely have a strong arm; Nixon has one but also anticipates where the throw should go in every situation. He's just as heady on the bases, even if he isn't much of a threat to steal.

2003 Outlook

On a team with more than its share of big stars, Nixon quietly plays an important supporting role. The only question is whether he will be able to learn to hit lefties. If he isn't, he eventually might slip into a platoon role. New manager Grady Little allowed him to play regularly last year, but might not show as much patience this season if Nixon fails to show progress. Nixon was eligible for arbitration over the winter, but the club was expected to keep him.

Position: RF/CF
Bats: L **Throws:** L
Ht: 6' 2" **Wt:** 211

Opening Day Age: 28
Born: 4/11/74 in Durham, NC
ML Seasons: 6

Boston

Overall Statistics

	G	AB	R	H	D	T	HR	RBI	SB	BB	SO	Avg	OBP	Slg
'02	152	532	81	136	36	3	24	94	4	65	109	.256	.338	.470
Car.	562	1906	319	516	118	20	78	294	23	261	386	.271	.359	.476

Where He Hits the Ball

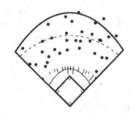
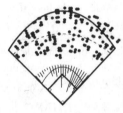

Vs. LHP   **Vs. RHP**

2002 Situational Stats

	AB	H	HR	RBI	Avg		AB	H	HR	RBI	Avg
Home	248	64	8	35	.258	LHP	116	27	3	15	.233
Road	284	72	16	59	.254	RHP	416	109	21	79	.262
First Half	277	75	10	37	.271	Sc Pos	131	35	6	67	.267
Scnd Half	255	61	14	57	.239	Clutch	72	16	4	15	.222

2002 Rankings (American League)

- 2nd in lowest percentage of swings on the first pitch (12.4)
- 4th in errors in right field (5) and lowest fielding percentage in right field (.982)
- Led the Red Sox in lowest percentage of swings on the first pitch (12.4)

2002 Season

Manny Ramirez had a fine 2002 season, driving in 107 runs in only 120 games and winning the American League batting title. Still, his season had its black marks. He missed six weeks in May and June with a broken finger as the result of an ill-advised headfirst slide into home, and he put his first-year manager on the spot when he didn't bother to run out a groundball in September as the team was falling out of contention.

Hitting

There is no safe way to pitch Ramirez. On an outside pitch, he can step into the ball and drive it to the opposite field with frightening power. On an inside pitch, he either can pull it to left, or keep his hands inside the ball and rip it the other way with equal force. When pitchers try to get him to chase balls outside the strike zone, he'll simply watch them go by until the pitcher comes in to him or walks him.

Baserunning & Defense

Ramirez is not an asset in the field or on the bases. His loping stride helps exaggerate the impression that he doesn't run hard, but he does tend to glide to the ball. Though his range is unimpressive, he plays the Green Monster adequately and throws fairly well. He's never been an aggressive baserunner, and hamstring and foot problems made him run more conservatively than ever last year.

2003 Outlook

Since he's never had anything close to an off year, the only real question with Ramirez is whether he'll be able to stay healthy. And while he's had his share of aches and pains over the last few campaigns, he's played enough to qualify for the batting title every year since 1995. In other words, he's as close as a superstar comes to money in the bank.

Position: LF/DH
Bats: R **Throws:** R
Ht: 6' 0" **Wt:** 213

Opening Day Age: 30
Born: 5/30/72 in Santo Domingo, DR
ML Seasons: 10
Pronunciation: ruh-MEER-ez

Overall Statistics

	G	AB	R	H	D	T	HR	RBI	SB	BB	SO	Avg	OBP	Slg
'02	120	436	84	152	31	0	33	107	0	73	85	.349	.450	.647
Car.	1229	4435	842	1400	301	13	310	1036	28	695	1012	.316	.411	.599

Where He Hits the Ball

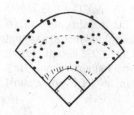

Vs. LHP   **Vs. RHP**

2002 Situational Stats

	AB	H	HR	RBI	Avg		AB	H	HR	RBI	Avg
Home	214	72	18	57	.336	LHP	73	32	6	21	.438
Road	222	80	15	50	.360	RHP	363	120	27	86	.331
First Half	156	53	9	38	.340	Sc Pos	108	47	9	71	.435
Scnd Half	280	99	24	69	.354	Clutch	56	16	3	10	.286

2002 Rankings (American League)

- 1st in batting average, on-base percentage, batting average with runners in scoring position and batting average on the road
- 2nd in slugging percentage, batting average at home and errors in left field (5)
- Led the Red Sox in home runs, walks, intentional walks (14), slugging percentage, HR frequency (13.2 ABs per HR), slugging percentage vs. lefthanded pitchers (.822), slugging percentage vs. righthanded pitchers (.612), on-base percentage vs. lefthanded pitchers (.534), on-base percentage vs. righthanded pitchers (.433), batting average at home, batting average on a 3-2 count (.355) and batting average with two strikes (.260)

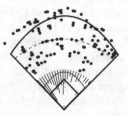

Ugueth Urbina

2002 Season

Early in 2002, Ugueth Urbina seemingly couldn't get his fastball beyond the upper-80s. This was especially troubling considering that the Yankees had cancelled a trade for him the previous summer based on the results of a physical. Urbina soon put those concerns to rest, though, recapturing his old heater while reeling off 20 consecutive scoreless appearances in May and June. He remained strong through the end of the year and ended up having one of his better seasons.

Pitching

With good command of his hard fastball and slider, Urbina is as tough on righthanded hitters as any short reliever in the game. Lefthanded hitters can hurt him, though, as he has trouble throwing his slider for strikes against them, mixing in changeups and splitters instead. He used to hurt himself with bases on balls on occasion, but last year he issued only 15 unintentional walks, by far his lowest total for a full season. That's a sign that he's starting to make the adjustments veteran pitchers must make as they begin to lose their dominance, although he still throws hard enough to work up in the zone effectively.

Defense

Urbina hasn't committed an error in five years, but has handled only 29 chances over that period—a natural result of his tendency to yield mostly strikeouts and flyballs. Baserunners always have run at will against him, and they stole off him less frequently last year only because he allowed fewer runners to reach first than he had in the past.

2003 Outlook

A free agent, Urbina's solid season eased concerns about his health. Having put in two quality seasons since twice undergoing elbow surgery in 2000, he's gone a long way toward reestablishing himself as one of the game's better short relievers.

Position: RP
Bats: R **Throws:** R
Ht: 6' 0" **Wt:** 205

Opening Day Age: 29
Born: 2/15/74 in Caracas, VZ
ML Seasons: 8
Pronunciation: ooo-GETT ooor-bee-NAH
Nickname: Oogy

Overall Statistics

	W	L	Pct.	ERA	G	GS	Sv	IP	H	BB	SO	HR	Ratio
'02	1	6	.143	3.00	61	0	40	60.0	44	20	71	8	1.07
Car.	32	33	.492	3.40	376	21	174	486.2	389	205	583	59	1.22

How Often He Throws Strikes

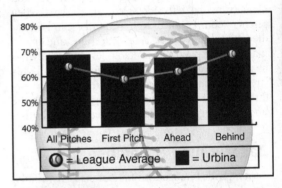

= League Average = Urbina

2002 Situational Stats

	W	L	ERA	Sv	IP		AB	H	HR	RBI	Avg
Home	1	4	3.66	19	32.0	LHB	113	29	6	15	.257
Road	0	2	2.25	21	28.0	RHB	105	15	2	8	.143
First Half	0	3	2.61	22	31.0	Sc Pos	51	9	1	16	.176
Scnd Half	1	3	3.41	18	29.0	Clutch	160	33	6	20	.206

2002 Rankings (American League)

- 3rd in saves and save opportunities (46)
- 5th in games finished (55), relief losses (6) and most strikeouts per nine innings in relief (10.6)
- Led the Red Sox in games pitched, saves, games finished (55), save opportunities (46), save percentage (87.0), blown saves (6), relief losses (6), relief ERA (3.00), lowest batting average allowed in relief (.202), most strikeouts per nine innings in relief (10.6) and fewest baserunners allowed per nine innings in relief (9.6)

Boston

Jason Varitek

2002 Season

Coming off a broken right elbow that wiped out half of his 2001 season, Jason Varitek faced questions concerning his throwing arm coming into 2002. Those concerns grew when he failed to catch a single one of the first 11 basestealers who tested him. He eventually put those fears to rest, though, performing up to his old standards behind the plate. Just as importantly, he stayed relatively healthy and caught 127 games. Still, it wasn't one of his better offensive seasons.

Hitting

The switch-hitting Varitek is equally effective from either side of the plate. He has decent power and can send balls off or over the Green Monster, even from the left side. He's at his best when pitchers come right in to him, but he can be handled when they work more carefully and try to make him expand the strike zone. Varitek always has been streaky, and one has to wonder if his streakiness can be linked to his willingness to play through injuries if possible. On days he isn't in the lineup, he gives the team a decent pinch-hitting option.

Baserunning & Defense

Varitek prides himself on his defense, justifiably. He works well communicating with pitchers and calling games, and his pitch-blocking skills give them the confidence to call for breaking balls in any situation. He throws well, although the staff's makeup doesn't allow him to compile a great caught-stealing percentage. On the bases, he's a typical catcher, although he'll occasionally surprise a pitcher who too conspicuously ignores him.

2003 Outlook

Going on age 31, Varitek isn't likely to get back to his peak numbers of a few years ago. As long as he's able to avoid major injuries, however, he likely will remain what he was last year—a defense-first receiver who also contributes with the bat. That style of play is more than acceptable to the Red Sox.

Position: C
Bats: B **Throws:** R
Ht: 6' 2" **Wt:** 237

Opening Day Age: 30
Born: 4/11/72 in Rochester, MI
ML Seasons: 6
Pronunciation: VARE-ih-tek

Overall Statistics

	G	AB	R	H	D	T	HR	RBI	SB	BB	SO	Avg	OBP	Slg
'02	132	467	58	124	27	1	10	61	4	41	95	.266	.332	.392
Car.	553	1794	233	473	121	5	54	260	8	185	344	.264	.335	.427

Where He Hits the Ball

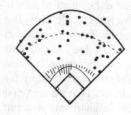 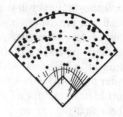

Vs. LHP   **Vs. RHP**

2002 Situational Stats

	AB	H	HR	RBI	Avg		AB	H	HR	RBI	Avg
Home	217	57	6	26	.263	LHP	118	31	2	21	.263
Road	250	67	4	35	.268	RHP	349	93	8	40	.266
First Half	249	67	6	31	.269	Sc Pos	136	32	1	50	.235
Scnd Half	218	57	4	30	.261	Clutch	66	20	2	11	.303

2002 Rankings (American League)

- 2nd in lowest percentage of runners caught stealing as a catcher (26.4)

Tim Wakefield

2002 Season

As he had for the previous few seasons, knuckle-baller Tim Wakefield continued to bounce between the rotation and long relief for the first half of 2002. He pitched better than he had in years, though—well enough to earn a spot in the rotation in late July. He took the opportunity and ran with it, going 6-1 with a 1.66 ERA over his last nine starts, ultimately placing fourth in the American League in ERA.

Pitching

Over the last two years, Wakefield has come to rely more and more on his curveball as his second pitch. It's by no means a beauty, but he can throw strikes with it, and it gives him a way to get ahead so he can go back to his main weapon, the knuckler. Like most pitchers of his type, he isn't quick to tire and is equally tough on hitters from either side of the plate. His ability to force batters to go after his offerings largely depends on his ability to get ahead in the count, so the larger strike zone over the last two years probably has helped him more than most pitchers.

Defense

Wakefield has a decent pickoff move and a compact stretch delivery, but there's only so much a knuckleballer can do, and he remains a fairly easy target for basestealers. He can handle himself in the field.

2003 Outlook

Instead of exercising a $3.8 million option for 2003, the Red Sox signed Wakefield to a three-year, $13.02 million deal. He will have a rotation spot right from the start, and in light of how well he's pitched the last two years, he easily could enjoy one of his best seasons. At the very least, he's probably more confident the club will not ship him back to the bullpen as soon as he starts to struggle. At age 36, he likely has at least a few more good seasons left.

Position: RP/SP
Bats: R **Throws:** R
Ht: 6' 2" **Wt:** 214

Opening Day Age: 36
Born: 8/2/66 in
Melbourne, FL
ML Seasons: 10

Overall Statistics

	W	L	Pct.	ERA	G	GS	Sv	IP	H	BB	SO	HR	Ratio
'02	11	5	.688	2.81	45	15	3	163.1	121	51	134	15	1.05
Car.	105	94	.528	4.25	357	220	21	1676.0	1619	695	1154	209	1.38

How Often He Throws Strikes

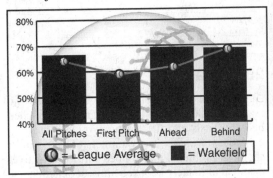

= League Average = Wakefield

2002 Situational Stats

	W	L	ERA	Sv	IP		AB	H	HR	RBI	Avg
Home	5	4	3.55	1	91.1	LHB	272	53	6	25	.195
Road	6	1	1.88	2	72.0	RHB	320	68	9	33	.213
First Half	2	3	2.90	3	71.1	Sc Pos	139	36	3	43	.259
Scnd Half	9	2	2.74	0	92.0	Clutch	106	23	2	13	.217

2002 Rankings (American League)

- 2nd in lowest batting average allowed (.204)
- 3rd in stolen bases allowed (21), lowest slugging percentage allowed (.333), lowest on-base percentage allowed (.276) and lowest batting average allowed vs. lefthanded batters
- 4th in ERA, balks (2), lowest batting average allowed vs. righthanded batters and most strikeouts per nine innings (7.4)
- Led the Red Sox in wild pitches (5), balks (2), lowest ERA on the road, lowest batting average allowed vs. lefthanded batters and relief innings (65.1)

Rolando Arrojo

Position: RP
Bats: R **Throws:** R
Ht: 6' 4" **Wt:** 236

Opening Day Age: 34
Born: 7/18/68 in Havana, Cuba
ML Seasons: 5
Pronunciation: ah-ROW-ho

Overall Statistics

	W	L	Pct.	ERA	G	GS	Sv	IP	H	BB	SO	HR	Ratio
'02	4	3	.571	4.98	29	8	1	81.1	83	27	51	7	1.35
Car.	40	42	.488	4.55	158	105	6	700.0	715	255	512	83	1.39

2002 Situational Stats

	W	L	ERA	Sv	IP		AB	H	HR	RBI	Avg
Home	2	2	6.10	0	31.0	LHB	163	51	3	22	.313
Road	2	1	4.29	1	50.1	RHB	145	32	4	25	.221
First Half	4	2	4.09	1	61.2	Sc Pos	84	26	2	41	.310
Scnd Half	0	1	7.78	0	19.2	Clutch	40	9	2	6	.225

2002 Season

As he'd done the year before, Rolando Arrojo began the 2002 season in the bullpen and pitched his way back into the rotation. Initially he succeeded as a starter last summer, only to suffer shoulder problems that robbed him of effectiveness and ultimately knocked him out of action. He also developed a disc problem in his back later on, and pitched less than 20 innings after the end of June.

Pitching & Defense

Arrojo throws sinkers and cutters at various speeds from various angles, using some of the same tricks as fellow countryman Orlando Hernandez. He makes it work well against righthanded hitters, but lefthanded hitters pick up the ball well against him and regularly punish him. Recurring shoulder miseries put his ability to stay in the rotation for any length of time very much in doubt. He's become proficient at cutting off the running game and always has performed adequately in the field.

2003 Outlook

A free agent, Arrojo has shown he still can be effective when healthy. He'll likely land a roster spot somewhere this spring if he's physically able.

Carlos Baerga

Position: DH/2B
Bats: B **Throws:** R
Ht: 5'11" **Wt:** 215

Opening Day Age: 34
Born: 11/4/68 in San Juan, PR
ML Seasons: 11
Pronunciation: by-AIR-ga

Overall Statistics

	G	AB	R	H	D	T	HR	RBI	SB	BB	SO	Avg	OBP	Slg
'02	73	182	17	52	11	0	2	19	6	7	20	.286	.316	.379
Car.	1353	4989	676	1452	257	17	126	705	58	260	531	.291	.330	.425

2002 Situational Stats

	AB	H	HR	RBI	Avg		AB	H	HR	RBI	Avg
Home	86	23	1	6	.267	LHP	49	11	0	3	.224
Road	96	29	1	13	.302	RHP	133	41	2	16	.308
First Half	132	40	2	16	.303	Sc Pos	49	11	0	17	.224
Scnd Half	50	12	0	3	.240	Clutch	40	10	0	5	.250

2002 Season

After being out of the majors for two years, Carlos Baerga made a moderately successful comeback with Boston last year. Though he was of limited use as a designated hitter and backup second baseman, he was one of the better pinch-hitters in the league, going 10-for-29 (.345) in that capacity. While he wasn't as productive in the second half, his enthusiasm was appreciated on the bench and in the clubhouse.

Hitting, Baserunning & Defense

Baerga is an aggressive line-drive hitter who makes good contact, but he no longer is much of an extra-base threat. Though nominally a switch-hitter, it's been years since he's been effective from the right side of the plate. He's still mobile enough to get by in occasional appearances at second base, and stole six bases in as many attempts last year before hamstring problems slowed him down.

2003 Outlook

As far as his on-field abilities are concerned, Baerga's usefulness extends only as far as being a lefthanded pinch-hitter. His success in that role last year might give him a chance to be asked back, but any extended slump easily could cost him his roster spot.

John Burkett

Position: SP
Bats: R **Throws:** R
Ht: 6' 3" **Wt:** 215

Opening Day Age: 38
Born: 11/28/64 in New Brighton, PA
ML Seasons: 14
Pronunciation: BURK-it

Overall Statistics

	W	L	Pct.	ERA	G	GS	Sv	IP	H	BB	SO	HR	Ratio
'02	13	8	.619	4.53	29	29	0	173.0	199	50	124	25	1.44
Car.	154	127	.548	4.25	413	393	1	2466.2	2664	653	1659	237	1.34

2002 Situational Stats

	W	L	ERA	Sv	IP		AB	H	HR	RBI	Avg
Home	5	3	2.98	0	81.2	LHB	352	98	15	53	.278
Road	8	5	5.91	0	91.1	RHB	341	101	10	31	.296
First Half	7	3	3.80	0	85.1	Sc Pos	181	44	4	56	.243
Scnd Half	6	5	5.24	0	87.2	Clutch	33	11	0	3	.333

2002 Season

Coming off one of his finest seasons in 2001, veteran John Burkett picked up right where he left off, winning his first seven decisions in 2002. And though he finished with a winning record, the lasting impression of his season was his brutal run in late July and August as the Red Sox' playoff hopes slowly slipped away. From the All-Star break through the end of August, Burkett was 3-4 with a 6.71 ERA.

Pitching & Defense

Burkett gets by with his stuff only on the strength of his outstanding command. His fastball is below average, but he sinks it, cuts it and generally keeps it off the heart of the plate. He'll mix in a changeup and a big, slow curve, mainly after he's gotten ahead. What his pickoff move lacks in quality, he makes up for in quantity—few pitchers throw over more often. He finishes his delivery in good position to field, but isn't all that quick off the mound.

2003 Outlook

Burkett has one more year left on his contract. The Red Sox may keep him on a tighter leash early in the year, in hopes of keeping him fresh later into the season.

Frank Castillo

Position: SP/RP
Bats: R **Throws:** R
Ht: 6' 1" **Wt:** 198

Opening Day Age: 33
Born: 4/1/69 in El Paso, TX
ML Seasons: 11
Pronunciation: cas-TEE-yoh

Overall Statistics

	W	L	Pct.	ERA	G	GS	Sv	IP	H	BB	SO	HR	Ratio
'02	6	15	.286	5.07	36	23	1	163.1	174	58	112	19	1.42
Car.	82	103	.443	4.55	294	267	2	1590.0	1655	500	1097	190	1.36

2002 Situational Stats

	W	L	ERA	Sv	IP		AB	H	HR	RBI	Avg
Home	2	10	5.89	1	84.0	LHB	288	81	9	49	.281
Road	4	5	4.20	0	79.1	RHB	346	93	10	44	.269
First Half	5	9	4.80	0	99.1	Sc Pos	145	46	4	74	.317
Scnd Half	1	6	5.48	1	64.0	Clutch	45	10	0	2	.222

2002 Season

Frank Castillo pitched decently over the first two months of the season, but everything fell apart for him in June and July, when he lost five straight decisions before losing his rotation spot. Demoted to long relief, he made little impact the rest of the way.

Pitching & Defense

Mixing it up is what Castillo does best. He throws a mid-80s cutter, a slow curve and a changeup to both sides of the plate. To be effective, he must throw strikes and work ahead. Last year he had problems with men on base, which led to a lot of big innings. With men aboard in 2002, hitters batted .340 and slugged .485 against him. His tendency to throw a lot of low offspeed stuff makes him easy to run on. An above-average fielder, he had his second straight errorless season last year.

2003 Outlook

After Castillo's two-year deal expired at season's end, the Red Sox re-signed him to a one-year, $800,000 contract. He may get more work as a reliever than a starter in 2003. Succeeding as a starter may depend on solving his problems pitching out of the stretch.

Boston

Tony Clark

Position: 1B
Bats: B **Throws:** R
Ht: 6' 7" **Wt:** 245

Opening Day Age: 30
Born: 6/15/72 in Newton, KS
ML Seasons: 8

Overall Statistics

	G	AB	R	H	D	T	HR	RBI	SB	BB	SO	Avg	OBP	Slg
'02	90	275	25	57	12	1	3	29	0	21	57	.207	.265	.291
Car.	862	3106	453	840	168	8	159	543	6	364	778	.270	.347	.483

2002 Situational Stats

	AB	H	HR	RBI	Avg		AB	H	HR	RBI	Avg
Home	121	26	1	15	.215	LHP	82	13	1	6	.159
Road	154	31	2	14	.201	RHP	193	44	2	23	.228
First Half	190	41	2	24	.216	Sc Pos	80	16	3	28	.200
Scnd Half	85	16	1	5	.188	Clutch	34	6	0	6	.176

2002 Season

Tony Clark's power stroke seemingly deserted him over the last two months of 2001 and he was waived by Detroit after that season ended. The Red Sox claimed him and he opened 2002 as their starting first baseman, but he started ice-cold. He'd gotten off to poor starts before, but this time he never pulled out of it, and by August he was riding the pine.

Hitting, Baserunning & Defense

In his heyday, Clark had good straightaway power from either side of the plate and produced enough hard liners to hit for a respectable average as well, despite his frequent strikeouts. His bat generated just 16 extra-base hits in 2002, and just four after the All-Star break. He doesn't move well on the bases or in the field, but has decent hands and an adequate arm.

2003 Outlook

Clark became a free agent over the winter and may have a hard time finding another opportunity. He has hit only four homers in his last 397 at-bats, so it's very much an open question whether he'll ever get his power stroke back, or even get the chance to.

Alan Embree

Position: RP
Bats: L **Throws:** L
Ht: 6' 2" **Wt:** 190

Opening Day Age: 33
Born: 1/23/70 in The Dalles, OR
ML Seasons: 9
Pronunciation: EMM-bree

Overall Statistics

	W	L	Pct.	ERA	G	GS	Sv	IP	H	BB	SO	HR	Ratio
'02	4	6	.400	2.18	68	0	2	62.0	47	20	81	6	1.08
Car.	22	25	.468	4.46	432	4	6	408.0	380	176	398	53	1.36

2002 Situational Stats

	W	L	ERA	Sv	IP		AB	H	HR	RBI	Avg
Home	3	2	1.18	2	38.0	LHB	96	15	3	14	.156
Road	1	4	3.75	0	24.0	RHB	131	32	3	13	.244
First Half	3	4	1.00	2	36.0	Sc Pos	70	13	1	19	.186
Scnd Half	1	2	3.81	0	26.0	Clutch	132	29	4	14	.220

2002 Season

Coming off a disastrous 2001 season and offseason elbow surgery, lefthander Alan Embree put together his best year yet in 2002. After getting off to a terrific start with the Padres, he was traded to Boston in June and quickly established himself as the top lefthander out of the Red Sox' bullpen.

Pitching & Defense

When he's right, Embree does it on sheer heat, relying almost exclusively on his mid-90s fastball. His fastball lacks movement, though, and his slider is nothing special, so he's vulnerable when physical problems sap his velocity. His repertoire induces few comebackers, but he handles what he gets to, although he erred for the first time in 10 years last season. His high-effort delivery allows basestealers to get a good jump.

2003 Outlook

Intent on staying in Boston, Embree never filed for free agency and agreed to a two-year, $5.5 million deal with the Red Sox in early November. His career record shows that he's capable of being very effective when he's in top condition, but it also shows that he's no sure bet to be at full strength in any given season.

Casey Fossum

Position: RP/SP
Bats: B **Throws:** L
Ht: 6' 1" **Wt:** 165

Opening Day Age: 25
Born: 1/6/78 in Cherry Hill, NJ
ML Seasons: 2

Overall Statistics

	W	L	Pct.	ERA	G	GS	Sv	IP	H	BB	SO	HR	Ratio
'02	5	4	.556	3.46	43	12	1	106.2	113	30	101	12	1.34
Car.	8	6	.571	3.87	56	19	1	151.0	157	50	127	16	1.37

2002 Situational Stats

	W	L	ERA	Sv	IP		AB	H	HR	RBI	Avg
Home	1	3	4.55	0	59.1	LHB	112	31	1	18	.277
Road	4	1	2.09	1	47.1	RHB	309	82	11	33	.265
First Half	2	1	3.00	1	33.0	Sc Pos	122	28	2	37	.230
Scnd Half	3	3	3.67	0	73.2	Clutch	42	12	1	8	.286

2002 Season

Young lefthander Casey Fossum began the year in the Red Sox' bullpen, but had a hard time finding a role. Sent down to Triple-A Pawtucket in June, he was recalled in July and inserted into the rotation, where he pitched fairly well, compiling a 3.65 ERA in 12 starts.

Pitching & Defense

Fossum relies primarily on a 90-MPH fastball and a sweeping curve. His low-three-quarters delivery makes his fastball appear to rise and often induces hitters to get under it. Toward the end of the year he began mixing in a cutter and a changeup. Slight of build, he routinely tired after as few as 60 pitches and rarely worked into the seventh inning. He doesn't have much of a pickoff move, but he gets the ball to the plate quickly enough to help his catcher get off a good throw. He has fielded his position capably thus far.

2003 Outlook

Despite Fossum's respectable performance as a starter late last year, it still isn't clear that he can hold up for an entire season in that role. The Red Sox likely will give him the chance to show he can in 2003.

Rickey Henderson (Hall of Famer)

Position: LF
Bats: R **Throws:** L
Ht: 5'10" **Wt:** 190

Opening Day Age: 44
Born: 12/25/58 in Chicago, IL
ML Seasons: 24

Overall Statistics

G	AB	R	H	D	T	HR	RBI	SB	BB	SO	Avg	OBP	Slg
72	179	40	40	6	1	5	16	8	38	47	.223	.369	.352
3051	10889	2288	3040	509	66	295	1110	1403	2179	1678	.279	.402	.419

2002 Situational Stats

	AB	H	HR	RBI	Avg		AB	H	HR	RBI	Avg
Home	86	17	1	6	.198	LHP	85	17	2	6	.200
Road	93	23	4	10	.247	RHP	94	23	3	10	.245
First Half	122	29	3	13	.238	Sc Pos	39	8	0	11	.205
Scnd Half	57	11	2	3	.193	Clutch	20	3	0	0	.150

2002 Season

He doesn't hit for much of an average any more, and he no longer is a basestealing force, but Rickey Henderson still is capable of getting on base and scoring runs in spot duty at the top of the order. That's what he did for the Red Sox last year, sharing time in left field.

Hitting, Baserunning & Defense

It's been a while since Henderson hit for a good average. One of the few weapons he has left at the plate is his ability to work a walk, and that alone is enough to make him a useful leadoff man, even if his average is low. In the second half of 2002, when his average was below the Mendoza Line, he still posted a .387 OBP. He's lost several steps but still has the speed and know-how to swipe a bag when necessary. His instinctive nature on the bases does not extend to the outfield, and his weak arm is an additional liability.

2003 Outlook

Henderson says he wants to play one more year. It probably will be somewhere other than Boston, after he complained late in the season about his lack of playing time. At age 44, he'll do well to match his performance from last year.

Dustin Hermanson

Position: RP
Bats: R **Throws:** R
Ht: 6' 2" **Wt:** 200

Opening Day Age: 30
Born: 12/21/72 in Springfield, OH
ML Seasons: 8

Overall Statistics

	W	L	Pct.	ERA	G	GS	Sv	IP	H	BB	SO	HR	Ratio
'02	1	1	.500	7.77	12	1	0	22.0	35	7	13	3	1.91
Car.	62	62	.500	4.30	215	156	4	1019.1	1031	372	695	130	1.38

2002 Situational Stats

	W	L	ERA	Sv	IP		AB	H	HR	RBI	Avg
Home	1	1	7.07	0	14.0	LHB	40	13	0	4	.325
Road	0	0	9.00	0	8.0	RHB	59	22	3	13	.373
First Half	0	0	-	0	0.0	Sc Pos	29	9	0	10	.310
Scnd Half	1	1	7.77	0	22.0	Clutch	28	15	1	6	.536

2002 Season

The 2002 season was a complete washout for Dustin Hermanson. Expected to fill a spot in Boston's rotation, he strained a groin muscle in his first start of the season (a game ultimately rained out) and didn't make it back until the second half. Soon after his first appearance back, he developed a staph infection in his left arm. He made it back for good in late August, but was unable to pitch his way back into the rotation.

Pitching & Defense

A healthy Hermanson features a low-90s fastball and a hard slider, plus a cutter and changeup. Stamina never has been a strength of his, as he is at his best through his first 75 pitches and tends to be more effective when given extra rest. He defends his position capably and has a good pick-off move for a righthander.

2003 Outlook

The Red Sox declined their $7.5 million option on Hermanson's contract for 2003. They didn't offer salary arbitration, so he probably is moving on. It's worth noting that Hermanson's never suffered a serious injury to his pitching arm and remains capable of reestablishing himself as a useful middle-of-the-rotation starter.

Rey Sanchez

Position: 2B/SS
Bats: R **Throws:** R
Ht: 5' 9" **Wt:** 175

Opening Day Age: 35
Born: 10/5/67 in Rio Piedras, PR
ML Seasons: 12
Pronunciation: RAY SAN-chezz

Overall Statistics

	G	AB	R	H	D	T	HR	RBI	SB	BB	SO	Avg	OBP	Slg
'02	107	357	46	102	12	3	1	38	2	17	31	.286	.318	.345
Car.	1274	4178	486	1149	170	27	13	338	53	199	438	.275	.311	.338

2002 Situational Stats

	AB	H	HR	RBI	Avg		AB	H	HR	RBI	Avg
Home	160	47	1	19	.294	LHP	77	21	0	7	.273
Road	197	55	0	19	.279	RHP	280	81	1	31	.289
First Half	154	49	1	19	.318	Sc Pos	87	28	0	37	.322
Scnd Half	203	53	0	19	.261	Clutch	41	11	0	6	.268

2002 Season

Apart from the five weeks he missed in midseason, Rey Sanchez was Boston's regular second baseman last year. Though he hadn't played full-time on the right side of the infield since 1995, he didn't miss a beat, remaining one of the majors' best defenders in the middle infield. He hit enough to avoid being a liability at the bottom of the order, particularly at home.

Hitting, Baserunning & Defense

The contact-oriented Sanchez always hits for a respectable average, but he generates little power and rarely works the count deep enough to draw a walk. He has decent speed and can play a small part in a team's running attack. In the field is where he really shines. He has good range, terrific hands and a strong enough arm to be a fine shortstop. He's perfectly suited for second base, where he turns the double play adeptly.

2003 Outlook

Sanchez did everything the Red Sox expected last year, but he is certain not return after the team traded for Todd Walker in December. Sanchez will have to shop himself around once again to clubs looking for a short-term solution at a middle-infield spot.

Other Boston Red Sox

Benny Agbayani (Pos: LF, Age: 31, Bats: R)

	G	AB	R	H	D	T	HR	RBI	SB	BB	SO	Avg	OBP	Slg
'02	61	154	15	35	6	0	4	27	1	16	40	.227	.298	.344
Car.	383	1091	145	299	57	6	39	156	16	139	246	.274	.362	.445

Agbayani fared better with the bat when Shea Stadium was his home than he did in his half-season with Colorado (.205/.266 OBP), and in late August he was claimed off waivers by Boston (.297/.395 OBP). 2003 Outlook: C

Shane Andrews (Pos: 3B, Age: 31, Bats: R)

	G	AB	R	H	D	T	HR	RBI	SB	BB	SO	Avg	OBP	Slg
'02	7	13	2	1	1	0	0	0	0	1	3	.077	.200	.154
Car.	569	1704	196	375	76	4	86	263	7	191	515	.220	.298	.421

Andrews was released by the Cards' Triple-A team in March 2001, but he returned in 2002 to have a solid season at Triple-A Pawtucket. He didn't do enough with his September callup to expect a return. 2003 Outlook: C

Willie Banks (Pos: RHP, Age: 34)

	W	L	Pct.	ERA	G	GS	Sv	IP	H	BB	SO	HR	Ratio
'02	2	1	.667	3.23	29	0	1	39.0	32	14	26	5	1.18
Car.	33	39	.458	4.75	181	84	2	610.1	632	302	428	65	1.53

Banks re-emerged with the Red Sox in 2002, though he had to clear waivers and return to Triple-A Pawtucket briefly twice en route to a solid season. He looks like he could be helpful again in 2003. 2003 Outlook: B

Kevin L. Brown (Pos: C, Age: 29, Bats: R)

	G	AB	R	H	D	T	HR	RBI	SB	BB	SO	Avg	OBP	Slg
'02	2	1	0	0	0	0	0	0	0	0	0	.000	.000	.000
Car.	85	189	30	48	12	2	7	31	0	14	59	.254	.311	.450

His days as catching prospect are gone, and he didn't do much at Triple-A Pawtucket to rekindle hopes. In 70 games there, he batted .243 with a .299 OBP and a .389 slugging mark. 2003 Outlook: C

Juan Diaz (Pos: 1B, Age: 29, Bats: R)

	G	AB	R	H	D	T	HR	RBI	SB	BB	SO	Avg	OBP	Slg
'02	4	7	2	2	1	0	1	2	0	1	2	.286	.375	.857
Car.	4	7	2	2	1	0	1	2	0	1	2	.286	.375	.857

Diaz hit 20 homers at Triple-A Pawtucket for a second straight year, but he had more at-bats and his hitting percentages were down from 2001. He's now 29, but Boston's questions at first base offer hope. 2003 Outlook: C

Rich Garces (Pos: RHP, Age: 31)

	W	L	Pct.	ERA	G	GS	Sv	IP	H	BB	SO	HR	Ratio
'02	0	1	.000	7.59	26	0	0	21.1	21	12	16	4	1.55
Car.	23	10	.697	3.74	287	0	7	341.1	290	164	296	32	1.33

Garces was terrific in the Boston pen from 1999-2001, going 19-3 with a 3.11 ERA. He struggled in 2002, and he was released when he wouldn't meet with the Sox after being designated for assignment in July. 2003 Outlook: B

Wayne Gomes (Pos: RHP, Age: 30)

	W	L	Pct.	ERA	G	GS	Sv	IP	H	BB	SO	HR	Ratio
'02	1	2	.333	4.64	20	0	1	21.1	20	12	15	2	1.50
Car.	30	23	.566	4.60	321	0	29	368.0	373	191	284	33	1.53

Gomes was cut by the Pirates in late April, and he signed on with Boston and was 5-2 (2.64) in 42 games at Triple-A Pawtucket. But can he put up those numbers in the majors? 2003 Outlook: C

Chris Haney (Pos: LHP, Age: 34)

	W	L	Pct.	ERA	G	GS	Sv	IP	H	BB	SO	HR	Ratio
'02	0	0	–	4.20	24	0	1	30.0	32	10	15	2	1.40
Car.	38	52	.422	5.07	196	125	1	824.2	924	286	442	94	1.47

Haney started strong at Triple-A Pawtucket. He pitched well in Boston in June (1.08), but faded in the second half (6.48) and was released. 2003 Outlook: C

Bob Howry (Pos: RHP, Age: 29)

	W	L	Pct.	ERA	G	GS	Sv	IP	H	BB	SO	HR	Ratio
'02	3	5	.375	4.19	67	0	0	68.2	67	21	45	9	1.28
Car.	14	20	.412	3.81	314	0	49	340.1	301	137	300	41	1.29

Howry had lost his velocity after having shoulder surgery following the 2000 season. He was in the 90-MPH range again after the trade that sent him to Boston. 2003 Outlook: B

Lou Merloni (Pos: 2B, Age: 31, Bats: R)

	G	AB	R	H	D	T	HR	RBI	SB	BB	SO	Avg	OBP	Slg
'02	84	194	28	48	12	2	4	18	1	20	35	.247	.332	.392
Car.	258	690	87	187	46	4	9	77	5	45	124	.271	.325	.388

Merloni played all four infield positions and a little outfield, recording the best overall fielding percentage of his career. 2003 Outlook: C

Doug Mirabelli (Pos: C, Age: 32, Bats: R)

	G	AB	R	H	D	T	HR	RBI	SB	BB	SO	Avg	OBP	Slg
'02	57	151	17	34	7	0	7	25	0	17	33	.225	.312	.411
Car.	274	700	74	161	36	2	26	97	1	95	185	.230	.328	.399

Mirabelli approached double-digit homers again and had an error-free season behind the plate as a part-time player. 2003 Outlook: C

Bry Nelson (Pos: 2B, Age: 29, Bats: B)

	G	AB	R	H	D	T	HR	RBI	SB	BB	SO	Avg	OBP	Slg
'02	25	34	6	9	3	0	0	2	1	4	1	.265	.342	.353
Car.	25	34	6	9	3	0	0	2	1	4	1	.265	.342	.353

Nelson played second, third, short and in the outfield at Triple-A Pawtucket. He's also batted .305 in Triple-A ball the last three seasons. 2003 Outlook: C

Darren Oliver (Pos: LHP, Age: 32)

	W	L	Pct.	ERA	G	GS	Sv	IP	H	BB	SO	HR	Ratio
'02	4	5	.444	4.66	14	9	0	58.0	70	27	32	7	1.67
Car.	71	65	.522	5.02	246	186	2	1154.0	1303	500	700	137	1.56

After having a 6.02 ERA with Texas in 2001, Oliver was good in April, but the Sox released him after posting an 8.14 ERA in five May starts. 2003 Outlook: C

Boston

Boston Red Sox Minor League Prospects

Organization Overview:

In 2002, the Red Sox continued a recent trend of trading minor league talent for major leaguers, dealing righthanders Brad Baker, Frank Francisco and Pacific Rim prospects Seung Song, Sun-Woo Kim and Byeong An to acquire veterans. So there's very little in the system that can make a significant contribution in the next year or so. Freddy Sanchez and Josh Hancock stand a chance to help out in 2003. Otherwise, the best news down on the farm is that the new ownership had a good first draft in which Boston selected outfielder Mike Goss, catcher Alberto Concepcion, third baseman Scott White and lefthanders Jon Lester and Tyler Pelland. For now, though, the new regime will have to trade and spend money in the free-agent market to fill holes.

Jorge de la Rosa

Position: P   **Opening Day Age:** 21
Bats: L **Throws:** L   **Born:** 4/5/81 in
Ht: 6' 1" **Wt:** 192   Monterrey, Mexico

Recent Statistics

	W	L	ERA	G	GS	Sv	IP	H	R	BB	SO	HR
2001 A Sarasota	0	1	1.21	12	0	2	29.2	13	7	12	27	0
2001 AA Trenton	1	3	5.84	29	0	0	37.0	56	35	20	27	4
2002 A Sarasota	7	3	3.65	23	23	0	120.2	105	53	52	95	10
2002 AA Trenton	1	2	5.50	4	4	0	18.0	17	12	9	15	0

De la Rosa signed with Arizona in 1998, but two years later had his contract transferred to his hometown Monterrey Sultans, a Mexican club with a working agreement with Arizona. When the agreement lapsed, the Sultans kept de la Rosa's rights, and the Red Sox bought them after his fastball jumped into the mid-90s late in 2000 in the Mexican Pacific League. The southpaw pitched in relief in 2001. Then pitching coordinator Glenn Gregson lobbied to try de la Rosa as a starter. He threw 93-94 MPH with better command of his fastball in 2002, and he mixed in a hard curve and a changeup that needs polish. He wore down and wasn't as sharp in four starts at Double-A Trenton. Still, the Red Sox were pleased with initial results.

Manny Delcarmen

Position: P   **Opening Day Age:** 21
Bats: R **Throws:** R   **Born:** 2/16/82 in Boston,
Ht: 6' 2" **Wt:** 190   MA

Recent Statistics

	W	L	ERA	G	GS	Sv	IP	H	R	BB	SO	HR
2001 R Red Sox	4	2	2.54	11	8	1	46.0	35	16	19	62	0
2002 A Augusta	7	8	4.10	26	24	0	136.0	124	77	56	136	15

A second-round pick in 2000, Delcarmen rifled a mid-90s fastball and a hard, three-quarter breaking ball at overmatched Rookie-level Gulf Coast hitters in his 2001 debut. While Delcarmen still threw fastballs by hitters in the Class-A Sally League last summer, he became much more consistent with his breaking pitch late in the season. Utilizing a changeup was a developmental objective for Delcarmen, and he made strides at mixing it into his arsenal. Better competition provided a stiff test in 2002, and he had to learn that the hard stuff isn't always the solution. The Red Sox are impressed with his competitive nature, live arm and high ceiling.

Phil Dumatrait

Position: P   **Opening Day Age:** 21
Bats: R **Throws:** L   **Born:** 7/12/81 in
Ht: 6' 2" **Wt:** 175   Bakersfield, CA

Recent Statistics

	W	L	ERA	G	GS	Sv	IP	H	R	BB	SO	HR
2001 R Red Sox	3	0	2.76	8	8	0	32.2	27	10	9	33	0
2001 A Lowell	1	1	3.48	2	2	0	10.1	9	4	4	15	0
2002 A Augusta	8	5	2.77	22	22	0	120.1	109	44	47	108	5
2002 A Sarasota	0	2	3.86	4	4	0	14.0	10	9	15	16	0

Dumatrait was the 22nd overall pick in 2000, and his 2001 season was slowed by shoulder tendinitis that kept him out until July. When he was ready, he displayed a 12-to-6 curveball that is his best pitch. He fanned 48 in 43 innings between Rookie ball in Florida and short-season Lowell. While Dumatrait prefers the curveball, he has a good fastball that he needs to call on more. Its velocity is just average, roughly 89-91 MPH, but it has good life and his command of it is solid. His changeup is not nearly as far along as his fastball and curve. He showed fatigue late in the year at high Class-A Sarasota, which wasn't surprising, considering it was the first time he put a full season together.

Josh Hancock

Position: P   **Opening Day Age:** 24
Bats: R **Throws:** R   **Born:** 4/11/78 in
Ht: 6' 3" **Wt:** 217   Cleveland, MS

Recent Statistics

	W	L	ERA	G	GS	Sv	IP	H	R	BB	SO	HR
2002 AA Trenton	3	4	3.61	15	14	1	84.2	82	40	18	69	9
2002 AAA Pawtucket	4	2	3.45	8	8	0	44.1	39	20	26	29	2
2002 AL Boston	0	1	3.68	3	1	0	7.1	5	3	2	6	1

Hancock doesn't make prospect lists, but this 1998 pick has climbed steadily through the system. He was hit in the face with a line drive at Double-A Trenton last June, but the gutsy Hancock missed only a month, moved on to Triple-A Pawtucket and debuted with Boston in September. He throws an above-average 91-93 MPH fastball. With the aid of Trenton pitching coach Mike Griffin and a little first-finger pressure, Hancock has added some life to his fastball and improved his command of it. He throws both a curve and changeup that can be above average, but they need to be more consistent pitches. November surgery for a partial muscle tear in his pelvic wall will sideline him for up to four months.

Hanley Ramirez

Position: SS   **Opening Day Age:** 19
Bats: R **Throws:** R   **Born:** 12/23/83 in
Ht: 6' 1" **Wt:** 174   Samana, DR

Recent Statistics

	G	AB	R	H	D	T	HR	RBI	SB	BB	SO	Avg
2002 R Red Sox	45	164	29	56	11	3	6	26	8	16	15	.341
2002 A Lowell	22	97	17	36	9	2	1	19	4	4	14	.371

The Red Sox signed the skinny but athletic switch-hitting shortstop in 2000. After another season as a switch-hitter in the Dominican, Ramirez abandoned hitting from the left side and his bat advanced quickly. Making his North American debut in 2002, he was able to connect on many types of pitches in various locations, calling on good bat speed and making adjustments you don't often see from young players. He has the tools—the arm, hands and quick feet—to play shortstop, plus the game awareness and instincts that enhance those tools. While he has maturity issues like young guys his age, his five-tool potential and his solid debut at two levels have the Red Sox excited about his future.

Freddy Sanchez

Position: SS   **Opening Day Age:** 25
Bats: R **Throws:** R   **Born:** 12/21/77 in
Ht: 5' 11" **Wt:** 185   Hollywood, CA

Recent Statistics

	G	AB	R	H	D	T	HR	RBI	SB	BB	SO	Avg
2002 AA Trenton	80	311	60	102	23	1	3	38	19	37	45	.328
2002 AAA Pawtucket	45	183	25	55	10	1	4	28	5	12	21	.301
2002 AL Boston	12	16	3	3	0	0	0	2	0	2	3	.188

A 2000 pick, Sanchez made good contact instantly at two Class-A stops in his debut season. He's continued to hit, advancing to Double-A Trenton in 2001 and batting better than .300 at both Trenton and Triple-A Pawtucket in 2002. While he's been a very aggressive hitter who has hit for average because of his quick hands and bat, Sanchez has worked hard at showing more discipline and working the count, and his walk rate rose late in 2002 at Pawtucket. Although he lacks quickness and doesn't run that well, he's a fairly dependable fielder with good instincts. On the cusp of reaching Boston, Sanchez played second base in winter ball this offseason. The pivot has been the most difficult thing to learn, but he has the work ethic and skills to handle the move.

Kelly Shoppach

Position: C   **Opening Day Age:** 22
Bats: R **Throws:** R   **Born:** 4/29/80 in Fort
Ht: 5' 11" **Wt:** 210   Worth, TX

Recent Statistics

	G	AB	R	H	D	T	HR	RBI	SB	BB	SO	Avg
2002 A Sarasota	116	414	54	112	35	1	10	66	2	59	112	.271

A 2001 second-round pick, Shoppach debuted last summer, displaying promising power in a pitchers' league, solid discipline and an idea of what to do at the plate. He tended to swing only at pitches he could handle, and he generated 35 doubles in the high Class-A Florida State League. He was an above-average defensive player behind the plate with an average arm but a quick release. He immediately proved to be one of the better game-callers in the system, demonstrating intelligence and an ability to work well with a pitching staff. He wore down a bit, so improved conditioning will help him weather the long season. Rehab work will be part of his offseason regimen, as Shoppach underwent September surgery to repair a small rotator cuff tear.

Kevin Youkilis

Position: 3B   **Opening Day Age:** 24
Bats: R **Throws:** R   **Born:** 3/15/79 in
Ht: 6' 1" **Wt:** 225   Cincinnatti, OH

Recent Statistics

	G	AB	R	H	D	T	HR	RBI	SB	BB	SO	Avg
2001 A Lowell	59	183	52	58	14	2	3	28	4	70	28	.317
2001 A Augusta	5	12	0	2	0	0	0	0	0	3	3	.167
2002 A Augusta	15	53	5	15	5	0	0	6	0	13	8	.283
2002 A Sarasota	76	268	45	79	16	0	3	48	0	49	37	.295
2002 AA Trenton	44	160	34	55	10	0	5	26	5	31	18	.344

He lacks the classic baseball body and the tools that make scouts drool, but Youkilis not only has hit since he was drafted in 2001, he also has drawn walks with a vengeance. A young player with his plate discipline and walk totals often strikes out a great deal, but his hand-eye coordination and advanced two-strike approach have produced very low strikeout numbers. He jumped to Double-A Trenton in a breakout 2002 season, and he showed more power with a quick bat and a little lift in his swing. While he's capable of playing first base, Youkilis still is targeted for third, where he is an adequate defender. He lacks first-step quickness, but has good hands and an average arm that is accurate.

Others to Watch

Elbow woes have dogged righty **Jerome Gamble** (22) in the minors, and he succumbed to Tommy John surgery in 2001. He returned last summer, featuring a 92-94 MPH fastball and a decent curve. He posted a 1.82 ERA in 14 starts for Class-A Augusta. . . A kick-return specialist at Jackson State, 2002 11th-round pick **Michael Goss** (22) flirted with the idea of an NFL career before signing late. A dislocated finger at short-season Lowell hampered his pro debut, but still the fleet-footed outfielder batted .398 and stole 14 bases in 21 games. He's very raw, but knows his future is built on stroking line drives and groundballs. . . No one in the Boston system has his arm strength, and righthander **Josh Thigpen** (20) throws in the mid-90s when he's healthy. A knot in his throwing shoulder bothered him for much of 2002, and it wasn't until late in the season that he was fine and did his best work at Class-A Augusta, going 6-6 with a 3.92 ERA. He may be moving to the Reds in the Todd Walker trade.

Boston

Comiskey Park

Offense

The outfield bleachers could be a dangerous place when the All-Star Game comes to Comiskey Park in July. There are few parks in baseball with more favorable hitting conditions. The Ballpark in Arlington and Coors Field were the only parks that yielded more home runs than Comiskey's 2.7 per game in 2002. Fences were moved in after the 2000 season, with the new dimensions especially benefiting pull hitters. This year's new, ivy-covered batter's eye in center field helps batters. White Sox hitters batted 23 points higher at home.

Defense

With the outfield wall lowered to only eight feet, vertical leap has become valuable for outfielders. Even Carlos Lee took away home runs last year. Groundskeeper Roger Bossard, who always does a good job, is guaranteed to have Comiskey in the best shape possible for the All-Stars.

Who It Helps the Most

Frank Thomas, who once said he lost 100 home runs playing at the new Comiskey, has hit 56 of 75 homers at home over the last three seasons. Magglio Ordonez and Paul Konerko also are comfortable swinging at Comiskey's fences. Jose Valentin proves the park is just as good for left-handed hitters.

Who It Hurts the Most

It's unfortunate that Comiskey's evolution into a hitters' park coincided with the recent influx of young pitching prospects. You also wonder if the Sox, like the Rockies in Coors Field, pay the price when they go on the road. The White Sox struggle to manufacture runs, which is partly why they are 20 games under .500 on the road the last two seasons.

Rookies & Newcomers

Joe Borchard, a switch-hitter with tons of raw power, seems well suited for Comiskey, but he must avoid swinging for the fences. He was a better overall hitter with Double-A Birmingham, playing in a pitchers' park, than at Triple-A Charlotte, where Knights Stadium is considered a launching pad.

Dimensions: LF-330, LCF-377, CF-400, RCF-372, RF-335

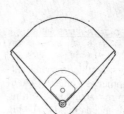

Capacity: 47,098

Elevation: 595 feet

Surface: Grass

Foul Territory: Average

Park Factors

2002 Season

	Home Games CWS	Opp	Total	Away Games CWS	Opp	Total	Index
G	72	72	144	72	72	144	
Avg	.284	.255	.269	.262	.264	.263	102
AB	2392	2447	4839	2519	2393	4912	99
R	427	331	758	342	368	710	107
H	679	623	1302	661	631	1292	101
2B	120	127	247	140	124	264	95
3B	10	7	17	15	9	24	72
HR	120	79	199	74	85	159	127
BB	237	241	478	233	229	462	105
SO	387	415	802	435	416	851	96
E	32	49	81	53	49	102	79
E-Infield	32	44	76	46	34	80	95
LHB-Avg	.293	.267	.277	.232	.286	.265	105
LHB-HR	30	46	76	22	43	65	123
RHB-Avg	.279	.244	.264	.276	.241	.262	101
RHB-HR	90	33	123	52	42	94	130

2001-2002

	Home Games CWS	Opp	Total	Away Games CWS	Opp	Total	Index
G	144	144	288	144	144	288	
Avg	.276	.262	.269	.267	.266	.267	101
AB	4795	4981	9776	4991	4765	9756	100
R	793	708	1501	689	713	1402	107
H	1324	1304	2628	1332	1269	2601	101
2B	249	261	510	285	251	536	95
3B	22	17	39	28	26	54	72
HR	218	180	398	162	147	309	129
BB	498	473	971	438	447	885	109
SO	820	838	1658	881	794	1675	99
E	84	101	185	101	93	194	95
E-Infield	78	86	164	84	74	158	104
LHB-Avg	.282	.265	.272	.249	.281	.268	101
LHB-HR	61	94	155	54	70	124	128
RHB-Avg	.273	.259	.267	.275	.252	.266	100
RHB-HR	157	86	243	108	77	185	129

2002 Rankings (American League)

- Second-highest walk factor
- Third-highest batting-average factor
- Third-highest run factor
- Third-highest home-run factor
- Third-highest RHB home-run factor
- Lowest error factor
- Third-lowest strikeout factor

Jerry Manuel

2002 Season

For a second straight season, Jerry Manuel was given a team that many picked to win the American League Central. It seemed especially winnable after Minnesota faded in the second half of the 2001 season and Cleveland streamlined over the offseason. But Manuel and pitching coach Nardi Contreras failed to prepare their pitching staff during spring training. The White Sox masked this fatal flaw by averaging 5.9 runs in their first 43 games and were tied for the Central lead as late as May 26. But a 13-24 stretch buried them before the All-Star break. When it seemed Manuel's job might be in jeopardy, he rallied his team to a .500 finish after a midseason purge of veterans.

Offense

Manuel may never have been more happy than in April, when Kenny Lofton and Ray. Durham allowed him to play the National League-style baseball he said he would implement when he arrived in Chicago in 1998. But the Sox finished the year waiting on three-run home runs. Lofton and Durham, who were traded in July, had 42 of the team's 75 stolen bases. No survivor was in double figures in steals.

Pitching & Defense

Year in and year out, Manuel is consistent with his quick hooks. Sometimes he goes too far. In the second game of 2002, he used five relievers in the seventh inning. Shouldn't he have been as worried about building the confidence of guys like Bob Howry as he was in protecting a 4-3 lead? All of Manuel's teams have been weak defensively, although this South Side trademark predates him. Royce Clayton and Joe Crede are the only above-average fielders he's had in his infield since Robin Ventura.

2003 Outlook

Manuel was ordered to shake up his coaching staff, losing Contreras during the season and third-base coach Wallace Johnson at season's end. That's a sure sign that Jerry Reinsdorf is running out of patience. If the White Sox don't contend into September, 2003 could mark the end of the Manuel era.

Born: 12/23/53 in Hahira, GA

Playing Experience: 1975-1982, Det, Mon, SD

Managerial Experience: 5 seasons

Manager Statistics

Year	Team, Lg	W	L	Pct	GB	Finish
2002	Chicago, AL	81	81	.500	13.5	2nd Central
5 Seasons		414	395	.512	–	–

2002 Starting Pitchers by Days Rest

	<=3	4	5	6+
White Sox Starts	0	87	51	16
White Sox ERA	–	5.37	4.53	4.03
AL Avg Starts	1	83	44	24
AL ERA	7.15	4.59	4.27	5.03

2002 Situational Stats

	Jerry Manuel	AL Average
Hit & Run Success %	32.1	36.0
Stolen Base Success %	70.8	68.1
Platoon Pct.	54.7	58.9
Defensive Subs	34	23
High-Pitch Outings	2	6
Quick/Slow Hooks	20/20	19/14
Sacrifice Attempts	76	53

2002 Rankings (American League)

- 1st in sacrifice bunt attempts
- 2nd in slow hooks and mid-inning pitching changes (198)
- 3rd in defensive substitutions, relief appearances (423), saves with over 1 inning pitched (10), first-batter platoon percentage and one-batter pitcher appearances (43)

Mark Buehrle

2002 Season

In recent decades, few young pitchers have had such easy success early on as the largely unadvertised, decidedly understated Mark Buehrle. He was named to the All-Star team and almost won 20 games in his second full season. In two summers he has a 35-20 record with mediocre teams. The Sox have been 40-26 in his starts and 124-134 behind anyone else in that stretch. Plus, he's evolved into an important voice in a clubhouse short of leaders.

Pitching

Buehrle simply works fast, uses his head and throws strikes with four different pitches. His fastball rarely hits above 91-92 MPH but gets in on the hands of righthanded hitters, perhaps because he keeps them off balance with a plus curveball and changeup. His cut fastball, a great pitch for him in 2001, wasn't as consistent last time around. Buehrle does a great job pitching ahead in the count, walking only 2.3 per nine innings last year. He's tough on lefthanded hitters but sometimes makes mistakes up in the strike zone to them.

Defense

Not much ever rattles Buehrle, but he does sometimes try to force the action on bunts and choppers. He cut down on his errors last season and has the potential to become a Gold Glove candidate. He's got such a great pickoff move that opponents almost never try to run against him. They were successful on only four of 14 stolen-base tries last year, and overall have been successful on only 36.7 percent of attempts in his career.

2003 Outlook

Buehrle suffered a bruised left shoulder after being hit by a Hideki Matsui line drive on an All-Star tour of Japan. The injury was not considered serious, but the Sox will breathe easier after seeing their ace back on the mound in spring training. He's proven himself to be a workhorse, ranking second in the AL with 34 starts and second with 239 innings last season. About the only thing he hasn't accomplished is a 20-win season. He'll have a shot at it provided he's healthy.

Position: SP
Bats: L **Throws:** L
Ht: 6' 2" **Wt:** 200

Opening Day Age: 24
Born: 3/23/79 in St. Charles, MO
ML Seasons: 3
Pronunciation: BURR-lee

Overall Statistics

	W	L	Pct.	ERA	G	GS	Sv	IP	H	BB	SO	HR	Ratio
'02	19	12	.613	3.58	34	34	0	239.0	236	61	134	25	1.24
Car.	39	21	.650	3.52	94	69	0	511.2	479	128	297	54	1.19

How Often He Throws Strikes

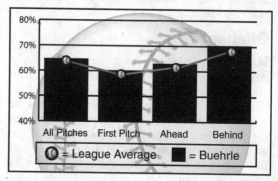

⊙ = League Average   ■ = Buehrle

2002 Situational Stats

	W	L	ERA	Sv	IP		AB	H	HR	RBI	Avg
Home	12	4	3.34	0	129.1	LHB	241	55	10	37	.228
Road	7	8	3.86	0	109.2	RHB	667	181	15	55	.271
First Half	12	6	3.57	0	128.2	Sc Pos	197	49	6	67	.249
Scnd Half	7	6	3.59	0	110.1	Clutch	47	14	3	7	.298

2002 Rankings (American League)

- 2nd in games started, complete games (5), shutouts (2) and innings pitched
- 3rd in batters faced (984) and lowest stolen-base percentage allowed (28.6)
- Led the White Sox in ERA, wins, games started, complete games (5), shutouts (2), innings pitched, hits allowed, pickoff throws (128), highest strikeout-walk ratio (2.2), lowest slugging percentage allowed (.405), lowest on-base percentage allowed (.308), highest groundball-flyball ratio allowed (1.5), most run support per nine innings (6.6), fewest home runs allowed per nine innings (.94) and fewest walks per nine innings (2.3)

Joe Crede

2002 Season

There's only one question about Joe Crede's year—why didn't the White Sox put in a call for him earlier? Crede played well enough in spring training to win at least a share of the third-base job, but was sent back to Triple-A Charlotte. He was among the International League's hitting leaders, yet stayed there until late July. He kept playing well after joining the Sox. Crede ended the season hitting .302 with 36 homers and 100 RBI between Charlotte and Chicago, establishing himself as a fixture in the White Sox' lineup.

Hitting

Crede has plenty of power but is at his best when he trusts his swing to take the ball to the right side or up the middle. He sometimes gets long with his swing and will go through stretches when he is vulnerable to strikeouts, but he has learned to make adjustments to get out of those funks. Crede likes to jump on the first pitch in the strike zone; he hit .476 when he put the first pitch into play after joining the Sox. He has not shown much ability to hit with two strikes.

Baserunning & Defense

He's not Robin Ventura, but he's close. Crede, who often was voted the best defensive third baseman in his league in the minors, played solid in the field. He has lots of range and does an excellent job coming in on grounders. He sometimes will try to force things, leading to errors, but should be a dramatic defensive upgrade at third. He is a below-average baserunner who pretty much can be ignored when he's on base.

2003 Outlook

Jerry Manuel is going to write Crede's name into the lineup as often as possible. He's a good bet to play 150 games if he is healthy and seems a good bet for 25 homers and 90 RBI. He'll go through some slumps but has shown the resilience to dig himself out of holes.

Position: 3B
Bats: R **Throws:** R
Ht: 6' 2" **Wt:** 195

Opening Day Age: 24
Born: 4/26/78 in Jefferson City, MO
ML Seasons: 3
Pronunciation: CREE-dee

Overall Statistics

	G	AB	R	H	D	T	HR	RBI	SB	BB	SO	Avg	OBP	Slg
'02	53	200	28	57	10	0	12	35	0	8	40	.285	.311	.515
Car.	77	264	31	73	12	1	12	45	1	11	54	.277	.305	.466

Where He Hits the Ball

 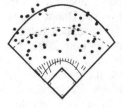

Vs. LHP   **Vs. RHP**

2002 Situational Stats

	AB	H	HR	RBI	Avg		AB	H	HR	RBI	Avg
Home	96	28	7	21	.292	LHP	54	14	3	9	.259
Road	104	29	5	14	.279	RHP	146	43	9	26	.295
First Half	0	0	0	0	-	Sc Pos	43	12	2	21	.279
Scnd Half	200	57	12	35	.285	Clutch	25	10	3	9	.400

2002 Rankings (American League)
- Did not rank near the top or bottom in any category

Chicago (AL)

Keith Foulke

2002 Season

Keith Foulke lost his closer's role after a horrible outing against the Yankees on May 29 and never got it back, despite an 0.74 ERA after the All-Star break. While he was sharing short-relief assignments with Damaso Marte and Antonio Osuna down the stretch, Foulke was especially effective. He didn't allow an earned run after August 17. Foulke did not fool hitters with his changeup as much as he had in previous seasons, in part because his fastball wasn't quite as good. But he threw strikes and bit his tongue, earning respect for the way he dealt with adversity.

Pitching

Have American League hitters begun to figure out Foulke? That would be an overstatement, but they did raise their batting average against him by 26 points from 2001. The OPS against him climbed from .535 to .592, which still is outstanding. Foulke's changeup remains among the best in baseball. He relies on it because he hasn't developed a consistent third pitch to go with his fastball-changeup combination. He is much more effective against righthanded hitters.

Defense

Foulke operates with dry hands. He hasn't committed an error since 1999, making 209 error-free appearances the last three seasons. He has enough confidence to take the easy out rather than take risks trying to get the lead runner. He generally is tough to run on, but didn't do quite as good of a job holding runners close last season.

2003 Outlook

Foulke, who might have had the best bad year of any pitcher in the big leagues, was traded to Oakland in a deal for Athletics closer Billy Koch in December. The change of scenery could be good for Foulke, who had lost Jerry Manuel's confidence. He'll have big shoes to fill in Oakland and needs a good year to take into the free-agent market. His value probably has peaked, but he could re-establish himself by helping Oakland get back to the playoffs.

Position: RP
Bats: R **Throws:** R
Ht: 6' 0" **Wt:** 210

Opening Day Age: 30
Born: 10/19/72 in Ellsworth AFB, SD
ML Seasons: 6
Pronunciation: FOLK

Overall Statistics

	W	L	Pct.	ERA	G	GS	Sv	IP	H	BB	SO	HR	Ratio
'02	2	4	.333	2.90	65	0	11	77.2	65	13	58	7	1.00
Car.	19	24	.442	3.36	357	8	100	490.2	399	121	458	52	1.06

How Often He Throws Strikes

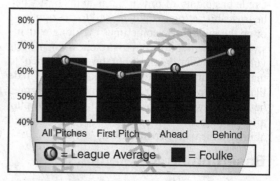

= League Average   = Foulke

2002 Situational Stats

	W	L	ERA	Sv	IP		AB	H	HR	RBI	Avg
Home	0	2	3.09	6	35.0	LHB	143	38	3	12	.266
Road	2	2	2.74	5	42.2	RHB	146	27	4	12	.185
First Half	1	4	4.83	9	41.0	Sc Pos	56	17	2	19	.304
Scnd Half	1	0	0.74	2	36.2	Clutch	128	35	3	17	.273

2002 Rankings (American League)

- 5th in fewest baserunners allowed per nine innings in relief (9.3)
- 10th in relief innings (77.2)
- Led the White Sox in saves, games finished (35), save opportunities (14), lowest batting average allowed vs. righthanded batters, lowest percentage of inherited runners scored (14.3), blown saves (3), relief losses (4), relief innings (77.2) and fewest baserunners allowed per nine innings in relief (9.3)

Jon Garland

2002 Season

Had the White Sox had a deeper starting rotation, Jon Garland would have been patted on the back for a 33-start, 192-inning year. But Todd Ritchie's collapse left the Sox needing someone to step up as a consistent winner and Garland failed to fill that bill. But unfair expectations aside, Garland did a good job. He took the ball every time and worked five-plus innings 27 times.

Pitching

Garland, the rare pitcher with an over-the-top sinker, is a little like a young Kevin Brown. His best pitch, the sinker, can be downright nasty. He has not shown the fifth gear that ultimately landed Brown that $105-million deal, however, almost never throwing harder than 92-93 MPH. But Garland might grow into it. He has improved his changeup but still needs a better curveball. He needs to change speeds and mix pitches better. In 2002 Garland was third in the AL in walks. When he doesn't command the count, hitters can lay off his sinker. That's why he's not more of a ground-ball pitcher.

Defense

Fielding is generally a problem for pitchers as tall as Garland, but he has worked to become at least adequate. He doesn't have the quickest hands, allowing many comebackers to skip into center field, but he did not commit an error last season. Garland gets the ball to home plate quickly, making it tough for opponents to steal bases against him.

2003 Outlook

Because Garland arrived in the big leagues when he was only 20, it's easy to forget that he still should be considered among the game's most valuable young pitchers. That value was borne out when he was almost traded for Anaheim's Darin Erstad before 2002. This guy will pitch at 23 next season and already has almost 400 innings of experience. The goal for him should be 15 victories and 200-plus innings.

Position: SP
Bats: R **Throws:** R
Ht: 6' 6" **Wt:** 205

Opening Day Age: 23
Born: 9/27/79 in Valencia, CA
ML Seasons: 3

Overall Statistics

	W	L	Pct.	ERA	G	GS	Sv	IP	H	BB	SO	HR	Ratio
'02	12	12	.500	4.58	33	33	0	192.2	188	83	112	23	1.41
Car.	22	27	.449	4.65	83	62	1	379.1	393	178	215	49	1.51

How Often He Throws Strikes

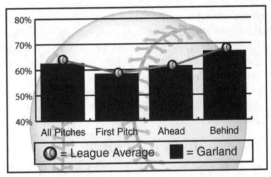

= League Average   = Garland

2002 Situational Stats

	W	L	ERA	Sv	IP		AB	H	HR	RBI	Avg
Home	7	7	4.00	0	96.2	LHB	413	119	14	53	.288
Road	5	5	5.16	0	96.0	RHB	315	69	9	38	.219
First Half	7	6	4.57	0	104.1	Sc Pos	164	45	6	62	.274
Scnd Half	5	6	4.58	0	88.1	Clutch	41	16	1	5	.390

2002 Rankings (American League)

- 1st in most GDPs induced per nine innings (1.5), fielding percentage at pitcher (1.000) and lowest strikeout-walk ratio (1.3)
- 2nd in GDPs induced (32) and highest walks per nine innings (3.9)
- 3rd in walks allowed
- 6th in highest on-base percentage allowed (.340)
- 7th in games started and highest ERA on the road
- Led the White Sox in walks allowed, hit batsmen (9), GDPs induced (32), most GDPs induced per GDP situation (19.0%) and most GDPs induced per nine innings (1.5)

Paul Konerko

2002 Season

After killing the ball all spring, Paul Konerko set the tone for his first All-Star season with a huge April. He cooled off in the second half, perhaps because he would take only two days off after badly injuring his left foot on a foul ball, but still finished with the best season of his career. It was hardly surprising. He relentlessly pushes himself every day of the season. His OPS has been between .844 and .863 for four years in a row. That's consistent.

Hitting

Sometimes it hurts to watch Konerko in the on-deck circle. He bends at the waist in a painful stretch but then still looks somewhat wooden at the plate. It doesn't show in his hitting, however. Konerko crushes most mistake pitches and has increased his bat speed slightly in recent seasons, becoming more effective against good fastballs. He has excellent plate coverage. Konerko does not walk a lot but is a good contact hitter for such a big man. He's a good first-pitch, fastball hitter.

Baserunning & Defense

With hard work, Konerko has become a solid fielder at first. His reactions seemed a tick quicker in 2002, when he made more diving stops, especially to his right, than ever before. He's a solid receiver of throws and has an above-average arm for a first baseman. He's a station-to-station runner who catches grief from teammates for his lack of speed.

2003 Outlook

Konerko was signed to a three-year, $23 million contract extension in mid-November. He's become a franchise cornerstone, but he may yet get caught up in a coming economic crunch. With fellow righthanded hitters Frank Thomas and Magglio Ordonez in the picture, it's possible the White Sox soon will have to choose between Konerko and Carlos Lee. Konerko is more entrenched, but the Sox are intrigued by the progress Lee made at the plate in 2002.

Position: 1B
Bats: R **Throws:** R
Ht: 6' 2" **Wt:** 215

Opening Day Age: 27
Born: 3/5/76 in Providence, RI
ML Seasons: 6
Pronunciation: kone-err-coe

Overall Statistics

	G	AB	R	H	D	T	HR	RBI	SB	BB	SO	Avg	OBP	Slg
'02	151	570	81	173	30	0	27	104	0	44	72	.304	.359	.498
Car.	673	2413	349	692	131	5	111	410	3	207	343	.287	.348	.483

Where He Hits the Ball

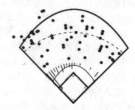 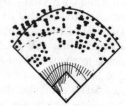

Vs. LHP   **Vs. RHP**

2002 Situational Stats

	AB	H	HR	RBI	Avg		AB	H	HR	RBI	Avg
Home	281	81	13	54	.288	LHP	122	34	5	19	.279
Road	289	92	14	50	.318	RHP	448	139	22	85	.310
First Half	326	107	20	71	.328	Sc Pos	178	54	9	80	.303
Scnd Half	244	66	7	33	.270	Clutch	64	22	1	10	.344

2002 Rankings (American League)

- 4th in lowest fielding percentage at first base (.993)
- 5th in errors at first base (8)
- Led the White Sox in singles, hit by pitch (9), highest percentage of swings put into play (50.3), batting average in the clutch, batting average on the road and batting average on a 3-2 count (.348)

Carlos Lee

2002 Season

Carlos Lee turned a corner. After a slow start that continued the downturn that began in 2001, he responded to some hands-on work by manager Jerry Manuel, who joined hitting coach Gary Ward in long sessions in the cage. Lee became a much tougher out, swinging through fewer pitches and taking many more pitches. He finished with more walks than strikeouts, a huge stride for a guy who had a strikeout-walk ratio of more than 5-1 as a rookie. Lee was especially impressive in September, hitting .316 and compiling a 1.113 OPS.

Hitting

Given the way opponents use to rave when Lee took batting practice, it's hard to believe he never has posted triple-digit RBI. He had tremendous bat speed when he arrived in the majors, but has lost some of it, perhaps because of the weight he has added. Lee was much more patient at the plate last season. He especially improved his approach against lefthanders, working the count and getting better pitches to hit. He hits the ball to all fields but shows more power when he pulls the ball.

Baserunning & Defense

Lee, a good athlete, stopped running last year. He was never on the disabled list but something seemed wrong. A converted third baseman, Lee is below average in left field, but reduced his errors in 2002. He catches the balls he gets to but often gets poor jumps. His arm is below average, but he gets his share of assists when teams try to run on him.

2003 Outlook

Lee may be moved to open up a spot for top prospect Joe Borchard, a switch-hitter who would break up the righthanded dominance in the lineup and improve the outfield defense. Lee is in the last year of his contract, but is under Sox control until 2005. He needs to go wire-to-wire with the improvement he showed in the second half to re-establish himself as a first-division player.

Position: LF
Bats: R **Throws:** R
Ht: 6' 2" **Wt:** 235

Opening Day Age: 26
Born: 6/20/76 in Aguadulce, Panama
ML Seasons: 4

Overall Statistics

	G	AB	R	H	D	T	HR	RBI	SB	BB	SO	Avg	OBP	Slg
'02	140	492	82	130	26	2	26	80	1	75	73	.264	.359	.484
Car.	569	2114	330	596	120	9	90	340	35	164	324	.282	.335	.475

Where He Hits the Ball

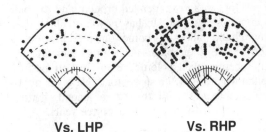

Vs. LHP   **Vs. RHP**

2002 Situational Stats

	AB	H	HR	RBI	Avg		AB	H	HR	RBI	Avg
Home	257	62	14	43	.241	LHP	112	33	3	13	.295
Road	235	68	12	37	.289	RHP	380	97	23	67	.255
First Half	273	68	13	41	.249	Sc Pos	118	32	7	56	.271
Scnd Half	219	62	13	39	.283	Clutch	56	15	2	5	.268

2002 Rankings (American League)

- 2nd in fielding percentage in left field (.996)
- 3rd in assists in left field (8)
- 4th in lowest groundball-flyball ratio (0.7)
- Led the White Sox in intentional walks (4), batting average vs. lefthanded pitchers and on-base percentage vs. lefthanded pitchers (.400)

Magglio Ordonez

Position: RF
Bats: R **Throws:** R
Ht: 6' 0" **Wt:** 210

Opening Day Age: 29
Born: 1/28/74 in
Caracas, VZ
ML Seasons: 6
Pronunciation:
or-DOAN-yez

2002 Season

For the first time since 1998, Magglio Ordonez wasn't on the American League All-Star team. Still, it was his best season yet for this superstar with a lunch pail mentality. Ordonez set career highs in doubles, homers, RBI and runs scored. He had 86 extra-base hits, and for the third consecutive season turned in an OPS better than .915. Few run producers were more consistent than Ordonez, who hit at least .281 every month.

Hitting

Like all great hitters, Ordonez has both an excellent eye and solid mechanics. He settles in at the plate in an unusual stance, with his weight on his back foot in an exaggerated crouch, and the ball jumps off his bat. He has power to all fields, though the bulk of his home runs in 2002 went to left. He has no problems against righthanders, hitting them as well as lefties. He jumps on the first pitch when it's in the strike zone. He gives pitchers nightmares with the bases loaded, batting .409-4-56 in 44 at-bats the last three years.

Baserunning & Defense

As Ordonez has improved as a run producer, he has become somewhat less likely to steal a base. He has average speed and does a good job scoring once he's on base. He has only average range in right but has developed the sit-slide into an art. His arm is average but he does a good job getting himself in position for throws.

2003 Outlook

Ordonez has replaced Frank Thomas as the biggest given in the White Sox' lineup. It appears only a serious injury could stop Ordonez from another 30-homer, 115-RBI season. He has two years and $23 million remaining on his contract. The Sox shouldn't wait too long to start trying to put together an extension that will keep him off the open market as a 30-year-old.

Overall Statistics

	G	AB	R	H	D	T	HR	RBI	SB	BB	SO	Avg	OBP	Slg
'02	153	590	116	189	47	1	38	135	7	53	77	.320	.381	.597
Car.	789	2999	497	916	186	10	149	567	73	260	336	.305	.362	.523

Where He Hits the Ball

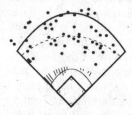
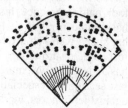

Vs. LHP   **Vs. RHP**

2002 Situational Stats

	AB	H	HR	RBI	Avg		AB	H	HR	RBI	Avg
Home	291	95	24	81	.326	LHP	125	36	9	28	.288
Road	299	94	14	54	.314	RHP	465	153	29	107	.329
First Half	315	96	15	67	.305	Sc Pos	180	57	12	99	.317
Scnd Half	275	93	23	68	.338	Clutch	62	16	3	8	.258

2002 Rankings (American League)

- 1st in slugging percentage vs. lefthanded pitchers (.624)
- 2nd in RBI and GDPs (21)
- 3rd in total bases (352), cleanup slugging percentage (.628), fielding percentage in right field (.986) and assists in right field (8)
- Led the White Sox in batting average, home runs, at-bats, runs scored, hits, doubles, total bases (352), RBI, GDPs (21), games played, slugging percentage, HR frequency (15.5 ABs per HR), batting average vs. righthanded pitchers, cleanup slugging percentage (.628), slugging percentage vs. righthanded pitchers (.589) and batting average at home
- Led AL right fielders in batting average, home runs and RBI

Todd Ritchie

2002 Season

With interleague play and one pool of umpires, changing leagues should be easier for pitchers than it once was. But Todd Ritchie is proof that American League teams still should think twice before adding pitchers from National League clubs. He absolutely got pounded after switching leagues, allowing opponents to hit .318 and posting a career-high 6.06 ERA. Lost in the final numbers is the fact that he actually got off to a pretty good start. He had a 3.32 ERA after nine starts, but it was 8.10 the rest of the way. Ritchie clearly was pitching in pain before an August trip to the disabled list with inflammation in his shoulder. It's possible health had as much to do with his problems as the superior lineups he faced in the AL.

Pitching

Ritchie is a classic power pitcher with a 93-94 MPH fastball and a hard slider. He fell behind too many hitters to be effective in 2002. His secondary pitches—curveball and changeup—work well for him only when he's ahead in the count. He needs to improve at least one of them to be more effective against lefthanded hitters, who looked like they were taking batting practice against him.

Defense

When it goes bad, it really goes bad. Ritchie is a good athlete and normally a solid fielder, but he even pressed defensively, which resulted in some costly errors. He also was an easy target for opposing basestealers, as he concentrated more on his mechanics than baserunners at times.

2003 Outlook

His pride damaged, Ritchie burns to redeem himself. It's unclear if he will return to the White Sox, who want him back but were not expected to offer him salary arbitration. He might benefit from a return to the NL, but Ritchie still wants to deliver for the Sox, who gave up Sean Lowe, Kip Wells and Josh Fogg to get him.

Position: SP
Bats: R **Throws:** R
Ht: 6' 3" **Wt:** 210

Opening Day Age: 31
Born: 11/7/71 in Portsmouth, VA
ML Seasons: 6

Overall Statistics

	W	L	Pct.	ERA	G	GS	Sv	IP	H	BB	SO	HR	Ratio
'02	5	15	.250	6.06	26	23	0	133.2	176	52	77	18	1.71
Car.	42	50	.457	4.65	175	113	0	799.0	881	246	497	96	1.41

How Often He Throws Strikes

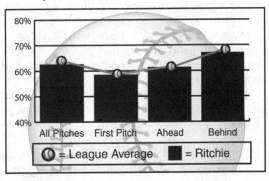

= League Average   = Ritchie

2002 Situational Stats

	W	L	ERA	Sv	IP		AB	H	HR	RBI	Avg
Home	4	5	6.24	0	57.2	LHB	301	105	13	72	.349
Road	1	10	5.92	0	76.0	RHB	252	71	5	25	.282
First Half	5	11	5.82	0	108.1	Sc Pos	151	56	5	74	.371
Scnd Half	0	4	7.11	0	25.1	Clutch	15	5	1	2	.333

2002 Rankings (American League)

- 2nd in lowest winning percentage, highest batting average allowed vs. lefthanded batters and highest batting average allowed with runners in scoring position
- 4th in losses and errors at pitcher (3)
- 5th in wild pitches (10)
- 10th in stolen bases allowed (15)
- Led the White Sox in losses and wild pitches (10)

Chicago (AL)

Aaron Rowand

2002 Season

Patience was required for Aaron Rowand. He was relegated to a reserve role for most of the season, getting only eight at-bats in April. He had a hard time keeping his batting stroke consistent with such erratic playing time and struggled just to keep his batting average above the Mendoza line. But Rowand seized the opportunity when Kenny Lofton was traded to San Francisco on July 29. He batted .291 after replacing Lofton in center field.

Hitting

Rowand isn't a big man but has plenty of strength, which allows him to drive the ball all around the park with a quick, if somewhat long, swing. Perhaps because he developed some bad habits while playing infrequently, he was somewhat tentative against righthanders last season, showing power only against lefties. He takes an aggressive approach to the plate and must learn to better work the count if he is to remain a regular. Rowand is an excellent bunter.

Baserunning & Defense

Rowand mostly was a corner outfielder in the minors. He became a center fielder out of necessity, as he wasn't going to unseat Magglio Ordonez or Carlos Lee. He doesn't have great range but is fearless chasing down balls. He has an average arm but was throwing well late in 2002, perhaps because he has developed excellent mechanics. He throws strikes to third base and home plate. While Rowand once stole 22 bases in the minors, he had no steals last year. He should run more as he gains experience.

2003 Outlook

Rowand may have cost himself his role as a regular by crashing on a dirk bike in the Nevada desert in November. He tore up his left shoulder badly and faces a tough rehabilitation from surgery to get ready for spring training. If he's not ready, the Sox will be quicker to give a job to top prospect Joe Borchard, who has been a minor league center fielder. Either way, Rowand must prove himself again to keep his spot in a crowded outfield.

Position: CF/LF
Bats: R **Throws:** R
Ht: 6' 1" **Wt:** 200

Opening Day Age: 25
Born: 8/29/77 in Portland, OR
ML Seasons: 2

Overall Statistics

	G	AB	R	H	D	T	HR	RBI	SB	BB	SO	Avg	OBP	Slg
'02	126	302	41	78	16	2	7	29	0	12	54	.258	.298	.394
Car.	189	425	62	114	21	2	11	49	5	27	82	.268	.325	.405

Where He Hits the Ball

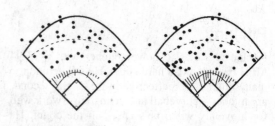

Vs. LHP	Vs. RHP

2002 Situational Stats

	AB	H	HR	RBI	Avg		AB	H	HR	RBI	Avg
Home	148	37	5	18	.250	LHP	98	26	5	13	.265
Road	154	41	2	11	.266	RHP	204	52	2	16	.255
First Half	87	18	1	6	.207	Sc Pos	61	18	0	17	.295
Scnd Half	215	60	6	23	.279	Clutch	38	9	1	5	.237

2002 Rankings (American League)

- 5th in sacrifice bunts (9)
- 8th in errors in center field (3)
- Led the White Sox in sacrifice bunts (9)

Frank Thomas

2002 Season

Either the torn right triceps injury that kept Frank Thomas out nearly all of 2001 was more devastating than most people acknowledged, or he may be done as a truly elite hitter. He was a disappointment across the board, though he showed flashes of his tremendous raw power. His batting average was the lowest of any season except '01 and he drove in the fewest runs of any season in which he played more than 135 games. He also set a career high for strikeouts. And Thomas was a headache for manager Jerry Manuel, distancing himself from teammates with extended clubhouse pouts and occasional late arrivals.

Hitting

Where Thomas once owned the strike zone, he now seems in daily negotiations with umpires. Where Thomas once punished lefthanders, he now seems tentative against them. But he still can fight off some tough pitches for opposite-field hits and will hit some monster home runs, most of which are pulled to left-center as pitchers try to bust him inside. Thomas opened his stance dramatically in 2000, when he hit .328-43-143. He experimented with stances throughout 2002, often going with a more upright approach. He's much more dangerous at Comiskey Park, where he's hit 56 of 75 homers since 2000.

Baserunning & Defense

Thomas never has had speed, but he used to take a base when a pitcher totally ignored him. Those days are gone, however. He played only four games at first base last season and committed two errors. While he's never been a good fielder, he makes an inviting target for infielders.

2003 Outlook

Thomas tested the free-agent market after Jerry Reinsdorf exercised the controversial "diminished skills" clause in his contract. It's clear the Sox would get rid of him if they could. He could stand to lose 25-35 pounds, and has vowed to get in better shape. Because of the contract issue, there is the danger that he may sulk through the remaining years of his new deal.

Position: DH
Bats: R **Throws:** R
Ht: 6' 5" **Wt:** 275

Opening Day Age: 34
Born: 5/27/68 in Columbus, GA
ML Seasons: 13
Nickname: Big Hurt

Overall Statistics

G	AB	R	H	D	T	HR	RBI	SB	BB	SO	Avg	OBP	Slg
148	523	77	132	29	1	28	92	3	88	115	.252	.361	.472
1698	6065	1168	1902	393	11	376	1285	32	1286	962	.314	.432	.568

Where He Hits the Ball

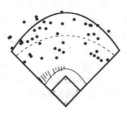 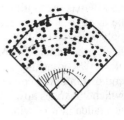

Vs. LHP   **Vs. RHP**

2002 Situational Stats

	AB	H	HR	RBI	Avg		AB	H	HR	RBI	Avg
Home	261	69	24	59	.264	LHP	117	25	6	19	.214
Road	262	63	4	33	.240	RHP	406	107	22	73	.264
First Half	293	70	14	54	.239	Sc Pos	153	41	10	69	.268
Scnd Half	230	62	14	38	.270	Clutch	67	18	4	11	.269

2002 Rankings (American League)

- 1st in most pitches seen per plate appearance (4.26) and lowest groundball-flyball ratio (0.4)
- 2nd in lowest percentage of extra bases taken as a runner (19.6)
- 4th in sacrifice flies (10)
- 5th in highest percentage of pitches taken (62.7)
- 7th in walks
- Led the White Sox in sacrifice flies (10), walks, strikeouts, pitches seen (2,676), most pitches seen per plate appearance (4.26), highest percentage of pitches taken (62.7) and lowest percentage of swings on the first pitch (17.4)

Chicago (AL)

Jose Valentin

2002 Season

Jose Valentin has the skills to be an all-around player, but has evolved into a platoon player who too often swings as hard as he can. His batting average continued a descent from the career-high .273 he put up in 2000, and he no longer was a threat on the bases. Valentin, who played almost exclusively against righthanders, played third base until Joe Crede's arrival in late July, after which he moved over to shortstop.

Hitting

Valentin always has been a better hitter from the left side, and has been so woeful righthanded that Jerry Manuel almost always sits him against lefties. He has the ability to cut down his swing and be a tough out, yet seems to go to that approach only when he has two strikes. He swings from his heels when there is no one on base, and he hit almost 90 points higher with men on in 2002. He comes through frequently with runners on base, which illustrates how effective he could be had he not fallen in love with the longball.

Baserunning & Defense

After struggling wherever he played in 2001, Valentin was surprisingly solid at third base. He showed good reactions on hard-hit balls and his above-average arm often allowed him to record outs after diving stops. At shortstop, Valentin is a well-known commodity. He will make spectacular plays and is an emotional leader in the infield, but he's cursed with bad hands. He made 36 errors in his one year as the Sox' primary shortstop.

2003 Outlook

This is a big year for Valentin, who is likely to open the year at shortstop. The Sox hold a contract option for 2004, so he'll need a good season to stay in their plans. Frequent leg injuries make you wonder if Valentin has played himself into the ground by never skipping winter ball in his native Puerto Rico.

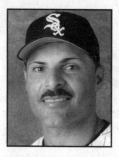

Position: 3B/SS
Bats: B **Throws:** R
Ht: 5'10" **Wt:** 185

Opening Day Age: 33
Born: 10/12/69 in Manati, PR
ML Seasons: 11
Pronunciation: VAL-en-teen

Overall Statistics

	G	AB	R	H	D	T	HR	RBI	SB	BB	SO	Avg	OBP	Slg
'02	135	474	70	118	26	4	25	75	3	43	99	.249	.311	.479
Car.	1165	3889	629	963	217	30	168	578	109	450	904	.248	.326	.448

Where He Hits the Ball

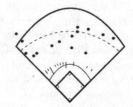 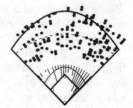

Vs. LHP   **Vs. RHP**

2002 Situational Stats

	AB	H	HR	RBI	Avg		AB	H	HR	RBI	Avg
Home	229	68	15	41	.297	LHP	46	7	1	4	.152
Road	245	50	10	34	.204	RHP	428	111	24	71	.259
First Half	269	67	12	43	.249	Sc Pos	94	33	4	49	.351
Scnd Half	205	51	13	32	.249	Clutch	60	13	2	7	.217

2002 Rankings (American League)

- 2nd in lowest batting average on the road
- 10th in batting average with runners in scoring position and errors at third base (11)
- Led the White Sox in batting average with runners in scoring position

Dan Wright

Position: SP
Bats: R **Throws:** R
Ht: 6' 5" **Wt:** 225

Opening Day Age: 25
Born: 12/14/77 in Longview, TX
ML Seasons: 2

2002 Season

Like Jon Garland, Dan Wright turned in an acceptable performance for a young starter. But its value wasn't truly appreciated. The White Sox, who had counted on Todd Ritchie to be the No. 2 starter, needed Wright or Garland to pitch like frontline starters to hide the lack of proven starters in a thin rotation. Wright won 14 games and made it through five innings in 27 of 33 starts. His high ERA was the result of too many big innings, many of which were the result of allowing 32 home runs.

Pitching

Perhaps because he's been so focused on not falling behind hitters, Wright rarely has shown the 95-MPH fastball he had in the minors. He often throws two-seam sinkers in the low 90s. That's more than enough velocity to set up his knuckle-curve, which is a plus pitch. Some think it would be even better if he made his delivery a little smoother. He's a good student and hard worker. While he hit six batters with pitches, coaches would like him to knock hitters off the plate more frequently, especially righthanded hitters. They often seemed comfortable against him.

Defense

Wright is an average fielder who allows a lot of grounders to go past him up the middle. He needs to work hard during spring training to either hold on runners better or shorten his time to home plate. Opponents were successful on almost 83 percent of their stolen-base attempts against him in 2002.

2003 Outlook

Like several other young Sox pitchers, Wright pitched better after former minor league pitching coordinator Don Cooper replaced Nardi Contreras as pitching coach. His strong September (4-1, 3.41) was no fluke. He's at least as good of a bet as Garland to develop into a long-term No. 2 starter behind Mark Buehrle, but it also wouldn't be shocking if he wound up one day as a closer.

Overall Statistics

	W	L	Pct.	ERA	G	GS	Sv	IP	H	BB	SO	HR	Ratio
'02	14	12	.538	5.18	33	33	0	196.1	200	71	136	32	1.38
Car.	19	15	.559	5.31	46	45	0	262.2	278	110	172	44	1.48

How Often He Throws Strikes

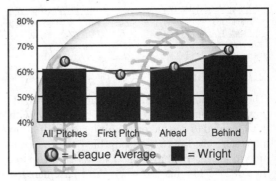

2002 Situational Stats

	W	L	ERA	Sv	IP		AB	H	HR	RBI	Avg
Home	7	6	5.44	0	92.2	LHB	413	106	18	58	.257
Road	7	6	4.95	0	103.2	RHB	348	94	14	47	.270
First Half	5	8	5.72	0	100.2	Sc Pos	174	49	9	72	.282
Scnd Half	9	4	4.61	0	95.2	Clutch	17	6	1	1	.353

2002 Rankings (American League)

- 1st in fielding percentage at pitcher (1.000)
- 2nd in highest stolen-base percentage allowed (82.6) and highest ERA at home
- 3rd in most home runs allowed per nine innings (1.47)
- 4th in home runs allowed and highest ERA
- 5th in wild pitches (10) and stolen bases allowed (19)
- 6th in highest walks per nine innings (3.3)
- Led the White Sox in home runs allowed, strikeouts, wild pitches (10), stolen bases allowed (19) and most strikeouts per nine innings (6.2)

Royce Clayton

Position: SS
Bats: R **Throws:** R
Ht: 6' 0" **Wt:** 185

Opening Day Age: 33
Born: 1/2/70 in Burbank, CA
ML Seasons: 12

Overall Statistics

	G	AB	R	H	D	T	HR	RBI	SB	BB	SO	Avg	OBP	Slg
'02	112	342	51	86	14	2	7	35	5	20	67	.251	.295	.365
Car.	1459	5151	659	1328	239	45	86	534	187	386	955	.258	.311	.372

2002 Situational Stats

	AB	H	HR	RBI	Avg		AB	H	HR	RBI	Avg
Home	163	45	4	14	.276	LHP	101	24	3	10	.238
Road	179	41	3	21	.229	RHP	241	62	4	25	.257
First Half	250	58	6	24	.232	Sc Pos	76	19	1	24	.250
Scnd Half	92	28	1	11	.304	Clutch	36	8	0	3	.222

2002 Season

The White Sox acquired him because of his fielding skills, but Royce Clayton's popularity with fans seemed to depend on his hitting. He got off to poor starts the last two seasons, but both times rallied to get his final average near his career mark. In 2002 he lost his job when third baseman Joe Crede was promoted to the majors, which moved Jose Valentin to shortstop. The Sox released Clayton on September 8.

Hitting, Baserunning & Defense

While his bat is suspect, Clayton remains an unusually reliable shortstop. He doesn't have quite as much range as he did when he was younger. Still, he was charged with only 12 errors in 242 games at short with the White Sox, including a streak of 69 consecutive games (67 in the field) without an error. While his arm is average, he does a good job turning double plays. Clayton no longer is a stolen-base threat.

2003 Outlook

Clayton will start again after signing a one-year, $1.75 million deal with the Brewers. He will replace free agent Jose Hernandez, who had one of the more productive bats on the Milwaukee roster.

Matt Ginter

Position: RP
Bats: R **Throws:** R
Ht: 6' 1" **Wt:** 220

Opening Day Age: 25
Born: 12/24/77 in Winchester, KY
ML Seasons: 3

Overall Statistics

	W	L	Pct.	ERA	G	GS	Sv	IP	H	BB	SO	HR	Ratio
'02	1	0	1.000	4.47	33	0	1	54.1	59	21	37	6	1.47
Car.	3	0	1.000	5.57	60	0	1	103.1	111	42	67	13	1.48

2002 Situational Stats

	W	L	ERA	Sv	IP		AB	H	HR	RBI	Avg
Home	1	0	4.10	0	26.1	LHB	111	38	2	23	.342
Road	0	0	4.82	1	28.0	RHB	101	21	4	21	.208
First Half	1	0	2.84	1	25.1	Sc Pos	61	25	4	39	.410
Scnd Half	0	0	5.90	0	29.0	Clutch	7	3	1	4	.429

2002 Season

Once considered a possible impact pitcher, Matt Ginter's star has faded. He failed to win a job in spring training but was promoted in early May. He returned to Triple-A Charlotte on June 12, but was back for good on June 24. Ginter performed mopup duties, working as many as four innings in a game, but briefly earned Jerry Manuel's confidence in setup situations before finishing badly.

Pitching & Defense

Ginter is pretty much a two-pitch pitcher, throwing a fastball in the low 90s and a hard slider. Because the slider is such a good pitch, he has more than enough stuff to be effective against righthanded hitters, but he must figure out how to neutralize lefthanded hitters. They aren't as quick to chase the slider and work their way into pitchers' counts. A big man, Ginter has slow reflexes on the mound.

2003 Outlook

Ginter once again must prove himself. He'll need to show improvement against lefthanders during spring training to earn a position on the staff. A former first-round pick, he's got the type of arm that interests other organizations and could benefit from a trade.

Gary Glover

Position: SP/RP
Bats: R **Throws:** R
Ht: 6' 5" **Wt:** 205

Opening Day Age: 26
Born: 12/3/76 in Cleveland, OH
ML Seasons: 3

Overall Statistics

	W	L	Pct.	ERA	G	GS	Sv	IP	H	BB	SO	HR	Ratio
'02	7	8	.467	5.20	41	22	1	138.1	136	52	70	21	1.36
Car.	12	13	.480	5.07	88	33	1	239.2	234	85	133	37	1.33

2002 Situational Stats

	W	L	ERA	Sv	IP		AB	H	HR	RBI	Avg
Home	4	4	4.84	1	67.0	LHB	304	85	17	45	.280
Road	3	4	5.55	0	71.1	RHB	233	51	4	33	.219
First Half	3	4	4.87	1	64.2	Sc Pos	118	34	2	49	.288
Scnd Half	4	4	5.50	0	73.2	Clutch	15	5	0	2	.333

2002 Season

After eight seasons of minor league work, Gary Glover did a decent job in the middle of the White Sox' pitching staff in 2002. He opened the season in the bullpen and finished it as a top setup man. In between he made 22 starts. He was much more effective out of the pen than in the rotation (7-7, 5.97), where he got knocked out before five innings eight times.

Pitching & Defense

Throwing strikes sometimes is a problem. Still, Glover can do a good job one time through the lineup as a two-pitch pitcher, throwing a low-90s fastball with a flat slider. He has been working on a splitter. Despite lots of work, his changeup has not become a reliable pitch, which is an issue if he is to succeed as a starter. He is an average fielder who needs to improve at either holding runners or speeding up his delivery. He's a fairly easy target for basestealers.

2003 Outlook

Glover goes to spring training as a likely long man, a candidate to pitch in the seventh and eighth innings. He can be valuable in either role but seems anxious to prove himself as a starter. It may take an emergency situation to get another shot in the White Sox' rotation.

Tony Graffanino

Position: 3B/2B
Bats: R **Throws:** R
Ht: 6' 1" **Wt:** 190

Opening Day Age: 30
Born: 6/6/72 in Amityville, NY
ML Seasons: 7
Pronunciation: graf-a-NEEN-oh

Overall Statistics

	G	AB	R	H	D	T	HR	RBI	SB	BB	SO	Avg	OBP	Slg
'02	70	229	35	60	12	4	6	31	2	22	38	.262	.329	.428
Car.	484	1193	183	308	60	12	25	126	23	123	243	.258	.329	.391

2002 Situational Stats

	AB	H	HR	RBI	Avg		AB	H	HR	RBI	Avg
Home	103	30	4	21	.291	LHP	92	24	4	10	.261
Road	126	30	2	10	.238	RHP	137	36	2	21	.263
First Half	158	45	4	27	.285	Sc Pos	51	16	1	24	.314
Scnd Half	71	15	2	4	.211	Clutch	38	11	1	4	.289

2002 Season

Tony Graffanino was having an excellent season when he tore up his right knee in a game on August 25. He had done a good job as Jose Valentin's third-base partner and coming off the bench. His hard-nosed approach always earns him respect. That, along with his reasonable salary, is why Jerry Reinsdorf calls him his favorite player.

Hitting, Baserunning & Defense

Graffanino took a more patient approach at the plate with the extended opportunity in 2002, chasing the first pitch less often than he did a couple of years ago. He also showed a little more power and his bat control makes him a good hit-and-run guy. Graffanino's trademark is the take-out slide at second base. He does not have much speed, however, and figures to be even more challenged after surgery. He is a reliable infielder. He lacks range but is fundamentally strong.

2003 Outlook

Graffanino underwent surgery to repair a torn knee ligament in August. He will be hard-pressed to be in baseball shape by the start of spring training. The addition of infielders Joe Crede, Willie Harris and D'Angelo Jimenez in the second half of 2002 could limit his role. He'll need to re-establish himself because he's in the last year of his contract.

Chicago (AL)

Willie Harris

Position: 2B
Bats: L **Throws:** R
Ht: 5' 9" **Wt:** 175

Opening Day Age: 24
Born: 6/22/78 in Cairo, GA
ML Seasons: 2

Overall Statistics

	G	AB	R	H	D	T	HR	RBI	SB	BB	SO	Avg	OBP	Slg
'02	49	163	14	38	4	0	2	12	8	9	21	.233	.270	.294
Car.	58	187	17	41	5	0	2	12	8	9	28	.219	.253	.278

2002 Situational Stats

	AB	H	HR	RBI	Avg		AB	H	HR	RBI	Avg
Home	82	18	2	5	.220	LHP	38	9	0	2	.237
Road	81	20	0	7	.247	RHP	125	29	2	10	.232
First Half	7	0	0	0	.000	Sc Pos	39	11	0	10	.282
Scnd Half	156	38	2	12	.244	Clutch	22	3	0	1	.136

2002 Season

Because they projected him only as a utilityman, the Orioles traded Willie Harris after a 2001 season in which he was a Double-A All-Star at second base. He immediately became the probable successor to free agent-in-waiting Ray Durham and fueled expectations by hitting .283 with 32 steals at Triple-A Charlotte. Harris got first crack at the job after Durham was traded, but didn't hit well and ended the season behind D'Angelo Jimenez.

Hitting, Baserunning & Defense

Harris has tremendous makeup as a 24th-rounder who reached the majors barely more than two years after he was drafted. His best tool is his speed. He has limited power but can drive pitchers' mistakes. He needs to improve his pitch recognition and do a much better job working walks. Harris has impressive range at second base and a decent arm. He also plays center field.

2003 Outlook

A good spring could earn Harris playing time, but his best chance to be a regular might come only if the Sox trade Jose Valentin and move Jimenez to shortstop. Otherwise Harris may grab a utility role. He might be best served by another 100-plus games in the minors.

D'Angelo Jimenez

Position: 2B/3B/SS
Bats: B **Throws:** R
Ht: 6' 0" **Wt:** 194

Opening Day Age: 25
Born: 12/21/77 in Santo Domingo, DR
ML Seasons: 3
Pronunciation: him-en-ez

Overall Statistics

	G	AB	R	H	D	T	HR	RBI	SB	BB	SO	Avg	OBP	Slg
'02	114	429	61	108	15	7	4	44	6	50	73	.252	.330	.347
Car.	207	757	109	201	36	7	7	81	8	92	145	.266	.344	.359

2002 Situational Stats

	AB	H	HR	RBI	Avg		AB	H	HR	RBI	Avg
Home	200	55	3	21	.275	LHP	138	36	0	11	.261
Road	229	53	1	23	.231	RHP	291	72	4	33	.247
First Half	321	77	3	33	.240	Sc Pos	95	27	2	39	.284
Scnd Half	108	31	1	11	.287	Clutch	64	16	0	6	.250

2002 Season

Two years in a row, D'Angelo Jimenez has been traded at midseason. In 2002 he went from San Diego, where he had spent a year as a regular, to the White Sox. He started 82 of 88 games for the Padres before the All-Star break, including 30 at third base, but was traded to the Sox for two minor leaguers on July 12. He regrouped in the minors and reached Chicago in late August. He played well enough to put himself into the Sox' plans for 2003.

Hitting, Baserunning & Defense

Jimenez, who was rated ahead of Alfonso Soriano as a Yankees prospect before a life-threatening car accident after the 1999 season, is a professional hitter who seldom gets himself out chasing bad pitches. He's a switch-hitter with some power from the left side of the plate. He has decent speed but hasn't emerged as a basestealing threat. Once rated the top defensive shortstop in the Triple-A International League, Jimenez was erratic there with San Diego and spent most of last season at second and third base.

2003 Outlook

Jimenez should be a regular with the Sox, either at second base or shortstop. He's a possibility for the leadoff spot.

Mark Johnson

Position: C
Bats: L **Throws:** R
Ht: 6' 0" **Wt:** 185

Opening Day Age: 27
Born: 9/12/75 in Wheat Ridge, CO
ML Seasons: 5

Overall Statistics

	G	AB	R	H	D	T	HR	RBI	SB	BB	SO	Avg	OBP	Slg
'02	86	263	31	55	8	1	4	18	0	30	52	.209	.297	.293
Car.	302	879	110	195	36	4	16	76	8	117	189	.222	.317	.327

2002 Situational Stats

	AB	H	HR	RBI	Avg		AB	H	HR	RBI	Avg
Home	128	23	1	7	.180	LHP	21	2	0	0	.095
Road	135	32	3	11	.237	RHP	242	53	4	18	.219
First Half	150	31	2	9	.207	Sc Pos	56	11	1	12	.196
Scnd Half	113	24	2	9	.212	Clutch	19	6	0	1	.316

2002 Season

Mark Johnson wound up as the Sox' primary catcher, starting 80 games. Despite the increased playing time, he failed to get into a comfort zone at the plate. To the contrary, he took a step backward, hitting .219 against righties. Johnson is the epitome of a receiver who works hard to help pitchers get outs.

Hitting, Baserunning & Defense

While he's never had power, Johnson does run into an occasional fastball. Pitchers know they'll get him out if they just throw strikes, as he often works into two-strike counts. Johnson has below-average speed but is a smart runner who seldom takes unnecessary risks. He has an average arm, but has developed a quick release and threw out 28 percent of basestealers last year, ranking eighth among the AL's 14 primary catchers.

2003 Outlook

Johnson was dealt to the Athletics to clear a path for catching prospect Miguel Olivo. Johnson will back up Ramon Hernandez in Oakland, but he could play a lot as the A's try to cut down on Hernandez' workload. It's possible that Johnson never again will get the chance he had in 2002, but there's no reason he can't have a long career as a lefthanded-hitting backup.

Damaso Marte

Position: RP
Bats: L **Throws:** L
Ht: 6' 2" **Wt:** 200

Opening Day Age: 28
Born: 2/14/75 in Santo Domingo, DR
ML Seasons: 3
Pronunciation: dah-MAH-so MAR-tay

Overall Statistics

	W	L	Pct.	ERA	G	GS	Sv	IP	H	BB	SO	HR	Ratio
'02	1	1	.500	2.83	68	0	10	60.1	44	18	72	5	1.03
Car.	1	3	.250	4.02	96	0	10	105.1	94	36	114	13	1.23

2002 Situational Stats

	W	L	ERA	Sv	IP		AB	H	HR	RBI	Avg
Home	1	0	1.39	5	32.1	LHB	101	15	2	11	.149
Road	0	1	4.50	5	28.0	RHB	115	29	3	14	.252
First Half	1	0	3.09	1	35.0	Sc Pos	58	15	0	18	.259
Scnd Half	0	1	2.49	9	25.1	Clutch	107	23	2	14	.215

2002 Season

The White Sox traded for Damaso Marte at the end of spring training. It may have been a career-turning break for Marte, who appeared headed for the minors with Pittsburgh. He made the most of his chance with his fourth organization, leading the team in appearances and earned run average. And Marte was one of three relievers who had 10-plus saves for Jerry Manuel. He compiled a 4-1 strikeout-walk ratio and appeared to get stronger as the season went on.

Pitching & Defense

Marte's best pitch is a low-90s fastball, but he breaks it up with a cut fastball and a slider, which acts like a slurve. He is learning to drop down against some hitters. While Marte has yet to commit an error in 96 big league games, he needs to pay more attention to runners. Teams learned he is slow to home plate and began to run on him.

2003 Outlook

Used as a setup man in the first half, Marte was 10-for-10 in save situations after Manuel turned to a bullpen by committee. The Sox believe he has the makings of a closer, but Billy Koch will get most of the 2003 saves. For Marte, durability will be a concern. He went to the Dominican Republic and worked as a starter in winter ball.

Chicago (AL)

Antonio Osuna

Position: RP
Bats: R **Throws:** R
Ht: 5'11" **Wt:** 205

Opening Day Age: 29
Born: 4/12/73 in
Sinaloa, Mexico
ML Seasons: 8
Pronunciation:
oh-SOO-na

Overall Statistics

	W	L	Pct.	ERA	G	GS	Sv	IP	H	BB	SO	HR	Ratio
'02	8	2	.800	3.86	59	0	11	67.2	64	28	66	1	1.36
Car.	32	23	.582	3.56	328	0	21	399.0	333	171	418	36	1.26

2002 Situational Stats

	W	L	ERA	Sv	IP		AB	H	HR	RBI	Avg
Home	5	0	2.57	5	35.0	LHB	120	30	0	17	.250
Road	3	2	5.23	6	32.2	RHB	136	34	1	16	.250
First Half	4	1	4.31	4	39.2	Sc Pos	77	20	0	31	.260
Scnd Half	4	1	3.21	7	28.0	Clutch	108	26	0	11	.241

2002 Season

Antonio Osuna bounced back well after surgery to repair a torn labrum in May 2001. He rehabbed hard and was ready to go in the spring. He not only re-established himself in the big leagues, he pitched so well that he earned Jerry Manuel's trust in save situations. He wound up as one of three Sox pitchers with double-figure save totals.

Pitching & Defense

Osuna, who once pumped high-octane gas for the Dodgers, got his fastball back into the mid-90s last season. He complements it with a slider and a screwball that acts like a changeup. Those pitches have become the equalizer he lacked when he was a young gun. He does an excellent job keeping pitches down in the strike zone, allowing only one home run in 2002. He can't be counted on to work back-to-back days because he often has high pitch counts. He has an average move to first.

2003 Outlook

Osuna will return to a setup role following the addition of Billy Koch. He could get an occasional save situation, but only a Koch injury would give him a shot at repeating his double-figure peformance. Osuna should have lots of good years left in him, especially if he keeps himself in decent shape.

Josh Paul

Position: C
Bats: R **Throws:** R
Ht: 6' 1" **Wt:** 200

Opening Day Age: 27
Born: 5/19/75 in
Evanston, IL
ML Seasons: 4

Overall Statistics

	G	AB	R	H	D	T	HR	RBI	SB	BB	SO	Avg	OBP	Slg
'02	33	104	11	25	4	0	0	11	2	9	22	.240	.302	.279
Car.	132	332	48	86	19	2	4	38	9	27	68	.259	.316	.364

2002 Situational Stats

	AB	H	HR	RBI	Avg		AB	H	HR	RBI	Avg
Home	37	9	0	5	.243	LHP	44	11	0	6	.250
Road	67	16	0	6	.239	RHP	60	14	0	5	.233
First Half	20	10	0	3	.500	Sc Pos	26	8	0	11	.308
Scnd Half	84	15	0	8	.179	Clutch	14	3	0	1	.214

2002 Season

After losing a positional battle to Mark Johnson in spring training, Josh Paul spent two months at Triple-A Charlotte. The regular playing time put him on track. He went 10-for-20 during a June stint when Sandy Alomar Jr. was on the DL. He received few opportunities the rest of the way, even after Alomar was traded. Paul hit .179 after rejoining the Sox in late July, and faded after prospect Miguel Olivo arrived in mid-September.

Hitting, Baserunning & Defense

Paul showed promising power in the minors, but it's been compromised since he broke the hamate bone in his right hand in 1997. He's a line-drive hitter with a decent idea of the strike zone, but seldom seems to drive the ball. Paul is a good athlete who could help off the bench if he hit better. He is a decent receiver with a below-average arm behind the plate. He has good speed and can play the outfield, and also is willing to try the infield.

2003 Outlook

With Olivo on his way, Paul needs a big spring to maintain his standing. If he goes back to Charlotte, he needs to do big things with his bat. Either way, this will be a critical year for Paul. If he doesn't show improvement, he could find himself on the outside looking in.

Other Chicago White Sox

Lorenzo Barcelo (Pos: RHP, Age: 25)

	W	L	Pct.	ERA	G	GS	Sv	IP	H	BB	SO	HR	Ratio
'02	0	1	.000	9.00	4	0	0	6.0	9	1	1	1	1.67
Car.	5	3	.625	4.50	43	1	0	66.0	67	18	42	7	1.29

Barcelo endured rotator cuff surgery in June 2001, and his recovery went slowly before he was shut down in May. Then he and GM Ken Williams sparred in the press about whether Barcelo returned too soon. 2003 Outlook: C

Rocky Biddle (Pos: RHP, Age: 26)

	W	L	Pct.	ERA	G	GS	Sv	IP	H	BB	SO	HR	Ratio
'02	3	4	.429	4.06	44	7	1	77.2	72	39	64	13	1.43
Car.	11	14	.440	5.23	78	32	1	229.0	240	99	156	34	1.48

Biddle had a respectable 3.48 ERA in seven starts for the Sox in 2002, and it will be interesting to see if he gets a chance to start after decent turns against the Yanks, Royals and Red Sox in September. 2003 Outlook: B

Jeff Liefer (Pos: 1B/LF/RF, Age: 28, Bats: L)

	G	AB	R	H	D	T	HR	RBI	SB	BB	SO	Avg	OBP	Slg
'02	76	204	28	47	8	0	7	26	0	19	60	.230	.295	.373
Car.	209	582	72	142	28	1	25	79	2	47	161	.244	.301	.424

His 18 homers in 254 at-bats in 2001 gave hope that he could be a solid part-time player with the Sox, but Liefer batted just .198 and slugged .264 in May, June and July. Where'd the power go? 2003 Outlook: B

Jim Parque (Pos: LHP, Age: 27)

	W	L	Pct.	ERA	G	GS	Sv	IP	H	BB	SO	HR	Ratio
'02	1	4	.200	9.95	8	4	0	25.1	34	16	13	11	1.97
Car.	30	33	.476	5.21	98	92	0	527.0	623	225	327	76	1.61

The White Sox hoped Parque could return and be productive after shoulder surgery in 2001, but he didn't have the velocity to survive in the majors. He'll be another year removed, yet face the same question. 2003 Outlook: C

Mike Porzio (Pos: LHP, Age: 30)

	W	L	Pct.	ERA	G	GS	Sv	IP	H	BB	SO	HR	Ratio
'02	2	2	.500	4.81	32	0	0	43.0	40	23	33	10	1.47
Car.	2	2	.500	5.77	48	0	0	57.2	61	33	43	15	1.63

Porzio made the club in the spring, but went to Triple-A Charlotte after a horrendous two weeks in early May. He returned in August, just before his 30th birthday, and posted a 3.49 ERA in the second half. 2003 Outlook: C

Kelly Wunsch (Pos: LHP, Age: 30)

	W	L	Pct.	ERA	G	GS	Sv	IP	H	BB	SO	HR	Ratio
'02	2	1	.667	3.41	50	0	0	31.2	26	19	22	3	1.42
Car.	10	5	.667	3.98	166	0	1	115.1	97	57	89	11	1.34

Wunsch had rotator cuff surgery in June 2001, and he didn't return to the Sox until late May. It took a while to regain his touch, but he posted a 2.04 ERA and .212 average against after the break. The Sox signed him for 2003 in November. 2003 Outlook: B

Chicago (AL)

Chicago White Sox Minor League Prospects

Organization Overview:

For years, the White Sox have been known for their organizational emphasis on pitching. That commitment paid off with the Sox getting 106 starts and 717 innings from pitchers under the age of 25 last season. But while pitchers were grabbing the attention, the Sox also were preparing an impressive group of minor league position players. Third baseman Joe Crede, second baseman-center fielder Willie Harris, outfielder Joe Borchard and catcher Miguel Olivo all had their moments in 2002. Those guys go to spring training with a chance to earn starting jobs. Competition for spots on the pitching staff will be fierce. The cast of pitchers who could contribute in 2003 includes Jon Rauch, Corwin Malone, Dave Sanders, Edwin Almonte and Josh Stewart.

Edwin Almonte

Position: P   **Opening Day Age:** 26
Bats: R **Throws:** R   **Born:** 12/17/76 in
Ht: 6' 3" **Wt:** 200   Santiago, DR

Recent Statistics

	W	L	ERA	G	GS	Sv	IP	H	R	BB	SO	HR
2001 AA Birmingham	1	4	1.49	54	0	36	66.1	58	16	16	62	4
2002 AAA Charlotte	2	3	2.24	50	0	26	60.1	52	16	12	56	6

Buckling down financially, the White Sox added only three players after rosters expanded in September. That bit of cost efficiency deprived Almonte of a promotion he had earned with a steady climb through the farm system. He used an outstanding changeup and a willingness to challenge hitters to compile 62 saves the last two seasons. After a trip to the Caribbean World Series, Almonte got hit hard with the Sox last spring. He is an aging prospect with borderline stuff—except the changeup—but so was Keith Foulke when he established himself. Mental toughness is an asset for this New Yorker, who is good enough to pitch in the bigs.

Joe Borchard

Position: OF   **Opening Day Age:** 24
Bats: B **Throws:** R   **Born:** 11/25/78 in
Ht: 6' 5" **Wt:** 220   Panorama City, CA

Recent Statistics

	G	AB	R	H	D	T	HR	RBI	SB	BB	SO	Avg
2002 A Winston-Sal	2	3	1	0	0	0	0	0	0	6	0	.000
2002 AAA Charlotte	117	438	62	119	35	2	20	59	2	49	139	.272
2002 AL Chicago	16	36	5	8	0	0	2	5	0	1	14	.222

Given $5.3 million to walk away from the chance to be a first-round NFL pick, the former Stanford quarterback has carried a heavy burden since arriving in the 2000 draft. Borchard, a power-hitting outfielder, has made the transition to full-time baseball player smoothly, but after two complete seasons in the minors, he has not smoothed all the rough edges off his game. Borchard

has tremendous power from both sides of the plate, a strong arm and surprising speed, but the Sox worry about his strikeout totals. He has played mostly center field in the minors but doesn't cover a lot of ground. His showing in spring training could determine whether he arrives for good in April or returns to Triple-A Charlotte to work on his plate discipline.

Kris Honel

Position: P   **Opening Day Age:** 20
Bats: R **Throws:** R   **Born:** 11/7/82 in
Ht: 6' 5" **Wt:** 190   Bourbonnais, IL

Recent Statistics

	W	L	ERA	G	GS	Sv	IP	H	R	BB	SO	HR
2001 R White Sox	2	0	1.80	3	1	0	10.0	9	3	3	8	0
2001 R Bristol	2	3	3.13	8	8	0	46.0	41	19	9	45	4
2002 A Kannapolis	9	8	2.82	26	26	0	153.1	128	57	52	152	12
2002 A Winston-Sal	0	0	1.69	1	1	0	5.1	3	2	3	2	0

Illinois is not exactly the cradle of pitchers. But Honel is showing that Chicago knew what it was doing when the team selected him 16th overall in 2001, higher than any Illinois high school pitcher had been taken in 19 years. He has a low-mileage arm, yet has gotten immediate results in his first two pro seasons. Honel's best pitch has long been a knuckle-curve, which acts like a slider. He had a low-90s fastball when he was drafted, but was effective pitching in the high 80s last year. He could dominate if his velocity increases. He'll probably spend 2003 in the high Class-A Carolina League, but could put himself in position to move fast.

Corwin Malone

Position: P   **Opening Day Age:** 22
Bats: R **Throws:** L   **Born:** 7/3/80 in Grove
Ht: 6' 3" **Wt:** 200   Hill, AL

Recent Statistics

	W	L	ERA	G	GS	Sv	IP	H	R	BB	SO	HR
2001 A Kannapolis	11	4	2.00	18	18	0	112.1	83	30	44	119	2
2001 A Winston-Sal	0	1	1.72	5	5	0	36.2	25	10	10	38	1
2001 AA Birmingham	0	0	2.33	4	4	0	19.1	8	5	12	20	2
2002 AA Birmingham	10	7	4.71	22	22	0	124.1	116	77	89	89	6

Malone made tremendous strides in 2000 and '01 before stalling somewhat last season. The one-time college recruit as a linebacker can overpower hitters with his fastball, even though it rarely exceeds 93 MPH, and his snappy curveball also is a plus pitch. The issues for Malone are control and consistency with his mechanics. He walked 6.4 per nine innings, which almost guarantees he'll return to Double-A Birmingham for the start of the season. But if he throws strikes, he won't stay there long. Malone's mentor in the system is Don Cooper, who is now the big league pitching coach. They will reunite in spring training, where Malone will be watched closely because last season ended with tenderness in his elbow, which was considered minor.

Arnaldo Munoz

Position: P	**Opening Day Age:** 20
Bats: L **Throws:** L	**Born:** 6/21/82 in Mao,
Ht: 5' 9" **Wt:** 170	DR

Recent Statistics

	W	L	ERA	G	GS	Sv	IP	H	R	BB	SO	HR
2001 A Kannapolis	6	3	2.49	60	0	12	79.2	41	24	42	115	2
2002 AA Birmingham	6	0	2.61	51	0	6	72.1	62	29	29	78	6

Basically unnoticed in his first two seasons, Munoz has used his Barry Zito-esque curveball to take the express train toward Comiskey Park. He looks like a major bullpen weapon and could help the White Sox in 2003. He opened the season as a 19-year-old in the Double-A Southern League and more than held his own, helping Birmingham to a title. Then he tore through the Dominican. He has averaged 11 strikeouts per nine innings in the minors and had a league-leading 60 Ks in his first 30 innings of winter ball. He's a baby-faced assassin who has the potential to give the Sox the kind of lift that Anaheim received from Francisco Rodriguez. Munoz could start in future years but appears plenty valuable out of the bullpen.

Miguel Olivo

Position: C	**Opening Day Age:** 24
Bats: R **Throws:** R	**Born:** 7/15/78 in Villa
Ht: 6' 1" **Wt:** 215	Vasquez, DR

Recent Statistics

	G	AB	R	H	D	T	HR	RBI	SB	BB	SO	Avg
2002 AA Birmingham	106	359	51	110	24	10	6	49	29	40	66	.306
2002 AL Chicago	6	19	2	4	1	0	1	5	0	2	5	.211

Acquired from Oakland two years ago for Chad Bradford, Olivo has developed into one of the top catching prospects in the majors. He always had a Pudge Rodriguez-style cannon for an arm, but more recently has answered questions about his abilities as a hitter. Olivo followed a strong showing in the Arizona Fall League by hitting .306 at Double-A Birmingham, leading the team to a championship. He hit four homers in the playoffs, earning MVP honors in the championship series. He stands out in an unsung cast of White Sox catchers, despite his inexperience and questions about his receiving skills. He could jump to the big leagues as a regular in 2003. If so, he seems a good bet to improve the offensive output from the catching spot.

Jon Rauch

Position: P	**Opening Day Age:** 24
Bats: R **Throws:** R	**Born:** 9/27/78 in
Ht: 6' 11" **Wt:** 230	Louisville, KY

Recent Statistics

	W	L	ERA	G	GS	Sv	IP	H	R	BB	SO	HR
2002 AL Chicago	2	1	6.59	8	6	0	28.2	28	26	14	19	7
2002 AAA Charlotte	7	8	4.28	19	19	0	109.1	91	60	42	97	14

At 6-foot-11, Rauch is the tallest player to ever reach the big leagues. He's not to be confused with Randy Johnson, however. Rauch throws in the low 90s and earned *Baseball America*'s Minor League Player of the Year distinction in 2000 because of his polish, not his power. His rise has been slowed both by shoulder surgery and some questionable usage by the White Sox. General manager Ken Williams pegged Rauch to open the 2002 season as the Sox' No. 5 starter, but manager Jerry Manuel used only four starters for much of April, getting Rauch only 1.1 innings of work in the first 15 days of the season. Rauch was ineffective when he was used, but came back to pitch well in September.

Dave Sanders

Position: P	**Opening Day Age:** 23
Bats: L **Throws:** L	**Born:** 8/29/79 in
Ht: 6' 0" **Wt:** 200	Oklahoma City, OK

Recent Statistics

	W	L	ERA	G	GS	Sv	IP	H	R	BB	SO	HR
2001 AA Birmingham	3	0	2.65	36	0	0	34.0	27	12	25	25	1
2002 AA Birmingham	3	1	1.84	47	0	0	63.2	56	17	28	61	3

No one in the White Sox' organization has come further than Sanders in the past year. While the former junior-college pitcher from Kansas was a high pick in the 1999 draft, he hadn't been considered a top prospect before 2002. But a strong showing at Double-A Birmingham and then in the Arizona Fall League has changed that. Some think Sanders needs only a solid spring to jump from Double-A ball to the big leagues as part of the Sox' bullpen. He can hit the low 90s, but his best pitch is a power slider that has earned him a strikeout per inning during his pro career. Sanders, a four-year honor roll student in high school, gets it.

Others to Watch

Righthander **Felix Diaz** (21) is the best prospect the Sox landed in a series of midseason trades that brought them several minor league pitchers. Diaz, considered a top prospect with the pitching-rich Giants, throws in the mid-90s but faces questions about his durability. . . **Andy Gonzalez** (21) is the prototype modern shortstop—a big, strong-armed man who should hit for power. He's played on the same team with fellow prospect Anthony Webster for two years and should make it three in a row. . . Infielder **Tim Hummel** (24) once appeared a likely successor to Ray Durham, but has fallen behind D'Angelo Jimenez and Willie Harris after a shaky year at Triple-A Charlotte. Some still expect him to re-establish himself as a .300 hitter in his second season there. That should get him to the big leagues. . . Lefthander **Royce Ring** (22), the Sox' top pick in the 2002 draft, was an All-American closer at San Diego State and could rise quickly through the system. . . He throws in the low 90s with an excellent slider. . . Center fielder **Anthony Webster** (19) has established himself as the organization's best athlete. He's also looked like a natural hitter in his first two pro seasons, hitting a combined .330 in rookie leagues. Webster could develop into an outstanding leadoff man, but has yet to be tested in a full-season league.

Jacobs Field

Offense

The Indians went 39-42 last year at Jacobs Field, their first losing season there since the ballpark opened in 1994. Their home batting average dropped 37 points and their homers fell by 21 in 2002, due more to a lack of talent than any ballpark changes. Jacobs Field still is a good home-run park. An average hitter can clear the fence in any part of the park. It is an especially good park for hitters who go to right field. The wind usually blows from left to right field and the outfield wall drops from 19 feet in left to nine feet in center and right. The lack of foul territory extends at-bats.

Defense

Along with replacing the infield and outfield grass after last season, the slippery outfield warning track was replaced with crushed brick. That will make outfielders happy throughout the American League. Outfielders have to work together to play the left-field wall because the bounces can be tricky. The right-field corner has some odd bounces, too. The infield grass is expected to remain thick, which will help infielders.

Who It Helps the Most

Most of the big guns who have thrived at the park are gone. Ellis Burks is a righthanded pull-hitter who has learned to clear the left-field wall. Despite an off year, Matt Lawton slugged .462 at home in 2002.

Who It Hurts the Most

Pitchers in love with their fastballs will get burned at Jacobs Field. Danys Baez gave up 10 of his 14 homers at home. C.C. Sabathia gave up 11 of his 17 homers there. The slow infield hurt Ricky Gutierrez and Travis Fryman, who together grounded into 14 double plays.

Rookies & Newcomers

Cliff Lee, Jason Davis, Brian Tallet, Ricardo Rodriguez and Billy Traber are five rookies expected to be in and out of the Tribe's rotation this season. They're going to have to learn how to hurl in a park built for offense. Patience is the key.

Dimensions: LF-325, LCF-370, CF-405, RCF-375, RF-325

Capacity: 43,368

Elevation: 660 feet

Surface: Grass

Foul Territory: Small

Park Factors

2002 Season

	Home Games Indians	Opp	Total	Away Games Indians	Opp	Total	Index
G	72	72	144	72	72	144	
Avg	.248	.274	.261	.257	.276	.266	98
AB	2372	2533	4905	2490	2397	4887	100
R	337	388	725	341	375	716	101
H	588	694	1282	639	661	1300	99
2B	120	151	271	114	135	249	108
3B	8	13	21	14	25	39	54
HR	85	71	156	93	60	153	102
BB	209	287	496	264	256	520	95
SO	435	533	968	453	398	851	113
E	43	65	108	55	32	87	124
E-Infield	38	58	96	47	30	77	125
LHB-Avg	.251	.288	.268	.252	.277	.264	102
LHB-HR	58	35	93	63	25	88	103
RHB-Avg	.245	.263	.255	.261	.275	.268	95
RHB-HR	27	36	63	30	35	65	99

2000-2002

	Home Games Indians	Opp	Total	Away Games Indians	Opp	Total	Index
G	215	215	430	217	217	434	
Avg	.275	.273	.274	.274	.273	.273	100
AB	7265	7623	14888	7643	7256	14899	101
R	1166	1125	2291	1168	1113	2281	101
H	2001	2078	4079	2092	1981	4073	101
2B	382	445	827	394	400	794	104
3B	33	39	72	50	52	102	71
HR	292	217	509	263	198	461	110
BB	768	832	1600	813	817	1630	98
SO	1348	1635	2983	1414	1458	2872	104
E	125	165	290	133	146	279	105
E-Infield	109	141	250	106	122	228	111
LHB-Avg	.278	.274	.276	.266	.285	.275	100
LHB-HR	170	100	270	143	83	226	115
RHB-Avg	.273	.272	.272	.280	.265	.272	100
RHB-HR	122	117	239	120	115	235	105

2002 Rankings (American League)
- Highest strikeout factor
- Second-highest infield-error factor
- Third-highest error factor
- Second-lowest triple factor
- Second-lowest RHB batting-average factor
- Third-lowest walk factor

Eric Wedge

2002 Season

The Indians named Eric Wedge manager in late October after he led Triple-A Buffalo to the International League playoffs for the second straight season. Wedge, who never has managed or coached in the big leagues, won 178 games at Buffalo in two years. The rebuilding Indians hired him because of his energy, aggressive nature and ability to keep young players focused. It served Wedge well that over the last two years he managed many of the prospects who will be playing in Cleveland in 2003.

Offense

Wedge likes to use the steal and hit-and-run. He did not sacrifice bunt much in two years at Buffalo, but his team was second in the International League last year in batting average while playing in pitcher-friendly Dunn Tire Park. Wedge isn't tied to righty vs. lefty matchups, but he will change his lineup if he feels a hitter's swing is a good match against a certain pitcher. He didn't have a lot of extra bodies at Buffalo to pinch-hit, but he likes to pinch-run and will exploit any weakness by the opposition.

Pitching & Defense

Handling the pitching staff will be Wedge's biggest challenge. The Indians' rotation will be young, so Wedge still will have to deal with strict pitch counts, despite moving from a developmental setting to one where winning is stressed. He likes a bullpen where everyone has a set role, but he showed that he can win without an established closer in 2002. Wedge didn't use the intentional walk much last year, preferring to let pitchers work their way out of jams. He set his own defense in Buffalo and will stress that his catchers and pitchers work hard to control the running game.

2003 Outlook

Wedge signed a two-year deal with two club options, so he'll get a chance to grow with the team. He'll be the youngest manager in the big leagues at 35, but the Indians feel he can make up for his lack of experience with his ability to reach and motivate players of all ages.

Born: 1/27/68 in Ft. Wayne, IN

Playing Experience: 1991-1994, Bos, Col

Managerial Experience: No major league managing experience

Manager Statistics (Joel Skinner)

Year	Team, Lg	W	L	Pct	GB	Finish
2002	Cleveland, AL	35	41	.461	20.5	3rd Central
1 Season		35	41	.461	–	

2002 Starting Pitchers by Days Rest

	<=3	4	5	6+
Indians Starts	1	35	17	15
Indians ERA	3.60	5.48	5.62	6.19
AL Avg Starts	1	83	44	24
AL ERA	7.15	4.59	4.27	5.03

2002 Situational Stats

	Joel Skinner	AL Average
Hit & Run Success %	61.5	36.0
Stolen Base Success %	71.9	68.1
Platoon Pct.	69.3	58.9
Defensive Subs	10	23
High-Pitch Outings	1	6
Quick/Slow Hooks	11/5	19/14
Sacrifice Attempts	32	53

2002 Rankings —Joel Skinner (American League)

- Did not rank near the top in any category

Danys Baez

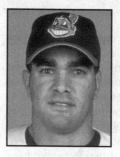

Position: SP/RP
Bats: R **Throws:** R
Ht: 6' 3" **Wt:** 225

Opening Day Age: 25
Born: 9/10/77 in Pinar del Rio, Cuba
ML Seasons: 2
Pronunciation: DAN-ees BUY-ez

2002 Season

Danys Baez made his first 26 appearances as a starter after impressing the Indians as a hard-throwing setup man in 2001. On August 27, he became the closer when Bob Wickman was shut down with a sore elbow. Baez went 9-10 as a starter and posted six saves in eight chances as a closer. He showed durability, pitching five or more innings in 23 of his 26 starts. But he had control problems and finished fourth in the American League with 82 walks.

Pitching

Baez is a fastball pitcher who can sink the ball, cut it or throw it straight. His fastball tops out at about 97 MPH, but he usually throws it 92-95 MPH as a reliever and 89-92 MPH as a starter. He basically was a fastball pitcher as a starter because his secondary pitches need work. Baez is more effective as a reliever because he'll use his split-finger pitch to offset the fastball. He wouldn't throw the splitter as a starter because it hurt his arm. His velocity was down when he was first moved to closer. Baez said it was because he had grown used to pacing himself as a starter.

Defense

Baez probably is the Indians' best fielding pitcher. He's quick off the mound and hustles to first. He'll make a bad throw occasionally when he tries to set up too fast. Baez controls the running game well. He has a quick move to the plate, getting the ball to the catcher in 1.3 seconds. He'll also use a slide step. Half of the runners who tried to steal on him (11 of 22) were thrown out.

2003 Outlook

Baez may settle in as the Indians' long-term closer. Wickman, who will miss this season because of elbow surgery, will be 35 and in the last year of his contract in 2004. The Indians liked the progress Baez was making as a starter, but feel he's better suited to close because of his personality and pitches. He's aggressive, likes to pitch often and is at his best in pressure situations.

Overall Statistics

	W	L	Pct.	ERA	G	GS	Sv	IP	H	BB	SO	HR	Ratio
'02	10	11	.476	4.41	39	26	6	165.1	160	82	130	14	1.46
Car.	15	14	.517	3.96	82	26	6	215.2	194	102	182	19	1.37

How Often He Throws Strikes

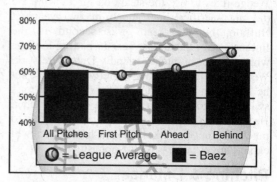

○ = League Average   ■ = Baez

2002 Situational Stats

	W	L	ERA	Sv	IP		AB	H	HR	RBI	Avg
Home	5	7	4.82	2	104.2	LHB	324	90	5	37	.278
Road	5	4	3.71	4	60.2	RHB	301	70	9	40	.233
First Half	7	6	4.22	0	96.0	Sc Pos	149	39	2	55	.262
Scnd Half	3	5	4.67	6	69.1	Clutch	47	10	1	6	.213

2002 Rankings (American League)

- 1st in highest walks per nine innings (4.5)
- 2nd in most pitches thrown per batter (3.98)
- 3rd in runners caught stealing (11)
- 4th in walks allowed and highest on-base percentage allowed (.347)
- 5th in lowest strikeout-walk ratio (1.6)
- 6th in highest ERA at home
- 7th in most strikeouts per nine innings (7.1) and lowest fielding percentage at pitcher (.935)
- Led the Indians in losses, hit batsmen (9), pickoff throws (83), runners caught stealing (11) and lowest batting average allowed vs. righthanded batters

Milton Bradley

2002 Season

The Indians gave Milton Bradley a chance to be their everyday center fielder, but he didn't stay healthy long enough to prove he can do the job. He was on the disabled list from May 2 to June 4 with a broken orbital bone around his left eye. He returned to the DL August 12-30 because of an emergency appendectomy. Bradley missed seven of the last eight games of the season with a strained muscle in his left side.

Hitting

The switch-hitting Bradley has the potential to be a middle-of-the-order hitter with power, but he needs to work harder and take instruction better. He hits for more power lefthanded, but for a higher average righthanded. He has a quick bat, but his lefthanded swing has holes. He's susceptible to breaking balls down in the strike zone and fastballs that climb the ladder. Bradley puts a lot of pressure on himself and it shows at the plate. He needs to relax his hands and hit the ball before it gets too deep into the strike zone.

Baserunning & Defense

Bradley has decent speed, but doesn't seem inclined to make basestealing a big part of his game. There were times he did not give a full effort running to first base, which angered the coaching staff. Defensively, he runs well and gets good jumps, but often doesn't take the right routes to balls. He charges balls well and has good jumping ability at the wall. Bradley's arm is above average and accurate, to which his nine assists in just 94 games attest.

2003 Outlook

When the Indians acquired Bradley from Montreal in 2001, they said he was a five-tool player who was going to help them rebuild. Bradley showed flashes of those tools, but he needs to do much more this year. He needs to stay healthy, work harder and avoid the mental funks that hurt his performance. The front office spent last year making excuses for Bradley's lack of hustle and moodiness. Now the Indians must get him to step up his game.

Position: CF
Bats: B **Throws:** R
Ht: 6' 0"   **Wt:** 190

Opening Day Age: 24
Born: 4/15/78 in Harbor City, CA
ML Seasons: 3

Overall Statistics

	G	AB	R	H	D	T	HR	RBI	SB	BB	SO	Avg	OBP	Slg
'02	98	325	48	81	18	3	9	38	6	32	58	.249	.317	.406
Car.	217	717	90	168	43	7	12	72	16	67	155	.234	.301	.364

Where He Hits the Ball

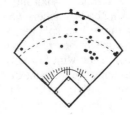
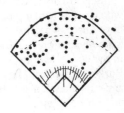

Vs. LHP   **Vs. RHP**

2002 Situational Stats

	AB	H	HR	RBI	Avg		AB	H	HR	RBI	Avg
Home	133	31	4	14	.233	LHP	99	29	1	11	.293
Road	192	50	5	24	.260	RHP	226	52	8	27	.230
First Half	163	38	4	15	.233	Sc Pos	78	18	3	28	.231
Scnd Half	162	43	5	23	.265	Clutch	39	4	0	3	.103

2002 Rankings (American League)

- 2nd in lowest batting average on a 3-2 count (.103)
- 5th in assists in center field (9)
- 6th in errors in center field (4)
- Led the Indians in batting average on an 0-2 count (.278)

Ellis Burks

2002 Season

If Ellis Burks can stay healthy, he'll hit. Last year he got 518 at-bats, the most since 1996, and produced one of his best seasons. He was especially effective after the All-Star break. Burks and Jim Thome helped prevent the rebuilding Indians from losing 100 games by giving them consistent offense in the middle of the lineup. Burks underwent surgery on his left shoulder in November, but should be ready in the spring.

Hitting

The line-drive hitting Burks has a short, quick swing. He's at his best when he uses the whole field, but he's become mostly a pull-hitter since coming to Cleveland. He's a good fastball hitter who crushes hanging breaking balls. Pitchers who have success against him throw him split-finger fastballs and breaking balls when they're behind in the count, and then come inside with fastballs. Burks, who makes enough contact to work the hit-and-run, handled lefties and righties efficiently and was dangerous with runners in scoring position in 2002.

Baserunning & Defense

Burks probably could hit until he's 45, but his knees won't let him. He's strong and well conditioned, but each knee has been operated on twice. At this stage of his career, they limit him to DH. Burks did play left field for six games when the Indians were on the road for interleague games. An experienced outfielder, Burks still moves well and has a decent arm. He runs the bases with abandon, slides hard into second base to break up a double play and gets to first base quickly. But when he runs too much, his knees swell and have to be drained.

2003 Outlook

Burks signed with the Indians to reach the post-season. After last season's rebuilding efforts, Burks hinted that he may ask to be traded to a contender. He's 38, in the last year of his contract and never has been to the World Series. Burks probably would be hard to deal until June or July. He's strictly an American League player who will make $6.5 million this year.

Position: DH
Bats: R **Throws:** R
Ht: 6' 2" **Wt:** 205

Opening Day Age: 38
Born: 9/11/64 in Vicksburg, MS
ML Seasons: 16

Overall Statistics

G	AB	R	H	D	T	HR	RBI	SB	BB	SO	Avg	OBP	Slg
138	518	92	156	28	0	32	91	2	44	108	.301	.362	.541
1934	7001	1220	2049	391	62	345	1177	178	763	1286	.293	.364	.514

Where He Hits the Ball

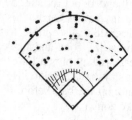 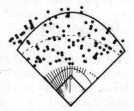

Vs. LHP   Vs. RHP

2002 Situational Stats

	AB	H	HR	RBI	Avg		AB	H	HR	RBI	Avg
Home	263	69	16	43	.262	LHP	136	43	9	19	.316
Road	255	87	16	48	.341	RHP	382	113	23	72	.296
First Half	279	75	16	43	.269	Sc Pos	130	48	7	59	.369
Scnd Half	239	81	16	48	.339	Clutch	55	18	5	12	.327

2002 Rankings (American League)

- 2nd in slugging percentage vs. lefthanded pitchers (.581)
- 4th in batting average on a 3-1 count (.643) and batting average on the road
- 5th in batting average with runners in scoring position
- 7th in batting average vs. lefthanded pitchers and on-base percentage vs. lefthanded pitchers (.400)
- 8th in HR frequency (16.2 ABs per HR)
- 10th in slugging percentage
- Led the Indians in batting average with runners in scoring position, slugging percentage vs. lefthanded pitchers (.581) and batting average on the road

Einar Diaz

2002 Season

Just when Einar Diaz seemed to be emerging as a catcher, he had the worst season of his career. He was battered in two home-plate collisions, breaking a rib April 20 and hyperextending his right elbow August 22. The second injury mercifully ended his season. The Indians believe he was hurt worse than he admitted when he broke the rib, and that it affected his game for the rest of the season.

Hitting

Diaz is a contact hitter who has turned pull-crazy the last two years. When the Indians had an All-Star lineup, pitchers would challenge him at the bottom of the order with fastballs, trying not to walk him. The Indians' lineup doesn't scare people as much now and pitchers are working Diaz harder. They're throwing him breaking balls and changeups instead of fastballs. He's not patient and dives into pitches, which robs him of power and results in weak grounders and flyballs. He grounded into 13 double plays last season.

Baserunning & Defense

Diaz' defense went the way of his offense in 2002. He made eight errors and was charged with eight passed balls. When his season ended in August, he had the second-worst fielding percentage of any regular catcher in the American League. He had problems blocking pitches in the dirt, reaching for them instead of moving his body in front of them. Diaz has a good arm, but his success rate throwing out runners fell from 35 percent to 27 percent between 2001 and last year. He stole 11 bases in 1999, but has just five since then.

2003 Outlook

The Indians believe Diaz' poor performance last season was due mostly to injury. So did the Texas Rangers, who acquired him in a four-player trade in early December to replace Pudge Rodriguez as their No. 1 catcher. The Rangers monitored Diaz' rehab in the Arizona Fall League, and are confident in his return to full speed. He still needs to find a safer way to block the plate and use the whole field when he hits, and the Rangers know that they aren't getting a star backstop. But it will be interesting to see what he can do over the course of a full season if he remains injury-free.

Position: C
Bats: R **Throws:** R
Ht: 5'10" **Wt:** 190

Opening Day Age: 30
Born: 12/28/72 in Chiriqui, Panama
ML Seasons: 7
Nickname: The Dream

Overall Statistics

	G	AB	R	H	D	T	HR	RBI	SB	BB	SO	Avg	OBP	Slg
'02	102	320	34	66	19	0	2	16	0	17	27	.206	.258	.284
Car.	456	1455	169	377	90	4	15	139	16	71	145	.259	.309	.357

Where He Hits the Ball

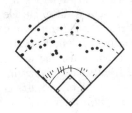
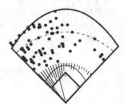

Vs. LHP　　　　**Vs. RHP**

2002 Situational Stats

	AB	H	HR	RBI	Avg		AB	H	HR	RBI	Avg
Home	139	37	1	8	.266	LHP	71	16	1	4	.225
Road	181	29	1	8	.160	RHP	249	50	1	12	.201
First Half	221	47	2	12	.213	Sc Pos	77	11	1	15	.143
Scnd Half	99	19	0	4	.192	Clutch	30	4	0	0	.133

2002 Rankings (American League)

- 2nd in errors at catcher (8)
- 3rd in highest percentage of runners caught stealing as a catcher (27.4) and most GDPs per GDP situation (20.3%)

Cleveland

Karim Garcia

2002 Season

One of the best moves the Indians made last year was reacquiring Karim Garcia after they released him in spring training. After the Yankees released him in July, the Indians quickly re-signed him. Garcia hit .396 (36-for-91) at Triple-A Buffalo and .299-16-52 in 197 at-bats after getting promoted to Cleveland on August 6. Garcia's 52 RBI were the most in the big leagues from August 6 through the end of the season.

Hitting

The Indians spent most of last season looking for a No. 5 hitter to protect Jim Thome. Garcia ended the search. He's a lefthanded hitter who can drive high fastballs out of the park. Most lefties are good low-ball hitters, but Garcia is different. He has spent most of his career as a pull-hitter, but over the last two years the Indians' minor league staff has worked hard with him to use the whole field. Lefties who change speeds have given him problems. Garcia, who reached the big leagues at 19, finally may be ready to establish himself.

Baserunning & Defense

Garcia can play all three outfield positions, but the Indians moved Matt Lawton to left field and handed Garcia the right-field job when he arrived in August. He has a strong, accurate arm and is faster than he appears. He can run down balls in the gap and get into the corner to keep doubles from becoming triples. In late August he was hobbled by an ankle injury that bothered him the rest of the year. Garcia isn't built for speed, but he won't clog the bases.

2003 Outlook

Garcia will report to spring training as the Indians' starting right fielder. In an organization devoid of young power hiitters, Garcia may have found a home. His biggest challenge will be proving he can be productive for a whole season. He had two strong months last year and 20 good games in 2001. The Indians showed their faith in Garcia by signing him to a one-year, $900,000 deal in December.

Position: RF
Bats: L **Throws:** L
Ht: 6' 0" **Wt:** 195

Opening Day Age: 27
Born: 10/29/75 in Ciudad Obregon, Mexico
ML Seasons: 8
Pronunciation: kuh-REEM

Overall Statistics

	G	AB	R	H	D	T	HR	RBI	SB	BB	SO	Avg	OBP	Slg
'02	53	202	30	60	8	0	16	52	0	6	41	.297	.314	.574
Car.	327	961	122	229	31	11	45	144	7	53	228	.238	.277	.434

Where He Hits the Ball

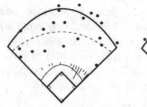 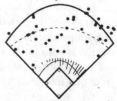

Vs. LHP   **Vs. RHP**

2002 Situational Stats

	AB	H	HR	RBI	Avg		AB	H	HR	RBI	Avg
Home	115	32	7	23	.278	LHP	72	20	5	21	.278
Road	87	28	9	29	.322	RHP	130	40	11	31	.308
First Half	5	1	0	0	.200	Sc Pos	53	15	5	34	.283
Scnd Half	197	59	16	52	.299	Clutch	30	9	4	13	.300

2002 Rankings (American League)

- Led the Indians in batting average on a 3-1 count (1.000)

Ricky Gutierrez

2002 Season

Before the 2002 season, the Indians signed Ricky Gutierrez to a three-year, $11 million contract and moved him from shortstop to second. But his first season, and perhaps his career, ended in August when he broke a season-long silence and told the Indians about a neck injury that he'd had since early April. Gutierrez needed a bone graft and two vertebrae in his neck fused. The injury helped explain Gutierrez' limited range at second base, struggles to catch popups and lack of speed.

Hitting

Gutierrez spent his whole big league career in the National League and had trouble adjusting to American League pitching. He's a line-drive, fast-ball hitter, but he saw a steady diet of breaking balls and changeups. Gutierrez is best suited as a No. 2 hitter because he's a good bunter, but the Indians used Omar Vizquel in that spot and Gutierrez' bunting ability was wasted. He showed little power after combining to hit 21 homers for the Cubs in 2000 and 2001. Gutierrez makes hard contact, but his lack of foot speed resulted in 14 GIDP in 2002.

Baserunning & Defense

Picture a slow man running in sand. That's how Gutierrez looked playing defense or running the bases. Worries that the converted shortstop could not turn the double play were unfounded, but his lack of range and speed made every grounder an adventure. Gutierrez had the misfortune of replacing Robbie Alomar, who won three straight Gold Gloves in front of Indians fans, and Gutierrez suffered in comparison. Gutierrez did score from first base on a triple on June 13, but pulled a groin and went on the disabled list.

2003 Outlook

Gutierrez underwent surgery October 7 and was in a neck brace until late November. Doctors told the Indians that there will be no gray area concerning his return. He'll either be able to play or he won't. The surgery took pressure off Gutierrez' spine, which had been causing numbness in his arms. If he can play, the Indians probably will move him to third base.

Position: 2B
Bats: R **Throws:** R
Ht: 6' 1" **Wt:** 190

Opening Day Age: 32
Born: 5/23/70 in Miami, FL
ML Seasons: 10
Pronunciation: goo-tee-AIR-ez

Overall Statistics

	G	AB	R	H	D	T	HR	RBI	SB	BB	SO	Avg	OBP	Slg
'02	94	353	38	97	13	0	4	38	0	20	48	.275	.325	.346
Car.	1058	3479	461	932	135	25	38	346	49	353	567	.268	.341	.354

Where He Hits the Ball

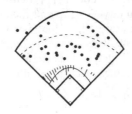

Vs. LHP   **Vs. RHP**

2002 Situational Stats

	AB	H	HR	RBI	Avg		AB	H	HR	RBI	Avg
Home	190	52	2	20	.274	LHP	89	33	1	14	.371
Road	163	45	2	18	.276	RHP	264	64	3	24	.242
First Half	245	61	2	14	.249	Sc Pos	82	24	1	34	.293
Scnd Half	108	36	2	24	.333	Clutch	33	11	1	6	.333

2002 Rankings (American League)

- 5th in errors at second base (11)
- 9th in most GDPs per GDP situation (17.3%) and lowest batting average on an 0-2 count (.059)
- Led the Indians in GDPs (14), highest groundball-flyball ratio (2.1), batting average vs. lefthanded pitchers and on-base percentage vs. lefthanded pitchers (.417)

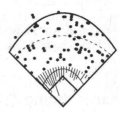

Cleveland

105

Matt Lawton

2002 Season

Matt Lawton endured an injury-plagued season. Acquired from the Mets in the Robbie Alomar trade, Lawton collected 17 runs and 14 RBI through the first 15 games before he separated his right shoulder diving for a ball on April 19. The injury turned him into a subpar outfielder and hurt his swing. He underwent surgery on September 17 to repair a torn labrum and rotator cuff.

Hitting

Lawton is a good hitter who uses the whole field and has enough power to hit 15-25 homers in a year, but he didn't look like it in 2002. Some of it was the shoulder injury. Some of it may have been the four-year, $27 million contract Lawton signed. It was his first multiyear deal, and there were times when Lawton did not look motivated. Pitchers who feed him fastballs early in the count and breaking balls late will get him out. Lawton, who batted leadoff in 66 games, is a patient hitter.

Baserunning & Defense

These were the most disappointing aspects of Lawton's game in 2002. After stealing 29 bases in 2001, he stole eight bases last year and was caught nine times. Normally a competent outfielder, Lawton looked lost with Cleveland. He opened the season in right field and covered little ground. Any ball hit down the right-field line had a chance to be a triple. He moved to left in August so he'd have a shorter throw home to protect his shoulder. The doctor who operated on Lawton said his shoulder was so damaged that it would have hurt him to run.

2003 Outlook

Lawton will need six to nine months to heal. He could be ready to play sometime in April. The Indians need him to come to camp in shape and focused. Lawton has made it clear that he doesn't want to go through the same kind of rebuilding program he did in Minnesota, but he may have no choice. Who's going to take a tired-looking outfielder with a bad shoulder and fat contract?

Position: RF/LF
Bats: L **Throws:** R
Ht: 5'10" **Wt:** 186

Opening Day Age: 31
Born: 11/3/71 in Gulfport, MS
ML Seasons: 8

Overall Statistics

	G	AB	R	H	D	T	HR	RBI	SB	BB	SO	Avg	OBP	Slg
'02	114	416	71	98	19	2	15	57	8	59	34	.236	.342	.399
Car.	933	3271	518	882	193	16	90	454	114	489	403	.270	.373	.421

Where He Hits the Ball

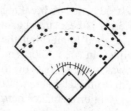 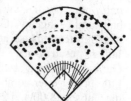

Vs. LHP   **Vs. RHP**

2002 Situational Stats

	AB	H	HR	RBI	Avg		AB	H	HR	RBI	Avg
Home	195	51	8	28	.262	LHP	118	21	5	16	.178
Road	221	47	7	29	.213	RHP	298	77	10	41	.258
First Half	289	71	10	37	.246	Sc Pos	96	23	5	42	.240
Scnd Half	127	27	5	20	.213	Clutch	48	11	1	8	.229

2002 Rankings (American League)

- 1st in lowest batting average vs. lefthanded pitchers
- 2nd in highest percentage of swings put into play (54.2) and errors in right field (6)
- 3rd in lowest batting average on the road
- 6th in lowest percentage of swings that missed (10.6), lowest batting average on a 3-1 count (.125) and lowest on-base percentage for a leadoff hitter (.341)
- 7th in highest percentage of pitches taken (62.1)
- Led the Indians in hit by pitch (8), highest percentage of pitches taken (62.1), highest percentage of swings put into play (54.2) and highest percentage of extra bases taken as a runner (58.6)

John McDonald

2002 Season

This was John McDonald's seventh season with the Indians' organization, and his first full season in the majors. The Indians could have given him the second-base job when they traded Robbie Alomar to the Mets, but they signed Ricky Gutierrez instead. When Gutierrez went on the disabled list August 15, McDonald went from utility infielder to starting second baseman. He hit .306 in July, but only .226 (30-for-133) after getting the job full-time.

Hitting

McDonald is a little guy who hits too many fly-balls with an uppercut swing. If he's going to be a starting second baseman, he has to play the game right. He has to hit behind the runner, sacrifice bunt and work the hit-and-run. McDonald has one big league homer, but that hasn't stopped him from swinging early and often. He goes to the plate with the idea of hitting line drives over the second baseman's head, but needs to be more patient. Pitchers set up McDonald with breaking balls and get him out on high fastballs.

Baserunning & Defense

McDonald is one of the best middle infielders in the American League. If not for Omar Vizquel, he'd probably be the starting shortstop. He has good range to his right and left and a strong arm. McDonald has exceptionally quick hands and feet. They allow him to turn the double play with ease and start the 4-6-3 double play from the hole between first and second. He can get down the right-field line to catch foul pops and is quick enough to catch balls in shallow right-center field. He's an average runner.

2003 Outlook

McDonald may be doomed to spend most of his career in the wrong organization. He was stuck behind Vizquel and Alomar for years. Now he'll compete with top-flight prospect Brandon Phillips for the second-base job this spring. If McDonald gets stronger and dedicates himself to being a small-ball, situational-type hitter, he may hold off Phillips for a year. If not, he's still good enough to make the club as an extra infielder.

Position: 2B/SS/3B
Bats: R **Throws:** R
Ht: 5'11" **Wt:** 175

Opening Day Age: 28
Born: 9/24/74 in New London, CT
ML Seasons: 4

Overall Statistics

	G	AB	R	H	D	T	HR	RBI	SB	BB	SO	Avg	OBP	Slg
'02	93	264	35	66	11	3	1	12	3	10	50	.250	.288	.326
Car.	137	316	38	79	12	3	1	12	3	11	61	.250	.287	.316

Where He Hits the Ball

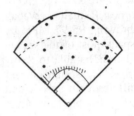 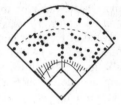

Vs. LHP   **Vs. RHP**

2002 Situational Stats

	AB	H	HR	RBI	Avg		AB	H	HR	RBI	Avg
Home	107	27	0	4	.252	LHP	69	16	1	8	.232
Road	157	39	1	8	.248	RHP	195	50	0	4	.256
First Half	91	25	0	7	.275	Sc Pos	61	14	0	11	.230
Scnd Half	173	41	1	5	.237	Clutch	31	3	0	2	.097

2002 Rankings (American League)

• Led the Indians in sacrifice bunts (7)

C.C. Sabathia

2002 Season

C.C. Sabathia, hung over from his rookie success in 2001, started last season poorly. He was a disappointing 6-7 with a 4.95 ERA at the All-Star break, but he turned his season around after failing to field a grounder against Seattle. The misplay made him realize that he was out of shape and needed to work harder. Sabathia went 7-2 with a 2.54 ERA in his last 11 starts of the season.

Pitching

Sabathia's struggles were rooted in three things—he didn't throw enough strikes, couldn't field his position because he was too heavy and couldn't stop the running game. He worked on each weakness and made significant progress by the end of the season. Sabathia throws a fastball, curveball and changeup. He was throwing 95-97 MPH by the end of the year, but spent most of the season throwing 93-95 MPH. When he is able to throw all three pitches for strikes, he's hard to hit because there's such a difference in speeds and action on his pitches. He had trouble controlling the strike zone and his emotions on the mound in 2002. He finished second in the American League with 88 walks.

Defense

As a rookie, Sabathia fielded his position well, but last year he came to camp pushing 300 pounds and lost agility and quickness. It wasn't until he started doing extra running between starts in the second half that he looked comfortable fielding his position. Basestealers went 19-for-28 against Sabathia, but after some tips from teammate Terry Mulholland, Sabathia gave up just one steal in his last 13 starts.

2003 Outlook

The Indians are counting on Sabathia, 22, to be their No. 1 starter. The talent is there. He's won 30 games in his first two years. But what about his maturity and commitment? If Sabathia is out of shape again this year, and is unable to pitch deep into games until the second half of the season, the Indians may regret the four-year, $9.5 million contract they gave him last February.

Position: SP
Bats: L **Throws:** L
Ht: 6' 7" **Wt:** 270

Opening Day Age: 22
Born: 7/21/80 in Vallejo, CA
ML Seasons: 2
Pronunciation: sa-BATH-ee-a

Overall Statistics

	W	L	Pct.	ERA	G	GS	Sv	IP	H	BB	SO	HR	Ratio
'02	13	11	.542	4.37	33	33	0	210.0	198	88	149	17	1.36
Car.	30	16	.652	4.38	66	66	0	390.1	347	183	320	36	1.36

How Often He Throws Strikes

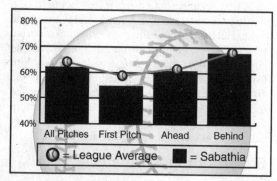

○ = League Average   ■ = Sabathia

2002 Situational Stats

	W	L	ERA	Sv	IP		AB	H	HR	RBI	Avg
Home	6	5	4.08	0	97.0	LHB	196	47	3	16	.240
Road	7	6	4.62	0	113.0	RHB	591	151	14	81	.255
First Half	6	7	4.95	0	103.2	Sc Pos	191	47	3	71	.246
Scnd Half	7	4	3.81	0	106.1	Clutch	27	5	0	0	.185

2002 Rankings (American League)

- 1st in balks (3)
- 2nd in walks allowed
- 3rd in highest walks per nine innings (3.8)
- 5th in stolen bases allowed (19)
- 6th in runners caught stealing (9) and GDPs induced (24)
- 7th in games started, fewest home runs allowed per nine innings (.73) and most GDPs induced per nine innings (1.0)
- Led the Indians in wins, losses, games started, innings pitched, hits allowed, batters faced (891), home runs allowed, walks allowed, strikeouts, balks (3), pitches thrown (3,379), stolen bases allowed (19) and GDPs induced (24)

Jim Thome

2002 Season

Thome had a dream season in his free-agent walk year. He hit a franchise-record 52 homers, led the American League in walks, finished second in on-base percentage and hit .300 for the first time since 1996. In a testament to his knowledge of the strike zone, Thome reduced his strikeouts from 185 in 2001 to 139 last year and reached base by walk or hit in his final 55 games.

Hitting

Thome has power to all parts of the park. He'll drive low breaking balls and changeups over the fence from center field to the right-field line. He can power outside fastballs over the left-field fence. Pitchers try to get him out with fastballs up and in. Thome is patient, drawing 100 or more walks in six of the last seven seasons. Teams try to stop him with infield shifts and lefthanded relievers. Lefties still give him fits, but he's learned to handle the shift.

Baserunning & Defense

Thome won't win many foot races, but he runs the bases well for a big man and can unleash a variety of slides to score on close plays at the plate. He's a solid first baseman whose range was limited last year by back spasms. Thome likes to dive for grounders to his left and right, which can bring on back pain. Thome handles foul pops well and starts the 3-6-3 double play quickly. He does have problems scooping throws in the dirt from his fellow infielders.

2003 Outlook

Cleveland ultimately lost a bidding war to Philadelphia for Thome. The Indians offered him slightly more than $60 million, but the Phillies won his services with a six-year, $85 million deal. Thome, one of the last links to the Tribe's World Series teams of 1995 and 1997, will be changing leagues in the prime of his career, and he will not have the designated hitter to fall back on if his back acts up. It may take awhile to adjust to National League pitching, but he's going to give the Phillies a dangerous lineup. While Cleveland without Thome is a frightening thought, the acquisition of Travis Hafner from Texas as a possible replacement was a good move.

Position: 1B/DH
Bats: L **Throws:** R
Ht: 6' 4" **Wt:** 220

Opening Day Age: 32
Born: 8/27/70 in Peoria, IL
ML Seasons: 12
Pronunciation: TOE-mee

Overall Statistics

G	AB	R	H	D	T	HR	RBI	SB	BB	SO	Avg	OBP	Slg
147	480	101	146	19	2	52	118	1	122	139	.304	.445	.677
1377	4640	917	1332	259	20	334	927	18	997	1377	.287	.414	.567

Where He Hits the Ball

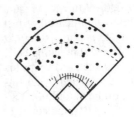 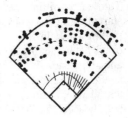

Vs. LHP   **Vs. RHP**

2002 Situational Stats

	AB	H	HR	RBI	Avg		AB	H	HR	RBI	Avg
Home	246	86	30	72	.350	LHP	159	39	12	32	.245
Road	234	60	22	46	.256	RHP	321	107	40	86	.333
First Half	273	76	26	60	.278	Sc Pos	120	41	13	71	.342
Scnd Half	207	70	26	58	.338	Clutch	53	17	3	13	.321

2002 Rankings (American League)

- 1st in walks, slugging percentage, HR frequency (9.2 ABs per HR), cleanup slugging percentage (.707), slugging percentage vs. righthanded pitchers (.766), on-base percentage vs. righthanded pitchers (.485), and batting average at home
- 2nd in home runs, intentional walks (18), on-base percentage, batting average vs. righthanded pitchers, errors at first base (10), lowest percentage of swings put into play (34.3) and lowest fielding percentage at first base (.991)
- 3rd in batting average on a 3-2 count (.362)
- Led AL first basemen in batting average, home runs and RBI

Cleveland

Omar Vizquel

2002 Season

The whispers began after the 2001 season that Omar Vizquel was on the decline. He dispelled those rumors last year with a comeback season that saw him set career highs in homers and RBI. After an offseason of weightlifting, Vizquel was hitting .312 with nine homers and 42 RBI through June 14. The fast start led to his third All-Star appearance, but Vizquel was denied a 10th straight Gold Glove when the award went to Alex Rodriguez.

Hitting

The switch-hitting Vizquel's biggest improvement came from the right side of the plate. Tutored by hitting coach Eddie Murray, Vizquel started using the whole field again instead of just pulling the ball. Pitchers try to take the sting out of his bat by getting him to lunge at breaking balls and changeups. When he stays back and keeps his swing short and compact, he's a much better hitter. Vizquel's career high in homers did not happen by accident. When he's ahead in the count 1-0, 2-0 or 3-1, he looks for a fastball that he can drive.

Baserunning & Defense

Vizquel still can steal a base, but his judgment and timing are not always the best. He hasn't been successful in 80 percent of his steals since 1999, but remains a daredevil who occasionally will attempt a straight steal of home. Defense still is the strongest part of Vizquel's game. He has a quick release that makes up for an average arm, but a quick runner can beat his throw to first. Vizquel is fearless on the double play and has remarkable range catching flyballs down the line or in shallow left field.

2003 Outlook

Vizquel is signed for two more years. He was disappointed when he didn't win the Gold Glove in 2002, but is driven by another goal. He knows he needs to keep playing at a high level to have a chance to make the Hall of Fame. Ozzie Smith opened the door for him last year, but it's up to Vizquel to walk through it.

Position: SS
Bats: B **Throws:** R
Ht: 5' 9" **Wt:** 175

Opening Day Age: 35
Born: 4/24/67 in Caracas, VZ
ML Seasons: 14
Pronunciation: viz-KELL

Overall Statistics

	G	AB	R	H	D	T	HR	RBI	SB	BB	SO	Avg	OBP	Slg
'02	151	582	85	160	31	5	14	72	18	56	64	.275	.341	.418
Car.	1926	7002	1004	1921	307	49	57	637	291	699	712	.274	.340	.357

Where He Hits the Ball

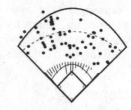

Vs. LHP   **Vs. RHP**

2002 Situational Stats

	AB	H	HR	RBI	Avg		AB	H	HR	RBI	Avg
Home	304	90	9	46	.296	LHP	171	48	3	22	.281
Road	278	70	5	26	.252	RHP	411	112	11	50	.273
First Half	305	87	10	47	.285	Sc Pos	118	36	3	54	.305
Scnd Half	277	73	4	25	.264	Clutch	77	26	1	13	.338

2002 Rankings (American League)

- 2nd in lowest percentage of swings that missed (8.3) and fielding percentage at shortstop (.990)
- 4th in sacrifice flies (10)
- Led the Indians in at-bats, hits, singles, doubles, triples, sacrifice bunts (7), sacrifice flies (10), stolen bases, caught stealing (10), hit by pitch (8), pitches seen (2,621), plate appearances (663), games played, stolen-base percentage (64.3), bunts in play (19), lowest percentage of swings that missed (8.3), steals of third (3), batting average in the clutch, on-base percentage for a leadoff hitter (.426), lowest percentage of swings on the first pitch (14.5) and batting average with two strikes (.219)

Mark Wohlers

2002 Season

Mark Wohlers continued his comeback from three years of hard times. Following a rocky first half, he went 3-3 with a 2.54 ERA and seven saves after the All-Star break. He led the Indians with 64 appearances and took over the closer's role from July 22 through August 27. Wohlers' save on July 22 against Oakland was his first in the big leagues since June 1998. Wohlers didn't allow a run in 14 appearances from July 11 through August 6.

Pitching

Wohlers doesn't throw as hard as he did when he was young, but his fastball still is a consistent 94-96 MPH. He throws a slider with a downward break and a good splitter between 88-91 MPH. Wohlers pitched 71.1 innings last year, his most since 1996, and held the Indians' bullpen together in the wake of trades and injuries. He struggled with his control, but first batters hit only .148 (9-for-61) against him. Wohlers probably never will be the dominant closer he was with Atlanta, but at 33 he may start a second career as a reliable setup man. He showed last year that his velocity and stuff improve the more he pitches.

Defense

When Wohlers is pitching, basestealers run wild. The opposition went 15-for-17 against him in 2002. It was the most steals against any reliever in the American League. As a closer, Wohlers could get away with ignoring the running game, but not as a setup man, when he's pitching in the seventh or eighth innings. He's not good with the glove either, making five errors over the last two seasons.

2003 Outlook

The Indians signed Wohlers to a two-year contract a year ago, which seemed excessive. There wasn't a big market for him, but the Indians did it nonetheless because they liked his arm. Now he could be the only experienced reliever in their bullpen. Wohlers will be the righthanded setup man, and could step in as closer if Danys Baez struggles. The Indians may get the most out of their investment.

Position: RP
Bats: R **Throws:** R
Ht: 6' 4" **Wt:** 207

Opening Day Age: 33
Born: 1/23/70 in Holyoke, MA
ML Seasons: 12
Pronunciation: WO-lers

Overall Statistics

	W	L	Pct.	ERA	G	GS	Sv	IP	H	BB	SO	HR	Ratio
'02	3	4	.429	4.79	64	0	7	71.1	71	26	46	6	1.36
Car.	39	29	.574	3.97	533	0	119	553.1	490	272	557	37	1.38

How Often He Throws Strikes

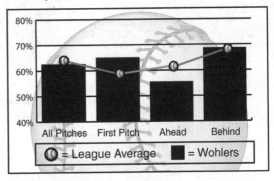

= League Average   = Wohlers

2002 Situational Stats

	W	L	ERA	Sv	IP		AB	H	HR	RBI	Avg
Home	3	2	4.38	1	39.0	LHB	117	30	5	21	.256
Road	0	2	5.29	6	32.1	RHB	155	41	1	20	.265
First Half	0	1	7.52	0	32.1	Sc Pos	89	25	3	37	.281
Scnd Half	3	3	2.54	7	39.0	Clutch	140	32	3	16	.229

2002 Rankings (American League)

- 5th in first batter efficiency (.148)
- 8th in highest relief ERA (4.79)
- 10th in stolen bases allowed (15)
- Led the Indians in games pitched, first batter efficiency (.148), blown saves (4), relief wins (3), relief losses (4), relief innings (71.1), relief ERA (4.79) and fewest baserunners allowed per nine innings in relief (12.6)

Cleveland

Dave Burba

Position: SP/RP
Bats: R **Throws:** R
Ht: 6' 4" **Wt:** 240

Opening Day Age: 36
Born: 7/7/66 in Dayton, OH
ML Seasons: 13
Pronunciation: BUR-ba

Overall Statistics

	W	L	Pct.	ERA	G	GS	Sv	IP	H	BB	SO	HR	Ratio
'02	5	5	.500	5.20	35	21	0	145.1	155	57	95	16	1.46
Car.	110	85	.564	4.52	443	232	1	1657.1	1665	717	1313	189	1.44

2002 Situational Stats

	W	L	ERA	Sv	IP		AB	H	HR	RBI	Avg
Home	3	1	6.21	0	75.1	LHB	295	73	7	31	.247
Road	2	4	4.11	0	70.0	RHB	280	82	9	51	.293
First Half	4	4	5.22	0	100.0	Sc Pos	146	47	4	64	.322
Scnd Half	1	1	5.16	0	45.1	Clutch	30	14	3	11	.467

2002 Season

Dave Burba started last season in Texas' rotation after spending the four previous years with Cleveland. He was 3-0 after his first eight starts, but then went into a four-game losing streak. The Rangers released him July 29, and on August 7 the Indians signed him to help stabilize a staff that seemed to change daily.

Pitching & Defense

Burba, on the downside of a good career, can help a team in a variety of roles. He has the durability and arm strength to start and is experienced as a reliever. He throws a fastball, sinker, slider, curveball and split. When he starts, he throws between 87 and 89 MPH. When he relieves, he's between 90 and 92. Burba tends to throw his splitter too much, which steals velocity from his fastball. He's a decent defender who controls the running game with a quick move to the plate.

2003 Outlook

The Indians, who like Burba's versatility and leadership, were considering re-signing him after he filed for free agency. They have a young staff and need some veterans to help them through the rebuilding process. Burba, still competitive, enjoys the role of team elder.

Greg LaRocca

Position: 3B
Bats: R **Throws:** R
Ht: 5'11" **Wt:** 185

Opening Day Age: 30
Born: 11/10/72 in Oswego, NY
ML Seasons: 2

Overall Statistics

	G	AB	R	H	D	T	HR	RBI	SB	BB	SO	Avg	OBP	Slg
'02	21	52	12	14	3	1	0	4	1	6	6	.269	.367	.365
Car.	34	79	13	20	5	1	0	6	1	7	10	.253	.330	.342

2002 Situational Stats

	AB	H	HR	RBI	Avg		AB	H	HR	RBI	Avg
Home	28	6	0	2	.214	LHP	18	6	0	2	.333
Road	24	8	0	2	.333	RHP	34	8	0	2	.235
First Half	0	0	0	0	–	Sc Pos	13	4	0	4	.308
Scnd Half	52	14	0	4	.269	Clutch	8	4	0	0	.500

2002 Season

Greg LaRocca, a career minor leaguer, spent the final six weeks of 2002 with the Indians as a utility player. He was promoted from Triple-A Buffalo when second baseman Ricky Gutierrez went on the disabled list in mid-August. La Rocca appeared in 15 games at third and three at second.

Hitting, Baserunning & Defense

LaRocca's best feature is his bat. He's short, powerfully built and has a line-drive swing. He was used mostly against lefthanders with the Indians and hit them well. LaRocca crowds the plate—he was hit 23 times at Buffalo last year—and has enough power to hit between 10 and 15 homers a year. He is a decent baserunner, stealing 32 bases over the last three years in the minors. If LaRocca plays every day, his defensive flaws will be exposed. He made six errors in 30 chances at third base for the Indians.

2003 Outlook

The Indians dropped LaRocca from the 40-man roster October 14, but invited him to spring training. LaRocca, 30, has played just 34 games in the majors in nine years. Last year he considered retiring. This year may be his last chance to see if he can stick in the big leagues.

Chris Magruder

Position: LF/RF/CF
Bats: B **Throws:** R
Ht: 5'11" **Wt:** 200

Opening Day Age: 25
Born: 4/26/77 in Tacoma, WA
ML Seasons: 2

Overall Statistics

	G	AB	R	H	D	T	HR	RBI	SB	BB	SO	Avg	OBP	Slg
'02	87	258	34	56	15	1	6	29	2	15	55	.217	.261	.353
Car.	104	287	37	61	15	1	6	30	2	16	60	.213	.257	.334

2002 Situational Stats

	AB	H	HR	RBI	Avg		AB	H	HR	RBI	Avg
Home	125	25	3	17	.200	LHP	91	25	3	11	.275
Road	133	31	3	12	.233	RHP	167	31	3	18	.186
First Half	110	24	3	13	.218	Sc Pos	74	14	2	21	.189
Scnd Half	148	32	3	16	.216	Clutch	41	6	0	3	.146

2002 Season

Chris Magruder spent more time in Cleveland than anticipated due to injuries to outfielders Milton Bradley and Matt Lawton. The switch-hitting Magruder made at least 16 starts at each outfield position. His double off Detroit's Jeff Weaver prevented the Indians from getting no-hit in May in Magruder's first game with the Tribe.

Hitting, Baserunning & Defense

Magruder has a blend of speed, defense and power, but it's probably not enough to play every day. It might not even be enough to stay in the big leagues. His swing gets long and slow, resulting in too many weak flyballs and grounders. Righthanders relying on offspeed pitches and fastballs out of the strike zone dominated him. His walk-strikeout ratio was terrible, which contributed to a woeful .261 on-base percentage. Magruder hustles to first and runs the bases hard. He's a decent outfielder with an average arm.

2003 Outlook

For Magruder to help the Indians this year, he needs to shorten his swing, handle the bat better and start bunting more, in order to bring in the first and third basemen and create some holes in the infield. He could find a home in the big leagues if he can hit between .270 and .280.

Chad Paronto

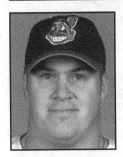

Position: RP
Bats: R **Throws:** R
Ht: 6' 5" **Wt:** 250

Opening Day Age: 27
Born: 7/28/75 in Woodsville, NH
ML Seasons: 2
Pronunciation: pah-RON-toe

Overall Statistics

	W	L	Pct.	ERA	G	GS	Sv	IP	H	BB	SO	HR	Ratio
'02	0	2	.000	4.04	29	0	0	35.2	34	11	23	3	1.26
Car.	1	5	.167	4.45	53	0	0	62.2	67	22	39	8	1.42

2002 Situational Stats

	W	L	ERA	Sv	IP		AB	H	HR	RBI	Avg
Home	0	1	1.77	0	20.1	LHB	53	12	2	11	.226
Road	0	1	7.04	0	15.1	RHB	84	22	1	13	.262
First Half	0	2	4.97	0	29.0	Sc Pos	44	9	1	19	.205
Scnd Half	0	0	0.00	0	6.2	Clutch	11	3	0	3	.273

2002 Season

The Indians claimed Chad Paronto off waivers from Baltimore after the 2001 season. He split last year between Cleveland and Triple-A Buffalo before his season ended July 29 with tendinitis in the right elbow. He had allowed just one run in his previous 11 appearances before getting injured.

Pitching & Defense

Paronto throws a 93-95 MPH fastball with heavy sink. The Indians like him as a middle- to late-inning reliever because he can get out of jams by striking out a batter with his slider or by throwing a double play-inducing sinker. He needs to work on a split-finger fastball or changeup. In his brief big league career, Paronto has done a good job against lefthanded hitters, but righties have worn him out. Defensively, Paronto is slow coming off the mound and doesn't field his position well. He did a good job controlling the running game.

2003 Outlook

If Paronto stays healthy, he could win a job in the Tribe's bullpen. The Indians like his makeup and his ability to pitch in pressure situations so much that they see him as a potential setup man. They're going to need a durable bullpen to carry a young starting rotation that will be working on pitch counts.

Cleveland

Jason Phillips

Position: SP
Bats: R **Throws:** R
Ht: 6' 6" **Wt:** 225

Opening Day Age: 29
Born: 3/22/74 in Williamsport, PA
ML Seasons: 2

Overall Statistics

	W	L	Pct.	ERA	G	GS	Sv	IP	H	BB	SO	HR	Ratio
'02	1	3	.250	4.97	8	6	0	41.2	41	20	23	7	1.46
Car.	1	3	.250	5.92	14	6	0	48.2	52	26	30	9	1.60

2002 Situational Stats

	W	L	ERA	Sv	IP		AB	H	HR	RBI	Avg
Home	1	2	4.68	0	25.0	LHB	93	23	5	14	.247
Road	0	1	5.40	0	16.2	RHB	65	18	2	8	.277
First Half	0	1	7.50	0	6.0	Sc Pos	38	8	1	15	.211
Scnd Half	1	2	4.54	0	35.2	Clutch	0	0	0	0	–

2002 Season

After making his big league debut with Pittsburgh in 1999, Jason Phillips didn't get back to the majors until the Indians recalled him July 6 from Triple-A Buffalo. Phillips pitched decently with the Indians, mostly as a starter, before he needed surgery on his right elbow in late August.

Pitching & Defense

With a history of arm problems, Phillips throws a sinking, 88-94 MPH fastball and an old-fashioned, top-to-bottom curveball. It's a unique combination because most pitchers who throw a sinker complement it with a slider. He also throws a cut fastball and a changeup. He's best suited for starting or long relief, but durability is a concern. Phillips showed command and control in 16 starts at Buffalo, but they were lacking in his Cleveland appearances. Phillips is a big man who is an average defender. He holds the ball and uses a slide step to slow the running game.

2003 Outlook

The Indians took Phillips off the 40-man roster following his elbow surgery, outrighted him to Buffalo and invited him to spring training. He's a long shot to make the club, but could help as a starter or long reliever in 2003. To do so, he must stay healthy, which has been a problem.

Jerrod Riggan

Position: RP
Bats: R **Throws:** R
Ht: 6' 3" **Wt:** 197

Opening Day Age: 28
Born: 5/16/74 in Brewster, WA
ML Seasons: 3
Pronunciation: RIG-gan

Overall Statistics

	W	L	Pct.	ERA	G	GS	Sv	IP	H	BB	SO	HR	Ratio
'02	2	1	.667	7.64	29	0	0	33.0	53	18	22	3	2.15
Car.	5	4	.556	5.01	65	0	0	82.2	98	42	64	8	1.69

2002 Situational Stats

	W	L	ERA	Sv	IP		AB	H	HR	RBI	Avg
Home	2	0	5.40	0	18.1	LHB	70	26	2	19	.371
Road	0	1	10.43	0	14.2	RHB	72	27	1	17	.375
First Half	1	1	7.65	0	20.0	Sc Pos	56	26	3	36	.464
Scnd Half	1	0	7.62	0	13.0	Clutch	14	6	0	4	.429

2002 Season

The Indians had a lot of disappointments last year and Jerrod Riggan was one of the biggest. He was acquired from the Mets in the Robbie Alomar trade in December, and the Indians felt he'd be a solid part of the bullpen. But he bounced between Cleveland and Triple-A Buffalo three times.

Pitching & Defense

Riggan throws a 92-94 MPH fastball that has no movement. Righthanders and lefties feasted on it. His best pitch is an 82-84 MPH splitter, but he couldn't throw it for strikes. The Mets used him as a late-inning reliever in 2001. The Indians used him more in middle relief and he wasn't able to adjust. When Riggan did get a chance to pitch in pressure situations, he tried too hard and the results were disastrous. The opposition hit .464 (26-for-56) against him with runners in scoring position. Riggan gets off the mound quickly and can control the running game.

2003 Outlook

The Indians believe Riggan is better than he pitched in 2002 because he couldn't be much worse. He has to reestablish his ability to throw strikes and get hitters out at the big league level. If he doesn't, he could be spending most of the season in Buffalo.

David Riske

Position: RP
Bats: R **Throws:** R
Ht: 6' 2" **Wt:** 175

Opening Day Age: 26
Born: 10/23/76 in Renton, WA
ML Seasons: 3
Pronunciation: RISK-ee

Overall Statistics

	W	L	Pct.	ERA	G	GS	Sv	IP	H	BB	SO	HR	Ratio
'02	2	2	.500	5.26	51	0	1	51.1	49	35	65	8	1.64
Car.	5	3	.625	4.76	89	0	2	92.2	89	59	110	13	1.60

2002 Situational Stats

	W	L	ERA	Sv	IP		AB	H	HR	RBI	Avg
Home	1	1	6.03	0	31.1	LHB	75	19	4	19	.253
Road	1	1	4.05	1	20.0	RHB	116	30	4	20	.259
First Half	1	2	5.86	1	27.2	Sc Pos	59	14	2	28	.237
Scnd Half	1	0	4.56	0	23.2	Clutch	48	8	0	11	.167

2002 Season

David Riske, on the verge of establishing himself as a big league reliever after a strong second half in 2001, was sidetracked by injuries and inconsistency last year. After a decent start, he slumped in May and June and went on the DL with back and hamstring problems. He rallied in September.

Pitching & Defense

Riske lives off his 92-93 MPH fastball. When he's healthy, he throws it with a deceptive motion to good spots. Riske's velocity was down last year and his control suffered. He threw a changeup in spring training, but abandoned it once the season started. He needs it to keep hitters off his fastball. Riske is a one-inning pitcher who is fearless in tight situations. The opposition hit .167 (2-for-12) against him with the bases loaded in 2002. Despite his injuries, Riske made the second-most appearances on the team. He needs to improve on stopping the running game.

2003 Outlook

The Indians know they didn't see the real David Riske last year. They believe he pitched most of the year injured. When healthy, he can pitch middle relief, set up and even close on occasion. After trading veteran relievers Paul Shuey and Ricardo Rincon last year, they need Riske to produce.

Lee Stevens

Position: 1B/LF
Bats: L **Throws:** L
Ht: 6' 4" **Wt:** 235

Opening Day Age: 35
Born: 10/3/67 in Kansas City, KS
ML Seasons: 10

Overall Statistics

	G	AB	R	H	D	T	HR	RBI	SB	BB	SO	Avg	OBP	Slg
'02	116	358	50	73	13	2	15	57	1	54	89	.204	.305	.377
Car.	1012	3332	440	847	185	15	144	531	9	345	832	.254	.323	.448

2002 Situational Stats

	AB	H	HR	RBI	Avg		AB	H	HR	RBI	Avg
Home	171	32	7	24	.187	LHP	73	10	3	9	.137
Road	187	41	8	33	.219	RHP	285	63	12	48	.221
First Half	222	42	10	33	.189	Sc Pos	89	22	7	44	.247
Scnd Half	136	31	5	24	.228	Clutch	68	14	2	10	.206

2002 Season

The Indians acquired Stevens from Montreal in the Bartolo Colon trade on June 27. The first baseman-outfielder was having a miserable year with the Expos and things didn't get much better with the Indians. He started out in a 5-for-40 slump and ended in a 3-for-28 slump. He played in his 1,000th game on September 8.

Hitting, Baserunning & Defense

Stevens, a big lefthanded hitter, has power, but didn't show much in 2002. Pitchers worked him inside on the hands and got him out with high fastballs. Lack of playing time hurt Stevens. After the trade, he received only 153 at-bats. He did go 5-for-10 as a pinch-hitter with the Indians. Stevens is a slow runner, but is a decent first baseman. He made 15 starts in the outfield with the Indians. They were his first outfield appearances since 1998. He did not receive any Gold Glove votes, but at least he didn't pull a muscle.

2003 Outlook

If Stevens gets regular playing time this year, he could hit 25 homers. But those kind of at-bats are unlikely because of his age. Stevens became a free agent at the end of the year, as the Indians cut their ties with him by not offering him arbitration.

Jake Westbrook

Position: RP
Bats: R **Throws:** R
Ht: 6' 3" **Wt:** 185

Opening Day Age: 25
Born: 9/29/77 in Athens, GA
ML Seasons: 3

Overall Statistics

	W	L	Pct.	ERA	G	GS	Sv	IP	H	BB	SO	HR	Ratio
'02	1	3	.250	5.83	11	4	0	41.2	50	12	20	6	1.49
Car.	5	9	.357	6.29	37	12	0	113.0	144	38	69	13	1.61

2002 Situational Stats

	W	L	ERA	Sv	IP		AB	H	HR	RBI	Avg
Home	0	2	7.66	0	24.2	LHB	89	26	4	22	.292
Road	1	1	3.18	0	17.0	RHB	80	24	2	15	.300
First Half	0	0	–	0	0.0	Sc Pos	52	17	3	31	.327
Scnd Half	1	3	5.83	0	41.2	Clutch	21	7	0	2	.333

2002 Season

Jake Westbrook really never got started last year. He underwent surgery on his right elbow on February 26 after a week of spring training. He rejoined the Indians on July 11, making 11 appearances, including four starts. His season ended after an August 25 start because of a bone bruise in his elbow.

Pitching & Defense

Westbrook throws a sinker, changeup and slider. When he starts, he throws a 91-92 MPH fastball. Westbrook is capable of going deep into games with a low pitch count when he's 100 percent. He can throw his sinker to both halves of the plate for strikes, and his changeup may be his best pitch. Westbrook's durability as a starter is questionable, so he may be better suited to the pen, where he could pitch two or three innings. Westbrook has good baseball instincts when it comes to fielding and controlling the running game.

2003 Outlook

Westbrook's days as a starter with the Indians probably are over. They like him in middle relief. He had success in that role in 2001, but hasn't been healthy enough to reclaim it. What he needs most of all is enough time in the big leagues to establish himself and show he can stay healthy.

Bob Wickman

Position: RP
Bats: R **Throws:** R
Ht: 6' 1" **Wt:** 240

Opening Day Age: 34
Born: 2/6/69 in Green Bay, WI
ML Seasons: 11

Overall Statistics

	W	L	Pct.	ERA	G	GS	Sv	IP	H	BB	SO	HR	Ratio
'02	1	3	.250	4.46	36	0	20	34.1	42	10	36	3	1.51
Car.	59	45	.567	3.68	627	28	156	863.0	854	367	639	61	1.41

2002 Situational Stats

	W	L	ERA	Sv	IP		AB	H	HR	RBI	Avg
Home	1	3	3.54	9	20.1	LHB	80	22	2	12	.275
Road	0	0	5.79	11	14.0	RHB	68	20	1	6	.294
First Half	0	2	3.99	19	29.1	Sc Pos	48	15	0	14	.313
Scnd Half	1	1	7.20	1	5.0	Clutch	96	27	2	15	.281

2002 Season

Until last season, Bob Wickman had never been on the disabled list. He went on it twice last summer and will miss 2003 as he recovers from ligament transplant surgery on his right elbow. Wickman's season ended on August 10, but he still went 20-for-22 in save situations.

Pitching & Defense

Wickman is a fastball-slider pitcher. When healthy, he throws between 89-92 MPH. Last year he hit 94 MPH often as he tried to compensate for his elbow pain by not throwing sliders. He has become a consistent closer over the last five years because he understands situations, studies hitters and has great location on his pitches. He's gone from being a starter to a setup man to a closer, and the transition has helped his control and command. Wickman can get beat to first base by a fast runner on an infield hit, but he'll catch what's hit to him.

2003 Outlook

Wickman knew he was hurt in spring training, but kept pitching in pain. Now, after Tommy John surgery in early December, he'll be out at least a year, and no one knows how effective he'll be when he returns at age 35 in 2004. Luckily for him, he signed a three-year, $16 million contract after the 2001 season.

Other Cleveland Indians

Chad Allen (Pos: LF, Age: 28, Bats: R)

	G	AB	R	H	D	T	HR	RBI	SB	BB	SO	Avg	OBP	Slg
'02	5	10	0	1	1	0	0	0	0	0	2	.100	.100	.200
Car.	214	716	91	195	38	5	14	73	15	59	142	.272	.329	.398

Allen played Triple-A ball with both the O's and Tribe in 2002, and batted .301 and slugged .487 with Triple-A Buffalo. His stay in Cleveland didn't impress, and he signed a minor league deal with the Marlins. 2003 Outlook: C

Brady Anderson (Pos: CF/LF, Age: 39, Bats: L)

	G	AB	R	H	D	T	HR	RBI	SB	BB	SO	Avg	OBP	Slg
	34	80	4	13	4	0	1	5	4	18	23	.163	.327	.250
	1834	6499	1062	1661	338	67	210	761	315	960	1190	.256	.362	.425

He drew walks to the very end, but Anderson hasn't made enough contact or shown enough power the last two years to have much value. If he has one last gasp, he'll show it to the Padres after signing a minor league contract. 2003 Outlook: C

Bruce Aven (Pos: LF, Age: 31, Bats: R)

	G	AB	R	H	D	T	HR	RBI	SB	BB	SO	Avg	OBP	Slg
'02	7	17	1	2	0	0	0	0	1	4	4	.118	.286	.118
Car.	259	609	85	166	33	2	20	103	6	57	135	.273	.343	.432

Aven had a promising season as a part-time player with Florida in 1999, but he hasn't hit much in major league stints since then. Aven gets a new chance after signing a minor league deal with the Jays. 2003 Outlook: C

Ben Broussard (Pos: LF, Age: 26, Bats: L)

	G	AB	R	H	D	T	HR	RBI	SB	BB	SO	Avg	OBP	Slg
'02	39	112	10	27	4	0	4	9	0	7	25	.241	.292	.384
Car.	39	112	10	27	4	0	4	9	0	7	25	.241	.292	.384

Acquired from Cincinnati for Russell Branyan last summer, Broussard is being groomed to play some outfield and first base. He can put the bat on the ball and draw walks. 2003 Outlook: C

Coco Crisp (Pos: CF, Age: 23, Bats: B)

	G	AB	R	H	D	T	HR	RBI	SB	BB	SO	Avg	OBP	Slg
'02	32	127	16	33	9	2	1	9	4	11	19	.260	.314	.386
Car.	32	127	16	33	9	2	1	9	4	11	19	.260	.314	.386

Crisp batted .310 and stole 30 bases at the Double-A level in 2002. Drawing more walks is critical for this speed demon, who was acquired from the Cards in the Chuck Finley deal. 2003 Outlook: C

Jason Davis (Pos: RHP, Age: 22)

	W	L	Pct.	ERA	G	GS	Sv	IP	H	BB	SO	HR	Ratio
'02	1	0	1.000	1.84	3	2	0	14.2	12	4	11	1	1.09
Car.	1	0	1.000	1.84	3	2	0	14.2	12	4	11	1	1.09

A 21st-rounder in 1999, Davis climbed quickly through the Cleveland system after debuting in 2000 and reaching Double-A Akron last summer. He made two solid September starts and could surprise. A real sleeper. 2003 Outlook: C

Sean DePaula (Pos: RHP, Age: 29)

	W	L	Pct.	ERA	G	GS	Sv	IP	H	BB	SO	HR	Ratio
'02	1	1	.500	12.79	5	0	0	6.1	11	3	8	3	2.21
Car.	1	1	.500	6.75	29	0	0	34.2	39	20	42	6	1.70

DePaula pitched impressively as a rookie, but arm problems have kept him from finding his way into the Cleveland bullpen. He signed a minor league deal with the Reds in November. 2003 Outlook: C

Ryan Drese (Pos: RHP, Age: 26)

	W	L	Pct.	ERA	G	GS	Sv	IP	H	BB	SO	HR	Ratio
'02	10	9	.526	6.55	26	26	0	137.1	176	62	102	15	1.73
Car.	11	11	.500	5.90	35	30	0	174.0	208	77	126	17	1.64

The Tribe hoped Drese's diverse arsenal would allow him to secure a spot in the rotation last summer, but beyond a 3-1 (3.44) performance in May, it wasn't pretty. In a four-player trade in December, Drese went to Texas, where he'll compete for work on a young, inexperienced pitching staff. 2003 Outlook: C

Todd Dunwoody (Pos: LF, Age: 27, Bats: L)

	G	AB	R	H	D	T	HR	RBI	SB	BB	SO	Avg	OBP	Slg
'02	2	6	0	0	0	0	0	0	0	0	3	.000	.000	.000
Car.	295	915	98	213	48	12	11	81	13	51	234	.233	.277	.348

Six hitless at-bats in 2002 leave him with a .211 average (91-for-431) over the last four major league seasons. He hasn't drawn walks or shown power, either. 2003 Outlook: C

Dave Elder (Pos: RHP, Age: 27)

	W	L	Pct.	ERA	G	GS	Sv	IP	H	BB	SO	HR	Ratio
'02	0	2	.000	3.13	15	0	0	23.0	18	14	23	1	1.39
Car.	0	2	.000	3.13	15	0	0	23.0	18	14	23	1	1.39

Already Cleveland has gotten the better end of last winter's John Rocker deal with Texas, as Elder came over and pitched better than Rocker. Elder is back for 2003 after signing a new minor league deal. 2003 Outlook: C

Travis Fryman (Pos: 3B, Age: 34, Bats: R)

	G	AB	R	H	D	T	HR	RBI	SB	BB	SO	Avg	OBP	Slg
	118	397	42	86	14	3	11	55	0	40	82	.217	.292	.350
	1698	6481	895	1776	345	40	223	1022	72	602	1369	.274	.336	.443

Injuries took their toll on a very consistent performer at third base throughout the 1990s. Fryman played 2002 in need of Tommy John surgery and announced his retirement in August. 2003 Outlook: D

Alex Herrera (Pos: LHP, Age: 26)

	W	L	Pct.	ERA	G	GS	Sv	IP	H	BB	SO	HR	Ratio
'02	0	0	—	0.00	5	0	0	5.1	3	1	5	0	0.75
Car.	0	0	—	0.00	5	0	0	5.1	3	1	5	0	0.75

Chicken pox and a family illness meant lost time in 2002, but a good season at Double-A Akron ended with five solid appearances in Cleveland. A better breaking ball could mean good things in the bullpen. 2003 Outook: C

Dave Maurer (Pos: LHP, Age: 28)

	W	L	Pct.	ERA	G	GS	Sv	IP	H	BB	SO	HR	Ratio
'02	0	1	.000	13.50	2	0	0	1.1	3	0	0	1	2.25
Car.	1	1	.500	6.00	19	0	0	21.0	26	9	17	4	1.67

After an impressive season as a reliever with Triple-A Buffalo, Maurer made two September appearances and had Tommy John surgery at the end of the month. He won't return to action until 2004. 2003 Outlook: D

Terry Mulholland (Pos: LHP, Age: 40)

	W	L	Pct.	ERA	G	GS	Sv	IP	H	BB	SO	HR	Ratio
'02	3	2	.600	5.70	37	3	0	79.0	101	21	38	15	1.54
Car.	116	127	.477	4.34	547	314	5	2291.1	2485	593	1204	252	1.34

Mulholland's been traded during the waning days of July four times since 1996, and it could happen again if the 40-year-old southpaw can pitch well enough in the spring to make a club. Cleveland, wanting a couple veterans on the staff to help the kids, offered him salary arbitration. 2003 Outlook: C

Heath Murray (Pos: LHP, Age: 29)

	W	L	Pct.	ERA	G	GS	Sv	IP	H	BB	SO	HR	Ratio
'02	0	2	.000	7.50	9	0	0	12.0	12	7	11	3	1.58
Car.	2	15	.118	6.41	88	15	0	158.2	204	94	94	24	1.88

Murray's terrific Triple-A numbers the last two seasons have not translated into major league success. He's posted a sub-6.00 ERA only once in four big league seasons, and that was a 5.76 mark in 1999. 2003 Outlook: C

Charles Nagy (Pos: RHP, Age: 35)

	W	L	Pct.	ERA	G	GS	Sv	IP	H	BB	SO	HR	Ratio
'02	1	4	.200	8.88	19	7	0	48.2	76	13	22	10	1.83
Car.	129	103	.556	4.51	313	297	0	1942.1	2173	583	1235	217	1.42

Pitching without cartilage in the elbow hasn't been easy. It's remarkable Nagy's doing it at all, but he posted an ERA worse than 8.00 for the second time in three years. It's been a gutsy battle. 2003 Outlook: C

Eddie Perez (Pos: C, Age: 34, Bats: R)

	G	AB	R	H	D	T	HR	RBI	SB	BB	SO	Avg	OBP	Slg
'02	42	117	6	25	9	0	0	4	0	5	25	.214	.252	.291
Car.	367	967	94	244	54	1	24	108	1	55	153	.252	.299	.385

Perez was traded to Cleveland late in spring training for a minor league outfielder. Josh Bard, Vic Martinez and Tim Laker will battle for catching duties in 2003, and Perez will look for a new employer this offseason. 2003 Outlook: C

Carl Sadler (Pos: LHP, Age: 26)

	W	L	Pct.	ERA	G	GS	Sv	IP	H	BB	SO	HR	Ratio
'02	1	2	.333	4.43	24	0	0	20.1	15	11	23	2	1.28
Car.	1	2	.333	4.43	24	0	0	20.1	15	11	23	2	1.28

Sadler was dependable between Double-A Akron and Triple-A Buffalo, posting a 2.22 ERA in 65 relief innings. He was solid in August with Cleveland (2.70 ERA in 11 games), but lost it in September. He'll be back. 2003 Outlook: C

Bill Selby (Pos: 3B/LF, Age: 32, Bats: L)

	G	AB	R	H	D	T	HR	RBI	SB	BB	SO	Avg	OBP	Slg
'02	65	159	15	34	7	2	6	21	0	15	27	.214	.278	.396
Car.	171	392	42	92	19	3	11	43	1	30	60	.235	.290	.383

The Tribe re-signed the utility infielder-outfielder in October, and he broke his hand in winter ball in November. He'll be ready in the spring, but it's a setback for an already-weak bat. 2003 Outlook: C

Roy Smith (Pos: RHP, Age: 26)

	W	L	Pct.	ERA	G	GS	Sv	IP	H	BB	SO	HR	Ratio
'02	0	0	–	3.00	4	1	0	6.0	9	5	2	1	2.33
Car.	0	0	–	5.24	13	1	0	22.1	28	19	4	1.93

Smith has been solid as a reliever in the Cleveland system the last three years, but his big league chance may come with Oakland after he was dealt to the A's for cash at the November GM meetings. 2003 Outlook: C

Earl Snyder (Pos: 1B, Age: 26, Bats: R)

	G	AB	R	H	D	T	HR	RBI	SB	BB	SO	Avg	OBP	Slg
'02	18	55	5	11	2	0	1	4	0	6	21	.200	.279	.291
Car.	18	55	5	11	2	0	1	4	0	6	21	.200	.279	.291

Acquired from the Mets in the Alomar deal, Snyder enjoyed a .263-19-66 season in 110 games at Triple-A Buffalo. He could join the Cleveland bench to provide some righthanded pop at third and in left. 2003 Outlook: B

Jaret Wright (Pos: RHP, Age: 27)

	W	L	Pct.	ERA	G	GS	Sv	IP	H	BB	SO	HR	Ratio
'02	2	3	.400	15.71	8	6	0	18.1	40	19	12	3	3.22
Car.	35	32	.522	5.50	98	96	0	515.2	552	268	360	60	1.59

Wright enjoyed a memorable debut during Cleveland's World Series run in 1997, but arm troubles and multiple surgeries have diminished his stuff. Years of rehab work couldn't keep Wright from an uncertain future as a free agent, but he has signed a one-year deal with the Padres. 2003 Outlook: C

Cleveland Indians Minor League Prospects

Organization Overview:

The sold-out games and perennial division titles are in the past, and the front office unloaded some of its aging talent in 2002. While few teams fared well dealing veterans for prospects, with a possible labor standoff threatening last year's postseason, Cleveland did a remarkable job replenishing its farm system with its trades. Dealing Bartolo Colon, Chuck Finley, Paul Shuey and Ricardo Rincon landed pitching prospects Cliff Lee, Ricardo Rodriguez and Francisco Cruceta, as well as position prospects Brandon Phillips, Luis Garcia, Covelli Crisp and Grady Sizemore. Lee and Rodriguez join Billy Traber and Brian Tallet as solid candidates to claim spots in the rebuilt Cleveland rotation. Other recent trade pickups, such as Alex Escobar and Earl Snyder, also could join the big club in 2003.

Josh Bard

Position: C   **Opening Day Age:** 25
Bats: B **Throws:** R   **Born:** 3/30/78 in Ithaca,
Ht: 6' 3" **Wt:** 215   NY

Recent Statistics

	G	AB	R	H	D	T	HR	RBI	SB	BB	SO	Avg
2002 AAA Buffalo	94	344	36	102	26	2	6	53	0	20	45	.297
2002 AL Cleveland	24	90	9	20	5	0	3	12	0	4	13	.222

In May 2001, Cleveland acquired Bard from the Rockies for outfielder Jacob Cruz, and the trade looks good for Cleveland. There's never been any doubt about Bard's catching and game-calling skills. He can catch in the majors and he'll fare well throwing out runners with his catch-and-throw technique. The question always has been whether Bard would hit enough in the majors, and the Indians believe he will because his makeup will make the difference. He's consistent from both sides of the plate as a hitter, and he started showing more power at Triple-A Buffalo in 2002. While he's a leader who is capable of running a pitching staff, Bard faces a big challenge in becoming familiar with major league hitters and the Cleveland staff.

Travis Hafner

Position: 1B   **Opening Day Age:** 25
Bats: L **Throws:** R   **Born:** 6/3/77 in
Ht: 6' 3" **Wt:** 240   Jamestown, ND

Recent Statistics

	G	AB	R	H	D	T	HR	RBI	SB	BB	SO	Avg
2002 AAA Oklahoma	110	401	79	137	22	1	21	77	2	79	76	.342
2002 AL Texas	23	62	6	15	4	1	1	6	0	8	15	.242

The minor league Player of the Year lists for 2002 inexplicably overlooked what Hafner did with Triple-A Oklahoma. He hit .342-21-77, while carrying a playoff team. Hafner is a rare offensive player: a power hitter with exceptional plate command and understanding of the strike zone. He is comfortable hitting deep in the count and has the natural strength to hit the ball hard to the opposite field. His speed is a drawback. Still, Cleveland may have gotten the best piece of a minor four-player trade with the Rangers in December. Hafner will compete with Ben Broussard for the first-base job vacated by Jim Thome.

Cliff Lee

Position: P   **Opening Day Age:** 24
Bats: L **Throws:** L   **Born:** 8/30/78 in Benton,
Ht: 6' 3" **Wt:** 190   AK

Recent Statistics

	W	L	ERA	G	GS	Sv	IP	H	R	BB	SO	HR
2002 AA Harrisburg	7	2	3.23	15	15	0	86.1	61	31	23	105	12
2002 AA Akron	2	1	5.40	3	3	0	16.2	11	11	10	18	1
2002 AAA Buffalo	3	2	3.77	8	8	0	43.0	36	18	22	30	7
2002 AL Cleveland	0	1	1.74	2	2	0	10.1	6	2	8	6	0

Acquired in last June's Bartolo Colon deal, Lee has terrific stuff with good movement and late action. Nearly all of his pitches can be above-average big league offerings if he is able to gain consistent command of them. He works with two-seam and four-seam fastballs, a slider, curve and changeup. The depth on his breaking stuff puts him a notch above the other lefthanders who are close to Cleveland. He calls on all of his pitches, but he needs to improve his pitch selection. He tends to turn to his fastball a bit too much. Throwing his breaking ball for a strike in pressure situations is something the Indians would like to see more frequently. He will compete for a rotation spot in the spring.

Victor Martinez

Position: C   **Opening Day Age:** 24
Bats: B **Throws:** R   **Born:** 12/23/78 in
Ht: 6' 2" **Wt:** 170   Ciudad Bolivar, VZ

Recent Statistics

	G	AB	R	H	D	T	HR	RBI	SB	BB	SO	Avg
2002 AA Akron	121	443	84	149	40	0	22	85	3	58	62	.336
2002 AL Cleveland	12	32	2	9	1	0	1	5	0	3	2	.281

Signed in 1996, Martinez has emerged as a top prospect with consecutive batting titles and MVP honors the last two summers in the high Class-A Carolina League and Double-A Eastern League. The switch-hitter is sound from both sides of the plate. Martinez is a hard worker, known for focusing on the little things no matter how good things are going. Behind the plate, he is a leader and an excellent receiver and game-caller. He only lacks top-flight arm strength, and he needs to quicken his release on his throws to counter basestealers. At the plate, he showed better discipline, but also was pitched around more often, so further refining his strike zone would help him against better pitching.

Cleveland

Brandon Phillips

Position: SS

Bats: R **Throws:** R

Ht: 5' 11" **Wt:** 185

Opening Day Age: 21

Born: 6/28/81 in Raleigh, NC

Recent Statistics

	G	AB	R	H	D	T	HR	RBI	SB	BB	SO	Avg
2002 AA Harrisburg	60	245	40	80	13	2	9	35	6	16	33	.327
2002 AAA Ottawa	10	35	1	9	4	0	1	5	0	2	6	.257
2002 AAA Buffalo	55	223	30	63	14	0	8	27	8	14	39	.283
2002 AL Cleveland	11	31	5	8	3	1	0	4	0	3	6	.258

Phillips was the most coveted of the three prospects acquired for Bartolo Colon. He's the heir to Omar Vizquel at short, a five-tool talent with above-average defensive skills. At the plate, he's hit for average despite being very young for his affiliation, and he has tantalizing power potential. He needs to walk more and spray the ball around the field consistently. With Vizquel at short, Phillips will compete for second-base duties in the spring. If he doesn't grab a regular job, he'll go to Triple-A Buffalo to play every day.

Ricardo Rodriguez

Position: P

Bats: R **Throws:** R

Ht: 6' 3" **Wt:** 165

Opening Day Age: 24

Born: 5/21/78 in Manga, DR

Recent Statistics

	W	L	ERA	G	GS	Sv	IP	H	R	BB	SO	HR
2002 AA Jacksnville	5	4	1.99	11	11	0	68.0	56	21	13	44	4
2002 AAA Las Vegas	1	0	3.86	2	2	0	11.2	13	5	5	7	1
2002 AAA Buffalo	3	1	3.60	4	4	0	25.0	26	10	7	14	1
2002 AL Cleveland	2	2	5.66	7	7	0	41.1	40	27	18	24	5

Signed by the Dodgers in 1996, Rodriguez spent three years in the Dominican Summer League before rocketing up the minor league ladder in three summers. He was 10-3 (1.88) at Rookie-level Great Falls in 2000, and 14-6 (3.21) at high Class-A Vero Beach in 2001, setting the stage for a 9-5 (2.58) season in the high minors and a trade to Cleveland in July. Rodriguez has a loose arm and solid command of a low-90s sinker, a sharp curve and a changeup. He exhibits confidence on the mound, as he has had experience against major league hitters in Dominican winter ball. He's a student of the game, a bright kid from a special family—one brother is a doctor and two others are in law school—and he'll compete for a rotation spot this spring.

Brian Tallet

Position: P

Bats: L **Throws:** L

Ht: 6' 7" **Wt:** 208

Opening Day Age: 25

Born: 9/21/77 in Midwest City, OK

Recent Statistics

	W	L	ERA	G	GS	Sv	IP	H	R	BB	SO	HR
2002 AA Akron	10	1	3.08	18	16	0	102.1	93	41	32	73	9
2002 AAA Buffalo	2	3	3.07	8	7	0	44.0	47	17	16	25	1
2002 AL Cleveland	1	0	1.50	2	2	0	12.0	9	3	4	5	0

A second-round pick in 2000, Tallet went from starting the title game of the 2000 College World Series to debuting as a pro at short-season Mahoning Valley. He was tough to hit in six starts and fanned better than a batter an inning. Tallet maintained that strikeout rate despite jumping to high Class-A Kinston in 2001, and in '02 he went 12-4 (3.07) between Double-A Akron and Triple-A Buffalo before making two decent starts in Cleveland. He calls on three pitches—a low-90s fastball, slider and a budding changeup that he throws with his fastball's arm slot and arm speed. He's using his secondary pitches more frequently. His command isn't great, but he'll be in the rotation mix in Cleveland.

Billy Traber

Position: P

Bats: L **Throws:** L

Ht: 6' 5" **Wt:** 205

Opening Day Age: 23

Born: 9/18/79 in Torrance, CA

Recent Statistics

	W	L	ERA	G	GS	Sv	IP	H	R	BB	SO	HR
2001 A St. Lucie	6	5	2.66	18	18	0	101.2	85	36	23	79	2
2001 AA Binghamton	4	3	4.43	8	8	0	42.2	50	25	13	45	4
2001 AAA Norfolk	0	1	1.29	1	1	0	7.0	5	3	0	0	0
2002 AA Akron	13	2	2.76	18	17	0	107.2	99	38	20	82	8
2002 AAA Buffalo	4	3	3.29	9	9	0	54.2	58	22	12	33	3

Perhaps the overlooked piece of the Robbie Alomar trade is Traber, the Mets' first-round pick in 2000. He signed late and didn't play until 2001. Traber debuted at high Class-A St. Lucie and advanced all the way to Triple-A Norfolk, on the strength of a four-pitch arsenal that includes an 89-91 MPH fastball, curve, changeup and splitter, his out pitch of choice. His sinker and curve also can deliver outs, and his changeup improved in 2002, though a drop in velocity for part of the year compromised his changeup's effectiveness. Traber also calls upon a deceptive two-part delivery. He stops briefly before his body jerks to the plate. He'll battle for a rotation spot in Cleveland.

Others to Watch

The one-time jewel of the Mets' system, center fielder **Alex Escobar** (24) was a key element of the Robbie Alomar trade in December 2001. Three months later he tore the ACL in his left knee and missed all of 2002. He is a five-tool player with great defensive skills, but poor command of the strike zone is limiting his bat. . . Cleveland's first-round pick last June, righthander **Jeremy Guthrie** (23), signed too late to play in 2002. Yet he was exceptional in the Arizona Fall League, showing terrific makeup in going after hitters. He touched 96 MPH and showed a good feel for a change-up and a solid breaking ball. . . After struggling as a hitter in his first two seasons, dependable shortstop **John Peralta** (20) made better contact and enjoyed a power surge at Double-A Akron in 2002, collecting 28 doubles and 15 homers in 470 at-bats. He has great poise and a quick stroke. . . Another midsummer acquisition from Montreal, lefthanded-hitting **Grady Sizemore** (20), is a pure athlete with a powerful and quick stroke, but a quiet body at the plate. He batted .343 at high Class-A Kinston after the trade, and he should hit more homers as he matures.

Comerica Park

Offense

The Tigers are bringing the fences in 20 feet in left-center field in 2003. It was just too difficult for major league hitters, even in this longball-dominated era, to reach the fences in left and center field. Originally the Tigers had hoped to build a National League-style team tailored to the dimensions at Comerica Park. As for right field, which has been inviting for lefthanded pull-hitters, there will be no changes.

Defense

The spacious outfield has been a dominant feature, but that changes with the fence moved in. The Tigers have struggled to find a center fielder who can cover an extraordinary amount of ground. Now it is not as much of a concern.

Who It Helps the Most

Lefthander Mike Maroth has done particularly well at Comerica Park, posting a 3.18 ERA in 11 starts. Bobby Higginson has a .309 career average there. Robert Fick hit 12 of 17 homers at home in 2002, though he hits many more doubles on the road. Moving the fence in should help a couple veteran righthanded hitters who have struggled in recent seasons, third baseman Dean Palmer and second baseman Damion Easley. The Tigers would like to unload their hefty salaries, but if they are with the club and stay healthy, moving in the fences should help both immensely.

Who It Hurts the Most

The park has been hard on righthanded power hitters, whose long flyballs have helped pitchers such as Maroth and Steve Sparks, guys who let hitters put the ball in play. How Maroth and Sparks will be affected by the closer fences remains to be seen.

Rookies & Newcomers

First baseman Carlos Pena, acquired by the Tigers from Oakland last July, should perform well at Comerica. When he hits the ball with power, he generally pulls it to right field. Young middle infielders Ramon Santiago and Omar Infante like to hit the ball to the opposite field and into the gaps, so they should fit the ballpark well.

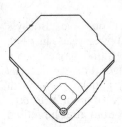

Dimensions: LF-345, LCF-395, CF-420, RCF-365, RF-330

Capacity: 40,120

Elevation: 585 feet

Surface: Grass

Foul Territory: Average

Park Factors

2002 Season

	Home Games Tigers	Opp	Total	Away Games Tigers	Opp	Total	Index
G	71	71	142	72	72	144	
Avg	.247	.280	.264	.252	.293	.272	97
AB	2347	2550	4897	2465	2436	4901	101
R	249	356	605	279	436	715	86
H	579	713	1292	621	713	1334	98
2B	92	144	236	153	162	315	75
3B	26	31	57	6	21	27	211
HR	57	55	112	56	97	153	73
BB	162	192	354	167	223	390	91
SO	396	363	759	503	352	855	89
E	63	33	96	71	35	106	92
E-Infield	50	24	74	54	31	85	88
LHB-Avg	.266	.282	.273	.268	.298	.282	97
LHB-HR	43	34	77	30	43	73	104
RHB-Avg	.225	.278	.255	.236	.289	.263	97
RHB-HR	14	21	35	26	54	80	44

2001-2002

	Home Games Tigers	Opp	Total	Away Games Tigers	Opp	Total	Index
G	143	143	286	144	144	288	
Avg	.255	.278	.267	.252	.295	.273	98
AB	4741	5053	9794	4985	4943	9928	99
R	558	713	1271	603	850	1453	88
H	1208	1405	2613	1258	1456	2714	97
2B	210	277	487	294	326	620	80
3B	66	58	124	21	39	60	209
HR	107	115	222	125	191	316	71
BB	372	447	819	368	457	825	101
SO	771	722	1493	980	740	1720	88
E	129	90	219	128	94	222	99
E-Infield	104	76	180	94	82	176	103
LHB-Avg	.272	.289	.280	.264	.290	.277	101
LHB-HR	70	77	147	60	87	147	100
RHB-Avg	.238	.270	.255	.242	.298	.270	94
RHB-HR	37	38	75	65	104	169	45

2002 Rankings (American League)

- Highest triple factor
- Lowest double factor
- Lowest walk factor
- Lowest RHB home-run factor
- Second-lowest run factor
- Second-lowest home-run factor
- Second-lowest strikeout factor

Detroit

Alan Trammell

2002 Season

Alan Trammell was a coach on Bruce Bochy's staff with the Padres the past three years. In 1999, Trammell was the Tigers' hitting coach when Larry Parrish was the manager. For two decades Trammell was an extremely popular player with the Tigers. He then turned down an offer to be a broadcaster to start at the bottom after he retired as a player in 1996. He spent two years scouting the minor leagues and for the amateur draft. He also visited each minor league stop in Detroit's system as an instructor. Although Trammell never has managed before, he's paid his dues.

Offense

Trammell's manager when he played, Sparky Anderson, played it safe when it came to stealing bases and using the hit-and-run. How Trammell approaches the little-ball game probably will be determined by his personnel. The Tigers don't have much speed, and bringing in the fences at Comerica Park may further emphasize home runs over small ball.

Pitching & Defense

Trammell obviously understands defensive play, and both Anderson and Bochy liked to experiment with players at different positions while Trammell was around them. How Trammell will handle a pitching staff is the big unknown. His pitching coach is Bob Cluck, who has worked in the Texas system recently and had a stint as Oakland's and Houston's pitching coach. Anderson gained the reputation as Captain Hook when he managed Cincinnati, but he stuck with starting pitchers longer when he managed the Tigers. Bochy is careful not to overwork his Padres starters.

2003 Outlook

Trammell's biggest challenge will be adjusting the Tigers' attitude. The clubhouse has run amok the last two years. To help in that regard, Trammell has hired former teammate Kirk Gibson as his bench coach. It should help that Gibson is close friends with Bobby Higginson, who has struggled as a team leader. As for wins and losses, Trammell is in a no-lose situation. Even if Detroit wins just 65 games this season, it would represent a 10-game improvement from 2002.

Born: 2/21/58 in Garden Grove, CA

Playing Experience: 1977-1996, Det

Managerial Experience: No major league managing experience

Manager Statistics (Luis Pujols)

Year	Team, Lg	W	L	Pct	GB	Finish
2002	Detroit, AL	55	100	.355	39.0	5th Central
1 Season		55	100	.355	–	–

2002 Starting Pitchers by Days Rest

	<=3	4	5	6+
Tigers Starts	0	78	41	28
Tigers ERA	–	5.78	4.59	3.95
AL Avg Starts	1	83	44	24
AL ERA	7.15	4.59	4.27	5.03

2002 Situational Stats

	Luis Pujols	AL Average
Hit & Run Success %	46.0	36.0
Stolen Base Success %	59.0	68.1
Platoon Pct.	57.3	58.9
Defensive Subs	11	23
High-Pitch Outings	12	6
Quick/Slow Hooks	10/19	19/14
Sacrifice Attempts	49	53

2002 Rankings —Luis Pujols (American League)

- 1st in hit-and-run success percentage and starts with over 120 pitches (12)
- 3rd in fewest caught stealings of third base (3), starting lineups used (126) and slow hooks

Matt Anderson

2002 Season

Matt Anderson was bothered by pain in his shoulder almost from the start of last season and never was able to get on track. He went on the disabled list in May with a torn muscle in his shoulder pit and he did not return until September, when he made only three appearances. It was a rare injury and it took Anderson longer to recover than originally had been anticipated. After leading the Tigers with 22 saves in 2001, Anderson didn't register one last season.

Pitching

Anderson is one of the hardest throwers in baseball. It is not uncommon for him to reach triple digits on the radar gun. He also has a nasty off-speed pitch, an 86-MPH knuckle-curve, which buckles the knees of hitters. Anderson does not take full advantage of his velocity, however, because he flies open early in his delivery and shows hitters the ball right away. His breaking ball is an effective pitch only if he gets ahead in the count, because it is difficult to throw consistently for strikes. He has worked on a split-finger pitch, but has not used it often.

Defense

Anderson is athletic. He has a loose, lanky frame and he runs well. In fact, he is one of the fastest runners on the Tigers. He has good hands and fields his position well. Anderson has a good pickoff move, but sometimes forgets about baserunners.

2003 Outlook

Entering last season, Anderson seemed to be on the verge of becoming one of baseball's better closers. But there seems to be a lack of maturity that is holding him back. The atmosphere surrounding the Tigers has not helped Anderson, but he needs to become more of a leader rather than a follower in that regard.

Position: RP
Bats: R **Throws:** R
Ht: 6' 4" **Wt:** 190

Opening Day Age: 26
Born: 8/17/76 in Louisville, KY
ML Seasons: 5

Overall Statistics

	W	L	Pct.	ERA	G	GS	Sv	IP	H	BB	SO	HR	Ratio
'02	2	1	.667	9.00	12	0	0	11.0	17	8	8	1	2.27
Car.	15	6	.714	4.84	222	0	23	223.1	205	137	207	22	1.53

How Often He Throws Strikes

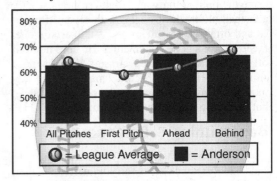

= League Average   = Anderson

2002 Situational Stats

	W	L	ERA	Sv	IP		AB	H	HR	RBI	Avg
Home	2	0	2.84	0	6.1	LHB	23	10	1	9	.435
Road	0	1	17.36	0	4.2	RHB	22	7	0	3	.318
First Half	2	1	7.56	0	8.1	Sc Pos	20	5	1	12	.250
Scnd Half	0	0	13.50	0	2.2	Clutch	16	9	1	7	.563

2002 Rankings (American League)

- Did not rank near the top or bottom in any category

Detroit

Damion Easley

2002 Season

Damion Easley strained his left oblique muscle during the opening week of the season and did not return until June 1. When he did, he immediately went into a long slump. The result was his worst season since early in his career with the Angels. It was the first time he did not reach double figures in home runs and stolen bases since 1996. In September, he often sat as the Tigers began to look at youngster Omar Infante as his possible replacement at second base.

Hitting

Easley is strong for a middle infielder and will drive the ball a long way. However, he is strictly a fastball hitter. He struggles with offspeed pitches and often chases them out of the strike zone. Easley is not a good clutch hitter. He does not foul off tough pitches to keep himself alive in those situations. His flaws become magnified at key moments. Easley has good balance in his stance, but his swing gradually has become longer.

Baserunning & Defense

The days when Easley is a consistent threat to steal bases are over. He is carrying more bulk than he did earlier in his career and does not run nearly as well. Hindered by the injury to his oblique muscle, he stole just one base last season. Defensively, Easley has good hands. He is not as fluid as some middle infielders, but he does make the routine play. He hangs in exceptionally well and does an excellent job of turning the double play.

2003 Outlook

The handwriting is on the wall for Easley in Detroit. The double-play combination of the future clearly is Ramon Santiago and Omar Infante, and the club would love to unload Easley. It is not that he does not present some value as a player, but the Tigers must pay him $6.5 million this season and in 2004. Given Easley's declining production, teams are not exactly lining up to acquire him. In addition, he has the power to decline a trade.

Position: 2B
Bats: R **Throws:** R
Ht: 5'11" **Wt:** 187

Opening Day Age: 33
Born: 11/11/69 in New York, NY
ML Seasons: 11

Overall Statistics

	G	AB	R	H	D	T	HR	RBI	SB	BB	SO	Avg	OBP	Slg
'02	85	304	29	68	14	1	8	30	1	27	43	.224	.307	.355
Car.	1191	4189	583	1066	223	21	119	506	105	399	731	.254	.332	.403

Where He Hits the Ball

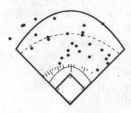 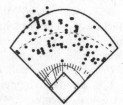

Vs. LHP   **Vs. RHP**

2002 Situational Stats

	AB	H	HR	RBI	Avg		AB	H	HR	RBI	Avg
Home	161	28	4	13	.174	LHP	67	21	4	9	.313
Road	143	40	4	17	.280	RHP	237	47	4	21	.198
First Half	108	21	4	10	.194	Sc Pos	69	12	1	19	.174
Scnd Half	196	47	4	20	.240	Clutch	54	13	1	2	.241

2002 Rankings (American League)

- 8th in errors at second base (9)
- 9th in hit by pitch (11)
- 10th in lowest batting average on a 3-1 count (.143)
- Led the Tigers in hit by pitch (11)

Robert Fick

2002 Season

Not everything former Detroit manager Phil Garner did was bad while he led the Tigers. It was Garner who, in an attempt to get Robert Fick's bat in the lineup every day, placed him in right field late in 2001 and throughout all of spring training last year. The move worked. Fick, who came up as a catcher-first baseman, played every day in right field and again was one of the Tigers' most productive hitters. Defensively, he played well enough to register 21 outfield assists.

Hitting

Fick has a quick, compact lefthanded stroke that serves him well at Comerica Park, where the right-field fence is reachable. Fick is at his best when he hits the ball to all fields. He is capable of going with the pitch, but sometimes tries to pull the ball too much. Fick knows the strike zone and recognizes pitches well. He also is effective against lefthanders. He is just a good all-around hitter who sometimes tries to do too much. Fick is prone to lengthy slumps for that reason.

Baserunning & Defense

Fick was surprisingly efficient in right field. He does not run well, nor does he get a particularly good jump, so his range is below average. Yet his throwing, inconsistent as a catcher, was accurate as an outfielder. The high number of assists is the result of opposing baserunners constantly testing out an inexperienced outfielder. Fick passed those tests consistently. While his range is limited, Fick's hands are good. He caught what he reached. At first base, Fick's footwork is poor. And the more he catches, the more his weaknesses get exposed.

2003 Outlook

The Tigers' clubhouse has not been the best, and Fick often falls in line with some of the players who have had their attitudes questioned. He needs to be smarter than that. As a good hitter who is limited defensively, he'd be a role player on a contending team. On a struggling team such as Detroit, Fick is one of the better players. October surgery to repair a torn labrum in his left shoulder isn't expected to affect his spring training.

Position: RF
Bats: L **Throws:** R
Ht: 6' 1" **Wt:** 200

Opening Day Age: 29
Born: 3/15/74 in Torrance, CA
ML Seasons: 5

Overall Statistics

	G	AB	R	H	D	T	HR	RBI	SB	BB	SO	Avg	OBP	Slg
'02	148	556	66	150	36	2	17	63	0	46	90	.270	.331	.433
Car.	360	1183	158	317	65	6	45	163	4	116	204	.268	.336	.447

Where He Hits the Ball

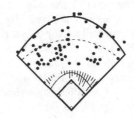 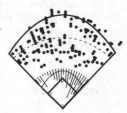

Vs. LHP **Vs. RHP**

2002 Situational Stats

	AB	H	HR	RBI	Avg		AB	H	HR	RBI	Avg
Home	279	76	12	34	.272	LHP	171	48	5	14	.281
Road	277	74	5	29	.267	RHP	385	102	12	49	.265
First Half	307	89	11	40	.290	Sc Pos	129	30	5	43	.233
Scnd Half	249	61	6	23	.245	Clutch	80	19	4	11	.238

2002 Rankings (American League)

- 1st in errors in right field (12), assists in right field (21) and lowest fielding percentage in right field (.963)
- 8th in GDPs (17)
- Led the Tigers in at-bats, runs scored, hits, doubles, total bases (241), walks, times on base (203), GDPs (17), pitches seen (2,406), plate appearances (614), games played, batting average vs. lefthanded pitchers, on-base percentage vs. lefthanded pitchers (.342), lowest percentage of swings on the first pitch (22.4) and batting average with two strikes (.230)

Detroit

Bobby Higginson

2002 Season

It was the second disappointing season in a row for Bobby Higginson. He was limited to 119 games because of a hamstring injury, which sidelined him for a month. He hit just 10 home runs and had only 63 RBI, numbers that pale in comparison to his best season in 2000, when he had 30 home runs and 102 RBI. Higginson also drew the ire of management with his constant complaining to the media about the sorry state of the Tigers while posting mediocre numbers himself. His reputation as clubhouse lawyer grew.

Hitting

Higginson has a quick bat. He is able to turn on a fastball and drive it. He has good knowledge of the strike zone and recognizes pitches well. He makes remarkably consistent contact for a hitter with good power. When Higginson slumps, usually it is because he tries to pull the ball too much. Among his many complaints are the dimensions of Comerica Park, which he once called Comerica National Park. But his lament rings a bit hollow because the right-field fence is quite reachable there and Higginson is a lefthanded pull-hitter. After all, he hit 30 home runs in 2000 while playing his home games there.

Baserunning & Defense

Higginson annually ranks among the league leaders in outfield assists. He has a strong and accurate throwing arm, although he is guilty of overthrowing the cutoff man at times. He has below-average speed for a major league outfielder. However, his instincts are good and he gets a good jump on the ball. Left field is particularly spacious at Comerica Park, but Higginson has handled it well. Although he has limited speed, Higginson has averaged 15.7 steals the last three seasons. He has a good feel for running the bases.

2003 Outlook

Higginson is the Tigers' top player, but his attitude is a concern. The years of losing have taken a toll on his approach to the game. His mentor is former teammate Kirk Gibson. Management is hoping that Gibson's appointment as bench coach will get Higginson turned around.

Position: LF
Bats: L **Throws:** R
Ht: 5'11" **Wt:** 202

Opening Day Age: 32
Born: 8/18/70 in Philadelphia, PA
ML Seasons: 8

Overall Statistics

	G	AB	R	H	D	T	HR	RBI	SB	BB	SO	Avg	OBP	Slg
'02	119	444	50	125	24	3	10	63	12	41	45	.282	.345	.417
Car.	1091	3967	611	1114	233	27	161	592	78	519	634	.281	.364	.475

Where He Hits the Ball

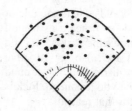 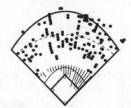

Vs. LHP   **Vs. RHP**

2002 Situational Stats

	AB	H	HR	RBI	Avg		AB	H	HR	RBI	Avg
Home	239	65	6	28	.272	LHP	133	32	1	15	.241
Road	205	60	4	35	.293	RHP	311	93	9	48	.299
First Half	208	60	5	30	.288	Sc Pos	93	34	0	47	.366
Scnd Half	236	65	5	33	.275	Clutch	66	12	0	6	.182

2002 Rankings (American League)

- 1st in errors in left field (7), assists in left field (15), lowest slugging percentage vs. left-handed pitchers (.286) and lowest fielding percentage in left field (.973)
- Led the Tigers in sacrifice flies (7), caught stealing (5), on-base percentage, lowest percentage of swings that missed (11.7), batting average with runners in scoring position, highest percentage of extra bases taken as a runner (57.5), on-base percentage vs. righthanded pitchers (.368) and batting average on a 3-2 count (.283)

Brandon Inge

2002 Season

Inge was beaten out for the starting catcher spot by Michael Rivera during spring training and was sent to Triple-A Toledo so he could play every day. When he returned, Inge was an improved hitter from the one who hit just .180 in 2001. He showed more power and continued to make strides as a receiver. Although Inge soon claimed the starting job, as the season moved on he was not able to sustain the improvements he made early in the season as a hitter.

Hitting

When Inge came up in the minor leagues, he used an inside-out stroke similar to that of Ivan Rodriguez. But when Inge reached the major leagues for the first time, he was unable to handle the inside fastball with that stroke. He abandoned it during the 2001 season and became totally confused. Last season, he went to a conventional approach and made strides. He still swings at and misses an inordinate number of pitches and lacks consistency. For a smaller player, Inge is strong, capable of driving the ball with authority.

Baserunning & Defense

A relief pitcher and shortstop at Virginia Commonwealth University, the athletic Inge has a strong arm and quick feet behind the plate. He is remarkably advanced for someone who has caught only a few years. He had a chronic problem with his left shoulder, which kept popping out of socket and hindered him all of last season. It made him struggle receiving pitches over his head. Inge also dropped too many pitches. He still needs work calling a game, but has made progress in that area. Inge runs well for a catcher, but is not a threat to steal bases.

2003 Outlook

Inge is being counted on as the Tigers' everyday catcher. In the right environment, Inge could prosper. He has the potential to be one of the best defensive catchers in baseball. He has a lot of holes as a hitter, but with time may develop successfully because of his strength and athleticism.

Position: C
Bats: R **Throws:** R
Ht: 5'11" **Wt:** 189

Opening Day Age: 25
Born: 5/19/77 in Lynchburg, VA
ML Seasons: 2

Overall Statistics

	G	AB	R	H	D	T	HR	RBI	SB	BB	SO	Avg	OBP	Slg
'02	95	321	27	65	15	3	7	24	1	24	101	.202	.266	.333
Car.	174	510	40	99	26	3	7	39	2	33	142	.194	.247	.298

Where He Hits the Ball

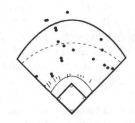 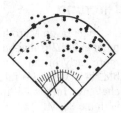

Vs. LHP   **Vs. RHP**

2002 Situational Stats

	AB	H	HR	RBI	Avg		AB	H	HR	RBI	Avg
Home	151	34	3	14	.225	LHP	70	16	3	6	.229
Road	170	31	4	10	.182	RHP	251	49	4	18	.195
First Half	151	38	6	13	.252	Sc Pos	73	16	1	16	.219
Scnd Half	170	27	1	11	.159	Clutch	63	12	2	6	.190

2002 Rankings (American League)

- 2nd in fielding percentage at catcher (.998)
- 10th in lowest batting average on an 0-2 count (.063)
- Led the Tigers in strikeouts and most pitches seen per plate appearance (4.21)

Detroit

Mike Maroth

2002 Season

Entering last season, Mike Maroth was an aging prospect who was losing stature within the Tigers' minor league system because of a poor showing at Triple-A Toledo in 2001. But after beginning last season by going 8-1 with a 2.82 ERA in 11 starts for Toledo, Maroth was called to the majors in early June. In his second big league start, he threw eight strong innings and beat the defending World Champion Diamondbacks on the road. That proved to the Tigers, and perhaps to Maroth himself because he has struggled with his confidence in the past, that he belongs in the major leagues. He was not spectacular the remainder of the season, but Maroth did hold his own.

Pitching

The big reason Maroth made a dramatic improvement in 2002 is that he started to challenge hitters more early in the count. When Maroth has trouble, it is when he falls behind and is forced to challenge hitters with his fastball, which usually is in the 88-MPH range. He has a good two-seam fastball that sinks away from righthanded hitters. He uses it to set up his changeup, which is an out pitch and probably Maroth's best offering. But there is some variety to his pitch menu. He also throws a cut fastball.

Defense

Maroth fields his position adequately. He moves well enough off the mound and did not make an error last year. He has a good pickoff move to first base and holds runners well.

2003 Outlook

Between Triple-A Toledo and the major leagues, Maroth was 14-11 in 2002. In the process, he displayed the type of consistency he had not showed previously in the minor leagues. If he continues to progress along the same line, he should begin the new season in Detroit's starting rotation.

Position: SP
Bats: L **Throws:** L
Ht: 6' 0" **Wt:** 180

Opening Day Age: 25
Born: 8/17/77 in Orlando, FL
ML Seasons: 1

Overall Statistics

	W	L	Pct.	ERA	G	GS	Sv	IP	H	BB	SO	HR	Ratio
'02	6	10	.375	4.48	21	21	0	128.2	136	36	58	7	1.34
Car.	6	10	.375	4.48	21	21	0	128.2	136	36	58	7	1.34

How Often He Throws Strikes

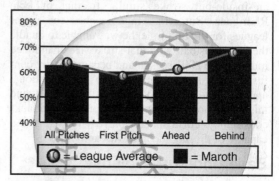

2002 Situational Stats

	W	L	ERA	Sv	IP		AB	H	HR	RBI	Avg
Home	5	4	3.18	0	76.1	LHB	115	29	1	12	.252
Road	1	6	6.36	0	52.1	RHB	377	107	6	42	.284
First Half	1	3	4.86	0	33.1	Sc Pos	106	34	2	48	.321
Scnd Half	5	7	4.34	0	95.1	Clutch	47	14	0	4	.298

2002 Rankings (American League)

- 1st in losses among rookies
- 5th in most GDPs induced per GDP situation (21.6%)
- Led the Tigers in runners caught stealing (4), GDPs induced (21), highest groundball-flyball ratio allowed (1.6), most GDPs induced per GDP situation (21.6%), lowest ERA at home and most GDPs induced per nine innings (1.5)

Carlos Pena

2002 Season

The Tigers acquired Carlos Pena from Oakland in early July, as part of a three-way trade that sent their best pitcher, Jeff Weaver, to the Yankees. It was the second time in 2002 that Pena, originally drafted by Texas, had been traded despite being considered one of the top prospects in baseball. In fact, he entered 2002 as the favorite to be named American League Rookie of the Year. After hitting four home runs in his first seven games with Oakland, Pena slumped badly and was sent to the minors on May 21. He did not return until he was traded to Detroit. With the Tigers he hit .253-12-36 in 273 at-bats.

Hitting

Pena can turn on a pitch over the heart of the plate and drive it with power. Most of his home runs are flyballs to right field. Pitchers tend to work him in the classic manner. They pound him with fastballs inside, a pitch Pena does not handle well, and then work him away with offspeed pitches. It's effective because Pena is not good at recognizing pitches. He is capable of using the entire field, but does not drive fastballs away to left field with authority as much as he should. While Pena swings at too many bad pitches and strikes out a lot, he hangs in well against lefthanded pitching.

Baserunning & Defense

A future Gold Glove winner, Pena is an exceptional fielder with extraordinary hands. He makes every type of play with fluidity and ease, fielding groundballs like a middle infielder and handling throws from across the diamond. He also has an outstanding arm for the position. Pena is a below-average runner who is not a threat to steal.

2003 Outlook

General Manager Dave Dombrowski acquired Pena because he feels Pena eventually will be a difference-maker on a contending team. He will play every day at first base, and the expectation is that Pena will display more consistency than he did during his up-and-down rookie season.

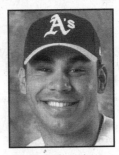

Position: 1B
Bats: L **Throws:** L
Ht: 6' 2" **Wt:** 210

Opening Day Age: 24
Born: 5/17/78 in Santo Domingo, DR
ML Seasons: 2
Pronunciation: PAIN-yuh

Overall Statistics

	G	AB	R	H	D	T	HR	RBI	SB	BB	SO	Avg	OBP	Slg
'02	115	397	43	96	17	4	19	52	2	41	111	.242	.316	.448
Car.	137	459	49	112	21	5	22	64	2	51	128	.244	.322	.455

Where He Hits the Ball

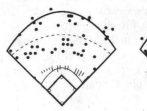

Vs. LHP   **Vs. RHP**

2002 Situational Stats

	AB	H	HR	RBI	Avg		AB	H	HR	RBI	Avg
Home	221	53	10	30	.240	LHP	132	35	8	23	.265
Road	176	43	9	22	.244	RHP	265	61	11	29	.230
First Half	128	30	7	18	.234	Sc Pos	80	19	5	29	.238
Scnd Half	269	66	12	34	.245	Clutch	52	13	4	10	.250

2002 Rankings (American League)

- 2nd in home runs among rookies (19) and fielding percentage at first base (.996)
- 3rd in lowest percentage of swings put into play (34.6)
- 5th in RBI among rookies (52) and highest percentage of swings that missed (27.6)
- 7th in slugging percentage vs. lefthanded pitchers (.538)
- Led the Tigers in slugging percentage (.462), HR frequency (22.8 ABs per HR) and slugging percentage vs. lefthanded pitchers (.500)

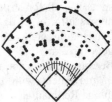

Detroit

129

Mark Redman

2002 Season

After being injured most of the 2001 season, Mark Redman put together a year that was his best in many ways. Whereas he had never pitched more than 151.1 innings before, he worked 203. His ERA was a career-best 4.21 and he threw the first three complete games of his major league career. In a 19-start span from April 28 through August 7, Redman was 7-6 with a 2.44 ERA. He had back-to-back complete-game victories to end May. Beyond that 19-game stretch, however, Redman was 1-9 with an 8.14 ERA.

Pitching

Redman is not overpowering. His fastball usually is in the high 80s, and when he is at his best, he spots it well for strikes early in the count. That allows him to set up his changeup, which is an outstanding pitch, later in the count. He also has a good breaking ball and a good feel for pitching. Because he does not throw that hard or have a lot of movement with his fastball, there are two things Redman cannot do. He cannot pitch from behind in the count. And he cannot pitch with his fastball up in the strike zone. Although he did surpass 200 innings in 2002, his durability is questionable. He ran out of steam late in the season and has been nagged by injury problems in the past.

Defense

Redman does not move well on the mound or have good hands. He made six errors in just 36 chances last season and he's started just three double plays his entire career. Redman does a respectable job holding runners. His delivery is quick to the plate and he uses the slide-step method at times to hold runners.

2003 Outlook

Redman had a good season for Minnesota in 2000, but the Twins could not get him out of town fast enough the following season. So the onus is on Redman to prove that he can put together back-to-back good seasons for the first time in his career.

Position: SP
Bats: L **Throws:** L
Ht: 6' 5" **Wt:** 245

Opening Day Age: 29
Born: 1/5/74 in San Diego, CA
ML Seasons: 4

Overall Statistics

	W	L	Pct.	ERA	G	GS	Sv	IP	H	BB	SO	HR	Ratio
'02	8	15	.348	4.21	30	30	0	203.0	211	51	109	15	1.29
Car.	23	30	.434	4.57	78	66	0	425.0	464	126	270	47	1.39

How Often He Throws Strikes

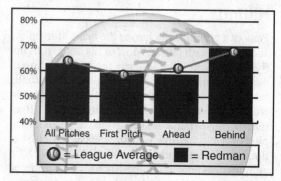

= League Average   = Redman

2002 Situational Stats

	W	L	ERA	Sv	IP		AB	H	HR	RBI	Avg
Home	4	6	3.29	0	98.1	LHB	190	55	4	26	.289
Road	4	9	5.07	0	104.2	RHB	598	156	11	66	.261
First Half	4	8	3.65	0	120.2	Sc Pos	188	55	3	73	.293
Scnd Half	4	7	5.03	0	82.1	Clutch	54	14	1	4	.259

2002 Rankings (American League)

- 1st in least run support per nine innings (3.7)
- 2nd in errors at pitcher (6) and lowest fielding percentage at pitcher (.833)
- 3rd in wild pitches (11)
- 4th in losses and fewest home runs allowed per nine innings (.67)
- 5th in fewest strikeouts per nine innings (4.8)
- 8th in lowest stolen-base percentage allowed (50.0), highest batting average allowed (.268) and highest ERA on the road
- Led the Tigers in wins, games started, complete games (3), innings pitched, strikeouts, wild pitches (11), pitches thrown (3,166) and fewest walks per nine innings (2.3)

Randall Simon

Position: DH/1B
Bats: L **Throws:** L
Ht: 6' 0" **Wt:** 230

Opening Day Age: 27
Born: 5/26/75 in Willemstad, Curacao
ML Seasons: 5

2002 Season

Given a chance to play regularly for the first time in his major league career, Randall Simon proved he can be effective. He hit .301 playing on a daily basis and also showed good power, leading the Tigers with 19 home runs and 82 RBI. Simon lived up to his reputation as a free swinger, walking just 13 times. Yet he struck out only 30 times. He did not figure much in the Tigers' plans at the start of the season, before injuries sidelined Dmitri Young, and Simon did not play as much after the Tigers traded for youngster Carlos Pena.

Hitting

Simon is a one-of-a-kind hitter. Literally, there is no one quite like him. He swings at everything with a vicious downward hack. His hand-eye coordination is extraordinary. That Simon can swing away and strike out as few times as he does speaks volumes. He will take a pitch off the ground and drive it. Pitchers deliberately do not throw the ball over the plate to Simon. It doesn't matter. He hits them anyway. The downside is the lack of walks. There are times when Simon should take a walk and does not, hurting his team.

Baserunning & Defense

Simon does not run well, nor is he a particularly good baserunner instinctively. He has to go station-to-station on the bases. Defensively, Simon's footwork is not good and his arm is considerably below average. Simon is short in terms of height for the position and does not present a good throwing target, though he does have decent hands.

2003 Outlook

There is a place in the major leagues for Simon, but it's in Pittsburgh and not Detroit, with the Tigers grooming young first basemen Carlos Pena and Eric Munson. Simon may be better coming off the bench, but on a below-average team like the Pirates, it looks like he will get most of the at-bats as the lefthanded half of a first-base platoon with Kevin Young.

Overall Statistics

	G	AB	R	H	D	T	HR	RBI	SB	BB	SO	Avg	OBP	Slg
'02	130	482	51	145	17	1	19	82	0	13	30	.301	.320	.459
Car.	321	986	109	301	48	3	30	149	2	46	86	.305	.336	.451

Where He Hits the Ball

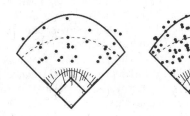

Vs. LHP   **Vs. RHP**

2002 Situational Stats

	AB	H	HR	RBI	Avg		AB	H	HR	RBI	Avg
Home	227	76	13	44	.335	LHP	141	36	3	14	.255
Road	255	69	6	38	.271	RHP	341	109	16	68	.320
First Half	278	78	10	47	.281	Sc Pos	117	37	5	61	.316
Scnd Half	204	67	9	35	.328	Clutch	70	22	1	8	.314

2002 Rankings (American League)

- 1st in fewest pitches seen per plate appearance (2.72) and highest percentage of swings on the first pitch (53.2)
- 5th in lowest cleanup slugging percentage (.422)
- 6th in errors at first base (7) and lowest on-base percentage vs. lefthanded pitchers (.266)
- Led the Tigers in batting average, home runs, singles, RBI, sacrifice flies (7), intentional walks (5), highest groundball-flyball ratio (1.8), highest percentage of swings put into play (52.5), batting average with the bases loaded (.455), batting average vs. righthanded pitchers, slugging percentage vs. righthanded pitchers (.510) and batting average at home

Detroit

131

Steve W. Sparks

2002 Season

After having the best season of his career in 2001, Steve Sparks took a step back last season. He won six fewer games, lost seven more and his ERA rose nearly two runs per game. After a solid start by Sparks, the season fell apart for him in May and June. In nine starts in those two months, Sparks was 1-6 with an 8.87 ERA. Sparks was better after that, but still wasn't able to match the magic he produced in 2001, when he led the American League in complete games.

Pitching

Sparks is a knuckleball specialist who throws the pitch at least 70 percent of the time. When he keeps his knuckler down, he is effective. When he gets it up, he tends to get hit hard. Sparks throws two different knuckleballs. One is slower and has more movement. The other is firmer, but has less break. Sparks has an 82-MPH fastball, which is just enough velocity to keep hitters off balance. Last season he started throwing a cut fastball, and he also has a serviceable curveball.

Defense

Sparks is an exceptional athlete. He has excellent hands and is very quick. Because of the nature of the knuckleball, he usually is in good fielding position after delivering it and snags balls hit back up the middle. He fields bunts and balls hit out in front of the plate well. Sparks is quick to home plate and has a good pickoff move.

2003 Outlook

Sparks is a dedicated, hardworking pitcher who is an asset to a pitching staff. His best role is probably as a spot starter and long reliever. However, on a club that is thin in starting pitching, he will take the ball every fifth day and eat up innings. His advancing age is not a factor because he is a knuckleballer. Plus, Sparks is in such great shape physically.

Position: SP
Bats: R **Throws:** R
Ht: 6' 0" **Wt:** 195

Opening Day Age: 37
Born: 7/2/65 in Tulsa, OK
ML Seasons: 7
Nickname: Sparky

Overall Statistics

	W	L	Pct.	ERA	G	GS	Sv	IP	H	BB	SO	HR	Ratio
'02	8	16	.333	5.52	32	30	0	189.0	238	67	98	23	1.61
Car.	56	63	.471	4.76	190	164	1	1092.0	1198	438	547	123	1.50

How Often He Throws Strikes

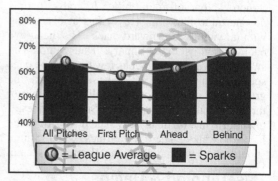

League Average = ● Sparks = ■

2002 Situational Stats

	W	L	ERA	Sv	IP		AB	H	HR	RBI	Avg
Home	3	7	5.05	0	87.1	LHB	371	111	10	61	.299
Road	5	9	5.93	0	101.2	RHB	407	127	13	69	.312
First Half	4	8	6.05	0	99.2	Sc Pos	240	72	7	103	.300
Scnd Half	4	8	4.94	0	89.1	Clutch	26	13	1	4	.500

2002 Rankings (American League)

- 1st in highest ERA, highest batting average allowed (.306), highest slugging percentage allowed (.486) and highest ERA on the road
- 2nd in losses, hits allowed, lowest strikeout-walk ratio (1.5), highest on-base percentage allowed (.366), highest batting average allowed vs. righthanded batters and fewest strikeouts per nine innings (4.7)
- 3rd in highest ERA at home
- 4th in balks (2)
- 5th in hit batsmen (12) and pickoff throws (124)
- Led the Tigers in wins, losses, games started, complete games (3) and hits allowed

Chris Truby

2002 Season

With Dean Palmer out for the season with injuries to his neck and throwing shoulder, the Tigers acquired Chris Truby from Montreal in May to fill the void. Truby made an immediate impact with the Tigers because he improved the defense on the left side of their infield, which kept him in the lineup virtually every day even though he was not hitting well. As the season wore on, though, his lack of production at the plate began to outweigh his contribution defensively, and he started less regularly even though third base was an obvious problem for the Tigers. Truby also was hindered by a rib injury that put him on the 15-day disabled list during July.

Hitting

Truby has struggled to duplicate what he did as a Houston rookie in 2000, when he hit .260 with 11 home runs and 59 RBI in just 258 at-bats. Truby's biggest flaw as a hitter is that he does not stay on the ball. He hooks off nearly every pitch. There are times when he hits the ball for surprising distance, but those times were fewer last season. His patience at the plate is alarming and his plate coverage is poor. Unless it's a fastball over the heart of the plate that he knows is coming, Truby is not an effective hitter.

Baserunning & Defense

Truby is a major league-caliber third baseman. He has good hands and good range. He makes the routine play consistently and occasionally will make a spectacular one. Truby has arm strength and throws accurately. On the Tigers, whose infield defense was exceptionally poor last season, Truby was as an exceptionally good defensive player.

2003 Outlook

It's a fact of life that good-field, no-hit third basemen are not exactly in demand. Truby has a good glove that can help any team. But his work with the bat last season would not be adequate for a middle infielder, let alone someone playing on the corner. He'll be in camp this spring, but he's a long shot to hit well enough to re-claim the third-base job.

Position: 3B
Bats: R **Throws:** R
Ht: 6' 2" **Wt:** 215

Opening Day Age: 29
Born: 12/9/73 in Palm Springs, CA
ML Seasons: 3

Overall Statistics

	G	AB	R	H	D	T	HR	RBI	SB	BB	SO	Avg	OBP	Slg
'02	124	382	35	82	18	4	4	22	2	10	98	.215	.238	.314
Car.	250	776	74	177	39	9	23	104	5	33	192	.228	.264	.390

Where He Hits the Ball

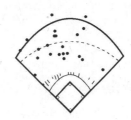 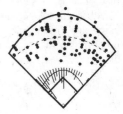

Vs. LHP   **Vs. RHP**

2002 Situational Stats

	AB	H	HR	RBI	Avg		AB	H	HR	RBI	Avg
Home	187	42	1	8	.225	LHP	68	14	1	5	.206
Road	195	40	3	14	.205	RHP	314	68	3	17	.217
First Half	232	55	4	15	.237	Sc Pos	89	14	0	16	.157
Scnd Half	150	27	0	7	.180	Clutch	62	5	0	2	.081

2002 Rankings (American League)

- 10th in errors at third base (11)

Dmitri Young

2002 Season

After signing a four-year, $28.5 million contract in February 2002, Young suffered through an injury-plagued season. He went on the disabled list in July because of a hernia condition that required surgery. When he was able to play, Young's numbers were not that far from what he had produced earlier in his career. He played mostly DH and first base, but also saw limited playing time in the outfield and at third base.

Hitting

Young is a classic fastball hitter who looks for first-pitch fastballs and often connects. He does not walk often. He has walked more than 40 times just once in a seven-year major league career. Mostly a gap-to-gap and line-drive hitter when he came up, Young has gotten stronger and gained home-run power over the years. He is a switch-hitter who is capable from both sides of the plate.

Baserunning & Defense

Each season, Young grows bigger physically. While that has helped him gain power as a hitter, it has limited his range in the field and speed on the bases. At this point of his career, Young ideally is a first baseman. His movement and arm strength are above average for the position. In the outfield and at third base, he is below average in both areas. He does have good hands. Young hustles on the bases. While he is not a base clogger, he is not a threat to steal, either.

2003 Outlook

Young brings energy to a team. He is a quality hitter and a veteran player who understands the game, but finding a spot for him in the lineup might be difficult because of youngsters Carlos Pena and Eric Munson. Young was in conflict with the Tigers' brass late last season over a possible move to third base, saying he was brought aboard to play first, his preferred position. Unfortunately for the Tigers, Young would be difficult to trade because of his big-money contract.

Position: DH/1B
Bats: B **Throws:** R
Ht: 6' 2" **Wt:** 235

Opening Day Age: 29
Born: 10/11/73 in Vicksburg, MS
ML Seasons: 7

Overall Statistics

	G	AB	R	H	D	T	HR	RBI	SB	BB	SO	Avg	OBP	Slg
'02	54	201	25	57	14	0	7	27	2	12	39	.284	.329	.458
Car.	745	2560	346	757	171	15	79	359	21	204	429	.296	.349	.467

Where He Hits the Ball

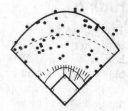

Vs. LHP **Vs. RHP**

2002 Situational Stats

	AB	H	HR	RBI	Avg		AB	H	HR	RBI	Avg
Home	122	32	5	14	.262	LHP	54	16	1	7	.296
Road	79	25	2	13	.316	RHP	147	41	6	20	.279
First Half	201	57	7	27	.284	Sc Pos	50	17	1	20	.340
Scnd Half	0	0	0	0	-	Clutch	34	8	0	2	.235

2002 Rankings (American League)

- 6th in lowest cleanup slugging percentage (.457)
- Led the Tigers in intentional walks (5) and cleanup slugging percentage (.457)

Juan Acevedo

Position: RP
Bats: R **Throws:** R
Ht: 6' 2" **Wt:** 228

Opening Day Age: 32
Born: 5/5/70 in Juarez, Mexico
ML Seasons: 7
Pronunciation: OSS-uh-vay-doe

Overall Statistics

	W	L	Pct.	ERA	G	GS	Sv	IP	H	BB	SO	HR	Ratio
'02	1	5	.167	2.65	65	0	28	74.2	68	23	43	4	1.22
Car.	27	35	.435	4.16	328	34	47	531.2	545	208	322	66	1.42

2002 Situational Stats

	W	L	ERA	Sv	IP		AB	H	HR	RBI	Avg
Home	1	1	0.78	16	46.1	LHB	140	37	3	20	.264
Road	0	4	5.72	12	28.1	RHB	136	31	1	13	.228
First Half	1	4	3.02	14	44.2	Sc Pos	77	18	1	29	.234
Scnd Half	0	1	2.10	14	30.0	Clutch	173	44	2	24	.254

2002 Season

After inconsistent seasons in recent years, Juan Acevedo became the Tigers' closer in 2002 and saved a career-high 28 games. He won the job when Matt Anderson went on the DL with a shoulder ailment and Acevedo performed well. He had a stretch during May and June in which he converted 10 straight save opportunities.

Pitching & Defense

Acevedo consistently throws his fastball 92-94 MPH. He adds some cutting and sinking action to it. Willing to challenge hitters, Acevedo succeeded in 2002 by reducing his walks considerably. In the past, he's found trouble by falling behind hitters and coming in with a pitch over the heart of the plate. Getting ahead of hitters kept Acevedo from being hurt as much by home runs. Although he has a stocky build, Acevedo is a decent athlete.

2003 Outlook

On a contender, Acevedo would be used as a setup man, not as a closer. He lacks command and that one dominating pitch that most closers possess. When he's good, though, Acevedo is very good. Look for the Tigers to move Anderson or rookie Franklyn German into the closer role. Acevedo wasn't offered salary arbitration by Detroit after he reportedly asked for closer's money.

Adam Bernero

Position: RP/SP
Bats: R **Throws:** R
Ht: 6' 4" **Wt:** 205

Opening Day Age: 26
Born: 11/28/76 in Los Gatos, CA
ML Seasons: 3
Pronunciation: bur-NAIR-o

Overall Statistics

	W	L	Pct.	ERA	G	GS	Sv	IP	H	BB	SO	HR	Ratio
'02	4	7	.364	6.20	28	11	0	101.2	128	31	69	17	1.56
Car.	4	8	.333	5.82	45	15	0	148.1	174	48	97	24	1.50

2002 Situational Stats

	W	L	ERA	Sv	IP		AB	H	HR	RBI	Avg
Home	1	4	9.00	0	44.0	LHB	224	72	10	42	.321
Road	3	3	4.06	0	57.2	RHB	190	56	7	28	.295
First Half	2	4	5.98	0	52.2	Sc Pos	108	36	1	46	.333
Scnd Half	2	3	6.43	0	49.0	Clutch	38	14	1	5	.368

2002 Season

Adam Bernero was called up to the Tigers from Triple-A Toledo on May 21. He promptly turned in two strong performances. But he was not able to sustain his effectiveness. After a string of up and mostly down performances, Bernero was demoted to the bullpen after giving up eight earned runs in 4.2 innings during a mid-July start against Minnesota. Bernero did pick up two victories in relief, but his ERA (5.30) still was high while working out of the bullpen.

Pitching & Defense

Bernero has more than enough in his arsenal to be an effective major league pitcher. He throws in the 92-MPH range with a fastball that has good sinking action. He also has a good breaking ball. His struggles primarily are with consistency. There are times when Bernero loses command of his fastball, falls behind in the count and is hit hard. He pitches as if he is unsure of himself at times.

2003 Outlook

Bernero helped himself last season by showing that he can pitch in relief. There are several young starting pitchers, who either are in the major leagues or knocking on the door, now ahead of Bernero in the Tigers' pecking order. His best chance likely lies in long relief.

Detroit

Jacob Cruz

Position: DH
Bats: L **Throws:** L
Ht: 6' 0" **Wt:** 210

Opening Day Age: 30
Born: 1/28/73 in Oxnard, CA
ML Seasons: 7

Overall Statistics

	G	AB	R	H	D	T	HR	RBI	SB	BB	SO	Avg	OBP	Slg
'02	35	88	12	24	3	1	2	6	3	13	20	.273	.377	.398
Car.	203	455	61	113	20	2	12	59	4	53	118	.248	.337	.380

2002 Situational Stats

	AB	H	HR	RBI	Avg		AB	H	HR	RBI	Avg
Home	31	8	0	1	.258	LHP	10	4	0	1	.400
Road	57	16	2	5	.281	RHP	78	20	2	5	.256
First Half	88	24	2	6	.273	Sc Pos	13	1	0	4	.077
Scnd Half	0	0	0	0	–	Clutch	10	0	0	1	.000

2002 Season

Signed by the Tigers as a minor league free agent during the offseason, Jacob Cruz hit safely in his first six games, batting .364, but that would be the highlight of his season. He played in just 35 games and got just 88 at-bats before his season ended in late June because of bone chips in his left elbow. He already had been on the disabled list for nearly three weeks in June with inflammation in his right knee.

Hitting, Baserunning & Defense

Cruz has some gap power, but that's just about his only asset at this stage of his career. He's mostly successful handling mediocre pitching. Cruz does not run well and his arm strength is average. He is a below-average outfielder defensively.

2003 Outlook

This is not the same player who came up with Cleveland and showed so much promise after he was acquired in a trade from San Francisco in 1998. Since tearing his ACL during the opening month of the 2000 season, the skills have not been there and he has been hurt a lot. Cruz refused a minor league assignment and became a free agent in October, so he's in search of a major league job for 2003.

Shane Halter

Position: SS/3B
Bats: R **Throws:** R
Ht: 6' 0" **Wt:** 180

Opening Day Age: 33
Born: 11/8/69 in LaPlata, MD
ML Seasons: 6

Overall Statistics

	G	AB	R	H	D	T	HR	RBI	SB	BB	SO	Avg	OBP	Slg
'02	122	410	46	98	22	6	10	39	0	39	92	.239	.309	.395
Car.	530	1425	158	367	83	16	29	154	14	112	307	.258	.315	.399

2002 Situational Stats

	AB	H	HR	RBI	Avg		AB	H	HR	RBI	Avg
Home	197	52	4	15	.264	LHP	107	26	2	7	.243
Road	213	46	6	24	.216	RHP	303	72	8	32	.238
First Half	206	52	4	21	.252	Sc Pos	83	18	2	26	.217
Scnd Half	204	46	6	18	.225	Clutch	58	12	1	5	.207

2002 Season

After putting together his best season in 2001 and being rewarded with a two-year, $3.5 million contract, Shane Halter struggled in 2002. He opened the year as the Tigers' regular shortstop, but lost his job to rookie Ramon Santiago in May. In just 81 games at short, Halter made 15 errors. He was not much better at third base with four errors in 30 games. His average fell from .284 in 2001 to .239 in '02, and his RBI total dropped from 65 to 39.

Hitting, Baserunning & Defense

Halter was seemingly heading nowhere until he began showing surprising power in 2001. He no longer is a typical weak-hitting utilityman. He had 51 extra-bases hits in '01 despite playing his home games at spacious Comerica Park. Even last season, when he slumped badly, Halter produced 38 extra-base hits. He plays a lot of positions, but none of them well. He was overmatched at shortstop last season, but he probably is an even worse third baseman. Halter does not run well.

2003 Outlook

Halter does have something to offer as a bench player, but he cannot be used every day at any position without being exposed defensively. He has some power, but is woefully inconsistent as a hitter.

Damian Jackson

Position: 2B
Bats: R **Throws:** R
Ht: 5'11" **Wt:** 185

Opening Day Age: 29
Born: 8/16/73 in Los Angeles, CA
ML Seasons: 7

Overall Statistics

	G	AB	R	H	D	T	HR	RBI	SB	BB	SO	Avg	OBP	Slg
'02	81	245	31	63	20	1	1	25	12	21	36	.257	.320	.359
Car.	512	1627	236	398	97	16	21	149	101	191	393	.245	.328	.363

2002 Situational Stats

	AB	H	HR	RBI	Avg		AB	H	HR	RBI	Avg
Home	109	22	0	10	.202	LHP	60	13	0	7	.217
Road	136	41	1	15	.301	RHP	185	50	1	18	.270
First Half	145	39	1	19	.269	Sc Pos	57	17	0	20	.298
Scnd Half	100	24	0	6	.240	Clutch	41	9	0	6	.220

2002 Season

Used mostly as a utility player, Jackson hit a career-best .257 in 81 games. His season got off to a slow start when he suffered a finger laceration in April while turning a double play at second base, his primary position. At the All-Star break, Jackson was on his way to his best season. He was hitting .269 and playing fairly regularly. After that, however, he got only 100 at-bats as Damion Easley came back from the disabled list and the Tigers called up prospect Omar Infante from Triple-A Toledo in September.

Hitting, Baserunning & Defense

Jackson's best asset is speed. He is capable of driving the ball up the gaps if ahead in the count and he sees a fastball over the heart of the plate. Jackson made better contact at the plate last season. His strikeout rate dropped considerably from 2001. He is a solid infielder who turns the double play well. His best position is second base, though he is capable of playing center field in a pinch.

2003 Outlook

The Tigers released Jackson because of a crowded infield in Detroit, with Easley and Shane Halter still under contract and the emergence of youngsters Infante and Ramon Santiago. Still, Jackson is a good utilityman with above-average speed.

George Lombard

Position: CF/LF
Bats: L **Throws:** R
Ht: 6' 0" **Wt:** 212

Opening Day Age: 27
Born: 9/14/75 in Atlanta, GA
ML Seasons: 4

Overall Statistics

	G	AB	R	H	D	T	HR	RBI	SB	BB	SO	Avg	OBP	Slg
'02	72	241	34	58	11	3	5	13	13	20	78	.241	.300	.373
Car.	111	292	45	66	11	3	6	16	20	22	95	.226	.284	.346

2002 Situational Stats

	AB	H	HR	RBI	Avg		AB	H	HR	RBI	Avg
Home	121	31	2	7	.256	LHP	33	5	0	2	.152
Road	120	27	3	6	.225	RHP	208	53	5	11	.255
First Half	50	15	2	5	.300	Sc Pos	36	7	0	6	.194
Scnd Half	191	43	3	8	.225	Clutch	34	5	0	1	.147

2002 Season

George Lombard began last season on the disabled list with Atlanta because of a strained right calf muscle. He went on a two-plus week rehab assignment in the minors before being traded to Detroit in exchange for minor league pitcher Kris Keller on June 19. After a slow start both at the plate and in the field, Lombard did well in July and August before fading in September.

Hitting, Baserunning & Defense

Lombard is strong, fast and athletic. The problem has been not translating that athleticism into baseball skills. He will hit the ball a mile one at-bat and not even come close to making contact the next. He will make a spectacular catch in the outfield, then take a bad route to a ball. At 27, and after nine seasons of pro baseball, Lombard still is a raw talent who needs to be more consistent and refined in every way.

2003 Outlook

Lombard will be given every opportunity to win a regular job, perhaps in center field. He started 40 games there and proved to be adequate, at least by the standards of the Tigers, who have struggled to fill that spot since the mid-1990s. His primary competition will come from trade acquisition Gene Kingsale and untested rookie Andres Torres.

Wendell Magee

Position: CF
Bats: R **Throws:** R
Ht: 6' 0" **Wt:** 227

Opening Day Age: 30
Born: 8/3/72 in
Hattiesburg, MS
ML Seasons: 7
Pronunciation:
muh-GHEE

Overall Statistics

	G	AB	R	H	D	T	HR	RBI	SB	BB	SO	Avg	OBP	Slg
'02	97	347	34	94	19	1	6	35	2	10	64	.271	.289	.383
Car.	386	1086	120	268	52	8	24	122	7	69	204	.247	.291	.376

2002 Situational Stats

	AB	H	HR	RBI	Avg		AB	H	HR	RBI	Avg
Home	161	47	3	20	.292	LHP	89	21	1	6	.236
Road	186	47	3	15	.253	RHP	258	73	5	29	.283
First Half	282	76	6	28	.270	Sc Pos	69	19	1	26	.275
Scnd Half	65	18	0	7	.277	Clutch	63	16	1	10	.254

2002 Season

Wendell Magee had his best season in the majors, reaching career bests in most offensive departments and starting more games in center field than any other Detroit player. He was hitting above .300 through June 18, but slumped the remainder of the season as the Tigers began looking at George Lombard and Hiram Bocachica in center field. Magee missed most of September because of surgery on his right big toe.

Hitting, Baserunning & Defense

Magee's skills are all average or below average. He does not run well enough to be the everyday center fielder on a good team. Patience at the plate is a problem. Magee walked just 10 times in 364 plate appearances last season. He is not that sure-handed with the balls he reaches. Magee makes more than his share of errors for an outfielder.

2003 Outlook

When his playing time shrank last season, Magee complained that he is tired of being labeled a fourth outfielder. But he is going to have to accept his role as a backup and play well when given a chance. There isn't a market for middle-aged players with a .247 lifetime batting average who do not realize their role. Magee was outrighted to the minor leagues following the season.

Dean Palmer

Position: DH
Bats: R **Throws:** R
Ht: 6' 1" **Wt:** 219

Opening Day Age: 34
Born: 12/27/68 in
Tallahassee, FL
ML Seasons: 13

Overall Statistics

G	AB	R	H	D	T	HR	RBI	SB	BB	SO	Avg	OBP	Slg
4	12	0	0	0	0	0	0	0	1	5	.000	.077	.000
1331	4816	731	1217	229	15	275	843	48	493	1304	.253	.326	.478

2002 Situational Stats

	AB	H	HR	RBI	Avg		AB	H	HR	RBI	Avg
Home	7	0	0	0	.000	LHP	7	0	0	0	.000
Road	5	0	0	0	.000	RHP	5	0	0	0	.000
First Half	12	0	0	0	.000	Sc Pos	1	0	0	0	.000
Scnd Half	0	0	0	0	–	Clutch	3	0	0	0	.000

2002 Season

It was the second nightmare season in a row for Dean Palmer because of ongoing problems with his throwing shoulder. He had surgery in July 2001 with the idea he definitely would be ready for spring training, but he was not. Every time Palmer thought he was ready, he would suffer another setback, including a neck injury. He began last season on the disabled list, and on April 14, just seven days after he was removed from the DL, Palmer went back on and did not play again.

Hitting, Baserunning & Defense

Even before the shoulder ailment, Palmer was a below-average third baseman defensively. Now there are concerns whether he will ever be able to play the position again. While he has played some first base in the past and could DH, the team has three first basemen, Carlos Pena, Eric Munson and Dmitri Young, already vying for at-bats. Palmer has established himself as a genuine power hitter. He strikes out too much, but has a live bat.

2003 Outlook

This is the final year of a five-year, $36 million contract. Palmer would be difficult to unload, so the Tigers would love to take advantage of his powerful bat and leadership in the clubhouse. The question is finding Palmer a position.

Craig Paquette

Position: 3B/1B
Bats: R **Throws:** R
Ht: 6' 0" **Wt:** 190

Opening Day Age: 34
Born: 3/28/69 in Long Beach, CA
ML Seasons: 10
Pronunciation: paw-KET

Overall Statistics

	G	AB	R	H	D	T	HR	RBI	SB	BB	SO	Avg	OBP	Slg
'02	72	252	20	49	14	1	4	20	1	10	53	.194	.223	.306
Car.	803	2558	302	615	128	10	99	377	27	120	615	.240	.275	.414

2002 Situational Stats

	AB	H	HR	RBI	Avg		AB	H	HR	RBI	Avg
Home	123	23	0	7	.187	LHP	59	16	0	3	.271
Road	129	26	4	13	.202	RHP	193	33	4	17	.171
First Half	182	37	4	18	.203	Sc Pos	55	11	1	15	.200
Scnd Half	70	12	0	2	.171	Clutch	38	9	1	3	.237

2002 Season

Signed to a two-year, $5 million contract in December 2002, Craig Paquette was expected to be a consistent contributor. Forced to open the season at third instead of the outfield, Paquette struggled. His batting average fell 88 points from 2001, and he made eight errors in 49 games at third. From June 27 until the end of the season, he had no homers and two RBI in 93 at-bats.

Hitting, Baserunning & Defense

Paquette has reached double figures in home runs six times in his major league career. But with the fences at Comerica Park so deep in left and center fields, he was totally overmatched by the size of his home stadium. He isn't patient and swings at too many pitches out of the strike zone. He also lacks the soft hands, good arm and range needed at third base. Paquette is better in the outfield, where he gets a decent jump, throws to the right base and is surehanded, although his lack of speed and arm strength are problems.

2003 Outlook

In the right situation, Paquette can be a valuable player. But he has to be a role player, which the Tigers found out the hard way. The one plus tool Paquette had going into last season was his bat, but now that is in question.

Ramon Santiago

Position: SS
Bats: B **Throws:** R
Ht: 5'11" **Wt:** 150

Opening Day Age: 23
Born: 8/31/79 in Las Matas de Farfan, DR
ML Seasons: 1

Overall Statistics

	G	AB	R	H	D	T	HR	RBI	SB	BB	SO	Avg	OBP	Slg
'02	65	222	33	54	5	5	4	20	8	13	48	.243	.306	.365
Car.	65	222	33	54	5	5	4	20	8	13	48	.243	.306	.365

2002 Situational Stats

	AB	H	HR	RBI	Avg		AB	H	HR	RBI	Avg
Home	120	26	3	8	.217	LHP	54	12	0	2	.222
Road	102	28	1	12	.275	RHP	168	42	4	18	.250
First Half	165	41	4	17	.248	Sc Pos	48	11	0	16	.229
Scnd Half	57	13	0	3	.228	Clutch	37	14	2	6	.378

2002 Season

After a quick start in the minors in 2002, Ramon Santiago caught the eye of Tigers officials, who were not pleased with the play of regular shortstop Shane Halter. That elicited a call for Santiago. He hit above .300 through May, but was not nearly as effective the remainder of the season. He missed five weeks in July and August because of a fractured right hamate bone.

Hitting, Baserunning & Defense

Santiago spent all of 2001 as a designated hitter for high Class-A Lakeland after surgery to repair a torn labrum late in the 2000 season. At one time, he had an exceptionally strong arm, but he needed to relearn his throwing mechanics following the surgery. His arm was adequate last season, but still is a long-range concern. Santiago has good range in the field and makes the routine play well. As a hitter, he has more power from the left side, but does not walk enough. Santiago has average speed for a major league middle infielder.

2003 Outlook

As long as Damion Easley still is with the Tigers, Santiago will have to battle with Omar Infante for playing time. If Easley goes, Infante will move to second base and Santiago will be the shortstop.

Jason Beverlin (Pos: RHP, Age: 29)

	W	L	Pct.	ERA	G	GS	Sv	IP	H	BB	SO	HR	Ratio
'02	0	3	.000	8.69	7	3	0	19.2	27	9	16	3	1.83
Car.	0	3	.000	8.69	7	3	0	19.2	27	9	16	3	1.83

Beverlin started the year with Cleveland's Triple-A Buffalo, pitching well in the rotation. After struggling in the majors, he was claimed off waivers by Detroit in July, but the Tribe has re-signed him. 2003 Outlook: C

Hiram Bocachica (Pos: CF/LF, Age: 27, Bats: R)

	G	AB	R	H	D	T	HR	RBI	SB	BB	SO	Avg	OBP	Slg
'02	83	168	26	37	7	0	8	17	3	10	41	.220	.264	.405
Car.	166	311	43	71	18	1	10	26	7	19	76	.228	.275	.389

Part-timer Bocachica showed a bit of a power surge between Los Angeles and Detroit last summer, but he still doesn't hit for average or draw walks, the two things he needs to do to play more. 2003 Outlook: C

Eric Eckenstahler (Pos: LHP, Age: 26)

	W	L	Pct.	ERA	G	GS	Sv	IP	H	BB	SO	HR	Ratio
'02	1	0	1.000	5.63	7	0	0	8.0	14	2	13	1	2.00
Car.	1	0	1.000	5.63	7	0	0	8.0	14	2	13	1	2.00

Eckenstahler was fine at Triple-A Toledo, though high walk numbers still plague him. He wasn't bad in Detroit, either, taking a couple of beatings that make the numbers look much worse. 2003 Outlook: C

Jeff Farnsworth (Pos: RHP, Age: 27)

	W	L	Pct.	ERA	G	GS	Sv	IP	H	BB	SO	HR	Ratio
'02	2	3	.400	5.79	44	0	0	70.0	100	29	28	6	1.84
Car.	2	3	.400	5.79	44	0	0	70.0	100	29	28	6	1.84

Farnsworth was a Double-A starter in 2001, but worked out of the Tigers' pen in '02 as a Rule 5 pickup. He posted a 1.80 ERA in May, but walks and too many hittable pitches were a year-long problem for him. 2003 Outlook: C

Seth Greisinger (Pos: RHP, Age: 27)

	W	L	Pct.	ERA	G	GS	Sv	IP	H	BB	SO	HR	Ratio
'02	2	2	.500	6.21	8	8	0	37.2	46	13	14	4	1.57
Car.	8	11	.421	5.37	29	29	0	167.2	188	61	80	21	1.49

Greisinger was a legit Tigers prospect before arm woes, including Tommy John surgery in 1999, sidetracked his career. He reached the majors again in 2002, but a tender shoulder was an issue. 2003 Outlook: C

Oscar Henriquez (Pos: RHP, Age: 29)

	W	L	Pct.	ERA	G	GS	Sv	IP	H	BB	SO	HR	Ratio
'02	1	1	.500	4.50	30	0	2	28.0	19	15	23	5	1.21
Car.	1	2	.333	6.06	49	0	2	52.0	47	30	45	9	1.48

Henriquez looked like a budding closer five years ago in the Houston system. He has struggled, but has a chance to stick in Detroit after 2002. Then he had arthroscopic elbow surgery for bone chips, though he should be ready in the spring. 2003 Outlook: C

Ryan Jackson (Pos: LF, Age: 31, Bats: L)

	G	AB	R	H	D	T	HR	RBI	SB	BB	SO	Avg	OBP	Slg
'02	4	6	0	2	1	1	0	0	0	1	2	.333	.429	.833
Car.	226	452	49	108	23	4	7	52	7	32	120	.239	.292	.354

Jackson got the call in June when Bobby Higginson was injured. Jackson's power and walks were down in Triple-A ball in 2002. He signed a minor league deal with the Rays in November. 2003 Outlook: C

Jason Jimenez (Pos: LHP, Age: 27)

	W	L	Pct.	ERA	G	GS	Sv	IP	H	BB	SO	HR	Ratio
'02	0	0	–	7.36	6	0	0	7.1	12	2	5	2	1.91
Car.	0	0	–	7.36	6	0	0	7.1	12	2	5	2	1.91

Jimenez was effective at Triple-A Durham for the Rays, but he was lost to the Tigers on waivers during the last week of the 2002 season. The lefty is in the 2003 mix to work in Detroit's bullpen. 2003 Outlook: C

Kris Keller (Pos: RHP, Age: 25)

	W	L	Pct.	ERA	G	GS	Sv	IP	H	BB	SO	HR	Ratio
'02	0	0	–	27.00	1	0	0	1.0	2	3	1	1	5.00
Car.	0	0	–	27.00	1	0	0	1.0	2	3	1	1	5.00

The young righthander reached Triple-A Toledo in 2001 and was better there in 2002. The Tigers dealt him to Atlanta for George Lombard in June, and Keller continued his tutoring at Triple-A Richmond. 2003 Outlook: C

Jose Lima (Pos: RHP, Age: 30)

	W	L	Pct.	ERA	G	GS	Sv	IP	H	BB	SO	HR	Ratio
'02	4	6	.400	7.77	20	12	0	68.1	86	21	33	12	1.57
Car.	63	74	.460	5.14	262	161	5	1138.0	1281	262	763	193	1.36

Moving to the spacious new Comerica Park from Houston didn't exactly turn Lima's career around. That may not bode well for his career. The Tigers gave up, releasing him in early September. 2003 Outlook: C

Shane Loux (Pos: RHP, Age: 23)

	W	L	Pct.	ERA	G	GS	Sv	IP	H	BB	SO	HR	Ratio
'02	0	3	.000	9.00	3	3	0	14.0	19	3	7	4	1.57
Car.	0	3	.000	9.00	3	3	0	14.0	19	3	7	4	1.57

Loux had his elbow cleaned out before the 2001 season, his first at Triple-A Toledo, and he's gone 21-21 (5.24) since then. The velocity and numbers were a bit better in 2002, so there's some hope. 2003 Outlook: C

Mitch Meluskey (Pos: C, Age: 29, Bats: B)

	G	AB	R	H	D	T	HR	RBI	SB	BB	SO	Avg	OBP	Slg
'02	8	27	3	6	0	0	0	1	0	5	3	.222	.353	.222
Car.	143	405	55	116	23	0	15	73	2	66	87	.286	.390	.454

His catching was nothing special, but Meluskey's bat was very enticing. Serious injuries wiped out two of the last three years, but the A's have signed him to a minor league deal. 2003 Outlook: C

Matt Miller (Pos: LHP, Age: 28)

	W	L	Pct.	ERA	G	GS	Sv	IP	H	BB	SO	HR	Ratio
'02	0	0	–	13.50	2	0	0	0.2	4	1	1	1	7.50
Car.	0	0	–	7.84	15	0	0	10.1	20	5	7	1	2.42

Miller had rotator cuff surgery in April and missed nearly the entire season. He had a chance to be a lefty in the Tigers' pen, but he now takes his game to Colorado after signing a minor league deal. 2003 Outlook: C

Craig Monroe (Pos: RF, Age: 26, Bats: R)

	G	AB	R	H	D	T	HR	RBI	SB	BB	SO	Avg	OBP	Slg
'02	13	25	3	3	1	0	1	1	0	0	5	.120	.154	.280
Car.	40	77	11	14	2	0	3	6	2	6	23	.182	.250	.325

Monroe has had solid seasons in Triple-A ball two years in a row, but he hasn't been the same hitter during a handful of callups over that span. He has a last chance to be part of the rebuilding. 2003 Outlook: C

Jose Paniagua (Pos: RHP, Age: 29)

	W	L	Pct.	ERA	G	GS	Sv	IP	H	BB	SO	HR	Ratio
'02	0	1	.000	5.83	41	0	1	41.2	50	15	34	10	1.56
Car.	18	21	.462	4.39	269	14	13	356.2	351	187	276	40	1.51

Dealt by the M's to Colorado last December, Paniagua never pitched in Denver, thanks to a March trade to Detroit. He still pitched like he was there, issuing 10 homers in 41.2 frames before his release. 2003 Outlook: C

Danny Patterson (Pos: RHP, Age: 32)

	W	L	Pct.	ERA	G	GS	Sv	IP	H	BB	SO	HR	Ratio
'02	0	2	.000	15.00	6	0	0	3.0	5	2	1	0	2.33
Car.	24	18	.571	4.07	294	0	4	325.0	359	92	207	27	1.39

Back pain was a problem in spring training, and a tender elbow developed the first week of the season. Patterson had Tommy John surgery in late June and may not resurface until 2004. 2003 Outlook: C

Terry Pearson (Pos: RHP, Age: 31)

	W	L	Pct.	ERA	G	GS	Sv	IP	H	BB	SO	HR	Ratio
'02	0	0	–	10.50	4	0	0	6.0	8	2	4	2	1.67
Car.	0	0	–	10.50	4	0	0	6.0	8	2	4	2	1.67

Pearson made his major league debut at age 30 when he made the Tigers out of spring training. He was gone before the month was out, but pitched OK in the high minors as an indy-league signee. 2003 Outook: C

Matt Perisho (Pos: LHP, Age: 27)

	W	L	Pct.	ERA	G	GS	Sv	IP	H	BB	SO	HR	Ratio
'02	0	0	–	8.71	5	0	0	10.1	16	6	3	2	2.13
Car.	4	14	.222	7.07	86	28	0	215.0	288	125	150	35	1.92

Perisho adapted well to a move to the bullpen over the last two summers of Triple-A ball. But in neither year did the success follow him to Detroit. The Rays have signed him to a minor league deal. 2003 Outlook: C

Brian Powell (Pos: RHP, Age: 29)

	W	L	Pct.	ERA	G	GS	Sv	IP	H	BB	SO	HR	Ratio
'02	1	5	.167	4.84	13	9	0	57.2	64	21	30	11	1.47
Car.	6	15	.286	5.94	41	31	0	175.2	204	73	93	37	1.58

Powell won 10 games and pitched decently at Triple-A Toledo, but he didn't dominate hitters, and that certainly was the case in Detroit as well. Lefties slugged .569 off him. 2003 Outlook: C

Erik Sabel (Pos: RHP, Age: 28)

	W	L	Pct.	ERA	G	GS	Sv	IP	H	BB	SO	HR	Ratio
'02	0	0	–	–	1	0	0	0.0	2	0	0	1	–
Car.	3	2	.600	5.02	50	0	0	61.0	71	18	31	10	1.46

Sabel looked like he was heading back to the majors with a solid 2001 at Arizona's Triple-A Tucson. He wasn't as effective at Tucson or Triple-A Toledo in 2002, and he didn't get anyone out in Detroit. 2003 Outlook: C

Oscar Salazar (Pos: 2B, Age: 24, Bats: R)

	G	AB	R	H	D	T	HR	RBI	SB	BB	SO	Avg	OBP	Slg
'02	8	21	2	4	1	0	1	3	0	1	2	.190	.227	.381
Car.	8	21	2	4	1	0	1	3	0	1	2	.190	.227	.381

Salazar was in the A's system until Detroit claimed him off waivers in January 2002. The Mets did the same last July, and Salazar didn't hit much between Double-A tenures with the Tigers and Mets. 2003 Outlook: C

Julio Santana (Pos: RHP, Age: 29)

	W	L	Pct.	ERA	G	GS	Sv	IP	H	BB	SO	HR	Ratio
'02	3	5	.375	2.84	38	0	0	57.0	49	28	38	8	1.35
Car.	14	26	.350	5.33	161	42	0	428.2	476	204	255	63	1.59

Santana enjoyed his best major league season in 2002, mostly because he wasn't throttled by the longball for the first time in his career. The big question is, can he do it again? Tough call. 2003 Outlook: C

Matt Walbeck (Pos: C, Age: 33, Bats: B)

	G	AB	R	H	D	T	HR	RBI	SB	BB	SO	Avg	OBP	Slg
'02	27	85	4	20	2	0	0	3	0	3	14	.235	.258	.259
Car.	623	1971	204	468	75	4	27	202	13	130	317	.237	.286	.321

Walbeck might have hit below the Mendoza line if not for a 10-for-20 stretch (.500) in August. He's the favorite to back up starter Brandon Inge behind the plate after re-signing with the Tigers. 2003 Outlook: C

Jamie Walker (Pos: LHP, Age: 31)

	W	L	Pct.	ERA	G	GS	Sv	IP	H	BB	SO	HR	Ratio
'02	1	1	.500	3.71	57	0	1	43.2	32	9	40	9	0.94
Car.	4	5	.444	5.45	113	2	1	104.0	108	32	79	20	1.35

The southpaw began a move to the bullpen in 2001 playing Triple-A ball. Walker was even better working strictly in relief last summer. He gave up lots of homers, but the strikeout-walk ratio was good. 2003 Outlook: C

Detroit Tigers Minor League Prospects

Organization Overview:

Trading 25-year-old ace Jeff Weaver was controversial, but the Tigers spruced up their system by acquiring prospects Carlos Pena, Jeremy Bonderman and Franklyn German. They picked up an everyday player, a potential rotation stud and a budding closer in the deal. Pena and German should provide immediate assistance to the rebuilding Tigers, as should young-sters Nate Cornejo, Andy Van Hekken, Fernando Rodney, Jason Jimenez, Ramon Santiago, Omar Infante, Brandon Inge and Eric Munson. Instant success may not be in the cards, but most of these young players should eventually contribute. Looking beyond 2003, more young pitching may follow, with prospects Bonderman, Preston Larrison and Kenny Baugh expected to anchor an impressive Double-A rotation.

Jeremy Bonderman

Position: P **Opening Day Age:** 20
Bats: R **Throws:** R **Born:** 10/28/82 in
Ht: 6' 1" **Wt:** 210 Kennewick, WA

Recent Statistics

	W	L	ERA	G	GS	Sv	IP	H	R	BB	SO	HR
2002 A Modesto	9	8	3.61	25	25	0	144.2	129	77	55	160	15
2002 A Lakeland	0	1	6.00	2	2	0	12.0	11	8	4	10	3

The former Oakland pick was named in the Jeff Weaver trade in August, a little more than a year after getting his GED as a high school junior in order to be eligible for the 2001 draft. With his low-90s heat, a hard break-ing pitch and an above-average changeup, Bonderman enjoyed an impressive debut for someone so young and inexperienced in the high Class-A California League. He immediately demonstrated solid command of his offerings and a good feel for pitching that allowed him to succeed against more advanced hitters. His package of skills suggests a very high ceiling. He'll head to Double-A Erie, and if he adjusts quickly to the higher level, he might make a mad dash to Detroit.

Nate Cornejo

Position: P **Opening Day Age:** 23
Bats: R **Throws:** R **Born:** 9/24/79 in
Ht: 6' 5" **Wt:** 240 Wellington, KS

Recent Statistics

	W	L	ERA	G	GS	Sv	IP	H	R	BB	SO	HR
2002 AL Detroit	1	5	5.04	9	9	0	50.0	63	33	18	23	6
2002 AAA Toledo	9	8	4.42	21	20	0	132.1	163	72	31	86	11

A supplemental first-round pick in 1998, Cornejo reached Double-A Jacksonville in 2000, exhibiting good command of an 89-92 MPH sinker that he mixed effectively with a plus breaking pitch. His velocity crept upward in his breakout 2001 season, when he was 16-3 (2.57) in the high minors, but the key to his suc-cess was the movement and location of both pitches. Both have life and can be difficult to control. He was-n't able to establish himself in the Detroit rotation last spring, and his troubles continued at Toledo. While Cornejo excelled at making his own adjustments to hit-ters and situations in 2001, his confidence suffered in '02. He must avoid trying to overpower hitters. When he attempts to get a little extra on his pitches, they lose sinking action and movement.

Franklyn German

Position: P **Opening Day Age:** 23
Bats: R **Throws:** R **Born:** 1/20/80 in San
Ht: 6' 4" **Wt:** 265 Cristobal, DR

Recent Statistics

	W	L	ERA	G	GS	Sv	IP	H	R	BB	SO	HR
2002 AA Midland	1	1	3.05	37	0	16	41.1	28	14	27	59	0
2002 AAA Toledo	1	1	1.59	23	0	13	22.2	15	4	7	31	0
2002 AL Detroit	1	0	0.00	7	0	1	6.2	3	0	2	6	0

Signed at age 16 by the A's in 1996, the 6-foot-4 German was a slender kid, but he's beefed up and now has a big frame that is ideal for his power stuff. He debuted that stuff with seven scoreless appearances for Detroit last September, just two months after being dealt to the Tigers in the Jeff Weaver trade. He can turn up the heat to 96-99 MPH and overpower hitters—as he did so well at Triple-A Toledo—and he also throws a nasty splitter with late action and an occasional slider. The slider could be a little more consistent, but other-wise, German is ready to grab a spot in the Detroit bullpen, where he will gain the experience that may lead to closer duties soon.

Omar Infante

Position: SS **Opening Day Age:** 21
Bats: R **Throws:** R **Born:** 12/26/81 in Puerto
Ht: 5' 9" **Wt:** 150 la Cruz, VZ

Recent Statistics

	G	AB	R	H	D	T	HR	RBI	SB	BB	SO	Avg
2002 AAA Toledo	120	436	49	117	16	8	4	51	19	28	49	.268
2002 AL Detroit	18	72	4	24	3	0	1	6	0	3	10	.333

Despite perennially being one of the youngest players in his league, in 2001 Infante was a disciplined hitter who manipulated his little-ball skills successfully at Double-A Erie. He got away from that approach last spring at Triple-A Toledo, but Syracuse manager Jose Malave, who had managed him in winter ball, told him to stop trying to pull pitches and focus on small ball. He improved in the second half and made a strong first impression in Detroit in September. Infante, a leader who is very instinctive on the diamond, is ready to take over at short in Detroit, with his great range and strong arm. He can be special if he draws more walks, perfects his little-ball skills and learns major league pitchers.

Eric Munson

Position: 1B
Bats: L **Throws:** R
Ht: 6' 3" **Wt:** 228

Opening Day Age: 25
Born: 10/3/77 in San
Diego, CA

Recent Statistics

	G	AB	R	H	D	T	HR	RBI	SB	BB	SO	Avg
2002 AAA Toledo	136	477	77	125	30	4	24	84	1	77	114	.262
2002 AL Detroit	18	59	3	11	0	0	2	5	0	6	11	.186

Munson was drafted third overall in 1999 for his power potential. He has an exceptionally quick bat, but a tendency to get pull-happy was an issue at Double-A Jacksonville in 2000 and during a brutal start at Triple-A Toledo in 2002. Munson also struggled with offspeed stuff and being pitched around as Toledo's key power threat. He was batting .192 through May, and former Tiger Al Kaline worked with him on his approach, emphasizing the need to drive pitches to all fields and to be selective and accept the walk. Munson enjoyed a strong second half. His strikeout-walk ratio was better than it was at Double-A Erie in 2001, signs of a more selective approach and a willingness to make adjustments. Munson was drafted as a catcher and has become an adequate first baseman, but he's being tried at third base in winter ball.

Fernando Rodney

Position: P
Bats: R **Throws:** R
Ht: 5' 11" **Wt:** 170

Opening Day Age: 26
Born: 3/18/77 in
Samana, DR

Recent Statistics

	W	L	ERA	G	GS	Sv	IP	H	R	BB	SO	HR
2002 AA Erie	1	0	1.33	21	0	11	20.1	14	4	5	18	0
2002 AL Detroit	1	3	6.00	20	0	0	18.0	25	15	10	10	2
2002 AAA Toledo	1	1	0.81	20	0	4	22.1	13	4	9	25	1

The hard-throwing Rodney was signed five years ago. A knock on him is that his fastball comes in straight, but it reaches the high 90s. And when Rodney's on, it doesn't matter if it's straight. His changeup came a long way in 2001, and both of his secondary pitches—his slider and particularly the changeup—were better in 2002. The key to all of his pitches is consistently using them effectively in the strike zone. Rodney's days as a starter are over. His future is in the pen, most likely as a setup man, or possibly as a closer.

Andres Torres

Position: OF
Bats: B **Throws:** R
Ht: 5' 10" **Wt:** 175

Opening Day Age: 25
Born: 1/26/78 in
Aguada, PR

Recent Statistics

	G	AB	R	H	D	T	HR	RBI	SB	BB	SO	Avg
2002 AAA Toledo	115	462	80	123	17	8	4	42	42	53	116	.266
2002 AL Detroit	19	70	7	14	1	1	0	3	2	6	16	.200

Growing up in Puerto Rico, the speedy Torres spent far more time on a running track than a baseball diamond, and since his fourth-round selection in 1998, he's exhibited a rawness that he's still refining. While his instincts are OK but not great, he's probably the hardest worker in the system. Torres is small but strong, and he can play the small-ball game, stroking liners, laying down bunts and working counts. He must focus on making more consistent contact. He has the capability to be a solid defender with his speed, but his reads and jumps still need work. If he can develop into a leadoff type who makes things happen, he could be the long-term answer in center field.

Andy Van Hekken

Position: P
Bats: R **Throws:** L
Ht: 6' 3" **Wt:** 175

Opening Day Age: 23
Born: 7/31/79 in Holland,
MI

Recent Statistics

	W	L	ERA	G	GS	Sv	IP	H	R	BB	SO	HR
2002 AA Erie	4	7	3.83	21	21	0	134.0	138	69	34	97	10
2002 AAA Toledo	5	0	1.82	7	7	0	49.1	41	14	11	19	4
2002 AL Detroit	1	3	3.00	5	5	0	30.0	38	13	6	5	2

While Fernando Rodney has relied mostly on heat, Van Hekken has called on poise, pitch movement, command and a competitive nature to climb the ladder. He's never dominated, but he makes the most of his stuff. Van Hekken's very effective with both his tailing fastball and curveball, and he commands the outer half of the strike zone successfully. He works inside as well, though mostly to keep hitters from focusing on the outside half. While he's mostly worked in the high 80s with his fastball, he was throwing 90-91 MPH in the spring before his velocity dropped off late in the year. Working on his conditioning during the offseason might counter a tendency to wear down. His changeup still needs work, but soon he'll get the chance to prove his stuff can retire major league hitters.

Others to Watch

Rigthander **Kenny Baugh** (24) showed solid command, good life on his fastball and effective arm action on his changeup after signing as Detroit's first-round pick in 2001. He worked a lot of innings that year and developed shoulder soreness that led to surgery last June. He didn't pitch in 2002, but Baugh should be ready for Double-A Erie in 2003. . . . A second-round pick in 2001, righthander **Preston Larrison** (22) called on a solid fastball with life and a good changeup to go 10-5 (2.39) at high Class-A Lakeland last summer. He takes his good command to Double-A Erie in 2003. . . . His tools aren't overwhelming, but **Cody Ross** (22) is a scrappy, Craig Biggio-type hitter with great instincts and a good arm in the outfield. He's not a big guy, but he has gap-to-gap power and hit his share of homers in a .280-19-72 season at Double-A Erie. . . . Second baseman **Michael Woods** (22), who posted a .393 OBP between two Class-A stops as a first-year pro in 2001, injured a knee in 2002 at high Class-A Lakeland. By year's end, he had arthroscopic procedures performed on both knees and lost most of a year of development. He should be ready to play in the spring.

Detroit

143

Ewing M. Kauffman Stadium

Offense

The lowering and moving in of outfield fences in 1995 have made Kauffman Stadium one of the most offense-friendly parks in baseball. Exceptional sight lines increase batting averages and help reduce strikeouts, while summer heat makes sure the ball carries well. The park positively influences nearly every aspect of offense. Recent additions of luxury boxes between the dugouts have reduced foul popups. Meanwhile, the deep center field adds triples and forces center fielders to play deep, increasing the number of singles hit in front of them—speedy outfielders are a must at Kauffman. While it's a symmetrical park, righthanded power hitters are aided by usually having a favorable wind towards left field.

Defense

Kauffman Stadium always has displayed some of the most immaculate field conditions in the game, giving infielders few bad-hop grounders. The slight angles of the outfield walls at the foul poles often turn singles into triples when the ball hugs the wall to scoot past unwary outfielders.

Who It Helps the Most

Nearly all hitters enjoy Kauffman, but especially those who pull the ball for power and those who hit line drives up the middle. Carlos Beltran and Mark Quinn are positively affected. Pitchers must keep the ball down to be successful.

Who It Hurts the Most

Power pitchers are hurt by the tendency of the ball to carry well, especially in the summertime. Those who work high in the strike zone will give up too many home runs to win consistently in Kansas City. Blake Stein *really* struggled at home with the Royals.

Rookies & Newcomers

Pitchers who rely on hard stuff, like Runelvys Hernandez and Ryan Bukvich, have to keep the ball down to succeed. The park will have less negative effects upon finesse pitchers like Chris George. It will help both Angel Berroa's batting average and Brandon Berger's power. Berroa's infield glovework will fare well at "The K."

Dimensions: LF-330, LCF-375, CF-400, RCF-375, RF-330

Capacity: 40,793

Elevation: 750 feet

Surface: Grass

Foul Territory: Average

Park Factors

2002 Season

	Home Games Royals	Opp	Total	Away Games Royals	Opp	Total	Index
G	72	72	144	72	72	144	
Avg	.272	.291	.282	.236	.266	.251	112
AB	2466	2637	5103	2444	2397	4841	105
R	372	433	805	276	347	623	129
H	671	767	1438	577	638	1215	118
2B	132	159	291	114	130	244	113
3B	23	14	37	16	16	32	110
HR	75	109	184	47	84	131	133
BB	236	243	479	229	244	473	96
SO	339	399	738	475	437	912	77
E	52	55	107	62	42	104	103
E-Infield	43	49	92	51	37	88	105
LHB-Avg	.272	.296	.284	.230	.267	.248	114
LHB-HR	36	49	85	24	36	60	134
RHB-Avg	.272	.286	.280	.241	.265	.253	110
RHB-HR	39	60	99	23	48	71	133

2000-2002

	Home Games Royals	Opp	Total	Away Games Royals	Opp	Total	Index
G	216	216	432	216	216	432	
Avg	.283	.291	.287	.258	.267	.262	109
AB	7442	7827	15269	7550	7140	14690	104
R	1120	1296	2416	970	1086	2056	118
H	2104	2279	4383	1946	1905	3851	114
2B	373	438	811	368	361	729	107
3B	60	50	110	41	42	83	128
HR	217	313	530	170	282	452	113
BB	628	791	1419	637	840	1477	92
SO	1039	1248	2287	1306	1191	2497	88
E	155	173	328	151	173	324	101
E-Infield	126	144	270	121	155	276	98
LHB-Avg	.280	.291	.287	.247	.268	.259	111
LHB-HR	64	151	215	65	132	197	104
RHB-Avg	.284	.291	.287	.264	.265	.265	109
RHB-HR	153	162	315	105	150	255	119

2002 Rankings (American League)

- Highest batting-average factor
- Highest run factor
- Highest hit factor
- Highest LHB batting-average factor
- Highest LHB home-run factor
- Second-highest RHB batting-average factor
- Second-highest RHB home-run factor
- Lowest strikeout factor

Tony Pena

2002 Season

The search for a new manager was short following Tony Muser's firing a month into last season. Royals GM Allard Baird got his first choice a few weeks later. Genial and approachable, Tony Pena quickly lived up to his reputation as a player's manager, providing a steadying influence on the team's younger members. Pena showed a strong developmental approach when handling youngsters, while leaving the veterans in familiar roles.

Offense

Pena is a firm believer in the value of speed. He prefers to force the issue, pressuring the defense by constantly using the hit-and-run and stealing bases. He's willing to take chances on the bases, and everybody is expected to participate in an aggressive running game. Pena showed a developmental style as he worked youngsters into the lineup carefully. Veterans are expected to play their way out of slumps. But Pena will briefly remove a struggling youngster to provide instruction, and then re-insert him a day later. He prefers set lineups with veterans who have well-defined roles, but otherwise uses platoon advantages.

Pitching & Defense

Tasked with helping develop the Royals' young rotation, Pena handled the younger starters carefully, limiting innings and stretching off-day schedules to prevent overuse. Only Paul Byrd regularly pitched deep into games. Pena tried to have youngsters leave on a high note instead of yanking them after they got into trouble. He prefers specific bullpen roles, including a definitive closer. He rarely uses pitchouts, preferring instead to defuse big innings by using an intentional walk to set up a double play.

2003 Outlook

Little is expected of a Royals team coming off the franchise's worst record, especially a club having many new faces and players in new roles. Focused upon rebuilding the team around its young rotation, they also hope to develop a closer from within, and Pena will be challenged to solve the second-base problem. Newcomers will be expected to adapt their existing talents to the club's pitching, speed and defensive approach.

Born: 6/04/57 in Monte Cristi, Dominican Republic

Playing Experience: 1980-1997, Pit, StL, Bos, Cle, CWS, Hou

Managerial Experience: 1 season

Manager Statistics

Year	Team, Lg	W	L	Pct	GB	Finish
2002	Kansas City, AL	49	77	.389	32.5	4th Central
1 Season		49	77	.389	–	–

2002 Starting Pitchers by Days Rest

	<=3	4	5	6+
Royals Starts	0	73	22	25
Royals ERA	–	5.05	5.24	6.21
AL Avg Starts	1	83	44	24
AL ERA	7.15	4.59	4.27	5.03

2002 Situational Stats

	Tony Pena	AL Average
Hit & Run Success %	38.0	36.0
Stolen Base Success %	65.0	68.1
Platoon Pct.	66.0	58.9
Defensive Subs	10	23
High-Pitch Outings	7	6
Quick/Slow Hooks	21/13	19/14
Sacrifice Attempts	58	53

2002 Rankings (American League)

- 1st in steals of home plate (1) and intentional walks (33)
- 2nd in hit-and-run attempts (92)
- 3rd in stolen base attempts (160) and double steals (4)

Carlos Beltran

2002 Season

Carlos Beltran followed his rebound 2001 campaign with another solid year at the plate and in the field. He became the first player in Royals history with three seasons of 100 RBI and 100 runs scored. Beltran came on strong in the second half, hitting 17 homers and driving in 58 runs after the All-Star break, and nearly reaching the 30-homer/30-steal level. His consistent hitting near the top of the order was one of the few bright spots in the Royals' otherwise dismal season.

Hitting

Beltran has the ability to hit for both power and average. He gradually has begun to trade some contact hitting for power by using more of an uppercut swing and becoming even more aggressive at the plate. He has a compact swing, which helps him make nice contact even though he lacks good strike-zone judgment. He looks fastball on every pitch and will chase bad breaking balls, especially down and away. Beltran handles all kinds of pitchers well, though he's displayed more power against finesse pitchers. He also had trouble against lefties last year, something that had not been a problem in the past. Opponents should avoid throwing a first-pitch fastball. He's a career .349 hitter when he puts the first pitch in play.

Baserunning & Defense

Beltran is an excellent baserunner. He uses his good speed well, running with his head up to take advantage of advancement opportunities without running into outs. He's enjoyed an excellent stolen-base success rate by stealing at the most opportune times. Beltran's speed comes in handy in center field. He glides smoothly through the outfield, covering lots of ground. He has an average arm for a center fielder, but often places high on outfield assist lists because he gets into good throwing position before catching flyballs.

2003 Outlook

Now that he's proven his consistency, Beltran will enter his prime years as a slightly flawed, multi-talented star. Developing better strike-zone judgment could permit him to have a huge year at the plate. The Royals soon will have a dilemma on their hands as he becomes eligible for free agency.

Position: CF/DH
Bats: B **Throws:** R
Ht: 6' 1" **Wt:** 190

Opening Day Age: 25
Born: 4/24/77 in Manati, PR
ML Seasons: 5
Pronunciation: BELL-tron

Overall Statistics

	G	AB	R	H	D	T	HR	RBI	SB	BB	SO	Avg	OBP	Slg
'02	162	637	114	174	44	7	29	105	35	71	135	.273	.346	.501
Car.	585	2347	393	665	123	33	82	365	109	207	459	.283	.341	.469

Where He Hits the Ball

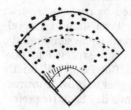 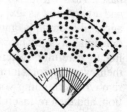

Vs. LHP   **Vs. RHP**

2002 Situational Stats

	AB	H	HR	RBI	Avg		AB	H	HR	RBI	Avg
Home	326	94	19	64	.288	LHP	163	40	8	24	.245
Road	311	80	10	41	.257	RHP	474	134	21	81	.283
First Half	327	83	12	47	.254	Sc Pos	161	51	12	79	.317
Scnd Half	310	91	17	58	.294	Clutch	103	29	6	20	.282

2002 Rankings (American League)

- 1st in games played, highest percentage of extra bases taken as a runner (76.4) and assists in center field (12)
- 2nd in stolen bases, pitches seen (2,854), errors in center field (7) and lowest fielding percentage in center field (.983)
- 5th in doubles, triples and plate appearances (722)
- Led the Royals in home runs, at-bats, runs scored, hits, doubles, triples, total bases (319), RBI, stolen bases, walks, times on base (249), strikeouts, pitches seen (2,854), plate appearances (722) and batting average with the bases loaded (.500)

Paul Byrd

2002 Season

Paul Byrd seemed to be doing a Steve Carlton impression for the Royals in 2002, trying to win almost every game himself. Byrd ended up with more than a quarter of the club's 62 victories. He finished among the league leaders in several categories and developed a cult following in Kansas City. The Royals adjusted their rotation in the season's second half to try to get him to 20 wins. While Byrd fell short, he still posted the best season of his career.

Pitching

Byrd has excellent control of a wide assortment of pitches. He'll use mid-80s fastballs spotted on the corners to get ahead of hitters, then toss sliders, screwballs, curves and changeups to get them to beat the ball into the ground. He has tried to improve his screwball as a weapon against left-handed hitters, who always have hit him much better than righthanders. Byrd has superior stamina—his success usually is determined by the first few innings. If he gets to the fourth or fifth frame without getting hit hard, he has a very good chance of finishing the game. He's been fragile over the course of a season, managing to make more than 16 starts in just two of eight big league campaigns.

Defense

Byrd is rather slow to react as a fielder. But he is fairly reliable once he gets to the ball and throws well to bases. He has worked to improve his pick-off move, a necessity since his reliance on off-speed stuff gives baserunners an edge. Byrd's best tool to control the running game has been to stay ahead in the count.

2003 Outlook

Although he said he wanted to return to Kansas City and the Royals made a contract offer, Byrd was expected to turn his big season into a big free-agency payday. Despite his success last year, he's a poor gamble for the long run. He's been plagued by shoulder injuries and inconsistency throughout his career. The challenge in 2003 is to prove he can succeed over the long haul.

Position: SP
Bats: R **Throws:** R
Ht: 6' 1" **Wt:** 185

Opening Day Age: 32
Born: 12/3/70 in Louisville, KY
ML Seasons: 8

Overall Statistics

	W	L	Pct.	ERA	G	GS	Sv	IP	H	BB	SO	HR	Ratio
'02	17	11	.607	3.90	33	33	0	228.1	224	38	129	36	1.15
Car.	52	46	.531	4.39	196	108	0	793.0	796	243	473	119	1.31

How Often He Throws Strikes

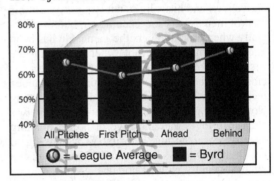

2002 Situational Stats

	W	L	ERA	Sv	IP		AB	H	HR	RBI	Avg
Home	8	5	4.29	0	109.0	LHB	472	127	17	48	.269
Road	9	6	3.54	0	119.1	RHB	403	97	19	54	.241
First Half	11	6	3.99	0	117.1	Sc Pos	153	47	8	69	.307
Scnd Half	6	5	3.81	0	111.0	Clutch	77	20	1	8	.260

2002 Rankings (American League)

- 1st in complete games (7) and fewest pitches thrown per batter (3.45)
- 2nd in shutouts (2), home runs allowed and fewest walks per nine innings (1.5)
- 4th in lowest groundball-flyball ratio allowed (0.8) and most home runs allowed per nine innings (1.42)
- 5th in highest strikeout-walk ratio (3.4)
- Led the Royals in ERA, wins, games started, innings pitched, batters faced (935), hit batsmen (7), strikeouts, runners caught stealing (6), GDPs induced (17) and winning percentage

Roberto Hernandez

2002 Season

Despite recording the 300th save of his major league career, 2002 was one of Roberto Hernandez' poorest seasons. A strained pitching elbow kept the usually durable reliever on the disabled list for a month to begin the campaign. A second-half slump in which he blew three straight chances and went almost a month without any saves was followed by just one save in September.

Pitching

Hernandez is all about throwing hard. His fastball sometimes touches 100 MPH, although it's more commonly in the upper 90s. He'll also throw a hard slider, and his splitter can be deadly. But his control increasingly has become a problem, especially when he first enters the game. He has been known to boil his own hot water by putting the first couple of hitters on base when coming in to close a game in the ninth inning. Hernandez recently has been used strictly as a one-inning closer. It's a good fit for his all-or-nothing power game. He loves the challenge of power pitching against power hitting, and always is looking to beat hitters with his best fastball. Hernandez can pitch frequently without noticeable effect, but he sometimes has problems working on consecutive days.

Defense

Often slow to recognize and field bunts, Hernandez also occasionally throws too hard to the bases, making for difficult chances for other infielders. Otherwise, he's a capable fielder. Because he is so focused on blowing away hitters, Hernandez sometimes forgets about baserunners, giving them a small advantage. Still, his strict reliance upon hard stuff also helps negate the running game.

2003 Outlook

Hernandez became a free agent during the offseason. After five years with some of baseball's worst teams, he wants to spend the last part of his career with contending clubs in hope of getting to the World Series. He no longer may display the consistency required of big league closers with first-division clubs, so he may have to settle for a setup job as he tries to get his ring.

Position: RP
Bats: R **Throws:** R
Ht: 6' 4" **Wt:** 250

Opening Day Age: 38
Born: 11/11/64 in Santurce, PR
ML Seasons: 12
Pronunciation: her-NAN-dezz

Overall Statistics

	W	L	Pct.	ERA	G	GS	Sv	IP	H	BB	SO	HR	Ratio
'02	1	3	.250	4.33	53	0	26	52.0	62	12	39	6	1.42
Car.	48	51	.485	3.22	696	3	320	775.0	698	305	716	62	1.29

How Often He Throws Strikes

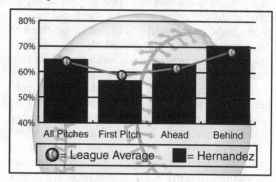

= League Average   ■ = Hernandez

2002 Situational Stats

	W	L	ERA	Sv	IP		AB	H	HR	RBI	Avg
Home	1	1	3.64	14	29.2	LHB	103	29	2	16	.282
Road	0	2	5.24	12	22.1	RHB	104	33	4	12	.317
First Half	1	2	3.86	14	25.2	Sc Pos	67	19	3	24	.284
Scnd Half	0	1	4.78	12	26.1	Clutch	133	43	3	18	.323

2002 Rankings (American League)

- 2nd in lowest save percentage (78.8)
- 3rd in highest batting average allowed in relief (.300)
- 4th in blown saves (7)
- 8th in save opportunities (33)
- 9th in saves
- 10th in games finished (42)
- Led the Royals in saves, games finished (42), save opportunities (33), save percentage (78.8) and blown saves (7)

Runelvys Hernandez

2002 Season

Runelvys Hernandez was yet another player revealed to be a few years older than originally listed. He began the season with two starts in the high Class-A Carolina League, then used an impressive first half at Double-A Wichita to jump straight into a big league rotation. He pitched fairly well for the Royals before developing a tired arm in August. Hernandez complained of a sore elbow, got some rest and came back to finish the season strong, nearly throwing a complete game in mid-September. The Royals were very pleased with his progress, clearly considering him a future member of their rotation.

Pitching

Hernandez has a power pitcher's build and delivery. He can work as a sinker/slider pitcher, but usually relies heavily upon a mid-90s, four-seam fastball. His changeup can be deceptive, though it's been an unreliable pitch thus far in the majors. Hernandez has displayed fairly good control for a power pitcher and is unafraid to challenge hitters with heat. He has not yet developed the stamina to regularly pitch deep into games. He usually had one bad inning in the middle of his starts that would derail his chance of going the distance. He runs a lot of high pitch counts, but doesn't walk a lot of batters because he can throw strikes when he needs to.

Defense

Hernandez occasionally looked lost in the field. He's quick off the mound and has a reliable glove, but he sometimes didn't know where to throw to. He has a good pickoff move and a deceptive delivery that helps tie baserunners to the bag.

2003 Outlook

Because of his tired arm in the latter part of last season, Hernandez was asked by the Royals to forego winter ball in his native Dominican Republic. He'll be a frontrunner for a rotation spot in 2003, with a goal of throwing 200 innings. The club hopes he'll continue to build his off-speed repertoire to supplement his four-seam fastball. He's considered one of the Royals' best pitching prospects and will be expected to produce in the big leagues right away.

Position: SP
Bats: R **Throws:** R
Ht: 6' 1" **Wt:** 205

Opening Day Age: 24
Born: 4/27/78 in Santo Domingo, DR
ML Seasons: 1

Overall Statistics

	W	L	Pct.	ERA	G	GS	Sv	IP	H	BB	SO	HR	Ratio
'02	4	4	.500	4.36	12	12	0	74.1	79	22	45	8	1.36
Car.	4	4	.500	4.36	12	12	0	74.1	79	22	45	8	1.36

How Often He Throws Strikes

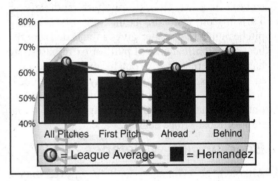

= League Average   = Hernandez

2002 Situational Stats

	W	L	ERA	Sv	IP		AB	H	HR	RBI	Avg
Home	2	4	4.31	0	48.0	LHB	162	49	6	19	.302
Road	2	0	4.44	0	26.1	RHB	127	30	2	13	.236
First Half	0	0	—	0	0.0	Sc Pos	68	18	0	20	.265
Scnd Half	4	4	4.36	0	74.1	Clutch	11	5	2	3	.455

2002 Rankings (American League)

• Did not rank near the top or bottom in any category

149

Raul Ibanez

2002 Season

It was a serendipitous season for Raul Ibanez, the former bench player and minor leaguer. He earned a full-time job and rewarded the Royals with one of the most unlikely 100-RBI seasons in the majors. He was especially dangerous after the All-Star break, hammering 16 homers and driving in 59 runs in July and August. Although a sprained left thumb slowed him in September, Ibanez easily finished with the best season of his career.

Hitting

Ibanez is constantly tinkering with his stance and swing. He's an excellent mistake hitter who has trouble against finesse pitchers and lefties. Thriving on fastballs, he'll fight off breaking pitches until the pitcher gives in and delivers the heater, which Ibanez will pull for extra bases. He has an uppercut swing, but he makes good contact. He hits a fair number of flyballs and occasionally gets into trouble by trying to hit the ball out of the park, although he managed to avoid that trap for most of last season.

Baserunning & Defense

Although he's versatile with the glove, Ibanez doesn't stand out at any one position. He has a subpar arm and doesn't read flyballs especially well, but he runs surprisingly well in the outfield. He isn't a good defensive first baseman and, in fact, suffered his thumb injury misplaying a poor throw. Ibanez was a catcher in the minors and has played some third base, too, so he can fill in at both spots in a pinch. Although he lacks bases-stealing speed, he runs the bases well, taking the extra base when needed.

2003 Outlook

Ibanez has earned his newfound fame and success the hard way, overcoming obstacles and molding himself into a consistent run producer. He's been able to make the necessary adjustments to remain successful, so he isn't likely to suffer a big setback in 2003. On the other hand, he won't sneak up on anyone this year. Ibanez will be expected to carry a large RBI burden in the middle of the Royals' batting order while serving as an occasional outfielder and DH.

Position: 1B/LF/DH/RF
Bats: L **Throws:** R
Ht: 6' 2" **Wt:** 200

Opening Day Age: 30
Born: 6/2/72 in Manhattan, NY
ML Seasons: 7
Pronunciation: e-BON-yez

Overall Statistics

	G	AB	R	H	D	T	HR	RBI	SB	BB	SO	Avg	OBP	Slg
'02	137	497	70	146	37	6	24	103	5	40	76	.294	.346	.537
Car.	472	1254	173	339	70	13	51	215	12	108	213	.270	.328	.469

Where He Hits the Ball

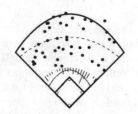
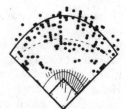

Vs. LHP **Vs. RHP**

2002 Situational Stats

	AB	H	HR	RBI	Avg		AB	H	HR	RBI	Avg
Home	264	79	14	60	.299	LHP	124	34	1	23	.274
Road	233	67	10	43	.288	RHP	373	112	23	80	.300
First Half	204	58	10	40	.284	Sc Pos	145	45	7	79	.310
Scnd Half	293	88	14	63	.300	Clutch	82	25	7	19	.305

2002 Rankings (American League)

- 1st in batting average on a 3-2 count (.434)
- 6th in triples
- 7th in batting average on a 3-1 count (.588)
- 8th in batting average with the bases loaded (.500) and slugging percentage vs. righthanded pitchers (.582)
- 10th in cleanup slugging percentage (.530)
- Led the Royals in batting average with the bases loaded (.500), batting average on a 3-1 count (.588), slugging percentage vs. righthanded pitchers (.582) and batting average on a 3-2 count (.434)

Chuck Knoblauch

2002 Season

Free agent Chuck Knoblauch was the Royals' biggest offseason acquisition last year. He was expected to carry the load as Kansas City's lead-off hitter. Instead, he almost disappeared, missing more than half of the season with a variety of injuries. His most notable ailment was a strained left forearm that nagged him for two months before he spent a six-week stint on the disabled list in midsummer. He was ineffective even in those rare times when he was in the lineup regularly. It easily was the worst season of Knoblauch's professional career.

Hitting

Usually a patient hitter, Knoblauch makes good contact. He tries to hit the ball on the ground to take advantage of his speed. He crowds the plate and attempts to work the count, using every opportunity to get on base. He's a good bunter and occasionally will lay one down for a hit. Knoblauch fares better when he hits to the opposite field, though he occasionally will turn on a pitch and pull it down the line for extra bases. He constantly looks fastball and can be frustrated by good offspeed stuff. He had unusual trouble against righthanders last year, after showing little platoon differentials in past seasons.

Baserunning & Defense

Knoblauch remains a top-notch baserunner who steals bases and takes every extra base possible, even though age and injuries have dampened his speed. He is a tentative outfielder who rarely gets good jumps on flyballs. He doesn't gauge the depth of flies well at all, although his speed lets him outrun some mistakes. Knoblauch's arm is below average, limiting him to left field.

2003 Outlook

The best approach for Knoblauch, who declared for free agency shortly after last season ended, would be to forget about 2002. He still has the speed and on-base ability to succeed as a leadoff hitter, and he still contributes enough offense to retain a starting job in left field. Provided he can remain healthy, Knoblauch should enjoy a big rebound in 2003.

Position: LF
Bats: R **Throws:** R
Ht: 5' 9" **Wt:** 175

Opening Day Age: 34
Born: 7/7/68 in Houston, TX
ML Seasons: 12
Pronunciation: NOB-lock
Nickname: Knobby

Overall Statistics

	G	AB	R	H	D	T	HR	RBI	SB	BB	SO	Avg	OBP	Slg
'02	80	300	41	63	9	0	6	22	19	28	32	.210	.284	.300
Car.	1632	6366	1132	1839	322	64	98	615	407	804	730	.289	.378	.406

Where He Hits the Ball

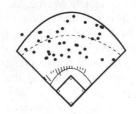
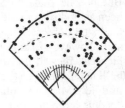

Vs. LHP	**Vs. RHP**

2002 Situational Stats

	AB	H	HR	RBI	Avg		AB	H	HR	RBI	Avg
Home	152	32	3	9	.211	LHP	78	18	1	2	.231
Road	148	31	3	13	.209	RHP	222	45	5	20	.203
First Half	150	25	3	14	.167	Sc Pos	65	7	1	17	.108
Scnd Half	150	38	3	8	.253	Clutch	45	13	0	4	.289

2002 Rankings (American League)

- 1st in lowest on-base percentage for a leadoff hitter (.262)
- 3rd in steals of third (8)
- 4th in stolen-base percentage (86.4)
- 6th in lowest batting average on an 0-2 count (.045)
- 7th in errors in left field (3) and assists in left field (5)
- Led the Royals in stolen-base percentage (86.4), most pitches seen per plate appearance (4.01), lowest percentage of swings that missed (6.7), steals of third (8) and lowest percentage of swings on the first pitch (13.7)

Brent Mayne

2002 Season

Despite a relatively poor batting average in 2002, Brent Mayne had a season very similar to any of his other previous 10 years outside of Coors Field. As the Royals' regular catcher, his main tasks were handling the club's young pitchers and chipping in an occasional key hit. He did his job at the plate and also helped some of the young hurlers make positive strides as big leaguers.

Hitting

Mayne is a patient, contact hitter whose power is limited to gap doubles and the rare pulled homer. Although he struggled when down in the count last year, he historically has been a good two-strike hitter who can handle breaking pitches. Because he makes decent contact, Mayne has been a good run producer from near the bottom of the batting order. He can be overmatched by hard stuff, however, as high fastballs can induce him to hit weak flies. If he can get around on the pitch, he'll pull the ball on the ground or hit liners up the middle. Mayne's platoon differentials have become more pronounced in recent years, as lefties increasingly have their way with him.

Baserunning & Defense

Defense is the primary purpose for having Mayne on a major league roster. He is considered a good handler of young pitchers, a reputation that was heavily tested by the Royals' youngsters in 2002. Mayne's mobility behind the plate, good mechanics and quick release mask a barely average arm. He runs better than expected, considering he's a catcher who will turn 35 in April 2003. He won't take unnecessary chances and occasionally will take an extra base when given an opportunity.

2003 Outlook

Mayne's chance to start in 2003 will depend largely upon his venue. His meager offensive abilities might fit a starter's role for a second-division club, or he could be relegated to a bench job for a contender. His success mostly will be judged by the relative success of others. If young pitchers on the staff develop, it will be a good season. Regardless, Mayne's career is winding down.

Position: C
Bats: L **Throws:** R
Ht: 6' 1" **Wt:** 190

Opening Day Age: 34
Born: 4/19/68 in Loma Linda, CA
ML Seasons: 13
Nickname: Mayner

Overall Statistics

	G	AB	R	H	D	T	HR	RBI	SB	BB	SO	Avg	OBP	Slg
'02	101	326	35	77	8	2	4	30	4	34	54	.236	.309	.310
Car.	1083	3052	306	818	155	6	32	352	17	311	480	.268	.336	.354

Where He Hits the Ball

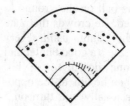

Vs. LHP   **Vs. RHP**

2002 Situational Stats

	AB	H	HR	RBI	Avg		AB	H	HR	RBI	Avg
Home	162	40	2	14	.247	LHP	68	11	1	2	.162
Road	164	37	2	16	.226	RHP	258	66	3	28	.256
First Half	141	29	0	8	.206	Sc Pos	83	20	1	23	.241
Scnd Half	185	48	4	22	.259	Clutch	56	13	3	5	.232

2002 Rankings (American League)

- 2nd in lowest batting average with two strikes (.087)
- 7th in errors at catcher (4) and lowest fielding percentage at catcher (.993)

Neifi Perez

2002 Season

Neifi Perez' season started negatively when it was revealed that he had lied about his age and was two years older than originally stated. He finished the year benched for refusing to enter a game as a substitute. In between, he earned the ire of Royals fans with lackadaisical play, such as failing to run out batted balls, making too many easy outs at the plate and too many errors on easy fielding plays. It was a terrible season for Perez.

Hitting

Perez is one of the most aggressive first-ball hitters in the game. Too often, he hits flies by trying to pull the ball instead of hitting it on the ground and using his speed. Power pitchers chew him up, especially after he falls behind flailing at pitches out of the strike zone. Swinging at the first hittable pitch in nearly every at-bat left Perez hitting from a hole most of last year, and he's an especially poor two-strike hitter. His occasional power usually comes batting righthanded. Although he showed few batting talents in 2002, he's a fine bunter.

Baserunning & Defense

Perez has great range at shortstop, displaying a strong, accurate arm. He's a slick fielder, when he tries. He's especially skilled at going into the hole or charging softly hit grounders. He tends to let up on "easy" plays, making too many nonchalant errors. He also tries to make flashy plays, such as barehanding grounders or unnecessarily taking double-play pivots himself instead of utilizing the second baseman. Perez has decent speed, but he is an awful baserunner who alternately tries to steal in poor situations, then doesn't take an extra base when appropriate.

2003 Outlook

It will be difficult for Perez to maintain a starting job without a complete overhaul of his attitude. He gets a new lease on life with the Giants, who claimed him off waivers in November. He has the talent to play regularly if he doesn't handicap himself with lazy play. Should his focus return, Perez can be a useful middle infielder who bats lower in the batting order.

Position: SS
Bats: B **Throws:** R
Ht: 6' 0" **Wt:** 175

Opening Day Age: 29
Born: 6/2/73 in Villa Mella, DR
ML Seasons: 7
Pronunciation: NAY-fee

Overall Statistics

	G	AB	R	H	D	T	HR	RBI	SB	BB	SO	Avg	OBP	Slg
'02	145	554	65	131	20	4	3	37	8	20	53	.236	.260	.303
Car.	862	3481	478	948	152	54	47	330	44	163	359	.272	.303	.388

Where He Hits the Ball

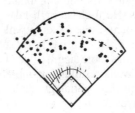

Vs. LHP   **Vs. RHP**

2002 Situational Stats

	AB	H	HR	RBI	Avg		AB	H	HR	RBI	Avg
Home	270	70	1	22	.259	LHP	154	35	2	10	.227
Road	284	61	2	15	.215	RHP	400	96	1	27	.240
First Half	335	77	2	25	.230	Sc Pos	122	27	0	32	.221
Scnd Half	219	54	1	12	.247	Clutch	92	14	1	6	.152

2002 Rankings (American League)

- 1st in bunts in play (38), lowest slugging percentage, lowest on-base percentage, lowest on-base percentage vs. lefthanded pitchers (.250) and lowest on-base percentage vs. righthanded pitchers (.264)
- 2nd in errors at shortstop (19), lowest HR frequency (184.7 ABs per HR), lowest slugging percentage vs. lefthanded pitchers (.312) and lowest slugging percentage vs. righthanded pitchers (.300)
- 3rd in lowest batting average, lowest batting average in the clutch and lowest fielding percentage at shortstop (.972)
- Led the Royals in singles, caught stealing (9) and bunts in play (38)

Joe Randa

2002 Season

Following an offseason conditioning program designed to strengthen a troublesome hamstring and help him lose some weight, Joe Randa enjoyed a fairly good start to 2002. He finished with his usual blend of useful batting average, occasional power and strong defense. Although his season totals were similar to recent years, he didn't do an especially good job of driving in runs over the second half. But Randa was a solid presence in the Royals' youthful clubhouse. Overall, it was another sturdy season from a reliable veteran.

Hitting

Randa is a dangerous fastball hitter who can be beaten with good breaking stuff but will make pitchers pay for mistakes. He'll chase high fastballs when down in the count, as he looks to pull the ball for extra bases in order to drive in runs. He increasingly has become more aggressive in his role as an RBI producer, resulting in more deep flyballs. His platoon differential gradually has expanded in recent years, and he now is a notably better hitter against lefthanders. Randa has developed a reputation for clutch hitting. He is susceptible to lengthy streaks, good and bad, although he is consistent year to year.

Baserunning & Defense

A steady, solid defender with good range at the hot corner, Randa nevertheless tends to make his few seasonal errors in bunches. He owns a strong, accurate arm and is quick to start double plays. Serious hamstring injuries have curtailed his aggressiveness on the bases, limiting him to station-to-station baserunning.

2003 Outlook

The Royals and Randa are a good fit. An adaptable, multitalented player, he's a steady performer who won't command a superstar's salary while providing useful hitting and solid defense. While Randa is signed through the 2003 season and hopes to finish his career in Kansas City, the Royals reportedly have dangled him in an offseason effort to dump salary. If he stays, Randa will be an important part of the Royals' everyday lineup and a defensive anchor on the infield.

Position: 3B/DH
Bats: R **Throws:** R
Ht: 5'11" **Wt:** 190

Opening Day Age: 33
Born: 12/18/69 in Milwaukee, WI
ML Seasons: 8
Nickname: The Joker

Overall Statistics

	G	AB	R	H	D	T	HR	RBI	SB	BB	SO	Avg	OBP	Slg
'02	151	549	63	155	36	5	11	80	2	46	69	.282	.341	.426
Car.	1024	3680	458	1050	209	31	78	515	41	288	493	.285	.340	.423

Where He Hits the Ball

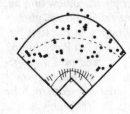 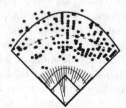

Vs. LHP   **Vs. RHP**

2002 Situational Stats

	AB	H	HR	RBI	Avg		AB	H	HR	RBI	Avg
Home	276	81	6	47	.293	LHP	131	42	2	19	.321
Road	273	74	5	33	.271	RHP	418	113	9	61	.270
First Half	277	80	8	52	.289	Sc Pos	150	40	2	66	.267
Scnd Half	272	75	3	28	.276	Clutch	93	24	1	12	.258

2002 Rankings (American League)

- 2nd in sacrifice flies (11) and fielding percentage at third base (.972)
- 6th in batting average vs. lefthanded pitchers
- Led the Royals in sacrifice flies (11), hit by pitch (9) and GDPs (13)

Jeff Suppan

2002 Season

Jeff Suppan was the Royals' most consistent pitcher for the previous three seasons, but he was anything but consistent in 2002. He surrendered his staff ace role to Paul Byrd and continued to give up too many hits, especially homers. A victory in Suppan's final start snapped a personal nine-game losing streak, but didn't prevent him from posting the worst season of his career.

Pitching

Suppan works steadily to spot a low-90s fastball, mixing in an occasional slider or changeup. He then uses his sharp-breaking curveball as an out pitch. He doesn't try to strike out batters and is very hittable. Therefore, he must keep his walks under control to limit baserunners, especially since he's vulnerable to the longball. He hung too many curves that were deposited in the seats last year. Free swingers have the most trouble with Suppan. Patient hitters can foul off his better curveballs and wait for a hanging breaking ball or a fastball over the plate. Usually strong for about six innings, Suppan historically becomes increasingly more hittable after about 75 pitches. He lacks the power stuff and stamina usually associated with aces.

Defense

Suppan is barely average as a fielder, though he has improved in fielding grounders hit back through the box. Although he makes a lot of throws to first to control the running game, he registered just three pickoffs last season, and his deliberate windup and reliance on offspeed stuff gives baserunners significant advantages.

2003 Outlook

Likely to command a big salary boost despite last year's struggles, Suppan is expected to leave Kansas City. If he's pitching for a strong team, he can fit more easily into a lower rotation role and could be a big winner. If he's miscast as an ace, however, Suppan again would be forced to try to perform beyond his abilities. Few pitchers have been as reliable as Suppan. He should rebound in 2003 to have a decent season as an innings-eater.

Position: SP
Bats: R **Throws:** R
Ht: 6' 2" **Wt:** 210

Opening Day Age: 28
Born: 1/2/75 in Oklahoma City, OK
ML Seasons: 8
Pronunciation: SUE-pon

Kansas City

Overall Statistics

	W	L	Pct.	ERA	G	GS	Sv	IP	H	BB	SO	HR	Ratio
'02	9	16	.360	5.32	33	33	0	208.0	229	68	109	32	1.43
Car.	49	64	.434	5.03	190	175	0	1088.1	1207	364	610	154	1.44

How Often He Throws Strikes

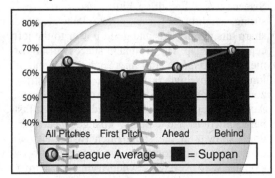

= League Average = Suppan

2002 Situational Stats

	W	L	ERA	Sv	IP		AB	H	HR	RBI	Avg
Home	8	4	4.89	0	99.1	LHB	424	117	12	54	.276
Road	1	12	5.71	0	108.2	RHB	398	112	20	58	.281
First Half	7	6	4.38	0	121.1	Sc Pos	176	55	7	81	.313
Scnd Half	2	10	6.65	0	86.2	Clutch	33	8	2	4	.242

2002 Rankings (American League)

- 2nd in losses and highest ERA
- 3rd in highest ERA on the road
- 4th in home runs allowed, errors at pitcher (3), highest slugging percentage allowed (.459) and fewest strikeouts per nine innings (4.7)
- 5th in hits allowed, wild pitches (10), highest batting average allowed (.279), highest ERA at home and most home runs allowed per nine innings (1.38)
- Led the Royals in losses, games started, hits allowed, walks allowed, hit batsmen (7), wild pitches (10), pitches thrown (3,440), lowest stolen-base percentage allowed (50.0) and most run support per nine innings (5.1)

155

Mike Sweeney

2002 Season

A cursory look at Mike Sweeney's 2002 season gives the impression he had another strong year, comparable to the previous three. Closer examination shows that he continues to improve as a hitter. Despite battling injury all year, Sweeney increased his slugging percentage, improved his strikeout-walk ratio and challenged for a batting title, all while hitting in an anemic Royals lineup. The only thing to slow him down was a strained left hip that cost him a month on the disabled list shortly after the All-Star break.

Hitting

Sweeney is a line-drive hitter who possesses a strong, slightly uppercut stroke that generates sharp hits to all fields and good power to the left-center field gap. He has made successful adjustments to offspeed stuff in recent years and no longer chases high fastballs. He has fine strike-zone judgment and makes excellent contact. Attack Sweeney carefully—avoid first-pitch fastballs, pitch to the corners, change speeds and don't show him the same pitch twice. He will expand his strike zone to drive in runs and occasionally will overswing when trying too hard to produce runs in a weak offense.

Baserunning & Defense

Sweeney's large build belies his decent speed. Despite his awkward appearance, he's a good baserunner who has some success as a basestealer and will take an extra base when opportunities occur. Although he's not Gold Glove material, he continues to make strides as a fielder. Last year he improved his throwing accuracy and continued to display adequate range afield.

2003 Outlook

Sweeney's success at producing runs is limited by his environment. He could produce some astounding offensive totals in the middle of a potent lineup. Instead, he'll remain the brightest light in a dim Royals lineup and one of the American League's most dangerous hitters this season. Sweeney is more likely to challenge for a batting title than a home-run crown, but he will be an effective hitter in either case.

Position: 1B/DH
Bats: R **Throws:** R
Ht: 6' 3" **Wt:** 225

Opening Day Age: 29
Born: 7/22/73 in Orange, CA
ML Seasons: 8

Overall Statistics

	G	AB	R	H	D	T	HR	RBI	SB	BB	SO	Avg	OBP	Slg
'02	126	471	81	160	31	1	24	86	9	61	46	.340	.417	.563
Car.	812	2914	470	899	187	3	123	521	39	309	317	.309	.379	.501

Where He Hits the Ball

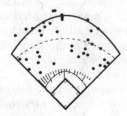 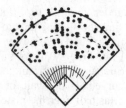

Vs. LHP **Vs. RHP**

2002 Situational Stats

	AB	H	HR	RBI	Avg		AB	H	HR	RBI	Avg
Home	239	79	14	52	.331	LHP	112	40	6	19	.357
Road	232	81	10	34	.349	RHP	359	120	18	67	.334
First Half	296	107	16	46	.361	Sc Pos	107	43	9	64	.402
Scnd Half	175	53	8	40	.303	Clutch	68	26	6	23	.382

2002 Rankings (American League)

- 1st in batting average vs. righthanded pitchers and assists at first base (105)
- 2nd in batting average and batting average with runners in scoring position
- 3rd in batting average on the road
- 4th in on-base percentage, batting average in the clutch and errors at first base (9)
- 5th in cleanup slugging percentage (.602) and batting average at home
- 6th in on-base percentage vs. righthanded pitchers (.418)
- Led the Royals in batting average, singles, intentional walks (10), slugging percentage, on-base percentage, HR frequency (19.6 ABs per HR), batting average with runners in scoring position and batting average in the clutch

Michael Tucker

2002 Season

Michael Tucker wasn't especially happy to learn he'd been traded back to the Royals during last offseason. But he made the most of his return. He was expected to be a fourth outfielder or possibly platoon in right field. But due to injuries to Mark Quinn and Chuck Knoblauch, Tucker wound up with almost full-time play and finished as one of the club's most consistent hitters. It was overall a fairly typical season for Tucker, and a good fit for the Royals.

Hitting

Tucker is a streaky hitter who goes through phases when he uses a big swing and tries to pull everything, resulting in some power but also big strikeout numbers. He tends to get caught up in battling pitchers who try to overpower him, and will chase fastballs up and out of the strike zone. He succeeds when shortening his stroke and trying to hit the ball to left and left-center, slashing liners instead of trying to hit the ball out of the yard. He always has had trouble against left-handers, and frequently has been platooned to limit his exposure to them. Tucker has not fared well coming off the bench or in sparse use. He needs regular work to stay sharp.

Baserunning & Defense

An outstanding baserunner, Tucker has above-average speed and uses it well on the bases and in the outfield. He's fast enough to succeed at any outfield spot. His arm is average, though barely adequate for right field. He can play on the infield, too, and did well enough in his short infield stints in 2002.

2003 Outlook

The Royals are considering several options at second base, and Tucker is in the mix. He originally was drafted as a shortstop and played second base as he came up through the minors. The club even tried him briefly at second near the end of last season. Although he didn't seem too keen on the idea, it might help him win more playing time, because as strictly an outfielder, Tucker most likely would platoon or come off the bench in 2003.

Position: RF/LF/DH/CF
Bats: L **Throws:** R
Ht: 6' 2" **Wt:** 195

Opening Day Age: 31
Born: 6/25/71 in South Boston, VA
ML Seasons: 8

Overall Statistics

	G	AB	R	H	D	T	HR	RBI	SB	BB	SO	Avg	OBP	Slg
'02	144	475	65	118	27	6	12	56	23	56	105	.248	.330	.406
Car.	1012	2906	449	751	147	37	93	369	95	334	700	.258	.339	.430

Where He Hits the Ball

 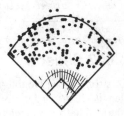

Vs. LHP   **Vs. RHP**

2002 Situational Stats

	AB	H	HR	RBI	Avg		AB	H	HR	RBI	Avg
Home	238	78	10	32	.328	LHP	77	16	3	10	.208
Road	237	40	2	24	.169	RHP	398	102	9	46	.256
First Half	222	52	4	23	.234	Sc Pos	113	26	2	37	.230
Scnd Half	253	66	8	33	.261	Clutch	79	21	3	9	.266

2002 Rankings (American League)

- 1st in lowest batting average on the road
- 5th in bunts in play (24)
- 6th in triples
- 7th in batting average on a 3-1 count (.588), batting average at home and highest percentage of swings on the first pitch (37.0)
- 8th in fewest GDPs per GDP situation (5.2%) and assists in right field (5)
- 9th in stolen bases, caught stealing (9) and lowest stolen-base percentage (71.9)
- Led the Royals in sacrifice bunts (7), caught stealing (9), fewest GDPs per GDP situation (5.2%) and batting average on a 3-1 count (.588)

Jeremy Affeldt

Position: RP
Bats: L **Throws:** L
Ht: 6' 4" **Wt:** 215

Opening Day Age: 23
Born: 6/6/79 in
Phoenix, AZ
ML Seasons: 1

Overall Statistics

	W	L	Pct.	ERA	G	GS	Sv	IP	H	BB	SO	HR	Ratio
'02	3	4	.429	4.64	34	7	0	77.2	85	37	67	8	1.57
Car.	3	4	.429	4.64	34	7	0	77.2	85	37	67	8	1.57

2002 Situational Stats

	W	L	ERA	Sv	IP		AB	H	HR	RBI	Avg
Home	1	2	6.87	0	36.2	LHB	92	26	3	15	.283
Road	2	2	2.63	0	41.0	RHB	218	59	5	25	.271
First Half	1	4	4.47	0	50.1	Sc Pos	106	25	4	33	.236
Scnd Half	2	0	4.94	0	27.1	Clutch	77	21	3	8	.273

2002 Season

A strong '01 at Double-A Wichita led to a '02 big
league debut for Jeremy Affeldt. He worked out of
the pen before replacing Bryan Rekar in the rotation in May. Starting led to a blister and a split nail
on his pitching hand, which cost him two months
before returning to the pen in August. It was a
cautiously optimistic start to his big league career.

Pitching & Defense

A typical lefty sinker/slider pitcher, Affeldt has a
90-MPH fastball with good movement and a hard-
breaking curve. But he lacks an effective changeup, which could help him keep batters from sitting
on his fastball. Affeldt hasn't learned how to pitch
to lefties, who hit better and for more power
against him last year. Stamina could be an issue
because of a recurring blister on his pitching hand.
His pickoff move still is a puzzle to most baserunners. Few tried to steal against him last year.

2003 Outlook

Because of the time lost to injury, and because the
Royals wanted to try him in short relief, Affeldt
went to the Dominican Winter League. But the
blister returned, ending his winter season and possibly his chance to make the Royals' rotation in
2003. Still, Affeldt is seen as an important element
of the Royals' 2003 staff.

Luis Alicea

Position: 2B/3B/DH
Bats: B **Throws:** R
Ht: 5' 9" **Wt:** 175

Opening Day Age: 37
Born: 7/29/65 in
Santurce, PR
ML Seasons: 13
Pronunciation:
al-a-SAY-a

Overall Statistics

	G	AB	R	H	D	T	HR	RBI	SB	BB	SO	Avg	OBP	Slg
'02	94	237	28	54	8	2	1	23	2	32	34	.228	.322	.291
Car.	1341	3971	551	1031	189	53	47	422	81	500	624	.260	.346	.369

2002 Situational Stats

	AB	H	HR	RBI	Avg		AB	H	HR	RBI	Avg
Home	116	32	0	13	.276	LHP	44	9	0	2	.205
Road	121	22	1	10	.182	RHP	193	45	1	21	.233
First Half	136	27	0	11	.199	Sc Pos	60	16	1	22	.267
Scnd Half	101	27	1	12	.267	Clutch	43	9	0	2	.209

2002 Season

For the second year in a row, Luis Alicea got more
playing time than expected in a reserve infielder
role. He spelled Carlos Febles at second base and
Joe Randa at third base. But Alicea had a weak
season at the plate and only was moderately useful
as a fielder. He declared for free agency after the
season.

Hitting, Baserunning & Defense

A slash-and-dash hitter, Alicea tries to line the ball
to the opposite field. He has virtually no power,
and he will chase pitches out of the strike zone.
Power pitchers give him too much to handle.
Alicea can play anywhere on the infield or in the
outfield. However, his lack of range at middle-
infield spots would be exposed in regular duty, and
his weak arm is insufficient for regular outfield
use. He still runs the bases aggressively, even
though his once above-average speed has evapo-
rated.

2003 Outlook

Alicea barely is clinging to his career at this point.
His value to a major league team lies in his versatility, although his specific skills are wearing thin.
If he remains in the big leagues another season, it
will be as a deep bench player for a second-division team. It probably won't be the Royals.

Miguel Asencio

Position: SP/RP
Bats: R **Throws:** R
Ht: 6' 2" **Wt:** 160

Opening Day Age: 22
Born: 9/29/80 in Villa Mella, DR
ML Seasons: 1

Overall Statistics

	W	L	Pct.	ERA	G	GS	Sv	IP	H	BB	SO	HR	Ratio
'02	4	7	.364	5.11	31	21	0	123.1	136	64	58	17	1.62
Car.	4	7	.364	5.11	31	21	0	123.1	136	64	58	17	1.62

2002 Situational Stats

	W	L	ERA	Sv	IP		AB	H	HR	RBI	Avg
Home	3	3	6.81	0	70.0	LHB	250	66	7	25	.264
Road	1	4	2.87	0	53.1	RHB	232	70	10	35	.302
First Half	1	2	5.79	0	46.2	Sc Pos	125	30	1	38	.240
Scnd Half	3	5	4.70	0	76.2	Clutch	5	0	0	0	.000

2002 Season

A Rule 5 selection from the Phillies, Miguel Asencio began his big league career in ignominious fashion, walking the first four batters he faced on 16 pitches. Things did get better, especially after he grabbed a rotation spot near the end of May. He showed signs of late-season fatigue, but was effective as a five-inning pitcher.

Pitching & Defense

Asencio has a decent low-90s fastball with good movement and an above-average changeup. He gets lots of grounders when his heater is moving. Command has been an issue. He would suddenly lose his touch in almost every game, and his command was especially poor pitching out of the bullpen. Consistency from one inning to the next is his biggest challenge. An athletic fielder who moves well to the ball, Asencio is a bit tentative throwing to bases. Baserunners take advantage of his below-average pickoff move.

2003 Outlook

Asencio needs to work on his stamina and command. The Royals sent him to winter ball after last season to help build arm strength. Now that his Rule 5 status has expired, Asencio could spend a significant part of 2003 in the minors developing more consistent command.

Brandon Berger

Position: RF/LF/DH
Bats: R **Throws:** R
Ht: 5'11" **Wt:** 205

Opening Day Age: 28
Born: 2/21/75 in Covington, KY
ML Seasons: 2

Overall Statistics

	G	AB	R	H	D	T	HR	RBI	SB	BB	SO	Avg	OBP	Slg
'02	51	134	16	27	5	1	6	17	1	8	32	.201	.255	.388
Car.	57	150	20	32	6	2	8	19	1	10	34	.213	.270	.440

2002 Situational Stats

	AB	H	HR	RBI	Avg		AB	H	HR	RBI	Avg
Home	65	16	5	13	.246	LHP	56	12	3	5	.214
Road	69	11	1	4	.159	RHP	78	15	3	12	.192
First Half	92	19	4	11	.207	Sc Pos	32	8	2	11	.250
Scnd Half	42	8	2	6	.190	Clutch	19	4	1	4	.211

2002 Season

Brandon Berger earned frequent traveler miles in 2002. He was optioned to Triple-A Omaha on three occasions, only to be recalled each time. He did exactly as expected while filling in for injured outfielders Chuck Knoblauch and Mark Quinn, hitting a few homers and playing useful defense as a corner outfielder.

Hitting, Baserunning & Defense

Although he isn't built like a slugger, Berger uses a big, uppercut swing. Unlike many rookie power hitters, he has handled breaking-ball pitchers better while having trouble with big league flamethrowers. His big swing generates both power and strikeouts. The challenge for Berger is to cut down on his big swing to make better contact without losing too much power. He has little speed and runs the bases conservatively. He lacks the range to play center field, and his average arm is exposed in right field.

2003 Outlook

September shoulder surgery to repair a rotator cuff tear could slow Berger in 2003. When he's recovered, he should challenge for a platoon role in the majors. His power makes him a useful bat off the bench, even if he doesn't win a full-time job.

Carlos Febles

Jason Grimsley

Position: 2B
Bats: R **Throws:** R
Ht: 5'11" **Wt:** 185

Opening Day Age: 26
Born: 5/24/76 in El Seybo, DR
ML Seasons: 5
Pronunciation: FAY-bless

Position: RP
Bats: R **Throws:** R
Ht: 6' 3" **Wt:** 205

Opening Day Age: 35
Born: 8/7/67 in Cleveland, TX
ML Seasons: 11

Overall Statistics

	G	AB	R	H	D	T	HR	RBI	SB	BB	SO	Avg	OBP	Slg
'02	119	351	44	86	16	4	4	26	16	41	63	.245	.336	.348
Car.	432	1460	224	368	60	18	24	135	60	150	267	.252	.332	.367

Overall Statistics

	W	L	Pct.	ERA	G	GS	Sv	IP	H	BB	SO	HR	Ratio
'02	4	7	.364	3.91	70	0	1	71.1	64	37	59	4	1.42
Car.	33	41	.446	4.77	362	72	4	749.0	751	410	505	64	1.55

2002 Situational Stats

	AB	H	HR	RBI	Avg		AB	H	HR	RBI	Avg
Home	157	42	2	16	.268	LHP	83	19	1	4	.229
Road	194	44	2	10	.227	RHP	268	67	3	22	.250
First Half	227	52	3	17	.229	Sc Pos	78	21	0	18	.269
Scnd Half	124	34	1	9	.274	Clutch	58	9	0	2	.155

2002 Situational Stats

	W	L	ERA	Sv	IP		AB	H	HR	RBI	Avg
Home	2	4	4.19	0	43.0	LHB	129	32	3	15	.248
Road	2	3	3.49	1	28.1	RHB	142	32	1	25	.225
First Half	3	4	5.06	0	32.0	Sc Pos	88	25	0	34	.284
Scnd Half	1	3	2.97	1	39.1	Clutch	158	39	3	23	.247

2002 Season

The 2002 season was yet another frustrating mix for Carlos Febles. He started off well enough, hitting .279 in April while scoring seven runs for the month and making all the plays in the field. But as his swing became less controlled, his strikeouts mounted. And after a few lackadaisical efforts in the field, Febles was demoted in August. He finished the year in a part-time role with the Royals.

Hitting, Baserunning & Defense

Pitch selection remains a struggle for Febles. He gives away too many at-bats by chasing high fastballs, resulting in too many easy flyball outs. His inability to make regular contact is exacerbated when he swings for the fences. He runs the bases aggressively, but must get on base more often to make use of his speed. Playing deep helps Febles display good range, especially to his left. He has an accurate arm and is adept at turning the double play.

2003 Outlook

At his best, Febles provides sharp defense, occasional power and dangerous speed on the bases. However, he rarely has been at, or even near, his best for any extended period. The promise of his 1999 rookie season has dissolved, and Febles now must produce from the outset to remain a regular.

2002 Season

Jason Grimsley, had a rollercoaster season in 2002. He lost time with a strained oblique muscle, then lost effectiveness due to a flaw in his delivery. Grimsley corrected the flaw and was more consistent in his setup role before drawing the ire of Royals fans for his prominent position in the labor strife. The booing seemed to negatively affect his overall performance.

Pitching & Defense

Grimsley works almost exclusively with two pitches—mid-90s fastballs and sinkers he uses to get groundballs. His occasional splitter has not been useful. Because he's ready to work every game, he fits the setup role well. But his lack of sharp control would hurt him in a lengthy closer role. Grimsley isn't a good fielder and has just an average move to first. He focuses too much on getting ahead of batters instead of holding runners.

2003 Outlook

With the expected departure of Roberto Hernandez via free agency, Grimsley could be in line to pick up saves for the Royals in 2003. More likely, though, he'll continue his setup work. It's a role in which Grimsley has succeeded and for which he's well suited. But he'll be an important bullpen contributor in any role.

A.J. Hinch

Position: C
Bats: R **Throws:** R
Ht: 6' 1" **Wt:** 205

Opening Day Age: 28
Born: 5/15/74 in Waverly, IA
ML Seasons: 5

Overall Statistics

	G	AB	R	H	D	T	HR	RBI	SB	BB	SO	Avg	OBP	Slg
'02	72	197	25	49	7	1	7	27	3	18	35	.249	.321	.401
Car.	319	868	96	192	24	2	29	101	13	68	192	.221	.284	.354

2002 Situational Stats

	AB	H	HR	RBI	Avg		AB	H	HR	RBI	Avg
Home	105	28	6	16	.267	LHP	76	21	2	6	.276
Road	92	21	1	11	.228	RHP	121	28	5	21	.231
First Half	117	28	5	19	.239	Sc Pos	37	9	3	20	.243
Scnd Half	80	21	2	8	.263	Clutch	32	8	1	7	.250

2002 Season

Persistence paid off for A.J. Hinch. He enjoyed his best season ever in the majors, albeit in a reserve role. Playing a couple of times per week behind Royals starter Brent Mayne, Hinch hit for a bit of power and produced a useful batting average for the first time in his major league career.

Hitting, Baserunning & Defense

Hinch will look for a first-pitch fastball to pull before settling into his usual patient approach. He's a good breaking-ball hitter who can be overpowered by hard throwers, especially right-handers. He has worked to improve his contact-hitting ability, and also has improved his situational hitting. Hinch calls a good game, but an average arm limits his success in the field. He has better speed than the average catcher, though it doesn't make him much of a basestealing threat.

2003 Outlook

Despite his unexpected success in 2002, Hinch must fight for a big league role. He elected to become a free agent after being optioned to Triple-A in October. He remains unproven as a regular and hasn't shown any extraordinary skills off the bench. Hinch is a replacement-level catcher whose playing time will be strictly dependent upon the needs of his organization in 2003.

Darrell May

Position: SP
Bats: L **Throws:** L
Ht: 6' 2" **Wt:** 184

Opening Day Age: 30
Born: 6/13/72 in San Bernardino, CA
ML Seasons: 4

Overall Statistics

	W	L	Pct.	ERA	G	GS	Sv	IP	H	BB	SO	HR	Ratio
'02	4	10	.286	5.35	30	21	0	131.1	144	50	95	28	1.48
Car.	6	12	.333	5.67	71	25	0	198.1	228	81	144	40	1.56

2002 Situational Stats

	W	L	ERA	Sv	IP		AB	H	HR	RBI	Avg
Home	3	2	4.85	0	59.1	LHB	139	40	6	24	.288
Road	1	8	5.75	0	72.0	RHB	381	104	22	53	.273
First Half	2	5	4.92	0	60.1	Sc Pos	125	39	5	50	.312
Scnd Half	2	5	5.70	0	71.0	Clutch	35	11	2	8	.314

2002 Season

Darrell May spent four seasons in Japan and led the Japanese Central League in strikeouts in 2001. He passed up significant money to return to the States and a chance to pitch in the majors again. He started slowly due to a groin strain that twice landed him on the disabled list. May lost his rotation job, but pitched well enough in relief to return to the rotation by season's end.

Pitching & Defense

May spots an upper-80s fastball and mixes in changeups and sliders to set up a sharp curve. Because he lacks a blazing fastball, he has to work the corners and stay ahead in the count in order to use his curve as an out pitch. When he falls behind, May is susceptible to the longball. His stuff is better suited to rotation duty, although he didn't show the ability to go more than six innings last year. He lacks an effective pickoff move and baserunners stole 13 times in 14 tries last year. May is not an adept fielder.

2003 Outlook

The Royals hoped to bring May back as a veteran lefty anchor for their developing young staff. Now that he has a full year back in the majors under his belt, May can concentrate on putting together a consistent season in a big league rotation.

Mark Quinn

Position: RF
Bats: R **Throws:** R
Ht: 6' 1" **Wt:** 195

Opening Day Age: 28
Born: 5/21/74 in La Miranda, CA
ML Seasons: 4

Overall Statistics

	G	AB	R	H	D	T	HR	RBI	SB	BB	SO	Avg	OBP	Slg
'02	23	76	9	18	4	0	2	11	2	5	15	.237	.301	.368
Car.	293	1089	153	307	72	5	45	167	17	56	186	.282	.324	.481

2002 Situational Stats

	AB	H	HR	RBI	Avg		AB	H	HR	RBI	Avg
Home	32	8	2	7	.250	LHP	23	8	1	6	.348
Road	44	10	0	4	.227	RHP	53	10	1	5	.189
First Half	76	18	2	11	.237	Sc Pos	21	5	0	8	.238
Scnd Half	0	0	0	0	–	Clutch	9	3	0	1	.333

2002 Season

A non-baseball related cracked rib sidelined Mark Quinn until mid-May. He then strained his left hamstring in June in a game, and later was lost for the season when he slipped on a curb and sprained his right ankle in August. Early in the year, his ribcage injury prevented him from swinging the bat. Later, his hamstring and ankle injuries kept him from running. It was a lost year for Quinn.

Hitting, Baserunning & Defense

One of baseball's most aggressive fastball hitters, Quinn frequently puts himself in a hole by swinging at bad pitches, trying to jack every ball out. He has developed a reputation for stubbornness in refusing to alter his batting approach. Quinn has above-average speed, but he hasn't made good choices about when to run. While he has a good arm and can be a decent outfielder, his focus often has been lacking on defense.

2003 Outlook

Quinn's career took a year off in 2002. When it resumes, which Quinn will return? He can hit for average and power, run and throw, and would be a valuable addition to any lineup. However, if he picks up where he left off, swinging for the fences and making mindless mistakes on the basepaths and in the outfield, he'll earn a place on the bench.

Shawn Sedlacek

Position: SP
Bats: R **Throws:** R
Ht: 6' 4" **Wt:** 200

Opening Day Age: 25
Born: 6/29/77 in Cedar Rapids, IA
ML Seasons: 1

Overall Statistics

	W	L	Pct.	ERA	G	GS	Sv	IP	H	BB	SO	HR	Ratio
'02	3	5	.375	6.72	16	14	0	84.1	99	36	52	16	1.60
Car.	3	5	.375	6.72	16	14	0	84.1	99	36	52	16	1.60

2002 Situational Stats

	W	L	ERA	Sv	IP		AB	H	HR	RBI	Avg
Home	1	4	9.33	0	36.2	LHB	173	56	10	31	.324
Road	2	1	4.72	0	47.2	RHB	154	43	6	26	.279
First Half	0	0	2.84	0	25.1	Sc Pos	80	27	3	40	.338
Scnd Half	3	5	8.39	0	59.0	Clutch	16	6	2	3	.375

2002 Season

Success at Double-A Wichita and Triple-A Omaha earned Shawn Sedlacek his first taste of the big leagues last June. But early success turned to disappointment later in the year and he was demoted to the bullpen. While there were some encouraging signs for Sedlacek, there were just as many indications that he was overmatched in the majors.

Pitching & Defense

Sharp control is central to Sedlacek's game. He throws an upper-80s fastball, sinker and slider, and he spots a straight-breaking curve. He uses a deceptive changeup as an out pitch. He doesn't yet have the power to blow away hitters, so he must change speeds to succeed. Nervousness contributed to some of his first-inning problems in 2002. He steadied considerably later in games. Sedlacek is a bit awkward as a fielder, though he held baserunners well enough last year.

2003 Outlook

Sedlacek remains a work in progress. He needs to spend the season building arm strength, refining his control and trying to add a little more pop to his heater. But the Royals' desperation for pitching may cause them to keep an unpolished Sedlacek on their staff all year, with potentially disappointing results.

Other Kansas City Royals

Jeff Austin (Pos: RHP, Age: 26)

	W	L	Pct.	ERA	G	GS	Sv	IP	H	BB	SO	HR	Ratio
'02	0	0	–	4.91	10	0	0	11.0	14	6	6	0	1.82
Car.	0	0	–	5.35	31	0	0	37.0	41	20	33	4	1.65

Austin beat a regular path between Kansas City and Omaha, but he didn't work much for the Royals. He pitched well at Triple-A Omaha, posting a 3.27 ERA working strictly as a reliever. May have found his niche. 2003 Outlook: C

Cory Bailey (Pos: RHP, Age: 32)

	W	L	Pct.	ERA	G	GS	Sv	IP	H	BB	SO	HR	Ratio
'02	3	4	.429	4.11	37	0	1	46.0	53	31	24	5	1.83
Car.	9	10	.474	3.96	172	0	1	207.0	208	116	150	13	1.57

Bailey was OK in the Royals' pen in 2001, but he was more hittable and wild last summer, and by midseason he was shipped out to Triple-A Omaha and he never returned. Now he's a free agent. 2003 Outlook: C

Juan Brito (Pos: C, Age: 23, Bats: R)

	G	AB	R	H	D	T	HR	RBI	SB	BB	SO	Avg	OBP	Slg
'02	9	23	1	7	2	0	0	1	0	0	3	.304	.304	.391
Car.	9	23	1	7	2	0	0	1	0	0	3	.304	.304	.391

Brito batted .304 during a month-long stay in May, but don't get excited. He has a .256 career average in six minor league seasons and he doesn't draw walks. He didn't walk once with the Royals. 2003 Outlook: C

Mike Caruso (Pos: SS, Age: 25, Bats: L)

	G	AB	R	H	D	T	HR	RBI	SB	BB	SO	Avg	OBP	Slg
'02	12	20	3	2	0	0	0	0	0	1	2	.100	.143	.100
Car.	281	1072	144	294	28	10	7	90	34	35	76	.274	.302	.339

In late June, Caruso made his first big league appearance since his White Sox days of 1999. While he batted .306 at Triple-A Omaha, he managed just two hits in 20 at-bats and was gone in early August. 2003 Outlook: C

Chad Durbin (Pos: RHP, Age: 25)

	W	L	Pct.	ERA	G	GS	Sv	IP	H	BB	SO	HR	Ratio
'02	0	1	.000	11.88	2	2	0	8.1	13	4	5	3	2.04
Car.	11	22	.333	6.01	48	47	0	262.0	306	106	140	43	1.57

Durbin started 2002 in the Royals' rotation, but after two rugged outings he was shipped off to Triple-A Omaha. By late April he had a tender elbow that led to September surgery. He's out all of next year. 2003 Outlook: D

Nate Field (Pos: RHP, Age: 27)

	W	L	Pct.	ERA	G	GS	Sv	IP	H	BB	SO	HR	Ratio
'02	0	0	–	9.00	5	0	0	5.0	8	3	3	2	2.20
Car.	0	0	–	9.00	5	0	0	5.0	8	3	3	2	2.20

Field debuted with five relief appearances for the Royals in April, but he spent the year in Triple-A ball. He joined Triple-A Columbus and struggled after the Yanks picked him up off waivers in June. 2003 Outlook: C

Aaron Guiel (Pos: RF, Age: 30, Bats: L)

	G	AB	R	H	D	T	HR	RBI	SB	BB	SO	Avg	OBP	Slg
'02	70	240	30	56	13	0	4	38	1	19	61	.233	.296	.338
Car.	70	240	30	56	13	0	4	38	1	19	61	.233	.296	.338

Guiel batted .353 and slugged .540 at Triple-A Omaha in 2002, his fifth Triple-A season. He got his first callup in June and batted .435 with 10 RBI in eight games that month before cooling off quickly. 2003 Outlook: C

Donzell McDonald (Pos: LF, Age: 28, Bats: B)

	G	AB	R	H	D	T	HR	RBI	SB	BB	SO	Avg	OBP	Slg
'02	10	22	3	4	2	0	0	1	1	4	5	.182	.296	.273
Car.	15	25	3	5	2	0	0	1	1	4	7	.200	.300	.280

While Donzell's career hitting percentages in the minors are better than brother Darnell's, who is in the Orioles system, his 2002 Triple-A percentages were not as good. Darnell may debut first. Donzell signed a minor league deal with Atlanta. 2003 Outlook: C

Scott Mullen (Pos: LHP, Age: 28)

	W	L	Pct.	ERA	G	GS	Sv	IP	H	BB	SO	HR	Ratio
'02	4	5	.444	3.15	44	0	0	40.0	40	13	21	5	1.33
Car.	4	5	.444	3.58	72	0	0	60.1	63	25	31	7	1.46

Walks became an issue late in 2002 with the Royals, but Mullen enjoyed a decent season split between Triple-A Omaha and Kansas City. He wasn't very effective against lefties, though. 2003 Outlook: C

Wes Obermueller (Pos: RHP, Age: 26)

	W	L	Pct.	ERA	G	GS	Sv	IP	H	BB	SO	HR	Ratio
'02	0	2	.000	11.74	2	2	0	7.2	14	2	5	3	2.09
Car.	0	2	.000	11.74	2	2	0	7.2	14	2	5	3	2.09

Obermueller went 14-5 (2.85) as a 25-year-old between high Class-A and Double-A stops in 2002, but with the Royals he was roughed up for 10 runs and three homers in two starts against guys more his own age. 2003 Outlook: C

Luis Ordaz (Pos: 2B, Age: 27, Bats: R)

	G	AB	R	H	D	T	HR	RBI	SB	BB	SO	Avg	OBP	Slg
'02	33	94	11	21	2	0	0	4	2	12	13	.223	.308	.245
Car.	205	438	51	96	13	0	0	30	12	34	53	.219	.276	.249

Ordaz did little for the Cubs' Triple-A Iowa club in the first half of the season. But he was cut loose and ripped it up at Triple-A Omaha (.309 average and .493 SLG) before arriving in Kansas City and showing his true colors. 2003 Outlook: C

Kit Pellow (Pos: 3B, Age: 29, Bats: R)

	G	AB	R	H	D	T	HR	RBI	SB	BB	SO	Avg	OBP	Slg
'02	29	63	6	15	1	0	1	5	1	9	21	.238	.342	.302
Car.	29	63	6	15	1	0	1	5	1	9	21	.238	.342	.302

Pellow has shown power and high strikeout totals in four Triple-A seasons. The power disappeared with the Royals, but he still struck out one of every three at-bats. At least he drew walks. 2003 Outlook: C

Chan Perry (Pos: 1B, **Age**: 30, **Bats**: R)

	G	AB	R	H	D	T	HR	RBI	SB	BB	SO	Avg	OBP	Slg
'02	5	11	0	1	0	0	0	3	0	0	1	.091	.091	.091
Car.	18	25	1	2	0	0	0	3	0	0	6	.080	.080	.080

The minor league vet dropped down to Double-A Wichita in 2002 and put up good numbers, but he managed just one hit in a second-half recall. But going 1-for-11 raised his career average by nine points. 2003 Outlook: C

Dan Reichert (Pos: RHP, **Age**: 26)

	W	L	Pct.	ERA	G	GS	Sv	IP	H	BB	SO	HR	Ratio
'02	3	5	.375	5.32	30	6	0	66.0	77	25	36	10	1.55
Car.	21	25	.457	5.53	109	51	2	379.0	413	215	227	41	1.66

Reichert hadn't pitched particularly well since a 9-2 run at Triple-A Omaha in 1999, and the Royals allowed the Devil Rays to claim him off waivers on September 20. 2003 Outlook: C

Bryan Rekar (Pos: RHP, **Age**: 30)

	W	L	Pct.	ERA	G	GS	Sv	IP	H	BB	SO	HR	Ratio
'02	0	2	.000	15.43	2	2	0	7.0	12	6	2	1	2.57
Car.	25	49	.338	5.62	131	108	0	655.0	788	208	383	99	1.52

Rekar arrived from the minors in late April, but after two brutal starts he was gone and was dealt to Colorado in May. Just the place for a guy with a 5.62 ERA, but free agency now gives him new life. 2003 Outlook: C

Brian Shouse (Pos: LHP, **Age**: 34)

	W	L	Pct.	ERA	G	GS	Sv	IP	H	BB	SO	HR	Ratio
'02	0	0	–	6.14	23	0	0	14.2	15	9	11	3	1.64
Car.	0	1	.000	6.41	36	0	0	26.2	31	15	19	6	1.73

After solid Triple-A seasons in 2000 and '01, Shouse made the Royals and pitched well in April. Elbow pain in May led to a DL stint, a bad year and eventually, his release. He and Texas agreed to a minor league deal. 2003 Outlook: C

Blake Stein (Pos: RHP, **Age**: 29)

	W	L	Pct.	ERA	G	GS	Sv	IP	H	BB	SO	HR	Ratio
'02	0	4	.000	7.91	27	2	1	46.2	59	27	42	6	1.84
Car.	21	28	.429	5.41	117	66	2	475.2	451	281	369	78	1.54

Other than a solid stint in August, when he posted a 1.35 ERA in nine games, Stein wasn't effective and the Royals finally cut ties when they released him in early September. 2003 Outlook: C

Mac Suzuki (Pos: RHP, **Age**: 27)

	W	L	Pct.	ERA	G	GS	Sv	IP	H	BB	SO	HR	Ratio
'02	0	2	.000	9.00	7	1	0	21.0	24	17	15	2	1.95
Car.	16	31	.340	5.72	117	67	0	465.2	501	265	327	67	1.64

Suzuki was a prospect nearly a decade ago, but he has never really had a good season in the minors or the majors. His second go-round with the Royals began in late May and was over just six weeks later. 2003 Outlook: C

Brad Voyles (Pos: RHP, **Age**: 26)

	W	L	Pct.	ERA	G	GS	Sv	IP	H	BB	SO	HR	Ratio
'02	0	2	.000	6.51	22	0	1	27.2	31	18	26	5	1.77
Car.	0	2	.000	5.84	29	0	1	37.0	36	26	32	6	1.68

Voyles' walk rate has been high throughout his pro career, and it was true at Triple-A Omaha and Kansas City in 2002, though Voyles did post five saves and 34 strikeouts in 32.1 frames with a 4.18 ERA at Omaha. 2003 Outlook: C

Dusty Wathan (Pos: C, **Age**: 29, **Bats**: R)

	G	AB	R	H	D	T	HR	RBI	SB	BB	SO	Avg	OBP	Slg
'02	3	5	1	3	1	0	0	1	0	0	1	.600	.667	.800
Car.	3	5	1	3	1	0	0	1	0	0	1	.600	.667	.800

Wathan got his first cup-of-coffee in the majors in 2002, and it was like celebrating with two chocolate donuts on the side. He doubled home a run in his first at-bat and was 3-for-5 on the season. 2003 Outlook: C

Kris Wilson (Pos: RHP, **Age**: 26)

	W	L	Pct.	ERA	G	GS	Sv	IP	H	BB	SO	HR	Ratio
'02	2	0	1.000	8.20	12	0	0	18.2	29	5	10	7	1.82
Car.	8	6	.571	5.32	61	15	1	162.1	199	48	94	36	1.52

Elbow tendinitis kept him off the mound until May, but Wilson posted a 2.30 ERA in 74.1 relief innings in the high minors. He wasn't effective in Kansas City, but a healthier Wilson in 2003 may be. 2003 Outlook: B

Kansas City Royals Minor League Prospects

Organization Overview:

With Kansas City focusing on developing pitching prospects, its steady production of position players gradually has depleted the farm system of potential big leaguers. Angel Berroa, Dee Brown and Ken Harvey will compete for major league jobs in 2003, while Alexis Gomez and Alejandro Machado are a few years away. The rest of the Royals' major league potential is tied up in their stable of young arms, most notably starter prospects Chris George, Jimmy Gobble, Kyle Snyder and Brian Sanches, and relief prospects Ryan Bukvich, Jeremy Hill and Mike MacDougal. The Royals have been using nearly all of their top draft picks on pitching since 1997, and they will be relying heavily upon that investment in 2003.

Angel Berroa

Position: SS
Bats: R **Throws:** R
Ht: 6' 0" **Wt:** 175
Opening Day Age: 25
Born: 1/27/78 in Santo Domingo, DR

Recent Statistics

	G	AB	R	H	D	T	HR	RBI	SB	BB	SO	Avg
2002 AAA Omaha	77	297	37	64	11	4	8	35	6	15	84	.215
2002 AL Kansas City	20	75	8	17	7	1	0	5	3	7	10	.227

Berroa had the kind of season in 2002 that can age a player quickly. Literally. First, his visa application revealed he was two years older than previously reported. Then he tore cartilage in his right knee, nearly wiping half of his campaign. Berroa is an aggressive hitter who possesses surprising power and above-average speed, although his baserunning instincts are poor. He will have to show far better plate discipline in the majors. Berroa has the defensive tools to succeed in the big leagues: a powerful arm and the range to make any play. He needs only to take more care on the routine plays to be among the better shortstops in the majors when he becomes the Royals' regular this season. The pressure will be on Berroa, as he'll be remembered as the compensation for the unpopular Johnny Damon trade.

Dee Brown

Position: OF
Bats: L **Throws:** R
Ht: 6' 0" **Wt:** 225
Opening Day Age: 25
Born: 3/27/78 in Bronx, NY

Recent Statistics

	G	AB	R	H	D	T	HR	RBI	SB	BB	SO	Avg
2002 AAA Omaha	121	458	66	126	23	1	17	75	10	44	111	.275
2002 AL Kansas City	16	51	5	12	3	1	1	7	0	4	20	.235

There's no mistaking that Brown is an athlete. His powerful build and good speed make an immediate impression. However, Brown has made little impact as a baseball player since his major league debut in 1998. He remains an aggressive hitter who alternately lets good pitches go by, then overswings at bad ones. He would benefit by shortening his stroke to make better contact and let his natural power drive the ball for extra bases. Despite his speed, Brown is a poor outfielder with a below-average arm, and he does not read flyballs well. But Brown likely will have a prominent role in the Royals' latest youth movement.

Ryan Bukvich

Position: P
Bats: R **Throws:** R
Ht: 6' 2" **Wt:** 250
Opening Day Age: 24
Born: 5/13/78 in Naperville, IL

Recent Statistics

	W	L	ERA	G	GS	Sv	IP	H	R	BB	SO	HR
2002 AA Wichita	1	1	1.31	23	0	8	34.1	17	8	15	47	0
2002 AAA Omaha	1	0	0.00	12	0	8	13.2	4	0	7	17	0
2002 AL Kansas City	1	0	6.12	26	0	0	25.0	26	19	19	20	2

Bukvich blasted through the upper minors last year, posting a sub-1.00 ERA and fanning 64 in 48 innings at Double-A Wichita and Triple-A Omaha before joining the Royals' pen in July. He works primarily with a mid-90s fastball, mixing in hard sliders and splitters. Control is the biggest problem for Bukvich, who occasionally overthrows his hard stuff. He has shown good composure under pressure in the minors, but he hasn't been tested in late, close games in the majors. Recent attempts by the Royals to develop their own closer have met with failure, so Bukvich will have to overcome long odds to grab the job in 2003. He likely will be given a baptism by fire, with Jeremy Hill and Mike MacDougal waiting in the wings should he stumble.

Chris George

Position: P
Bats: L **Throws:** L
Ht: 6' 2" **Wt:** 200
Opening Day Age: 23
Born: 9/16/79 in Houston, TX

Recent Statistics

	W	L	ERA	G	GS	Sv	IP	H	R	BB	SO	HR
2002 AAA Omaha	6	12	5.87	22	21	0	127.1	145	86	65	94	15
2002 AL Kansas City	0	4	5.60	6	6	0	27.1	37	17	8	13	2

Chris George often has been compared to Tom Glavine as he has advanced through the Royals' system, but George fell on hard times in 2002. Some scouts feel he tried too hard to rack up strikeouts and left too many hittable pitches up in the zone. The comparisons to Glavine come from George's moving, low-90s fastball, top-notch changeup and above-average slider, and his advanced knowledge of how to pitch. While 2002 was a setback, George still has the potential to become a No. 1 or 2 starter in the majors. A focus on pitching to his strengths by changing speeds and location could quickly restore his top-prospect status.

Jimmy Gobble

Position: P		**Opening Day Age:** 21	
Bats: L **Throws:** L		**Born:** 7/19/81 in Bristol, TN	
Ht: 6' 3" **Wt:** 190			

Recent Statistics

	W	L	ERA	G	GS	Sv	IP	H	R	BB	SO	HR
2001 A Wilmington	10	6	2.55	27	27	0	162.1	134	58	33	154	8
2002 AA Wichita	5	7	3.38	13	13	0	69.1	71	29	19	52	3

If Chris George doesn't meet the challenge, perhaps this fellow lefty will. Gobble also has a moving, low-90s fastball which he complements with an outstanding curveball. Gobble reached Double-A for the first time in 2002, but his season was cut short by trips to the disabled list with a groin injury. Although he wasn't a big winner at Wichita, he did strike out nearly three times as many batters as he walked, and he kept the ball in the yard at one of the Texas League's better power parks. Gobble needs another full season in the high minors to develop more stamina, and also to refine his command before challenging for a big league job late in 2003.

Alexis Gomez

Position: OF		**Opening Day Age:** 22	
Bats: L **Throws:** L		**Born:** 8/6/80 in Loma de Cabrera, DR	
Ht: 6' 2" **Wt:** 180			

Recent Statistics

	G	AB	R	H	D	T	HR	RBI	SB	BB	SO	Avg
2002 AA Wichita	114	461	72	136	21	8	14	75	36	45	84	.295
2002 AL Kansas City	5	10	0	2	0	0	0	0	0	0	2	.200

Only chicken pox slowed Gomez in 2002. He hit for power and average, and stole everything that wasn't nailed down in finishing among the Double-A Texas League leaders in most offensive categories. Gomez covers a lot of ground in center field and displays a good arm. Like many Royals prospects, though, Gomez lacks plate discipline. He has been prone to inconsistency, but that is partly due to being one of the youngest regulars at each level he has visited. The Royals see him as a raw talent who just needs experience—they won't rush him to the majors just yet. Gomez will start 2003 in Triple-A Omaha, and should challenge for a regular job in 2004.

Ken Harvey

Position: 1B		**Opening Day Age:** 25	
Bats: R **Throws:** R		**Born:** 3/1/78 in Los Angeles, CA	
Ht: 6' 2" **Wt:** 240			

Recent Statistics

	G	AB	R	H	D	T	HR	RBI	SB	BB	SO	Avg
2001 A Wilmington	35	137	22	52	9	1	6	27	3	13	21	.380
2001 AA Wichita	79	314	54	106	20	3	9	63	3	18	60	.338
2001 AL Kansas City	4	12	1	3	2	0	0	2	0	0	4	.250
2002 AAA Omaha	128	488	75	135	30	1	20	75	8	42	87	.277

You can't help but think "power hitter" when looking at the burly Harvey, but it would be more appropriate to see Mo Vaughn or Frank Thomas, who both developed primarily as line-drive hitters before displaying their power in the majors. Harvey is a pure hitter who has hit for a high average at almost every level in his minor league career before having a breakout showing in the Arizona Fall League. He credits his success to tweaking his swing at the end of the 2002 season and refocusing on making contact. A nagging toe injury has slowed Harvey on the bases and in the field. He's not a bad baserunner, but is barely adequate around the bag at first base. Harvey is expected to challenge for a share of the big league DH job in 2003.

Jeremy Hill

Position: P		**Opening Day Age:** 25	
Bats: R **Throws:** R		**Born:** 8/8/77 in Dallas, TX	
Ht: 5' 10" **Wt:** 185			

Recent Statistics

	W	L	ERA	G	GS	Sv	IP	H	R	BB	SO	HR
2002 AA Wichita	4	7	2.36	56	0	19	76.1	61	26	32	80	4
2002 AL Kansas City	0	1	3.86	10	0	0	9.1	8	4	8	7	1

Beginning his pro career as a catcher has stunted Hill's development as a pitcher. Thus he has just one major league pitch, a mid-90s fastball, and his hard slider is still subpar. Still, Hill made spectacular progress through the minors, blowing away hitters at Double-A Wichita in 2002 to earn his major league debut in just his second year as a pro pitcher. He wasn't overmatched in Kansas City, and had just one bad outing in 10 September appearances. Like fellow Kansas City relief prospect Ryan Bukvich, Hill hasn't been tested in late, close games in the majors, although he brings a competitive fire necessary to all successful closers.

Others to Watch

The conversion to short relief for **Mike MacDougal** (26) continued with six September major league outings in 2002. He has a lively fastball, but the mid-90s offering has been tough to corral, leading him to walk more than a batter per inning last year. In winter ball, his work as a closer continued, and his fastball reached the upper-90s with improved command. MacDougal will battle Ryan Bukvich and Jeremy Hill for the big league closer's job. . . The Royals lack middle-infield talent, and they might get some help if they can wait until **Alejandro Machado** (20) is ready. Machado held his own—and then some—last year in the high Class-A Carolina League at the tender age of 20, leading his team in average while stealing 20 bases. He projects as a big league second baseman who runs well and hits for average. . . Righthander **Brian Sanches** (24) had more success in his second try at the Double-A level in 2002, leading the Wranglers in victories and strikeouts. Sanches works with a 90-MPH sinking fastball to set up an outstanding curveball. . . Fresh off Tommy John surgery in 2001, righthander **Kyle Snyder** (25) rebounded in six outings for Double-A Wichita and seven more impressive outings in the Arizona Fall League. Snyder has a mid-90s fastball and useful offspeed stuff, and he shows great poise on the mound.

Hubert H. Humphrey Metrodome

Offense

The American League Central champs have been built to play in the Dome, featuring a lineup heavy on lefthanded hitters who can take advantage of the short right-field fence, and with better-than-average speed at most positions. Contrary to popular perception, the Dome isn't a home-run haven. Instead, it favors hitters with gap power and the speed to stretch singles into doubles. The Twins tied Boston for the American League lead in doubles and were fourth in the AL in triples.

Defense

It's equally true that the Twins have been built to play a solid defensive game at the Dome. The slick artificial turf requires excellent range and quickness up the middle, and the Twins have that in the double-play combination of Luis Rivas and Cristian Guzman and center fielder Torii Hunter. The turf also requires quickness at the corners, and Corey Koskie, Doug Mientkiewicz and Jacque Jones fit the desired mold.

Who It Helps the Most

The Dome favors lefthanded hitters capable of bouncing line drives off—or over—the blue tarp that hangs atop the short right-field fence. The righthanded-hitting Hunter has the speed to take advantage of turf hits and gap doubles. Pitchers who succeed there have excellent control and keep the ball down. Control artist Brad Radke has a career 3.97 ERA at the Dome.

Who It Hurts the Most

Righthanded hitters with marginal speed who try too hard to hit home runs will not benefit from the Dome's quirks. A case in point in 2002 was Dustan Mohr, who hit .216 with three homers at home. Michael Cuddyer hit .231 with two homers. Righthanded pitchers have to learn how to use the Dome to their advantage.

Rookies & Newcomers

In need of righthanded punch, the Twins are going to give Cuddyer a shot at winning the right-field job in the spring. Matthew LeCroy, another young righthanded power hitter, might unseat lefthanded David Ortiz as the designated hitter.

Dimensions: LF-343, LCF-385, CF-408, RCF-367, RF-327

Capacity: 48,678

Elevation: 815 feet

Surface: Turf

Foul Territory: Average

Minnesota

Park Factors

2002 Season

	Home Games Twins	Opp	Total	Away Games Twins	Opp	Total	Index
G	72	72	144	71	71	142	
Avg	.279	.251	.265	.271	.274	.272	97
AB	2432	2521	4953	2523	2435	4958	99
R	357	287	644	336	348	684	93
H	678	634	1312	684	666	1350	96
2B	174	132	306	137	122	259	118
3B	22	17	39	9	13	22	177
HR	63	66	129	89	96	185	70
BB	217	195	412	204	197	401	103
SO	452	472	924	505	417	922	100
E	30	51	81	39	53	92	87
E-Infield	25	43	68	34	47	81	83
LHB-Avg	.287	.254	.273	.274	.295	.283	96
LHB-HR	30	34	64	54	49	103	64
RHB-Avg	.268	.249	.257	.266	.257	.261	99
RHB-HR	33	32	65	35	47	82	77

2000-2002

	Home Games Twins	Opp	Total	Away Games Twins	Opp	Total	Index
G	216	216	432	215	215	430	
Avg	.276	.272	.274	.269	.273	.271	101
AB	7317	7708	15025	7612	7303	14915	100
R	1073	1050	2123	988	1062	2050	103
H	2019	2098	4117	2048	1993	4041	101
2B	481	435	916	420	377	797	114
3B	66	52	118	43	38	81	145
HR	176	240	416	218	275	493	84
BB	701	595	1296	666	659	1325	97
SO	1355	1476	2831	1479	1183	2662	106
E	116	163	279	150	157	307	90
E-Infield	94	138	232	131	138	269	86
LHB-Avg	.288	.281	.285	.274	.282	.277	103
LHB-HR	98	110	208	133	115	248	85
RHB-Avg	.259	.267	.264	.262	.266	.265	100
RHB-HR	78	130	208	85	160	245	82

2002 Rankings (American League)

- Second-highest triple factor
- Third-highest double factor
- Third-highest walk factor
- Lowest home-run factor
- Second-lowest LHB home-run factor
- Third-lowest hit factor
- Third-lowest infield-error factor
- Third-lowest LHB batting-average factor

Ron Gardenhire

2002 Season

It wasn't always smooth sailing for rookie manager Ron Gardenhire. The Twins had to overcome injuries to starting pitchers Joe Mays, Brad Radke and Eric Milton, as well as regulars Luis Rivas, Corey Koskie and David Ortiz. Gardenhire deserves credit for creating an atmosphere in which young players like J.C. Romero, Johan Santana, Kyle Lohse, Dustan Mohr and Bobby Kielty thrived. In the end, the Twins coasted to the division title, getting a double-digit lead for the first time on July 15 and stretching the margin to as much as 17 games.

Offense

The Twins scored enough runs to win, although it's a bit of a mystery how. The tablesetters, Jacque Jones and Cristian Guzman, lack patience and had dismal on-base percentages. And the club is top-heavy with lefthanded hitters. A major problem is the fact that the lineup is filled with free swingers who lack patience, and those failings showed in the ALCS loss to Anaheim.

Pitching & Defense

The foundation of the Twins' success is defense, with center fielder Torii Hunter and first baseman Doug Mientkiewicz among the best at their positions in the majors. The Twins' defense is built for the Dome's artificial surface, relying on speed up the middle. Starting pitching was expected to be the key to Minnesota's success, but Gardenhire showed he was not afraid to call upon the bullpen to help save the injury-plagued rotation. Eddie Guardado set a team record with 45 saves, and J.C. Romero, LaTroy Hawkins and Johan Santana had solid seasons.

2003 Outlook

The Twins were the class of the American League Central last season, despite a combined 13-13 record from Radke (9-5) and Mays (4-8). If Mays can bounce back to his 17-win form of 2001, and Radke has his normal season, the club should win another AL Central title. The question is whether tight-fisted owner Carl Pohlad will spend enough to keep the roster intact. Young players such as Santana, Michael Cuddyer and Matt LeCroy may be asked to shoulder a bigger load in 2003.

Born: 10/24/57 in Butzbach, West Germany

Playing Experience: 1981-1985, NYM

Managerial Experience: 1 season

Manager Statistics

Year	Team, Lg	W	L	Pct	GB	Finish
2002	Minnesota, AL	94	67	.584	–	1st Central
1 Season		94	67	.584	–	–

2002 Starting Pitchers by Days Rest

	<=3	4	5	6+
Twins Starts	2	94	34	22
Twins ERA	16.71	4.57	3.74	4.05
AL Avg Starts	1	83	44	24
AL ERA	7.15	4.59	4.27	5.03

2002 Situational Stats

	Ron Gardenhire	AL Average
Hit & Run Success %	24.2	36.0
Stolen Base Success %	56.0	68.1
Platoon Pct.	68.9	58.9
Defensive Subs	41	23
High-Pitch Outings	4	6
Quick/Slow Hooks	27/12	19/14
Sacrifice Attempts	49	53

2002 Rankings (American League)

- 1st in steals of home plate (1), squeeze plays (6), quick hooks and starts on three days rest
- 2nd in double steals (5), sacrifice-bunt percentage (85.7%), defensive substitutions, relief appearances (435) and 2+ pitching changes in low-scoring games (37)
- 3rd in hit-and-run attempts (91)

Cristian Guzman

2002 Season

Cristian Guzman looked like a budding star when he earned a spot on the 2001 All-Star team. But the shortstop now is more enigma than All-Star, a player of immense physical talent whose lack of consistency might keep him from realizing his potential. He's also injury prone, suffering from knee and shoulder problems the last two seasons. Team officials questioned Guzman's work ethic early last season, and his effort did improve during the second half. But the overall numbers were down in 2002.

Hitting

Guzman has power, combining for 34 triples and 18 home runs in the 2000 and 2001 seasons. But he became more of a slap hitter last season. With his tremendous speed, Guzman should be a better hitter on turf. But surprisingly, in 2002 he had a .266 average on turf and a .280 mark on natural grass. His biggest shortcoming at the plate is his lack of patience. He has the physical gifts to be a leadoff hitter, but he walked only 17 times in 656 plate appearances last season. He's a good fastball hitter, but when he falls behind in the count, he'll chase pitches outside the zone.

Baserunning & Defense

Guzman has the speed to be a tremendous threat on the bases, but he needs to get his knees fully healthy and improve his basestealing technique. His success rate dropped from 76 percent in 2001 to 48 percent last season. He has exceptional range defensively, and appeared to regain strength in his injured right shoulder as the season progressed. The rap on Guzman has been that he'll make the great play, then boot a routine grounder because of his lackadaisical style. Still, he reduced his errors from 21 in 2001 to 12 last year.

2003 Outlook

Guzman should rebound in 2003. He has the physical ability to hit .300 with power, but he needs to develop a more consistent approach to his job. If he dedicates himself to returning to his 2001 form, Guzman will be among the league's elite shortstops. Otherwise, he may remain the enigma that he was for much of 2002.

Position: SS
Bats: B **Throws:** R
Ht: 6' 0" **Wt:** 195

Opening Day Age: 25
Born: 3/21/78 in Santo Domingo, DR
ML Seasons: 4
Pronunciation: GOOZ-mahn

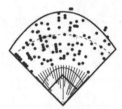

Minnesota

Overall Statistics

	G	AB	R	H	D	T	HR	RBI	SB	BB	SO	Avg	OBP	Slg
'02	148	623	80	170	31	6	9	59	12	17	79	.273	.292	.385
Car.	553	2167	296	570	96	43	28	190	74	106	348	.263	.299	.386

Where He Hits the Ball

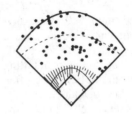

Vs. LHP   **Vs. RHP**

2002 Situational Stats

	AB	H	HR	RBI	Avg		AB	H	HR	RBI	Avg
Home	302	82	6	33	.272	LHP	214	55	5	25	.257
Road	321	88	3	26	.274	RHP	409	115	4	34	.281
First Half	346	89	4	31	.257	Sc Pos	150	39	1	43	.260
Scnd Half	277	81	5	28	.292	Clutch	96	26	3	19	.271

2002 Rankings (American League)

- 2nd in caught stealing (13) and lowest stolen-base percentage (48.0)
- 3rd in lowest on-base percentage
- 4th in highest groundball-flyball ratio (2.0) and highest percentage of swings put into play (53.4)
- Led the Twins in at-bats, singles, triples, sacrifice bunts (8), caught stealing (13), plate appearances (656), highest groundball-flyball ratio (2.0), bunts in play (23), highest percentage of swings put into play (53.4) and batting average on an 0-2 count (.255)

Torii Hunter

2002 Season

First-year manager Ron Gardenhire made it clear to Torii Hunter that the club would accept strikeouts in exchange for power. It proved to be good tradeoff. Hunter let his natural ability take over and didn't fret about his failure to make contact, as he frequently did under former manager Tom Kelly. The result: the center fielder had career highs in batting average, doubles, home runs and RBI. Those numbers, combined with his defense, have made Hunter one of the league's best all-around outfielders.

Hitting

Hunter remains a work in progress at the plate. His lack of patience continues to be a problem. Once he falls behind in the count, he'll chase anything near the strike zone, meaning he sees a steady diet of curves and sliders off the outside corner of the plate. He has become adept at hitting curves that hang over the plate, but more often than not he'll chase pitches outside the strike zone. Hunter batted .155 after he fell behind in the count 0-and-2. He counters by being aggressive early on in the count, which is when he's most dangerous.

Baserunning & Defense

For years the Twins have touted Hunter as a five-tool player, and in this case the scouting report has proven to be correct. He has excellent speed, allowing him to steal a career-high 23 bases in 31 attempts last season. Defensively, he is without peer among American League outfielders. He gets an exceptional jump, attacks flyballs with reckless abandon and possesses a strong, accurate throwing arm. These abilities garnered Hunter another Gold Glove in 2002.

2003 Outlook

Hunter is such a marvelous athlete that it's difficult to tell what his ceiling might be. He made a significant jump offensively in 2002, and his improvement as a hitter may continue. Hunter looks capable of hitting .300 with 30 homers and 30 steals. It's not unreasonable to think he can be a 40-40 player. The trick will be increasing his patience at the plate without curbing his aggressive swing.

Position: CF
Bats: R **Throws:** R
Ht: 6' 2" **Wt:** 205

Opening Day Age: 27
Born: 7/18/75 in Pine Bluff, AR
ML Seasons: 6

Overall Statistics

	G	AB	R	H	D	T	HR	RBI	SB	BB	SO	Avg	OBP	Slg
'02	148	561	89	162	37	4	29	94	23	35	118	.289	.334	.524
Car.	537	1862	267	505	101	18	70	267	46	110	389	.271	.317	.458

Where He Hits the Ball

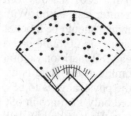 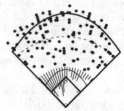

Vs. LHP   **Vs. RHP**

2002 Situational Stats

	AB	H	HR	RBI	Avg		AB	H	HR	RBI	Avg
Home	290	97	13	54	.334	LHP	169	50	6	23	.296
Road	271	65	16	40	.240	RHP	392	112	23	71	.286
First Half	337	103	20	61	.306	Sc Pos	160	41	8	59	.256
Scnd Half	224	59	9	33	.263	Clutch	94	23	5	16	.245

2002 Rankings (American League)

- 3rd in batting average at home
- 5th in fielding percentage in center field (.992)
- 6th in assists in center field (7)
- Led the Twins in home runs, doubles, RBI, stolen bases, GDPs (17), slugging percentage, HR frequency (19.3 ABs per HR), stolen-base percentage (74.2), steals of third (3), highest percentage of extra bases taken as a runner (62.9) and batting average at home
- Led AL center fielders in home runs

Jacque Jones

2002 Season

One of Ron Gardenhire's first moves as manager was to name Jacque Jones his everyday leadoff hitter. The left fielder had been in danger of becoming a platoon player under former manager Tom Kelly because of his failure to hit lefthanded pitching. Jones struggled against lefties again in 2002, batting just .213. But his power and excellent defense in left field were adequate tradeoffs. He had 11 homers leading off games and led Minnesota in games, runs, hits, total bases and outfield assists.

Hitting

Jones likely never will be your prototypical lead-off hitter. He seldom walks, doesn't steal bases, strikes out too much and probably should be platooned more. What he provides is offensive punch at the leadoff position. Jones' biggest shortcoming remains his tendency to swing at anything near the strike zone when he gets behind in the count. In 2002 batted .133 with 56 strikeouts in 105 at-bats after falling behind 0-and-2, and a .154 mark after a 1-and-2 count. When he's ahead in the count and can sit on a fastball, he has the power to drive the pitch.

Baserunning & Defense

Jones has better-than-average speed, but he stole just six bases in 13 attempts last season. He needs to work on his technique and get a better jump if that total is going to rise. Defensively he's among the league's best left fielders. He's a former center fielder who has good speed and gets an excellent jump on the ball. He also has an above-average throwing arm.

2003 Outlook

Jones was eligible for arbitration for the first time this offseason, and the Twins were expected to pay what it takes to keep him in the lineup. The biggest question is whether he'll be back in the leadoff spot, although the free-swinging Twins don't have a lot of other options. If Jones is going to continue to bat leadoff, he needs to show improved patience at the plate. He'll turn 28 in late April, and the Twins need to see that Jones can improve on his shortcomings.

Position: LF
Bats: L **Throws:** L
Ht: 5'10" **Wt:** 176

Opening Day Age: 27
Born: 4/25/75 in San Diego, CA
ML Seasons: 4

Overall Statistics

	G	AB	R	H	D	T	HR	RBI	SB	BB	SO	Avg	OBP	Slg
'02	149	577	96	173	37	2	27	85	6	37	129	.300	.341	.511
Car.	547	1897	273	546	112	9	69	254	28	119	395	.288	.331	.465

Where He Hits the Ball

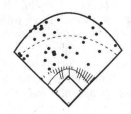
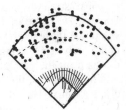

Vs. LHP   **Vs. RHP**

2002 Situational Stats

	AB	H	HR	RBI	Avg		AB	H	HR	RBI	Avg
Home	282	76	6	37	.270	LHP	160	34	3	17	.213
Road	295	97	21	48	.329	RHP	417	139	24	68	.333
First Half	341	97	13	55	.284	Sc Pos	128	45	6	59	.352
Scnd Half	236	76	14	30	.322	Clutch	77	23	3	11	.299

2002 Rankings (American League)

- 2nd in batting average vs. righthanded pitchers, errors in left field (5), assists in left field (11), highest percentage of swings that missed (30.1) and lowest fielding percentage in left field (.986)
- Led the Twins in runs scored, hits, doubles, total bases (295), times on base (212), strikeouts, games played, batting average with runners in scoring position, on-base percentage for a leadoff hitter (.346) and slugging percentage vs. righthanded pitchers (.580)
- Led AL left fielders in batting average and home runs

Corey Koskie

2002 Season

Corey Koskie appeared to be on his way to stardom after the 2001 season, when he became the first Twins player since Gary Gaetti in 1987 to surpass 25 homers and 100 RBI. He also stole 27 bases and scored 100 runs. But Koskie took a large step backward last season, especially in the area of run production. His home-run and RBI numbers dipped, and he batted only .256 with runners in scoring position. He was bothered by several nagging injuries, including a hamstring pull that landed him on the disabled list in May.

Hitting

The former hockey player from Canada has the physical strength and power swing to hit 30 homers. He's one of the few Twins hitters who should be more aggressive in his approach, especially early in the count. Koskie frequently looks too hard for the perfect pitch, which ends up putting him in a hole that forces him to hit the pitcher's best stuff. He's almost always more successful if he tries to drive the first strike he sees. Koskie has power to all fields. He's an excellent low-ball hitter with a quick bat for a big man.

Baserunning & Defense

Koskie's no speedster, but he's a smart baserunner who swiped 27 bases in 33 attempts in 2001. Last season Koskie stole 10 bases in 21 attempts, which is probably closer to his true ability as a basestealing threat. He makes good decisions on the bases, taking the extra base when it's there. He came to the majors extremely rough defensively, and there were doubts he would field well enough to play every day. But he's a tireless worker who has improved his defense to the point where he deserves Gold Glove consideration.

2003 Outlook

The Twins naturally hope that 2002 was just a blip on the radar screen of Koskie's career. He's certain to start again at third base and bat somewhere in the middle of the order. He'll need to improve upon his .253 average against lefthanded pitchers and increase his run-production numbers, but his resume suggests he'll do just that.

Position: 3B
Bats: L **Throws:** R
Ht: 6' 3" **Wt:** 217

Opening Day Age: 29
Born: 6/28/73 in Anola, MB, Canada
ML Seasons: 5
Pronunciation: KOSS-key

Overall Statistics

	G	AB	R	H	D	T	HR	RBI	SB	BB	SO	Avg	OBP	Slg
'02	140	490	71	131	37	3	15	69	10	72	127	.267	.368	.447
Car.	567	1897	294	538	127	9	62	297	46	259	431	.284	.375	.458

Where He Hits the Ball

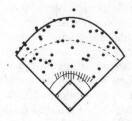 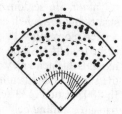

Vs. LHP　　　　**Vs. RHP**

2002 Situational Stats

	AB	H	HR	RBI	Avg		AB	H	HR	RBI	Avg
Home	240	72	6	38	.300	LHP	.162	41	5	15	.253
Road	250	59	9	31	.236	RHP	328	90	10	54	.274
First Half	262	71	8	37	.271	Sc Pos	133	34	2	51	.256
Scnd Half	228	60	7	32	.263	Clutch	74	20	5	20	.270

2002 Rankings (American League)

- 1st in lowest stolen-base percentage (47.6)
- 3rd in fielding percentage at third base (.969)
- 4th in highest percentage of swings that missed (27.8)
- 5th in caught stealing (11)
- 6th in lowest percentage of swings put into play (35.6)
- 9th in errors at third base (12), lowest batting average on the road and highest percentage of swings on the first pitch (36.5)
- Led the Twins in doubles, times on base (212) and pitches seen (2,325)

Joe Mays

Position: SP
Bats: B **Throws:** R
Ht: 6' 1" **Wt:** 185

Opening Day Age: 27
Born: 12/10/75 in Flint, MI
ML Seasons: 4

2002 Season

After his 17-victory season of 2001, Joe Mays was widely acclaimed to have the best stuff among Twins starters. Minnesota officials were so impressed that they signed Mays to a hefty four-year contract. But Mays hit a sizeable bump on the road to stardom in 2002, when an elbow injury sidelined him for more than three months. The righthander returned to the rotation in late July, showing flashes of brilliance (a two-hit shutout on August 16 to defeat Boston's Pedro Martinez), but he was unable to sustain the consistency he showed in 2001.

Pitching

Mays at his best relies on a darting sinker that stays low in the strike zone. Everything Mays throws has excellent movement, including a fastball that hits the low 90s. He'll mix in a curve and change to keep hitters honest. But it's the sinker that sets his stuff apart. Team officials convinced him in 2001 to stop trying to hit corners and finesse hitters, and just throw the sinker for strikes. The movement on the pitch was so good that Mays often was overpowering. The elbow injury took an obvious toll in 2002. After his return in July, he allowed hits and homers at a significantly higher rate than in 2001.

Defense

Mays is only an average athlete, and it shows in his fielding. He has six career errors in 144 total chances, for an uninspiring .958 fielding percentage. He has learned to control his emotions on the mound, and that's helped him reduce his mental miscues. Although he has only an average move to first base, he works quickly and is seldom hurt by stolen bases.

2003 Outlook

Mays probably will begin the season as the team's No. 3 starter. If his elbow is sound, following November surgery to repair a bone spur, he eventually could move to the top of the staff again. Last summer there were games his sinker was as good as it was in 2001, and other games when the pitch lacked movement. The Twins hope a winter of rest and rehabilitation will be the cure.

Overall Statistics

	W	L	Pct.	ERA	G	GS	Sv	IP	H	BB	SO	HR	Ratio
'02	4	8	.333	5.38	17	17	0	95.1	113	25	38	14	1.45
Car.	34	47	.420	4.38	131	99	0	660.1	690	223	378	83	1.38

How Often He Throws Strikes

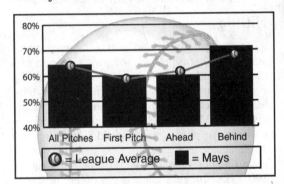

= League Average   = Mays

2002 Situational Stats

	W	L	ERA	Sv	IP		AB	H	HR	RBI	Avg
Home	2	2	4.21	0	51.1	LHB	222	61	10	33	.275
Road	2	6	6.75	0	44.0	RHB	165	52	4	19	.315
First Half	0	2	11.57	0	11.2	Sc Pos	87	32	4	37	.368
Scnd Half	4	6	4.52	0	83.2	Clutch	17	6	0	1	.353

2002 Rankings (American League)

• Did not rank near the top or bottom in any category

Doug Mientkiewicz

2002 Season

Doug Mientkiewicz' performance in 2002 was a mixed bag. His batting average dropped 45 points from his .306 mark of 2001, and most of his power numbers took a corresponding dip. But he batted a solid .306 with runners in scoring position, while increasing his walks and decreasing his strikeouts. And his true value to the team is his glovework at first base, which again was worthy of several SportsCenter highlight films. Mientkiewicz played much of the year with nagging injuries, the most serious of which was a bothersome left wrist. For the second straight year he wore down, batting .177 during the final month in 2001 and .193 in September of last season.

Hitting

A fundamentally sound hitter, Mientkiewicz never is going to produce the power desired of a corner infielder. Yet he has the ability to hit for average with gap power. With his quick wrists, Mientkiewicz is capable of pulling inside pitches toward the Metrodome's short right-field fence or lash outside pitches to left field. He's hit much better at home, where his .293 average was 66 points higher than his average on the road in 2002. His slugging mark is 56 points higher at home over his career.

Baserunning & Defense

Mientkiewicz isn't fast, but he's quick and has excellent instincts defensively. He makes as many diving stops of hard-hit balls as any American League first baseman, and his excellent glove has saved the Twins a run or two in numerous games. He lacks the speed to be an effective basestealer, but he's aggressive when running the basepaths. He is smart enough to take the extra base whenever possible.

2003 Outlook

Mientkiewicz' strength is his glove, and that's reason enough to keep him in the lineup on a daily basis. His patience at the plate and his average with runners in scoring position attest to the fact that he's more valuable offensively than his meager power totals would indicate. The biggest question is how to keep him strong over the course of an entire season.

Position: 1B
Bats: L **Throws:** R
Ht: 6' 2" **Wt:** 200

Opening Day Age: 28
Born: 6/19/74 in Toledo, OH
ML Seasons: 5
Pronunciation: mint-KAY-vich

Overall Statistics

	G	AB	R	H	D	T	HR	RBI	SB	BB	SO	Avg	OBP	Slg
'02	143	467	60	122	29	1	10	64	1	74	69	.261	.365	.392
Car.	423	1376	172	374	90	5	27	176	5	188	215	.272	.363	.403

Where He Hits the Ball

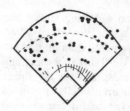
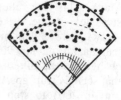

Vs. LHP   **Vs. RHP**

2002 Situational Stats

	AB	H	HR	RBI	Avg		AB	H	HR	RBI	Avg
Home	242	71	6	35	.293	LHP	152	39	4	22	.257
Road	225	51	4	29	.227	RHP	315	83	6	42	.263
First Half	263	67	3	38	.255	Sc Pos	111	34	4	54	.306
Scnd Half	204	55	7	26	.270	Clutch	71	17	2	12	.239

2002 Rankings (American League)

- 4th in fielding percentage at first base (.996)
- Led the Twins in walks, intentional walks (8), lowest percentage of swings that missed (11.1) and lowest percentage of swings on the first pitch (18.9)

Eric Milton

2002 Season

Eric Milton was in the midst of his best stretch of the season when he suffered a knee injury warming up before a start in early August. The left-hander missed a month, and for the most part struggled after his return to the rotation. In his seven starts prior to the injury, Milton was 5-1 with a 2.77 ERA, allowing just seven walks while striking out 47 in 52 innings. Those are the stretches that tantalize, and suggest that Milton has the right stuff to be a staff ace. There are other stretches when Milton is inconsistent with his location, however, resulting in a high number of home runs.

Pitching

Milton's bread and butter is a 94-MPH fastball that he moves in and out. He's at his best when he's hitting the inside corners with that fastball, then mixing in a hard slider and better-than-average curve that he throws at different speeds. Milton has been working on his changeup, and a better offspeed pitch would increase his effectiveness. His slider breaks down and in on righthanded hitters, which is a key reason they batted just .249 against him in 2002. As good as Milton's stuff is, consider this: in five full major league seasons, only once has he had an ERA under 4.49. And only once has he allowed fewer hits than innings pitched. Those numbers attest largely to his inability to consistently locate his fastball.

Defense

Milton is a solid fielder who made only one error last season and has just five miscues in his five major league seasons. He is starting to pitch with a veteran's presence, and he seldom makes mental mistakes in his defensive decision-making. He has a good move to first and is difficult for runners to steal against.

2003 Outlook

The wait goes on for Milton to harness his ability over a full season. Milton can be as dominating as any lefty in the league when he's on. But inconsistency continues to be his biggest enemy. The Twins hope this will be the year he puts the whole package together, but then again, they've been waiting on that for several seasons.

Position: SP
Bats: L **Throws:** L
Ht: 6' 3" **Wt:** 220

Opening Day Age: 27
Born: 8/4/75 in State College, PA
ML Seasons: 5

Overall Statistics

	W	L	Pct.	ERA	G	GS	Sv	IP	H	BB	SO	HR	Ratio
'02	13	9	.591	4.84	29	29	0	171.0	173	30	121	24	1.19
Car.	56	51	.523	4.80	163	162	0	970.1	985	268	708	147	1.29

How Often He Throws Strikes

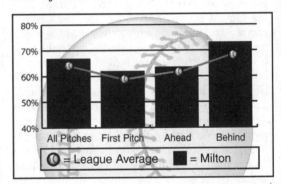

= League Average ■ = Milton

2002 Situational Stats

	W	L	ERA	Sv	IP		AB	H	HR	RBI	Avg
Home	7	6	4.23	0	110.2	LHB	111	34	9	27	.306
Road	6	3	5.97	0	60.1	RHB	559	139	15	63	.249
First Half	10	6	5.21	0	115.2	Sc Pos	135	52	7	66	.385
Scnd Half	3	3	4.07	0	55.1	Clutch	38	7	2	3	.184

2002 Rankings (American League)

- 2nd in lowest groundball-flyball ratio allowed (0.7)
- 3rd in highest strikeout-walk ratio (4.0) and fewest walks per nine innings (1.6)
- 6th in highest ERA
- 8th in most pitches thrown per batter (3.84)
- 10th in lowest on-base percentage allowed (.291), highest slugging percentage allowed (.433), least run support per nine innings (4.7) and lowest fielding percentage at pitcher (.944)
- Led the Twins in losses and complete games (2)

David Ortiz

2002 Season

David Ortiz posted good numbers during the second half of 2002. That's the good news. The bad news is that the designated hitter landed on the disabled list for the third time in his major league career, undergoing left knee surgery to remove bone chips in mid-April. Ortiz also flashed a couple of glaring deficiencies: a .242 average with runners in scoring position and a .203 average against lefthanders. The full-time DH for most of the season, he was platooned for much of the postseason.

Hitting

Potential always has been more intriguing than the present reality with Ortiz. He looks like a player who has all the tools to be a 30-plus home-run hitter in the majors. Injuries certainly have been a factor in preventing him from reaching that level, but so have long periods of inconsistency. He will hit the ball to all fields, but has trouble getting around on good inside fastballs, which has hurt his ability to take advantage of the Metrodome's short right-field fence. Ortiz has struggled against lefthanded pitching, and he has hit less than .245 with runners in scoring position in each of the last two campaigns.

Baserunning & Defense

The reason Ortiz became a DH at a young age was his poor defense at first base. He has very limited range and only an average glove. Doug Mientkiewicz offers a dramatic improvement. Ortiz' lack of speed is a evident on the bases. He isn't going to get many steals, but his instincts and judgment on the bases have improved over the past two seasons.

2003 Outlook

There's a chance that Ortiz won't be with the club in 2003. The DH is eligible for arbitration after last season, and his home-run total could net him a contract in the $2 million range. Several team officials don't believe Ortiz is worth it, and they believe that Matthew LeCroy, given the opportunity, would be as productive as Ortiz in the DH role. On the flip side, the club is reluctant to give up on Ortiz because he could land with another club and finally realize his 30-homer potential.

Position: DH/1B
Bats: L **Throws:** L
Ht: 6' 4" **Wt:** 230

Opening Day Age: 27
Born: 11/18/75 in Santo Domingo, DR
ML Seasons: 6
Pronunciation: or-TEEZ

Overall Statistics

	G	AB	R	H	D	T	HR	RBI	SB	BB	SO	Avg	OBP	Slg
'02	125	412	52	112	32	1	20	75	1	43	87	.272	.339	.500
Car.	455	1477	215	393	108	3	58	238	4	186	339	.266	.348	.461

Where He Hits the Ball

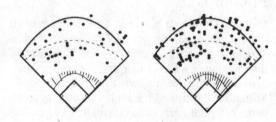

Vs. LHP   **Vs. RHP**

2002 Situational Stats

	AB	H	HR	RBI	Avg		AB	H	HR	RBI	Avg
Home	187	52	5	29	.278	LHP	118	24	5	18	.203
Road	225	60	15	46	.267	RHP	294	88	15	57	.299
First Half	183	44	5	33	.240	Sc Pos	124	30	3	51	.242
Scnd Half	229	68	15	42	.297	Clutch	58	17	4	12	.293

2002 Rankings (American League)

- 2nd in lowest on-base percentage vs. left-handed pitchers (.256)
- 5th in lowest batting average vs. lefthanded pitchers
- 9th in sacrifice flies (8)
- Led the Twins in sacrifice flies (8), most pitches seen per plate appearance (4.13), fewest GDPs per GDP situation (5.6%), cleanup slugging percentage (.517) and batting average with two strikes (.234)

A.J. Pierzynski

2002 Season

Early in the 2000 season, the Twins demoted A.J. Pierzynski from Triple-A to Double-A ball, a move generally reserved for non-prospects. In Pierzynski's case it was intended as a work-ethic wakeup call. He clearly got the message. Last summer Pierzynski batted .300 and earned a spot on the American League All-Star team for the first time. He hit well against both lefthanded and righthanded pitchers, and batted .319 with runners in scoring position. He also improved his defensive skills behind the plate, showing what it takes to be a No. 1 catcher at the major league level.

Hitting

Unorthodox would be a mild way to describe the lefthanded hitter's style. Pierzynski swings at anything moving near the strike zone, but somehow manages to be a decent contact hitter who hits for average. Not the way you'd teach it, but for him it works. The aggressive approach results in very few walks, but his clutch hitting is a compensating factor. The Twins believe Pierzynski eventually will hit at least 20 homers. For now he has gap power, and he frequently slaps the ball where it's pitched.

Baserunning & Defense

Pierzynski has the speed you'd expect from a catcher, meaning he's no threat to steal. But he is an aggressive baserunner with good instincts. Pierzynski has learned to use the nuances of the Dome, hitting five of his six triples in 2002 at home. He's made dramatic improvement behind the plate, especially in the area of blocking low pitches. He cut his error total from 10 in 2001 to three last year. He has a decent arm, and threw out 25 percent of potential basestealers in 2002.

2003 Outlook

Pierzynksi, the team's No. 1 catcher, will be only 26 when the 2003 season opens, and he appears capable of holding the starting backstop job for several seasons. That poses an intriguing competition in two or three years, when super-prospect Joe Mauer is due to arrive in the majors. Pierzynski has shown that Mauer is going to have to be as good as advertised to be the No. 1 catcher in Minnesota.

Position: C
Bats: L **Throws:** R
Ht: 6' 3" **Wt:** 220

Opening Day Age: 26
Born: 12/30/76 in Bridgehampton, NY
ML Seasons: 5
Pronunciation: PEER-zin-skee

Overall Statistics

	G	AB	R	H	D	T	HR	RBI	SB	BB	SO	Avg	OBP	Slg
'02	130	440	54	132	31	6	6	49	1	13	61	.300	.334	.439
Car.	293	941	121	278	71	9	15	119	3	36	138	.295	.332	.438

Where He Hits the Ball

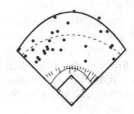 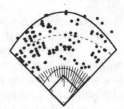

Vs. LHP   **Vs. RHP**

2002 Situational Stats

	AB	H	HR	RBI	Avg		AB	H	HR	RBI	Avg
Home	221	68	2	25	.308	LHP	89	24	2	13	.270
Road	219	64	4	24	.292	RHP	351	108	4	36	.308
First Half	244	78	6	32	.320	Sc Pos	113	36	0	37	.319
Scnd Half	196	54	0	17	.276	Clutch	75	24	0	5	.320

2002 Rankings (American League)

- 4th in fielding percentage at catcher (.996)
- 6th in triples
- 9th in hit by pitch (11)
- Led the Twins in batting average, triples, hit by pitch (11) and batting average in the clutch

Brad Radke

2002 Season

It was a bittersweet year for Brad Radke, who failed to win 10 games for the first time in his major league career. Still, he rebounded with a pair of victories over Oakland in the ALDS. His regular season was disrupted by a groin injury that resulted in two separate stints on the disabled list. When he was healthy he was typical Radke, relying on control to give his team a shot at winning most of his starts. He's had problems with fatigue in recent seasons, losing velocity on his fastball late in the year. But in 2002, Radke had a strong September and an even stronger October. Maybe the midsummer shutdown did him a favor.

Pitching

Radke relies on one of the game's smoothest deliveries and control of four pitches—fastball, curve, slider and change—to keep hitters off balance. His fastball hits the low 90s and is the pitch that sets up everything else. When the righthander gets ahead in the count, his changeup becomes his best pitch. Radke isn't overpowering and is extremely hittable when he doesn't pitch to spots. Opponents hit .365 with runners in scoring position in 2002. But Radke always compensates with control; he allowed just six walks in 217 at-bats to righthanded batters.

Defense

The righthander's defense is like his pitching: he seldom does anything to beat himself. Radke is quick and surehanded defensively, making just three errors in 356 total chances in his major league career. He has a good mound presence and seldom makes a mental gaffe. He does an excellent job of holding runners on, making him extremely difficult for would-be thieves.

2003 Outlook

Radke is more Mr. Consistency than he is staff ace, although you can bet he'll be the Opening Day starter for the seventh time in his major league career. By now the pattern is well defined, so look for 12-15 victories, an ERA around 4.00 and an extremely low walk total. The victory total will increase if he receives better-than-average run support.

Position: SP
Bats: R **Throws:** R
Ht: 6' 2" **Wt:** 188

Opening Day Age: 30
Born: 10/27/72 in Eau Claire, WI
ML Seasons: 8
Pronunciation: RAD-key

Overall Statistics

	W	L	Pct.	ERA	G	GS	Sv	IP	H	BB	SO	HR	Ratio
'02	9	5	.643	4.72	21	21	0	118.1	124	20	62	12	1.22
Car.	102	100	.505	4.30	252	251	0	1656.0	1761	336	1004	214	1.27

How Often He Throws Strikes

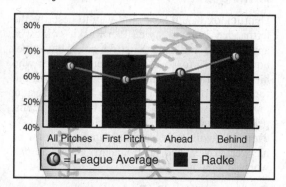

= League Average   ■ = Radke

2002 Situational Stats

	W	L	ERA	Sv	IP		AB	H	HR	RBI	Avg
Home	5	1	3.02	0	62.2	LHB	239	59	7	32	.247
Road	4	4	6.63	0	55.2	RHB	217	65	5	30	.300
First Half	4	2	5.23	0	51.2	Sc Pos	96	35	3	49	.365
Scnd Half	5	3	4.32	0	66.2	Clutch	10	3	0	2	.300

2002 Rankings (American League)

- 6th in highest batting average allowed vs. righthanded batters
- Led the Twins in complete games (2), highest groundball-flyball ratio allowed (1.0), lowest stolen-base percentage allowed (50.0), fewest pitches thrown per batter (3.53) and most GDPs induced per nine innings (0.8)

Rick Reed

Pinpoint Control

2002 Season

Rick Reed showed last season why the Twins were willing to deal All-Star outfielder Matt Lawton for the righthander during the 2001 stretch drive. A disappointment in Minnesota in '01, Reed was the anchor of the 2002 staff after injuries felled Brad Radke, Eric Milton and Joe Mays. Reed led the club in victories, games started and innings pitched. His forte is control, and he led the league in fewest walks per nine innings (1.24). Reed had several superb stretches where he carried the staff. He went 4-1 (3.58) in his first seven starts, and was 6-1 (1.57) in seven starts between August 13 and September 14.

Pitching

Reed and teammate Brad Radke are so similar in style that the Twins wouldn't start them back-to-back in postseason play. Like Radke, Reed does not have dominating stuff, but rather relies on control and a varied assortment of pitches. Reed's fastball is generally in the 90-91 MPH range, and he has to hit the corners to be effective. His best pitch is his sinker. When he's throwing his fastball and sinker for strikes, his changeup and slider become effective. Balls leave the yard when he gets his pitches up in the zone. For Reed, everything comes back to control. He's the active major league leader in fewest walks per nine innings at 1.63 (minimum 1,000 innings).

Defense

Reed is a decent athlete who is relatively sure-handed on grounders back to the mound. He did make two errors last season, but has only 11 in 314 chances in his career. He's very good at holding baserunners, with a quick move to first and a quick delivery.

2003 Outlook

Reed's future with the Twins is linked to the team's payroll. The righthander will be paid $8 million in 2003, and that might be too much for owner Carl Pohlad, especially when the club has a cheaper alternative in young lefty Johan Santana. The front office certainly would like to have Reed back after his strong performance in the 2002 season.

Position: SP
Bats: R **Throws:** R
Ht: 6' 1" **Wt:** 195

Opening Day Age: 37
Born: 8/16/65 in Huntington, WV
ML Seasons: 14

Overall Statistics

	W	L	Pct.	ERA	G	GS	Sv	IP	H	BB	SO	HR	Ratio
'02	15	7	.682	3.78	33	32	0	188.0	192	26	121	32	1.16
Car.	87	64	.576	3.93	246	224	1	1410.2	1446	256	899	192	1.21

How Often He Throws Strikes

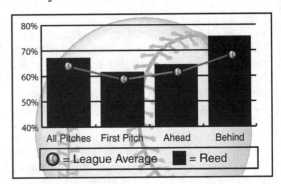

2002 Situational Stats

	W	L	ERA	Sv	IP		AB	H	HR	RBI	Avg
Home	8	4	3.90	0	90.0	LHB	405	106	25	56	.262
Road	7	3	3.67	0	98.0	RHB	335	86	7	26	.257
First Half	6	5	4.62	0	97.1	Sc Pos	138	39	5	47	.283
Scnd Half	9	2	2.88	0	90.2	Clutch	41	12	3	3	.293

2002 Rankings (American League)

- 1st in fewest walks per nine innings (1.2)
- 2nd in highest strikeout-walk ratio (4.7), most home runs allowed per nine innings (1.53) and fewest GDPs induced per nine innings (0.4)
- 4th in home runs allowed and lowest fielding percentage at pitcher (.933)
- Led the Twins in wins, games started, complete games (2), innings pitched, hits allowed, home runs allowed, pickoff throws (56), highest strikeout-walk ratio (4.7), lowest on-base percentage allowed (.288), most run support per nine innings (6.1) and fewest walks per nine innings (1.2)

Minnesota

(chart legend: ⊙ = League Average   ■ = Reed)

Luis Rivas

2002 Season

The tone for a disappointing summer was set when Luis Rivas was hit by a pitch and fractured his left wrist in the second game of the season. The second baseman played in just 93 games and never fulfilled the promise of his rookie campaign in 2001. Rivas batted .285 after the All-Star break that year, and the Twins figured he might develop into a .300 hitter with gap power. Maybe that is too optimistic. One way Rivas did not disappoint was defensively. His quickness and range in the field make him one of the league's top second basemen.

Hitting

Like his double-play partner, Cristian Guzman, Rivas has the physical tools to be a leadoff hitter, but his lack of patience and knowledge of the strike zone won't allow it. He actually regressed in patience in 2002, drawing a walk every 16.6 at-bats after coaxing a free pass every 14.1 at-bats as a rookie. Rivas strikes out too much for a middle infielder who has the speed to make things happen just by putting the ball in play. He needs to improve his bat control and take advantage of the Metrodome's slick artificial turf. But his batting average was 49 points lower at the Dome than on the road last season.

Baserunning & Defense

A converted shortstop, Rivas has mastered the pivot at second base. His quickness and range make him an ideal second baseman on artificial turf. He's also surehanded and possesses a strong arm. He stole just nine bases last season after swiping 31 as a rookie. While Rivas needs to improve his technique, he has the speed to steal 40 or more. He's an aggressive baserunner and generally makes the correct decision in going for an extra base.

2003 Outlook

Rivas still is a mainstay of the Twins' everyday lineup, and will get ample opportunity to show that last season's offensive shortcomings were an aberration. But he needs to become a more patient and intelligent hitter to do that. He also must become more of a contact hitter when he's playing on turf.

Position: 2B
Bats: R **Throws:** R
Ht: 5'11" **Wt:** 175

Opening Day Age: 23
Born: 8/30/79 in La Guaira, VZ
ML Seasons: 3
Pronunciation: REE-vas

Overall Statistics

	G	AB	R	H	D	T	HR	RBI	SB	BB	SO	Avg	OBP	Slg
'02	93	316	46	81	23	4	4	35	9	19	51	.256	.305	.392
Car.	262	937	124	249	48	11	11	88	42	61	154	.266	.315	.376

Where He Hits the Ball

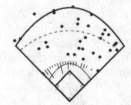 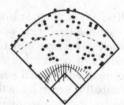

Vs. LHP   **Vs. RHP**

2002 Situational Stats

	AB	H	HR	RBI	Avg		AB	H	HR	RBI	Avg
Home	171	40	2	19	.234	LHP	107	25	3	10	.234
Road	145	41	2	16	.283	RHP	209	56	1	25	.268
First Half	102	28	0	11	.275	Sc Pos	84	22	1	29	.262
Scnd Half	214	53	4	24	.248	Clutch	51	13	1	7	.255

2002 Rankings (American League)

- 2nd in most GDPs per GDP situation (23.1%)
- 6th in sacrifice bunts (8)
- Led the Twins in sacrifice bunts (8)

Eddie Guardado

Position: RP
Bats: R **Throws:** L
Ht: 6' 0" **Wt:** 194

Opening Day Age: 32
Born: 10/2/70 in Stockton, CA
ML Seasons: 10
Pronunciation: gwar-DAH-doe

Overall Statistics

	W	L	Pct.	ERA	G	GS	Sv	IP	H	BB	SO	HR	Ratio
'02	1	3	.250	2.93	68	0	45	67.2	53	18	70	9	1.05
Car.	33	42	.440	4.67	573	25	75	632.1	612	254	545	92	1.37

2002 Situational Stats

	W	L	ERA	Sv	IP		AB	H	HR	RBI	Avg
Home	1	1	2.68	22	37.0	LHB	57	15	1	6	.263
Road	0	2	3.23	23	30.2	RHB	190	38	8	17	.200
First Half	1	2	2.85	26	41.0	Sc Pos	43	9	3	15	.209
Scnd Half	0	1	3.04	19	26.2	Clutch	178	40	7	20	.225

2002 Season

Eyebrows were raised when rookie skipper Ron Gardenhire named Eddie Guardado as his closer before the 2002 season. He wasn't the prototypical righty with a dominant pitch. Yet, he set a team record with 45 saves. Opponents batted just .215 against him, and he averaged 2.39 walks and 9.3 strikeouts per nine innings.

Pitching & Defense

The lefty compensates for his lack of an out pitch with variety, excellent control and an aggressive attitude. He'll hit corners with his 93-MPH fastball, and he keeps batters off balance with a splitfinger fastball, slider and curve. He added the splitter last season, primarily to use against righties, and it proved to be extremely effective. He's not a great athlete, but he's a veteran who fields his position well. He has a compact delivery and is tough to steal on.

2003 Outlook

Guardado has gotten better with age, and there's no reason to believe that his 2002 season was a fluke. He didn't have an ERA under 3.90 in any of his first eight major league seasons. But in his last two campaigns, he's had a 3.22 mark in 135 games. "Everyday Eddie" has the perfect temperament for a closer and a durable arm.

LaTroy Hawkins

Position: RP
Bats: R **Throws:** R
Ht: 6' 5" **Wt:** 204

Opening Day Age: 30
Born: 12/21/72 in Gary, IN
ML Seasons: 8

Overall Statistics

	W	L	Pct.	ERA	G	GS	Sv	IP	H	BB	SO	HR	Ratio
'02	6	0	1.000	2.13	65	0	0	80.1	63	15	63	5	0.97
Car.	35	54	.393	5.38	292	98	42	740.2	887	275	457	101	1.57

2002 Situational Stats

	W	L	ERA	Sv	IP		AB	H	HR	RBI	Avg
Home	4	0	1.64	0	38.1	LHB	129	29	3	16	.225
Road	2	0	2.57	0	42.0	RHB	161	34	2	15	.211
First Half	3	0	1.52	0	53.1	Sc Pos	72	17	3	26	.236
Scnd Half	3	0	3.33	0	27.0	Clutch	116	24	3	14	.207

2002 Season

No Twins player had a better comeback season than LaTroy Hawkins, who lost his closer's job, his control and his confidence in 2001. He revamped his mechanics under new pitching coach Rick Anderson, and the results were eye-popping. He averaged five less walks per nine innings over 2001, and opponents hit just .217 against him. He started the season pitching mostly in mopup situations, but by season's end was the club's top righthanded setup man.

Pitching & Defense

The mechanical changes added several MPH to Hawkins' fastball. He hit 97-98 MPH fairly consistently late in the season, and when he keeps that pitch low and in the strike zone, he's effective. Hawkins also developed a decent slider and throws a curve and change. He has quick reflexes and fields his position well.

2003 Outlook

There's no reason to believe that Hawkins can't build on his success of last season. Confidence is the key. Anderson, in addition to re-tooling Hawkins' mechanics, made him believe that he has the stuff to succeed. He simply has to locate his pitches. The Twins picked up the $3 million option on his contract for 2003.

Denny Hocking

Position: 2B/SS/3B
Bats: B **Throws:** R
Ht: 5'10" **Wt:** 183

Opening Day Age: 32
Born: 4/2/70 in Torrance, CA
ML Seasons: 10
Pronunciation: HAWK-ing

Overall Statistics

	G	AB	R	H	D	T	HR	RBI	SB	BB	SO	Avg	OBP	Slg
'02	102	260	28	65	13	0	2	25	0	24	44	.250	.310	.323
Car.	793	2016	251	511	99	15	22	193	36	173	375	.253	.312	.350

2002 Situational Stats

	AB	H	HR	RBI	Avg		AB	H	HR	RBI	Avg
Home	109	27	1	10	.248	LHP	76	26	0	12	.342
Road	151	38	1	15	.252	RHP	184	39	2	13	.212
First Half	175	45	2	19	.257	Sc Pos	67	16	0	23	.239
Scnd Half	85	20	0	6	.235	Clutch	48	13	0	5	.271

2002 Season

Denny Hocking was widely acclaimed as one of the game's best utility men in 2000, but his stock and statistics have nose-dived since then. In 2002, Hocking posted his lowest batting average since 1998, doubled his error total (10) over any previous major league season and failed to steal a base.

Hitting, Baserunning & Defense

Hocking still has value because he can play every position except catcher and pitcher. Plus, he's a switch-hitter who over the course of his career has hit from both sides equally well. There was a time the Twins were comfortable with Hocking in the leadoff position, but that's no longer the case. These days he has trouble against good fastball pitchers, and he appears to have lost a step on the bases. He still has decent range and a better-than-average arm defensively. His best position is second base, but he's capable at short, third and all three outfield spots.

2003 Outlook

The Twins' lack of middle-infield depth means Hocking will be back in his familiar utility role. He and the Twins agreed on a $1.1 million contract for 2003. But he needs to reverse his declining production if he's going to stick around beyond this season.

Mike Jackson

Position: RP
Bats: R **Throws:** R
Ht: 6' 2" **Wt:** 215

Opening Day Age: 38
Born: 12/22/64 in Houston, TX
ML Seasons: 16

Overall Statistics

	W	L	Pct.	ERA	G	GS	Sv	IP	H	BB	SO	HR	Ratio
'02	2	3	.400	3.27	58	0	0	55.0	59	13	29	5	1.31
Car.	60	67	.472	3.35	960	7	142	1141.2	928	449	980	120	1.21

2002 Situational Stats

	W	L	ERA	Sv	IP		AB	H	HR	RBI	Avg
Home	1	1	3.81	0	28.1	LHB	69	19	2	9	.275
Road	1	2	2.70	0	26.2	RHB	139	40	3	13	.288
First Half	2	2	2.23	0	36.1	Sc Pos	54	9	0	14	.167
Scnd Half	0	1	5.30	0	18.2	Clutch	117	36	3	13	.308

2002 Season

The veteran reliever started strong, and for half a season, Mike Jackson was the Twins' top righthanded setup man. He exhibited excellent control of his trademark hard slider. But a shoulder problem landed him on the disabled list in late July, and Jackson's numbers soared after the All-Star break.

Pitching & Defense

Jackson's age and the health of his right arm are big question marks. He missed the entire 2000 season after undergoing shoulder surgery, and had his worst major league season in 2001 with Houston. His shoulder problems of 2002 were not considered serious, so he still might be productive. When he gets ahead in the count, the slider is an effective pitch, as evidenced by these 2002 numbers: opponents batted .158 after an 0-and-2 count and .140 after starting 1-and-2. Jackson is an adequate fielder who is difficult to steal on.

2003 Outlook

The Twins have decided not to pursue Jackson for 2003. The club believes it has several righthanders in the minors ready to pitch in the majors. Jackson's second-half numbers won't help him draw a big contract, but he once again could be a bargain for a team seeking veteran relief help.

Bobby Kielty

Position: RF/CF
Bats: B **Throws:** R
Ht: 6' 1" **Wt:** 215

Opening Day Age: 26
Born: 8/5/76 in Fontana, CA
ML Seasons: 2
Pronunciation: KELL-tee

Overall Statistics

	G	AB	R	H	D	T	HR	RBI	SB	BB	SO	Avg	OBP	Slg
'02	112	289	49	84	14	3	12	46	4	52	66	.291	.405	.484
Car.	149	393	57	110	22	3	14	60	7	60	91	.280	.378	.458

2002 Situational Stats

	AB	H	HR	RBI	Avg		AB	H	HR	RBI	Avg
Home	126	36	8	24	.286	LHP	91	24	4	14	.264
Road	163	48	4	22	.294	RHP	198	60	8	32	.303
First Half	154	49	5	27	.318	Sc Pos	79	22	2	30	.278
Scnd Half	135	35	7	19	.259	Clutch	60	17	4	10	.283

2002 Season

At the very least Bobby Kielty showed that he can be a valuable fourth outfielder in the majors. He's solid in almost every aspect of the game. The Twins like that he's a switch-hitter who can play all three outfield positions. On top of that, he posted creditable numbers for a player seeing his first extended action at the major league level.

Hitting, Baserunning & Defense

Kielty is a patient hitter with a good knowledge of the strike zone, which makes him something of an anomaly among his free-swinging teammates. He's a good fastball hitter who is patient enough to lay off breaking balls that would give him trouble. Kielty's strength is his all-around ability. He has decent power and speed and should hit at least .280. Defensively he gets a good jump on the ball and has an accurate throwing arm.

2003 Outlook

The one statistic that could net Kielty more playing time is his .405 OBP in 2002. It's not out of the question that Kielty could win the starting right-field job in spring training and get a look as the team's leadoff hitter. Still, it works against him that he hit better from the left side in 2002. The Twins have a surplus of lefthanded hitters and are seeking righthanded-hitting punch for 2003.

Matthew LeCroy

Position: DH
Bats: R **Throws:** R
Ht: 6' 2" **Wt:** 225

Opening Day Age: 27
Born: 12/13/75 in Belton, SC
ML Seasons: 3
Pronunciation: LEE-croy

Overall Statistics

	G	AB	R	H	D	T	HR	RBI	SB	BB	SO	Avg	OBP	Slg
'02	63	181	19	47	11	1	7	27	0	13	38	.260	.306	.448
Car.	134	388	43	93	26	1	15	56	0	30	84	.240	.295	.428

2002 Situational Stats

	AB	H	HR	RBI	Avg		AB	H	HR	RBI	Avg
Home	82	21	2	11	.256	LHP	90	26	5	16	.289
Road	99	26	5	16	.263	RHP	91	21	2	11	.231
First Half	112	35	4	18	.313	Sc Pos	48	12	5	23	.250
Scnd Half	69	12	3	9	.174	Clutch	34	6	1	2	.176

2002 Season

Matthew LeCroy started the season in the minors, but early injuries and the team's season-long problems against lefthanded pitching opened the door for him. He didn't exactly bust through the opening though, but he batted .289 with a homer every 18 at-bats against lefthanders. He slumped in the second half.

Hitting, Baserunning & Defense

LeCroy's future rests squarely on his power production. He lacks footspeed and is a below-average defensive player, although he offers versatility. He was drafted as a catcher and can fill in behind the plate, but his defensive shortcomings moved him to first base. LeCroy has 30-homer potential, but he also has trouble catching up with good fastballs and needs to refine his knowledge of the strike zone.

2003 Outlook

LeCroy will be getting a serious look in spring training, based on his numbers against lefthanded pitching. There's a decent chance that regular DH David Ortiz won't return in 2003, which would make LeCroy the frontrunner for the DH job. If LeCroy can supply righthanded power—one of the team's biggest holes in 2002—he'll get plenty of playing time.

Kyle Lohse

Position: SP
Bats: R **Throws:** R
Ht: 6' 2" **Wt:** 190

Opening Day Age: 24
Born: 10/4/78 in Chico, CA
ML Seasons: 2
Pronunciation: loshe

Overall Statistics

	W	L	Pct.	ERA	G	GS	Sv	IP	H	BB	SO	HR	Ratio
'02	13	8	.619	4.23	32	31	0	180.2	181	70	124	26	1.39
Car.	17	15	.531	4.72	51	47	0	271.0	283	99	188	42	1.41

2002 Situational Stats

	W	L	ERA	Sv	IP		AB	H	HR	RBI	Avg
Home	6	5	4.70	0	90.0	LHB	341	105	13	44	.308
Road	7	3	3.77	0	90.2	RHB	357	76	13	38	.213
First Half	8	5	5.25	0	97.2	Sc Pos	165	35	7	54	.212
Scnd Half	5	3	3.04	0	83.0	Clutch	21	11	3	6	.524

2002 Season

Kyle Lohse was a key reason the Twins were able to overcome injuries to starters Brad Radke, Eric Milton and Joe Mays. The Twins' No. 5 starter finished second on the club in innings and strikeouts and tied for second in wins. He worked at least six innings in 18 of his 31 starts, and generally pitched well enough to give his team a chance to win. He limited opponents to a .225 batting average after the All-Star break.

Pitching & Defense

Lohse's improvement can be traced to better control of his fastball, the pitch that sets up an outstanding curve and decent slider. He has gained a couple ticks on his fastball, which now hits 93-94 MPH. Lefthanded hitters gave him trouble, and he needs an improved changeup to keep them off balance. He is a good athlete who fields his position well and holds runners close.

2003 Outlook

Lohse was the odd man out when the Twins went to a four-man rotation for the playoffs. He should be a mainstay of next season's rotation, however, and could find himself promoted to the No. 4 spot if the club opts to trade Rick Reed and his $8 million salary. Lohse has a major league arm, and he should continue to improve.

Dustan Mohr

Position: RF/LF
Bats: R **Throws:** R
Ht: 6' 0" **Wt:** 210

Opening Day Age: 26
Born: 6/19/76 in Hattiesburg, MS
ML Seasons: 2

Overall Statistics

	G	AB	R	H	D	T	HR	RBI	SB	BB	SO	Avg	OBP	Slg
'02	120	383	55	103	23	2	12	45	6	31	86	.269	.325	.433
Car.	140	434	61	115	25	2	12	49	7	36	103	.265	.322	.415

2002 Situational Stats

	AB	H	HR	RBI	Avg		AB	H	HR	RBI	Avg
Home	199	43	3	23	.216	LHP	133	27	3	11	.203
Road	184	60	9	22	.326	RHP	250	76	9	34	.304
First Half	226	67	7	27	.296	Sc Pos	99	26	2	32	.263
Scnd Half	157	36	5	18	.229	Clutch	53	14	2	8	.264

2002 Season

Dustan Mohr has come a long way since he was released by the Cleveland organization in 2000. He was the Twins' starting right fielder for much of the first half of last season, then saw his playing time decline because of a second-half slide. He batted just .209 in August and September.

Hitting, Baserunning & Defense

Mohr has a quick, compact swing that produces line-drive power. He needs to be more selective, because he strikes out too much for someone with marginal pop. One thing that hurt Mohr, especially in the second half, was his failure to hit lefthanded pitching. That's a mystery in light of his success against righthanded pitchers. Mohr is the team's best defensive right fielder. He has an accurate arm and gets a good jump on the ball. He's not a speedster, but he is aggressive on the bases.

2003 Outlook

Mohr will be in a three-player battle for the starting right-field job with Michael Cuddyer and Bobby Kielty. Cuddyer figures to be the frontrunner, because he has the righthanded power the Twins are seeking. Mohr's lack of power and his second-half slide force him to have a strong spring to earn regular playing time in 2003.

J.C. Romero

Position: RP
Bats: B **Throws:** L
Ht: 5'11" **Wt:** 195

Opening Day Age: 26
Born: 6/4/76 in Rio Piedras, PR
ML Seasons: 4

Overall Statistics

	W	L	Pct.	ERA	G	GS	Sv	IP	H	BB	SO	HR	Ratio
'02	9	2	.818	1.89	81	0	1	81.0	62	36	76	3	1.21
Car.	12	13	.480	4.68	112	22	1	213.1	218	90	169	21	1.44

2002 Situational Stats

	W	L	ERA	Sv	IP		AB	H	HR	RBI	Avg
Home	5	0	1.48	1	42.2	LHB	125	27	0	8	.216
Road	4	2	2.35	0	38.1	RHB	166	35	3	16	.211
First Half	4	1	2.06	0	48.0	Sc Pos	94	16	1	22	.170
Scnd Half	5	1	1.64	1	33.0	Clutch	188	41	1	16	.218

2002 Season

There was no more pleasant surprise on the roster than J.C. Romero, who became the team's top setup man. He was such a disappointment in 2001 that after he was optioned to the minors that July, the club declined to extend him a September recall. The lefthander improved upon his 2001 opponents' batting average by 64 points.

Pitching & Defense

Romero's strengths are his fastball, which hits the mid-90s, and a hard slider. What helped him turn the corner last season was the addition of a changeup that kept batters from sitting on his heater. Romero's stuff was nasty in 2002. When he went up 0-and-1 on hitters, they batted just .132. After an 0-2 count, his opponents' average dipped to .089. He also stranded 44 of 54 (81 percent) inherited baserunners. He's a good athlete who fields his position well. The lefty has a good move to first, and has improved his slide step with runners aboard.

2003 Outlook

Romero was so effective last season against both righthanded and lefthanded batters that the Twins used him as their No.1 setup man, regardless of who was scheduled to be at the plate. He figures to be in the same role in 2003.

Johan Santana

Position: SP/RP
Bats: L **Throws:** L
Ht: 6' 0" **Wt:** 195

Opening Day Age: 24
Born: 3/13/79 in Tovar Merida, VZ
ML Seasons: 3

Overall Statistics

	W	L	Pct.	ERA	G	GS	Sv	IP	H	BB	SO	HR	Ratio
'02	8	6	.571	2.99	27	14	1	108.1	84	49	137	7	1.23
Car.	11	9	.550	4.58	72	23	1	238.0	236	119	229	24	1.49

2002 Situational Stats

	W	L	ERA	Sv	IP		AB	H	HR	RBI	Avg
Home	5	2	2.43	0	55.2	LHB	77	15	0	7	.195
Road	3	4	3.59	1	52.2	RHB	319	69	7	25	.216
First Half	4	1	2.45	0	40.1	Sc Pos	88	20	2	25	.227
Scnd Half	4	5	3.31	1	68.0	Clutch	25	2	0	0	.080

2002 Season

It appeared Johan Santana would spend most of 2002 in the minors, but by season's end he was a key member of the postseason staff after working as both a starter and reliever. He was effective in both roles, going 7-4 (3.13) as a starter and posting a 2.67 ERA in relief. While he ranked fifth on the team in innings, Santana led the club in strikeouts and posted 11.38 strikeouts per nine innings.

Pitching & Defense

Santana has a good fastball and hard slider, but until last season he didn't have the command or offspeed pitch to take advantage of his hard stuff. Santana arrived from the minors in late May with a much-improved changeup that made his fastball and slider more effective. Santana is a decent athlete, but needs to improve defensively. He has five errors in 42 chances in his short career. He does do an adequate job of holding runners on.

2003 Outlook

While Santana is a central figure in the Twins' long-term plans, his immediate role is uncertain. If Rick Reed returns to the club, Santana might start the season in the bullpen. That would give the Twins three lefties in the pen. Still, Santana's stuff is too good to spend much more time working as a long reliever.

Casey Blake (**Pos**: 3B, **Age**: 29, **Bats**: R)

	G	AB	R	H	D	T	HR	RBI	SB	BB	SO	Avg	OBP	Slg
'02	9	20	2	4	1	0	0	1	0	2	7	.200	.273	.250
Car.	49	112	12	26	6	0	2	7	3	11	33	.232	.304	.339

Blake has batted .309 with a fair share of extra-base hits and walks in each of the last two seasons at Triple-A Edmonton, but he hasn't been able to crack a Minnesota roster beaming with prospects. 2003 Outlook: C

Jay Canizaro (**Pos**: 2B, **Age**: 29, **Bats**: R)

	G	AB	R	H	D	T	HR	RBI	SB	BB	SO	Avg	OBP	Slg
'02	38	112	14	24	8	1	0	11	0	10	22	.214	.280	.304
Car.	195	596	73	149	35	3	10	68	5	44	119	.250	.303	.369

After missing '01 with a torn right ACL, Canizaro played when Luis Rivas broke his forearm in April. He didn't hit and was sent to Triple-A Edmonton. The Rays signed him to a minor league deal. 2003 Outlook: C

Jack Cressend (**Pos**: RHP, **Age**: 27)

	W	L	Pct.	ERA	G	GS	Sv	IP	H	BB	SO	HR	Ratio
'02	0	1	.000	5.91	23	0	0	32.0	40	19	22	6	1.84
Car.	3	3	.500	4.59	78	0	0	102.0	110	41	68	12	1.48

Cressend surfaced in May 2001 and was a pleasant surprise for the Twins. Last summer was a nightmare, as he struggled before enduring shoulder surgery in September. Cleveland has claimed him off waivers. 2003 Outlook: C

Tony Fiore (**Pos**: RHP, **Age**: 31)

	W	L	Pct.	ERA	G	GS	Sv	IP	H	BB	SO	HR	Ratio
'02	10	3	.769	3.16	48	2	0	91.0	74	43	55	10	1.29
Car.	11	5	.688	4.05	66	2	0	115.2	104	55	71	13	1.37

Fiore took over Cressend's role of surprise contributor, arriving in early April from Triple-A Edmonton and working effectively out of the pen. He won nine games and posted a 2.79 ERA as a reliever. 2003 Outlook: B

Kevin Frederick (**Pos**: RHP, **Age**: 26)

	W	L	Pct.	ERA	G	GS	Sv	IP	H	BB	SO	HR	Ratio
'02	0	0	–	10.03	8	0	0	11.2	13	10	5	3	1.97
Car.	0	0	–	10.03	8	0	0	11.2	13	10	5	3	1.97

Frederick features a solid fastball-slider combo, but he allowed too many hits and didn't throw enough strikes at Edmonton in 2002. He can work 2-3 days in a row and could land in the Twins' pen. 2003 Outlook: C

Matt Kinney (**Pos**: RHP, **Age**: 26)

	W	L	Pct.	ERA	G	GS	Sv	IP	H	BB	SO	HR	Ratio
'02	2	7	.222	4.64	14	12	0	66.0	78	33	45	13	1.68
Car.	4	9	.308	4.82	22	20	0	108.1	119	58	69	20	1.63

Once a heralded prospect, Kinney throws in the mid-90s, but he hasn't done much since going 6-1 (2.71) at Double-A New Britain early in 2000. A second chance in 2002 ended with a shoulder strain and DL stop. In November he was dealt to Milwaukee, where he'll compete for a rotation spot. 2003 Outlook: C

David Lamb (**Pos**: SS, **Age**: 27, **Bats**: B)

	G	AB	R	H	D	T	HR	RBI	SB	BB	SO	Avg	OBP	Slg
'02	7	10	0	1	0	0	0	0	0	0	2	.100	.100	.100
Car.	69	139	19	30	5	1	1	13	0	11	21	.216	.273	.288

Light-hitting Lamb enjoyed a career year at Triple-A Edmonton, earning his third cup of coffee in the majors. The big payoff came when Denny Hocking was injured and Lamb took his place on the ALCS roster. He was released after the playoffs. 2003 Outlook: C

Travis Miller (**Pos**: LHP, **Age**: 30)

	W	L	Pct.	ERA	G	GS	Sv	IP	H	BB	SO	HR	Ratio
'02	0	0	–	4.50	5	0	0	4.0	5	2	3	0	1.75
Car.	7	18	.280	5.05	203	14	1	267.1	331	113	199	27	1.66

The southpaw pitched for three Triple-A clubs in 2002 after he was waived by the Twins in June and the Cubs in August. He signed with Cleveland and finished the year at Triple-A Buffalo. Prospects fading. 2003 Outlook: C

Warren Morris (**Pos**: 2B, **Age**: 29, **Bats**: L)

	G	AB	R	H	D	T	HR	RBI	SB	BB	SO	Avg	OBP	Slg
'02	4	7	0	0	0	0	0	0	0	0	1	.000	.000	.000
Car.	343	1149	139	305	57	5	20	127	12	127	176	.265	.339	.376

The former Pirate signed with the Twins in spring training and made the roster, but was banished two weeks later after going 0-for-7. The Tigers signed him to a minor league deal in December. 2003 Outlook: C

Tom Prince (**Pos**: C, **Age**: 38, **Bats**: R)

	G	AB	R	H	D	T	HR	RBI	SB	BB	SO	Avg	OBP	Slg
'02	51	125	14	28	7	1	4	16	1	14	26	.224	.317	.392
Car.	487	1142	108	238	64	4	22	134	8	100	245	.208	.285	.329

Prince had a typical season in 2002, except he played in a postseason for the first time in 16 big league seasons. He will stay with Minnesota, where he has six homers in 159 Metrodome at-bats. 2003 Outlook: C

Jose Rodriguez (**Pos**: LHP, **Age**: 28)

	W	L	Pct.	ERA	G	GS	Sv	IP	H	BB	SO	HR	Ratio
'02	0	1	.000	18.00	6	0	0	4.0	12	6	1	0	4.50
Car.	0	1	.000	9.00	12	0	0	8.0	14	9	3	0	2.88

The 27-year-old southpaw didn't fare well in trials with both St. Louis and Minnesota, and his big opportunity ended with an inflamed vein in his throwing arm, which required blood thinners. 2003 Outlook: C

Todd Sears (**Pos**: 1B, **Age**: 27, **Bats**: L)

	G	AB	R	H	D	T	HR	RBI	SB	BB	SO	Avg	OBP	Slg
'02	7	12	2	4	2	0	0	0	0	0	1	.333	.333	.500
Car.	7	12	2	4	2	0	0	0	0	0	1	.333	.333	.500

Sears has hit for average and power in two Triple-A seasons since arriving from the Rockies in the Todd Walker deal. With 100 RBI in 2002, Sears may find a role in Minnesota if vets are dealt to save cash. 2003 Outlook: C

Mike Trombley (Pos: RHP, Age: 35)

	W	L	Pct.	ERA	G	GS	Sv	IP	H	BB	SO	HR	Ratio
'02	0	1	.000	15.75	5	0	0	4.0	10	1	3	2	2.75
Car.	37	47	.440	4.48	509	36	44	795.2	800	319	672	114	1.41

Trombley was released by the Dodgers at the end of spring training, and the Twins picked him up to help out in the pen. Originally with the Twins, he couldn't rekindle the magic and was released in June. 2003 Outlook: D

Javier Valentin (Pos: C, Age: 27, Bats: B)

	G	AB	R	H	D	T	HR	RBI	SB	BB	SO	Avg	OBP	Slg
'02	4	4	0	2	0	0	0	0	0	0	0	.500	.500	.500
Car.	141	391	34	90	19	2	8	46	0	33	72	.230	.288	.350

Valentin was traded to Milwaukee in mid-November. The Brewers' catching job is wide open, and Valentin has an excellent shot to grab at least a chunk of it. He's a capable hitter—much better than his main competitor, Robert Machado—and easily could wind up handling the bulk of the catching chores. 2003 Outlook: B

Bob Wells (Pos: RHP, Age: 36)

	W	L	Pct.	ERA	G	GS	Sv	IP	H	BB	SO	HR	Ratio
'02	2	1	.667	5.90	48	0	0	58.0	78	16	30	8	1.62
Car.	40	28	.588	5.03	414	21	15	635.2	688	200	417	101	1.40

Wells gave the Twins solid seasons in 1999 and 2000, but he's been more hittable the last two years and struggled while Minnesota was winning the AL Central crown. The Twins did not pick up the 2003 option on his contract, making him a free agent. 2003 Outlook: C

Minnesota Twins Minor League Prospects

Organization Overview:

The wave of kids arriving from the farm system continued in 2002. In 1999, Corey Koskie, Cristian Guzman, Torii Hunter, Jacque Jones and Joe Mays became fixtures in Minnesota. David Ortiz, Luis Rivas, A.J. Pierzynski and Doug Mientkiewicz soon followed, setting the stage for a promising 2001 campaign. Bobby Kielty, Kyle Lohse, Johan Santana, Michael Cuddyer, Matt LeCroy and Dustan Mohr played key roles in Minnesota's run to the postseason last summer, and the core is now settling in for what could be a long run of big league success. With mashers Michael Restovich, Justin Morneau and Joe Mauer expected to fit into the mix at some point, the Twins soon may feature a power-laden lineup reminiscent of the 1960s.

Grant Balfour

Position: P   **Opening Day Age:** 25
Bats: R **Throws:** R   **Born:** 12/30/77 in
Ht: 6' 2" **Wt:** 175   Sydney, Australia

Recent Statistics

	W	L	ERA	G	GS	Sv	IP	H	R	BB	SO	HR
2001 AA New Britain	2	1	1.08	35	0	13	50.0	26	6	22	72	1
2001 AL Minnesota	0	0	13.50	2	0	0	2.2	3	4	3	2	2
2001 AAA Edmonton	2	2	5.51	11	0	0	16.1	18	11	10	17	2
2002 AAA Edmonton	2	4	4.16	58	0	8	71.1	60	34	30	88	3

The Twins have made a splash in Australia, and in 1997 they signed Balfour. At the time he was a skinny kid who didn't throw hard, but the fitness buff is much stronger now. More consistent mechanics have him throwing a low-90s fastball, which he complements with an impressive slider that is his out pitch. Since 2001, he's been effective as both a setup man and closer in the high minors. His walks at Triple-A Edmonton were a bit high in 2002, and his changeup remains a work in progress. And although he projects more as a setup man in the majors, Balfour has proven durable and capable of working on consecutive nights. He could fit into the Twins' bullpen in 2003.

Michael Cuddyer

Position: OF-1B   **Opening Day Age:** 24
Bats: R **Throws:** R   **Born:** 3/27/79 in Norfolk,
Ht: 6' 2" **Wt:** 215   VA

Recent Statistics

	G	AB	R	H	D	T	HR	RBI	SB	BB	SO	Avg
2002 AAA Edmonton	86	330	70	102	16	9	20	53	12	36	79	.309
2002 AL Minnesota	41	112	12	29	7	0	4	13	2	8	30	.259

A 1997 first-round pick, Cuddyer made a fairly smooth transition from shortstop to third base in 1999. His power dropped off at Double-A New Britain in 2000, however, when Cuddyer said he had mechanical problems with his swing. He got back on track in 2001, returning to Double-A ball and turning on the power.

With Corey Koskie lodged at third base, Cuddyer has moved to the outfield and completed the transition at Triple-A Edmonton in 2002. He has an above-average arm and average speed, and his defensive game in the outfield has improved, though his ability to read and get good jumps on flyballs should improve further with more experience. He hit for both average and power at Edmonton, and the Twins hope he'll do the same as their starting right fielder in 2003.

Adam Johnson

Position: P   **Opening Day Age:** 23
Bats: R **Throws:** R   **Born:** 7/12/79 in San
Ht: 6' 2" **Wt:** 210   Jose, CA

Recent Statistics

	W	L	ERA	G	GS	Sv	IP	H	R	BB	SO	HR
2001 AA New Britain	5	6	3.82	18	18	0	113.0	105	53	39	110	10
2001 AL Minnesota	1	2	8.28	7	4	0	25.0	32	25	13	17	6
2001 AAA Edmonton	1	1	5.70	4	4	0	23.2	19	15	10	25	0
2002 AAA Edmonton	13	8	5.47	27	27	0	151.1	182	96	55	112	25

A first-round pick in 2000, Johnson departed Cal State Fullerton as the school's strikeout king and debuted by fanning 92 batters in 69.1 innings at high Class-A Fort Myers. He averaged a strikeout an inning as a second-year pro at Double-A New Britain and Triple-A Edmonton in 2001, calling on three solid pitches: a low-90s fastball, slider and a nasty changeup. He struggled early in 2002 at Edmonton, favoring a power approach over successfully mixing his pitches. Once he focused on pitching rather than challenging hitters, he rebounded from his rough start. He has the stuff to be a starter, but closing still may be in his future. He has a closer's mentality from his days as a finisher in college.

Joe Mauer

Position: C   **Opening Day Age:** 19
Bats: L **Throws:** R   **Born:** 4/19/83 in St.
Ht: 6' 4" **Wt:** 215   Paul, MN

Recent Statistics

	G	AB	R	H	D	T	HR	RBI	SB	BB	SO	Avg
2001 R Elizabethtn	32	110	14	44	6	2	0	14	4	19	10	.400
2002 A Quad City	110	411	58	124	23	1	4	62	0	61	42	.302

The first overall pick in 2001, Mauer adjusted quickly to the wood bat and faster pitching. His impressive swing sprayed line drives all over the field at Class-A Quad City in 2002. Mauer exhibited a good knowledge of the strike zone and an affinity for making adjustments. Defensively, he was solid behind the plate with a take-charge attitude. The Twins believe his game-calling may be the aspect of his game that improved the most last summer. Mauer has a dedication to his craft that should pay big dividends for him. He was sidelined by a double hernia late in the season, but after six weeks of rehab, he was ready for instructional league.

Justin Morneau

Position: 1B   **Opening Day Age:** 21
Bats: L **Throws:** R   **Born:** 5/15/81 in New
Ht: 6' 4" **Wt:** 205   Westminster, BC

Recent Statistics

	G	AB	R	H	D	T	HR	RBI	SB	BB	SO	Avg
2001 A Quad City	64	236	50	84	17	2	12	53	0	26	38	.356
2001 A Ft. Myers	53	197	25	58	10	3	4	40	0	24	41	.294
2001 AA New Britain	10	38	3	6	1	0	0	4	0	3	8	.158
2002 AA New Britain	126	494	72	147	31	4	16	80	7	42	88	.298

Morneau compares favorably to fellow Twins prospect Joe Mauer as a potential star with the bat, and he should hit for average and power in the majors. He has a sweet lefthanded swing and a well-developed knowledge of the strike zone. The Canadian native got off to a slow start in 2002, when he lost 20-plus pounds to a bacterial virus that shut him down in the spring. Still, he enjoyed a .298-16-80 season at Double-A New Britain and finished the year in the Triple-A playoffs. He was drafted as a catcher and spent a year in the outfield, so he's still finding his way around the first-base bag. With his big body, he's strictly a first baseman now.

Michael Restovich

Position: OF   **Opening Day Age:** 24
Bats: R **Throws:** R   **Born:** 1/3/79 in
Ht: 6' 4" **Wt:** 233   Rochester, MN

Recent Statistics

	G	AB	R	H	D	T	HR	RBI	SB	BB	SO	Avg
2002 AAA Edmonton	138	518	95	148	32	7	29	98	11	53	151	.286
2002 AL Minnesota	8	13	3	4	0	0	1	1	1	1	4	.308

Restovich is an impressive athlete who may have as much raw power as any prospect in the Twins' system. He enjoyed a power surge at Double-A New Britain in 2001, and posted even higher totals in runs, hits, homers, RBI and the three hitting percentages at Triple-A Edmonton last summer. His strikeout numbers indicate he needs more work learning the strike zone, and he must recognize and adjust more quickly to the steady diet of breaking stuff that pitchers feed him out of the zone. Although he was drafted as a first baseman, Restovich runs well for a big man and has become a very good all-around outfielder. He can play both left and right, which may aid his cause in Minnesota.

Juan Rincon

Position: P   **Opening Day Age:** 24
Bats: R **Throws:** R   **Born:** 1/23/79 in
Ht: 5' 11" **Wt:** 190   Maracaibo, VZ

Recent Statistics

	W	L	ERA	G	GS	Sv	IP	H	R	BB	SO	HR
2002 AAA Edmonton	7	4	4.78	19	16	0	101.2	111	56	35	75	12
2002 AL Minnesota	0	2	6.28	10	3	0	28.2	44	23	9	21	5

Signed in November 1996, Rincon has relied on a moving 91-92 MPH fastball and hard slider to dominate hitters. Lacking a polished changeup caught up with him at Double-A New Britain in 2000. It was a better pitch during Rincon's second go-round at New Britain in 2001, when he successfully set up hitters en route to a 14-6 season. He still needs to call on his changeup more often. In 2002, Rincon was promoted to Minnesota when injuries plagued the pitching staff. When he was sent back to Triple-A Edmonton, Twins manager Ron Gardenire encouraged him to work on his changeup and use it more in game situations. If Rincon is ready for the majors in 2003, it's likely he will serve as a swing man, much as Johan Santana did in 2002.

Michael Ryan

Position: OF   **Opening Day Age:** 25
Bats: L **Throws:** R   **Born:** 7/6/77 in Indiana,
Ht: 5' 10" **Wt:** 185   PA

Recent Statistics

	G	AB	R	H	D	T	HR	RBI	SB	BB	SO	Avg
2002 AAA Edmonton	131	540	92	141	36	6	31	101	4	55	124	.261
2002 AL Minnesota	7	11	3	1	0	0	0	0	0	0	2	.091

A 1996 fifth-round pick, Ryan debuted by batting just .197 for the Twins' Gulf Coast League rookie club. He quickly developed a propensity to hit near .300 and draw walks, but he soon was lost among the power prospects that came into the system. He spent a season at second base and a few at third, but eventually Ryan found his niche in the outfield. He's not a true center fielder, but played there in 2002 at Triple-A Edmonton, where he set career highs in runs, homers and RBI. While he's not as gifted as the young power guys, he has a steadfast desire to improve. Ryan has a sweet left-handed swing, but strikes out too often. If he can come off the bench and hit, he has a chance to stick with Minnesota as a spare outfielder.

Others to Watch

Southpaw **Ricky Barrett** (22) impressed in the Rookie-level Appy League, using all of his pitches, showing good composure and an idea about pitching. He was 7-1 with a league-leading 1.27 ERA for Elizabethton. . . Righthander **J.D. Durbin** (21) called on a low-90s fastball and an impressive curveball that is his out pitch to go 13-4 (3.19) at Class-A Quad City. He led the Midwest League with 163 strikeouts in 161 innings. . . First baseman **Dusty Gomon** (20) is a big-time power prospect who batted .302, and slugged .568 with Rookie-level Elizabethton in 2002. He also was good around the first-base bag. . . Australian lefty **Brad Thomas** (25) set up hitters effectively with fastball strikes early in the count at Double-A New Britain in 2001, but fell behind hitters too often in the Triple-A Edmonton rotation last summer. Still, he has good stuff and cuts and sinks an above-average fastball. . . **Scott Tyler** (20) is a 6-foot-6, 215-pounder who has the ceiling to be the complete package as a pitcher. He is quite raw, but already the big righthander throws a low-90s fastball and a good curveball. He also takes the mound with a game plan.

Yankee Stadium

Offense

Asymmetrical Yankee Stadium remains true to its reputation as a lefthander's park. Pull-hitting power hitters from that side derive the biggest advantage. Righhanded power hitters can be frustrated unless they're able to pull the ball right down the line.

Defense

In this park, left field is not the place to try to hide an outfielder with limited mobility. Balls that split the gap and disappear into Death Valley routinely clear the bases and often go for triples, so it's imperative to cut off as many as possible. The long infield grass allows middle infielders to get to more balls, so it helps for them to have strong enough arms to make plays on the ones they get to. Southpaws have enjoyed pitching here because the righthanded-hitting lineups they face are at a disadvantage.

Who It Helps the Most

Roger Clemens has pitched very well here, as have lefties Andy Pettitte, David Wells and Mike Stanton. Shane Spencer is one of the Yankees' few righthanded hitters who hits better here. Lefthanded-hitting Jason Giambi hit well here in his first season. Rookie Nick Johnson hit for a better average at home and may take advantage of the short porch in right as his power develops.

Who It Hurts the Most

Surprisingly, Robin Ventura did not hit well in his first season at the Stadium, but Rondell White's struggles were less remarkable. Alfonso Soriano, whose power is to the deepest part of the park, has hit for better power and average on the road in his two full seasons.

Rookies & Newcomers

Jeff Weaver did not pitch well here last year, but mostly because of a couple of bad outings. There's nothing to keep him from winning here. Raul Mondesi, who came over in midseason, isn't well suited to hit at Yankee Stadium and may have a tough time adjusting. Rookie Juan Rivera's power might be stunted a little bit.

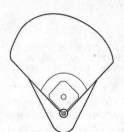

Dimensions: LF-318, LCF-399, CF-408, RCF-385, RF-314

Capacity: 57,478

Elevation: 55 feet

Surface: Grass

Foul Territory: Small

Park Factors

2002 Season

	Home Games			Away Games			
	Yankees	Opp	Total	Yankees	Opp	Total	Index
G	71	71	142	72	72	144	
Avg	.274	.245	.259	.276	.262	.269	96
AB	2407	2506	4913	2579	2488	5067	98
R	386	298	684	411	305	716	97
H	660	614	1274	711	653	1364	95
2B	125	133	258	149	141	290	92
3B	6	9	15	4	13	17	91
HR	95	66	161	104	57	161	103
BB	281	154	435	288	190	478	94
SO	494	550	1044	537	473	1010	107
E	50	55	105	60	38	98	109
E-Infield	43	42	85	50	30	80	108
LHB-Avg	.275	.234	.255	.276	.239	.259	98
LHB-HR	52	32	84	57	22	79	107
RHB-Avg	.274	.253	.263	.275	.278	.277	95
RHB-HR	43	34	77	47	35	82	99

2000-2002

	Home Games			Away Games			
	Yankees	Opp	Total	Yankees	Opp	Total	Index
G	214	214	428	216	216	432	
Avg	.277	.251	.264	.271	.266	.269	98
AB	7211	7500	14711	7680	7366	15046	99
R	1164	954	2118	1129	1006	2135	100
H	1994	1886	3880	2082	1960	4042	97
2B	391	373	764	414	404	818	96
3B	23	24	47	26	44	70	69
HR	303	217	520	264	198	462	115
BB	801	608	1409	766	677	1443	100
SO	1321	1620	2941	1509	1474	2983	101
E	147	160	307	158	140	298	104
E-Infield	127	117	244	138	120	258	95
LHB-Avg	.278	.248	.264	.271	.255	.263	100
LHB-HR	172	99	271	135	86	221	125
RHB-Avg	.275	.254	.264	.271	.274	.273	97
RHB-HR	131	118	249	129	112	241	106

2002 Rankings (American League)

- Second-lowest hit factor
- Second-lowest walk factor
- Third-lowest batting-average factor
- Third-lowest RHB batting-average factor

Joe Torre

2002 Season

It's to Joe Torre's credit that there was no lingering hangover last spring from the Yankees' stunning loss in Game 7 of the previous fall's World Series. The club had been loaded up with an influx of talent, and under Torre it played up to expectations. The Yanks cruised to another division title with the best record in the majors, and the only blemish was a surprising loss in the ALDS to an Angels team destined for greater things.

Offense

Torre adapted to his more power-laden lineup last year, turning Alfonso Soriano and Derek Jeter loose on the basepaths but letting his run producers do the rest. He called for fewer bunts and sacrifices than he had in the past. With one of his weakest benches in years, he did little in-game maneuvering. Though he encourages his hitters to be patient and make the pitcher work, he won't force the philosophy on a player who is unable or unwilling to adopt it.

Pitching & Defense

Torre has innate trust in his veteran pitchers, but not as much with a young, unfamiliar pitcher such as Jeff Weaver. He's willing to use the intentional walk to get a more favorable matchup in situations that obviously call for it. His relievers' roles usually are well-defined, although he's not afraid to define them unconventionally, such as bringing in his closer in the eighth.

2003 Outlook

What Torre brings to the Yankees is a steady hand at the helm, no matter how rough the sailing gets, which was helpful in 2002 and may be required again this year. The front office brought in new regulars last year at five positions, and Torre was able to make the transition appear seamless. He may need to oversee a similar turnover this spring, but the most critical performers will remain, as will the high expectations.

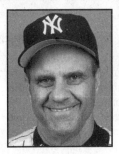

Born: 7/18/40 in Brooklyn, NY

Playing Experience: 1960-1977, Mil, Atl, StL, NYM

Managerial Experience: 21 seasons

Manager Statistics

Year	Team, Lg	W	L	Pct	GB	Finish
2002	New York, AL	103	58	.640	–	1st East
21 Seasons		1579	1448	.522	–	–

2002 Starting Pitchers by Days Rest

	<=3	4	5	6+
Yankees Starts	2	65	61	24
Yankees ERA	4.63	4.21	4.03	3.32
AL Avg Starts	1	83	44	24
AL ERA	7.15	4.59	4.27	5.03

2002 Situational Stats

	Joe Torre	AL Average
Hit & Run Success %	31.7	36.0
Stolen Base Success %	72.5	68.1
Platoon Pct.	62.2	58.9
Defensive Subs	27	23
High-Pitch Outings	8	6
Quick/Slow Hooks	15/15	19/14
Sacrifice Attempts	35	53

2002 Rankings (American League)

- 1st in intentional walks (33), starts on three days rest and saves with over 1 inning pitched (13)
- 2nd in steals of third base (18)
- 3rd in stolen-base percentage, starts with over 120 pitches (8) and 2+ pitching changes in low-scoring games (33)

New York (AL)

Roger Clemens

2002 Season

If Roger Clemens' 2002 season was a disappointment, it's only because his super 20-3 record the season before might have made it seem like he hadn't lost a thing. He wasn't able to keep up the pace in 2002, but his season actually was quite good for someone who turned 40 in August. It would have been even better if a strained groin hadn't sapped him of effectiveness and cost him a few starts in midsummer.

Pitching

Clemens has yielded remarkably little to age. He still brings mid-90s heat with regularity, and has the same impeccable command of it he's always had. He can throw his four-seamer past hitters or get them to chase his hard splitter down and out of the zone. His other weapons include a two-seamer, a slider and a changeup. Lefthanded hitters actually find him tougher because he relies more heavily on his two best pitches against them. Baserunners can drive him to distraction at times.

Defense

Since Clemens isn't quick to the plate and throws splitters in the dirt in predictable counts, basestealers regularly take liberties. He throws over time and again, and even picks off a runners now and then, but he still hardly slows them down. His age shows most in the field, where he's always been somewhat heavy-legged, although he did enjoy his first errorless season in 13 years last year.

2003 Outlook

Now only seven wins shy of 300, Clemens is a free agent. He's spoken many times of his desire to spend more time with his family, and he's never been content with anything shy of excellence, so it's a very real possibility that this could be his final season, if he chooses to come back at all. If his increasingly troublesome leg muscles cooperate, he very well could go out with one last quality season.

Position: SP
Bats: R **Throws:** R
Ht: 6' 4" **Wt:** 235

Opening Day Age: 40
Born: 8/4/62 in Dayton, OH
ML Seasons: 19
Nickname: Rocket

Overall Statistics

W	L	Pct.	ERA	G	GS	Sv	IP	H	BB	SO	HR	Ratio
13	6	.684	4.35	29	29	0	180.0	172	63	192	18	1.31
293	151	.660	3.15	574	573	0	4067.0	3478	1321	3909	297	1.18

How Often He Throws Strikes

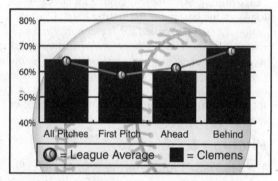

	All Pitches	First Pitch	Ahead	Behind

= League Average ■ = Clemens

2002 Situational Stats

	W	L	ERA	Sv	IP		AB	H	HR	RBI	Avg
Home	9	1	2.84	0	101.1	LHB	363	80	9	31	.220
Road	4	5	6.29	0	78.2	RHB	325	92	9	47	.283
First Half	8	3	4.20	0	113.2	Sc Pos	163	42	4	60	.258
Scnd Half	5	3	4.61	0	66.1	Clutch	34	5	0	1	.147

2002 Rankings (American League)

- 1st in pickoff throws (157) and fielding percentage at pitcher (1.000)
- 2nd in strikeouts, wild pitches (14), stolen bases allowed (23) and most strikeouts per nine innings (9.6)
- 3rd in highest stolen-base percentage allowed (82.1) and fewest GDPs induced per nine innings (0.4)
- 6th in highest strikeout-walk ratio (3.0) and most pitches thrown per batter (3.90)
- Led the Yankees in walks allowed, strikeouts, wild pitches (14), pickoff throws (157), stolen bases allowed (23), lowest ERA at home and most strikeouts per nine innings (9.6)

Jason Giambi

2002 Season

In his first season in pinstripes, Jason Giambi did not disappoint, placing in the top five in the American League in runs scored, home runs, RBI, walks, on-base percentage and slugging percentage. Known as an often-vocal clubhouse presence in Oakland, he was more restrained in New York and had no problem fitting into the Yankees' more serene atmosphere. Batting third or fourth in the order, he was a perfect fit in the lineup, too.

Hitting

Giambi is capable of reaching the fences from left-center to the right-field foul pole. Last year, moving to Yankee Stadium, he understandably made more of an effort to pull the ball. It paid off, as he hit well in his new home park. Strong and patient, he generally takes the first strike but will punish a pitcher who starts him with a get-ahead fastball. Much of his confidence and willingness to wait out a pitcher stems from his ability to hit with two strikes—he's a respectable .244 hitter with two strikes for his career. He's a pronounced flyball hitter, and southpaws do not faze him.

Baserunning & Defense

A reliable first baseman with average range, Giambi is bothered from time to time by minor hamstring problems and sometimes is used as a DH to keep him fresh. He also isn't pushed to overextend himself on the basepaths, though he has little speed to put to use there anyway. He always hustles but rarely tries to go farther than he ought to.

2003 Outlook

Giambi improved steadily over his first few years in the league and has plateaued at the superstar level. Now 32, he figures to stay there for several more years. The only thing that might slow him down is an injury, but he's proven to be consistently durable.

Position: 1B/DH
Bats: L **Throws:** R
Ht: 6' 3" **Wt:** 235

Opening Day Age: 32
Born: 1/8/71 in West Covina, CA
ML Seasons: 8
Pronunciation: gee-OM-bee

New York (AL)

Overall Statistics

	G	AB	R	H	D	T	HR	RBI	SB	BB	SO	Avg	OBP	Slg
'02	155	560	120	176	34	1	41	122	2	109	112	.314	.435	.598
Car.	1108	3958	721	1224	262	8	228	797	11	695	714	.309	.416	.552

Where He Hits the Ball

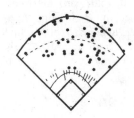 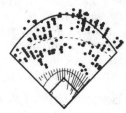

Vs. LHP   **Vs. RHP**

2002 Situational Stats

	AB	H	HR	RBI	Avg		AB	H	HR	RBI	Avg
Home	273	91	19	63	.333	LHP	154	46	9	32	.299
Road	287	85	22	59	.296	RHP	406	130	32	90	.320
First Half	314	100	22	71	.318	Sc Pos	144	49	11	80	.340
Scnd Half	246	76	19	51	.309	Clutch	72	20	7	18	.278

2002 Rankings (American League)

- 1st in times on base (300) and pitches seen (2,892)
- 2nd in walks, most pitches seen per plate appearance (4.20), cleanup slugging percentage (.640) and on-base percentage vs. righthanded pitchers (.448)
- 3rd in hit by pitch (15) and on-base percentage
- 4th in home runs, runs scored, slugging percentage, highest percentage of pitches taken (62.7), slugging percentage vs. righthanded pitchers (.626) and batting average at home
- Led the Yankees in home runs, RBI, walks, hit by pitch (15), times on base (300), slugging percentage, on-base percentage and HR frequency (13.7 ABs per HR)

Derek Jeter

2002 Season

The only things that could be considered disappointing about Derek Jeter's 2002 season were that he hit under .300 for the first time in five years and his club failed to make it back to the World Series. Otherwise, it was a typical season for Jeter, who regularly reached base and scored runs, stole bases and hardly ever missed a game.

Hitting

Jeter is a terrific No. 2 hitter. He combines a good average and batting eye with a willingness to take a pitch to help a basestealer and an ability to hit the ball through the right side. He has respectable power and is especially adept at staying inside the ball and driving it to right field, particularly on inside fastballs. He's much more of a line-drive hitter than a flyball hitter, and many of his hits come on hard grounders through the infield. His bat control enables him to protect the plate well with two strikes.

Baserunning & Defense

No one will deny that Jeter is a tremendous athlete with a powerful arm, strong fundamentals and terrific instincts. Nonetheless, he lets more balls go through than someone with his tools ought to (as was apparent in the ALDS, for example). Overall, he is a good defensive shortstop, but to deserve a Gold Glove he must improve his footwork and positioning. A terrific baserunner with very good speed, Jeter finished third in the league in steals and had the majors' best stolen-base percentage.

2003 Outlook

Apart from being one of the best all-around shortstops in the majors, Jeter has every right to be called one of the most consistent and reliable players in the game. He's set the bar high for himself, but he plays up to that standard every year and can be expected to do so again this season.

Position: SS
Bats: R **Throws:** R
Ht: 6' 3" **Wt:** 195

Opening Day Age: 28
Born: 6/26/74 in Pequannock, NJ
ML Seasons: 8
Pronunciation: JEE-ter

Overall Statistics

	G	AB	R	H	D	T	HR	RBI	SB	BB	SO	Avg	OBP	Slg
'02	157	644	124	191	26	0	18	75	32	73	114	.297	.373	.421
Car.	1093	4388	839	1390	214	38	117	563	167	470	785	.317	.389	.463

Where He Hits the Ball

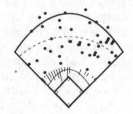 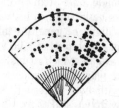

Vs. LHP   **Vs. RHP**

2002 Situational Stats

	AB	H	HR	RBI	Avg		AB	H	HR	RBI	Avg
Home	297	84	8	31	.283	LHP	124	39	5	13	.315
Road	347	107	10	44	.308	RHP	520	152	13	62	.292
First Half	349	109	12	43	.312	Sc Pos	147	47	4	57	.320
Scnd Half	295	82	6	32	.278	Clutch	84	20	2	11	.238

2002 Rankings (American League)

- 1st in stolen-base percentage (91.4)
- 2nd in singles, plate appearances (730) and highest groundball-flyball ratio (2.2)
- 3rd in runs scored, stolen bases and batting average on an 0-2 count (.333)
- 4th in at-bats
- 5th in lowest fielding percentage at shortstop (.977)
- 6th in times on base (271), pitches seen (2,724), steals of third (5) and on-base percentage vs. lefthanded pitchers (.410)
- Led the Yankees in singles, games played, highest groundball-flyball ratio (2.2), stolen-base percentage (91.4), bunts in play (9) and batting average on an 0-2 count (.333)

Raul Mondesi

2002 Season

It was a painful year for Raul Mondesi all around. The Blue Jays traded him to the Yankees in July for very little, wanting only to get out from under his contract. Soon after arriving in New York, he had a collision with an outfield wall, the effects of which he was still feeling six weeks later. Playing with a sore knee, chest, neck and shoulder, his average fell to a career-low .232—though it should be noted that his average actually was lower *before* the collision.

Hitting

Mondesi's approach is to go up there hacking, which makes him dangerous on the first pitch but increasingly vulnerable on longer counts. Always looking to pull, he can be made to chase breaking balls or pitches out of the strike zone. Though he's continued to bat in the middle of the order on the strength of his reputation, he no longer hits righthanders well enough to help there.

Baserunning & Defense

Mondesi has surprising speed for a man his size, and his stolen bases are not mere window dressing—a good chunk of them do come at opportune times. He runs the bases with abandon and it can be far from pleasant to get in his way. His throwing arm is one of the most respected in the majors, and baserunners almost never challenge him. He has good range in right and can fill in in center if needed.

2003 Outlook

Mondesi is due to receive $13 million this year (a percentage of which is slated to be paid by Toronto), and while the Yankees reportedly want to move him, they might have to eat a lot of his salary in order to do so. He's carrying extra weight and it wouldn't be surprising if aches and pains eat into his playing time and production.

Position: RF/DH/CF
Bats: R **Throws:** R
Ht: 5'11" **Wt:** 230

Opening Day Age: 32
Born: 3/12/71 in San Cristobal, DR
ML Seasons: 10
Pronunciation: MON-de-see

Overall Statistics

	G	AB	R	H	D	T	HR	RBI	SB	BB	SO	Avg	OBP	Slg
'02	146	569	90	132	34	1	26	88	15	59	103	.232	.308	.432
Car.	1307	5016	799	1385	272	44	240	757	207	394	967	.276	.331	.491

Where He Hits the Ball

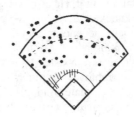 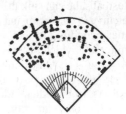

Vs. LHP   **Vs. RHP**

2002 Situational Stats

	AB	H	HR	RBI	Avg		AB	H	HR	RBI	Avg
Home	284	67	16	51	.236	LHP	135	33	8	20	.244
Road	285	65	10	37	.228	RHP	434	99	18	68	.228
First Half	318	73	16	50	.230	Sc Pos	166	40	5	62	.241
Scnd Half	251	59	10	38	.235	Clutch	90	16	1	3	.178

2002 Rankings (American League)

- 1st in lowest batting average (.232)
- 3rd in lowest batting average vs. righthanded pitchers (.228) and lowest fielding percentage in right field (.978)
- 4th in errors in right field (5)
- 5th in assists in right field (7) and lowest on-base percentage vs. righthanded pitchers (.295)
- Led the Yankees in fewest GDPs per GDP situation (4.3%)

Mike Mussina

2002 Season

It's rare to call an 18-win season frustrating, but that's exactly what last year was for Mike Mussina. He went through a four-month stretch from late April through late August in which he struggled to find any sort of consistency, performing at well below his accustomed level yet picking up victories nonetheless. To his credit, he eventually pulled out of it, and ultimately provided his usual 200-plus innings, but for Mussina it was a trying year.

Pitching

Mussina has good stuff and locates it with purpose and precision. Throwing mostly low-90s fastballs, he can sink the ball or cut it. He also has a curve, a changeup and a knuckle-curve, and can make good use of any of them, depending on the hitter and which pitch is working best for him on a given day. One thing he does consistently is keep the ball away from righthanded hitters. Hitters from either side of the plate find him equally tough to solve. He normally has good stamina, but having to pitch out of trouble more often last season sometimes wore him down a bit. Few pitchers can match his reliability—he's never had a major arm injury and seldom misses a start.

Defense

Mussina does just about everything well in the field, from fielding his position to holding baserunners. A good athlete and five-time Gold Glover, he committed only one error all year. Basestealers were only 6-for-16 against him.

2003 Outlook

It's hard to imagine Mussina again slipping into a prolonged funk, especially since there seemed to be nothing wrong with him physically. Even at age 34, he remains perfectly capable of having the 20-win season that has eluded him to this point in his career.

Position: SP
Bats: L **Throws:** R
Ht: 6' 2" **Wt:** 185

Opening Day Age: 34
Born: 12/8/68 in Williamsport, PA
ML Seasons: 12
Pronunciation: myoo-SEE-nuh
Nickname: Moose

Overall Statistics

	W	L	Pct.	ERA	G	GS	Sv	IP	H	BB	SO	HR	Ratio
'02	18	10	.643	4.05	33	33	0	215.2	208	48	182	27	1.19
Car.	182	102	.641	3.54	355	355	0	2454.0	2305	557	1931	257	1.17

How Often He Throws Strikes

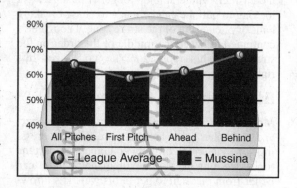

= League Average ■ = Mussina

2002 Situational Stats

	W	L	ERA	Sv	IP		AB	H	HR	RBI	Avg
Home	7	8	4.25	0	112.1	LHB	444	114	16	53	.257
Road	11	2	3.83	0	103.1	RHB	379	94	11	40	.248
First Half	12	3	4.54	0	115.0	Sc Pos	147	42	5	59	.286
Scnd Half	6	7	3.49	0	100.2	Clutch	46	16	0	5	.348

2002 Rankings (American League)

- 2nd in shutouts (2)
- 3rd in strikeouts and most strikeouts per nine innings (7.6)
- 4th in runners caught stealing (10), highest strikeout-walk ratio (3.8) and lowest stolen-base percentage allowed (37.5)
- 7th in games started and most run support per nine innings (6.3)
- Led the Yankees in losses, games started, shutouts (2), innings pitched, batters faced (886), home runs allowed, pitches thrown (3,354), runners caught stealing (10), highest strikeout-walk ratio (3.8) and lowest stolen-base percentage allowed (37.5)

Andy Pettitte

2002 Season

For a while, it looked like Andy Pettitte's 2002 season might be a disaster. He was shut down with a sore elbow after only three starts, and it was two months before he worked his way back. He didn't get his second victory of the season until the last day of June, but he made up for it with a huge second half, winning 11 of 13 decisions and finishing with the lowest ERA among the club's starters. Unfortunately, he had one of his worst starts of the second half in the ALDS.

Pitching

Pettitte handcuffs righthanded hitters by running his cut fastball in on their hands. His changeup is a good second pitch, and he makes more extensive use of his four-seamer and sinker against left-handed hitters. As the strike zone has expanded upward over the last two years, he's worked his four-seamer upstairs more often, cutting his walks but getting fewer groundballs. He's still primarily a groundball pitcher, though, and is able to escape jams by inducing more than his share of twin-killings. Hitters rarely are able to take him out of the park.

Defense

Known for having one of the best pickoff moves in the game, Pettitte is very tough to run on and places among the leaders in pickoffs every season. He's also an active, alert fielder who consistently helps himself with the glove.

2003 Outlook

The Yankees didn't cut costs by cutting Pettitte, instead picking up the $11.5 million option they held for 2003. Until last year, Pettitte never had missed significant time with an arm injury. He proved over the second half that he'd put his elbow problems behind him, so there's every reason to think he'll deliver another Pettitte-quality healthy season this year.

Position: SP
Bats: L **Throws:** L
Ht: 6' 5" **Wt:** 225

Opening Day Age: 30
Born: 6/15/72 in Baton Rouge, LA
ML Seasons: 8
Pronunciation: PET-it

Overall Statistics

	W	L	Pct.	ERA	G	GS	Sv	IP	H	BB	SO	HR	Ratio
'02	13	5	.722	3.27	22	22	0	134.2	144	32	97	6	1.31
Car.	128	70	.646	3.93	250	243	0	1584.1	1674	529	1095	122	1.39

How Often He Throws Strikes

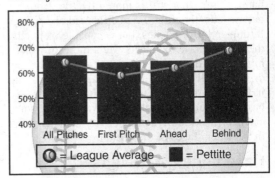

◯ = League Average   ■ = Pettitte

2002 Situational Stats

	W	L	ERA	Sv	IP		AB	H	HR	RBI	Avg
Home	8	2	3.48	0	67.1	LHB	102	26	2	12	.255
Road	5	3	3.07	0	67.1	RHB	427	118	4	39	.276
First Half	2	3	4.74	0	38.0	Sc Pos	118	31	3	44	.263
Scnd Half	11	2	2.70	0	96.2	Clutch	39	9	0	0	.231

2002 Rankings (American League)

- 9th in complete games (3) and winning percentage
- Led the Yankees in ERA, complete games (3), GDPs induced (16), lowest slugging percentage allowed (.365), highest groundball-flyball ratio allowed (1.3), lowest ERA on the road, fewest home runs allowed per nine innings (.40) and most GDPs induced per nine innings (1.1)

Jorge Posada

2002 Season

It was an often-painful season for Jorge Posada. Coming off right shoulder surgery, he battled soreness early in the year after being hit on the same shoulder by a foul ball. In August and September, a sore left knee hampered him. And in between, he was cracked on the head several times by batters' follow-throughs. He still managed to post another fine offensive year, driving in a career-high 99 runs, although he did go homerless in his last 36 games.

Hitting

The switch-hitting Posada has improved as a left-handed hitter, but still is more effective from his natural side, the right. From either side he swings through a lot of pitches, but is capable of juicing the ball when he connects. He's more of a pull-hitter from the right side. From the left he can drive the ball into the left-field gap as well as pull it. His homers typically come in bunches. He also has an aptitude for waiting out walks. Like some catchers, his offensive productivity tends to suffer in the latter stages of the season.

Baserunning & Defense

Posada's physical problems showed up mainly in his baserunning and defensive work. The shoulder problem affected his throwing accuracy early in the year, and the knee problem slowed his release and affected his pitch-blocking in the second half. He led American League catchers in errors for the second consecutive year and wasn't successful throwing out runners. He'd always run well for catcher, but last year he attempted only one steal and led the league in grounding into double plays.

2003 Outlook

Posada fell one inning short of leading the majors in innings caught, and it seemed to catch up with him. If the Yankees can give him more rest, he actually might wind up with better numbers. Even if they don't, he should remain one of the best offensive catchers in baseball.

Position: C
Bats: B **Throws:** R
Ht: 6' 2" **Wt:** 205

Opening Day Age: 31
Born: 8/17/71 in Santurce, PR
ML Seasons: 8
Pronunciation: hor-hay po-sa-da

Overall Statistics

	G	AB	R	H	D	T	HR	RBI	SB	BB	SO	Avg	OBP	Slg
'02	143	511	79	137	40	1	20	99	1	81	143	.268	.370	.468
Car.	724	2439	366	653	157	5	105	425	7	381	648	.268	.369	.465

Where He Hits the Ball

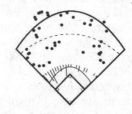 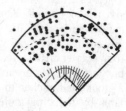

Vs. LHP	Vs. RHP

2002 Situational Stats

	AB	H	HR	RBI	Avg		AB	H	HR	RBI	Avg
Home	249	67	12	51	.269	LHP	135	44	5	25	.326
Road	262	70	8	48	.267	RHP	376	93	15	74	.247
First Half	282	75	15	58	.266	Sc Pos	155	48	10	83	.310
Scnd Half	229	62	5	41	.271	Clutch	79	28	2	16	.354

2002 Rankings (American League)

- 1st in GDPs (23), errors at catcher (12) and lowest fielding percentage at catcher (.988)
- Led the Yankees in intentional walks (9), GDPs (23) and batting average with the bases loaded (.579)
- Led AL catchers in batting average, home runs and RBI

Mariano Rivera

2002 Season

In the 2001 World Series, Mariano Rivera's shield of postseason invulnerability was pierced. Then last year, his seeming indestructibility vanished as well. After never having suffered an arm injury in his career, he strained his shoulder in July. He missed two weeks, made five more appearances and reinjured it, finally returning only a couple of weeks before the playoffs. He pitched as well as ever when healthy, converting 28 of 32 save opportunities.

Pitching

Rivera's signature pitch is a cut fastball in the upper 90s. It runs away from righthanded hitters, who find it hard to pull, and runs in on the fists of lefthanded hitters, who have trouble getting around on it. He'll also mix in a straight four-seamer. Being so hard to hit allows him to go right at hitters, minimizing walks. His cutter induces a lot of weakly hit balls, but fewer outright swings and misses than other closers' strikeout pitches. Rivera thus gets more groundballs but fewer strikeouts than most closers. Before his shoulder woes, he often was asked to go more than one inning, and had no problem doing so.

Defense

Athletic and agile, Rivera fields his position well. The fact that he muffed two of 11 fielding chances last year is more an aberration than a lingering effect of his World Series error from the year before. Holding runners is not a strength of his, but getting the out at the plate sure works for him.

2003 Outlook

After a winter of rest, Rivera's arm troubles hopefully are behind him. The Yankees are hoping he'll be his old self from start to finish this year, but only time will tell. The club may limit him to an inning at a time in an effort to keep him healthy, which wouldn't affect his overall numbers much.

Position: RP
Bats: R **Throws:** R
Ht: 6' 2" **Wt:** 185

Opening Day Age: 33
Born: 11/29/69 in Panama City, Panama
ML Seasons: 8

Overall Statistics

	W	L	Pct.	ERA	G	GS	Sv	IP	H	BB	SO	HR	Ratio
'02	1	4	.200	2.74	45	0	28	46.0	35	11	41	3	1.00
Car.	38	27	.585	2.60	448	10	243	579.0	454	167	519	34	1.07

How Often He Throws Strikes

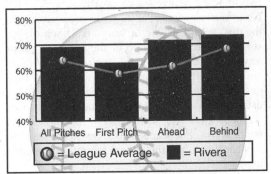

= League Average   = Rivera

2002 Situational Stats

	W	L	ERA	Sv	IP		AB	H	HR	RBI	Avg
Home	1	2	2.66	9	20.1	LHB	83	15	1	13	.181
Road	0	2	2.81	19	25.2	RHB	89	20	2	10	.225
First Half	1	3	1.47	21	30.2	Sc Pos	48	13	2	22	.271
Scnd Half	0	1	5.28	7	15.1	Clutch	133	25	2	19	.188

2002 Rankings (American League)

- 5th in save percentage (87.5)
- 7th in saves, first batter efficiency (.182) and fewest GDPs induced per GDP situation (2.8%)
- 9th in save opportunities (32)
- Led the Yankees in saves, save opportunities (32), lowest batting average allowed vs. left-handed batters, save percentage (87.5), first batter efficiency (.182), blown saves (4) and relief losses (4)

Alfonso Soriano

2002 Season

Many expected Alfonso Soriano to reach stardom, but few expected it to happen so suddenly, so soon. Moving up to the leadoff spot, he put up power numbers few second basemen had ever attained, all while batting .300 and leading the league in stolen bases. He led the majors in runs scored and extra-base hits, and missed a rare 40-40 season by a single homer.

Hitting

Some hitters are just not born to be patient. Soriano tried to lay off the first pitch in 2001, but last year the Yankees turned him loose and he batted .464 and slugged .825 on the first offering. Notoriously aggressive, he will chase pitches in the dirt, yet is capable of stinging a pitch off his shoetops. Standing on top of the plate, he whips around a long, heavy bat with his incredibly strong wrists, generating exceptional power. He's deadly on fastballs in any location, and pitchers usually try to tie him up inside and then feed him offspeed stuff. He strikes out a lot and almost never walks, but seems to be one of the few hitters capable of putting up great numbers nonetheless.

Baserunning & Defense

In his second year as a second baseman, Soriano's defense improved a lot. Though he led major league second basemen in errors for the second straight season, the bulk of them came early in the year. He has good range and a strong arm, but needs to improve his reliability and his double-play pivot. Fast and fearless on the bases, he likes to run on the first pitch and will try to steal third if a pitcher lets him.

2003 Outlook

Only 25 this year, Soriano now needs to smooth out the bumps in his fielding. He's already an offensive star and ought to stay at this level for years to come.

Position: 2B
Bats: R **Throws:** R
Ht: 6' 1" **Wt:** 180

Opening Day Age: 25
Born: 1/7/78 in San Pedro de Macoris, DR
ML Seasons: 4
Pronunciation: soar-ee-ah-no

Overall Statistics

	G	AB	R	H	D	T	HR	RBI	SB	BB	SO	Avg	OBP	Slg
'02	156	696	128	209	51	2	39	102	41	23	157	.300	.332	.547
Car.	345	1328	212	373	88	5	60	179	86	53	300	.281	.314	.490

Where He Hits the Ball

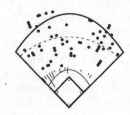

Vs. LHP   **Vs. RHP**

2002 Situational Stats

	AB	H	HR	RBI	Avg		AB	H	HR	RBI	Avg
Home	335	94	17	49	.281	LHP	133	42	8	19	.316
Road	361	115	22	53	.319	RHP	563	167	31	83	.297
First Half	368	116	20	51	.315	Sc Pos	140	46	8	64	.329
Scnd Half	328	93	19	51	.284	Clutch	97	31	1	12	.320

2002 Rankings (American League)

- 1st in at-bats, runs scored, hits, stolen bases, plate appearances (741), steals of third (9), errors at second base (23) and lowest fielding percentage at second base (.968)
- 2nd in total bases (381), caught stealing (13) and strikeouts
- 3rd in doubles, highest percentage of extra bases taken as a runner (69.5), slugging percentage vs. lefthanded pitchers (.571) and lowest percentage of pitches taken (42.7)
- 4th in lowest on-base percentage for a leadoff hitter (.329)
- Led the Yankees in at-bats, runs scored, hits, doubles, triples, total bases (381), sacrifice flies (7), stolen bases, caught stealing (13), strikeouts and plate appearances (741)

Robin Ventura

2002 Season

Taking over as the Yankees' third baseman, Robin Ventura had a respectable season, though it could have been better, as he hit only two homers over his last 33 games. Despite his late slump and low average, he contributed in his usual ways, with solid if unspectacular glovework, lefthanded power and plenty of walks.

Hitting

A patient hitter with a smooth stroke, Ventura likes the ball out over the plate and is capable of reaching the fences from left-center to the right-field line. For a lefthanded hitter, Ventura hangs in well against most southpaws, although he's been given more and more days off against them in recent seasons to help keep him fresh. Moving to Yankee Stadium last season, he seemed to become more pull-conscious, which pitchers sometimes used to their advantage against him. He's often excessively patient in his first at-bat of a game against a pitcher, but more aggressive and more effective in subsequent at-bats against them. He's been prone to lengthy slumps over the last few seasons as nagging injuries have lingered at times.

Baserunning & Defense

A six-time Gold Glover, Ventura had an off year in the field by his own standards. His 23 errors represented his highest total since 1992. He's lost a step of range and some zip on his throws, but still is one of the better gloves at his position. Few are better at charging and bare-handing bunts. The best that can be said about his baserunning is that he's well aware of his limitations.

2003 Outlook

After making $8.25 million in 2002, Ventura became a free agent before deciding to return to the Yankees on a one-year, $5 million contract. The Bronx is where he wanted to be. Ventura may be at the point in his career where he'll help the team most in a slightly reduced role.

Position: 3B
Bats: L **Throws:** R
Ht: 6' 1" **Wt:** 198

Opening Day Age: 35
Born: 7/14/67 in Santa Maria, CA
ML Seasons: 14

Overall Statistics

	G	AB	R	H	D	T	HR	RBI	SB	BB	SO	Avg	OBP	Slg
'02	141	465	68	115	17	0	27	93	3	90	101	.247	.368	.458
Car.	1839	6520	945	1753	317	13	275	1099	24	995	1061	.269	.364	.448

Where He Hits the Ball

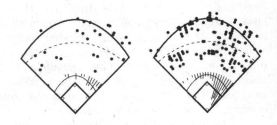

Vs. LHP   **Vs. RHP**

2002 Situational Stats

	AB	H	HR	RBI	Avg		AB	H	HR	RBI	Avg
Home	223	52	9	36	.233	LHP	101	22	8	23	.218
Road	242	63	18	57	.260	RHP	364	93	19	70	.255
First Half	262	69	19	62	.263	Sc Pos	145	37	6	65	.255
Scnd Half	203	46	8	31	.227	Clutch	70	14	6	12	.200

2002 Rankings (American League)

- 1st in errors at third base (23) and lowest fielding percentage at third base (.941)
- 6th in walks
- 7th in lowest batting average at home
- 9th in most pitches seen per plate appearance (4.04)
- 10th in intentional walks (9), HR frequency (17.2 ABs per HR) and lowest batting average
- Led the Yankees in intentional walks (9)

Rondell White

2002 Season

In many ways, 2002 was the worst season of left fielder Rondell White's career. After signing a two-year deal with the Yankees, he got off to a slow start before rupturing a tendon in his left middle finger in June. He kept playing but never got his bat going, and by the time the playoffs came he'd been reduced to a part-time role.

Hitting

White is an aggressive line-drive hitter with fairly good power to all fields. He doesn't hit enough flyballs to be a consistent home-run threat, but he'd always hit for a good average until last year. Drawing walks is not part of his game, and he'll chase fastballs up and out of the strike zone. He's always hit well against southpaws, and continued to do so last year even as he struggled badly against righthanded pitchers. He likes to jump on the first pitch and does his best hitting early in the count. He's always drawn too few walks to be an ideal leadoff man, and hasn't had quite enough power to be a top-flight run producer. So when he doesn't hit for a good average, he fills no useful role at all.

Baserunning & Defense

White still has good speed, but years of knee problems have rendered him a nonthreat to steal and a much less aggressive baserunner overall for someone with his ability. He puts his mobility to good use in the outfield, where he has above-average range. His notoriously weak throwing arm is a major liability, even in left field.

2003 Outlook

The outlook for White is the same as it's always been: he's capable of putting up good numbers if he can stay healthy, but his injury history makes that unlikely. Still, with the money the Yankees have invested in him, they likely will have to give him every chance to rebound if they are unable to trade him.

Position: LF/DH
Bats: R **Throws:** R
Ht: 6' 1" **Wt:** 225

Opening Day Age: 31
Born: 2/23/72 in Milledgeville, GA
ML Seasons: 10

Overall Statistics

	G	AB	R	H	D	T	HR	RBI	SB	BB	SO	Avg	OBP	Slg
'02	126	455	59	109	21	0	14	62	1	25	86	.240	.288	.378
Car.	982	3601	529	1038	207	24	134	503	90	256	648	.288	.343	.471

Where He Hits the Ball

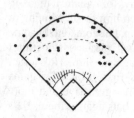 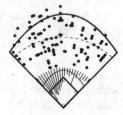

Vs. LHP   **Vs. RHP**

2002 Situational Stats

	AB	H	HR	RBI	Avg		AB	H	HR	RBI	Avg
Home	214	49	5	24	.229	LHP	105	30	3	14	.286
Road	241	60	9	38	.249	RHP	350	79	11	48	.226
First Half	261	67	9	38	.257	Sc Pos	138	29	2	45	.210
Scnd Half	194	42	5	24	.216	Clutch	68	15	3	13	.221

2002 Rankings (American League)
- 1st in fielding percentage in left field (1.000)
- 2nd in lowest batting average vs. righthanded pitchers and lowest on-base percentage vs. righthanded pitchers (.269)
- 3rd in lowest batting average with runners in scoring position
- 4th in lowest slugging percentage vs. righthanded pitchers (.354)

Bernie Williams

2002 Season

It's a significant testament to Bernie Williams that he accomplished as much as he did last year despite two bad shoulders. He required cortisone shots in each shoulder just a couple of weeks into the season, and needed daily treatment for the rest of the year, but ended up playing 154 games and finishing third in the American League batting race.

Hitting

Williams has enough power to hit cleanup, but he always has been more of a line-drive hitter than one who lofted the ball. Last year, with his bad shoulders sapping his strength, that tendency was more pronounced than ever. A patient hitter, he's quite able to pull the ball with authority, but is willing to go up the middle or the other way if that's how he's pitched. He's a true switch-hitter, equally proficient from either side of the plate.

Baserunning & Defense

The part of Williams' game his shoulders affected the most was his defense. His weak throwing arm was even worse than usual, especially early in the season. Though he moves smoothly, he doesn't get the best jumps and a lot of balls fall in front of him. Knee and hamstring problems may have been partly to blame, but it seems the day is drawing near when he'll need to be moved to left field. Never an instinctive baserunner despite good speed, he took fewer chances last year.

2003 Outlook

A winter of rehab work hopefully will rebuild the strength in Williams' shoulders. If so, he can be expected to get his home-run total back up to its usual levels. Even if he isn't able to do that, he's still a key part of the Yankees' offense because of his ability to get on base. Getting him out of center may help him stay healthier overall.

Position: CF
Bats: B **Throws:** R
Ht: 6' 2" **Wt:** 205

Opening Day Age: 34
Born: 9/13/68 in San Juan, PR
ML Seasons: 12

Overall Statistics

	G	AB	R	H	D	T	HR	RBI	SB	BB	SO	Avg	OBP	Slg
'02	154	612	102	204	37	2	19	102	8	83	97	.333	.415	.493
Car.	1537	5958	1066	1833	353	52	226	998	138	827	927	.308	.392	.498

Where He Hits the Ball

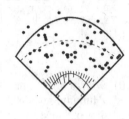 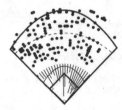

Vs. LHP   **Vs. RHP**

2002 Situational Stats

	AB	H	HR	RBI	Avg		AB	H	HR	RBI	Avg
Home	284	88	13	39	.310	LHP	164	58	4	22	.354
Road	328	116	6	63	.354	RHP	448	146	15	80	.326
First Half	324	101	11	45	.312	Sc Pos	174	65	5	84	.374
Scnd Half	288	103	8	57	.358	Clutch	84	33	2	17	.393

2002 Rankings (American League)

- 2nd in times on base (290), batting average in the clutch, on-base percentage vs. lefthanded pitchers (.430) and batting average on the road
- 3rd in batting average, hits, singles, batting average vs. lefthanded pitchers and errors in center field (5)
- 4th in GDPs (19), batting average with runners in scoring position and lowest fielding percentage in center field (.986)
- 5th in on-base percentage, highest ground ball-flyball ratio (1.9) and batting average on an 0-2 count (.308)
- Led the Yankees in batting average, triples and lowest percentage of swings that missed (17.7)

Orlando Hernandez

Position: SP
Bats: R **Throws:** R
Ht: 6' 2" **Wt:** 220

Opening Day Age: 33
Born: 10/11/69 in Havana, Cuba
ML Seasons: 5
Pronunciation: her-NAN-dezz

Overall Statistics

	W	L	Pct.	ERA	G	GS	Sv	IP	H	BB	SO	HR	Ratio
'02	8	5	.615	3.64	24	22	1	146.0	131	36	113	17	1.14
Car.	53	38	.582	4.04	124	121	1	791.2	707	268	619	105	1.23

2002 Situational Stats

	W	L	ERA	Sv	IP		AB	H	HR	RBI	Avg
Home	5	2	3.43	1	76.0	LHB	286	64	12	37	.224
Road	3	3	3.86	0	70.0	RHB	270	67	5	20	.248
First Half	5	2	2.89	1	62.1	Sc Pos	125	26	4	39	.208
Scnd Half	3	3	4.20	0	83.2	Clutch	44	5	1	2	.114

2002 Season

After missing half of 2001 with a toe injury, Orlando Hernandez endured a tumultuous 2002 season as well. He started off hot but missed six weeks with a strained back in May and June. After he returned, Jeff Weaver was acquired, and Hernandez reportedly refused to move to the bullpen. A crisis was averted only when Weaver pitched his way into the pen himself. Hernandez pitched unspectacularly for the rest of the year and was left out of the postseason rotation.

Pitching & Defense

Hernandez always seems to be pulling new tricks out of his bag. Last year it was an eephus-like changeup to go with his fastball, curve, slider and variety of arm angles. For the first time in El Duque's major league career, lefties did not hit him hard. He always has been tough on righthanded hitters. Controlling the running game still is a problem, although he did better last year by varying his normally big leg kick. He's a fine fielder.

2003 Outlook

Unless the Yankees non-tender him, Hernandez probably will be back in pinstripes in 2003. But only Roger Clemens leaving New York would ensure him a rotation spot. He's capable of having a good year if healthy.

Sterling Hitchcock

Position: RP
Bats: L **Throws:** L
Ht: 6' 0" **Wt:** 205

Opening Day Age: 31
Born: 4/29/71 in Fayetteville, NC
ML Seasons: 11

Overall Statistics

	W	L	Pct.	ERA	G	GS	Sv	IP	H	BB	SO	HR	Ratio
'02	1	2	.333	5.49	20	2	0	39.1	57	15	31	4	1.83
Car.	68	69	.496	4.77	242	189	3	1176.2	1261	431	915	162	1.44

2002 Situational Stats

	W	L	ERA	Sv	IP		AB	H	HR	RBI	Avg
Home	1	1	5.79	0	23.1	LHB	57	18	1	8	.316
Road	0	1	5.06	0	16.0	RHB	118	39	3	18	.331
First Half	1	0	7.48	0	21.2	Sc Pos	61	20	1	21	.328
Scnd Half	0	2	3.06	0	17.2	Clutch	24	11	0	4	.458

2002 Season

The Yankees got virtually nothing out of left-hander Sterling Hitchcock last year. A strained groin and lower back kept him out until mid-May, and the back injury bothered him for the rest of the season and shelved him again for six weeks in midsummer. Even when active, he did little more than make occasional appearances in long relief.

Pitching & Defense

Last year was Hitchcock's first full season back from Tommy John surgery, and it was hard to tell how well he'd recovered, considering his other ailments. He used to get strikeouts with a 90-MPH fastball and hard splitter, but last year his fastball was ordinary and his splitter lacked bite. At times he lost confidence in his fastball and pitched backwards, nibbling with curves and changeups. He's easy to run on, though few did so last year because the game seldom was close when he was pitching. His glove is average.

2003 Outlook

Last year, Hitchcock had to prove his arm had recovered. Now he must prove his back is healthy too. He'll get every chance to do so, since he's signed to a lucrative contract through 2003.

Nick Johnson

Position: 1B/DH
Bats: L **Throws:** L
Ht: 6' 3" **Wt:** 224

Opening Day Age: 24
Born: 9/19/78 in
Sacramento, CA
ML Seasons: 2

Overall Statistics

	G	AB	R	H	D	T	HR	RBI	SB	BB	SO	Avg	OBP	Slg
'02	129	378	56	92	15	0	15	58	1	48	98	.243	.347	.402
Car.	152	445	62	105	17	0	17	66	1	55	113	.236	.341	.389

2002 Situational Stats

	AB	H	HR	RBI	Avg		AB	H	HR	RBI	Avg
Home	190	51	7	36	.268	LHP	63	11	2	13	.175
Road	188	41	8	22	.218	RHP	315	81	13	45	.257
First Half	249	58	11	41	.233	Sc Pos	98	29	6	45	.296
Scnd Half	129	34	4	17	.264	Clutch	59	17	2	8	.288

2002 Season

Nick Johnson's long-delayed arrival ultimately wasn't all that eventful. He served as the Yankees' designated hitter for most of the year, playing first base when Jason Giambi was given a day off from playing the field. Johnson had a slow first half, but started to pick it up after the All-Star break before suffering a bone bruise in his left wrist that kept him out a month. He returned in September but never got back in the groove.

Hitting, Baserunning & Defense

An extremely patient hitter, Johnson consistently found himself behind in the count when major league pitchers were much more willing than minor leaguers had been to come right at him. He fared poorly in limited at-bats against southpaws, but had no such problem in the minors and isn't expected to need to be platooned. He showed good skills around the bag when asked to play first and runs fairly well for a man his size.

2003 Outlook

Johnson is capable of doing a lot more than he showed in 2002. It could come together for him quickly once he shows pitchers he no longer will let them get ahead in the count at will.

Steve Karsay

Position: RP
Bats: R **Throws:** R
Ht: 6' 3" **Wt:** 215

Opening Day Age: 31
Born: 3/24/72 in
Flushing, NY
ML Seasons: 8
Pronunciation:
CAR-say

Overall Statistics

	W	L	Pct.	ERA	G	GS	Sv	IP	H	BB	SO	HR	Ratio
'02	6	4	.600	3.26	78	0	12	88.1	87	30	65	7	1.32
Car.	31	38	.449	3.88	321	40	41	565.2	582	187	435	51	1.36

2002 Situational Stats

	W	L	ERA	Sv	IP		AB	H	HR	RBI	Avg
Home	2	1	2.74	7	46.0	LHB	136	33	6	20	.243
Road	4	3	3.83	5	42.1	RHB	201	54	1	20	.269
First Half	3	3	3.20	3	50.2	Sc Pos	104	22	1	31	.212
Scnd Half	3	1	3.35	9	37.2	Clutch	182	49	3	22	.269

2002 Season

In his first year in pinstripes, Steve Karsay gave the Yankees just what they'd expected. He served as the Yankees' primary righthanded setup man and even filled in for Mariano Rivera when the Yankees' closer went down late in the year.

Pitching & Defense

With excellent command of a moving mid- to upper-90s fastball, Karsay gets plenty of strikeouts and groundballs. His hard curve is a reliable second pitch, and he rarely goes to his splitter or changeup. He issued only 16 unintentional walks last year. His main weakness is that he tends to lose effectiveness over the course of the season. He can field his position decently, but baserunners stole 11 bases off him without being caught in 2002.

2003 Outlook

The question with Karsay always has been whether his rebuilt elbow can hold up under regular work, but he's had four strong years in a row to ease that concern. Now the issue is his back, which he originally hurt in a game in late August. The injury resurfaced while working out on a treadmill in October, and Karsay had surgery for a herniated disc in November. He should be ready by spring, but back injuries bear watching.

Ramiro Mendoza

Position: RP
Bats: R **Throws:** R
Ht: 6' 2" **Wt:** 195

Opening Day Age: 30
Born: 6/15/72 in Los Santos, Panama
ML Seasons: 7

Overall Statistics

	W	L	Pct.	ERA	G	GS	Sv	IP	H	BB	SO	HR	Ratio
'02	8	4	.667	3.44	62	0	4	91.2	102	16	61	8	1.29
Car.	54	34	.614	4.08	277	57	16	698.2	766	154	413	68	1.32

2002 Situational Stats

	W	L	ERA	Sv	IP		AB	H	HR	RBI	Avg
Home	4	2	4.17	1	45.1	LHB	165	43	4	18	.261
Road	4	2	2.72	3	46.1	RHB	206	59	4	31	.286
First Half	6	2	3.17	1	54.0	Sc Pos	117	28	1	41	.239
Scnd Half	2	2	3.82	3	37.2	Clutch	140	38	3	17	.271

2002 Season

It's a thankless job, but Ramiro Mendoza does it well. He did it again last year, taking over for starters who were knocked out early or couldn't carry a lead all the way to the setup corps. Though his role lacks prestige, Mendoza made a solid contribution by preventing games from getting out of hand and by allowing the rest of the relief corps to stick to their given roles.

Pitching & Defense

A pure sinkerballer, Mendoza simply comes in, throws strikes and gets grounders, regardless of the batter or situation. He also throws a four-seamer and a change, mostly for show. He came through the minors as a starter and is capable of working several innings at a time. Years of flagging down the comebackers he induces has trained him well, and he's gotten better at holding runners.

2003 Outlook

Mendoza became a free agent after the season, and while the Yankees would like to bring him back, he may move on in hopes of getting a chance to start. He could be a decent third or fourth starter for a team with a good defensive infield.

Shane Spencer

Position: RF/LF
Bats: R **Throws:** R
Ht: 5'11" **Wt:** 225

Opening Day Age: 31
Born: 2/20/72 in Key West, FL
ML Seasons: 5

Overall Statistics

	G	AB	R	H	D	T	HR	RBI	SB	BB	SO	Avg	OBP	Slg
'02	94	288	32	71	15	2	6	34	0	31	62	.247	.324	.375
Car.	345	1091	148	287	54	7	43	167	5	94	228	.263	.324	.444

2002 Situational Stats

	AB	H	HR	RBI	Avg		AB	H	HR	RBI	Avg
Home	125	36	5	22	.288	LHP	75	20	1	8	.267
Road	163	35	1	12	.215	RHP	213	51	5	26	.239
First Half	186	46	5	24	.247	Sc Pos	64	15	3	30	.234
Scnd Half	102	25	1	10	.245	Clutch	48	12	2	12	.250

2002 Season

It was a year of missed opportunities for Shane Spencer. He had several chances to take control of the right-field job, but ill-timed slumps and injuries thwarted him. A sprained wrist in June helped precipitate the acquisition of Raul Mondesi, which left Spencer filling in during Rondell White's injuries. A pulled hamstring virtually ended Spencer's season in late August.

Hitting, Baserunning & Defense

Spencer punishes lefthanders but doesn't hit righthanders well enough to play every day. A good fastball hitter, he's prone to chasing pitches out of the strike zone after he falls behind. A decent outfielder, his range is a bit short for Yankee Stadium's spacious left field, and his arm is accurate but not ideal for right field. He has decent speed but runs conservatively.

2003 Outlook

Unlike last year, Spencer could go into the season well down the depth chart. That could change, but the club first would have to find a taker for either Mondesi or White, both expensive commodities, and top prospect Juan Rivera would have to flop.

Mike Stanton (Rubber Arm)

Position: RP
Bats: L **Throws:** L
Ht: 6' 1" **Wt:** 215

Opening Day Age: 35
Born: 6/2/67 in Houston, TX
ML Seasons: 14

Overall Statistics

	W	L	Pct.	ERA	G	GS	Sv	IP	H	BB	SO	HR	Ratio
'02	7	1	.875	3.00	79	0	6	78.0	73	28	44	4	1.29
Car.	53	37	.589	3.77	835	1	71	823.2	785	308	688	70	1.33

2002 Situational Stats

	W	L	ERA	Sv	IP			AB	H	HR	RBI	Avg
Home	3	0	3.46	3	41.2	LHB		123	33	2	19	.268
Road	4	1	2.48	3	36.1	RHB		162	40	2	15	.247
First Half	3	1	2.37	1	49.1	Sc Pos		90	19	2	31	.211
Scnd Half	4	0	4.08	5	28.2	Clutch		141	37	1	16	.262

2002 Season

Rubber-armed reliever Mike Stanton had another busy season out of the Yankees' pen last year. As usual, he served as New York's primary lefthanded setup man, and he even was pressed into service as a co-closer late in the year when Mariano Rivera was sidelined. He finished second in the majors in appearances by a southpaw.

Pitching & Defense

Though he's a lefty, Stanton is much better suited to be a full-fledged setup man than a specialist. First, he's not any tougher on lefthanded hitters than he is on righthanded ones. Plus, he thrives on frequent work and can pitch several days in a row, even while pitching an inning at a time. He throws in the low 90s, mixing in splitters and sliders. He's an average fielder but holds runners very well and is tough to run on.

2003 Outlook

A free agent after six solid seasons in the Bronx, Stanton's services are in demand after the Yankees reportedly forced his hand with a contract offer that required an immediate response, didn't offer salary arbitration and quickly signed southpaw Chris Hammond. As long as he's used in his optimal role, Stanton ought to remain a valuable part of his new team's relief corps.

John Vander Wal

Position: RF/DH
Bats: L **Throws:** L
Ht: 6' 1" **Wt:** 197

Opening Day Age: 36
Born: 4/29/66 in Grand Rapids, MI
ML Seasons: 12

Overall Statistics

	G	AB	R	H	D	T	HR	RBI	SB	BB	SO	Avg	OBP	Slg
'02	84	219	30	57	17	1	6	20	1	23	58	.260	.327	.429
Car.	1213	2373	322	627	143	17	81	381	37	335	574	.264	.354	.441

2002 Situational Stats

	AB	H	HR	RBI	Avg		AB	H	HR	RBI	Avg
Home	104	28	2	8	.269	LHP	21	5	0	1	.238
Road	115	29	4	12	.252	RHP	198	52	6	19	.263
First Half	145	40	3	16	.276	Sc Pos	54	7	0	13	.130
Scnd Half	74	17	3	4	.230	Clutch	28	7	0	1	.250

2002 Season

John Vander Wal had a hard time finding a way to contribute last year. He spent most of the first half platooning in right field, but was relegated to the bench after Raul Mondesi was acquired in July. Vander Wal was known as a top pinch-hitter in the National League, but found few opportunities off the bench in his first season in the American League.

Hitting, Baserunning & Defense

Vander Wal is a low-ball hitter with fairly good straightaway power. Southpaws have given him trouble in the infrequent chances he's had against them. He has the rare ability to hit just as well when coming off the bench cold. A passable corner outfielder, he can fill in at first base if needed. He's a decent baserunner with average speed.

2003 Outlook

Vander Wal's contract was up over the winter and he almost certainly wasn't going to return to the Bronx. It may be hard for him to find another chance to play semi-regularly. His pinch-hitting skills are sure to land him a job somewhere, though.

Jeff Weaver

Position: SP
Bats: R **Throws:** R
Ht: 6' 5" **Wt:** 200

Opening Day Age: 26
Born: 8/22/76 in
Northridge, CA
ML Seasons: 4

Overall Statistics

	W	L	Pct.	ERA	G	GS	Sv	IP	H	BB	SO	HR	Ratio
'02	11	11	.500	3.52	32	25	2	199.2	193	48	132	16	1.21
Car.	44	54	.449	4.30	126	117	2	792.2	809	224	534	88	1.30

2002 Situational Stats

	W	L	ERA	Sv	IP		AB	H	HR	RBI	Avg
Home	6	6	4.51	1	101.2	LHB	387	90	6	29	.233
Road	5	5	2.48	1	98.0	RHB	385	103	10	47	.268
First Half	7	8	3.43	0	128.2	Sc Pos	166	43	6	57	.259
Scnd Half	4	3	3.68	2	71.0	Clutch	123	37	3	12	.301

2002 Season

Going from the hapless Tigers to the defending AL champions in midseason was supposed to give Jeff Weaver a big boost, but it didn't quite work out that way. After a strong first half with Detroit, he was hit hard in his first month with the Yankees, spent most of August in the bullpen, and made a pair of spot starts in September.

Pitching & Defense

Weaver historically is tough on righthanded hitters, running his low to mid-90s fastball in on their hands and following with hard sliders. Lefthanded hitters had given him trouble until last year, when he started to make good use of a two-seamer against them. He's prone to the longball when he gets the ball up. Big and strong, Weaver is capable of pitching deep into games consistently. His concentration lapses were less frequent last year as he fielded his position decently and vastly improved his effectiveness at controlling the running game.

2003 Outlook

Weaver's conspicuous struggles in New York helped obscure the fact that he cut more than a half-run off his 2001 ERA. Still only 26, he'll almost certainly be back in the rotation this year and very well could enjoy his best season yet.

David Wells

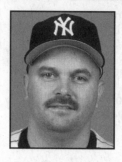

Position: SP
Bats: L **Throws:** L
Ht: 6' 4" **Wt:** 240

Opening Day Age: 39
Born: 5/20/63 in
Torrance, CA
ML Seasons: 16
Nickname: Boomer

Overall Statistics

	W	L	Pct.	ERA	G	GS	Sv	IP	H	BB	SO	HR	Ratio
'02	19	7	.731	3.75	31	31	0	206.1	210	45	137	21	1.24
Car.	185	121	.605	4.05	526	356	13	2613.2	2672	604	1772	306	1.25

2002 Situational Stats

	W	L	ERA	Sv	IP		AB	H	HR	RBI	Avg
Home	8	4	3.83	0	94.0	LHB	202	43	5	19	.213
Road	11	3	3.69	0	112.1	RHB	610	167	16	68	.274
First Half	9	5	3.66	0	113.0	Sc Pos	180	45	5	63	.250
Scnd Half	10	2	3.86	0	93.1	Clutch	46	11	2	5	.239

2002 Season

Going on age 39 and coming off back surgery that had wiped out half of his 2001 season, David Wells signed an incentive-laden deal to return to New York. Despite his usual quota of off-field flare-ups, he unarguably got the job done on the field. He wouldn't have won a team-high 19 games if he hadn't received the majors' best run support by far. But the bottom line was that he provided exactly what's come to be expected: 200 reasonably effective innings.

Pitching & Defense

Wells always has had a knack for not just throwing strikes, but throwing quality strikes. He comes right at hitters, getting ahead with his high-80s fastball to set up his sweeping curve. He doesn't hurt himself with walks, and his efficiency enables him to pitch into the seventh inning with regularity. He's a passable fielder but is easy to run against.

2003 Outlook

It's safe to say Wells won't approach 20 wins again, but he's shown he's still a capable mid-rotation starter. Even at age 40, he might have another solid season or two left in the tank.

Alex Arias (Pos: 3B, Age: 35, Bats: R)

	G	AB	R	H	D	T	HR	RBI	SB	BB	SO	Avg	OBP	Slg
'02	6	7	0	0	0	0	0	0	0	1	2	.000	.125	.000
Car.	775	1773	203	470	84	6	18	196	10	181	211	.265	.338	.350

Arias had managed at least 100 plate appearances in 10 straight seasons before 2002. He was cut by Seattle in the spring and played in both the O's and Yankees' systems. He's 35 and nearing the end. 2003 Outlook: C

Alberto Castillo (Pos: C, Age: 33, Bats: R)

	G	AB	R	H	D	T	HR	RBI	SB	BB	SO	Avg	OBP	Slg
'02	15	37	3	5	1	1	0	4	0	1	12	.135	.158	.216
Car.	332	790	66	173	25	1	8	69	2	74	172	.219	.289	.284

His at-bats and batting average declined for a third straight season, and he's been below the Mendoza Line in consecutive seasons. He's a free agent again, which now looks like a perennial condition. 2003 Outlook: C

Randy Choate (Pos: LHP, Age: 27)

	W	L	Pct.	ERA	G	GS	Sv	IP	H	BB	SO	HR	Ratio
'02	0	0	–	6.04	18	0	0	22.1	18	15	17	1	1.48
Car.	3	2	.600	4.31	77	0	0	87.2	66	50	64	4	1.32

Lefties hit just .107 (3-for-28) against him, but otherwise he was ineffective enough that he bounced between New York and Triple-A Columbus and pitched just one inning in New York after the break. 2003 Outlook: C

Ron Coomer (Pos: 3B/1B/DH, Age: 36, Bats: R)

	G	AB	R	H	D	T	HR	RBI	SB	BB	SO	Avg	OBP	Slg
'02	55	148	14	39	7	0	3	17	0	6	23	.264	.290	.372
Car.	842	2894	322	797	147	8	88	434	13	167	410	.275	.314	.423

After several seasons as a regular in Minnesota, Coomer saw his at-bats drop significantly with the Yanks in 2002. Only in his rookie season did he get fewer ABs and he's team shopping again for '03, though the Yanks offered salary arbitration. 2003 Outlook: C

Adrian Hernandez (Pos: RHP, Age: 28)

	W	L	Pct.	ERA	G	GS	Sv	IP	H	BB	SO	HR	Ratio
'02	0	1	.000	12.00	2	1	0	6.0	10	6	9	2	2.67
Car.	0	4	.000	5.46	8	4	0	28.0	25	16	19	9	1.46

The Yanks found out Hernandez was four years older last winter. He wasn't able to turn the corner in his second go-round in '02 at Triple-A Columbus. He's signed for two more years, but. . . 2003 Outlook: C

Brandon Knight (Pos: RHP, Age: 27)

	W	L	Pct.	ERA	G	GS	Sv	IP	H	BB	SO	HR	Ratio
'02	0	0	–	11.42	7	0	0	8.2	11	5	7	2	1.85
Car.	0	0	–	10.71	11	0	0	19.1	29	8	14	7	1.91

Knight was reasonably effective at Triple-A Columbus, but he allowed runs in four of his seven appearances in New York and didn't take advantage of injuries to Yankees hurlers. 2003 Outlook: C

Jay Tessmer (Pos: RHP, Age: 31)

	W	L	Pct.	ERA	G	GS	Sv	IP	H	BB	SO	HR	Ratio
'02	0	0	–	6.75	2	0	0	1.1	0	2	0	0	1.50
Car.	1	0	1.000	7.71	22	0	0	23.1	29	11	14	5	1.71

Tessmer made the roster out of spring training, but he simply was holding a spot for injured Ramiro Mendoza. Tessmer was far more hittable at the Triple-A level than in previous years and never returned. 2003 Outlook: C

Marcus Thames (Pos: RF, Age: 26, Bats: R)

	G	AB	R	H	D	T	HR	RBI	SB	BB	SO	Avg	OBP	Slg
'02	7	13	2	3	1	0	1	2	0	0	4	.231	.231	.538
Car.	7	13	2	3	1	0	1	2	0	0	4	.231	.231	.538

Thames is a tools guy who didn't progress much until 2001, when he had more plate patience and a better approach, and it meant a lot more power. But he regressed, batting .207 in Triple-A ball at age 25. 2003 Outlook: C

Mike Thurman (Pos: RHP, Age: 29)

	W	L	Pct.	ERA	G	GS	Sv	IP	H	BB	SO	HR	Ratio
'02	1	0	1.000	5.18	12	2	0	33.0	45	12	23	2	1.73
Car.	26	36	.419	5.05	105	87	0	493.2	537	190	296	59	1.47

The Yankees gave the Montreal product a minor league deal, and he didn't impress when called upon early in the season. Hitters batted .328 against him, though he posted a decent 3.60 ERA after the break. He's a free agent again. 2003 Outlook: C

Chris Widger (Pos: C, Age: 31, Bats: R)

	G	AB	R	H	D	T	HR	RBI	SB	BB	SO	Avg	OBP	Slg
'02	21	64	4	19	5	0	0	5	0	2	9	.297	.338	.375
Car.	488	1490	147	361	84	7	50	188	10	114	318	.242	.300	.409

Widger received the fewest at-bats he's seen since he was a rookie in 1996, but he hit fairly well during his brief stay in New York. The Yankees re-signed him in early December. 2003 Outlook: B

Gerald Williams (Pos: RF, Age: 36, Bats: R)

	G	AB	R	H	D	T	HR	RBI	SB	BB	SO	Avg	OBP	Slg
'02	33	17	6	0	0	0	0	0	2	2	4	.000	.105	.000
Car.	1045	2869	443	739	172	16	80	348	99	169	492	.258	.304	.412

For most of his career, Williams had value because he could hit lefties for average and power, but that ability has dried up. He may have closed out his major league career where it began by going hitless in 2002. 2003 Outlook: C

Enrique Wilson (Pos: 3B/SS, Age: 29, Bats: B)

	G	AB	R	H	D	T	HR	RBI	SB	BB	SO	Avg	OBP	Slg
'02	60	105	17	19	2	2	2	11	1	8	22	.181	.239	.295
Car.	384	1009	117	258	53	5	13	95	10	64	134	.256	.298	.357

Wilson's star was rising a few years ago, but he has batted just .201 over the last two seasons and his known age jumped from 26 to 28 last winter, when tougher requirements to get work visas were put into effect. The Yankees have signed him for the 2003 season. 2003 Outlook: C

New York (AL)

New York Yankees Minor League Prospects

Organization Overview:

For so long, the Yankees seemed to have it all: a major league club that made its way to the World Series nearly every year, and a farm system so rich that the front office was more inclined to *trade* kids to fill holes than *use* kids to fill them. The outlook isn't nearly as bright as it was a year or two ago, after a few more trades, a couple of key injuries and the 2002 struggles of high-minors prospects Adrian Hernandez, Drew Henson, Erick Almonte and Marcus Thames. That's not to say that there isn't plenty of legitimate talent in the Yankees' system. But for now, the organization fits more in the middle of the major league pack after being one of the better systems in the game for a number of years.

Jason Anderson

Position: P **Opening Day Age:** 23
Bats: L **Throws:** R **Born:** 6/9/79 in Danville,
Ht: 6' 0" **Wt:** 170 IL

Recent Statistics

	W	L	ERA	G	GS	Sv	IP	H	R	BB	SO	HR
2001 A Greensboro	7	9	3.76	23	19	1	124.1	127	68	40	101	9
2001 A Staten Isla	5	1	1.70	7	7	0	47.2	32	9	12	56	2
2002 A Tampa	4	2	4.07	12	3	1	24.1	27	13	3	22	2
2002 AA Norwich	1	1	0.93	16	0	2	19.1	14	2	5	21	1
2002 AAA Columbus	5	1	3.15	26	0	7	34.1	26	13	11	28	3

Anderson went 29-5 for the Illini as a college starter. His success made him a 10th-round pick in 2000, but it didn't follow him in his first two years in the Yankees' system. As a starter, he threw in the low 90s and used four decent pitches. He was moved to the bullpen just for the short-season New York-Penn League playoffs in his debut year, and his velocity jumped roughly five MPH. So after two seasons stuck in Class-A ball, Anderson moved to the pen in 2002 and rose quickly to Triple-A Columbus. He showed more velocity in relief, and his work at Double-A Norwich and Columbus have him in line to battle for a job in the Bronx.

Danny Borrell

Position: P **Opening Day Age:** 24
Bats: L **Throws:** L **Born:** 1/24/79 in
Ht: 6' 3" **Wt:** 195 Lansdale, PA

Recent Statistics

	W	L	ERA	G	GS	Sv	IP	H	R	BB	SO	HR
2001 A Tampa	7	9	3.97	22	20	0	111.0	109	58	38	84	6
2002 A Tampa	4	1	2.33	7	6	0	38.2	33	11	10	44	0
2002 AA Norwich	9	4	2.31	21	20	0	128.1	116	44	39	91	5

A second-round pick out of Wake Forest in 2000, Borrell was more raw than a lot of college pitchers because of the time he spent as a slugging first baseman and outfielder. Despite being shut down during the second half of 2001 because of shoulder pain, the 6-foot-3 lefty has advanced quickly, calling on a low-90s fastball, a polished changeup and a decent curveball. The curve isn't as far along as his other pitches, but Borrell can work his stuff effectively on both sides of the plate. While allowing just five home runs in 167 innings at high Class-A Tampa and Double-A Norwich in 2002, Borrell went 13-5 with a 2.32 ERA. Borrell doesn't have that exceptional punch-out pitch, so he'll have to have solid command of his offerings to succeed.

Brandon Claussen

Position: P **Opening Day Age:** 23
Bats: L **Throws:** L **Born:** 5/1/79 in Rapid
Ht: 6' 2" **Wt:** 175 City, SD

Recent Statistics

	W	L	ERA	G	GS	Sv	IP	H	R	BB	SO	HR
2001 A Tampa	5	2	2.73	8	8	0	56.0	47	21	13	69	2
2001 AA Norwich	9	2	2.13	21	21	0	131.1	101	42	55	151	6
2002 AAA Columbus	2	8	3.28	15	15	0	93.1	85	47	46	73	4

A 34-round pick, Claussen was a draft-and-follow who had an impressive debut at short-season Staten Island in 1999. His progress then slowed until he went 14-4 (2.31) between high Class-A Tampa and Double-A Norwich in 2001, when he led the minor leagues with 220 strikeouts in 187 innings. Claussen bumped up the velocity a bit on his above-average cut fastball. He also added some bite to his slider, an out pitch that ranks among the best breaking balls in the system. His workload, though, may have contributed to elbow woes that led to Tommy John surgery last June. Claussen will miss most or all of 2003.

Julio DePaula

Position: P **Opening Day Age:** 23
Bats: R **Throws:** R **Born:** 7/27/79 in Sabana
Ht: 6' 1" **Wt:** 160 Grande, DR

Recent Statistics

	W	L	ERA	G	GS	Sv	IP	H	R	BB	SO	HR
2001 A Asheville	1	1	3.78	3	3	0	16.2	19	13	2	26	3
2001 A Greensboro	6	1	2.75	8	8	0	55.2	35	19	21	67	2
2001 A Tampa	9	5	3.58	16	13	0	83.0	65	43	53	77	3
2002 AA Norwich	14	6	3.45	27	26	0	175.0	141	74	52	152	11

DePaula was traded to the Yankees for Triple-A reliever Craig Dingman in April 2001, because Colorado wanted a pitcher who was closer to helping the major league staff. DePaula may be the guy who is closer now, after going 29-12 (3.36) between two Class-A teams and Double-A Norwich in two years with the Yankees. He features deceptive arm action on a moving low-90s fastball, slider and changeup. His improved secondary pitches and a better sense of changing speeds effectively sparked a strong finish in 2002. He was more efficient with his pitches and worked deeper into games. And he used his secondary pitches when he fell behind hitters. DePaula has emerged as one of New York's top pitching prospects.

Drew Henson

Position: 3B
Bats: R **Throws:** R
Ht: 6' 5" **Wt:** 222
Opening Day Age: 23
Born: 2/13/80 in San Diego, CA

Recent Statistics

	G	AB	R	H	D	T	HR	RBI	SB	BB	SO	Avg
2002 AAA Columbus	128	471	68	113	30	4	18	65	2	37	151	.240
2002 AL New York	3	1	1	0	0	0	0	0	0	0	1	.000

A 1998 pick, Henson flirted with a football career at Michigan until a year ago. It took a six-year, $17 million contract in 2001 to get his baseball career on track, but it hasn't come easy. While there's little doubt about his athleticism, power potential and high ceiling, Henson has a long swing, lacks plate discipline and struggles to recognize offspeed pitches, often making him an easy target for Triple-A pitchers. Defensively, he's improved and features a strong arm, but his troubles at the plate suggest he was rushed to Triple-A Columbus in 2001, when he had just 289 at-bats in high Class-A ball and 306 Double-A at-bats.

Andy Phillips

Position: 2B
Bats: R **Throws:** R
Ht: 6' 0" **Wt:** 205
Opening Day Age: 25
Born: 4/6/77 in Tuscaloosa, AL

Recent Statistics

	G	AB	R	H	D	T	HR	RBI	SB	BB	SO	Avg
2001 AA Norwich	51	183	23	49	9	2	6	25	1	21	54	.268
2001 A Tampa	75	288	43	87	17	4	11	50	3	25	95	.302
2002 AA Norwich	73	272	58	83	24	2	19	51	4	33	56	.305
2002 AAA Columbus	51	205	32	54	11	1	9	36	0	10	46	.263

A 1999 pick who played at Alabama, Phillips made contact and drew walks in a solid debut at short-season Staten Island. He wasn't young for the league and didn't jump onto prospect lists, but Phillips continued a steady climb that led to an impressive .287-28-87 season between Double-A Norwich and Triple-A Columbus in 2002. His walk rate dropped at Columbus, where he posted a .296 OBP, a sign he may need more Triple-A time. Phillips is blocked by Alfonso Soriano's emergence at second base. Defensively, Phillips is adequate at second after a move from third base two years ago. He doesn't excel at a position, so his future may be as a utilityman. He must show enough plate discipline to tap into his budding power in the majors.

Juan Rivera

Position: OF
Bats: R **Throws:** R
Ht: 6' 2" **Wt:** 170
Opening Day Age: 24
Born: 7/3/78 in Guarenas, VZ

Recent Statistics

	G	AB	R	H	D	T	HR	RBI	SB	BB	SO	Avg
2002 AAA Columbus	65	265	40	86	21	1	8	47	5	13	39	.325
2002 AL New York	28	83	9	22	5	0	1	6	1	6	10	.265
2002 R Yankees	4	13	1	4	2	0	0	4	0	2	3	.308

Signed in 1996, Rivera debuted in North America by leading the Rookie-level Gulf Coast League in homers and RBI in 1998. He made little progress the next two years at high Class-A Tampa, but Rivera clobbered the ball at Double-A Norwich in 2001. He continued his tear at Triple-A Columbus, finishing the year at .322-28-98. After ripping it up at Columbus early in 2002, Rivera took over in right field for New York. Three days after he was recalled, however, he fractured a kneecap and was lost for seven weeks, setting the stage for the Raul Mondesi trade. His 2003 fate is unclear, but Rivera now is a solid defender with a terrific arm. In recent seasons he's learned to recognize and handle off-speed stuff and to drive the ball to all fields.

Bronson Sardinha

Position: SS/OF
Bats: L **Throws:** R
Ht: 6' 1" **Wt:** 195
Opening Day Age: 19
Born: 4/6/83 in Honolulu, HI

Recent Statistics

	G	AB	R	H	D	T	HR	RBI	SB	BB	SO	Avg
2001 R Yankees	55	188	42	57	14	3	4	27	11	28	51	.303
2002 A Greensboro	93	342	49	90	13	0	12	44	15	34	78	.263
2002 A Staten Isla	36	124	25	40	8	0	4	16	4	24	36	.323

The Honolulu-born shortstop was the third Sardinha to be drafted, but Bronson bypassed a chance to follow his two older brothers to Pepperdine. He was a Rookie-level Gulf Coast League All-Star as an 18-year-old in his debut season in 2001, and showed his quick stroke and advanced approach to hitting at two Class-A stops in 2002. During the season, with the Yankees convinced he wasn't well suited to play shortstop, Sardinha was moved from his natural position to left field, where his athleticism, baseball instincts and strong arm made for a fairly smooth transition. His bat should be ready for high Class-A Tampa in 2003, and the Yankees may try him in center field there.

Others to Watch

Middle infielder **Robinson Cano** (20) showed his quick bat and an innate ability to adjust to pitches with his hands last summer at two Class-A stops. He batted .276 and collected 25 doubles, 10 triples and 15 homers between Staten Island and Greensboro. . . Dominican outfielder **Rudy Guillen** (19) created a buzz in the Rookie-level Gulf Coast League in 2002. Signed in 2000, Guillen put his five-tool promise on display in North America, batting .306 and posting a .351 OBP in 59 games. . . Lefthander **Sean Henn** (21) is a 6-foot-5 power pitcher who was lost to Tommy John surgery for all of 2002. He was impressive at short-season Staten Island in 2001 before the injury, and he'll be ready to go again this spring. . . Taiwan native **Chien-Ming Wang** (23) was signed in 2000, but missed all of 2001 with a shoulder problem. He returned to short-season Staten Island last summer, rekindling his low-90s fastball and the late break of a wicked slider. He also mixes in a solid splitter and changeup, and his command of all four pitches is advanced for his age.

New York (AL)

Network Associates Coliseum

Offense

As good as the Athletics played at home in 2001 (53-28), winning their final 17 home games, they were able to improve the mark by a game in 2002, establishing themselves as one of the toughest home clubs in baseball. Home runs are more prevalent at Network Associates Coliseum than in the years prior to the enclosing of center field, which does indeed allow the ball to carry. A seemingly benign popup can drift into the stands.

Defense

The Net has a ton of foul territory, and that generally helps the defense. Though the gaps are wide, the enclosed outfield helps lift a flyball from time to time, to the pitcher's chagrin. The infield is thick grass with a crisscross cut. The summer sun, especially in the outfield, can be deadly.

Who It Helps the Most

Line-drive and gap hitters do well in Oakland, while hitters who either get under the pitch or hit down on it suffer as a result of those same gaps and that thick grass. In general, the park picks on lefthanded and righthanded hitters the same way (though lefties got a bit of a lift last season), making it much more of a pitchers' paradise than a hitters' haven.

Who It Hurts the Most

Flyball pitchers can get caught when the thin night air arrives, surrendering home runs on flies that normally would be caught. At the plate, sometimes a foul ball will be caught when it would be lost in the stands at another venue.

Rookies & Newcomers

Oakland is stacked with young players. With the emergence of Mark Ellis last season, most of the big league roster spots will be manned by players who now have at least one major league season under their belt. Righthanded-hitting Eric Byrnes, who has shown leadoff potential in the minors, batted .351 and slugged .649 in 37 at-bats at home in 2002. Young second baseman Esteban German fell off the prospect radar when he didn't fare well anywhere in a brief look.

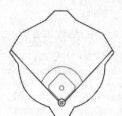

Dimensions: LF-330, LCF-362, CF-400, RCF-362, RF-330

Capacity: 43,662

Elevation: 25 feet

Surface: Grass

Foul Territory: Large

Park Factors

2002 Season

	Home Games			Away Games			
	Athletics	Opp	Total	Athletics	Opp	Total	Index
G	72	72	144	72	72	144	
Avg	.263	.248	.255	.254	.260	.257	99
AB	2401	2476	4877	2547	2442	4989	98
R	363	302	665	334	300	634	105
H	631	613	1244	647	636	1283	97
2B	123	123	246	117	123	240	105
3B	15	9	24	11	17	28	88
HR	104	61	165	79	62	141	120
BB	287	196	483	252	232	484	102
SO	434	483	917	447	427	874	107
E	43	49	92	45	39	84	110
E-Infield	35	39	74	38	32	70	106
LHB-Avg	.277	.254	.267	.243	.257	.248	107
LHB-HR	59	25	84	44	25	69	125
RHB-Avg	.247	.243	.245	.267	.263	.265	93
RHB-HR	45	36	81	35	37	72	115

2000-2002

	Home Games			Away Games			
	Athletics	Opp	Total	Athletics	Opp	Total	Index
G	216	216	432	215	215	430	
Avg	.261	.249	.255	.269	.272	.270	94
AB	7183	7530	14713	7675	7308	14983	98
R	1156	910	2066	1205	994	2199	94
H	1877	1876	3753	2062	1987	4049	92
2B	356	359	715	432	361	793	92
3B	33	30	63	34	39	73	88
HR	301	186	487	270	210	480	103
BB	926	636	1562	868	735	1603	99
SO	1378	1441	2819	1435	1308	2743	105
E	157	135	292	157	131	288	101
E-Infield	123	105	228	129	109	238	95
LHB-Avg	.274	.251	.264	.274	.271	.273	97
LHB-HR	172	71	243	162	91	253	97
RHB-Avg	.247	.248	.247	.262	.272	.268	92
RHB-HR	129	115	244	108	119	227	110

2002 Rankings (American League)
- Second-highest LHB batting-average factor
- Third-highest strikeout factor
- Third-highest LHB home-run factor
- Lowest RHB batting-average factor

Ken Macha

2002 Season

The karmic principle of "What goes around, comes around," must be spinning wildly in Ken Macha's head. That is because not long ago there was talk that Oakland GM Billy Beane would jump ship to Boston, the team with which Beane refused to allow Macha to discuss a managing job just a year earlier. Since the issue of Beane's tenure has been resolved, Macha, who managed in the high minors for the Red Sox between 1995-98, can look forward to managing in Oakland with the bulk of the front office and support staff intact.

Offense

If Macha, who knows his players well, can retain hitting coach Thad Bosley, the team should be fine. Bosley, who understands putting the Athletics' "selectivity at the plate" program into practical use as well as anyone, should help the offense get to the next level. Macha's style may be a bit more "hands on" than his predecessor's, but Bosley's success with the team's offense is pretty well documented, and Macha probably will yield to his hitting wizard, provided he returns to the club.

Pitching & Defense

Macha will want to retain both pitching coach Rick Peterson and third base-infield coach Ron Washington (who is signed). Peterson, whose family relocated to New Jersey during the 2002 season, might prefer to coach for Art Howe and work closer to home. That could strike a blow to the Athletics' staff, although the troika of Tim Hudson, Mark Mulder and Barry Zito are now seasoned vets. Washington is much more likely to stay with the club and is invaluable with his savvy in relating to the players.

2003 Outlook

Macha certainly has to be surprised by the odd twists of fate that allowed him a first managing opportunity right in his own current backyard, after so many interviews elsewhere over the past couple of years. With Beane still holding the reins, Macha will get a chance to adjust to his new gig. Still, he inherits a very good team and will be expected to win.

Born: 9/29/50 in Monroeville, PA

Playing Experience: 1974-1981, Pit, Mon, Tor

Managerial Experience: No major league managing experience

Manager Statistics (Art Howe)

Year	Team, Lg	W	L	Pct	GB	Finish
2002	Oakland, AL	103	59	.636	–	1st West
12 Seasons		992	951	.511	–	–

2002 Starting Pitchers by Days Rest

	<=3	4	5	6+
Athletics Starts	0	100	32	23
Athletics ERA	–	3.19	3.25	6.55
AL Avg Starts	1	83	44	24
AL ERA	7.15	4.59	4.27	5.03

2002 Situational Stats

	Art Howe	AL Average
Hit & Run Success %	29.4	36.0
Stolen Base Success %	69.7	68.1
Platoon Pct.	56.0	58.9
Defensive Subs	43	23
High-Pitch Outings	2	6
Quick/Slow Hooks	12/7	19/14
Sacrifice Attempts	29	53

2002 Rankings —Art Howe (American League)

- 1st in fewest caught stealings of third base (2), sacrifice-bunt percentage (86.2%), defensive substitutions and 2+ pitching changes in low-scoring games (44)
- 2nd in fewest caught stealings of second base (18), first-batter platoon percentage and one-batter pitcher appearances (46)
- 3rd in intentional walks (32), pinch-hitters used (126) and mid-inning pitching changes (191)

Oakland

Eric Chavez

2002 Season

Eric Chavez followed his breakthrough 2001 season with one revealing small areas of improvement that will push him to a new level of consistency. His run and RBI totals, along with his batting average, dipped a little last season, despite his career high in home runs. He also walked 24 more times than in '01 and logged a career high in at-bats. Chavez also smoked during postseason, hitting .381-1-5 before the Athletics were knocked out.

Hitting

A fine natural hitter with excellent power, Chavez made great strides in his plate discipline last season, improving his on-base numbers from the previous season. Lefthanded pitching is his Achilles' heel, but utilizing that patience against southpaws will bring those numbers up again. At the plate, Chavez has quick wrists and a fast bat. He can drive the ball to any field with aplomb. The best part is that, at age 25, he still is learning. He led all regular MLB third sackers in total bases and homers in 2002.

Baserunning & Defense

Chavez won a Gold Glove in 2001. He also won the award in 2002 despite a drop in numbers. He plays a shallow third, reacts well, and possesses a strong arm that is quick to first. Chavez has very good speed and not only can swipe a bag, but also runs the bases very well. He has yet to crack 100 runs, but that is just a matter of time. If basestealing was a key component of the Athletics' game, he could hit double digits in swipes.

2003 Outlook

Watch the numbers continue to get better across the board, as Chavez goes into his peak production years with an already-impressive dossier. He should hit cleanup all year, protecting his left-side compatriot Miguel Tejada, and Chavez again should top both the 30-homer and 100-RBI marks.

Position: 3B
Bats: L **Throws:** R
Ht: 6' 1" **Wt:** 206

Opening Day Age: 25
Born: 12/7/77 in Los Angeles, CA
ML Seasons: 5
Pronunciation: shah-VEZ

Overall Statistics

	G	AB	R	H	D	T	HR	RBI	SB	BB	SO	Avg	OBP	Slg
'02	153	585	87	161	31	3	34	109	8	65	119	.275	.348	.513
Car.	588	2039	320	561	122	10	105	365	20	217	373	.275	.344	.499

Where He Hits the Ball

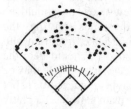 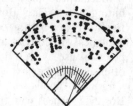

Vs. LHP   **Vs. RHP**

2002 Situational Stats

	AB	H	HR	RBI	Avg		AB	H	HR	RBI	Avg
Home	285	76	17	60	.267	LHP	163	34	6	27	.209
Road	300	85	17	49	.283	RHP	422	127	28	82	.301
First Half	306	83	20	58	.271	Sc Pos	167	52	7	71	.311
Scnd Half	279	78	14	51	.280	Clutch	84	24	5	16	.286

2002 Rankings (American League)

- 5th in errors at third base (17), fielding percentage at third base (.961) and lowest on-base percentage vs. lefthanded pitchers (.261)
- 6th in intentional walks (13) and lowest batting average vs. lefthanded pitchers
- 7th in home runs
- Led the Athletics in home runs, stolen bases, intentional walks (13), strikeouts, slugging percentage, HR frequency (17.2 ABs per HR), cleanup slugging percentage (.481) and slugging percentage vs. righthanded pitchers (.571)

Ray Durham

2002 Season

By midseason the biggest hole in the Oakland lineup was the leadoff spot. A number of players tried to fill the bill, but no one adequately delivered the desired on-base numbers and speed. So, Billy Beane pulled off another jaw-dropping swap, acquiring the dependable Ray Durham from Chicago for the stretch run. Durham stepped in, supplying speed and savvy to the top of the order, as he proved to be a valuable cog in the Oakland offense during the second half.

Hitting

A versatile hitter, Durham can use his speed dashing out of the batter's box or just as easily turn on a pitch and drive it into the stands. A switch-hitter, he is able to use the entire field, although he hits righthanders for much better average and power. Durham has good power to the gaps. He can be streaky but is a big-time player who wants to win, as his .292 average with runners in scoring position last year suggests.

Baserunning & Defense

Blessed with excellent speed, Durham is a formidable basestealer and baserunner. He can beat out an infield hit or leg out a triple with equal skill. Durham improved his stealing percentage from 69 percent in 2001 to 78 percent last season. The defensive skills, which never were a strength, now elude him—at least at second base. He spent the bulk of his time in Oakland as the designated hitter, spelling Mark Ellis at second only on occasion.

2003 Outlook

Durham moved across the bay in December, signing a three-year, $20.1 million deal with the Giants. He will be the starting second baseman for San Francisco if the team can't come to terms with Jeff Kent. Or Durham could end up in the outfield if Kent returns. Durham has some pop and could be the answer to the Giants' long-standing leadoff problems. His defense up the middle won't be a revelation, but he should score a lot of runs hitting in front of Barry Bonds and could deliver 20-20 totals.

Position: 2B/DH
Bats: B **Throws:** R
Ht: 5' 8" **Wt:** 180

Opening Day Age: 31
Born: 11/30/71 in Charlotte, NC
ML Seasons: 8

Overall Statistics

	G	AB	R	H	D	T	HR	RBI	SB	BB	SO	Avg	OBP	Slg
'02	150	564	114	163	34	6	15	70	26	73	93	.289	.374	.450
Car.	1200	4698	827	1306	263	57	112	506	225	508	792	.278	.352	.430

Where He Hits the Ball

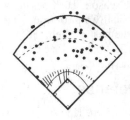
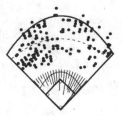

Vs. LHP **Vs. RHP**

2002 Situational Stats

	AB	H	HR	RBI	Avg		AB	H	HR	RBI	Avg
Home	256	77	11	39	.301	LHP	145	37	3	16	.255
Road	308	86	4	31	.279	RHP	419	126	12	54	.301
First Half	283	81	7	43	.286	Sc Pos	130	38	4	55	.292
Scnd Half	281	82	8	27	.292	Clutch	67	19	1	9	.284

2002 Rankings (American League)

- 2nd in highest percentage of extra bases taken as a runner (72.6) and errors at second base (17)
- 4th in sacrifice bunts (10)
- 5th in most pitches seen per plate appearance (4.07) and batting average on an 0-2 count (.308)
- 6th in triples (6)
- 7th in runs scored (114)
- 8th in stolen bases (26), pitches seen (2,682), steals of third (3) and on-base percentage for a leadoff hitter (.357)
- 9th in stolen-base percentage (78.8)
- Led the Athletics in triples (4) and highest percentage of extra bases taken as a runner (66.7)

Oakland

Jermaine Dye

2002 Season

Recovering from an ugly leg injury sustained during an equally ugly loss to the Yankees during the 2001 playoffs, Jermaine Dye didn't start a game for the Athletics until the end of April. Once in the order, it took him awhile to get into the groove, but Dye excelled during the second half, belting 18 long flies and driving in 53 runs as he held down the No. 5 spot in the batting order.

Hitting

Coming from the free-swinging Royals during the 2001 season, Dye tried to embrace Oakland's code of patience at the plate. However, despite the slow start, Dye's on-base numbers were very similar for each half of last season. He does have excellent power and is basically a pull-hitter. Dye can turn on a pitch with the best of them. Hitting behind the duo of Miguel Tejada and Eric Chavez adds to Dye's danger at the plate.

Baserunning & Defense

Dye is blessed with good speed. He was careful with his running for a large part of the season, due to the injury he sustained in the 2001 playoffs. As a result, his steal totals were down, but as a baserunner, Dye was on target for 100 runs if he had had a full season of play. He is an excellent defensive player with a strong and accurate arm that keeps opposing teams honest when the ball is hit to right.

2003 Outlook

The real Jermaine Dye began to show himself after the All-Star break last season. Even though the coming season will be his third with Oakland, he still has not spent a full spring training and regular season in the Athletics' lineup. With that stability in 2003—health permitting—Dye should be able to duplicate the stellar 1999-2000 numbers that established him as one of the top young players in the game.

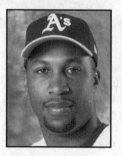

Position: RF/DH
Bats: R **Throws:** R
Ht: 6' 5"   **Wt:** 220

Opening Day Age: 29
Born: 1/28/74 in Vacaville, CA
ML Seasons: 7

Overall Statistics

	G	AB	R	H	D	T	HR	RBI	SB	BB	SO	Avg	OBP	Slg
'02	131	488	74	123	27	1	24	86	2	52	108	.252	.333	.459
Car.	837	3065	450	858	178	13	134	511	18	272	602	.280	.340	.478

Where He Hits the Ball

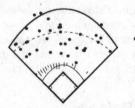

Vs. LHP   **Vs. RHP**

2002 Situational Stats

	AB	H	HR	RBI	Avg		AB	H	HR	RBI	Avg
Home	236	54	13	42	.229	LHP	99	21	1	5	.212
Road	252	69	11	44	.274	RHP	389	102	23	81	.262
First Half	224	54	6	33	.241	Sc Pos	132	33	5	59	.250
Scnd Half	264	69	18	53	.261	Clutch	61	12	2	9	.197

2002 Rankings (American League)

- 1st in lowest cleanup slugging percentage (.371)
- 2nd in lowest fielding percentage in right field (.972)
- 4th in most pitches seen per plate appearance (4.12) and errors in right field (5)
- 6th in lowest percentage of swings on the first pitch (14.0) and lowest batting average at home
- Led the Athletics in sacrifice flies (5)

Mark Ellis

2002 Season

Oakland hitting coach Thad Bosley pointed out Mark Ellis as "something special" during the Arizona Fall League following the 2001 season. Right "Bos" was, as Ellis emerged from the back of the pack to claim the second-base job in early June. Once he cracked the lineup, Ellis never looked back, supplying steady and improving play in the field and at the dish.

Hitting

As a minor leaguer, Ellis' numbers suggested a perfect fit in the Oakland scheme, as, for example, his 78 walks to 72 whiffs at high Class-A Wilmington in 2000 would indicate. Ellis also showed a good stick (.302) and a little power (six homers and 27 doubles) during that stint. One of the great things about Ellis' 2002 performance with Oakland was that he showed he is capable of totals even better than his first-year stats. Blessed with a terrific work ethic and a quick learning curve, Ellis logged a .397 OBP during the final month of the season. Ellis proved he adjusts readily at the plate, and he should continue to improve as a hitter.

Baserunning & Defense

Ellis, who averaged 23 swipes over each of his three minor league seasons, has very good speed and is a smart baserunner. He was caught twice last season in six major league attempts. But the running game is not at the center of the Oakland offense, and Ellis' total does not suggest his ability. In the field, Ellis is steady and a quick study. Despite being a shortstop during his previous minor league campaigns, Ellis made the adjustment to second with fluidity. By season's end, he was turning dazzling double plays with Miguel Tejada on a regular basis.

2003 Outlook

Ellis has nowhere to go but up, now that he owns the second-base job. Look for quantum leaps in several offensive categories, including swipes, doubles, runs and on-base and slugging percentages.

Position: 2B
Bats: R **Throws:** R
Ht: 5'11" **Wt:** 180

Opening Day Age: 25
Born: 6/6/77 in Rapid City, SD
ML Seasons: 1

Overall Statistics

	G	AB	R	H	D	T	HR	RBI	SB	BB	SO	Avg	OBP	Slg
'02	98	345	58	94	16	4	6	35	4	44	54	.272	.359	.394
Car.	98	345	58	94	16	4	6	35	4	44	54	.272	.359	.394

Where He Hits the Ball

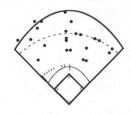

Vs. LHP   **Vs. RHP**

2002 Situational Stats

	AB	H	HR	RBI	Avg		AB	H	HR	RBI	Avg
Home	159	47	6	24	.296	LHP	54	16	2	9	.296
Road	186	47	0	11	.253	RHP	291	78	4	26	.268
First Half	105	26	2	9	.248	Sc Pos	71	23	2	31	.324
Scnd Half	240	68	4	26	.283	Clutch	43	10	2	8	.233

2002 Rankings (American League)

- 3rd in batting average among rookies
- 6th in sacrifice bunts (8) and fewest GDPs per GDP situation (4.9%)
- 8th in errors at second base (9)
- 10th in on-base percentage for a leadoff hitter (.347) and lowest on-base percentage for a leadoff hitter (.347)
- Led the Athletics in triples, sacrifice bunts (8), bunts in play (13) and batting average at home

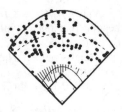

Oakland

Scott Hatteberg

2002 Season

A lot of eyebrows were raised when Oakland signed Scott Hatteberg, ostensibly to replace defecting stud Jason Giambi. Though Hatteberg hardly could be expected to assemble numbers like his illustrious predecessor, he was solid at first base, logging career highs in games, at-bats, homers, RBI and just about everything. He also hit the spectacular game-winning homer in the Athletics' 20th straight victory in September.

Hitting

When GM Billy Beane signed Hatteberg, he likely was eyeing the .367 on-base percentage the former catcher earned while with the Red Sox in 1999. Beane obviously knew what he was seeing, as Hatteberg proved to a be a perfect fit, even besting that mark while walking 12 more times than he whiffed in 2002. That patience correspondingly helped Hatteberg's power numbers, but Hatteberg also is adept at going up the middle as well as using right field to move runners along.

Baserunning & Defense

Third-base coach Ron Washington suggested that no one expected Hatteberg, a converted backstop, to play as well as he did, either at the plate or in the field. He committed only five errors while serving as the first baseman for 91 games, the most games he has played at one spot since 1998, let alone at a new position. Hatteberg does not have a lot of speed, but he is a smart and selfless player whom the team declares "a winner" no matter what aspect of the game you are talking about.

2003 Outlook

Oakland already has picked up Hatteberg's option for 2003 and is looking to sign him beyond that. Knowing he has a set role should help him improve on his fine 2002 totals, but Hatteberg probably will not see more than 430 or so at-bats over the course of the year. Those plate appearances will be key to the Athletics' success.

Position: 1B/DH
Bats: L **Throws:** R
Ht: 6' 1" **Wt:** 210

Opening Day Age: 33
Born: 12/14/69 in Salem, OR
ML Seasons: 8
Pronunciation: hatt-EH-berg

Overall Statistics

	G	AB	R	H	D	T	HR	RBI	SB	BB	SO	Avg	OBP	Slg
'02	136	492	58	138	22	4	15	61	0	68	56	.280	.374	.433
Car.	590	1802	221	488	108	6	49	220	1	243	265	.271	.361	.419

Where He Hits the Ball

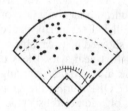 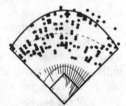

Vs. LHP   **Vs. RHP**

2002 Situational Stats

	AB	H	HR	RBI	Avg		AB	H	HR	RBI	Avg
Home	229	65	8	28	.284	LHP	86	20	4	12	.233
Road	263	73	7	33	.278	RHP	406	118	11	49	.291
First Half	259	70	11	34	.270	Sc Pos	132	33	5	44	.250
Scnd Half	233	68	4	27	.292	Clutch	60	18	1	8	.300

2002 Rankings (American League)

- 1st in lowest percentage of swings on the first pitch (9.5)
- 3rd in most pitches seen per plate appearance (4.15) and highest percentage of pitches taken (64.5)
- 5th in lowest percentage of swings that missed (10.2)
- 6th in highest percentage of swings put into play (52.3)
- Led the Athletics in triples, highest percentage of pitches taken (64.5), lowest percentage of swings that missed (10.2), highest percentage of swings put into play (52.3), lowest percentage of swings on the first pitch (9.5) and batting average on a 3-2 count (.321)

Ramon Hernandez

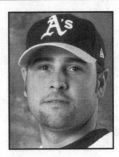

2002 Season

One of the players with the most unrealized potential on the Athletics, Ramon Hernandez and his 2002 offensive season fell short of expectations. Though he continued to be a dependable presence behind the plate, his offensive totals dropped across the board, save a stable (but low) on-base percentage. He came around in the second half, but his numbers dipped again in September and he had little impact during the postseason.

Hitting

As a third-year starter, Hernandez struggled at the plate throughout the year, rather than just during the first half, which had been his pattern. Usually adept at going the other way, in pressure situations and with two strikes, Hernandez struggled with his stance and simply didn't produce. After the break he worked at a more upright position in the box and that helped him for a time. In the end, Hernandez did his best hitting with no one out (.304-3-10) and in late-and-close situations (.283-0-2). He improved his strikeout-walk numbers a bit over his 2001 totals.

Baserunning & Defense

Despite his offensive struggles, Hernandez made a quantum leap in his defense against the stolen base in 2002, nailing 32 percent of would-be stealers (compared to 25 percent in 2001 and 22 percent in 2000). His defensive game has improved each year and he posted a career-best fielding percentage last summer. Hernandez is not much of a threat on the bases.

2003 Outlook

Firmly entrenched as the catcher, Hernandez clearly has made strides behind the plate both with his defense and his ability to work with those fabulous Oakland starters. Even though his offensive numbers took a hit last year, he still wasn't far off from his production of previous seasons and he is approaching his prime. He's just 26 years old, so anticipating some improvement on all fronts in the coming season is not a stretch.

Position: C
Bats: R **Throws:** R
Ht: 6' 0" **Wt:** 210

Opening Day Age: 26
Born: 5/20/76 in Caracas, VZ
ML Seasons: 4
Pronunciation: ruh-MOWN

Overall Statistics

	G	AB	R	H	D	T	HR	RBI	SB	BB	SO	Avg	OBP	Slg
'02	136	403	51	94	20	0	7	42	0	43	64	.233	.313	.335
Car.	455	1411	171	348	71	0	39	185	3	136	207	.247	.318	.380

Where He Hits the Ball

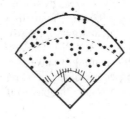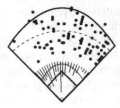

Vs. LHP   **Vs. RHP**

2002 Situational Stats

	AB	H	HR	RBI	Avg		AB	H	HR	RBI	Avg
Home	209	48	3	27	.230	LHP	109	28	3	11	.257
Road	194	46	4	15	.237	RHP	294	66	4	31	.224
First Half	211	47	4	23	.223	Sc Pos	97	24	1	32	.247
Scnd Half	192	47	3	19	.245	Clutch	46	13	0	2	.283

2002 Rankings (American League)

- 3rd in errors at catcher (7) and lowest batting average with two strikes (.130)
- 4th in lowest batting average on a 3-2 count (.125)
- 6th in lowest fielding percentage at catcher (.992)
- Led the Athletics in highest groundball-flyball ratio (1.4) and batting average with the bases loaded (.500)

Tim Hudson

2002 Season

Despite a win total that was lower than in either of his previous two seasons, there were signs in Tim Hudson's 2002 campaign that point to improvement. First, he set a career high in innings pitched. And though he also reached a high in hits allowed, his total walks allowed dropped, as did his earned runs and home runs allowed. Though Hudson struggled some over the first half, particularly in May, he was as effective as ever after the break and was lights out over 11 August and September starts (8-0, 1.75).

Pitching

Tenacious is probably the best way to describe Hudson and his approach to pitching, as he simply will not give in. Add to that a 92-MPH fastball, a change, a slider, and a splitter that gets hitters to commit despite a propensity to find dirt. Hudson also manages to hide what's coming, thanks to a delivery that is similar irrespective of the pending pitch. He is the guy you want to give the ball to if a big game is on the line.

Defense

Hudson takes every aspect of his game seriously, and holding runners and manning the leather are not exceptions. Last season he successfully handled all 53 balls hit his way for a perfect 1.000 fielding percentage. He was the best among Oakland starters at preventing the steal—a marked improvement over 2001—as he allowed just five steals after being victimized 24 times the year before.

2003 Outlook

Based upon his past success, it is hard to imagine that Hudson could improve, but in each of the past three seasons he has hit a rocky handful of starts early in the year. As he gains more experience and confidence, Hudson is more likely to stay in control over the course of a full season. He is durable and dependable. And his main competition for a Cy Young Award sits on his home bench.

Position: SP
Bats: R **Throws:** R
Ht: 6' 1" **Wt:** 164

Opening Day Age: 27
Born: 7/14/75 in Columbus, GA
ML Seasons: 4

Overall Statistics

	W	L	Pct.	ERA	G	GS	Sv	IP	H	BB	SO	HR	Ratio
'02	15	9	.625	2.98	34	34	0	238.1	237	62	152	19	1.25
Car.	64	26	.711	3.42	122	122	0	812.0	743	277	634	71	1.26

How Often He Throws Strikes

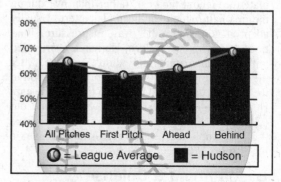

= League Average ■ = Hudson

2002 Situational Stats

	W	L	ERA	Sv	IP		AB	H	HR	RBI	Avg
Home	7	4	2.76	0	127.0	LHB	484	137	15	53	.283
Road	8	5	3.23	0	111.1	RHB	418	100	4	23	.239
First Half	6	7	3.44	0	130.2	Sc Pos	191	44	4	56	.230
Scnd Half	9	2	2.42	0	107.2	Clutch	73	22	1	3	.301

2002 Rankings (American League)

- 1st in GDPs induced (35) and fielding percentage at pitcher (1.000)
- 2nd in games started, shutouts (2) and most GDPs induced per nine innings (1.3)
- 3rd in innings pitched, hits allowed, highest groundball-flyball ratio allowed (2.0) and fewest pitches thrown per batter (3.49)
- Led the Athletics in complete games (4), shutouts (2), innings pitched, hits allowed, batters faced (983), wild pitches (7), highest groundball-flyball ratio allowed (2.0), lowest stolen-base percentage allowed (38.5), fewest home runs allowed per nine innings (.72) and most GDPs induced per nine innings (1.3)

Billy Koch

2002 Season

There were grumblings in Oakland when the team let Jason Isringhausen depart and traded for Billy Koch in December 2001. Koch's durability was suspect, and so was his ability to shut down the opposition. Koch turned out to be invaluable during the Athletics' record-setting 20-game win streak, saving nine contests and winning another three. In August he saved an unbelievable 11 games over 18 innings, with an 0.50 ERA. So much for the doubting Thomases.

Pitching

Koch brings heat, no doubt about it. More important, he wants to pitch, and is ready to, every day. His fastball clocks at 100 MPH, and he has a good sinker and slider. He also possesses a fine curve that he should use more often. When it is breaking, all of Koch's pitches fall into place and his stuff is truly electric. Koch has worked on coming more overhand with his delivery, which has strengthened his arm and made him a lot more durable. A power pitcher, Koch can be prone to the longball.

Defense

As a closer, Koch does not pay that much attention to baserunners, and they take advantage. Considering he is a fairly big guy, Koch gets off the hill quickly and has become an adept fielder, handling 26 chances last season without making an error.

2003 Outlook

Koch was packaged as part of a six-player trade with the White Sox in early December, a deal that brought closer Keith Foulke to the Bay and also freed up some future cash for the Athletics. The White Sox experienced plenty of closer problems in 2002, and Koch should help resolve that issue in '03. He throws hard and did pitch a lot of innings last year for a closer, but if he stays healthy, Koch should be a solid member of a team that looks to rebound from a very disappointing 2002 campaign. He won't benefit nearly as much from the starters in Chicago as he did from the members of the Oakland rotation, but Koch still is a top-flight stopper who will help the Sox try to regain some championship momentum.

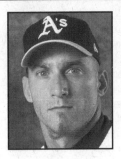

Position: RP
Bats: R **Throws:** R
Ht: 6' 3" **Wt:** 215

Opening Day Age: 28
Born: 12/14/74 in Rockville Center, NY
ML Seasons: 4
Pronunciation: KOTCH

Overall Statistics

	W	L	Pct.	ERA	G	GS	Sv	IP	H	BB	SO	HR	Ratio
'02	11	4	.733	3.27	84	0	44	93.2	73	46	93	7	1.27
Car.	22	17	.564	3.48	277	0	144	305.1	275	127	265	25	1.32

How Often He Throws Strikes

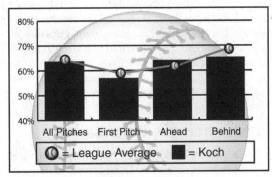

◯ = League Average   ■ = Koch

2002 Situational Stats

	W	L	ERA	Sv	IP		AB	H	HR	RBI	Avg
Home	9	2	2.88	21	50.0	LHB	152	36	3	14	.237
Road	2	2	3.71	23	43.2	RHB	189	37	4	24	.196
First Half	5	1	3.35	20	48.1	Sc Pos	102	20	3	31	.196
Scnd Half	6	3	3.18	24	45.1	Clutch	252	53	5	28	.210

2002 Rankings (American League)

- 1st in games pitched, games finished (79), relief wins (11) and relief innings (93.2)
- 2nd in saves and save opportunities (50)
- 4th in winning percentage and save percentage (88.0)
- 7th in blown saves (6)
- Led the Athletics in saves, stolen bases allowed (10), lowest batting average allowed vs. righthanded batters, blown saves (6), relief losses (4), lowest batting average allowed in relief (.214) and most strikeouts per nine innings in relief (8.9)

Oakland

Terrence Long

2002 Season

Terrence Long's 2002 season was a peculiar combination of disappointments and achievements. For a second consecutive season he played in all 162 of his team's games, increased his homer total over 2001 by four, and covered a lot more ground on defense than ever before. Yet his three hitting percentages took huge hits as his numbers declined through the final three months of the season, a frustrating trend that continued into the postseason.

Hitting

Long generally is regarded as one of the Athletics who has unfulfilled potential. Sadly, 2002 did not reveal much progress. He has solid power and can hit for the gaps, but he gets caught guessing at pitches during tough spells, and that contributes to some rough runs at the plate. Whereas lefties have given him the most trouble in the past, both righthanders and southpaws gave him grief last season.

Baserunning & Defense

Long has very good speed, but his basestealing also took a huge hit in 2002, as he was nailed trying to swipe six of nine times. Similarly, his run totals also were down, but that is largely attributable to the big drop in his on-base numbers. Defensively, Long performed admirably in trying to step into the center-field shoes of departed Johnny Damon, but he really plays his best defense in left.

2003 Outlook

Long is a talented and sensitive player, a hard worker who likely is as disappointed in his offensive dropoff in 2002 as anyone. Despite the fact that he played every day, he just couldn't get the breaks he did in previous seasons. With his talent, a much better year lies ahead. The one unanswered question is whether it will be in left or center field, which depends on whether general manager Billy Beane can acquire an affordable and useful center fielder during the offseason.

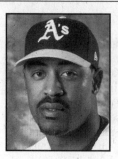

Position: CF
Bats: L **Throws:** L
Ht: 6' 1" **Wt:** 202

Opening Day Age: 27
Born: 2/29/76 in Montgomery, AL
ML Seasons: 4

Overall Statistics

	G	AB	R	H	D	T	HR	RBI	SB	BB	SO	Avg	OBP	Slg
'02	162	587	71	141	32	4	16	67	3	48	96	.240	.298	.390
Car.	465	1803	265	487	103	12	46	232	17	143	278	.270	.323	.417

Where He Hits the Ball

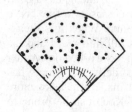

Vs. LHP　　　　**Vs. RHP**

2002 Situational Stats

	AB	H	HR	RBI	Avg		AB	H	HR	RBI	Avg
Home	294	78	9	37	.265	LHP	156	39	3	15	.250
Road	293	63	7	30	.215	RHP	431	102	13	52	.237
First Half	319	79	7	42	.248	Sc Pos	129	29	3	44	.225
Scnd Half	268	62	9	25	.231	Clutch	82	21	0	5	.256

2002 Rankings (American League)

- 1st in games played, errors in center field (8) and lowest fielding percentage in center field (.980)
- 5th in lowest batting average, lowest on-base percentage and lowest batting average on the road
- 6th in lowest batting average with runners in scoring position and lowest batting average vs. righthanded pitchers
- 7th in lowest on-base percentage vs. righthanded pitchers (.300)
- 8th in GDPs (17) and lowest slugging percentage
- Led the Athletics in doubles, triples, caught stealing (6) and games played

Mark Mulder

2002 Season

Mark Mulder followed up his breakthrough 21-8 season in 2001 with an equally fine 19-7 record last summer. Just how impressive that 2002 mark is cannot be seen on the surface. Mulder spent a month—from April 12 to May 10—on the disabled list with a sore left forearm, and he ended up making four fewer starts than he did in 2001. It mattered little to opposing hitters, however, who saw the same stellar stuff. Mulder showed his emergence was no fluke, as he held his own as a member of the best starting trio in the majors.

Pitching

Mulder's fastball clocks in the low 90s, and he uses the same delivery with a splitter that keeps hitters guessing. Both, especially the fastball, have great movement. When Mulder adds a change and slider to the mix, it is easy to understand how he gets the best of hitters. At 6-foot-6, Mulder also is able to exploit the downward angle that his height and the mound provide. Despite the arm troubles early on, Mulder still was able to exceed 200 innings for the second straight season.

Defense

Holding baserunners is not among the strengths of the Athletics' hurlers, and seven of 16 basestealers were successful against the lefty in 2002. Mulder is an excellent fielder, initiating three double plays and executing 45 total chances last season without committing an error.

2003 Outlook

After suffering from arm troubles last spring, Mulder came back with a vengeance. But expect the lefty to have learned just how fragile a pitcher's life can be. A smart player, Mulder likely will watch his wing closely from now on. On the near end, that means another season with more than 15 wins. On the long end, it means he is planning to stick around for a long time.

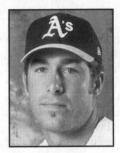

Position: SP
Bats: L **Throws:** L
Ht: 6' 6" **Wt:** 215

Opening Day Age: 25
Born: 8/5/77 in South Holland, IL
ML Seasons: 3

Overall Statistics

	W	L	Pct.	ERA	G	GS	Sv	IP	H	BB	SO	HR	Ratio
'02	19	7	.731	3.47	30	30	0	207.1	182	55	159	21	1.14
Car.	49	25	.662	3.98	91	91	0	590.2	587	175	400	59	1.29

How Often He Throws Strikes

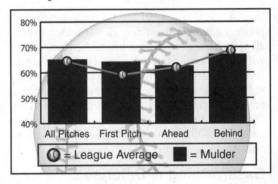

= League Average   = Mulder

2002 Situational Stats

	W	L	ERA	Sv	IP		AB	H	HR	RBI	Avg
Home	7	3	3.27	0	99.0	LHB	172	42	5	18	.244
Road	12	4	3.66	0	108.1	RHB	614	140	16	61	.228
First Half	9	5	3.99	0	90.1	Sc Pos	152	39	4	54	.257
Scnd Half	10	2	3.08	0	117.0	Clutch	71	12	6	7	.169

2002 Rankings (American League)

- 1st in fielding percentage at pitcher (1.000)
- 2nd in fewest pitches thrown per batter (3.49)
- 4th in wins
- 5th in winning percentage and highest groundball-flyball ratio allowed (1.6)
- 6th in runners caught stealing (9) and lowest stolen-base percentage allowed (43.8)
- 7th in hit batsmen (11), lowest batting average allowed (.232), lowest slugging percentage allowed (.366) and fewest GDPs induced per nine innings (0.6)
- Led the Athletics in hit batsmen, wild pitches (7), runners caught stealing (9) and highest strikeout-walk ratio (2.9)

Oakland

223

2002 Season

Perhaps the biggest question in Oakland entering the 2002 season was, "Can someone step into Jason Giambi's role?" As the Athletics struggled through the month of May, it seemed as if the answer was no. Then, late in the month, Art Howe moved shortstop Miguel Tejada into the No. 3 slot in the order. Tejada responded with an MVP campaign, including his first .300-30-100 season and his first with 200 hits. During the Athletics' unbelievable 20-game run in August and September, he provided late-inning, game-winning hits in two of the streak's final three contests.

Hitting

In 2002 Tejada established himself among the premier hitters in the game. He hit with power to all fields and was consistent, going three games without a hit only once all year. His power stroke favors left field, and Tejada can drive a ball over the fence in the deepest part of the park. It was in pressure situations that Tejada shined in 2002, hitting .373 with runners in scoring position and two outs, and .409 with the bases juiced. In short, he now can hit anywhere off of anybody.

Baserunning & Defense

Fleet afoot, Tejada cracked the 100-run mark in '02 for the third consecutive season. And he stole seven bases while being caught only twice. In the field, he was a revelation, appearing in highlight films on a nightly basis with acrobatic leaps and dives and a stellar arm. Tejada increased his total assists by 31 over 2001 and participated in 106 double plays, while logging only 19 errors, the fewest of his career.

2003 Outlook

It is hard to imagine Tejada improving on his 2002 MVP numbers, but remember, he still is just 26 years old and heading into his peak years of productivity. Though his walks remain low, he has reduced his strikeout total in each of the last two seasons, and his '02 marks in batting average, on-base percentage and slugging percentage all were career highs. At some point this progression will level out, but probably not in 2003.

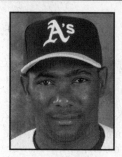

Position: SS
Bats: R **Throws:** R
Ht: 5' 9" **Wt:** 200

Opening Day Age: 26
Born: 5/25/76 in Bani, DR
ML Seasons: 6
Pronunciation: mee-GHEL tay-HA-duh

Overall Statistics

	G	AB	R	H	D	T	HR	RBI	SB	BB	SO	Avg	OBP	Slg
'02	162	662	108	204	30	0	34	131	7	38	84	.308	.354	.508
Car.	774	2948	476	791	149	11	129	498	39	234	477	.268	.330	.458

Where He Hits the Ball

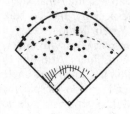 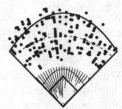

Vs. LHP   **Vs. RHP**

2002 Situational Stats

	AB	H	HR	RBI	Avg		AB	H	HR	RBI	Avg
Home	329	92	17	64	.280	LHP	137	39	9	26	.285
Road	333	112	17	67	.336	RHP	525	165	25	105	.314
First Half	360	106	15	59	.294	Sc Pos	176	66	9	93	.375
Scnd Half	302	98	19	72	.325	Clutch	98	32	4	18	.327

2002 Rankings (American League)

- 1st in games played
- 2nd in at-bats, GDPs (21) and errors at short stop (19)
- 3rd in hits, RBI, batting average with runners in scoring position and batting average with two strikes (.265)
- Led the Athletics in batting average, home runs, runs scored, singles, RBI, total bases (336), hit by pitch (11), times on base (253), plate appearances (715), steals of third (3), batting average with runners in scoring position, batting average vs. lefthanded pitchers, batting average vs. righthanded pitchers, on-base percentage vs. lefthanded pitchers (.342) and batting average on the road

Barry Zito

2002 Season

Barry Zito clearly marches to the beat of his own drum. So it was easy for some to dismiss the left-hander as either flaky or a flash in the pan after his very good 2001 season. Zito's first 20-win season, however, has shattered any doubts, as Zito led the league in wins and was among the leaders in nearly every other pitching category. At season's end he won the American League's Cy Young Award.

Pitching

Zito, ever cool, relies on three pitches to manipulate hitters—a change, a fastball that just nibbles at 90 MPH and a knee-buckling 12-to-6. And a manipulation it often seems. When he is on, Zito pretty much can put any of the three pitches wherever he chooses, whenever he chooses. The curve is the key to his success. When it is breaking sharply, it is a thing of beauty to all except those facing it. Without it, Zito can be hit. However, he is one of those pitchers who must be nailed when the opportunity presents itself, as he will gain command of all three at some point in a game.

Defense

For a lefty, Zito doesn't strike much fear in the eyes of baserunners who manage to get to first base—he tied with Billy Koch for the most swipes allowed (10) among all Oakland pitchers. He is adequate defensively, but committed three errors in just 45 chances in 2002. Zito's defense should improve; he is the kind of player who wants to excel at every aspect of his game.

2003 Outlook

It is hard to think in terms of "the sky is the limit." But for the 24-year-old lefty, who is coming off a season most pitchers only dream about, that is the story. Zito's concentration and smarts, coupled with that brilliant troika of pitches, make him the most likely candidate in the majors to toss a no-hitter.

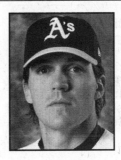

Position: SP
Bats: L **Throws:** L
Ht: 6' 4" **Wt:** 215

Opening Day Age: 24
Born: 5/13/78 in Las Vegas, NV
ML Seasons: 3

Overall Statistics

	W	L	Pct.	ERA	G	GS	Sv	IP	H	BB	SO	HR	Ratio
'02	23	5	.821	2.75	35	35	0	229.1	182	78	182	24	1.13
Car.	47	17	.734	3.04	84	84	0	536.1	430	203	465	48	1.18

How Often He Throws Strikes

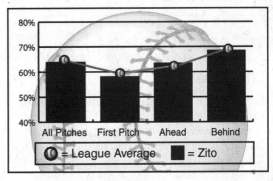

= League Average   = Zito

2002 Situational Stats

	W	L	ERA	Sv	IP		AB	H	HR	RBI	Avg
Home	11	1	2.56	0	112.1	LHB	171	47	7	14	.275
Road	12	4	2.92	0	117.0	RHB	665	135	17	54	.203
First Half	11	3	3.49	0	121.1	Sc Pos	162	30	4	44	.185
Scnd Half	12	2	1.92	0	108.0	Clutch	38	9	2	3	.237

2002 Rankings (American League)

- 1st in wins, games started, pitches thrown (3,690) and lowest batting average allowed with runners in scoring position
- 2nd in winning percentage and lowest batting average allowed vs. righthanded batters
- 3rd in ERA, strikeouts, pickoff throws (138), most run support per nine innings (6.8) and lowest groundball-flyball ratio allowed (0.7)
- Led the Athletics in walks allowed, stolen bases allowed (10), runners caught stealing (9), lowest batting average allowed (.218), lowest on-base percentage allowed (.289), lowest ERA at home, lowest ERA on the road, and most strikeouts per nine innings (7.1)

Oakland

Chad Bradford

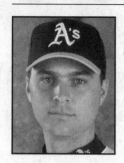

Position: RP
Bats: R **Throws:** R
Ht: 6' 5" **Wt:** 203

Opening Day Age: 28
Born: 9/14/74 in
Jackson, MS
ML Seasons: 5

Overall Statistics

	W	L	Pct.	ERA	G	GS	Sv	IP	H	BB	SO	HR	Ratio
'02	4	2	.667	3.11	75	0	2	75.1	73	14	56	2	1.15
Car.	9	4	.692	3.32	154	0	4	160.0	163	33	110	9	1.23

2002 Situational Stats

	W	L	ERA	Sv	IP		AB	H	HR	RBI	Avg
Home	3	0	2.61	1	38.0	LHB	90	24	0	11	.267
Road	1	2	3.62	1	37.1	RHB	198	49	2	25	.247
First Half	4	2	1.71	1	42.0	Sc Pos	85	25	1	33	.294
Scnd Half	0	0	4.86	1	33.1	Clutch	113	29	0	13	.257

2002 Season

In 2002 Chad Bradford justified the team's patience with him, stepping into the setup role and logging career highs in most categories. Bradford was untouchable over the first half, and though he struggled in August and September, he rebounded with three shutout innings in the postseason.

Pitching & Defense

One of the keys to Oakland's pitching success is how difficult it is to face Bradford's submarine style after looking at the team's more conventional starters. Bradford's fastball, which tops out at around 84 MPH, confounds hitters with its rising action. He also mixes in a nice curve and change. Bradford gets into trouble when his fastball rises too much. He records most of his outs via the groundball, so Bradford gets to handle the results of his pitching handiwork and almost always makes the play. He also holds runners well.

2003 Outlook

Bradford likely will use the offseason to rest his arm, which seemed to tire in 2002 under the rigors of a full season of setup work. Oakland has several good arms in the pen capable of filling several relief roles, and Bradford is as critical as any of them. He goes into 2003 as the man most likely to hand the ball to closer Keith Foulke.

Aaron Harang

Position: SP
Bats: R **Throws:** R
Ht: 6' 7" **Wt:** 240

Opening Day Age: 24
Born: 5/9/78 in San
Diego, CA
ML Seasons: 1

Overall Statistics

	W	L	Pct.	ERA	G	GS	Sv	IP	H	BB	SO	HR	Ratio
'02	5	4	.556	4.83	16	15	0	78.1	78	45	64	7	1.57
Car.	5	4	.556	4.83	16	15	0	78.1	78	45	64	7	1.57

2002 Situational Stats

	W	L	ERA	Sv	IP		AB	H	HR	RBI	Avg
Home	2	3	3.05	0	41.1	LHB	156	37	1	19	.237
Road	3	1	6.81	0	37.0	RHB	143	41	6	17	.287
First Half	3	2	2.84	0	44.1	Sc Pos	79	20	2	29	.253
Scnd Half	2	2	7.41	0	34.0	Clutch	3	0	0	0	.000

2002 Season

Aaron Harang is another of the rabbits GM Billy Beane pulls from an Athletics cap each season. Harang began the season at Double-A Midland (2-0, 1.08 over three starts). He quickly was promoted to Triple-A Sacramento (3-2, 1.77 over seven outings) before settling into the Athletics' rotation while struggling Cory Lidle reassembled his game.

Pitching & Defense

Harang is a strikeout guy, but his fastball clocks only in the 89-92 MPH range. He complements it with a slider and a change. He is a high-ball hurler, which makes him vulnerable to both the homer and the walk. Because he is a big man, Harang doesn't get off the mound quickly. He generally is surehanded with the balls he can field and is good at holding baserunners.

2003 Outlook

Harang came out of nowhere in 2001. From June through August of 2002, he was an important cog in the Oakland starting five, but he struggled as hitters learned his game. And once Lidle returned to form, Harang was out of the rotation. He probably faces time at Sacramento to start 2003, as a way to get regular work.

Cory Lidle

Traded To BLUE JAYS

Position: SP
Bats: R **Throws:** R
Ht: 5'11" **Wt:** 192

Opening Day Age: 31
Born: 3/22/72 in Hollywood, CA
ML Seasons: 5
Pronunciation: LIE-dell

Overall Statistics

	W	L	Pct.	ERA	G	GS	Sv	IP	H	BB	SO	HR	Ratio
'02	8	10	.444	3.89	31	30	0	192.0	191	39	111	17	1.20
Car.	33	24	.579	3.96	150	73	2	563.1	569	137	349	60	1.25

2002 Situational Stats

	W	L	ERA	Sv	IP		AB	H	HR	RBI	Avg
Home	4	6	3.75	0	108.0	LHB	391	97	11	36	.248
Road	4	4	4.07	0	84.0	RHB	349	94	6	36	.269
First Half	2	7	5.30	0	88.1	Sc Pos	155	37	4	52	.239
Scnd Half	6	3	2.69	0	103.2	Clutch	32	6	1	1	.188

2002 Season

Coming off a career year in 2001, when he settled into a terrific Oakland rotation, Cory Lidle hit a wall during the first half of 2002 and endured a hot and cold season. As good as he was over 45.1 August innings (5-0, 0.20 ERA), he was just as bad in May (0-2, 8.71) and June (1-2, 5.04).

Pitching & Defense

Lidle throws a hard, sinking fastball, complemented by a splitter that tails downward, and the combo makes him an effective groundball pitcher when he's on. He also throws a change and curve. When he keeps the ball down, Lidle is as tough as they come. He fields his position adequately, getting to a fair amount of balls hit his way. Lidle could improve at holding runners, who stole successfully nine of 14 times against him last season.

2003 Outlook

Lidle lost his starting job to Aaron Harang in June and trade talk began bubbling. In July, Lidle began to get his game together and eventually finished with respectable totals. Still, the pitching-rich A's looked ahead at salary considerations, and Lidle was swapped to the Jays in mid-November. He should be the No. 2 or 3 starter in Toronto, though his stats could suffer away from Oakland's spacious, pitcher-friendly park.

Ted Lilly

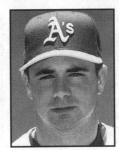

Position: SP
Bats: L **Throws:** L
Ht: 6' 0" **Wt:** 185

Opening Day Age: 27
Born: 1/4/76 in Lameta, CA
ML Seasons: 4

Overall Statistics

	W	L	Pct.	ERA	G	GS	Sv	IP	H	BB	SO	HR	Ratio
'02	5	7	.417	3.69	22	16	0	100.0	80	31	77	15	1.11
Car.	10	14	.417	4.92	64	40	0	252.1	244	96	228	43	1.35

2002 Situational Stats

	W	L	ERA	Sv	IP		AB	H	HR	RBI	Avg
Home	1	3	5.29	0	49.1	LHB	78	12	2	6	.154
Road	4	4	2.13	0	50.2	RHB	295	68	13	33	.231
First Half	3	6	3.40	0	76.2	Sc Pos	69	12	3	21	.174
Scnd Half	2	1	4.63	0	23.1	Clutch	26	4	2	3	.154

2002 Season

Ted Lilly began the year as arguably the No. 6 starter on the Yankees. Thanks to injuries, he made 11 starts (3-6, 3.40) for New York, pitching much better than the totals suggest, before a three-way deal dropped him into the middle of the Oakland rotation. Lilly won his first two starts before a tender shoulder forced him on the disabled list in late July. He returned in September and made the postseason roster.

Pitching & Defense

A control pitcher, Lilly falls just short of delivering a fastball in the 90s, but does possess an excellent change to go with a curve with good break. Baserunners who reach are able to take advantage of his delivery. Lilly, who primarily is a flyball pitcher and therefore doesn't see a lot of chances, nevertheless fields his position well. He didn't commit an error in 2002.

2003 Outlook

Everything looked so promising as the 2002 season progressed, but it got away from him when he developed a sore shoulder. During his rehab, Lilly worked with Oakland pitching coach Rick Peterson to change his delivery and reduce the strain on his shoulder. Lilly should add another quality arm to the best rotation in baseball in 2003.

Oakland

John Mabry

Position: 1B/LF/RF
Bats: L **Throws:** R
Ht: 6' 4" **Wt:** 210

Opening Day Age: 32
Born: 10/17/70 in Wilmington, DE
ML Seasons: 9
Pronunciation: MAY-bree

Overall Statistics

	G	AB	R	H	D	T	HR	RBI	SB	BB	SO	Avg	OBP	Slg
'02	110	214	28	59	13	1	11	43	1	15	42	.276	.321	.500
Car.	924	2575	292	699	142	4	66	328	7	195	503	.271	.324	.407

2002 Situational Stats

	AB	H	HR	RBI	Avg		AB	H	HR	RBI	Avg
Home	104	32	8	22	.308	LHP	26	5	1	2	.192
Road	110	27	3	21	.245	RHP	188	54	10	41	.287
First Half	89	33	3	20	.371	Sc Pos	62	20	3	33	.323
Scnd Half	125	26	8	23	.208	Clutch	36	12	1	11	.333

2002 Season

Oakland's Billy Beane has made a number of moves, but perhaps none caused more stir than his swapping of Jeremy Giambi to Philadelphia for utilityman John Mabry. And perhaps no move ignited his team more, as the sub-.500 Athletics went 25-6 immediately after Mabry's arrival and the last Giambi departed. Mabry also caught fire, hitting .381 his first full month with the club and setting a career high in slugging.

Hitting, Baserunning & Defense

Considered the ultimate role player by Oakland insiders, Mabry can play the corners in either the infield or the outfield and comes to the park prepared. He gets playing time in a platoon role because he has excellent power against righties. He is a conscientious hitter, though, and gets quality at-bats no matter who he is facing. Mabry doesn't have a lot of speed. On the bases he plays it smart and stays out of trouble.

2003 Outlook

Mabry is someone Oakland would like to have back in 2003, but that isn't likely after he wasn't offered salary arbitration. So the A's must find someone else who can spell the corner outfielders and infielders in the field, and supply a solid left-handed stick with some pop off the bench.

Jim Mecir

Position: RP
Bats: B **Throws:** R
Ht: 6' 1" **Wt:** 230

Opening Day Age: 32
Born: 5/16/70 in Queens, NY
ML Seasons: 8
Pronunciation: mah-SEAR

Overall Statistics

	W	L	Pct.	ERA	G	GS	Sv	IP	H	BB	SO	HR	Ratio
'02	6	4	.600	4.26	61	0	1	67.2	68	29	53	5	1.43
Car.	26	23	.531	3.70	316	0	9	399.0	358	173	342	30	1.33

2002 Situational Stats

	W	L	ERA	Sv	IP		AB	H	HR	RBI	Avg
Home	5	2	5.68	0	31.2	LHB	108	22	3	14	.204
Road	1	2	3.00	1	36.0	RHB	155	46	2	21	.297
First Half	3	1	4.65	0	40.2	Sc Pos	97	19	0	27	.196
Scnd Half	3	3	3.67	1	27.0	Clutch	167	47	3	23	.281

2002 Season

After a fine second half in 2001, Jim Mecir seemed poised to grab the spotlight in 2002 as the setup man. There was even thought that should new closer Billy Koch falter, Mecir might bag that job. But Mecir struggled, posting ERAs well above 5.00 in three of six months and blowing five of six save chances. He often found himself just spot pitching to lefties, thanks to his scroogie.

Pitching & Defense

Mecir's screwball ties up lefties all right. Sadly, righthanded hitters knocked him around in 2002, and that was the source of a lot of his problems. His fastball registers in the low 90s, and Mecir also has a pretty good slider, but he lives and dies with the screwball. A typical reliever, Mecir pays little attention to baserunners, so they run at will when he is on the hill. He fields his position very well, however.

2003 Outlook

Mecir was hoping to bounce back to his pre-2002 form, but he is expected to miss the first two months of the season after being injured playing with his children and needing knee surgery in the fall. Still, Mecir's prior success handling hitters from either side of the plate should make him a valuable strategic cog when he's healthy again.

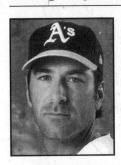

Greg Myers

Position: C
Bats: L **Throws:** R
Ht: 6' 2" **Wt:** 225

Opening Day Age: 36
Born: 4/14/66 in Riverside, CA
ML Seasons: 15

Overall Statistics

	G	AB	R	H	D	T	HR	RBI	SB	BB	SO	Avg	OBP	Slg
'02	65	144	15	32	5	0	6	21	0	26	36	.222	.341	.382
Car.	973	2683	282	670	129	7	72	342	3	228	477	.250	.307	.384

2002 Situational Stats

	AB	H	HR	RBI	Avg		AB	H	HR	RBI	Avg
Home	55	14	2	10	.255	LHP	25	5	0	2	.200
Road	89	18	4	11	.202	RHP	119	27	6	19	.227
First Half	92	22	5	16	.239	Sc Pos	47	8	2	15	.170
Scnd Half	52	10	1	5	.192	Clutch	37	9	1	9	.243

2002 Season

Affectionately referred to as "Crash" for obvious theatrical reasons, Greg Myers filled a void perfectly when Oakland signed him as a free agent in June 2001. In 2002 he continued to play that part, spelling starter Ramon Hernandez and often catching Barry Zito's starts. Myers supplied occasional power, sometimes in a game-winning fashion, in his genial low-key way.

Hitting, Baserunning & Defense

As the lefthanded-hitting backstop, Myers generally doesn't face lefthanded hurlers unless he is starting a day game following a night game. Myers draws walks and has good power, and he struggles in pressure situations in general. Myers has no speed and generally merits a substitute when he gets on and the situation warrants it. He is an excellent defensive backstop with a better-than-average arm.

2003 Outlook

While Myers fit into the youthful mix well and was a fine tutor for a number of the young pitchers and catchers on the Oakland roster, the Athletics declined to pick up a $1.1 million option for 2003. The veteran catcher signed a one-year, $800,000 deal to join a young Toronto club.

Adam Piatt

Position: LF/RF
Bats: R **Throws:** R
Ht: 6' 2" **Wt:** 205

Opening Day Age: 27
Born: 2/8/76 in Chicago, IL
ML Seasons: 3
Pronunciation: pie-at

Overall Statistics

	G	AB	R	H	D	T	HR	RBI	SB	BB	SO	Avg	OBP	Slg
'02	55	137	18	32	8	0	5	18	2	12	33	.234	.303	.401
Car.	151	389	51	99	18	6	10	47	2	48	103	.254	.339	.409

2002 Situational Stats

	AB	H	HR	RBI	Avg		AB	H	HR	RBI	Avg
Home	79	19	3	11	.241	LHP	43	10	2	6	.233
Road	58	13	2	7	.224	RHP	94	22	3	12	.234
First Half	122	30	4	15	.246	Sc Pos	35	8	1	13	.229
Scnd Half	15	2	1	3	.133	Clutch	17	3	1	3	.176

2002 Season

Once again, Adam Piatt had a season that saw many ups and downs. He started the season at Triple-A Sacramento, came up in May, and claimed an outfield spot, only to slump and return to the minors in late July. By September Piatt was back in a support role, supplying some power down the stretch and making the postseason roster.

Hitting, Baserunning & Defense

Piatt has good power and has delivered some terrific numbers in the minors, but aside from a couple of flashes, he continues to struggle at the plate in the majors. Selectivity seems to be at the heart of Piatt's struggles, but the ability is there. He has very good speed and can swipe a base, but for now, getting on is presenting a roadblock to displaying that ability. Piatt, a converted third sacker, made strides as an outfielder and also logged a game at first, committing no errors in the field.

2003 Outlook

Piatt's offensive totals have been a disappointment, but openings with the possible retirement of David Justice and the departure of Ray Durham present another opportunity to start. A more likely scenario points to a role-playing job, spelling the corners in both the outfield and the infield.

Oakland

Ricardo Rincon

Position: RP
Bats: L **Throws:** L
Ht: 5' 9" **Wt:** 187

Opening Day Age: 32
Born: 4/13/70 in Veracruz, Mexico
ML Seasons: 6
Pronunciation: rin-CONE

Overall Statistics

	W	L	Pct.	ERA	G	GS	Sv	IP	H	BB	SO	HR	Ratio
'02	1	4	.200	4.18	71	0	1	56.0	47	11	49	4	1.04
Car.	11	18	.379	3.45	354	0	21	299.2	250	122	284	25	1.24

2002 Situational Stats

	W	L	ERA	Sv	IP		AB	H	HR	RBI	Avg
Home	1	1	4.26	1	31.2	LHB	118	24	2	12	.203
Road	0	3	4.07	0	24.1	RHB	86	23	2	16	.267
First Half	0	3	3.23	0	30.2	Sc Pos	56	16	0	23	.286
Scnd Half	1	1	5.33	1	25.1	Clutch	92	19	2	15	.207

2002 Season

As the A's headed into late summer, it became clear to management that the squad lacked effective lefties in the pen. So, it was exit the ineffective Mike Magnante, and enter Ricardo Rincon, acquired from the Indians at the trade deadline. Rincon filled the void admirably, notching a 3.10 ERA, saving a game and whiffing 19 batters over the 20.1 situational innings he hurled for Oakland.

Pitching & Defense

Rincon's fastball hits the gun at around 92 MPH and carries some sink with it. He also tosses an excellent hard slider and has very good control. He held lefthanded hitters to an .083 average during his Oakland stint. Rincon also has proved to be durable and can work on back-to-back days. He holds runners reasonably well and is a fine fielder, having committed just three errors over his 354 major league games.

2003 Outlook

Rincon is signed with the Athletics through the 2003 season. He should enjoy a full year in the Oakland pen as the lefthanded setup man. In a good pitchers' park with solid starters and hitters joining him on the roster, Rincon can expect a season equaling or exceeding the two good ones he logged in Cleveland in 2000 and 2001.

Olmedo Saenz

Position: 1B/3B
Bats: R **Throws:** R
Ht: 5'11" **Wt:** 221

Opening Day Age: 32
Born: 10/8/70 in Chitre Herrera, Panama
ML Seasons: 5
Pronunciation: SIGNS

Overall Statistics

	G	AB	R	H	D	T	HR	RBI	SB	BB	SO	Avg	OBP	Slg
'02	68	156	15	43	10	1	6	18	1	13	31	.276	.354	.468
Car.	352	944	131	249	61	5	35	124	3	79	187	.264	.345	.450

2002 Situational Stats

	AB	H	HR	RBI	Avg		AB	H	HR	RBI	Avg
Home	88	26	3	8	.295	LHP	63	20	4	10	.317
Road	68	17	3	10	.250	RHP	93	23	2	8	.247
First Half	105	32	4	12	.305	Sc Pos	34	7	1	12	.206
Scnd Half	51	11	2	6	.216	Clutch	30	5	1	3	.167

2002 Season

Olmedo Saenz must feel snakebit as a utilityman who performs well as a part-timer. With the departure of Jason Giambi, it looked like Saenz might have positioned himself to be next in line for the Oakland first-base job. But Scott Hatteberg was signed and Saenz kept his utility role. He missed a month late in the year to a finger injury before rupturing his Achilles tendon in Game 1 of the American League Division Series.

Hitting, Baserunning & Defense

Saenz logged a career low in at-bats last season, although when he played, his slugging and on-base numbers were good. He has good power and hits lefties better than righthanders. Saenz is a pull-hitter who drives the ball to the left side. He is not much of a baserunner or stealer. He can cover both infield corners and is a good first baseman.

2003 Outlook

The Athletics declined to pick up their $1.2 million option on Saenz' contract. He faces a six-month rehab from his postseason injury, which may have figured in the decision, but the team also may prefer someone who can cover the middle-infield positions. Saenz can be a valuable bench player, but his injury clouds his free-agent status.

Other Oakland Athletics

Micah Bowie (Pos: LHP, Age: 28)

	W	L	Pct.	ERA	G	GS	Sv	IP	H	BB	SO	HR	Ratio
'02	2	0	1.000	1.50	13	0	0	12.0	12	8	8	1	1.67
Car.	4	7	.364	8.57	27	11	0	63.0	93	42	49	10	2.14

Bowie rekindled some of his minor league promise with a solid start at Triple-A Sacramento as a reliever, and he arrived in late July. He was used conservatively in the A's pen and wasn't bad. 2003 Outlook: C

Eric Byrnes (Pos: LF/RF, Age: 27, Bats: R)

	G	AB	R	H	D	T	HR	RBI	SB	BB	SO	Avg	OBP	Slg
'02	90	94	24	23	4	2	3	11	3	4	17	.245	.291	.426
Car.	119	142	38	35	5	2	6	16	6	8	24	.246	.306	.437

Through hard work, Byrnes developed some patience and advanced despite lacking strong tools. He's struggled in Oakland and his patience slipped at Triple-A Sacramento in '02. A possible reserve outfielder. 2003 Outlook: C

Mike Colangelo (Pos: LF, Age: 26, Bats: R)

	G	AB	R	H	D	T	HR	RBI	SB	BB	SO	Avg	OBP	Slg
'02	20	23	2	4	1	0	0	0	0	1	2	.174	.240	.217
Car.	71	116	12	27	4	3	2	8	0	10	32	.233	.305	.371

He's hit for average and drawn walks in the minors, but injuries have stalled his career. He made a big league roster in the spring for the first time, but he struggled and was gone by May. 2003 Outlook: C

Jose Flores (Pos: 2B, Age: 29, Bats: R)

	G	AB	R	H	D	T	HR	RBI	SB	BB	SO	Avg	OBP	Slg
'02	7	3	2	0	0	0	0	0	0	1	1	.000	.400	.000
Car.	7	3	2	0	0	0	0	0	0	1	1	.000	.400	.000

Flores has batted .300 with a .394 OBP over the last two Triple-A seasons, and his ability to play around the infield and in the outfield may open a reserve role for him. 2003 Outlook: C

Mike Fyhrie (Pos: RHP, Age: 33)

	W	L	Pct.	ERA	G	GS	Sv	IP	H	BB	SO	HR	Ratio
'02	2	4	.333	4.44	16	4	0	48.2	46	20	29	3	1.36
Car.	2	11	.154	4.00	84	11	0	175.1	183	67	109	16	1.43

He was effective in 13 starts at Triple-A Sacramento, his first gig as a starter since 1999. He struggled in the A's rotation in April and May, but was good in brief bullpen stints late in the year. 2003 Outlook: C

Esteban German (Pos: 2B, Age: 25, Bats: R)

	G	AB	R	H	D	T	HR	RBI	SB	BB	SO	Avg	OBP	Slg
'02	9	35	4	7	0	0	0	0	1	4	11	.200	.300	.200
Car.	9	35	4	7	0	0	0	0	1	4	11	.200	.300	.200

After posting impressive OBPs in the minors, German was given the second-base job when Frank Menechino was shipped out, but he failed and Mark Ellis stole the job. Lack of position flexibility hurts German. 2003 Outlook: C

Jason Grabowski (Pos: LF, Age: 26, Bats: L)

	G	AB	R	H	D	T	HR	RBI	SB	BB	SO	Avg	OBP	Slg
'02	4	8	3	3	1	1	0	1	0	3	1	.375	.545	.750
Car.	4	8	3	3	1	1	0	1	0	3	1	.375	.545	.750

Finding him a position has been a problem, but he keeps hitting for average and drawing walks. He showed more pop at Triple-A Sacramento in 2002, and may find work as a part-time player in Oakland. 2003 Outlook: B

Erik Hiljus (Pos: RHP, Age: 30)

	W	L	Pct.	ERA	G	GS	Sv	IP	H	BB	SO	HR	Ratio
'02	3	3	.500	6.50	9	9	0	45.2	52	21	29	11	1.60
Car.	8	3	.727	4.79	34	20	0	124.0	134	48	99	21	1.47

Hiljus seemed to finally make it, going 5-0 with a 3.95 ERA as a starter in 2001, but he wasn't effective early in 2002 and was sent to the minors in late May. He was not any better at Triple-A Sacramento. 2003 Outlook: C

David Justice (Pos: LF/RF/DH, Age: 36, Bats: L)

	G	AB	R	H	D	T	HR	RBI	SB	BB	SO	Avg	OBP	Slg
'02	118	398	54	106	18	3	11	49	4	70	66	.266	.376	.410
Car.	1610	5625	929	1571	280	24	305	1017	53	903	999	.279	.378	.500

While his plate patience still is a constant, Justice does not display as much power as he did a few years ago. He enjoyed his first year in Oakland, but hinted at retirement late in the season and shortly after the A's were eliminated from the playoffs. That might have been losing "talking," and a productive Justice could resurface somewhere this spring. 2003 Outlook: B

Mike Magnante (Pos: LHP, Age: 37)

	W	L	Pct.	ERA	G	GS	Sv	IP	H	BB	SO	HR	Ratio
'02	0	2	.000	5.97	32	0	0	28.2	38	11	11	2	1.71
Car.	26	32	.448	4.08	484	19	3	617.2	666	234	347	45	1.46

Despite a solid 2001 season with the A's, he wasn't effective in 2002 and was released in July. He signed on with the Dodgers' Triple-A team in mid-August but did not make it to LA. He may be done. 2003 Outlook: C

Cody McKay (Pos: C, Age: 29, Bats: L)

	G	AB	R	H	D	T	HR	RBI	SB	BB	SO	Avg	OBP	Slg
'02	2	3	0	2	0	0	0	2	0	0	1	.667	.500	.667
Car.	2	3	0	2	0	0	0	2	0	0	1	.667	.500	.667

McKay has hit for an OK average with a little pop in the high minors, but doesn't draw walks. He debuted in the majors with the A's, but Milwaukee has signed him and added him to the 40-man roster. 2003 Outlook: C

Frank Menechino (Pos: 2B, Age: 32, Bats: R)

	G	AB	R	H	D	T	HR	RBI	SB	BB	SO	Avg	OBP	Slg
'02	38	132	22	27	7	0	3	15	0	20	32	.205	.312	.326
Car.	252	757	135	180	38	3	21	101	3	119	178	.238	.353	.379

He got off to a slow start along with the A's, and he was shipped to the minors as part of the purge that moved Jeremy Giambi to Philadelphia in May. Mark Ellis may block Menechino from ever returning. 2003 Outlook: C

Larry Sutton (**Pos**: 1B, **Age**: 32, **Bats**: L)

	G	AB	R	H	D	T	HR	RBI	SB	BB	SO	Avg	OBP	Slg
'02	7	19	3	2	0	0	1	3	0	1	8	.105	.150	.263
Car.	244	567	63	134	23	2	12	77	4	54	100	.236	.302	.347

Sutton put up his best Triple-A numbers and hitting percentages since 1997, but once again he didn't capitalize on his big league chance. His 93 Triple-A walks opened a door, but is it still open? Boston signed him to a minor league deal. 2003 Outlook: C

Jeff Tam (**Pos**: RHP, **Age**: 32)

	W	L	Pct.	ERA	G	GS	Sv	IP	H	BB	SO	HR	Ratio
'02	1	2	.333	5.13	40	0	0	40.1	56	13	14	2	1.71
Car.	7	10	.412	3.57	207	0	6	226.2	231	73	120	13	1.34

Tam managed to stick for two seasons in Oakland, 2000 and 2001, but in 2002 he was more hittable and bounced between the A's and Triple-A Sacramento, where he posted a 5.59 ERA. The Blue Jays signed him shortly after the postseason. 2003 Outlook: B

Randy Velarde (**Pos**: 2B, **Age**: 40, **Bats**: R)

	G	AB	R	H	D	T	HR	RBI	SB	BB	SO	Avg	OBP	Slg
'02	56	133	22	30	8	0	2	8	3	15	32	.226	.325	.331
Car.	1273	4244	633	1171	214	23	100	445	78	463	853	.276	.352	.408

Velarde's playing time and hitting percentages took a dive in 2002, and he hinted he might retire after the A's were eliminated from the playoffs. He turned 40 soon after the A's elimination. 2003 Outlook: D

Mike Venafro (**Pos**: LHP, **Age**: 29)

	W	L	Pct.	ERA	G	GS	Sv	IP	H	BB	SO	HR	Ratio
'02	2	2	.500	4.62	47	0	0	37.0	45	14	16	5	1.59
Car.	13	10	.565	4.06	259	0	5	221.2	226	85	114	13	1.40

His best season was his rookie year in 1999, and he's been in steady decline since then. He worked his lowest innings total in '02, thanks to an August stay in the minors. Being a lefty may buy time. 2003 Outlook: C

Oakland Athletics Minor League Prospects

Organization Overview:

The names at the top of prospect lists have changed, but the Athletics' system still has big-time talent to get excited about. Offseason trades that netted closer Billy Koch and top hitting prospect Carlos Pena cost the A's 2002 Rookie of the Year Eric Hinske, Justin Miller, Ryan Ludwick, Jason Hart and Mario Ramos. Then in July, Pena and promising righthanders Jeremy Bonderman and Franklyn German were moved in a three-team trade for lefthander Ted Lilly and top Yankees prospects Jason Arnold and John-Ford Griffin. Now there's an impressive array of young pitching on the cusp of the rotation behind Barry Zito, Tim Hudson, Mark Mulder and Lilly. It includes Arnold, Rich Harden, John Rheinecker, Mike Wood and Bert Snow.

Jason Arnold

Position: P **Opening Day Age:** 23
Bats: R **Throws:** R **Born:** 5/2/79 in
Ht: 6' 3" **Wt:** 210 Melbourne, FL

Recent Statistics

	W	L	ERA	G	GS	Sv	IP	H	R	BB	SO	HR
2001 A Staten Isla	7	2	1.50	10	10	0	66.0	35	13	15	74	2
2002 A Tampa	7	1	2.48	13	13	0	80.0	64	27	22	83	2
2002 AA Norwich	1	2	4.15	3	3	0	17.1	17	14	5	18	1
2002 AA Midland	5	1	2.33	10	10	0	58.0	42	22	24	53	2

The Yankees' second-round pick in 2001, Arnold was moved in the three-team Jeff Weaver trade and reached Double-A ball in his first full season as a pro. The righthander dominated hitters in the New York-Penn League in 2001, calling on a deceptive motion, mid-90s heat, an advanced palmball with splitter action and a slider. The A's believe Arnold tended to pitch a bit backwards, favoring his offspeed stuff over his fastball, but in 2002 he used his fastball more effectively with better command. He has settled at 91-92 MPH with more movement on the pitch. Although Arnold was 5-1 (2.33) at Double-A Midland after he was dealt to Oakland, the A's plan to give him plenty of time to adjust to better hitters at Triple-A Sacramento.

Freddie Bynum

Position: SS-2B **Opening Day Age:** 23
Bats: L **Throws:** R **Born:** 3/15/80 in Wilson,
Ht: 6' 1" **Wt:** 175 NC

Recent Statistics

	G	AB	R	H	D	T	HR	RBI	SB	BB	SO	Avg
2001 A Modesto	120	440	59	115	19	7	2	46	28	41	95	.261
2002 A Visalia	135	539	83	165	26	5	3	56	41	64	116	.306

The A's second-round pick in 2000, Bynum jumped to high Class-A Modesto for his first full pro season in 2001. The game was too fast for him at first, but he came around and finished strong. He returned to the California League last summer and his true ability began to emerge. He has the tools to be a leadoff type with impressive defensive skills. He has learned to drive the ball consistently the other way and move it all over the field. While his error total was high at Visalia, he plays well at both second and short with good range, hands and a strong arm. The A's want him to improve his pitch-to-pitch focus at the plate, while taking more pitches and improving his OBP.

Bobby Crosby

Position: SS **Opening Day Age:** 23
Bats: R **Throws:** R **Born:** 1/12/80 in
Ht: 6' 3" **Wt:** 195 Lakewood, CA

Recent Statistics

	G	AB	R	H	D	T	HR	RBI	SB	BB	SO	Avg
2001 A Modesto	11	38	7	15	5	0	1	3	0	3	8	.395
2002 A Modesto	73	280	47	86	17	2	2	38	5	33	43	.307
2002 AA Midland	59	228	31	64	16	0	7	31	9	19	41	.281

A 2001 first-round pick from Long Beach State, Crosby is a natural baseball player with good instincts and power potential. He's part of the bigger breed of shortstops coming into the game. His style is a bit rigid and isn't always pretty, and he needs to work on improving his range. After debuting with a .395 average in just 11 games at high Class-A Modesto in 2001, Crosby reached Double-A Midland last summer and handled the quicker game. He's beginning to show power by getting better extension on his swing, keeping the bat barrel in the zone longer and getting more loft. He must work counts better to improve his OBP.

John-Ford Griffin

Position: OF **Opening Day Age:** 23
Bats: L **Throws:** L **Born:** 11/19/79 in
Ht: 6' 2" **Wt:** 215 Sarasota, FL

Recent Statistics

	G	AB	R	H	D	T	HR	RBI	SB	BB	SO	Avg
2001 A Staten Isla	66	238	46	74	17	1	5	43	10	40	41	.311
2002 A Tampa	65	255	32	68	16	1	3	31	1	29	45	.267
2002 AA Norwich	18	67	17	22	3	0	5	10	0	8	13	.328
2002 AA Midland	2	7	0	1	0	0	0	0	0	0	3	.143

The Yankees' first-rounder in 2001, after hitting better than .400 in three seasons at Florida State, Griffin also came over in the Jeff Weaver deal. He demonstrated a mature approach to hitting in his 2001 debut at short-season Staten Island. His ability to make quick adjustments at the plate makes the most of his sweet swing and terrific bat speed, and this strong gap-to-gap hitter should show more home-run power as he matures. Defensively, he needs to work on his overall game, including routes and throwing, to become an everyday left fielder in the majors. A below-average arm because of shoulder surgery in college limits him to left.

Oakland

Rich Harden

Position: P
Bats: L **Throws:** R
Ht: 6' 1" **Wt:** 180

Opening Day Age: 21
Born: 11/30/81 in Victoria, BC

Recent Statistics

	W	L	ERA	G	GS	Sv	IP	H	R	BB	SO	HR
2001 A Vancouver	2	4	3.39	18	14	0	74.1	47	29	38	100	3
2002 A Visalia	4	3	2.91	12	12	0	67.2	49	27	24	85	4
2002 AA Midland	8	3	2.95	16	16	0	85.1	67	33	52	102	7

A 17th-round pick in 2000, Harden debuted in 2001 as a draft-and-follow. That year he dominated hitters at short-season Vancouver. He advanced to Double-A Midland in his first full pro season by successfully mixing an impressive arsenal with good command, en route to a 12-6 (2.94) season between high Class-A Visalia and Midland. He has the potential to be a No. 1 or 2 starter because of an above-average 93-95 MPH fastball and a slider that has a chance to be above average. He also works with an 84-85 MPH two-seamer, a split-finger pitch and changeup. He may start 2003 at Triple-A Sacramento, and he must fine-tune the sequence of pitches he uses to move on to Oakland.

John Rheinecker

Position: P
Bats: L **Throws:** L
Ht: 6' 2" **Wt:** 215

Opening Day Age: 23
Born: 5/29/79 in Belleville, IL

Recent Statistics

	W	L	ERA	G	GS	Sv	IP	H	R	BB	SO	HR
2001 A Vancouver	0	1	1.59	6	5	0	22.2	13	5	4	17	0
2001 A Modesto	0	1	6.30	2	2	0	10.0	10	7	5	5	1
2002 A Visalia	3	0	2.31	9	9	0	50.2	41	16	10	62	2
2002 AA Midland	7	7	3.38	20	20	0	128.0	137	63	24	100	7

A supplemental first-rounder in 2001, Rheinecker advanced to high Class-A Modesto in his debut season on the strength of a moving low-90s fastball and a pair of solid breaking pitches. His curveball is the best breaking ball in the system, and it helped him advance to Double-A Midland in his second season. The southpaw also calls on a good cutter that is effective against righthanded hitters. He has a good pitch combination and a feel for using it. Although he goes after hitters, perfecting his sequence of pitches is key to moving forward. At times he throws too many pitches, and it isn't a case of trying to strike out hitters. The A's would like him to work longer in games by reducing his pitch counts to individual batters.

Joe Valentine

Position: P
Bats: R **Throws:** R
Ht: 6' 2" **Wt:** 195

Opening Day Age: 23
Born: 12/24/79 in Las Vegas, NV

Recent Statistics

	W	L	ERA	G	GS	Sv	IP	H	R	BB	SO	HR
2001 A Kannapolis	2	2	2.93	30	0	14	30.2	21	10	10	33	0
2001 A Winston-Sal	5	1	1.01	27	0	8	44.2	18	7	27	50	0
2002 AA Birmingham	4	1	1.97	55	0	36	59.1	36	16	30	63	1

The White Sox dealt Valentine to Oakland in December's Billy Koch-Keith Foulke trade, but it's the Tigers who must regret not hanging onto him as a Rule 5 pick a year ago. Valentine returned to the White Sox' system to tie the Double-A Southern League save record in 2002, when he anchored the bullpen of Birmingham's championship team. While minor league closers are taken with a grain of salt, Valentine's stuff is legit. He's a fastball-slider pitcher who can hit the mid-90s to set up a plus slider. He held opponents to a .173 average in Double-A ball and has allowed only 89 hits in 159.2 innings over the last three seasons. Control can be an issue at times, but he's got an above-average knack for escape. Valentine may be groomed to replace Foulke as Oakland's closer someday.

Mike Wood

Position: P
Bats: R **Throws:** R
Ht: 6' 3" **Wt:** 175

Opening Day Age: 22
Born: 4/26/80 in West Palm Beach, FL

Recent Statistics

	W	L	ERA	G	GS	Sv	IP	H	R	BB	SO	HR
2001 A Vancouver	2	0	1.25	5	2	0	21.2	17	4	4	24	0
2001 A Modesto	4	3	3.09	10	9	0	58.1	46	22	10	52	6
2002 A Modesto	3	3	3.48	7	7	0	41.1	41	17	6	50	4
2002 AA Midland	11	3	3.15	17	17	0	105.2	103	41	29	63	8

A 2001 pick, Wood arrived from the University of North Florida with a reputation of working in the low 90s. The A's have doubts he ever threw that hard consistently, but Wood has been successful calling on a hard-sinking 86-87 MPH fastball, a slider, splitter and changeup. He's the most consistent strike-thrower in the system. After going 11-3 (3.15) at Double-A Midland last summer, he has a 20-9 (3.01) record as a pro. His sinker-slider combo draws comparisons to Tim Hudson's, though Hudson has extra zip on his sinker. Wood's is a good pitch, but the challenge will be getting hitters out with it at higher levels. Although he may succeed with the velocity he has, adding a little would make him a potential No. 1 or 2 starter.

Others to Watch

One of the A's rare high school picks among the system's top prospects, **Matt Allegra** (21) changed his batting approach in instructional league after his 2000 debut and enjoyed a power surge at short-season Vancouver in 2001. There have been lots of strikeouts, but he made better contact and didn't swing so wildly during a .281-20-93 season at high Class-A Visalia in 2002. . . A supplemental first-round pick last June, catcher **Jeremy Brown** (23) had one of the better pro debuts among college talent in the draft. He spent 10 games at short-season Vancouver, where he batted .286 with a .487 OBP, before enjoying a .310-10-40 campaign with tons of walks at high Class-A Visalia. . . Righthander **Bert Snow** (26) had the best slider in the system before Tommy John surgery sidetracked him in 2001. The pitch lacked its customary tightness during his 2002 return, and regaining command of his pitches also is an ongoing project.

Safeco Field

Offense

Ever since it opened in mid-1999, Safeco Field has been one of the top pitchers' parks in baseball. They say it's due to the air and the glare. Though the roof is retractable, the open-sided park remains subject to the cool Pacific breeze even when the roof is closed. This keeps balls from carrying, particularly to left field. Batters complain about distracting glare and shadows in the batter's eye in center field, and say it's worst during afternoon starts and when the roof is open.

Defense

The deep alleys give the center fielder plenty of territory to cover, and put enough of a responsibility on the corner outfielders that it's hard to hide a defensive liability there. Pitchers who put the ball in play—particularly flyball hurlers—are less likely to run into problems here. Young pitchers are able to adjust to the majors more easily.

Who It Helps the Most

Virtually all pitchers are assisted by Safeco. Jamie Moyer has thrived here, adjusting his style to get more flyballs. Ryan Franklin has pitched with more confidence and effectiveness at Safeco. Joel Pineiro has found it easier to pitch aggressively here, which has compounded his effectiveness.

Who It Hurts the Most

The glare has the most extreme impact on Mike Cameron, who has a minor problem with the vision in his right eye. Cameron would hit for a better average and more power in almost any other park. Jeff Cirillo had the lowest home batting average of any major league regular last year. Part of that may have been psychological, especially after he had gotten used to hitting at Coors Field. Ben Davis, Ruben Sierra, John Olerud and Dan Wilson all suffer to varying extents.

Rookies & Newcomers

Randy Winn, who hit well in Tropicana Field over the last two years and had become more of a flyball hitter in recent seasons, probably will have difficulty adjusting. Rafael Soriano, an extreme flyball pitcher, didn't pitch well here last year but probably will if given a greater opportunity.

Dimensions: LF-331, LCF-390, CF-405, RCF-387, RF-327

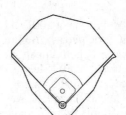

Capacity: 47,116

Elevation: -2 feet

Surface: Grass

Foul Territory: Average

Park Factors

2002 Season

	Home Games Mariners	Opp	Total	Away Games Mariners	Opp	Total	Index
G	72	72	144	72	72	144	94
Avg	.265	.255	.260	.288	.265	.277	94
AB	2391	2511	4902	2554	2435	4989	98
R	327	306	633	403	348	751	84
H	633	641	1274	736	646	1382	92
2B	105	126	231	145	135	280	84
3B	17	3	20	10	11	21	97
HR	55	73	128	78	91	169	77
BB	308	217	525	257	190	447	120
SO	442	506	948	446	434	880	110
E	37	56	93	40	52	92	101
E-Infield	30	49	79	30	47	77	103
LHB-Avg	.274	.264	.269	.308	.276	.292	92
LHB-HR	21	41	62	40	37	77	81
RHB-Avg	.256	.247	.252	.271	.255	.263	96
RHB-HR	34	32	66	38	54	92	74

2001-2002

	Home Games Mariners	Opp	Total	Away Games Mariners	Opp	Total	Index
G	144	144	288	144	144	288	94
Avg	.275	.240	.257	.290	.257	.274	94
AB	4805	4962	9767	5193	4872	10065	97
R	722	559	1281	824	659	1483	86
H	1323	1191	2514	1506	1253	2759	91
2B	243	238	481	291	266	557	89
3B	30	9	39	29	27	56	72
HR	121	133	254	151	173	324	81
BB	585	409	994	534	413	947	108
SO	857	969	1826	906	908	1814	104
E	67	117	184	80	116	196	94
E-Infield	56	99	155	63	104	167	93
LHB-Avg	.286	.249	.267	.302	.270	.287	93
LHB-HR	43	72	115	56	74	130	91
RHB-Avg	.266	.232	.249	.279	.246	.263	95
RHB-HR	78	61	139	95	99	194	74

2002 Rankings (American League)

- Highest walk factor
- Second-highest strikeout factor
- Lowest batting-average factor
- Lowest run factor
- Lowest hit factor
- Second-lowest LHB batting-average factor
- Third-lowest double factor
- Third-lowest home-run factor

Seattle

Bob Melvin

2002 Season

New Seattle manager Bob Melvin spent 2001 and 2002 as the Diamondbacks' bench coach. Before that, he was Phil Garner's bench coach in Milwaukee (1999) and Detroit (2000). Melvin's only managerial experience was in the Arizona Fall League, but as Brenly's bench coach, he was said to have been given significant in-game responsibilities. He also was a part-time catcher for seven different major league teams from 1985-1994. Melvin certainly has some big shoes to fill in taking over for Lou Piniella, who guided the Mariners to three division crowns between 1995 and 2001.

Offense

Melvin has said that he sees the M's as a National League-style team, so the running game should remain in high gear. He's also said he believes in using his bench, which should ensure that Mark McLemore and Desi Relford continue to see plenty of playing time. One of Melvin's biggest challenges will be to get Jeff Cirillo back on track; Melvin coached him in 1999, during Cirillo's better days in Milwaukee, and might hold the key.

Pitching & Defense

With the pitching staff, Melvin may have to work one or two youngsters, including Rafael Soriano, Ryan Franklin and the recovering Gil Meche, into the starting rotation. He'll also have to be careful to keep from leaning too hard on young Joel Pineiro. Melvin will be inheriting a strong bullpen, as well as one of the league's better defensive units. One challenge will be to give Ben Davis enough playing time to develop while relying on Dan Wilson to guide the staff's young pitchers.

2003 Outlook

Melvin takes over a team long on both talent and expectations. Seattle's ability to re-sign Edgar Martinez, John Olerud and Jamie Moyer goes a long way toward framing Melvin's priorities as the club heads into spring training. He will direct a club with speed, with Ichiro and Randy Winn at the top of the order, and Mike Cameron and super reserve Mark McLemore providing zip lower in the lineup.

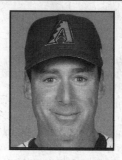

Born: 10/28/1961 in Palo Alto, CA

Playing Experience: 1985-1994, Det, SF, Bal, KC, Bos, NYY, CWS

Managerial Experience: No major league managing experience

Manager Statistics (Lou Piniella)

Year	Team, Lg	W	L	Pct	GB	Finish
2002	Seattle, AL	93	69	.574	10.0	3rd West
16 Seasons		1319	1135	.537	–	–

2002 Starting Pitchers by Days Rest

	<=3	4	5	6+
Mariners Starts	0	97	38	19
Mariners ERA	–	4.18	4.70	4.02
AL Avg Starts	1	83	44	24
AL ERA	7.15	4.59	4.27	5.03

2002 Situational Stats

	Lou Piniella	AL Average
Hit & Run Success %	43.8	36.0
Stolen Base Success %	70.3	68.1
Platoon Pct.	64.0	58.9
Defensive Subs	32	23
High-Pitch Outings	8	6
Quick/Slow Hooks	22/11	19/14
Sacrifice Attempts	62	53

2002 Rankings—Lou Piniella (American League)

- 1st in stolen base attempts (195), steals of second base (116), steals of third base (21), double steals (10) and starting lineups used (128)
- 3rd in hit-and-run success percentage, quick hooks and starts with over 120 pitches (8)

Bret Boone

2002 Season

Coming off a third-place finish in the American League MVP balloting, Bret Boone took a big tumble in the first half of 2002, taking a .229 average into the All-Star break. He returned to his 2001 form in the second half and finished with totals that were respectable but disappointing nonetheless. To his credit, no matter how badly he struggled at the plate, his smooth glovework never wavered.

Hitting

Boone's opposite-field power is among the best in the game, and over the last two years he's learned to take full advantage of it. When Boone returned to the American League in 2001, pitchers who habitually worked off the outside corner to power hitters soon learned they were playing right into his hands. He also is deadly on pitches down and in, staying inside the ball very well. There was no obvious explanation for his first-half struggles, though some chalked it up to the long hot and cold spells he's been prone to throughout his career.

Baserunning & Defense

With soft hands, a good double-play pivot and an arm strong enough for shortstop, Boone is an elite defensive second baseman. He won his second Gold Glove in 2002 after leading AL second basemen in fielding percentage. He also stole 12 bases in 17 attempts, but the majority of them came as the tail runner on double-steals. He has average speed at best, though he generally runs the bases intelligently.

2003 Outlook

It may be that Boone will spend the rest of his career trying to duplicate his magical 2001 season. That may never happen, but if he simply does what he did last year—drive in 100 runs and play Gold Glove defense—he'll remain a key contributor with the Mariners.

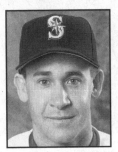

Position: 2B
Bats: R **Throws:** R
Ht: 5'10" **Wt:** 190

Opening Day Age: 33
Born: 4/6/69 in El Cajon, CA
ML Seasons: 11

Overall Statistics

	G	AB	R	H	D	T	HR	RBI	SB	BB	SO	Avg	OBP	Slg
'02	155	608	88	169	34	3	24	107	12	53	102	.278	.339	.462
Car.	1385	5142	709	1371	286	20	186	784	64	400	970	.267	.323	.439

Where He Hits the Ball

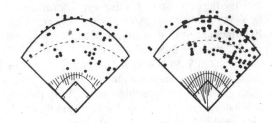

Vs. LHP   **Vs. RHP**

2002 Situational Stats

	AB	H	HR	RBI	Avg		AB	H	HR	RBI	Avg
Home	298	84	13	53	.282	LHP	149	44	8	26	.295
Road	310	85	11	54	.274	RHP	459	125	16	81	.272
First Half	328	75	12	53	.229	Sc Pos	171	52	6	82	.304
Scnd Half	280	94	12	54	.336	Clutch	91	28	4	20	.308

2002 Rankings (American League)

- 1st in fielding percentage at second base (.989)
- Led the Mariners in total bases (281), RBI and highest percentage of extra bases taken as a runner (58.7)
- Led AL second basemen in RBI

Mike Cameron

2002 Season

It was a frustrating season for Mike Cameron, not because he played poorly, but rather because everyone knew he was capable of doing more. His average was low and strikeouts came in bunches, even though he continued to hit for power, draw walks and steal bases. He also played center field as well as ever, though he failed to repeat as a Gold Glover.

Hitting

Cameron always has been strikeout-prone, but it's become a more serious problem over the last two years. In 2002 he led the American League in strikeouts by not an inconsiderable margin, which was the biggest reason his average fell off. Since he swings through so many pitches, he's especially vulnerable with two strikes. He has very good power, though, especially to the left-field alley. He also is able to lay off most pitches out of the strike zone, drawing more than his share of walks. Batting sixth, he's something of a hybrid, driving in whatever runners are left for him, and then running the bases aggressively while the bottom third of the order bats.

Baserunning & Defense

In the field, there's nothing Cameron can't do, whether it's turning his back to a drive and chasing it down, climbing a wall to take away a home run, or outrunning a drive in the gap. His strong arm is an asset as well. He has both the quickness and the straight-ahead speed to steal a lot of bases while rarely being caught. As a basestealer, he's not as effective against lefthanded pitchers.

2003 Outlook

The Mariners would love for Cameron to bring his average back up, but there's little reason to think he'll be able to as long as he plays at Safeco. Even so, he'll remain a valuable player, low batting average and all.

Position: CF
Bats: R **Throws:** R
Ht: 6' 2" **Wt:** 195

Opening Day Age: 30
Born: 1/8/73 in LaGrange, GA
ML Seasons: 8

Overall Statistics

	G	AB	R	H	D	T	HR	RBI	SB	BB	SO	Avg	OBP	Slg
'02	158	545	84	130	26	5	25	80	31	79	176	.239	.340	.442
Car.	905	2994	493	747	154	31	113	434	177	402	833	.249	.343	.435

Where He Hits the Ball

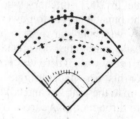

Vs. LHP   **Vs. RHP**

2002 Situational Stats

	AB	H	HR	RBI	Avg		AB	H	HR	RBI	Avg
Home	262	57	7	31	.218	LHP	142	34	10	29	.239
Road	283	73	18	49	.258	RHP	403	96	15	51	.238
First Half	299	65	15	51	.217	Sc Pos	140	32	5	54	.229
Scnd Half	246	65	10	29	.264	Clutch	90	14	1	5	.156

2002 Rankings (American League)

- 1st in strikeouts
- 2nd in lowest batting average at home
- 3rd in errors in center field (5)
- 4th in stolen bases and lowest batting average
- 5th in batting average on a 3-1 count (.632), lowest batting average in the clutch, lowest fielding percentage in center field (.988) and lowest batting average with two strikes (.137)
- Led the Mariners in home runs, stolen bases, strikeouts, pitches seen (2,601), games played, HR frequency (21.8 ABs per HR), stolen-base percentage (79.5), most pitches seen per plate appearance (4.06) and batting average on a 3-1 count (.632)

Jeff Cirillo

Position: 3B/1B
Bats: R **Throws:** R
Ht: 6' 1" **Wt:** 190

Opening Day Age: 33
Born: 9/23/69 in
Pasadena, CA
ML Seasons: 9
Pronunciation:
suh-RILL-o

2002 Season

Everyone expected that Jeff Cirillo's average would drop a few points as he moved from Colorado to Seattle's pitcher-oriented Safeco Field, but no one expected him to suffer through the worst offensive season of his career. Cirillo always has demanded a lot from himself, and when he didn't hit early on, manager Lou Piniella added to the pressure. Cirillo only grew more confused at the plate, and never came out of his funk.

Hitting

When he's going well, Cirillo is a line-drive hitter who makes excellent contact and uses the whole field, and his ability to hit with two strikes gives him the confidence to wait out a pitcher. His entire approach seemed to collapse last year as he became more tentative and lost the ability to protect the plate and wait for his pitch. He became defensive, swinging not to miss, and all but stopped hitting the ball with authority. He went homerless in his last 78 games.

Baserunning & Defense

Even last year, Cirillo's defense remained top-notch. A pitcher in college, Cirillo has one of the strongest infield arms around and is capable of gunning the ball to first from just about any position. He has good hands and reactions, and while he's lost a little range, he charges bunts as well as ever. He runs decently but didn't steal many bases last year after American League pitchers caught on to them.

2003 Outlook

If anyone has a chance to be reinvigorated by Seattle's change of managers, it's Cirillo. New manager Bob Melvin was a Brewers coach in Cirillo's final year with Milwaukee, at a time when he was his most productive. On the other hand, Cirillo's been in decline for a few years now, something that was masked for a time by Coors Field. He probably will bounce back somewhat, but he may never be the hitter he once was.

Overall Statistics

	G	AB	R	H	D	T	HR	RBI	SB	BB	SO	Avg	OBP	Slg
'02	146	485	51	121	20	0	6	54	8	31	67	.249	.301	.328
Car.	1230	4422	678	1345	285	19	100	624	55	471	574	.304	.374	.445

Where He Hits the Ball

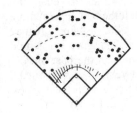 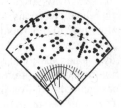

Vs. LHP   **Vs. RHP**

2002 Situational Stats

	AB	H	HR	RBI	Avg		AB	H	HR	RBI	Avg
Home	226	49	2	21	.217	LHP	148	45	4	20	.304
Road	259	72	4	33	.278	RHP	337	76	2	34	.226
First Half	285	70	6	39	.246	Sc Pos	128	35	2	48	.273
Scnd Half	200	51	0	15	.255	Clutch	70	17	0	7	.243

2002 Rankings (American League)

- 1st in fielding percentage at third base (.973), lowest batting average vs. righthanded pitchers, lowest slugging percentage vs. righthanded pitchers (.285) and lowest batting average at home
- 2nd in sacrifice bunts (13)
- 3rd in lowest slugging percentage and lowest on-base percentage vs. righthanded pitchers (.275)
- 4th in lowest HR frequency (80.8 ABs per HR)
- 6th in lowest on-base percentage
- 7th in bunts in play (22)
- Led the Mariners in sacrifice bunts (13), hit by pitch (9) and bunts in play (22)

2002 Season

Coming off his best season, Mariners ace Freddy Garcia kept rolling along during the first half of 2002, taking an 11-5 won-lost record into the All-Star break. Then it suddenly all fell apart for him, as he suffered a puzzling disintegration in the second half. Making it all the more baffling was that the problem apparently was not physical, making it tough to pinpoint. No one felt the frustration more keenly than Garcia.

Pitching

Some felt that Garcia's struggles resulted from his inability to get his curve over. If that were the case, it's odd that it would have such an impact, since his low-90s fastball and superb changeup are reliable weapons. He left the ball up a lot more often in 2002, particularly late in games. It may have been a simple case of fatigue, since he'd always had excellent stamina in the past but did not display it as often last year, even as the team continued to lean on him to go deep into games. That's understandable, though—with a good pitcher's build and a long, loose arm, he always projects strength and power.

Defense

At times, Garcia's frustration was evident in his fielding, as he sometimes failed to keep his mind on the play at hand. He showed the year before that he's capable of fielding his position well when focused. On the other hand, he did make progress in slowing down the running game in 2002.

2003 Outlook

The Mariners can only hope that whatever was bothering Garcia last summer won't be an issue this season. Unless he was hiding an injury, it's hard to imagine he won't be able to return to form as one of the league's elite righthanders.

Position: SP
Bats: R **Throws:** R
Ht: 6' 4" **Wt:** 235

Opening Day Age: 26
Born: 6/10/76 in Caracas, VZ
ML Seasons: 4

Overall Statistics

	W	L	Pct.	ERA	G	GS	Sv	IP	H	BB	SO	HR	Ratio
'02	16	10	.615	4.39	34	34	0	223.2	227	63	181	30	1.30
Car.	60	29	.674	3.83	122	121	0	788.0	743	286	593	80	1.31

How Often He Throws Strikes

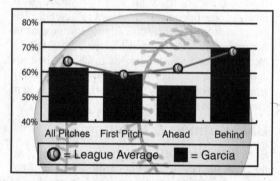

Ⓚ = League Average   ■ = Garcia

2002 Situational Stats

	W	L	ERA	Sv	IP		AB	H	HR	RBI	Avg
Home	8	5	4.18	0	112.0	LHB	482	123	17	58	.255
Road	8	5	4.59	0	111.2	RHB	392	104	13	43	.265
First Half	11	5	3.44	0	128.1	Sc Pos	188	47	2	68	.250
Scnd Half	5	5	5.66	0	95.1	Clutch	42	7	1	3	.167

2002 Rankings (American League)

- 1st in highest stolen-base percentage allowed (90.0)
- 2nd in games started and pitches thrown (3,607)
- 4th in errors at pitcher (3) and lowest fielding percentage at pitcher (.933)
- 5th in batters faced (955), strikeouts and most strikeouts per nine innings (7.3)
- 6th in hits allowed
- Led the Mariners in wins, losses, hits allowed, home runs allowed, walks allowed, strikeouts, most run support per nine innings (6.0) and most strikeouts per nine innings (7.3)

Carlos Guillen

2002 Season

Two months into the 2002 season, Carlos Guillen was hitting better than .300 with uncharacteristic power and was well on his way to his best season yet. On May 31, though, he squared to bunt and was hit on the left hand, spraining his ring finger. When he returned 10 days later, he was unable to bat righthanded for several weeks. Even after resuming switch-hitting in late July, he never got his stroke back.

Hitting

Guillen played the second half of 2001 weakened by tuberculosis, so it wasn't a complete surprise when he showed more power early in 2002. He's a spray-type hitter from either side of the plate, although he is a bit more disciplined from the left side. He was drawing more walks last year before he got hurt. He's also a capable bunter. The question always has been whether he would develop enough to be moved up from the bottom of the order to the No. 2 spot; the early results in 2002 were promising.

Baserunning & Defense

Though rarely spectacular, Guillen is a solid defender who makes all the plays. A good first step gives him ample range, and his arm is strong enough to makes plays from the hole. His errors nearly doubled last year, but his injured left hand may have been a factor. His straight-ahead speed is above average but not good enough for him to be much of a basestealing threat.

2003 Outlook

For the second straight year, Guillen showed flashes but wasn't able to show what he could do in a full, healthy season. There's no reason to assume his health problems will continue, so this could be the year he emerges as more of an offensive threat.

Position: SS
Bats: B **Throws:** R
Ht: 6' 1" **Wt:** 202

Opening Day Age: 27
Born: 9/30/75 in Maracay, VZ
ML Seasons: 5
Pronunciation: GEY-un

Overall Statistics

	G	AB	R	H	D	T	HR	RBI	SB	BB	SO	Avg	OBP	Slg
'02	134	475	73	124	24	6	9	56	4	46	91	.261	.326	.394
Car.	379	1277	201	332	61	13	22	159	11	131	248	.260	.328	.380

Where He Hits the Ball

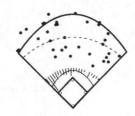 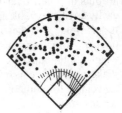

Vs. LHP   **Vs. RHP**

2002 Situational Stats

	AB	H	HR	RBI	Avg		AB	H	HR	RBI	Avg
Home	249	68	4	27	.273	LHP	122	27	3	16	.221
Road	226	56	5	29	.248	RHP	353	97	6	40	.275
First Half	247	71	7	36	.287	Sc Pos	129	34	1	45	.264
Scnd Half	228	53	2	20	.232	Clutch	84	29	2	15	.345

2002 Rankings (American League)

- 2nd in lowest fielding percentage at shortstop (.966)
- 4th in errors at shortstop (18) and lowest slugging percentage vs. lefthanded pitchers (.328)
- 6th in triples
- 10th in lowest batting average vs. lefthanded pitchers and lowest on-base percentage vs. lefthanded pitchers (.280)

Edgar Martinez

2002 Season

Edgar Martinez really only had a half-season last year. He ruptured a tendon behind his left knee in early April and missed almost all of the first half, but returned to his customary cleanup spot in late June and hit almost as well as usual. Just as importantly, he was able to play every day for the last three months of the season without any further physical problems.

Hitting

A powerful, patient hitter, Martinez seems to approach every at-bat with a plan, and afterward it often looks like he got the pitch he'd been looking for. He has excellent plate coverage, and lines an outside pitch over the right-field wall just as easily as he can yank an inside pitch into the seats in left field. He takes the first pitch so often that pitchers sometimes just lay one in there, only to watch it go out. Martinez can afford to take a strike or two because he has terrific bat control, especially for someone who hits the ball hard so consistently.

Baserunning & Defense

Martinez' legs are prone to muscle pulls, which is why the M's try to keep him healthy by using him in the field as little as possible. He's played a handful of games at first over the last few years and probably still can fill in there in an emergency. He almost never tries to steal a base or stretch a hit.

2003 Outlook

The Mariners re-signed Martinez to a one-year deal for 2003. Even at age 40, he still can swing the bat. The bigger question is whether he'll be able to avoid the injuries that have cost him 95 games over the last two seasons. In order to stay fresh, he might need to be given more days off than he's used to receiving.

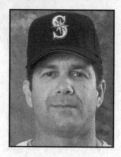

Position: DH
Bats: R **Throws:** R
Ht: 5'11" **Wt:** 210

Opening Day Age: 40
Born: 1/2/63 in New York, NY
ML Seasons: 16

Overall Statistics

G	AB	R	H	D	T	HR	RBI	SB	BB	SO	Avg	OBP	Slg
97	328	42	91	23	0	15	59	1	67	69	.277	.403	.485
1769	6230	1102	1973	466	15	273	1100	48	1133	1000	.317	.424	.528

Where He Hits the Ball

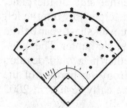 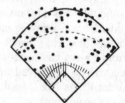

Vs. LHP   **Vs. RHP**

2002 Situational Stats

	AB	H	HR	RBI	Avg		AB	H	HR	RBI	Avg
Home	165	50	9	33	.303	LHP	85	26	6	14	.306
Road	163	41	6	26	.252	RHP	243	65	9	45	.267
First Half	84	22	3	13	.262	Sc Pos	89	23	1	40	.258
Scnd Half	244	69	12	46	.283	Clutch	49	17	2	11	.347

2002 Rankings (American League)

- 6th in highest percentage of pitches taken (62.5)
- 8th in lowest cleanup slugging percentage (.466)
- 10th in batting average in the clutch
- Led the Mariners in on-base percentage, batting average in the clutch, batting average with the bases loaded (.571), slugging percentage vs. lefthanded pitchers (.612) and on-base percentage vs. lefthanded pitchers (.469)

Jamie Moyer

2002 Season

Coming off his first 20-win season in 2001, Jamie Moyer's win total fell to 13 even though the overall quality of his work hardly dropped off at all. He had a shot to reach 20 wins again as late as mid-August, but he went 1-4 with a 5.09 ERA over his last nine starts. Despite that, Moyer posted a career-low 3.32 ERA and nearly set a new career high in innings pitched, all at age 39.

Pitching

Changing speeds and locating with pinpoint precision, Moyer shows how effective a pitcher can be without being able to throw any harder than the mid-80s. Righthanded hitters can't help falling for his terrific changeup, which fades off the outside corner while dropping into the dirt. Against lefties he works inside with fastballs before coming back with his big, looping curve. While Moyer's in the process of setting up his offspeed pitches, hitters often get to his fastball and hit it in the air, but he generally locates well enough to keep the ball in the park.

Defense

The lefthander has developed a decent pickoff move and is a bit tougher than average to run against. He finishes his delivery square to the plate and gets to everything hit anywhere near him. The consummate veteran, he rarely makes mental or physical errors.

2003 Outlook

Moyer was the last of Seattle's core of free agents to re-sign. He agreed to a three-year, $15.5 million contract in early December. Getting a three-year deal as a 40th birthday present may seem foolish, as few pitchers are able to maintain their effectiveness into their forties, but Moyer could lose quite a bit and still be useful. He's always pitched well at Safeco, and he'll stay in the home park that contains the many flyballs he allows.

Position: SP
Bats: L **Throws:** L
Ht: 6' 0" **Wt:** 175

Opening Day Age: 40
Born: 11/18/62 in Sellersville, PA
ML Seasons: 16

Overall Statistics

	W	L	Pct.	ERA	G	GS	Sv	IP	H	BB	SO	HR	Ratio
'02	13	8	.619	3.32	34	34	0	230.2	198	50	147	28	1.08
Car.	164	125	.567	4.14	439	387	0	2522.2	2586	714	1528	295	1.31

How Often He Throws Strikes

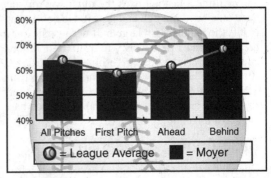

◉ = League Average   ■ = Moyer

2002 Situational Stats

	W	L	ERA	Sv	IP		AB	H	HR	RBI	Avg
Home	5	5	3.18	0	130.0	LHB	293	81	12	38	.276
Road	8	3	3.49	0	100.2	RHB	567	117	16	45	.206
First Half	8	4	3.20	0	129.1	Sc Pos	140	33	9	58	.236
Scnd Half	5	4	3.46	0	101.1	Clutch	55	9	0	2	.164

2002 Rankings (American League)

- 2nd in games started and shutouts (2)
- 3rd in lowest batting average allowed vs. righthanded batters
- 4th in complete games (4), innings pitched and lowest on-base percentage allowed (.278)
- 5th in lowest batting average allowed (.230)
- 6th in lowest slugging percentage allowed (.366) and fewest walks per nine innings (2.0)
- Led the Mariners in hit batsmen (9), runners caught stealing (6), lowest batting average allowed (.230), lowest slugging percentage allowed (.366) and lowest on-base percentage allowed (.278)

Position: 1B
Bats: L **Throws:** L
Ht: 6' 5" **Wt:** 220

Opening Day Age: 34
Born: 8/5/68 in Seattle, WA
ML Seasons: 14
Pronunciation: OLE-le-RUDE

2002 Season

One has to wonder if John Olerud is human, since he never has an off year. But he can't be a machine either, because every machine eventually breaks down. Olerud's 2002 season offered no new clues to this timeless conundrum, as Olerud once again played every day, made all the plays, and nearly matched his career norms in virtually every offensive category. And, of course, he did it as quietly and unobtrusively as possible.

Hitting

Olerud covers the plate very well with a smooth, controlled stroke. He waits on the ball very well, and can line a fastball hard the other way or stay back on a breaking ball and golf it. He consistently hits the ball hard, in large part because he has a great eye and often works himself into hitters' counts. Lefthanders can give him a little trouble, particularly hard throwers that can keep him from getting on top of the ball. While southpaws may sap his power overall, he still is able to reach base against them enough to help.

Baserunning & Defense

One suspects that the last time Olerud made a fundamental mistake in the field, his Little League coach called him aside and showed him the right way to do it. At a position where handling a large number of chances efficiently is the most important criterion, Olerud is one of the most efficient of all. He was rewarded for his efforts with his second Gold Glove last year. He has very little speed but seldom makes foolish decisions on the bases.

2003 Outlook

After entering the offseason as a free agent, Olerud decided to stay close to home by inking a two-year, $15.4 million contract in early December. While Safeco Field shaves points off his average, he continues to produce and everyone knows exactly what to expect out of him.

Overall Statistics

G	AB	R	H	D	T	HR	RBI	SB	BB	SO	Avg	OBP	Slg
154	553	85	166	39	0	22	102	0	98	66	.300	.403	.490
1868	6455	1012	1934	438	12	229	1062	11	1114	868	.300	.404	.478

Where He Hits the Ball

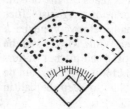 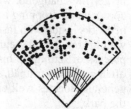

Vs. LHP   **Vs. RHP**

2002 Situational Stats

	AB	H	HR	RBI	Avg		AB	H	HR	RBI	Avg
Home	273	75	9	48	.275	LHP	164	47	3	33	.287
Road	280	91	13	54	.325	RHP	389	119	19	69	.306
First Half	306	96	15	54	.314	Sc Pos	151	47	5	75	.311
Scnd Half	247	70	7	48	.283	Clutch	87	30	4	26	.345

2002 Rankings (American League)

- 1st in sacrifice flies (12), highest percentage of pitches taken (66.4) and highest percentage of swings put into play (56.8)
- 2nd in assists at first base (101)
- 3rd in lowest percentage of swings on the first pitch (12.5) and fielding percentage at first base (.996)
- 4th in GDPs (19)
- Led the Mariners in doubles, walks, GDPs (19), slugging percentage, cleanup slugging percentage (.497), slugging percentage vs. righthanded pitchers (.517), on-base percentage vs. righthanded pitchers (.414) and batting average on a 3-2 count (.283)

Joel Pineiro

2002 Season

Despite his fine performance in 2001, Joel Pineiro began 2002 in the bullpen, waiting for a rotation spot to open up. One did in late April, and from that point to the end of the season he arguably was the team's most consistent starter. He put up 20 quality starts in 28 tries and had poor back-to-back starts only a couple of times all year.

Pitching

None of Pineiro's pitches are tremendous, but he gets a lot out of them by locating them with precision. He tries to get ahead with a low-90s fastball and a sinking two-seamer, and finish hitters off with his overhand curve, changeup and slider. He's always around the plate and can be hit, but rarely beats himself with bases on balls. He seemed to save his best for when he got into jams last year. Young and physically unimposing, he was stronger in the first half and when he pitched on longer rest.

Defense

Pineiro proved himself to be a quite capable fielder last year. He doesn't have a great pickoff move and is little better than average at stopping the running game, but he made progress in that regard over the course of the season.

2003 Outlook

Though Pineiro can be expected to be in the rotation all year, he may have a hard time duplicating last year's success right away. He'll need to build his stamina a little more in order to keep from wearing down during six months of starting. Also, he can't expect to pitch out of jams as successfully as he did last year. The proven route to success is to get into fewer jams in the first place.

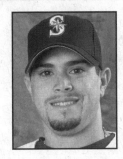

Position: SP
Bats: R **Throws:** R
Ht: 6' 1" **Wt:** 180

Opening Day Age: 24
Born: 9/25/78 in Rio Piedras, PR
ML Seasons: 3

Overall Statistics

	W	L	Pct.	ERA	G	GS	Sv	IP	H	BB	SO	HR	Ratio
'02	14	7	.667	3.24	37	28	0	194.1	189	54	136	24	1.25
Car.	21	9	.700	3.08	62	40	0	289.0	264	88	202	29	1.22

How Often He Throws Strikes

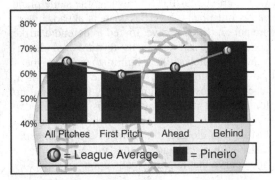

= League Average   = Pineiro

2002 Situational Stats

	W	L	ERA	Sv	IP		AB	H	HR	RBI	Avg
Home	7	3	2.55	0	98.2	LHB	397	107	14	41	.270
Road	7	4	3.95	0	95.2	RHB	342	82	10	30	.240
First Half	9	3	2.70	0	100.0	Sc Pos	150	29	5	45	.193
Scnd Half	5	4	3.82	0	94.1	Clutch	39	9	3	4	.231

2002 Rankings (American League)

- 2nd in lowest ERA at home and lowest batting average allowed with runners in scoring position
- 5th in most GDPs induced per nine innings (1.1)
- 8th in ERA and highest stolen-base percentage allowed (76.5)
- 9th in GDPs induced (23)
- 10th in most pitches thrown per batter (3.80)
- Led the Mariners in ERA, wild pitches (8), stolen bases allowed (13), GDPs induced (23), lowest ERA at home and lowest batting average allowed with runners in scoring position

Kazuhiro Sasaki

2002 Season

For the first two months of 2002, Kazuhiro Sasaki was as untouchable as a pitcher can be, notching 20 consecutive scoreless appearances. He took a sub-2.00 ERA into September, but came down with a sore elbow and was ineffective the rest of the way. It was a fine season for him overall, but it hurt that he was unable to contribute when the team was fighting for its survival in the wild-card race.

Pitching

One of the most effective strikeout pitches in the game is Sasaki's tumbling splitter. He sets it up with high-90s fastballs thrown on the same plane as his out pitch. Once Sasaki gets ahead, hitters are put on the defensive, forced to defend a strike zone that Sasaki lengthens upward and downward. This allows him to minimize walks; eight of the 20 he allowed last year came in September, when he'd lost something off his fastball and no longer could get ahead with it consistently. He can be vulnerable to the longball when he leaves a fastball too close to the heart of the plate, especially with a lefthanded hitter up. He also has a good curve that he rarely calls upon.

Defense

Sasaki gets a large percentage of strikeouts and flyballs, so he handles fewer chances afield; he botched two of 16 last year. Basestealers found him easy to run on in his rookie year, but he's tightened up his control of the running game considerably since then.

2003 Outlook

Sasaki had surgery after the season to remove a bone chip from his elbow. He's expected to recover fully, and if he does, the 35-year-old should have several more good seasons ahead. On the other hand, his September performance showed how quickly he can lose his edge when his fastball loses a couple of feet.

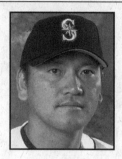

Position: RP
Bats: R **Throws:** R
Ht: 6' 4" **Wt:** 220

Opening Day Age: 35
Born: 2/22/68 in Sendai, Japan
ML Seasons: 3
Nickname: Daimajin
Pronunciation: kaz-oo-hero sa-sa-key

Overall Statistics

	W	L	Pct.	ERA	G	GS	Sv	IP	H	BB	SO	HR	Ratio
'02	4	5	.444	2.52	61	0	37	60.2	44	20	73	6	1.05
Car.	6	14	.300	2.98	193	0	119	190.0	134	62	213	22	1.03

How Often He Throws Strikes

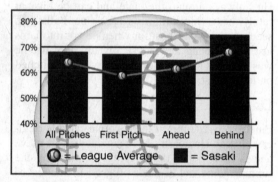

= League Average ◼ = Sasaki

2002 Situational Stats

	W	L	ERA	Sv	IP			AB	H	HR	RBI	Avg
Home	2	4	3.03	20	32.2	LHB		116	24	2	13	.207
Road	2	1	1.93	17	28.0	RHB		103	20	4	9	.194
First Half	2	3	1.36	21	33.0	Sc Pos		46	8	0	15	.174
Scnd Half	2	2	3.90	16	27.2	Clutch		152	35	5	21	.230

2002 Rankings (American League)

- 1st in blown saves (8)
- 3rd in most strikeouts per nine innings in relief (10.8)
- 5th in games finished (55) and save opportunities (45)
- 6th in saves, lowest batting average allowed in relief (.201) and lowest save percentage (82.2)
- Led the Mariners in saves, games finished (55), save opportunities (45), save percentage (82.2), blown saves (8), relief losses (5) and most strikeouts per nine innings in relief (10.8)

Ichiro Suzuki

2002 Season

Expectations were high in 2002 for the American League's reigning MVP and Rookie of the Year, and for the first half of the season Ichiro lived up to them, taking a .357 average into the All-Star break. In the second half, though, it was a different story. For whatever reason, he wasn't the same hitter. Even so, he finished with fine overall numbers and won his second consecutive Gold Glove.

Hitting

The game's preeminent contact hitter, Suzuki waits on the ball so long it often seems he takes two steps up the line and then flicks the ball into left field on his way to first. He hits the ball mostly on the ground, collecting hits on grounders that find holes and beating out plenty that don't. He was much more patient at the plate during the first half last year, but got away from that in the second half. One second-half change that was even more apparent was his tendency—seemingly by choice—to drive the ball more often. He certainly is capable of doing so effectively, but in the past he had been more choosy in picking his spots. Even when he wasn't going as well in the second half, pitchers still respected him, as Suzuki led the American League by a wide margin with 27 intentional walks.

Baserunning & Defense

Suzuki perhaps has the league's best combination of pure speed and first-step quickness. It makes him a terrific baserunner and basestealer, though for some reason he attempted only 15 steals in the second half and was thrown out on six of those chances. In the outfield, he's a natural center fielder who would play center on almost any other team. His powerful arm is well-known and rarely challenged.

2003 Outlook

Was Suzuki trying to hit for power in the second half? If so, will he keep trying, or will he go back to the style that had worked so well before? And if he keeps trying, might he succeed? Anything is possible. The only thing that's safe to say is that he'll remain a superstar.

Position: RF
Bats: L **Throws:** R
Ht: 5' 9" **Wt:** 160

Opening Day Age: 29
Born: 10/22/73 in Kasugai, Japan
ML Seasons: 2
Pronunciation: ee-chee-row

Overall Statistics

	G	AB	R	H	D	T	HR	RBI	SB	BB	SO	Avg	OBP	Slg
'02	157	647	111	208	27	8	8	51	31	68	62	.321	.388	.425
Car.	314	1339	238	450	61	16	16	120	87	98	115	.336	.385	.441

Where He Hits the Ball

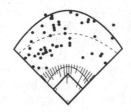 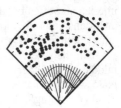

Vs. LHP   **Vs. RHP**

2002 Situational Stats

	AB	H	HR	RBI	Avg		AB	H	HR	RBI	Avg
Home	321	99	4	27	.308	LHP	180	64	3	19	.356
Road	326	109	4	24	.334	RHP	467	144	5	32	.308
First Half	347	124	2	28	.357	Sc Pos	119	43	1	42	.361
Scnd Half	300	84	6	23	.280	Clutch	104	32	0	13	.308

2002 Rankings (American League)

- 1st in singles, caught stealing (15), intentional walks (27), highest groundball-flyball ratio (2.5), steals of third (9), on-base percentage for a leadoff hitter (.383) and fielding percentage in right field (.991)
- 2nd in hits, batting average vs. lefthanded pitchers and batting average with two strikes (.268)
- 3rd in at-bats, triples, plate appearances (728), assists in right field (8) and lowest HR frequency (80.9 ABs per HR)
- Led the Mariners in batting average, at-bats, runs scored, hits, singles, triples, stolen bases, caught stealing (15), intentional walks (27), times on base (281) and plate appearances (728)

Dan Wilson

2002 Season

Veteran receiver Dan Wilson had his best offensive season in five years last year, hitting a career-high .295. As usual, though, his biggest contributions came on defense. Handling a pitching staff where it seemed every important pitcher relied heavily on some sort of breaking ball or offspeed pitch that was most effective when thrown in the dirt, Wilson never shied away from calling for the right pitch. He seldom let the ball go to the screen and gave his pitchers the confidence to keep the ball down.

Hitting

Wilson's solid year at the plate resulted from enjoying a season largely free of the nagging injuries that often befall catchers and had affected his offensive production in the past. He is a somewhat defensive hitter who takes a controlled cut. As such, he's best at hitting high fastballs up the middle or the other way, and Wilson protects the plate well with two strikes. He doesn't have a good eye, though, and is prone to chasing breaking balls down and away. He is a capable bunter.

Baserunning & Defense

Wilson is valued for his wide range of defensive skills, including his ability to call a game, his pitch-blocking skills and his accurate throwing arm. He committed only two errors in 2002, and even more impressively, had only two passed balls. He has more speed than most catchers, but not nearly enough to be any sort of basestealing threat.

2003 Outlook

Wilson was re-signed to a two-year deal over the winter, but that doesn't necessarily mean he'll continue to handle the bulk of the Mariners' catching chores. Expect him to cede an increasing share of the work to young Ben Davis.

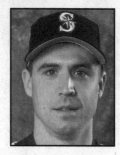

Position: C
Bats: R **Throws:** R
Ht: 6' 3" **Wt:** 214

Opening Day Age: 34
Born: 3/25/69 in Barrington, IL
ML Seasons: 11

Overall Statistics

	G	AB	R	H	D	T	HR	RBI	SB	BB	SO	Avg	OBP	Slg
'02	115	359	35	106	16	1	6	44	1	18	81	.295	.326	.396
Car.	1089	3524	384	936	183	11	82	441	23	239	644	.266	.314	.394

Where He Hits the Ball

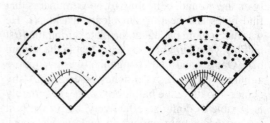

Vs. LHP	Vs. RHP

2002 Situational Stats

	AB	H	HR	RBI	Avg		AB	H	HR	RBI	Avg
Home	178	47	3	19	.264	LHP	104	30	3	14	.288
Road	181	59	3	25	.326	RHP	255	76	3	30	.298
First Half	185	58	3	26	.314	Sc Pos	106	26	1	34	.245
Scnd Half	174	48	3	18	.276	Clutch	43	14	2	4	.326

2002 Rankings (American League)

- 3rd in fielding percentage at catcher (.997)
- 6th in lowest batting average with the bases loaded (.111)
- 9th in sacrifice flies (8)
- Led the Mariners in batting average on an 0-2 count (.265)

James Baldwin

Position: SP
Bats: R **Throws:** R
Ht: 6' 3" **Wt:** 235

Opening Day Age: 31
Born: 7/15/71 in
Southern Pines, NC
ML Seasons: 8

Overall Statistics

	W	L	Pct.	ERA	G	GS	Sv	IP	H	BB	SO	HR	Ratio
'02	7	10	.412	5.28	30	23	0	150.0	179	49	88	26	1.52
Car.	79	69	.534	5.02	226	200	0	1245.0	1355	461	807	186	1.46

2002 Situational Stats

	W	L	ERA	Sv	IP		AB	H	HR	RBI	Avg
Home	4	5	4.29	0	86.0	LHB	297	96	11	36	.323
Road	3	5	6.61	0	64.0	RHB	303	83	15	51	.274
First Half	6	6	4.54	0	103.0	Sc Pos	144	45	6	57	.313
Scnd Half	1	4	6.89	0	47.0	Clutch	26	8	2	6	.308

2002 Season

Last winter, righthander James Baldwin signed a one-year free-agent deal to come to Seattle. He began the year as the Mariners' fourth starter and pitched indifferently over the first half. After the All-Star Game he had several rough starts and was removed from the rotation in mid-August. He hardly pitched the rest of the year.

Pitching & Defense

Baldwin had shoulder surgery two winters ago, and ever since then he's struggled to develop a consistent style. His curve lacks the snap it once had, and his 90-MPH fastball and cutter are hittable, so he has trouble putting hitters away. To survive, he's learned to move the ball around, but that only goes so far, especially on nights when he lacks his good command. He used to be rather error-prone in the field, but enjoyed his first errorless season last year. He's also become very good at holding baserunners close.

2003 Outlook

The Mariners declined to pick up Baldwin's $4 million option for 2003, making him a free agent. He'll catch on somewhere, but his inability to stay in the rotation for a strong Mariners team in a pitchers' park doesn't bode well.

Ben Davis

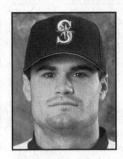

Position: C
Bats: B **Throws:** R
Ht: 6' 4" **Wt:** 214

Opening Day Age: 26
Born: 3/10/77 in
Chester, PA
ML Seasons: 5

Overall Statistics

	G	AB	R	H	D	T	HR	RBI	SB	BB	SO	Avg	OBP	Slg
'02	80	228	24	59	10	1	7	43	1	18	58	.259	.313	.404
Car.	338	1073	121	260	50	2	26	144	8	123	275	.242	.320	.365

2002 Situational Stats

	AB	H	HR	RBI	Avg		AB	H	HR	RBI	Avg
Home	102	22	1	14	.216	LHP	51	12	0	6	.235
Road	126	37	6	29	.294	RHP	177	47	7	37	.266
First Half	126	29	1	18	.230	Sc Pos	70	21	5	40	.300
Scnd Half	102	30	6	25	.294	Clutch	55	13	1	10	.236

2002 Season

With last winter's trade, Ben Davis went from San Diego, where he was the starting catcher, to Seattle, where Dan Wilson was the established first-stringer. Davis handled the smaller role as well as could have been expected, though, catching about a third of the time while showing development at the plate.

Hitting, Baserunning & Defense

Davis took a more aggressive approach at the plate last year, and it worked for him. He also showed better pop from the left side, after having shown slightly more extra-base power from the right side in past seasons. He finished strongly, avoiding the second-half slumps that have bothered him in seasons where he's caught a lot of games. He always had a strong arm, and improved footwork helped him post a more respectable caught-stealing percentage of 34.3 in 2002. He's otherwise above average defensively, if a bit unrefined at times. Speed is not part of his game.

2003 Outlook

The Mariners have re-signed Wilson, but they still consider Davis their catcher of the future. Expect him to gradually take over a bigger share of the catching chores over the next few seasons.

Seattle

John Halama

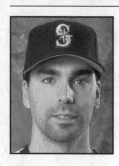

Position: RP/SP
Bats: L **Throws:** L
Ht: 6' 5" **Wt:** 210

Opening Day Age: 31
Born: 2/22/72 in
Brooklyn, NY
ML Seasons: 5
Pronunciation:
ha-LA-ma

Overall Statistics

	W	L	Pct.	ERA	G	GS	Sv	IP	H	BB	SO	HR	Ratio
'02	6	5	.545	3.56	31	10	0	101.0	112	33	70	9	1.44
Car.	42	32	.568	4.54	136	87	0	589.1	680	184	333	66	1.47

2002 Situational Stats

	W	L	ERA	Sv	IP		AB	H	HR	RBI	Avg
Home	4	1	3.86	0	51.1	LHB	134	33	5	13	.246
Road	2	4	3.26	0	49.2	RHB	265	79	4	25	.298
First Half	4	2	2.56	0	63.1	Sc Pos	86	24	3	30	.279
Scnd Half	2	3	5.26	0	37.2	Clutch	35	9	0	3	.257

2002 Season

For John Halama, 2002 was very much like the year before. He failed to hold onto a spot in the starting rotation and bounced back and forth between there and long relief. He even was sent down to the minors for a couple of weeks in August. He had the lowest ERA of his career, but was inconsistent when given chances to start.

Pitching & Defense

Halama is the stereotypical finesse lefty, working around his lack of a major league fastball by offering up curves, sinkers and changeups at different speeds and locations. For some reason, he's usually less effective against lefthanded hitters. Long relief agreed with him because he has trouble maintaining his effectiveness for more than a few innings. He has an excellent pickoff move and is very tough to run against. Fielding his position well comes naturally to him.

2003 Outlook

The Mariners may choose to non-tender Halama, having given him ample chances to prove himself as a starter. He's not well suited to any particular role, so finding a niche may be an uphill battle for him no matter where he ends up.

Shigetoshi Hasegawa

Position: RP
Bats: R **Throws:** R
Ht: 5'11" **Wt:** 178

Opening Day Age: 34
Born: 8/1/68 in Kobe, Japan
ML Seasons: 6
Pronunciation:
shig-eh-toe-shi hoss-eh-gawa

Overall Statistics

	W	L	Pct.	ERA	G	GS	Sv	IP	H	BB	SO	HR	Ratio
'02	8	3	.727	3.20	53	0	1	70.1	60	30	39	4	1.28
Car.	38	30	.559	3.76	340	0	8	512.2	496	200	339	62	1.36

2002 Situational Stats

	W	L	ERA	Sv	IP		AB	H	HR	RBI	Avg
Home	5	2	3.86	0	35.0	LHB	116	33	1	19	.284
Road	3	1	2.55	1	35.1	RHB	136	27	3	11	.199
First Half	4	1	1.01	1	35.2	Sc Pos	67	18	1	26	.269
Scnd Half	4	2	5.45	0	34.2	Clutch	108	23	1	9	.213

2002 Season

Signed as a free agent, Shigetoshi Hasegawa gave the Mariners a big boost over the first half of the season, replacing the injured Jeff Nelson as the club's top righthanded setup man. Hasegawa faltered in August and September, ceding his role back to Nelson, but overall it was one of his best years.

Pitching & Defense

Hasegawa has good command of an average fastball, a forkball and a slider. With no one on base, Hasegawa works up and down, but in double-play situations, he goes for groundballs and gets them, inducing a remarkable 13 twin-killings in 2002. He is not a strikeout pitcher by any stretch, and he's sharpest when he gets a day off between appearances. Not a single base was stolen off him last year, and only one was even attempted. He's a fine fielder.

2003 Outlook

Hasegawa was intent on returning and quickly re-signed with the Mariners after the season without pursuing free agency. Since his style contrasts sharply with Nelson's, the club might mix and match them in the seventh and eighth innings.

Mark McLemore

Position: LF/3B/CF
Bats: B **Throws:** R
Ht: 5'11" **Wt:** 207

Opening Day Age: 38
Born: 10/4/64 in San Diego, CA
ML Seasons: 17

Overall Statistics

	G	AB	R	H	D	T	HR	RBI	SB	BB	SO	Avg	OBP	Slg
'02	104	337	54	91	17	2	7	41	18	61	63	.270	.380	.395
Car.	1656	5633	880	1468	226	45	49	557	267	796	879	.261	.351	.343

2002 Situational Stats

	AB	H	HR	RBI	Avg		AB	H	HR	RBI	Avg
Home	166	45	4	21	.271	LHP	33	5	1	10	.152
Road	171	46	3	20	.269	RHP	304	86	6	31	.283
First Half	225	67	6	33	.298	Sc Pos	69	20	4	36	.290
Scnd Half	112	24	1	8	.214	Clutch	48	13	0	6	.271

2002 Season

Mark McLemore's role with the Mariners continued to change in 2002 as the team's needs changed. He'd spent 2001 as the club's regular non-regular, splitting time between several different positions, but last year, he mainly platooned in left field, batting second against righthanded pitchers. He was in the midst of another fine year before missing almost all of September with elbow and groin injuries.

Hitting, Baserunning & Defense

A switch-hitter, McLemore is better from the left side and gets most of his at-bats against righthanders. A spray hitter, his ability to work walks and move runners makes him a good fit in the No. 2 hole. He has good range in left and always has been a good defensive second baseman. He also can fill it at third or move over to center in a pinch. Nagging injuries slowed him a bit last year, but he still was able to steal a base when it counted.

2003 Outlook

The acquisition of Randy Winn to play left field should free up McLemore to return to the role in which he was so valuable in 2001. Now 38 and more susceptible to minor injuries, he may play a bit less but should remain productive.

Jeff Nelson

Position: RP
Bats: R **Throws:** R
Ht: 6' 8" **Wt:** 235

Opening Day Age: 36
Born: 11/17/66 in Baltimore, MD
ML Seasons: 11

Overall Statistics

	W	L	Pct.	ERA	G	GS	Sv	IP	H	BB	SO	HR	Ratio
'02	3	2	.600	3.94	41	0	2	45.2	36	27	55	4	1.38
Car.	42	37	.532	3.28	644	0	23	666.1	530	358	703	44	1.33

2002 Situational Stats

	W	L	ERA	Sv	IP		AB	H	HR	RBI	Avg
Home	1	1	4.44	1	24.1	LHB	76	17	1	6	.224
Road	2	1	3.38	1	21.1	RHB	87	19	3	12	.218
First Half	1	1	6.75	0	14.2	Sc Pos	55	9	2	15	.164
Scnd Half	2	1	2.61	2	31.0	Clutch	84	23	1	10	.274

2002 Season

Jeff Nelson redeemed his 2002 season with strong work down the stretch. His year got off to a rocky start before he underwent elbow surgery in May. He returned in late June and took awhile to come around, but he eventually found his groove in August and September, reclaiming his role as the Mariners' top righthanded setup man.

Pitching & Defense

Nelson's out pitch is a big-breaking slider that starts out looking like a strike and winds up completely out of a batter's reach. Righthanded hitters find his funky sidearm delivery especially tough. He's always hard to hit but gives up his share of walks when he can't get hitters to chase his slider. He holds batters fairly well, but his slider is a good pitch to run on. He's a capable fielder who rarely hurts himself with the glove, though he hasn't had more than a dozen total chances in a season since 1997.

2003 Outlook

Having a healthy Jeff Nelson all season should make a big difference to the Seattle bullpen this year. He's getting up there in years, but he showed late last season that he still can be as unhittable as ever.

Desi Relaford

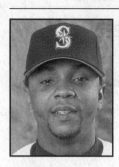

Position:
SS/3B/LF/2B/RF
Bats: B **Throws:** R
Ht: 5' 9" **Wt:** 174

Opening Day Age: 29
Born: 9/16/73 in
Valdosta, GA
ML Seasons: 7

Overall Statistics

	G	AB	R	H	D	T	HR	RBI	SB	BB	SO	Avg	OBP	Slg
'02	112	329	55	88	13	2	6	43	10	33	51	.267	.339	.374
Car.	597	1823	234	453	93	12	25	199	53	195	323	.248	.329	.354

2002 Situational Stats

	AB	H	HR	RBI	Avg			AB	H	HR	RBI	Avg
Home	147	40	1	21	.272	LHP	89	18	1	7	.202
Road	182	48	5	22	.264	RHP	240	70	5	36	.292
First Half	166	45	2	25	.271	Sc Pos	80	22	0	35	.275
Scnd Half	163	43	4	18	.264	Clutch	63	20	2	12	.317

2002 Season

Desi Relaford plugged just about every hole the Mariners sprung last year. When shortstop Carlos Guillen had a hand injury during the first half, Relaford filled in. Later, when Jeff Cirillo fell out of favor, Relaford was the one who picked up the slack at third. He also backed up second base and the outfield corners. With his contributions in the field, at the plate and on the bases, he was by far the club's most valuable reserve.

Hitting, Baserunning & Defense

After coming to the majors as a very weak hitter, the switch-hitting Relaford has become a rather proficient hitter from the left side. He remains streaky but can drive the ball at times. He also can lay down a bunt or work a walk. He has the quick feet of a shortstop and an arm more than strong enough for third. He played the outfield for the first time last year and acquitted himself well in left and right. He accelerates quickly and is one of the fastest baserunners on the team.

2003 Outlook

Relaford is well suited to the role he was given last year. Playing a single position would be a waste of his versatility, so he probably will continue to get plenty of playing time between several different spots.

Arthur Rhodes

Position: RP
Bats: L **Throws:** L
Ht: 6' 2" **Wt:** 205

Opening Day Age: 33
Born: 10/24/69 in Waco, TX
ML Seasons: 12

Overall Statistics

	W	L	Pct.	ERA	G	GS	Sv	IP	H	BB	SO	HR	Ratio
'02	10	4	.714	2.33	66	0	2	69.2	45	13	81	4	0.83
Car.	66	48	.579	4.34	447	61	14	829.1	717	370	820	94	1.31

2002 Situational Stats

	W	L	ERA	Sv	IP		AB	H	HR	RBI	Avg
Home	7	2	2.82	2	38.1	LHB	120	19	1	20	.158
Road	3	2	1.72	0	31.1	RHB	121	26	3	10	.215
First Half	5	1	2.76	1	32.2	Sc Pos	51	15	2	26	.294
Scnd Half	5	3	1.95	1	37.0	Clutch	196	37	3	23	.189

2002 Season

For the second straight year, Arthur Rhodes was one of the top lefthanded setup men in baseball. He was second in the majors with 10 victories in relief, and tied for second in the American League with 27 holds. Lefthanded hitters batted just .158 against him, and he was one of the top relievers with a .187 opponents' average overall.

Pitching & Defense

Rhodes works mostly with a mid-90s fastball and hard slider. He works up and down with the heater and has good enough control of it to get ahead and force batters to chase either the slider or a fastball up and out of the zone. In double-play situations, he's able to get grounders by keeping the ball down and using his curve and changeup. Only three bases have been stolen off him in the last three years, and Rhodes hasn't committed an error since 1998.

2003 Outlook

Rhodes has one more year left on his contract with Seattle and should continue to see similar late-inning work. With closer Kazuhiro Sasaki coming off elbow surgery to remove bone chips, Rhodes might be asked to step in temporarily if Sasaki's arm is slow to come around.

Ruben Sierra

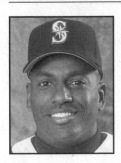

Position: LF/DH
Bats: B **Throws:** R
Ht: 6' 1" **Wt:** 215

Opening Day Age: 37
Born: 10/6/65 in Rio Piedras, PR
ML Seasons: 16

Overall Statistics

	G	AB	R	H	D	T	HR	RBI	SB	BB	SO	Avg	OBP	Slg
'02	122	419	47	113	23	0	13	60	4	31	66	.270	.319	.418
Car.	1898	7232	994	1950	386	57	276	1181	139	545	1089	.270	.317	.453

2002 Situational Stats

	AB	H	HR	RBI	Avg		AB	H	HR	RBI	Avg
Home	218	54	6	23	.248	LHP	143	38	1	14	.266
Road	201	59	7	37	.294	RHP	276	75	12	46	.272
First Half	291	87	11	51	.299	Sc Pos	142	36	4	48	.254
Scnd Half	128	26	2	9	.203	Clutch	69	17	1	7	.246

2002 Season

Signed to play left field, Ruben Sierra hit well as a DH for most of the first half while Edgar Martinez was on the disabled list. After Martinez returned, Sierra slumped and began to get crowded out. He strained his quadriceps in August and played infrequently over the final six weeks of the season.

Hitting, Baserunning & Defense

Historically, Sierra has been a better hitter from the right side. He still hits for a decent average from that side, but now has better power from the left. His lack of plate discipline can be exploited by a pitcher who makes him expand the zone. His speed no longer is above average, and his defensive skills have eroded to the point that former manager Lou Piniella was reluctant to let him do more than DH.

2003 Outlook

Sierra became a free agent over the winter. His bat might be useful in a part-time role, and he might bounce back a bit if he's able to land in a better ballpark, but at age 37, his body probably is not up to playing every day.

Ismael Valdes

Position: SP
Bats: R **Throws:** R
Ht: 6' 4" **Wt:** 225

Opening Day Age: 29
Born: 8/21/73 in Ciudad Victoria, Mexico
ML Seasons: 9
Pronunciation: EES-mah-ALE val-DEZ

Overall Statistics

	W	L	Pct.	ERA	G	GS	Sv	IP	H	BB	SO	HR	Ratio
'02	8	12	.400	4.18	31	31	0	196.0	194	47	102	26	1.23
Car.	80	86	.482	3.76	255	228	1	1491.2	1458	423	1032	172	1.26

2002 Situational Stats

	W	L	ERA	Sv	IP		AB	H	HR	RBI	Avg
Home	5	5	4.44	0	93.1	LHB	411	105	15	44	.255
Road	3	7	3.94	0	102.2	RHB	344	89	11	41	.259
First Half	5	6	3.91	0	99.0	Sc Pos	145	40	7	60	.276
Scnd Half	3	6	4.45	0	97.0	Clutch	42	10	1	3	.238

2002 Season

Ismael Valdes signed a one-year deal with the Rangers last winter, and generally pitched decently for them, despite a wide assortment of minor injuries. He was dealt to Seattle in August and did the same for the Mariners, although he was bombed in his last start after the club had been eliminated from contention.

Pitching & Defense

With an average fastball and a fairly good curve, Valdes needs to have good command to be effective. He has it more often than not, but he's prone to all sorts of aches and pains—including chronic blisters—that can throw off his command just enough to keep him from staying ahead in the count. He'll mix in a slider and changeup for show. He's an adequate fielder who has become quite adept at controlling the running game by throwing to first repeatedly and getting the ball to the plate quickly.

2003 Outlook

Valdes now is in the same situation he was in last winter, looking for a team that needs middle-of-the-rotation help. At this point, his best-case scenario is to stay healthy enough to throw 200 decent innings.

Other Seattle Mariners

Paul Abbott (Pos: RHP, Age: 35)

	W	L	Pct.	ERA	G	GS	Sv	IP	H	BB	SO	HR	Ratio
'02	1	3	.250	11.96	7	5	0	26.1	40	20	22	5	2.28
Car.	39	24	.619	4.63	132	85	0	577.0	529	309	418	71	1.45

After going 17-4 in 2001, a torn labrum led to June surgery in '02. Abbott faces an uncertain 2003 after being released. The M's can't bring him back until May 15, and his health still may be an issue. 2003 Outlook: C

Willie Bloomquist (Pos: LF, Age: 25, Bats: R)

	G	AB	R	H	D	T	HR	RBI	SB	BB	SO	Avg	OBP	Slg
'02	12	33	11	15	4	0	0	7	3	5	2	.455	.526	.576
Car.	12	33	11	15	4	0	0	7	3	5	2	.455	.526	.576

Bloomquist had an OK season at Triple-A Tacoma, but turned red-hot with Seattle, swinging with authority and giving the struggling M's a lift. Able to play several positions, he's up for a utility role. 2003 Outlook: C

Pat Borders (Pos: C, Age: 39, Bats: R)

	G	AB	R	H	D	T	HR	RBI	SB	BB	SO	Avg	OBP	Slg
'02	4	4	0	2	1	0	0	1	0	0	1	.500	.500	.750
Car.	1010	3056	267	784	156	12	67	328	6	149	508	.257	.292	.381

Borders, who turns 40 in May, spent his third straight season playing Triple-A ball. Talk about resisting retirement, considering that at best he'd be a third-string catcher in the majors. 2003 Outlook: C

Doug Creek (Pos: LHP, Age: 34)

	W	L	Pct.	ERA	G	GS	Sv	IP	H	BB	SO	HR	Ratio
'02	3	2	.600	5.82	52	0	0	55.2	57	35	56	10	1.65
Car.	7	14	.333	5.29	238	3	1	253.1	222	180	263	40	1.59

The Mariners traded for Creek in July, probably because lefties have a .210 average against him lifetime. But they slugged .432 against him in an off year. The Jays gave him a one-year deal this fall. 2003 Outlook: B

Brian Fitzgerald (Pos: LHP, Age: 28)

	W	L	Pct.	ERA	G	GS	Sv	IP	H	BB	SO	HR	Ratio
'02	0	0	–	8.53	6	0	0	6.1	11	2	3	2	2.05
Car.	0	0	–	8.53	6	0	0	6.1	11	2	3	2	2.05

Fitzgerald was recalled early in the year and got roughed up. He wasn't much better at Triple-A Tacoma before he was claimed off waivers by the Rockies in August. 2003 Outlook: C

Ryan Franklin (Pos: RHP, Age: 30)

	W	L	Pct.	ERA	G	GS	Sv	IP	H	BB	SO	HR	Ratio
'02	7	5	.583	4.02	41	12	0	118.2	117	22	65	14	1.17
Car.	12	6	.667	3.89	85	12	0	208.1	203	54	131	29	1.23

Franklin has quietly and steadily served in a middle relief role for the Mariners the last two years. He even stepped into a starting role briefly in 2002, going 4-5 with a 3.91 ERA in 12 starts. 2003 Outlook: B

Charles Gipson (Pos: LF/RF, Age: 30, Bats: R)

	G	AB	R	H	D	T	HR	RBI	SB	BB	SO	Avg	OBP	Slg
'02	79	72	22	17	5	2	0	8	4	9	14	.236	.329	.361
Car.	331	296	72	70	14	7	0	27	12	28	65	.236	.312	.331

Gipson has spent the entire year in the majors the last two seasons, accumulating a total of 136 at-bats in 173 games primarily as a defensive replacement. He's batted .228 over that span. 2003 Outlook: C

Justin Kaye (Pos: RHP, Age: 26)

	W	L	Pct.	ERA	G	GS	Sv	IP	H	BB	SO	HR	Ratio
'02	0	0	–	12.00	3	0	0	3.0	6	1	3	0	2.33
Car.	0	0	–	12.00	3	0	0	3.0	6	1	3	0	2.33

Kaye was better at Triple-A Tacoma in 2001 than he was last summer, but he got a brief first taste of the majors in May. He has a good slider, but a better fastball would help his cause. The Red Sox signed him to a minor league deal in November. 2003 Outlook: C

Julio Mateo (Pos: RHP, Age: 25)

	W	L	Pct.	ERA	G	GS	Sv	IP	H	BB	SO	HR	Ratio
'02	0	0	–	4.29	12	0	0	21.0	20	12	15	2	1.52
Car.	0	0	–	4.29	12	0	0	21.0	20	12	15	2	1.52

Mateo pitched in the high minors for the first time in 2002, handling the Double-A and Triple-A levels quite well and not embarrassing himself in Seattle in three trips to the majors during the season. 2003 Outlook: C

Jose Offerman (Pos: 1B/DH, Age: 34, Bats: B)

	G	AB	R	H	D	T	HR	RBI	SB	BB	SO	Avg	OBP	Slg
'02	101	284	48	66	12	1	5	31	9	37	38	.232	.320	.335
Car.	1488	5404	807	1483	235	69	53	502	171	732	866	.274	.361	.373

Offerman escaped Boston after he refused to enter an August contest as a pinch-hitter. The M's picked him up off waivers, but he wasn't helpful down the stretch. The free agent's big-money days are over. 2003 Outlook: C

Scott Podsednik (Pos: LF, Age: 27, Bats: L)

	G	AB	R	H	D	T	HR	RBI	SB	BB	SO	Avg	OBP	Slg
'02	14	20	2	4	0	0	1	5	0	4	6	.200	.320	.350
Car.	19	26	3	5	0	1	1	8	0	4	7	.192	.290	.385

Podsednik has posted OK numbers in his first two Triple-A seasons. He hasn't hit for average in two brief stints in Seattle, but he has eight RBI in 26 at-bats. The Brewers claimed him off waivers in October. 2003 Outlook: C

Luis Ugueto (Pos: DH/2B, Age: 24, Bats: B)

	G	AB	R	H	D	T	HR	RBI	SB	BB	SO	Avg	OBP	Slg
'02	62	23	19	5	0	0	1	1	8	2	8	.217	.280	.348
Car.	62	23	19	5	0	0	1	1	8	2	8	.217	.280	.348

Ugueto was a Rule 5 pickup from the Marlins a year ago. He aced out Alex Arias for a roster spot with a decent spring and stayed all year, except for a three-week stint on the disabled list. 2003 Outlook: C

Mark Watson (**Pos**: LHP, **Age**: 29)

	W	L	Pct.	ERA	G	GS	Sv	IP	H	BB	SO	HR	Ratio
'02	1	0	1.000	18.00	3	0	0	4.0	8	4	1	1	3.00
Car.	1	1	.500	12.19	9	0	0	10.1	20	6	5	1	2.52

His second cup-of-coffee last July didn't go any better than his first in 2000. Like many 2002 playoff pitchers, Watson took a beating from Anaheim. The Reds have signed him to a minor league deal. 2003 Outlook: C

Ron Wright (**Pos**: DH, **Age**: 27, **Bats**: R)

	G	AB	R	H	D	T	HR	RBI	SB	BB	SO	Avg	OBP	Slg
'02	1	3	0	0	0	0	0	0	0	0	1	.000	.000	.000
Car.	1	3	0	0	0	0	0	0	0	0	1	.000	.000	.000

Back problems sidetracked a promising career a few years ago, but Wright got his first cup-of-coffee in the majors in the midst of two solid Triple-A seasons in a row. He was gone before it cooled. 2003 Outlook: C

Seattle

Seattle Mariners Minor League Prospects

Organization Overview:

While injuries ruined the 2002 season for pitchers Ryan Anderson, Cha Baek, Jeff Heaverlo and Matt Thornton, some of the sting might have been taken out of those losses by the emergence of potential star Jose Lopez. The Mariners have developed a reputation for international signings from the Pacific Rim, ranging from Japanese stars Ichiro Suzuki and Kazuhiro Sasaki to minor leaguers from Korea and Australia. But keep an eye on this teenage shortstop from Venezuela. And despite the injuries, the Mariners still may get 2003 pitching help from Rafael Soriano, Aaron Taylor and the up-and-coming Clint Nageotte.

Shin-Soo Choo

Position: OF   **Opening Day Age:** 20
Bats: L **Throws:** L   **Born:** 7/13/82 in Pusan,
Ht: 5' 11" **Wt:** 178   Korea

Recent Statistics

	G	AB	R	H	D	T	HR	RBI	SB	BB	SO	Avg
2001 R Mariners	51	199	51	60	10	10	4	35	12	34	49	.302
2001 A Wisconsin	3	13	1	6	0	0	0	3	2	1	9	.462
2002 A Wisconsin	119	420	69	127	24	8	6	48	34	70	98	.302
2002 A San Berndno	11	39	14	12	5	1	1	9	3	9	9	.308

The Mariners signed Choo in August 2000, and he adjusted quickly to life and baseball in the United States. He led the Rookie-level Arizona League in runs, triples and walks in his 2001 debut, displaying his line-drive stroke and advanced plate patience. The Mariners believe the muscular Choo, who has good tools, will add more pop as he gets older. He easily handled the move to full-season ball last summer, earning a roster spot in the 2002 Futures Game. Choo made good progress on adjusting to offspeed stuff, but he still must work on his approach to breaking balls and changeups to reduce his strikeouts. While he lacks top-flight speed, he has the instincts to steal bases and play center field. He played center at both Class-A stops in 2002, although he's more comfortable in right.

Kenny Kelly

Position: OF   **Opening Day Age:** 24
Bats: R **Throws:** R   **Born:** 1/26/79 in Plant
Ht: 6' 3" **Wt:** 180   City, FL

Recent Statistics

	G	AB	R	H	D	T	HR	RBI	SB	BB	SO	Avg
2001 AA San Antonio	121	478	72	125	20	5	11	46	18	45	111	.262
2002 AAA Tacoma	122	391	51	97	13	10	11	53	11	26	93	.248

A Tampa Bay second-rounder in 1997, Kelly played pro ball and college football until he abandoned quarterbacking duties at Miami early in 2000. He has terrific tools—impressive bat speed, solid range, running ability and a strong arm—but he's lost development time to

football. The Mariners acquired Kelly in April 2001, and he began showing progress and more power during the second half of the season at Double-A San Antonio. He didn't come on nearly as much at Triple-A Tacoma in 2002. Making consistent contact and plate discipline still are areas that need work. He excels at hitting the fastball, but must improve against breaking balls. Defensively, he is much more advanced.

Jose Lopez

Position: SS   **Opening Day Age:** 19
Bats: R **Throws:** R   **Born:** 11/24/83 in
Ht: 6' 2" **Wt:** 170   Anzoategui, VZ

Recent Statistics

	G	AB	R	H	D	T	HR	RBI	SB	BB	SO	Avg
2001 A Everett	70	289	42	74	15	0	2	20	13	13	44	.256
2002 A San Berndno	123	522	82	169	39	5	8	60	31	27	45	.324

Signed in 2000, Lopez debuted in the short-season Northwest League in 2001 as the youngest player in the circuit. He was the league's best defensive shortstop, featuring the soft hands, range, arm and agility to excel at the position. Lopez also fared well enough with the bat to jump to high Class-A San Bernardino for his first full pro season last summer. The teenager was one of the league's youngest players, but that didn't keep him from making good contact and showing more power. He worked the learning curve all season, continually making adjustments and proving instinctive. His dramatic leap forward guarantees that Lopez will remain one of the youngest players in his league.

Clint Nageotte

Position: P   **Opening Day Age:** 22
Bats: R **Throws:** R   **Born:** 10/25/80 in
Ht: 6' 4" **Wt:** 200   Parma, OH

Recent Statistics

	W	L	ERA	G	GS	Sv	IP	H	R	BB	SO	HR
2001 A Wisconsin	11	8	3.13	28	26	0	152.1	141	65	50	187	10
2002 A San Berndno	9	6	4.54	29	29	0	164.2	153	101	68	214	10

A 1999 fifth-round pick, Nageotte emerged as one of the best pitching prospects in the Class-A Midwest League in 2001. He displayed above-average pitches in his low-90s fastball and nasty slider, going 11-8 (3.13) and leading the circuit with 187 strikeouts in 152.1 innings. After a strong follow-up at high Class-A San Bernardino in 2002, when he set the club strikeout record, his fastball-slider combo is close to major league-ready. The fastball tops out at 93-94 MPH, and only his command of its release point is creating inconsistency with the pitch. His changeup isn't as far along and his overall command still needs some fine-tuning before Nageotte is ready to help in Seattle. His aggressive and competitive nature serves him well on the mound.

Chris Snelling

Position: OF
Bats: L **Throws:** L
Ht: 5' 10" **Wt:** 165

Opening Day Age: 21
Born: 12/3/81 in North Miami, FL

Recent Statistics

	G	AB	R	H	D	T	HR	RBI	SB	BB	SO	Avg
2002 AA San Antonio	23	89	10	29	9	2	1	12	5	12	11	.326
2002 AL Seattle	8	27	2	4	0	0	1	3	0	2	4	.148

Signed in 1999, Snelling has great makeup, phenomenal instincts and an all-out, play-to-win approach. He also has an advanced ability to make contact and hit for average, plus he draws walks, shows gap power, flashes some range and plays solid defense. He's batted better than .300 in every minor league season. It didn't matter that he broke his thumb in spring training and made his Double-A debut on May 2. Snelling thrived against Double-A pitching, though big leaguers cooled him off after his recall by pounding him inside. Soon after his callup, Snelling tore the ACL in his left knee and had surgery, but he should be ready before camp breaks. A number of injuries have slowed his progress.

Rafael Soriano

Position: P
Bats: R **Throws:** R
Ht: 6' 1" **Wt:** 175

Opening Day Age: 23
Born: 12/19/79 in San Jose, DR

Recent Statistics

	W	L	ERA	G	GS	Sv	IP	H	R	BB	SO	HR
2002 AA San Antonio	2	3	2.31	10	8	0	46.2	32	13	15	52	6
2002 AL Seattle	0	3	4.56	10	8	1	47.1	45	25	16	32	8

Once a light-hitting outfielder, Soriano became a pitcher prior to the 1999 season. He not only had a better feel for pitching than expected, but also a moving mid-90s fastball that initially generated lots of strikeouts. He lacked secondary pitches early on, but he's been a dominant pitcher for two minor league seasons now with an impressive fastball-slider combo that is major league-caliber. Soriano also pitches inside and works both sides of the plate aggressively. He's getting more consistent with his changeup, a pitch he's always had a feel for but has lacked command. Overall consistency is all that's keeping him from sticking in Seattle. While he was nearly perfect in relief with the Mariners, Soriano could work his way into the Seattle rotation.

Jamal Strong

Position: OF
Bats: R **Throws:** R
Ht: 5' 10" **Wt:** 175

Opening Day Age: 24
Born: 8/5/78 in Pasadena, CA

Recent Statistics

	G	AB	R	H	D	T	HR	RBI	SB	BB	SO	Avg
2001 A Wisconsin	51	184	41	65	12	1	0	19	35	40	27	.353
2001 A San Berndno	81	331	74	103	11	2	0	32	47	51	60	.311
2002 AA San Antonio	127	503	63	140	16	5	1	31	46	62	87	.278

Drafted in 2000, Strong lacks extra-base pop, but calls on impressive little-ball skills. He's a good center fielder who has terrific speed and can run the ball down. He has a bit of an inside-out swing, which he uses to hit the ball on the ground. With a .406 career OBP in the minors, Strong has shown he can draw walks. Once on base, he's dangerous. Strong has averaged 63 steals a year in three seasons and stole 46 in 2002 at the Double-A level. Learning to read pitchers on steal attempts is ongoing. Strong got off to a slow start at San Antonio last summer, but worked hard to rebound under the guidance of coaches. His OBP dipped below .400 for the first time, and consistently getting on base in the high minors is his ticket to Seattle.

Aaron Taylor

Position: P
Bats: R **Throws:** R
Ht: 6' 7" **Wt:** 230

Opening Day Age: 25
Born: 8/20/77 in Valdosta, GA

Recent Statistics

	W	L	ERA	G	GS	Sv	IP	H	R	BB	SO	HR
2002 AA San Antonio	4	3	2.34	61	0	24	77.0	51	28	34	93	5
2002 AL Seattle	0	0	9.00	5	0	0	5.0	8	5	0	6	2

A Braves pick in 1996, Taylor left the Mariners' camp during spring training in 2001, frustrated by his lack of progress and a career 6.26 ERA, mostly as a starter. He returned a week later and his career turned around with a solid 2001 season in the Class-A Wisconsin bullpen. Better command has helped Taylor since he quit and went home. He wasn't getting his slider and splitter over the plate consistently and was relying too much on his mid-90s fastball early in 2002 at Double-A San Antonio. Hitters were attacking his heater, but eventually he called on his slider and splitter successfully. With the progress he made mixing his pitches, this future closer soon may be in the Seattle pen. Consistent command of all three pitches is the key.

Others to Watch

Southpaw **Ryan Anderson** (23) and righthanders **Cha Baek** (22) and **Jeff Heaverlo** (25) endured lost seasons in 2002, due to injuries. Anderson, once known for a lively mid-90s fastball and devastating curve, has had surgery for a torn labrum in each of the last two springs. By mid-November, Anderson was throwing at distances of 80 feet, but not working off a mound. He won't be rushed. Baek, who throws a low-90s fastball and late-breaking slider, had Tommy John surgery during the 2001 season and is on course to return in 2003. Heaverlo, a polished college pitcher with a good sinker, followed three solid minor league seasons with labrum surgery early in 2002. He worked off a mound in instructional league and should be ready for spring training. . . Aussie lefthander **Travis Blackley** (20) underwent surgery for bone chips a year ago, but he rebounded strongly from extensive rehab to post a 3.49 ERA and fan 152 in 121.1 innings at high Class-A San Bernardino in 2002. His fastball comes in at 88-89 MPH, and he has a good breaking ball, changeup and feel for pitching.

Seattle

257

Tropicana Field

Offense

Five years is enough time to prove that Tropicana Field is not going to be the offensive bandbox that many had envisioned. While the Devil Rays' impotent offensive teams haven't helped the equation, the number of dingers and doubles hit there usually ends up being in the middle of the league. There have been an abundance of triples as a result of deep gaps and oddly angled walls.

Defense

While Tropicana features an unusual combination of a FieldTurf playing surface and all-dirt base paths, there have not been a lot of problems or complaints with the fast infield, though some opponents have trouble the first time in. There *are* problems with the outfield, both with balls bouncing off the catwalks and balls being lost against the off-white roof. The large outfield surface begs for speedy defenders.

Who It Helps the Most

The player who had the best stats at Tropicana Field no longer plays there, as Randy Winn was sent to Seattle in the deal for manager Lou Piniella. The dimensions have been favorable to lefthander Aubrey Huff, who hit 17 of his 23 homers there. Lefthanded pitcher Joe Kennedy also has learned to pitch effectively there, using the roomy outfield to his advantage.

Who It Hurts the Most

Ben Grieve should benefit from the dimensions, but his numbers were much better on the road. The tricky outfield configuration also makes it tougher for him defensively. The somewhat fast infield has made it more difficult for Brent Abernathy and other infielders who don't have great range. Closer Esteban Yan also has struggled at home.

Rookies & Newcomers

Carl Crawford's July arrival showed the immense benefit of having athletic players, as he covered the spacious gaps and used the large field to his advantage. Center fielder Rocco Baldelli should enjoy the same advantages, as will right fielder Josh Hamilton if he ever gets over his injuries.

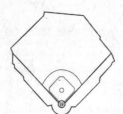

Dimensions: LF-315, LCF-370, CF-404, RCF-370, RF-322

Capacity: 43,772

Elevation: 15 feet

Surface: Turf

Foul Territory: Average

Park Factors

2002 Season

	Home Games			Away Games			
	Devil Rays	Opp	Total	Devil Rays	Opp	Total	Index
G	72	72	144	71	71	142	
Avg	.264	.268	.266	.239	.293	.266	100
AB	2492	2585	5077	2445	2383	4828	104
R	308	406	714	287	421	708	99
H	659	694	1353	585	698	1283	104
2B	125	148	273	126	150	276	94
3B	16	14	30	13	8	21	136
HR	54	88	142	63	105	168	80
BB	206	288	494	201	270	471	100
SO	488	455	943	503	364	867	103
E	49	39	88	61	45	106	82
E-Infield	43	35	78	50	37	87	88
LHB-Avg	.274	.291	.282	.253	.309	.279	101
LHB-HR	35	50	85	32	50	82	98
RHB-Avg	.256	.251	.253	.227	.281	.255	99
RHB-HR	19	38	57	31	55	86	63

2000-2002

	Home Games			Away Games			
	Devil Rays	Opp	Total	Devil Rays	Opp	Total	Index
G	215	215	430	215	215	430	
Avg	.260	.272	.266	.250	.283	.266	100
AB	7297	7708	15005	7436	7173	14609	103
R	920	1179	2099	904	1197	2101	100
H	1900	2097	3997	1861	2030	3891	103
2B	397	440	837	346	416	762	107
3B	37	46	83	24	33	57	142
HR	172	274	446	194	282	476	91
BB	673	750	1423	618	801	1419	98
SO	1389	1401	2790	1484	1166	2650	103
E	157	126	283	174	130	304	93
E-Infield	139	113	252	144	111	255	99
LHB-Avg	.267	.278	.273	.263	.299	.281	97
LHB-HR	75	128	203	78	124	202	97
RHB-Avg	.256	.267	.261	.241	.270	.255	102
RHB-HR	97	146	243	116	158	274	87

2002 Rankings (American League)

- Third-highest hit factor
- Third-highest triple factor
- Second-lowest error factor
- Second-lowest RHB home-run factor

Lou Piniella

2002 Season

Lou Piniella knew that short of a World Series championship, there was no way the 2002 Mariners could followup the success of the 2001 team. And as much as he pushed the players—and the front office—the reality was that last year's team wasn't good enough to get it done. Piniella did what he could, but the injuries and inconsistent performances robbed him of too many weapons.

Offense

Piniella likes to make things happen, and it will be interesting to see how the young Devil Rays respond. Piniella's Mariners led the league in steals of third and double steals and were among the more successful hit-and-run squads. It's likely he will try to do similar things in Tampa, attempting to take advantage of what speed the team has while making up for a lack of power. Piniella and hitting coach Lee Elia likely will have a big impact on the mental approach of the young hitters, preaching patience and discipline.

Pitching & Defense

Piniella is said to have mellowed in recent years, and that may be a good thing for the young Tampa Bay pitchers who are going to test his patience. Too often last season, Devil Rays hurlers lacked aggressiveness and tried to nibble too much. Under Piniella, they either will go after the batters or go somewhere else. Piniella also knows the value of a strong defense, and he will sacrifice some offense for it. His first priority was to find a strong defensive shortstop with good range, knowing that will help the pitching staff.

2003 Outlook

As much excitement and enthusiasm the hiring of Piniella has generated, the reality is that it is going to be another long year in Tampa Bay as the Rays cut payroll and build toward 2004 and beyond. But Piniella never has accepted losing before, and he's not going to start now, even at age 59. The Rays are not going to compete, but they'll soon be better than expected, and that really won't be a surprise.

Born: 8/28/43 in Tampa, FL

Playing Experience: 1964-1984, Bal, Cle, KC, NYY

Managerial Experience: 16 seasons

Manager Statistics

Year	Team, Lg	W	L	Pct	GB	Finish
2002	Seattle, AL	93	69	.574	10.0	3rd West
16 Seasons		1319	1135	.537	–	–

2002 Starting Pitchers by Days Rest

	<=3	4	5	6+
Mariners Starts	0	97	38	19
Mariners ERA	–	4.18	4.70	4.02
AL Avg Starts	1	83	44	24
AL ERA	7.15	4.59	4.27	5.03

2002 Situational Stats

	Lou Piniella	AL Average
Hit & Run Success %	43.8	36.0
Stolen Base Success %	70.3	68.1
Platoon Pct.	64.0	58.9
Defensive Subs	32	23
High-Pitch Outings	8	6
Quick/Slow Hooks	22/11	19/14
Sacrifice Attempts	62	53

2002 Rankings (American League)

- 1st in stolen base attempts (195), steals of second base (116), steals of third base (21), double steals (10) and starting lineups used (128)
- 3rd in hit-and-run success percentage, quick hooks and starts with over 120 pitches (8)

Brent Abernathy

2002 Season

Brent Abernathy got the chance to be the every-day second baseman, but he didn't make the most of the opportunity and ended up on the bench on several occasions. After hitting .281 through a decent first six weeks, Abernathy struggled for most of the rest of the way. The hits he did get primarily were singles, as his .311 slugging percentage was the second lowest among all American League regulars.

Hitting

Abernathy is the kind of player who doesn't impress with a particular tool or dazzling skill. Rather, he gets by with desire and hustle—and results. His key to offensive success has been putting the ball in play, using all fields and finding ways to get on base. Whether he was trying to do too much last season, or trying too much to do something different, remains to be seen. The bottom line is that he is going to have to get back to his game, especially making better use of the opposite field. Abernathy doesn't have much power and occasionally can be knocked off the plate. He still ranked as one of the team's best clutch hitters, however.

Baserunning & Defense

Much like at the plate, Abernathy does not dazzle with a singular defensive skill. He doesn't have great range or great hands or great feet or a great arm, but he finds a way to get the job done. He has improved at turning the double play and has the smarts to compensate for physical shortcomings with better positioning. His baseball instincts make him a better baserunner than would be expected, with the potential to average 15-20 steals a season.

2003 Outlook

This will be a key year for Abernathy, who was close to being sent down midway through last season. He is going to have to show that he can do all the little things to help, whether he is batting at the top or bottom of the order or providing steady defense in the field, and continue to improve.

Position: 2B
Bats: R **Throws:** R
Ht: 6' 1" **Wt:** 191

Opening Day Age: 25
Born: 9/23/77 in Atlanta, GA
ML Seasons: 2

Overall Statistics

	G	AB	R	H	D	T	HR	RBI	SB	BB	SO	Avg	OBP	Slg
'02	117	463	46	112	18	4	2	40	10	25	46	.242	.288	.311
Car.	196	767	89	194	35	5	7	73	18	52	81	.253	.304	.339

Where He Hits the Ball

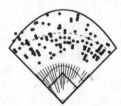

Vs. LHP   **Vs. RHP**

2002 Situational Stats

	AB	H	HR	RBI	Avg		AB	H	HR	RBI	Avg
Home	235	59	2	20	.251	LHP	79	16	1	8	.203
Road	228	53	0	20	.232	RHP	384	96	1	32	.250
First Half	317	82	2	25	.259	Sc Pos	113	34	0	36	.301
Scnd Half	146	30	0	15	.205	Clutch	88	26	0	12	.295

2002 Rankings (American League)

- 1st in lowest HR frequency (231.5 ABs per HR)
- 2nd in lowest slugging percentage and lowest on-base percentage
- 3rd in lowest slugging percentage vs. righthanded pitchers (.310) and lowest fielding percentage at second base (.979)
- 4th in errors at second base (12) and lowest on-base percentage vs. righthanded pitchers (.294)
- Led the Devil Rays in sacrifice bunts (8), highest percentage of swings put into play (52.2) and lowest percentage of swings on the first pitch (21.8)

Steve Cox

2002 Season

For a guy who spent his whole career waiting for the chance to be an everyday major league first baseman, Steve Cox did not exactly take advantage of the opportunity. After a tremendous start, he fell into a slump that seemed to last the rest of the season. Cox hit .156 September, when he primarily was limited to DH duties because of a sore left arch. He finished with a disappointing .254 mark, though he was second on the team with 72 RBI.

Hitting

Cox is not your typical slugging first baseman. He doesn't have big-time power, but his swing is sweet enough that he should be able to put up some big numbers—similar, perhaps, to Mark Grace. To do so, Cox has to take full advantage of his RBI opportunities. He led the Rays with 28 game-tying or go-ahead RBI despite hitting just .208 with runners in scoring position. Surprisingly, he struggled mightily against left-handers, with a .197 average that was second worst in the league. Better command of the strike zone would be a solid step in the right direction. Cox has something of an unusual stance, holding his hands high and usually going without batting gloves (also like Grace).

Baserunning & Defense

Cox is a solid defensive player, but his range seemed limited in the second half last season, perhaps a result of nagging soreness in his left arch. He made only one error in his first 74 games, and seven overall, ranking sixth in the league with a .993 fielding percentage. Cox doesn't have much speed, but is a solid fundamental baserunner.

2003 Outlook

Cox apparently no longer fits into the team's plans, and the Devil Rays sold his rights to the Yokohama Bay Bears in Japan. His departure follows a breakout offensive year by Aubrey Huff, who will take over as the everyday first baseman. Greg Vaughn will handle DH duties. That would leave Cox, who can't play any other position, without a major league job, but he'll be paid handsomely for two or three years in Japan.

Position: 1B/DH
Bats: L **Throws:** L
Ht: 6' 4" **Wt:** 225

Opening Day Age: 28
Born: 10/31/74 in Delano, CA
ML Seasons: 4

Overall Statistics

	G	AB	R	H	D	T	HR	RBI	SB	BB	SO	Avg	OBP	Slg
'02	148	560	65	142	30	1	16	72	5	60	116	.254	.330	.396
Car.	378	1239	146	324	72	2	39	158	8	130	240	.262	.340	.417

Where He Hits the Ball

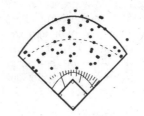

Vs. LHP   **Vs. RHP**

2002 Situational Stats

	AB	H	HR	RBI	Avg		AB	H	HR	RBI	Avg
Home	270	67	4	31	.248	LHP	152	30	4	22	.197
Road	290	75	12	41	.259	RHP	408	112	12	50	.275
First Half	316	88	10	42	.278	Sc Pos	159	33	2	51	.208
Scnd Half	244	54	6	30	.221	Clutch	96	21	0	11	.219

2002 Rankings (American League)

- 2nd in lowest batting average with runners in scoring position and lowest batting average vs. lefthanded pitchers
- 3rd in lowest fielding percentage at first base (.993)
- 4th in assists at first base (86) and lowest on-base percentage vs. lefthanded pitchers (.260)
- 6th in errors at first base (7)
- Led the Devil Rays in sacrifice flies (6)

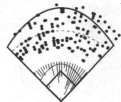

Tampa Bay

Chris Gomez

2002 Season

Chris Gomez seemed to do about everything the Devil Rays could have asked in 2002. He hit .265 with a team shortstop-record 10 homers and 46 RBI, and his .980 fielding percentage was the sixth-best figure among American League shortstops. He also was healthy the entire season. In essence, after several seasons cut short because of knee injuries, he reestablished himself as a major league starter.

Hitting

Gomez came to the Devil Rays in July 2001 with a reputation as little more than a typical National League No. 8 singles hitter. But he made a decision to take a more aggressive approach at the plate and it has paid off. He can be overmatched at times by an overpowering fastball, and the Rays occasionally made an effort to protect him, but Gomez usually found a way to put the ball in play and produce runs. He occasionally gets in trouble by being too pull-conscious.

Baserunning & Defense

In his one and a half seasons with the Devil Rays, Gomez definitely has lived up to his reputation as a shortstop who can make all the routine plays. His shortcoming is a lack of range, perhaps exacerbated by the fast infield at Tropicana Field. He pretty much can handle everything hit at him, but it is rare when he goes in the hole or up the middle for a spectacular play. The knee surgeries robbed him of some speed, but he improved enough to hit three triples for the first time since 1998. He's no threat to steal.

2003 Outlook

For all the good that Gomez did for the Devil Rays, they released him the day after the season ended rather than picking up a reasonable $2 million 2003 option. Given that the Rays don't have anyone nearly as dependable in their system, it seemed like a surprising move. Gomez most likely will end up going to spring training somewhere else as a backup or utilityman, and then try to win a starting job.

Position: SS
Bats: R **Throws:** R
Ht: 6' 1" **Wt:** 185

Opening Day Age: 31
Born: 6/16/71 in Los Angeles, CA
ML Seasons: 10

Overall Statistics

	G	AB	R	H	D	T	HR	RBI	SB	BB	SO	Avg	OBP	Slg
'02	130	461	51	122	31	3	10	46	1	21	58	.265	.305	.410
Car.	1022	3332	374	844	176	13	51	359	26	316	612	.253	.322	.360

Where He Hits the Ball

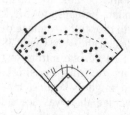 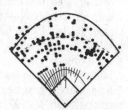

Vs. LHP   **Vs. RHP**

2002 Situational Stats

	AB	H	HR	RBI	Avg			AB	H	HR	RBI	Avg
Home	232	61	2	19	.263		LHP	87	15	1	8	.172
Road	229	61	8	27	.266		RHP	374	107	9	38	.286
First Half	267	70	7	23	.262		Sc Pos	117	29	1	35	.248
Scnd Half	194	52	3	23	.268		Clutch	105	29	2	6	.276

2002 Rankings (American League)

- 6th in fielding percentage at shortstop (.980)
- Led the Devil Rays in lowest percentage of swings that missed (11.6) and batting average on a 3-2 count (.279)

Ben Grieve

2002 Season

When the question is asked, What happened to Ben Grieve? the Devil Rays only can hope there eventually is an answer, because they sure don't know. Grieve followed his dismal 2001 Tampa Bay debut with an even worse 2002 performance, setting career lows with a .251 average, 62 runs and 64 RBI. The only positive was an increase in home runs, from 11 to 19.

Hitting

Grieve has the physical size, a strong baseball background and a smooth natural swing. He also has a track record after averaging .278, 24 home runs and 93 RBI in his three full seasons in Oakland. So what is the problem? To start with, Grieve is too passive, and too picky, at the plate. He took 61.5 percent of his pitches (eighth highest in the American League) and 63 of his 121 strikeouts were called. He also has become extremely vulnerable to lefthanded pitchers. Finally, he is not getting much lift on the ball, evidenced by a 2.08 groundball-flyball ratio that was third highest in the league. In 2001, he admitted to trying too many adjustments at the plate. Last season, he primarily stuck with the same approach, but never was consistently hot.

Baserunning & Defense

As an outfielder, Grieve makes a pretty good case for keeping the DH. He is slow in the field, is neither smooth nor instinctive and does not throw well. On most flyballs, he takes the military approach—it's not a job, it's an adventure. The lack of speed limits what he can do on the bases, too. Former manager Hal McRae tried to run him often in hopes of making him more aggressive.

2003 Outlook

This is the final year of Grieve's contract, which at least makes it possible for the Devil Rays to trade him, though it won't be easy given his $5.25 million salary. There is talk of moving him to left field in an effort to minimize his defensive liability. The hope is that, at 26, he somehow finds his old offensive form.

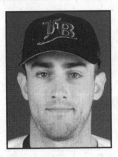

Position: RF/DH
Bats: L **Throws:** R
Ht: 6' 4" **Wt:** 216

Opening Day Age: 26
Born: 5/4/76 in Arlington, TX
ML Seasons: 6
Pronunciation: greev

Overall Statistics

	G	AB	R	H	D	T	HR	RBI	SB	BB	SO	Avg	OBP	Slg
'02	136	482	62	121	30	0	19	64	8	69	121	.251	.353	.432
Car.	775	2780	412	756	168	5	106	439	24	390	666	.272	.368	.450

Where He Hits the Ball

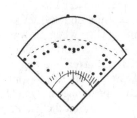

Vs. LHP   **Vs. RHP**

2002 Situational Stats

	AB	H	HR	RBI	Avg		AB	H	HR	RBI	Avg
Home	248	56	7	36	.226	LHP	131	29	2	14	.221
Road	234	65	12	28	.278	RHP	351	92	17	50	.262
First Half	283	72	10	38	.254	Sc Pos	126	30	2	41	.238
Scnd Half	199	49	9	26	.246	Clutch	84	18	0	11	.214

2002 Rankings (American League)

- 2nd in fielding percentage in right field (.988)
- 3rd in highest groundball-flyball ratio (2.1), lowest percentage of extra bases taken as a runner (24.4) and lowest slugging percentage vs. lefthanded pitchers (.313)
- 4th in lowest batting average at home
- 6th in assists in right field (6)
- Led the Devil Rays in walks, hit by pitch (8), highest groundball-flyball ratio (2.1), highest percentage of pitches taken (61.5) and cleanup slugging percentage (.500)

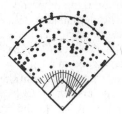

Tampa Bay

Toby Hall

2002 Season

Toby Hall's mistake going into last season was believing the hype. It took a brutal first two months and a four-week banishment to Triple-A Durham, but he eventually got straightened out and returned to doing what the Devil Rays expected of him. He hit .309 after being recalled on June 25, enough to hike his average to a respectable .258 by the end of the year.

Hitting

Hall got to the majors by being a tough out and hitting the ball hard. He got away from that approach early in the season, chasing too many bad pitches and becoming extremely vulnerable to breaking balls and offspeed pitches, especially from lefthanders. He already had endured an 0-for-28 stretch and was hitting .187 when he was sent down on May 28. The demotion turned out to be a good move, because Hall relaxed and began swinging with confidence again. He struck out only once per 13.1 plate appearances, which would have been the third-best ratio in the league had he qualified for the leader board. There still were some concerns, such as his puzzling .200 average against lefties, but his .322 mark with men in scoring position was encouraging.

Baserunning & Defense

Hall got into some bad habits early last season, and it showed in his poor efforts at blocking pitches, as well as his off-target throws. Some intense sessions with former bullpen coach Glenn Ezell got him back on track, and Hall looked to again be on the verge of stardom as the season ended. With Ezell gone, the burden will be on Hall to remain consistent and avoid the defensive lapses. Like most catchers, he doesn't run well.

2003 Outlook

Long-time starting catcher John Flaherty wasn't offered salary arbitration and isn't expected back. That isn't surprising, as Hall clearly is one of the Devil Rays' prized building blocks, and his progress will be seen as a barometer of their progress under new manager Lou Piniella. Hall is one of the team's hopes for future success, and a .300 average with 20 home runs would be a reassuring sign.

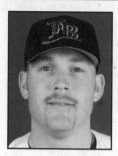

Position: C
Bats: R **Throws:** R
Ht: 6' 3" **Wt:** 240

Opening Day Age: 27
Born: 10/21/75 in Tacoma, WA
ML Seasons: 3

Overall Statistics

	G	AB	R	H	D	T	HR	RBI	SB	BB	SO	Avg	OBP	Slg
'02	85	330	37	85	19	1	6	42	0	17	27	.258	.293	.376
Car.	138	530	66	143	35	1	11	73	2	22	43	.270	.302	.402

Where He Hits the Ball

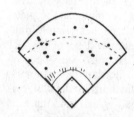 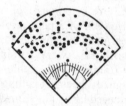

Vs. LHP   **Vs. RHP**

2002 Situational Stats

	AB	H	HR	RBI	Avg		AB	H	HR	RBI	Avg
Home	168	44	2	16	.262	LHP	65	13	1	4	.200
Road	162	41	4	26	.253	RHP	265	72	5	38	.272
First Half	165	34	3	21	.206	Sc Pos	87	28	4	39	.322
Scnd Half	165	51	3	21	.309	Clutch	52	16	0	5	.308

2002 Rankings (American League)

- 1st in batting average on a 3-1 count (.750)
- 3rd in batting average with the bases loaded (.571)
- 4th in most GDPs per GDP situation (18.9%) and lowest fielding percentage at catcher (.989)
- 5th in errors at catcher (6)
- Led the Devil Rays in batting average with the bases loaded (.571) and batting average on a 3-1 count (.750)

Aubrey Huff

2002 Season

Aubrey Huff was a final spring-training cut, and he missed the first three weeks of the Triple-A season recovering from surgery after being struck in the eye with a ball. But he still ended up having a pretty good all-around year. Huff joined the Devil Rays on May 28 and never stopped hitting. His .313 average would have been seventh in the American League had he made eight more plate appearances, and he was one of just a handful of players in the past decade to lead his team in homers after starting the season in the minors.

Hitting

Huff showed significant improvement in his third major league stint, eliminating most of the holes in his game and handling pretty much anything thrown at him. He hit for average and for power, didn't strike out much and had no problem with lefthanded pitchers, posting a .307 average that was second only to Ichiro among AL lefthanded batters. Huff has a long swing, but his biggest flaw was his impatience in not letting the game come to him, evidenced by a low total of 37 walks. Once he learns to not give away so many at-bats, he may join the ranks of the league's elite young stars.

Baserunning & Defense

Huff is not yet a smooth defensive player, but he improved enough at first base that he does not hurt his team. By the end of last season he even started to look comfortable there. He also can play third base, but not well enough to do so on more than a spot basis. Huff is not fast, but with continued work on his physical condition, he is capable of holding his own on the bases.

2003 Outlook

First base will be Huff's 2003 position after the Devil Rays sold the rights to Steve Cox to a Japanese team. Huff will be counted on heavily in the middle of the batting order. His 2002 performance has team officials excited that he will continue to develop into one of the game's top pure hitters, and just as importantly, that his defense won't hold him back.

Position: DH/1B/3B
Bats: L **Throws:** R
Ht: 6' 4" **Wt:** 231

Opening Day Age: 26
Born: 12/20/76 in Marion, OH
ML Seasons: 3

Overall Statistics

	G	AB	R	H	D	T	HR	RBI	SB	BB	SO	Avg	OBP	Slg
'02	113	454	67	142	25	0	23	59	4	37	55	.313	.364	.520
Car.	263	987	121	279	57	1	35	118	5	65	145	.283	.327	.449

Where He Hits the Ball

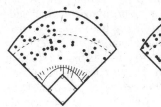
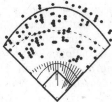

Vs. LHP   **Vs. RHP**

2002 Situational Stats

	AB	H	HR	RBI	Avg		AB	H	HR	RBI	Avg
Home	235	77	17	40	.328	LHP	127	39	4	15	.307
Road	219	65	6	19	.297	RHP	327	103	19	44	.315
First Half	141	39	7	17	.277	Sc Pos	128	33	2	33	.258
Scnd Half	313	103	16	42	.329	Clutch	72	25	2	7	.347

2002 Rankings (American League)

- 5th in most GDPs per GDP situation (18.7%)
- 8th in GDPs (17) and batting average at home
- 9th in batting average in the clutch
- 10th in batting average vs. lefthanded pitchers and errors at first base (5)
- Led the Devil Rays in batting average, home runs, intentional walks (7), GDPs (17), slugging percentage, on-base percentage, HR frequency (19.7 ABs per HR), batting average vs. righthanded pitchers, highest percentage of extra bases taken as a runner (56.3), slugging percentage vs. righthanded pitchers (.526), on-base percentage vs. righthanded pitchers (.365), batting average at home, batting average on the road and batting average with two strikes (.226)

Joe Kennedy

2002 Season

Joe Kennedy continued to impress, going 8-11 on a team that was 51 games under .500, and only falling short of 200 innings because his last start was rained out. He allowed three earned runs or less in 18 of his 30 starts and had five complete games. He also shared the American League lead in pickoffs and finished second to Texas' Chan Ho Park with 16 hit batters.

Pitching

Kennedy presents a tough challenge for even the best hitters with a combination of good stuff and a somewhat funky across-the-body delivery. He mixes two- and four-seam fastballs that regularly are clocked in the low 90-MPH range and seem to sneak in on hitters, a big-breaking curveball and a consistent changeup. A key is to have command of the curveball, which not only is an effective strikeout pitch, but also prevents batters from sitting on the fastball. He also was working on a slider. Kennedy is something of a control freak, averaging about 2.5 walks per nine innings. And better conditioning may help; he won just once in his last eight starts.

Defense

Kennedy is a much better fielder than he showed, as his 10 errors were the most by a pitcher since Melido Perez did the same in 1992. Kennedy's problem is a combination of trying to do too much and rushing what he does. He has a tremendous pickoff move, but it will be a challenge to see if he can improve it as runners become more aware of him and cautious about running.

2003 Outlook

Kennedy has won 15 major league games so far, all before turning 24. With a one-and-a-half season apprenticeship out of the way, it's time for him to step up and take his place among the top young lefthanders in the game. He may not be the Devil Rays' No. 1 starter this season, but he likely will be their *best* starter.

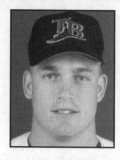

Position: SP
Bats: R   **Throws:** L
Ht: 6' 4"   **Wt:** 237

Opening Day Age: 23
Born: 5/24/79 in La Mesa, CA
ML Seasons: 2

Overall Statistics

	W	L	Pct.	ERA	G	GS	Sv	IP	H	BB	SO	HR	Ratio
'02	8	11	.421	4.53	30	30	0	196.2	204	55	109	23	1.32
Car.	15	19	.441	4.50	50	50	0	314.1	326	89	187	39	1.32

How Often He Throws Strikes

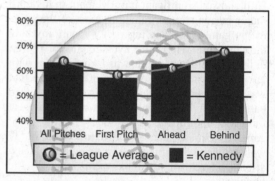

= League Average   ■ = Kennedy

2002 Situational Stats

	W	L	ERA	Sv	IP		AB	H	HR	RBI	Avg
Home	4	6	3.51	0	92.1	LHB	172	47	7	28	.273
Road	4	5	5.43	0	104.1	RHB	586	157	16	75	.268
First Half	5	7	4.33	0	116.1	Sc Pos	168	54	7	78	.321
Scnd Half	3	4	4.82	0	80.1	Clutch	65	17	2	9	.262

2002 Rankings (American League)

- 1st in errors at pitcher (10) and lowest fielding percentage at pitcher (.756)
- 2nd in complete games (5) and hit batsmen (16)
- 5th in highest batting average allowed with runners in scoring position
- Led the Devil Rays in ERA, wins, complete games (5), hit batsmen (16), highest strikeout-walk ratio (2.0), lowest on-base percentage allowed (.328), lowest ERA at home, most run support per nine innings (5.4), fewest home runs allowed per nine innings (1.05) and fewest walks per nine innings (2.5)

Jared Sandberg

2002 Season

Turning the third-base job over to Jared Sandberg was something of a hit-or-miss proposition for the Devil Rays. Actually, it ended up being both. Sandberg hit 18 home runs in 401 plate appearances, an impressive total for a 24-year-old in his first extended major league action. But he struck out 139 times, a massive total for any player at any level. However, the power potential was enough to keep the nephew of former Cubs star Ryne Sandberg in the lineup.

Hitting

Even though he struck out so often (the fourth-highest ratio of strikeouts-plate appearances of *all time* among batters with at least 400 PA in a season), Sandberg might benefit from being more aggressive. Too often, he put himself in a defensive position by falling behind early in the count. He missed on 40.6 percent of his swings last season—the highest percentage in the majors—and thus had the second-lowest percentage of swings put into play (29.1 percent). When he does swing, Sandberg needs to make more of an effort to use the middle of the field, as well as the opposite field. He is plenty strong and can catch up with just about any fastball, but he must begin to realize he doesn't need to pull everything.

Baserunning & Defense

What helps make Sandberg's high-frequency strikeout totals more tolerable is his smooth defensive play at third. He has soft hands, a strong arm, good instincts and a sense of calm about him that make him a plus defensive player. He made 14 errors, but he has the potential to cut down on that total with added work and experience. He doesn't have much speed, but he uses everything he has to be a decent baserunner.

2003 Outlook

All indications are that new manager Lou Piniella will give Sandberg an ample chance to show he belongs as a major league starter at the hot corner. The key will be for Sandberg to improve his plate discipline and cut down on his strikeouts, while still giving the Devil Rays middle-of-the-order-type production.

Position: 3B
Bats: R **Throws:** R
Ht: 6' 3" **Wt:** 226

Opening Day Age: 25
Born: 3/2/78 in Olympia, WA
ML Seasons: 2

Overall Statistics

	G	AB	R	H	D	T	HR	RBI	SB	BB	SO	Avg	OBP	Slg
'02	102	358	55	82	21	1	18	54	3	39	139	.229	.305	.444
Car.	141	494	68	110	28	1	19	69	4	49	184	.223	.294	.399

Where He Hits the Ball

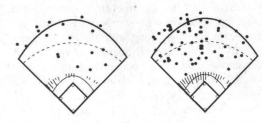

Vs. LHP   Vs. RHP

2002 Situational Stats

	AB	H	HR	RBI	Avg		AB	H	HR	RBI	Avg
Home	197	43	10	33	.218	LHP	86	18	4	6	.209
Road	161	39	8	21	.242	RHP	272	64	14	48	.235
First Half	135	32	7	17	.237	Sc Pos	103	25	5	38	.243
Scnd Half	223	50	11	37	.224	Clutch	65	15	1	10	.231

2002 Rankings (American League)

- 1st in batting average on a 3-1 count (.750), highest percentage of swings that missed (40.6) and lowest percentage of swings put into play (29.1)
- 5th in strikeouts
- 7th in errors at third base (14)
- 10th in lowest batting average with two strikes (.148)
- Led the Devil Rays in strikeouts, most pitches seen per plate appearance (4.02) and batting average on a 3-1 count (.750)

Tampa Bay

Tanyon Sturtze

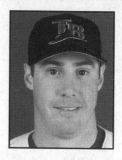

Position: SP
Bats: R **Throws:** R
Ht: 6' 5" **Wt:** 221

Opening Day Age: 32
Born: 10/12/70 in Worcester, MA
ML Seasons: 7
Pronunciation: STURTS

2002 Season

Everything Tanyon Sturtze did in 2002 seemed to go wrong, so much so that by the end of the long season he had made history. Sturtze became the first pitcher to lead the American League in losses (18), hits allowed (271), runs (141) and walks (89). Only three NL pitchers ever did it, the last being Phil Niekro in 1979. Sturtze went 15 starts before his first win, allowed a team-record 33 home runs and gave up more than 10 hits six times.

Pitching

As bad as Sturtze's numbers were, he really wasn't pitching *that* badly. Many times, one bad pitch would spoil an inning, or even a game. Sturtze keeps it simple with a basic repertoire of two- and four-seam fastballs, along with a slider and splitter. His low-90s fastball doesn't overpower hitters, and sometimes he has to be reminded of that; he needs to do a better job of keeping the ball down and hitting his spots. What he needs most is a dependable out pitch, such as a splitter he could bury when necessary. Sturtze proved his durability—and made a statement about his character—by making 33 starts and logging 224 innings despite the dismal numbers he was putting up. There has been some thought of making him a short reliever in an attempt to take advantage of his competitiveness.

Defense

A former basketball player and converted infielder, Sturtze is an excellent athlete. He can do a lot of things to help himself, such as fielding his area, making strong throws and covering the bases properly. In 2000 and 2001, Sturtze had allowed consistently high stolen-base percentages on his watch, but he was much improved against the running game last year.

2003 Outlook

Someone is going to give Sturtze a chance, and the odds are strong that he is going to redeem himself. The Devil Rays have flirted with the idea of making him a reliever, and that talk could resurface if they bring him back and the team can come up with five other starters.

Overall Statistics

	W	L	Pct.	ERA	G	GS	Sv	IP	H	BB	SO	HR	Ratio
'02	4	18	.182	5.18	33	33	0	224.0	271	89	137	33	1.61
Car.	22	33	.400	5.07	119	72	1	539.1	610	223	318	74	1.54

How Often He Throws Strikes

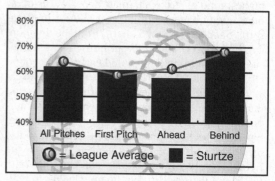

○ = League Average   ■ = Sturtze

2002 Situational Stats

	W	L	ERA	Sv	IP			AB	H	HR	RBI	Avg
Home	3	7	4.81	0	127.1	LHB		443	143	22	68	.323
Road	1	11	5.68	0	96.2	RHB		454	128	11	64	.282
First Half	1	9	4.52	0	121.1	Sc Pos		230	73	5	96	.317
Scnd Half	3	9	5.96	0	102.2	Clutch		82	24	5	12	.293

2002 Rankings (American League)

- 1st in losses, hits allowed, batters faced (1,008), walks allowed, runners caught stealing (15), lowest winning percentage and highest on-base percentage allowed (.369)
- 2nd in highest batting average allowed (.302), highest slugging percentage allowed (.480) and least run support per nine innings (3.9)
- 3rd in home runs allowed, pitches thrown (3,576) and highest ERA
- 4th in complete games (4), balks (2), lowest strikeout-walk ratio (1.5), highest ERA on the road and highest walks per nine innings (3.6)
- Led the Devil Rays in losses, games started, innings pitched, hits allowed, batters faced (1,008) and home runs allowed

Paul Wilson

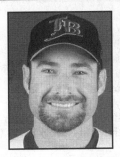

Position: SP
Bats: R **Throws:** R
Ht: 6' 5" **Wt:** 214

Opening Day Age: 30
Born: 3/28/73 in Orlando, FL
ML Seasons: 4

2002 Season

Paul Wilson had another solid season, although he seemed to tire during the final month. He was 6-8 with a 3.80 ERA through his first 24 starts, but keep in mind that four of those wins did come at the expense of Baltimore. He then went 0-4 with an 11.57 ERA in his final six outings. He fell just short of 200 innings, though he still managed to allow 219 hits.

Pitching

Wilson committed himself last spring to becoming predominantly a sinkerball pitcher, and he made the transition fairly smoothly. The only problems occurred on the days when the ball wouldn't sink and he had to feel his way through the game, fighting a tendency to nibble. Wilson doesn't have dominating stuff, but he can be a solid starter when he mixes in some changeups, sliders and an occasional curveball. Although Devil Rays coaches thought he was tired at the end of the season, Wilson's career-high 193.2 innings should have eliminated any questions about the health of his arm.

Defense

Wilson is a good athlete who is in excellent shape. He can help himself by coming off the mound well. He handled a respectable total of 39 chances last year, and was part of four double plays. He also is very determined and very intense in all facets of the game. Though he allowed just eight stolen bases while on the mound last year, he still could benefit from holding runners on a little better. He has yet to pick off a baserunner at the big league level.

2003 Outlook

The Devil Rays faced a financial decision on Wilson, but there was no question that he pitched well enough to be in somebody's rotation. The Florida native liked pitching in Tampa Bay well enough that he was hoping to work out a deal to stay. If so, he'll be expected to provide innings as well as leadership to young starters such as Dewon Brazelton.

Overall Statistics

	W	L	Pct.	ERA	G	GS	Sv	IP	H	BB	SO	HR	Ratio
'02	6	12	.333	4.83	30	30	0	193.2	219	67	111	29	1.48
Car.	20	37	.351	4.86	104	87	0	545.0	579	206	379	66	1.44

How Often He Throws Strikes

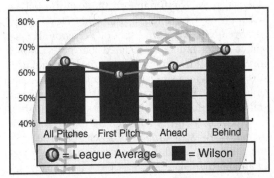

80%
70%
60%
50%
40%

All Pitches First Pitch Ahead Behind

◎ = League Average ■ = Wilson

2002 Situational Stats

	W	L	ERA	Sv	IP		AB	H	HR	RBI	Avg
Home	3	7	4.61	0	97.2	LHB	359	111	13	50	.309
Road	3	5	5.06	0	96.0	RHB	404	108	16	56	.267
First Half	2	6	4.28	0	107.1	Sc Pos	170	50	6	70	.294
Scnd Half	4	6	5.53	0	86.1	Clutch	66	18	1	8	.273

2002 Rankings (American League)

- 2nd in pickoff throws (141)
- 3rd in highest slugging percentage allowed (.478) and highest on-base percentage allowed (.352)
- 4th in hit batsmen (13), highest batting average allowed (.287) and highest stolen-base percentage allowed (80.0)
- 6th in most home runs allowed per nine innings (1.35)
- 7th in highest ERA, lowest winning percentage, lowest strikeout-walk ratio (1.7) and least run support per nine innings (4.4)
- Led the Devil Rays in pickoff throws (141) and highest groundball-flyball ratio allowed (1.2)

Randy Winn

Traded To MARINERS

2002 Season

Randy Winn established himself not only as an everyday player last season, but also as an extraordinary player. Winn was selected to the American League All-Star team for the first time and was voted the Devil Rays' MVP. He set a new franchise record with 181 hits in a season. With one more hit, he also would have finished with his first .300 average.

Hitting

Winn once was projected as a slap-hitting leadoff man, but he has developed into an all-around hitter, adding enough power to hit 14 home runs. He seemed most comfortable in the leadoff slot but was productive enough that the Devil Rays dropped him to the third spot on occasion. He is a much better hitter righthanded, but he is able to drive the ball from both sides of the plate and uses his speed to turn singles into doubles and doubles into triples. He was one of only two players to rank in the top 10 in the AL in singles, doubles and triples. Winn is an effective bunter, and he occasionally will drop one down for a hit. The best thing he could do to improve his numbers is walk more.

Baserunning & Defense

Winn does not have a strong arm, but he has learned to compensate with positioning and anticipation. He ranked third in the AL with 13 outfield assists last season. Similarly, he is not a particularly smooth outfielder, occasionally taking circuitous routes to flyballs, but he usually recovers to make the play. Center field seemed particularly challenging. Winn is a fast baserunner, but he doesn't steal enough to take full advantage of his speed. Confidence may be an issue there.

2003 Outlook

Winn would have been a key piece of the Devil Rays' lineup in 2003, playing center field and batting leadoff. Instead, he will be a complementary part in Seattle—probably playing left field and possibly batting second—after being traded as the compensation for manager Lou Piniella. The move should benefit Winn, as he figures to be part of a winning team for the first time in his career.

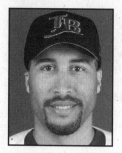

Position: CF
Bats: B **Throws:** R
Ht: 6' 2" **Wt:** 197

Opening Day Age: 28
Born: 6/9/74 in Los Angeles, CA
ML Seasons: 5

Overall Statistics

	G	AB	R	H	D	T	HR	RBI	SB	BB	SO	Avg	OBP	Slg
'02	152	607	87	181	39	9	14	75	27	55	109	.298	.360	.461
Car.	519	1836	264	513	94	28	24	182	80	165	347	.279	.342	.400

Where He Hits the Ball

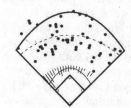 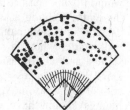

Vs. LHP   **Vs. RHP**

2002 Situational Stats

	AB	H	HR	RBI	Avg		AB	H	HR	RBI	Avg
Home	320	104	9	48	.325	LHP	144	50	4	16	.347
Road	287	77	5	27	.268	RHP	463	131	10	59	.283
First Half	335	104	7	42	.310	Sc Pos	133	42	6	64	.316
Scnd Half	272	77	7	33	.283	Clutch	117	43	3	16	.368

2002 Rankings (American League)

- 2nd in triples
- 4th in batting average vs. lefthanded pitchers, on-base percentage for a leadoff hitter (.375), fielding percentage in center field (.992) and assists in center field (10)
- 5th in steals of third (6) and slugging percentage vs. lefthanded pitchers (.549)
- 6th in batting average in the clutch
- 7th in stolen bases
- Led the Devil Rays in at-bats, runs scored, hits, singles, doubles, triples, total bases (280), RBI, stolen bases, caught stealing (8), times on base (242), pitches seen (2,612), plate appearances (674), games played, stolen-base percentage (77.1), bunts in play (15) and steals of third (6)

Esteban Yan

2002 Season

Esteban Yan didn't get any better in his second full season as a closer. He tied for the American League lead with eight blown saves, and also posted the lowest save percentage (.704). He finally was stripped of exclusive closer duties because of his inconsistent performance. On the positive side, Yan made it through a season without injury for the first time since 1998.

Pitching

Yan has the necessary physical tools to be a closer—a fastball that is regularly in the 95-96 MPH range and can hit 98, a slider that can be nasty at times and a splitter that can be simply unhittable. But he can't execute on a consistent basis, leading to continued questions as to whether he has the makeup and mental toughness to be successful in pressure situations. He tends to get out of control and rush his delivery, making for outings that start well and quickly blow up. When he is going good, he can run off several strong outings in a row. But when he struggles, it tends to carry over, such as an August stretch when he blew four saves in five outings.

Defense

Yan is big, slow, and not particularly well-coordinated, so he is not much of a fielder. Plus his violent delivery doesn't usually leave him in good fielding position, making him vulnerable to bunts. Yan has not erred in two years, but he has not logged many chances, either. He showed improvement at holding runners on, however, and allowed just one stolen base all year.

2003 Outlook

There is some thought that Yan is better suited as a setup man, but the Devil Rays don't have that luxury. If they pay the arbitration-inflated price to bring him back, they are going to need him to be a closer and can only hope he will be more consistent. New manager Lou Piniella isn't likely to tolerate anything less.

Position: RP
Bats: R **Throws:** R
Ht: 6' 4" **Wt:** 255

Opening Day Age: 27
Born: 6/22/75 in Campina del Seibo, DR
ML Seasons: 7
Pronunciation: YAHN

Overall Statistics

	W	L	Pct.	ERA	G	GS	Sv	IP	H	BB	SO	HR Ratio
'02	7	8	.467	4.30	55	0	19	69.0	70	29	53	10	1.43
Car.	26	31	.456	5.26	273	23	42	437.2	480	165	362	68	1.47

How Often He Throws Strikes

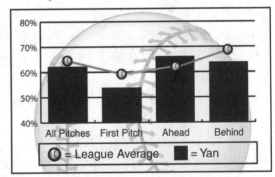

= League Average   = Yan

2002 Situational Stats

	W	L	ERA	Sv	IP		AB	H	HR	RBI	Avg
Home	5	6	4.76	6	39.2	LHB	128	35	8	27	.273
Road	2	2	3.68	13	29.1	RHB	142	35	2	8	.246
First Half	4	4	5.03	11	34.0	Sc Pos	72	20	3	26	.278
Scnd Half	3	4	3.60	8	35.0	Clutch	196	52	5	24	.265

2002 Rankings (American League)

- 1st in blown saves (8), relief losses (8) and lowest save percentage (70.4)
- 8th in relief wins (7)
- 9th in games finished (47) and first batter efficiency (.196)
- Led the Devil Rays in games pitched, saves, games finished (47), save opportunities (27), save percentage (70.4), first batter efficiency (.196), blown saves (8), relief wins (7), relief losses (8), relief innings (69.0) and lowest batting average allowed in relief (.259)

Tampa Bay

Wilson Alvarez

Position: RP/SP
Bats: L **Throws:** L
Ht: 6' 1" **Wt:** 245

Opening Day Age: 33
Born: 3/24/70 in
Maracaibo, VZ
ML Seasons: 11

Overall Statistics

	W	L	Pct.	ERA	G	GS	Sv	IP	H	BB	SO	HR	Ratio
'02	2	3	.400	5.28	23	10	1	75.0	80	36	56	13	1.55
Car.	88	80	.524	4.03	273	234	2	1508.0	1404	744	1130	166	1.42

2002 Situational Stats

	W	L	ERA	Sv	IP		AB	H	HR	RBI	Avg
Home	1	1	6.27	0	33.0	LHB	77	23	4	17	.299
Road	1	2	4.50	1	42.0	RHB	217	57	9	25	.263
First Half	2	2	5.56	0	45.1	Sc Pos	74	21	4	31	.284
Scnd Half	0	1	4.85	1	29.2	Clutch	34	5	0	4	.147

2002 Season

Just making it to the mound for his first start was a victory for Wilson Alvarez, who missed the entire 2000 and 2001 seasons because of left shoulder surgery. Alvarez was on the DL twice more last season for unrelated reasons and lost his spot in the rotation, but by the end of the year had evolved into a successful reliever.

Pitching & Defense

Alvarez' best performances came when he had the confidence to use his low-90s fastball to set up his offspeed stuff. When he came back from the DL the second time in August and was moved to the bullpen, he seemed to find himself, pitching aggressively with his fastball in the 88-90 MPH range and a complementary changeup and curveball. Physical conditioning always has been a battle for Alvarez, and it can affect him in the field. He has a passable pickoff move, and has done a good job of controlling the running game.

2003 Outlook

The Rays couldn't wait to part ways with Alvarez, releasing him the day after the season ended. While his five-year stay was considered a waste, Alvarez showed enough as a reliever over the final two months that he should be able to help some team as a middle reliever and spot starter.

Jason Conti

Position: CF/RF/LF
Bats: L **Throws:** R
Ht: 5'11" **Wt:** 175

Opening Day Age: 28
Born: 1/27/75 in
Pittsburgh, PA
ML Seasons: 3
Pronunciation:
CON-tie

Overall Statistics

	G	AB	R	H	D	T	HR	RBI	SB	BB	SO	Avg	OBP	Slg
'02	78	222	26	57	15	2	3	21	4	18	55	.257	.315	.383
Car.	130	317	38	79	19	5	4	36	7	26	87	.249	.310	.379

2002 Situational Stats

	AB	H	HR	RBI	Avg		AB	H	HR	RBI	Avg
Home	107	25	2	12	.234	LHP	30	11	1	3	.367
Road	115	32	1	9	.278	RHP	192	46	2	18	.240
First Half	116	26	1	10	.224	Sc Pos	59	14	1	19	.237
Scnd Half	106	31	2	11	.292	Clutch	36	7	0	1	.194

2002 Season

Jason Conti made his first Opening Day roster and spent his first full season in the major leagues, but he didn't get to play much. He showed surprising power and a strong arm, while spending most of his time in right and center field.

Hitting, Baserunning & Defense

Conti is a contact hitter who could bat at the top of the order if he walked more. He has the power to hit the ball into the gap and the speed to take advantage of doing so, but he would be more of an offensive threat if he made better use of the opposite field. He also seems to be something of a streak hitter, which is tough for someone who doesn't play much. While Conti has above-average speed, he doesn't steal a lot of bases, which may be a matter of confidence or circumstance. His speed makes him a strong defensive outfielder, and he has a plus arm.

2003 Outlook

If nothing else, Conti should be insurance for the Devil Rays in case left fielder Carl Crawford or top minor league prospect Rocco Baldelli are not ready to play at the big league level. Even if they are, Conti should have a chance to contribute as a fourth outfielder and defensive replacement for Ben Grieve.

Carl Crawford

Position: LF
Bats: L **Throws:** L
Ht: 6' 2" **Wt:** 219

Opening Day Age: 21
Born: 8/5/81 in
Houston, TX
ML Seasons: 1

Overall Statistics

	G	AB	R	H	D	T	HR	RBI	SB	BB	SO	Avg	OBP	Slg
'02	63	259	23	67	11	6	2	30	9	9	41	.259	.290	.371
Car.	63	259	23	67	11	6	2	30	9	9	41	.259	.290	.371

2002 Situational Stats

	AB	H	HR	RBI	Avg		AB	H	HR	RBI	Avg
Home	121	36	1	15	.298	LHP	60	12	0	7	.200
Road	138	31	1	15	.225	RHP	199	55	2	23	.276
First Half	0	0	0	0	–	Sc Pos	67	22	1	28	.328
Scnd Half	259	67	2	30	.259	Clutch	33	5	0	7	.152

2002 Season

Carl Crawford won the International League Rookie of the Year Award based on his three-plus months with Triple-A Durham, then was promoted on July 20 and named the Devil Rays' Most Outstanding Rookie. At 20 years and 349 days, Crawford was the youngest ever to play for the Devil Rays.

Hitting, Baserunning & Defense

Crawford is a fast runner, good contact hitter and fine defensive player. He hasn't shown much power yet, but the team is confident that will come. Until then, he'll make do with hitting the ball on the ground and down the lines and using his speed to force mistakes. All that will keep Crawford from being a 50-plus stolen base guy is familiarity with pitchers and enough opportunities. He's graceful and acrobatic in the field, and has a strong enough arm to be an impact player.

2003 Outlook

Crawford is one of the Devil Rays' prized athletic prospects. There is talk of moving him from left field to right to take better advantage of his speed and arm. Crawford struggled a bit last season once opponents got a look at him, but Tampa Bay officials were not worried and predict that stardom won't be far off.

John Flaherty

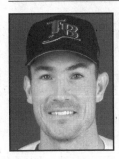

Position: C
Bats: R **Throws:** R
Ht: 6' 1" **Wt:** 196

Opening Day Age: 35
Born: 10/21/67 in New
York, NY
ML Seasons: 11
Nickname: Flash

Overall Statistics

	G	AB	R	H	D	T	HR	RBI	SB	BB	SO	Avg	OBP	Slg
'02	76	281	27	73	20	0	4	33	2	15	50	.260	.296	.374
Car.	913	3013	282	768	154	3	68	354	10	160	444	.255	.293	.376

2002 Situational Stats

	AB	H	HR	RBI	Avg		AB	H	HR	RBI	Avg
Home	141	41	4	20	.291	LHP	56	14	1	4	.250
Road	140	32	0	13	.229	RHP	225	59	3	29	.262
First Half	149	38	3	18	.255	Sc Pos	66	19	1	27	.288
Scnd Half	132	35	1	15	.265	Clutch	53	12	0	4	.226

2002 Season

John Flaherty handled the transition from starter to backup well despite inconsistent usage. He finished with a .260 average and 20 doubles, posting a 12-game hitting streak along the way. A slight fracture on the tip of his left middle finger caused him to miss the last 11 games.

Hitting, Baserunning & Defense

Flaherty is at his best when he hits the ball where it is pitched and uses all fields, but he has gotten away from that approach at times and tries to overcompensate by making too many adjustments. His handling of pitchers and game-calling ability are excellent, making him a favorite of many veterans. His arm still is strong, though he needs an occasional brushup on fundamentals to avoid bad habits that drag his defensive numbers down. Like most catchers, Flaherty isn't much of a baserunner, though he did have two steals last season.

2003 Outlook

After five long seasons with Tampa, Flaherty filed for free agency, hoping to find either a starting job or an opportunity to be a backup on a championship-caliber club. The Rays made an initial attempt to bring him back, but he wasn't interested. His skills and professional approach will make him a valuable addition for some team.

Tampa Bay

Travis Harper

Position: RP
Bats: R **Throws:** R
Ht: 6' 4" **Wt:** 192

Opening Day Age: 26
Born: 5/21/76 in Harrisonburg, VA
ML Seasons: 3

Overall Statistics

	W	L	Pct.	ERA	G	GS	Sv	IP	H	BB	SO	HR	Ratio
'02	5	9	.357	5.46	37	7	1	85.2	101	27	60	14	1.49
Car.	6	13	.316	5.41	45	14	1	124.2	146	45	76	24	1.53

2002 Situational Stats

	W	L	ERA	Sv	IP		AB	H	HR	RBI	Avg
Home	4	2	4.70	0	46.0	LHB	163	49	10	33	.301
Road	1	7	6.35	1	39.2	RHB	186	52	4	24	.280
First Half	3	5	3.57	1	45.1	Sc Pos	101	23	1	36	.228
Scnd Half	2	4	7.59	0	40.1	Clutch	99	32	4	20	.323

2002 Season

Travis Harper was the most versatile, if not most valuable, pitcher on the Tampa Bay staff last season. After beginning the season with Triple-A Durham, he made seven starts and 30 relief appearances for the Rays. While he won two of the starts, he consistently was more effective out of the pen, going 3-5 with a save and a 3.81 ERA that was the best of the team's regular relievers.

Pitching & Defense

Harper doesn't dominate with any one pitch, but rather is successful by using his full repertoire— low-90s fastball, curve, changeup, slider—hitting his spots and changing speeds. Locating the off-speed pitches has been key, and he seems to have realized how imperative it is that he keep the ball down. Harper would like to be a starter, but he is more effective in short bursts as hitters seemed to get better swings against him the second or third time through the lineup. He did a fine job keeping opposing baserunners in check last year.

2003 Outlook

Harper is intense and determined, and he seemed to learn a lot in 2002. Now the Devil Rays will have to figure out whether to be satisfied with using him as a middle reliever, or to push things and give him another chance as a starter.

Russ Johnson

Position: 3B
Bats: R **Throws:** R
Ht: 5'10" **Wt:** 198

Opening Day Age: 30
Born: 2/22/73 in Baton Rouge, LA
ML Seasons: 6

Overall Statistics

	G	AB	R	H	D	T	HR	RBI	SB	BB	SO	Avg	OBP	Slg
'02	45	111	15	24	5	0	1	12	5	16	22	.216	.320	.288
Car.	342	818	112	217	44	2	14	97	16	104	169	.265	.349	.375

2002 Situational Stats

	AB	H	HR	RBI	Avg		AB	H	HR	RBI	Avg
Home	57	15	0	6	.263	LHP	24	5	1	3	.208
Road	54	9	1	6	.167	RHP	87	19	0	9	.218
First Half	93	20	1	11	.215	Sc Pos	29	8	1	12	.276
Scnd Half	18	4	0	1	.222	Clutch	26	5	0	1	.192

2002 Season

Russ Johnson won the starting third-base job in spring training, but a right foot injury in late March changed everything. He was on the DL until April 15, struggled when he got back, lost his job, played sparingly, left the team mysteriously in July, resurfaced in mid-August after being treated for what he said was anxiety and depression, and rejoined the team September 7.

Hitting, Baserunning & Defense

Johnson has a good eye, surprising power and decent speed. He can handle just about any fastball and knows how to prolong an at-bat by working the count. Johnson came up as a shortstop and still considers himself capable of playing there, but his range and arm make him more suited to play second and third. He plays the game hard, and that shows in all facets, including his baserunning.

2003 Outlook

Johnson was outrighted to Triple-A Durham after the season to create a roster spot, but he has a $775,000 contract for 2003 and could be back on the Tampa Bay bench. If not, he'll probably end up helping some team. There are going to be some questions about him given the time he missed last season and the personal reasons behind it.

Ryan Rupe

Position: SP
Bats: R **Throws:** R
Ht: 6' 5" **Wt:** 248

Opening Day Age: 28
Born: 3/31/75 in Houston, TX
ML Seasons: 4
Pronunciation: roop

Overall Statistics

	W	L	Pct.	ERA	G	GS	Sv	IP	H	BB	SO	HR	Ratio
'02	5	10	.333	5.60	15	15	0	90.0	83	25	67	11	1.20
Car.	23	37	.383	5.84	85	83	0	466.2	501	161	348	77	1.42

2002 Situational Stats

	W	L	ERA	Sv	IP			AB	H	HR	RBI	Avg
Home	3	7	4.25	0	65.2	LHB	183	45	7	32	.246
Road	2	3	9.25	0	24.1	RHB	158	38	4	23	.241
First Half	5	9	5.54	0	87.2	Sc Pos	91	28	2	42	.308
Scnd Half	0	1	7.71	0	2.1	Clutch	6	2	0	1	.333

2002 Season

Ryan Rupe looked like a totally different pitcher during much of the season, learning to become primarily a sinkerball pitcher. He started the campaign 3-1 and was 5-5 with a 4.88 ERA at the end of May, but irritation in his right knee became a bigger problem. He finally had surgery August 21 to smooth out cartilage under the kneecap.

Pitching & Defense

Rupe is big and strong, like a classic power pitcher, but he accepted the reality that he doesn't have the velocity to throw the ball by major league hitters. Instead, he bought into former pitching coach Jackie Brown's idea to make the best of his 87-88 MPH fastball by repeatedly pounding the bottom of the strike zone with a heavy sinker. Once he got that down, Rupe was able to make better use of his changeup and slider. He still has to learn to keep his emotions in check and not get overexcited, especially when fielding a ball.

2003 Outlook

By having the surgery in August, Rupe is expected to be fully ready for spring training. But the Rays released him in a November roster shuffle and he was claimed by the Red Sox. Boston was eager to sign him and quick to say he figured heavily in its pitching plans.

Andy Sheets

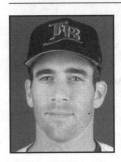

Position: 2B/SS
Bats: R **Throws:** R
Ht: 6' 2" **Wt:** 192

Opening Day Age: 31
Born: 11/19/71 in Baton Rouge, LA
ML Seasons: 7

Overall Statistics

	G	AB	R	H	D	T	HR	RBI	SB	BB	SO	Avg	OBP	Slg
'02	41	149	18	37	4	0	4	22	2	12	41	.248	.301	.356
Car.	356	960	118	207	38	3	19	113	16	76	275	.216	.271	.321

2002 Situational Stats

	AB	H	HR	RBI	Avg		AB	H	HR	RBI	Avg
Home	79	20	1	10	.253	LHP	41	11	0	3	.268
Road	70	17	3	12	.243	RHP	108	26	4	19	.241
First Half	0	0	0	0	–	Sc Pos	43	12	3	21	.279
Scnd Half	149	37	4	22	.248	Clutch	23	6	2	8	.261

2002 Season

Andy Sheets earned another chance in the big leagues with a strong first four months at Triple-A Durham (including a .294 average and 69 RBI in 98 games). He was promoted July 20 and took advantage of the callup by proving to be a valuable utility infielder for the Rays.

Hitting, Baserunning & Defense

The biggest improvement Sheets made was at the plate, where he turned into a more aggressive hitter who showed some power. He said the change was more in his approach than anything technical, and it clearly worked, though he still can be overpowered by a good fastball. Sheets is a steady defender who can make all the routine plays, but he rarely does anything spectacular. He is versatile enough to play all four infield positions but is best suited to be in the middle. Sheets also is the type of player who usually makes a positive contribution when he is on the basepaths.

2003 Outlook

Expected to be in the Tampa Bay mix for a middle-infield spot, either as a starter or a reserve, Sheets will play for the Hiroshima Carp of Japan's Central League in 2003, after the Rays sold his rights to the Carp.

Tampa Bay

Greg Vaughn

Position: DH/LF
Bats: R **Throws:** R
Ht: 6' 0" **Wt:** 206

Opening Day Age: 37
Born: 7/3/65 in
Sacramento, CA
ML Seasons: 14
Pronunciation:
von

Overall Statistics

	G	AB	R	H	D	T	HR	RBI	SB	BB	SO	Avg	OBP	Slg
'02	69	251	28	41	10	2	8	29	3	41	82	.163	.286	.315
Car.	1709	6066	1009	1468	281	23	352	1067	121	857	1500	.242	.337	.470

2002 Situational Stats

	AB	H	HR	RBI	Avg		AB	H	HR	RBI	Avg
Home	116	22	1	15	.190	LHP	50	4	1	1	.080
Road	135	19	7	14	.141	RHP	201	37	7	28	.184
First Half	251	41	8	29	.163	Sc Pos	87	14	1	19	.161
Scnd Half	0	0	0	0	–	Clutch	39	9	2	8	.231

2002 Season

The highlight of 2002 for Greg Vaughn was a four-homer, six-RBI weekend in Baltimore in mid-May. Otherwise, it was a lost season for the once-proud slugger. He didn't play again after bruising his right shoulder June 22 at Colorado. At the time of the injury, he had the lowest average and most strikeouts (82) in the AL.

Hitting, Baserunning & Defense

The days when Vaughn would torment pitchers by waiting for a fat fastball and muscling it out of the ballpark appear to be gone. His bat has slowed and much of his power has been stripped by the residual effects of a series of shoulder injuries. Vaughn has deceptive speed, especially home to first, but leg muscle pulls and strains have limited him. He has resisted the move to DH, but his spotty, though determined, defense and inability to throw hard make the shift a virtual necessity.

2003 Outlook

The Rays would like to dump his $9.25 million salary, but that's unlikely after back-to-back injury-shortened seasons. At least they have a place to use him after selling the rights to first baseman Steve Cox to Japan. Getting Vaughn into the lineup as the DH creates the possibility of a hot start, which may make a July deal feasible.

Victor Zambrano

Position: RP/SP
Bats: R **Throws:** R
Ht: 6' 0" **Wt:** 203

Opening Day Age: 27
Born: 8/6/75 in Los
Teques, VZ
ML Seasons: 2

Overall Statistics

	W	L	Pct.	ERA	G	GS	Sv	IP	H	BB	SO	HR	Ratio
'02	8	8	.500	5.53	42	11	1	114.0	120	68	73	15	1.65
Car.	14	10	.583	4.79	78	11	3	165.1	158	86	131	21	1.48

2002 Situational Stats

	W	L	ERA	Sv	IP		AB	H	HR	RBI	Avg
Home	2	3	6.79	0	51.2	LHB	195	57	6	28	.292
Road	6	5	4.48	1	62.1	RHB	237	63	9	48	.266
First Half	3	4	5.93	0	41.0	Sc Pos	148	36	4	61	.243
Scnd Half	5	4	5.30	1	73.0	Clutch	90	24	3	18	.267

2002 Season

Based on an impressive 2001, Tampa Bay expected Victor Zambrano to be a star in the bullpen. Instead, he struggled mightily. He was sent down once and was about to go down a second time when he was moved to the rotation in early August. He turned out to be surprisingly effective in that role, going 4-4 with a 4.27 ERA in 11 starts.

Pitching & Defense

Zambrano probably has the best pure stuff of anyone on the Rays' staff: a low to mid-90s fastball, a changeup that freezes lefthanders and a nasty slider. But getting him to use his stuff, and getting him to believe that he can be successful by using it, have been big problems. Devil Rays coaches tried to simplify things by having him focus solely on location, and it appeared to help. Zambrano is a former infielder, so his defense usually is very good.

2003 Outlook

The Rays need help in the rotation and in the bullpen, so it may come down to where Zambrano feels most comfortable and looks more likely to succeed. He said at the end of last season he would like to remain a starter. Figuring out how to get the best out of him should be a top priority of new pitching coach Chris Bosio.

Other Tampa Bay Devil Rays

Brandon Backe (Pos: RHP, **Age**: 24)

	W	L	Pct.	ERA	G	GS	Sv	IP	H	BB	SO	HR	Ratio
'02	0	0	–	6.92	9	0	0	13.0	15	7	6	3	1.69
Car.	0	0	–	6.92	9	0	0	13.0	15	7	6	3	1.69

Backe got his first taste of the major leagues in a short stay with the Devil Rays after the All-Star break. He doesn't have much experience, so another year or two in the minors may be necessary. 2003 Outlook: C

Lance Carter (Pos: RHP, **Age**: 28)

	W	L	Pct.	ERA	G	GS	Sv	IP	H	BB	SO	HR	Ratio
'02	2	0	1.000	1.33	8	0	2	20.1	15	5	14	2	0.98
Car.	2	1	.667	2.10	14	0	2	25.2	18	8	17	4	1.01

Carter was impressive in eight September appearances, posting a 1.33 ERA and two saves over 20.1 innings. The righthander is versatile and the Devil Rays may choose to groom him into a closer. 2003 Outlook: C

Jesus Colome (Pos: RHP, **Age**: 25)

	W	L	Pct.	ERA	G	GS	Sv	IP	H	BB	SO	HR	Ratio
'02	2	7	.222	8.27	32	0	0	41.1	56	33	33	6	2.15
Car.	4	10	.286	5.60	62	0	0	90.0	93	58	64	14	1.68

A year ago the hard-throwing Colome seemed poised to become the Rays' closer, but he regressed in 2002. Plus he aged two years when his visa was processed last spring. His star isn't as shiny now. 2003 Outlook: B

Luis de los Santos (Pos: RHP, **Age**: 25)

	W	L	Pct.	ERA	G	GS	Sv	IP	H	BB	SO	HR	Ratio
'02	0	3	.000	11.57	3	3	0	14.0	24	4	7	5	2.00
Car.	0	3	.000	11.57	3	3	0	14.0	24	4	7	5	2.00

After missing two years with arm troubles, de los Santos was impressive in Triple-A last season, going 9-2 with a 2.42 ERA in 24 games. However, he got shelled in three starts with Tampa. 2003 Outlook: C

Felix Escalona (Pos: SS/2B, **Age**: 24, **Bats**: R)

	G	AB	R	H	D	T	HR	RBI	SB	BB	SO	Avg	OBP	Slg
'02	59	157	17	34	8	2	0	9	7	3	44	.217	.262	.293
Car.	59	157	17	34	8	2	0	9	7	3	44	.217	.262	.293

Escalona was with the Devil Rays all of last season despite batting a dismal .217. If he hopes to regain his reserve infielder role again in 2003, he will need to improve on those numbers. 2003 Outlook: C

Lee Gardner (Pos: RHP, **Age**: 28)

	W	L	Pct.	ERA	G	GS	Sv	IP	H	BB	SO	HR	Ratio
'02	1	1	.500	4.05	12	0	0	13.1	12	8	8	3	1.50
Car.	1	1	.500	4.05	12	0	0	13.1	12	8	8	3	1.50

Other than two short stints with Tampa Bay, Gardner spent the bulk of 2002 in Triple-A, posting a 2.36 ERA in 45 games. He refused an assignment in September and became a free agent. 2003 Outlook: C

Paul Hoover (Pos: C, **Age**: 26, **Bats**: R)

	G	AB	R	H	D	T	HR	RBI	SB	BB	SO	Avg	OBP	Slg
'02	5	17	1	3	0	0	0	2	0	0	5	.176	.176	.176
Car.	8	21	2	4	0	0	0	2	0	0	6	.190	.190	.190

Hoover is a good defensive catcher and is surprisingly quick on the bases. However, his problem has been reaching base, posting OBPs of .260 and .285 the last two years at Triple-A Durham. The Marlins have signed him to a minor league deal. 2003 Outlook: C

Delvin James (Pos: RHP, **Age**: 25)

	W	L	Pct.	ERA	G	GS	Sv	IP	H	BB	SO	HR	Ratio
'02	0	3	.000	6.55	8	6	0	34.1	40	15	17	5	1.60
Car.	0	3	.000	6.55	8	6	0	34.1	40	15	17	5	1.60

James spent time on the DL last season with right shoulder tendinitis. His season then was cut short when he was shot in the left shoulder. He is expected to be ready for spring training. 2003 Outlook: C

Steve Kent (Pos: LHP, **Age**: 24)

	W	L	Pct.	ERA	G	GS	Sv	IP	H	BB	SO	HR	Ratio
'02	0	2	.000	5.65	34	0	1	57.1	67	38	41	6	1.83
Car.	0	2	.000	5.65	34	0	1	57.1	67	38	41	6	1.83

After three years in Class-A, Kent made the jump to the major leagues, spending the entire 2002 season with the Devil Rays. He was waived in November and claimed by the Seattle Mariners. 2003 Outlook: C

Tom Martin (Pos: LHP, **Age**: 32)

	W	L	Pct.	ERA	G	GS	Sv	IP	H	BB	SO	HR	Ratio
'02	0	0	–	16.20	2	0	0	1.2	5	1	1	0	3.60
Car.	8	5	.615	5.45	122	0	2	132.0	154	64	87	14	1.65

Martin was limited to just six appearances last season—four in Triple-A, two with the Devil Rays—because of a strained rotator cuff. He was released in September and became a free agent. 2003 Outlook: C

Dave McCarty (Pos: LF, **Age**: 33, **Bats**: R)

	G	AB	R	H	D	T	HR	RBI	SB	BB	SO	Avg	OBP	Slg
'02	25	66	5	9	1	0	2	4	0	6	19	.136	.230	.242
Car.	504	1285	150	303	55	7	31	148	8	107	313	.236	.298	.362

McCarty possesses power in his bat, but his tendency to strike out too often has prevented him from becoming an everyday player. He signed a minor league deal with the A's following the 2002 season. 2003 Outlook: C

Travis Phelps (Pos: RHP, **Age**: 25)

	W	L	Pct.	ERA	G	GS	Sv	IP	H	BB	SO	HR	Ratio
'02	1	2	.333	4.78	26	0	0	37.2	30	27	36	7	1.51
Car.	3	4	.429	3.97	75	0	5	99.2	83	51	90	13	1.34

Phelps split last season between the Devil Rays and their Triple-A affiliate, posting similar numbers at both levels. With a little more experience, he should be a staple in the Tampa Bay pen. 2003 Outlook: C

Tampa Bay

Damian Rolls (Pos: RF, **Age**: 25, **Bats**: R)

	G	AB	R	H	D	T	HR	RBI	SB	BB	SO	Avg	OBP	Slg
'02	21	89	15	26	6	1	0	6	2	3	16	.292	.330	.382
Car.	106	329	48	89	17	2	2	18	14	13	64	.271	.302	.353

Rolls looked to be the Devil Rays' future second baseman in 2001, but was ousted by Brent Abernathy. Since that time, Rolls has been getting work in the outfield. He could battle for a reserve spot in 2003. 2003 Outlook: C

Bobby Smith (Pos: 3B, **Age**: 28, **Bats**: R)

	G	AB	R	H	D	T	HR	RBI	SB	BB	SO	Avg	OBP	Slg
'02	18	63	4	11	2	0	1	6	0	3	25	.175	.212	.254
Car.	258	826	88	192	29	4	21	107	11	70	268	.232	.297	.354

Smith was released by Tampa Bay after batting just .175 over the first month of the 2002 campaign. He then signed a minor league contract with the Brewers and hit just .239 with Triple-A Indianapolis. 2003 Outlook: C

Jason Smith (Pos: 3B, **Age**: 25, **Bats**: L)

	G	AB	R	H	D	T	HR	RBI	SB	BB	SO	Avg	OBP	Slg
'02	26	65	9	13	1	2	1	6	3	2	24	.200	.224	.323
Car.	28	66	9	13	1	2	1	6	3	2	25	.197	.221	.318

Smith has adequate speed and possesses decent power for a middle infielder. He could see time with Tampa Bay in 2003, but still needs some work. Another year spent mostly in Triple-A is likely. 2003 Outlook: C

Jorge Sosa (Pos: RHP, **Age**: 25)

	W	L	Pct.	ERA	G	GS	Sv	IP	H	BB	SO	HR	Ratio
'02	2	7	.222	5.53	31	14	0	99.1	88	54	48	16	1.43
Car.	2	7	.222	5.53	31	14	0	99.1	88	54	48	16	1.43

After struggling as an outfielder in Rookie and Class-A ball for four years, Sosa was converted into a pitcher. He made his major league debut in 2002, appearing in 31 games. He still is a bit green. 2003 Outlook: C

Jason Tyner (Pos: LF, **Age**: 25, **Bats**: L)

	G	AB	R	H	D	T	HR	RBI	SB	BB	SO	Avg	OBP	Slg
'02	44	168	17	36	2	1	0	9	7	7	19	.214	.249	.238
Car.	199	688	77	175	14	6	0	43	45	27	77	.254	.287	.292

Tyner posted respectable numbers in 2001, including 31 stolen bases. However, a sore knee slowed him in 2002, and he spent most of the year in Triple-A. He is a career .307 batter in the minors. 2003 Outlook: C

Organization Overview:

The baby boom in Tampa Bay got underway in 2002, as homegrown prospects Aubrey Huff, Jared Sandberg, Carl Crawford, Toby Hall and Joe Kennedy settled into regular duty with the Rays. It's been the Rays' tendency to draft tools-rich but raw talent that required loads of development time, so few minor leaguers have had an impact in the franchise's brief history. But that's changing, and guys like Rocco Baldelli, Jason Standridge, Dewon Brazelton and recent trade acquisitions Nick Bierbrodt and Antonio Perez also are knocking on the door as 2003 approaches.

Rocco Baldelli

Position: OF   **Opening Day Age:** 21
Bats: R **Throws:** R   **Born:** 9/25/81 in
Ht: 6' 4" **Wt:** 187   Woonsocket, RI

Recent Statistics

	G	AB	R	H	D	T	HR	RBI	SB	BB	SO	Avg
2001 A Chrlstn (SC)	113	406	58	101	23	6	8	55	25	23	89	.249
2002 A Bakersfield	77	312	63	104	19	1	14	51	21	18	63	.333
2002 AA Orlando	17	70	10	26	3	1	2	13	3	5	11	.371
2002 AAA Durham	23	96	13	28	6	1	3	7	2	0	23	.292

The Rays' first-round pick in 2000, Baldelli is a five-tool prospect who advanced by leaps and bounds as a hitter last summer. Prior to the season, his numbers did not reflect the talents of a guy with a quick bat, good hands and power potential. Baldelli improved markedly at adjusting to pitchers and being more selective with his swings. Still, he didn't walk at Triple-A Durham and needs to show more plate patience. Continually adjusting to pitchers and learning how to approach different counts will speed his rise to Tampa. Defensively, the athletic center fielder has good speed and a clear path to regular work with the Rays when he is ready.

Nick Bierbrodt

Position: P   **Opening Day Age:** 24
Bats: L **Throws:** L   **Born:** 5/16/78 in
Ht: 6' 5" **Wt:** 214   Tarzana, CA

Recent Statistics

	W	L	ERA	G	GS	Sv	IP	H	R	BB	SO	HR
2001 AA El Paso	2	1	1.37	4	4	0	19.2	13	3	6	18	1
2001 AAA Tucson	4	1	2.18	7	6	0	45.1	48	15	9	56	0
2001 NL Arizona	2	5	8.22	5	5	0	23.0	29	21	12	17	6
2001 AL Tampa Bay	3	4	4.55	11	11	0	61.1	71	38	27	56	11
2002 A Chrlstn (SC)	0	0	3.60	1	1	0	5.0	5	4	2	2	0

Arizona's first-ever pick in 1996, Bierbrodt's ascent to the majors was slow. He debuted in 2001 before he was dealt to the Rays that July in a trade for Albie Lopez. Bierbrodt was inconsistent in the Rays' rotation, but was certain of a 2002 spot until he lost all control and walked or hit most of the spring-training batters he faced. He didn't face hitters again until May. In the minors in early June, Bierbrodt was shot twice—in his non-throwing arm and chest—sitting in a taxi in Charleston, S.C. He's working out and should be throwing with Rays pitching coach Chris Bosio in December. If he has no offseason complications, Bierbrodt will try to rekindle his low-90s sinker, a budding slider and a changeup that had been his best pitch.

Dewon Brazelton

Position: P   **Opening Day Age:** 22
Bats: R **Throws:** R   **Born:** 6/16/80 in
Ht: 6' 4" **Wt:** 214   Tullahoma, TN

Recent Statistics

	W	L	ERA	G	GS	Sv	IP	H	R	BB	SO	HR
2002 AA Orlando	5	9	3.33	26	26	0	146.0	129	69	67	109	7
2002 AAA Durham	1	0	0.00	1	1	0	5.0	5	0	1	6	0
2002 AL Tampa Bay	0	1	4.85	2	2	0	13.0	12	7	6	5	3

Picked third overall in 2001, Brazelton signed in August and soon joined the Rays because his contract put him on the big league roster on September 1. He didn't pitch in a game, but used the time to clean up his mechanics and tinker with his changeup. Brazelton started slowly at Double-A Orlando in 2002, needing time to adapt to the heavier pitching schedule and facing better hitters. He finished strong, adding a slider that needs fine-tuning. His changeup was his best pitch, and he throws a moving low-90s fastball that can be tough to command. Brazelton learned from his big league experience, which he can take to camp to make further adjustments to major league hitters.

Gerardo Garcia

Position: P   **Opening Day Age:** 23
Bats: R **Throws:** R   **Born:** 2/13/80 in
Ht: 6' 0" **Wt:** 160   Nuevo Leon, Mexico

Recent Statistics

	W	L	ERA	G	GS	Sv	IP	H	R	BB	SO	HR
2002 AA Orlando	2	1	2.79	10	4	0	38.2	24	14	12	28	4
2002 AAA Durham	2	7	6.50	15	15	0	63.2	79	48	30	50	5

Before the 2002 season, Garcia was acquired from the Mexico City Tigers, with which the Rays have a working agreement. He worked as a starter and reliever for the Tigers in 2001, playing a key role for the Mexican League champions. He pitched well at Double-A Orlando, getting his feet wet and earning a berth in the 2002 Futures Game. He didn't fare as well at Triple-A Durham, but he took a no-hitter into the seventh inning of the deciding game of the International League championship series. He's a savvy pitcher who changes speeds well and works with four pitches—fastball, curve, slider and straight change—and he can snap off the breaking balls. Garcia has the power stuff to be a closer if needed, but he'll first get an opportunity to join the Rays as a starter.

Tampa Bay

Josh Hamilton

Position: OF   **Opening Day Age:** 21
Bats: L **Throws:** L   **Born:** 5/21/81 in Raleigh,
Ht: 6' 4" **Wt:** 209   NC

Recent Statistics

	G	AB	R	H	D	T	HR	RBI	SB	BB	SO	Avg
2001 AA Orlando	23	89	5	16	5	0	0	4	2	5	22	.180
2001 A Chrlstn (SC)	4	11	3	4	1	0	1	2	0	2	3	.364
2002 A Bakersfield	56	211	32	64	14	1	9	44	10	20	46	.303

Selected first overall in 1999, Hamilton is another five-tool prospect with the Rays, but injuries have kept him from reaching the majors by now. A car accident during spring training in 2001 began a series of back and leg ailments that led to a lost season. Three trips to the disabled list last year ended with arthroscopic cleanups of his left shoulder and left elbow in July. Still, Hamilton produced quality numbers in a short time with a sweet lefthanded stroke that will generate even more power in time. He mostly was a designated hitter in 2002, but he has the tools to be a solid right fielder in the majors. A lengthy stretch of good health and performance could move the gifted Hamilton into the Rays' outfield.

Seth McClung

Position: P   **Opening Day Age:** 22
Bats: R **Throws:** R   **Born:** 2/7/81 in
Ht: 6' 6" **Wt:** 235   Lewisburg, WV

Recent Statistics

	W	L	ERA	G	GS	Sv	IP	H	R	BB	SO	HR
2001 A Chrlstn (SC)	10	11	2.79	28	28	0	164.1	142	72	53	165	6
2002 A Bakersfield	3	2	2.92	7	7	0	37.0	35	16	11	48	1
2002 AA Orlando	5	7	5.37	20	19	0	114.0	138	74	53	64	12

A high school pick in 1999, the big righthander has the thick thighs and build of a power pitcher. McClung commands a mid-90s fastball that can creep close to 100 MPH. His plus curveball improved in 2002, and at times is as good as the fastball. His changeup lags behind his other pitches. McClung fanned 165 in 164.1 innings at Class-A Charleston in 2001, and his strikeout rate was even better at high Class-A Bakersfield last year before jumping to Double-A Orlando. He must continue adjusting to better hitters and master working in different situations. McClung won't be rushed, giving him time to learn the art of pitching.

Antonio Perez

Position: SS   **Opening Day Age:** 23
Bats: R **Throws:** R   **Born:** 1/26/80 in Bani,
Ht: 5' 11" **Wt:** 175   DR

Recent Statistics

	G	AB	R	H	D	T	HR	RBI	SB	BB	SO	Avg
2001 AA San Antonio	5	21	3	3	0	0	0	0	0	0	7	.143
2002 AA San Antonio	72	240	30	62	8	2	2	24	15	11	64	.258
2002 R Mariners	6	15	3	5	1	0	1	3	4	4	2	.333

Another five-tool guy—this one a shortstop—but he's already been traded to Seattle for Ken Griffey Jr. and dealt to the Rays along with the rights to Lou Piniella.

After the Griffey deal in February 2000, Perez broke out with a .276-17-63 season that included a .376 OBP at high Class-A Lancaster. A broken bone in his right wrist limited him to five games in 2001. A hamate bone injury in the same wrist cost him two months last season. Not only has he lost development time, he added 18 months to his age when he secured his working visa for 2002. Before his injuries, he made consistent contact and started showing power. Perez, a solid fielder with good range and a strong arm, must prove his wrist and bat are ready to move toward Tampa Bay.

Jason Standridge

Position: P   **Opening Day Age:** 24
Bats: R **Throws:** R   **Born:** 11/9/78 in
Ht: 6' 4" **Wt:** 230   Birmingham, AL

Recent Statistics

	W	L	ERA	G	GS	Sv	IP	H	R	BB	SO	HR
2002 AAA Durham	10	9	3.12	29	29	0	173.0	168	71	64	111	12
2002 AL Tampa Bay	0	0	9.00	1	0	0	3.0	7	3	4	1	1

A first-round pick in 1997, Standridge endured a disappointing '98 campaign before benefiting from a switch to a lower arm slot the next spring. He responded with a 13-5 (2.57) season for two Class-A clubs in 1999. The change gave his low-90s fastball better sink, and it's a solid pitch to go along with a sharp-breaking curveball that is his out pitch. His changeup continues to improve. His second go-round at Triple-A Durham last summer went much better than the first, as Standridge was a more refined pitcher with much better stamina, which allowed him to be more successful over a full season. Further refining his command around the strike zone will prepare him for major league hitters.

Others to Watch

The Rays' fourth-round pick last June, outfielder **Wes Bankston** (19) recognized pitches well and hit fastballs and breaking stuff. He made adjustments within at-bats and showed good plate discipline in a .301-18-57 debut season at Rookie-level Princeton. . . A 2001 pick, outfielder **Jonny Gomes** (22) used a quick bat and raw power to lead the Rookie-level Appy League with 16 homers. He jumped to high Class-A Bakersfield and homered 30 times in 2002. Gomes also fanned 173 times in 134 games, but his hitting percentages were solid and the Rays anticipate a drop in his strikeout-homer ratio. . . A second-rounder in 2002, outfielder **Jason Pridie** (19) is a solid player with good tools and a nice stroke. He's a strong guy who makes good contact. Pridie enjoyed a .368-7-33 season in 67 games for Rookie-level Princeton, then batted .344 in eight games at short-season Hudson Valley. . . Drafted second overall last June, **B.J. Upton** (18) has five-tool potential as a shortstop. He'll debut this spring after signing in September. Upton's a fine athlete *and* baseball player with an innate ability to play the game. He has a strong arm, a spray approach to hitting and power potential, plus exceptional speed.

The Ballpark in Arlington

Offense

The Rangers and their opponents combined for a major league high 245 homers and also scored 11.8 runs per game at The Ballpark last season. On the road, the Rangers and their opponents combined for 179 homers and 9.5 runs per game. Balls hit from right-center to the foul line get into a jet stream and go out at an alarming rate. The outfield gaps are vast, making this a good doubles park.

Defense

It is hard to hide a poor defensive player at The Ballpark. The power gaps are spacious, putting a premium on fast outfielders with strong arms. Playing the infield becomes an adventure as the season progresses. The Texas heat bakes the grass, giving the infield the speed of an artificial-turf surface without the consistent bounces.

Who It Helps the Most

During his first stay with the Rangers, Rafael Palmeiro sat in on design sessions for the new park. Whether he exerted undue influence is not known, but The Ballpark favors lefthanded hitters who lift the ball. No lefthanded hitter lifts the ball more than Palmeiro.

Who It Hurts the Most

What was Chan Ho Park thinking when he left friendly Dodger Stadium to join the Rangers as a free agent last season? Park is ineffective away from Dodger Stadium, a fact that was painfully obvious last year. Park went 6-4 with a 6.84 ERA and 12 homers allowed in 72.1 innings at The Ballpark. Flyballs that went nowhere in the dead night air of Los Angeles landed 20 rows back at The Ballpark.

Rookies & Newcomers

Since moving into The Ballpark, the Rangers have loaded up on lefthanded hitters. They have two promising third basemen who hit from the left side: Hank Blalock and Mark Teixeira, a switch-hitter. Teixeira, the fifth pick overall in the 2001 draft, is on the verge of passing Blalock.

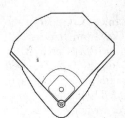

Dimensions: LF-332, LCF-390, CF-400, RCF-381, RF-325

Capacity: 49,115

Elevation: 551 feet

Surface: Grass

Foul Territory: Average

Park Factors

2002 Season

	Home Games			Away Games			
	Rangers	Opp	Total	Rangers	Opp	Total	Index
G	72	72	144	72	72	144	
Avg	.282	.278	.280	.253	.265	.259	108
AB	2440	2579	5019	2549	2417	4966	101
R	421	425	846	322	364	686	123
H	689	718	1407	645	640	1285	109
2B	141	167	308	132	145	277	110
3B	13	20	33	12	19	31	105
HR	123	99	222	83	72	155	142
BB	258	286	544	231	308	539	100
SO	429	486	915	482	431	913	99
E	39	44	83	48	47	95	87
E-Infield	29	35	64	40	39	79	81
LHB-Avg	.285	.268	.275	.255	.268	.262	105
LHB-HR	43	43	86	28	37	65	126
RHB-Avg	.281	.287	.284	.252	.262	.256	111
RHB-HR	80	56	136	55	35	90	154

2000-2002

	Home Games			Away Games			
	Rangers	Opp	Total	Rangers	Opp	Total	Index
G	217	217	434	214	214	428	
Avg	.287	.287	.287	.265	.285	.274	105
AB	7426	7893	15319	7593	7250	14843	102
R	1247	1308	2555	1049	1211	2260	111
H	2133	2266	4399	2009	2064	4073	107
2B	429	530	959	426	448	874	106
3B	42	56	98	30	51	81	117
HR	326	298	624	255	253	508	119
BB	800	841	1641	703	866	1569	101
SO	1259	1319	2578	1402	1215	2617	95
E	166	155	321	145	149	294	108
E-Infield	135	129	264	118	130	248	105
LHB-Avg	.286	.288	.287	.272	.288	.280	102
LHB-HR	136	135	271	107	108	215	117
RHB-Avg	.289	.287	.288	.259	.282	.271	106
RHB-HR	190	163	353	148	145	293	120

2002 Rankings (American League)

- Highest home-run factor
- Highest RHB batting-average factor
- Highest RHB home-run factor
- Second-highest batting-average factor
- Second-highest run factor
- Second-highest hit factor
- Second-highest LHB home-run factor
- Second-lowest infield-error factor

Buck Showalter

2002 Season

After modestly successful stints as skipper of the Yankees and Diamondbacks from 1992-2000, Buck Showalter worked as an ESPN analyst for the second consecutive season in 2002. He used the time in front of the camera to his advantage. He worked at his job and added to his information bank. He lost out to Tony Pena when Kansas City hired a new manager, but the Rangers scooped Showalter up shortly after the end of the regular season.

Offense

Showalter returns to the American League, but he always was an NL-type manager. His New York team in 1995 reached the playoffs despite the AL's third-lowest homer total. The key was to apply pressure by getting runners on base. Showalter wants the free-swinging Rangers to take more walks and become more conscious of on-base percentage. He likes to stay with a set lineup; he used 99 lineups, third fewest in the NL, with Arizona in 2000.

Pitching & Defense

Showalter will let the starting pitcher go as deep as possible. The 1995 Yankees had the AL's second-highest complete-game total with 18. His 2000 Arizona team led the NL with 16 complete games. Of course, those clubs had proven lead horses such as Jack McDowell, David Cone, Randy Johnson and Curt Schilling in the rotation. Showalter's new club will test his desire to keep a light hand on the bullpen to have fresh relievers late in the season. If it comes down to a debate of offense vs. defense, he will stay with the better defensive player. That goes against GM John Hart's philosophy.

2003 Outlook

This is the third massive building project of Showalter's managerial career. He took over the Yankees in 1992 after a 91-loss season and put the expansion Diamondbacks into the playoffs during their second season. But the Rangers may be Showalter's hardest project to date, as his previous teams had a better core of talent.

Born: 5/23/56 in DeFuniak Springs, FL

Playing Experience: No major league playing experience

Managerial Experience: 7 seasons

Manager Statistics

Year	Team, Lg	W	L	Pct	GB	Finish
2000	Arizona, NL	85	77	.525	12.0	3rd West
7 Seasons		563	504	.528	–	–

2002 Starting Pitchers by Days Rest

	<=3	4	5	6+
Rangers Starts	1	89	24	36
Rangers ERA	15.00	5.38	4.67	5.52
AL Avg Starts	1	83	44	24
AL ERA	7.15	4.59	4.27	5.03

2002 Situational Stats

	Jerry Narron	AL Average
Hit & Run Success %	30.3	36.0
Stolen Base Success %	64.6	68.1
Platoon Pct.	51.6	58.9
Defensive Subs	24	23
High-Pitch Outings	8	6
Quick/Slow Hooks	25/11	19/14
Sacrifice Attempts	59	53

2002 Rankings—Jerry Narron (American League)

- 1st in starting lineups used (128), relief appearances (487), mid-inning pitching changes (238) and one-batter pitcher appearances (49)
- 2nd in pinch-hitters used (131) and quick hooks
- 3rd in starts with over 120 pitches (8) and starts on three days rest

Hank Blalock

Position: 3B
Bats: L **Throws:** R
Ht: 6' 1" **Wt:** 192

Opening Day Age: 22
Born: 11/21/80 in San Diego, CA
ML Seasons: 1

2002 season

Hank Blalock continued a year-long surge with a strong spring training that forced the Rangers to make him the Opening Day third baseman at age 21, *without* the benefit of any Triple-A seasoning. But he simply was not ready once the real games began. He swung at too many first pitches and was hitting only .200 with one homer and nine extra-base hits in 100 at-bats when he returned to the minors in mid-May. Blalock showed *some* improvement when he joined back up with the parent club in September, hitting a modest .234. But he still lacked power and stroked only two extra-base hits in 47 big league at-bats in September.

Hitting

The aggressiveness that made Blalock an elite prospect in the minors worked against him in the majors. He regularly chased the first pitch, and teams took advantage of his overzealous approach by putting him in early holes. He had a 1-2 count in 48 of his 147 at-bats with Texas. The abundance of bad counts zapped Blalock's power, and he often was reduced to defensive swings. He also had trouble staying on the pitch against lefthanders, whom he had handled quite nicely at Double-A Tulsa in 2001. In the end, the Rangers admitted they probably rushed Blalock.

Baserunning & Defense

Blalock played better than expected at third base. Defense is not his calling card, however, and the Rangers are flirting with the idea of converting him into a power-hitting, run-producing second baseman, a la Jeff Kent. Texas had Blalock man the keystone several times at Triple-A Oklahoma last year. Blalock has below-average speed, but he understands how to run the bases.

2003 Outlook

Blalock remains a coveted talent. When Cleveland shopped righthander Bartolo Colon last year, the Rangers would not include Blalock in a proposed deal. The rising presence of third baseman Mark Teixeira could affect Blalock's status in the organization, however. Blalock could be moved to second, or the Rangers could trade him for a needed center fielder or catcher.

Overall Statistics

	G	AB	R	H	D	T	HR	RBI	SB	BB	SO	Avg	OBP	Slg
'02	49	147	16	31	8	0	3	17	0	20	43	.211	.306	.327
Car.	49	147	16	31	8	0	3	17	0	20	43	.211	.306	.327

Where He Hits the Ball

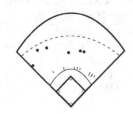
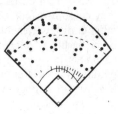

Vs. LHP   **Vs. RHP**

2002 Situational Stats

	AB	H	HR	RBI	Avg		AB	H	HR	RBI	Avg
Home	79	19	2	10	.241	LHP	30	2	0	3	.067
Road	68	12	1	7	.176	RHP	117	29	3	14	.248
First Half	100	20	1	6	.200	Sc Pos	36	7	0	12	.194
Scnd Half	47	11	2	11	.234	Clutch	27	5	0	2	.185

2002 Rankings (American League)

- Did not rank near the top or bottom in any category

Frank Catalanotto

2002 Season

Injuries blunted the momentum Frank Catalanotto built during a strong 2001. He missed a total of 85 games during two stays on the disabled list in 2002 because of back and hand injuries. Unlike 2001, when he challenged for a batting title, Catalanotto never got hot. He had his average at .300 or higher for only three days all season.

Hitting

Catalanotto has an opposite-field swing but also can drive the ball. He is comfortable hitting deep in the count, which made him an effective leadoff hitter last season—he had a .366 on-base percentage when batting in the No. 1 spot in the lineup. The Rangers used nine other leadoff hitters, and they combined for a .281 OBP at No. 1. Among other things, Catalanotto excels at getting on base by being hit by pitches. But his average dropped 61 points last season in part because he did not produce as well at home. He hit .345 at The Ballpark in Arlington in 2001, but fell to .254 there last season.

Baserunning & Defense

Catalanotto, who has lost weight since leaving Detroit, runs better than advertised. He has 24 stolen bases in 34 attempts during the last two seasons and can score from first on a double. The problem is that the Rangers cannot find a full-time position for Catalanotto. His best spot is first base, but Texas is overloaded there. He is eager but limited on defense at second base and left field. He makes the plays on what balls he gets to, but his range is below average. And his arm strength has not been the same since shoulder surgery in 1997.

2003 Outlook

This could be time the for the Rangers to cash in on Catalanotto's value. They cannot find a full-time spot for him, and his versatility and ability to hit off the bench make him better suited for the National League. If he stays in Texas, he will continue to bounce around the lineup. Catalanotto also must find a way to stay healthy, as he has missed more than 100 games during three DL stays in the last three years.

Position: LF/2B/1B
Bats: L **Throws:** R
Ht: 5'11" **Wt:** 195

Opening Day Age: 28
Born: 4/27/74 in Smithtown, NY
ML Seasons: 6
Pronunciation: ca-tal-a-NAH-tow

Overall Statistics

	G	AB	R	H	D	T	HR	RBI	SB	BB	SO	Avg	OBP	Slg
'02	68	212	42	57	16	6	3	23	9	25	27	.269	.364	.443
Car.	506	1482	240	439	94	15	41	182	36	127	213	.296	.362	.463

Where He Hits the Ball

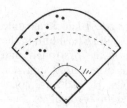
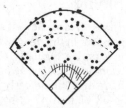

Vs. LHP   **Vs. RHP**

2002 Situational Stats

	AB	H	HR	RBI	Avg		AB	H	HR	RBI	Avg
Home	114	29	2	15	.254	LHP	26	6	0	4	.231
Road	98	28	1	8	.286	RHP	186	51	3	19	.274
First Half	122	32	2	14	.262	Sc Pos	46	16	0	19	.348
Scnd Half	90	25	1	9	.278	Clutch	39	9	1	5	.231

2002 Rankings (American League)

- 6th in triples and on-base percentage for a leadoff hitter (.366)
- Led the Rangers in stolen bases, lowest percentage of swings that missed (12.6), highest percentage of swings put into play (48.7) and on-base percentage for a leadoff hitter (.366)

Carl Everett

2002 Season

As was also the case for big-name teammates Ivan Rodriguez and Juan Gonzalez, Carl Everett had another turbulent and disappointing season. Everett went on the disabled list twice because of leg problems, and now has played as many as 135 games only once in the last five years. He refused to go to the minors on an rehabilitation assignment after his second disabled-list stay. Everett went 1-for-4 on Opening Day, but did not have his average above .200 thereafter until August 2.

Hitting

While with Boston, Everett hit .329 with 24 homers and 69 RBI in 289 at-bats during the first half of 2000 and made the American League All-Star team that year. He has not approached that level since, and has hit only .262 with 40 homers and 159 RBI during the past two and a half seasons. He starts his swing early to catch up to the fastball, making him vulnerable to offspeed pitches. A switch-hitter, Everett's swing from the right side is useless. He has hit only .206 against left-handers in the last two seasons.

Baserunning & Defense

Everett had surgery to remove damaged cartilage from the right knee in December 2001, and took an inordinate time to recover and get back into playing shape. The Rangers tried Everett in center field, but his lack of range was stunning. Texas opponents posted 10 triples in the 24 games that Everett started in center. He is nothing more than an average left fielder at this stage. Everett's stolen-base total dropped for the third consecutive season, down to two.

2003 Outlook

This is the final season of Everett's contract, which qualifies as good news either way for the Rangers. They can be free of his salary ($9.15 million) at the end of 2003, and in the meantime should get a better performance from him this year. Everett had a breakthrough campaign with Houston in 1999, when he was in the final year of a contract.

Position: RF/CF/LF/DH
Bats: B **Throws:** R
Ht: 6' 0" **Wt:** 215

Opening Day Age: 31
Born: 6/3/71 in Tampa, FL
ML Seasons: 10

Texas

Overall Statistics

	G	AB	R	H	D	T	HR	RBI	SB	BB	SO	Avg	OBP	Slg
'02	105	374	47	100	16	0	16	62	2	33	77	.267	.333	.439
Car.	949	3204	490	887	189	20	133	545	93	302	736	.277	.347	.473

Where He Hits the Ball

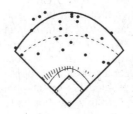 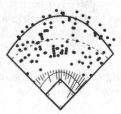

Vs. LHP   **Vs. RHP**

2002 Situational Stats

	AB	H	HR	RBI	Avg		AB	H	HR	RBI	Avg
Home	180	52	11	42	.289	LHP	91	20	4	11	.220
Road	194	48	5	20	.247	RHP	283	80	12	51	.283
First Half	166	32	6	20	.193	Sc Pos	112	34	6	48	.304
Scnd Half	208	68	10	42	.327	Clutch	68	15	1	7	.221

2002 Rankings (American League)

- 5th in lowest percentage of swings put into play (35.5)
- 7th in errors in left field (3)
- 10th in highest percentage of swings that missed (25.9)

Juan Gonzlaez

2002 Season

The increasingly brittle Juan Gonzalez again spent the majority of his time out of the lineup. Gonzalez had problems with his right hand after being jammed on a pitch by Oakland's Chad Bradford in the third game of the season. He did not return after July 30 because of torn muscle fibers and a strained ligament in the right thumb. He appeared in only 70 games and joined just a handful of players in big league history to have a drop-off of 100 RBI or more in consecutive seasons. Gonzalez has played in more than 140 games just twice in the last eight years.

Hitting

The early-season thumb injury robbed Gonzalez of his power. He had a stretch of 80 at-bats without a homer and posted a career-low .451 slugging percentage for the year. When he is healthy, he can be a dominant run producer. He has exceptional plate coverage and good power to the opposite field. His career-long problem is a remarkable lack of familiarity with the strike zone. For more than a decade, Gonzalez has chased breaking pitches out of the zone, and some things just never seem to change—he drew just 17 walks in 296 trips to the plate in 2002.

Baserunning & Defense

Gonzalez showed renewed interest in playing right field last season. He still cautiously approaches balls and always knows where the wall is, but he threw well enough to have a team-high nine assists despite logging just 62 games in the outfield. Injuries have cut into his speed, but he rarely makes mistakes on the bases.

2003 Outlook

Though his body does not seem to cooperate as well as it should, Gonzalez is only 33 years old and is far from finished. When he had a poor season with Detroit in 2000, he bounced back with a strong year for Cleveland in '01. The incentive of playing for a contract should motivate him in 2003, but the status of his thumb remains a concern. He wanted to play winter ball in his homeland this offseason, but getting medical clearance to play seemed unlikely in December.

Position: RF
Bats: R **Throws:** R
Ht: 6' 3" **Wt:** 220

Opening Day Age: 33
Born: 10/16/69 in Vega Baja, PR
ML Seasons: 14
Nickname: Igor

Overall Statistics

	G	AB	R	H	D	T	HR	RBI	SB	BB	SO	Avg	OBP	Slg
	70	277	38	78	21	1	8	35	2	17	56	.282	.324	.451
	1573	6101	995	1805	367	23	405	1317	25	434	1181	.296	.344	.563

Where He Hits the Ball

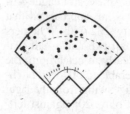 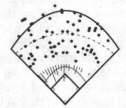

Vs. LHP   **Vs. RHP**

2002 Situational Stats

	AB	H	HR	RBI	Avg		AB	H	HR	RBI	Avg
Home	137	42	4	20	.307	LHP	81	29	3	10	.358
Road	140	36	4	15	.257	RHP	196	49	5	25	.250
First Half	198	61	6	24	.308	Sc Pos	64	21	1	25	.328
Scnd Half	79	17	2	11	.215	Clutch	56	16	1	6	.286

2002 Rankings (American League)

- 2nd in assists in right field (9)
- 4th in lowest cleanup slugging percentage (.419)
- 10th in most GDPs per GDP situation (17.2%)
- Led the Rangers in batting average vs. left-handed pitchers, slugging percentage vs. left-handed pitchers (.580) and on-base percentage vs. lefthanded pitchers (.384)

Todd Hollandsworth

2002 season

The Rangers were so eager to rid themselves of outfielder Gabe Kapler that they sent him to Colorado as part of a deadline deal for Todd Hollandsworth, who himself was headed to free agency. While with the Rangers, Hollandsworth had another stay on the disabled list—his ninth in the last eight seasons. He is a capable player, but he seemingly did not fit on a team already stacked with injury-plagued corner outfielders. He hit just .258 in 39 games for Texas and his bat showed little pop once removed from Coors Field.

Hitting

Hollandsworth's offensive numbers deserve a second look. In the last two seasons, he hit .369 at Coors Field and The Ballpark in Arlington, a pair of playpens for hitters. In all other venues, he has produced at a meager .239 pace. His swing can become complicated because he incorporates so much of his body. He uses a relatively short bat, so he also has difficulties covering the outside corner of the plate.

Baserunning & Defense

The Rangers tried to justify the Kapler trade by playing Hollandsworth in center field. He is solid fundamentally, but lacks the range needed to play the position on a full-time basis. He is best suited for left field, where his merely average arm is not taxed as heavily. Hollandsworth suffered nerve damage and stress fractures in the right shin during the 2001 season, and he has not fully regained his speed. He no longer appears to be a double-digit stolen-base threat.

2003 Outlook

Hollandsworth will make a fine complementary player for some team, just not the Rangers. He did not show enough during a two-month trial to make them change their plans and keep him. Ultimately, his biggest contribution to Texas was giving them a way out of Kapler's deal.

Position: LF/RF/CF
Bats: L **Throws:** L
Ht: 6' 2" **Wt:** 207

Opening Day Age: 29
Born: 4/20/73 in Dayton, OH
ML Seasons: 8
Pronunciation: HAHL-enz-worth

Overall Statistics

	G	AB	R	H	D	T	HR	RBI	SB	BB	SO	Avg	OBP	Slg
'02	134	430	55	122	27	1	16	67	8	40	98	.284	.344	.463
Car.	747	2288	338	637	128	14	74	288	68	190	502	.278	.334	.444

Where He Hits the Ball

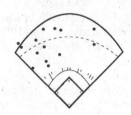 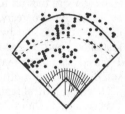

Vs. LHP   Vs. RHP

2002 Situational Stats

	AB	H	HR	RBI	Avg		AB	H	HR	RBI	Avg
Home	193	69	11	40	.358	LHP	57	13	1	5	.228
Road	237	53	5	27	.224	RHP	373	109	15	62	.292
First Half	246	73	9	41	.297	Sc Pos	114	33	6	50	.289
Scnd Half	184	49	7	26	.266	Clutch	64	12	2	6	.188

2002 Rankings (American League)
- Did not rank near the top or bottom in any category

Texas

Kevin Mench

2002 Season

Rookie Kevin Mench had a cup-of-coffee in April and May, but he returned to the majors to stay in mid-June and produced 14 homers and 50 RBI in his final 321 at-bats. He stayed in the lineup in September despite a wrist injury, however, and hit only .192 with no homers and seven RBI for 73 at-bats during the month. Mench showed no signs of nervousness, but veterans wondered if he was having too much fun. He began making mental mistakes late in the season and was briefly benched by former manager Jerry Narron.

Hitting

The bullish Mench likes the ball down and understands how to foul off tough pitches to get the one he wants. He also gears up for the fastball. In less than two weeks, he twice homered on 98-MPH fastballs from Houston closer Billy Wagner. Teams picked up on that, and Mench had late-season difficulty with offspeed pitches. He hit only .221 with a .301 slugging percentage in his final 136 at-bats. He must make the adjustment to a steadier diet of breaking balls in 2003.

Baserunning & Defense

Mench is a far better left fielder than Pete Incaviglia, to whom he is compared because of similar barrel-chested body shapes. Mench has adequate speed, arm strength and defensive instincts. That made his odd baserunning all the more puzzling. He sometimes lost concentration on the bases and ran into six outs. Like Incaviglia, he is of little or no threat to steal.

2003 Outlook

Mench could be a major factor in a core of talent produced by the farm system. The question is whether he will avoid "big head" syndrome and realize that just getting to the majors does not guarantee that he will stay there. According to one teammate, Mench was a "2-and-10" rookie; "Been here two months and acts like he's been here 10 years," the teammate said.

Position: RF/LF
Bats: R **Throws:** R
Ht: 6' 0" **Wt:** 215

Opening Day Age: 25
Born: 1/7/78 in Wilmington, DE
ML Seasons: 1

Overall Statistics

	G	AB	R	H	D	T	HR	RBI	SB	BB	SO	Avg	OBP	Slg
'02	110	366	52	95	20	2	15	60	1	31	83	.260	.327	.448
Car.	110	366	52	95	20	2	15	60	1	31	83	.260	.327	.448

Where He Hits the Ball

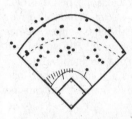 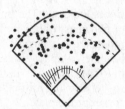

Vs. LHP   **Vs. RHP**

2002 Situational Stats

	AB	H	HR	RBI	Avg		AB	H	HR	RBI	Avg
Home	194	54	8	41	.278	LHP	108	29	8	21	.269
Road	172	41	7	19	.238	RHP	258	66	7	39	.256
First Half	129	37	9	29	.287	Sc Pos	91	29	3	43	.319
Scnd Half	237	58	6	31	.245	Clutch	66	18	4	14	.273

2002 Rankings (American League)

- 2nd in RBI among rookies
- 3rd in home runs among rookies
- 4th in batting average on an 0-2 count (.324) and assists in left field (6)
- 5th in batting average among rookies
- 7th in fewest GDPs per GDP situation (4.9%)
- Led the Rangers in fewest GDPs per GDP situation (4.9%), batting average on an 0-2 count (.324) and batting average on a 3-2 count (.257)

Rafael Palmeiro

2002 Season

Rafael Palmeiro gets better with age and has become a legitimate Hall of Fame candidate. He had his eighth consecutive season with at least 38 homers since turning 30, and now sits at 490 home runs for his career. Not bad for someone who had only 25 homers in his first 874 major league at-bats. Opponents respect Palmeiro. Alex Rodriguez batted ahead of him and received only 12 intentional walks. Palmeiro had *16* intentional walks.

Hitting

Palmeiro made a conscious decision to sacrifice average for power and has become a confirmed pull-hitter. The power production rose as the average dropped. He has had only one .300 season in the last seven years. Early in his career, Palmeiro drove the ball to the opposite-field gap and was a doubles-oriented .300 hitter. In his eagerness to pull the ball now, however, Palmeiro is vulnerable to offspeed pitches away. But with 500 homers clearly in sight, it is unlikely that he will change the approach to help his average.

Baserunning & Defense

Palmeiro had season-long leg ailments last season. Combined with a balky right knee, that made him painfully slow. He clogged the bases, rarely advancing more than one sack at a time. He also needed time off from his duties at first base for the sake of his legs. Palmeiro still can handle the balls he reaches, and he throws well for a first baseman.

2003 Outlook

Paul Molitor is the only player of this generation to improve after age 30 as much as Palmeiro has. There is no reason to doubt Palmeiro will pass the 500-homer barrier in 2003—and keep on going. He needs more time at designated hitter, and his name is sure to surface in trade talks if the club tanks early. Palmeiro can become a free agent after this season, and at some point the Rangers will need to decide when to go younger, and cheaper, at the position.

Position: 1B/DH
Bats: L **Throws:** L
Ht: 6' 0" **Wt:** 190

Opening Day Age: 38
Born: 9/24/64 in Havana, Cuba
ML Seasons: 17
Pronunciation: pahl-MARE-oh
Nickname: Raffy

Overall Statistics

G	AB	R	H	D	T	HR	RBI	SB	BB	SO	Avg	OBP	Slg
155	546	99	149	34	0	43	105	2	104	94	.273	.391	.571
2413	8992	1456	2634	522	36	490	1575	91	1140	1167	.293	.373	.522

Where He Hits the Ball

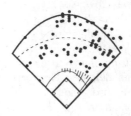 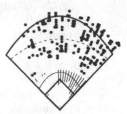

Vs. LHP   **Vs. RHP**

2002 Situational Stats

	AB	H	HR	RBI	Avg		AB	H	HR	RBI	Avg
Home	284	84	23	54	.296	LHP	159	35	10	33	.220
Road	262	65	20	51	.248	RHP	387	114	33	72	.295
First Half	276	73	21	50	.264	Sc Pos	144	37	5	58	.257
Scnd Half	270	76	22	55	.281	Clutch	84	25	8	15	.298

2002 Rankings (American League)

- 2nd in lowest groundball-flyball ratio (0.5)
- 3rd in home runs, walks and HR frequency (12.7 ABs per HR)
- 4th in intentional walks (16)
- 5th in slugging percentage vs. righthanded pitchers (.615), on-base percentage vs. righthanded pitchers (.420), assists at first base (84) and lowest percentage of extra bases taken as a runner (26.9)
- Led the Rangers in doubles, sacrifice flies (7), most pitches seen per plate appearance (4.02), highest percentage of pitches taken (59.1) and cleanup slugging percentage (.582)

Chan Ho Park

2002 Season

Chan Ho Park wilted under the culture shock of pitching in the American League for the first time in his career. Park never adapted to the stacked lineups, which prevented him from cruising through the lower part of the order as he did in the NL with Los Angeles. He also was troubled by the windy and hot Texas climate, a spring-training hamstring injury and irregular blisters on his pitching hand. The result was the highest ERA (5.75) among American Leaguers with 140 innings in 2002, and only nine wins despite having a lead in 18 of his starts.

Pitching

In the NL, Park had electric stuff. He left it behind. Park's velocity was down so much, barely hitting 90 MPH in some games, that many scouts wondered if he was pitching hurt. Park had back problems near the end of his stay with the Dodgers, and the hamstring injury affected his balance and drive in his delivery. He became more and more reluctant to throw the fastball, and turned into little more than a breaking-ball pitcher. He lacked an out pitch and built up high pitch counts early in games. Park failed to make it past the fifth inning in eight of his 25 starts.

Defense

Opponents tried to steal a base only nine times against Park last season, but that number is deceptive. Most of the time, teams were playing with a lead and shut down the running game against him. The hamstring injury hampered Park's ability to field his position, and his assist total plummeted in 2002.

2003 Outlook

The Rangers again will try to make Park their ace, but it may be a losing battle. Park never liked the attention of being the No. 1 starter when circumstances forced the job upon him down the stretch with Los Angeles in 2001, and he never came close to taking on the role last season. With Park under contract for four more seasons, the Rangers have to find a way to fix that. The alternative is another free-agent bust.

Position: SP
Bats: R **Throws:** R
Ht: 6' 2" **Wt:** 204

Opening Day Age: 29
Born: 6/30/73 in Kong Ju City, South Korea
ML Seasons: 9

Overall Statistics

	W	L	Pct.	ERA	G	GS	Sv	IP	H	BB	SO	HR	Ratio
'02	9	8	.529	5.75	25	25	0	145.2	154	78	121	20	1.59
Car.	89	62	.589	4.01	246	201	0	1329.1	1155	638	1219	144	1.35

How Often He Throws Strikes

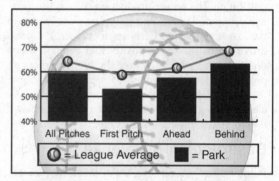

= League Average ■ = Park

2002 Situational Stats

	W	L	ERA	Sv	IP		AB	H	HR	RBI	Avg
Home	6	4	6.84	0	72.1	LHB	328	94	12	55	.287
Road	3	4	4.66	0	73.1	RHB	236	60	8	33	.254
First Half	3	4	8.01	0	57.1	Sc Pos	146	41	8	67	.281
Scnd Half	6	4	4.28	0	88.1	Clutch	25	5	0	1	.200

2002 Rankings (American League)

- 1st in hit batsmen (17)
- 5th in walks allowed
- 9th in wild pitches (9)
- Led the Rangers in walks allowed, hit batsmen (17), strikeouts, wild pitches (9), most run support per nine innings (6.4) and most strikeouts per nine innings (7.5)

Alex Rodriguez

Position: SS
Bats: R **Throws:** R
Ht: 6' 3" **Wt:** 210

Opening Day Age: 27
Born: 7/27/75 in New York, NY
ML Seasons: 9
Pronunciation: rod-RI-guez
Nickname: A-Rod

2002 Season

Alex Rodriguez continued to live up to the unrealistic demands created by his $252 million contract. He put together the most dominant offensive season in history by a shortstop, and also played Gold Glove defense while appearing in every game. Rodriguez led the American League in home runs and RBI, but a September slump dropped him out of the top 10 for batting. He did not play well in Texas' most important games of the season, however. He hit .185 in the 1-6 start that doomed the club, and batted only .197 in the final 20 contests, all against AL West teams jockeying for playoff position.

Hitting

Rodriguez won a batting title with a .358 mark in 1996 with Seattle. Asked to be more of a run producer with Texas, A-Rod added more lift to his swing and has produced back-to-back 50-homer seasons. The tradeoff has been an average that has dropped below .320 each season, and his strikeouts have risen accordingly. Unlike Barry Bonds, Rodriguez makes outs. He has three consecutive seasons of more than 120 strikeouts. Moving to The Ballpark in Arlington has helped inflate his numbers. In two seasons with Texas, Rodriguez has 60 homers and 147 RBI at home and 49 homers and 130 RBI on the road.

Baserunning & Defense

Rodriguez ranks among the game's smartest players, and his intelligence shows on the bases. He makes good decisions and runs well without having exceptional speed. Despite playing on a difficult natural surface at home, Rodriguez made only 10 errors to earn his first AL Gold Glove at short. He will not show off his arm like other shortstops, but he has the ability to always have just enough on his throw to get the out.

2003 Outlook

Many still feel that Rodriguez caused his own problems by choosing to take the money rather than staying with a competitive team in Seattle. He has kept up a brave front in the face of two consecutive last-place finishes with Texas, but how long can he keep his focus in a situation that has little hope for immediate improvement?

Overall Statistics

	G	AB	R	H	D	T	HR	RBI	SB	BB	SO	Avg	OBP	Slg
'02	162	624	125	187	27	2	57	142	9	87	122	.300	.392	.623
Car.	1114	4382	885	1354	255	16	298	872	160	472	869	.309	.380	.579

Where He Hits the Ball

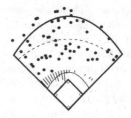
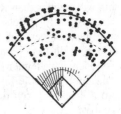

Vs. LHP   **Vs. RHP**

2002 Situational Stats

	AB	H	HR	RBI	Avg		AB	H	HR	RBI	Avg
Home	313	101	34	82	.323	LHP	159	38	8	24	.239
Road	311	86	23	60	.277	RHP	465	149	49	118	.320
First Half	328	100	27	73	.305	Sc Pos	153	56	17	87	.366
Scnd Half	296	87	30	69	.294	Clutch	96	24	7	23	.250

2002 Rankings (American League)

- 1st in home runs, total bases (389), RBI and games played
- 2nd in runs scored, HR frequency (10.9 ABs per HR) and slugging percentage vs. righthanded pitchers (.682)
- 3rd in times on base (284), pitches seen (2,812) and slugging percentage
- 4th in plate appearances (725) and fielding percentage at shortstop (.987)
- 5th in highest percentage of extra bases taken as a runner (61.8)
- Led the Rangers in home runs, at-bats, runs scored, hits, total bases (389), RBI, stolen bases, hit by pitch (10), times on base (284), strikeouts, pitches seen (2,812) and plate appearances (725)

Ivan Rodriguez

2002 Season

Injuries cut into Ivan Rodriguez' playing time for the third consecutive season. He missed 47 games during the first half of 2002 because of a herniated disc in his lower back and was hindered by the condition upon his return. Rodriguez' injuries all seem to be related to his heavy workload as a catcher. He appeared in more than 140 games annually from 1996-99, but he has not avoided the disabled list since. Offense remains a strength, however. He has hit .300 or better in each of the past eight seasons.

Hitting

Few regulars in the majors swing at more bad pitches than Rodriguez. But no one does more with bad pitches than Rodriguez. There are drawbacks to the let-no-pitch-pass approach. Rodriguez' career high for walks is 38, and he has posted an on-base percentage of more than .360 just once. His tendency to hit pitchers' pitches makes him a double-play threat. He has grounded into at least a dozen double plays in seven consecutive seasons, and has 74 double-play grounders in the last four years alone. Those outs take their toll on a club.

Baserunning & Defense

The back problem produced a noticeable slide in Rodriguez' defense last season. He had difficulty getting down to block pitches in the dirt, and the Rangers led the American League in wild pitches with 84. Kansas City had the second-highest total at 68. Rodriguez threw out 13 of 39 runners, well below his career rate of 46.1 percent. And helping pitchers through tough spots never has been Rodriguez' strength. He has curtailed his running and had five fewer steals in the last three seasons combined (20) than he swiped in 1999 alone.

2003 Outlook

At age 31, Rodriguez enters the danger zone for catchers. He has caught 1,426 games, and the body begins to break down after that much work. A position switch might prolong Rodriguez the offensive player, but he wants to play out his career as a catcher. The free-agent market for Rodriguez seems small, but someone will commit to keeping him behind the plate.

Position: C
Bats: R **Throws:** R
Ht: 5' 9" **Wt:** 205

Opening Day Age: 31
Born: 11/30/71 in Vega Baja, PR
ML Seasons: 12
Pronunciation: rod-RI-gez
Nickname: Pudge

Overall Statistics

	G	AB	R	H	D	T	HR	RBI	SB	BB	SO	Avg	OBP	Slg
'02	108	408	67	128	32	2	19	60	5	25	71	.314	.353	.542
Car.	1479	5656	852	1723	344	28	215	829	80	304	763	.305	.342	.489

Where He Hits the Ball

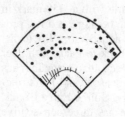
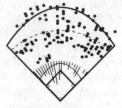

Vs. LHP   **Vs. RHP**

2002 Situational Stats

	AB	H	HR	RBI	Avg		AB	H	HR	RBI	Avg
Home	212	75	15	41	.354	LHP	108	33	4	15	.306
Road	196	53	4	19	.270	RHP	300	95	15	45	.317
First Half	151	44	6	23	.291	Sc Pos	98	25	6	42	.255
Scnd Half	257	84	13	37	.327	Clutch	69	22	3	12	.319

2002 Rankings (American League)

- 3rd in errors at catcher (7)
- 4th in lowest percentage of pitches taken (43.6)
- 5th in lowest fielding percentage at catcher (.990)
- Led the Rangers in batting average and batting average at home

Kenny Rogers

2002 Season

Kenny Rogers underwent surgery in July 2001 to remove a rib that had been pinching an artery and causing a circulation problem. After a lengthy rehab, his velocity increased by about five MPH, allowing him once again to work both sides of the plate rather than relying only on a sinker. He led the Rangers' staff in wins and innings in 2002 by a wide margin, and pitched well in a home park known to help hitters. Rogers had to deal with a flurry of trade talk near the deadline. He rejected a deal to Cincinnati but accepted a move to Boston. That deal fell through because the Red Sox would not give up lefthander Casey Fossum.

Pitching

Once upon a time, Rogers threw hard. Those days are long gone, and he gets by on guile and breaking pitches. One aspect of Rogers' game has not changed, however. He refuses to give in to hitters no matter the count. He will try a breaking pitch on 3-1 rather than lob in a fastball. Because of that determination, Rogers finished tied for eighth in the American League in walks. He showed the best way to pitch at The Ballpark in Arlington is to keep the ball on the ground. Rogers had the AL's fourth-highest groundball-flyball ratio last season, at 2.02.

Defense

No AL pitcher fields his position as well as Rogers, and he pocketed his second Gold Glove in the past three seasons. He functions as a fifth infielder, cutting off balls up the middle and taking away the bunt. He sometimes tries to do too much as a fielder and forces throws. He holds runners so well and has such a deceptive pickoff move that no one tried to steal second base against him last season.

2003 Outlook

Rogers has pitched more than 190 innings in four of the last five seasons. He is 38, but he could pitch about three to four years with his effortless style. Rogers filed for free agency, and he seems certain to go elsewhere after rejecting a significant offer from the Rangers in December.

Position: SP
Bats: L **Throws:** L
Ht: 6' 1" **Wt:** 217

Opening Day Age: 38
Born: 11/10/64 in Savannah, GA
ML Seasons: 14
Nickname: The Gambler

Texas

Overall Statistics

	W	L	Pct.	ERA	G	GS	Sv	IP	H	BB	SO	HR	Ratio
'02	13	8	.619	3.84	33	33	0	210.2	212	70	107	21	1.34
Car.	145	106	.578	4.20	589	304	28	2260.0	2305	848	1422	225	1.40

How Often He Throws Strikes

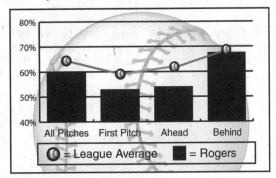

O = League Average   ■ = Rogers

2002 Situational Stats

	W	L	ERA	Sv	IP		AB	H	HR	RBI	Avg
Home	4	4	3.65	0	101.0	LHB	176	34	6	17	.193
Road	9	4	4.02	0	109.2	RHB	636	178	15	69	.280
First Half	9	5	3.57	0	113.1	Sc Pos	191	54	3	60	.283
Scnd Half	4	3	4.16	0	97.1	Clutch	62	17	2	7	.274

2002 Rankings (American League)

- 1st in lowest stolen-base percentage allowed (0.0) and fewest strikeouts per nine innings (4.6)
- 2nd in lowest batting average allowed vs. lefthanded batters
- 3rd in most GDPs induced per nine innings (1.2) and lowest strikeout-walk ratio (1.5)
- Led the Rangers in ERA, wins, games started, complete games (2), innings pitched, hits allowed, batters faced (892), home runs allowed, pitches thrown (3,338), pickoff throws (116), winning percentage and lowest ERA at home

Michael Young

2002 Season

General Manager John Hart wanted Frank Catalanotto for his offense at second base. But former manager Jerry Narron stuck with Michael Young, and Young claimed the position with Gold Glove-level defense. Young proved to be one of the most, if not *the* most, athletic second basemen in the American League, and he has the strongest arm. He raised his batting average by 13 points from his rookie season but still had too many strikeouts for a bottom-of-the-order hitter.

Hitting

Young must bring his swing under control and recognize that he will get by with singles, not homers. He struck out 112 times in 2002 while drawing just 41 walks. Of the 23 AL players with at least 110 strikeouts last year, he was the only one who did not hit at least 15 home runs. The experiment of Young as leadoff hitter did not work. He hit only .213 with a .263 on-base percentage for 39 starts in the No. 1 spot. He has the speed to bunt for hits if he shows a willingness to develop that part of his offensive game.

Baserunning & Defense

Young is an exceptional second baseman. He finished second to Seattle's Bret Boone in fielding percentage among AL second basemen, but he also had 81 more chances. Young has more range to his left but still moves well to his right. His arm strength, which reminds scouts of former Gold Glove winner Manny Trillo, shows on double plays. Young and shortstop Alex Rodriguez formed the AL's best middle-infield combination. Though he has the speed to steal bases, Young must refine his technique—he was caught stealing (seven) more times than he was successful (six) in 2002.

2003 Outlook

As long as Hart wants offense from second base, Young will have to keep proving himself. There continues to be talk in the organization that Young could be the answer to the long-term problem in center field. If that move is made, that could open up the possibility of super-prospect Hank Blalock relocating from third base to the keystone.

Position: 2B/SS
Bats: R **Throws:** R
Ht: 6' 1" **Wt:** 190

Opening Day Age: 26
Born: 10/19/76 in Covina, CA
ML Seasons: 3

Overall Statistics

	G	AB	R	H	D	T	HR	RBI	SB	BB	SO	Avg	OBP	Slg
'02	156	573	77	150	26	8	9	62	6	41	112	.262	.308	.382
Car.	264	961	134	246	44	12	20	111	9	67	204	.256	.303	.389

Where He Hits the Ball

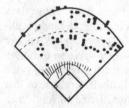
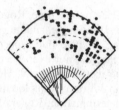

Vs. LHP **Vs. RHP**

2002 Situational Stats

	AB	H	HR	RBI	Avg		AB	H	HR	RBI	Avg
Home	267	75	3	34	.281	LHP	155	45	2	11	.290
Road	306	75	6	28	.245	RHP	418	105	7	51	.251
First Half	280	73	7	36	.261	Sc Pos	128	34	1	46	.266
Scnd Half	293	77	2	26	.263	Clutch	86	20	1	9	.233

2002 Rankings (American League)

- 2nd in sacrifice bunts (13), fielding percentage at second base (.988) and lowest on-base percentage for a leadoff hitter (.263)
- 3rd in triples
- 4th in lowest slugging percentage
- Led the Rangers in singles, triples, sacrifice bunts (13), caught stealing (7), highest groundball-flyball ratio (1.6) and bunts in play (15)

Francisco Cordero

Position: RP
Bats: R **Throws:** R
Ht: 6' 2" **Wt:** 200

Opening Day Age: 27
Born: 5/11/75 in Santo Domingo, DR
ML Seasons: 4
Pronunciation: cor-DER-oh

Overall Statistics

	W	L	Pct.	ERA	G	GS	Sv	IP	H	BB	SO	HR	Ratio
'02	2	0	1.000	1.79	39	0	10	45.1	33	13	41	2	1.01
Car.	5	5	.500	3.94	118	0	10	144.0	142	81	110	15	1.55

2002 Situational Stats

	W	L	ERA	Sv	IP		AB	H	HR	RBI	Avg
Home	1	0	1.66	5	21.2	LHB	74	14	1	9	.189
Road	1	0	1.90	5	23.2	RHB	88	19	1	6	.216
First Half	0	0	3.15	3	20.0	Sc Pos	36	10	1	14	.278
Scnd Half	2	0	0.71	7	25.1	Clutch	69	15	1	10	.217

2002 Season

Francisco Cordero finally showed the ability that made him the key to the nine-player deal that sent outfielder Juan Gonzalez to Detroit in 1999. Cordero stepped in as the Rangers' closer after others went down because of injury or poor performance. Cordero had 10 saves in 12 chances and was scored on only once in his last 21 appearances, a span of 21.1 innings.

Pitching & Defense

Cordero showed a dominant slider and also broke out a cut fastball that helped him against lefthanded hitters. His top velocity stayed in the mid-90s range, but his ball is heavy and hard to lift. The key for Texas was the fact that he threw strikes. The club attributed the improvement primarily to better concentration. Like most late-innings pitchers, Cordero holds runners pretty well, though he prefers to go all out against the hitter rather than use a slide step to slow the runner.

2003 Outlook

With Jeff Zimmerman out until at least the All-Star break, Cordero begins 2003 as Texas' closer. If he shows the same concentration and slider that he displayed last season, he could keep the job for a long time. A healthy Zimmerman paired with Cordero could be a dynamic late-game duo.

Doug Davis

Position: SP
Bats: R **Throws:** L
Ht: 6' 4" **Wt:** 190

Opening Day Age: 27
Born: 9/21/75 in Sacramento, CA
ML Seasons: 4

Overall Statistics

	W	L	Pct.	ERA	G	GS	Sv	IP	H	BB	SO	HR	Ratio
'02	3	5	.375	4.98	10	10	0	59.2	67	22	28	7	1.49
Car.	21	21	.500	5.03	72	53	0	347.0	408	149	212	38	1.61

2002 Situational Stats

	W	L	ERA	Sv	IP		AB	H	HR	RBI	Avg
Home	1	2	4.19	0	19.1	LHB	74	18	2	11	.243
Road	2	3	5.36	0	40.1	RHB	157	49	5	23	.312
First Half	3	5	4.98	0	59.2	Sc Pos	58	17	0	25	.293
Scnd Half	0	0	—	0	0.0	Clutch	6	0	0	0	.000

2002 Season

Doug Davis never found a common ground with pitching coach Oscar Acosta, and neither lasted the 2002 season. When Davis slumped after going 2-0 with a 1.88 ERA in his first three starts, Acosta determined that he was timid. An 11-game winner with a last-place team in 2001, Davis found himself in the minors by the end of May.

Pitching & Defense

Davis' stuff is average, but he helps himself by hiding the ball well in his delivery. He struggled all spring to find a pitch to complement his cut fastball. He needs something to work the outside corner of the plate against righthanders. Davis finishes his delivery in poor fielding position and has been hurt by his inability to handle balls up the middle. He has four errors in only 64 career chances. He has a decent pickoff move, but didn't have much chance to display it last year.

2003 Outlook

No one will benefit from the change in managers to Buck Showalter more than Davis. Showalter refuses to believe a pitcher who won 11 games in 2001 cannot be helpful this season. Davis will get every chance to work his way back into the Texas rotation.

Bill Haselman

Position: C
Bats: R **Throws:** R
Ht: 6' 3" **Wt:** 225

Opening Day Age: 36
Born: 5/25/66 in Long Branch, NJ
ML Seasons: 12
Pronunciation: HASS-el-man

Overall Statistics

	G	AB	R	H	D	T	HR	RBI	SB	BB	SO	Avg	OBP	Slg
'02	69	179	16	44	7	0	3	18	0	11	25	.246	.297	.335
Car.	585	1603	185	416	94	3	47	210	9	114	299	.260	.311	.410

2002 Situational Stats

	AB	H	HR	RBI	Avg		AB	H	HR	RBI	Avg
Home	73	18	1	6	.247	LHP	47	17	1	8	.362
Road	106	26	2	12	.245	RHP	132	27	2	10	.205
First Half	144	35	3	16	.243	Sc Pos	55	13	1	14	.236
Scnd Half	35	9	0	2	.257	Clutch	23	7	0	1	.304

2002 Season

A herniated disc in the lower back of starting catcher Ivan Rodriguez forced Texas to call upon Bill Haselman more than planned. He proved to be an adequate replacement, and the Rangers were 22-28 in his starts compared to 50-62 in all other games. Haselman's strength is his ability to work with young pitchers on the mental and physical aspects of the game.

Hitting, Baserunning & Defense

Haselman can catch up to a fastball and has doubles power. He also can handle lefthanded pitching but struggles against righthanders. He is a lifetime .301 hitter in 529 at-bats against lefties, but has just a .239 mark against righties. He is a good receiver but does not throw well, due to two major arm surgeries in the last three years. It takes at least two hits to score him from first, and he hasn't stolen a base since 1999.

2003 Outlook

In their never-ending quest for offense from every position, the Rangers kept Todd Greene as the backup catcher and did not pick up an option on Haselman. A team that wants a veteran catcher to handle young pitchers should look no further than Haselman, who remains serviceable as long as he stays in the 250-275 at-bat range.

Danny Kolb

Position: RP
Bats: R **Throws:** R
Ht: 6' 4" **Wt:** 215

Opening Day Age: 28
Born: 3/29/75 in Sterling, IL
ML Seasons: 4

Overall Statistics

	W	L	Pct.	ERA	G	GS	Sv	IP	H	BB	SO	HR	Ratio
'02	3	6	.333	4.22	34	0	1	32.0	27	22	20	1	1.53
Car.	5	7	.417	5.01	68	0	1	79.0	80	49	50	5	1.63

2002 Situational Stats

	W	L	ERA	Sv	IP		AB	H	HR	RBI	Avg
Home	3	2	5.65	0	14.1	LHB	55	16	1	8	.291
Road	0	4	3.06	1	17.2	RHB	64	11	0	9	.172
First Half	0	0	—	0	0.0	Sc Pos	39	8	0	13	.205
Scnd Half	3	6	4.22	1	32.0	Clutch	74	20	1	11	.270

2002 Season

The oft-injured Danny Kolb made it back to the majors after a two-year recovery from Tommy John surgery and a partially torn rotator cuff. He pitched 46.1 innings in the majors and the minors after June 25, and stayed healthy. He even saw action in four games for Texas with a save on the line, and converted one of those opportunities.

Pitching & Defense

Kolb consistently throws in the low 90-MPH range, and his sinking fastball has hard late movement in on righthanded hitters. He needs a better offspeed pitch to use against lefties, who batted .291 against him last year, 119 points higher than the mark posted by righties. Kolb has not been tested in the field very much in the majors, though he has yet to be charged with a big league error. He does have trouble slowing baserunners.

2003 Outlook

The Rangers envision Kolb as a setup reliever, but he must stay healthy. He has yet to work more than 32.0 major league innings in a single season, and he will be 28 years old on March 29. The club believes Kolb will be stronger after a year of rehabilitating from shoulder surgery, but in his last 27 appearances in 2002, Kolb was just 2-6 with a 4.91 ERA.

Mike Lamb

Position: 1B/DH/3B/LF
Bats: L **Throws:** R
Ht: 6' 1" **Wt:** 195

Opening Day Age: 27
Born: 8/9/75 in West Covina, CA
ML Seasons: 3

Overall Statistics

	G	AB	R	H	D	T	HR	RBI	SB	BB	SO	Avg	OBP	Slg
'02	115	314	54	89	13	0	9	33	0	33	48	.283	.354	.411
Car.	329	1091	161	313	56	2	19	115	2	81	135	.287	.341	.394

2002 Situational Stats

	AB	H	HR	RBI	Avg		AB	H	HR	RBI	Avg
Home	154	44	7	19	.286	LHP	38	8	0	4	.211
Road	160	45	2	14	.281	RHP	276	81	9	29	.293
First Half	181	54	4	18	.298	Sc Pos	63	17	2	24	.270
Scnd Half	133	35	5	15	.263	Clutch	55	12	0	5	.218

2002 Season

For the third consecutive year, the Rangers went with another third baseman on Opening Day only to return to Mike Lamb early in the season. The club believes his future is as a utility player, with catcher one of the potential spots he could fill in a pinch. Lamb, who had one disastrous start at catcher, is cool to the idea and still thinks of himself as an everyday player.

Hitting, Baserunning & Defense

Lamb hits for average with a funky swing—lower body moving to pull while his upper body heads to the opposite field—but he has lacked power. He had a career-high nine homers in 2002, but that lifted his lifetime total to just 19 in 1,091 at-bats. Those types of numbers simply won't cut it for a full-time corner infielder. Lamb also lacks the power to offset his defense at third base. He still has footwork problems that lead to poor throws. His work at first base and left field was not much better. He's also nothing special on the basepaths.

2003 Outlook

Lamb could help a team as a bench player, but he first must accept the role to be any good at it. With Hank Blalock and Mark Teixeira on the horizon, Lamb's chances of being the full-time third baseman with Texas are nil.

Herbert Perry

Position: 3B/1B
Bats: R **Throws:** R
Ht: 6' 2" **Wt:** 225

Opening Day Age: 33
Born: 9/15/69 in Live Oak, FL
ML Seasons: 7

Overall Statistics

	G	AB	R	H	D	T	HR	RBI	SB	BB	SO	Avg	OBP	Slg
'02	132	450	64	124	24	1	22	77	4	34	66	.276	.333	.480
Car.	469	1538	227	427	99	5	50	227	12	114	269	.278	.339	.446

2002 Situational Stats

	AB	H	HR	RBI	Avg		AB	H	HR	RBI	Avg
Home	216	57	9	40	.264	LHP	127	33	6	22	.260
Road	234	67	13	37	.286	RHP	323	91	16	55	.282
First Half	211	59	10	38	.280	Sc Pos	120	30	6	54	.250
Scnd Half	239	65	12	39	.272	Clutch	77	19	1	7	.247

2002 Season

Herbert Perry eventually filled the void created when rookie Hank Blalock could not hold the third-base job. Perry altered his swing and set career highs for homers and RBI. He also avoided the leg injuries that have marred his career and appeared in a personal-record 132 games.

Hitting, Baserunning & Defense

A confirmed pull-hitter, Perry became more conscious of using the opposite field and also added a lift to his swing. That cost him some points off his batting average but added unexpected power. Perry's .480 slugging percentage was 48 points higher than his previous career average. Leg injuries have left him with below-average speed, and he is a prime double-play candidate when he hits the ball on the ground. Perry's arm is accurate, but his range at third base is below average. In the last three seasons, he has 34 errors in 291 games at the hot corner.

2003 Outlook

The Rangers worked out a two-year, $3 million contract extension with Perry in early September. For a reasonable price, he gives them insurance at third base should either Blalock or Mark Teixeira not be ready, as well as an extra righthanded bat and a strong, positive voice in the clubhouse.

Jay Powell

Position: RP
Bats: R **Throws:** R
Ht: 6' 4" **Wt:** 225

Opening Day Age: 31
Born: 1/9/72 in
Meridian, MS
ML Seasons: 8

Overall Statistics

	W	L	Pct.	ERA	G	GS	Sv	IP	H	BB	SO	HR	Ratio
'02	3	2	.600	3.44	51	0	0	49.2	50	24	35	5	1.49
Car.	32	22	.593	3.77	433	0	22	456.1	443	223	365	32	1.46

2002 Situational Stats

	W	L	ERA	Sv	IP		AB	H	HR	RBI	Avg
Home	0	1	4.50	0	28.0	LHB	72	16	2	12	.222
Road	3	1	2.08	0	21.2	RHB	126	34	3	20	.270
First Half	1	1	7.45	0	9.2	Sc Pos	69	17	2	27	.246
Scnd Half	2	1	2.48	0	40.0	Clutch	103	30	2	15	.291

2002 Season

A torn tendon in his right middle finger forced Jay Powell to miss the first 10 weeks of the 2002 season. He never found a rhythm until early August, when he allowed only two earned runs in a stretch of 15.2 innings. The Rangers had expected Powell to handle the eighth inning with a lead, and they never found an adequate replacement.

Pitching & Defense

When healthy, Powell gets good sinking movement on the fastball. The pitch helped him against lefthanded hitters more last year than in recent seasons. His pitching style makes him vulnerable to balls getting through the infield in late-game situations. In the last two years, he has allowed 32 of 74 inherited runners to score. Powell has been known to panic on fielding plays, but that did not happen last season. He holds runners well and is better than average to the plate.

2003 Outlook

The Rangers will try again to make Powell their eighth-inning pitcher, with the early save chances going to Francisco Cordero. At least the club knows Powell should not be intimidated by his home park—in the last two seasons, Powell has called three hitter-friendly venues home: Houston, Colorado and Texas.

John Rocker

Position: RP
Bats: R **Throws:** L
Ht: 6' 4" **Wt:** 225

Opening Day Age: 28
Born: 10/17/74 in
Statesboro, GA
ML Seasons: 5

Overall Statistics

	W	L	Pct.	ERA	G	GS	Sv	IP	H	BB	SO	HR	Ratio
'02	2	3	.400	6.66	30	0	1	24.1	29	13	30	5	1.73
Car.	13	22	.371	3.40	278	0	88	254.1	198	161	332	23	1.41

2002 Situational Stats

	W	L	ERA	Sv	IP		AB	H	HR	RBI	Avg
Home	2	0	5.14	1	14.0	LHB	33	12	3	15	.364
Road	0	3	8.71	0	10.1	RHB	64	17	2	7	.266
First Half	2	3	6.66	1	24.1	Sc Pos	34	9	3	19	.265
Scnd Half	0	0	—	0	0.0	Clutch	63	19	3	16	.302

2002 Season

John Rocker may have blown his last chance. This time the reason was performance, not behavior. He opened the season as the Texas closer because of injuries, but was sent to the minors after converting only one of three chances. Rocker balked at the move and went off for a week of work with former major league pitching coach Tom House. The results were no better, and he later did a three-week stint in the minors. He did not pitch after July 3 because of shoulder soreness.

Pitching & Defense

Rocker's velocity was down during spring training and never returned to past levels. He tried to get by with a slider, but the pitch lacked bite. Opponents hit .299 against Rocker, not the kind of figure a team is looking for from its closer. When he had 62 saves with Atlanta in 1999-2000, opponents hit only .193 against him. Rocker does nothing to help himself on the mound, and in the last two seasons he has committed five errors on just 19 chances.

2003 Outlook

Texas General Manager John Hart traded for Rocker twice in less than a year. Even Hart is not willing to be fooled a third time. Rocker will be hard-pressed to find a job.

Todd Van Poppel

Position: RP
Bats: R **Throws:** R
Ht: 6' 5" **Wt:** 240

Opening Day Age: 31
Born: 12/9/71 in
Hinsdale, IL
ML Seasons: 9

Overall Statistics

	W	L	Pct.	ERA	G	GS	Sv	IP	H	BB	SO	HR	Ratio
'02	3	2	.600	5.45	50	0	1	72.2	80	29	85	14	1.50
Car.	33	45	.423	5.50	295	82	4	743.1	757	414	605	113	1.58

2002 Situational Stats

	W	L	ERA	Sv	IP		AB	H	HR	RBI	Avg
Home	2	1	5.40	1	43.1	LHB	127	37	6	16	.291
Road	1	1	5.52	0	29.1	RHB	164	43	8	36	.262
First Half	1	0	4.31	1	39.2	Sc Pos	91	26	8	44	.286
Scnd Half	2	2	6.82	0	33.0	Clutch	44	16	2	8	.364

2002 Season

Todd Van Poppel became the highest-paid mopup reliever in baseball history in 2002. In the first season of a three-year, $7.5 million contract, Van Poppel worked his way into "lost causes" duty. He entered the game with a lead or tie only 16 times in 50 appearances. The Rangers were 16-34 when Van Poppel pitched last year. The Chicago Cubs were 20-39 in his appearances in 2001.

Pitching & Defense

Van Poppel pitches high in the zone, and he did not have the stuff to get away with that last season. He led American League relievers in homers allowed with 14 in only 72.2 innings. He junked the curveball for the slider as his breaking pitch while with the Cubs, but he was inconsistent with that offering. Van Poppel is slow to the plate, and opponents notched 11 steals in 12 tries in 2002. A generally steady fielder, he bounced back after a subpar performance with the glove in 2001 to turn in another errorless showing last year.

2003 Outlook

The Rangers have their long reliever for the next two seasons. They will use Van Poppel in crucial situations only as a last resort. His contract remains one of the most staggering overpayments in recent years.

Jeff Zimmerman

Position: RP
Bats: R **Throws:** R
Ht: 6' 1" **Wt:** 200

Opening Day Age: 30
Born: 8/9/72 in
Kelowna, BC, Canada
ML Seasons: 3

Overall Statistics

	W	L	Pct.	ERA	G	GS	Sv	IP	H	BB	SO	HR	Ratio
'02					Did Not Play								
Car.	17	12	.586	3.27	196	0	32	228.2	178	73	213	29	1.10

2002 Situational Stats

	W	L	ERA	Sv	IP		AB	H	HR	RBI	Avg
Home	—	—	—	—	—	LHB	—	—	—	—	—
Road	—	—	—	—	—	RHB	—	—	—	—	—
First Half	—	—	—	—	—	Sc Pos	—	—	—	—	—
Scnd Half	—	—	—	—	—	Clutch	—	—	—	—	—

2002 Season

Scheduled to be the closer after converting his final 17 save chances in 2001, Jeff Zimmerman never made it to the mound. After two months of treatment and rehab, the Rangers determined he had blown out his elbow. Zimmerman underwent Tommy John surgery in July. The good news for Zimmerman is orthopedists have become so good at the surgery that most subjects now return with stronger arms and better velocity.

Pitching & Defense

The Rangers expect Zimmerman to have the same slider as before. He throws the slider to hitters from both sides of the plate. Zimmerman does not really need the extra velocity that Tommy John recipients show. When he throws the slider too hard, it flattens out and stays on a single plane. He ends his delivery in good fielding position. Not surprisingly, he focuses more on the hitter than the runner in late-game situations.

2003 Outlook

The Rangers are eyeing Zimmerman to return sometime around the All-Star break. They will ease him back into the bullpen, but believe he can be a closer again by the end of the season. If his recovery hinges on work ethic, he will be back before even the most-optimistic expectations.

Other Texas Rangers

Juan Alvarez (Pos: LHP, Age: 29)

	W	L	Pct.	ERA	G	GS	Sv	IP	H	BB	SO	HR	Ratio
'02	0	4	.000	4.76	52	0	0	39.2	35	21	30	7	1.41
Car.	0	5	.000	5.73	71	0	0	48.2	50	32	36	10	1.68

Alvarez assisted an injury-depleted Texas pen and had an OK rookie season as a 28-year-old. He endured a rough spot in late July and had a 12.71 ERA in September, possibly hastening his release in November. 2003 Outlook: C

Rob Bell (Pos: RHP, Age: 26)

	W	L	Pct.	ERA	G	GS	Sv	IP	H	BB	SO	HR	Ratio
'02	4	3	.571	6.22	17	15	0	94.0	113	35	70	16	1.57
Car.	16	21	.432	5.95	70	68	0	384.0	419	172	279	80	1.54

Bell was a promising pitcher a few years ago, but has not turned the corner. Texas would love to see him step up with holes in its rotation. He was 6-0 (3.67) in the high minors, but it was ugly in Texas. 2003 Outlook: C

Reynaldo Garcia (Pos: RHP, Age: 28)

	W	L	Pct.	ERA	G	GS	Sv	IP	H	BB	SO	HR	Ratio
'02	0	0	–	31.50	3	0	0	2.0	7	1	2	3	4.00
Car.	0	0	–	31.50	3	0	0	2.0	7	1	2	3	4.00

Garcia was solid as a swingman at Double-A Tulsa, and even better working only in the pen in his first Triple-A exposure with Oklahoma. He got lit up twice in three midseason appearances and was gone. 2003 Outlook: C

Todd Greene (Pos: C/1B, Age: 31, Bats: R)

	G	AB	R	H	D	T	HR	RBI	SB	BB	SO	Avg	OBP	Slg
'02	42	112	15	30	5	0	10	19	0	2	23	.268	.282	.580
Car.	300	888	107	217	42	0	42	122	5	35	181	.244	.277	.434

Greene hit 17 Triple-A homers in 277 at-bats and 10 more with the Rangers in just 112 at-bats. He slugged .584 for the season, but his .282 OBP with Texas, 23-2 strikeout-walk ratio and poor arm tell another story. 2003 Outlook: C

Rusty Greer (Pos: LF/DH, Age: 34, Bats: L)

	G	AB	R	H	D	T	HR	RBI	SB	BB	SO	Avg	OBP	Slg
'02	51	199	24	59	9	2	1	17	1	19	17	.296	.356	.377
Car.	1027	3829	643	1166	258	25	119	614	31	519	555	.305	.387	.478

Greer is paying for an all-out hustling career. He had November surgery to repair his left rotator cuff, which will keep him out all of 2003. Plus he faces Tommy John surgery as well as knee and hip procedures. 2003 Outlook: D

Hideki Irabu (Pos: RHP, Age: 33)

	W	L	Pct.	ERA	G	GS	Sv	IP	H	BB	SO	HR	Ratio
'02	3	8	.273	5.74	38	2	16	47.0	51	16	30	11	1.43
Car.	34	35	.493	5.15	126	80	16	514.0	547	175	405	91	1.40

A disappointment for the Yanks and Expos, who gave up Ted Lilly to get him from New York, Irabu had a brief run as the Texas closer in 2002, but blood clots in his lungs ended his season in July. He signed a one-year deal with Hanshin of the Japanese Central League in December. 2003 Outlook: D

Dan Miceli (Pos: RHP, Age: 32)

	W	L	Pct.	ERA	G	GS	Sv	IP	H	BB	SO	HR	Ratio
'02	0	2	.000	8.64	9	0	0	8.1	13	3	5	1	1.92
Car.	33	38	.465	4.78	448	9	32	502.1	507	225	454	65	1.46

It's been a long, slow slide since he was a Padres bullpen stud in 1998. His only bright spot has been a 2.21 ERA with Colorado in 2001. The pitching-needy Rangers cut him in May last year. 2003 Outlook: C

Chris Michalak (Pos: LHP, Age: 32)

	W	L	Pct.	ERA	G	GS	Sv	IP	H	BB	SO	HR	Ratio
'02	0	2	.000	4.40	13	0	0	14.1	20	10	5	1	2.09
Car.	8	11	.421	4.66	53	18	1	156.1	186	69	77	21	1.63

Michalak has a 5.24 career ERA as a reliever, with more walks than strikeouts. He worked in relief only with Texas last summer, and by June he was pitching in Boston's Triple-A Pawtucket rotation, going 5-9 (5.77). 2003 Outlook: C

Calvin Murray (Pos: CF, Age: 31, Bats: R)

	G	AB	R	H	D	T	HR	RBI	SB	BB	SO	Avg	OBP	Slg
'02	48	89	16	13	5	1	0	1	4	7	17	.146	.216	.225
Car.	277	628	106	145	33	4	8	53	22	70	111	.231	.314	.334

Injuries in the Rangers' outfield spurred his trade from the Giants to Texas in late April. He went to Triple-A Oklahoma in June and fractured a kneecap in July. 2003 has to be a better year. 2003 Outlook: C

Aaron Myette (Pos: RHP, Age: 25)

	W	L	Pct.	ERA	G	GS	Sv	IP	H	BB	SO	HR	Ratio
'02	2	5	.286	10.06	15	12	0	48.1	64	41	48	11	2.17
Car.	6	12	.333	7.88	40	30	0	147.1	175	96	127	25	1.84

In December, Myette was dealt to Cleveland, where there are open rotation spots but plenty of solid prospects in the running. Myette has the arm, but hasn't shown the command he needs in recent major league trials with the White Sox and Texas. Cleveland wants to use him in the pen. 2003 Outlook: C

C.J. Nitkowski (Pos: LHP, Age: 30)

	W	L	Pct.	ERA	G	GS	Sv	IP	H	BB	SO	HR	Ratio
'02	0	1	.000	2.63	12	0	0	13.2	11	13	14	0	1.76
Car.	16	31	.340	5.28	282	44	3	433.0	457	237	314	53	1.60

He signed three minor league deals for 2002 and finally surfaced with Texas. The good news: he averaged a strikeout an inning. The bad news: almost a walk per, too. He re-upped with another minor league pact. 2003 Outlook: C

Hector Ortiz (Pos: C, Age: 33, Bats: R)

	G	AB	R	H	D	T	HR	RBI	SB	BB	SO	Avg	OBP	Slg
'02	7	14	1	3	1	0	1	2	0	1	1	.214	.267	.500
Car.	93	260	29	75	13	1	1	18	1	18	33	.288	.339	.358

Ortiz was traded by the Royals to Texas in April after Ivan Rodriguez was sidelined by a herniated disk. His stay as Bill Haselman's backup was brief. He was gone by mid-May and released in July. 2003 Outlook: C

Dennys Reyes (**Pos**: LHP, **Age**: 25)

	W	L	Pct.	ERA	G	GS	Sv	IP	H	BB	SO	HR	Ratio
'02	4	4	.500	5.33	58	5	0	82.2	98	45	59	10	1.73
Car.	15	21	.417	4.56	253	27	2	355.1	358	213	332	32	1.61

Reyes went from Colorado to Texas with Todd Hollandsworth in a July deadline deal, but he was better and less homer-prone in Denver. He had a 4.25 ERA in relief, so he may stick in the Texas pen. 2003 Outlook: B

Ruben Rivera (**Pos**: CF, **Age**: 29, **Bats**: R)

	G	AB	R	H	D	T	HR	RBI	SB	BB	SO	Avg	OBP	Slg
'02	69	158	17	33	4	0	4	14	4	17	45	.209	.302	.310
Car.	631	1536	231	334	65	11	62	199	49	180	496	.217	.309	.395

Stealing a Derek Jeter glove didn't end his career, but his hitting percentages with Texas were among his worst after the Yankees released him. A once-promising career nears its end at age 29. 2003 Outlook: C

Rich Rodriguez (**Pos**: LHP, **Age**: 40)

	W	L	Pct.	ERA	G	GS	Sv	IP	H	BB	SO	HR	Ratio
'02	3	2	.600	5.40	36	0	1	16.2	14	11	12	1	1.50
Car.	31	22	.585	3.81	606	2	8	637.0	638	260	393	62	1.41

Rodriguez turns 40 in March, hasn't had a strong season since 1998 and had shoulder trouble in '02. But being lefthanded, he's got as many lives as Bob McClure, and he's six years younger than Jesse Orosco. 2003 Outlook: C

Donnie Sadler (**Pos**: SS/3B/LF/CF, **Age**: 27, **Bats**: R)

	G	AB	R	H	D	T	HR	RBI	SB	BB	SO	Avg	OBP	Slg
'02	73	98	16	16	2	1	0	7	5	7	19	.163	.231	.204
Car.	322	613	97	126	22	6	5	41	21	41	122	.206	.262	.285

He's batted .162 and .163 the last two years with nary a hitting percentage near .300. He hasn't produced for three teams in those two years, including the Rangers, who have signed him to a new minor league deal. 2003 Outlook: C

Rudy Seanez (**Pos**: RHP, **Age**: 34)

	W	L	Pct.	ERA	G	GS	Sv	IP	H	BB	SO	HR	Ratio
'02	1	3	.250	5.73	33	0	0	33.0	28	24	40	5	1.58
Car.	17	16	.515	4.49	275	0	11	278.2	242	154	278	29	1.42

Seanez came back from Tommy John surgery in 2000 to have a terrific 2001, but arm trouble and a herniated disk that led to June surgery derailed him last summer. Good health is key for Seanez, who signed a minor league deal to stay with Texas. 2003 Outlook: C

Anthony Telford (**Pos**: RHP, **Age**: 37)

	W	L	Pct.	ERA	G	GS	Sv	IP	H	BB	SO	HR	Ratio
'02	2	1	.667	6.46	20	0	1	23.2	30	15	19	3	1.90
Car.	22	25	.468	4.17	333	9	8	455.1	475	176	331	48	1.43

After a brief, rugged stop in Montreal in 2001, Telford enjoyed a decent start at Triple-A Oklahoma in '02. He was recalled and made three scoreless appearances in May before the roof fell in on him. 2003 Outlook: C

Steve Woodard (**Pos**: RHP, **Age**: 27)

	W	L	Pct.	ERA	G	GS	Sv	IP	H	BB	SO	HR	Ratio
'02	0	0	—	6.62	14	0	0	17.2	20	8	14	4	1.58
Car.	31	36	.463	4.93	155	94	0	649.2	759	144	452	87	1.39

The bright moments have been few since he debuted with eight innings of one-hit ball and 12 whiffs in 1997. He spent time in two other systems in '02 after an early June release. The BoSox inked him in November. 2003 Outlook: C

Texas Rangers Minor League Prospects

Organization Overview:

On the final day of the 2001 season, Rangers owner Tom Hicks cited a poor farm system as his main reason for firing then-GM Doug Melvin. That showed how out of touch Hicks was with his organization, or that he is getting poor advice from outsiders. Melvin performed the difficult juggling act of trying to win in the majors and build in the minors. A few months into last season, Hicks realized the truth. Melvin had left behind a good player-development system, and it was time for the club to use those players. Righthanders Joaquin Benoit and Colby Lewis and outfielder Kevin Mench received extended time. Michael Young showed himself to be a Gold Glove-quality second baseman. There are more players coming. The Rangers have two premier third-base prospects in Hank Blalock and Mark Teixeira. The organization still needs to show it can produce pitchers, but there are arms loaded with potential.

Joaquin Benoit

Position: P **Opening Day Age:** 25
Bats: R **Throws:** R **Born:** 7/26/77 in
Ht: 6' 3" **Wt:** 205 Santiago, DR

Recent Statistics

	W	L	ERA	G	GS	Sv	IP	H	R	BB	SO	HR
2002 AAA Oklahoma	8	4	3.56	16	16	0	98.2	74	42	37	103	8
2002 AL Texas	4	5	5.31	17	13	1	84.2	91	51	58	59	6
2002 A Charlotte	0	0	0.00	1	1	0	5.0	1	0	3	8	0

Given extended major league exposure for the first time, Benoit frustrated the Rangers with his inconsistency. He produced several dazzling games but also failed to make it past the fifth inning in seven of his 13 starts. He pitched six innings in consecutive starts only once. The first inning usually was the key. If Benoit started well, he performed well. If he had early troubles, he could not find a way to fix them and was gone in a hurry. Benoit has a good fastball to go with a plus slider, and both pitches are hard to lift. He gave up only six homers in 335 at-bats with Texas in 2002. His downfall was poor command, and he allowed 6.17 walks per nine innings. This is a make-or-break season for Benoit with Texas, as he is out of minor league options.

Jason Hart

Position: 1B **Opening Day Age:** 25
Bats: R **Throws:** R **Born:** 9/5/77 in Walnut
Ht: 6' 4" **Wt:** 240 Creek, CA

Recent Statistics

	G	AB	R	H	D	T	HR	RBI	SB	BB	SO	Avg
2002 AAA Oklahoma	134	514	78	135	32	1	25	83	1	68	122	.263
2002 AL Texas	10	15	2	4	3	0	0	0	0	2	7	.267

The similarities between Travis Hafner and Hart were hard to ignore, and Hafner getting traded to Cleveland may open up a roster spot in Texas for the large, power-hitting Hart. His righthanded bat may earn some DH duty and a little outfield time in 2003, even though he has a long swing and is prone to striking out. In 2002, he notched his fourth consecutive 100-strikeout season, fanning 122 times at Triple-A Oklahoma. He rose to prominence with a 30-homer, 121-strikeout performance in the offense-crazed Double-A Texas League in 2000. At the Triple-A level, he has hit only .255 with 231 strikeouts in 1,026 at-bats for his career. To give Hart a better chance of playing in the majors, the Rangers moved him from first base to left field last season, and he proved to be adequate in the outfield. Hart will play somewhere in the big leagues, and with Hafner's departure, it may be in Texas.

Ben Kozlowski

Position: P **Opening Day Age:** 22
Bats: L **Throws:** L **Born:** 8/16/80 in St.
Ht: 6' 6" **Wt:** 220 Petersburg, FL

Recent Statistics

	W	L	ERA	G	GS	Sv	IP	H	R	BB	SO	HR
2002 A Myrtle Beach	0	1	4.50	1	1	0	4.0	4	5	3	3	0
2002 A Charlotte	4	4	2.05	21	12	0	79.0	63	31	25	76	2
2002 AA Tulsa	4	2	1.90	8	8	0	52.0	28	12	22	41	3
2002 AL Texas	0	0	6.30	2	2	0	10.0	11	7	11	6	3

General Manager John Hart had a brutal first season with Texas, but he did make one good move. Hart was able to pry a legitimate promising lefthander from Atlanta for lefthander Andy Pratt, who had been removed from the 40-man roster for reasons that remain fuzzy. Kozlowski went from Class-A Charlotte to Double-A Tulsa to two late-season starts with the Rangers. He went 8-7 with a 2.07 ERA and a .195 opponents' batting average at two levels of the minors. Kozlowski has a low-90s fastball, good command of the curveball and exceptional deception in his arms-and-legs delivery. He is also a competitor of the highest order. Kozlowski found a changeup during the season and must continue to refine that pitch when he returns to the minors this season.

Colby Lewis

Position: P **Opening Day Age:** 23
Bats: R **Throws:** R **Born:** 8/2/79 in
Ht: 6' 4" **Wt:** 215 Bakersfield, CA

Recent Statistics

	W	L	ERA	G	GS	Sv	IP	H	R	BB	SO	HR
2002 AL Texas	1	3	6.29	15	4	0	34.1	42	26	26	28	4
2002 AAA Oklahoma	5	6	3.63	20	20	0	106.2	100	49	28	99	4

Of the many mistakes made by the Rangers' front office last season, the handling of Lewis ranks near the top. A top rotation prospect, Lewis made the team out of spring training as a reliever and worked in clutch situations because veterans failed. He was not ready for that work and had his development delayed by two trips between the majors and the minors. The Rangers finally decided to keep Lewis in a rotation, and he dominated in the final month with Triple-A Oklahoma. Lewis has a high-90s fastball and a sharp, knee-buckling curveball. When Lewis worked in relief, Oakland's Terrence Long compared him to Anaheim closer Troy Percival. The Rangers learned their lesson the hard way and will not use Lewis in the bullpen again. He is one more good spring away from opening the season in the rotation of the parent club.

Ryan Ludwick

Position: OF **Opening Day Age:** 24
Bats: R **Throws:** L **Born:** 7/13/78 in Satellite
Ht: 6' 3" **Wt:** 203 Beach, FL

Recent Statistics

	G	AB	R	H	D	T	HR	RBI	SB	BB	SO	Avg
2002 AAA Oklahoma	78	305	62	87	27	4	15	52	2	38	76	.285
2002 AL Texas	23	81	10	19	6	0	1	9	2	7	24	.235

Injuries threaten to ruin Ludwick's career. He had a stress fracture in his back while with Oakland in 2001, and he missed the final two months of last season because of a fracture in his left hip that required surgery. The club is not certain how much, if at all, the surgery will affect Ludwick's speed, but it cannot help. When healthy, he is a solid fundamental outfielder with a good arm, but he lacks the speed to play center full time, as he showed in 21 starts at the position last season. On offense, Ludwick needs to make better contact and do more with two strikes; he tends to give away at-bats when behind in the count. He had 24 strikeouts and drew only seven walks during his 2002 cup-of-coffee with the Rangers.

Mario Ramos

Position: P **Opening Day Age:** 25
Bats: L **Throws:** L **Born:** 10/19/77 in
Ht: 6' 0" **Wt:** 180 Aurora, IL

Recent Statistics

	W	L	ERA	G	GS	Sv	IP	H	R	BB	SO	HR
2001 AA Midland	8	1	3.07	15	15	0	93.2	71	37	28	68	7
2001 AAA Sacramento	8	3	3.14	13	13	0	80.1	74	32	27	82	5
2002 AAA Oklahoma	3	8	7.40	34	19	0	121.2	162	107	53	75	20

A 1999 pick of the A's, Ramos debuted with an impressive 14-5 (2.66) season between high Class-A Modesto and Double-A Midland in 2000. His advanced fastball-changeup combo was as good as ever in 2001, when he was 16-4 (3.10) at Midland and Triple-A Sacramento. The big difference, though, was an improved curveball that had more action. Plus, his cut fastball is a difficult pitch for hitters to pick up. Ramos was dealt to Texas in last January's Carlos Pena trade, and the Rangers saw him lose command of his fastball and flounder at Triple-A Oklahoma in 2002. As a finesse guy, he has to command his pitches to succeed. Ramos, known for doing his homework to prepare for hitters he will face,

rallied in the Arizona Fall League and is back in the organization's good graces.

Mark Teixeira

Position: 3B **Opening Day Age:** 22
Bats: B **Throws:** R **Born:** 4/11/80 in
Ht: 6' 2" **Wt:** 215 Annapolis, MD

Recent Statistics

	G	AB	R	H	D	T	HR	RBI	SB	BB	SO	Avg
2002 A Charlotte	38	150	32	48	10	2	9	41	2	21	24	.320
2002 AA Tulsa	48	171	31	54	11	3	10	28	3	25	36	.316

When the Rangers had the fifth pick overall in the 2001 draft, the public clamored for a major league-ready pitcher. Then-scouting director Tim Hallgren ignored those cries and made the right choice in Teixeira, the best college hitter of this generation. His debut delayed by a spring-training elbow injury, Teixeira batted .318 with 19 homers, 69 RBI and a .592 slugging percentage in 321 at-bats at the Class-A and Double-A levels last season. A switch-hitter, Teixeira has the same swing and production from both sides. He lacks the instinctive movements of a natural third baseman and could be forced to move to first. Teixeira was pulled out of action from the Arizona Fall League in mid-November due to an abdominal strain, but the injury did not appear to be serious. There certainly is nothing wrong with the bat, which should appear in the majors this season.

Others to Watch

Injuries ravaged the Rangers' minor league pitchers last season. The club is increasingly worried that oft-injured righthander **Jovanny Cedeno** (23) is not strong enough to survive. More shoulder woes limited Cedeno to five innings in the Rookie-level Gulf Coast League, and he has only 14.2 innings to show for the last two years. . . Righthander **Ryan Dittfurth** (23) had the first injury problem (shoulder) of his career and lasted only 41.1 innings with Double-A Tulsa. The Rangers expect Dittfurth to be ready in the spring. . . A reliever with a low-90s fastball and super slider, righthander **Travis Hughes** (24) moved into the Double-A Tulsa rotation in 2002 and went 9-7 (3.52). An improving changeup and better command will push him toward Texas. . . Oakland threw catcher **Gerald Laird** (23) into last January's six-player deal because it did not believe he could play in the majors. Laird's offense improved at Double-A Tulsa, and Texas believes he can be at least a serviceable major league backup. . . Outfielder **Laynce Nix** (22) is the second coming of Rusty Greer with more advanced offensive skills at this stage of his career. Nix led the high Class-A Florida State League in RBI with 110 and finished second in homers with 21 while stealing 17 bases in 18 tries and playing excellent defense in center. . . Lefthander **C.J. Wilson** (22) followed the same path as fellow lefthander Ben Kozlowski and had a better record. Wilson, in his first full season as a pitcher, went a combined 11-2 with a combined 3.08 ERA at Class-A and Double-A.

SkyDome

Offense

SkyDome can be a home-run hitters' park, but it generally favors contact hitters due to the fast, bouncy artificial turf. When the retractable roof is closed, especially after the long winter, batted balls soar through stagnant atmosphere. With the roof open, wind funnels over the third-base side grandstand and generally boosts balls hit to right and right-center field. The currents can take the steam out of balls to left-center, but pulled balls to left are relatively unaffected.

Defense

Defenses are most vulnerable up the middle and to the expansive alleys due to the presence of turf. When the Jays won the World Series in 1992 and 1993, they were exceedingly strong up the middle with Gold Glove-caliber defenders Devon White in center, Roberto Alomar at second base and Manny Lee/Tony Fernandez at shortstop.

Who It Helps the Most

Line-drive gap hitters and groundball hitters have advantages. Leadoff hitter Shannon Stewart averaged .351 and .319 at home the past two seasons and Dave Berg hit .324 in 2002, compared with .217 on the road. Ace Roy Halladay, who can induce popups with his high fastball, had a 2.56 ERA at SkyDome.

Who It Hurts the Most

Flyball hitters such as Jose Cruz Jr., whose average was .226 at home. Sinkerball pitchers fare none too well at SkyDome due to the turf. Chris Carpenter had a 4.83 ERA at home in 2001, 5.25 in '02. Steve Parris, a pitcher who needs to keep the ball low in the zone, had a 6.04 home ERA.

Rookies & Newcomers

Rookie Eric Hinske, at .304, averaged 49 points better at home. Starter Justin Miller went 5-1, 3.97 ERA. Reliever Cliff Politte was 2-1 with a 2.93 ERA and miniscule 1.13 WHIP. Mark Hendrickson was 2-0 in home games with a 2.57 ERA.

Dimensions: LF-328, LCF-375, CF-400, RCF-375, RF-328

Capacity: 50,516

Elevation: 300 feet

Surface: Turf

Foul Territory: Large

Park Factors

2002 Season

	Home Games TOR	Opp	Total	Away Games TOR	Opp	Total	Index
G	72	72	144	72	72	144	
Avg	.270	.267	.269	.256	.274	.265	102
AB	2432	2533	4965	2553	2444	4997	99
R	370	374	744	372	379	751	99
H	657	677	1334	653	669	1322	101
2B	151	154	305	126	129	255	120
3B	19	9	28	16	17	33	85
HR	92	78	170	75	80	155	110
BB	226	263	489	230	268	498	99
SO	483	455	938	544	437	981	96
E	47	51	98	50	41	91	108
E-Infield	43	42	85	45	35	80	106
LHB-Avg	.260	.279	.271	.261	.287	.276	98
LHB-HR	42	43	85	37	44	81	110
RHB-Avg	.276	.256	.267	.253	.259	.255	104
RHB-HR	50	35	85	38	36	74	112

2000-2002

	Home Games TOR	Opp	Total	Away Games TOR	Opp	Total	Index
G	216	216	432	215	215	430	
Avg	.272	.273	.272	.261	.279	.270	101
AB	7346	7667	15013	7676	7350	15026	99
R	1100	1141	2241	1062	1084	2146	104
H	1995	2093	4088	2003	2051	4054	100
2B	426	483	909	374	404	778	117
3B	37	32	69	46	36	82	84
HR	293	234	527	267	248	515	102
BB	659	726	1385	657	721	1378	101
SO	1377	1394	2771	1542	1282	2824	98
E	137	144	281	142	132	274	102
E-Infield	125	118	243	115	111	226	107
LHB-Avg	.273	.281	.277	.272	.291	.282	98
LHB-HR	142	115	257	137	125	262	100
RHB-Avg	.271	.266	.269	.254	.268	.260	103
RHB-HR	151	119	270	130	123	253	105

2002 Rankings (American League)

- Highest double factor
- Third-highest RHB batting-average factor

Carlos Tosca

2002 Season

Carlos Tosca took over from Buck Martinez on June 3, becoming the club's ninth manager. He is the fifth native Cuban to manage in the big leagues. After the All-Star break, he guided the young club to a 44-32 record. Three weeks into his tenure, Tosca made an impression on the clubhouse by benching right fielder Raul Mondesi for two games. Mondesi, who'd shown for up late for a pre-series meeting in Tampa Bay, was traded to the Yankees not long afterwards. Star first baseman Carlos Delgado endorsed Tosca, saying the manager backed up pledges such as using bench players at least twice per week. General manager J.P. Ricciardi gave him credit for improving the clubhouse atmosphere.

Offense

In spite of a strikeout-prone batting order, the club is attempting to embrace the Oakland philosophy by improving on-base percentage with patience at the plate, then going for the big hit. While his predecessor encouraged an aggressive style of play, Tosca has de-emphasized the stolen base. Tosca's hit-and-run attempts resulted in success 43.6 percent of the time, sixth among all AL skippers. By comparison, Martinez' hit-and-run success rate was 10.6. Tosca keeps his bench fresh.

Pitching & Defense

Projected over a full season, Tosca would have ranked among the top five AL managers in mid-inning changes and one-batter appearances. He also would have been second only to Gardenhire in all of baseball in quick hooks for starters, with 25. Outside of Roy Halladay, the Jays did not get much from their rotation. Halladay led the league in innings, though Tosca became protective of his arm in September.

2003 Outlook

On September 3, Tosca and his coaching staff agreed to a two-year contract extension through 2004. The challenge now will be dealing with the heightened expectations created by the club's strong finish in 2002.

Born: 9/29/53 in Pinar del Rio, Cuba

Playing Experience: No major league playing experience

Managerial Experience: 1 season

Manager Statistics

Year	Team, Lg	W	L	Pct	GB	Finish
2002	Toronto, AL	58	51	.532	25.5	3rd East
1 Season		58	51	.532	–	–

2002 Starting Pitchers by Days Rest

	<=3	4	5	6+
Blue Jays Starts	0	70	17	19
Blue Jays ERA	–	4.89	3.27	5.93
AL Avg Starts	1	83	44	24
AL ERA	7.15	4.59	4.27	5.03

2002 Situational Stats

	Carlos Tosca	AL Average
Hit & Run Success %	43.6	36.0
Stolen Base Success %	77.8	68.1
Platoon Pct.	48.7	58.9
Defensive Subs	16	23
High-Pitch Outings	1	6
Quick/Slow Hooks	17/12	19/14
Sacrifice Attempts	15	53

2002 Rankings (American League)

- 1st in stolen-base percentage and fewest caught stealings of second base (7)

Jose Cruz

2002 Season

Coming off a 30-30 season in 2001, Jose Cruz had to make room for Vernon Wells in spring training by moving from center to left field. Then a rib-cage strain delayed Cruz' preparation by forcing him out of Grapefruit League play. Struggling from the outset, he was hitting .150 after 10 games and never did raise his average above .250. Just when his bat was beginning to show signs of consistency with five multihit games in a span of 10, Cruz severely sprained his left ankle on August 9 and was out until mid-September.

Hitting

A switch-hitter, Cruz shows impressive power from the left side. He tends to spread the ball around more from the other side of the plate, though his average against lefties fell to .225 in 2002. He's an outstanding fastball hitter, especially high in the zone, and at times he demonstrates some ability to hit the changeup. Most dangerous when hitting the ball up the middle, Cruz is nonetheless tempted to pull, especially when batting lefthanded. Most pitchers will try to tease him with fastballs outside the strike zone and get him out with the change or breaking ball over the plate. Cruz drew 71 walks in 2000, but as his career has progressed, he has indicated a preference to swing aggressively and his strikeout ratios reflect the approach.

Baserunning & Defense

Seemingly born and raised with sharp instincts, Cruz is an outstanding runner capable of stealing 30 bases annually. A versatile outfielder, he has acquired the knack of catching balls hit over his head and gets a good jump laterally, though he could improve chasing down balls hit in front of him. His arm is strong and accurate.

2003 Outlook

After the trade of Raul Mondesi to the Yankees, Cruz moved from left to right field and played the position convincingly. After earning $3.7 million in the second year of a two-year contract in 2002, Cruz once again became the subject of trade rumors. The cost-cutting Jays were expected to shop him vigorously during the offseason.

Position: LF/RF/CF
Bats: B **Throws:** R
Ht: 6' 0" **Wt:** 210

Opening Day Age: 28
Born: 4/19/74 in Arroyo, PR
ML Seasons: 6

Overall Statistics

	G	AB	R	H	D	T	HR	RBI	SB	BB	SO	Avg	OBP	Slg
'02	124	466	64	114	26	5	18	70	7	51	106	.245	.317	.438
Car.	747	2742	424	689	148	21	134	389	86	329	680	.251	.330	.467

Where He Hits the Ball

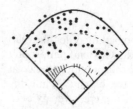
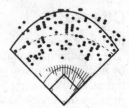

Vs. LHP   **Vs. RHP**

2002 Situational Stats

	AB	H	HR	RBI	Avg		AB	H	HR	RBI	Avg
Home	230	52	11	37	.226	LHP	142	32	3	15	.225
Road	236	62	7	33	.263	RHP	324	82	15	55	.253
First Half	322	73	13	45	.227	Sc Pos	125	35	3	46	.280
Scnd Half	144	41	5	25	.285	Clutch	57	13	0	4	.228

2002 Rankings (American League)

- 1st in lowest batting average with the bases loaded (.000)
- 4th in lowest batting average with two strikes (.130)
- 5th in lowest batting average at home
- 7th in lowest on-base percentage vs. lefthanded pitchers (.275)
- 8th in assists in right field (5) and lowest batting average
- 9th in lowest batting average on a 3-2 count (.140)
- Led the Blue Jays in highest percentage of extra bases taken as a runner (53.5)

Carlos Delgado

2002 Season

Carlos Delgado struggled through much of 2001 and '02 to rediscover his high-average, big-power form. With six homers and a .323 average on April 25, he seemed to be on track. However, while the first baseman delivered another seven homers in May, his overall average dropped to .251 and the slump was on. Midway through an impotent summer by his standards, Delgado ended a club-record run of 432 consecutive games played on August 4 and went on the disabled list five days later with a lower back strain. Upon returning, he looked like the Delgado of 2000, with hits in 18 of his final 20 games.

Hitting

Late in 2000 or early in 2001, Delgado became snared by a mechanical fault in his stance. He couldn't find a way out of it until late last season. His front-to-back weight shift had become slightly exaggerated and in unknowingly moving too far back, he would be obliged to hurry forward as the pitch approached. As a result, he made contact while leaning over his front foot too often and lost power. Pitchers complicated things by changing their pattern, staying away with offspeed material or busting him up and in with fastballs. He reacted by trying to pull, whereas he is most dangerous when driving the middle-away fastballs toward the alleys. He'll crush mistake breaking balls and sliders, in addition to the low fastball.

Baserunning & Defense

Delgado isn't quick off the mark, but he runs the bases well once up to speed. Defensively, he lacks range to his right, but he made several outstanding plays along the line last year and has improved an ability to scoop the short-hop throws from infielders. His arm is adequate.

2003 Outlook

While rediscovering his 2000 swing late in the season, Delgado also found renewed inspiration in the club's late-season run. Given reasonable protection in the batting order, he should put up robust numbers. Delgado would be unlikely to waive the no-trade clause in his contract unless the club regresses. If the club is struggling in mid-summer, trade talk will be rekindled.

Position: 1B
Bats: L **Throws:** R
Ht: 6' 3" **Wt:** 230

Opening Day Age: 30
Born: 6/25/72 in Aguadilla, PR
ML Seasons: 10
Pronunciation: del-GAH-doh

Overall Statistics

	G	AB	R	H	D	T	HR	RBI	SB	BB	SO	Avg	OBP	Slg
'02	143	505	103	140	34	2	33	108	1	102	126	.277	.406	.549
Car.	1134	3980	698	1118	279	10	262	814	9	649	990	.281	.390	.554

Where He Hits the Ball

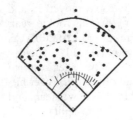 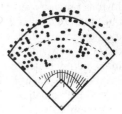

Vs. LHP **Vs. RHP**

2002 Situational Stats

	AB	H	HR	RBI	Avg		AB	H	HR	RBI	Avg
Home	240	68	17	51	.283	LHP	172	41	4	29	.238
Road	265	72	16	57	.272	RHP	333	99	29	79	.297
First Half	308	75	18	62	.244	Sc Pos	143	44	8	75	.308
Scnd Half	197	65	15	46	.330	Clutch	79	16	5	13	.203

2002 Rankings (American League)

- 1st in errors at first base (12) and lowest fielding percentage at first base (.991)
- 2nd in intentional walks (18)
- 3rd in slugging percentage vs. righthanded pitchers (.646), on-base percentage vs. righthanded pitchers (.444) and assists at first base (95)
- Led the Blue Jays in home runs, runs scored, RBI, sacrifice flies (8), walks, hit by pitch (13), times on base (255), slugging percentage, on-base percentage, HR frequency (15.3 ABs per HR), batting average on a 3-1 count (.520), cleanup slugging percentage (.549) and on-base percentage vs. righthanded pitchers (.444)

Kelvim Escobar

2002 Season

General manager J.P. Ricciardi traded Billy Koch to Oakland to obtain third baseman Eric Hinske and give Kelvim Escobar the opportunity to finish games. Nothing if not inconsistent throughout his career, Escobar showed flashes of both brilliance and incompetence in his first full season as the closer. The hard-throwing righthander recorded 38 saves but suffered seven losses and eight blown saves. Six of the eight missed chances occurred when he pitched without a day's rest. He finished with promising strength, however, and established a personal high with 76 appearances.

Pitching

In four previous seasons, Escobar moved in and out of the rotation. Only in 1997, his rookie year, did he perform strictly in relief prior to 2002. As a starter, Escobar had experienced difficulty maintaining concentration, so the idea was to maximize his talent by letting him overpower hitters in short situations. He throws a two-seam and four-seam fastball (93-97 MPH), a splitter at 88 MPH and a curve in the mid-80s. Last season, he added an 88-90 MPH cutter. However, concentration continues to be Escobar's greatest challenge. He tends to lapse into mechanical faults in the midst of an outing, leading to a sudden and frustrating loss of control. What results is the base on balls, and all too often a home run. That said, he did show signs of overcoming a nasty habit of slowing his pace with runners aboard, and held opponents to a .242 average with runners in scoring position despite issuing 21 walks in 117 such plate appearances.

Defense

Escobar is very quick off the mound. He gets to batted balls easily and covers first base well. He has committed just three errors in 260 big league games. His move to first is above average, which helps him to keep runners honest.

2003 Outlook

After six years of experimentation, Escobar has proven most promising in short relief. Toronto is confident his delivery mechanics will become more consistent, which would allow Escobar to become one of the league's premier closers.

Position: RP
Bats: R **Throws:** R
Ht: 6' 1" **Wt:** 210

Opening Day Age: 26
Born: 4/11/76 in La Guaira, VZ
ML Seasons: 6

Overall Statistics

	W	L	Pct.	ERA	G	GS	Sv	IP	H	BB	SO	HR	Ratio
'02	5	7	.417	4.27	76	0	38	78.0	75	44	85	10	1.53
Car.	45	46	.495	4.66	260	75	54	668.2	657	316	585	69	1.46

How Often He Throws Strikes

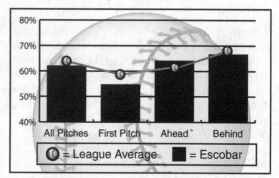

= League Average   = Escobar

2002 Situational Stats

	W	L	ERA	Sv	IP			AB	H	HR	RBI	Avg
Home	4	3	3.98	22	40.2	LHB		163	40	5	20	.245
Road	1	4	4.58	16	37.1	RHB		142	35	5	21	.246
First Half	4	4	4.87	14	40.2	Sc Pos		95	23	1	28	.242
Scnd Half	1	3	3.62	24	37.1	Clutch		204	52	8	34	.255

2002 Rankings (American League)

- 1st in blown saves (8)
- 2nd in games finished (68) and relief losses (7)
- 3rd in save opportunities (46)
- 5th in games pitched and saves
- 7th in save percentage (82.6) and relief innings (78.0)
- Led the Blue Jays in games pitched, saves, games finished (68), save opportunities (46), save percentage (82.6), blown saves (8), relief wins (5), relief losses (7), relief innings (78.0) and most strikeouts per nine innings in relief (9.8)

Roy Halladay

2002 Season

Roy Halladay established himself as Toronto's ace while threatening to win 20 games for the first time. With a 1-1 record through his first six starts, Halladay reeled off wins in 13 of his next 16 decisions to complete a remarkable metamorphosis. In spring training 2001, the Jays sent the former first-round pick back to Class-A, where he began to restructure his delivery and regain confidence after a wicked 2000 season (4-7, 10.64 ERA). Last season, he led American League pitchers in innings while placing fifth in ERA, sixth in strikeouts and 10th in batting average against.

Pitching

Halladay has learned to harness the intensity that once bedeviled him. The key for him was to master control of his fastball, especially when under pressure. Last season his strikeout-walk ratio nearly reached 3:1—previously in his career, the ratio barely exceeded 1.5:1 despite possession of top-shelf stuff. His four-seam fastball ranges between 92-95 MPH with late sink, and his cutter runs at an 89-92 MPH clip. Halladay also throws a big curve. His splitter developed well enough over the past year to become part of his regular arsenal. His competitiveness comes through in his road record (9-1), his aggressive approach and his endurance.

Defense

Halladay's pickoff move is average, and he's not especially quick to the plate. Runners stole 21 bases against him last year, most successfully when a righthander was at bat. A fine all-around athlete, Halladay is agile for his size and fields balls hit to both sides of the mound adeptly. He covers first base in plenty of time.

2003 Outlook

The ace of a relatively inexperienced starting staff, Halladay has found his groove at the major league level. An All-Star last season, he's expected to be a consistent 200-inning, 15-20 game winner. He earned $2.56 million in 2002 at the end of a multiyear contract. Though he made his debut with the Jays in 1998, he has less than four years of major league service and remains under the team's control for at least three more seasons.

Position: SP
Bats: R **Throws:** R
Ht: 6' 6" **Wt:** 230

Opening Day Age: 25
Born: 5/14/77 in Denver, CO
ML Seasons: 5
Pronunciation: HAL-luh-day

Overall Statistics

	W	L	Pct.	ERA	G	GS	Sv	IP	H	BB	SO	HR	Ratio
'02	19	7	.731	2.93	34	34	0	239.1	223	62	168	10	1.19
Car.	37	24	.607	4.11	108	83	1	575.2	592	210	403	48	1.39

How Often He Throws Strikes

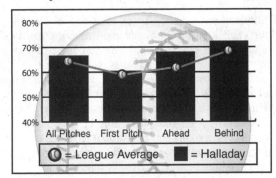

= League Average ■ = Halladay

2002 Situational Stats

	W	L	ERA	Sv	IP		AB	H	HR	RBI	Avg
Home	10	6	2.56	0	123.0	LHB	475	123	6	51	.259
Road	9	1	3.33	0	116.1	RHB	438	100	4	35	.228
First Half	9	4	3.06	0	126.2	Sc Pos	245	61	1	73	.249
Scnd Half	10	3	2.80	0	112.2	Clutch	83	19	1	6	.229

2002 Rankings (American League)

- 1st in innings pitched and fewest home runs allowed per nine innings (.38)
- 2nd in games started, batters faced (993) and highest groundball-flyball ratio allowed (2.7)
- 3rd in stolen bases allowed (21) and lowest ERA at home
- Led the Blue Jays in ERA, wins, hits allowed, strikeouts, pitches thrown (3,500), runners caught stealing (7), GDPs induced (24), winning percentage, highest strikeout-walk ratio (2.7), lowest batting average allowed (.244), lowest slugging percentage allowed (.333), lowest on-base percentage allowed (.297), lowest ERA on the road and most strikeouts per nine innings (6.3)

Eric Hinske

2002 Season

Obtained from Oakland in the Billy Koch trade, Eric Hinske delivered as advertised, with a surprising 24 home runs, 64 extra-base hits and better-than-adequate defense at third base. Named AL Rookie of the Year by both the BBWAA and Sporting News, Hinske hit .306 with runners on base and .308 with teammates in scoring position. The willingness to wait for his pitch allowed managers Buck Martinez and Carlos Tosca to insert Hinske into the No. 2 slot of the batting order, a black hole for Toronto since Roberto Alomar's departure after the 1995 season.

Hitting

Showing the patience Tosca is asking of his hitters, Hinske drew 77 walks and drove the ball to all fields. As pitchers adjust, he may have to pick spots to be more aggressive, as he batted just .207 with none on and none out. A more significant challenge is mastering the lefthanded pitcher. Hinske is a low-ball hitter, preferring his pitches middle-away on the plate. But he also proved capable of making the adjustment to inside offerings. He demonstrated the ability to hit changeups and breaking balls, though he'll likely see more of both in his second season.

Baserunning & Defense

Inconsistent throwing early in the season caused concern, until Hinske was schooled to get his feet set before the launch. The mechanics fixed, his play at third base improved considerably. With quick feet for his size, he moves well and makes the slow-roller play very well. His arm strength is slightly above average, and he can put a little extra mustard on the ball when required. On the bases, he is an extremely instinctive runner who has good speed.

2003 Outlook

An intense competitor, Hinske quickly took on a leadership role alongside Carlos Delgado in spite of his rookie status. The starting third baseman for the 2003 Blue Jays likely will bat in the No. 2 spot during his sophomore season. His position in the order and his ability to wait out pitchers should insulate Hinske somewhat against a steadier diet of offspeed stuff.

Position: 3B
Bats: L **Throws:** R
Ht: 6' 2" **Wt:** 225

Opening Day Age: 25
Born: 8/5/77 in Menasha, WI
ML Seasons: 1
Pronunciation: hin-SKEE

Overall Statistics

	G	AB	R	H	D	T	HR	RBI	SB	BB	SO	Avg	OBP	Slg
'02	151	566	99	158	38	2	24	84	13	77	138	.279	.365	.481
Car.	151	566	99	158	38	2	24	84	13	77	138	.279	.365	.481

Where He Hits the Ball

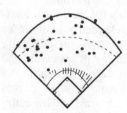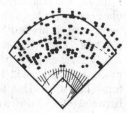

Vs. LHP   **Vs. RHP**

2002 Situational Stats

	AB	H	HR	RBI	Avg		AB	H	HR	RBI	Avg
Home	276	84	15	44	.304	LHP	124	25	4	17	.202
Road	290	74	9	40	.255	RHP	442	133	20	67	.301
First Half	286	78	14	46	.273	Sc Pos	133	41	4	54	.308
Scnd Half	280	80	10	38	.286	Clutch	83	22	7	16	.265

2002 Rankings (American League)

- 1st in home runs among rookies and RBI among rookies
- 2nd in batting average among rookies
- 3rd in errors at third base (20), lowest batting average vs. lefthanded pitchers and lowest fielding percentage at third base (.946)
- 7th in strikeouts
- 8th in batting average with the bases loaded (.500)
- Led the Blue Jays in doubles, strikeouts, pitches seen (2,542), plate appearances (650) and stolen-base percentage (92.9)

Orlando Hudson

Position: 2B
Bats: B **Throws:** R
Ht: 6' 0" **Wt:** 185

Opening Day Age: 25
Born: 12/12/77 in Darlington, SC
ML Seasons: 1

2002 Season

Touted highly after a strong 2001 minor league season, Orlando Hudson struggled at spring training and became an early demotion. At Triple-A Syracuse, he averaged .305, with 10 homers and a .363 on-base percentage in 100 games to earn a July 24 promotion. The second baseman's impact was immediate, with a nine-game hit streak July 30 to August 7 and standout defense at second base. He cooled slightly but still finished at .276 with a .319 on-base percentage in 54 games.

Hitting

A switch-hitter, Hudson had success batting left-handed but struggled from the right side. As his hitting mechanics and approach are about the same from both sides, his first-year lefty/righty splits may prove to be an oddity over time. He works best when determined to hit liners gap to gap, going with the pitch. Hudson struggled when pressing to hit for power yet showed the confidence to hit under pressure, with a .347 mark when runners were in scoring position.

Baserunning & Defense

Hudson has good instincts for the game and finds ways to help a team win with the glove. Voted best defensive third baseman in the Class-A Florida State League in 2000, Hudson was converted to second in 2001 at Double-A to exploit his quickness. He has very good range to his glove side and will stray far down the first-base line to make standout catches. Range to his backhand side is above average as well, but it can get better. His footwork and ability to turn the double play got better as the season progressed, and he shows no fear of standing in. As a baserunner, he was prone to the occasional costly blunder but appears to learn from experience.

2003 Outlook

Hudson is one of an exciting crop of young players brought into the organization by Vice President Tim Wilken. Hudson won the regular second-base job last season and batted mostly seventh and eighth in the order. He has the physical assets required to one day be a leadoff hitter.

Overall Statistics

	G	AB	R	H	D	T	HR	RBI	SB	BB	SO	Avg	OBP	Slg
'02	54	192	20	53	10	5	4	23	0	11	27	.276	.319	.443
Car.	54	192	20	53	10	5	4	23	0	11	27	.276	.319	.443

Where He Hits the Ball

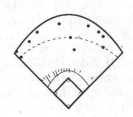 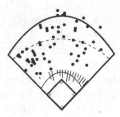

Vs. LHP   **Vs. RHP**

2002 Situational Stats

	AB	H	HR	RBI	Avg		AB	H	HR	RBI	Avg
Home	102	28	2	10	.275	LHP	49	9	0	4	.184
Road	90	25	2	13	.278	RHP	143	44	4	19	.308
First Half	0	0	0	0	—	Sc Pos	49	17	1	18	.347
Scnd Half	192	53	4	23	.276	Clutch	26	8	0	1	.308

2002 Rankings (American League)

- 6th in lowest batting average on a 3-1 count (.125)

Esteban Loaiza

2002 Season

Esteban Loaiza had what's become a typical season, mixing the occasionally brilliant outing with a bundle of mediocre to poor starts. He gave up 1.3 hits per inning and averaged 6.05 innings per outing. He pitched better at SkyDome (5-4, 4.90) than on the road (4-6, 6.90).

Pitching

Loaiza has an outstanding ability to locate his pitches somewhere in the strike zone, but it's his location within the zone that gets him into trouble. Strange as it sounds, scouts say Loaiza throws *too many* strikes. When he expands the zone by working the corners and wasting the occasional pitch, he is much more effective. As it is, hitters sit back and wait for their pitch, without being intimidated. His repertoire includes a two-seam and four-seam fastball running 88-92 MPH, an 80-MPH changeup and an 82-84 MPH slider. He added a cutter midway through the season, and turned in a strong showing in August before faltering in September. A naturally fluid delivery keeps his arm in good shape. Otherwise, coaches involved with Loaiza throughout his career have been dismayed by dubious work habits in between starts. It is commonly believed that he has the ability to steady the roller-coaster performances and become a reliable 12-15 game winner, and so he tantalizes and frustrates.

Defense

Loaiza finishes his motion in ideal position to field batted balls, cover first or run to the plate. A good, agile athlete with a sure glove, he plays the position well, but is prone to a mental lapse from time to time. He does a very good job of controlling the running game.

2003 Outlook

A free agent following the expiration of his two-year contract that paid $5.8 million last season, Loaiza declared free agency and wasn't expected to land back in Toronto. Some club, somewhere, will install him in the rotation and await the breakthrough season that never seems to come. If he applies himself strictly to the job, Loaiza is capable of 175 innings and 12-15 wins.

Position: SP
Bats: R **Throws:** R
Ht: 6' 3" **Wt:** 205

Opening Day Age: 31
Born: 12/31/71 in Tijuana, Mexico
ML Seasons: 8
Pronunciation: s-TAY-bahn low-EYE-zah

Overall Statistics

	W	L	Pct.	ERA	G	GS	Sv	IP	H	BB	SO	HR	Ratio
'02	9	10	.474	5.71	25	25	0	151.1	192	38	87	18	1.52
Car.	69	73	.486	4.88	235	202	1	1253.2	1470	357	758	161	1.46

How Often He Throws Strikes

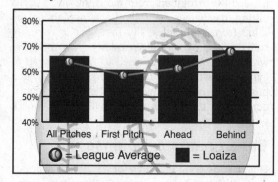

= League Average   = Loaiza

2002 Situational Stats

	W	L	ERA	Sv	IP		AB	H	HR	RBI	Avg
Home	5	4	4.90	0	90.0	LHB	325	100	8	44	.308
Road	4	6	6.90	0	61.1	RHB	296	92	10	46	.311
First Half	3	5	5.78	0	62.1	Sc Pos	160	59	4	71	.369
Scnd Half	6	5	5.66	0	89.0	Clutch	31	8	2	4	.258

2002 Rankings (American League)

- 3rd in highest batting average allowed vs. righthanded batters and highest batting average allowed with runners in scoring position
- 4th in highest ERA at home
- 9th in complete games (3)
- Led the Blue Jays in losses, complete games (3), pickoff throws (57), fewest pitches thrown per batter (3.50), most run support per nine innings (6.2) and fewest walks per nine innings (2.3)

Justin Miller

2002 Season

Acquired from Oakland with third baseman Eric Hinske in exchange for closer Billy Koch, Justin Miller shuttled between Triple-A Syracuse (eight starts, 3-2, 1.61 ERA) and Toronto. On August 9, he came up to the parent club to stay. Used both in the bullpen and rotation, Miller went 8-5 with a 5.32 ERA as a starting pitcher, in 18 games. His hurdle was getting past the first inning, a frame which saw him yield 19 earned runs and 23 walks.

Pitching

The Oakland organization envisioned Miller as a power pitcher reliant on the four-seam fastball. With Toronto, he dropped his arm angle slightly to regain the movement on his pitches, thus feeding a strength. He also lowered his hands in the set position later in the season to relax his upper body and get the ball out quicker. This technique discourages his arm from lagging. His two-seam fastball is a heavy sinker timed at 88-92 MPH with good life. He also uses a four-seamer, especially when having difficulty locating the two-seamer. His out pitch—the slider—made the difference in his third and final callup to Toronto in 2002. It's hard with a good tilt at 85-87 MPH. For variance, he's been working on a changeup and a splitter.

Defense

Surprisingly athletic, as a fielder Miller is ranked a 4 on a scale of 1-to-5 in scouts' notebooks. He has a good move to first but needs to improve the time of his delivery to the plate with runners aboard. Runners were successful 11 times and caught just four times on Miller's watch last year.

2003 Outlook

With a team that needs starting pitching, Miller will be given a full chance at a spot in the starting rotation. He was rushed in 2002 but showed improvement in the second half of the season. He learned to trust his stuff and became more consistent with the lower arm slot.

Position: SP
Bats: R **Throws:** R
Ht: 6' 2" **Wt:** 195

Opening Day Age: 25
Born: 8/27/77 in Torrance, CA
ML Seasons: 1

Toronto

Overall Statistics

	W	L	Pct.	ERA	G	GS	Sv	IP	H	BB	SO	HR	Ratio
'02	9	5	.643	5.54	25	18	0	102.1	103	66	68	12	1.65
Car.	9	5	.643	5.54	25	18	0	102.1	103	66	68	12	1.65

How Often He Throws Strikes

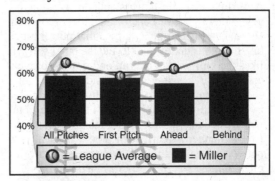

2002 Situational Stats

	W	L	ERA	Sv	IP		AB	H	HR	RBI	Avg
Home	5	1	3.97	0	56.2	LHB	189	56	7	41	.296
Road	4	4	7.49	0	45.2	RHB	196	47	5	24	.240
First Half	4	4	6.51	0	55.1	Sc Pos	114	29	5	52	.254
Scnd Half	5	1	4.40	0	47.0	Clutch	15	3	0	2	.200

2002 Rankings (American League)

- 5th in wins among rookies
- 7th in hit batsmen (11)
- Led the Blue Jays in walks allowed, hit batsmen (11), wild pitches (6) and most GDPs induced per nine innings (1.4)

Josh Phelps

2002 Season

When he was slamming homers at Double-A Tennessee in 2001, the knock on Josh Phelps was that his swing was too long for a successful ride in the majors. He proved otherwise, hitting immediately upon being promoted July 2. He maintained a .300 or better average through his first 17 games, dropped to a season low of .269 on August 16, and wound up at .309. Over a 162-game schedule, the DH's numbers projected to 33 home runs, 44 doubles and 127 RBI.

Hitting

When in a rhythm, Phelps actually has a compact, powerful swing. He'll overswing on occasion, but day to day he proved one of the club's most consistent batters. Definitely a potential power hitter, his strength is up the middle and the other way. He likes the ball middle-out, up and down, so pitchers react by busting him inside. But Phelps showed the capacity to adjust. He can be tempted by the high-and-away fastball out of the zone, which accounts in part for a high strikeout ratio. He was dangerous early in the count and with runners on base. He hit .480 when he put the first pitch in play.

Baserunning & Defense

On the bases, Phelps has decent speed for his size but is no threat to steal and was prone to rookie mistakes. In the minors, he played catcher and first base. He was thought to have a future as a catcher in spite of his height and mediocre arm, but now the Blue Jays regard him only as a third, emergency receiver. As an infielder, Phelps lacked range.

2003 Outlook

Unlike many young players, Phelps can handle the time in between at-bats as a DH. This will be his primary role. The Blue Jays flirted with the idea of sending him to instructional league to get him some experience at first base, but a lingering knee problem shelved that plan. Still, there's a lot of excitement about his home-run potential after his first full season.

Position: DH
Bats: R **Throws:** R
Ht: 6' 3" **Wt:** 220

Opening Day Age: 24
Born: 5/12/78 in Anchorage, AK
ML Seasons: 3

Overall Statistics

	G	AB	R	H	D	T	HR	RBI	SB	BB	SO	Avg	OBP	Slg
'02	74	265	41	82	20	1	15	58	0	19	82	.309	.362	.562
Car.	83	278	44	82	20	1	15	59	1	21	88	.295	.351	.536

Where He Hits the Ball

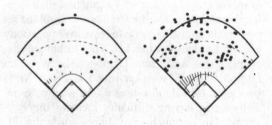

Vs. LHP   **Vs. RHP**

2002 Situational Stats

	AB	H	HR	RBI	Avg		AB	H	HR	RBI	Avg
Home	118	33	6	25	.280	LHP	49	14	1	10	.286
Road	147	49	9	33	.333	RHP	216	68	14	48	.315
First Half	27	10	0	3	.370	Sc Pos	80	29	2	39	.363
Scnd Half	238	72	15	55	.303	Clutch	31	10	2	8	.323

2002 Rankings (American League)

- 3rd in home runs among rookies and RBI among rookies
- 5th in batting average with the bases loaded (.545)
- Led the Blue Jays in batting average with runners in scoring position and batting average on the road

Shannon Stewart

2002 Season

After slumping in May while sharing the primary DH duties with Raul Mondesi, Shannon Stewart recovered his batting stroke after being returned to the outfield. He hit one point above his career average for the season, and just 10 points under his 1999-2001 rate of .313. Stewart's power output and stolen bases dropped in '02, but he was very steady when given the chance to play in the field. As a DH, he averaged .239, while as an outfielder he hit .330.

Hitting

When allowed to lead off and play in left field, Stewart is a relentlessly consistent hitting machine. Unlike many hitters, there is little fluctuation in many of his splits, especially his marks against left- and righthanded pitchers. This is because pitchers have discovered there is no common way to retire him. He can hit the low ball and high ball, fastball, breaking ball and changeup. Stewart has good power to the opposite field, and he drives the ball to both alleys. Many scouts and coaches regard him as the prototypical No. 3 hitter, but Stewart hasn't taken especially well to the role during several experiments.

Baserunning & Defense

Stewart has scored 100 runs in four consecutive seasons, so he knows his way around the diamond. His basestealing totals have fallen off dramatically, however, from 51 in 1998 to a career-low 14 for a full season in 2002. He has only average range in left field, and a weak throwing arm does little to intimidate opposing runners.

2003 Outlook

Offensively and defensively, there is no reason to suspect Stewart will depart from his established pattern. Given health and a position in the field over a full season, he'll post close to 200 hits and 100 runs, plus 15-20 homers and double-digit stolen bases. Off the field, an attempt to negotiate a multiyear contract prior to the 2002 season failed and the sides settled for a one-year, $4.25 million arrangement. Stewart was bound to be shopped around over the winter unless a multiyear contract was negotiated.

Position: LF/DH
Bats: R **Throws:** R
Ht: 6' 1" **Wt:** 210

Opening Day Age: 29
Born: 2/25/74 in Cincinnati, OH
ML Seasons: 8

Overall Statistics

	G	AB	R	H	D	T	HR	RBI	SB	BB	SO	Avg	OBP	Slg
'02	141	577	103	175	38	6	10	45	14	54	60	.303	.371	.442
Car.	784	3147	534	951	196	30	66	321	162	288	404	.302	.369	.446

Where He Hits the Ball

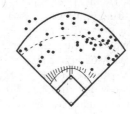 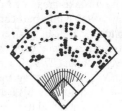

Vs. LHP	**Vs. RHP**

2002 Situational Stats

	AB	H	HR	RBI	Avg		AB	H	HR	RBI	Avg
Home	279	89	4	25	.319	LHP	129	39	3	10	.302
Road	298	86	6	20	.289	RHP	448	136	7	35	.304
First Half	288	83	4	20	.288	Sc Pos	117	33	2	35	.282
Scnd Half	289	92	6	25	.318	Clutch	71	24	0	5	.338

2002 Rankings (American League)

- 3rd in on-base percentage for a leadoff hitter (.379)
- 6th in triples
- 8th in singles and GDPs (17)
- Led the Blue Jays in batting average, runs scored, hits, singles, doubles, triples, stolen bases, GDPs (17), lowest percentage of swings that missed (12.2), highest percentage of swings put into play (48.7), batting average in the clutch, batting average with the bases loaded (.750), on-base percentage for a leadoff hitter (.379), batting average on a 3-2 count (.324) and batting average with two strikes (.236)

Toronto

Vernon Wells

2002 Season

Vernon Wells' first full season in the majors netted 100 RBI at age 23, the youngest to reach that vaunted plateau in franchise history. He drove in 64 runs in a 76-game stretch that went from the beginning of July all the way to late September. He also drove in 41 teammates in his final 40 road games. Wells was most successful in the No. 5 and 6 holes of the batting order, with 49 RBI and a combined average at those spots of just above .300. Defensively, he established himself as a future Gold Glove candidate.

Hitting

A line-drive hitter, Wells feasts on low fastballs and mistake breaking balls. He hits finesse pitchers very hard, but can struggle versus power pitchers. He can be overly aggressive at the plate, as he tries to prevent the count from running deep. He drew just 27 walks in nearly 650 plate appearances. By exhibiting more patience at the plate, Wells could push his batting average into the .300 range. A cerebral type, he learns quickly. The first time he faced a pitcher in a game, he averaged .248; the third time up against the same pitcher, his average jumped to .342. And with runners on base, Wells posted a .301 mark.

Baserunning & Defense

A smart runner with good speed, Wells seems to lack the quick jump of prolific basestealers. He swiped nine bags in 2002, but he was caught four times. In the outfield, though, Wells *does* seem to get good jumps on the ball, and he makes the spectacular catches look routine by covering a lot of ground and hauling in the liners with a sure glove.

2003 Outlook

Wells will enter his second full season in the big leagues, likely batting behind Carlos Delgado in the fifth or sixth spot of the order. Wells' biggest challenge will be to achieve greater consistency, and his track record in the minors suggests he'll do just that. He is capable of averaging at least .280 with 20 homers.

Position: CF/RF
Bats: R **Throws:** R
Ht: 6' 1" **Wt:** 225

Opening Day Age: 24
Born: 12/8/78 in Shreveport, LA
ML Seasons: 4

Overall Statistics

	G	AB	R	H	D	T	HR	RBI	SB	BB	SO	Avg	OBP	Slg
'02	159	608	87	167	34	4	23	100	9	27	85	.275	.305	.457
Car.	216	794	109	220	47	4	25	114	15	36	118	.277	.308	.441

Where He Hits the Ball

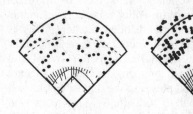

Vs. LHP   **Vs. RHP**

2002 Situational Stats

	AB	H	HR	RBI	Avg		AB	H	HR	RBI	Avg
Home	292	78	10	42	.267	LHP	154	40	4	29	.260
Road	316	89	13	58	.282	RHP	454	127	19	71	.280
First Half	304	80	10	42	.263	Sc Pos	178	49	8	76	.275
Scnd Half	304	87	13	58	.286	Clutch	80	15	1	7	.188

2002 Rankings (American League)

- 2nd in assists in center field (11)
- 3rd in fielding percentage in center field (.995)
- 6th in games played
- 7th in lowest on-base percentage and fewest pitches seen per plate appearance (3.42)
- 8th in batting average on an 0-2 count (.298)
- Led the Blue Jays in at-bats, total bases (278), sacrifice flies (8), caught stealing (4), games played and batting average on an 0-2 count (.298)

Chris Woodward

Position: SS
Bats: R **Throws:** R
Ht: 6' 0" **Wt:** 185

Opening Day Age: 26
Born: 6/27/76 in
Covina, CA
ML Seasons: 4
Nickname: Woody

2002 Season

A 54th-round draft pick in 1994, Chris Woodward emerged over former first-round pick Felipe Lopez for the starting shortstop position in the middle of the season. Nicknamed Woody, Woodward hit .344 combined in June and July despite missing nearly three weeks with a strained groin and strained right hamstring. He continued to hit well through August, recording the 11th three-homer performance in club history on August 7 versus Seattle.

Hitting

Wiry and athletic, Woodward possesses very good hand strength, which enables above-average bat speed. Formerly, a mechanical defect caused him to lose power. But last year, Woodward adjusted his swing to bring the bat on a more level, direct path, and good things happened. He'll hit balls anywhere in the strike zone, often with surprising pop. His weakness is the fastball up and away, and he can be lured to swing at low breaking pitches outside of the strike zone. Lefthanders bother Woodward as well, and held him to a .149 average last season. A line-drive hitter, Woodward took more pitches per plate appearance (3.91) than the previous season, with good results.

Baserunning & Defense

A heady runner with good speed, Woodward stole just three bases in 2002. But he flashes the ability to steal 10-20 bases per season if given the opportunity. Defensively, he has mediocre range to both his right and left, and possesses an average arm. But he turns the double play crisply and positions himself very well in the field.

2003 Outlook

The starting shortstop job is Woodward's to lose. He took a lot of opponents by surprise with his power last season, and all for the bargain rate of $235,000. His confidence boosted, look for him to hit with a quiet efficiency. He'll be placed toward the bottom of the order, though the No. 2 hole is possible on occasion.

Overall Statistics

	G	AB	R	H	D	T	HR	RBI	SB	BB	SO	Avg	OBP	Slg
'02	90	312	48	86	13	4	13	45	3	26	72	.276	.330	.468
Car.	178	505	74	123	24	6	18	66	4	39	120	.244	.297	.422

Where He Hits the Ball

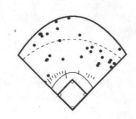
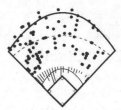

Vs. LHP   **Vs. RHP**

2002 Situational Stats

	AB	H	HR	RBI	Avg		AB	H	HR	RBI	Avg
Home	159	46	9	26	.289	LHP	74	11	0	3	.149
Road	153	40	4	19	.261	RHP	238	75	13	42	.315
First Half	58	16	3	5	.276	Sc Pos	84	23	0	29	.274
Scnd Half	254	70	10	40	.276	Clutch	37	10	2	4	.270

2002 Rankings (American League)

- 8th in errors at shortstop (13)
- 9th in sacrifice flies (8)
- Led the Blue Jays in sacrifice flies (8) and batting average vs. righthanded pitchers

Dave Berg

Position:
2B/3B/SS/1B/RF
Bats: R **Throws:** R
Ht: 5'11" **Wt:** 196

Opening Day Age: 32
Born: 9/3/70 in
Roseville, CA
ML Seasons: 5

Overall Statistics

	G	AB	R	H	D	T	HR	RBI	SB	BB	SO	Avg	OBP	Slg
'02	109	374	42	101	26	2	4	39	0	26	57	.270	.322	.382
Car.	463	1285	151	350	81	5	14	122	8	118	247	.272	.337	.376

2002 Situational Stats

	AB	H	HR	RBI	Avg		AB	H	HR	RBI	Avg
Home	185	60	3	28	.324	LHP	106	28	2	10	.264
Road	189	41	1	11	.217	RHP	268	73	2	29	.272
First Half	202	51	4	16	.252	Sc Pos	90	25	0	32	.278
Scnd Half	172	50	0	23	.291	Clutch	55	16	1	6	.291

2002 Season

Dave Berg equaled a career high by playing in 109 games in 2002. A valued utility player, he started at seven different positions: 43 at second, 11 at shortstop, 18 at third, nine in right, seven at first, eight at DH and one in left. Despite the constant shuffling, he kept his concentration at the plate and produced respectable numbers.

Hitting, Baserunning & Defense

Berg has a good understanding of how pitchers work him. His approach centers around hitting the ball up the middle and the other way. An outstanding situational hitter, he'll sacrifice points off his batting average to advance runners. He was one of the team's best hit-and-run batters. He understands how to play different positions and sets himself according to the pitcher's approach. He handled low throws at first base well and was able to start the double play from first. He isn't particularly fast, but knows how to run the bases.

2003 Outlook

Berg's experience and work ethic should be a valuable asset on a team that has become younger and is building for the future. Entering his free-agency season, he should see spot duty at several positions and is likely to receive in the range of 350 at-bats.

Chris Carpenter

Position: SP
Bats: R **Throws:** R
Ht: 6' 6" **Wt:** 215

Opening Day Age: 27
Born: 4/27/75 in Exeter, NH
ML Seasons: 6

Overall Statistics

	W	L	Pct.	ERA	G	GS	Sv	IP	H	BB	SO	HR	Ratio
'02	4	5	.444	5.28	13	13	0	73.1	89	27	45	11	1.58
Car.	49	50	.495	4.83	152	135	0	870.2	984	331	612	111	1.51

2002 Situational Stats

	W	L	ERA	Sv	IP		AB	H	HR	RBI	Avg
Home	2	2	5.25	0	24.0	LHB	164	54	8	24	.329
Road	2	3	5.29	0	49.1	RHB	127	35	3	16	.276
First Half	1	1	6.59	0	27.1	Sc Pos	74	20	5	32	.270
Scnd Half	3	4	4.50	0	46.0	Clutch	21	4	1	3	.190

2002 Season

Much was expected from Chris Carpenter in his fifth full season with the Jays, but he wasn't right from the beginning and ultimately succumbed to shoulder surgery after 13 starts. Normally a workhorse, he gave up 89 hits, 11 homers and 27 walks in only 73.1 innings.

Pitching & Defense

Carpenter mixes a 92-93 MPH fastball with a sweeping curve, a cutter and changeup. When the curve is on, he freezes batters; when it's not, he banks on a fastball that can lack movement and command. Delivering from the three-quarters position, he fought a tendency to drop down in the midst of a game. When healthy, Carpenter has a good move to first and gives his catchers a good shot at basestealers with a quick delivery. He is athletic off the mound, and hasn't erred in the past two seasons.

2003 Outlook

Carpenter likely won't be ready to pitch until late in the year, if then. While the Jays tried to keep their rehabbing free agent in the fold, Carpenter reached an agreement with St. Louis on a one-year, $1 million deal that includes a 2004 club option.

Felix Heredia

Position: RP
Bats: L **Throws:** L
Ht: 6' 0" **Wt:** 190

Opening Day Age: 27
Born: 6/18/75 in Barahona, DR
ML Seasons: 7
Pronunciation: heh-RAY-dee-ah

Overall Statistics

	W	L	Pct.	ERA	G	GS	Sv	IP	H	BB	SO	HR	Ratio
'02	1	2	.333	3.61	53	0	0	52.1	51	26	31	5	1.47
Car.	22	15	.595	4.69	392	2	5	330.0	329	178	279	30	1.54

2002 Situational Stats

	W	L	ERA	Sv	IP		AB	H	HR	RBI	Avg
Home	1	0	3.81	0	28.1	LHB	85	19	3	14	.224
Road	0	2	3.38	0	24.0	RHB	114	32	2	19	.281
First Half	0	2	4.68	0	32.2	Sc Pos	60	18	3	27	.300
Scnd Half	1	0	1.83	0	19.2	Clutch	43	15	3	13	.349

2002 Season

Acquired from the Cubs in exchange for shortstop Alex Gonzalez, Felix Heredia worked primarily in middle relief and as a situational lefty. Confined almost exclusively to the situational role in the second half, he went 1-0 with an 1.83 ERA in 23 games and recorded 17 scoreless outings in 18 appearances. In 14 combined outings in August and September, he allowed a total of nine hits.

Pitching & Defense

Heredia relies on a fastball that fluctuates between the high 80s and low 90s, as well as a changeup that will dive away from lefthanded batters. He held lefty hitters to a .224 average last year. He allows a lot of baserunners but can escape jams with the occasional strikeout. Still, 13 of 38 (34.2 percent) inherited runners in 2002 came around to score. Heredia's follow-through does not leave him in a very desirable fielding position, though he did set a career high with nine assists last year.

2003 Outlook

After finding success as a situational lefty in Toronto's bullpen, Heredia declared free agency. The club anticipated his loss, signing Doug Creek as insurance in late October. Heredia will serve in middle relief or a setup role wherever he lands.

Ken Huckaby

Position: C
Bats: R **Throws:** R
Ht: 6' 1" **Wt:** 205

Opening Day Age: 32
Born: 1/27/71 in San Leandro, CA
ML Seasons: 2
Pronunciation: HUCK-a-be

Overall Statistics

	G	AB	R	H	D	T	HR	RBI	SB	BB	SO	Avg	OBP	Slg
'02	88	273	29	67	6	1	3	22	0	9	44	.245	.270	.308
Car.	89	274	29	67	6	1	3	22	0	9	45	.245	.269	.307

2002 Situational Stats

	AB	H	HR	RBI	Avg		AB	H	HR	RBI	Avg
Home	140	40	1	15	.286	LHP	62	17	0	3	.274
Road	133	27	2	7	.203	RHP	211	50	3	19	.237
First Half	79	23	1	8	.291	Sc Pos	68	14	2	19	.206
Scnd Half	194	44	2	14	.227	Clutch	31	7	0	1	.226

2002 Season

The Jays got a lot of mileage out of a 31-year-old rookie. Ken Huckaby started the season at Triple-A Syracuse and was first called up on May 8. He made a handful of starts behind the plate before he was sent back down to the minors on May 21. Huckaby was called up again on June 4 for good, and ended up making 88 appearances (77 starts) behind the plate for the Blue Jays.

Hitting, Baserunning & Defense

A line-drive hitter without much power, Huckaby goes mostly to the opposite field. He is a good situational hitter, especially when the hit-and-run is on. Still, Huckaby is in the majors for his abilities behind the plate. He sets a low target, calls a decisive game and has a strong throwing arm. He is prone to the passed ball, finishing just one short of the franchise record with 13. Though he's no threat to steal, Huckaby goes hard from the batter's box and had an inside-the-park homer.

2003 Outlook

Huckaby fills a valuable role while prospect Kevin Cash develops. In spite of the passed balls, Huckaby earned the trust of the starting pitchers. If Cash progresses as hoped, Huckaby could return to a backup role or find himself back down in the minors by midseason.

Felipe Lopez

Position: SS
Bats: B **Throws:** R
Ht: 6' 0" **Wt:** 185

Opening Day Age: 22
Born: 5/12/80 in Bayamon, PR
ML Seasons: 2

Overall Statistics

	G	AB	R	H	D	T	HR	RBI	SB	BB	SO	Avg	OBP	Slg
'02	85	282	35	64	15	3	8	34	5	23	90	.227	.287	.387
Car.	134	459	56	110	20	7	13	57	9	35	129	.240	.293	.399

2002 Situational Stats

	AB	H	HR	RBI	Avg		AB	H	HR	RBI	Avg
Home	126	26	5	14	.206	LHP	66	20	3	14	.303
Road	156	38	3	20	.244	RHP	216	44	5	20	.204
First Half	258	60	8	31	.233	Sc Pos	68	17	2	26	.250
Scnd Half	24	4	0	3	.167	Clutch	51	13	1	9	.255

2002 Season

Felipe Lopez began 2002 as the starting shortstop but lost his job to backup Chris Woodward. Lopez was sent to Triple-A Syracuse in mid-July and brought back up at the beginning of September. In 43 games for Syracuse, Lopez averaged .318 with 11 doubles and three home runs.

Hitting, Baserunning & Defense

A switch-hitter, Lopez averaged .309 from the right side and .201 lefthanded last year. Quick hands and strong wrists give him surprising pop. Even so, power pitchers exploit his tendency to go after the high fastball, and get him out with a breaking ball out of the zone. He thus far has lacked the plate discipline to succeed in the majors. A five-tool player, Lopez has above-average range and a strong arm. Last season at short, he made eight errors in 320 chances for a .975 fielding percentage. On the bases, he has the speed to steal more often.

2003 Outlook

Lopez already has proven capable of hitting Triple-A pitching, but with Woodward having the shortstop's job to lose, Hinske now established at third and Orlando Hudson looking like the second baseman of the future, Lopez either takes a utility role, returns to the minors or gets traded.

Steve Parris

Position: SP
Bats: R **Throws:** R
Ht: 6' 0" **Wt:** 195

Opening Day Age: 35
Born: 12/17/67 in Joliet, IL
ML Seasons: 7

Overall Statistics

	W	L	Pct.	ERA	G	GS	Sv	IP	H	BB	SO	HR	Ratio
'02	5	5	.500	5.97	14	14	0	75.1	96	35	48	13	1.74
Car.	44	46	.489	4.67	129	122	0	709.2	786	275	465	102	1.50

2002 Situational Stats

	W	L	ERA	Sv	IP		AB	H	HR	RBI	Avg
Home	3	1	6.04	0	22.1	LHB	164	56	6	21	.341
Road	2	4	5.94	0	53.0	RHB	142	40	7	23	.282
First Half	1	2	3.45	0	28.2	Sc Pos	75	20	3	31	.267
Scnd Half	4	3	7.52	0	46.2	Clutch	0	0	0	0	–

2002 Season

Coming off September 2001 shoulder surgery a little earlier than expected, Steve Parris returned on June 16 and started his 2002 season promisingly. He won five of his first seven decisions, but he struggled for consistent command after the All-Star break (4-3, 7.52). The Jays shut him down for good after an August 28 appearance with what was termed as a "dead arm."

Pitching & Defense

Parris has above-average command of a fastball that usually runs in the high 80s and can reach 92 MPH. He also throws a 75-77 MPH breaking ball and an 80-MPH changeup. By concentrating on changing speeds more often, he could improve his ability to keep hitters off balance. As it is, he relies on moving his fastball around the strike zone, and they wait for the pitch in their zone. Parris is efficient in the field, and has helped turn 11 double plays in his career.

2003 Outlook

A determined competitor and positive clubhouse influence, Parris made $3.4 million in the final season of his contract with the Blue Jays. With the condition of his shoulder uncertain and the team bent on developing young pitchers, it is unlikely that Parris will be re-signed.

Cliff Politte

Position: RP
Bats: R **Throws:** R
Ht: 5'11" **Wt:** 185

Opening Day Age: 29
Born: 2/27/74 in St. Louis, MO
ML Seasons: 5
Pronunciation: po-LEET

Overall Statistics

	W	L	Pct.	ERA	G	GS	Sv	IP	H	BB	SO	HR	Ratio
'02	3	3	.500	3.67	68	0	1	73.2	57	28	72	5	1.15
Car.	12	12	.500	4.26	124	16	1	213.1	200	96	182	23	1.39

2002 Situational Stats

	W	L	ERA	Sv	IP		AB	H	HR	RBI	Avg
Home	2	1	2.93	0	40.0	LHB	125	34	4	16	.272
Road	1	2	4.54	1	33.2	RHB	145	23	1	13	.159
First Half	3	2	4.82	0	37.1	Sc Pos	61	17	1	23	.279
Scnd Half	0	1	2.48	1	36.1	Clutch	148	31	1	13	.209

2002 Season

Having fallen out of favor in Philadelphia, Cliff Politte was obtained for veteran lefthanded reliever Dan Plesac on May 26. He fit in nicely as Paul Quantrill's replacement, setting up for closer Kelvim Escobar. Nineteen of his 25 holds preceded Escobar saves. He had 18 strikeouts in his final 13 innings and allowed about a baserunner per inning in his stint with Toronto (38 hits, 19 walks, 1 hit batsman in 57.1 innings).

Pitching & Defense

Politte could mature into a closer. He has excellent command of an overpowering four-seam fastball that is clocked regularly at 96 MPH and goes up to 98. He hits both sides of the plate, up and down. His slider runs 88-90 MPH, and he works in a two-seam fastball and a changeup. In his few chances, he showed well as a fielder. He is quick to the plate with a simple delivery and can get the ball home in 1.2 seconds, which should make him difficult to run on.

2003 Outlook

Though some believe he would make a reliable second or third starter in the rotation, Politte likely will continue in the setup role. As Escobar is more effective with one day's rest, Politte may get the occasional save opportunity.

Corey Thurman

Position: RP
Bats: R **Throws:** R
Ht: 6' 1" **Wt:** 215

Opening Day Age: 24
Born: 11/5/78 in Augusta, GA
ML Seasons: 1

Overall Statistics

	W	L	Pct.	ERA	G	GS	Sv	IP	H	BB	SO	HR	Ratio
'02	2	3	.400	4.37	43	1	0	68.0	65	45	56	11	1.62
Car.	2	3	.400	4.37	43	1	0	68.0	65	45	56	11	1.62

2002 Situational Stats

	W	L	ERA	Sv	IP		AB	H	HR	RBI	Avg
Home	1	1	3.93	0	36.2	LHB	123	29	5	17	.236
Road	1	2	4.88	0	31.1	RHB	139	36	6	16	.259
First Half	1	2	3.02	0	41.2	Sc Pos	88	19	3	24	.216
Scnd Half	1	1	6.49	0	26.1	Clutch	30	9	1	3	.300

2002 Season

Corey Thurman's 43 appearances surpassed Jim Acker's 38 in 1983 to establish a team record for a Rule 5 draftee. Acquired from Kansas City, Thurman made the jump from Double-A starter to major league reliever. He had an 0.69 ERA in June but allowed eight home runs in his final 11 outings.

Pitching & Defense

With excellent arm speed from a high three-quarter arm slot, Thurman relies heavily on a change-up that takes on parachute action at the plate. He has exceptional command of the pitch for a young pitcher and uses it in combination with a four-seam fastball. He has trouble commanding his curve. He also has worked on a slider but hasn't used it much. His fielding is adequate. A high leg kick hampers his ability to hold runners.

2003 Outlook

His future in the rotation, Thurman will need work to be ready for a starting role, meaning he could begin the season at Triple-A Syracuse now that Kansas City has lost the right to reclaim him. He allowed five runs in three-plus innings in his only start, September 2 against the White Sox. He needs to throw his curve consistently for strikes, or develop another pitch.

Pete Walker

Position: SP/RP
Bats: R **Throws:** R
Ht: 6' 2" **Wt:** 195

Opening Day Age: 33
Born: 4/8/69 in Beverly, MA
ML Seasons: 5

Overall Statistics

	W	L	Pct.	ERA	G	GS	Sv	IP	H	BB	SO	HR	Ratio
'02	10	5	.667	4.36	38	20	1	140.1	145	51	80	18	1.40
Car.	11	5	.688	4.66	57	20	1	170.0	185	63	92	22	1.46

2002 Situational Stats

	W	L	ERA	Sv	IP		AB	H	HR	RBI	Avg
Home	6	3	4.84	0	80.0	LHB	271	78	11	41	.288
Road	4	2	3.73	1	60.1	RHB	264	67	7	35	.254
First Half	3	0	2.98	1	48.1	Sc Pos	134	39	8	64	.291
Scnd Half	7	5	5.09	0	92.0	Clutch	40	12	0	4	.300

2002 Season

At the tender age of 33, Pete Walker was claimed off waivers from the Mets' organization as a reliever on May 3 and wound up making his first 20 major league starts for Toronto. He made 10 appearances out of the Blue Jays' bullpen before his first start, and was quite effective in his relief role. Toronto then went 12-8 in his starts, and he won seven of his final 10 decisions in a span of 12 outings. As a starter, he was 9-5 with a 4.79 ERA, and as a reliever he went 1-0, 2.46.

Pitching & Defense

Walker comes right at hitters with a low-90s fastball, as well as a sinker, breaking ball and changeup. He has good control, and the groundball pitcher gets out of jams with the sinking fastball that helped to produce 17 double plays last year. Because Walker induced 29 more grounders than flyballs last year, naturally he was much more effective on grass (3.27 ERA) than artificial turf (4.86). He committed his first two big league errors last year, but opposing baserunners were not much better than .500 against him.

2003 Outlook

Having earned the major league minimum, Walker is a candidate for a back-of-the-rotation berth in Toronto, or a spot in the pen.

Tom Wilson

Position: C/DH/1B
Bats: R **Throws:** R
Ht: 6' 3" **Wt:** 220

Opening Day Age: 32
Born: 12/19/70 in Fullerton, CA
ML Seasons: 2

Overall Statistics

	G	AB	R	H	D	T	HR	RBI	SB	BB	SO	Avg	OBP	Slg
'02	96	265	33	68	10	0	8	37	0	28	79	.257	.334	.385
Car.	105	286	37	72	10	0	10	41	0	29	84	.252	.328	.392

2002 Situational Stats

	AB	H	HR	RBI	Avg		AB	H	HR	RBI	Avg
Home	136	38	6	19	.279	LHP	83	28	3	17	.337
Road	129	30	2	18	.233	RHP	182	40	5	20	.220
First Half	153	37	5	21	.242	Sc Pos	76	22	3	32	.289
Scnd Half	112	31	3	16	.277	Clutch	45	14	2	8	.311

2002 Season

Obtained in a trade from Oakland in January 2002, Tom Wilson opened the season as a platoon partner of Darrin Fletcher, who retired in July. As Ken Huckaby assumed more of the catching duties later in the season, Wilson was used at first base and DH. After a solid May, he fell off in June and July but finished strong after the All-Star break.

Hitting, Baserunning & Defense

Wilson works the count well and sees a lot of pitches, averaging 4.25 pitches per appearance. The righthanded-hitting Wilson has some power to the opposite field. He excels against lefthanded pitching, but struggled against righties last year. As a baserunner, Wilson is a minor league vet who knows what he's doing and won't clog up the basepaths. Behind the plate, he threw out just 20 percent of attempted basestealers. The staff had an ERA of 5.07 with him, versus 4.28 with Huckaby.

2003 Outlook

The Blue Jays seemed content with the stop-gap complement of Wilson and Huckaby behind the plate, which would allow prospect Kevin Cash to start 2003 at Triple-A Syracuse. Wilson offers more offensive pop and Huckaby supplies superior defense. Still, the Jays signed Greg Myers to a one-year deal in December.

Brian Bowles (Pos: RHP, Age: 26)

	W	L	Pct.	ERA	G	GS	Sv	IP	H	BB	SO	HR	Ratio
'02	2	1	.667	4.05	17	0	0	20.0	13	14	19	0	1.35
Car.	2	1	.667	3.42	19	0	0	23.2	17	15	23	0	1.35

His walk totals have been a bit high, but Bowles has posted a 3.10 ERA and 20 saves over the last two seasons at Triple-A Syracuse. He showed the Jays enough that he may have a role in the bullpen in 2003. 2003 Outlook: C

Scott Cassidy (Pos: RHP, Age: 27)

	W	L	Pct.	ERA	G	GS	Sv	IP	H	BB	SO	HR	Ratio
'02	1	4	.200	5.73	58	0	0	66.0	52	32	48	12	1.27
Car.	1	4	.200	5.73	58	0	0	66.0	52	32	48	12	1.27

Cassidy has overcome diabetes and a lack of prospect status, and he surfaced in the Jays' pen in 2002. He was more effective in the first half, but he may have the guts and know-how to make it. 2003 Outlook: C

Brian Cooper (Pos: RHP, Age: 28)

	W	L	Pct.	ERA	G	GS	Sv	IP	H	BB	SO	HR	Ratio
'02	0	1	.000	14.04	2	2	0	8.1	14	4	3	5	2.16
Car.	5	11	.313	5.86	29	23	0	136.2	152	61	61	28	1.56

A castoff from the Angels farm system, Cooper was beat up in two April starts and never returned to Toronto. His best numbers at the Triple-A level came during his first exposure in 1999, so time's running out. 2003 Outlook: C

Bob File (Pos: RHP, Age: 26)

	W	L	Pct.	ERA	G	GS	Sv	IP	H	BB	SO	HR	Ratio
'02	0	1	.000	18.90	5	0	0	3.1	8	2	2	0	3.00
Car.	5	4	.556	3.94	65	0	0	77.2	65	31	40	6	1.24

After a solid rookie season in 2001, File looked like the Jays' setup man until he injured his ribcage in late March, missed two months and later injured an ankle and his lower back. He never got on track. 2003 Outlook: B

Darrin Fletcher (Pos: C, Age: 36, Bats: L)

	G	AB	R	H	D	T	HR	RBI	SB	BB	SO	Avg	OBP	Slg
'02	45	127	8	28	6	0	3	22	0	4	13	.220	.239	.339
Car.	1245	3902	377	1048	214	8	124	583	2	255	399	.269	.318	.423

Fletcher batted .320 and slugged .514 in his best big league season in 2000, but slipped to .226 and .353 in 2001. He was off to an even poorer start in '02 before retiring near the end of July. 2003 Outlook: D

Jason Kershner (Pos: LHP, Age: 26)

	W	L	Pct.	ERA	G	GS	Sv	IP	H	BB	SO	HR	Ratio
'02	0	1	.000	4.88	25	0	1	24.0	20	14	18	3	1.42
Car.	0	1	.000	4.88	25	0	1	24.0	20	14	18	3	1.42

After four solid months at San Diego's Triple-A Portland, Kershner was promoted to the Padres in late July. He posted a 3.15 ERA over the final two months, and the Blue Jays picked him up off waivers. 2003 Outlook: B

Joe Lawrence (Pos: 2B, Age: 26, Bats: R)

	G	AB	R	H	D	T	HR	RBI	SB	BB	SO	Avg	OBP	Slg
'02	55	150	16	27	4	0	2	15	2	16	38	.180	.262	.247
Car.	55	150	16	27	4	0	2	15	2	16	38	.180	.262	.247

Lawrence always had a promising bat, but he hasn't hit as well since a wrist injury in 2001. He's been bounced around different positions, and now he joins Milwaukee on a minor league contract. 2003 Outlook: C

Brian Lesher (Pos: 1B, Age: 32, Bats: R)

	G	AB	R	H	D	T	HR	RBI	SB	BB	SO	Avg	OBP	Slg
'02	24	38	2	5	1	0	0	2	0	4	15	.132	.209	.158
Car.	108	263	31	59	10	2	9	38	5	19	65	.224	.275	.380

Lesher won a utility job in the spring, but didn't stick around long. He didn't hit or walk when the Jays called again in August. 2003 Outlook: C

Brandon Lyon (Pos: RHP, Age: 23)

	W	L	Pct.	ERA	G	GS	Sv	IP	H	BB	SO	HR	Ratio
'02	1	4	.200	6.53	15	10	0	62.0	78	19	30	14	1.56
Car.	6	8	.429	5.40	26	21	0	125.0	141	34	65	20	1.40

In 2001, Lyon dashed to Toronto, going 10-3 in the high minors. He struggled in '02, however, and Boston claimed him off waivers in October. 2003 Outlook: C

Luke Prokopec (Pos: RHP, Age: 25)

	W	L	Pct.	ERA	G	GS	Sv	IP	H	BB	SO	HR	Ratio
'02	2	9	.182	6.78	22	12	0	71.2	90	25	41	19	1.60
Car.	11	17	.393	5.30	56	37	0	231.0	255	74	144	48	1.42

After the Jays dealt for the coveted Prokopec a year ago, his bad year ended in September shoulder surgery. He's out most or all of 2003, but LA inked him to a two-year minor league pact. 2003 Outlook: C

Pedro Swann (Pos: DH, Age: 32, Bats: L)

	G	AB	R	H	D	T	HR	RBI	SB	BB	SO	Avg	OBP	Slg
'02	13	12	3	1	0	0	0	1	0	1	6	.083	.154	.083
Car.	17	14	3	1	0	0	0	1	0	1	8	.071	.133	.071

Swann's .290 career average and .366 OBP in the minors are indicative of his recent Triple-A seasons, but he fanned six times in 12 at-bats with the Jays, mostly as a pinch-hitter. 2003 Outlook: C

Scott Wiggins (Pos: LHP, Age: 27)

	W	L	Pct.	ERA	G	GS	Sv	IP	H	BB	SO	HR	Ratio
'02	0	0	–	3.38	3	0	0	2.2	5	1	3	1	2.25
Car.	0	0	–	3.38	3	0	0	2.2	5	1	3	1	2.25

Wiggins was acquired for Raul Mondesi in July, and he reached Toronto in September. He must build on his decent second half. 2003 Outlook: C

Dewayne Wise (Pos: RF, Age: 25, Bats: L)

	G	AB	R	H	D	T	HR	RBI	SB	BB	SO	Avg	OBP	Slg
'02	42	112	14	20	4	1	3	13	5	4	15	.179	.207	.313
Car.	70	134	17	23	4	1	3	13	6	5	20	.172	.207	.284

Wise finally showed some plate patience, but it didn't carry into his stint with the Jays after he was recalled in July. A bench role is possible. 2003 Outlook: C

Toronto

Toronto Blue Jays Minor League Prospects

Organization Overview:

New GM J.P. Ricciardi began overhauling the major league roster. Billy Koch was dealt to Oakland for Eric Hinske, arguably the best 2002 rookie in the majors, and Justin Miller, who won nine games for the Jays. Alex Gonzalez, Paul Quantrill and Raul Mondesi also were moved, and prospects Orlando Hudson, Josh Phelps, Vernon Wells and Chris Woodward joined Hinske as regulars. The rebuilding continues with Jayson Werth and Kevin Cash likely to move into the 2003 lineup. There's plenty of young pitching that may arrive the next few seasons, and the Jays' 2002 draft—the first executed by the new regime—features college talent that impressed last year.

Kevin Cash

Position: C | **Opening Day Age:** 25
Bats: R **Throws:** R | **Born:** 12/6/77 in Tampa,
Ht: 6' 0" **Wt:** 185 | FL

Recent Statistics

	G	AB	R	H	D	T	HR	RBI	SB	BB	SO	Avg
2002 AA Tennessee	55	213	38	59	15	1	8	44	5	36	44	.277
2002 AAA Syracuse	67	236	27	52	18	0	10	26	0	25	72	.220
2002 AL Toronto	7	14	1	2	0	0	0	0	1	4	.143

Cash hadn't done any catching before filling in in an emergency in the Cape Cod League in 1999, and soon after the Jays signed him as an undrafted free agent and sent the Florida State product to Class-A ball to catch. Now he's the best defensive catcher in the system, featuring excellent receiving skills and a terrific arm. He's in line to take over catching duties in Toronto, and he mostly needs to bone up on handling major league pitchers to be ready. A successful gap hitter, Cash must focus on spraying the ball and avoid becoming pull-conscious. His plate discipline dropped off against Triple-A pitching in 2002, and more Triple-A experience will help him prepare for hitting in Toronto.

Vinny Chulk

Position: P | **Opening Day Age:** 24
Bats: R **Throws:** R | **Born:** 12/19/78 in Miami,
Ht: 6' 2" **Wt:** 190 | FL

Recent Statistics

	W	L	ERA	G	GS	Sv	IP	H	R	BB	SO	HR
2001 A Dunedin	1	2	3.12	16	1	1	34.2	38	16	13	50	2
2001 AAA Syracuse	1	0	1.50	5	0	0	6.0	5	1	4	3	0
2001 AA Tennessee	2	5	3.14	24	1	2	43.0	34	15	8	43	5
2002 AA Tennessee	13	5	2.96	25	24	1	152.0	133	55	53	108	12
2002 AAA Syracuse	0	1	5.79	2	1	0	4.2	6	6	6	2	0

A 12th-round pick in 2000, Chulk quickly showed he could throw three pitches from three different arm slots. He favors a three-quarters slot that gives his low-90s fastball plenty of sinking action, and he also calls on a slider and changeup. After working in the pen at high Class-A Dunedin and Double-A Tennessee in 2001, Chulk returned to starting in '02 and improved the command of his plus fastball. His slider was better as well, but he still must focus on throwing strikes with it. His changeup needs work. A year at Triple-A Syracuse will fine-tune it. Chulk averaged more than six innings per start last summer, a sign of his physical strength.

Gabe Gross

Position: OF | **Opening Day Age:** 23
Bats: L **Throws:** R | **Born:** 10/21/79 in
Ht: 6' 3" **Wt:** 205 | Baltimore, MD

Recent Statistics

	G	AB	R	H	D	T	HR	RBI	SB	BB	SO	Avg
2001 A Dunedin	35	126	23	38	9	2	4	15	4	26	29	.302
2001 AA Tennessee	11	41	8	10	1	0	3	11	0	6	12	.244
2002 AA Tennessee	112	403	57	96	17	5	10	54	8	53	71	.238

A pure hitter drafted 15th overall in 2001, Gross seemed to adjust quickly to the wood bat. He batted .302 with a .426 OBP in his debut at high Class-A Dunedin. But Gross got off to a very slow start at Double-A Tennessee in '02, batting less than .200 over the first two months. Early on, the league's hurlers made adjustments to him faster than he did to them. Even while he struggled, Gross demonstrated decent discipline and plate coverage, and his controlled approach helped him recover as the season progressed. The Jays credit him with working hard through tough times, yet his season stalled when he fouled a ball off his shin and missed the final month of the season. Gross is an adequate corner outfielder who has a strong arm.

Mark Hendrickson

Position: P | **Opening Day Age:** 28
Bats: L **Throws:** L | **Born:** 6/23/74 in Mount
Ht: 6' 9" **Wt:** 230 | Vernon, WA

Recent Statistics

	W	L	ERA	G	GS	Sv	IP	H	R	BB	SO	HR
2002 AAA Syracuse	7	5	3.52	19	14	0	92.0	90	38	22	68	12
2002 AL Toronto	3	0	2.45	16	4	0	36.2	25	11	12	21	1

Hendrickson played four NBA seasons between 1996 and 2000. Former Jays scouting director Tim Wilken liked his athleticism, and the Jays drafted him in 1997. They let him play basketball and Hendrickson didn't come to camp until the NBA season ended for three years. Despite being 28, he is a "young" pitcher by virtue of not working lots of innings as a minor leaguer. He throws a solid fastball, a good changeup and a slider that he cuts. His big frame generates very good deception that makes life difficult for hitters, but as they adjust to seeing him, he'll need a better slider. The Jays would like to keep Hendrickson a starter, but his fate may be decided by the Jays' activity in the free-agent market this offseason.

Alexis Rios

Position: OF
Bats: R **Throws:** R
Ht: 6' 5" **Wt:** 178

Opening Day Age: 22
Born: 2/18/81 in Coffee, AL

Recent Statistics

	G	AB	R	H	D	T	HR	RBI	SB	BB	SO	Avg
2001 A Christn (WV)	130	480	40	126	20	9	2	58	22	25	59	.263
2002 A Dunedin	111	456	60	139	22	8	3	61	14	27	55	.305

While the Jays took heat for drafting Rios as a less-costly first-round pick in 1999, today they view him as one of their top prospects, one who may develop into a star outfielder. His large but lanky frame may add another 30-40 pounds as he matures. He makes good contact with a short, easy stroke, and more power will come. He matched his career total of three homers early in the 2002 season, but didn't hit another after breaking his hand running the bases in May. He missed just three weeks and played through pain, yet hit the ball well. Drawing more walks would elevate his offensive game. In the field, he is a good outfielder with above-average speed and arm strength. He can play all three outfield spots but soon may be limited to a corner.

Mike Smith

Position: P
Bats: R **Throws:** R
Ht: 5' 11" **Wt:** 195

Opening Day Age: 25
Born: 9/19/77 in Norwood, MA

Recent Statistics

	W	L	ERA	G	GS	Sv	IP	H	R	BB	SO	HR
2002 AAA Syracuse	8	4	3.48	20	20	0	121.2	106	51	43	76	10
2002 AL Toronto	0	3	6.62	14	6	0	35.1	43	28	20	16	3

A fifth-round pick in 2000, Smith reached Double-A Tennessee barely more than a year after signing. The 5-foot-11 Smith is a bulldog who pitches like a big man with his power stuff. He called on his low-90s fastball and hard slider—both solid offerings—at Triple-A Syracuse in 2002, but his control remains an issue. His command of the slider still needs work, as he discovered during a 2002 major league initiation in which Smith often fell behind hitters. His changeup progressed well at Syracuse, and although his Triple-A strikeout rate was down, his stuff, tenacity and feel for pitching work for him. Smith simply needs to throw his offerings for strikes more consistently.

Jayson Werth

Position: OF
Bats: R **Throws:** R
Ht: 6' 5" **Wt:** 190

Opening Day Age: 23
Born: 5/20/79 in Springfield, IL

Recent Statistics

	G	AB	R	H	D	T	HR	RBI	SB	BB	SO	Avg
2002 AAA Syracuse	127	443	65	114	25	2	18	82	24	67	125	.257
2002 AL Toronto	15	46	4	12	2	1	0	6	1	6	11	.261

Werth was drafted as a catcher in 1997. Despite his 6-foot-5 frame, he displays an athleticism and quickness that has allowed the Jays to move him to the outfield since acquiring him from Baltimore in 2000. Initially Werth was successful as a contact hitter with solid plate discipline. But he found a power stroke in the second half of 2001 and he continued to show his budding power at Triple-A Syracuse last summer. While Werth's average took a dip there, the Jays were pleased with his first exposure to Triple-A ball, in light of his full-time move to the outfield. He's an above-average runner who's in the spring mix for right-field duty in Toronto. His swing was a bit long during his major league debut in September, and pitchers found holes. Shortening his stroke will be a training camp priority.

Others to Watch

The Jays' first-round pick last June, University of North Carolina shortstop **Russ Adams** (22) split time at short-season Auburn and high Class-A Dunedin, posting a .386 OBP in his first taste of the pro game. . . After a 15-6 (3.37) season that produced league MVP honors at Double-A Tennessee in 2001, **Chris Baker** (25) experienced shoulder soreness and a loss of velocity at Triple-A Syracuse. He was 4-7 (4.33) before undergoing surgery in early August. . . Slender righthander **Pasqual Coco** (25) has a good fastball-changeup combo, but perfecting a breaking pitch hasn't gone well and he has stalled at Triple-A Syracuse. Another opportunity awaits. Coco could end up in the pen. . . As a teenager at short-season Auburn, **Brandon League** (20) called on his overpowering arm and OK command to go 7-2 (3.15). He needs to throw more strikes, particularly with his slider. When his command shows marked improvement, League will be on his way. . . A native of the Netherland Antilles, **Diegomar Markwell** (22) is a 6-foot-2 southpaw who gets hitters out with a solid curve and an average fastball. He changes speeds effectively and works hitters in and out. In 2002, he went 13-9 (4.38) and shared the league lead in wins with teammate Vinny Chulk at Double-A Tennessee. . . A supplemental first-round pick in 2000, righty **Dustin McGowan** (21) has a great pitcher's body and power stuff. He was downright wild in 2001, but he threw a lot more strikes in going 11-10 (4.19) at Class-A Charleston in 2002. Still, his command is inconsistent. . . . Lefthanded-hitting **Dominic Rich** (23) is a gap hitter who makes consistent contact with the bat. He was one of the better hitters in the high Class-A Florida State League, batting .345 with a .437 OBP in 95 games, and he held his own upon reaching Double-A Tennessee. His defensive game at second base is less advanced, and a move to the outfield is possible. . . Righthander **Francisco Rosario** (22) dominated two Class-A leagues (9-4, 1.94) in 2002 and emerged as one of Toronto's best pitching prospects, thanks mostly to dramatic improvement in his command. He effectively mixed an improved slider with his mid-90s fastball and changeup. A torn elbow ligament in the Arizona Fall League led to October surgery, and Rosario will be sidelined for much of 2003.

National League Players

Bank One Ballpark

Offense

With the second-highest altitude in the majors (Atlanta is about 40 feet lower), Bank One Ballpark is a good hitters' park. If the roof is open—usually during the first six weeks of the season, and perhaps the last week—the ball tends to carry better. Gap-to-gap the park is fairly large, but down the lines hitters can reach the seats with relative ease.

Defense

The left-field fence is low enough for outfielders to take away home runs, but a good center fielder is important at BOB because of the large area to cover and some tricky angles and overhangs. With the roof closed most of the time, it is difficult to grow grass. Thus, late in the season there tends to be divots taken out by diving outfielders, and some rough spots on grounders in the outfield. The infield can get hard at times.

Who It Helps the Most

Power hitters who can pull the ball down either line will find the park to their liking. Steve Finley and Tony Womack have fared better at home in each of the past two seasons.

Who It Hurts the Most

Flyball pitchers can get in trouble, especially with the roof open. Curt Schilling asked for it to be closed for all his starts early in '02, but after fan backlash, the team reverted to using fan comfort as the deciding factor on the status of the roof.

Rookies & Newcomers

Rookie first baseman Lyle Overbay sprays line drives with some power, so he should not be affected much by Bank One Ballpark. A candidate for the 2003 rotation, righthander John Patterson earned both of his major league wins and posted a 1.76 ERA in four home appearances in his 2002 big league debut. He was more homer-prone on the road, but he'll have to work effectively around the strike zone to avoid having hitters exploit the park's higher altitude and lighter air. Mike Koplove, who was effective in the pen as a rookie last year, showed it can be done. He was 4-1 with a 3.03 ERA in 29 relief appearances at home.

Dimensions: LF-330, LCF-374, CF-407, RCF-374, RF-334

Capacity: 49,033

Elevation: 1090 feet

Surface: Grass

Foul Territory: Average

Park Factors

2002 Season

	Home Games Dbacks	Opp	Total	Away Games Dbacks	Opp	Total	Index
G	72	72	144	72	72	144	
Avg	.284	.248	.266	.248	.247	.248	107
AB	2413	2549	4962	2485	2361	4846	102
R	415	313	728	319	284	603	121
H	686	632	1318	617	584	1201	110
2B	131	127	258	116	101	217	116
3B	25	22	47	14	8	22	209
HR	79	73	152	70	71	141	105
BB	331	195	526	255	179	434	118
SO	432	623	1055	486	541	1027	100
E	43	45	88	37	59	96	92
E-Infield	39	37	76	30	51	81	94
LHB-Avg	.286	.263	.277	.260	.260	.260	107
LHB-HR	45	25	70	41	32	73	98
RHB-Avg	.282	.240	.256	.233	.240	.237	108
RHB-HR	34	48	82	29	39	68	114

2000-2002

	Home Games Dbacks	Opp	Total	Away Games Dbacks	Opp	Total	Index
G	219	219	438	219	219	438	
Avg	.283	.257	.270	.250	.248	.249	108
AB	7357	7644	15001	7639	7214	14853	101
R	1193	1003	2196	1025	899	1924	114
H	2080	1963	4043	1907	1786	3693	109
2B	396	359	755	366	315	681	110
3B	62	52	114	48	25	73	155
HR	256	267	523	249	221	470	110
BB	843	624	1467	774	635	1409	103
SO	1288	1737	3025	1462	1719	3181	94
E	128	129	257	127	152	279	92
E-Infield	118	104	222	111	125	236	94
LHB-Avg	.293	.257	.279	.258	.260	.259	108
LHB-HR	137	98	235	141	84	225	107
RHB-Avg	.270	.257	.262	.239	.241	.240	109
RHB-HR	119	169	288	108	137	245	114

2002 Rankings (National League)
- Highest triple factor
- Highest walk factor
- Third-highest run factor

Bob Brenly

2002 Season

Bob Brenly became the second manager since the start of divisional play to win titles in his first two seasons (Larry Dierker was the other). Arizona followed up its 2001 World Series march with an even better regular season, winning 98 games and repeating as National League West champions. Brenly had to cope with a flurry of injuries early in the year and again late. But without infielder Craig Counsell and outfielders Danny Bautista and Luis Gonzalez, the team was swept by St. Louis in the NLDS. Brenly also was part of the All-Star Game fiasco, when both teams ran out of players and a tie was declared.

Offense

Brenly prefers to be aggressive on the bases, but the veteran-laden Diamondbacks don't have as much speed as he prefers. He excels at his timing when calling for the hit-and-run. He likes to alternate left- and righthanded hitters in the lineup, when possible, but also varies his lineup—he used 141 different batting orders last year, most in the majors. His players need to be prepared for changing spots in the lineup or inconsistent roles.

Pitching & Defense

Brenly will rely on aces Randy Johnson and Curt Schilling, shifting the pitching rotation to get those two as many starts as possible. That means other starters will have to adjust their throwing schedules. Relievers also have constantly shifting roles. As on offense, Brenly likes to ride the "hot hand" with relievers, so at times a pitcher can be overused or go a long time without working, which can hurt effectiveness. He often uses relievers for just one batter. Brenly will take chances by moving a player out of position at times to strengthen the lineup.

2003 Outlook

The Diamondbacks' roster likely will change considerably heading into this season, so Brenly will have some added challenges in his third year. How he handles extraneous players in the infield will be a test. This is the third season of Brenly's three-year contract; the team holds an option for 2004.

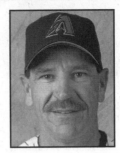

Born: 2/25/54 in Coshocton, OH

Playing Experience: 1981-1989, SF, Tor

Managerial Experience: 2 seasons

Arizona

Manager Statistics

Year	Team, Lg	W	L	Pct	GB	Finish
2002	Arizona, NL	98	64	.605	–	1st West
2 Seasons		190	134	.586	–	–

2002 Starting Pitchers by Days Rest

	<=3	4	5	6+
Diamondbacks Starts	1	114	16	24
Diamondbacks ERA	3.60	3.58	2.81	4.87
NL Avg Starts	1	88	42	21
NL ERA	3.18	4.22	4.14	4.58

2002 Situational Stats

	Bob Brenly	NL Average
Hit & Run Success %	45.0	36.5
Stolen Base Success %	66.7	68.3
Platoon Pct.	62.0	52.7
Defensive Subs	22	19
High-Pitch Outings	14	7
Quick/Slow Hooks	14/12	24/11
Sacrifice Attempts	87	95

2002 Rankings (National League)

- 1st in fewest caught stealings of third base (1), hit-and-run success percentage, starting lineups used (141), starts with over 140 pitches (1), saves with over 1 inning pitched (11) and one-batter pitcher appearances (49)
- 2nd in pinch-hitters used (300) and starts with over 120 pitches (14)
- 3rd in starts on three days rest and first-batter platoon percentage

Miguel Batista

2002 Season

After beginning the season as the odd man out in Arizona's starting staff, Miguel Batista moved into the rotation because of Brian Anderson's ineffectiveness. Batista remained there when Todd Stottlemyre's injuries flared up again. He ended up making 29 starts and pitched a bit better than his 8-9 record would indicate; the Diamondbacks were 7-5 in his 12 no-decisions, and two of the losses were 1-0 games in which Batista did not allow a run. He set career highs in innings pitched and strikeouts, but was hit pretty hard in an NLDS loss to the Cardinals.

Pitching

Batista throws a 92-94 MPH fastball and also has a sinker, a rare curve and an occasional splitter. He likes to cut his fastball. In fact, he sometimes gets stubborn and overuses his cutter, which he offers up in the 88-91 MPH range. Some days, he has a hard time throwing the pitch for a strike, which leads to hitters' counts and short outings. Batista tends to work a lot of deep counts and thus cannot be counted on for more than six or seven innings per start.

Defense & Hitting

Batista has improved his delivery time and ability to hold runners, but he still is below average when it comes to controlling opposing running games. He also is a below-average fielder. His offense has improved greatly, however. Once one of the worst hitting pitchers in the majors, he now makes more consistent contact and generates a few more line drives.

2003 Outlook

Batista's role seems assured heading into 2003, as he will be a starter for Arizona from the get-go. Depending upon how Arizona fills the final hole in its rotation, Batista could end up in the No. 3 spot. His arm has been durable to this point in his career, and he should have no problem with the added responsibility. The Diamondbacks hold an option for 2004 on Batista, so he will be given every chance to prove his value to the club in 2003.

Position: SP
Bats: R **Throws:** R
Ht: 6' 2" **Wt:** 195

Opening Day Age: 32
Born: 2/19/71 in Santo Domingo, DR
ML Seasons: 8
Pronunciation: bah-TEESE-tah

Overall Statistics

	W	L	Pct.	ERA	G	GS	Sv	IP	H	BB	SO	HR	Ratio
'02	8	9	.471	4.29	36	29	0	184.2	172	70	112	12	1.31
Car.	32	41	.438	4.62	218	92	1	708.2	706	324	460	71	1.45

How Often He Throws Strikes

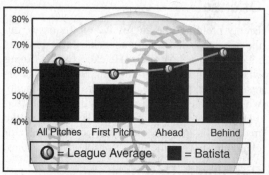

2002 Situational Stats

	W	L	ERA	Sv	IP		AB	H	HR	RBI	Avg
Home	4	1	4.26	0	74.0	LHB	334	90	7	43	.269
Road	4	8	4.31	0	110.2	RHB	367	82	5	41	.223
First Half	4	5	4.85	0	91.0	Sc Pos	168	48	2	68	.286
Scnd Half	4	4	3.75	0	93.2	Clutch	54	10	1	5	.185

2002 Rankings (National League)

- 2nd in fewest home runs allowed per nine innings (.58)
- 3rd in balks (2)
- 5th in highest groundball-flyball ratio allowed (1.7) and highest stolen-base percentage allowed (85.7)
- 8th in wild pitches (9) and lowest strikeout-walk ratio (1.6)
- Led the Diamondbacks in wild pitches (9), highest groundball-flyball ratio allowed (1.7), fewest home runs allowed per nine innings (.58) and most GDPs induced per nine innings (0.8)

Danny Bautista

2002 Season

Danny Bautista was signed to a three-year, $9 million contract in December 2001 and was handed the right-field job after the departure of Reggie Sanders. Bautista got off to a hot start and appeared to be on his way to justifying the deal, but then his season ended abruptly on May 22. Bautista suffered a severe injury to his left shoulder while attempting to make a diving catch, and he required surgery to repair a large tear in his left labrum, a tear in the anterior capsule, a ligament tear and a bruised humerus bone. Bautista made a good recovery and could have been on the roster if Arizona had advanced past the first round of the playoffs.

Hitting

Playing every day seemed to give Bautista more confidence last year, and he showed more power than he had as a career fourth outfielder. He was slugging an even .500 when his season ended. Still, he is mostly a free-swinging, line-drive hitter who will generate doubles but won't lift the ball enough to be a big home-run producer. Bautista doesn't walk much, but he does not strike out at an extremely high rate, either.

Baserunning & Defense

Bautista is an above-average outfielder with good range and a very strong arm. He racked up a total of 10 outfield assists for Arizona in limited action in 2000 and 2001. However, he has trouble harnessing his throws and often will overthrow cutoff men, allowing other runners to move up a base. He has good speed and can steal a base when called upon.

2003 Outlook

Bautista's shoulder is expected to be fully recovered in time for spring training. So Arizona is counting on him to be a steady performer in right field. Bautista has batted .313 and slugged .483 since coming to the Diamondbacks in a June 2000 trade, and only poor health should keep him from reaching career highs in games and at-bats in 2003.

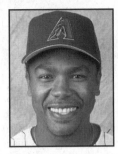

Position: RF
Bats: R **Throws:** R
Ht: 5'11" **Wt:** 204

Opening Day Age: 30
Born: 5/24/72 in Santo Domingo, DR
ML Seasons: 10
Pronunciation: BAW-tee-sta

Overall Statistics

	G	AB	R	H	D	T	HR	RBI	SB	BB	SO	Avg	OBP	Slg
'02	40	154	22	50	5	2	6	23	4	11	21	.325	.367	.500
Car.	666	1694	224	453	78	15	47	218	28	93	293	.267	.306	.414

Where He Hits the Ball

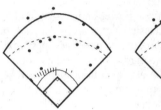
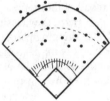

Vs. LHP   **Vs. RHP**

2002 Situational Stats

	AB	H	HR	RBI	Avg		AB	H	HR	RBI	Avg
Home	79	32	4	17	.405	LHP	47	17	4	11	.362
Road	75	18	2	6	.240	RHP	107	33	2	12	.308
First Half	154	50	6	23	.325	Sc Pos	43	13	1	15	.302
Scnd Half	0	0	0	0	–	Clutch	15	5	0	2	.333

2002 Rankings (National League)

- Did not rank near the top or bottom in any category

Craig Counsell

2002 Season

When Matt Williams was injured in spring training, Craig Counsell became Arizona's primary third baseman. When Williams returned after the All-Star break, Counsell rotated infield positions, mainly between shortstop and third. But he began feeling numbness in his right arm on August 9 and eventually was diagnosed with a pinched nerve in his neck. The injury required surgery to fuse together two vertebrae, and Counsell missed the postseason.

Hitting

Despite an unusual approach at the plate—he begins his stance with the bat held high over his left shoulder—Counsell is effective. He sprays the ball without much power and is a good clutch hitter. He is the classic singles-and-doubles hitter whose slugging percentages never are much higher than his on-base marks. Counsell has good bat control and can be asked to bunt or hit-and-run. However, he can run into trouble when trying to make contact against good lefthanded breaking balls. Not a single one of his 13 career homers have come against a southpaw.

Baserunning & Defense

Counsell has excellent baseball instincts and runs the bases well. He can swipe a base, though he's not often called upon to do so. He is sure-handed and can play any infield position. Counsell's best position is second base. He is a very good third baseman, and despite a below-average arm for the position, is capable at shortstop.

2003 Outlook

Counsell's neck is expected to be healed in time for the 2003 season. But where he plays remains to be seen, since Arizona may have the same quandary it had in the second half of last season: four players for three infield positions. But the Diamondbacks like Counsell's winning instincts, and they should find a place for him to play on a fairly regular basis.

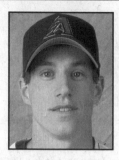

Position: 3B/SS/2B
Bats: L **Throws:** R
Ht: 6' 0" **Wt:** 175

Opening Day Age: 32
Born: 8/21/70 in South Bend, IN
ML Seasons: 7
Nickname: Rudy

Overall Statistics

	G	AB	R	H	D	T	HR	RBI	SB	BB	SO	Avg	OBP	Slg
'02	112	436	63	123	22	1	2	51	7	45	52	.282	.348	.351
Car.	569	1720	249	468	87	12	13	167	21	210	234	.272	.353	.359

Where He Hits the Ball

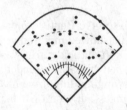 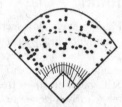

Vs. LHP   **Vs. RHP**

2002 Situational Stats

	AB	H	HR	RBI	Avg		AB	H	HR	RBI	Avg
Home	211	54	0	22	.256	LHP	145	39	0	20	.269
Road	225	69	2	29	.307	RHP	291	84	2	31	.289
First Half	327	92	1	45	.281	Sc Pos	110	40	1	48	.364
Scnd Half	109	31	1	6	.284	Clutch	56	15	1	7	.268

2002 Rankings (National League)

- 4th in batting average on a 3-1 count (.667)
- 5th in highest percentage of pitches taken (62.9) and batting average with runners in scoring position
- 7th in highest percentage of swings put into play (54.3)
- Led the Diamondbacks in highest percentage of pitches taken (62.9), batting average with runners in scoring position, batting average with the bases loaded (.462), batting average on the road, lowest percentage of swings on the first pitch (11.6), batting average on a 3-2 count (.333) and batting average with two strikes (.241)

Steve Finley

Position: CF
Bats: L **Throws:** L
Ht: 6' 2" **Wt:** 195

Opening Day Age: 38
Born: 3/12/65 in Union City, TN
ML Seasons: 14

2002 Season

After his typical slow start, Steve Finley finished with a .287 average, his highest mark since 1996. From May 11 on, Finley batted .303 with 17 homers and 74 RBI in 406 at-bats. He matched his career best with 65 walks and stole 16 bases, also his most since '96. Finley's durability continued to be on display, as he played 150 games, marking the eighth consecutive year that he logged time in 139 or more contests. On September 13, he collected his 2,000th career hit.

Hitting

Against righthanded pitching, Finley looks to pull balls that are middle and in. He will take lefthanders the other way at times. He has good power on balls down in the strike zone, and usually puts together a good at-bat in clutch situations. He also regained some of the pop that he seemed to have lost in 2001, and reached the 25-homer mark for the fifth time in his big league career.

Baserunning & Defense

Nearing 40, Finley has not slowed down on the bases or in the field. A smart baserunner, he can steal bases when called upon. He is an above-average center fielder who catches balls on the run instead of making highlight-film dives because he gets good reads off the bat. He made just two errors in 144 games in center in 2002. He will have lapses at times—running a slightly wrong route, for example—but not often.

2003 Outlook

Finley's four-year deal expired after last season, but he turned down a more lucrative offer from the Giants to stay with the Diamondbacks. He agreed to a two-year deal worth $11.25 million in early December. Finley is dedicated in his physical conditioning so, despite occasional bumps and bruises, he should be able to sustain his level of play for most or all of the contract.

Overall Statistics

	G	AB	R	H	D	T	HR	RBI	SB	BB	SO	Avg	OBP	Slg
'02	150	505	82	145	24	4	25	89	16	65	73	.287	.370	.499
Car.	1980	7327	1153	2018	353	98	227	907	281	646	993	.275	.335	.443

Where He Hits the Ball

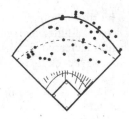
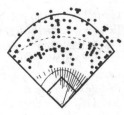

Vs. LHP   **Vs. RHP**

2002 Situational Stats

	AB	H	HR	RBI	Avg		AB	H	HR	RBI	Avg
Home	264	84	14	46	.318	LHP	158	47	9	30	.297
Road	241	61	11	43	.253	RHP	347	98	16	59	.282
First Half	268	76	13	42	.284	Sc Pos	147	42	4	58	.286
Scnd Half	237	69	12	47	.291	Clutch	74	22	2	7	.297

2002 Rankings (National League)

- 4th in lowest percentage of swings on the first pitch (15.2) and fielding percentage in center field (.994)
- 6th in stolen-base percentage (80.0)
- Led the Diamondbacks in slugging percentage and stolen-base percentage (80.0)

Arizona

Luis Gonzalez

2002 Season

Perhaps pressing in hopes that the Diamondbacks would extend his contract beyond 2003, Luis Gonzalez was not up to his 2001 standards for most of last year, especially in the first half. His home runs dropped from 57 to 28 and his slugging percentage from .688 to .498. In the season's final week, Gonzalez suffered a separated left shoulder in an outfield collision that required surgery and also kept him out of the playoffs. Gonzalez did manage to collect his 1,000th RBI last year, and he now sits just one home run shy of 250 for his career.

Hitting

Gonzalez has the power to hit the ball out to left field, but he has become a dead pull-hitter, and his power totals have consequently increased. Teams often employ a Barry Bonds-type shift when Gonzalez is at the plate, with the shortstop up the middle or on the right side. He is best pitched up and in; lefthanders can get him with breaking balls away. Gonzalez has a good eye for the strike zone, and his strikeout totals continue to remain modest even as his power numbers have increased.

Baserunning & Defense

Gonzalez plays a deep left field and ranges well laterally and toward the fence. He has a knack for making sliding grabs on popups, but balls do drop in front of him in short left. Gonzalez' arm seems to be getting weaker and good runners can go from first to third on him. He has only average speed, but he makes good decisions and swiped nine bases in 11 tries last year.

2003 Outlook

The Diamondbacks expect Gonzalez to recover fully in time for spring training. However, his September shoulder injury was considered severe, and there may be lingering effects. If he returns to full health, Gonzalez could benefit from better protection in the batting order, which would force teams to throw him strikes. But if the team holds off on signing him past 2003, Gonzalez could wind up pressing again.

Position: LF
Bats: L **Throws:** R
Ht: 6' 2" **Wt:** 195

Opening Day Age: 35
Born: 9/3/67 in Tampa, FL
ML Seasons: 13

Overall Statistics

	G	AB	R	H	D	T	HR	RBI	SB	BB	SO	Avg	OBP	Slg
'02	148	524	90	151	19	3	28	103	9	97	76	.288	.400	.496
Car.	1747	6229	968	1783	384	54	249	1020	110	749	846	.286	.366	.485

Where He Hits the Ball

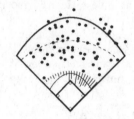

Vs. LHP   **Vs. RHP**

2002 Situational Stats

	AB	H	HR	RBI	Avg		AB	H	HR	RBI	Avg
Home	248	67	11	49	.270	LHP	191	52	10	41	.272
Road	276	84	17	54	.304	RHP	333	99	18	62	.297
First Half	307	85	16	58	.277	Sc Pos	151	53	6	75	.351
Scnd Half	217	66	12	45	.304	Clutch	80	17	1	11	.213

2002 Rankings (National League)

- 2nd in fielding percentage in left field (.985)
- 5th in sacrifice flies (7) and lowest cleanup slugging percentage (.481)
- 7th in errors in left field (4)
- 8th in batting average with runners in scoring position, on-base percentage vs. righthanded pitchers (.412) and lowest percentage of swings on the first pitch (18.3)
- Led the Diamondbacks in home runs, total bases (260), RBI, sacrifice flies (7), walks, intentional walks (8), times on base (253), on-base percentage, HR frequency (18.7 ABs per HR), slugging percentage vs. righthanded pitchers (.523) and on-base percentage vs. righthanded pitchers (.412)

Rick Helling

Position: SP
Bats: R **Throws:** R
Ht: 6' 3" **Wt:** 220

Opening Day Age: 32
Born: 12/15/70 in
Devils Lake, ND
ML Seasons: 9

2002 Season

Signed to a one-year deal with an option after David Wells reneged on a handshake deal, Rick Helling put together a year better than his statistics might indicate. He allowed two earned runs or fewer in 15 of his starts (a better percentage than Curt Schilling) and was 9-2 when Arizona provided him with two or more runs of support. He lost out to Miguel Batista in the decision for a No. 3 starter in the playoffs, but he was a pleasant surprise that helped enable the team to get to the postseason in the first place.

Pitching

Helling throws a fastball, curve, slider and changeup, but he has to keep his straight fastball on the edges of the strike zone in order to be truly effective. Not doing so results in his propensity for allowing home runs. He yielded 31 longballs last year—the third time in the past four seasons that he finished above the 30 mark. Helling has good break on his curve, and his other offspeed pitches look like fastballs coming out of his hand. He tends to allow a high number of hits, but has the poise to pitch out of jams.

Defense & Hitting

Helling fields his position well and has a fair pick-off move and quick delivery to the plate. He does an excellent job of keeping opposing running games in check. After four-plus years in the American League, Helling managed just two hits in 46 at-bats last season. But he showed signs of being a decent bunter and will draw an occasional walk.

2003 Outlook

Arizona declined a 2003 option on Helling for $6.5 million, allowing him to become a free agent. Disappointed in the Diamondbacks' lack of confidence in him, Helling is expected to sign elsewhere. He is a reliable, durable pitcher who can eat up innings and put together a winning record for a good team.

Overall Statistics

	W	L	Pct.	ERA	G	GS	Sv	IP	H	BB	SO	HR	Ratio
'02	10	12	.455	4.51	30	30	0	175.2	180	48	120	31	1.30
Car.	82	70	.539	4.72	231	201	0	1287.1	1309	484	886	208	1.39

How Often He Throws Strikes

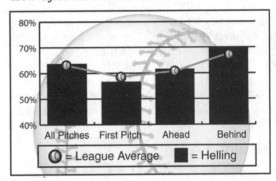

2002 Situational Stats

	W	L	ERA	Sv	IP		AB	H	HR	RBI	Avg
Home	4	6	5.98	0	84.1	LHB	315	89	14	43	.283
Road	6	6	3.15	0	91.1	RHB	366	91	17	45	.249
First Half	7	7	4.70	0	105.1	Sc Pos	157	36	10	62	.229
Scnd Half	3	5	4.22	0	70.1	Clutch	32	6	2	2	.188

2002 Rankings (National League)

- 1st in lowest groundball-flyball ratio allowed (0.7), highest ERA at home and most home runs allowed per nine innings (1.59)
- 2nd in home runs allowed
- 3rd in lowest stolen-base percentage allowed (33.3)
- 4th in highest slugging percentage allowed (.470)
- 7th in most run support per nine innings (5.7) and fewest GDPs induced per nine innings (0.6)
- Led the Diamondbacks in losses, home runs allowed and lowest stolen-base percentage allowed (33.3)

Randy Johnson

2002 Season

Randy Johnson earned his record-tying fourth straight National League Cy Young Award by leading the Senior Circuit in wins (a career high), ERA, strikeouts, innings pitched and complete games. He paced the majors in strikeouts for the eighth time, tying the record held by Walter Johnson, and won his fourth ERA title. And his 45 victories over the past two seasons ties teammate Curt Shilling (also 45 in 2001-02) for the most in consecutive years since Jim Palmer went 23-11 and 22-13 in 1976.

Pitching

As if his 97-MPH (or more) fastball and a slider that reaches 90 MPH were not enough, Johnson also has a split-finger pitch he uses as a sort of changeup. At 86-88 MPH, he uses the splitter with two strikes as an out pitch. He also has a two-seam fastball he can throw in when trying to induce a groundball. More often than in the past, Johnson's slider is not as sharp-breaking on some days.

Defense & Hitting

Johnson is not a very good fielder, with a tendency for errant throws. He's been charged with at least two errors in each of the past four years. Johnson will pick some runners off when they take off on his first movement, and basestealers were only slightly better than 50 percent against him last year. Johnson has worked hard on his hitting and can put a mistake pitch in play. He struggles running the bases, however, and is a below-average bunter.

2003 Outlook

If his lower back isn't a problem—it acted up a couple of times last year—Johnson is in excellent physical condition, despite the fact that he's approaching 40. He will have subpar stuff on occasion, but always seems to bounce back strong in his next start. This is the last (option) year of Johnson's contract with Arizona, but he seems to want to play past this season.

Position: SP
Bats: R **Throws:** L
Ht: 6'10" **Wt:** 232

Opening Day Age: 39
Born: 9/10/63 in Walnut Creek, CA
ML Seasons: 15
Nickname: Big Unit

Overall Statistics

W	L	Pct.	ERA	G	GS	Sv	IP	H	BB	SO	HR	Ratio
24	5	.828	2.32	35	35	0	260.0	197	71	334	26	1.03
224	106	.679	3.06	436	426	2	3008.1	2310	1231	3746	267	1.18

How Often He Throws Strikes

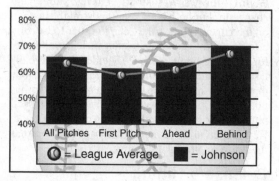

| = League Average | = Johnson |

2002 Situational Stats

	W	L	ERA	Sv	IP		AB	H	HR	RBI	Avg
Home	14	3	2.12	0	157.1	LHB	140	31	5	11	.221
Road	10	2	2.63	0	102.2	RHB	805	166	21	62	.206
First Half	12	3	2.47	0	138.2	Sc Pos	185	27	3	42	.146
Scnd Half	12	2	2.15	0	121.1	Clutch	104	20	1	4	.192

2002 Rankings (National League)

- 1st in ERA, wins, complete games (8), innings pitched, batters faced (1,035), strikeouts, pitches thrown (3,996), winning percentage, lowest batting average allowed (.208), lowest ERA at home, lowest batting average allowed with runners in scoring position, and most strikeouts per nine innings (11.6)
- 2nd in games started, shutouts (4), runners caught stealing (15) and highest strikeout-walk ratio (4.7)
- 3rd in balks (2), lowest on-base percentage allowed (.273) and lowest ERA on the road

Byung-Hyun Kim

2002 Season

With Matt Mantei working back from Tommy John surgery, Byung-Hyun Kim was Arizona's closer. He showed no ill effects from his 2001 World Series meltdowns, setting a Diamondbacks record for saves and making the All-Star team. Kim finished strong, with a 1.05 ERA over his final 22 outings, including 8.2 scoreless innings at the end of the regular season. However, he endured yet another rough postseason outing, surrendering two hits and three walks in one inning in the Game 3 loss to the Cardinals in the NLDS.

Pitching

Kim can throw up to 93 MPH from a sidearm delivery, offering a unique mix of arm angle and velocity. He also has a wicked slider that he can even throw as a riser. Righthanders have a hard time picking up the ball. Against lefthanders, Kim's slider breaks into the bat, but he has a good changeup—68-70 MPH with a drop. He gets in trouble when he doesn't throw strikes, and that often is a product of Kim trying to nibble and get a strikeout rather than let hitters try to make contact with his stuff.

Defense & Hitting

Kim is a good athlete who can spear balls hit back at him, but he sometimes gets sloppy on his throws. He has been charged with an error in each of the past three seasons, but to his credit he was involved in a pair of double plays in 2002. Kim does not hold runners very well, but he has improved in that area. He has two career hits but has an ugly swing.

2003 Outlook

Kim has expressed a desire to be a starter, but the Diamondbacks seem reluctant to let hitters see him a few times a game and test his stamina. Kim certainly has the pitches to be a good closer, but if Mantei is healthy, Arizona could be tempted to deal the arbitration-eligible Kim.

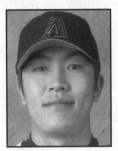

Position: RP
Bats: R **Throws:** R
Ht: 5'11" **Wt:** 177

Opening Day Age: 24
Born: 1/19/79 in Gwangju, South Korea
ML Seasons: 4
Pronunciation: bee-YUNG hee-YUN

Overall Statistics

	W	L	Pct.	ERA	G	GS	Sv	IP	H	BB	SO	HR	Ratio
'02	8	3	.727	2.04	72	0	36	84.0	64	26	92	5	1.07
Car.	20	17	.541	3.21	236	1	70	280.0	194	136	347	26	1.18

How Often He Throws Strikes

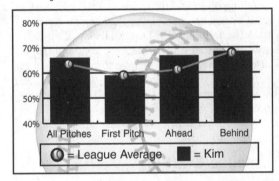

 = League Average ■ = Kim

2002 Situational Stats

	W	L	ERA	Sv	IP			AB	H	HR	RBI	Avg
Home	5	0	1.47	18	43.0	LHB		141	31	3	12	.220
Road	3	3	2.63	18	41.0	RHB		167	33	2	14	.198
First Half	3	1	2.34	22	50.0	Sc Pos		87	18	2	22	.207
Scnd Half	5	2	1.59	14	34.0	Clutch		205	35	4	22	.171

2002 Rankings (National League)

- 1st in relief wins (8)
- 4th in games finished (66)
- 7th in save opportunities (42), blown saves (6), relief innings (84.0) and lowest save percentage (85.7)
- Led the Diamondbacks in games pitched, saves, games finished (66), save opportunities (42), lowest batting average allowed vs. righthanded batters, save percentage (85.7), lowest percentage of inherited runners scored (20.6), blown saves (6), relief losses (3), relief innings (84.0), relief ERA (2.04), lowest batting average allowed in relief (.208) and most strikeouts per nine innings in relief (9.9)

Curt Schilling

2002 Season

Determined to carry over his stellar effort from the 2001 postseason, Curt Schilling made yet another strong run at the National League Cy Young Award with a career-high 23 wins. He won a personal-best nine straight decisions in the first half, and flirted with the chance to post more wins than walks for an entire season. His strikeout-walk ratio was the second best ever for a starting pitcher. Despite those accomplishments, Schilling again finished second to teammate Randy Johnson in the eyes of Cy Young voters.

Pitching

Schilling often will throw his fastball 93-94 MPH until he reaches a crucial spot, when he can reach back for a 97-98 MPH heater. His No. 2 pitch is a split-finger that usually has very good tumble. He also has a curveball, which he throws early in the count as a surprise pitch to try to get a called strike, and a slider, which he will use in varying proportions. Schilling excels at changing the hitter's eye level with the high fastball and the diving splitter.

Defense & Hitting

Schilling has a quick delivery that makes it tough for runners to steal bases. Only 15 baserunners attempted to steal against him last year, and six of those thieves were caught. Defensively, he is fundamentally sound—he has just one error in the past five years. Schilling is a good bunter and decent hitter for a pitcher.

2003 Outlook

Perhaps a second second-place finish in the Cy Young Award voting will motivate Schilling even further. He already has an intense routine of preparation, which involves studying video—via CD-ROM—of opposing hitters' at-bats against him in the past, and it is being reported that he will pursue what the team calls "a rigorous off-season fitness program." Schilling enters every game with a detailed plan of attack, and that should continue to serve him well. He is signed through 2004.

Position: SP
Bats: R **Throws:** R
Ht: 6' 4" **Wt:** 231

Opening Day Age: 36
Born: 11/14/66 in Anchorage, AK
ML Seasons: 15
Pronunciation: SHILL-ing

Overall Statistics

	W	L	Pct.	ERA	G	GS	Sv	IP	H	BB	SO	HR	Ratio
'02	23	7	.767	3.23	36	35	0	259.1	218	33	316	29	0.97
Car.	155	108	.589	3.36	426	314	13	2418.0	2142	571	2348	246	1.12

How Often He Throws Strikes

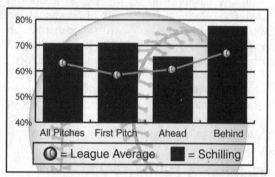

= League Average   = Schilling

2002 Situational Stats

	W	L	ERA	Sv	IP		AB	H	HR	RBI	Avg
Home	11	4	3.24	0	130.2	LHB	451	109	14	46	.242
Road	12	3	3.22	0	128.2	RHB	523	109	15	44	.208
First Half	14	3	3.08	0	140.1	Sc Pos	146	38	5	59	.260
Scnd Half	9	4	3.40	0	119.0	Clutch	109	25	4	13	.229

2002 Rankings (National League)

- 1st in highest strikeout-walk ratio (9.6), lowest on-base percentage allowed (.251), fewest walks per nine innings (1.1) and fielding percentage at pitcher (1.000)
- 2nd in wins, games started, innings pitched, batters faced (1,017), strikeouts, pitches thrown (3,721) and most strikeouts per nine innings (11.0)
- 3rd in complete games (5), winning percentage and fewest GDPs induced per nine innings (0.4)
- Led the Diamondbacks in games started and hits allowed

Junior Spivey

2002 Season

A candidate for the 25th spot on the roster when spring training began, Junior Spivey played well in the Cactus League and earned the spot at second base after injuries to Matt Williams and Jay Bell. Spivey was picked for the All-Star Game and wound up leading the team in average, runs, hits, doubles and being hit by pitch. However, his average was 54 points lower in the second half, as he showed the effects of playing a full major league season for the first time.

Hitting

Spivey is strong and has a quick bat, and he shows no fear as a hitter. He stands close to the plate, which helps him against breaking balls, and is slightly open so he can turn on inside pitches. He was plunked 16 times last year, good for fourth most in the National League. Spivey primarily is a pull-hitter, but he flashes some power to right-center field. His power totals should increase as he gains experience, and 20 home runs should be well within his reach.

Baserunning & Defense

A good athlete, Spivey has above-average speed and could be a 20-steal player. On defense he has excellent range, especially on popups, but he needs to refine his skills. He sometimes makes ill-advised decisions, such as rushing a throw when he has no real chance at making the out. Spivey has a two-step exchange on the double play and could stand to speed things up on the pivot.

2003 Outlook

Spivey seems a fixture in the crowded Arizona infield, thanks to his blossoming skills and his injection of speed and energy into the lineup. Now conditioned to a 162-game season, he should be better able to pace himself for the long haul. He also should continue to adapt to major league pitching. He certainly has the potential to repeat as an All-Star.

Position: 2B
Bats: R   **Throws:** R
Ht: 6' 0"   **Wt:** 185

Opening Day Age: 28
Born: 1/28/75 in Oklahoma City, OK
ML Seasons: 2
Pronunciation: spy-VEE

Overall Statistics

	G	AB	R	H	D	T	HR	RBI	SB	BB	SO	Avg	OBP	Slg
'02	143	538	103	162	34	6	16	78	11	65	100	.301	.389	.476
Car.	215	701	136	204	40	9	21	99	14	88	147	.291	.381	.464

Where He Hits the Ball

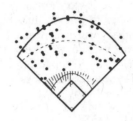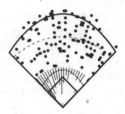

Vs. LHP	Vs. RHP

2002 Situational Stats

	AB	H	HR	RBI	Avg		AB	H	HR	RBI	Avg
Home	264	84	9	44	.318	LHP	170	55	11	29	.324
Road	274	78	7	34	.285	RHP	368	107	5	49	.291
First Half	268	88	9	46	.328	Sc Pos	135	39	1	56	.289
Scnd Half	270	74	7	32	.274	Clutch	81	24	1	10	.296

2002 Rankings (National League)
- 2nd in lowest fielding percentage at second base (.977)
- 3rd in errors at second base (15)
- 4th in hit by pitch (16)
- 7th in on-base percentage vs. lefthanded pitchers (.441)
- 8th in runs scored
- 9th in slugging percentage vs. lefthanded pitchers (.612)
- Led the Diamondbacks in runs scored, hits, doubles, hit by pitch (16), strikeouts and on-base percentage vs. lefthanded pitchers (.441)

Arizona

Matt Williams

2002 Season

A broken left leg and dislocated left ankle suffered early in spring training kept Matt Williams out until the All-Star break. He was eased back into the lineup for four weeks, then became a regular again after Craig Counsell's neck injury. He even moved into the cleanup spot on a handful of occasions after Arizona lost Luis Gonzalez to a shoulder injury. Williams' batting average fell to its lowest level in more than a decade, but he actually homered more frequently (once every 17.9 at-bats) than in any year since his big 1999 season.

Hitting

Williams still is a dangerous hitter if he gets the pitch he is looking for. He will try to shorten his swing so he can react better to pitches, but is mostly geared for the fastball, which he can hit out of the park if located anywhere from the middle of the plate in. Williams also still can hammer a hanging breaking ball. He needs healthy legs to give him a base to drive the ball, however.

Baserunning & Defense

His range is a bit down from his best years, but Williams continues to be a very good third baseman. He has good reactions and excellent hands, then a quick release with an accurate arm still strong enough for the position. He now has below-average range, but he does a solid job of getting to everything he's supposed to snag around the third-base bag. Williams' leg problems keep him from being a basestealing threat, but he is a smart baserunner.

2003 Outlook

As has been the case the past four years, if Williams is healthy he can be a productive player. But he has a continuing history of lower-body injuries. This will be the final season of the five-year extension he signed after being traded to Arizona, and it appears he will spend it in Phoenix after a Williams-Larry Walker deal fell apart late in 2002. Williams, though, may have to share playing time at third base with Craig Counsell.

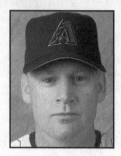

Position: 3B
Bats: R **Throws:** R
Ht: 6' 2" **Wt:** 219

Opening Day Age: 37
Born: 11/28/65 in Bishop, CA
ML Seasons: 16

Overall Statistics

G	AB	R	H	D	T	HR	RBI	SB	BB	SO	Avg	OBP	Slg
60	215	29	56	7	2	12	40	3	21	41	.260	.324	.479
1822	6866	980	1845	329	35	374	1202	53	453	1337	.269	.316	.490

Where He Hits the Ball

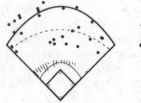 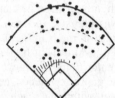

Vs. LHP   **Vs. RHP**

2002 Situational Stats

	AB	H	HR	RBI	Avg		AB	H	HR	RBI	Avg
Home	98	34	7	26	.347	LHP	83	24	8	18	.289
Road	117	22	5	14	.188	RHP	132	32	4	22	.242
First Half	0	0	0	0	-	Sc Pos	70	19	3	30	.271
Scnd Half	215	56	12	40	.260	Clutch	32	7	2	5	.219

2002 Rankings (National League)

- Did not rank near the top or bottom in any category

Tony Womack

2002 Season

As has become the norm for Tony Womack, he once again came on strong in the second half of the season. In mid-May, he was batting .234 and was dropped from the leadoff spot all the way down to eighth in the Arizona batting order. But Womack heated up a bit in late July and quickly moved back to the top of the order. He tied his career high with 57 RBI, but his strikeout rate also jumped up over his 2001 figure.

Hitting

Womack finally has begun to utilize his speed by bunting for hits, although he will always punch the ball toward third base rather than take it with him. He also slashes the ball to the left side more often, but will hit lazy flies to left on a pitch up and away. Womack can be quick and dangerous on pitches down and in, which is how he gets his occasional home run. For the second straight year he struggled mightily against lefties, and his average versus southpaws is just .205 during that span.

Baserunning & Defense

Despite still possessing very good speed, Womack is cautious as a basestealer. He waits for spots he feels sure he can advance, rather than running at any chance. He barely topped the 70-percent success rate on his stolen-base attempts last year. On defense, Womack has nervous hands and feet, and he struggles more with hard-hit balls than slow rollers. He tends to leave his feet while trying to turn double plays, resulting in weak throws. Womack's errors tend to come in bunches.

2003 Outlook

Womack has one more year on his deal with Arizona and is the incumbent at shortstop, although Craig Counsell and Alex Cintron could fight for playing time at the position. Counsell is the best alternative in the leadoff spot, so Womack again should bat first, seventh or eighth in the lineup.

Position: SS
Bats: L **Throws:** R
Ht: 5' 9" **Wt:** 170

Opening Day Age: 33
Born: 9/25/69 in Danville, VA
ML Seasons: 9
Pronunciation: WO-mack

Overall Statistics

	G	AB	R	H	D	T	HR	RBI	SB	BB	SO	Avg	OBP	Slg
'02	153	590	90	160	23	5	5	57	29	46	80	.271	.325	.353
Car.	919	3664	552	1004	143	51	28	288	296	243	486	.274	.321	.364

Where He Hits the Ball

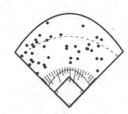 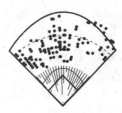

Vs. LHP   **Vs. RHP**

2002 Situational Stats

	AB	H	HR	RBI	Avg		AB	H	HR	RBI	Avg
Home	304	97	4	40	.319	LHP	182	39	0	10	.214
Road	286	63	1	17	.220	RHP	408	121	5	47	.297
First Half	324	83	1	27	.256	Sc Pos	139	40	2	53	.288
Scnd Half	266	77	4	30	.289	Clutch	77	25	1	7	.325

2002 Rankings (National League)

- 3rd in lowest slugging percentage vs. left-handed pitchers (.253) and lowest fielding percentage at shortstop (.964)
- 4th in lowest batting average on the road
- 5th in steals of third (5), lowest percentage of swings on the first pitch (16.2) and errors at shortstop (20)
- 6th in singles and caught stealing (12)
- Led the Diamondbacks in at-bats, singles, stolen bases, caught stealing (12), pitches seen (2,528), plate appearances (652), games played, bunts in play (28), steals of third (5) and highest percentage of extra bases taken as a runner (62.9)

Arizona

Brian Anderson

Position: SP/RP
Bats: R **Throws:** L
Ht: 6' 1" **Wt:** 183

Opening Day Age: 30
Born: 4/26/72 in
Portsmouth, VA
ML Seasons: 10

Overall Statistics

	W	L	Pct.	ERA	G	GS	Sv	IP	H	BB	SO	HR	Ratio
'02	6	11	.353	4.79	35	24	0	156.0	174	32	81	23	1.32
Car.	61	58	.513	4.72	218	182	1	1152.2	1275	237	549	197	1.31

2002 Situational Stats

	W	L	ERA	Sv	IP		AB	H	HR	RBI	Avg
Home	3	5	4.27	0	78.0	LHB	159	48	6	18	.302
Road	3	6	5.31	0	78.0	RHB	453	126	17	59	.278
First Half	4	7	5.09	0	88.1	Sc Pos	129	40	5	50	.310
Scnd Half	2	4	4.39	0	67.2	Clutch	21	4	0	0	.190

2002 Season

After going 0-1 with an 8.36 ERA in his first three starts, Brian Anderson was sent to the bullpen. He rejoined the rotation when Todd Stottlemyre went on the disabled list, but only as Arizona's de facto fifth starter. Every time the Diamondbacks had a day off in the second half, Anderson's turn was skipped so Randy Johnson and Curt Schilling could pitch every fifth day. Anderson's season ended September 21 when Colorado's Ben Petrick hit a line drive that broke Anderson's left foot.

Pitching, Defense & Hitting

Anderson throws a fastball, a cutter/slider and a changeup, which is his best pitch. He uses the fastball to set up the change, but he needs to come inside to keep righthanded hitters from leaning out over the plate and looking for the changeup. He does not often come inside for strikes. Anderson is a steady if unspectacular fielder with a very good pickoff move—his eight pickoffs last year tied for third in the National League. He also can handle the bat well and even pinch-run.

2003 Outlook

Anderson is a free agent, but he has been offered salary arbitration by Arizona. His foot should be healed in time for this season, and he could be a decent No. 4 or 5 starter wherever he lands.

Greg Colbrunn

Position: 1B
Bats: R **Throws:** R
Ht: 6' 0" **Wt:** 212

Opening Day Age: 33
Born: 7/26/69 in
Fontana, CA
ML Seasons: 11
Pronunciation:
COAL-brun

Overall Statistics

	G	AB	R	H	D	T	HR	RBI	SB	BB	SO	Avg	OBP	Slg
'02	72	171	30	57	16	2	10	27	0	13	19	.333	.378	.626
Car.	950	2684	329	782	154	11	95	414	29	165	423	.291	.341	.463

2002 Situational Stats

	AB	H	HR	RBI	Avg		AB	H	HR	RBI	Avg
Home	81	27	3	12	.333	LHP	117	43	7	21	.368
Road	90	30	7	15	.333	RHP	54	14	3	6	.259
First Half	94	28	3	15	.298	Sc Pos	41	11	1	15	.268
Scnd Half	77	29	7	12	.377	Clutch	23	8	1	2	.348

2002 Season

In the National League in 2002, only Barry Bonds had a better average against lefthanded pitching than did Greg Colbrunn. Colbrunn made 36 starts at first base for Arizona, and he usually batted fourth when he was in the lineup. He also hit .364 as a pinch-hitter, giving him a .319 career mark in that role. On September 18, he became just the second Diamondback to hit for the cycle when he collected five hits and a pair of homers against the Padres.

Hitting, Baserunning & Defense

Colbrunn's quick bat gives him the ability to turn around any fastball. He feasts on fastballs from the middle in, and he has good home-run power. He also has improved his ability to make solid contact on balls away from him. Colbrunn is limited but capable at first base. Third base should be nothing more than an emergency role for him. He is not fast, but he's smart on the basepaths.

2003 Outlook

Since he knows how to fill a part-time/pinch-hitting role—and is willing to accept it—Colbrunn is a valuable player for a contending team. He was a free agent after the season, and Arizona will try to re-sign him. But with first base already crowded, he likely could find more playing time elsewhere.

David Dellucci

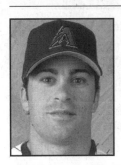

Position: RF/LF
Bats: L **Throws:** L
Ht: 5'11" **Wt:** 198

Opening Day Age: 29
Born: 10/31/73 in Baton Rouge, LA
ML Seasons: 6
Pronunciation: duh-LOO-chee

Overall Statistics

	G	AB	R	H	D	T	HR	RBI	SB	BB	SO	Avg	OBP	Slg
'02	97	229	34	56	11	2	7	29	2	28	55	.245	.326	.402
Car.	450	1048	137	288	51	17	24	140	9	102	250	.275	.344	.425

2002 Situational Stats

	AB	H	HR	RBI	Avg		AB	H	HR	RBI	Avg
Home	102	27	2	18	.265	LHP	27	3	0	3	.111
Road	127	29	5	11	.228	RHP	202	53	7	26	.262
First Half	69	16	2	8	.232	Sc Pos	61	15	0	20	.246
Scnd Half	160	40	5	21	.250	Clutch	42	10	2	9	.238

2002 Season

David Dellucci began the season as a bench player and was on the disabled list when right fielder Danny Bautista suffered season-ending injuries in May. He then got some time in right field, although most of the right-field duties went to Quinton McCracken. Dellucci did contribute with some key pinch-hits—including doubles off Eric Gagne and Robb Nen—down the stretch, but his .245 batting average was well below his career mark entering the season.

Hitting, Baserunning & Defense

Dellucci can hammer inside fastballs, and as a pinch-hitter he usually gets a pitch to hit. He is vulnerable when hurlers work him away, and he struggles against good lefties. Dellucci isn't much above average as a baserunner, but he always hustles. He's not afraid to get his uniform dirty if that's what it takes to make a catch. He has a poor arm, and his outfield assists are rare.

2003 Outlook

Eligible for arbitration yet still thought of as a reserve, Dellucci could price himself out of a spot with the Diamondbacks. He has proven he can handle a pinch-hitting role well. Although only 29, he probably will have to accept a bench role on a contending team.

Erubiel Durazo

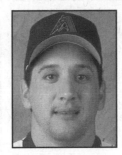

Position: 1B
Bats: L **Throws:** L
Ht: 6' 3" **Wt:** 240

Opening Day Age: 29
Born: 1/23/74 in Hermosillo, Mexico
ML Seasons: 4
Pronunciation: eh-ROO-bee-el du-RAH-zo

Overall Statistics

	G	AB	R	H	D	T	HR	RBI	SB	BB	SO	Avg	OBP	Slg
'02	76	222	46	58	12	2	16	48	0	49	60	.261	.395	.550
Car.	287	748	146	208	38	4	47	149	2	137	195	.278	.390	.528

2002 Situational Stats

	AB	H	HR	RBI	Avg		AB	H	HR	RBI	Avg
Home	120	34	11	33	.283	LHP	54	9	2	5	.167
Road	102	24	5	15	.235	RHP	168	49	14	43	.292
First Half	92	22	8	21	.239	Sc Pos	70	15	4	29	.214
Scnd Half	130	36	8	27	.277	Clutch	43	15	6	17	.349

2002 Season

Two stints on the disabled list kept Erubiel Durazo from fulfilling the promise he showed in spring training. When healthy, he usually platooned at first base with Greg Colbrunn. Durazo had a three-homer, nine-RBI night in his second game of the season on May 17. But he homered just once in his final 80 at-bats, and when the team tried him in right field after Luis Gonzalez' season-ending injury, Durazo's left elbow could not handle the longer throws and he begged off.

Hitting, Baserunning & Defense

Durazo has a good eye for the strike zone and the quick, short swing and pure power to hit homers to any field. At times he loses concentration, especially when he's hot at the plate, and gets over-anxious. He is purely a station-to-station runner who never is asked to steal. Durazo has unsure hands at first base and is tentative on throws.

2003 Outlook

With Mark Grace returning and prospect Lyle Overbay on the way, Arizona is ready to deal Durazo. He might benefit from a change of scenery and would be a good DH in the American League. He has the tools to be a middle-of-the-order power threat, but he has a fragile makeup and needs to be handled properly.

Mike Fetters

Position: RP
Bats: R **Throws:** R
Ht: 6' 4" **Wt:** 239

Opening Day Age: 38
Born: 12/19/64 in Van Nuys, CA
ML Seasons: 14

Overall Statistics

	W	L	Pct.	ERA	G	GS	Sv	IP	H	BB	SO	HR	Ratio
'02	3	3	.500	4.09	65	0	0	55.0	53	37	53	4	1.64
Car.	31	40	.437	3.76	592	6	99	692.0	674	336	503	60	1.46

2002 Situational Stats

	W	L	ERA	Sv	IP		AB	H	HR	RBI	Avg
Home	2	0	4.88	0	27.2	LHB	62	19	1	8	.306
Road	1	3	3.29	0	27.1	RHB	148	34	3	23	.230
First Half	1	0	3.23	0	30.2	Sc Pos	68	19	2	29	.279
Scnd Half	2	3	5.18	0	24.1	Clutch	101	25	3	14	.248

2002 Season

Mike Fetters was having a solid season as Pittsburgh's setup man when Arizona, needing middle-relief help, sent hard-throwing prospect Duaner Sanchez to the Pirates for Fetters. He became a fan favorite in Arizona with his intense scowl and pre-pitch head snap toward the plate, but he also pitched well. His year-end statistics were skewed drastically by his final three outings (two innings, 11 hits, nine earned runs).

Pitching, Defense & Hitting

Fetters gets his fastball up to 93 MPH. He also mixes in a 90-MPH sinker, as well as a split-finger and curveball, both of which are above average. He keeps everything down and thus gets a lot of groundballs. But when hitters are patient, Fetters can struggle to find the strike zone. He has an excellent pickoff move, which will work a few times a year. In 592 career big league games, he has yet to make an appearance at the plate.

2003 Outlook

Arizona declined its $2.75 million option on Fetters, but it was thought the D-backs might try to work out a lesser deal. That's dead now that they didn't offer salary arbitration. He knows how to pitch and can be a useful setup or middle-relief righthander.

Mark Grace

Position: 1B
Bats: L **Throws:** L
Ht: 6' 2" **Wt:** 200

Opening Day Age: 38
Born: 6/28/64 in Winston-Salem, NC
ML Seasons: 15

Overall Statistics

G	AB	R	H	D	T	HR	RBI	SB	BB	SO	Avg	OBP	Slg
124	298	43	75	19	0	7	48	2	46	30	.252	.351	.386
2179	7930	1166	2418	506	45	170	1130	70	1059	627	.305	.385	.444

2002 Situational Stats

	AB	H	HR	RBI	Avg		AB	H	HR	RBI	Avg
Home	127	31	4	23	.244	LHP	81	26	3	16	.321
Road	171	44	3	25	.257	RHP	217	49	4	32	.226
First Half	194	49	5	34	.253	Sc Pos	99	28	1	40	.283
Scnd Half	104	26	2	14	.250	Clutch	61	11	2	9	.180

2002 Season

Mark Grace spent time as Arizona's regular first baseman when Erubiel Durazo was not healthy, but otherwise was a bench player for the first time in his career. Used sparingly over the final two months, primarily as a pinch-hitter and late-inning defensive replacement, the 15-year veteran found it hard to get in a groove. He finished with the lowest batting average of his career, 55 points below his previous overall mark.

Hitting, Baserunning & Defense

Grace's bat has slowed to the point where he does not often drive the ball with authority, either to left field *or* to right. He swings defensively with two strikes in an effort to avoid strikeouts and to try to put the ball in play, but he succeeds less than in the past. Grace's defense is still solid and heady, although his hands are not quite as good. He is a slow, but smart, baserunner.

2003 Outlook

Although he admits he no longer can play 130 games, Grace likely will return to the Diamondbacks this season. He agreed to forgo a $3 million option for 2003, and is expected to re-sign with the team at a lower price tag. Arizona wants him to continue to be a positive presence in the clubhouse and to tutor prospect Lyle Overbay.

Mike Koplove

Position: RP
Bats: R **Throws:** R
Ht: 6' 0" **Wt:** 170

Opening Day Age: 26
Born: 8/30/76 in Philadelphia, PA
ML Seasons: 2

Overall Statistics

	W	L	Pct.	ERA	G	GS	Sv	IP	H	BB	SO	HR	Ratio
'02	6	1	.857	3.36	55	0	0	61.2	47	23	46	2	1.14
Car.	6	2	.750	3.39	64	0	0	71.2	55	32	60	3	1.21

2002 Situational Stats

	W	L	ERA	Sv	IP		AB	H	HR	RBI	Avg
Home	4	1	3.03	0	35.2	LHB	69	12	0	3	.174
Road	2	0	3.81	0	26.0	RHB	152	35	2	15	.230
First Half	0	0	2.16	0	16.2	Sc Pos	54	12	0	15	.222
Scnd Half	6	1	3.80	0	45.0	Clutch	86	13	1	7	.151

2002 Season

Called up in early June when lefty Eddie Oropesa was sent down, Mike Koplove stayed for the rest of the season and filled a variety of roles for the Diamondbacks. At times—even in the same week—Koplove could be a long reliever, the setup man or a righthanded specialist. Koplove had a 1.81 ERA in late August but then showed signs of overuse, and a 17.05 ERA over his final six outings skewed his final season totals.

Pitching, Defense & Hitting

Koplove has good life on his sidearm pitches and is especially tough on righthanders. He can throw an up-and-away riser, an 88-90 MPH running fastball and a slider. He adds a changeup against lefthanded hitters, often placing it neatly out of the strike zone. Koplove is a good fielder off the mound who could take a decent swing if called upon.

2003 Outlook

His versatility and durability make Koplove a good bet to make the club out of spring training this year. If Arizona deals one of its closers (Byung-Hyun Kim or Matt Mantei), Koplove could fill the righthanded setup role. His workload needs to be monitored more closely than last year to avoid a similar late-season collapse.

Quinton McCracken

Position: RF/CF
Bats: B **Throws:** R
Ht: 5' 7" **Wt:** 173

Opening Day Age: 33
Born: 3/16/70 in Wilmington, NC
ML Seasons: 8
Nickname: Q, Coo Coo

Overall Statistics

	G	AB	R	H	D	T	HR	RBI	SB	BB	SO	Avg	OBP	Slg
'02	123	349	60	108	27	8	3	40	5	32	68	.309	.367	.458
Car.	631	1815	288	519	97	25	17	198	75	172	340	.286	.348	.395

2002 Situational Stats

	AB	H	HR	RBI	Avg		AB	H	HR	RBI	Avg
Home	169	59	1	25	.349	LHP	144	44	0	11	.306
Road	180	49	2	15	.272	RHP	205	64	3	29	.312
First Half	144	47	1	11	.326	Sc Pos	74	25	0	32	.338
Scnd Half	205	61	2	29	.298	Clutch	59	17	0	7	.288

2002 Season

After being let go by the Devil Rays, Cardinals and Twins in the span of two years, Quinton McCracken came to Diamondbacks camp as a non-roster invitee and made the team after a flurry of injuries. When right fielder Danny Bautista went down in late May, McCracken became a key player and wound up starting 78 games. Along the way, he set career highs in both batting average and slugging percentage.

Hitting, Baserunning & Defense

McCracken hits about the same from either side, although his power comes when he bats lefthand-ed. He controls the bat well, can bunt and hit to all fields, and has made himself a tough out. He can be vulnerable to breaking pitches and will rack up a fair number of strikeouts as his exposure increas-es. A threat to steal early in his career, McCracken hasn't put up big numbers in that category since he tore his right ACL in 1999. He has an average arm and can play anywhere in the outfield.

2003 Outlook

Since he can switch-hit and play all three outfield positions, McCracken is a valuable fourth out-fielder for the Diamondbacks.

Damian Miller

Traded To CUBS

Position: C
Bats: R **Throws:** R
Ht: 6' 2" **Wt:** 218

Opening Day Age: 33
Born: 10/13/69 in La Crosse, WI
ML Seasons: 6

Overall Statistics

	G	AB	R	H	D	T	HR	RBI	SB	BB	SO	Avg	OBP	Slg
'02	101	297	40	74	22	0	11	42	0	38	88	.249	.340	.434
Car.	492	1531	185	412	99	2	50	207	3	141	375	.269	.334	.434

2002 Situational Stats

	AB	H	HR	RBI	Avg		AB	H	HR	RBI	Avg
Home	153	39	4	18	.255	LHP	91	25	2	11	.275
Road	144	35	7	24	.243	RHP	206	49	9	31	.238
First Half	224	59	9	36	.263	Sc Pos	80	18	2	31	.225
Scnd Half	73	15	2	6	.205	Clutch	37	5	0	0	.135

2002 Season

Damian Miller began the season as Arizona's regular catcher, was picked to the All-Star team and then wound up starting just one of the Diamondbacks' three playoff games. He was batting .259 with nine homers and 36 RBI when he went on the DL in late July. When he came back, Chad Moeller had taken over as Randy Johnson's personal catcher and Rod Barajas was still Miguel Batista's personal backstop. As a result, Miller started just 24 of the team's final 75 games.

Hitting, Baserunning & Defense

Miller is best when he hits the ball to all fields, but he will chase pitches that are high and away. His offensive numbers, while not eye-catching, have been consistent throughout his career. He's a good receiver who calls a good game, is excellent at blocking balls, has a quick release and accurate arm. Miller is an average runner for a catcher.

2003 Outlook

Miller was traded to the Cubs in November for two minor leaguers, then signed to a two-year, $5.7 million deal. Miller should be an effective No. 1 catcher for the Cubs, as he offers decent offensive potential and good defense. The only question is his health; he tends to have minor injuries, especially late in the season.

Chad Moeller

Position: C
Bats: R **Throws:** R
Ht: 6' 3" **Wt:** 210

Opening Day Age: 28
Born: 2/18/75 in Upland, CA
ML Seasons: 3
Pronunciation: MOLE-er

Overall Statistics

	G	AB	R	H	D	T	HR	RBI	SB	BB	SO	Avg	OBP	Slg
'02	37	105	10	30	11	1	2	16	0	17	23	.286	.385	.467
Car.	110	289	31	70	14	3	4	27	1	32	68	.242	.317	.353

2002 Situational Stats

	AB	H	HR	RBI	Avg		AB	H	HR	RBI	Avg
Home	56	18	2	11	.321	LHP	25	3	1	1	.120
Road	49	12	0	5	.245	RHP	80	27	1	15	.338
First Half	0	0	0	0	—	Sc Pos	29	9	0	13	.310
Scnd Half	105	30	2	16	.286	Clutch	10	3	0	0	.300

2002 Season

Chad Moeller made Arizona's Opening Day roster, was sent down two weeks into the season and returned in mid-July when Damian Miller went on the disabled list. Moeller also took over as Randy Johnson's personal catcher. Moeller went 9-for-20 in September, including a two-homer game on the season's final day, to raise his average to .286.

Hitting, Baserunning & Defense

Based on his success in the minor leagues, Moeller could develop into a decent offensive catcher with gap power. He needs to improve his contact ratio against major league pitching, however. He won't do any damage on the basepaths, either good or bad. Moeller's strength is his rapport with pitchers. His dedication to working with his battery-mate and his receiving skills are appreciated. He has a below-average throwing arm, but works well behind the plate.

2003 Outlook

Moeller and Rod Barajas could share time at catcher for the Diamondbacks, who traded Damian Miller to the Cubs in November. Moeller ended last season as the personal catcher for Johnson and John Patterson, so if that continues, he would be Arizona's starter for at least 40 percent of the games.

Other Arizona Diamondbacks

Rod Barajas (**Pos**: C, **Age**: 27, **Bats**: R)

	G	AB	R	H	D	T	HR	RBI	SB	BB	SO	Avg	OBP	Slg
'02	70	154	12	36	10	0	3	23	1	10	25	.234	.288	.357
Car.	131	289	25	60	14	0	8	38	1	15	56	.208	.252	.339

After batting just .171 before the All-Star break, Barajas hit .306 thereafter. With Damian Miller dealt to Chicago, Barajas and Chad Moeller are expected to share catching duties for Arizona. 2003 Outlook: B

Jay Bell (**Pos**: 3B, **Age**: 37, **Bats**: R)

	G	AB	R	H	D	T	HR	RBI	SB	BB	SO	Avg	OBP	Slg
	32	49	3	8	1	0	2	11	0	5	9	.163	.250	.306
	1991	7282	1112	1942	393	67	195	857	91	831	1405	.267	.344	.419

Injuries delayed Bell's debut with Arizona until after the All-Star break last season, and he didn't have a starting job when he returned. He also didn't hit, and might decide to retire. 2003 Outlook: C

Chris Donnels (**Pos**: 3B, **Age**: 36, **Bats**: L)

	G	AB	R	H	D	T	HR	RBI	SB	BB	SO	Avg	OBP	Slg
'02	74	80	5	19	4	1	3	16	0	10	14	.238	.312	.425
Car.	450	798	83	186	36	5	17	86	5	103	165	.233	.319	.355

Donnels signed a minor league deal with the Diamondbacks last winter and performed OK as a left-handed bat off the bench. He may have a similar role in 2003 after inking another minor league contract with Arizona. 2003 Outlook: C

Felix Jose (**Pos**: RF, **Age**: 37, **Bats**: B)

	G	AB	R	H	D	T	HR	RBI	SB	BB	SO	Avg	OBP	Slg
'02	13	19	5	5	0	0	2	4	0	4	8	.263	.360	.579
Car.	729	2509	321	702	134	14	53	318	102	197	504	.280	.333	.408

Jose just won't go away. Every couple years, it seems, he returns to the majors to make a cameo. He's played in Korea and Japan in recent years, and looks like he still can hit. 2003 Outlook: C

Danny Klassen (**Pos**: 3B, **Age**: 27, **Bats**: R)

	G	AB	R	H	D	T	HR	RBI	SB	BB	SO	Avg	OBP	Slg
'02	4	3	0	1	0	0	0	0	0	0	1	.333	.333	.333
Car.	63	188	25	41	5	1	5	16	2	17	58	.218	.290	.335

Although Klassen should be in the prime of his career, it's hard to see much progress. Injuries haven't helped, but the best he might be able to hope for is to carve out a utility role. 2003 Outlook: C

Mark Little (**Pos**: RF/LF/CF, **Age**: 30, **Bats**: R)

	G	AB	R	H	D	T	HR	RBI	SB	BB	SO	Avg	OBP	Slg
'02	79	130	28	27	5	3	0	7	2	15	34	.208	.327	.292
Car.	137	227	46	57	11	3	3	20	8	18	59	.251	.339	.366

Little was traded from the Rockies to the Mets to the Diamondbacks in the space of a month last summer. He doesn't do anything exceptionally well, which may make it difficult to keep a bench job. 2003 Outlook: C

Matt Mantei (**Pos**: RHP, **Age**: 29)

	W	L	Pct.	ERA	G	GS	Sv	IP	H	BB	SO	HR	Ratio
'02	2	2	.500	4.73	31	0	0	26.2	28	12	26	3	1.50
Car.	8	11	.421	3.78	219	0	60	230.2	172	152	293	18	1.40

The D-Backs hope Mantei can return to closing after missing almost all of 2001 because of elbow surgery. He stayed healthy the second half of last season, which has Arizona thinking about dealing closer Byung-Hyun Kim. For Mantei, though, injuries may always be a concern. 2003 Outlook: B

Mike Morgan (**Pos**: RHP, **Age**: 43)

	W	L	Pct.	ERA	G	GS	Sv	IP	H	BB	SO	HR	Ratio
'02	1	1	.500	5.29	29	0	0	34.0	41	9	13	7	1.47
Car.	141	186	.431	4.23	597	411	8	2772.1	2943	938	1403	270	1.40

Morgan pitched only once more for Arizona after bruising his knee last June. Now 43 years of age and seven years removed from his last sub-4.00 ERA, he's again testing the free-agent waters. 2003 Outlook: C

Mike Myers (**Pos**: LHP, **Age**: 33)

	W	L	Pct.	ERA	G	GS	Sv	IP	H	BB	SO	HR	Ratio
'02	4	3	.571	4.38	69	0	4	37.0	39	17	31	2	1.51
Car.	12	19	.387	4.23	545	0	14	340.1	324	166	306	37	1.44

Myers was traded from Colorado to Arizona last winter. He should be able to keep a job as long as he can handle lefthanded batters, and the Diamondbacks have picked up his option for this season. 2003 Outlook: B

Eddie Oropesa (**Pos**: LHP, **Age**: 31)

	W	L	Pct.	ERA	G	GS	Sv	IP	H	BB	SO	HR	Ratio
'02	2	0	1.000	10.30	32	0	0	25.1	39	15	18	6	2.13
Car.	3	0	1.000	7.92	62	0	0	44.1	55	32	33	7	1.96

Oropesa somehow remained undefeated last year, despite some wretched numbers. He's lefthanded and Cuban, which might mean more than it should to some teams. 2003 Outlook: C

Jose Parra (**Pos**: RHP, **Age**: 30)

	W	L	Pct.	ERA	G	GS	Sv	IP	H	BB	SO	HR	Ratio
'02	0	1	.000	3.21	16	0	0	14.0	13	11	8	0	1.71
Car.	6	12	.333	6.33	69	19	0	167.2	211	73	103	31	1.69

After struggling a bit with control during his brief time with the Diamondbacks last spring, Parra refused to be reassigned to the minors and became a free agent. 2003 Outlook: C

Bret Prinz (**Pos**: RHP, **Age**: 25)

	W	L	Pct.	ERA	G	GS	Sv	IP	H	BB	SO	HR	Ratio
'02	0	2	.000	9.45	20	0	0	13.1	23	10	10	1	2.48
Car.	4	3	.571	4.31	66	0	9	54.1	56	29	37	5	1.56

After a nice debut season in 2001, Prinz couldn't make it out of April before getting demoted last season. A key will be how well he rebounds against righthanded batters. 2003 Outlook: B

Arizona

Armando Reynoso (**Pos**: RHP, **Age**: 36)

	W	L	Pct.	ERA	G	GS	Sv	IP	H	BB	SO	HR	Ratio
'02	0	0	–	10.80	2	0	0	1.2	3	1	2	0	2.40
Car.	68	62	.523	4.74	198	186	1	1079.2	1185	376	554	138	1.45

After battling shoulder problems in 2001 and recovering from neck surgery, Reynoso pitched very little in 2002. The Diamondbacks re-signed him to a minor league deal in December, but he'll have to prove he's healthy. 2003 Outlook: C

Todd Stottlemyre (**Pos**: RHP, **Age**: 37)

	W	L	Pct.	ERA	G	GS	Sv	IP	H	BB	SO	HR	Ratio
'02	0	2	.000	7.52	5	4	0	20.1	26	7	12	4	1.62
Car.	138	121	.533	4.28	372	339	1	2191.2	2200	816	1587	246	1.38

After battling arm problems almost from the day he arrived in Arizona in 1999, Stottlemyre has decided to retire. He finishes with 26 fewer career wins (138) than his father (164). 2003 Outlook: D

Greg Swindell (**Pos**: LHP, **Age**: 38)

	W	L	Pct.	ERA	G	GS	Sv	IP	H	BB	SO	HR	Ratio
'02	0	2	.000	6.27	34	0	0	33.0	38	5	23	9	1.30
Car.	123	122	.502	3.86	664	269	7	2233.1	2313	501	1542	262	1.26

Swindell had two stints on the disabled list due to shoulder tendinitis and back problems last season. He also had problems with lefthanded batters, as they hit .339 with good power against him. 2003 Outlook: B

Arizona Diamondbacks Minor League Prospects

Organization Overview:

Six years after their first draft, the Diamondbacks finally have top-to-bottom depth in their farm system. This year's Triple-A Tucson team, for the first time, will feature more homegrown prospects than six-year free agents signed to round out the roster. That team will have many of the same players from last year's Double-A El Paso club, which was second in the Texas League with 76 victories. Most of the pitching talent will be at the higher levels, including a group from that El Paso team (Oscar Villarreal, Mike Gosling, Brandon Webb, Brian Bruney and Jesus Silva). The offensive talent in the organization primarily is at the corner positions. One theme in the system is a group of possible impact offensive players who are suspect on defense at their current position, and thus may have to move: second baseman Scott Hairston, third baseman Chad Tracy, left fielder Jesus Cota and shortstop Sergio Santos.

Brian Bruney

Position: P
Bats: R **Throws:** R
Ht: 6' 3" **Wt:** 220

Opening Day Age: 21
Born: 2/17/82 in Astoria, OR

Recent Statistics

	W	L	ERA	G	GS	Sv	IP	H	R	BB	SO	HR
2001 A South Bend	1	4	4.13	26	0	8	32.2	24	19	19	40	1
2001 A Yakima	1	2	5.14	15	0	2	21.0	19	14	11	28	2
2002 A South Bend	4	3	1.68	37	0	10	48.1	37	15	17	54	1
2002 AA El Paso	0	2	2.92	10	0	0	12.1	11	5	4	14	1

A strong effort in the Arizona Fall League (0.00 ERA in 16 appearances) has vaulted Bruney, along with Jesus Silva, to the top of the Diamondbacks' relief prospects. Bruney was a 12th-round selection in 2000 who threw 98-99 MPH out of high school, but with more mechanics. Smoothed out a bit, he throws 94-95 MPH with good movement and a slider. His velocity could still improve—he did not turn 21 until February—and if he throws more strikes, he could be dominating.

Jesus Cota

Position: 1B
Bats: L **Throws:** R
Ht: 6' 3" **Wt:** 215

Opening Day Age: 21
Born: 11/7/81 in Tucson, AZ

Recent Statistics

	G	AB	R	H	D	T	HR	RBI	SB	BB	SO	Avg
2001 R Missoula	75	272	74	100	22	0	16	71	2	56	52	.368
2002 A Lancaster	135	540	73	151	33	3	16	101	0	38	121	.280

Cota led the high Class-A California League with 101 RBI last year while switching positions, from first to left field—mainly because of the depth of first basemen in the organization (Erubiel Durazo, Lyle Overbay, etc.). Cota shows some similarities to Durazo: a short-armed, lefthanded swing that allows him to go the other

way with power. And at 21, Cota could get even stronger and learn to pull the ball more. Left field may be a stretch, but his bat will get him to the big leagues as an offensive left fielder, first baseman or DH. He needs to cut down on his strikeouts.

Mike Gosling

Position: P
Bats: L **Throws:** L
Ht: 6' 2" **Wt:** 215

Opening Day Age: 22
Born: 9/23/80 in Salt Lake City, UT

Recent Statistics

	W	L	ERA	G	GS	Sv	IP	H	R	BB	SO	HR
2002 AA El Paso	14	5	3.13	27	27	0	166.2	149	66	62	115	7

The polished Gosling is a fast-rising prospect who has average stuff—89-91 MPH fastball, curve and improving changeup—but he has an excellent feel for pitching. His strength is his poise; he needs to work on defense and holding runners. Gosling is a long shot to make the team out of spring training, but he conceivably could pitch his way into the majors by summer. A second-round pick from Stanford, Gosling signed late after the 2001 draft for $2 million, Thus he did not make his pro debut until 2002. But despite being pushed to Double-A El Paso, Gosling responded brilliantly. He earned Organization Pitcher of the Year honors by going 14-5 with a 3.13 ERA, ranking third in the Texas League in innings and ERA.

Scott Hairston

Position: 2B
Bats: R **Throws:** R
Ht: 6' 0" **Wt:** 190

Opening Day Age: 22
Born: 5/25/80 in Oro Valley, AZ

Recent Statistics

	G	AB	R	H	D	T	HR	RBI	SB	BB	SO	Avg
2001 R Missoula	74	291	81	101	16	6	14	65	2	38	50	.347
2002 A South Bend	109	394	79	131	35	4	16	72	9	58	74	.332
2002 A Lancaster	18	79	20	32	11	1	6	26	1	6	16	.405

While Hairston's defense is an issue, his offense is not—he is the best overall hitter in the Diamondbacks' system. He has power to all fields and a quick bat that allows him to wait on the pitch and still drive it. Hairston also has shown excellent judgment of the strike zone. He tied for the minor league lead last year with 73 extra-base hits between two Class-A stops, hitting a combined .345. He also has decent speed, a stole nine bases at Class-A South Bend last year. If Hairston can become adequate at second base, he could be a Jeff Kent-type impact middle infielder. But for now, Hairston needs refinement defensively—with both his footwork and his hands—on grounders and turning double plays, which leads to the thought he may wind up in the outfield.

Lyle Overbay

Position: 1B   **Opening Day Age:** 26
Bats: L **Throws:** L   **Born:** 1/28/77 in
Ht: 6' 2" **Wt:** 215   Centralia, WA

Recent Statistics

	G	AB	R	H	D	T	HR	RBI	SB	BB	SO	Avg
2002 AAA Tucson	134	525	83	180	40	0	19	109	0	42	86	.343
2002 NL Arizona	10	10	0	1	0	0	0	.1	0	0	5	.100

With Mark Grace taking on a part-time role for his final season and Erubiel Durazo expected to be traded, Overbay can step in as Arizona's regular first baseman. With a flat swing, he is a line-drive, spray hitter who may have to develop big league power. Overbay has proven himself on every level, batting .345 in his minor league career, but he looked overmatched at times in his September 2002 callup (1-for-10). Overbay is an average first baseman, but he is expected to be tutored by Grace. It should be noted that although Overbay is in just his fifth pro season, he will be 26 before spring training opens (he was drafted as a 22-year-old college senior).

John Patterson

Position: P   **Opening Day Age:** 25
Bats: R **Throws:** R   **Born:** 1/30/78 in Orange,
Ht: 6' 6" **Wt:** 200   TX

Recent Statistics

	W	L	ERA	G	GS	Sv	IP	H	R	BB	SO	HR
2002 AAA Tucson	10	5	4.23	19	18	0	112.2	117	59	45	104	14
2002 NL Arizona	2	0	3.23	7	5	0	30.2	27	11	7	31	7

A long comeback from Tommy John surgery culminated with Patterson's callup last year. He made three mid-summer starts while Rick Helling was on the DL, and came back up again in September. With Helling not expected back, Patterson—one of the 1996 "loophole" free agents, an Expos first-round pick who signed with the Diamondbacks for $6.075 million—can step into the rotation. Patterson, 6-foot-6, throws 92-93 MPH and is successful when he changes the hitter's eye level by moving the fastball up and down and mixing in a very good, over-the-top curveball. He also has a changeup he can use against lefties. Last year's experience should help him be poised this season, despite high expectations.

Chad Tracy

Position: 3B   **Opening Day Age:** 22
Bats: L **Throws:** R   **Born:** 5/22/80 in
Ht: 6' 2" **Wt:** 200   Charlotte, NC

Recent Statistics

	G	AB	R	H	D	T	HR	RBI	SB	BB	SO	Avg
2001 A Yakima	10	36	2	10	1	0	0	5	1	3	5	.278
2001 A South Bend	54	215	43	73	11	0	4	36	3	19	19	.340
2002 AA El Paso	129	514	80	177	39	5	8	74	2	38	51	.344

Tracy could be the first position player from the 2001 draft to reach the majors. A selective hitter, he led the Double-A Texas League in average (.344), hits (177) and doubles (39) last year. Like Overbay, Tracy is a pure lefthanded hitter, although Tracy has shown less home-run power so far. He throws righthanded and thus has more positions to choose from, but he has a ways to go to become a decent third baseman (26 errors in 2002). Tracy was assigned to the Arizona Fall League but only lasted a week because of a sore right shoulder. He is expected to be ready for spring training.

Oscar Villarreal

Position: P   **Opening Day Age:** 21
Bats: L **Throws:** R   **Born:** 11/22/81 in
Ht: 6' 1" **Wt:** 190   Monterrey, Mexico

Recent Statistics

	W	L	ERA	G	GS	Sv	IP	H	R	BB	SO	HR
2001 AA El Paso	6	9	4.41	27	27	0	140.2	154	96	63	108	10
2002 AA El Paso	6	3	3.74	14	12	0	84.1	73	36	26	85	2
2002 AAA Tucson	3	3	4.36	10	10	0	64.0	68	33	22	40	8

Some believe Villarreal has the best arm in the organization, and by the end of last season he was a 20-year-old Triple-A pitcher. Villarreal struck out 125 in 148.1 combined innings, with just 48 walks. Despite his smallish size (6-foot-1, 190 pounds), Villareal can throw up to 95 MPH, with a slider, and he could develop into a true big league power pitcher. He also has a two-seam sinking fastball. He, too, could be a midseason big league arrival if he matures and improves his focus. He has a tendency to pitch into trouble and to try to trick hitters too often.

Others to Watch

Shortstop **Alex Cintron** (24) likely will be Arizona's utility infielder this year, and he is well suited to the role. Cintron is a switch-hitter who can run and play all three infield positions capably. He showed better patience in his callups last year. . . Another righty, **Andrew Good** (23) came back from Tommy John surgery to have a strong 2002 in Double-A. He relies on control, with his best pitch a changeup. . . Second baseman **Matt Kata** (25) is a switch-hitter who could be a major league utilityman. He led the Double-A Texas League in runs last year. . . **Sergio Santos** (19), a shortstop who was last year's first-round pick, may have to move to third base eventually. But he showed good offensive potential in his pro debut (.302 with six homers in August for Rookie-level Missoula). . . Righthander **Jesus Silva** (20) throws in the mid-90s but has yet to develop a second pitch. Because of that and his ability to throw very hard for brief outings, he is definitely suited to closing rather than starting. . . RHP **Brandon Webb** (23) was fourth last year in the Double-A Texas League in ERA and third in strikeouts. He has a power sinker and could be a back-end starter or setup reliever. . . Outfielder **Marland Williams** (21) has the best speed in the organization. He stole 51 bases and hit eight triples in 70 games for short-season Yakima last year.

Turner Field

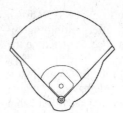

Offense

Turner Field is considered a pitchers' park and ranks in the middle of the pack in terms of run production. Lefthanded hitters love taking cuts in Atlanta. While the fence down the right field line is an average 330 feet, the power alley juts out to 390 feet, creating considerable room for balls to fall for hits. The Braves' lefthanded swingers produced roughly twice as many homers at home than on the road last year, while also producing a higher batting average. Righthanded hitters have tended to produce a few more homers in Braves road games than at Turner on an annual basis.

Defense

For the fifth time in six seasons, the Braves led the National League in pitching, posting a 3.13 ERA, which was 0.41 better than second-place San Francisco. Turner Field plays a role in that success. While the ball carries well during the summer months, steady breezes through the opening in center field keep pitches in the park during April and May. Turner Field also has deep alleys and a large outfield, though the Braves employ Andruw Jones in center to run down nearly everything hit from gap to gap.

Who It Helps the Most

Chipper Jones has hit well at home since Turner Field was built, and he continued that trend last year, batting 37 points higher in Atlanta than on the road. Lefthanded hitter Matt Franco used his line-drive swing and the ballpark's spacious right field to hit 55 points higher at home.

Who It Hurts the Most

Gary Sheffield, who bats from the right side, hit .272 at Turner Field, 64 points lower than his average on the road. Darren Bragg also had more success on the road, hitting .312 in away games compared to .207 at home.

Rookies & Newcomers

Trey Hodges has the best chance among first-year players to break into the Atlanta rotation. Hodges spent September with the Braves and enjoyed the comforts of home, posting a 3.00 ERA at Turner Field, as opposed to a 7.94 mark on the road.

Dimensions: LF-335, LCF-380, CF-401, RCF-390, RF-330

Capacity: 50,091

Elevation: 1050 feet

Surface: Grass

Foul Territory: Average

Park Factors

2002 Season

	Home Games Braves	Opp	Total	Away Games Braves	Opp	Total	Index
G	72	72	144	71	71	142	
Avg	.261	.243	.252	.252	.244	.248	102
AB	2361	2480	4841	2496	2350	4846	99
R	321	257	578	286	258	544	105
H	617	603	1220	628	573	1201	100
2B	118	119	237	122	95	217	109
3B	13	12	25	9	16	25	100
HR	74	58	132	68	55	123	107
BB	243	236	479	250	268	518	93
SO	433	450	883	485	469	954	93
E	52	52	104	50	48	98	105
E-Infield	46	46	92	42	35	77	118
LHB-Avg	.274	.250	.262	.260	.236	.248	106
LHB-HR	24	16	40	12	17	29	138
RHB-Avg	.255	.240	.247	.248	.248	.248	100
RHB-HR	50	42	92	56	38	94	98

2000-2002

	Home Games Braves	Opp	Total	Away Games Braves	Opp	Total	Index
G	216	216	432	215	215	430	
Avg	.267	.251	.259	.257	.249	.253	102
AB	7107	7459	14566	7506	7139	14645	99
R	988	860	1848	972	844	1816	101
H	1899	1875	3774	1927	1776	3703	101
2B	346	322	668	371	310	681	99
3B	35	26	61	33	40	73	84
HR	228	198	426	228	198	426	101
BB	700	676	1376	753	676	1429	97
SO	1275	1445	2720	1477	1443	2920	94
E	163	188	351	147	159	306	114
E-Infield	147	158	305	123	133	256	119
LHB-Avg	.269	.270	.270	.256	.250	.253	106
LHB-HR	66	79	145	60	63	123	117
RHB-Avg	.266	.241	.253	.257	.248	.253	100
RHB-HR	162	119	281	168	135	303	94

2002 Rankings (National League)
- Third-highest infield-error factor
- Third-highest LHB home-run factor
- Third-lowest strikeout factor

Atlanta

Bobby Cox

2002 Season

Bobby Cox was named Sporting News' National League Manager of the Year after putting together another masterful performance. He became the first NL skipper to win 100 games five times. He's also just the 12th manager in major league history to reach 1,800 victories. While having to juggle the back end of the rotation and an infield that failed to find consistency at first and second base, Cox guided the Braves to their 11th straight division crown, a professional sports record.

Offense

Cox employs a conservative approach while playing to his team's strengths. The home run always has been a part of his strategy, resulting in a more station-to-station approach than most NL clubs. While Cox did not hit-and-run a lot, his success rate of 44.3 percent was second best in the league. Cox never has been shy about platooning players, and traditionally favors veterans over youngsters. He also plays the percentages, loading the batting order with 96.6 percent righthanded hitters when facing lefthanded starters in 2002.

Pitching & Defense

Cox has different approaches with different pitchers. He'll let veterans such as Tom Glavine and Greg Maddux provide input, but is quick to pull younger hurlers such as Jason Marquis and Damian Moss. Cox takes full advantage of his bullpen and prefers to have six situational relievers with defined roles before employing the designated closer. He also wants experienced defensive players, and will go with a struggling hitter, such as Vinny Castilla, if he's providing solid glovework.

2003 Outlook

Cox' last 12 full-season teams have finished in first place, dating to the 1985 season when he guided Toronto to the American League East flag. While he has his critics for winning just one World Series title, Cox gets the most out of his team by treating his players equally and maintaining a calm and professional atmosphere over the course of the campaign. With no manager more secure in his job, he should have the Braves back in the playoff hunt this season.

Born: 5/21/41 in Tulsa, OK

Playing Experience: 1968-1969, NYY

Managerial Experience: 21 seasons

Manager Statistics

Year	Team, Lg	W	L	Pct	GB	Finish
2002	Atlanta, NL	101	59	.631	–	1st East
21 Seasons		1805	1404	.562	–	–

2002 Starting Pitchers by Days Rest

	<=3	4	5	6+
Braves Starts	6	102	21	24
Braves ERA	1.57	2.92	3.87	5.90
NL Avg Starts	1	88	42	21
NL ERA	3.18	4.22	4.14	4.58

2002 Situational Stats

	Bobby Cox	NL Average
Hit & Run Success %	44.3	36.5
Stolen Base Success %	66.1	68.3
Platoon Pct.	47.6	52.7
Defensive Subs	15	19
High-Pitch Outings	5	7
Quick/Slow Hooks	32/6	24/11
Sacrifice Attempts	89	95

2002 Rankings (National League)

- 1st in pitchouts with a runner moving (8), starts on three days rest and 2+ pitching changes in low-scoring games (54)
- 2nd in hit-and-run success percentage and pitchouts (52)
- 3rd in quick hooks, relief appearances (469) and saves with over 1 inning pitched (9)

Vinny Castilla

2002 Season

Although he played solid defense, Vinny Castilla failed to live up to the Braves' expectations after signing as a free agent prior to last season. He battled an ailing right wrist and posted the lowest full-season batting average and power numbers of his career. He went a career-high 256 at-bats, from June 11 to September 13, without hitting a home run, and drove in just eight runs in July and August combined.

Hitting

Castilla's struggles centered on his lack of patience and his determination to pull every pitch. He fell into the habit of swinging at anything close to the strike zone instead of waiting for his pitch. Most scouts agree that Castilla's bat speed has slowed considerably over the past two years. Not only does he have difficulty catching up to average fastballs, pitchers toy with his aggressiveness by striking him out on breaking balls as much as a foot off the plate. As a result, Castilla ranked last in the National League in on-base percentage, pitches per plate appearance and percentage of pitches taken.

Baserunning & Defense

Atlanta manager Bobby Cox believes Castilla is the best defensive third baseman in the league. Castilla does a fantastic job of positioning himself correctly on most plays. He has good range, a strong and accurate arm, and makes near perfect throws to second base on around-the-horn double plays. He set a franchise record for third basemen while leading the circuit with a .982 fielding percentage. He has below-average speed and doesn't excel on the basepaths.

2003 Outlook

Castilla looked more like the washed-up hitter he appeared to be with Tampa Bay in early 2001 than the more effective power threat he was later in the year with the Astros. With Castilla owed $4 million this season, the Braves are stuck with the declining slugger. If his bat can produce any memories of his days in Colorado and Houston, Castilla won't hurt the Braves due to his steady glovework at the hot corner.

Position: 3B
Bats: R **Throws:** R
Ht: 6' 1" **Wt:** 205

Opening Day Age: 35
Born: 7/4/67 in Oaxaca, Mexico
ML Seasons: 12
Pronunciation: cas-TEE-yah

Overall Statistics

	G	AB	R	H	D	T	HR	RBI	SB	BB	SO	Avg	OBP	Slg
'02	143	543	56	126	23	2	12	61	4	22	69	.232	.268	.348
Car.	1330	4928	665	1388	232	21	246	805	28	294	739	.282	.324	.487

Where He Hits the Ball

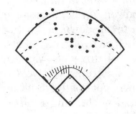

Vs. LHP   **Vs. RHP**

2002 Situational Stats

	AB	H	HR	RBI	Avg		AB	H	HR	RBI	Avg
Home	256	57	5	25	.223	LHP	76	17	2	10	.224
Road	287	69	7	36	.240	RHP	467	109	10	51	.233
First Half	318	78	9	45	.245	Sc Pos	160	32	3	48	.200
Scnd Half	225	48	3	16	.213	Clutch	92	18	0	6	.196

2002 Rankings (National League)

- 1st in fielding percentage at third base (.982), lowest on-base percentage, fewest pitches seen per plate appearance (3.12), lowest percentage of pitches taken (39.5), lowest on-base percentage vs. righthanded pitchers (.268), lowest batting average at home and highest percentage of swings on the first pitch (52.7)
- 2nd in lowest batting average
- 4th in lowest batting average vs. righthanded pitchers
- Led the Braves in sacrifice flies (6) and GDPs (22)

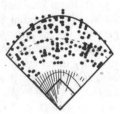

Atlanta

Rafael Furcal

2002 Season

As Rafael Furcal goes, so goes the Atlanta offense. After missing the second half of 2001 with a separated shoulder, the shortstop overcame a sluggish start last year. From May 1 until the end of the season, the Braves went 56-8 when Furcal scored at least one run. He tied a major league record on April 21 when he became the first Braves player since 1956 to hit three triples in one game.

Hitting

Furcal is capable of using his outstanding speed and deft handling of the bat to his advantage. He ranked second in the National League last year with 21 bunt hits, and third with 38 infield hits. He also has surprising power. Yet his occasional pop has Furcal reluctant to cut down on his big swing and alter his approach on two-strike counts, resulting in an excessive 114 strikeouts. He also isn't patient at the plate. His overaggressiveness gets him behind in the count constantly, resulting in poor contact on pitchers' pitches and a miserable .323 on-base percentage.

Baserunning & Defense

Furcal has quick feet, outstanding range and one of the strongest arms among major league shortstops. Rusty early last season, he committed 13 errors in his first 38 games before settling down. He can be too aggressive in charging balls on in-between hops, instead of waiting and trusting his arm. Opponents tried to shut down Furcal on the basepaths with slide steps and pitchouts, and were successful by nabbing him 15 times in 42 stolen base attempts. After struggling while sliding feet-first, Furcal returned to his headfirst slide despite separating his shoulder while doing so in 2001.

2003 Outlook

The Braves believe Furcal can be the long-term answer at shortstop, but would like for the diminutive player to hone his skills to his greatest advantage. When he plays under control, Furcal is the most athletic shortstop in franchise history and a true tablesetter atop the Atlanta lineup. Yet in order for that scenario to remain intact, he must do the little things on a consistent basis or risk losing his job.

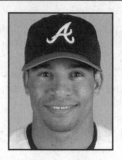

Position: SS
Bats: B **Throws:** R
Ht: 5'10" **Wt:** 165

Opening Day Age: 24
Born: 8/24/78 in Loma de Cabrera, DR
ML Seasons: 3
Pronunciation: fur-CALL

Overall Statistics

	G	AB	R	H	D	T	HR	RBI	SB	BB	SO	Avg	OBP	Slg
'02	154	636	95	175	31	8	8	47	27	43	114	.275	.323	.387
Car.	364	1415	221	398	70	12	16	114	89	140	250	.281	.347	.382

Where He Hits the Ball

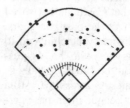 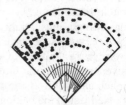

Vs. LHP   **Vs. RHP**

2002 Situational Stats

	AB	H	HR	RBI	Avg		AB	H	HR	RBI	Avg
Home	322	91	4	24	.283	LHP	111	32	1	12	.288
Road	314	84	4	23	.268	RHP	525	143	7	35	.272
First Half	357	102	4	25	.286	Sc Pos	118	36	1	38	.305
Scnd Half	279	73	4	22	.262	Clutch	88	25	0	11	.284

2002 Rankings (National League)

- 1st in lowest batting average with the bases loaded (.000)
- 2nd in at-bats, triples, caught stealing (15), bunts in play (53), errors at shortstop (27), batting average on a 3-2 count (.380) and lowest fielding percentage at shortstop (.963)
- 3rd in plate appearances (693), highest percentage of extra bases taken as a runner (67.4) and lowest stolen-base percentage (64.3)
- Led the Braves in runs scored, singles, triples, stolen bases, caught stealing (15), pitches seen (2,638), lowest percentage of swings that missed (12.4), steals of third (3) and on-base percentage for a leadoff hitter (.323)

Tom Glavine

2002 Season

Tom Glavine is giving new meaning to the term "stopper." In 16 outings following an Atlanta loss last year, Glavine went 10-3 with a 1.58 ERA. He got off to a great start by winning 11 of his first 13 decisions, and finished with a 2.96 ERA, his lowest since 1998. Glavine moved into ninth place on the all-time list for wins by a lefthander, and his total of 233 victories over the past 14 years is tops among southpaws.

Pitching

Glavine altered his approach during 2002. After pitching primarily away and getting the called outside strike, he started working both sides of the plate and moving his pitches in and out of the strike zone, with many of his strikeouts coming on fastballs that cut across the inside corner. Glavine's velocity remains an unimpressive 87-89 MPH, but his fastball is plenty hard due to his outstanding changeup. He also has added a couple of variations to his traditional offerings, among them an average curveball and slider, and does an impressive job of mixing his pitches. Glavine keeps his pitches low, which helped him record the 2,000th strikeout of his career last season.

Defense & Hitting

Greg Maddux receives the Gold Glove hardware, but Glavine is equally efficient with the leather. His quick reflexes and sure hands have compiled a perfect fielding record each of the past three seasons. He also does a laudable job of holding runners, with five pickoffs last year. A good hitter, Glavine had his toughest year at the plate, recording just seven hits, although he tied for third in the National League with 13 sacrifice bunts.

2003 Outlook

Glavine joined Maddux in filing for free agency, and the lefthander moved quickly and signed a three-year, $35 million contract with the Mets in December. Glavine's value cannot be overstated as a durable southpaw who topped the NL in starts last year. He remains a premier hurler, making the necessary adjustments, possessing an outstanding repertoire, and displaying an unmatched desire to succeed. He should remain a No. 1-type starter for a couple more years.

Position: SP
Bats: L **Throws:** L
Ht: 6' 0" **Wt:** 185

Opening Day Age: 37
Born: 3/25/66 in Concord, MA
ML Seasons: 16
Pronunciation: GLAV-in

Overall Statistics

W	L	Pct.	ERA	G	GS	Sv	IP	H	BB	SO	HR	Ratio
18	11	.621	2.96	36	36	0	224.2	210	78	127	21	1.28
242	143	.629	3.37	505	505	0	3344.2	3174	1140	2054	247	1.29

How Often He Throws Strikes

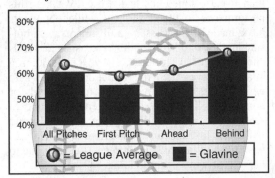

2002 Situational Stats

	W	L	ERA	Sv	IP		AB	H	HR	RBI	Avg
Home	9	6	3.18	0	124.1	LHB	164	40	6	21	.244
Road	9	5	2.69	0	100.1	RHB	668	170	15	50	.254
First Half	11	4	2.27	0	130.2	Sc Pos	192	37	0	46	.193
Scnd Half	7	7	3.93	0	94.0	Clutch	40	13	0	5	.325

2002 Rankings (National League)

- 1st in games started, runners caught stealing (16) and fielding percentage at pitcher (1.000)
- 3rd in ERA, sacrifice bunts (13) and lowest batting average allowed with runners in scoring position
- 4th in wins, pitches thrown (3,577), lowest ERA on the road and fewest strikeouts per nine innings (5.1)
- 5th in innings pitched and batters faced (936)
- Led the Braves in sacrifice bunts (13), wins, losses, games started, complete games (2), innings pitched, hits allowed, batters faced (936), home runs allowed, hit batsmen (8), pitches thrown (3,577), runners caught stealing (16) and lowest ERA on the road

Atlanta

Andruw Jones

Position: CF
Bats: R **Throws:** R
Ht: 6' 1" **Wt:** 210

Opening Day Age: 25
Born: 4/23/77 in Willemstad, Curacao
ML Seasons: 7

2002 Season

Andruw Jones got off to a strong start before struggling through the summer months and finishing on a high note. His batting average peaked at .301 in early June, leading to his second All-Star invitation. His average then plummeted more than 50 points while he battled a strained left shoulder and neck and a jammed wrist during the second half. He still managed to homer in four consecutive at-bats in early September and posted his first three-homer game on September 25.

Hitting

After having the game come so easy to him for so many years, Jones has had difficulty taking his performance to the next level while opponents have made the necessary adjustments. An outstanding natural athlete, Jones crushes fastballs and most mistake pitches. However, he joins a host of Braves in being impatient at the plate while trying to pull everything to left field for home runs. The free swinger remains prone to striking out on low-and-away breaking balls, and will chase fastballs up in the strike zone. He also has tired and faltered late in recent seasons due to his lack of winter conditioning.

Baserunning & Defense

Jones has outstanding speed and a loose, fluid stride. He's the best defensive center fielder of the current era, making the spectacular catch as well as running down most everything hit into either gap. His five assists are misleading because few teams will risk running on Jones' cannon-like arm and pinpoint accuracy. While he has plus speed, he's not a great basestealer. He also experiences lapses of concentration on the basepaths and isn't known for getting quick jumps.

2003 Outlook

Jones is maddeningly inconsistent to those who keep expecting him to take the final step into superstardom. His defense may be unmatched, and he's averaged 35 homers and 101 RBI over the past three years, but his career average is just .267. Some observers believe his career-best 83 walks in 2002 is a sign that Jones slowly is developing into the great all-around player his obvious tools indicate he should be.

Overall Statistics

	G	AB	R	H	D	T	HR	RBI	SB	BB	SO	Avg	OBP	Slg
'02	154	560	91	148	34	0	35	94	8	83	135	.264	.366	.513
Car.	981	3520	574	940	188	23	185	559	114	377	745	.267	.342	.491

Where He Hits the Ball

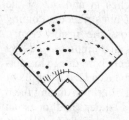
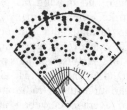

Vs. LHP **Vs. RHP**

2002 Situational Stats

	AB	H	HR	RBI	Avg		AB	H	HR	RBI	Avg
Home	286	77	18	48	.269	LHP	79	18	2	14	.228
Road	274	71	17	46	.259	RHP	481	130	33	80	.270
First Half	328	85	19	54	.259	Sc Pos	167	43	10	61	.257
Scnd Half	232	63	16	40	.272	Clutch	91	15	4	12	.165

2002 Rankings (National League)

- 5th in fielding percentage in center field (.993)
- 6th in highest percentage of swings that missed (28.8)
- Led the Braves in home runs, sacrifice flies (6), strikeouts and HR frequency (16.0 ABs per HR)
- Led NL center fielders in home runs and RBI

Chipper Jones

2002 Season

Chipper Jones didn't let his unselfish move from third base to left field have any effect on his offensive output. After enduring an atypical power slump at midseason, when he hit just four homers during a 59-game stretch, he rebounded to go deep 17 times following the All-Star break. He reached the 100-RBI plateau for the seventh straight season, becoming only the fifth player in National League history to attain the feat.

Hitting

Jones remains one of the most prolific switch-hitters in the game, hitting well over .300 from both sides of the plate. He has strong, quick hands that allow him to drive the ball. A perfectionist regarding his swing, Jones is prone to mild slumps when his mechanics go slightly awry. He went through a stretch last summer when he bent his back too much, resulting in a longer swing. But a call to his father, as usual, corrected the problem. Jones has one of the best batting eyes in the game, leading to 57 walks in his last 63 games.

Baserunning & Defense

Jones has stolen as many as 25 bases in the big leagues, but maintains only slightly above-average speed since suffering a serious knee injury in 1994. He's a smart baserunner and does an effective job taking the extra base. Although he made seven errors, Jones improved in left field as last season progressed. He led Atlanta outfielders with eight assists. While his ultimate destination may be first base, Jones has enough athleticism to do at least an average job at any defensive position.

2003 Outlook

Few players in the majors are more underrated from a national standpoint than Jones. He ranks among the league leaders in numerous offensive categories on an annual basis, yet rarely is mentioned when the topic is centered on the game's premier performers. Despite the relative anonymity, Jones should maintain his lofty numbers this year for Atlanta, whether he remains in left field or returns to the infield for the retooling Braves.

Position: LF
Bats: B **Throws:** R
Ht: 6' 4" **Wt:** 210

Opening Day Age: 30
Born: 4/24/72 in DeLand, FL
ML Seasons: 9

Overall Statistics

	G	AB	R	H	D	T	HR	RBI	SB	BB	SO	Avg	OBP	Slg
'02	158	548	90	179	35	1	26	100	8	107	89	.327	.435	.536
Car.	1252	4589	863	1419	272	24	253	837	114	759	698	.309	.404	.544

Where He Hits the Ball

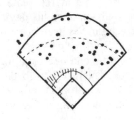

Vs. LHP   **Vs. RHP**

2002 Situational Stats

	AB	H	HR	RBI	Avg		AB	H	HR	RBI	Avg
Home	260	90	17	64	.346	LHP	100	32	4	15	.320
Road	288	89	9	36	.309	RHP	448	147	22	85	.328
First Half	313	96	9	51	.307	Sc Pos	136	41	8	68	.301
Scnd Half	235	83	17	49	.353	Clutch	81	23	4	15	.284

2002 Rankings (National League)

- 3rd in on-base percentage
- 4th in walks, intentional walks (23), times on base (288), on-base percentage vs. righthanded pitchers (.442) and errors in left field (7)
- 5th in batting average, batting average vs. righthanded pitchers, batting average at home, assists in left field (8) and lowest fielding percentage in left field (.975)
- Led the Braves in batting average, hits, doubles, total bases (294), RBI, times on base (288), games played, slugging percentage, batting average vs. righthanded pitchers, cleanup slugging percentage (.566), slugging percentage vs. righthanded pitchers (.542) and batting average at home

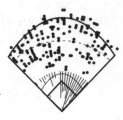

Atlanta

Javy Lopez

Position: C
Bats: R **Throws:** R
Ht: 6' 3" **Wt:** 225

Opening Day Age: 32
Born: 11/5/70 in Ponce, PR
ML Seasons: 11
Pronunciation: HAH-vee LOE-pezz

2002 Season

Javy Lopez entered last season with a .287 career batting average. But he hit more than 50 points below that figure in 2002 while also posting just 11 home runs. Part of his difficulties can be attributed to the strained AC joint he suffered in his right shoulder on July 21. Still, his final home run last season gave him 171 in his career, enabling Lopez to pass Del Crandall for the most round-trippers by a catcher in franchise history.

Hitting

In the past two seasons, Lopez has gone from one of the league's best offensive catchers to an overall mediocre receiver. His drop in production is centered on his lack of discipline at the plate. Although he's been a free swinger since his days in the minors, the 11-year veteran has been guessing at pitches and hacking at anything close to the strike zone instead of waiting and reacting to offerings in his comfort zone. The result has been a drop in batting average, power production and confidence. He's still capable of hitting the longball, however, especially on low fastballs.

Baserunning & Defense

Lopez hasn't regained the quickness he lost after undergoing knee surgery in 2000. Although he was bothered by his shoulder injury during last year's second half, his footwork and overall technique improved in 2002. Even so, Lopez can be lackadaisical about blocking balls in the dirt, and his game-calling abilities leave something to be desired. His arm angle was inconsistent on throws to second, causing many tosses to bounce, and he managed to retire just 29.9 percent of basestealers. Lopez' speed is barely average for a catcher, and he's prone to making mental mistakes on the basepaths.

2003 Outlook

Lopez had a player's option for 2003 worth $7 million, a deal the catcher couldn't refuse. The Braves have always recognized his limitations, but are baffled by his rapid decline with the bat. As a result, Lopez' career is at a crossroads. Despite his struggles, he'll serve as Atlanta's primary catcher for the 10th consecutive season.

Overall Statistics

	G	AB	R	H	D	T	HR	RBI	SB	BB	SO	Avg	OBP	Slg
'02	109	347	31	81	15	0	11	52	0	26	63	.233	.299	.372
Car.	1027	3546	419	998	161	11	171	585	8	238	638	.281	.332	.478

Where He Hits the Ball

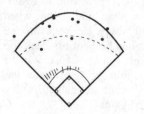 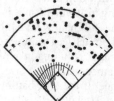

Vs. LHP **Vs. RHP**

2002 Situational Stats

	AB	H	HR	RBI	Avg		AB	H	HR	RBI	Avg
Home	162	45	1	17	.278	LHP	51	13	2	11	.255
Road	185	36	10	35	.195	RHP	296	68	9	41	.230
First Half	227	56	6	31	.247	Sc Pos	98	28	6	42	.286
Scnd Half	120	25	5	21	.208	Clutch	58	15	1	11	.259

2002 Rankings (National League)

- 1st in lowest fielding percentage at catcher (.986)
- 3rd in errors at catcher (10)

Greg Maddux

2002 Season

Nagging injuries, including an inflamed back muscle that sent him to the disabled list for the first time in his career, hampered Greg Maddux throughout last season. Nevertheless, he remained the master of consistency by reaching the 15-win mark for the 15th consecutive year, joining Cy Young as the lone members of the exclusive club.

Pitching

Maddux is a cerebral assassin on the mound. He knows his strengths and limitations as well as those of every hitter. That knowledge allows him to be more efficient than any hurler, resulting in the fewest pitches per start (77.9) in the National League. The righthander possesses pinpoint control, gets ahead in the count and mixes his pitches as well as anyone. He rarely tops the high 80s with his fastball, but his outstanding movement on the pitch produces groundball outs. Maddux also throws a cut fastball and a plus changeup at any time in the count. He refuses to waste pitches or give in to hitters, instead opting to keep his offerings low in the strike zone while moving his pitches off both corners of the plate.

Defense & Hitting

Maddux almost ignores baserunners, which allows them to run at will. Defensively, he's won 13 straight Gold Gloves—deserving them all—and remains one of the most nimble fielders by leading NL pitchers with 3.16 chances per nine innings. Maddux has quick reflexes and bounces off the mound well to field bunts and cover first base. The righthander also continues to help himself with the lumber, posting 11 hits and nine sacrifice bunts last season.

2003 Outlook

Maddux currently has 273 career victories, which ties Red Ruffing for 28th on the all-time list. He is testing free agency for the second time in his career and was looking for a deal that should be his final contract. Regardless of his destination, the righthander has at least a couple seasons left as a consistent starter near the top of a rotation, someone who will give his team at least six quality innings every outing.

Position: SP
Bats: R **Throws:** R
Ht: 6' 0" **Wt:** 185

Opening Day Age: 36
Born: 4/14/66 in San Angelo, TX
ML Seasons: 17
Pronunciation: MADD-ucks

Overall Statistics

	W	L	Pct.	ERA	G	GS	Sv	IP	H	BB	SO	HR	Ratio
'02	16	6	.727	2.62	34	34	0	199.1	194	45	118	14	1.20
Car.	273	152	.642	2.83	539	535	0	3750.1	3400	805	2641	210	1.12

How Often He Throws Strikes

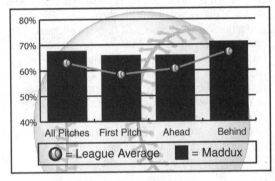

2002 Situational Stats

	W	L	ERA	Sv	IP		AB	H	HR	RBI	Avg
Home	11	3	2.48	0	112.1	LHB	327	76	6	29	.232
Road	5	3	2.79	0	87.0	RHB	427	118	8	31	.276
First Half	8	2	2.81	0	102.2	Sc Pos	172	37	4	49	.215
Scnd Half	8	4	2.42	0	96.2	Clutch	38	13	2	4	.342

2002 Rankings (National League)

- 1st in fewest pitches thrown per batter (3.23)
- 2nd in ERA and highest groundball-flyball ratio allowed (2.2)
- 3rd in pickoff throws (157) and stolen bases allowed (24)
- 4th in games started, most GDPs induced per GDP situation (22.0%), lowest ERA at home, fewest home runs allowed per nine innings (.63) and fewest walks per nine innings (2.0)
- Led the Braves in pickoff throws (157), stolen bases allowed (24), GDPs induced (24), fewest home runs allowed per nine innings (.63), most GDPs induced per nine innings (1.1) and fewest walks per nine innings (2.0)

Atlanta

Jason Marquis

2002 Season

Jason Marquis earned Atlanta's No. 4 starter job in spring training, before inconsistency led to frustration. After a strong start, he battled tendinitis in his right shoulder that landed him on the disabled list from April 15 to May 11. The righthander allowed two runs or less in 12 of 22 starts, but surrendered five or more in seven outings. He also gave up 26 earned runs in his final seven starts, covering 25.2 innings.

Pitching

Marquis has one of the premier arms in the league and the overall ability to emerge as a power pitcher. His fastball has plus movement and sits in the 94-96 MPH range. He also throws a hard slider and a modest changeup, and does an adequate job of mixing those tosses. Marquis' problems center on a lack of control. He admits that he thinks too much about his mechanics while on the mound instead of focusing on the situation. He also tends to get stubborn and is slow to make adjustments, which resulted in extended troubles during his first full season as a starter. Scouts remain concerned that the torque he places on his arm could lead to problems down the road.

Defense & Hitting

Experience has enabled Marquis to improve both his fielding and hitting. He committed one error in 29 chances last season, and looked more comfortable getting off the mound to cover bunts as well as first base. For a righthanded pitcher, he does a good job of holding baserunners, with only three of seven basestealers having success. Marquis posted five hits, including the first home run of his professional career.

2003 Outlook

The Braves still have hope for Marquis, and manager Bobby Cox vows to remain patient. But the fact remains that the righthander has yet to establish himself as a dependable starter in the major leagues. Marquis is an aggressive pitcher with a bulldog mentality. He continues to show flashes of brilliance with his outstanding arm. Those glimpses lead to the promise that someday he could emerge as a No. 3 starter.

Position: SP
Bats: L **Throws:** R
Ht: 6' 1" **Wt:** 210

Opening Day Age: 24
Born: 8/21/78 in Manhasset, NY
ML Seasons: 3
Pronunciation: mar-KEE

Overall Statistics

	W	L	Pct.	ERA	G	GS	Sv	IP	H	BB	SO	HR	Ratio
'02	8	9	.471	5.04	22	22	0	114.1	127	49	84	19	1.54
Car.	14	15	.483	4.28	75	38	0	267.0	263	120	199	37	1.43

How Often He Throws Strikes

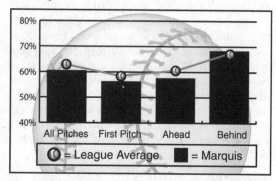

= League Average   ■ = Marquis

2002 Situational Stats

	W	L	ERA	Sv	IP		AB	H	HR	RBI	Avg
Home	5	4	4.58	0	59.0	LHB	209	61	7	21	.292
Road	3	5	5.53	0	55.1	RHB	239	66	12	39	.276
First Half	6	4	3.95	0	73.0	Sc Pos	94	31	2	38	.330
Scnd Half	2	5	6.97	0	41.1	Clutch	14	4	1	2	.286

2002 Rankings (National League)

- Led the Braves in most run support per nine innings (5.7)

Kevin Millwood

2002 Season

Kevin Millwood proved his right shoulder was healthy and responded with his best season since 1999. The righthander was 2-5 with a 4.92 ERA after a loss at Colorado on May 18. But he rebounded to go 16-3 with a 2.64 ERA in his final 25 starts, allowing two earned runs or less in 19 of those outings. He concluded his strong showing with two impressive outings against the Giants in the National League Division Series.

Pitching

After compensating for his aching shoulder the past two years, Millwood worked out a hitch in his delivery that included bringing his hands too high when beginning his windup. By lowering his hands, he had the best command of his career, particularly with his heavy, 91-93 MPH fastball. He also added a changeup, regained the feel for his curveball to the point where it is one of the best in the NL, and threw inside more often. His slider became more consistent, thereby giving opponents other pitches to think about and keeping them off balance. Millwood's pitches have a heavy, sinking action.

Defense & Hitting

Millwood is adequate defensively but isn't in the class of Greg Maddux and Tom Glavine. Millwood's slow delivery and average pickoff move allow basestealers to get good jumps. Maddux was the only Atlanta pitcher to surrender more steals than the 21 Millwood gave up in 22 attempts. Millwood has become a good hitter, posting 14 hits last year, including five doubles, a homer and 11 RBI.

2003 Outlook

Millwood gave every indication by the end of last season that he is ready to handle the responsibilities associated with being a No. 2 starter. Nagging injuries marred his progress for two years, but the righthander looks more like the hurler capable of filling John Smoltz' former power slot in the rotation. The 28-year-old Millwood is entering the prime of his career and finally appears capable of taking the next step.

Position: SP
Bats: R **Throws:** R
Ht: 6' 4" **Wt:** 220

Opening Day Age: 28
Born: 12/24/74 in Gastonia, NC
ML Seasons: 6

Overall Statistics

	W	L	Pct.	ERA	G	GS	Sv	IP	H	BB	SO	HR	Ratio
'02	18	8	.692	3.24	35	34	0	217.0	186	65	178	16	1.16
Car.	75	46	.620	3.73	168	160	0	1004.1	918	303	840	105	1.22

How Often He Throws Strikes

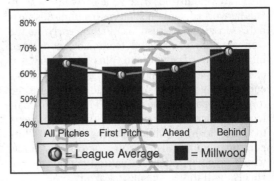

= League Average ■ = Millwood

2002 Situational Stats

	W	L	ERA	Sv	IP		AB	H	HR	RBI	Avg
Home	7	6	3.21	0	103.2	LHB	380	94	8	35	.247
Road	11	2	3.26	0	113.1	RHB	429	92	8	40	.214
First Half	6	5	3.79	0	111.2	Sc Pos	155	36	1	51	.232
Scnd Half	12	3	2.65	0	105.1	Clutch	40	10	2	4	.250

2002 Rankings (National League)

- 1st in highest stolen-base percentage allowed (95.5)
- 3rd in lowest slugging percentage allowed (.337)
- 4th in wins and games started
- 5th in lowest on-base percentage allowed (.292)
- 6th in stolen bases allowed (21) and fewest home runs allowed per nine innings (.66)
- Led the Braves in wins, hit batsmen (8), strikeouts, highest strikeout-walk ratio (2.7), lowest slugging percentage allowed (.337), lowest on-base percentage allowed (.292) and most strikeouts per nine innings (7.4)

Atlanta

Damian Moss

2002 Season

When Greg Maddux went on the disabled list in early April, the Braves received an unexpected boost once Damian Moss stepped into the rotation. The lefthander became the first Atlanta rookie in 19 seasons to win at least 12 games, a total that tied for fourth among first-year pitchers in the National League. He allowed two earned runs or fewer in 19 of 29 starts.

Pitching

Moss' emergence can be attributed to his improved command. He led the Triple-A International League in walks in 2000 and had difficulty finding the strike zone early last season. But he worked hard on spotting his high-80s fastball. Moss didn't trust his pitches early in the campaign, before several teammates convinced him that his fastball and plus changeup had enough movement, and his curveball was sharp enough, to get hitters out. Instead of trying to be too fine by painting the corners, Moss began challenging hitters. As a result, he limited opponents to a .221 average while allowing only 7.03 hits per nine innings. He throws across his body, which gives his pitches a natural cutting action. He also will throw a changeup at any time.

Defense & Hitting

Moss holds runners better than any Atlanta pitcher. He has a couple of different pickoff moves and an excellent hesitation that freezes baserunners. The lefty picked off nine runners, and only eight basestealers were successful in their attempts. Despite having good quickness around the mound, Moss is only an average fielder. His success at the plate also is no better than average.

2003 Outlook

A native of Australia, Moss had been considered a top prospect after signing as a 16-year-old in 1993. He developed slowly before undergoing reconstructive elbow surgery in 1998. He has made incredible progress since then and enters the 2003 season as a key part of Atlanta's rotation. While he must keep making adjustments, Moss has shown he has the savvy and ability to build on his rookie campaign.

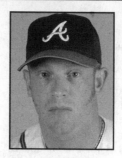

Position: SP
Bats: R **Throws:** L
Ht: 6' 0" **Wt:** 187

Opening Day Age: 26
Born: 11/24/76 in Darlinghurst, Australia
ML Seasons: 2

Overall Statistics

	W	L	Pct.	ERA	G	GS	Sv	IP	H	BB	SO	HR	Ratio
'02	12	6	.667	3.42	33	29	0	179.0	140	89	111	20	1.28
Car.	12	6	.667	3.40	38	30	0	188.0	143	98	119	21	1.28

How Often He Throws Strikes

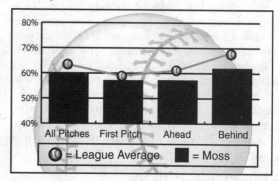

= League Average   = Moss

2002 Situational Stats

	W	L	ERA	Sv	IP		AB	H	HR	RBI	Avg
Home	5	2	3.36	0	77.2	LHB	103	17	2	7	.165
Road	7	4	3.46	0	101.1	RHB	530	123	18	65	.232
First Half	4	3	3.38	0	88.0	Sc Pos	142	29	4	51	.204
Scnd Half	8	3	3.46	0	91.0	Clutch	27	9	0	4	.333

2002 Rankings (National League)

- 1st in ERA among rookies
- 2nd in lowest batting average allowed vs. lefthanded batters, lowest strikeout-walk ratio (1.2) and highest walks per nine innings (4.5)
- 3rd in wild pitches (13) and balks (2)
- 4th in lowest batting average allowed with runners in scoring position and wins among rookies
- Led the Braves in walks allowed, wild pitches (13), balks (2), lowest batting average allowed (.221) and lowest stolen-base percentage allowed (42.1)

Gary Sheffield

2002 Season

After a rocky experience in Los Angeles, Gary Sheffield found bliss in Atlanta. He struggled with injuries early last season and endured the worst slump of his career. He went hitless in a span of 29 at-bats and failed to drive in a run during a nine-game stretch, causing his average to fall to .203 in May. Sheffield bounced back to reach base in a team-record 52 straight games from May 28 to July 27, and paced the National League with 23 game-winning RBI.

Hitting

Sheffield has incredible quickness and great bat speed that allows him to drive the ball to all fields, although nearly all of his homers come when he pulls pitches to left. He has the eye and discipline of a batting champion and rarely chases outside pitches. While he can be fooled with low and outside breaking balls, Sheffield makes pitchers pay with offerings left hanging or over the plate. He also thrives in pressure situations, ranking fourth last year with a .367 batting average with runners in scoring position.

Baserunning & Defense

Sheffield may no longer pile up 25 steals the way he did in 1990, but maintains good speed and an excellent knowledge of how to run the bases. He picked his spots last year to succeed on 12 of 14 stolen base attempts. Sheffield is adequate defensively. He doesn't have a quick first step, and he allows many soft hits to land in front of him and near the right field line. He has an above-average arm with good accuracy, and accumulated seven assists last season.

2003 Outlook

Although the Braves expected a little more power production from Sheffield compared to what they received, he's an intimidating presence in the middle of their lineup and provides excellent protection for Chipper Jones. Opposing teams subtly pitched around Sheffield at times last year, which played a role in his failing to equal the 38 homers and 103 RBI he averaged the previous three campaigns. Those numbers, however, should be attainable this year for the Atlanta cleanup hitter.

Position: RF
Bats: R **Throws:** R
Ht: 6' 0" **Wt:** 205

Opening Day Age: 34
Born: 11/18/68 in Tampa, FL
ML Seasons: 15

Overall Statistics

G	AB	R	H	D	T	HR	RBI	SB	BB	SO	Avg	OBP	Slg
135	492	82	151	26	0	25	84	12	72	53	.307	.404	.512
1727	6153	1064	1819	319	21	340	1100	182	1024	741	.296	.399	.520

Where He Hits the Ball

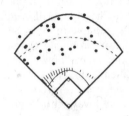

Vs. LHP	Vs. RHP

2002 Situational Stats

	AB	H	HR	RBI	Avg		AB	H	HR	RBI	Avg
Home	224	61	10	37	.272	LHP	82	24	2	8	.293
Road	268	90	15	47	.336	RHP	410	127	23	76	.310
First Half	275	73	15	46	.265	Sc Pos	120	44	8	62	.367
Scnd Half	217	78	10	38	.359	Clutch	70	25	6	14	.357

2002 Rankings (National League)

- 1st in batting average on an 0-2 count (.333)
- 3rd in batting average on the road
- 4th in batting average with runners in scoring position
- 5th in lowest fielding percentage in right field (.984)
- Led the Braves in hit by pitch (11), stolen-base percentage (85.7), highest percentage of pitches taken (58.6), highest percentage of swings put into play (48.8), batting average with runners in scoring position, batting average in the clutch, lowest percentage of swings on the first pitch (19.9) and batting average with two strikes (.256)

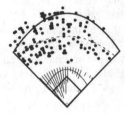

Atlanta

John Smoltz

2002 Season

Signed to a three-year, $30 million contract prior to last season, John Smoltz proved to be as valuable as a closer as he was as a Cy Young Award-winning starter. After an inconsistent April and May, Smoltz dominated unlike any closer in Braves history. He established a National League record with 55 saves, and the Braves went undefeated in his last 49 appearances.

Pitching

Smoltz is one of the game's premier competitors and the possessor of two of baseball's nastiest pitches. He throws his 97-98 MPH fastball harder than ever, while his 88-89 MPH slider looks like his heater before the bottom drops out. He also had success with his split-finger fastball again after abandoning the pitch a couple of years ago when he was bothered by arm problems. Smoltz has put his changeup and knuckleball on the shelf, preferring instead to challenge hitters with his power pitches. His command remains precise, and he throws hard enough to get away with leaving pitches up in the strike zone on occasion. Combine his ability to change the batter's eye level with his overpowering stuff, and Smoltz can be nearly impossible to hit.

Defense & Hitting

Smoltz is one of the Braves' best athletes, which is obvious with his fielding and hitting abilities. He has soft hands and runs extremely well, allowing him to cover everything in front of the mound as well as first base. While Smoltz batted only two times as a closer last season, he's a career .173 hitter with five homers and 51 RBI.

2003 Outlook

Even though the Braves couldn't be any happier to have Smoltz to call upon in the ninth inning, the righthander longs to start again. The free agency of Greg Maddux and Tom Glavine and the offseason activity of the Braves will determine Smoltz' future, but the plan calls for him to remain in the bullpen. He's more likely to deliver 40 saves than 15 wins.

Position: RP
Bats: R **Throws:** R
Ht: 6' 3" **Wt:** 220

Opening Day Age: 35
Born: 5/15/67 in Warren, MI
ML Seasons: 14

Overall Statistics

	W	L	Pct.	ERA	G	GS	Sv	IP	H	BB	SO	HR	Ratio
'02	3	2	.600	3.25	75	0	55	80.1	59	24	85	4	1.03
Car.	163	118	.580	3.34	467	361	65	2553.2	2204	808	2240	206	1.18

How Often He Throws Strikes

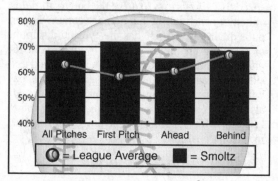

Graph values (All Pitches, First Pitch, Ahead, Behind):

Ⓞ = League Average   ■ = Smoltz

2002 Situational Stats

	W	L	ERA	Sv	IP		AB	H	HR	RBI	Avg
Home	3	2	4.10	24	37.1	LHB	141	30	1	17	.213
Road	0	0	2.51	31	43.0	RHB	146	29	3	14	.199
First Half	1	2	4.44	31	48.2	Sc Pos	70	19	1	25	.271
Scnd Half	2	0	1.42	24	31.2	Clutch	225	45	2	24	.200

2002 Rankings (National League)

- 1st in saves, save opportunities (59) and save percentage (93.2)
- 2nd in games finished (68)
- 5th in first batter efficiency (.149)
- 7th in fewest baserunners allowed per nine innings in relief (9.3)
- 10th in most strikeouts per nine innings in relief (9.5)
- Led the Braves in games pitched, saves, games finished (68), save opportunities (59), save percentage (93.2), relief innings (80.1) and most strikeouts per nine innings in relief (9.5)

Henry Blanco

Position: C
Bats: R **Throws:** R
Ht: 5'11" **Wt:** 220

Opening Day Age: 31
Born: 8/29/71 in Caracas, VZ
ML Seasons: 5
Pronunciation: BLAHN-ko

Overall Statistics

	G	AB	R	H	D	T	HR	RBI	SB	BB	SO	Avg	OBP	Slg
'02	81	221	17	45	9	1	6	22	0	20	51	.204	.267	.335
Car.	369	1087	110	241	63	7	26	113	4	124	222	.222	.300	.364

2002 Situational Stats

	AB	H	HR	RBI	Avg		AB	H	HR	RBI	Avg
Home	106	20	4	13	.189	LHP	38	8	2	7	.211
Road	115	25	2	9	.217	RHP	183	37	4	15	.202
First Half	96	18	2	8	.188	Sc Pos	54	10	1	16	.185
Scnd Half	125	27	4	14	.216	Clutch	30	8	2	6	.267

2002 Season

Acquired from the Brewers in a three-player deal during spring training, Henry Blanco served as Javy Lopez' backup and as Greg Maddux' personal catcher. The defensive specialist worked extensively with Atlanta's younger pitchers. Blanco struggled to hit .200, though he did manage to hit .267 in clutch situations.

Hitting, Baserunning & Defense

Blanco is one of the premier defensive catchers in the major leagues, and the possessor of one its strongest throwing arms. He threw out 19 of 56 basestealers last year. But that becomes more impressive since he caught Maddux, who basically ignores runners. Blanco attracts raves for his game-calling skills and his ability to block pitches in the dirt. Offensively, the pull hitter makes poor contact but has above-average power, with more than a third of his hits going for extra bases in each of the past four seasons. His catcher's speed means he's a station-to-station baserunner.

2003 Outlook

Blanco's inability to hit with any consistency has kept him from becoming anything more than a reserve in the major leagues. He's a solid addition to any team, although he must be careful about pricing himself out of the market as a free agent.

Mark DeRosa

Position: 2B/SS
Bats: R **Throws:** R
Ht: 6' 1" **Wt:** 205

Opening Day Age: 28
Born: 2/26/75 in Passaic, NJ
ML Seasons: 5

Overall Statistics

	G	AB	R	H	D	T	HR	RBI	SB	BB	SO	Avg	OBP	Slg
'02	72	212	24	63	9	2	5	23	2	12	24	.297	.339	.429
Car.	172	400	62	115	18	2	8	46	4	26	47	.288	.339	.403

2002 Situational Stats

	AB	H	HR	RBI	Avg		AB	H	HR	RBI	Avg
Home	87	28	3	9	.322	LHP	58	17	1	5	.293
Road	125	35	2	14	.280	RHP	154	46	4	18	.299
First Half	58	20	0	7	.345	Sc Pos	44	14	0	17	.318
Scnd Half	154	43	5	16	.279	Clutch	37	11	0	3	.297

2002 Season

With Marcus Giles ailing and Rafael Furcal struggling last May, Mark DeRosa earned the Braves' starting job at shortstop, only to succumb to damaged ligaments in his right ankle shortly after. DeRosa underwent surgery and missed two months before returning to give the Braves a lift off the bench and as an occasional starter.

Hitting, Baserunning & Defense

DeRosa is a selective contact hitter with surprising power and the ability to drive the ball into the gaps. Though not particularly fast, he's an aggressive baserunner who gets good jumps and knows when to take the extra base. DeRosa has good range, excellent hands and above-average arm strength. He does a consistent job of turning double plays from both middle infield positions. He also played third base and both corner outfield positions in 2002.

2003 Outlook

A shortstop throughout his professional career, DeRosa saw limited activity at second base before toiling for 32 games at the position last season. After going with Giles early and Keith Lockhart late in the campaign, the Braves appear willing to give DeRosa a well-deserved first shot at second base in 2003.

Julio Franco

Position: 1B
Bats: R **Throws:** R
Ht: 6' 1" **Wt:** 188

Opening Day Age: 44
Born: 8/23/58 in San Pedro de Macoris, DR
ML Seasons: 18

Overall Statistics

	G	AB	R	H	D	T	HR	RBI	SB	BB	SO	Avg	OBP	Slg
'02	125	338	51	96	13	1	6	30	5	39	75	.284	.357	.382
Car.	2041	7672	1168	2300	352	48	150	1022	265	802	1101	.300	.366	.417

2002 Situational Stats

	AB	H	HR	RBI	Avg		AB	H	HR	RBI	Avg
Home	165	46	3	18	.279	LHP	76	29	3	14	.382
Road	173	50	3	12	.289	RHP	262	67	3	16	.256
First Half	184	49	3	17	.266	Sc Pos	88	20	1	23	.227
Scnd Half	154	47	3	13	.305	Clutch	64	16	2	4	.250

2002 Season

Julio Franco continued to prove there's life in the major leagues after 40, platooning with Matt Franco at first base. The former Mexican League player started 72 games overall, and hit .315 in his final 72 contests. Franco tied for the team lead with seven pinch-hits, and recorded the 1,000th RBI of his career.

Hitting, Baserunning & Defense

Franco is a versatile hitter who batted everywhere from second to seventh in the lineup. He has an unorthodox swing and stance, which begins with the bat wrapped across the top of his head and his knees close together. When in sync, Franco produces line drives and sends many pitches to the opposite field. He runs well for his age and is smart on the basepaths. He also is a consistent defensive player with decent range and the ability to handle all types of throws.

2003 Outlook

Franco continues to prove he can play. The Braves have expressed interest in bringing him back in the same role. Based on his performance last year, Franco can produce a decent average as a part-time starter while providing some pop off the pines.

Matt Franco

Position: 1B
Bats: L **Throws:** R
Ht: 6' 1" **Wt:** 210

Opening Day Age: 33
Born: 8/19/69 in Santa Monica, CA
ML Seasons: 7

Overall Statistics

	G	AB	R	H	D	T	HR	RBI	SB	BB	SO	Avg	OBP	Slg
'02	81	205	25	65	15	4	6	30	1	27	31	.317	.395	.517
Car.	549	843	99	228	38	6	19	102	2	113	132	.270	.356	.397

2002 Situational Stats

	AB	H	HR	RBI	Avg		AB	H	HR	RBI	Avg
Home	86	30	3	15	.349	LHP	6	2	0	0	.333
Road	119	35	3	15	.294	RHP	199	63	6	30	.317
First Half	56	20	5	13	.357	Sc Pos	53	16	3	26	.302
Scnd Half	149	45	1	17	.302	Clutch	25	5	0	5	.200

2002 Season

The last cut of spring training, Matt Franco hit well at Triple-A Richmond and earned a May 29 promotion to Atlanta. He platooned with Julio Franco at first base and provided several clutch hits, including the first grand slam of his career.

Hitting, Baserunning & Defense

Franco is a leader by example with his exemplary work habits. After hitting almost exclusively against righthanders early in his career, Franco batted well over .300 against lefthanders as well as righties last year. He's an excellent fastball hitter with good power to all fields, and will make pitchers pay when they try to get ahead in the count with heat down the middle. Franco isn't fast, but is aggressive on the basepaths and ranked second on the team with four triples. He did a solid job at first base and is capable as a corner outfielder, even though his arm is a bit erratic.

2003 Outlook

Franco is a solid role player and an ideal complement on a championship-caliber club. He platoons without complaint, provides a potent bat off the pines and can start if needed for an extended period before his weaknesses become exposed. He's a Bobby Cox type of player and should find himself in a similar role with the Braves once again.

Marcus Giles

Position: 2B
Bats: R **Throws:** R
Ht: 5' 8" **Wt:** 180

Opening Day Age: 24
Born: 5/18/78 in San Diego, CA
ML Seasons: 2

Overall Statistics

	G	AB	R	H	D	T	HR	RBI	SB	BB	SO	Avg	OBP	Slg
'02	68	213	27	49	10	1	8	23	1	25	41	.230	.315	.399
Car.	136	457	63	113	20	3	17	54	3	53	78	.247	.327	.416

2002 Situational Stats

	AB	H	HR	RBI	Avg		AB	H	HR	RBI	Avg
Home	110	25	4	15	.227	LHP	38	6	1	1	.158
Road	103	24	4	8	.233	RHP	175	43	7	22	.246
First Half	152	36	5	12	.237	Sc Pos	50	9	2	14	.180
Scnd Half	61	13	3	11	.213	Clutch	45	11	3	7	.244

2002 Season

Marcus Giles endured a season to forget. After hitting .237 during the first two months as Atlanta's second baseman, Giles severely sprained his right ankle and went on the disabled list for six weeks. The injury, coupled with the death of a daughter born prematurely, landed Giles in Triple-A. He returned to Atlanta in August and hit .213 in 26 games.

Hitting, Baserunning & Defense

Giles is an offensive player with a powerful, compact stroke that produces line drives to all fields. While he struggled with runners in scoring position last year, he thrives in tight situations and is confident, enabling him to be effective off the bench. He has average speed but knows when to take an extra base. His hands are not soft and his arm is average, but he turns the double play well. His range at second base is more than adequate due to his quick first step.

2003 Outlook

With less than two full years in the major leagues, Giles' future is uncertain. He will have to reclaim his job at second base from a variety of contenders and could see action at both second and third base. With his ability to hit, Giles should garner a significant role at some point this season.

Chris Hammond

Position: RP
Bats: L **Throws:** L
Ht: 6' 1" **Wt:** 195

Opening Day Age: 37
Born: 1/21/66 in Atlanta, GA
ML Seasons: 10

Overall Statistics

	W	L	Pct.	ERA	G	GS	Sv	IP	H	BB	SO	HR	Ratio
'02	7	2	.778	0.95	63	0	0	76.0	53	31	63	1	1.11
Car.	53	57	.482	4.25	254	136	1	919.2	955	344	576	82	1.41

2002 Situational Stats

	W	L	ERA	Sv	IP		AB	H	HR	RBI	Avg
Home	3	0	1.36	0	33.0	LHB	92	16	1	8	.174
Road	4	2	0.63	0	43.0	RHB	180	37	0	11	.206
First Half	6	2	1.60	0	45.0	Sc Pos	78	13	1	19	.167
Scnd Half	1	0	0.00	0	31.0	Clutch	115	25	0	5	.217

2002 Season

Chris Hammond was considered retired from baseball after the 1998 season, but the lefthander returned to the minors in 2001 and received a non-roster invitation to Atlanta's camp last spring. He responded by joining Dennis Eckersley and Ferdie Schupp as the only pitchers in major league history to throw at least 70 innings and post an ERA below one.

Pitching, Defense & Hitting

Hammond's success centered on mixing his killer changeup and average fastball and slider with amazing effectiveness. His changeup is one of the best in baseball and makes his 85-MPH fastball look 5 MPH faster. He throws his moving heater on the inside corner of the plate with precision. An average fielder and good hitter, he's superb at holding runners on base with a deceptive pickoff move.

2003 Outlook

After allowing no earned runs in his final 32 outings, Hammond the free agent inspired the Yankees to give him a generous two-year deal. As a lefthander capable of bridging the gap between the starter and closer, the new-and-improved Hammond should remain a key bullpen ingredient for the foreseeable future.

Atlanta

367

Darren Holmes

Position: RP
Bats: R **Throws:** R
Ht: 6' 0" **Wt:** 202

Opening Day Age: 36
Born: 4/25/66 in
Asheville, NC
ML Seasons: 12

Overall Statistics

	W	L	Pct.	ERA	G	GS	Sv	IP	H	BB	SO	HR	Ratio
'02	2	2	.500	1.81	55	0	1	54.2	41	12	47	3	0.97
Car.	34	31	.523	4.25	509	6	59	638.0	662	245	535	58	1.42

2002 Situational Stats

	W	L	ERA	Sv	IP		AB	H	HR	RBI	Avg
Home	1	0	1.72	0	31.1	LHB	74	17	1	6	.230
Road	1	2	1.93	1	23.1	RHB	121	24	2	6	.198
First Half	2	1	1.51	1	35.2	Sc Pos	41	5	0	7	.122
Scnd Half	0	1	2.37	0	19.0	Clutch	67	17	1	6	.254

2002 Season

After sitting out the 2001 season due to major back surgery, Darren Holmes made a remarkable recovery and emerged as one of the stalwarts of a strong Atlanta bullpen. His 1.81 ERA ranked third among National League relievers. A 20-day stint on the disabled list in July with a lacerated right thumb served as his lone setback.

Pitching, Defense & Hitting

Holmes' best pitch is an over-the-top curveball that freezes hitters. The curve serves as an excellent complement to his 91-92 MPH fastball, decent changeup and sharp slider. He has excellent command of all his pitches, and didn't walk a batter until his 20th appearance last season. Holmes does a decent job of keeping the opposing running game in check, but he's a poor fielder who made three errors in 16 chances. He didn't bat in 2002, and his hitting prowess is worse than his fielding.

2003 Outlook

A free agent, Holmes signed a one-year deal with Atlanta to stay close to his North Carolina home. As a former closer, he brings determination to the setup role while giving hitters a variety of pitches to think about. Holmes should remain effective for a few more seasons, provided he stays healthy.

Kerry Ligtenberg

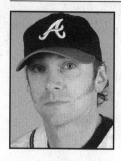

Position: RP
Bats: R **Throws:** R
Ht: 6' 2" **Wt:** 215

Opening Day Age: 31
Born: 5/11/71 in Rapid
City, SD
ML Seasons: 5
Pronunciation:
lite-en-berg

Overall Statistics

	W	L	Pct.	ERA	G	GS	Sv	IP	H	BB	SO	HR	Ratio
'02	3	4	.429	2.97	52	0	0	66.2	52	33	51	6	1.28
Car.	12	12	.500	3.04	254	0	44	266.2	208	115	256	27	1.21

2002 Situational Stats

	W	L	ERA	Sv	IP		AB	H	HR	RBI	Avg
Home	2	2	3.76	0	38.1	LHB	98	21	3	11	.214
Road	1	2	1.91	0	28.1	RHB	146	31	3	12	.212
First Half	2	3	2.35	0	38.1	Sc Pos	69	9	3	15	.130
Scnd Half	1	1	3.81	0	28.1	Clutch	49	8	2	6	.163

2002 Season

Kerry Ligtenberg overcame his traditional slow start in April to record his lowest ERA since 1998. Throughout his career, the righthander's ERA in April is 5.82, compared to 2.63 in all other months. He didn't allow an earned run from April 23 to June 7, a span of 11 outings.

Pitching, Defense & Hitting

Ligtenberg's aggressive approach tied him for second in the National League in first-batter efficiency by allowing only six hits in 42 at-bats. His pitches have a good sinking action that force hitters to keep the ball on the ground. His best pitch is a split-finger fastball, but he mixes a slider and four-seam fastball that touches the low 90s. He's an average fielder and quick to the plate, although basestealers succeeded on seven of nine attempts last year. His mediocre batting skills were not showcased in 2002.

2003 Outlook

Since June of 2001, Lightenberg has surrendered only 29 earned runs in 87 appearances, covering 108.2 innings. With that consistency, he should resume his stellar showings in middle relief.

Mike Remlinger

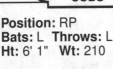

Position: RP
Bats: L **Throws:** L
Ht: 6' 1" **Wt:** 210

Opening Day Age: 37
Born: 3/23/66 in
Middletown, NY
ML Seasons: 10
Pronunciation:
REM-lin-jurr

Overall Statistics

	W	L	Pct.	ERA	G	GS	Sv	IP	H	BB	SO	HR	Ratio
'02	7	3	.700	1.99	73	0	0	68.0	48	28	69	3	1.12
Car.	44	41	.518	3.80	439	59	16	711.1	624	349	682	80	1.37

2002 Situational Stats

	W	L	ERA	Sv	IP		AB	H	HR	RBI	Avg
Home	2	0	2.27	0	31.2	LHB	68	16	1	8	.235
Road	5	3	1.73	0	36.1	RHB	174	32	2	11	.184
First Half	6	0	1.48	0	42.2	Sc Pos	61	13	0	15	.213
Scnd Half	1	3	2.84	0	25.1	Clutch	170	32	1	13	.188

2002 Season

For the fourth time in as many seasons, Mike Remlinger was the key to Atlanta's strong bullpen. The lefty surrendered one earned run over 30 outings from May 16 to July 26. His 1.99 ERA ranked seventh among NL relievers and earned him his first All-Star Game appearance.

Pitching, Defense & Hitting

Remlinger has a deep repertoire, including a late-breaking slider that held righties to a .184 average in '02. He throws a 90-92 MPH fastball with good movement and an effective changeup. His success depends on getting ahead in the count by challenging hitters. He holds runners with a deceptive delivery and pickoff move, allowing only two stolen bases over the past three seasons. His defense is average at best, and he's a poor batter.

2003 Outlook

The Cubs gave Remlinger a three-year, $10.65 million deal over the winter, and it's safe to say they didn't pay all that money to have him pitch middle relief. At the very least, he'll share the closer role with Antonio Alfonseca. He may get the majority of the save chances, but it's just as likely that the Cubs will sign a closer. He's never been a full-time closer, but he's capable of thriving in the role.

Tim Spooneybarger

Position: RP
Bats: R **Throws:** R
Ht: 6' 3" **Wt:** 190

Opening Day Age: 23
Born: 10/21/79 in San Diego, CA
ML Seasons: 2

Overall Statistics

	W	L	Pct.	ERA	G	GS	Sv	IP	H	BB	SO	HR	Ratio
'02	1	0	1.000	2.63	51	0	1	51.1	38	26	33	4	1.25
Car.	1	1	.500	2.60	55	0	1	55.1	43	28	36	4	1.28

2002 Situational Stats

	W	L	ERA	Sv	IP		AB	H	HR	RBI	Avg
Home	0	0	1.46	0	24.2	LHB	60	9	0	2	.150
Road	1	0	3.71	1	26.2	RHB	124	29	4	15	.234
First Half	0	0	2.95	0	21.1	Sc Pos	42	9	0	12	.214
Scnd Half	1	0	2.40	1	30.0	Clutch	85	16	2	6	.188

2002 Season

Tim Spooneybarger spent April and early May in Atlanta before toiling for more than six weeks at Triple-A. He then established himself in the Braves' bullpen during the campaign's final three months. The righthander held opponents to a .207 batting average, and didn't allow a run in 29 of his last 33 games.

Pitching, Defense & Hitting

Spooneybarger's forte is the incredible movement on all of his pitches. From a deceptive delivery, he throws a hard curveball along with a two-seam fastball that acts like a splitter. His four-seam fastball has a little hop and clocks consistently in the 92-94 MPH range. His performance increased proportionally with his confidence as the season progressed. Spooneybarger is a decent fielder who made one error in 13 chances. As a situational reliever, he's not very familiar with the lumber.

2003 Outlook

The Braves tried to make Spooneybarger a starter at the Class-A level in 2000, but he's blossomed since moving back to the bullpen. He may take on a key role in Florida's pen after being dealt to the Marlins in Atlanta's Mike Hampton deal in November.

Atlanta

Darren Bragg (Pos: RF/LF/CF, Age: 33, Bats: L)

	G	AB	R	H	D	T	HR	RBI	SB	BB	SO	Avg	OBP	Slg
'02	109	212	34	57	15	2	3	15	5	24	52	.269	.347	.401
Car.	765	2198	307	569	137	12	42	242	53	281	501	.259	.346	.389

After losing B.J. Surhoff for the season, the Braves called up Bragg from the minors to serve as their fourth outfielder. He topped 200 at-bats and hit a respectable .269 in the role. He is a free agent, but the Braves offered salary arbitration. 2003 Outlook: C

Joey Dawley (Pos: RHP, Age: 31)

	W	L	Pct.	ERA	G	GS	Sv	IP	H	BB	SO	HR	Ratio
'02	0	0	–	0.00	1	0	0	0.1	0	0	1	0	0.00
Car.	0	0	–	0.00	1	0	0	0.1	0	0	1	0	0.00

After 10 years in the minors, Dawley may be ready to make the jump. The righthander was solid with Triple-A Richmond in 2002, going 9-7 with a 2.63 ERA in 24 games, including 23 starts. 2003 Outlook: C

John Ennis (Pos: RHP, Age: 23)

	W	L	Pct.	ERA	G	GS	Sv	IP	H	BB	SO	HR	Ratio
'02	0	0	–	4.50	1	1	0	4.0	5	3	1	0	2.00
Car.	0	0	–	4.50	1	1	0	4.0	5	3	1	0	2.00

Ennis went 9-9 with a 4.18 ERA in 26 starts at Double-A last season. With Tom Glavine gone and Greg Maddux still unsigned, Ennis could be a part of the Braves' starting rotation in 2003. 2003 Outlook: C

John Foster (Pos: LHP, Age: 24)

	W	L	Pct.	ERA	G	GS	Sv	IP	H	BB	SO	HR	Ratio
'02	1	0	1.000	10.80	5	0	0	5.0	6	6	6	3	2.40
Car.	1	0	1.000	10.80	5	0	0	5.0	6	6	6	3	2.40

Foster made his major league debut early last season, but spent most of the year at Triple-A Richmond. The lefthander is 22-13 with a 2.80 ERA in 161 appearances over four minor league seasons. 2003 Outlook: C

Jesse Garcia (Pos: 2B, Age: 29, Bats: R)

	G	AB	R	H	D	T	HR	RBI	SB	BB	SO	Avg	OBP	Slg
'02	39	61	6	12	1	0	0	5	0	0	14	.197	.197	.213
Car.	92	112	17	20	1	0	2	7	6	4	20	.179	.207	.241

Garcia has split time between Atlanta and Triple-A Richmond the past two seasons. He hit .300 with Richmond and showed some power, but could not echo the performance with Atlanta. 2003 Outlook: C

Kevin Gryboski (Pos: RHP, Age: 29)

	W	L	Pct.	ERA	G	GS	Sv	IP	H	BB	SO	HR	Ratio
'02	2	1	.667	3.48	57	0	0	51.2	50	37	33	6	1.68
Car.	2	1	.667	3.48	57	0	0	51.2	50	37	33	6	1.68

Acquired from the Mariners, Gryboski enjoyed an impressive rookie season with Atlanta. Despite missing a month with a sore elbow, he appeared in 57 games, picking up two wins while posting a 3.48 ERA. 2003 Outlook: B

Wes Helms (Pos: 1B/3B, Age: 26, Bats: R)

	G	AB	R	H	D	T	HR	RBI	SB	BB	SO	Avg	OBP	Slg
'02	85	210	20	51	16	0	6	22	1	11	57	.243	.283	.405
Car.	198	444	50	104	27	3	17	60	2	32	119	.234	.287	.423

Helms has struggled to find a role with the Braves because of inconsistency. The team has experiment with him at first base and in the outfield in addition to his natural third base. He re-signed with Atlanta in December. 2002 Outlook: B

Ryan Langerhans (Pos: LF, Age: 23, Bats: L)

	G	AB	R	H	D	T	HR	RBI	SB	BB	SO	Avg	OBP	Slg
'02	1	1	0	0	0	0	0	0	0	0	0	.000	.000	.000
Car.	1	1	0	0	0	0	0	0	0	0	0	.000	.000	.000

Langerhans spent most of 2002 in Double-A, batting .251 in 109 games. With a little more experience, he could supply the Braves with a quality lefthanded bat off the bench in the coming years. 2003 Outlook: C

Keith Lockhart (Pos: 2B, Age: 38, Bats: L)

	G	AB	R	H	D	T	HR	RBI	SB	BB	SO	Avg	OBP	Slg
'02	128	296	34	64	13	3	5	32	0	27	50	.216	.282	.331
Car.	917	2173	272	568	112	16	41	260	30	182	249	.261	.318	.384

Lockhart appeared in 128 games, starting 72, after signing a minor league deal with the Braves last winter. He struggled, batting just .216. The 38-year-old again is a free agent and could re-sign. 2003 Outlook: C

Albie Lopez (Pos: RHP, Age: 31)

	W	L	Pct.	ERA	G	GS	Sv	IP	H	BB	SO	HR	Ratio
'02	1	4	.200	4.37	30	4	0	55.2	66	18	39	1	1.51
Car.	43	56	.434	4.73	282	92	4	818.2	897	326	543	105	1.49

The Braves signed Lopez to a one-year deal last winter in hopes of using him as their fifth starter. However, an early-season groin injury and lingering shoulder tendinitis limited his time. 2003 Outlook: C

Andy Pratt (Pos: LHP, Age: 23)

	W	L	Pct.	ERA	G	GS	Sv	IP	H	BB	SO	HR	Ratio
'02	0	0	–	6.75	1	0	0	1.1	1	4	1	0	3.75
Car.	0	0	–	6.75	1	0	0	1.1	1	4	1	0	3.75

Pratt was 4-2 with a 3.10 ERA in six starts with Triple-A Richmond. He struck out 36 and walked just nine in 40.2 innings. Making the Braves rotation in 2003 is doubtful, but he is only 23. 2003 Outlook: C

Aaron Small (Pos: RHP, Age: 31)

	W	L	Pct.	ERA	G	GS	Sv	IP	H	BB	SO	HR	Ratio
'02	0	0	–	27.00	1	0	0	0.1	2	2	1	0	12.00
Car.	15	10	.600	5.27	139	3	4	201.2	243	94	113	19	1.67

Small appeared in one game with the Braves in April before being designated for assignment. He spent the rest of the season in the minors, going 0-3 with a 6.39 ERA for Triple-A Richmond. 2003 Outlook: C

B.J. Surhoff (**Pos**: 1B, **Age**: 38, **Bats**: L)

	G	AB	R	H	D	T	HR	RBI	SB	BB	SO	Avg	OBP	Slg
'02	25	75	5	22	5	0	0	9	1	9	5	.293	.369	.360
Car.	2029	7293	951	2048	397	39	170	1028	137	570	732	.281	.331	.416

Surhoff hit .293, but was limited to just 25 games in 2002, having his season cut short by a torn ligament in his right knee. At 38, he may not have much left in the tank. 2003 Outlook: C

Steve Torrealba (**Pos**: C, **Age**: 25, **Bats**: R)

	G	AB	R	H	D	T	HR	RBI	SB	BB	SO	Avg	OBP	Slg
'02	13	17	1	1	0	0	0	1	0	3	4	.059	.200	.059
Car.	15	19	1	2	0	0	0	1	0	3	4	.105	.227	.105

Torrealba has displayed skills on defense, but the catcher has yet to find his groove at the plate. In eight minor league seasons, he has batted a disappointing .243. The Cardinals signed him to a minor league deal. 2003 Outlook: C

Atlanta Braves Minor League Prospects

Organization Overview:

No team has been more dedicated to player development over the past decade than the Braves. The system has been productive in developing players for the major league roster and providing trade bait for established veterans during the team's record 11 consecutive division titles. While the upper reaches of the organization have been a little bare of late, three consecutive deep drafts conducted by scouting director Roy Clark have left the Braves with an incredible amount of talent in the lower reaches of the minors, highlighted by young pitching. Both of Atlanta's Class-A affiliates featured stacked rotations last year, while the Rookie-level clubs in the Appalachian and Gulf Coast leagues had a similar situation with promising arms such as Anthony Lerew, Dan Meyer, Manuel Mateo and Kyle Davies.

Matt Belisle

Position: P **Opening Day Age:** 22
Bats: R **Throws:** R **Born:** 6/6/80 in Austin,
Ht: 6' 3" **Wt:** 195 TX

Recent Statistics

	W	L	ERA	G	GS	Sv	IP	H	R	BB	SO	HR
2002 AA Greenville	5	9	4.35	26	26	0	159.1	162	91	39	123	18

Belisle experienced an inconsistent first half at Double-A Greenville last year before putting things together down the stretch. The righthander missed all of the 2001 campaign after undergoing surgery to repair a ruptured disc in his back. His rustiness was apparent early last year, but Belisle is a tenacious pitcher with a low-to-mid 90s fastball, along with a changeup and slider. He possesses excellent command of all three pitches and mixes them well to keep hitters off balance. Drafted in the second round in 1998, Belisle is on the verge of polishing the rough edges of his game before making his push for the major league rotation.

Wilson Betemit

Position: SS **Opening Day Age:** 21
Bats: B **Throws:** R **Born:** 11/2/81 in Santo
Ht: 6' 2" **Wt:** 155 Domingo, DR

Recent Statistics

	G	AB	R	H	D	T	HR	RBI	SB	BB	SO	Avg
2001 A Myrtle Beach	84	318	38	88	20	1	7	43	8	23	71	.277
2001 AA Greenville	47	183	22	65	14	0	5	19	6	12	36	.355
2001 NL Atlanta	8	3	1	0	0	0	0	0	1	2	3	.000
2002 AAA Richmond	93	343	43	84	17	1	8	34	8	34	82	.245
2002 R Braves	7	19	2	5	4	0	0	2	1	5	2	.263

After blazing through the organization in 2001, Betemit battled nagging injuries last season that included a strained back, bruised foot and sprained ankle. While he wound up having a disappointing season at Triple-A Richmond, batting just .245 with eight homers and 34 RBI, Betemit's future remains bright. He's a five-tool

talent whose skills still are blossoming. He hits to all fields from both sides of the plate and is adding power as his 21-year-old body continues to mature. His glove at shortstop is steady, and he brings a strong arm and soft hands to the position. Betemit should regroup this year and once again contend for a spot on the Atlanta roster by the end of the season.

Jung Bong

Position: P **Opening Day Age:** 22
Bats: L **Throws:** L **Born:** 7/15/80 in Seoul,
Ht: 6' 3" **Wt:** 175 South Korea

Recent Statistics

	W	L	ERA	G	GS	Sv	IP	H	R	BB	SO	HR
2002 AA Greenville	7	8	3.25	27	17	2	122.0	136	59	45	107	6
2002 NL Atlanta	0	1	7.50	1	1	0	6.0	8	5	2	4	0

Bong received his first start in the major leagues early last season when the Braves were faced with a shortage of starters. While he was with Atlanta for little more than 24 hours, Bong proved that his future lies at the game's top level. He spent most of last year at Double-A Greenville, going into a tailspin shortly after returning from the majors, before working out his control problems in the bullpen. He finished the campaign on a strong note with a 7-8 record and 3.25 ERA in 27 appearances. Command of his pitches is the key to Bong's game. He throws an excellent changeup with a high-80s fastball and a decent curveball. A native of Korea, Bong has the potential to be a solid No. 3 or 4 starter in the major leagues.

Trey Hodges

Position: P **Opening Day Age:** 24
Bats: R **Throws:** R **Born:** 6/29/78 in
Ht: 6' 3" **Wt:** 187 Houston, TX

Recent Statistics

	W	L	ERA	G	GS	Sv	IP	H	R	BB	SO	HR
2002 AAA Richmond	15	9	3.19	28	28	0	172.1	158	66	56	116	9
2002 NL Atlanta	2	0	5.40	4	0	0	11.2	16	7	2	6	2

Hodges has raced through the Atlanta organization since he was drafted in the 17th round out of LSU in 2000. He was named the high Class-A Carolina League Pitcher of the Year after going 15-8 with a 2.76 ERA in 2001. He then led the Triple-A International League with 15 victories in 2002. Hodges may not be overpowering, but he has good movement on his pitches and maintains excellent command. His fastball resides in the low 90s, and he mixes it well with a changeup, slider and a slow curveball that improved immensely last season. Hodges wasn't overmatched during four appearances in Atlanta in September, giving up only four hits and one run in his last two outings. He will be a candidate in 2003 to become the Braves' No. 5 starter.

Andy Marte

Position: 3B **Opening Day Age:** 19
Bats: R **Throws:** R **Born:** 10/21/83 in Villa
Ht: 6' 1" **Wt:** 185 Tapia, DR

Recent Statistics

	G	AB	R	H	D	T	HR	RBI	SB	BB	SO	Avg
2001 R Danville	37	125	12	25	6	0	1	12	3	20	45	.200
2002 A Macon	126	488	69	137	32	4	21	105	2	41	114	.281

The Braves believe they may have found their future third baseman based on the way Marte developed at Class-A Macon last season. He led the South Atlantic League with 105 RBI while hitting 21 homers. Signed out of the Dominican Republic for $600,000 in 2000, Marte is a classic power-hitting third baseman with soft hands and excellent reflexes. He won't celebrate his 20th birthday until October 21, which will make him one of the youngest players this year in either the high Class-A Carolina League or the Double-A Southern League. Marte is on the fast track to the major leagues and should be knocking on the door in the near future.

Kenny Nelson

Position: P **Opening Day Age:** 21
Bats: R **Throws:** R **Born:** 8/26/81 in Clinton,
Ht: 6' 2" **Wt:** 200 MD

Recent Statistics

	W	L	ERA	G	GS	Sv	IP	H	R	BB	SO	HR
2001 A Macon	12	8	3.93	25	24	0	151.0	144	76	57	154	16
2002 A Myrtle Beach	11	5	1.72	23	23	0	135.2	98	37	44	105	4
2002 R Braves	0	0	0.00	3	3	0	5.0	1	0	1	7	0

Aside from a five-inning rehab stint in the Rookie-level Gulf Coast League, Nelson spent the entire 2002 season at high Class-A Myrtle Beach and topped the minor leagues with a 1.66 ERA. The overpowering righthander got better as the season progressed, allowing just one earned run over his last four starts. His biggest step came in reducing his home runs allowed. After surrendering 16 roundtrippers in 2001, Nelson gave up only four last season, including none in his final seven outings. He was a second-round draft pick in 2000 and throws a heavy 93-95 MPH fastball, along with an improving changeup and curveball. Nelson could be less than a full season from the major leagues.

Billy Sylvester

Position: P **Opening Day Age:** 26
Bats: R **Throws:** R **Born:** 10/1/76 in
Ht: 6' 5" **Wt:** 218 Darlington, SC

Recent Statistics

	W	L	ERA	G	GS	Sv	IP	H	R	BB	SO	HR
2001 AA Greenville	1	0	2.37	26	0	12	30.1	18	8	24	41	3
2001 AAA Richmond	0	4	5.11	36	0	11	37.0	28	21	27	41	2
2002 AAA Richmond	0	0	3.86	7	0	1	9.1	10	4	5	5	1
2002 AA Greenville	2	3	3.47	51	0	25	49.1	31	20	32	48	6

Free agency figures to take its toll on the Atlanta bullpen prior to the 2003 season. One of the first places the Braves will look for a replacement will be the righthanded Sylvester, who has become one of the most consistent closers in the organization. He spent most of last season at Double-A Greenville and posted 25 saves. Signed as a nondrafted free agent in 1997, Sylvester emerged as a closer at high Class-A Myrtle Beach with 16 saves in 2000, before saving 23 games between Greenville and Triple-A Richmond in 2001. While he has battled control problems at times, Sylvester has an excellent 93-95 MPH fastball, a sharp-breaking curveball and an average splitter.

Adam Wainwright

Position: P **Opening Day Age:** 21
Bats: R **Throws:** R **Born:** 8/30/81 in
Ht: 6' 6" **Wt:** 190 Brunswick, GA

Recent Statistics

	W	L	ERA	G	GS	Sv	IP	H	R	BB	SO	HR
2001 A Macon	10	10	3.77	28	28	0	164.2	144	89	48	184	9
2002 A Myrtle Beach	9	6	3.31	28	28	0	163.1	149	67	66	167	7

Wainwright has been one of the top pitching prospects in the minors since the Braves drafted him in the first round in 2000. In his first full professional season, in 2001, he registered 184 strikeouts while going 10-10 with a 3.77 ERA at Class-A Macon. Wainwright then made the jump to high Class-A Myrtle Beach last season and posted a 9-6 mark. Hitters have a hard time making consistent contact with his low-90s fastball and its excellent movement. His curveball and changeup also are outstanding offerings and keep hitters off balance. At 6-foot-6, Wainwright has an intimidating presence on the mound as well as the overall stuff to pile up innings at higher levels.

Others to Watch

Mike Hessman (25) ranked second in the Triple-A International League last year with 26 home runs. A third baseman who also is adept at handling the chores at first base and left field, Hessman has the makings of a power-hitting corner infielder if he can continue to improve upon making consistent contact at the plate. . . Shortstop **Kelly Johnson** (21) stumbled last year at high Class-A Myrtle Beach after putting together one of the brighter offensive shows in 2001 at Class-A Macon. A supplemental first-round pick in 2000, Johnson was named the top prospect in the Southern Atlantic League in 2001 after hitting .289 with 23 home runs, 66 RBI and 25 stolen bases. . . Lefthander **Horacio Ramirez** (23) missed most of the 2001 season due to reconstructive elbow surgery. He then battled through a dead arm shortly after reporting to Double-A Greenville last summer. A fifth-round draft pick in 1997, Ramirez got stronger as last season progressed and tied for the team lead with nine wins. . . Third baseman **Scott Thorman** (21) overwhelmed Class-A South Atlantic League pitching last year. Atlanta's second first-round draft pick in 2000, he missed all of 2001 after undergoing shoulder surgery. The lefthanded hitter moved from third base to first base after the operation, yet still is capable of throwing the ball more than 90 MPH.

Wrigley Field

Offense

Last year was the second summer in a row that Wrigley's friendly winds were far less prevalent than normal. Wrigley has more variability in terms of temperature and wind than the average major league park, and it isn't terribly unusual for it to favor the pitcher over the course of an entire season, as it has done in each of the last two seasons. Nothing has changed, though, and chances are it will revert to form next year if the weather is more typical. The small foul area and unusually short alleys make it a good hitters' park and home-run park.

Defense

The long grass helps groundball pitchers and can disguise an infielder's lack of range. The center fielder is required to cover less territory here than in any other major league park. It helps to have a strong arm in right, as the right-field corner is a lot deeper than normal.

Who It Helps the Most

Hitters who can take advantage of the alleys and groundball pitchers who can avoid home runs and keep the ball on the infield are served well at Wrigley. Alex Gonzalez hit 13 of his 18 homers here. Antonio Alfonseca, a groundballer, pitched very well here in his first season as a Cub. Jon Lieber has thrived here via the Ferguson Jenkins route, minimizing walks so as to hold most of the inevitable home runs to solo shots.

Who It Hurts the Most

Corey Patterson hasn't hit well here, which is curious, since he's tried to take a power hitter's approach. Matt Clement fits the profile of the type of pitcher who ought to succeed here, but didn't get results last year. Mark Prior, on the other hand, is a flyball pitcher and paid for it at times in 2002, although it shouldn't prevent him from developing.

Rookies & Newcomers

First baseman Hee Seop Choi is the kind of power hitter who should thrive here. Bobby Hill should do all right as long as he tries to hit the ball over the infield as well as through it.

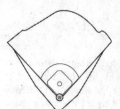

Dimensions: LF-355, LCF-368, CF-400, RCF-368, RF-353

Capacity: 39,111

Elevation: 595 feet

Surface: Grass

Foul Territory: Small

Park Factors

2002 Season

	Home Games Cubs	Opp	Total	Away Games Cubs	Opp	Total	Index
G	75	75	150	75	75	150	
Avg	.236	.243	.240	.253	.266	.259	92
AB	2467	2568	5035	2618	2473	5091	99
R	305	342	647	336	358	694	93
H	583	623	1206	662	659	1321	91
2B	107	125	232	129	130	259	91
3B	13	10	23	16	19	35	66
HR	88	93	181	90	58	148	124
BB	286	265	551	255	289	544	102
SO	580	680	1260	591	549	1140	112
E	58	42	100	49	51	100	100
E-Infield	48	36	84	43	42	85	99
LHB-Avg	.236	.247	.241	.251	.277	.263	92
LHB-HR	38	35	73	43	30	73	101
RHB-Avg	.237	.239	.238	.255	.258	.256	93
RHB-HR	50	58	108	47	28	75	146

2000-2002

	Home Games Cubs	Opp	Total	Away Games Cubs	Opp	Total	Index
G	221	221	442	221	221	442	
Avg	.255	.243	.249	.252	.272	.262	95
AB	7284	7572	14856	7680	7403	15083	98
R	987	994	1981	1037	1169	2206	90
H	1858	1838	3696	1937	2013	3950	94
2B	332	351	683	394	408	802	86
3B	37	24	61	42	56	98	63
HR	246	257	503	270	253	523	98
BB	842	810	1652	782	848	1630	103
SO	1553	1852	3405	1604	1634	3238	107
E	134	148	282	156	145	301	94
E-Infield	105	125	230	131	125	256	90
LHB-Avg	.242	.239	.240	.232	.279	.255	94
LHB-HR	85	95	180	112	114	226	79
RHB-Avg	.264	.245	.254	.265	.267	.266	96
RHB-HR	161	162	323	158	139	297	112

2002 Rankings (National League)

- Second-highest strikeout factor
- Second-highest RHB home-run factor
- Third-highest home-run factor
- Third-lowest batting-average factor
- Third-lowest hit factor
- Third-lowest RHB batting-average factor

Dusty Baker

2002 Season

Dusty Baker's experiences last year couldn't have been more different than that of the Cubs. Baker led the strong but hardly-feared Giants to a wild-card berth, won the National League pennant and came within a handful of outs of winning the World Series. The Cubs, on the other hand, came into the year with several key additions and high expectations, but immediately flopped.

Offense

Baker's overriding philosophy is to keep his players productive by keeping them in a good frame of mind. That can mean juggling the batting order if things aren't going well, even if the batting order isn't necessarily the problem. With regard to strategic decisions, he's within the bounds of convention, although he may rely on one-run strategies a bit less now that he's in Wrigley Field instead of pitcher-friendly Pac Bell. He very rarely has put a completely untested player into the everyday lineup, so it's hard to say how he might handle the situation if rookie Hee Seop Choi struggles. Baker's ability to be patient with youngsters also may be tested with Bobby Hill and Corey Patterson.

Pitching & Defense

Baker has pushed his starters fairly hard, but he also recognized that he needed to take it easier on guys with less stamina such as Kirk Rueter. Baker could have several young starters in the rotation, so it will be important to nurture the ones who need to be protected. Baker also must completely sort out the bullpen. Though he was accused of overusing his relievers at times, he did a good job overall of handling the Giants' pen. Perhaps he can do for a hard thrower like Kyle Farnsworth or Frank Beltran what he did for Felix Rodriguez.

2003 Outlook

Baker comes in with an enviable resume and inherits a team with great young talent. Still, he faces new challenges. He'll need to do something he never had to do in San Francisco—start a number of young players in key roles. He will have to balance the team's long-term future against its immediate needs. This year, the former issue probably deserves the highest priority.

Born: 6/15/49 in Riverside, CA

Playing Experience: 1968-1986, Atl, LA, SF, Oak

Managerial Experience: 10 seasons

Manager Statistics

Year	Team, Lg	W	L	Pct	GB	Finish
2002	San Francisco, NL	95	66	.590	2.5	2nd West
10 Seasons		840	715	.540	–	–

2002 Starting Pitchers by Days Rest

	<=3	4	5	6+
Giants Starts	0	90	52	14
Giants ERA	–	3.88	3.85	4.30
NL Avg Starts	1	88	42	21
NL ERA	3.18	4.22	4.14	4.58

2002 Situational Stats

	Dusty Baker	NL Average
Hit & Run Success %	35.8	36.5
Stolen Base Success %	77.9	68.3
Platoon Pct.	42.0	52.7
Defensive Subs	16	19
High-Pitch Outings	19	7
Quick/Slow Hooks	22/9	24/11
Sacrifice Attempts	92	95

2002 Rankings (National League)

- 1st in stolen-base percentage, fewest caught stealings of second base (20), fewest caught stealings of third base (1) and starts with over 120 pitches (19)

Chicago (NL)

Antonio Alfonseca

2002 Season

The Cubs acquired Antonio Alfonseca from Florida shortly before Opening Day to replace closer Tom Gordon, who'd suffered a serious shoulder injury a few weeks earlier. Alfonseca filled the void capably in the first half of 2002, although save opportunities were few and far between. He ran into control problems during a very rough stretch in July and August, however, and by September the club seemed to lose faith in him.

Position: RP
Bats: R **Throws:** R
Ht: 6' 5" **Wt:** 250

Opening Day Age: 30
Born: 4/16/72 in La Romana, DR
ML Seasons: 6
Pronunciation: AL-fon-say-ka
Nickname: Pulpo, Dragonslayer

Pitching

Few pitchers rely as heavily on one pitch as Alfonseca does on his mid-90s power sinker. He gives righthanded hitters fits by buzzing it in on their fists. Lefthanded hitters are more apt to see some of his other pitches, like his four-seamer, slider and changeup. He never has come up with an effective approach to them, and they continued to hound him last year. He can be hit, but rarely is hit solidly, so he gets fewer strikeouts than the typical closer but a huge number of groundballs. Though he's said to thrive on frequent work, in each of the past two seasons he's been at his worst when used on consecutive days.

Defense & Hitting

Alfonseca doesn't hold runners all that well, and basestealers had an easier time against him last year without Charles Johnson around to protect him. A big man, Alfonseca doesn't move that well but handles what he gets to. He got his first two major league hits last year, and they might be his last for a while.

2003 Outlook

Alfonseca's disastrous second half all but forced the Cubs' hand, and his tenure as the main man in Chicago expired when the team signed free-agent reliever Mike Remlinger over the winter. Remlinger may secure the job himself, or he may share it with Alfonseca. It's just as likely the Cubs will sign a closer and have Remlinger and Alfonseca share setup duties, though both would pick up the odd save from time to time.

Overall Statistics

	W	L	Pct.	ERA	G	GS	Sv	IP	H	BB	SO	HR	Ratio
'02	2	5	.286	4.00	66	0	19	74.1	73	36	61	5	1.47
Car.	20	29	.408	3.81	340	0	121	380.0	413	147	259	35	1.47

How Often He Throws Strikes

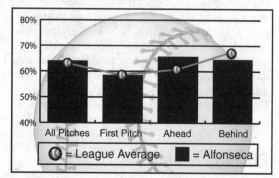

2002 Situational Stats

	W	L	ERA	Sv	IP		AB	H	HR	RBI	Avg
Home	2	0	1.91	13	37.2	LHB	125	38	3	24	.304
Road	0	5	6.14	6	36.2	RHB	159	35	2	18	.220
First Half	1	1	2.61	11	38.0	Sc Pos	103	23	1	34	.223
Scnd Half	1	4	5.45	8	36.1	Clutch	171	44	4	30	.257

2002 Rankings (National League)
- 1st in blown saves (9) and lowest save percentage (67.9)
- 10th in games finished (55)
- Led the Cubs in saves, games finished (55), save opportunities (28), save percentage (67.9) and blown saves (9)

Moises Alou

2002 Season

Signed to a three-year deal in December 2001 to play left field and bat fifth, Moises Alou was seen as the final component that would make the Cubs' heart of the order one the most fearsome around. The plan failed, and the one player who fell the shortest of expectations was Alou. Bothered by a strained calf and sore back, he contributed next to nothing over the first seven weeks of the season as the Cubs fell hopelessly behind. Alou recovered somewhat over the second half, but it still was the least productive season of his career.

Hitting

Alou is known as one of the best fastball hitters in the majors, and he excels at jumping on the first pitch when pitchers try to get ahead with one. He's primarily a pull-hitter, but is capable of hitting the ball hard up the middle or the other way. He had been one of the best hitters in baseball against southpaws until last year, when physical problems seemed to affect him across the board. Being aggressive early in the count keeps his walks and strikeouts down.

Baserunning & Defense

Alou has lost a step or two to leg injuries over the years and isn't quite as aggressive on the bases as he once was. He's still capable of swiping an occasional base, however, and was successful on all eight steal attempts last year. He has average range for a left fielder. His arm is more than strong enough for the position but not always accurate. He posted six assists from left field in 2002.

2003 Outlook

As he showed in the second half last year, Alou still is capable of being a productive hitter when healthy. However, he has missed 92 games over the last three seasons since coming back from a knee injury that wiped out his 1999 campaign, and he'll turn 37 this summer. He likely will bounce back somewhat if his body allows, but it's far from a given.

Position: LF
Bats: R **Throws:** R
Ht: 6' 3" **Wt:** 220

Opening Day Age: 36
Born: 7/3/66 in Atlanta, GA
ML Seasons: 11
Pronunciation: MOY-zes ah-LOO

Overall Statistics

	G	AB	R	H	D	T	HR	RBI	SB	BB	SO	Avg	OBP	Slg
'02	132	484	50	133	23	1	15	61	8	47	61	.275	.337	.419
Car.	1313	4722	746	1430	283	30	217	895	89	493	639	.303	.368	.513

Where He Hits the Ball

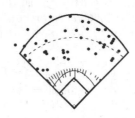

Vs. LHP   **Vs. RHP**

2002 Situational Stats

	AB	H	HR	RBI	Avg		AB	H	HR	RBI	Avg
Home	207	59	7	27	.285	LHP	115	37	2	12	.322
Road	277	74	8	34	.267	RHP	369	96	13	49	.260
First Half	242	61	8	27	.252	Sc Pos	128	28	1	39	.219
Scnd Half	242	72	7	34	.298	Clutch	85	16	1	7	.188

2002 Rankings (National League)

- 1st in fielding percentage in left field (.990)
- 3rd in batting average with the bases loaded (.500)
- 6th in highest percentage of swings on the first pitch (39.3)
- 7th in lowest batting average on a 3-2 count (.108)
- 10th in assists in left field (6) and fewest pitches seen per plate appearance (3.31)
- Led the Cubs in GDPs (15), highest percentage of swings put into play (48.2), batting average with the bases loaded (.500) and batting average at home

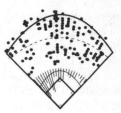

Chicago (NL)

Mark Bellhorn

2002 Season

One of the most pleasant surprises in baseball last year was Mark Bellhorn. The Cubs had obtained the switch-hitting infielder from the Athletics the previous winter. He came into the 2002 campaign with a career average below .200 and barely made the Opening Day roster. Playing all over the infield, he hit for decent power in the first half and won the second-base job in July, later shifting to third. He even served as the leadoff man for part of the year.

Hitting

From either side of the plate, Bellhorn's defining characteristic is his willingness to take a pitch, even a strike. It's a double-edged sword, as it helps him work a lot of walks but often leaves him in two-strike situations. He has good power as both a lefty and righty from straightaway center to the foul line. He's a pronounced pull-hitter from the right side; from the left, he's an extreme fly-ball hitter who likes the ball out over the plate. His emphasis on power and his inability to shorten up with two strikes probably will prevent him from ever hitting for a good average.

Baserunning & Defense

Bellhorn has experience at both second and third and performed adequately at both spots, showing average range and decent hands. His arm is strong enough for the hot corner, and his double-play pivot was fairly good at the keystone. He even held his own at shortstop and first. He runs fairly well and has stolen a few bases in the past, but he was successful just three times after hurting his wrist stealing a base in May.

2003 Outlook

Despite his success last year, it's far from certain that Bellhorn will play regularly this year. Highly anticipated prospect Bobby Hill's late-season success at second probably means the only open position for Bellhorn will be third base. Whether he's a starter or a regular non-regular, Bellhorn should continue to produce.

Position: 2B/3B/1B/SS
Bats: B **Throws:** R
Ht: 6' 1" **Wt:** 205

Opening Day Age: 28
Born: 8/23/74 in Boston, MA
ML Seasons: 5

Overall Statistics

	G	AB	R	H	D	T	HR	RBI	SB	BB	SO	Avg	OBP	Slg
'02	146	445	86	115	24	4	27	56	7	76	144	.258	.374	.512
Car.	272	768	133	179	35	7	34	80	16	120	261	.233	.342	.430

Where He Hits the Ball

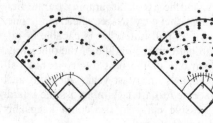

Vs. LHP   **Vs. RHP**

2002 Situational Stats

	AB	H	HR	RBI	Avg		AB	H	HR	RBI	Avg
Home	213	53	15	28	.249	LHP	122	37	10	24	.303
Road	232	62	12	28	.267	RHP	323	78	17	32	.241
First Half	163	43	11	27	.264	Sc Pos	97	24	6	33	.247
Scnd Half	282	72	16	29	.255	Clutch	91	18	3	7	.198

2002 Rankings (National League)

- 2nd in on-base percentage for a leadoff hitter (.389)
- 4th in slugging percentage vs. lefthanded pitchers (.672)
- 6th in most pitches seen per plate appearance (4.21)
- 7th in strikeouts
- 8th in highest percentage of pitches taken (61.2) and lowest groundball-flyball ratio (0.8)
- Led the Cubs in caught stealing (5), strikeouts, most pitches seen per plate appearance (4.21), highest percentage of pitches taken (61.2), on-base percentage for a leadoff hitter (.389) and highest percentage of extra bases taken as a runner (53.8)

Matt Clement

Position: SP
Bats: R **Throws:** R
Ht: 6' 3" **Wt:** 213

Opening Day Age: 28
Born: 8/12/74 in McCandless Township, PA
ML Seasons: 5
Pronunciation: clu-MENT

2002 Season

For the second straight season, Matt Clement was traded just days before Opening Day. This time he went to the Cubs, where he broke out with the kind of season his previous two employers had expected but never had received from him. He cut nearly a run and a half off his ERA and was among the league leaders in strikeouts and opponent batting average. He went 12-11 for a team that lost 95 games, and with a better team behind him, he could have been an even bigger winner.

Pitching

Clement always has had terrific stuff—perhaps *too* good. His low-90s sinking fastball and hard slider have so much action that he'd long struggled to keep from falling behind in the count. Last year he became more consistent with his command of the fastball, and being able to pitch from ahead in the count made all the difference. He also throws a straight four-seamer and a changeup. Stamina had been a problem in the past, but Clement maintained his stuff late into games much more effectively last year as well. He also stayed cooler under pressure, pitching out of jams rather than yielding to frustration.

Defense & Hitting

Clement has no pickoff move—he throws over less frequently than any major league starter—but controls the running game very well by getting the ball to the plate quickly. He's otherwise adequate in the field, but no more. Bunting is his only skill at the plate; he's one of the absolute worst-hitting pitchers in the majors. He struck out 34 times last year, the third-highest total in the majors among pitchers.

2003 Outlook

Every indication is that Clement has turned the corner and matured into the pitcher he's always had the potential to become. He could be a fine pitcher and a consistent winner even if he never goes beyond the level he reached last year. He likely has many good years ahead of him.

Overall Statistics

	W	L	Pct.	ERA	G	GS	Sv	IP	H	BB	SO	HR	Ratio
'02	12	11	.522	3.60	32	32	0	205.0	162	85	215	18	1.20
Car.	46	50	.479	4.55	132	130	0	773.2	733	388	667	73	1.45

How Often He Throws Strikes

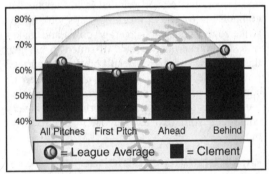

2002 Situational Stats

	W	L	ERA	Sv	IP		AB	H	HR	RBI	Avg
Home	6	6	4.57	0	106.1	LHB	341	75	7	34	.220
Road	6	5	2.55	0	98.2	RHB	411	87	11	40	.212
First Half	6	6	3.85	0	110.0	Sc Pos	153	36	3	53	.235
Scnd Half	6	5	3.32	0	95.0	Clutch	21	8	1	3	.381

2002 Rankings (National League)

- 1st in lowest ERA on the road
- 3rd in lowest batting average allowed (.215)
- 4th in shutouts (2), strikeouts, lowest slugging percentage allowed (.344) and most strikeouts per nine innings (9.4)
- 7th in lowest on-base percentage allowed (.299), lowest batting average allowed vs. righthanded batters and lowest fielding percentage at pitcher (.939)
- Led the Cubs in sacrifice bunts (10), wins, losses, winning percentage, lowest stolen-base percentage allowed (54.5) and lowest batting average allowed vs. righthanded batters

Chicago (NL)

Alex Gonzalez

2002 Season

The Cubs hardly could have been surprised with what they got from Alex Gonzalez. After coming over in an offseason trade from Toronto that sent Felix Heredia and Jim Deschaine north of the border, Gonzalez did exactly what had been expected of him. He provided strong defense at short and occasional power at the plate. The former was much more valuable than the latter, but that is precisely why Chicago acquired him.

Hitting

Gonzalez has decent power and likes the fastball from the middle in. He hasn't progressed offensively since coming to the majors eight years ago, and the biggest reason for that is his unchecked compulsion to chase breaking balls out of the strike zone. It keeps his average down and makes him strikeout-prone, so he's ill-suited to hit near the top of the order. He doesn't have quite enough power to be useful in an RBI spot either, so he can't really play a key offensive role. On the other hand, he has decent pop for a shortstop and is very consistent from year to year. He's also an adept bunter.

Baserunning & Defense

While he remained one of the top defensive shortstops in baseball, last year Gonzalez had to make adjustments while moving from SkyDome's artificial turf to Wrigley's long grass. It didn't take him long to learn that he had to charge some balls more aggressively. He tied a career high with 21 errors, but displayed more range than any Cubs shortstop had shown in a long time. His strong arm helps him make plays from the hole. He runs fairly well and can steal an occasional base, though he rarely was asked to do so last year.

2003 Outlook

Now going on age 30, Gonzalez no longer is seen as potential unfulfilled. He is what he is, and can be trusted to play to that level. At least for the time being, the Cubs seem satisfied with that.

Position: SS
Bats: R **Throws:** R
Ht: 6' 0" **Wt:** 200

Opening Day Age: 29
Born: 4/8/73 in Miami, FL
ML Seasons: 9

Overall Statistics

	G	AB	R	H	D	T	HR	RBI	SB	BB	SO	Avg	OBP	Slg
'02	142	513	58	127	27	5	18	61	5	46	136	.248	.312	.425
Car.	1032	3771	465	925	199	25	101	411	90	303	894	.245	.306	.392

Where He Hits the Ball

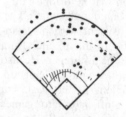
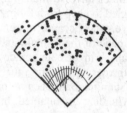

Vs. LHP   **Vs. RHP**

2002 Situational Stats

	AB	H	HR	RBI	Avg		AB	H	HR	RBI	Avg
Home	249	61	13	34	.245	LHP	114	27	5	16	.237
Road	264	66	5	27	.250	RHP	399	100	13	45	.251
First Half	253	58	9	31	.229	Sc Pos	125	28	3	41	.224
Scnd Half	260	69	9	30	.265	Clutch	93	30	5	14	.323

2002 Rankings (National League)

- 4th in errors at shortstop (21)
- 5th in lowest fielding percentage at shortstop (.965)
- 7th in lowest on-base percentage vs. righthanded pitchers (.304)
- 10th in lowest batting average
- Led the Cubs in triples

Bobby Hill

2002 Season

On the second try, Bobby Hill got it right. Called up in May to play second base while Delino DeShields was injured, Hill hit .182 and was sent back down when DeShields returned a month later. Recalled in late August and reinstalled at second and the leadoff spot, Hill batted .314 and finally showed the form that had made him one of the Cubs' top prospects.

Hitting

The switch-hitting Hill takes a leadoff man's approach, working the count and just looking to make contact. He was even too passive at times, letting hittable pitches pass and winding up in a lot of two-strike counts. That approach led to more strikeouts than a hitter of his type should have. He stays within himself, however, and doesn't get into trouble by trying to power up. He can bunt for a hit or just to move a runner up. With the Cubs, he hit much better from the right side, but that probably was a fluke, as his splits have been quite balanced in the minors over the last two years.

Baserunning & Defense

Hill's quickness on the bases is another reason he's well suited to hit at the top of the order. He didn't run much with the Cubs last year, but in the minors he's been not only a good basestealer, but also an excellent percentage basestealer. He's also a very reliable second baseman with decent range and a good double-play pivot.

2003 Outlook

Hill goes into the season as the Cubs' leadoff hitter and second baseman. He probably won't be an All-Star, at least for now, but he should be solid all-around and contribute in a number of ways. The only caveat is that the Cubs might be tempted to send him down if he again starts slowly.

Position: 2B
Bats: B **Throws:** R
Ht: 5'10" **Wt:** 190

Opening Day Age: 24
Born: 4/3/78 in San Jose, CA
ML Seasons: 1

Overall Statistics

	G	AB	R	H	D	T	HR	RBI	SB	BB	SO	Avg	OBP	Slg
'02	59	190	26	48	7	2	4	20	6	17	42	.253	.327	.374
Car.	59	190	26	48	7	2	4	20	6	17	42	.253	.327	.374

Where He Hits the Ball

 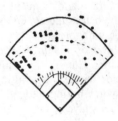

Vs. LHP **Vs. RHP**

2002 Situational Stats

	AB	H	HR	RBI	Avg		AB	H	HR	RBI	Avg
Home	82	21	1	10	.256	LHP	52	17	0	5	.327
Road	108	27	3	10	.250	RHP	138	31	4	15	.225
First Half	88	16	2	7	.182	Sc Pos	40	9	1	15	.225
Scnd Half	102	32	2	13	.314	Clutch	36	13	1	4	.361

2002 Rankings (National League)

- 4th in batting average on a 3-1 count (.667)
- Led the Cubs in batting average in the clutch and batting average on a 3-1 count (.667)

Todd Hundley

2002 Season

Todd Hundley's second season in Chicago was a replay of the first. He chafed under his limited playing time, but when he did play, he did little to merit a bigger role. With a lucrative multiyear deal, his struggles made him virtually untradeable and caused friction between a front office that had signed him and a manager that didn't want to play him. Even the normally-forgiving fans at Wrigley continued to make him the object of their scorn. He hit just .199 in a Cubs uniform.

Hitting

Lefthanded power is the one thing Hundley still can provide. It comes at a cost, however: a low average and frequent strikeouts. He tries to pull the ball in the air, and pitchers predictably counter with breaking balls and offspeed pitches to throw off his timing. Though nominally a switch-hitter, Hundley is so much weaker from the right side that at times during his career he's given up switch-hitting altogether. He's essentially a platoon player.

Baserunning & Defense

Hundley's surgically-rebuilt throwing arm is a major liability, one that basestealers exploit at every opportunity. With runners on base, he overcompensates by calling for too many fastballs, sometimes drawing the ire of his pitchers and managers. Other physical problems have eroded his pitch-blocking skills. He hasn't tripled or stolen a base in years, and some first basemen don't even bother holding him on. Even apart from the decline in his skills, it seems he's no longer physically able to go behind the plate on a regular basis.

2003 Outlook

Hundley's trade to Los Angeles could work out well for him. It freed him from a frustrating all-around situation in Chicago, and might give him the chance to play a position to which he's better suited, first base. In the right frame of mind, he could be a productive hitter again, although he probably will need to be platooned. None of that will matter, however, if Hundley no longer is physically able to do the job, which remains a real possibility.

Position: C
Bats: B **Throws:** R
Ht: 5'11" **Wt:** 200

Opening Day Age: 33
Born: 5/27/69 in Martinsville, VA
ML Seasons: 13

Overall Statistics

	G	AB	R	H	D	T	HR	RBI	SB	BB	SO	Avg	OBP	Slg
'02	92	266	32	56	8	0	16	35	0	32	80	.211	.301	.421
Car.	1204	3736	493	877	166	7	200	588	14	445	975	.235	.319	.444

Where He Hits the Ball

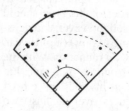 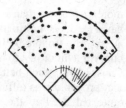

Vs. LHP   **Vs. RHP**

2002 Situational Stats

	AB	H	HR	RBI	Avg		AB	H	HR	RBI	Avg
Home	124	26	8	16	.210	LHP	46	10	2	6	.217
Road	142	30	8	19	.211	RHP	220	46	14	29	.209
First Half	132	25	7	18	.189	Sc Pos	73	13	3	19	.178
Scnd Half	134	31	9	17	.231	Clutch	50	10	0	4	.200

2002 Rankings (National League)

- 1st in lowest batting average on an 0-2 count (.000) and lowest batting average with two strikes (.116)
- 2nd in errors at catcher (11)
- 4th in lowest percentage of runners caught stealing as a catcher (26.0)

Fred McGriff

2002 Season

In his first full season with the Cubs, Fred McGriff was supposed to hit cleanup between Sammy Sosa and Moises Alou, forming an unstoppable heart of the order. It didn't happen. Over the Cubs' first 40 games, McGriff batted .209 with three homers, and the Cubs went 13-27 to fall 12 games back in the NL Central. McGriff eventually hit enough to get his numbers close to his usual levels, but he did most of his damage long after the team's season had been written off. He did manage to pass one milestone (1,500 RBI) and close in on another (500 home runs).

Hitting

Most modern sluggers generate power with bulging biceps and hip torque, but McGriff does it with good, old-fashioned arm extension. He has very good straightaway power on pitches on the outer half of the plate, and can golf a ball down and in. He's at his best when he's ahead in the count and able to look for a ball in a particular zone, but he doesn't hit well when he has to defend the plate with two strikes. Lefthanders gave him trouble last year, but that's likely an aberration, since he's always hit them fairly well.

Baserunning & Defense

McGriff looks like he ought to be able to run a little, but his speed has slipped to below average. He isn't a threat to run, and in each of the past two years he's scored nearly half his runs on his own homers. He's also been thrown out in six of the past nine times he's attempted to swipe a base. McGriff has fairly good hands at first base but doesn't move too well there either, and his arm is poor.

2003 Outlook

A free agent after the Cubs declined his $8.5 million option for 2003, McGriff is only 22 homers short of the vaunted 500 mark. He may be 39, but he's also coming off four consecutive 100-RBI seasons, so someone is sure to take a chance that he has at least one more good year left in him.

Position: 1B
Bats: L **Throws:** L
Ht: 6' 3" **Wt:** 225

Opening Day Age: 39
Born: 10/31/63 in Tampa, FL
ML Seasons: 17
Nickname: Crime Dog

Overall Statistics

G	AB	R	H	D	T	HR	RBI	SB	BB	SO	Avg	OBP	Slg
146	523	67	143	27	2	30	103	1	63	99	.273	.353	.505
2347	8388	1310	2403	424	24	478	1503	72	1265	1797	.286	.380	.514

Where He Hits the Ball

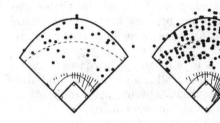

Vs. LHP   **Vs. RHP**

2002 Situational Stats

	AB	H	HR	RBI	Avg		AB	H	HR	RBI	Avg
Home	238	65	11	51	.273	LHP	141	30	2	22	.213
Road	285	78	19	52	.274	RHP	382	113	28	81	.296
First Half	302	79	17	55	.262	Sc Pos	158	48	6	73	.304
Scnd Half	221	64	13	48	.290	Clutch	90	26	5	18	.289

2002 Rankings (National League)

- 3rd in lowest percentage of extra bases taken as a runner (30.2)
- 6th in errors at first base (7)
- 7th in slugging percentage vs. righthanded pitchers (.571) and fielding percentage at first base (.993)
- Led the Cubs in sacrifice flies (5), batting average vs. righthanded pitchers, cleanup slugging percentage (.523), slugging percentage vs. righthanded pitchers (.571) and on-base percentage vs. righthanded pitchers (.375)

Chicago (NL)

Corey Patterson

2002 Season

Young center fielder Corey Patterson's first full season in the majors had its ups and downs. Most of the ups came early on. He began the year as the leadoff hitter and showed much-improved plate patience in April, drawing 10 walks in 23 games while batting .333 and stealing seven bases. He soon slipped back into his old habits, however, and his production sank. After the All-Star break he was dropped to the lower half of the order, and by the end of the year he was swinging at everything and hitting very little.

Hitting

Patterson has decent power, but it's interfered with his development because he tries to use it too often. He often becomes overly pull-conscious and opens up too soon, pulling off the ball. His recklessly aggressive approach regardless of the count leads to few walks and frequent strikeouts. He's a good fastball hitter but by the end of the year pitchers had discovered they could get him to chase pitches up and out of the zone. He struggled badly against lefthanders for the third season in a row.

Baserunning & Defense

Patterson puts his speed to good use in center field and on the bases. He's a rangy flycatcher with a good throwing arm, and had good success stealing bases before he was moved down in the order and stopped running. Still, an expectation of 20-25 steals annually is not a stretch.

2003 Outlook

He's only 23, so Patterson has plenty of time to smooth over his rough edges. His flaws are obvious, but so is his talent. How far he goes will depend on how he addresses the holes in his offensive game. At worst, the Cubs will have a platoon center fielder who plays good defense and makes occasional contributions with the bat. At best, they'll have a quality center fielder for many years to come.

Position: CF
Bats: L **Throws:** R
Ht: 5' 9" **Wt:** 175

Opening Day Age: 23
Born: 8/13/79 in Atlanta, GA
ML Seasons: 3

Overall Statistics

	G	AB	R	H	D	T	HR	RBI	SB	BB	SO	Avg	OBP	Slg
'02	153	592	71	150	30	5	14	54	18	19	142	.253	.284	.392
Car.	223	765	106	186	34	5	20	70	23	28	189	.243	.278	.379

Where He Hits the Ball

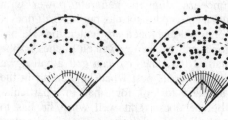

Vs. LHP   Vs. RHP

2002 Situational Stats

	AB	H	HR	RBI	Avg		AB	H	HR	RBI	Avg
Home	307	72	7	22	.235	LHP	149	28	2	14	.188
Road	285	78	7	32	.274	RHP	443	122	12	40	.275
First Half	316	87	7	31	.275	Sc Pos	132	30	5	40	.227
Scnd Half	276	63	7	23	.228	Clutch	99	21	3	9	.212

2002 Rankings (National League)

- 1st in lowest on-base percentage vs. lefthanded pitchers (.215)
- 3rd in stolen-base percentage (85.7), lowest on-base percentage and lowest batting average vs. lefthanded pitchers
- 4th in lowest percentage of pitches taken (45.3) and lowest slugging percentage vs. lefthanded pitchers (.262)
- Led the Cubs in at-bats, singles, doubles, triples, sacrifice flies (5), stolen bases, hit by pitch (8), games played, highest groundball-flyball ratio (1.5), stolen-base percentage (85.7), bunts in play (20) and fewest GDPs per GDP situation (7.6%)

Mark Prior

2002 Season

Mark Prior, one of the most heralded college pitchers of all time and the second overall pick in the 2001 draft, made good on his promise last year. He rocketed through the minors in seven weeks and made his major league debut May 22 with a 10-strikeout performance. He would record five more double-digit strikeout games before a hamstring injury ended his season a month early. He had 13 quality starts in 19 outings and deserved a much better record than his final 6-6 mark. He struck out 11.34 batters per nine innings, a mark that would have placed him second in the National League behind Randy Johnson had Prior worked enough innings to qualify.

Pitching

Prior has a mid-90s fastball and a hard curve, but his biggest weapon is his impeccable command. He's able to work the black like a veteran. The only complaint was that he sometimes worked too carefully to major league hitters, running up his pitch counts unnecessarily. He doesn't yet have the stamina to be able to afford to do that, as he gave up nine of his 14 homers after reaching the 90-pitch mark and had a lot of high-pitch outings for a 21-year-old.

Defense & Hitting

Prior already is one of the best-hitting pitchers in the majors. He had three home runs in 19 at-bats before his callup, and batted .171 with four doubles for the Cubs. He hasn't yet learned to bunt well, though. He also must work on paying more attention to baserunners.

2003 Outlook

The sky's the limit for Prior. It seems the only thing that could stop him is an arm injury, a possibility that can't be dismissed out of hand after the high number of pitches he threw last year. At the same time, his hamstring injury might have kept him from being pushed too far, and his arm has been healthy. His first full season in the majors in 2003 ought to be very good.

Position: SP
Bats: R **Throws:** R
Ht: 6' 5" **Wt:** 225

Opening Day Age: 22
Born: 9/7/80 in San Diego, CA
ML Seasons: 1

Overall Statistics

	W	L	Pct.	ERA	G	GS	Sv	IP	H	BB	SO	HR	Ratio
'02	6	6	.500	3.32	19	19	0	116.2	98	38	147	14	1.17
Car.	6	6	.500	3.32	19	19	0	116.2	98	38	147	14	1.17

How Often He Throws Strikes

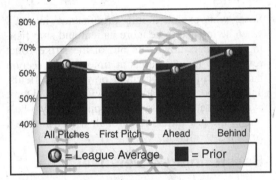

2002 Situational Stats

	W	L	ERA	Sv	IP		AB	H	HR	RBI	Avg
Home	4	3	3.56	0	68.1	LHB	186	38	7	19	.204
Road	2	3	2.98	0	48.1	RHB	248	60	7	23	.242
First Half	2	2	3.98	0	52.0	Sc Pos	102	18	3	28	.176
Scnd Half	4	4	2.78	0	64.2	Clutch	26	9	2	3	.346

2002 Rankings (National League)

- 7th in lowest batting average allowed vs. left-handed batters
- Led the Cubs in ERA, stolen bases allowed (13), lowest batting average allowed vs. left-handed batters, lowest batting average allowed with runners in scoring position and most strikeouts per nine innings (11.3)

Chicago (NL)

Sammy Sosa

2002 Season

It was supposed to be the year when teams no longer could pitch around Sammy Sosa. With Fred McGriff and Moises Alou hitting behind him, Sosa was going to feel less pressure to expand his strike zone and be more willing to take a walk. Instead, the Cubs' season went down the tubes so quickly that by the second half, there was little left to play for except personal goals. Bothered by a toe problem in August and a back injury in September, Sosa pressed to reach the 50-homer plateau for the fifth straight season and came up just short.

Hitting

Sosa, who exploded into prominence in 1998 when he learned to be more patient and stop fishing for sliders down and out of the strike zone, reverted to his old habits at times in the second half. He still has frightening power to all fields, and is especially deadly on low pitches. Don't ever assume he'll let a cripple pitch go by—he's one of the few hitters in baseball who will take a rip at a 3-0 offering.

Baserunning & Defense

Once a consistent basestealing threat, Sosa has added so much upper-body bulk over the last few years that he no longer has the quickness to steal bases effectively. He still runs fairly well, however, and has learned his limitations on the bases without abandoning his aggressiveness. He's become fairly reliable in right field, and still has good range and a strong arm.

2003 Outlook

Hopefully Sosa's back problems and second-half slide are not signs of things to come, but on the other hand, he's now 34. It wouldn't be all that surprising to see him drop off a little bit or suffer a few more nagging injuries than he has in the past. That said, he's still clearly one of the premier power hitters in baseball. It also will be interesting to see how Sosa's production is affected by the presence of new skipper Dusty Baker, who knows a thing or two about managing a team with a superstar power hitter.

Position: RF
Bats: R **Throws:** R
Ht: 6' 0" **Wt:** 220

Opening Day Age: 34
Born: 11/12/68 in San Pedro de Macoris, DR
ML Seasons: 14

Overall Statistics

G	AB	R	H	D	T	HR	RBI	SB	BB	SO	Avg	OBP	Slg
150	556	122	160	19	2	49	108	2	103	144	.288	.399	.594
1875	7026	1215	1955	297	43	499	1347	233	738	1834	.278	.348	.546

Where He Hits the Ball

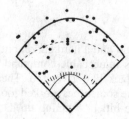

Vs. LHP	Vs. RHP

2002 Situational Stats

	AB	H	HR	RBI	Avg		AB	H	HR	RBI	Avg
Home	279	74	24	46	.265	LHP	101	37	11	19	.366
Road	277	86	25	62	.310	RHP	455	123	38	89	.270
First Half	306	94	28	58	.307	Sc Pos	121	32	13	61	.264
Scnd Half	250	66	21	50	.264	Clutch	96	23	7	16	.240

2002 Rankings (National League)

- 1st in home runs and runs scored
- 2nd in HR frequency (11.3 ABs per HR), slugging percentage vs. lefthanded pitchers (.733), on-base percentage vs. lefthanded pitchers (.526) and highest percentage of swings that missed (31.6)
- 3rd in batting average vs. lefthanded pitchers, errors in right field (6) and lowest fielding percentage in right field (.980)
- Led the Cubs in batting average, home runs, runs scored, hits, total bases (330), RBI, walks, intentional walks (15), times on base (266), strikeouts, pitches seen (2,695), plate appearances (666), slugging percentage, on-base percentage and HR frequency (11.3 ABs per HR)

Kerry Wood

2002 Season

On the surface, it might have looked like Kerry Wood made no progress last year, but that wasn't the case. He made several subtle but potentially important improvements, and perhaps even more importantly, he didn't miss a single start due to arm problems. The fact that he topped the 200-inning plateau for the first time as a big leaguer was reason alone for the Cubs to consider his season a success. He also pitched better than his won-lost record; he could have won several more games if his runs of support hadn't come in bunches.

Pitching

With a fastball in the mid- to upper 90s, Wood works up in the zone as effectively as any pitcher. Last year he reworked his hard curve, getting less downward action but more lateral break. The adjustment helped him to earn more called strikes, enabling him to cut his walks and work more efficiently. He also throws a tight slider and what is perhaps the fastest straight changeup in the majors (at 86-88 MPH, it's roughly equivalent to a Jamie Moyer fastball). He made better use of his breaking pitches in double-play situations, inducing 23 twin-killings, more than he'd gotten in his first three years combined.

Defense & Hitting

Among righthanders, Wood has one of the best pickoff moves in the majors. He has to, since his high leg kick allows runners to get a good jump. In the field, he's athletic and alert, and he knows what to do with the ball when he gets it. He can't be taken for granted at the plate, where he handles the bat well when hitting or bunting and even flashes occasional power. Wood homered for the fourth time in his career last year.

2003 Outlook

Ever since Wood burst onto the scene, it's looked like it would be only a matter of time before he would become a big winner. He's now proven his arm is sound, and he's made the refinements necessary to get to the next level. This well could be his year.

Position: SP
Bats: R **Throws:** R
Ht: 6' 5" **Wt:** 230

Opening Day Age: 25
Born: 6/16/77 in Irving, TX
ML Seasons: 4

Overall Statistics

	W	L	Pct.	ERA	G	GS	Sv	IP	H	BB	SO	HR	Ratio
'02	12	11	.522	3.66	33	33	0	213.2	169	97	217	22	1.24
Car.	45	30	.600	3.75	110	110	0	691.2	525	361	799	69	1.28

How Often He Throws Strikes

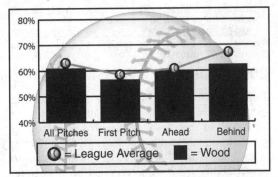

2002 Situational Stats

	W	L	ERA	Sv	IP		AB	H	HR	RBI	Avg
Home	4	5	3.71	0	89.2	LHB	363	81	8	34	.223
Road	8	6	3.63	0	124.0	RHB	401	88	14	47	.219
First Half	8	5	4.12	0	107.0	Sc Pos	176	32	3	52	.182
Scnd Half	4	6	3.21	0	106.2	Clutch	45	10	2	5	.222

2002 Rankings (National League)

- 1st in hit batsmen (16) and fielding percentage at pitcher (1.000)
- 2nd in lowest batting average allowed with runners in scoring position
- 3rd in walks allowed, strikeouts and lowest groundball-flyball ratio allowed (0.8)
- Led the Cubs in wins, losses, games started, complete games (4), innings pitched, hits allowed, batters faced (895), home runs allowed, walks allowed, hit batsmen (16), strikeouts, wild pitches (8), pitches thrown (3,384), stolen bases allowed (13), GDPs induced (23), winning percentage, most run support per nine innings (5.9) and most GDPs induced per nine innings (1.0)

Chicago (NL)

Jason Bere

Position: SP
Bats: R **Throws:** R
Ht: 6' 3" **Wt:** 225

Opening Day Age: 31
Born: 5/26/71 in
Cambridge, MA
ML Seasons: 10
Pronunciation:
ber-AY

Overall Statistics

	W	L	Pct.	ERA	G	GS	Sv	IP	H	BB	SO	HR	Ratio
'02	1	10	.091	5.67	16	16	0	85.2	98	28	65	13	1.47
Car.	71	65	.522	5.14	209	201	0	1104.1	1090	624	919	145	1.55

2002 Situational Stats

	W	L	ERA	Sv	IP		AB	H	HR	RBI	Avg
Home	0	8	6.89	0	47.0	LHB	141	46	5	22	.326
Road	1	2	4.19	0	38.2	RHB	197	52	8	33	.264
First Half	1	9	5.18	0	81.2	Sc Pos	80	27	2	39	.338
Scnd Half	0	1	15.75	0	4.0	Clutch	20	9	1	6	.450

2002 Season

Jason Bere hit rock bottom in 2002, pitching inconsistently over the first half and missing almost all of the second half with a slow-healing groin strain. It was a big comedown for a pitcher who had slowly worked his way back to respectability by 2001 after years of struggling. Though partly a victim of circumstance, Bere ended up posting the lowest winning percentage in all of baseball last year among pitchers with at least 10 decisions.

Pitching, Defense & Hitting

Arm problems interrupted Bere's career in 1996. He finally has regained his low-90s fastball, but hasn't ever gotten back the tight curveball that made him so effective his first two years in the league. Now his second pitch is a fosh. He's fairly tough on righthanded hitters, but lefty swingers give him problems. Two times through the order is about all he's good for. He's a decent fielder who's average at holding the running game, and he's become a somewhat useful hitter and bunter.

2003 Outlook

A free agent, Bere will try to land a spot with a team looking for back-of-the-rotation help. His arm has been healthy for the last few years, so he could provide some passable bulk innings.

Joe Borowski

Position: RP
Bats: R **Throws:** R
Ht: 6' 2" **Wt:** 240

Opening Day Age: 31
Born: 5/4/71 in
Bayonne, NJ
ML Seasons: 6

Overall Statistics

	W	L	Pct.	ERA	G	GS	Sv	IP	H	BB	SO	HR	Ratio
'02	4	4	.500	2.73	73	0	2	95.2	84	29	97	10	1.18
Car.	9	12	.429	3.73	131	1	2	166.1	168	73	131	17	1.45

2002 Situational Stats

	W	L	ERA	Sv	IP		AB	H	HR	RBI	Avg
Home	3	1	2.04	0	53.0	LHB	148	31	4	11	.209
Road	1	3	3.59	2	42.2	RHB	204	53	6	31	.260
First Half	2	4	3.26	2	49.2	Sc Pos	94	22	1	29	.234
Scnd Half	2	0	2.15	0	46.0	Clutch	127	33	1	14	.260

2002 Season

When Joe Borowski signed a minor league contract with the Cubs before the 2002 season, he was a 30-year-old indy league vet with a career ERA above 5.00 in 70.2 major league innings. He landed the final spot on the Cubs' roster coming out of spring training, however, and wound up being their most effective reliever. Serving as their main righthanded setup man, he posted a 2.73 ERA and threw the third-most innings of any major league reliever. His ERA was 10th best among NL pitchers who worked at least 75 innings in 2002.

Pitching, Defense & Hitting

Borowski works in and out with a low-90s fastball, a slider and a changeup. He's effective against hitters from either side but can be vulnerable to the longball when he gets the ball up. Going more than an inning at a time is not a problem for him. He is easy to run on but is a reliable fielder. He had a couple of hits last year but has little experience at the plate.

2003 Outlook

Despite his surprising season, Borowski wasn't quite as terrific as his ERA made him seem, and a mark in the mid-threes would have been more in order. He'll likely drop off a bit this year, but he still could remain a useful setup man.

Roosevelt Brown

Position: LF/CF
Bats: L **Throws:** R
Ht: 5'10" **Wt:** 205

Opening Day Age: 27
Born: 8/3/75 in Vicksburg, MS
ML Seasons: 4

Overall Statistics

	G	AB	R	H	D	T	HR	RBI	SB	BB	SO	Avg	OBP	Slg
'02	111	204	14	43	12	0	3	23	2	23	50	.211	.299	.314
Car.	228	442	44	111	32	2	11	69	3	36	98	.251	.311	.407

2002 Situational Stats

	AB	H	HR	RBI	Avg		AB	H	HR	RBI	Avg
Home	117	27	2	12	.231	LHP	20	4	0	3	.200
Road	87	16	1	11	.184	RHP	184	39	3	20	.212
First Half	110	21	2	14	.191	Sc Pos	52	14	1	18	.269
Scnd Half	94	22	1	9	.234	Clutch	46	6	0	5	.130

2002 Season

After tearing up the minors and hitting well in limited major league action in 2000 and 2001, Roosevelt Brown made the Cubs' Opening Day roster as a backup outfielder. He played some in April while Moises Alou was out, but Brown didn't hit and was relegated to the bench. He was one of the Cubs' top pinch-hitters and performed capably in that role, but didn't hit at all when given occasional chances to start. His .211 overall batting average matched that of Cubs teammate Todd Hundley.

Hitting, Baserunning & Defense

Brown's bat is what got him to the majors. An aggressive pull-hitter with gap power, he's capable of hitting better than he did last year but probably not well enough to hold down a corner-outfield spot. Lefthanders have not given him problems in the minors. He has the range to play the outfield corners, but he is stretched to cover center and his arm is not a strength.

2003 Outlook

At age 27 with his major league clock ticking, Brown opted to sign on with the Orix Blue Wave of the Japanese Pacific League in November.

Juan Cruz

Position: RP
Bats: R **Throws:** R
Ht: 6' 2" **Wt:** 165

Opening Day Age: 24
Born: 10/15/78 in Bonao, DR
ML Seasons: 2

Overall Statistics

	W	L	Pct.	ERA	G	GS	Sv	IP	H	BB	SO	HR	Ratio
'02	3	11	.214	3.98	45	9	1	97.1	84	59	81	11	1.47
Car.	6	12	.333	3.74	53	17	1	142.0	124	76	120	15	1.41

2002 Situational Stats

	W	L	ERA	Sv	IP		AB	H	HR	RBI	Avg
Home	3	5	3.09	0	55.1	LHB	148	37	3	22	.250
Road	0	6	5.14	1	42.0	RHB	201	47	8	28	.234
First Half	1	10	4.75	0	66.1	Sc Pos	95	22	1	37	.232
Scnd Half	2	1	2.32	1	31.0	Clutch	94	23	7	13	.245

2002 Season

After looking sharp in eight late-season starts during the 2001 campaign, Juan Cruz opened 2002 in the Cubs' starting rotation. He dropped his first seven decisions, however, often coming out of the game after only a few innings. When he developed a sore arm in May, the club moved the rail-thin youngster to the bullpen as a precaution. He took to his new assignment and pitched quite well from June 1 on.

Pitching, Defense & Hitting

Cruz doesn't look like he has the build to generate much velocity, but his fastball hits the mid-90s. He complements it with a hard sinker and a straight change. He surrendered too many home runs last year and will need to work the outer parts of the plate more effectively. He doesn't have a good pickoff move, but while basestealers have run on him often, they haven't been very successful. Cruz falls off the mound toward first at the end of his delivery, which doesn't help him in the field.

2003 Outlook

Cruz has the talent to be an effective pitcher, but it remains to be seen what his role will be. If he fills out and his arm stays healthy, it will make it easier for the club to put him back into the rotation.

Chicago (NL)

Kyle Farnsworth

Position: RP
Bats: R **Throws:** R
Ht: 6' 4" **Wt:** 235

Opening Day Age: 26
Born: 4/14/76 in
Wichita, KS
ML Seasons: 4

Overall Statistics

	W	L	Pct.	ERA	G	GS	Sv	IP	H	BB	SO	HR	Ratio
'02	4	6	.400	7.33	45	0	1	46.2	53	24	46	9	1.65
Car.	15	30	.333	5.12	194	26	4	335.2	348	155	297	59	1.50

2002 Situational Stats

	W	L	ERA	Sv	IP		AB	H	HR	RBI	Avg
Home	1	4	9.00	1	22.0	LHB	79	31	5	31	.392
Road	3	2	5.84	0	24.2	RHB	102	22	4	18	.216
First Half	2	1	4.60	0	15.2	Sc Pos	60	22	5	45	.367
Scnd Half	2	5	8.71	1	31.0	Clutch	98	28	5	27	.286

2002 Season

It's hard to fall as far, as fast as Kyle Farnsworth did last year. Coming off a strong 2001 campaign, he broke his foot in April and was sidelined until June. After he returned, he fell into a rut that seemed to deepen with each appearance. Opponents hit .293 against him for the season, and *slugged* .558. Along the way, he was disciplined several times for showing up late to games.

Pitching, Defense & Hitting

The oddest thing about Farnsworth's slump is that he was getting hit hard even as he continued to throw in the upper 90s. True, his command wavered, and his hard splitter was not the reliable second pitch it had been the year before, but some could only conclude that he must have been tipping his pitches. Farnsworth had particular trouble against lefthanded hitters and pitching out of the stretch. He's exceedingly easy to run on, doesn't field well and can't hit a lick.

2003 Outlook

The Cubs may be running out of patience with Farnsworth, but if they do, there is sure to be plenty of other teams that will take a chance on him turning it around. Whether he'll be able to do that is anyone's guess.

Joe Girardi

Position: C
Bats: R **Throws:** R
Ht: 5'11" **Wt:** 200

Opening Day Age: 38
Born: 10/14/64 in
Peoria, IL
ML Seasons: 14
Pronunciation:
jeh-RAR-dee

Overall Statistics

	G	AB	R	H	D	T	HR	RBI	SB	BB	SO	Avg	OBP	Slg
'02	90	234	19	53	10	1	1	13	1	16	35	.226	.275	.291
Car.	1261	4104	453	1097	186	26	36	421	44	276	603	.267	.316	.352

2002 Situational Stats

	AB	H	HR	RBI	Avg		AB	H	HR	RBI	Avg
Home	110	25	0	8	.227	LHP	64	11	0	5	.172
Road	124	28	1	5	.226	RHP	170	42	1	8	.247
First Half	135	32	0	5	.237	Sc Pos	52	13	0	11	.250
Scnd Half	99	21	1	8	.212	Clutch	33	9	0	1	.273

2002 Season

It says a lot about Joe Girardi that even at age 37, while batting .226 with one home run, he caught more innings for the Cubs than Todd Hundley, the power hitter with the big contract. Girardi contributed little at the plate but was valued for his leadership as co-captain and his ability to work with the team's pitchers.

Hitting, Baserunning & Defense

Even at his peak, Girardi's only real offensive contribution was a respectable batting average, and he no longer provides even that. He can bunt when called upon to do so. His pitch-blocking skills give his batterymates the confidence to throw breaking balls in the dirt. He also communicates well with pitchers and is respected for his game-calling skills. He no longer runs that well, even for a catcher.

2003 Outlook

Girardi's contract was up at the end of last season and he is a free agent. In November, the Cubs traded for Diamondbacks catcher Damian Miller and Milwaukee backstop Paul Bako. Even with Todd Hundley traded to the Dodgers, it's unlikely Girardi will be back in Chicago, as the Cubs did not offer him arbitration. It's possible he might have a hard time hooking on anywhere this season.

Chad Hermansen
Traded To DODGERS

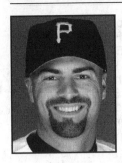

Position: CF/RF
Bats: R **Throws:** R
Ht: 6' 2" **Wt:** 192

Opening Day Age: 25
Born: 9/10/77 in Salt Lake City, UT
ML Seasons: 4

Overall Statistics

	G	AB	R	H	D	T	HR	RBI	SB	BB	SO	Avg	OBP	Slg
'02	100	237	25	49	14	1	8	18	7	22	82	.207	.276	.376
Car.	174	460	47	92	22	2	13	32	9	36	156	.200	.260	.341

2002 Situational Stats

	AB	H	HR	RBI	Avg		AB	H	HR	RBI	Avg
Home	112	24	4	6	.214	LHP	45	8	1	4	.178
Road	125	25	4	12	.200	RHP	192	41	7	14	.214
First Half	164	34	6	14	.207	Sc Pos	40	5	0	7	.125
Scnd Half	73	15	2	4	.205	Clutch	43	3	1	1	.070

2002 Season

Longtime prospect Chad Hermansen got his most extensive big league trial last year—not because he deserved to, but because he was out of options. He missed the first six weeks of the season with a strained buttocks muscle but was handed the Pirates' center-field job when he returned. A slump cost him the job by July, however, and at the trade deadline he was dealt to the Cubs, where he mostly rode the bench.

Hitting, Baserunning & Defense

Hermansen hit fairly well in the high minors at a young age, but his offensive development has stalled over the last three years. He simply swings through too many pitches, and he never has developed an eye for his pitch. When he does make contact, he pulls the ball in the air with acceptable power. Hermansen is athletic enough to cover center field, where his throwing arm is an asset. He's been a decent basestealer in the minors.

2003 Outlook

He was dealt to the Dodgers in a December salary dump deal. While Hermansen might secure a final roster spot because of his low salary, last year's struggles didn't help his chances. Minor league contracts may be in his future, and his best big league opportunity may be in his past.

Jon Lieber

Position: SP
Bats: L **Throws:** R
Ht: 6' 2" **Wt:** 230

Opening Day Age: 32
Born: 4/2/70 in Council Bluffs, IA
ML Seasons: 9
Pronunciation: LEE-ber

Overall Statistics

	W	L	Pct.	ERA	G	GS	Sv	IP	H	BB	SO	HR	Ratio
'02	6	8	.429	3.70	21	21	0	141.0	153	12	87	15	1.17
Car.	86	83	.509	4.18	272	225	2	1510.1	1603	311	1121	188	1.27

2002 Situational Stats

	W	L	ERA	Sv	IP		AB	H	HR	RBI	Avg
Home	4	2	3.09	0	70.0	LHB	273	84	11	36	.308
Road	2	6	4.31	0	71.0	RHB	280	69	4	22	.246
First Half	6	6	3.38	0	117.0	Sc Pos	114	27	2	40	.237
Scnd Half	0	2	5.25	0	24.0	Clutch	52	11	1	4	.212

2002 Season

Coming off his first 20-win season, Jon Lieber was expected to give the Cubs plenty of quality innings again last year. It raised little concern when the durable righthander missed a start in April with a sore elbow, and he rebounded to pitch well for most of the first half. In August, the pain got to be too much, and it turned out that his elbow ligament was so inflamed that Tommy John surgery was required.

Pitching, Defense & Hitting

Before the injury, Lieber used his terrific slider and immaculate control to dominate righthanded hitters. Righties have hit just .239 off him for his career. Lefthanded swingers were his nemesis, however, finding his average fastball and change-up easy to hit. Lieber doesn't look that athletic but moves decently and fields his position well. His slide step is so effective that runners stole only five bases off him over the last two years. He's become a creditable hitter and decent bunter.

2003 Outlook

The Cubs declined to pick up Lieber's $6.25 million option for 2003, making him a free agent. If he pitches at all this year, it won't be until late in the season, and he almost certainly won't make much of an impact until 2004 at the earliest.

Chicago (NL)

Chris Stynes

Position: 3B/2B
Bats: R **Throws:** R
Ht: 5'10" **Wt:** 205

Opening Day Age: 30
Born: 1/19/73 in
Queens, NY
ML Seasons: 8

Overall Statistics

	G	AB	R	H	D	T	HR	RBI	SB	BB	SO	Avg	OBP	Slg
'02	98	195	25	47	9	1	5	26	1	21	29	.241	.314	.374
Car.	616	1721	264	492	77	6	39	176	46	134	209	.286	.341	.406

2002 Situational Stats

	AB	H	HR	RBI	Avg		AB	H	HR	RBI	Avg
Home	91	20	1	11	.220	LHP	96	23	3	12	.240
Road	104	27	4	15	.260	RHP	99	24	2	14	.242
First Half	110	24	4	14	.218	Sc Pos	50	16	1	20	.320
Scnd Half	85	23	1	12	.271	Clutch	43	10	0	6	.233

2002 Season

In a way, Chris Stynes was victimized by Mark Bellhorn's breakout season last year. When third baseman Bill Mueller was hurt in April, Bellhorn and Stynes filled in, but only Bellhorn hit. When Mueller returned and second baseman Delino DeShields was cut, Bellhorn moved to second and Stynes remained on the bench. He did well as a pinch-hitter, batting .308 in that role, but he contributed little else.

Hitting, Baserunning & Defense

Stynes is a line-drive hitter who uses the whole field. He seemed to get away from his natural style and tried to loft the ball at times last year, without success. He's capable of playing second or third, although his arm is not strong enough for him to play third regularly. He has good hands and decent range at either spot. His speed is unremarkable, and while he runs aggressively he no longer tries to steal bases.

2003 Outlook

Stynes became a free agent after the season. Though he's coming off a down year, his career average of .286 and ability to pinch-hit and play second and third should enable him to find a job somewhere as a reserve.

Carlos Zambrano

Position: SP/RP
Bats: R **Throws:** R
Ht: 6' 5" **Wt:** 250

Opening Day Age: 21
Born: 6/1/81 in Puerto
Cabello, VZ
ML Seasons: 2

Overall Statistics

	W	L	Pct.	ERA	G	GS	Sv	IP	H	BB	SO	HR	Ratio
'02	4	8	.333	3.66	32	16	0	108.1	94	63	93	9	1.45
Car.	5	10	.333	4.42	38	17	0	116.0	105	71	97	11	1.52

2002 Situational Stats

	W	L	ERA	Sv	IP		AB	H	HR	RBI	Avg
Home	2	5	4.09	0	66.0	LHB	163	34	2	19	.209
Road	2	3	2.98	0	42.1	RHB	237	60	7	28	.253
First Half	1	1	2.88	0	25.0	Sc Pos	108	28	2	36	.259
Scnd Half	3	7	3.89	0	83.1	Clutch	29	8	0	0	.276

2002 Season

Rookie Carlos Zambrano started the season slowly but closed it with a rush. He spent the first half in the bullpen and on disabled list, but joined the rotation in July and allowed two earned runs or fewer in 11 of his 16 starts. His 3.66 ERA was the fourth-best figure on the team among pitchers who worked at least 50 innings last year.

Pitching, Defense & Hitting

Zambrano possesses a rare combination of velocity and movement. With a sinking fastball in the mid- to upper 90s and a very good slider, his arsenal resembles that of teammate Matt Clement. Like a young Clement, he is tough to hit and gets strikeouts and groundballs, but sometimes fights his control. He fielded his position very well and controlled the running game effectively—five of 12 basestealers were thrown out on his watch in 2002. He showed no aptitude at the plate, with one hit, 15 strikeouts and two sacrifices in 30 at-bats.

2003 Outlook

Zambrano goes into 2003 with a firm hold on a rotation spot. He may struggle with command and consistency at times, but his good games should outnumber the bad. Long-term, he could mature into a special pitcher.

Other Chicago Cubs

Alan Benes (Pos: RHP, Age: 31)

	W	L	Pct.	ERA	G	GS	Sv	IP	H	BB	SO	HR	Ratio
'02	2	2	.500	4.35	7	7	0	39.1	42	12	32	3	1.37
Car.	29	25	.537	4.42	108	66	0	470.2	456	206	381	57	1.41

Although Alan didn't have the kind of resurrection his brother Andy did with St. Louis, Alan still pitched well in five of seven starts for the Cubs late last season. 2003 Outlook: C

Scott Chiasson (Pos: RHP, Age: 25)

	W	L	Pct.	ERA	G	GS	Sv	IP	H	BB	SO	HR	Ratio
'02	0	0	–	23.14	4	0	0	4.2	11	6	3	2	3.64
Car.	1	1	.500	11.12	10	0	0	11.1	16	8	9	4	2.12

Chiasson pitched well in 2001, when he rose from Double-A to the majors. But things didn't go right last season, as he was knocked around on the mound and then had Tommy John surgery. 2003 Outlook: C

Will Cunnane (Pos: RHP, Age: 28)

	W	L	Pct.	ERA	G	GS	Sv	IP	H	BB	SO	HR	Ratio
'02	1	1	.500	5.47	16	0	0	26.1	27	13	30	5	1.52
Car.	10	9	.526	5.36	155	12	0	241.2	280	118	203	33	1.65

Cunnane signed a minor league contract with the Cubs last offseason. In his limited exposure after getting promoted in August, he shut down righthanded batters but was hit hard by lefties. 2003 Outlook: C

Delino DeShields (Pos: 2B, Age: 34, Bats: L)

	G	AB	R	H	D	T	HR	RBI	SB	BB	SO	Avg	OBP	Slg
'02	67	146	20	28	6	1	3	10	10	21	38	.192	.292	.308
Car.	1615	5779	872	1548	244	74	80	561	463	754	1061	.268	.352	.377

With Mark Bellhorn providing nice power and prospect Bobby Hill another alternative at second base, the Cubs released DeShields last August. It would help if DeShields could keep his average above .200. 2003 Outlook: C

Courtney Duncan (Pos: RHP, Age: 28)

	W	L	Pct.	ERA	G	GS	Sv	IP	H	BB	SO	HR	Ratio
'02	0	0	–	0.00	2	0	0	2.1	2	1	1	0	1.29
Car.	3	3	.500	4.80	38	0	0	45.0	44	26	50	5	1.56

Duncan was placed on the disabled list on two occasions in 2001, due to a back strain and then shoulder tendinitis. He seemed healthy last year, but was back in the minors for most of the campaign. 2003 Outlook: C

Angel Echevarria (Pos: 1B/RF, Age: 31, Bats: R)

	G	AB	R	H	D	T	HR	RBI	SB	BB	SO	Avg	OBP	Slg
'02	50	98	14	30	7	0	3	21	0	8	17	.306	.351	.469
Car.	328	543	70	152	32	0	21	90	1	46	104	.280	.343	.455

Echevarria left the Brewers and signed a minor league contract with the Cubs last offseason. Recalled in June, he spent the rest of the year on the Cubs' roster, hitting fairly well in a reserve role. 2003 Outlook: C

Mario Encarnacion (Pos: LF, Age: 27, Bats: R)

	G	AB	R	H	D	T	HR	RBI	SB	BB	SO	Avg	OBP	Slg
'02	3	7	0	0	0	0	0	0	0	2	3	.000	.222	.000
Car.	23	69	3	14	1	0	0	3	2	7	17	.203	.276	.217

The Cubs acquired Encarnacion off waivers from the Rockies last spring. After a brief period in the majors, he was demoted to Triple-A. He has not shown much power during his stints in the majors. 2003 Outlook: C

Darren Lewis (Pos: LF/CF, Age: 35, Bats: R)

	G	AB	R	H	D	T	HR	RBI	SB	BB	SO	Avg	OBP	Slg
'02	58	79	7	19	3	1	0	7	1	7	11	.241	.326	.304
Car.	1354	4081	607	1021	137	37	27	342	247	403	514	.250	.323	.322

After the Cubs traded Lewis to the Pirates in exchange for Chad Hermansen at last year's trading deadline, Lewis decided to retire. Lewis played for seven teams in a major league career covering 13 seasons. 2003 Outlook: D

Ron Mahay (Pos: LHP, Age: 31)

	W	L	Pct.	ERA	G	GS	Sv	IP	H	BB	SO	HR	Ratio
'02	2	0	1.000	8.59	11	0	0	14.2	13	8	14	6	1.43
Car.	9	2	.818	4.53	114	3	2	147.0	137	77	121	27	1.46

Mahay was hurt by the home run in a rough stretch with the Cubs last May, just before going on the disabled list with tendinitis. He pitched well at Triple-A and signed with Texas in November. 2003 Outlook: C

Pat Mahomes (Pos: RHP, Age: 32)

	W	L	Pct.	ERA	G	GS	Sv	IP	H	BB	SO	HR	Ratio
'02	1	1	.500	3.86	16	2	0	32.2	36	17	23	3	1.62
Car.	42	38	.525	5.49	299	62	5	686.2	719	380	439	114	1.60

Mahomes pitched most of last season at Triple-A. He did OK in relief in a couple stints with the Cubs, and even made two starts in late September. He became a free agent after the season. 2003 Outlook: C

Mike Mahoney (Pos: C, Age: 30, Bats: R)

	G	AB	R	H	D	T	HR	RBI	SB	BB	SO	Avg	OBP	Slg
'02	16	29	2	6	3	0	0	3	0	1	10	.207	.233	.310
Car.	20	36	3	8	4	0	0	4	0	2	10	.222	.282	.333

A 39th-round draft choice of the Braves in 1995, Mahoney generally hasn't hit for a high average or outstanding power as a pro. His three-RBI game for the Cubs last September may be his career highlight. 2003 Outlook: C

Augie Ojeda (Pos: SS, Age: 28, Bats: B)

	G	AB	R	H	D	T	HR	RBI	SB	BB	SO	Avg	OBP	Slg
'02	30	70	4	13	4	0	0	4	1	5	5	.186	.247	.243
Car.	136	291	30	59	12	2	3	24	2	27	34	.203	.274	.289

After spending 2001 and most of the first few months of 2002 with the Cubs, Ojeda returned to the minors. With a set of skills that is less than overwhelming, he may struggle to get back to the bigs. 2003 Outlook: C

Chicago (NL)

Kevin Orie (**Pos**: 3B, **Age**: 30, **Bats**: R)

	G	AB	R	H	D	T	HR	RBI	SB	BB	SO	Avg	OBP	Slg
'02	13	32	4	9	3	0	0	5	0	1	4	.281	.306	.375
Car.	316	1015	117	253	64	6	22	116	5	94	163	.249	.320	.389

Orie returned to his original organization last year, and even saw his first big league action since 1999. But he played most of the season at Triple-A, where he showed the most power of his career. 2003 Outlook: C

Donovan Osborne (**Pos**: LHP, **Age**: 33)

	W	L	Pct.	ERA	G	GS	Sv	IP	H	BB	SO	HR	Ratio
'02	0	1	.000	6.19	11	0	0	16.0	19	10	13	1	1.81
Car.	47	46	.505	3.96	154	138	0	856.0	870	241	548	97	1.30

Osborne is an injury waiting to happen. He returned to the majors last year for the first time since 1999, only to land on the disabled list with a strained muscle in May. He was released in September. 2003 Outlook: C

Jesus Sanchez (**Pos**: LHP, **Age**: 28)

	W	L	Pct.	ERA	G	GS	Sv	IP	H	BB	SO	HR	Ratio
'02	0	0	–	12.96	8	0	0	8.1	15	10	6	4	3.00
Car.	23	32	.418	5.20	150	80	0	502.1	535	268	374	77	1.60

Sanchez didn't fool many major league hitters in April and September last year. In between, he wasn't much better at Triple-A, allowing a nasty home-run rate. The Astros signed him to a minor league deal in December. 2003 Outlook: C

Chicago Cubs Minor League Prospects

Organization Overview:

The arrival of Mark Prior and Bobby Hill last season was further evidence of a burgeoning Chicago farm system that has been recognized as one of baseball's best the past few years. Hee Seop Choi will be expected to step into the regular lineup this year, while Steve Smyth and Francis Beltran could win roles on the pitching staff. Several additional candidates are in line for at least a September cameo. Astute scouting has culled talent from Latin America to East Asia to keep the system replenished, and last year was no exception. Cubs affiliates won championships in the Rookie-level Arizona League and short-season Northwest League, and according to *Baseball America* polls, claimed the top prospect in both circuits. In particular, Chicago has accumulated a wealth of strong arms that promises to bolster its pitching staff in the years to come.

Francis Beltran

Position: P   **Opening Day Age:** 23
Bats: R **Throws:** R   **Born:** 11/29/79 in Santo
Ht: 6' 5" **Wt:** 220   Domingo, DR

Recent Statistics

	W	L	ERA	G	GS	Sv	IP	H	R	BB	SO	HR
2002 AA West Tenn	2	2	2.59	39	0	23	41.2	28	14	19	43	2
2002 NL Chicago	0	0	7.50	11	0	0	12.0	14	11	16	11	2

Signed out of the Dominican Republic in 1996, Beltran was returned to the bullpen with the Double-A West Tennessee Diamond Jaxx last year and suddenly blossomed in the closer's role, posting 23 saves in 39 appearances. He's been clocked as high as 97 MPH on his fastball, which regularly hits near the 95-MPH mark and has sharp, late movement. He's been moved up the system fairly quickly the past few years, though in several promotions to the Cubs last year he had trouble finding the plate. Beltran will need to work on his control and command of his slider and changeup, but the Cubs feel that will come with experience. They view him as a potential closer of the near future.

Matt Bruback

Position: P   **Opening Day Age:** 24
Bats: R **Throws:** R   **Born:** 1/12/79 in Scott
Ht: 6' 7" **Wt:** 215   Airforce Base, IL

Recent Statistics

	W	L	ERA	G	GS	Sv	IP	H	R	BB	SO	HR
2001 A Daytona	6	3	3.00	14	14	0	84.0	70	33	21	87	3
2001 AA West Tenn	2	5	9.00	9	9	0	38.0	58	44	20	43	3
2002 AA West Tenn	9	7	3.16	28	28	0	174.0	157	70	48	158	9

Tall and lanky, Bruback is another pitcher who was aggressively moved up the chain in the Cubs' farm system, and he's proven to be something of a late-bloomer. After a rough baptism to Double-A ball at West Tennessee in 2001, he responded to the challenge last

year, leading the league with 158 strikeouts and tossing a career-high 174 innings. He mixes a 90-91 MPH fastball with a sinker, slider and change, and generally moves the ball low in the strike zone. At age 24, he's topped out in velocity, but with improved command of his repertoire and his resiliency, a future in the Cubs' bullpen, if not in the rotation, may not be far off.

Hee Seop Choi

Position: 1B   **Opening Day Age:** 24
Bats: L **Throws:** L   **Born:** 3/16/79 in Chun-
Ht: 6' 5" **Wt:** 235   Nam, Korea

Recent Statistics

	G	AB	R	H	D	T	HR	RBI	SB	BB	SO	Avg
2002 AAA Iowa	135	478	94	137	24	3	26	97	3	95	119	.287
2002 NL Chicago	24	50	6	9	1	0	2	4	0	7	15	.180

Having recovered from a 2001 hand and wrist injury, Choi terrorized the Triple-A Pacific Coast League last year and was called up to the parent club in September. He displayed a slick glove, but only occasional flashes of his power potential at the plate with the Cubs. He needs more exposure to lefthanded pitching to combat problems with the inside fastball, but it has been pointed out that aside from Barry Bonds, almost everyone will experience those troubles. Choi shows unusual patience at the plate. His ability to take pitches to the opposite field with authority will be a plus at Wrigley Field, where the jet stream often is directed to left-center. His .345-8-17 showing (25 games) in the Arizona Fall League may be the fine-tuning he needs.

Nic Jackson

Position: OF   **Opening Day Age:** 23
Bats: L **Throws:** R   **Born:** 9/25/79 in
Ht: 6' 3" **Wt:** 205   Richmond, VA

Recent Statistics

	G	AB	R	H	D	T	HR	RBI	SB	BB	SO	Avg
2001 A Daytona	131	503	87	149	30	6	19	85	24	39	96	.296
2002 AA West Tenn	32	131	18	38	9	1	3	20	8	6	23	.290

Jackson's progress was waylaid last year at Double-A West Tennessee when he suffered a fractured leg that ended his season after just 32 games. Before that, he was on the fast track to the big leagues, bringing an intriguing package to the plate—a .300 bat with power and speed on the bases. It's good news for the Cubs, then, that he has recovered after a fall season in the Mexican Pacific League. Jackson will need to improve his strikeout and walk ratios before he makes the next big step, but his compelling combination of power, speed and athleticism make him one of the more exciting prospects in the Cubs' system. There are some questions about his arm, but the organization projects him as being able to handle any of the outfield positions.

David Kelton

Position: 3B
Bats: R **Throws:** R
Ht: 6' 3" **Wt:** 205

Opening Day Age: 23
Born: 12/17/79 in
Dothan, AL

Recent Statistics

	G	AB	R	H	D	T	HR	RBI	SB	BB	SO	Avg
2001 AA West Tenn	58	224	33	70	9	4	12	45	1	24	55	.313
2002 AA West Tenn	129	498	68	130	28	6	20	79	12	52	129	.261

Kelton came back from a wrist ailment that cut short his 2001 debut in Double-A to tie for the Southern League home-run title in 2002. His overall production was down from the previous year's aborted season, but a lot of that could be attributed to rehab and his trials in the field, which resulted in his being bounced from third base to the outfield to first. A teammate of Nic Jackson's in Guasave of the Mexican Pacific League last fall, Kelton was moved back to third. After the switch, he seemed to regain his confidence, making very few of the type of throwing errors that were his bane since shoulder surgery in high school. The Cubs, who have had a long-standing hole at the hot corner, will have him under the microscope, as his short, powerful stroke already is considered major league-caliber.

Luis Montanez

Position: SS
Bats: R **Throws:** R
Ht: 6' 2" **Wt:** 185

Opening Day Age: 21
Born: 12/15/81 in
Bayamon, PR

Recent Statistics

	G	AB	R	H	D	T	HR	RBI	SB	BB	SO	Avg
2001 A Lansing	124	499	70	127	33	6	5	54	20	34	121	.255
2002 A Daytona	124	487	69	129	21	5	4	59	14	44	89	.265

The Cubs' first choice in the 2000 draft, Montanez saw his power numbers take a dip as a 20-year-old in the high Class-A Florida State League, but he made significant progress controlling the strike zone. He cut down his strikeouts by 35 percent. His coaches—who are loath to tinker with his smooth, level swing—are pleased with that progress, as well as his improvement in the field, where he again made far fewer errors in the second half after acclimating himself to a new league. He continued to work on his game in the Puerto Rican League over the winter, where he has hit well against strong competition.

Andy Sisco

Position: P
Bats: L **Throws:** L
Ht: 6' 9" **Wt:** 260

Opening Day Age: 20
Born: 1/13/83 in
Steamboat Springs, CO

Recent Statistics

	W	L	ERA	G	GS	Sv	IP	H	R	BB	SO	HR
2001 R Cubs	1	0	5.24	10	7	0	34.1	36	28	10	31	1
2002 A Boise	7	2	2.43	14	14	0	77.2	51	23	39	101	3

As the Cubs' second pick of the 2001 draft after Mark Prior, Sisco could make it a celebrated one. The 6-foot-9 lefty has scouts thinking he may be something spe-

cial. He was named the best prospect of the short-season Northwest League, where he surrendered just 5.9 hits and struck out 11.7 batters per nine innings. He possesses an instinctive touch on the mound that belies his 19 years, and when the coaches helped tighten his delivery, everything fell into place. He throws mid-90s heat that promises to increase with maturity, along with a splitter, curve and a developing change. He just needs his reps, which includes avoiding injury. A good athlete with a strong work ethic, he has the highest ceiling in the stable of Cubs pitching prospects.

Steve Smyth

Position: P
Bats: L **Throws:** L
Ht: 6' 1" **Wt:** 195

Opening Day Age: 24
Born: 6/3/78 in Brawley,
CA

Recent Statistics

	W	L	ERA	G	GS	Sv	IP	H	R	BB	SO	HR
2002 AA West Tenn	4	4	3.58	11	11	0	73.0	62	34	18	74	7
2002 AAA Iowa	3	2	5.81	6	6	0	31.0	35	21	10	25	4
2002 NL Chicago	1	3	9.35	8	7	0	26.0	34	28	10	16	9

It probably was unfair that the Cubs promoted Smyth when their rotation was depleted last year. He was a year removed from rotator cuff surgery, and was admittedly tired from 100-plus minor league innings, which affected both his velocity and command. It served to make for a rude welcome to the majors, where he surrendered nine homers in 26 innings and posted a 9.35 ERA. Cubs officials feel that he has regained his form from two years ago (when he was the ERA king of the Double-A Southern League), and that the real Steve Smyth will show up this year—with a 90-93 MPH fastball to go with a full slider-curve-change complement. He'll have a shot at a rotation slot, but he also could serve as a lefthanded setup man.

Others to Watch

Righthanded starter **Angel Guzman** (21) improved on his curve to go with a mid-90s fastball, resulting in a 11-4, 2.19 combined record in Class-A. . . Six-foot-8 southpaw **Luke Hagerty** (22) limited opposing batters to just three hits per game while posting a 1.13 ERA in the short-season Northwest League, and fanned 10 in the clinching game of a three-game playoff sweep. . . **Brendan Harris** (22) hit a combined .328 and slugged .533 with a .389 on-base percentage, all while moving from Class-A to Double-A ball and splitting time between second and third base. . . Rookie-level Mesa lefty **Justin Jones** already is sneaky fast in the low 90s at age 18, whiffing 11.3 per nine innings. He exhibits excellent command and poise for his age. . . Eighteen-year-old center-fielder **Felix Pie** copped co-MVP and top prospect honors in the Rookie-level Arizona League after hitting .321 with 17 steals and 13 triples in just 218 at-bats. . . Korean import **Jae-Kuk Ryu** (19), a 6-foot-3 righty, sported a mid-90s fastball along with a good curve and change in his first full season stateside, and he exhibits a good grasp of pitching know-how.

Great American Ball Park

Offense

With fair dimensions, including some old-fashioned touches such as a replication of Crosley Field's right-field terrace, Great American Ball Park should be a good offensive stadium. The team is waiting to see how the wind will play in the new park. The stadium faces in a different direction than Cinergy Field, and wind currents may aid more balls at Great American. The new stadium also has a grass surface that the Reds believe will play fast and true.

Defense

A key will be how the infielders adapt to the playing surface. Newly planted grass surfaces often have needed time to become "bad-hop proof." However, the Reds' field was laid last fall and should be completely settled when the season opens. Bullpens, which had been on the field at Cinergy Field, are now out of play, making the pursuit of foul flies much easier.

Who It Helps the Most

Cincinnati's array of young hitters can reach the seats in any park. Great American's right-field area could become a favorite target for sluggers like Adam Dunn and Ken Griffey Jr. And with reachable power alleys to all fields, the Reds' lineup shouldn't be affected at all.

Who It Hurts the Most

The Reds have struggled at home the past three years, a quirk that likely will be corrected in the new atmosphere. Cincinnati's pitching staff has lacked power pitchers in its starting rotation, something that can translate into home runs in what is likely to be an offensive stadium. However, most ballclubs get a boost from a new home and the Reds expect to benefit.

Rookies & Newcomers

Great American Ball Park ultimately may help the Reds the most by generating the extra revenue needed for the team to compete more aggressively in the free-agent market. Success could allow them to keep more of their young players, rather than shuffle rosters due to budget concerns.

Dimensions: LF-328, LCF-379, CF-404, RCF-370, RF-325

Capacity: 42,000

Elevation: 550 feet

Surface: Grass

Foul Territory: Average

Park Factors

2002 Season (Cinergy Field)

	Home Games			Away Games			
	Reds	Opp	Total	Reds	Opp	Total	Index
G	75	75	150	75	75	150	
Avg	.267	.279	.273	.244	.259	.252	109
AB	2487	2681	5168	2586	2505	5091	102
R	372	383	755	302	321	623	121
H	664	747	1411	632	649	1281	110
2B	165	148	313	114	127	241	128
3B	3	11	14	18	13	31	44
HR	83	103	186	79	57	136	135
BB	316	241	557	236	271	507	108
SO	522	486	1008	588	430	1018	98
E	49	43	92	64	50	114	81
E-Infield	36	37	73	49	41	90	81
LHB-Avg	.278	.283	.281	.262	.266	.264	106
LHB-HR	36	43	79	34	31	65	123
RHB-Avg	.259	.276	.268	.230	.254	.242	111
RHB-HR	47	60	107	45	26	71	145

2001-2002 (Cinergy Field)

	Home Games			Away Games			
	Reds	Opp	Total	Reds	Opp	Total	Index
G	150	150	300	147	147	294	
Avg	.266	.279	.273	.254	.266	.260	105
AB	5047	5374	10421	5105	4936	10041	102
R	697	792	1489	654	681	1335	109
H	1342	1502	2844	1295	1312	2607	107
2B	318	319	637	238	266	504	122
3B	8	21	29	34	28	62	45
HR	159	201	360	166	133	299	116
BB	525	483	1008	451	506	957	101
SO	1021	936	1957	1156	852	2008	94
E	113	102	215	128	106	234	90
E-Infield	89	86	175	101	91	192	89
LHB-Avg	.287	.282	.284	.275	.274	.274	104
LHB-HR	73	87	160	87	70	157	100
RHB-Avg	.251	.278	.265	.237	.260	.249	107
RHB-HR	86	114	200	79	63	142	134

2002 Rankings (National League)

- Highest double factor
- Second-highest run factor
- Second-highest home-run factor
- Second-highest RHB batting-average factor
- Third-highest batting-average factor
- Third-highest hit factor
- Third-highest RHB home-run factor
- Second-lowest triple factor

Cincinnati

Bob Boone

2002 Season

Bob Boone endured another frustrating season in which he never could field a consistent lineup due to a steady stream of injuries. He hasn't had the benefit of a healthy Ken Griffey Jr. for two years now. Boone also had to assimilate a string of new players, particularly several new pitchers as the year wore on. However, he did succeed in getting a handle on some of the newcomers, which should help entering this year.

Offense

Without having a set lineup, Boone constantly juggled his batting order. He also took a look at new combinations, such as Aaron Boone at shortstop and Russell Branyan at third base. Boone continues to search for a set leadoff hitter. He likes to innovate, using squeezes and sacrifices, as well as putting runners into motion as his personnel allows. However, he also has the potential of a big-bomb offense, with all the power possibly ready to deliver.

Pitching & Defense

Due to all the injuries and all the problems in his starting rotation, Boone has become a master at juggling his relievers for matchup advantages. At the same time, he's done a better job of not overworking his relievers unnecessarily. He was willing to convert Danny Graves into a starting pitcher and to try Scott Williamson as a closer. Those moves could pay big dividends this season. When he has the choice, Boone seems more likely to come down on the side of offense rather than defense when making his lineup and substitutions. He's very hands-on in terms of pitch-calling and demands much from his catchers.

2003 Outlook

Until Boone is given a full deck with which to play, it's difficult to judge him in the Reds' job. He also never has had the luxury of a legitimate group of starting pitchers. However, there are ingredients in place this year for a more reliable rotation. If he gets his lineup intact and healthy, Boone could have a team with which he shows how he manages while in contention.

Born: 11/19/47 in San Diego, CA

Playing Experience: 1972-1990, Phi, Cal, KC

Managerial Experience: 5 seasons

Manager Statistics

Year	Team, Lg	W	L	Pct	GB	Finish
2002	Cincinnati, NL	78	84	.481	19.0	3rd Central
5 Seasons		325	386	.457	–	–

2002 Starting Pitchers by Days Rest

	<=3	4	5	6+
Reds Starts	0	86	43	23
Reds ERA	–	4.62	4.34	5.94
NL Avg Starts	1	88	42	21
NL ERA	3.18	4.22	4.14	4.58

2002 Situational Stats

	Bob Boone	NL Average
Hit & Run Success %	32.4	36.5
Stolen Base Success %	69.0	68.3
Platoon Pct.	48.9	52.7
Defensive Subs	11	19
High-Pitch Outings	3	7
Quick/Slow Hooks	32/12	24/11
Sacrifice Attempts	125	95

2002 Rankings (National League)

- 2nd in steals of third base (16), sacrifice bunt attempts and starting lineups used (130)
- 3rd in stolen base attempts (168), steals of second base (100) and quick hooks

Aaron Boone

2002 Season

Healthy through a full season for the first time, Aaron Boone had his breakthrough power campaign that was long awaited. He nearly doubled his previous career high in home runs, and he also reached a personal highs in several other offensive categories. Unfortunately, the burst of power corresponded with a drop of 50 points from Boone's 2001 batting average. But in a year full of Reds injuries, he played in every game and was the club's leading run producer.

Hitting

Boone has added nearly 20 pounds of muscle over the last few years, and he's become a legitimate power hitter. He looks for fastballs early in the count and is much more anxious to jerk balls than he was in prior years. The flip side of that strategy is more strikeouts and less consistent contact. Boone rarely takes counts deep and will chase off-speed stuff out of the strike zone. However, the change in philosophy resulted in 66 extra-base hits last year, production that the Reds clearly will be happy with in any season.

Baserunning & Defense

Despite speed that is just slightly above average, Boone enjoyed a remarkable year with stolen bases, leading the Reds with 32 steals in 40 attempts. He uses good judgment on the basepaths and is aggressive about trying to take the extra base. He has greatly improved his footwork and range at third base, and his throwing arm usually is accurate. Boone also was tried for several games at shortstop last season. Though lacking superior range at the position, he handled himself adequately.

2003 Outlook

Cincinnati would like to see Boone improve his average from last year, when he hit better than .250 in only one month of the campaign. However, he has taken his power production to another plateau and is in the middle of his physical prime. With a healthy lineup around him, Boone could be a 30-homer, 100-RBI threat for the next several seasons.

Position: 3B/SS
Bats: R **Throws:** R
Ht: 6' 2" **Wt:** 200

Opening Day Age: 30
Born: 3/9/73 in La Mesa, CA
ML Seasons: 6

Overall Statistics

	G	AB	R	H	D	T	HR	RBI	SB	BB	SO	Avg	OBP	Slg
'02	162	606	83	146	38	2	26	87	32	56	111	.241	.314	.439
Car.	562	1980	266	536	122	11	68	297	68	156	354	.271	.333	.446

Where He Hits the Ball

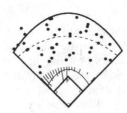 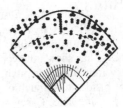

Vs. LHP   **Vs. RHP**

2002 Situational Stats

	AB	H	HR	RBI	Avg		AB	H	HR	RBI	Avg
Home	310	76	14	51	.245	LHP	150	35	4	24	.233
Road	296	70	12	36	.236	RHP	456	111	22	63	.243
First Half	319	75	12	45	.235	Sc Pos	159	37	4	54	.233
Scnd Half	287	71	14	42	.247	Clutch	100	28	6	17	.280

2002 Rankings (National League)

- 1st in games played
- 2nd in steals of third (7) and errors at third base (20)
- 3rd in lowest fielding percentage at third base (.954) and lowest batting average on a 3-2 count (.082)
- 5th in lowest batting average
- 6th in stolen bases and stolen-base percentage (80.0)
- 7th in at-bats
- Led the Reds in home runs, total bases (266), RBI, stolen bases, plate appearances (685), games played, stolen-base percentage (80.0) and steals of third (7)

Cincinnati

Sean Casey

2002 Season

A beaning and shoulder troubles cost Sean Casey a quarter of last season, which ended up being the worst of his young career. He lost three games in mid-April when he was plunked in the head by a Robert Person pitch, and later found himself on the shelf for nearly three weeks in July after tearing a muscle in his left shoulder. He batted only .237 after the All-Star break. He also struggled late in games. While he was a .300 hitter over the first six innings, he produced an anemic .178 average from the seventh inning on. He ended up missing the season's final four weeks due to the shoulder injury, which required surgery in mid-September.

Hitting

The book on Casey always has been to crowd him inside with hard stuff. He sits on the plate and never has shown the consistency or willingness to try and pull inside pitches. So he gets a steady diet of inside stuff, much of which he fights off to the opposite field. Casey struggled last year against lefthanded pitching, and his lack of power remained a concern. He doesn't lift many balls and is vulnerable to pitches up in the strike zone. His home runs and slugging percentage have declined in each of the past three seasons.

Baserunning & Defense

Casey's speed is below average, and he is only an occasional threat to steal a base. He also is an inconsistent first baseman. Though he has improved his work around the bag, his range remains poor and at times he's erratic when required to throw the ball. Casey does a good job of picking balls in the dirt, however.

2003 Outlook

Even with its new ballpark, Cincinnati remains limited in its payroll and Casey annually is a prime candidate to be moved. When he was hitting above .300, many clubs found him desirable, despite the lack of home runs. However, his market value suffered from his down season, and a first baseman who doesn't show power isn't always coveted. So the Reds have a major decision to make with Casey.

Position: 1B
Bats: L **Throws:** R
Ht: 6' 4" **Wt:** 225

Opening Day Age: 28
Born: 7/2/74 in Willingboro, NJ
ML Seasons: 6
Pronunciation: KAY-see

Overall Statistics

	G	AB	R	H	D	T	HR	RBI	SB	BB	SO	Avg	OBP	Slg
'02	120	425	56	111	25	0	6	42	2	43	47	.261	.334	.362
Car.	651	2344	342	708	161	6	71	368	7	243	325	.302	.373	.467

Where He Hits the Ball

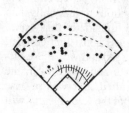   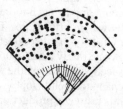

Vs. LHP   **Vs. RHP**

2002 Situational Stats

	AB	H	HR	RBI	Avg		AB	H	HR	RBI	Avg
Home	207	56	3	21	.271	LHP	130	30	2	16	.231
Road	218	55	3	21	.252	RHP	295	81	4	26	.275
First Half	294	80	5	34	.272	Sc Pos	108	22	1	35	.204
Scnd Half	131	31	1	8	.237	Clutch	63	10	2	7	.159

2002 Rankings (National League)

- 5th in lowest fielding percentage at first base (.993)
- 6th in batting average on an 0-2 count (.303) and errors at first base (7)
- 7th in lowest batting average in the clutch
- 8th in lowest batting average with runners in scoring position
- Led the Reds in highest groundball-flyball ratio (1.6) and batting average on an 0-2 count (.303)

Ryan Dempster

2002 Season

The Reds picked up Ryan Dempster last July in a trade with Florida. He had been acquired as a key to what the Reds hoped would be a playoff run, but he instead struggled after arriving with the team. He compiled an ERA of nearly 10.00 over his first seven outings with Cincinnati, and won only twice in his first 10 Reds starts. He finally found himself in September, when he went 3-0. He finished with more than 200 innings pitched for the third straight year.

Pitching

Dempster has nasty stuff, including a 95-MPH fastball and a hard slider that hits the high 80s. He also has developed a good straight change. However, as his high ERA suggests, he labors with command and constantly has struggled with mechanics. After coming to the Reds, pitching coach Don Gullett worked with Dempster on shortening his stride home and finding a consistent release point. It took some time for the adjustments to take hold, but when they did, Dempster had consistency with his heavy sinker and cut down on his walks. He also began regaining the aggressiveness that had been lost during the course of the past year and a half.

Defense & Hitting

His constant tinkering with his delivery has made Dempster inconsistent in his ability to hold runners. He fields his position adequately. After making seven errors between 2000 and 2001, he did not commit any miscues last season. He occasionally can help himself with the bat, and is an especially competent bunter.

2003 Outlook

The early returns on Dempster were not good for the Reds. However, this still could be a pickup that pays major dividends. He has long been considered an ace in waiting who needed to develop better command and mechanics. Those are things Gullett is good at teaching, and Dempster might have a nice career ahead of him. He has the stuff to be No. 1 or 2 starter and a consistent 16-18 game winner.

Position: SP
Bats: R **Throws:** R
Ht: 6' 3" **Wt:** 215

Opening Day Age: 25
Born: 5/3/77 in Sechelt, BC, Canada
ML Seasons: 5

Overall Statistics

	W	L	Pct.	ERA	G	GS	Sv	IP	H	BB	SO	HR	Ratio
'02	10	13	.435	5.38	33	33	0	209.0	228	93	153	28	1.54
Car.	47	48	.495	4.81	139	136	0	848.1	874	433	694	106	1.54

How Often He Throws Strikes

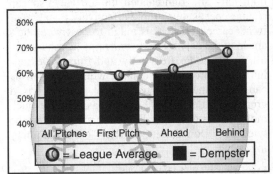

= League Average   = Dempster

2002 Situational Stats

	W	L	ERA	Sv	IP		AB	H	HR	RBI	Avg
Home	7	4	4.80	0	95.2	LHB	358	119	14	56	.332
Road	3	9	5.88	0	113.1	RHB	439	109	14	59	.248
First Half	5	8	4.79	0	120.1	Sc Pos	199	58	9	87	.291
Scnd Half	5	5	6.19	0	88.2	Clutch	44	16	1	6	.364

2002 Rankings (National League)

- 1st in fielding percentage at pitcher (1.000) and highest slugging percentage allowed (.472)
- 2nd in highest batting average allowed (.286), highest on-base percentage allowed (.365) and highest ERA on the road (5.88)
- 3rd in runners caught stealing (13) and highest ERA (5.38)
- 4th in lowest stolen-base percentage allowed (35.0)
- 5th in complete games (4), hits allowed (228) and walks allowed (93)
- 6th in home runs allowed (28), highest ERA at home (4.80) and highest walks per nine innings (4.0)

Cincinnati

Elmer Dessens

2002 Season

Elmer Dessens ranked among the National League's ERA leaders for much of last season. That success was a reflection of how consistently he pitched throughout much of the year, before minor injuries cost him starts. However, Dessens' solid pitching didn't translate into many wins, which was due in part to both a lack of run support and his inability to last into the late innings.

Pitching

Dessens has as effective a cut fastball as any pitcher in the league. He mixes it with a good sinker to give him two reliable weapons against both left- and righthanded hitters. He also can change speeds much more effectively than earlier in his career. Dessens is tough to beat when he's ahead in the count. However, teams learned to lay off cutters more frequently and forced Dessens into more predictable counts, which is when he can be vulnerable. His control has improved greatly, a reflection of how he has become much more consistent with his mechanics under the tutelage of Don Gullett, the Reds' excellent pitching coach.

Defense & Hitting

Dessens has developed a very good slide step that speeds up his delivery and can make him tough for baserunners to read. He is a good fielder who doesn't get rattled in pressure defensive situations. He also has worked hard to become a competitive hitter. He can be counted on to put the ball in play in the majority of his at-bats.

2003 Outlook

Though hardly among baseball's elite pitching names, Dessens has begun carving out a reputation as someone who keeps his team in virtually every game he works. That is a highly valuable commodity, especially for a team like Cincinnati, which constantly seems to be groping for solutions to starting pitcher problems. Dessens is one hurler the Reds can depend on, and he could be a 15-game winner with good support.

Position: SP
Bats: R **Throws:** R
Ht: 6' 0" **Wt:** 187

Opening Day Age: 31
Born: 1/13/72 in Hermosillo, Mexico
ML Seasons: 6
Pronunciation: dah-SENZ

Overall Statistics

	W	L	Pct.	ERA	G	GS	Sv	IP	H	BB	SO	HR	Ratio
'02	7	8	.467	3.03	30	30	0	178.0	173	49	93	24	1.25
Car.	30	35	.462	4.29	165	88	1	633.1	696	177	364	78	1.38

How Often He Throws Strikes

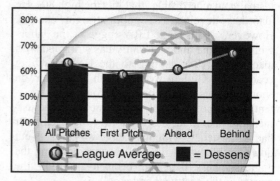

= League Average ■ = Dessens

2002 Situational Stats

	W	L	ERA	Sv	IP		AB	H	HR	RBI	Avg
Home	4	5	3.53	0	86.2	LHB	315	77	7	30	.244
Road	3	3	2.56	0	91.1	RHB	358	96	17	38	.268
First Half	5	4	2.91	0	105.1	Sc Pos	126	35	7	43	.278
Scnd Half	2	4	3.22	0	72.2	Clutch	25	8	4	6	.320

2002 Rankings (National League)

- 2nd in lowest ERA on the road
- 3rd in fewest strikeouts per nine innings (4.7)
- 6th in ERA and least run support per nine innings (4.1)
- 8th in lowest stolen-base percentage allowed (50.0)
- 10th in most home runs allowed per nine innings (1.21)
- Led the Reds in ERA, home runs allowed, hit batsmen (7), stolen bases allowed (8), runners caught stealing (8), lowest batting average allowed (.257) and lowest ERA at home

Adam Dunn

2002 Season

Adam Dunn excited Reds fans with his debut in 2001, when he slugged 19 homers after his July callup. But on the road to Cooperstown that many have predicted for him, Dunn hit a major pothole last season. He fell into a huge second-half slump, batting only .190 after the All-Star break, with just nine home runs and 17 RBI over that span. For the season, he ranked among the major league leaders in both walks and strikeouts.

Hitting

Dunn is very selective for such a young, powerful hitter, which accounts for his high walk totals. However, he can have trouble catching up to inside fastballs, and National League pitchers pounded him inside with increasing regularity. He also has holes that can be exploited with change-ups, and he is prone to chasing pitches when he gets behind in the count. At times he is too picky about waiting for a perfect pitch to drive, and he took far too many called strikes. Dunn has big-time strength and can hit the ball out to any part of the ballpark, including the opposite field.

Baserunning & Defense

There are few more imposing baserunners than the hard-charging Dunn. He is a legitimate stolen-base threat and is very aggressive about taking extra bases. He still can be crude in the outfield, where he made nine total errors last year, high for an outfielder with his average range. His arm is of average strength. He also saw extensive action at first base in 2002, where he committed six more miscues.

2003 Outlook

Dunn's impressive talent wasn't enough to prevent him from coming back to earth. The question for him now is whether he makes the necessary adjustments to get himself back on track. He has an excellent work ethic and immense talent, attributes that should allow him to resume his climb into the game's elite. Dunn has the unique combination of power and skill to someday be a 40-homer, .300-hitting monster.

Position: LF/1B/RF
Bats: L **Throws:** R
Ht: 6' 6" **Wt:** 240

Opening Day Age: 23
Born: 11/9/79 in Houston, TX
ML Seasons: 2

Overall Statistics

	G	AB	R	H	D	T	HR	RBI	SB	BB	SO	Avg	OBP	Slg
'02	158	535	84	133	28	2	26	71	19	128	170	.249	.400	.454
Car.	224	779	138	197	46	3	45	114	23	166	244	.253	.391	.493

Where He Hits the Ball

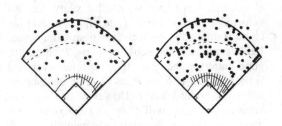

Vs. LHP   **Vs. RHP**

2002 Situational Stats

	AB	H	HR	RBI	Avg		AB	H	HR	RBI	Avg
Home	256	66	13	40	.258	LHP	169	43	11	27	.254
Road	279	67	13	31	.240	RHP	366	90	15	44	.246
First Half	283	85	17	54	.300	Sc Pos	130	27	4	42	.208
Scnd Half	252	48	9	17	.190	Clutch	88	18	6	13	.205

2002 Rankings (National League)

- 1st in errors in left field (8) and lowest fielding percentage in left field (.962)
- 2nd in strikeouts and most pitches seen per plate appearance (4.28)
- 3rd in walks, pitches seen (2,893) and assists in left field (9)
- 4th in cleanup slugging percentage (.595)
- 5th in lowest percentage of swings put into play (33.5)
- 6th in games played
- Led the Reds in home runs, runs scored, caught stealing (9), walks, intentional walks (13), times on base (270), strikeouts, pitches seen (2,893) and most pitches seen per plate appearance (4.28)

Shawn Estes

2002 Season

Whether in New York with the Mets or in Cincinnati with the Reds, Shawn Estes couldn't win last year. He earned only five victories in his 29 total starts, with only one coming after he joined the Reds. While with New York, he had a stretch of six straight starts (and 11 of 12) in which his team didn't win. It says something about his season that Estes' most memorable moment was throwing a pitch behind Roger Clemens in a Mets-Yankees interleague game when his teammates all wanted him to hit The Rocket.

Pitching

Estes' stuff has teased people for years. But his velocity has leveled out in the high 80s, and his command, always suspect, just hasn't improved. He has an assortment of weapons, including a good cutter, a changeup that he turns over and sinks and a 12-to-6 curve that can be devastating when it's under control. However, no one ever knows what Estes will bring to the mound on a given day. He also seems fragile mentally and is prone to allowing a big inning. He can be over-powering for four or five frames but then suddenly unravel when facing his first trouble in a game.

Defense & Hitting

Estes' delivery sometimes leaves him out of position. He tends to make erratic plays when he rushes. He holds runners fairly well and his pickoff move can be effective. Once a decent hitter, he's become a virtual automatic out at the plate, though one of his three hits last year was a home run that came against the Yankees amid the interleague circus surrounding Clemens' appearance versus the Mets.

2003 Outlook

The Reds appear to have little interest in keeping Estes, a free agent. And he faced a long winter looking for a job. Eventually, some team will take a chance on a lefthander who is only 30 years old and can show effective stuff. However, Estes needs a good season to revive what is fast becoming a washed-out career.

Position: SP
Bats: R **Throws:** L
Ht: 6' 2" **Wt:** 200

Opening Day Age: 30
Born: 2/18/73 in San Bernardino, CA
ML Seasons: 8
Pronunciation: EST-us
Nickname: Buck

Overall Statistics

	W	L	Pct.	ERA	G	GS	Sv	IP	H	BB	SO	HR	Ratio
'02	5	12	.294	5.10	29	29	0	160.2	171	83	109	13	1.58
Car.	69	62	.527	4.37	189	189	0	1150.2	1116	604	904	87	1.49

How Often He Throws Strikes

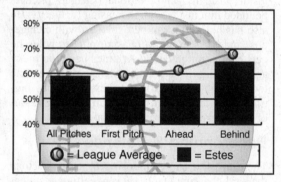

= League Average = Estes

2002 Situational Stats

	W	L	ERA	Sv	IP		AB	H	HR	RBI	Avg
Home	3	5	3.94	0	98.1	LHB	130	39	2	19	.300
Road	2	7	6.93	0	62.1	RHB	478	132	11	67	.276
First Half	3	7	4.81	0	97.1	Sc Pos	175	55	4	72	.314
Scnd Half	2	5	5.54	0	63.1	Clutch	22	5	1	1	.227

2002 Rankings (National League)

- 1st in lowest winning percentage (.294)
- 2nd in highest batting average allowed with runners in scoring position (.314)
- 5th in GDPs induced (26)
- 6th in errors at pitcher (3)
- 9th in stolen bases allowed (20)
- 10th in walks allowed (83)

Danny Graves

2002 Season

Danny Graves had another solid season as one of the National League's better closers. He joined John Franco as the only Reds relievers to record at least 30 saves on three occasions. However, after earning 32 saves in 39 opportunities, Graves finished the year in a new starting pitcher role. He made four late-season starts and fared well, winning his only decision and allowing just four runs in 19 innings.

Pitching

The Reds were ecstatic at how well Graves adapted to his first opportunity to start in the majors. They feel that with an offseason of conditioning and a full spring to prepare, he has the stuff to be a quality starter. As a closer, Graves came at every hitter with his mid-90s sinker. It's a pitch that should suit him well as a starter, too. However, over the last two years, he's also developed a quality straight change, as well as large-breaking slider that he can spot on the corners. The key for him always has been getting ahead in the count, and it certainly will be a deciding factor as a starter, where he can't afford to pitch behind too many hitters.

Defense & Hitting

One area in which Graves showed improvement last year was holding runners, which had not been a priority when working as a closer. He registered his first career pickoff and allowed only one successful stolen base on his watch in 2002. He has good reactions with the glove, and has shown some flashes of power at the plate. He could end up being a solid hitting pitcher as he prepares for the additional at-bats he'll get as a starter.

2003 Outlook

With all their starting pitching problems and potential bullpen depth, the Reds feel it's a good gamble to hand a spot in their rotation to Graves. He has the stuff and mentality to be a big winner. If he can make the transition, he could be the kind of consistent winner Cincinnati desperately has been trying to find for years. He also could make himself very expensive, since he is a year away from free agency.

Position: RP
Bats: R **Throws:** R
Ht: 6' 0" **Wt:** 185

Opening Day Age: 29
Born: 8/7/73 in Saigon, Vietnam
ML Seasons: 7

Overall Statistics

	W	L	Pct.	ERA	G	GS	Sv	IP	H	BB	SO	HR	Ratio
'02	7	3	.700	3.19	68	4	32	98.2	99	25	58	7	1.26
Car.	35	21	.625	3.42	367		4129	518.1	499	192	306	42	1.33

How Often He Throws Strikes

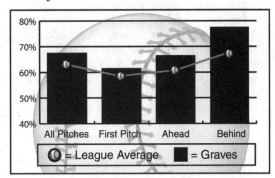

○ = League Average   ■ = Graves

2002 Situational Stats

	W	L	ERA	Sv	IP		AB	H	HR	RBI	Avg
Home	1	3	4.34	11	47.2	LHB	151	41	3	22	.272
Road	6	0	2.12	21	51.0	RHB	224	58	4	34	.259
First Half	3	3	2.96	26	51.2	Sc Pos	102	27	2	48	.265
Scnd Half	4	0	3.45	6	47.0	Clutch	213	57	4	35	.268

2002 Rankings (National League)

- 1st in highest percentage of inherited runners scored (57.5)
- 3rd in lowest save percentage (82.1)
- 6th in blown saves (7) and fewest strikeouts per nine innings in relief (5.2)
- 7th in relief wins (6)
- 10th in save opportunities (39)
- Led the Reds in saves, games finished (54), save opportunities (39), winning percentage, highest strikeout-walk ratio (2.3), lowest slugging percentage allowed (.365), lowest on-base percentage allowed (.311), highest groundball-flyball ratio allowed (2.2) and fewest pitches thrown per batter (3.29)

Ken Griffey Jr.

2002 Season

For a second straight season, Ken Griffey Jr. was reduced to being a non-factor by a series of injuries that had him on and off the disabled list. His ailments included a dislocated right kneecap and a strained right hamstring. He produced career lows in most significant offensive categories, managed fewer than 200 at-bats and went through the entire season without any sustained hot streak.

Hitting

It's difficult to believe that Griffey's skills have begun to go backward. However, it also is alarming to see him generate so little extra-base power. His bat often seems to have slowed down. In addition, he is much more vulnerable to inside hard stuff than at any time in his career. Griffey sometimes can fall off pitches, which results in too many weakly hit balls to the left side of the diamond. At his best, he can turn around any fastball and has home-run power to any field. However, for the past few years he has shown a pronounced uppercut as he concentrated more on home runs.

Baserunning & Defense

Griffey has stolen a total of nine bases over the past three years, a stat that almost looks like a typographical error. He no longer is a dangerous baserunner, though he still can turn it on when an extra base is needed. His outfield skills remain as good as anyone's, when he's healthy.

2003 Outlook

Griffey has fallen off the radar screen and has something to prove at 33 years of age. Once considered an automatic Hall of Famer, Griffey faces a lot of questions from baseball people, who privately feel he hasn't been as serious about conditioning as he should. Barry Bonds is a good example of a highly skilled player who took his game to another level in his mid-30s. Griffey has the skills to do the same, but it comes down to staying healthy and getting into better shape.

Position: CF
Bats: L **Throws:** L
Ht: 6' 3" **Wt:** 205

Opening Day Age: 33
Born: 11/21/69 in Donora, PA
ML Seasons: 14
Nickname: Junior, The Kid

Overall Statistics

G	AB	R	H	D	T	HR	RBI	SB	BB	SO	Avg	OBP	Slg
70	197	17	52	8	0	8	23	1	28	39	.264	.358	.426
1861	6913	1237	2039	370	35	468	1358	176	913	1212	.295	.379	.562

Where He Hits the Ball

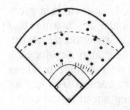 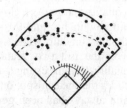

Vs. LHP   **Vs. RHP**

2002 Situational Stats

	AB	H	HR	RBI	Avg		AB	H	HR	RBI	Avg
Home	117	29	4	17	.248	LHP	60	13	1	7	.217
Road	80	23	4	6	.288	RHP	137	39	7	16	.285
First Half	74	18	2	4	.243	Sc Pos	38	8	1	15	.211
Scnd Half	123	34	6	19	.276	Clutch	37	10	1	5	.270

2002 Rankings (National League)

- Led the Reds in batting average on a 3-1 count (.500)

Austin Kearns

Position: RF/LF
Bats: R **Throws:** R
Ht: 6' 3" **Wt:** 220

Opening Day Age: 22
Born: 5/20/80 in Lexington, KY
ML Seasons: 1

2002 Season

A strained left hamstring last August cost Austin Kearns a chance to make a run at the National League Rookie of the Year Award. The injury caused him to miss the season's final five weeks. Still, he impressed with the way he was able to rebound from a June slump to bat .361 after the All-Star break. He showed he could handle both left- and righthanded pitching, and he posted impressive numbers both home and away. He finished the year with a .315 average that led NL rookies.

Hitting

Kearns is the total package. Though he doesn't have the explosive power of Adam Dunn, Kearns definitely is capable of hitting at least 25 to 30 home runs as he matures physically and as he learns to choose which pitches to drive. He also is likely to become an extra-base machine because of his strength to all fields and his very good management of the strike zone for such a young player. He is susceptible to being jammed because he crowds the plate and hangs in against all pitching. He also will take his share of walks and already has demonstrated the ability to limit strikeouts and make consistent contact.

Baserunning & Defense

Kearns has stolen as many as 21 bases in a minor league season, so he has some ability on the bases, even though his speed is average. He can play either left or right field with solid range. He also logged six games in center in 2002. He has a very good throwing arm and nice outfield mechanics.

2003 Outlook

Jot Kearns' name in the Reds' lineup for the next several years. He is a potential All-Star and batting champion with all-around ability and a very mature work ethic. Staying healthy may be his only question, as he missed part of 2001 due to injury, and was bit by the injury bug last year as well. However, the Reds expect him to be a franchise cornerstone for the next decade.

Overall Statistics

	G	AB	R	H	D	T	HR	RBI	SB	BB	SO	Avg	OBP	Slg
'02	107	372	66	117	24	3	13	56	6	54	81	.315	.407	.500
Car.	107	372	66	117	24	3	13	56	6	54	81	.315	.407	.500

Where He Hits the Ball

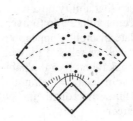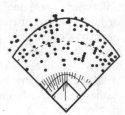

Vs. LHP   **Vs. RHP**

2002 Situational Stats

	AB	H	HR	RBI	Avg		AB	H	HR	RBI	Avg
Home	185	58	7	30	.314	LHP	91	30	2	9	.330
Road	187	59	6	26	.316	RHP	281	87	11	47	.310
First Half	214	60	8	29	.280	Sc Pos	97	26	4	42	.268
Scnd Half	158	57	5	27	.361	Clutch	68	24	1	6	.353

2002 Rankings (National League)

- 1st in batting average among rookies
- 2nd in home runs among rookies and RBI among rookies
- 6th in errors in right field (4) and assists in right field (7)
- 8th in batting average in the clutch
- Led the Reds in batting average, slugging percentage, on-base percentage, batting average with runners in scoring position, batting average in the clutch, batting average vs. left handed pitchers, batting average vs. righthanded pitchers, on-base percentage vs. lefthanded pitchers (.474), batting average on the road and batting average with two strikes (.239)

Cincinnati

Barry Larkin

2002 Season

Another series of injuries continued to erode the late career of Barry Larkin. Limited by assorted ailments, he never could generate any consistency, and his on-base percentage dipped into the low .300s. While Larkin managed 37 doubles, his production numbers were otherwise down from his previous standards. Nevertheless, after missing much of 2001 due to a groin pull and hernia surgery, he was able to play at least 145 games for only the sixth time in his career.

Hitting

Larkin still shows flashes of the bat speed and aggressiveness that made him such a star. Unfortunately, we don't see that ability on a regular basis. He too often seems vulnerable to average hard stuff, and his plate discipline appears to have suffered due to his lack of reliable playing time. Meanwhile, Larkin has fallen into the habit of lifting too many balls instead of being the slashing, line-drive machine that distinguished him for so much of his career.

Baserunning & Defense

Larkin remains a high-percentage basestealer, and his speed when going from first to third remains very close to what it was in his prime. But he's a shadow of his former self in the field. His range at shortstop no longer is what it used to be, and he doesn't make plays that used to look routine. His arm always has been one of the best, but recent shoulder trouble has cut down on his accuracy.

2003 Outlook

Larkin underwent surgery on his right big toe following last season, but he should be ready to go by spring training. This could be his last hurrah. The questionable contract extension given him three years ago expires after this season. Larkin will turn 39 early in 2003, and unless he comes back with a monster year, the first year in Cincinnati's new ballpark could be the last one for the long-time Reds captain.

Position: SS
Bats: R **Throws:** R
Ht: 6' 0" **Wt:** 185

Opening Day Age: 38
Born: 4/28/64 in Cincinnati, OH
ML Seasons: 17

Overall Statistics

	G	AB	R	H	D	T	HR	RBI	SB	BB	SO	Avg	OBP	Slg
'02	145	507	72	124	37	2	7	47	13	44	57	.245	.305	.367
Car.	1999	7350	1235	2172	410	72	188	898	375	883	746	.296	.372	.448

Where He Hits the Ball

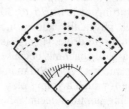 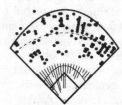

Vs. LHP   **Vs. RHP**

2002 Situational Stats

	AB	H	HR	RBI	Avg		AB	H	HR	RBI	Avg
Home	274	66	4	28	.241	LHP	122	23	3	11	.189
Road	233	58	3	19	.249	RHP	385	101	4	36	.262
First Half	288	72	5	26	.250	Sc Pos	113	26	1	41	.230
Scnd Half	219	52	2	21	.237	Clutch	78	18	0	9	.231

2002 Rankings (National League)

- 1st in lowest on-base percentage for a leadoff hitter (.259)
- 2nd in highest percentage of extra bases taken as a runner (67.5)
- 3rd in fielding percentage at shortstop (.979)
- 4th in lowest batting average vs. lefthanded pitchers
- 5th in sacrifice flies (7)
- 7th in lowest batting average
- 9th in steals of third (4) and lowest on-base percentage
- Led the Reds in sacrifice flies (7), GDPs (13), highest percentage of swings put into play (51.6), highest percentage of extra bases taken as a runner (67.5) and lowest percentage of swings on the first pitch (21.3)

Chris Reitsma

2002 Season

A hard-luck pitcher when he was a member of Cincinnati's rotation, Chris Reitsma went through a stretch of 13 starts last year when he won only once. He then spent a good portion of August in the minors before returning to the parent club to pitch exclusively out of the bullpen over the season's final six weeks. He was a success out of the bullpen, allowing runs in just two of 11 relief appearances.

Pitching

Reitsma throws a heavy sinker that touches the 95-MPH range. It's a pitch he used the majority of the time, particularly when he was working in a relief role. He also throws a riding four-seamer, and he has developed a very effective changeup, which he turns over with a slight screwball effect. He is much more aggressive in relief situations and more economical in his pitches, going right after hitters. Reitsma also seems to have more consistent velocity when working in a relief stint than when he's used as a starter. He is prone to occasional wild pitches when he overthrows his sinker.

Defense & Hitting

Reitsma holds runners fairly well with his slide step and pickoff move. But he eventually is slow coming to the plate. He handles himself well defensively, committing his first and only error in the big leagues last season. He's not much of a factor as a hitter, as he managed just three hits in 30 at-bats in 2002.

2003 Outlook

On a pitching staff with few givens, Reitsma is another of the Reds' projects. His winning percentage over the past two years is the worst of any National League hurler (minimum 25 decisions). But while Reitsma's record doesn't show it, he's capable of being a serviceable starting pitcher. Still, sentiment seems to be growing to bring him to spring training as a reliever, where his good stuff could make him a very effective setup man and occasional closer should Scott Williamson falter.

Position: SP/RP
Bats: R **Throws:** R
Ht: 6' 5" **Wt:** 215

Opening Day Age: 25
Born: 12/31/77 in Minneapolis, MN
ML Seasons: 2
Pronunciation: REETS-muh

Overall Statistics

	W	L	Pct.	ERA	G	GS	Sv	IP	H	BB	SO	HR	Ratio
'02	6	12	.333	3.64	32	21	0	138.1	144	45	84	17	1.37
Car.	13	27	.325	4.58	68	50	0	320.1	353	94	180	40	1.40

How Often He Throws Strikes

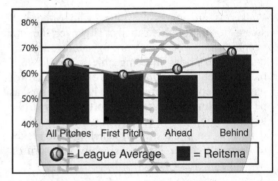

○ = League Average ■ = Reitsma

2002 Situational Stats

	W	L	ERA	Sv	IP		AB	H	HR	RBI	Avg
Home	4	7	3.75	0	72.0	LHB	230	61	10	28	.265
Road	2	5	3.53	0	66.1	RHB	310	83	7	38	.268
First Half	3	7	3.45	0	94.0	Sc Pos	144	40	6	53	.278
Scnd Half	3	5	4.06	0	44.1	Clutch	50	15	0	3	.300

2002 Rankings (National League)

- 4th in lowest winning percentage
- Led the Reds in losses

Todd Walker

2002 Season

Todd Walker seemed to have found a home in Cincinnati, where he gave the Reds a second straight solid season as their everyday second baseman after the Reds acquired him midway through the 2001 campaign. He led all Reds batters in hits, falling one point shy of .300 when he closed in a rush with a .380 average in September. Walker easily was the Reds' most effective lead-off man. He batted .297 in the No. 1 spot, compared to a .178 mark for all others used in the role. He also led Cincinnati in doubles and was among the team leaders in runs scored.

Hitting

Walker is an aggressive hitter who often will swing at first-pitch fastballs. However, he has become more adept at working counts. He has made great strides in being able to handle left-handed pitching. In addition, his extra-base power has grown considerably over the last two years, as he has become stronger and shortened his stroke to allow him to drive pitches into the gaps. He is dangerous on pitches away, which he often takes to deep left-center. He occasionally will turn on an inside pitch for power.

Baserunning & Defense

The Reds have worked with Walker to pick his spots on the bases better, and he has become a serviceable basestealer. He always looks to take the extra base and will challenge outfielders with his above-average speed. Walker has worked especially hard on improving his defensive skills and has made himself into a solid second baseman. His range is average, but he is surehanded and can turn the double play with consistency.

2003 Outlook

Walker's career had hit the skids three years ago when then-Twins manager Tom Kelly buried him in Minnesota. However, Walker has worked himself back to being a solid everyday player, and he should be just entering his prime. The Red Sox will benefit from that fact, dealing two minor league players to be named to the Reds for Walker in December. He potentially is a .300-hitting second baseman with decent power, and there aren't many of those in the game.

Position: 2B
Bats: L **Throws:** R
Ht: 6' 0" **Wt:** 190

Opening Day Age: 29
Born: 5/25/73 in Bakersfield, CA
ML Seasons: 7

Overall Statistics

	G	AB	R	H	D	T	HR	RBI	SB	BB	SO	Avg	OBP	Slg
'02	155	612	79	183	42	3	11	64	8	50	81	.299	.353	.431
Car.	749	2708	384	791	179	17	58	313	62	242	383	.292	.349	.435

Where He Hits the Ball

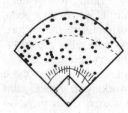 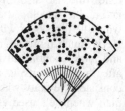

Vs. LHP   **Vs. RHP**

2002 Situational Stats

	AB	H	HR	RBI	Avg		AB	H	HR	RBI	Avg
Home	298	95	7	39	.319	LHP	158	44	2	17	.278
Road	314	88	4	25	.280	RHP	454	139	9	47	.306
First Half	311	88	5	31	.283	Sc Pos	150	40	4	53	.267
Scnd Half	301	95	6	33	.316	Clutch	97	23	1	11	.237

2002 Rankings (National League)

- 1st in fielding percentage at second base (.989)
- 5th in doubles
- 6th in at-bats, hits and singles
- 9th in errors at second base (8)
- Led the Reds in at-bats, hits, singles, doubles, lowest percentage of swings that missed (12.5), on-base percentage for a leadoff hitter (.340) and batting average at home

Russell Branyan

Position: LF/3B/1B
Bats: L **Throws:** R
Ht: 6' 3" **Wt:** 195

Opening Day Age: 27
Born: 12/19/75 in
Warner Robins, GA
ML Seasons: 5
Pronunciation:
BRAN-yen

Overall Statistics

	G	AB	R	H	D	T	HR	RBI	SB	BB	SO	Avg	OBP	Slg
'02	134	378	50	86	13	1	24	56	4	51	151	.228	.320	.458
Car.	326	928	134	213	38	5	61	154	5	114	380	.230	.317	.478

2002 Situational Stats

	AB	H	HR	RBI	Avg		AB	H	HR	RBI	Avg
Home	158	25	5	16	.158	LHP	60	14	7	13	.233
Road	220	61	19	40	.277	RHP	318	72	17	43	.226
First Half	218	47	11	26	.216	Sc Pos	103	19	5	30	.184
Scnd Half	160	39	13	30	.244	Clutch	56	15	4	12	.268

2002 Season

Finally given up on by Cleveland, Russell Branyan got a chance to play regularly for the Reds and showed flashes of his prodigious power. Branyan was traded to Cincinnati in June and finished third on the club with 16 home runs, even though he played only 84 games for the Reds. He saw action at first and third base, as well as in left field.

Hitting, Baserunning & Defense

Branyan's power and strikeout totals continue to be eye-popping. He fanned 151 times in 378 at-bats last year while still showing no signs of adjusting his big swing. He has trouble laying off high fastballs, and he remains very vulnerable to breaking balls. Branyan has average speed and stole four bases in seven attempts last season. He has an erratic arm at third base and limited range both in the outfield and at third. His first-base skills remain raw.

2003 Outlook

Someday, Branyan can be a 40-plus home-run hitter. But whatever future he has is tied directly to how well he can reduce his strikeouts. And his progress could be on hold after a winter ball shoulder injury required surgery. He may not be at full strength when this season begins.

Bruce Chen

Position: RP
Bats: L **Throws:** L
Ht: 6' 2" **Wt:** 210

Opening Day Age: 25
Born: 6/19/77 in
Panama City, Panama
ML Seasons: 5

Overall Statistics

	W	L	Pct.	ERA	G	GS	Sv	IP	H	BB	SO	HR	Ratio
'02	2	5	.286	5.56	55	6	0	77.2	85	43	80	16	1.65
Car.	20	18	.526	4.53	139	59	0	429.0	408	184	380	77	1.38

2002 Situational Stats

	W	L	ERA	Sv	IP		AB	H	HR	RBI	Avg
Home	2	2	4.25	0	42.1	LHB	115	29	2	17	.252
Road	0	3	7.13	0	35.1	RHB	195	56	14	35	.287
First Half	2	4	6.27	0	51.2	Sc Pos	75	21	3	35	.280
Scnd Half	0	1	4.15	0	26.0	Clutch	25	5	3	7	.200

2002 Season

It's hard to believe that at one time many baseball people considered Bruce Chen to be the jewel of the Atlanta Braves' farm system. Four organizations later, he wound up being used as a middle reliever for Cincinnati last season. It was a role in which he enjoyed some success, posting a relief ERA under 4.00 with the Reds. Cincinnati had acquired Chen in a deal with Montreal in June.

Pitching, Defense & Hitting

Chen doesn't have overpowering stuff and he's never been able to pitch inside consistently with either his sinking fastball or curve. However, he showed signs of being tough on lefties as long as he kept the ball down. Chen can get strikeouts in key spots, but his control can be erratic, especially in pressure spots. He does a decent job of controlling the running game and had seven pickoffs in 2001. He also has improved himself as a hitter.

2003 Outlook

The Reds think Chen is young enough to be salvaged as a useful pitcher. They likely will put him in the mix for a job in the rotation, knowing they have the alternative of using him out of the bullpen, where he showed some promise last year.

Joey Hamilton

Position: RP/SP
Bats: R **Throws:** R
Ht: 6' 4" **Wt:** 240

Opening Day Age: 32
Born: 9/9/70 in
Statesboro, GA
ML Seasons: 9
Nickname: Big Daddy

Overall Statistics

	W	L	Pct.	ERA	G	GS	Sv	IP	H	BB	SO	HR	Ratio
'02	4	10	.286	5.27	39	17	1	124.2	136	50	85	11	1.49
Car.	74	73	.503	4.38	239	209	1	1330.0	1387	488	887	127	1.41

2002 Situational Stats

	W	L	ERA	Sv	IP		AB	H	HR	RBI	Avg
Home	0	5	5.37	0	65.1	LHB	228	69	8	37	.303
Road	4	5	5.16	1	59.1	RHB	260	67	3	35	.258
First Half	3	6	5.21	0	86.1	Sc Pos	139	45	6	65	.324
Scnd Half	1	4	5.40	1	38.1	Clutch	67	18	1	9	.269

2002 Season

A strong spring training performance earned Joey Hamilton a spot in the Reds' season-opening starting rotation. In fact, he was the Opening Day starter against the Cubs. However, after a solid first six weeks, he began going backward. And after winning only three of 17 starts, Hamilton was sent to the bullpen in the first week of August.

Pitching, Defense & Hitting

Hamilton once had one of the better sinking fastballs in baseball, but that was a long time ago. His velocity is down to the high 80s, and he's never been able to develop the kind of consistent off-speed pitch to keep hitters from sitting on his fastball. He still gets his share of groundballs, however. Hamilton is just an average fielder, though he holds runners fairly well. He always has been a weak hitter, opening his career with a revealing 0-for-57 streak at the plate.

2003 Outlook

Hamilton did serviceable work as a middle and long reliever after being dumped from the Reds' rotation. He registered four holds and his first major league save in 2002. While it seemed unlikely he would be re-signed, Hamilton was offered salary arbitration by the Reds.

Jimmy Haynes

Position: SP
Bats: R **Throws:** R
Ht: 6' 4" **Wt:** 219

Opening Day Age: 30
Born: 9/5/72 in
LaGrange, GA
ML Seasons: 8

Overall Statistics

	W	L	Pct.	ERA	G	GS	Sv	IP	H	BB	SO	HR	Ratio
'02	15	10	.600	4.12	34	34	0	196.2	210	81	126	21	1.48
Car.	61	74	.452	5.24	204	181	1	1091.1	1214	537	705	131	1.60

2002 Situational Stats

	W	L	ERA	Sv	IP		AB	H	HR	RBI	Avg
Home	6	5	4.46	0	82.2	LHB	328	92	10	46	.280
Road	9	5	3.87	0	114.0	RHB	427	118	11	36	.276
First Half	10	6	4.44	0	103.1	Sc Pos	151	41	5	55	.272
Scnd Half	5	4	3.76	0	93.1	Clutch	15	6	1	4	.400

2002 Season

After losing 17 games for Milwaukee in 2001, Jimmy Haynes signed a minor league deal with the Reds before making their rotation last spring. Haynes wound up as one of Cincinnati's most reliable arms. He set career highs in games started and wins, and established himself as a solid major league starter.

Pitching, Defense & Hitting

Like so many other pitchers, it has taken Haynes several seasons to begin harnessing his considerable ability. He is in the low 90s with both his four-seam and two-seam fastballs, which he now throws the majority of time. He mixes in a big-breaking curve and a split, and he also has started throwing a straight change. Haynes has improved holding runners, and he logged a pair of pickoffs last season. He is a good athlete off the mound and has made himself a useful hitter. He led Reds pitchers with six RBI last season.

2003 Outlook

Although Cincinnati obtained Haynes at a bargain price, the Reds knew his breakthrough season was going to cost them. The two sides agreed to a two-year, $5 million pact in early December. The team now hopes Haynes could be ready to start putting together 15-17 win seasons with regularity.

Jason LaRue

Position: C
Bats: R **Throws:** R
Ht: 5'11" **Wt:** 200

Opening Day Age: 29
Born: 3/19/74 in
Houston, TX
ML Seasons: 4
Pronunciation:
la-RUE

Overall Statistics

	G	AB	R	H	D	T	HR	RBI	SB	BB	SO	Avg	OBP	Slg
'02	113	353	42	88	17	1	12	52	1	27	117	.249	.324	.405
Car.	301	905	105	216	48	3	32	117	8	70	274	.239	.312	.404

2002 Situational Stats

	AB	H	HR	RBI	Avg		AB	H	HR	RBI	Avg
Home	176	46	5	25	.261	LHP	92	19	2	5	.207
Road	177	42	7	27	.237	RHP	261	69	10	47	.264
First Half	191	46	2	24	.241	Sc Pos	99	25	5	42	.253
Scnd Half	162	42	10	28	.259	Clutch	61	15	1	12	.246

2002 Season

Jason LaRue handled the majority of the Reds' catching chores last season. He established a career high with 52 RBI and reached double figures in homers for a second straight year. LaRue also remained one of the tougher catchers to try to run on, as he threw out 42.4 percent of opposing basestealers. His season ended a week early due to hernia surgery.

Hitting, Baserunning & Defense

LaRue is a good fastball hitter who is dangerous when pitches are left over the inner half of the plate. He has trouble with breaking balls and he'll also chase pitches away. In addition, his big swing can be vulnerable to hard stuff up in the strike zone. While LaRue has average speed, his quick release and accurate arm are anything but average. He is one of the best at shutting down the running game.

2003 Outlook

With young catching on the way, the Reds were expected to shop LaRue, who is getting expensive as he enters his arbitration years. He often has locked horns with manager Bob Boone over the handling of pitchers. But LaRue's power and throwing ability could make him attractive to another club.

Brian Moehler

Position: SP
Bats: R **Throws:** R
Ht: 6' 3" **Wt:** 235

Opening Day Age: 31
Born: 12/31/71 in
Rockingham, NC
ML Seasons: 7
Pronunciation:
MOLE-er

Overall Statistics

	W	L	Pct.	ERA	G	GS	Sv	IP	H	BB	SO	HR	Ratio
'02	3	5	.375	4.86	13	12	0	63.0	78	13	31	11	1.44
Car.	50	56	.472	4.52	141	140	0	852.1	964	238	464	106	1.41

2002 Situational Stats

	W	L	ERA	Sv	IP		AB	H	HR	RBI	Avg
Home	2	2	4.02	0	40.1	LHB	125	37	7	18	.296
Road	1	3	6.35	0	22.2	RHB	133	41	4	16	.308
First Half	1	0	0.00	0	7.0	Sc Pos	69	17	2	21	.246
Scnd Half	2	5	5.46	0	56.0	Clutch	2	1	0	1	.500

2002 Season

After nearly a year and a half of shoulder troubles, Brian Moehler returned and made just three appearances for Detroit before getting traded to the Reds. He then won only two of nine starts for Cincinnati, spending some time on the disabled list due to weakness in his shoulder. However, despite his poor record and high ERA, Moehler displayed flashes of effectiveness, including a strong outing versus Houston when he went seven innings for one of his victories.

Pitching, Defense & Hitting

Moehler mixes a good sinker with a cut fastball that occasionally can be an effective weapon against lefthanded hitters. He also has a serviceable change. He doesn't overpower anyone with his average velocity, but Moehler usually is around the plate and can have good command with all his pitches. He is just an adequate fielder, and he's still looking for his first major league hit.

2003 Outlook

The Reds didn't offer salary arbitration to Moehler, so he will be moving on. With another winter of conditioning, he could be the solid mid-rotation type that he was before his injury problems. He won 47 games for Detroit from 1997 to 2000, reaching double figures each year.

Cincinnati

<table>
<tr><th colspan="2"></th></tr>
</table>

John Riedling

Position: RP
Bats: R **Throws:** R
Ht: 5'11" **Wt:** 190

Opening Day Age: 27
Born: 8/29/75 in Fort Lauderdale, FL
ML Seasons: 3
Pronunciation: READ-ling

Overall Statistics

	W	L	Pct.	ERA	G	GS	Sv	IP	H	BB	SO	HR	Ratio
'02	2	4	.333	2.70	33	0	0	46.2	39	26	30	2	1.39
Car.	6	6	.500	2.54	75	0	2	95.2	72	48	71	4	1.25

2002 Situational Stats

	W	L	ERA	Sv	IP		AB	H	HR	RBI	Avg
Home	2	1	2.36	0	26.2	LHB	75	24	2	9	.320
Road	0	3	3.15	0	20.0	RHB	92	15	0	1	.163
First Half	0	0	1.93	0	14.0	Sc Pos	39	7	0	7	.179
Scnd Half	2	4	3.03	0	32.2	Clutch	76	20	0	3	.263

2002 Season

John Riedling missed most of 2001 due to shoulder trouble. But he returned last June to be an effective member of the Reds' bullpen. He fashioned a solid ERA and showed he was healthy by making 33 appearances. Although he returned to the 15-day disabled list with a strained groin in August, he allowed just a .212 batting average during the season's second half.

Pitching, Defense & Hitting

Still regaining his arm strength, Riedling can touch the mid-90s with his fastball. At times he has a devastating splitter, but his command often wavers with all of his pitches. He also has had problems maintaining a consistent release point. If he gets ahead of hitters, Riedling usually puts them away. He holds runners fairly well but is not likely to be much of a factor as a hitter. He has struck out in all four of his major league at-bats.

2003 Outlook

Another of the Reds' hard-throwing question marks, Riedling will be in the mix as a candidate for setup work in the late innings this year. He needs to establish himself with a full, healthy season before being considered a possible closer down the road.

Scott Sullivan

Position: RP
Bats: R **Throws:** R
Ht: 6' 3" **Wt:** 210

Opening Day Age: 32
Born: 3/13/71 in Carrollton, AL
ML Seasons: 8

Overall Statistics

	W	L	Pct.	ERA	G	GS	Sv	IP	H	BB	SO	HR	Ratio
'02	6	5	.545	6.06	71	0	1	78.2	93	31	78	15	1.58
Car.	31	24	.564	3.93	444	0	9	613.0	550	225	521	75	1.26

2002 Situational Stats

	W	L	ERA	Sv	IP		AB	H	HR	RBI	Avg
Home	4	2	5.03	1	48.1	LHB	126	45	7	26	.357
Road	2	3	7.71	0	30.1	RHB	190	48	8	30	.253
First Half	5	2	4.45	1	54.2	Sc Pos	95	30	5	41	.316
Scnd Half	1	3	9.75	0	24.0	Clutch	147	45	4	21	.306

2002 Season

Though he pitched through shoulder troubles to remain one baseball's busiest relievers, Scott Sullivan's performance suffered on the way to his worst season in the majors. His ERA was nearly twice as high as his career mark entering last season, and he allowed significantly more hits than innings pitched. He also pitched fewer than 100 innings for the first time in five years.

Pitching, Defense & Hitting

Sullivan never regained the bite on his 90-plus, sidearm, sinking fastball. Without the sinker, he doesn't have an adequate weapon against righthanded hitters. He still is seeking to gain better command with his cutter. Sullivan often will fall off to the first-base side of the mound and put himself out of position defensively. He made three errors in just 11 total chances last year. He holds runners adequately and rarely hits.

2003 Outlook

There have been some concerns that Sullivan's heavy workload may have taken a toll on his arm. However, if he regains strength in his throwing arm and stays healthy, he is one of baseball's most valuable relievers, as he can eat middle and late innings. His contract runs through this season, with an option for 2004.

Gabe White

Position: RP
Bats: L **Throws:** L
Ht: 6' 2" **Wt:** 204

Opening Day Age: 31
Born: 11/20/71 in
Sebring, FL
ML Seasons: 8

Overall Statistics

	W	L	Pct.	ERA	G	GS	Sv	IP	H	BB	SO	HR	Ratio
'02	6	1	.857	2.98	62	0	0	54.1	49	10	41	3	1.09
Car.	28	22	.560	4.28	356	15	16	456.0	426	120	383	74	1.20

2002 Situational Stats

	W	L	ERA	Sv	IP		AB	H	HR	RBI	Avg
Home	3	1	5.14	0	28.0	LHB	89	18	1	8	.202
Road	3	0	0.68	0	26.1	RHB	116	31	2	12	.267
First Half	4	1	2.58	0	45.1	Sc Pos	55	16	0	16	.291
Scnd Half	2	0	5.00	0	9.0	Clutch	108	25	2	5	.231

2002 Season

The Reds re-acquired Gabe White last December in a deal with the Rockies. He bounced back from an off year in Colorado by dramatically reducing the longball. White again ranked as one of the top lefthanded middle relievers in baseball, despite missing time due to a broken toe and strained groin. He tied for the team lead in relief wins and appeared in at least 60 games for the fourth time in the past five years.

Pitching, Defense & Hitting

Working with Reds pitching coach Don Gullett, White smoothed his mechanics and in the process regained command of his good changeup. White also throws his fastball inside much more often than he used to, making him more effective against righthanded hitters. He has a quick delivery home, which helps to keep the running game in check, and he fields his position well. In his situational role, he rarely hits.

2003 Outlook

A workhorse who re-established himself last year, White likely will hold a key role in the setup end of what is likely to be a revamped Reds bullpen. Tireless lefties with good control like White always will find work. He's signed through this season, and his contract has an option for 2004.

Scott Williamson

Position: RP
Bats: R **Throws:** R
Ht: 6' 0" **Wt:** 185

Opening Day Age: 27
Born: 2/17/76 in Fort
Polk, LA
ML Seasons: 4

Overall Statistics

	W	L	Pct.	ERA	G	GS	Sv	IP	H	BB	SO	HR	Ratio
'02	3	4	.429	2.92	63	0	8	74.0	46	36	84	5	1.11
Car.	20	19	.513	2.89	175	10	33	280.0	193	156	327	20	1.25

2002 Situational Stats

	W	L	ERA	Sv	IP		AB	H	HR	RBI	Avg
Home	3	2	3.38	4	40.0	LHB	101	20	3	12	.198
Road	0	2	2.38	4	34.0	RHB	153	26	2	14	.170
First Half	2	2	4.86	0	33.1	Sc Pos	71	15	2	22	.211
Scnd Half	1	2	1.33	8	40.2	Clutch	119	22	2	14	.185

2002 Season

After missing most of 2001, Scott Williamson made the long road back from reconstructive elbow surgery and had a strong year for the Reds. He seemed to get better as last season progressed, allowing a .158 batting average after the All-Star break. He finished the campaign as Cincinnati's closer, converting eight of 10 save opportunities after Danny Graves moved into the starting rotation in September.

Pitching, Defense & Hitting

Williamson had his velocity back into the mid-90s last year. Even more importantly, he began regaining the bite on his electric slider by the final third of the season. He has a closer's aggressive mentality and can be a major strikeout pitcher when healthy. He's fanned more than 10 batters per nine innings during his big league career. He gathers himself in his delivery and is easy to run on. Williamson has little experience or skill as a hitter. He hasn't made any plate appearances since 2000.

2003 Outlook

With his elbow healthy and the closer's job his to lose, Williamson's career could be back on track. Few pitchers in baseball possess his overpowering stuff. If he stays healthy and continues to improve his command, Williamson can be a top stopper.

Cincinnati

Other Cincinnati Reds

Jose Acevedo (Pos: RHP, Age: 25)

	W	L	Pct.	ERA	G	GS	Sv	IP	H	BB	SO	HR	Ratio
'02	4	2	.667	7.23	6	5	0	23.2	28	12	14	8	1.69
Car.	9	9	.500	5.79	24	23	0	119.2	129	46	82	25	1.46

Acevedo opened last season in the Reds' rotation, but soon pitched his way to the minors, where he was more effective. He doesn't seem to have much margin for error, and home runs have hurt him. 2003 Outlook: B

Carlos Almanzar (Pos: RHP, Age: 29)

	W	L	Pct.	ERA	G	GS	Sv	IP	H	BB	SO	HR	Ratio
'02	0	1	.000	2.31	8	1	0	11.2	6	5	7	0	0.94
Car.	6	10	.375	5.02	137	1	0	161.1	176	56	123	25	1.44

Almanzar missed much of last season due to injury. He can be used against lefthanded hitters and can be effective as a situational reliever. The Reds re-signed him to a minor league deal for this season. 2003 Outlook: C

Juan Castro (Pos: SS/2B, Age: 30, Bats: R)

	G	AB	R	H	D	T	HR	RBI	SB	BB	SO	Avg	OBP	Slg
'02	54	82	5	18	3	0	2	11	0	7	18	.220	.278	.329
Car.	444	980	96	207	40	6	11	70	1	67	187	.211	.260	.298

A strained hamstring delayed Castro's Reds debut until June last season. He's signed through 2004, but it's hard to see what he adds, at least offensively. Defensive versatility may be his best asset. 2003 Outlook: C

Gookie Dawkins (Pos: SS, Age: 23, Bats: R)

	G	AB	R	H	D	T	HR	RBI	SB	BB	SO	Avg	OBP	Slg
'02	31	48	2	6	2	0	0	0	2	6	21	.125	.222	.167
Car.	52	96	8	16	4	0	0	3	2	8	32	.167	.238	.208

Once thought by some to be the Reds' shortstop of the future, Dawkins now looks like he never may be more than a utilityman. He's still young enough to improve, but his offense needs a boost. 2003 Outlook: C

Jared Fernandez (Pos: RHP, Age: 31)

	W	L	Pct.	ERA	G	GS	Sv	IP	H	BB	SO	HR	Ratio
'02	1	3	.250	4.44	14	8	0	50.2	59	24	36	5	1.64
Car.	1	4	.200	4.43	19	10	0	63.0	72	30	41	6	1.62

Fernandez isn't a dominating sort, but he has experience as a starter and reliever. While he controlled lefthanded hitters when working for the Reds last season, he was hurt by righthanded batters. 2003 Outlook: C

Jose Guillen (Pos: RF, Age: 26, Bats: R)

	G	AB	R	H	D	T	HR	RBI	SB	BB	SO	Avg	OBP	Slg
'02	85	240	25	57	7	0	8	31	4	14	43	.238	.287	.367
Car.	614	2050	239	533	102	12	52	268	14	96	379	.260	.305	.398

For a guy who's supposedly still only 26, Guillen sure has bounced around. He washed through the Tampa Bay, Arizona and Colorado organizations in the past year alone, and the Reds signed him last August. In December, he signed a $500,000 deal for 2003 that is not guaranteed. 2003 Outlook: B

Ruben Mateo (Pos: RF, Age: 25, Bats: R)

	G	AB	R	H	D	T	HR	RBI	SB	BB	SO	Avg	OBP	Slg
'02	46	86	11	22	6	0	2	7	0	6	20	.256	.319	.395
Car.	170	543	77	143	31	3	15	57	10	29	110	.263	.316	.414

Mateo's star has been dimmed by injuries. He's young enough to rebound, and he did hit better at Triple-A last season. 2003 Outlook: C

Corky Miller (Pos: C, Age: 27, Bats: R)

	G	AB	R	H	D	T	HR	RBI	SB	BB	SO	Avg	OBP	Slg
'02	39	114	9	29	10	0	3	15	0	9	20	.254	.328	.421
Car.	56	163	14	38	12	0	6	22	1	13	36	.233	.308	.417

Miller's offense took a big leap forward in 2001. He has an average arm and decent feet, and he wouldn't be a bad option as a backup catcher. 2003 Outlook: C

Luis Pineda (Pos: RHP, Age: 28)

	W	L	Pct.	ERA	G	GS	Sv	IP	H	BB	SO	HR	Ratio
'02	1	3	.250	4.18	26	2	0	32.1	25	24	31	4	1.52
Car.	1	4	.200	4.44	42	2	0	50.2	41	38	44	6	1.56

Pineda was part of the trade with Detroit involving Juan Encarnacion. Pineda missed much of 2002 due to rotator cuff and labrum problems, but the Reds have re-signed him to a minor league contract. 2003 Outlook: C

Jose Rijo (Pos: RHP, Age: 37)

	W	L	Pct.	ERA	G	GS	Sv	IP	H	BB	SO	HR	Ratio
'02	5	4	.556	5.14	31	9	0	77.0	89	20	38	13	1.42
Car.	116	91	.560	3.24	376	269	3	1880.0	1710	663	1606	147	1.26

Rijo won last season for the first time since 1995. He's not the overpowering sort he was before his elbow problems. He's testing free agency. 2003 Outlook: B

Jose Silva (Pos: RHP, Age: 29)

	W	L	Pct.	ERA	G	GS	Sv	IP	H	BB	SO	HR	Ratio
'02	1	0	1.000	4.24	12	0	0	23.1	25	10	6	3	1.50
Car.	25	28	.472	5.41	154	53	4	427.1	507	154	298	47	1.55

Silva missed large chunks of the season due to elbow surgery and shoulder tendinitis. He signed with the A's in November. 2003 Outlook: C

Kelly Stinnett (Pos: C, Age: 33, Bats: R)

	G	AB	R	H	D	T	HR	RBI	SB	BB	SO	Avg	OBP	Slg
'02	34	93	10	21	5	0	3	13	2	15	25	.226	.333	.376
Car.	521	1486	176	350	68	4	51	178	10	155	412	.236	.321	.390

Stinnett's sore throwing elbow kept him out of the Reds' lineup for all but one game in the first half last year. He's signed through this season and should contribute, if healthy. 2003 Outlook: B

Reggie Taylor (Pos: CF/LF, Age: 26, Bats: L)

	G	AB	R	H	D	T	HR	RBI	SB	BB	SO	Avg	OBP	Slg
'02	135	287	41	73	15	4	9	38	11	14	79	.254	.291	.429
Car.	149	305	43	74	15	4	9	38	12	15	88	.243	.280	.407

A first-round pick of the Phillies in 1995, Taylor didn't develop as hoped. He had a decent '02 season for Cincinnati, however, flashing power and speed. 2003 Outlook: B

Cincinnati Reds Minor League Prospects

Organization Overview:

Although Cincinnati stumbled in the second half and finished six games under .500, the Reds showed nice progress in 2002, improving by 12 games from the year before. In fact, only the Angels (24 games), Expos (15) and Braves (13) increased their wins by a larger margin. Furthermore, for the second consecutive year, the Reds promoted an exciting talent who offers even greater hope for the future. Austin Kearns followed Adam Dunn's impressive debut in 2001 by leading the Reds with a .315 batting average last season. While another impact performer may not be on the immediate horizon, Brandon Larson and Wily Mo Pena figure to see action this year. Actually, the Reds' system may be stronger and deeper on the pitching side, where a key contributor probably has a better chance of developing, though perhaps not in 2003.

Bobby Basham

Position: P **Opening Day Age:** 23
Bats: R **Throws:** R **Born:** 3/7/80 in Raleigh,
Ht: 6' 3" **Wt:** 205 NC

Recent Statistics

	W	L	ERA	G	GS	Sv	IP	H	R	BB	SO	HR
2001 R Billings	1	2	4.85	6	6	0	29.2	36	23	17	37	2
2002 A Dayton	6	4	1.64	13	13	0	87.2	64	25	9	97	4

After a fairly lackluster debut in the Rookie-level Pioneer League in 2001, Basham burst through with an outstanding campaign in the Class-A Midwest League last year. Check out his hit, walk and strikeout ratios. He allowed fewer than eights hits plus walks per nine innings, as he demonstrated plus command of an 88-92 MPH fastball. His out pitch is a hard slider with good depth that he'll throw for strikes. A pulled ribcage muscle troubled him, but Basham came back to strike out 13 and walk none in the game that clinched the high Class-A California League championship for Stockton. He was quite a story in 2002, and could be headed for Double-A or even Triple-A this season.

Edwin Encarnacion

Position: 3B **Opening Day Age:** 20
Bats: R **Throws:** R **Born:** 1/7/83 in La
Ht: 6' 1" **Wt:** 175 Romana, DR

Recent Statistics

	G	AB	R	H	D	T	HR	RBI	SB	BB	SO	Avg
2001 A Savannah	45	170	23	52	9	2	4	25	3	12	34	.306
2001 A Dayton	9	37	2	6	2	0	1	6	0	1	5	.162
2001 R Billings	52	211	27	55	8	2	5	26	8	15	29	.261
2002 A Dayton	136	517	80	146	32	4	17	73	25	40	108	.282

Encarnacion arrived in the Reds' organization in the 2001 deal with Texas that involved Rob Bell and Ruben Mateo. Encarnacion is one of the more exciting players in the Reds' system. His power continues to progress, and he succeeded in the Class-A Midwest League while still a teenager last season. He made more errors at third base than he probably will in the future, in part because he didn't utilize his legs as well as he could have when throwing. But he's a terrific athlete who was playing shortstop at the end of the year. A shortstop with his special bat would be quite a package. He's a player to watch, most likely in the high Class-A Carolina League.

Ty Howington

Position: P **Opening Day Age:** 22
Bats: B **Throws:** L **Born:** 11/4/80 in
Ht: 6' 5" **Wt:** 225 Vancouver, Washington

Recent Statistics

	W	L	ERA	G	GS	Sv	IP	H	R	BB	SO	HR
2001 A Dayton	4	0	1.15	6	6	0	39.0	15	7	9	47	0
2001 A Mudville	3	2	2.43	7	7	0	37.0	33	18	20	44	2
2001 AA Chattanooga	1	3	3.27	7	7	0	41.1	36	18	24	38	3
2002 AA Chattanooga	1	5	5.12	15	15	0	65.0	65	39	33	51	5
2002 A Stockton	1	1	3.09	2	2	0	11.2	7	6	4	9	1

Howington has been bothered by injuries since being selected in the first round of the 1999 draft. He's undergone elbow surgery in the past, and endured a rough 2002, battling weakness in his shoulder and flexibility problems. He was shut down late in the year. Howington's fastball tops out in the low 90s, and he shows a plus changeup. He's working on his curveball and could control the running game better. Innings obviously are a key to his development. The fast track that he appeared to be on may have slowed, though the Reds expect him to rebound.

Brandon Larson

Position: 3B **Opening Day Age:** 26
Bats: R **Throws:** R **Born:** 5/24/76 in San
Ht: 6' 0" **Wt:** 210 Angelo, TX

Recent Statistics

	G	AB	R	H	D	T	HR	RBI	SB	BB	SO	Avg
2002 AAA Louisville	80	297	47	101	20	1	25	69	1	24	70	.340
2002 NL Cincinnati	23	51	8	14	2	0	4	13	1	6	10	.275

The climb has been slow for Larson, who was selected in the first round in 1997. He seemed to languish in the minors before his breakthrough campaign last year. Larson led Triple-A Louisville in home runs while playing in only 80 games. He then provided some pop for the Reds when he wasn't spending separate stints on the disabled list with a broken toe and broken hand. He exhibits good power to all fields and runs well for his size. A shortstop at LSU, he's a decent defensive third baseman who can play first base and left field as well. He's also learning second base, which would make him even more valuable as he competes for a major league job this spring.

Cincinnati

Dustin Moseley

Position: P   **Opening Day Age:** 21
Bats: R **Throws:** R   **Born:** 12/26/81 in
Ht: 6' 4" **Wt:** 197   Texarkana, AR

Recent Statistics

	W	L	ERA	G	GS	Sv	IP	H	R	BB	SO	HR
2001 A Dayton	10	8	4.20	25	25	0	148.0	158	83	42	108	10
2002 A Stockton	6	3	2.74	14	14	0	88.2	60	28	21	80	3
2002 AA Chattanooga	5	6	4.13	13	13	0	80.2	91	47	37	52	5

The Reds selected Moseley with one of the picks acquired for losing Juan Guzman. He's shown great maturity at a young age, exhibiting a strong work ethic and a great desire to compete. It doesn't hurt that he boasts a fastball that reaches the low 90s, a plus breaking ball and good command, too. He didn't turn 21 until after last season, yet held his own when promoted to Double-A. Moseley still has adjustments to make, which should come as he throws more innings and gains experience. But his ceiling is high, and he has the ability to be a No. 2 or 3 starter in the big leagues.

Ranier Olmedo

Position: SS   **Opening Day Age:** 21
Bats: R **Throws:** R   **Born:** 5/31/81 in
Ht: 5' 11" **Wt:** 155   Maracay, VZ

Recent Statistics

	G	AB	R	H	D	T	HR	RBI	SB	BB	SO	Avg
2001 A Mudville	129	536	57	131	23	4	0	28	38	24	121	.244
2002 AA Chattanooga	132	478	62	118	21	1	3	30	15	53	86	.247

Venezuela has produced its share of slick-fielding shortstops, including Reds great Dave Concepcion. Olmedo looks like he can be a worthy successor to that lineage, at least defensively. He's a special athlete who possesses plus range, good hands and a strong arm. His shortstop play is so good that it isn't out of the question he could be summoned to the big leagues in a pinch. His offense is another matter, however. He picked up switch-hitting only a couple years ago, and he continues to exhibit little power. One good sign was that he walked more often in 2002. Olmedo plays the game the right way and was fairly young to be playing at Double-A last season. But he'll need to hit better if he's going to be anything more than just another Rey Ordonez.

Wily Mo Pena

Position: OF   **Opening Day Age:** 21
Bats: R **Throws:** R   **Born:** 1/23/82 in Laguna
Ht: 6' 3" **Wt:** 215   Salada, DR

Recent Statistics

	G	AB	R	H	D	T	HR	RBI	SB	BB	SO	Avg
2002 AA Chattanooga	105	388	47	99	23	1	11	47	8	36	126	.255
2002 NL Cincinnati	13	18	1	4	0	0	1	1	0	0	11	.222

Pena tore a hamstring in the Arizona Fall League and may not be ready to open 2003. When he is, his contract calls for him to play in the majors this season. Whether he assumes a role more important than the 25th man on Cincinnati's roster is another matter. Sure, he might be the most gifted athlete in the organization. He shows off-the-chart power, and is thought capable of hitting 30-40 homers and stealing the same number of bases annually. Well, maybe some day. Those skills weren't readily apparent at Double-A last year, and he still can use work on staying on the fastball longer.

Dane Sardinha

Position: C   **Opening Day Age:** 23
Bats: R **Throws:** R   **Born:** 4/8/79 in Honolulu,
Ht: 5' 11" **Wt:** 205   HI

Recent Statistics

	G	AB	R	H	D	T	HR	RBI	SB	BB	SO	Avg
2001 A Mudville	109	422	45	99	24	2	9	55	0	12	97	.235
2002 AA Chattanooga	106	394	34	81	20	0	4	40	0	14	114	.206

It isn't often that you'll find a prospect whose on-base and slugging percentages fall below .300. But Sardinha's defensive ability may be enough to compensate for any offensive deficiency. In fact, he's major league-caliber as a catch-and-throw guy right now. In an emergency, the Reds may not hesitate to call him up. But in such a case he'd likely be overmatched in the batter's box. Still, there are things Sardinha does that indicate he might get better with the stick. He has a soft front side, meaning he has good balance and uses his hands, and he will drive the ball the other way. He's a little quiet and laid back, and could stand to get more assertive and take greater control of the game when working behind the plate.

Others to Watch

Righthander **Dave Gil** (24) conquered Double-A, but stalled at Triple-A last year. He's a good athlete with plus command of an 88-92 MPH fastball. He's worked on staying on top of his slider, resulting in better tilt. . . Righthander **Josh Hall** (22) powers his 88-92 MPH fastball down in the zone. He repeats a good delivery and boasts one of the best curveballs in the organization. . . The Reds acquired righthander **Luke Hudson** (25) from the Rockies in the trade involving Pokey Reese following the 2001 season. Hudson pitched as a starter and reliever at Triple-A last year, striking out more than a batter per inning. . . Lefthander **John Koronka** (22) was unbeaten in 11 decisions at high Class-A Stockton last year, but found Double-A more challenging (2-8). He features a major league change-up. He's the kind of guy who may have to pitch at each level. . . Righthander **Mike Neu** (25) saved the title game of 1999 College World Series for the University of Miami. His 5-foot-10 stature may be the primary reason he wasn't drafted until the 29th round that year, but he's averaged more than 12 strikeouts per nine innings as a pro. He reached Triple-A and worked in the Arizona Fall League in 2002. . . Outfielder **Steve Smitherman** (24) produced an MVP-caliber season in the high Class-A California League while performing in a pitchers' park. He's a strong athlete with good power potential who already hits lots of doubles.

Coors Field

Offense

The Rockies constantly have looked for ways to calm down the offense at Coors Field. It hasn't worked. Last season, they built a climate-controlled room in which to store baseballs. There was a slight decrease in offense, but that was more due to the fact that the Rockies didn't have a power-laden lineup. The Rockies continue to have the biggest home-road offensive differential in baseball.

Defense

Manager Clint Hurdle makes no secret that the offensive nature of Coors makes defense vital. The outfield is a challenge because of its size and the way the ball carries. Outfielders often make the mistake of playing too deep. Teams need to concede that balls down the lines are doubles, and bunch their outfielders to take away those bloopers over short and second, and also to minimize balls getting through the alleys. Infielders live in danger, as the grass plays more like turf.

Who It Helps the Most

It's hard to be a hitter who doesn't get a lift from Coors Field. The park is particularly suited for line-drive, gap hitters. Although the alleys are big, the ball carries so well that there are more gap homers at Coors than in other ballparks.

Who It Hurts the Most

Mike Hampton was a perfect example of the Coors Field hangover. He was 4-3 at home last year, but went 3-12 with a road ERA of 6.44, the highest in baseball. Hitters can suffer, too. Juan Pierre hit for average but never hit a home run at Coors, prompting the Rockies to deal him, because they feel they need a power threat at every spot in the lineup.

Rookies & Newcomers

Aaron Cook is this year's homegrown pitcher, set to follow in the footsteps of Jason Jennings. Like Jennings in 2001, Cook opened last season at Double-A, dominated and moved to Triple-A before finishing with Colorado. The Rockies shut him down in the final weeks to avoid overworking him and also to preserve his rookie status.

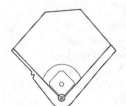

Dimensions: LF-347, LCF-390, CF-415, RCF-375, RF-350

Capacity: 50,449

Elevation: 5280 feet

Surface: Grass

Foul Territory: Average

Park Factors

2002 Season

	Home Games Rockies	Opp	Total	Away Games Rockies	Opp	Total	Index
G	72	72	144	72	72	144	
Avg	.310	.279	.294	.236	.270	.253	116
AB	2442	2543	4985	2447	2405	4852	103
R	435	419	854	259	361	620	138
H	756	709	1465	577	649	1226	119
2B	141	142	283	108	121	229	120
3B	26	17	43	12	16	28	149
HR	83	120	203	51	80	131	151
BB	232	243	475	204	267	471	98
SO	403	424	827	541	381	922	87
E	49	51	100	42	40	82	122
E-Infield	41	38	79	36	32	68	116
LHB-Avg	.332	.286	.309	.265	.284	.274	113
LHB-HR	41	48	89	27	30	57	147
RHB-Avg	.295	.274	.284	.215	.262	.240	119
RHB-HR	42	72	114	24	50	74	153

2000-2002

	Home Games Rockies	Opp	Total	Away Games Rockies	Opp	Total	Index
G	222	222	444	222	222	444	
Avg	.326	.290	.308	.248	.260	.253	121
AB	7764	7930	15694	7639	7285	14924	105
R	1531	1398	2929	922	1031	1953	150
H	2534	2299	4833	1891	1892	3783	128
2B	489	475	964	361	413	774	118
3B	95	52	147	45	49	94	149
HR	303	367	670	182	243	425	150
BB	762	823	1585	708	783	1491	101
SO	1220	1389	2609	1522	1318	2840	87
E	142	197	339	129	147	276	123
E-Infield	111	153	264	110	132	242	109
LHB-Avg	.341	.284	.316	.269	.267	.268	118
LHB-HR	164	142	306	110	93	203	142
RHB-Avg	.313	.293	.302	.228	.255	.243	124
RHB-HR	139	225	364	72	150	222	157

2002 Rankings (National League)

- Highest batting-average factor
- Highest run factor
- Highest hit factor
- Highest home-run factor
- Highest error factor
- Highest LHB batting-average factor
- Highest RHB batting-average facto
- Lowest strikeout factor

Clint Hurdle

2002 Season

On April 26, Clint Hurdle became the fourth manager in franchise history, replacing Buddy Bell, who was in his third season with the team. The Rockies were 6-16 at the time and responded with a 21-9 stretch, equaling the best 30-game effort in franchise history. By season's end, the Rockies had gone 67-73 under Hurdle. Most importantly, they regained an edge at Coors Field, going 44-27 at home under Hurdle's direction.

Offense

Hurdle understands Coors Field as well as anyone. He had been the Rockies hitting coach since 1997 before being promoted to the managerial role, and was on the staff of each of the three previous Rockies managers. He stresses contact and hitting the ball up the middle, having learned as a young player from the likes of Hal McRae. Hurdle shows signs of being more aggressive on the bases, along the lines of original Rockies manager Don Baylor, who time has proved had a good feel for what it takes to maximize the homefield advantage at Coors.

Pitching & Defense

Hurdle hired Bob Apodaca after the season, his pitching coach in four of the six years Hurdle managed in the minor leagues, and will give Apodaca control of the staff. Hurdle realizes the mental demands that Coors creates, and brought in a pitching-oriented bullpen coach, Rick Matthews, to help Apodaca. Hurdle wants to develop an approach in which the Rockies' starters go deeper into games on the road, saving the relievers, who will have to assume a bigger workload at Coors.

2003 Outlook

The Rockies have made a major concession. Instead of apologizing for Coors Field and its offensive madness, they're looking to exploit the opportunities to dominate teams. They traded veterans with long-term contracts, trying to create more of a hunger in the clubhouse. The key for the team being competitive will be what Rookie of the Year Jason Jennings and fellow rookie Denny Stark do for an encore.

Born: 7/30/57 in Big Rapids, MI

Playing Experience: 1977-1987, KC, Cin, NYM, StL

Managerial Experience: 1 season

Manager Statistics

Year	Team, Lg	W	L	Pct	GB	Finish
2002	Colorado, NL	67	73	.479	25.0	4th West
1 Season		67	73	.479	–	–

2002 Starting Pitchers by Days Rest

	<=3	4	5	6+
Rockies Starts	0	70	54	11
Rockies ERA	–	5.27	4.69	4.99
NL Avg Starts	1	88	42	21
NL ERA	3.18	4.22	4.14	4.58

2002 Situational Stats

	Clint Hurdle	NL Average
Hit & Run Success %	34.0	36.5
Stolen Base Success %	66.2	68.3
Platoon Pct.	51.3	52.7
Defensive Subs	23	19
High-Pitch Outings	3	7
Quick/Slow Hooks	14/18	24/11
Sacrifice Attempts	51	95

2002 Rankings (National League)

- 1st in sacrifice-bunt percentage (88.2%)
- 2nd in slow hooks
- 3rd in defensive substitutions

Sandy Alomar Jr.

2002 Season

Colorado was desperate for catching help when they acquired Alomar from the White Sox in a late July trade. The White Sox were anxious enough to move the veteran that they even picked up the final two months of Alomar's salary. He played more regularly with Colorado, though it may have affected him. He hit only .221 in his last 32 games with the Rockies.

Hitting

Alomar's experience makes him an average big league hitter. He understands what it takes to be successful, and has a feel for how pitchers are approaching him. But he is not going to provide great run production. The aches and pains of a career behind the plate have taken a toll, and it is noticeable in Alomar's reduced power. He isn't going to catch up with the premiere hard throwers, though he will feast on mediocre pitchers because he's content to put the ball in play. If a pitcher makes a big mistake, Alomar still can jump on it.

Baserunning & Defense

Alomar once was among the elite defensive catchers, but skills do erode over time. He has limited use of his bottom half. Continual knee problems don't allow him to move around like he once did. Alomar's throwing, more than anything, has been affected by his lack of spring. He still receives the ball well, blocks balls in the dirt and cherishes the chance to work a young pitcher through the game. Alomar understands what needs to be done when he's on the bases. However, those legs just don't always meet expectations, and the third base coach has to be aware of that.

2003 Outlook

A free agent, Alomar wants to stay in the game when he's done playing, which is why he figures to hang on as long as he can. He's no longer a player that a team can count on for 100-plus games behind the plate. He would be best used two or three times a week. That would keep him fresh and keep some life in his bat.

Position: C
Bats: R **Throws:** R
Ht: 6' 5" **Wt:** 235

Opening Day Age: 36
Born: 6/18/66 in Salinas, PR
ML Seasons: 15
Pronunciation: AL-uh-mar

Overall Statistics

	G	AB	R	H	D	T	HR	RBI	SB	BB	SO	Avg	OBP	Slg
'02	89	283	29	79	14	1	7	37	0	9	33	.279	.302	.410
Car.	1152	3932	463	1081	217	10	104	517	25	189	440	.275	.312	.415

Where He Hits the Ball

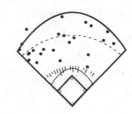 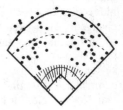

Vs. LHP   **Vs. RHP**

2002 Situational Stats

	AB	H	HR	RBI	Avg			AB	H	HR	RBI	Avg
Home	156	40	5	28	.256		LHP	81	20	1	10	.247
Road	127	39	2	9	.307		RHP	202	59	6	27	.292
First Half	134	41	7	24	.306		Sc Pos	74	19	1	29	.257
Scnd Half	149	38	0	13	.255		Clutch	40	9	0	1	.225

2002 Rankings (National League)

- Led the Rockies in batting average with the bases loaded (.500)

2002 Season

Mike Hampton received the largest guarantee ever for a pitcher—$121 million over eight years—to sign with Colorado before the 2001 season. It wasn't worth it. After going 9-2 with a 2.98 ERA, making him the first pitcher in franchise history to be selected to the All-Star team, he has been 12-26 with a 6.62 ERA since. A sprained ligament in his right foot cut last season short.

Pitching

Hampton's success was built off a hard sinker. But he got away from throwing that pitch with Colorado, going to a 93-MPH, four-seam fastball that he tries to run in on the hands of righthanded hitters. He also will use a slider, curveball and changeup. He's begun throwing across his body so much that he can't get in on righthanders, which is why he had to try the cutter instead of the sinker. The out-of-whack mechanics affected his command and stamina, and can be blamed, more than Coors Field, for his mediocrity.

Defense & Hitting

Hampton is a wonderful athlete. He has excellent reactions and will field anything hit back up the middle. He also comes off the mound quickly and makes batters pay for poor bunts. Hampton likes to get the lead man in sacrifice situations. He is quick to the plate and has a good move to first, making him one of the most difficult pitchers in the National League to steal against. And he's a legitimate threat with the bat. He can hit-and-run, drive the ball in the alleys, and is one of the fastest runners in the majors.

2003 Outlook

Hampton needed a change of scenery, and he got one when he was traded to Atlanta in November. He let Coors Field get into his head, and it affected him on the road as well as at home. He competes well and has legitimate stuff, but needs to regain confidence in his abilities. He may not be a staff ace because his mechanics make him inconsistent. But he is a quality No. 2 starter.

Position: SP
Bats: R **Throws:** L
Ht: 5'10" **Wt:** 180

Opening Day Age: 30
Born: 9/9/72 in Brooksville, FL
ML Seasons: 10

Overall Statistics

	W	L	Pct.	ERA	G	GS	Sv	IP	H	BB	SO	HR	Ratio
'02	7	15	.318	6.15	30	30	0	178.2	228	91	74	24	1.79
Car.	106	81	.567	3.98	303	249	1	1642.1	1698	665	1048	143	1.44

How Often He Throws Strikes

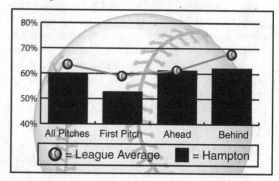

= League Average   = Hampton

2002 Situational Stats

	W	L	ERA	Sv	IP		AB	H	HR	RBI	Avg
Home	4	3	5.68	0	69.2	LHB	170	64	10	38	.376
Road	3	12	6.44	0	109.0	RHB	559	164	14	85	.293
First Half	5	9	6.73	0	104.1	Sc Pos	219	65	4	92	.297
Scnd Half	2	6	5.33	0	74.1	Clutch	16	8	3	3	.500

2002 Rankings (National League)

- 1st in most GDPs induced per nine innings (1.4), highest ERA, lowest strikeout-walk ratio (0.8), highest batting average allowed (.313), highest on-base percentage allowed (.390), highest ERA on the road, highest batting average allowed vs. lefthanded batters, and highest walks per nine innings (4.6)
- 2nd in fewest strikeouts per nine innings (3.7)
- 3rd in balks (2), GDPs induced (28), lowest winning percentage and highest slugging percentage allowed (.471)
- Led the Rockies in losses, hits allowed, batters faced (838), walks allowed, fewest pitches thrown per batter (3.58) and fewest home runs allowed per nine innings (1.21)

Todd Helton

Position: 1B
Bats: L **Throws:** L
Ht: 6' 2" **Wt:** 204

Opening Day Age: 29
Born: 8/20/73 in Knoxville, TN
ML Seasons: 6

Colorado

2002 Season

Todd Helton had what he considered an off season in 2002. That probably says it all about his abilities. In addition, though Helton had to settle for a .329 average, 73 extra-base hits, 109 RBI and a team-high 99 walks, he did so while playing with a bone spur in his right elbow and a benign tumor in his back. Surgery in October cleared up the elbow problem, and a winter workout routine should ease the back problems.

Hitting

Helton is a hitting coach's dream. He has a max-effort swing with the ability to wait to commit. As a kid, Helton's father worked with him in the garage on hitting the opposite way, and the attribute serves him well. He has the strength to drive the ball out to any field, and has made the adjustments to be able to yank the ball or drive it the other way. He has the patience to wait on breaking balls, and is not intimidated by lefthanded pitchers.

Baserunning & Defense

Although Helton won Gold Gloves in 2001 and 2002, he's not a dazzling first baseman. He is more of a workman. However, he does take care of business. He has soft hands and can dig throws out of the dirt. He has the initial reaction that expands his range, and he's aggressive in bunt situations. Helton loves to go for the lead runner in sacrifice situations, and has the arm strength and accuracy to do it. He's a below-average runner out of the blocks, but is solid average once he gets going, and isn't afraid to take the extra base.

2003 Outlook

Helton is the heart of the Rockies' present and future. He's going to play first base and hit third or fourth virtually every day. In an offseason filled with talk about moving long-term contracts, not a mention was made about a deal involving Helton, who is signed through 2011. A first-round draft choice in 1995, he's the first homegrown All-Star in franchise history.

Overall Statistics

	G	AB	R	H	D	T	HR	RBI	SB	BB	SO	Avg	OBP	Slg
'02	156	553	107	182	39	4	30	109	5	99	91	.329	.429	.577
Car.	821	2921	582	973	230	15	186	623	27	429	398	.333	.419	.613

Where He Hits the Ball

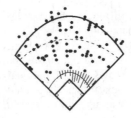
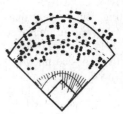

Vs. LHP	**Vs. RHP**

2002 Situational Stats

	AB	H	HR	RBI	Avg		AB	H	HR	RBI	Avg
Home	275	104	18	65	.378	LHP	199	65	11	46	.327
Road	278	78	12	44	.281	RHP	354	117	19	63	.331
First Half	306	106	16	63	.346	Sc Pos	138	46	8	76	.333
Scnd Half	247	76	14	46	.308	Clutch	80	18	0	6	.225

2002 Rankings (National League)

- 1st in batting average at home
- 3rd in sacrifice flies (10), batting average vs. righthanded pitchers and assists at first base (112)
- Led the Rockies in home runs, runs scored, hits, total bases (319), RBI, sacrifice flies (10), walks, intentional walks (21), times on base (286), pitches seen (2,675), plate appearances (668), games played, on-base percentage, batting average on an 0-2 count (.286), cleanup slugging percentage (.535), slugging percentage vs. lefthanded pitchers (.573), on-base percentage vs. lefthanded pitchers (.437) and batting average with two strikes (.263)
- Led NL first basemen in batting average and RBI

Jason Jennings

2002 Season

Jason Jennings won a four-man battle for a spot in the Rockies' rotation last spring. The righthander then pitched so well that he was the overwhelming choice for the National League Rookie of the Year, the first pitcher in franchise history to get serious consideration for a postseason award. Jennings broke the Rockies' rookie record with 16 wins, and came within one victory of tying the team's overall single-season record.

Pitching

Jennings is a masterful pitcher. He has a sinker, slider and changeup, and he mixes them well. His sinker is consistently in the 89-91 MPH range, which is where he needs to stay to keep it working. What really made a difference for him last year was an improved changeup. With his sinker and slider both being down in the zone, he needs the offspeed pitch to help control opponents' bat speed. Jennings not only throws strikes, but quality strikes. He doesn't back down from challenges, which is why he was able to cope with Coors Field.

Defense & Hitting

Jennings' bulky lower body belies his athletic ability. He has a chance to eventually win a Gold Glove award. He has quick feet and a quick move to first base, which keeps runners close and helps the catcher. He comes off the mound swiftly and has soft hands. He is a legitimate threat with the bat. The opposition doesn't work around the No. 8 hitter when Jennings is in the lineup. A cleanup hitter at Baylor, he has worked to stay sharp at the plate.

2003 Outlook

Jennings brings back memories of Rick Reuschel, with his easy delivery, hard sinker and athletic abilities wrapped up in that bulky body. Jennings will face a major test this year. He was the No. 5 starter to open 2002, which provided favorable matchups. He'll likely be the No. 1 guy this year, and will be going up against the top pitchers from other teams more often.

Position: SP
Bats: L **Throws:** R
Ht: 6' 2" **Wt:** 242

Opening Day Age: 24
Born: 7/17/78 in Dallas, TX
ML Seasons: 2

Overall Statistics

	W	L	Pct.	ERA	G	GS	Sv	IP	H	BB	SO	HR	Ratio
'02	16	8	.667	4.52	32	32	0	185.1	201	70	127	26	1.46
Car.	20	9	.690	4.53	39	39	0	224.2	243	89	153	28	1.48

How Often He Throws Strikes

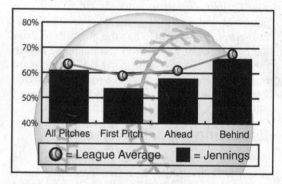

2002 Situational Stats

	W	L	ERA	Sv	IP		AB	H	HR	RBI	Avg
Home	9	4	5.65	0	94.0	LHB	298	89	8	40	.299
Road	7	4	3.35	0	91.1	RHB	420	112	18	52	.267
First Half	9	4	4.85	0	94.2	Sc Pos	167	42	4	60	.251
Scnd Half	7	4	4.17	0	90.2	Clutch	7	0	0	0	.000

2002 Rankings (National League)

- 1st in wins among rookies
- 2nd in most run support per nine innings (6.5) and highest ERA at home
- 3rd in most GDPs induced per nine innings (1.2) and highest on-base percentage allowed (.349)
- 4th in ERA among rookies and losses among rookies
- Led the Rockies in wins, games started, innings pitched, home runs allowed, strikeouts, wild pitches (10), pitches thrown (3,028), pickoff throws (58), runners caught stealing (4), lowest ERA on the road and most strikeouts per nine innings (6.2)

Jose Jimenez

2002 Season

Jose Jimenez blossomed in his third year as a closer. Not only did he earn 41 saves, he continued to get the job done on the road while also showing he could handle Coors Field. For the first time with the Rockies, he posted a lower home than road ERA, which is an accomplishment at Colorado's altitude. What's more, he converted 23 of 27 save opportunities at Coors.

Pitching

Jimenez is a sinking fastball and slider pitcher who will show a four-seam fastball on occasion. He never has mastered an offspeed pitch. That's why he was moved out of the starting rotation. His fastball is solid in the low-90 MPH range with plus sinking action. He can get himself in trouble with his four-seam fastball, because it's straight and tends to find the middle of the plate. He doesn't know how to pitch up. His command is key. When he's on, he pounds the zone down and gets plenty of groundballs. If he gets the ball up, however, he gets beat. He can get into ruts when he loses his command for a day or two. Jimenez has particular problems when he hangs his slider, which are magnified in the light air of Colorado.

Defense & Hitting

Jimenez is an aggressive fielder. However, he can create problems because he gets overanxious and will throw without planting himself, which leads to errors. The closer does have a slide step that he will use, and he needs it. He is too slow to the plate to keep opponents from stealing. He's wasting everybody's time if he picks up a bat.

2003 Outlook

Jimenez has handled the conversion from starter to closer quite well. His performance last season has put him into the closer mindset. The truth is, however, that on a good team he probably would be a setup man who can close games in an emergency. He doesn't have that strikeout pitch teams like to see from their closer. As a guy who's better suited to setup work but is in line for closer money, Jimenez reportedly has been on the trading block this offseason. If he is dealt, Todd Jones could take over closing duties.

Position: RP
Bats: R **Throws:** R
Ht: 6' 3" **Wt:** 228

Opening Day Age: 29
Born: 7/7/73 in San Pedro de Macoris, DR
ML Seasons: 5
Pronunciation: he-MEN-ez

Overall Statistics

	W	L	Pct.	ERA	G	GS	Sv	IP	H	BB	SO	HR	Ratio
'02	2	10	.167	3.56	74	0	41	73.1	76	11	47	7	1.19
Car.	21	27	.438	4.51	235	31	82	383.1	390	140	253	33	1.38

How Often He Throws Strikes

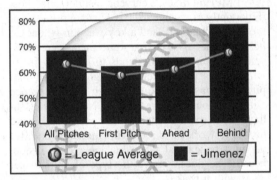

◎ = League Average   ■ = Jimenez

2002 Situational Stats

	W	L	ERA	Sv	IP		AB	H	HR	RBI	Avg
Home	1	4	2.90	23	40.1	LHB	139	37	4	16	.266
Road	1	6	4.36	18	33.0	RHB	148	39	3	19	.264
First Half	2	5	3.30	23	43.2	Sc Pos	77	22	2	27	.286
Scnd Half	0	5	3.94	18	29.2	Clutch	186	54	5	29	.290

2002 Rankings (National League)

- 1st in games finished (69) and relief losses (10)
- 6th in saves and save opportunities (47)
- 7th in save percentage (87.2) and blown saves (6)
- Led the Rockies in saves, games finished (69), save opportunities (47), save percentage (87.2), blown saves (6), relief losses (10) and relief ERA (3.56)

Denny Neagle

2002 Season

Denny Neagle felt abused and asked to be traded after manager Clint Hurdle put him in the bullpen last July. However, Neagle admits the move made him more aggressive and helped him recapture his changeup. He went 4-2 with a 1.93 ERA in his first seven starts after returning to the rotation. He struggled at the end of the season, but that was blamed on a bone chip in his elbow, which was removed with arthroscopic surgery in early October.

Pitching

Neagle features an 86-MPH fastball that will hit 90-91 MPH at times, a curveball, slider, and, most importantly, a changeup. His changeup is one of the best in baseball, and a key weapon whenever he's had success. But for some unanswered reason, it's a pitch that he tends to get away from, which leads to disaster. Although he's a flyball pitcher, it hasn't made that much of a difference with the Rockies. Most of all, Neagle needs to have his command. He has to work quickly, and he has to work inside to righthanded hitters. But he must be careful when he does come inside, because he doesn't have the type of stuff to get away with mistakes.

Defense & Hitting

Neagle isn't really quick to the plate, though he understands the importance of giving his catcher a chance. He will hold the ball, keeping the baserunner guessing, in order to prevent good jumps. Neagle is a good athlete and fields his position well, particularly in bunt situations. He's one of the rare pitchers who takes pride in his hitting, a residue of his time in Atlanta. He is a likely hit-and-run candidate in bunt situations.

2003 Outlook

Neagle still might be traded. He would be a bottom-of-the-rotation lefthander on a quality team, but is being paid as a top-of-the-rotation guy. He has three years and $37 million remaining on his current deal. He can handle bullpen duty, as much as he doesn't like it, because with his changeup he is more effective against righthanded than lefthanded hitters.

Position: SP
Bats: L **Throws:** L
Ht: 6' 3" **Wt:** 225

Opening Day Age: 34
Born: 9/13/68 in Annapolis, MD
ML Seasons: 12
Pronunciation: NAY-gull

Overall Statistics

	W	L	Pct.	ERA	G	GS	Sv	IP	H	BB	SO	HR	Ratio
'02	8	11	.421	5.26	35	28	0	164.1	170	63	111	26	1.42
Car.	122	88	.581	4.17	385	279	3	1855.0	1840	582	1394	238	1.31

How Often He Throws Strikes

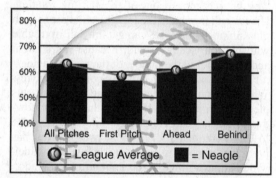

2002 Situational Stats

	W	L	ERA	Sv	IP		AB	H	HR	RBI	Avg
Home	3	5	5.16	0	89.0	LHB	149	47	10	29	.315
Road	5	6	5.38	0	75.1	RHB	491	123	16	66	.251
First Half	4	6	6.06	0	95.0	Sc Pos	159	47	6	69	.296
Scnd Half	4	5	4.15	0	69.1	Clutch	43	18	1	8	.419

2002 Rankings (National League)

- 3rd in highest ERA at home and least run support per nine innings (3.9)
- 4th in highest ERA, highest stolen-base percentage allowed (86.4) and most home runs allowed per nine innings (1.42)
- 7th in highest slugging percentage allowed (.459) and highest batting average allowed with runners in scoring position
- 8th in hit batsmen (10)
- 10th in stolen bases allowed (19) and highest on-base percentage allowed (.338)
- Led the Rockies in home runs allowed, hit batsmen (10) and stolen bases allowed (19)

Jay Payton

2002 Season

Acquired in late July in a five-player deal that sent John Thomson to the Mets, Jay Payton gave the Rockies a righthanded bat they needed so badly. Payton hit .335 in 47 games with the Rockies, including .473 at Coors Field, where he drove in 19 runs in 21 games. At season's end, however, he had once again fallen victim to a nagging injury, as he was sidelined by a pulled ribcage muscle.

Hitting

The tools are there, though the results haven't always been. Payton is a line-drive hitter with the ability to drive balls in the gaps. He has a short swing that generates power, but will fall into major slumps when he gets overanxious on sliders. He has slightly above-average power potential, but with his line-drive nature and the elements at Coors, he could become the next Dante Bichette or Jeffrey Hammonds. Payton is best suited to the No. 2 slot, where his speed and ability to hit the other way can be maximized.

Baserunning & Defense

Payton has the speed to play center field, but gets so-so breaks on balls. Adjusting to the way the ball carries at Coors took a little longer than anticipated. He is not afraid to make the diving play, though that's where the nagging injuries come up again. He throws a tad above average, and he does throw to the right base and does hit cutoff men. Payton has plus speed, but never has refined the art of stealing bases. It's a part of his game that still can be advanced.

2003 Outlook

Payton fits very much into the Rockies' everyday plans. He has the ability to play center field, but his arm strength might make him the perfect left fielder for Coors Field. That's where the Rockies need someone with center-field range and an arm that's slightly better than average. Payton gives manager Clint Hurdle lineup flexibility with his ability to hit anywhere from first through seventh.

Position: CF/LF
Bats: R **Throws:** R
Ht: 5'10" **Wt:** 185

Opening Day Age: 30
Born: 11/22/72 in Zanesville, OH
ML Seasons: 5

Overall Statistics

	G	AB	R	H	D	T	HR	RBI	SB	BB	SO	Avg	OBP	Slg
'02	134	445	69	135	20	7	16	59	7	29	54	.303	.351	.488
Car.	415	1324	179	378	61	9	41	156	17	78	172	.285	.329	.438

Where He Hits the Ball

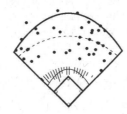
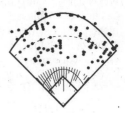

Vs. LHP   **Vs. RHP**

2002 Situational Stats

	AB	H	HR	RBI	Avg		AB	H	HR	RBI	Avg
Home	224	76	9	33	.339	LHP	135	34	4	13	.252
Road	221	59	7	26	.267	RHP	310	101	12	46	.326
First Half	217	58	7	26	.267	Sc Pos	93	30	3	42	.323
Scnd Half	228	77	9	33	.338	Clutch	89	23	4	10	.258

2002 Rankings (National League)

- 4th in batting average on an 0-2 count (.311)
- 6th in triples (7), batting average at home (.339) and assists in center field (7)

Juan Pierre

2002 Season

Maybe it's a tribute to Juan Pierre that in a year when he hit .287 and finished second in the National League with 47 stolen bases, the general conversation revolved around what was wrong with him. Even though he picked up the pace with a .422 average in September, he was traded to Florida in a six-player deal after the season.

Hitting

Pierre is the ultimate little-ball player, recording only 26 extra-base hits in 592 at-bats last season. He hits the ball on the ground and runs. He has shown signs of being able to turn on an inside fastball and drive it into the corner, but most often is content with slapping the ball the other way. He has to adjust his approach—moving up on the plate a couple of inches would help—because teams defense him well. He is an excellent bunter who is working to perfect the two-strike bunt.

Baserunning & Defense

Pierre's game is his legs. He runs well above average. He knows that stealing bases is a key component of his game, and is working to become more aggressive. He studies pitchers and made strides in getting better jumps, which allowed him to steal bases at a more successful rate. Pierre struggled in center field when he first came up, but he has addressed his shortcomings and has worked hard to become a solid center fielder. His arm strength is well below average. He's never going to have a rocket, though he's made strides in quickening his release and getting to balls quicker to slow down baserunners.

2003 Outlook

Pierre's game will fit much better into the elements of Florida's Pro Player Stadium. He was miscast in Colorado, where a player should have a chance to drive the ball out of the ballpark. Pierre will be near the top of the lineup and figures to be given the green light to run by manager Jeff Torborg.

Position: CF
Bats: L **Throws:** L
Ht: 6' 0" **Wt:** 180

Opening Day Age: 25
Born: 8/14/77 in Mobile, AL
ML Seasons: 3
Pronunciation: pee-AIR

Overall Statistics

	G	AB	R	H	D	T	HR	RBI	SB	BB	SO	Avg	OBP	Slg
'02	152	592	90	170	20	5	1	35	47	31	52	.287	.332	.343
Car.	359	1409	224	434	48	16	3	110	100	85	96	.308	.356	.371

Where He Hits the Ball

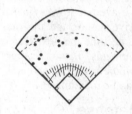 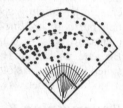

Vs. LHP   **Vs. RHP**

2002 Situational Stats

	AB	H	HR	RBI	Avg		AB	H	HR	RBI	Avg
Home	296	97	0	17	.328	LHP	126	37	0	3	.294
Road	296	73	1	18	.247	RHP	466	133	1	32	.285
First Half	358	97	0	17	.271	Sc Pos	113	38	0	33	.336
Scnd Half	234	73	1	18	.312	Clutch	79	21	0	6	.266

2002 Rankings (National League)

- 1st in bunts in play (62) and highest percentage of extra bases taken as a runner (72.5)
- 2nd in singles, stolen bases, highest groundball-flyball ratio (3.2) and lowest HR frequency (592.0 ABs per HR)
- 3rd in fielding percentage in center field (.995)
- Led the Rockies in at-bats, singles, sacrifice bunts (8), stolen bases, caught stealing (12), hit by pitch (9), highest groundball-flyball ratio (3.2), stolen-base percentage (79.7), bunts in play (62), lowest percentage of swings that missed (8.5), on-base percentage for a leadoff hitter (.334) and highest percentage of extra bases taken as a runner (72.5)

Denny Stark

2002 Season

Denny Stark was beaten out during spring training for the No. 5 spot in Colorado's rotation. By the middle of May, however, he had found his way back to the big leagues. He started briefly, made a visit to the bullpen, and finally returned to the rotation, where he was a pleasant surprise. He was 8-1 at Coors Field, where his 3.21 ERA was the lowest ever for a Rockies pitcher who made at least 10 starts or pitched at least 50 innings at Coors in a season.

Pitching

Stark has the basic fastball, slider and changeup assortment. The fastball is in the 87-91 MPH range with sink. He has an arm action that is testimony to the surgery he underwent three years ago, which creates concerns about his longevity. However, he pitches with a lot of heart. He's not particularly deceptive in his delivery, but has late movement and throws hitters off. He has the command to exploit a hitter's weakness. An opponent that will take pitches can get Stark in trouble.

Defense & Hitting

Stark is a better athlete than his body indicates. He could dunk a basketball when he was at the University of Toledo. He moves quickly off the mound on bunt plays and isn't afraid to make the play on the lead runner. He will quicken his stride and give the catcher at least a shot at throwing out runners. Having spent his entire career in the Seattle organization before 2002, Stark didn't work much on his hitting. By season's end, however, he showed he could handle a bat and gave promise of eventually contributing to the lineup.

2003 Outlook

Stark has staked claim to a spot in Colorado's rotation. In a perfect world, he would be a No. 4 or 5 starter, which would give him an edge in most matchups. With the Rockies, however, he is going to be fitted into the No. 2 slot behind Jason Jennings. While that could be asking a bit too much, given Stark's competitive nature, don't bet against him.

Position: SP/RP
Bats: R **Throws:** R
Ht: 6' 2" **Wt:** 210

Opening Day Age: 28
Born: 10/27/74 in Edgerton, OH
ML Seasons: 3

Overall Statistics

	W	L	Pct.	ERA	G	GS	Sv	IP	H	BB	SO	HR	Ratio
'02	11	4	.733	4.00	32	20	0	128.1	108	64	64	25	1.34
Car.	12	5	.706	4.76	41	23	0	149.1	139	72	80	30	1.41

How Often He Throws Strikes

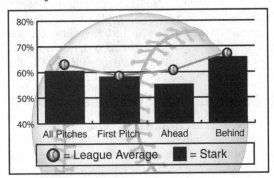

= League Average   = Stark

2002 Situational Stats

	W	L	ERA	Sv	IP		AB	H	HR	RBI	Avg
Home	8	1	3.21	0	84.0	LHB	184	42	13	34	.228
Road	3	3	5.48	0	44.1	RHB	295	66	12	32	.224
First Half	4	1	3.07	0	44.0	Sc Pos	100	25	4	38	.250
Scnd Half	7	3	4.48	0	84.1	Clutch	17	5	0	1	.294

2002 Rankings (National League)
- 4th in winning percentage
- Led the Rockies in ERA, winning percentage, lowest batting average allowed (.225), lowest slugging percentage allowed (.428), lowest ERA at home and most run support per nine innings (6.5)

Juan Uribe

Great Range

2002 Season

Uribe had a torrid beginning, hitting .373 in April. And he had a solid ending, batting .314 in September. In between, however, he hit .193, and created concerns that he was rushed to the big leagues. Uribe was allowed to play through the struggles because the Rockies didn't have a capable backup, and wound up playing 155 games.

Hitting

The biggest question Uribe faces is whether he'll hit enough to play every day. He has a two-piece swing, bringing his bat back, stopping, and starting over again. There is no fluidity. He is young, so he could adjust. He has a problem with breaking balls, which is compounded by the fact he doesn't force pitchers to throw strikes. He was particularly exposed on the road. Uribe is a good bunter, but has hit his way into the No. 8 slot, where bunting isn't as much of a factor.

Baserunning & Defense

Uribe likes to run the bases. However, he is not a blazer and never will be a huge basestealing threat. He is a plus runner though, and the speed shows up when he hits the ball in the gaps. He has 18 triples in 839 big league at-bats. Uribe has special defensive skills. Scouts rate his arm, range and hands near the top of the scale. He reads the ball very well off the bat, but has to concentrate better. All but a handful of his errors come on routine plays, as he tends to get a little lackadaisical.

2003 Outlook

Uribe is an everyday player, if for no other reason than his defensive skills. But he'll have to show some improvement with the bat if he's going to avoid a return to the minors. He's too young and too skilled to even think about making him a bench player. He has the offensive pop and speed that would project as a potential No. 2 hitter. However, he'll have to make more consistent contact to avoid being buried at the bottom of the lineup.

Position: SS
Bats: R **Throws:** R
Ht: 5'11" **Wt:** 173

Opening Day Age: 23
Born: 7/22/79 in Bani, DR
ML Seasons: 2
Pronunciation: ooh-REE-bay

Overall Statistics

	G	AB	R	H	D	T	HR	RBI	SB	BB	SO	Avg	OBP	Slg
'02	155	566	69	136	25	7	6	49	9	34	120	.240	.286	.341
Car.	227	839	101	218	40	18	14	102	12	42	175	.260	.299	.400

Where He Hits the Ball

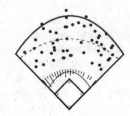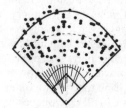

Vs. LHP   **Vs. RHP**

2002 Situational Stats

	AB	H	HR	RBI	Avg		AB	H	HR	RBI	Avg
Home	299	84	4	36	.281	LHP	141	34	1	18	.241
Road	267	52	2	13	.195	RHP	425	102	5	31	.240
First Half	337	82	3	27	.243	Sc Pos	124	31	2	42	.250
Scnd Half	229	54	3	22	.236	Clutch	83	21	1	11	.253

2002 Rankings (National League)

- 1st in lowest batting average on a 3-1 count (.000) and lowest batting average on the road
- 2nd in errors at shortstop (27)
- 3rd in lowest percentage of pitches taken (44.9)
- 4th in lowest batting average, lowest on-base percentage and lowest on-base percentage vs. righthanded pitchers (.288)
- 5th in lowest slugging percentage
- 6th in triples, lowest slugging percentage vs. righthanded pitchers (.346) and lowest fielding percentage at shortstop (.966)
- Led the Rockies in triples, strikeouts and steals of third (4)

Larry Walker

Position: RF
Bats: L **Throws:** R
Ht: 6' 3" **Wt:** 233

Opening Day Age: 36
Born: 12/1/66 in Maple Ridge, BC, Canada
ML Seasons: 14

2002 Season

Larry Walker secured his position as the most productive Canadian-born hitter in major league history last season. In his eighth year with the Rockies, he hit .300 for the seventh time and drove in at least 100 runs for the fifth time. However, he continued to battle left elbow problems that limited his power to 26 homers, continuing an every-other-year pattern of reduced home-run production.

Hitting

Walker is a complete hitter, his body permitting. But injuries have limited his playing time and power. Despite a long swing, he's quick and strong enough to handle just about any type of pitching. Walker has the power to hit the ball out to all fields. He has no fear of being hit by a pitch, so he hangs in at the plate, and he's one of the better lefthanded hitters versus southpaws.

Baserunning & Defense

Walker is a Gold Glove-caliber right fielder. He has wonderful instincts, getting impressive jumps on balls. His arm isn't as strong as it used to be, but he gets rid of the ball quickly and throws to the right base consistently. Runners don't take chances because Walker anticipates so well. His instincts and anticipation carry over to his baserunning. A plus runner, especially for someone his size, he consistently takes the extra base. He comes under fire for not always hustling to first on groundballs, which will cost him several times a season.

2003 Outlook

Walker is one of the most talented players in the National League. He's not its best player, in part because he doesn't play enough. His 136 games last year—122 of them starts—marked the eighth time in the past 10 seasons that he failed to play at least 140 games. It's not realistic to think a 36-year-old Walker is suddenly going to become an iron man. Still, he should put up numbers that will rank among the game's best.

Overall Statistics

	G	AB	R	H	D	T	HR	RBI	SB	BB	SO	Avg	OBP	Slg
'02	136	477	95	161	40	4	26	104	6	65	73	.338	.421	.602
Car.	1663	5880	1152	1863	410	50	335	1133	215	725	1023	.317	.398	.574

Where He Hits the Ball

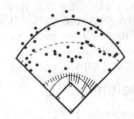

Vs. LHP   **Vs. RHP**

2002 Situational Stats

	AB	H	HR	RBI	Avg		AB	H	HR	RBI	Avg
Home	243	88	18	66	.362	LHP	166	56	5	40	.337
Road	234	73	8	38	.312	RHP	311	105	21	64	.338
First Half	274	96	20	67	.350	Sc Pos	114	41	4	68	.360
Scnd Half	203	65	6	37	.320	Clutch	77	36	6	23	.468

2002 Rankings (National League)

- 1st in batting average in the clutch and assists in right field (14)
- 2nd in batting average and batting average at home
- 3rd in slugging percentage
- Led the Rockies in doubles, HR frequency (18.3 ABs per HR), fewest GDPs per GDP situation (7.1%), batting average with runners in scoring position, batting average vs. left handed pitchers, batting average vs. righthanded pitchers, slugging percentage vs. righthanded pitchers (.640), on-base percentage vs. righthanded pitchers (.437), batting average on the road and batting average on a 3-2 count (.325)

Todd Zeile

2002 Season

Todd Zeile was all the Rockies could have expected after they acquired him a year ago from the New York Mets. He wasn't spectacular, but he gave them a professional hitter who filled the void at third base. Surgery that removed bone chips from his right elbow allowed him to get extension with his swing that was missing in 2001, and he rebounded with solid run production.

Hitting

Zeile is one of the game's ultimate guess hitters. He isn't afraid to sit on a pitch, and he isn't afraid to hit down in the count. He rarely swings at first pitches. However, he will change that approach against the elite pitchers, looking for that first-pitch fastball and hoping to get a good swing. He showed he still can drive the ball last season, and he fit well into Coors Field, where he could take advantage of the large outfield gaps.

Baserunning & Defense

After two years at first base with the Mets, Zeile returned to third base last season. The Rockies didn't have an alternative, and to Zeile's credit, he accepted the challenge. Still, defense can be a problem for him. He has to cheat in because of a lack of arm strength, which restricts his already limited range. The first-step quickness also isn't there. His arm is accurate, but there isn't a lot of carry. While Zeile is below average in terms of speed, he has a feel for the game and will take the extra base.

2003 Outlook

Zeile's days as an everyday player most likely are over. The Rockies let him go as a free agent. He could help an American League team as a DH, or provide a righthanded bat off the bench that also can fill in at third base or first base if needed. He's a good student of the game, which should help him adapt to a diminished role. However, that will mean dealing with a diminished salary from the $6 million he earned last year.

Position: 3B
Bats: R **Throws:** R
Ht: 6' 1" **Wt:** 200

Opening Day Age: 37
Born: 9/9/65 in Van Nuys, CA
ML Seasons: 14
Pronunciation: ZEAL

Overall Statistics

G	AB	R	H	D	T	HR	RBI	SB	BB	SO	Avg	OBP	Slg
144	506	61	138	23	0	18	87	1	66	92	.273	.353	.425
1921	6926	916	1855	371	21	233	1033	52	867	1142	.268	.349	.428

Where He Hits the Ball

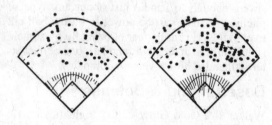

Vs. LHP   **Vs. RHP**

2002 Situational Stats

	AB	H	HR	RBI	Avg		AB	H	HR	RBI	Avg
Home	248	78	11	56	.315	LHP	146	40	4	23	.274
Road	258	60	7	31	.233	RHP	360	98	14	64	.272
First Half	289	84	13	54	.291	Sc Pos	152	46	10	77	.303
Scnd Half	217	54	5	33	.249	Clutch	67	14	2	7	.209

2002 Rankings (National League)

- 1st in most pitches seen per plate appearance (4.31), highest percentage of pitches taken (65.2), lowest percentage of swings on the first pitch (10.6), errors at third base (21) and lowest fielding percentage at third base (.942)
- 2nd in GDPs (27)
- 5th in sacrifice flies (7)
- 6th in highest groundball-flyball ratio (1.8)
- 8th in most GDPs per GDP situation (19.7%) and lowest batting average on the road
- Led the Rockies in GDPs (27), most pitches seen per plate appearance (4.31), highest percentage of pitches taken (65.2) and lowest percentage of swings on the first pitch (10.6)

Gary Bennett

Position: C
Bats: R **Throws:** R
Ht: 6' 0" **Wt:** 208

Opening Day Age: 30
Born: 4/17/72 in
Waukegan, IL
ML Seasons: 7

Overall Statistics

	G	AB	R	H	D	T	HR	RBI	SB	BB	SO	Avg	OBP	Slg
'02	90	291	26	77	10	2	4	26	1	15	45	.265	.314	.354
Car.	219	632	60	164	25	3	9	66	1	51	107	.259	.321	.351

2002 Situational Stats

	AB	H	HR	RBI	Avg		AB	H	HR	RBI	Avg
Home	144	43	2	15	.299	LHP	63	23	1	7	.365
Road	147	34	2	11	.231	RHP	228	54	3	19	.237
First Half	149	38	3	12	.255	Sc Pos	61	16	2	24	.262
Scnd Half	142	39	1	14	.275	Clutch	35	9	1	4	.257

2002 Season

In his 13th professional season, Gary Bennett had his most productive big league campaign. He saw his most extensive duty in the majors, appearing in 90 games, only 39 fewer than his previous career total. He shared the Rockies' catching duties with an assortment of other receivers.

Hitting, Baserunning & Defense

Bennett became an offensive contributor when he spread out his stance and concentrated on hitting the ball up the middle. While he'll put the ball in play, there's not a lot of power. He's going to hit at the bottom of the lineup. He does a decent job of handling a pitching staff. Veterans Mike Hampton and Denny Neagle, in particular, liked throwing to Bennett. He is a soft receiver, and has the quickness to block balls. Bennett has solid arm strength. He's not going to get the premier thieves, but will keep a team honest in its bases-tealing. He's a below-average runner who isn't going to take chances on the bases.

2003 Outlook

Bennett's ideal role is the one he had last year, when he started 85 games. He will wear down if he's asked to play more extensively. He'll turn 31 in April, and never has been asked to carry the load, even in the minor leagues.

Brent Butler

Position: 2B/3B/SS
Bats: R **Throws:** R
Ht: 6' 0" **Wt:** 180

Opening Day Age: 25
Born: 2/11/78 in
Laurinburg, NC
ML Seasons: 2

Overall Statistics

	G	AB	R	H	D	T	HR	RBI	SB	BB	SO	Avg	OBP	Slg
'02	113	344	55	89	18	4	9	42	2	10	40	.259	.287	.413
Car.	166	463	72	118	25	5	10	56	3	17	47	.255	.287	.395

2002 Situational Stats

	AB	H	HR	RBI	Avg		AB	H	HR	RBI	Avg
Home	185	57	7	32	.308	LHP	76	18	1	7	.237
Road	159	32	2	10	.201	RHP	268	71	8	35	.265
First Half	119	37	4	17	.311	Sc Pos	76	25	3	34	.329
Scnd Half	225	52	5	25	.231	Clutch	50	12	1	7	.240

2002 Season

Brent Butler opened last season with the Rockies because the team was on the road and it initially went with 11 pitchers. He was shuttled to Triple-A on a couple occasions, returning to the majors for good in mid-June.

Hitting, Baserunning & Defense

Butler primarily is a contact hitter. But throw him a fastball and beware, especially at Coors Field. He showed unexpected power last season, but he needs to work counts better and get better reads on breaking pitches. He had problems trying to take extra bases early last season, but showed better judgment when he returned to the big leagues in June. He's an average runner and has to maximize that ability. Butler plays solid defense, particularly at second base. He hangs in well on the double play. He has the arm but not the bat to play third.

2003 Outlook

Butler's versatility makes him an excellent utility player. That's the role the Rockies prefer for him, but unless they find a second baseman in the off-season, he and Pablo Ozuna are in the mix for the starting second-base job. While he could fill in at third, Butler doesn't have the range to play extensively at shortstop, his original position. He'll also get some exposure in the outfield in 2003.

Shawn Chacon

Position: SP
Bats: R **Throws:** R
Ht: 6' 3" **Wt:** 212

Opening Day Age: 25
Born: 12/23/77 in Anchorage, AK
ML Seasons: 2
Pronunciation: cha-CONE

Overall Statistics

	W	L	Pct.	ERA	G	GS	Sv	IP	H	BB	SO	HR	Ratio
'02	5	11	.313	5.73	21	21	0	119.1	122	60	67	25	1.53
Car.	11	21	.344	5.35	48	48	0	279.1	279	147	201	51	1.53

2002 Situational Stats

	W	L	ERA	Sv	IP		AB	H	HR	RBI	Avg
Home	3	4	6.47	0	57.0	LHB	204	65	14	36	.319
Road	2	7	5.05	0	62.1	RHB	259	57	11	37	.220
First Half	3	6	4.96	0	74.1	Sc Pos	118	32	6	48	.271
Scnd Half	2	5	7.00	0	45.0	Clutch	9	4	1	1	.444

2002 Season

Shawn Chacon opened last season as Colorado's No. 4 starter, but ended it at Triple-A. He was disabled with a strained pectoral muscle in early May and struggled when he returned. He wasn't asked to rejoin the Rockies in September.

Pitching, Defense & Hitting

Chacon grew up in Colorado, so maybe that's why he throws a curveball at altitude and it works. The problem last year was that his fastball disappeared. As a rookie, he was constantly in the 89-93 MPH range. But he lost a good five miles in 2002. He obviously didn't have confidence in the pitch, because he tried to work away instead of challenging hitters. He has a slider and change, but they're secondary pitches. He's worked to become an adequate hitter, but still can't lay down the bunt consistently. He's a good enough athlete that he should become a solid fielder.

2003 Outlook

Chacon has to prove he deserves a spot in a big league rotation. He did it two years ago, when he made an emergency start and never went back down. Last year, however, he let the opportunity slip away. A lot will be determined by Chacon's attitude, and if he will fight to regain his job. Mike Hampton's departure opens the door for him.

Brian Fuentes

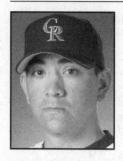

Position: RP
Bats: L **Throws:** L
Ht: 6' 4" **Wt:** 220

Opening Day Age: 27
Born: 8/9/75 in Merced, CA
ML Seasons: 2
Pronunciation: foo-WHEN-tayz

Overall Statistics

	W	L	Pct.	ERA	G	GS	Sv	IP	H	BB	SO	HR	Ratio
'02	2	0	1.000	4.73	31	0	0	26.2	25	13	38	4	1.43
Car.	3	1	.750	4.70	41	0	0	38.1	31	21	48	6	1.36

2002 Situational Stats

	W	L	ERA	Sv	IP		AB	H	HR	RBI	Avg
Home	2	0	3.31	0	16.1	LHB	42	16	3	10	.381
Road	0	0	6.97	0	10.1	RHB	58	9	1	7	.155
First Half	0	0	11.25	0	4.0	Sc Pos	28	8	0	11	.286
Scnd Half	2	0	3.57	0	22.2	Clutch	10	3	0	1	.300

2002 Season

Brian Fuentes came to the Rockies from Seattle prior to last season as part of the package for Jeff Cirillo. Fuentes then made four tours with the big league team. Given a chance to pitch regularly in his final callup, he showed improved command, walking six and striking out 25 in 18.2 innings.

Pitching, Defense & Hitting

Fuentes has an unorthodox delivery that is pseudo-submarine. He describes it as the action of throwing a Frisbee. He has surprising velocity for his style, hitting 92 MPH at times with his fastball. With consistent work, he showed solid command and an ability to hit the third base side of the plate. His ball is fairly straight, but he throws it past hitters because of the deception in his delivery. He needs to tighten his slider. He is slow to the plate, and with his arm action even a slide step wouldn't help much. He hasn't batted in the big leagues.

2003 Outlook

Fuentes showed enough in his final promotion last season to be counted on for an expanded role in the late innings. He might even get to close a few games if he comes in and pitches well in the eighth inning. The key will be his continued effectiveness against righthanded hitters.

Todd Jones

Position: RP
Bats: B **Throws:** R
Ht: 6' 3" **Wt:** 230

Opening Day Age: 34
Born: 4/24/68 in
Marietta, GA
ML Seasons: 10

Overall Statistics

	W	L	Pct.	ERA	G	GS	Sv	IP	H	BB	SO	HR	Ratio
'02	1	4	.200	4.70	79	0	1	82.1	84	28	73	10	1.36
Car.	36	37	.493	3.75	607	0	184	681.0	650	313	613	62	1.41

2002 Situational Stats

	W	L	ERA	Sv	IP		AB	H	HR	RBI	Avg
Home	1	3	6.63	0	38.0	LHB	146	34	2	14	.233
Road	0	1	3.05	1	44.1	RHB	166	50	8	34	.301
First Half	1	1	4.00	1	45.0	Sc Pos	83	26	5	43	.313
Scnd Half	0	3	5.54	0	37.1	Clutch	199	44	5	25	.221

2002 Season

Todd Jones turned his setup role with the Rockies into an opportunity to resurrect his career. Don't be deceived by his 6.63 ERA at Coors Field. Five rough outings in the 37 appearances he made there really hurt him. He handled the challenge well, shaking off bad outings and not letting them compound. He pitched in a career-high 79 games.

Pitching, Defense & Hitting

Jones is a rare late-inning reliever who will mix three pitches. He has a curveball and changeup to go with his fastball, which came back last season and was a solid low-90s MPH pitch. He showed that a good curveball can master the altitude. Jones has the command that allows him to get by with a fastball that doesn't have a lot of movement. He is adequate fielding his position. His delivery to the plate is a natural slide step, which helps him control the running game somewhat. He struck out twice in three at-bats last year.

2003 Outlook

The Rockies wasted no time exercising Jones' $3 million option for 2003. He gives them excellent bullpen protection, and most likely will get a chance to return to closing games, at least in a committee type of setup. He shared the American League lead with 42 saves in 2000.

Gabe Kapler

Position: LF/RF/CF
Bats: R **Throws:** R
Ht: 6' 2" **Wt:** 208

Opening Day Age: 27
Born: 8/31/75 in
Hollywood, CA
ML Seasons: 5
Pronunciation:
CAP-ler

Overall Statistics

	G	AB	R	H	D	T	HR	RBI	SB	BB	SO	Avg	OBP	Slg
'02	112	315	37	88	16	4	2	34	11	16	53	.279	.313	.375
Car.	499	1683	236	458	99	11	51	221	55	162	258	.272	.335	.435

2002 Situational Stats

	AB	H	HR	RBI	Avg		AB	H	HR	RBI	Avg
Home	165	47	1	19	.285	LHP	100	25	0	7	.250
Road	150	41	1	15	.273	RHP	215	63	2	27	.293
First Half	171	45	0	14	.263	Sc Pos	70	25	0	30	.357
Scnd Half	144	43	2	20	.299	Clutch	53	17	0	6	.321

2002 Season

Gabe Kapler has the size, strength and speed that makes scouts drool. But he continued to fall short of expectations last season. He hit only two home runs, and both of those came after the Rockies acquired him from Texas in a trade that sent Todd Hollandsworth to the Rangers.

Hitting, Baserunning & Defense

Kapler has become so muscle-bound that it ties up his swing. The benefit he derives from his strength isn't balls flying over fences, but jam shots he's able to flip over infielders' heads. He has a two-part, mechanical swing. He has no chance against elite pitchers, because his swing is too long and slow. Kapler can run and is a threat to take an extra base or steal whenever he manages to get on. He has the tools to play all three outfield positions, but his lack of instincts are glaring in center field. He has plenty of arm strength and rarely throws to the wrong base.

2003 Outlook

Colorado was able to get Texas to pick up half of Kapler's $3.1 million salary for this season, which allows the Rockies to be comfortable with Kapler as a fourth outfielder. It should be a good spot for him.

Jose Ortiz

Position: 2B
Bats: R **Throws:** R
Ht: 5'10" **Wt:** 182

Opening Day Age: 25
Born: 6/13/77 in Santo Domingo, DR
ML Seasons: 3

Overall Statistics

	G	AB	R	H	D	T	HR	RBI	SB	BB	SO	Avg	OBP	Slg
'02	65	192	22	48	7	1	1	12	2	16	30	.250	.315	.313
Car.	136	449	68	109	15	2	14	51	6	35	74	.243	.305	.379

2002 Situational Stats

	AB	H	HR	RBI	Avg		AB	H	HR	RBI	Avg
Home	98	24	1	7	.245	LHP	43	10	0	1	.233
Road	94	24	0	5	.255	RHP	149	38	1	11	.255
First Half	160	39	1	9	.244	Sc Pos	50	10	1	11	.200
Scnd Half	32	9	0	3	.281	Clutch	25	9	0	1	.360

2002 Season

Jose Ortiz was the Rockies' Opening Day second baseman, but he landed on the DL with a strained hamstring in June and spent some time in Triple-A on a rehab assignment. He regained some offensive hope at Colorado Springs, where he also saw action at third base. When the Rockies recalled him in September, however, Ortiz was reluctant to make the position change.

Hitting, Baserunning & Defense

Ortiz previously had shown one of the quicker bats in baseball, which translated into nice power. However, he bulked up after the 2001 season and became so tight in his upper body that he lost that quickness. Add in that Ortiz never has shown any desire to go to the right side, and he became an offensive liability. If he doesn't hit, he isn't going to play. He's a below-average runner, and his defense is weak. He has stiff hands and slow feet, though his arm is a plus for a second baseman.

2003 Outlook

Ortiz was released and most likely will wind up in Japan, where he'll have a chance to catch up with the fastball. He must regain the ability to play shortstop, his original position, and work to become adequate at third base in order to become more useful as a major leaguer.

Ben Petrick

Position: LF/C
Bats: R **Throws:** R
Ht: 6' 0" **Wt:** 200

Opening Day Age: 25
Born: 4/7/77 in Salem, OR
ML Seasons: 4
Pronunciation: PEET-rick

Overall Statistics

	G	AB	R	H	D	T	HR	RBI	SB	BB	SO	Avg	OBP	Slg
'02	38	95	10	20	3	1	5	11	0	9	33	.211	.283	.421
Car.	194	547	96	145	31	5	23	82	5	70	146	.265	.350	.466

2002 Situational Stats

	AB	H	HR	RBI	Avg		AB	H	HR	RBI	Avg
Home	50	14	4	9	.280	LHP	52	13	4	5	.250
Road	45	6	1	2	.133	RHP	43	7	1	6	.163
First Half	47	7	0	4	.149	Sc Pos	25	1	0	5	.040
Scnd Half	48	13	5	7	.271	Clutch	10	3	2	4	.300

2002 Season

Ben Petrick bounced between Triple-A and the big leagues once again, reaffirming that he can handle minor league pitching. More importantly, he gave up catching and made the conversion to the outfield. By season's end he had shown he could play all three outfield spots.

Hitting, Baserunning & Defense

The question for Petrick is whether shedding the challenge of catching will allow him to finally relax. He has a short swing and possesses the gap power that would seem ideal for Coors Field. However, he can be overpowered inside and has been exploited by big league pitchers, who have learned that he can handle breaking pitches. The move to the outfield should help save Petrick's legs. He's a plus runner who can steal bases. He adapted quickly to the outfield, and actually played center field very well. He's not afraid to dive, but has to learn when it's a bad risk.

2003 Outlook

Petrick no longer is the pride of the organization. Although he's going to have to earn a spot on a big league roster, he would provide a luxury for his team. Now listed as an outfielder, he also can be a third catcher. He's said he would enjoy an occasional game or two behind the plate.

Terry Shumpert

Position: 2B
Bats: R **Throws:** R
Ht: 6' 0" **Wt:** 198

Opening Day Age: 36
Born: 8/16/66 in Paducah, KY
ML Seasons: 13

Overall Statistics

	G	AB	R	H	D	T	HR	RBI	SB	BB	SO	Avg	OBP	Slg
'02	106	234	30	55	12	1	6	21	4	21	41	.235	.304	.372
Car.	795	1885	281	481	104	24	47	216	84	156	352	.255	.316	.411

2002 Situational Stats

	AB	H	HR	RBI	Avg		AB	H	HR	RBI	Avg
Home	109	35	4	13	.321	LHP	85	25	3	11	.294
Road	125	20	2	8	.160	RHP	149	30	3	10	.201
First Half	137	35	3	12	.255	Sc Pos	57	10	1	15	.175
Scnd Half	97	20	3	9	.206	Clutch	48	13	1	1	.271

2002 Season

Terry Shumpert completed his third full year in the big leagues since former Rockies GM Bob Gebhard made him a player-coach at Triple-A Colorado Springs. Shumpert showed his versatility, starting at second base, shortstop, left field and right field, and also seeing time at third base.

Hitting, Baserunning & Defense

The key to Shumpert is not overexposing him. He still can hit the fastball, which makes him valuable coming off the bench. He isn't a real home run threat, but will drive the ball into the gaps. He is a notch below average defensively, though he can fill in at second and short. He's also worked hard the last four years to make himself an adequate left fielder, giving his manager an additional option. Shumpert is an average runner with decent instincts on the bases. He can steal if he isn't watched closely, and will take the extra base.

2003 Outlook

The Rockies have been Shumpert's fifth organization. Though he's a free agent, he's old enough and has bounced around enough that he accepts the role of being a bench player. That attitude, combined with the fact that he makes the commitment to be in shape, will keep him around for several more years.

Justin Speier

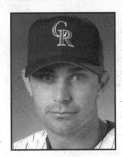

Position: RP
Bats: R **Throws:** R
Ht: 6' 4" **Wt:** 205

Opening Day Age: 29
Born: 11/6/73 in Walnut Creek, CA
ML Seasons: 5
Pronunciation: SPY-er

Overall Statistics

	W	L	Pct.	ERA	G	GS	Sv	IP	H	BB	SO	HR	Ratio
'02	5	1	.833	4.33	63	0	1	62.1	51	19	47	9	1.12
Car.	16	9	.640	4.63	202	0	1	256.2	234	93	217	46	1.27

2002 Situational Stats

	W	L	ERA	Sv	IP		AB	H	HR	RBI	Avg
Home	4	1	6.40	0	32.1	LHB	104	25	4	11	.240
Road	1	0	2.10	1	30.0	RHB	132	26	5	19	.197
First Half	3	0	3.00	1	27.0	Sc Pos	60	13	1	21	.217
Scnd Half	2	1	5.35	0	35.1	Clutch	95	20	2	14	.211

2002 Season

Justin Speier established himself as a key part of the Rockies late-inning relief brigade. He showed that he was durable and resilient, making a career-high 63 appearances. He worked more than an inning on 12 occasions, and less than an inning only 16 times. He was effective enough against lefthanded hitters to be kept in to face them in key situations.

Pitching, Defense & Hitting

Speier lives with two basic pitches—a fastball that will touch 95 MPH but usually is 91-93, and a split-finger. He does have a slider, but it just gets him in trouble. He has learned to throw strikes more consistently, which has created more key opportunities. His split is especially hard to pick up with his funky delivery. Speier has energy on the mound, which gives him a chance to make that tough defensive play. He has problems holding runners because he's so upright in the stretch position. He's 3-for-15 as a hitter in the big leagues.

2003 Outlook

Speier will be slated for setup duty in 2003, but could get a bigger challenge. With his type of stuff, he figures to get a chance to close out some games, even if they require more than one inning of work.

Other Colorado Rockies

Mark Corey (Pos: RHP, Age: 28)

	W	L	Pct.	ERA	G	GS	Sv	IP	H	BB	SO	HR	Ratio
'02	0	3	.000	8.59	26	0	0	22.0	32	16	21	9	2.18
Car.	0	3	.000	9.13	28	0	0	23.2	37	19	24	9	2.37

Corey came back from a seizure suffered in June before being traded from the Mets to the Rockies in late July. He was stung by the longball with Colorado, but was sharp in the minors the past two years. 2003 Outlook: C

Scott Elarton (Pos: RHP, Age: 27)

	W	L	Pct.	ERA	G	GS	Sv	IP	H	BB	SO	HR	Ratio
'02						Did Not Play							
Car.	32	23	.582	4.91	124	71	3	506.1	495	206	395	76	1.38

Elarton missed the entire 2002 season after undergoing shoulder surgery. He won 17 games for Houston as recently as 2000, but his career has been headed in the wrong direction since. 2003 Outlook: B

Bobby Estalella (Pos: C, Age: 28, Bats: R)

	G	AB	R	H	D	T	HR	RBI	SB	BB	SO	Avg	OBP	Slg
'02	38	112	17	23	8	0	8	25	0	14	33	.205	.285	.491
Car.	252	737	106	162	42	5	39	122	4	108	224	.220	.320	.449

Estalella was called up to the Rockies in May and shared the catching duties before undergoing July surgery on his non-throwing shoulder. 2003 Outlook: C

Randy Flores (Pos: LHP, Age: 27)

	W	L	Pct.	ERA	G	GS	Sv	IP	H	BB	SO	HR	Ratio
'02	0	2	.000	7.45	28	2	1	29.0	40	16	14	7	1.93
Car.	0	2	.000	7.45	28	2	1	29.0	40	16	14	7	1.93

The Rockies acquired Flores off waivers from the Rangers last July. His major league existence may lie as a lefthanded arm in the bullpen. 2003 Outlook: C

Ross Gload (Pos: 1B, Age: 26, Bats: L)

	G	AB	R	H	D	T	HR	RBI	SB	BB	SO	Avg	OBP	Slg
'02	26	31	4	8	1	0	1	4	0	3	7	.258	.324	.387
Car.	44	62	8	14	1	1	2	7	0	6	17	.226	.290	.371

Gload can play first base or a corner outfield spot. Except for a 31-homer season in 2000, he's demonstrated good but not great power. 2003 Outlook: C

Mike James (Pos: RHP, Age: 35)

	W	L	Pct.	ERA	G	GS	Sv	IP	H	BB	SO	HR	Ratio
'02	0	0	–	5.56	13	0	0	11.1	12	5	10	2	1.50
Car.	16	14	.533	3.67	288	0	11	314.0	285	149	247	30	1.38

After making 91 appearances for the Cardinals between 2000 and 2001, James didn't make it out of May with Colorado last year. He's constantly battled injuries, and has signed with Tampa Bay. 2003 Outlook: C

Sean Lowe (Pos: RHP, Age: 32)

	W	L	Pct.	ERA	G	GS	Sv	IP	H	BB	SO	HR	Ratio
'02	5	3	.625	5.79	51	1	0	79.1	101	41	64	9	1.79
Car.	22	14	.611	4.80	220	22	3	395.1	430	173	260	44	1.53

Lowe was part of the Todd Ritchie trade last offseason. The Rockies scooped him up, but later declined a contract option. 2003 Outlook: B

Walt McKeel (Pos: C, Age: 31, Bats: R)

	G	AB	R	H	D	T	HR	RBI	SB	BB	SO	Avg	OBP	Slg
'02	5	13	1	4	0	0	0	0	0	0	3	.308	.308	.308
Car.	11	16	1	4	0	0	0	0	0	0	4	.250	.250	.250

McKeel's major league existence last season consisted of two weeks between Bobby Estalella's injury and Sandy Alomar Jr.'s acquisition. Now a free agent, McKeel needs another break to return to the bigs. 2003 Outlook: C

Kent Mercker (Pos: LHP, Age: 35)

	W	L	Pct.	ERA	G	GS	Sv	IP	H	BB	SO	HR	Ratio
'02	3	1	.750	6.14	58	0	0	44.0	55	22	37	12	1.75
Car.	66	62	.516	4.38	424	150	19	1113.1	1117	510	750	129	1.46

After missing the 2001 season following a cerebral hemorrhage in 2000, Mercker set a personal high by pitching in 58 games. In that sense, last season was a success, despite the high ERA. 2003 Outlook: C

Chris Nichting (Pos: RHP, Age: 36)

	W	L	Pct.	ERA	G	GS	Sv	IP	H	BB	SO	HR	Ratio
'02	1	1	.500	4.46	29	0	0	36.1	40	5	25	7	1.24
Car.	1	4	.200	5.22	92	0	1	112.0	144	31	78	16	1.56

Nichting posted his first major league victory at age 36 last year. After a 0.60 ERA in his first 11 appearances, he struggled thereafter. He was even worse in the minors, and later became a free agent. 2003 Outlook: C

Greg Norton (Pos: 3B/1B, Age: 30, Bats: B)

	G	AB	R	H	D	T	HR	RBI	SB	BB	SO	Avg	OBP	Slg
'02	113	168	19	37	8	1	7	37	2	24	52	.220	.314	.405
Car.	567	1386	183	342	72	8	53	195	11	170	348	.247	.330	.425

Norton got off to a bad start last year, batting .176 before the All-Star break. While he also struggled at Coors, Norton's versatility in the field and switch-hitting bat should keep a bench role for him. 2003 Outlook: B

Jason Romano (Pos: 2B/LF/CF, Age: 23, Bats: R)

	G	AB	R	H	D	T	HR	RBI	SB	BB	SO	Avg	OBP	Slg
'02	47	91	17	23	4	1	0	5	6	7	24	.253	.303	.319
Car.	47	91	17	23	4	1	0	5	6	7	24	.253	.303	.319

Romano is a decent prospect whom the Rockies acquired in the Todd Hollandsworth trade last July. Romano hit well against righthanders and played five positions in the majors. 2003 Outlook: B

Victor Santos (Pos: RHP, Age: 26)

	W	L	Pct.	ERA	G	GS	Sv	IP	H	BB	SO	HR	Ratio
'02	0	4	.000	10.38	24	2	0	26.0	41	22	25	3	2.42
Car.	2	6	.250	5.10	57	9	0	102.1	103	71	77	12	1.70

The Rockies acquired Santos in a trade with Detroit last March. He failed to impress in his two months with Colorado, and was torched in two starts. He signed a minor league deal with Texas after the season. 2003 Outlook: C

Colorado Rockies Minor League Prospects

Organization Overview:

The Rockies finally began to see the payoff for their emphasis on pitching in the amateur draft. Jason Jennings, their No. 1 choice in 1999 and one of nine pitchers the Rockies have selected in the first round since they began taking part in the draft in 1992, was the National League Rookie of the Year. And there is more where Jennings came from. Aaron Cook figures to open 2003 in the rotation, with Jason Young expected to join the big league team at some point, and Chin-Hui Tsao is on a schedule that could bring him to Coors Field by season's end. Cook and Young were both selected for last year's Futures Game, held the Sunday before the All-Star Game in Milwaukee. And the Rockies added another pitcher with their No. 1 pick in 2002—lefthander Jeff Francis.

J.D. Closser

Position: C
Bats: B **Throws:** R
Ht: 5' 10" **Wt:** 195

Opening Day Age: 23
Born: 1/15/80 in Beech Grove, IN

Recent Statistics

	G	AB	R	H	D	T	HR	RBI	SB	BB	SO	Avg
2001 A Lancaster	128	468	85	136	26	6	21	87	6	65	106	.291
2002 AA Carolina	95	315	43	89	27	1	13	62	9	44	69	.283

The switch-hitting Closser is strong, with a quick swing from both sides of the plate. He was acquired along with Jack Cust from Arizona in the Mike Myers trade prior to last season. Closser can get himself in trouble by becoming too pull-conscious and losing any chance he has to cover the outside part of the plate. He would help himself if he had better pitch selection and took more pitches to force hurlers to make mistakes. However, Closser does have the bat speed to be a power threat. He benefited from playing for a former catcher, P.J. Carey, at Double-A Carolina last year, and made big strides in his receiving and handling of pitches. Closser needs to smooth out his footwork on throws to second.

Aaron Cook

Position: P
Bats: R **Throws:** R
Ht: 6' 3" **Wt:** 175

Opening Day Age: 24
Born: 2/8/79 in Ft. Campbell, KY

Recent Statistics

	W	L	ERA	G	GS	Sv	IP	H	R	BB	SO	HR
2002 AA Carolina	7	2	1.42	14	14	0	95.0	73	24	19	58	4
2002 AAA Col Sprngs	4	4	3.78	10	10	0	64.1	67	40	18	32	6
2002 NL Colorado	2	1	4.54	9	5	0	35.2	41	18	13	14	4

In his sixth year in the organization, and first above Class-A, Cook took charge. He went from Double-A, where he was voted the best pitching prospect in the Southern League, to Triple-A and finally the majors. He has a dominating hard sinker that sits between 94-97

MPH, and he throws quality strikes. He needs to clean up his offspeed pitch, which is critical for success at Coors. Cook was a second-round draft pick out of high school in 1997. He was shut down in mid-September last year to preserve his rookie status for 2003. He is set for one of the five spots in the Rockies' rotation this season, where he will join Jason Jennings and Denny Stark, last year's rookie sensations.

Jack Cust

Position: OF
Bats: L **Throws:** R
Ht: 6' 1" **Wt:** 205

Opening Day Age: 24
Born: 1/16/79 in Flemington, NJ

Recent Statistics

	G	AB	R	H	D	T	HR	RBI	SB	BB	SO	Avg
2002 AAA Col Sprngs	105	359	74	95	24	0	23	55	6	83	121	.265
2002 NL Colorado	35	65	8	11	2	0	1	8	0	12	32	.169

Cust is a well-known minor league power hitter, but he doesn't show the aggressiveness and quickness that translates into big league success. He gets plenty of publicity, but he hit only .265 at Triple-A Colorado Springs. A former first-round draft choice of Arizona, Cust takes too many pitches and hasn't shown the ability to pull the ball. Big league pitchers can pound him inside. His defense is suspect. He takes poor routes on flyballs, doesn't move well and misses cutoff men with his throws. He figures to go back to Colorado Springs for another year of seasoning, in hopes of regaining his trade value if he isn't dealt. He showed last season he isn't ready for the majors.

Choo Freeman

Position: OF
Bats: R **Throws:** R
Ht: 6' 2" **Wt:** 200

Opening Day Age: 23
Born: 10/20/79 in Pine Bluff, AR

Recent Statistics

	G	AB	R	H	D	T	HR	RBI	SB	BB	SO	Avg
2001 A Salem	132	517	63	124	16	5	8	42	19	31	108	.240
2002 AA Carolina	124	430	81	125	18	6	12	64	15	64	101	.291

Freeman had a breakout season at Double-A Carolina in 2002, after spending two years at the Class-A level. A sandwich pick between the first and second rounds in 1998, Freeman was the Mudcats' most consistent player last season. He was both a midseason and postseason Southern League All-Star. He is diligent about his daily routine in the cage before batting practice. A wide receiver recruit of Texas A&M out of high school, Freeman instead opted to sign with the Rockies. He has excellent first-step quickness and gets good initial reads on flyballs. His arm strength has improved and is playable. But his offensive potential will be the key. Scouts compared him to Ellis Burks and Torii Hunter last year.

Rene Reyes

Position: OF-1B | **Opening Day Age:** 25
Bats: B **Throws:** R | **Born:** 2/21/78 in Isla
Ht: 5' 11" **Wt:** 213 | Margarita, VZ

Recent Statistics

	G	AB	R	H	D	T	HR	RBI	SB	BB	SO	Avg
2001 A Asheville	128	484	71	156	27	2	11	61	53	28	80	.322
2002 AA Carolina	123	455	64	133	33	4	14	54	10	29	69	.292

Reyes battled major injury problems earlier in his career, which forced him to give up catching, his original position. It also has left him often overlooked when evaluating Rockies prospects. However, Reyes has the biggest upside of any offensive player in the organization. On a Double-A Carolina team brimming with prospects, the switch-hitter had the most physical ability. And last season, thanks to prodding from teammate Tino Sanchez, Reyes began to develop a good work ethic. While he can play first base, he runs too well to not be in the outfield. He is a line-drive hitter with home-run power and stolen-base ability. He finished third in the Class-A South Atlantic League in stolen bases in 2001. Reyes could be in the big league picture by season's end.

Chin-Hui Tsao

Position: P | **Opening Day Age:** 21
Bats: R **Throws:** R | **Born:** 6/2/81 in Hua-lien,
Ht: 6' 2" **Wt:** 178 | Taiwan

Recent Statistics

	W	L	ERA	G	GS	Sv	IP	H	R	BB	SO	HR
2001 A Salem	0	4	4.67	4	4	0	17.1	23	11	5	18	1
2002 A Tri-City	0	0	0.00	3	3	0	11.0	6	2	2	16	0
2002 A Salem	4	2	2.09	9	9	0	47.1	34	13	12	45	3

After missing most of 2001 following reconstructive elbow surgery, Tsao returned to the mound in mid-2002. He appeared briefly at short-season Tri-City, and then joined the rotation at high Class-A Salem. Tsao pitched so well—he was 3-1 with a 0.81 ERA in five August starts—that the plan was to have him promoted to Double-A Carolina for the playoffs. However, he had some forearm stiffness and the Rockies didn't want to take any risks. Tsao averages 93 MPH with his fastball, and can touch 96. His changeup and slider are plus pitches. He was restricted from throwing his slider to protect his arm, but he has developed a useable curveball. He will open this season at Double-A Tulsa.

Cory Vance

Position: P | **Opening Day Age:** 23
Bats: L **Throws:** L | **Born:** 6/20/79 in Dayton,
Ht: 6' 1" **Wt:** 195 | OH

Recent Statistics

	W	L	ERA	G	GS	Sv	IP	H	R	BB	SO	HR
2002 AA Carolina	10	8	3.77	25	25	0	150.1	142	73	76	114	8
2002 NL Colorado	0	0	6.75	2	1	0	4.0	4	3	4	1	2

Vance had a strong second half at Double-A Carolina last season because he began to throw strikes with his fastball. It earned him a cameo appearance in the big leagues in September, when the Rockies had to shut down veterans Denny Neagle and Mike Hampton, and decided to rest rookie Aaron Cook. The lefthanded Vance will average 87-89 MPH with his fastball and touch 92-93 MPH. He always has had enough of a fastball to go with his good curveball and decent changeup, but inconsistent fastball location held him back. A fourth-round draft choice in 2000, he led the Atlantic Coast Conference with 13 wins that year. Vance will make the move to Triple-A this season.

Jason Young

Position: P | **Opening Day Age:** 23
Bats: R **Throws:** R | **Born:** 9/28/79 in
Ht: 6' 5" **Wt:** 214 | Oakland, CA

Recent Statistics

	W	L	ERA	G	GS	Sv	IP	H	R	BB	SO	HR
2001 A Salem	6	7	3.44	17	17	0	104.2	104	47	28	91	8
2002 AA Carolina	7	4	2.64	14	14	0	88.2	71	30	30	76	1
2002 AAA Col Sprngs	6	5	4.97	13	13	0	79.2	87	52	38	74	10

Young was a second-round pick out of Stanford in 2000, but signed too late to play that year. He then had his pro debut in 2001 cut short by elbow soreness. However, Young was healthy last season and moved quickly. He opened the season at Double-A and finished at Triple-A. He would have been called up in September except for the threat of a work stoppage and the fact that Young didn't have to be protected on the 40-man roster. He sits in the low 90s with his fastball, and complements it with a hard slider and changeup. Aaron Cook's rise provides a motivation for Young, who has been Cook's roommate in the minor leagues the last two years.

Others to Watch

Third baseman **Garrett Atkins** (23) was moved from first base last season. After first-half troubles, he settled down in the second half. He has good plate patience and is learning to go the other way. . . Third baseman **Jeff Baker** (21) figures to be on the fast track now that he's signed. The Rockies fourth-round choice out of Clemson last June, he was the best power prospect in the draft. . . Shortstop **Clint Barmes** (24) emerged as an everyday prospect last season after previously being considered a utility player. He has shown solid defensive skills, and last year began to drive the ball and show plus power for a middle infielder. . . Lefthander **Jeff Francis** (22), Colorado's No. 1 draft choice last June, had his season cut short after being hit in the face with a line drive. He has a live arm and command, and figures to move quickly. . . First baseman **Brad Hawpe** (23) shows hitting instincts. He's aware that his path to the big leagues could be blocked by Todd Helton, and was playing the outfield part-time in Venezuela. . . Second baseman **Jayson Nix** (20) made a smooth transition from short to second. He has a good feel for the offensive game and shows power potential.

Pro Player Stadium

Offense

Marlins hitters continued to come to terms with their home park, which does them few favors in the power department. Despite the midseason trades that cost them Cliff Floyd in favor of Juan Encarnacion, they wound up hitting 14 points higher at home. They averaged 4.56 runs per game at home, compared with 4.07 on the road.

Defense

Everybody talks about the Green Monster and the Crawford Boxes, but the Pro has its own significant challenge in left-center. The Teal Tower, a 26.5-foot-high out-of-town scoreboard, causes its share of crazy caroms. Center fielders also must run down balls in the Bermuda Triangle in deep left-center, and right field is extremely spacious. The infield and outfield grass is among the fastest in the league.

Who It Helps the Most

Pitchers in general and flyball pitchers in particular. The spacious dimensions and thick air keep balls in the park that get out easily in other venues. Ace A.J. Burnett's ERA was a run and a half better at home, where he allowed just three of his 12 homers. Extra-base hits, especially triples, remained plentiful, much to the delight of speedsters like Luis Castillo (16 of his 25 extra-base hits at home).

Who It Hurts the Most

Derrek Lee hit 52 points higher at home, but more than two-thirds of his 27 homers came on the road. The Pro robs him of his power to right-center. Andy Fox hit 17 points lower at home, while Mike Redmond hit 23 points lower at home. Rookie righthander Josh Beckett saw his ERA drop by more than two runs away from home.

Rookies & Newcomers

Righthander Justin Wayne, in a five-start September audition, saw his ERA drop by nearly three-and-a-half runs on the road. Reliever Blaine Neal posted a 1.96 ERA at home but saw that figure rise to 3.68 on the road.

Dimensions: LF-330, LCF-385, CF-404, RCF-385, RF-345

Capacity: 36,331

Elevation: 10 feet

Surface: Grass

Foul Territory: Average

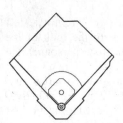

Florida

Park Factors

2002 Season

	Home Games Marlins	Opp	Total	Away Games Marlins	Opp	Total	Index
G	72	72	144	72	72	144	
Avg	.270	.255	.262	.252	.273	.262	100
AB	2398	2522	4920	2488	2402	4890	101
R	342	322	664	278	373	651	102
H	647	644	1291	627	656	1283	101
2B	130	133	263	117	130	247	106
3B	22	20	42	8	16	24	174
HR	63	58	121	67	84	151	80
BB	294	291	585	226	277	503	116
SO	497	556	1053	517	437	954	110
E	43	47	90	49	56	105	86
E-Infield	31	39	70	43	51	94	74
LHB-Avg	.261	.254	.257	.255	.301	.284	90
LHB-HR	11	20	31	12	36	48	61
RHB-Avg	.273	.256	.265	.251	.253	.252	105
RHB-HR	52	38	90	55	48	103	89

2000-2002

	Home Games Marlins	Opp	Total	Away Games Marlins	Opp	Total	Index
G	215	215	430	217	217	434	
Avg	.264	.251	.258	.256	.276	.266	97
AB	7137	7427	14564	7585	7228	14813	99
R	968	953	1921	928	1138	2066	94
H	1887	1865	3752	1939	1997	3936	96
2B	376	380	756	391	392	783	98
3B	54	66	120	26	53	79	154
HR	197	195	392	223	238	461	86
BB	771	851	1622	651	878	1529	108
SO	1515	1631	3146	1605	1302	2907	110
E	132	143	275	165	157	322	86
E-Infield	109	116	225	137	134	271	84
LHB-Avg	.279	.252	.262	.265	.288	.279	94
LHB-HR	47	64	111	49	98	147	74
RHB-Avg	.259	.251	.255	.252	.268	.259	99
RHB-HR	150	131	281	174	140	314	93

2002 Rankings (National League)

- Second-highest walk factor
- Third-highest triple factor
- Third-highest strikeout factor
- Second-lowest home-run factor
- Second-lowest infield-error factor
- Second-lowest LHB home-run factor
- Third-lowest error factor
- Third-lowest LHB batting-average factor

Jeff Torborg

2002 Season

After managing four months in Montreal, Jeff Torborg came south along with the bulk of the Expos' front office and uniformed personnel. He quickly took to his new group. Despite a handful of key injuries, including a sprained left thumb that limited catcher Charles Johnson's effectiveness all year, Torborg had the Marlins in first place for nine days in the middle of May. Soon thereafter, pitcher Brad Penny was lost for six-plus weeks and shortstop Alex Gonzalez (shoulder) was lost for the season. The Marlins were never the same after that, especially on the road.

Offense

Owing to Torborg's roots with the Go-Go Dodgers of the mid-1960s, the Marlins placed a newfound emphasis on the running game. Florida led the majors in stolen bases with 177, which was 26 percent more than the closest rival, the Royals. Torborg also showed a willingness from the start to experiment with his batting order. He tried nine different starters in the No. 2 slot, including a resistant Preston Wilson. He tried six different starting cleanup hitters and six different starters in the No. 3 hole.

Pitching & Defense

Torborg didn't tinker much with his lineup for defensive purposes, preferring to stick with his starters. He had one of the slowest hooks in the league, especially when it came to ace A.J. Burnett. He allowed Burnett to exceed 120 pitches on 10 occasions. Torborg opened the year at a disadvantage following the trade of Antonio Alfonseca. When the bullpen-by-committee approach was getting wracked early on, he installed Vladimir Nunez as the closer and he flourished for the next two months. When Nunez hit a rough patch, Torborg went to Braden Looper.

2003 Outlook

Despite his long-running friendship with Marlins owner Jeffrey Loria, Torborg was not granted an extension. He enters the final year of his three-year contract. Torborg claimed not to be bothered by the arrangement, saying contract status alone won't make players respect you. From all indications, he still has the respect of his players.

Born: 11/26/41 in Westfield, NJ

Playing Experience: 1964-1973, LA, Cal

Managerial Experience: 10 seasons

Manager Statistics

Year	Team, Lg	W	L	Pct	GB	Finish
2002	Florida, NL	79	83	.488	23.0	4th East
10 Seasons		618	696	.470	–	–

2002 Starting Pitchers by Days Rest

	<=3	4	5	6+
Marlins Starts	0	93	33	25
Marlins ERA	–	4.16	4.61	5.61
NL Avg Starts	1	88	42	21
NL ERA	3.18	4.22	4.14	4.58

2002 Situational Stats

	Jeff Torborg	NL Average
Hit & Run Success %	39.0	36.5
Stolen Base Success %	70.8	68.3
Platoon Pct.	43.1	52.7
Defensive Subs	13	19
High-Pitch Outings	13	7
Quick/Slow Hooks	32/15	24/11
Sacrifice Attempts	82	95

2002 Rankings (National League)

- 1st in stolen base attempts (250), steals of second base (152), steals of third base (24) and double steals (8)
- 2nd in steals of home plate (1) and hit-and-run attempts (105)
- 3rd in squeeze plays (10), slow hooks, quick hooks and starts with over 120 pitches (13)

Josh Beckett

Position: SP
Bats: R **Throws:** R
Ht: 6' 5" **Wt:** 216

Opening Day Age: 22
Born: 5/15/80 in Spring, TX
ML Seasons: 2

Florida

2002 Season

After a four-start taste of the majors at the end of his widely acclaimed 2001 minor league season, Josh Beckett was the chalk favorite for National League Rookie of the Year. Instead, he suffered through a maddening series of setbacks, all attributable not to the shoulder problems that dogged him two years earlier but to persistent blisters on the middle finger of his pitching hand. Virtually every possible remedy was tried as Beckett endured three stints on the disabled list with the recurring blisters. Opinions were solicited from, among others, Nolan Ryan and Al Leiter, both blister sufferers early in their careers.

Pitching

Even when his finger cooperated, Beckett was surprisingly inconsistent. When he's on, he throws a two-seamer in the low 90s and a four-seamer at 96-98 MPH. His 12-to-6 curve has great break and fools as many umpires as it buckles hitters' knees. His changeup still needs work. Beckett is extremely competitive and tends to get down on himself when things aren't going well. He was hit particularly hard on a couple of occasions, after which there was speculation he was tipping his pitches. He shot down those theories, refusing to embrace any excuse.

Defense & Hitting

Beckett is a good athlete with solid instincts in the field. Though just an average fielder, he does a good job of covering first and backing up home and third. He is a poor hitter and tends to be slow to home plate, but is learning to compensate in other ways. He varies his hold times well and he'll showcase a slide step early in games, simply to put that thought in opposing managers' minds.

2003 Outlook

Beckett is still under the Marlins' control after completing a four-year, $7 million big league contract he received upon signing as the No. 2 overall pick in the 1999 draft. Along with A.J. Burnett, Beckett is considered one of two untouchables on the fluid Marlins roster. He is correctly viewed as a championship piece, but his blister problems must be remedied.

Overall Statistics

	W	L	Pct.	ERA	G	GS	Sv	IP	H	BB	SO	HR	Ratio
'02	6	7	.462	4.10	23	21	0	107.2	93	44	113	13	1.27
Car.	8	9	.471	3.62	27	25	0	131.2	107	55	137	16	1.23

How Often He Throws Strikes

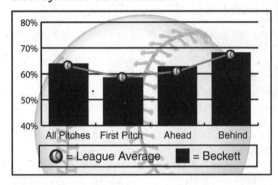

2002 Situational Stats

	W	L	ERA	Sv	IP		AB	H	HR	RBI	Avg
Home	3	4	5.25	0	48.0	LHB	195	48	9	27	.246
Road	3	3	3.17	0	59.2	RHB	206	45	4	25	.218
First Half	2	3	3.86	0	53.2	Sc Pos	89	26	1	35	.292
Scnd Half	4	4	4.33	0	54.0	Clutch	13	3	0	4	.231

2002 Rankings (National League)

- Led the Marlins in stolen bases allowed (12), highest strikeout-walk ratio (2.6), lowest ERA on the road and most strikeouts per nine innings (9.4)

A.J. Burnett

2002 Season

After suffering through two straight years of freak injuries that short-circuited his development, A.J. Burnett stayed healthy through mid-August and flourished. With the help of new pitching coach Brad Arnsberg, he adopted a Kevin Brown-style leg turn in his delivery at spring training and something clicked. He was among the most durable starters in the majors, ranking behind only Randy Johnson in total pitches thrown and pitches per start through the first five months. A late-season bone bruise in his pitching elbow landed him on the disabled list, but he was able to return to the rotation by season's end.

Pitching

Burnett's fastball alone is a devastating weapon. Throwing freer and easier than ever after the spring adjustment, he hit 96 MPH with regularity with his underrated two-seamer, and had several four-seamers clocked at 101. His curve is a classic over-the-top pitch, but he also learned to drop his arm slot and create a sweeping angle that enabled him to go down and in to lefties. His changeup, thrown in the mid-80s, is a work in progress. His deception with the pitch must improve, and the same goes for his confidence in using it.

Defense & Hitting

Burnett, a former star basketball player in high school, is a decent fielder and good all-around athlete. His career batting average is .128, but he is among the club's better sacrifice bunters. He has excellent instincts in general. He must improve his work against the running game, including varying his holds.

2003 Outlook

Eligible for salary arbitration for the first time, Burnett stood to make a substantial raise. His salary likely will fall in the $2 million range, but the Marlins were determined to hold onto him. He almost certainly will make his first Opening Day start and again serve as the club's workhorse. His maturity has improved to the point where he must be considered a candidate to not only throw a second no-hitter but also contend for his first Cy Young Award in the near future.

Position: SP
Bats: R **Throws:** R
Ht: 6' 4" **Wt:** 229

Opening Day Age: 26
Born: 1/3/77 in North Little Rock, AR
ML Seasons: 4

Overall Statistics

	W	L	Pct.	ERA	G	GS	Sv	IP	H	BB	SO	HR	Ratio
'02	12	9	.571	3.30	31	29	0	204.1	153	90	203	12	1.19
Car.	30	30	.500	3.82	78	76	0	501.2	415	242	421	43	1.31

How Often He Throws Strikes

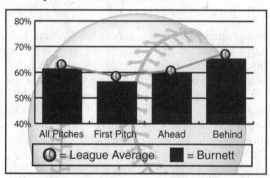

League Average / Burnett — All Pitches, First Pitch, Ahead, Behind

2002 Situational Stats

	W	L	ERA	Sv	IP		AB	H	HR	RBI	Avg
Home	7	3	2.55	0	102.1	LHB	359	87	5	34	.242
Road	5	6	4.06	0	102.0	RHB	373	66	7	44	.177
First Half	8	6	3.31	0	133.1	Sc Pos	174	50	3	63	.287
Scnd Half	4	3	3.30	0	71.0	Clutch	73	13	1	5	.178

2002 Rankings (National League)

- 1st in shutouts (5), wild pitches (14), lowest slugging percentage allowed (.309), lowest batting average allowed vs. righthanded batters, fewest home runs allowed per nine innings (.53) and lowest fielding percentage at pitcher (.886)
- 2nd in complete games (7), lowest batting average allowed (.209), errors at pitcher (4) and least run support per nine innings (3.7)
- Led the Marlins in ERA, wins, games started, innings pitched, batters faced (844), walks allowed, strikeouts, wild pitches (14), pitches thrown (3,248), pickoff throws (71), winning percentage and lowest ERA at home

Luis Castillo

Position: 2B
Bats: B **Throws:** R
Ht: 5'11" **Wt:** 190

Opening Day Age: 27
Born: 9/12/75 in San Pedro de Macoris, DR
ML Seasons: 7
Pronunciation: ca-STEE-yo

2002 Season

Luis Castillo became the focus of national attention with a 35-game hitting streak that broke the records for second basemen and Latin American players. The whole experience seemed to improve Castillo's self-esteem, long a problem for the Dominican. After bidding for his first batting title in the first half, Castillo tailed off to a .260 average after the break. He played through some nagging injuries, including a torn labrum in his left hip that would require offseason surgery.

Hitting

Once a basket case with runners in scoring position, Castillo now ranks among the club's most reliable situational hitters. A natural righthanded hitter, the switch-hitting Castillo batted 32 points higher from that side. From the right side he likes to turn on fastballs in, preferably thigh-high. He can handle offspeed stuff down in the zone as well, but struggles with fastballs up. He stands on top of the plate and likes to flick outer-half fastballs the other way. He can be jammed with fastballs or quality breaking stuff.

Baserunning & Defense

Castillo won his second NL stolen-base crown in three seasons, narrowly holding off Juan Pierre. His speed is a legitimate game-changing weapon. He made 13 errors for the second straight year but saw his range factor drop by more than six percent. He has perhaps the strongest arm in the league at his position, and handles feeds and pivots with ease. Once reluctant to dive to his left following a history of left shoulder problems, he improved his coverage to that side.

2003 Outlook

Coming off the hip surgery, Castillo figured to miss the first part of spring training. He typically comes in 10 pounds heavy, so his conditioning will have to be monitored. The Marlins were expected to hold onto him using the money they saved by unloading the salaries of Preston Wilson and Charles Johnson, even though Castillo's five-plus arbitration status could push his salary north of $5 million. If nothing else, Castillo and new teammate Juan Pierre should form the most exciting basestealing duo in baseball.

Overall Statistics

	G	AB	R	H	D	T	HR	RBI	SB	BB	SO	Avg	OBP	Slg
'02	146	606	86	185	18	5	2	39	48	55	76	.305	.364	.361
Car.	704	2749	413	790	87	25	8	155	229	330	469	.287	.364	.346

Where He Hits the Ball

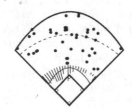 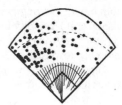

Vs. LHP   **Vs. RHP**

2002 Situational Stats

	AB	H	HR	RBI	Avg		AB	H	HR	RBI	Avg
Home	306	94	0	21	.307	LHP	158	52	1	10	.329
Road	300	91	2	18	.303	RHP	448	133	1	29	.297
First Half	337	115	2	23	.341	Sc Pos	117	33	1	37	.282
Scnd Half	269	70	0	16	.260	Clutch	95	36	0	7	.379

2002 Rankings (National League)

- 1st in singles, stolen bases and highest groundball-flyball ratio (3.4)
- 2nd in caught stealing (15) and batting average in the clutch
- 3rd in lowest slugging percentage vs. righthanded pitchers (.339)
- Led the Marlins in at-bats, bunts in play (24), highest percentage of pitches taken (60.7), lowest percentage of swings that missed (9.2), highest percentage of swings put into play (52.2), batting average vs. lefthanded pitchers, on-base percentage for a leadoff hitter (.363), batting average on the road, lowest percentage of swings on the first pitch (17.8), batting average on a 3-2 count (.320) and batting average with two strikes (.259)

Juan Encarnacion

2002 Season

Acquired from the Tigers in a winter deal for Dmitri Young, Juan Encarnacion had a solid first half with the Reds. Just when he was putting down roots in Cincinnati, the Reds moved him to the Marlins in an eight-player, three-team deal that also saw Wilton Guerrero, prospect Ryan Snare and former All-Star righthander Ryan Dempster change addresses. Encarnacion impressed the Marlins with his five-tool potential, but his production dropped off after the break.

Hitting

Never the most patient hitter, Encarnacion set a career-high for walks, along with homers, RBI and runs scored. A classic mistake hitter, he likes to jump on hanging breaking balls. He can handle the medium-velocity fastball on the inner half, but he struggles to lay off eye-level fastballs. Pitchers are able to bust him inside with quality heaters, then put him away with tight breaking balls on the outer half. He did his best work in the No. 6 slot but remains an intriguing possibility as a No. 2 hitter.

Baserunning & Defense

Encarnacion notched his first 20-20 season, a level he should reach annually with his combination of power and speed. His career stolen-base success rate is nearly 72 percent. He is an above-average outfielder with a plus arm, although he could stand to be more accurate. He saw the bulk of his early-season time with the Reds in center in place of Ken Griffey Jr., but Encarnacion stayed largely in right for the Marlins. He appears equally adept at both spots, with a slight edge to center in terms of the routes he takes.

2003 Outlook

A four-plus arbitration-eligible, Encarnacion could see his salary double from the $1.55 million he made last year. The Marlins view him as a key component in their revamping of a mature roster in terms of service time. The unloading of Preston Wilson and Charles Johnson gives Florida the monetary means to bring Encarnacion back, and he will be the starting right fielder next to new center fielder Juan Pierre.

Position: RF/CF
Bats: R **Throws:** R
Ht: 6' 3" **Wt:** 215

Opening Day Age: 27
Born: 3/8/76 in Las Matas de Farfan, DR
ML Seasons: 6
Pronunciation: en-car-NAH-see-own

Overall Statistics

	G	AB	R	H	D	T	HR	RBI	SB	BB	SO	Avg	OBP	Slg
'02	152	584	77	.158	22	5	24	85	21	46	113	.271	.324	.449
Car.	596	2254	299	608	106	29	77	309	89	124	452	.270	.314	.445

Where He Hits the Ball

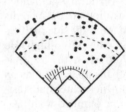 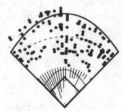

Vs. LHP   **Vs. RHP**

2002 Situational Stats

	AB	H	HR	RBI	Avg		AB	H	HR	RBI	Avg
Home	293	76	8	41	.259	LHP	133	31	5	15	.233
Road	291	82	16	44	.282	RHP	451	127	19	70	.282
First Half	321	89	16	51	.277	Sc Pos	152	39	4	57	.257
Scnd Half	263	69	8	34	.262	Clutch	91	23	2	11	.253

2002 Rankings (National League)

- 4th in lowest percentage of extra bases taken as a runner (32.7)
- 5th in sacrifice flies (7)
- 6th in errors in right field (4) and assists in right field (7)
- 8th in lowest on-base percentage vs. lefthanded pitchers (.276)
- 9th in lowest stolen-base percentage (70.0)
- Led the Marlins in batting average on an 0-2 count (.300)

Alex Gonzalez

2002 Season

The top spring project for new coaches Ozzie Guillen and Perry Hill, Alex Gonzalez made considerable progress in two key areas: attitude and concentration. He carried that newfound zest into the season before suffering a freak injury on May 18 in San Francisco. Stationed close to second base on the Barry Bonds Shift, Gonzalez tried to make an awkward stop across his body of a Bonds' smash to his right. Gonzalez landed hard on his left shoulder, suffering a severe separation. Originally expected to miss four to six weeks, he was recalled from a rehab assignment in mid-July and underwent season-ending surgery.

Hitting

Never a very patient hitter, Gonzalez was making some progress in that area before getting hurt. He was on pace to blow away his career-best of 30 walks. He likes low fastballs down the middle but struggles with fastballs up and breaking balls away. He prefers hitting second but batted just .189 in that role. He did his best work in the No. 7 hole, where he can whale away without much regard for situations or setting up his teammates.

Baserunning & Defense

Merely a decent baserunner, Gonzalez lacks the instincts and daring to change a game with his feet. His speed is good enough, but he has just 15 stolen bases in 24 career attempts. He showed much-improved footwork in the field, especially on routine plays. He has a plus arm and a quick release. His range is tremendous to both sides and extends into the outfield, where he runs down popups with the best of them. He could improve at charging balls.

2003 Outlook

Typically the type to play winter ball back home in Venezuela, Gonzalez was stuck with a winter of rehab work instead. He was expected to be ready by the early part of spring training, where he will battle his replacement, Andy Fox, for the starting job. Gonzalez was due another raise as a four-plus arbitration guy, and he soon could grow too expensive for the Marlins' low-rent tastes.

Position: SS
Bats: R **Throws:** R
Ht: 6' 0" **Wt:** 200

Opening Day Age: 26
Born: 2/15/77 in Cagua, VZ
ML Seasons: 5

Overall Statistics

	G	AB	R	H	D	T	HR	RBI	SB	BB	SO	Avg	OBP	Slg
'02	42	151	15	34	7	1	2	18	3	12	32	.225	.296	.325
Car.	457	1697	199	408	90	14	35	174	15	79	359	.240	.284	.372

Where He Hits the Ball

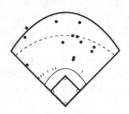 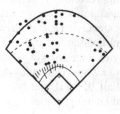

Vs. LHP   **Vs. RHP**

2002 Situational Stats

	AB	H	HR	RBI	Avg		AB	H	HR	RBI	Avg
Home	76	17	1	10	.224	LHP	30	6	1	7	.200
Road	75	17	1	8	.227	RHP	121	28	1	11	.231
First Half	151	34	2	18	.225	Sc Pos	40	8	1	16	.200
Scnd Half	0	0	0	0	–	Clutch	21	6	2	9	.286

2002 Rankings (National League)

- Led the Marlins in batting average with the bases loaded (.333)

Charles Johnson

2002 Season

Charles Johnson sprained his left thumb in a freak collision at first base just one week into spring games and never got in sync. He wound up with career lows in batting average, homers and RBI. Because he wasn't hitting, he ceded more playing time to backup Mike Redmond. Because of that inactivity, Johnson failed to shed the in-season weight he typically does and became noticeably slower behind the plate. Back spasms also flared up several times in the second half.

Hitting

Johnson's woes didn't start last season. They actually began in mid-July 2001, shortly after he made his second All-Star team. He likes fastballs down and middle-away, where he can get his arms extended. He can drive balls to right-center but not enough of those cleared the fence. He struggles with breaking balls down and fastballs up in the zone. His swing became long in the second half of 2001 and has yet to shorten up for more than a few games here or there.

Baserunning & Defense

Among the slowest players in the majors, Johnson is nothing more than station-to-station on the bases. A big surprise in his decline was the slide in his defense. He reaches for too many balls, failing to get in good blocking position the way he did early in his career. His throwing remains strong, but has slipped. His game-calling also has come under criticism, and his catcher's ERA was more than a half-run higher than Redmond's.

2003 Outlook

Along with center fielder Preston Wilson, Johnson was atop the club's offseason to-deal list. The Marlins killed both birds with one stone in mid-November as part of a whirlwind three-team deal that sent both Johnson and Wilson to the Rockies, Mike Hampton to the Braves and netted Florida both Juan Pierre and Tim Spooneybarger. Coors Field could be just the answer for a four-time Gold Glover whose skills and hunger obviously had slipped, but he has a lot of ground to make up after last season's sharp drop-off.

Position: C
Bats: R **Throws:** R
Ht: 6' 3" **Wt:** 250

Opening Day Age: 31
Born: 7/20/71 in Fort Pierce, FL
ML Seasons: 9

Overall Statistics

	G	AB	R	H	D	T	HR	RBI	SB	BB	SO	Avg	OBP	Slg
'02	83	244	18	53	19	0	6	36	0	31	61	.217	.301	.369
Car.	952	3129	369	777	167	4	134	457	3	368	811	.248	.329	.433

Where He Hits the Ball

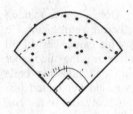
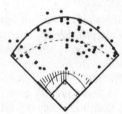

Vs. LHP   **Vs. RHP**

2002 Situational Stats

	AB	H	HR	RBI	Avg		AB	H	HR	RBI	Avg
Home	131	29	2	24	.221	LHP	51	14	1	9	.275
Road	113	24	4	12	.212	RHP	193	39	5	27	.202
First Half	154	34	3	20	.221	Sc Pos	69	16	1	30	.232
Scnd Half	90	19	3	16	.211	Clutch	37	5	0	5	.135

2002 Rankings (National League)

- 1st in lowest batting average on a 3-1 count (.000)
- 4th in fielding percentage at catcher (.994)

Derrek Lee

Position: 1B
Bats: R **Throws:** R
Ht: 6' 5" **Wt:** 248

Opening Day Age: 27
Born: 9/6/75 in
Sacramento, CA
ML Seasons: 6

2002 Season

Derrek Lee had another typical Derrek Lee season. Nothing about it seemed remarkable, but when it was over he had set career highs in runs, RBI, walks, on-base percentage and stolen bases. He overcame a slow start which saw him hitting .229 on June 1, but he kept plugging away. Lee played every game for the first time, stretched his consecutive-games streak to 209 and now has missed just seven games the past three seasons.

Hitting

Lee exceeded his previous career high by 35 walks but also struck out once every 3.5 at-bats, the worst rate of his career for a full season. This happened as he grew more comfortable working deep counts and spitting at borderline pitches, some of which became called third strikes. He likes thigh-high fastballs and can turn on the inside fastball. He can drive balls to right-center if they're out over the plate and has good power that way. He struggles with high fastballs that are just out of the zone and still chases good breaking balls. His power numbers would almost certainly be better if he were freed from Pro Player Stadium, where he hit just a third of his homers.

Baserunning & Defense

Turned loose for the first time on the bases, Lee fell one steal short of his first 20-20 season. He is very agile for such a tall man and runs the bases with good instincts. Defensively, many feel he has surpassed J.T. Snow and Todd Helton, and that Lee deserved his first Gold Glove for his work last season. Lee made a career-high 12 errors, but he saved at least that many for his teammates with a huge wingspan and soft hands. He has an accurate arm and positions himself well.

2003 Outlook

Lee is due another substantial raise through salary arbitration, which could put him in the $4 million range. Still, with plans to increase their payroll to the $48 million range, the Marlins expected to keep their slugging first baseman. The extra cash that was freed up when Preston Wilson and Charles Johnson were shipped to Colorado also should come in handy towards keeping Lee in South Florida for at least another season.

Overall Statistics

	G	AB	R	H	D	T	HR	RBI	SB	BB	SO	Avg	OBP	Slg
'02	162	581	95	157	35	7	27	86	19	98	164	.270	.378	.494
Car.	711	2345	340	614	131	16	99	329	30	284	627	.262	.346	.458

Where He Hits the Ball

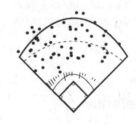
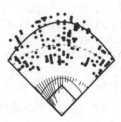

Vs. LHP   **Vs. RHP**

2002 Situational Stats

	AB	H	HR	RBI	Avg			AB	H	HR	RBI	Avg
Home	279	83	9	38	.297		LHP	125	33	6	18	.264
Road	302	74	18	48	.245		RHP	456	124	21	68	.272
First Half	323	86	17	50	.266		Sc Pos	155	38	3	53	.245
Scnd Half	258	71	10	36	.275		Clutch	96	25	1	10	.260

2002 Rankings (National League)

- 1st in games played and assists at first base (121)
- 2nd in pitches seen (2,896)
- 3rd in strikeouts and lowest fielding percentage at first base (.992)
- 4th in errors at first base (12)
- 6th in triples
- 7th in plate appearances (688), most pitches seen per plate appearance (4.21) and lowest stolen-base percentage (67.9)
- Led the Marlins in home runs, runs scored, total bases (287), walks, times on base (260) and on-base percentage vs. lefthanded pitchers (.391)

Mike Lowell

2002 Season

Mike Lowell exploded in the first half of 2002 to make the All-Star team for the first time. A freak accident just before the break, in which he suffered a badly bruised hip while sliding onto a bat mistakenly left at home plate, cost him valuable momentum. He finally sat out after making 111 straight starts, then fell into a lengthy tailspin that included a .145 batting average in August. He rallied in September, hitting five homers in the final week.

Hitting

Lowell is a marked flyball hitter who likes the ball middle-in and thigh high. He is a good lowball hitter but struggles with fastballs up and good breaking balls away. Lowell has an excellent feel for situational hitting and a nose for the RBI. He did his best work in the Nos. 4 and 5 slots in the batting order, but struggled when asked to hit third ahead of Cliff Floyd.

Baserunning & Defense

Lowell is notoriously slow and even makes jokes at his own expense, but he is an intelligent baserunner who rarely makes needless outs and typically scores when he should. His defense gets a little better every year, to the point where National League managers ranked him behind only Scott Rolen at the position. Lowell showed an improved first step and the ability to make the acrobatic play. His arm is solid and accurate and he makes good use of scouting reports to position himself well.

2003 Outlook

Due to make $3.7 million in the final year of a three-year deal, Lowell was being shopped around in an effort to find a cheaper alternative. But the Marlins cut a big chunk of payroll when they sent Preston Wilson and Charles Johnson to Colorado. Lowell would still just be a five-year arbitration case at season's end, so it looks like Florida will be holding on to one of its most productive, respected and recognizable players.

Position: 3B
Bats: R **Throws:** R
Ht: 6' 3" **Wt:** 217

Opening Day Age: 29
Born: 2/24/74 in San Juan, PR
ML Seasons: 5

Overall Statistics

	G	AB	R	H	D	T	HR	RBI	SB	BB	SO	Avg	OBP	Slg
'02	160	597	88	165	44	0	24	92	4	65	92	.276	.346	.471
Car.	551	1979	259	540	134	0	76	330	9	188	316	.273	.339	.456

Where He Hits the Ball

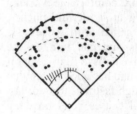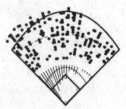

Vs. LHP   **Vs. RHP**

2002 Situational Stats

	AB	H	HR	RBI	Avg		AB	H	HR	RBI	Avg
Home	292	81	13	47	.277	LHP	145	37	4	13	.255
Road	305	84	11	45	.275	RHP	452	128	20	79	.283
First Half	338	105	14	58	.311	Sc Pos	157	42	3	64	.268
Scnd Half	259	60	10	34	.232	Clutch	100	24	4	13	.240

2002 Rankings (National League)

- 1st in sacrifice flies (11)
- 2nd in doubles
- 3rd in lowest groundball-flyball ratio (0.6)
- 4th in games played and fielding percentage at third base (.969)
- 5th in lowest cleanup slugging percentage (.481) and lowest percentage of extra bases taken as a runner (35.4)
- 6th in errors at third base (14)
- Led the Marlins in RBI and sacrifice flies (11)

Kevin Millar

2002 Season

Kevin Millar got off to a decent start, then missed a month with a strained muscle in his left side. He struggled through the middle two months before rallying to hit a combined .378 in August and September. He began the year in right field but moved to left in late April at the suggestion of then-left fielder Cliff Floyd. Handling the massive right-field area at Pro Player Stadium eventually proved too much for Millar, a converted infielder.

Hitting

Millar punishes fastballs out over the plate, where he can get his arms extended. He can drive balls to right field when he's at his best. When he struggles, he's too quick and pulls lots of balls foul. He struggles with balls up and in, which he frequently pops up when in a funk. He'll swing through fastballs in his eyes and breaking balls away. After proving himself among the Marlins' best clutch hitters the past couple years, he hit just .253 with runners in scoring position. He is a patient hitter who enjoys working a count, waiting for a pitcher to make a mistake.

Baserunning & Defense

Playing for a go-go manager in Jeff Torborg, Millar might appear miscast. He has one stolen base in three career attempts, but finds plenty of other ways to compensate. He's largely a station-to-station runner on the basepaths. His defense has improved to the point where he won't hurt you in left field, although he won't win any Gold Gloves out there either. Making shorter throws after the move to left seemed to agree with him as well, as he made four assists in left. He played just two games apiece at third and first, his natural positions.

2003 Outlook

Millar just completed a two-year, $1.6 million contract and was eligible for a sizeable raise through salary arbitration. His name was mentioned in at least one early-winter trade rumor, but the Marlins chose to unload the more-expensive Preston Wilson instead. Millar will be the starting left fielder, and his bat, professionalism and clubhouse presence will be greatly valued.

Position: LF/RF
Bats: R **Throws:** R
Ht: 6' 0" **Wt:** 210

Opening Day Age: 31
Born: 9/24/71 in Los Angeles, CA
ML Seasons: 5
Pronunciation: mi-LAR

Overall Statistics

	G	AB	R	H	D	T	HR	RBI	SB	BB	SO	Avg	OBP	Slg
'02	126	438	58	134	41	0	16	57	0	40	74	.306	.366	.509
Car.	500	1499	205	443	111	12	59	251	1	156	255	.296	.367	.504

Where He Hits the Ball

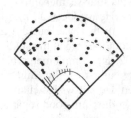 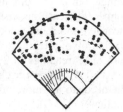

Vs. LHP   **Vs. RHP**

2002 Situational Stats

	AB	H	HR	RBI	Avg		AB	H	HR	RBI	Avg
Home	231	77	11	38	.333	LHP	104	33	3	9	.317
Road	207	57	5	19	.275	RHP	334	101	13	48	.302
First Half	193	52	5	19	.269	Sc Pos	99	25	0	34	.253
Scnd Half	245	82	11	38	.335	Clutch	64	20	1	6	.313

2002 Rankings (National League)

- 7th in doubles
- 8th in batting average at home
- Led the Marlins in batting average and batting average at home

Brad Penny

2002 Season

Coming off a season in which he was the Marlins' most consistent starter, Brad Penny took a step back in 2002. His conditioning became an issue because of a bout with the flu that limited his endurance, and he spent six-plus weeks on the disabled list at midseason with biceps tendinitis. His best month was August, when he posted four quality starts, but he faded down the stretch. He continued to dominate the Expos, but take out his five starts against Montreal and his ERA jumped to 5.06.

Pitching

Penny relies on a heavy sinker in the 91-92 MPH range, but he can dial up his four-seamer into the upper 90s when he wishes. He has been a bit too worried about his velocity in the past, but did a better job of pitching without looking at the stadium radar readings in 2002. He complements his fastball with a power curve and a good changeup he needs to use more often. He throws his change in the 81-82 MPH range, giving him good separation. His sinker is such a good weapon, he'll throw it 70 percent of the time.

Defense & Hitting

Penny tends to get predictable in his hold times, which makes him susceptible to the running game. Too often he's a "bump and go" guy, which allows smart basestealers to time their break. He's just an average fielder, lacking first-step quickness. Once he gets going, however, he's not slow. He's a decent hitter with gap power but needs to improve his bunting.

2003 Outlook

Like many of the Marlins who were due their first big raise through salary arbitration, Penny's future with the club was made a bit more secure when Florida dumped the salaries of Preston Wilson and Charles Johnson. If the Marlins do keep Penny in the fold, they would like to see him drop about 10 pounds and renew his commitment to an undeniable talent. He still could turn into a big winner if he gets his health and his fire back.

Position: SP
Bats: R **Throws:** R
Ht: 6' 4" **Wt:** 247

Opening Day Age: 24
Born: 5/24/78 in Broken Arrow, OK
ML Seasons: 3

Overall Statistics

	W	L	Pct.	ERA	G	GS	Sv	IP	H	BB	SO	HR	Ratio
'02	8	7	.533	4.66	24	24	0	129.1	148	50	93	18	1.53
Car.	26	24	.520	4.26	78	77	0	454.0	451	164	327	46	1.35

How Often He Throws Strikes

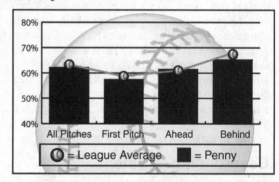

= League Average   = Penny

2002 Situational Stats

	W	L	ERA	Sv	IP		AB	H	HR	RBI	Avg
Home	4	1	4.18	0	56.0	LHB	231	68	9	30	.294
Road	4	6	5.03	0	73.1	RHB	282	80	9	41	.284
First Half	3	3	5.14	0	49.0	Sc Pos	129	34	3	48	.264
Scnd Half	5	4	4.37	0	80.1	Clutch	24	4	0	0	.167

2002 Rankings (National League)

- Led the Marlins in home runs allowed

Julian Tavarez

2002 Season

Acquired from the Cubs in the final week before the end of spring training, Julian Tavarez was thrust into an impossible situation. He was the only big leaguer the Marlins received in exchange for closer Antonio Alfonseca and righthander Matt Clement. Tavarez suffered by comparison, especially after a strained throwing shoulder forced him onto the disabled list three starts into the season. His ERA after two months was 9.09, but Tavarez went from putrid to merely inconsistent thereafter. He had two separate stretches of five quality starts in six-start spans and ate up innings for an injury-ravaged rotation.

Pitching

Tavarez is a sinker-slider guy who can rush it up to home plate as high as 95 MPH. Typically, he sits in the 88-92 MPH range with tremendous movement. He throws his changeup at 80 MPH with great life to both sides of the plate. He has a sweeping slider that he spots well, but he tends to leave it up in the zone too often. That's been a problem with his changeup as well. He'll throw the backdoor slider to lefties, who give him fits. He is a battler who seems to improve his concentration with runners on base.

Defense & Hitting

Tavarez is a good athlete who can make acrobatic plays in the field but also can botch the routine play. He's been known to bounce balls to first on purpose, and not just when playing on turf. He can be quick to home plate but too often lapses into a high leg kick that leaves him an easy mark for basestealers. He is a poor hitter with an awkward, slashing stroke, but he does a good job getting down sacrifice bunts.

2003 Outlook

A free agent after his two-year contract ended, Tavarez was not expected to return. After bouncing around to four different clubs in the past four years, he was likely to find a fifth home this winter, albeit at a much lower salary than the $3.1 million he earned last year.

Position: SP
Bats: L **Throws:** R
Ht: 6' 2" **Wt:** 195

Opening Day Age: 29
Born: 5/22/73 in Santiago, DR
ML Seasons: 10
Pronunciation: JOOL-ee-en tah-VAR-rez

Overall Statistics

	W	L	Pct.	ERA	G	GS	Sv	IP	H	BB	SO	HR	Ratio
'02	10	12	.455	5.39	29	27	0	153.2	188	74	67	9	1.70
Car.	60	45	.571	4.61	427	79	2	867.2	972	348	492	75	1.52

How Often He Throws Strikes

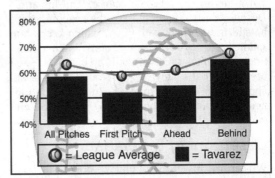

2002 Situational Stats

	W	L	ERA	Sv	IP		AB	H	HR	RBI	Avg
Home	5	5	4.08	0	92.2	LHB	300	100	3	39	.333
Road	5	7	7.38	0	61.0	RHB	310	88	6	50	.284
First Half	7	4	5.81	0	79.0	Sc Pos	205	64	4	79	.312
Scnd Half	3	8	4.94	0	74.2	Clutch	17	3	0	0	.176

2002 Rankings (National League)

- 2nd in errors at pitcher (4)
- 3rd in hit batsmen (15), balks (2) and highest batting average allowed with runners in scoring position
- 8th in highest batting average allowed vs. lefthanded batters
- Led the Marlins in losses, hits allowed, GDPs induced (23), highest groundball-flyball ratio allowed (1.9), fewest home runs allowed per nine innings (.53) and most GDPs induced per nine innings (1.3)

Preston Wilson

2002 Season

A second straight down year for Preston Wilson left the Marlins with serious doubts about their center fielder. Manager Jeff Torborg tried to use Wilson's speed in the No. 2 hole in the batting order, but that experiment fell apart quickly. No longer considered a cleanup hitter, Wilson bounced around the order before settling in at No. 3 after the midseason trade of Cliff Floyd. Wilson was bothered by nagging injuries to his wrist and hamstring but never went on the disabled list.

Hitting

A classic mistake hitter, Wilson likes fastballs down the middle where he can extend his arms. Despite constant harping from the coaching staff, he still tries to pull everything, which keeps him saddled with hefty strikeout totals. Pitchers routinely get him out with fastballs up in the zone and breaking balls away. Wilson's situational approach remains abysmal—he hit .200 with runners in scoring position and .167 with RISP and two outs.

Baserunning & Defense

Wilson had his third straight 20-homer, 20-steal season, but it was an empty achievement. He notched his 20th stolen base on August 20, then had no more attempts the rest of the way as his stat-sheet motives were exposed. His speed is his biggest asset in the outfield, where he can close with the best of them and regularly outruns mistakes. Poor jumps and odd routes are part of the package. He had a career-low eight assists to go with six errors.

2003 Outlook

As part of the three-team deal that sent Mike Hampton to Atlanta, the Marlins dumped both Wilson and Charles Johnson on Colorado. With $27.5 million and three years left on his contract, Wilson figured to be hard to move, but the Rockies seemed even more desperate to rid themselves of Hampton's burgeoning price tag. At 28 and coming off two straight down seasons, Wilson is at a career crossroads, but Coors Field certainly could turn his slide around. The Rockies are sure to lean on Wilson's speed to man the vast center field at Coors.

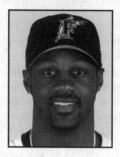

Position: CF
Bats: R **Throws:** R
Ht: 6' 2" **Wt:** 213

Opening Day Age: 28
Born: 7/19/74 in Bamberg, SC
ML Seasons: 5

Overall Statistics

	G	AB	R	H	D	T	HR	RBI	SB	BB	SO	Avg	OBP	Slg
'02	141	510	80	124	22	2	23	65	20	58	140	.243	.329	.429
Car.	596	2116	318	555	110	11	104	331	88	201	611	.262	.333	.472

Where He Hits the Ball

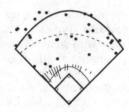 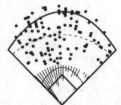

Vs. LHP   **Vs. RHP**

2002 Situational Stats

	AB	H	HR	RBI	Avg		AB	H	HR	RBI	Avg
Home	237	62	8	31	.262	LHP	120	29	8	18	.242
Road	273	62	15	34	.227	RHP	390	95	15	47	.244
First Half	304	73	14	41	.240	Sc Pos	135	27	5	42	.200
Scnd Half	206	51	9	24	.248	Clutch	75	22	6	17	.293

2002 Rankings (National League)

- 1st in errors in center field (6)
- 2nd in lowest fielding percentage in center field (.981)
- 4th in assists in center field (8) and lowest stolen-base percentage (64.5)
- 5th in lowest batting average with runners in scoring position
- 6th in lowest batting average and lowest batting average on the road
- 8th in batting average on a 3-1 count (.600)
- 9th in caught stealing (11) and steals of third (4)
- 10th in strikeouts
- Led the Marlins in GDPs (17) and slugging percentage vs. lefthanded pitchers (.492)

Armando Almanza

Position: RP
Bats: L **Throws:** L
Ht: 6' 3" **Wt:** 240

Opening Day Age: 30
Born: 10/26/72 in El Paso, TX
ML Seasons: 4

Overall Statistics

	W	L	Pct.	ERA	G	GS	Sv	IP	H	BB	SO	HR	Ratio
'02	3	2	.600	4.34	51	0	2	45.2	36	23	57	8	1.29
Car.	9	7	.563	4.36	184	0	2	148.2	116	101	168	20	1.46

2002 Situational Stats

	W	L	ERA	Sv	IP			AB	H	HR	RBI	Avg
Home	1	2	4.24	1	23.1	LHB		55	14	0	5	.255
Road	2	0	4.43	1	22.1	RHB		106	22	8	19	.208
First Half	2	2	4.50	1	20.0	Sc Pos		45	9	2	17	.200
Scnd Half	1	0	4.21	1	25.2	Clutch		69	15	1	8	.217

2002 Season

Still rusty after offseason arthroscopic surgery to remove bone chips from his throwing elbow, Armando Almanza didn't join the big league roster until the third week of May. He allowed just one run over his first 10 appearances and proved a valuable late-game option the rest of the way. Take away two messy outings against the Mets and his ERA would have been 2.64.

Pitching, Defense & Hitting

Almanza retains a live arm that can pump fastballs at 92-96 MPH. He elevates his four-seamer well, getting overanxious hitters to climb the ladder, producing a marked flyball ratio. That also helps his big-breaking overhand curve. His changeup is much improved, as evidenced by the fact that righthanders posted an on-base percentage that was nearly 150 points lower than lefties. Almanza moves well on his feet and is very aware of situations and limitations. He holds runners well, but is 0-for-4 at the plate in his career.

2003 Outlook

Almanza is arbitration-eligible for the first time but still figures to be a sub-$1 million commodity. He is likely to remain the top short relief option from the left side, with a chance to notch the rare save should matchups dictate.

Andy Fox

Position: SS
Bats: L **Throws:** R
Ht: 6' 4" **Wt:** 202

Opening Day Age: 32
Born: 1/12/71 in Sacramento, CA
ML Seasons: 7

Overall Statistics

	G	AB	R	H	D	T	HR	RBI	SB	BB	SO	Avg	OBP	Slg
'02	133	435	55	109	14	5	4	41	31	49	94	.251	.338	.333
Car.	660	1762	232	435	60	16	29	159	73	189	359	.247	.333	.348

2002 Situational Stats

	AB	H	HR	RBI	Avg		AB	H	HR	RBI	Avg
Home	219	53	3	22	.242	LHP	88	13	0	6	.148
Road	216	56	1	19	.259	RHP	347	96	4	35	.277
First Half	232	58	1	23	.250	Sc Pos	101	30	2	38	.297
Scnd Half	203	51	3	18	.251	Clutch	75	14	0	7	.187

2002 Season

Coming off a nightmare season marred by a broken finger on his right hand, Andy Fox used a winter-ball stint in Puerto Rico to rediscover his batting stroke and confidence. That proved key when starting shortstop Alex Gonzalez went down with a shoulder injury seven weeks into the season and left Fox in the lineup for the rest of the year.

Hitting, Baserunning & Defense

Fox hit eight points higher against lefties than righties before last season, when he struggled against them. He likes medium-velocity fastballs out over the plate but at times thinks opposite field too much. He struggles with fastballs up and in and offspeed stuff down in the zone, especially split-finger pitches from righties. Fox has above-average speed and has improved footwork in the field, where he has an accurate arm and makes up for below-average range with sound positioning.

2003 Outlook

The Marlins exercised a 2003 option in Fox' contract for $800,000, leaving him a low-budget alternative to Gonzalez. With Gonzalez again eligible for arbitration, there was a chance he might be non-tendered, leaving Fox as the starter. At the very least, Fox figured to provide sound insurance should Gonzalez have trouble in the spring.

Graeme Lloyd

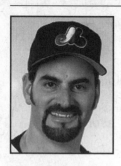

Position: RP
Bats: L **Throws:** L
Ht: 6' 7" **Wt:** 225

Opening Day Age: 35
Born: 4/9/67 in
Geelong, Victoria,
Australia
ML Seasons: 9
Pronunciation: gram

Overall Statistics

	W	L	Pct.	ERA	G	GS	Sv	IP	H	BB	SO	HR	Ratio
'02	4	5	.444	5.21	66	0	5	57.0	67	19	37	6	1.51
Car.	29	32	.475	3.91	516	0	17	485.1	492	147	279	49	1.32

2002 Situational Stats

	W	L	ERA	Sv	IP		AB	H	HR	RBI	Avg
Home	3	1	4.97	2	25.1	LHB	86	28	2	14	.326
Road	1	4	5.40	3	31.2	RHB	139	39	4	25	.281
First Half	2	3	5.87	5	30.2	Sc Pos	73	27	2	34	.370
Scnd Half	2	2	4.44	0	26.1	Clutch	75	26	4	17	.347

2002 Season

Graeme Lloyd endured an erratic year, registering four saves in April and weathering two months with an ERA of 9.00 or higher. He was traded to Florida at midseason in an eight-player, three-team deal and was very upset. He challenged the deal in arbitration but lost when it was determined he lost his limited no-trade clause when his agents missed an offseason filing deadline.

Pitching, Defense & Hitting

Lloyd survives by changing the hitter's eye level with an extremely high arm slot and great downward tilt. His fastball is just 88-89 MPH but he uses a cut fastball to both lefties and righties, although lefties hit 45 points higher against him. He has a loopy curveball and a changeup as well, but has been tinkering with a potentially devastating palmball that features knuckleball action. Though a decent athlete, he is a below-average fielder. Despite a high leg kick, he controls the running game with a slide step.

2003 Outlook

Lloyd was a free agent after finishing out a three-year, $9 million contract originally signed with Marlins owner Jeffrey Loria when he was in Montreal. Lloyd isn't expected to return, but he still can help some team as a situational lefty.

Braden Looper

Position: RP
Bats: R **Throws:** R
Ht: 6' 3" **Wt:** 220

Opening Day Age: 28
Born: 10/28/74 in
Weatherford, OK
ML Seasons: 5

Overall Statistics

	W	L	Pct.	ERA	G	GS	Sv	IP	H	BB	SO	HR	Ratio
'02	2	5	.286	3.14	78	0	13	86.0	73	28	55	8	1.17
Car.	13	13	.500	3.71	298	0	18	310.2	308	126	190	27	1.40

2002 Situational Stats

	W	L	ERA	Sv	IP		AB	H	HR	RBI	Avg
Home	1	1	1.17	8	46.0	LHB	144	40	4	17	.278
Road	1	4	5.40	5	40.0	RHB	173	33	4	15	.191
First Half	0	3	3.88	0	46.1	Sc Pos	81	19	2	23	.235
Scnd Half	2	2	2.27	13	39.2	Clutch	191	43	4	19	.225

2002 Season

When Antonio Alfonseca was traded to the Cubs five days before the start of the regular season, Braden Looper was left to head up the closing committee. He blew his only two save chances in the first week and soon moved back into his customary setup role. To Looper's credit, he didn't sulk, and when Vladimir Nunez faltered at midseason, Looper was perfect in 13 save chances from July 20 on.

Pitching, Defense & Hitting

Looper is blessed with an overpowering sinker he throws at 95-97 MPH. At times he can get away with throwing almost exclusively sinkers, but he has grown more comfortable with the cut fastball he worked on with pitching coach Brad Arnsberg. The cutter also gave him an option to use against lefties. Looper has a decent pickoff move but could do better holding runners. He's a good athlete but is 0-for-5 in his career with the bat.

2003 Outlook

Looper will report to spring training as the undisputed closer. He will earn a minimum of $1.6 million in the final year of a three-year deal, with the chance to push that to $2.4 million with incentives. At last, the prototypical closer will get a chance to prove he deserves that tag.

Mike Mordecai

Position: 3B/SS
Bats: R **Throws:** R
Ht: 5'10" **Wt:** 185

Opening Day Age: 35
Born: 12/13/67 in Birmingham, AL
ML Seasons: 9
Pronunciation: more-dah-KYE

Overall Statistics

	G	AB	R	H	D	T	HR	RBI	SB	BB	SO	Avg	OBP	Slg
'02	93	151	19	37	8	0	0	11	2	13	27	.245	.313	.298
Car.	657	1187	139	295	68	7	21	119	10	98	221	.249	.307	.371

2002 Situational Stats

	AB	H	HR	RBI	Avg		AB	H	HR	RBI	Avg
Home	63	17	0	7	.270	LHP	78	22	0	5	.282
Road	88	20	0	4	.227	RHP	73	15	0	6	.205
First Half	74	15	0	4	.203	Sc Pos	33	9	0	11	.273
Scnd Half	77	22	0	7	.286	Clutch	40	8	0	2	.200

2002 Season

Traded at midseason in the eight-player deal that sent Cliff Floyd to Montreal, Mike Mordecai fit in well in his new surroundings. He seemed to fall out of favor with Expos manager Frank Robinson but didn't have to convince Marlins skipper Jeff Torborg, who had him in Montreal, of his value. Still, Mordecai posted his lowest batting average in three years and took his fewest at-bats since an injury-plagued 1998 campaign.

Hitting, Baserunning & Defense

At the plate, Mordecai likes fastballs up and out over the plate and has the ability to go the other way. He finished up with a strong September, by far his best month. Extremely versatile, Mordecai played five different positions. He compensates for an average arm by studying tendencies. A natural shortstop, he also has become comfortable at third, where he gave Mike Lowell an occasional break. Mordecai has quick feet and turns the double play well at both middle-infield spots. A smart baserunner, he isn't much of a stolen-base threat.

2003 Outlook

Mordecai will make $500,000 in the final year of a two-year, $1 million contract. Along with Andy Fox, he gives the Marlins a couple of solid utility options.

Vladimir Nunez

Position: RP
Bats: R **Throws:** R
Ht: 6' 4" **Wt:** 240

Opening Day Age: 28
Born: 3/15/75 in Havana, Cuba
ML Seasons: 5
Pronunciation: NOON-yez

Overall Statistics

	W	L	Pct.	ERA	G	GS	Sv	IP	H	BB	SO	HR	Ratio
'02	6	5	.545	3.41	77	0	20	97.2	80	37	73	8	1.20
Car.	17	26	.395	4.35	194	27	21	372.0	349	157	270	40	1.36

2002 Situational Stats

	W	L	ERA	Sv	IP		AB	H	HR	RBI	Avg
Home	4	3	4.06	11	51.0	LHB	162	31	2	14	.191
Road	2	2	2.70	9	46.2	RHB	195	49	6	26	.251
First Half	4	3	3.65	18	49.1	Sc Pos	100	24	2	31	.240
Scnd Half	2	2	3.17	2	48.1	Clutch	236	57	5	31	.242

2002 Season

Vladimir Nunez entered the year with one career save, but he inherited the closer's role after the spring-training trade of Antonio Alfonseca and the early-season flameout of Braden Looper. Nunez blew just two of his first 17 save chances until running into a rough patch in mid-June. Within a month, he had lost the closer's job to Looper.

Pitching, Defense & Hitting

Durable as they come, Nunez has a 93-94 MPH fastball that he should challenge hitters with more often. He'll work away to righties with his four-seamer and can start a two-seamer in against lefties and let it tail back over the plate. He possesses a nasty splitter and a good slider but falls behind in counts too much. He has largely curbed a long-standing tendency to drop his arm angle when he gets in trouble. He has a good move to first and a slide step but doesn't pay much attention to base-runners. He is a good athlete and a good fielder.

2003 Outlook

Nunez, eligible for salary arbitration for the first time, should finally see his paycheck push into seven figures. Because he's durable enough to pitch two or more innings at a time, which he did 23 times last year, he will be counted on to set up Looper.

Florida

Eric Owens

Position: LF/RF/CF
Bats: R **Throws:** R
Ht: 6' 0" **Wt:** 208

Opening Day Age: 32
Born: 2/3/71 in Danville, VA
ML Seasons: 8

Overall Statistics

	G	AB	R	H	D	T	HR	RBI	SB	BB	SO	Avg	OBP	Slg
'02	131	385	44	104	15	5	4	37	26	31	33	.270	.324	.366
Car.	695	2112	276	556	80	16	25	194	115	172	260	.263	.320	.352

2002 Situational Stats

	AB	H	HR	RBI	Avg		AB	H	HR	RBI	Avg
Home	174	49	2	17	.282	LHP	94	25	1	6	.266
Road	211	55	2	20	.261	RHP	291	79	3	31	.271
First Half	239	68	3	27	.285	Sc Pos	104	28	0	28	.269
Scnd Half	146	36	1	10	.247	Clutch	75	17	0	6	.227

2002 Season

After a miserable first year in South Florida, outfielder Eric Owens returned sleeker and with an improved attitude. As a result, he quickly won the confidence of new manager Jeff Torborg. He had a big May filling in for injured starter Kevin Millar but saw his playing time decrease markedly in the second half.

Hitting, Baserunning & Defense

Owens returned to the speed-based game his skills require. His groundball-flyball ratio climbed back to 2.73:1, and he cut his strikeout rate nearly in half. He likes high fastballs but struggles with fastballs on his hands and breaking pitches away. He ranked among the NL's top 15 in infield hits and stolen bases, showing a strong first step and good instincts on the bases. Though he would seem a perfect No. 2 hitter, he did his best work when batting sixth or seventh. He can play all three outfield spots and has an average arm.

2003 Outlook

Coming off a season in which he made $2 million, Owens is a fifth-year arbitration-eligible who could prove too expensive for the Marlins. Having re-established himself as a useful fourth outfielder at the very least, he might fit better as a reserve with a contending team.

Carl Pavano

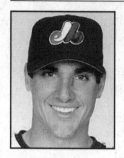

Position: SP/RP
Bats: R **Throws:** R
Ht: 6' 5" **Wt:** 230

Opening Day Age: 27
Born: 1/8/76 in New Britain, CT
ML Seasons: 5

Overall Statistics

	W	L	Pct.	ERA	G	GS	Sv	IP	H	BB	SO	HR	Ratio
'02	6	10	.375	5.16	37	22	0	136.0	174	45	92	19	1.61
Car.	27	37	.422	4.71	103	86	0	514.1	569	173	345	60	1.44

2002 Situational Stats

	W	L	ERA	Sv	IP		AB	H	HR	RBI	Avg
Home	2	4	5.10	0	72.1	LHB	252	90	8	30	.357
Road	4	6	5.23	0	63.2	RHB	304	84	11	38	.276
First Half	3	8	6.30	0	74.1	Sc Pos	143	41	1	45	.287
Scnd Half	3	2	3.79	0	61.2	Clutch	43	14	1	2	.326

2002 Season

Carl Pavano went 3-8 with a 6.11 ERA in his first 14 starts for the Expos, earning a June demotion to Triple-A Ottawa. Three weeks later, he was dealt to the Marlins in the Cliff Floyd trade, where he was reunited with former pitching coach Brad Arnsberg. Pavano made progress and earned an eight-start audition down the stretch.

Pitching, Defense & Hitting

Pavano is a groundball pitcher with a plus four-seamer that can reach 95-96 MPH and a two-seamer that sits in the low 90s and shows great run to both sides of the plate. His slider can be short, quick and late-breaking, but he gets in trouble when he drops his arm slot and the pitch flattens out. When it's on, the slider carries an almost cutter-like tilt and can be hard to pick up. He is a below-average fielder with a slow lower half. He wasn't victimized much by the stolen base despite a high leg kick and slow times to the plate. He can swing the bat and is a good bunter.

2003 Outlook

A fourth-year arbitration-eligible, Pavano should see his salary rise into the $1.75 million range. Finally healthy after a history of shoulder and elbow problems, he is penciled into the back of the starting rotation.

Mike Redmond

Position: C
Bats: R **Throws:** R
Ht: 5'11" **Wt:** 208

Opening Day Age: 31
Born: 5/5/71 in Seattle, WA
ML Seasons: 5

Overall Statistics

	G	AB	R	H	D	T	HR	RBI	SB	BB	SO	Avg	OBP	Slg
'02	89	256	19	78	15	0	2	28	0	21	34	.305	.372	.387
Car.	345	967	87	287	45	1	9	96	0	78	116	.297	.362	.373

2002 Situational Stats

	AB	H	HR	RBI	Avg		AB	H	HR	RBI	Avg
Home	123	36	1	17	.293	LHP	70	20	1	6	.286
Road	133	42	1	11	.316	RHP	186	58	1	22	.312
First Half	130	42	1	15	.323	Sc Pos	66	20	0	23	.303
Scnd Half	126	36	1	13	.286	Clutch	56	16	1	6	.286

2002 Season

With starting catcher Charles Johnson suffering through the worst season of his career, Mike Redmond stepped up from his caddy role to assume a near-equal platoon. While remaining respectful of his friend and former minor league teammate, Redmond also out produced the two-time All-Star, both at the plate and behind it.

Hitting, Baserunning & Defense

Pesky as they come, Redmond hit better than .300 for the fourth time in five MLB seasons. He drove opposing pitchers crazy with his opposite-field approach. He rarely strikes out but can be overpowered by mid-90s fastballs. Pitchers love throwing to Redmond, who calls a great game, frames pitches, blocks balls and throws out nearly 40 percent of opposing basestealers. He became the personal receiver for the top two starters on the staff, A.J. Burnett and Ryan Dempster. Redmond hustles on the bases but was caught in the only two stolen-base attempts of his career.

2003 Outlook

With the Marlins sending Johnson to Colorado, Redmond becomes the regular backstop in Florida. He could see action in 110-120 games. Due a raise as a fourth-year arbitration-eligible, he also could see his $650,000 salary double.

Michael Tejera

Position: RP/SP
Bats: L **Throws:** L
Ht: 5' 9" **Wt:** 175

Opening Day Age: 26
Born: 10/18/76 in Havana, Cuba
ML Seasons: 2
Pronunciation: te-HAIR-a

Overall Statistics

	W	L	Pct.	ERA	G	GS	Sv	IP	H	BB	SO	HR	Ratio
'02	8	8	.500	4.45	47	18	1	139.2	144	60	95	17	1.46
Car.	8	8	.500	4.75	50	19	1	146.0	154	65	102	18	1.50

2002 Situational Stats

	W	L	ERA	Sv	IP		AB	H	HR	RBI	Avg
Home	7	3	3.68	0	93.0	LHB	114	26	4	15	.228
Road	1	5	5.98	1	46.2	RHB	422	118	13	48	.280
First Half	5	1	2.87	1	62.2	Sc Pos	129	31	3	42	.240
Scnd Half	3	7	5.73	0	77.0	Clutch	52	9	1	3	.173

2002 Season

Two years removed from ligament-replacement surgery on his pitching elbow, Michael Tejera enjoyed a surprising rookie season. He notched his first career save, his first eight big league wins, and he won the faith of manager Jeff Torborg. Tejera moved into the rotation in June and spent three months there before wearing down.

Pitching, Defense & Hitting

Despite an average fastball that sits in the 88-91 MPH range, Tejera isn't afraid to challenge hitters. He goes after righties with a plus changeup and limits lefties with a big-bending curve and tight slider. Though in excellent shape, he tends to wear down in the middle innings. The best athlete on the Marlins pitching staff, Tejera was a center fielder back in Cuba. He had one of two homers by Marlins pitchers and runs the bases well enough to serve as an occasional pinch-runner. He holds runners well and has so much confidence in his fielding, he sometimes is too overaggressive.

2003 Outlook

Having shown he can either start or relieve, Tejera is a valuable commodity. He is penciled into the rotation, where he likely would be the only left-hander. Best of all for the Marlins, he doesn't make much more than the minimum.

Other Florida Marlins

Brian Banks (Pos: RF, Age: 32, Bats: B)

	G	AB	R	H	D	T	HR	RBI	SB	BB	SO	Avg	OBP	Slg
'02	20	28	3	9	1	0	1	4	0	1	6	.321	.345	.464
Car.	181	346	51	87	13	1	9	41	6	37	91	.251	.321	.373

Banks has prospered in the Marlins' system, a dangerous hitter since signing in May 2001. The switch-hitter has batted .302 with 42 homers in 231 games with Triple-A Calgary. He could replace Tim Raines on the roster. Outlook: B

Toby Borland (Pos: RHP, Age: 33)

	W	L	Pct.	ERA	G	GS	Sv	IP	H	BB	SO	HR	Ratio
'02	1	0	1.000	5.27	15	0	0	13.2	14	5	11	3	1.39
Car.	10	8	.556	4.17	182	0	8	241.2	242	126	189	20	1.52

Borland appeared in a career-high 69 games with the Phillies in 1996. Since then, he has pitched in just 55 big league games over six seasons. His best years may be behind him, but he signed another minor league deal with Florida. 2003 Outlook: C

Homer Bush (Pos: 2B, Age: 30, Bats: R)

	G	AB	R	H	D	T	HR	RBI	SB	BB	SO	Avg	OBP	Slg
'02	63	132	16	30	2	0	1	7	4	5	25	.227	.266	.265
Car.	400	1267	174	363	50	5	11	115	64	57	236	.287	.325	.360

Bush showed some promise with the Blue Jays in 1999, batting .320 in 128 games. He has battled injuries since, and has been unable to get back on track. The Padres signed him to a minor league deal. 2003 Outlook: C

Ramon Castro (Pos: C, Age: 27, Bats: R)

	G	AB	R	H	D	T	HR	RBI	SB	BB	SO	Avg	OBP	Slg
'02	54	101	11	24	4	0	6	18	0	14	24	.238	.322	.455
Car.	135	317	25	71	12	0	10	37	0	41	75	.224	.310	.356

With Charles Johnson's trade to the Rockies, Castro will see more time behind the plate in 2003. His power numbers have improved, but he needs to find some consistency. 2003 Outlook: C

Vic Darensbourg (Pos: LHP, Age: 32)

	W	L	Pct.	ERA	G	GS	Sv	IP	H	BB	SO	HR	Ratio
'02	1	2	.333	6.14	42	0	0	48.1	61	26	33	10	1.80
Car.	7	15	.318	5.00	271	0	2	264.2	276	115	215	29	1.48

Darensbourg was traded to Rockies in November after posting a 6.14 ERA in 42 relief appearances in 2002. The thin air in Colorado likely will not assist him in improving those numbers. 2003 Outlook: B

Hansel Izquierdo (Pos: RHP, Age: 26)

	W	L	Pct.	ERA	G	GS	Sv	IP	H	BB	SO	HR	Ratio
'02	2	0	1.000	4.55	20	2	0	29.2	33	21	20	2	1.82
Car.	2	0	1.000	4.55	20	2	0	29.2	33	21	20	2	1.82

It took Izquierdo nearly seven years to get out of Class-A ball, but he debuted in the majors last season. He signed a minor league deal with Boston in October. 2003 Outlook: C

Gary Knotts (Pos: RHP, Age: 26)

	W	L	Pct.	ERA	G	GS	Sv	IP	H	BB	SO	HR	Ratio
'02	3	1	.750	4.40	28	0	0	30.2	21	16	21	6	1.21
Car.	3	2	.600	4.66	30	1	0	36.2	28	17	30	7	1.23

Knotts recorded a 3.29 ERA with Florida in April, but a 14.54 ERA the next month forced the team to assign him to the minors. Recalled in September and back on track, he posted a 2.13 ERA. 2003 Outlook: C

Oswaldo Mairena (Pos: LHP, Age: 28)

	W	L	Pct.	ERA	G	GS	Sv	IP	H	BB	SO	HR	Ratio
'02	2	3	.400	5.35	31	0	0	33.2	38	12	21	7	1.49
Car.	2	3	.400	6.06	33	0	0	35.2	45	14	21	8	1.65

Mairena was recalled by the Marlins after posting a 1.59 ERA in Triple-A ball during the month of April. However, after suffering an abdominal injury in June, the lefthander struggled the rest of the year. 2003 Outlook: C

Marty Malloy (Pos: 2B, Age: 30, Bats: L)

	G	AB	R	H	D	T	HR	RBI	SB	BB	SO	Avg	OBP	Slg
'02	24	25	1	3	0	0	0	1	0	2	8	.120	.185	.120
Car.	35	53	4	8	1	0	1	2	0	4	10	.151	.211	.226

Malloy, who has 11 minor league seasons under his belt, has seen limited duty in the major leagues. After refusing assignment in June, he became a free agent and signed a minor league deal with the Reds. 2003 Outlook: C

Kevin Olsen (Pos: RHP, Age: 26)

	W	L	Pct.	ERA	G	GS	Sv	IP	H	BB	SO	HR	Ratio
'02	0	5	.000	4.53	17	8	0	55.2	57	31	38	5	1.58
Car.	0	5	.000	3.82	21	10	0	70.2	68	33	51	5	1.43

The Marlins have allowed Olsen to get his feet wet in the majors each of the last two seasons, using him in relief, and also as a spot starter. Olsen should emerge as a No. 4 or 5 starter very soon. 2003 Outlook: C

Pablo Ozuna (Pos: 2B, Age: 28, Bats: R)

	G	AB	R	H	D	T	HR	RBI	SB	BB	SO	Avg	OBP	Slg
'02	34	47	4	13	2	2	0	3	1	1	3	.277	.300	.404
Car.	48	71	6	21	3	2	0	3	2	1	5	.296	.311	.394

Ozuna is a consistent hitter with enough power to get by. He also has good speed on the bases. Dealt to the Rockies in a six-player deal in November, Ozuna may make the big league roster. He will compete for the second-base job if the Rocks don't acquire a veteran. 2003 Outlook: C

Tim Raines (Pos: LF, Age: 43, Bats: B)

	G	AB	R	H	D	T	HR	RBI	SB	BB	SO	Avg	OBP	Slg
	98	89	9	17	3	0	1	7	0	22	19	.191	.351	.258
	2502	8872	1571	2605	430	113	170	980	808	1330	966	.294	.385	.425

After more than two decades in the major leagues, Raines announced his retirement following 2002. He finishes his career as a .294 hitter with 2,605 hits, 170 home runs and 980 RBI. 2003 Outlook: D

Nate Robertson (**Pos**: LHP, **Age**: 25)

	W	L	Pct.	ERA	G	GS	Sv	IP	H	BB	SO	HR	Ratio
'02	0	1	.000	11.88	6	1	0	8.1	15	4	3	3	2.28
Car.	0	1	.000	11.88	6	1	0	8.1	15	4	3	3	2.28

Robertson was 10-9 with a 3.42 ERA in 27 starts with Double-A Portland last season before a September callup by the Marlins. He still needs some work and should spend the 2003 season at Triple-A Calgary. 2003 Outlook: C

Nate Teut (**Pos**: LHP, **Age**: 27)

	W	L	Pct.	ERA	G	GS	Sv	IP	H	BB	SO	HR	Ratio
'02	0	1	.000	9.82	2	1	0	7.1	13	3	4	0	2.18
Car.	0	1	.000	9.82	2	1	0	7.1	13	3	4	0	2.18

Teut was acquired from the Chicago Cubs last winter and spent most of the 2002 season in Triple-A ball, going 5-6 with a 5.28 ERA in 27 games, including 19 starts. Another young arm in the Marlins' system. 2003 Outlook: C

Florida Marlins Minor League Prospects

Organization Overview:

New Marlins owner Jeffrey Loria placed a priority on filling some perceived gaps in an already strong farm system. Deals that sent off big leaguers Antonio Alfonseca, Matt Clement, Ryan Dempster and Cliff Floyd brought the likes of lefties Dontrelle Willis and Ryan Snare, righthanders Justin Wayne and Don Levinski, and catcher Ryan Jorgensen in return. While the flow of young pitching appears strong, cheap help in the field should be on the way soon, as well. Venezuelan third baseman Miguel Cabrera, first basemen Adrian Gonzalez and Jason Stokes and second baseman Jesus Medrano have shown intriguing potential. Meanwhile, it could be put-up-or-shut-up time for long-ballyhooed outfielder Abraham Nunez and a number of others in the system.

Miguel Cabrera

Position: SS   **Opening Day Age:** 19
Bats: R **Throws:** R   **Born:** 4/18/83 in
Ht: 6' 2" **Wt:** 185   Maracay, Venezuela

Recent Statistics

	G	AB	R	H	D	T	HR	RBI	SB	BB	SO	Avg
2001 A Kane County	110	422	61	113	19	4	7	66	3	37	76	.268
2002 A Jupiter	124	489	77	134	43	1	9	75	10	38	85	.274

Signed out of Venezuela in 1999 for a national record $1.9 million, Cabrera has done nothing to disappoint. A natural shortstop, he took well to a shift to third base last spring. He has played winter ball in Venezuela and, despite being one of the youngest players in the league, more than held his own. Cabrera does everything with apparent ease, including driving the ball with authority into both gaps and producing runs in RBI situations. He has a good idea of the strike zone for such a young player. He has plus range and arm strength, and should make the move to Double-A this year.

Adrian Gonzalez

Position: 1B   **Opening Day Age:** 20
Bats: L **Throws:** L   **Born:** 5/8/82 in San
Ht: 6' 2" **Wt:** 190   Diego, CA

Recent Statistics

	G	AB	R	H	D	T	HR	RBI	SB	BB	SO	Avg
2001 A Kane County	127	516	86	161	37	1	17	103	5	57	83	.312
2002 AA Portland	138	508	70	135	34	1	17	96	6	54	112	.266

The top overall pick in the 2000 draft, Gonzalez signed for $3 million. He roared through the Class-A Midwest League in his first full season but took a bit of a step back after making the jump to the Double-A Eastern League. He seemed too power-conscious at times, an approach that goes poorly with his fill-the-gaps game. His defense remains outstanding. A planned trip to the Arizona Fall League was canceled after he was hit on the right wrist near the end of the season. The pain persisted and Gonzalez had to wear a cast for two weeks before being shut down. He should be fine by spring, when he'll bid for a promotion to Triple-A.

Rob Henkel

Position: P   **Opening Day Age:** 24
Bats: R **Throws:** L   **Born:** 8/3/78 in La Mesa,
Ht: 6' 2" **Wt:** 210   CA

Recent Statistics

	W	L	ERA	G	GS	Sv	IP	H	R	BB	SO	HR
2001 R Marlins	1	3	1.52	9	8	0	29.2	17	9	11	38	0
2001 A Utica	0	0	4.32	3	3	0	8.1	7	4	6	11	0
2001 A Kane County	0	0	4.50	1	1	0	4.0	6	3	1	2	0
2002 A Jupiter	8	3	2.51	14	12	0	75.1	55	22	22	82	4
2002 AA Portland	5	4	3.86	13	13	0	70.0	54	31	27	68	6

Before returning for his senior year at UCLA, Henkel turned down $700,000 from the Mets, who took him in the 20th round in 1999. After signing for $650,000 in September 2000, Henkel spent nearly a year fighting a balky pitching shoulder that caused his velocity to drop from 93-95 MPH to the low 80s. He worked hard to strengthen the shoulder and gradually saw his velocity climb back up to 89-92 MPH. He dominated the high Class-A Florida State League to earn a midseason promotion to Double-A. He showed a much-improved changeup to go with his signature pitch, a devastating knuckle-curve with a late, quick break. A survivor of Tommy John surgery, Henkel has a tremendous work ethic and projects as No. 2 or 3 starter. He is a candidate to break into the big league bullpen this spring.

Blaine Neal

Position: P   **Opening Day Age:** 24
Bats: L **Throws:** R   **Born:** 4/6/78 in Marlton,
Ht: 6' 5" **Wt:** 205   NJ

Recent Statistics

	W	L	ERA	G	GS	Sv	IP	H	R	BB	SO	HR
2002 AAA Calgary	3	1	2.90	29	0	11	31.0	27	11	15	26	2
2002 NL Florida	3	0	2.73	32	0	0	33.0	32	12	14	33	1

Neal spent four separate stints with the Marlins in 2002, going back and forth on the shuttle to Triple-A Calgary. He pitched well at both places, showing enough potential to earn a full shot in a setup role this year. A fourth-round pick, Neal's development was stunted by mysterious elbow problems his first two pro seasons. The Marlins tried him at first base, but he flopped there as well. Nearly released after the '98 season, he underwent arthroscopic surgery to remove several large bone spurs and shave down part of a bone to relieve pressure on a nerve. That led to his re-emergence as a pitching prospect. Neal comes right at hitters with a 93-95 MPH fastball with late movement. He has a short, quick curveball and a strong pitcher's frame.

Abraham Nunez

Position: OF **Opening Day Age:** 26
Bats: B **Throws:** R **Born:** 2/5/77 in Haina,
Ht: 6' 2" **Wt:** 186 DR

Recent Statistics

	G	AB	R	H	D	T	HR	RBI	SB	BB	SO	Avg
2002 AAA Calgary	129	428	68	107	24	5	21	60	31	51	112	.250
2002 NL Florida	19	17	2	2	0	0	0	1	0	0	5	.118

Originally signed by the Diamondbacks, Nunez moved to the Marlins in December 1999 as the player to be named in the Matt Mantei deal. He was found to be three years older than believed last winter. Nunez is a five-tool player with plus power from both sides of the plate. His throwing shoulder is back to full strength after a nagging injury limited him mostly to DH duties in 2000. He has the arm and range to play either center or right field. He will take pitches and has shown the ability to draw walks. Strikeouts remain a concern, as does overswinging. He received a 19-game audition after a September callup and didn't do much, but he still could force his way into the outfield rotation next year.

Jason Stokes

Position: 1B **Opening Day Age:** 21
Bats: R **Throws:** R **Born:** 1/23/82 in Irving,
Ht: 6' 4" **Wt:** 225 TX

Recent Statistics

	G	AB	R	H	D	T	HR	RBI	SB	BB	SO	Avg
2001 A Utica	35	130	12	30	2	1	6	19	0	11	48	.231
2002 A Kane County	97	349	73	119	25	0	27	75	1	47	96	.341

Signed for $2.027 million as a second-rounder in 2000, Stokes' first full season in the minor leagues was an unmitigated success. Everybody knew about his power, but he showed an advanced knowledge of hitting that few expected to see so early in his career. Stokes' performance at Class-A Kane County was all the more impressive considering he was playing much of the year with nagging pain in his left wrist. Stokes was shut down near the end of his season so he could undergo surgery to remove a cyst on the outside of the wrist. His lower back, which had been a problem in 2001, responded well to a return to first base after a failed experiment in left field.

Justin Wayne

Position: P **Opening Day Age:** 23
Bats: R **Throws:** R **Born:** 4/16/79 in
Ht: 6' 3" **Wt:** 205 Honolulu, HI

Recent Statistics

	W	L	ERA	G	GS	Sv	IP	H	R	BB	SO	HR
2002 AA Harrisburg	5	2	2.37	17	17	0	98.2	74	41	32	47	7
2002 AA Portland	3	3	4.85	7	7	0	42.2	43	26	13	30	3
2002 AAA Calgary	0	1	6.35	2	2	0	11.1	8	8	6	10	3
2002 NL Florida	2	3	5.32	5	5	0	23.2	22	16	13	16	3

Wayne was one of two pitching prospects the Marlins received from the Expos in the blockbuster that sent Cliff Floyd back to his original organization. The righthander is a personal favorite of Marlins owner Jeffrey Loria, whose Expos took him with the fifth overall pick in 2000. Wayne, a Stanford product, signed for a franchise-record $2.95 million bonus and dominated in the first half at Double-A. He didn't do as well in a brief taste at Triple-A and showed only flashes in a five-start September audition in the bigs. Wayne pitches at 87-88 MPH and doesn't get many strikeouts, but he keeps hitters off balance with pinpoint control. He has a plus curveball and an improving changeup.

Dontrelle Willis

Position: P **Opening Day Age:** 21
Bats: L **Throws:** L **Born:** 1/12/82 in
Ht: 6' 4" **Wt:** 195 Oakland, CA

Recent Statistics

	W	L	ERA	G	GS	Sv	IP	H	R	BB	SO	HR
2001 A Boise	8	2	2.98	15	15	0	93.2	76	36	19	77	1
2002 A Kane County	10	2	1.83	19	19	0	127.2	91	29	21	101	3
2002 A Jupiter	2	0	1.80	5	5	0	30.0	24	7	3	27	2

Willis was the key player in the controversial spring deal that sent pitchers Antonio Alfonseca and Matt Clement to the Cubs. A former eighth-round pick, Willis dominated at Class-A Kane County. He earned a late-season promotion to high Class-A Jupiter, where he continued to distinguish himself. He was shut down near the end with shoulder tendinitis, but he pitched at instructional league without incident. Willis' improved fastball tops out at 94 MPH, and he mixes in a solid curve and changeup. His biggest weapon, however, is the deception he creates with an unorthodox delivery. He elicits tons of groundballs and awkward swings and could open the year at Double-A. Despite his age, Willis has an advanced knowledge of pitching and knows how to set hitters up.

Others to Watch

Righty **Denny Bautista** (20) has been mentored by fellow Dominican Pedro Martinez and shows similar flair. Bautista struggled with his mechanics and missed a month with shoulder tendinitis, but his 94-96 MPH fastball and plus curve make him an intriguing prospect. . . Righthander **Don Levinski** (20), named in the Cliff Floyd deal, was shut down for the final month with a slight rotator cuff problem. He was fine by instructional league and should build on a dominant season in the Class-A Midwest League. Levinski has a 92-94 MPH fastball and good feel. . . **Jesus Medrano** (24) finished out his year in the Arizona Fall League after a scare at Double-A Portland, where he was struck in the temple by an errant throw during pregame. He sustained a concussion. Medrano is rated the fastest player in the system, plays a solid second base and has some gap power. . . Lefthandeder **Ryan Snare** (24) was acquired from the Reds in the Ryan Dempster deal. Snare has a plus curveball, a solid-average fastball and could challenge for a bullpen role this season. He has shown the ability to start or relieve.

Minute Maid Park

Offense

When Minute Maid Park opened in 2000, it looked like one of the best hitters' parks in baseball outside of the Rockies. But its offensive tendencies generally have diminished over the past two years. The park still tends to favor hitters, but the Astros and their opponents combined for more homers in Houston road games last season. While the Crawford Boxes in left field would seem an inviting target, lefthanded hitters get the biggest longball boost at Minute Maid.

Defense

A number of weird angles along the outfield wall have the potential to create interesting caroms. One of Minute Maid's most distinctive features is "Tal's Hill" in center field, which seemed to come into play more often last year. That may be due to pitchers trying to funnel hits to that deep part of the park. Strikeouts have been reduced compared to the previous experience at the Astrodome.

Who It Helps the Most

The batting averages of Lance Berkman, Brad Ausmus and Jose Vizcaino all prospered at home last year. Berkman's power remained relatively unaffected, however. Roy Oswalt and Peter Munro, who get their share of grounders, posted better ERAs at home than on the road. Octavio Dotel, a flyball pitcher, nevertheless has compiled a 1.62 home ERA over the past two seasons.

Who It Hurts the Most

Although Richard Hidalgo hit 11 of his 15 homers away from Minute Maid last year, that probably was an aberration, and he hit just .218 on the road. Billy Wagner's home ERA since 2001 (3.26) is nearly twice as high as his mark on the road (1.79).

Rookies & Newcomers

Jason Lane might have the best chance at carving out playing time, though the Astros may need to move an outfielder. Lane has the power to reach Minute Maid's seats. Brad Lidge and Jeriome Robertson also might get the opportunity to prove Minute Maid isn't the nightmare for pitchers it first appeared to be.

Dimensions: LF-315, LCF-362, CF-435, RCF-373, RF-326

Capacity: 40,950

Elevation: 22 feet

Surface: Grass

Foul Territory: Average

Park Factors

2002 Season

	Home Games Astros	Opp	Total	Away Games Astros	Opp	Total	Index
G	75	75	150	75	75	150	
Avg	.284	.256	.270	.238	.259	.248	109
AB	2524	2596	5120	2558	2458	5016	102
R	380	312	692	318	314	632	109
H	717	665	1382	608	637	1245	111
2B	142	143	285	132	143	275	102
3B	18	10	28	13	22	35	78
HR	83	60	143	73	72	145	97
BB	289	218	507	251	275	526	94
SO	488	575	1063	549	539	1088	96
E	41	49	90	38	43	81	111
E-Infield	34	37	71	32	34	66	108
LHB-Avg	.299	.272	.285	.262	.269	.266	107
LHB-HR	42	25	67	26	32	58	114
RHB-Avg	.275	.246	.261	.225	.253	.238	110
RHB-HR	41	35	76	47	40	87	85

2000-2002

	Home Games Astros	Opp	Total	Away Games Astros	Opp	Total	Index
G	222	222	444	222	222	444	
Avg	.281	.268	.274	.257	.264	.261	105
AB	7461	7837	15298	7696	7430	15126	101
R	1251	1140	2391	1072	1027	2099	114
H	2093	2099	4192	1981	1961	3942	106
2B	428	416	844	388	397	785	106
3B	61	50	111	33	49	82	134
HR	307	294	601	263	253	516	115
BB	866	710	1576	828	772	1600	97
SO	1475	1687	3162	1602	1513	3115	100
E	142	148	290	157	147	304	95
E-Infield	121	119	240	131	123	254	94
LHB-Avg	.297	.291	.293	.273	.271	.272	108
LHB-HR	101	138	239	74	108	182	134
RHB-Avg	.274	.252	.264	.251	.258	.254	104
RHB-HR	206	156	362	189	145	334	106

2002 Rankings (National League)

- Second-highest batting-average factor
- Second-highest hit factor
- Second-highest LHB batting-average factor
- Third-highest RHB batting-average factor
- Third-lowest RHB home-run factor

Jimy Williams

2002 Season

His Houston tenure didn't start well, as Lance Berkman was the only consistent run producer early on, and Jeff Bagwell and Craig Biggio started slowly. Spring injuries hampered starters Shane Reynolds and Wade Miller, and the Astros were below .500 until surging in early July. They were 36-20 in July and August, sparked by solid pitching from Miller, Roy Oswalt and rookie Kirk Saarloos, and they climbed within reach of the NL Central lead before falling off in September.

Offense

The offense generated more concerns than expected. A surgically repaired shoulder troubled Bagwell, and questions lingered whether Biggio's bat is in decline. Daryle Ward didn't provide what Moises Alou did before he left, and Richard Hidalgo went deeper into a two-year funk. Hidalgo expressed his displeasure with news that he would platoon with Orlando Merced, but otherwise, the team adjusted to Williams' tendency to give his reserves more playing time than other managers. Williams struggled to find an effective leadoff hitter, and in the National League, only the Reds (.293) recorded a lower OBP out of the No. 1 hole that the Astros (.313).

Pitching & Defense

Former Houston manager Larry Dierker tended to let his starters battle through trouble spots, but Williams is more inclined to go to his bullpen. No NL manager generated as many relief appearances in '02, and he went to the well even though the pen struggled early on in the season. Williams also spent time trying to fill the last couple of rotation spots with a host of youngsters after Shane Reynolds went down for the season. Defensively, Williams likes to make substitutions late in games, though his first Astros roster didn't have many candidates to fill such roles.

2003 Outlook

Biggio's season improved after he moved from the leadoff spot into the No. 2 spot. Bagwell's shoulder should be better and the young pitchers are another year older. Williams' second go-round may go better, no matter what the Astros do during the offseason.

Born: 10/04/43 in Santa Maria, CA

Playing Experience: 1966-1967, StL

Managerial Experience: 10 seasons

Manager Statistics

Year	Team, Lg	W	L	Pct	GB	Finish
2002	Houston, NL	84	78	.519	13.0	2nd Central
10 Seasons		779	671	.537	–	–

2002 Starting Pitchers by Days Rest

	<=3	4	5	6+
Astros Starts	2	77	56	16
Astros ERA	1.59	3.83	4.17	4.26
NL Avg Starts	1	88	42	21
NL ERA	3.18	4.22	4.14	4.58

2002 Situational Stats

	Jimy Williams	NL Average
Hit & Run Success %	25.0	36.5
Stolen Base Success %	72.4	68.3
Platoon Pct.	55.3	52.7
Defensive Subs	23	19
High-Pitch Outings	2	7
Quick/Slow Hooks	32/4	24/11
Sacrifice Attempts	89	95

2002 Rankings (National League)

- 1st in relief appearances (480)
- 2nd in stolen-base percentage, fewest caught stealings of second base (22), pitchouts with a runner moving (6) and starts on three days rest
- 3rd in fewest caught stealings of third base (3), pitchouts (50), defensive substitutions, quick hooks and mid-inning pitching changes (164)

Houston

Brad Ausmus

2002 Season

Brad Ausmus was determined to prove his season-long 2001 hitting slump was an aberration, and he did so by just missing his career average of .259. A sore elbow coming out of training camp slowed him defensively early, but he recovered enough to win his second straight Gold Glove, committing just three errors in 1,079 innings. His .997 fielding percentage second among all National League catchers who played at least 81 games behind the plate.

Hitting

Ausmus struggled at the plate until July, when old friend Moises Alou gave him one of Alou's bats to use during a series in Chicago. Ausmus caught fire after that, hitting .306 in June and .272 in July. The greater weight of the bat seemed to help him stay back on his swing. Or perhaps it was psychological. Ausmus admitted he wasn't sure which, but he stayed with the larger bat through the rest of the season and doesn't plan to give it up. He sprayed his hits around the park more, as opposed to hitting to right field as he did in the past.

Baserunning & Defense

Ausmus almost began the year on the DL, but he decided to try and play through his elbow soreness and his caught-stealing figures suffered early. Still, he ended up nabbing 30 of 96 baserunners attempting to steal—no National League catcher threw out more would-be thieves (although his 31.6-percent success ratio trailed five NL backstops). Ausmus blocks the plate better than most catchers and his handling of the young Astros pitchers was credited with helping convert this team to the quirky dimensions of Minute Maid Park. An athletic, smart baserunner, he has good speed for a catcher.

2003 Outlook

Ausmus seems completely readjusted to playing in Houston again after two seasons in Detroit. The Astros love the way he handles the young, wide-eyed pitchers they have brought up the last two years, and they were glad he chose to take the $5.5 million option to re-sign with them shortly after the club declined to pick up its more expensive option of $7 million.

Position: C
Bats: R **Throws:** R
Ht: 5'11" **Wt:** 200

Opening Day Age: 33
Born: 4/14/69 in New Haven, CT
ML Seasons: 10
Pronunciation: AHHS-muss

Overall Statistics

	G	AB	R	H	D	T	HR	RBI	SB	BB	SO	Avg	OBP	Slg
'02	130	447	57	115	19	3	6	50	2	38	71	.257	.322	.353
Car.	1171	3877	499	1004	179	27	59	383	80	385	642	.259	.331	.365

Where He Hits the Ball

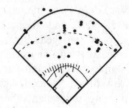
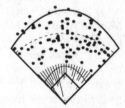

Vs. LHP   **Vs. RHP**

2002 Situational Stats

	AB	H	HR	RBI	Avg		AB	H	HR	RBI	Avg
Home	198	62	4	28	.313	LHP	88	27	3	12	.307
Road	249	53	2	22	.213	RHP	359	88	3	38	.245
First Half	223	59	3	19	.265	Sc Pos	102	28	3	44	.275
Scnd Half	224	56	3	31	.250	Clutch	70	9	0	6	.129

2002 Rankings (National League)

- 1st in GDPs (30) and most GDPs per GDP situation (28.6%)
- 2nd in fielding percentage at catcher (.997)
- Led the Astros in GDPs (30), highest ground-ball-flyball ratio (1.7) and highest percentage of swings put into play (48.5)

Jeff Bagwell

2002 Season

It was largely another typical Jeff Bagwell season, starting very slowly and finishing up strong. But this time his surgically repaired shoulder seemed to bother him considerably, and his perennial early-season problems with his unorthodox swing lingered uncharacteristically into midseason. He still finished very close to posting a seventh straight 30-homer, 100-RBI, 100-runs scored, 100-walks season. He's the only player in MLB history to have six straight such campaigns.

Hitting

Neither Bagwell's stance nor his swing are things of beauty, and neither will be on any instructional videos. His feet spread wide, knees bent in a compact crouch, he swings inside out with fierce power. He often goes after first-pitch fastballs, but then becomes more selective and works the count in his favor most of the time. But he had fits last year getting into the precise groove he needs to feel comfortable. The sore shoulder also seemed to affect that quest for comfort, not to mention a shift from third to fourth in the lineup, and he did not start feeling right until July.

Baserunning & Defense

The shoulder bothered Bagwell most while throwing, and early in the season he struggled to find a comfortable release. He concentrated more on his fielding and had only seven errors—tying his career low. But he's not quite as quick as he was in the past and got to fewer balls. His baserunning still is an example for younger players. Bagwell reads pitchers and knows the arm of every outfielder, picking his spots well for advancing bases and for steals.

2003 Outlook

Bagwell never complained about the pain he suffered last season and is resigned to the fact his shoulder never again will be 100 percent. But a full year after the surgery and with continued off-season rehab, it should be at least 50 percent better than last year. Barring further physical problems, Bagwell will surpass the 2,000-hit and 400-home run plateaus this season, and he shows no signs of slipping from his diverse contributions.

Position: 1B
Bats: R **Throws:** R
Ht: 6' 0" **Wt:** 215

Opening Day Age: 34
Born: 5/27/68 in Boston, MA
ML Seasons: 12
Pronunciation: BAG-well

Overall Statistics

G	AB	R	H	D	T	HR	RBI	SB	BB	SO	Avg	OBP	Slg
158	571	94	166	33	2	31	98	7	101	130	.291	.401	.518
1795	6520	1293	1969	427	28	380	1321	185	1199	1287	.302	.414	.551

Where He Hits the Ball

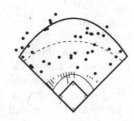 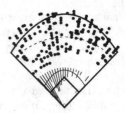

Vs. LHP   **Vs. RHP**

2002 Situational Stats

	AB	H	HR	RBI	Avg		AB	H	HR	RBI	Avg
Home	294	88	16	54	.299	LHP	108	36	10	24	.333
Road	277	78	15	44	.282	RHP	463	130	21	74	.281
First Half	307	83	15	49	.270	Sc Pos	148	45	7	67	.304
Scnd Half	264	83	16	49	.314	Clutch	80	21	3	12	.263

2002 Rankings (National League)

- 3rd in slugging percentage vs. lefthanded pitchers (.685)
- 4th in sacrifice flies (9) and assists at first base (111)
- 5th in pitches seen (2,745), on-base percentage vs. lefthanded pitchers (.459) and fielding percentage at first base (.995)
- 6th in plate appearances (691), games played and errors at first base (7)
- Led the Astros in singles, sacrifice flies (9), strikeouts, pitches seen (2,745), games played, slugging percentage vs. lefthanded pitchers (.685), on-base percentage vs. left-handed pitchers (.459) and batting average on the road
- Led NL first basemen in home runs

Lance Berkman

2002 Season

Lance Berkman had another dazzling season, and was the Astros' lone consistent run producer early in the year. Only the fifth switch-hitter ever to hit 40 or more home runs in a season, Berkman also seemed to become more comfortable at his new home in center field. He was one of the team's ironmen, shrugging off minor knee and hamstring problems to register a team-high 158 games (tied with Jeff Bagwell). He hit his 100th homer in his 452nd game as an Astro, becoming the fastest in club history to reach that plateau.

Hitting

Berkman is so intense and such a good athlete that he seems to adjust almost effortlessly to all changes. He was moved into the No. 3 spot (from No. 4) early by manager Jimy Williams, and responded immediately. Berkman's only problem last season was a lower batting average, as he finished 39 points below his phenomenal 2001 season. That seemed the result of an old dilemma: trouble hitting from the right side. His overall power numbers didn't suffer, however, leaving observers to wonder what he might do if he gets his righthanded hitting going again.

Baserunning & Defense

Berkman's basestealing improved last season, as he seemed to take a cue from Bagwell and pick his spots well. He stole eight of 12 and never will be a big threat, but his baserunning also seemed to improve. He has good speed and a quick first step. He moved from left to center for most of the year and used his athleticism and speed to make some sparkling over-the-shoulder and diving catches. His arm is only average, but he has greatly improved his throws to the cutoff man.

2003 Outlook

The sky continues to be the limit for Berkman, who seems destined to be an annual MVP candidate. His future would be better in left field, but he's an adequate center fielder if the team doesn't trade for one. Never a power hitter from the right side, Berkman is likely to improve in that area, with the possibility of becoming a potential .300-50-150 man in the process.

Position: CF/LF/RF
Bats: B **Throws:** L
Ht: 6' 1" **Wt:** 220

Opening Day Age: 27
Born: 2/10/76 in Waco, TX
ML Seasons: 4

Overall Statistics

	G	AB	R	H	D	T	HR	RBI	SB	BB	SO	Avg	OBP	Slg
'02	158	578	106	169	35	2	42	128	8	107	118	.292	.405	.578
Car.	462	1601	302	487	120	8	101	336	26	267	333	.304	.406	.578

Where He Hits the Ball

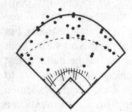 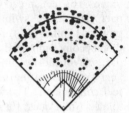

Vs. LHP **Vs. RHP**

2002 Situational Stats

	AB	H	HR	RBI	Avg		AB	H	HR	RBI	Avg
Home	294	94	20	61	.320	LHP	129	31	2	14	.240
Road	284	75	22	67	.264	RHP	449	138	40	114	.307
First Half	310	91	29	81	.294	Sc Pos	144	52	10	81	.361
Scnd Half	268	78	13	47	.291	Clutch	76	23	4	19	.303

2002 Rankings (National League)

- 1st in RBI
- 3rd in home runs, total bases (334), cleanup slugging percentage (.596), slugging percentage vs. righthanded pitchers (.639) and lowest fielding percentage in center field (.983)
- 4th in walks, plate appearances (692) and HR frequency (13.8 ABs per HR)
- Led the Astros in home runs, at-bats, runs scored, hits, total bases (334), RBI, walks, intentional walks (20), times on base (280), plate appearances (692), games played, slugging percentage, on-base percentage, HR frequency (13.8 ABs per HR) and highest percentage of pitches taken (57.5)

Craig Biggio

2002 Season

Craig Biggio had a nightmarish first half of the season by his own admission. He was beset by off-field personal tragedies, including the deaths of a close family friend and Darryl Kile. He seemed to pull out of it in July and August, but then had a disastrous .187 September to finish at .253, a full 35 points below his career average.

Hitting

Many thought Biggio's bat speed had slowed early in the season and questioned whether he was washed up. But a .330 mark in July seemed to belie that contention. His well-known ability to turn on inside pitches still seemed lacking all season, and his renowned hit-by-pitch total also was down to only 17. He hit a miserable .229 with men on third and only .270 with men in scoring position. His 58 total RBI also were below his career average. He seemed content at the No. 2 spot in the lineup, though the team never really found a true leadoff hitter to replace him.

Baserunning & Defense

Biggio still is not close to the basestealing threat he was before major knee surgery in 2000. But last season he showed a keener sense of picking his spots and successfully stole 16 of 18 attempts. His defense also is considerably more limited. His range is diminished, and he hasn't had a good double-play connection in three seasons. But his surehanded glovework continues to be consistent; his .988 fielding percentage was third-best among National League regulars at the keystone in 2002.

2003 Outlook

After Biggio played in a club-record 15th season last year, Biggio is at a crossroads in his career. In the offseason, the club declined to rework his contract, which is up after this season. The Astros seemed to be sending a clear message that they want to know if he still has it. If Biggio doesn't bounce back with a big season, many observers wonder if the 2003 campaign will be his last.

Position: 2B
Bats: R **Throws:** R
Ht: 5'11" **Wt:** 185

Opening Day Age: 37
Born: 12/14/65 in Smithtown, NY
ML Seasons: 15
Pronunciation: BIDG-ee-oh

Overall Statistics

G	AB	R	H	D	T	HR	RBI	SB	BB	SO	Avg	OBP	Slg
145	577	96	146	36	3	15	58	16	50	111	.253	.330	.404
2100	7960	1401	2295	473	49	195	869	381	963	1257	.288	.377	.434

Where He Hits the Ball

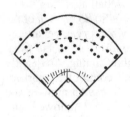 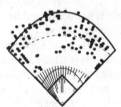

Vs. LHP	**Vs. RHP**

2002 Situational Stats

	AB	H	HR	RBI	Avg		AB	H	HR	RBI	Avg
Home	300	82	7	33	.273	LHP	115	21	2	8	.183
Road	277	64	8	25	.231	RHP	462	125	13	50	.271
First Half	309	78	7	33	.252	Sc Pos	122	33	2	42	.270
Scnd Half	268	68	8	25	.254	Clutch	76	24	2	15	.316

2002 Rankings (National League)

- 2nd in lowest batting average vs. lefthanded pitchers
- 3rd in hit by pitch (17) and fielding percentage at second base (.988)
- 6th in lowest slugging percentage vs. left-handed pitchers (.270)
- 7th in lowest batting average on the road
- 8th in lowest on-base percentage for a leadoff hitter (.313)
- 9th in errors at second base (8)
- Led the Astros in doubles, sacrifice bunts (9), stolen bases, hit by pitch (17), stolen-base percentage (88.9), bunts in play (12), steals of third (2) and highest percentage of extra bases taken as a runner (59.6)

Octavio Dotel

Position: RP
Bats: R **Throws:** R
Ht: 6' 0" **Wt:** 200

Opening Day Age: 29
Born: 11/25/73 in
Santo Domingo, DR
ML Seasons: 4
Pronunciation:
dough-TEL

2002 Season

Many thought Octavio Dotel was the best reliever in all of baseball last year, and his stats were startling. He was second in the majors in relief innings pitched (97.1) and first in relief strikeouts (118). At times he was overpowering, like in the month of August when he allowed only one earned run in 18 innings. He also led the team with a 1.85 ERA. Once an unwilling reliever, Dotel seemed to embrace the role last year and was a dominating setup man for Billy Wagner. Their 1-2 combination was one of the best in baseball.

Pitching

Dotel has an exploding fastball that hits 96-98 MPH regularly, and he uses it 80-85 percent of the time. It often rises, and few hitters can get around on it. He seemed more comfortable in his usual role of pitching the eighth inning, frequently going three-and-out. Dotel's control was markedly better last season, and that gave him more and more confidence in his fastball. He allowed only 27 walks, with only two wild pitches. He got away from his curve in favor of the slider, though the team would like to see him use both pitches. While he was caught off-guard when occasionally asked to close, he still was successful in six of 10 save situations.

Defense & Hitting

Dotel has good quickness off the mound to cover first and field bunts. But because he strikes out so many hitters, he has few chances to prove his prowess in the field. He does not pay much attention to the running game and his hitting never was a strong suit, but neither are much of a factor in his current role.

2003 Outlook

The Astros are grooming Dotel to someday be Wagner's successor as a closer, and they think he will be one of the game's best when it happens. For now, he's content to fill the setup role and step in with an occasional save appearance. The righty-lefty combination of Dotel and Wagner in the final two innings of games is proving to be increasingly unbeatable.

Overall Statistics

	W	L	Pct.	ERA	G	GS	Sv	IP	H	BB	SO	HR	Ratio
'02	6	4	.600	1.85	83	0	6	97.1	58	27	118	7	0.87
Car.	24	19	.558	3.86	213	34	24	412.2	333	184	490	50	1.25

How Often He Throws Strikes

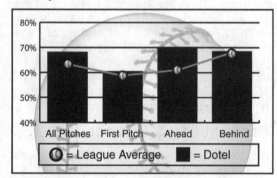

2002 Situational Stats

	W	L	ERA	Sv	IP		AB	H	HR	RBI	Avg
Home	5	1	1.53	5	53.0	LHB	153	29	2	10	.190
Road	1	3	2.23	1	44.1	RHB	182	29	5	18	.159
First Half	5	3	2.48	2	54.1	Sc Pos	75	11	2	22	.147
Scnd Half	1	1	1.05	4	43.0	Clutch	231	42	5	22	.182

2002 Rankings (National League)

- 1st in lowest batting average allowed in relief (.173)
- 2nd in games pitched, holds (31), relief innings (97.1), most strikeouts per nine innings in relief (10.9) and fewest baserunners allowed per nine innings in relief (8.2)
- 4th in lowest batting average allowed vs. left-handed batters and relief ERA (1.85)
- Led the Astros in ERA, games pitched, holds (31), highest strikeout-walk ratio (4.4), lowest batting average allowed (.173), lowest slugging percentage allowed (.275), lowest on-base percentage allowed (.239) and lowest ERA at home

Richard Hidalgo

2002 Season

Things went from bad in 2001 to worse last season to even *worse* in the offseason. Richard Hidalgo returned home to Venezuela and was shot in the left arm during an attempted car-jacking in November. The on-field problems last year reached such proportions that he finally was platooned with Orlando Merced, something Hidalgo didn't take well. He had a postgame chair-throwing tirade in the locker room, and suggested after the season that a trade may benefit him. He struggled to a .235 average and has had only 34 home runs and 128 RBI combined the last two years since signing a $32 million, four-year contract.

Hitting

When he stays back and waits on pitches, Hidalgo shows flashes of his ability. But he usually regresses to lunging and pulling the ball down the left-field line. His impatience led to 85 strikeouts and only 43 walks in 2002. Hidalgo had a few stretches when it appeared he might come out of his two-year long slump, but they never lasted. He then hit .149 in July and August combined, and finally went on the disabled list with a strained right hip. He appeared only twice after returning September 9, as team officials thought he was hopelessly locked in a downward spiral.

Baserunning & Defense

Hidalgo has lost the speed that once made him a good baserunner, a modest basestealing threat and a much better outfielder. Whether he has too much weight or has lost flexibility through too much weightlifting (which the club believes), the fact remains that he has slowed considerably both on the basepaths and in the field. He still has a remarkable arm that few teams ever challenge.

2003 Outlook

With $22 million left in the last two years of the back-loaded contract, Hidalgo has become almost untradable. The problems with the offseason shooting also could affect him this season, as doctors are uncertain how he will come back from some nerve damage in the left arm. The Astros have few options other than to continue to platoon Hidalgo, and hope he finally returns to his 2000 form.

Position: RF
Bats: R **Throws:** R
Ht: 6' 3" **Wt:** 220

Opening Day Age: 27
Born: 7/2/75 in Caracas, VZ
ML Seasons: 6
Pronunciation: HUH-dahl-go

Overall Statistics

	G	AB	R	H	D	T	HR	RBI	SB	BB	SO	Avg	OBP	Slg
'02	114	388	54	91	17	4	15	48	6	43	85	.235	.319	.415
Car.	614	2114	330	577	133	12	102	347	34	230	430	.273	.353	.492

Where He Hits the Ball

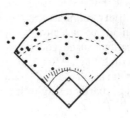 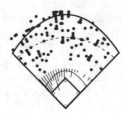

Vs. LHP   **Vs. RHP**

2002 Situational Stats

	AB	H	HR	RBI	Avg		AB	H	HR	RBI	Avg
Home	182	46	4	24	.253	LHP	76	20	3	11	.263
Road	206	45	11	24	.218	RHP	312	71	12	37	.228
First Half	293	76	13	42	.259	Sc Pos	115	27	1	32	.235
Scnd Half	95	15	2	6	.158	Clutch	57	12	4	12	.211

2002 Rankings (National League)

- 1st in fielding percentage in right field (.995)
- 3rd in lowest batting average on an 0-2 count (.043)
- 9th in lowest batting average with two strikes (.148)
- Led the Astros in triples and steals of third (2)

Julio Lugo

2002 Season

Julio Lugo had another enigmatic season in the field and at the plate, but team officials seemed satisfied. Bothered by a sore shoulder, he had a lackluster spring and lost the starting job to slick-fielding Adam Everett. But after Everett couldn't hit, Lugo stepped in and initially was impressive, hitting .319 in May. But he cooled off and finished at .261 before having his season cut short when he broke his forearm when hit by a pitch August 12.

Hitting

Lugo is a streaky hitter who falls into bad habits and can have horrendous stretches, as he did in June when he hit .197. He has very good bat speed, but his lack of selectivity still is a problem. He walked only 28 times in 322 at-bats and struck out 74 times. He has excellent speed and occasionally will get on with a drag bunt. After a long stretch without a home run, he also regained some pop in his bat, though he's primarily a singles hitter to all fields.

Baserunning & Defense

The Astros would love to let Lugo lead off permanently, but he has not shown the patience at the plate or the consistency to stay there. Despite his speed, he also has failed to show good decision making on the basepaths. His defense improved in 2002, as he led National League shortstops who logged at least 600 innings in fewest errors. But that statistic is a bit misleading because Lugo still had trouble turning the double play and his range is average at best.

2003 Outlook

Astros officials seem committed to Lugo remaining the team's shortstop for the moment, if not the future. Everett still has the latter tag if he can ever hit better than his slight weight. For now, Lugo likely will start at short since he's inexpensive, young and improving. When Everett is ready, Lugo probably will become a utility infielder who occasionally spends some time in the outfield.

Position: SS
Bats: R **Throws:** R
Ht: 6' 1"   **Wt:** 170

Opening Day Age: 27
Born: 11/16/75 in Barahona, DR
ML Seasons: 3

Overall Statistics

	G	AB	R	H	D	T	HR	RBI	SB	BB	SO	Avg	OBP	Slg
'02	88	322	45	84	15	1	8	35	9	28	74	.261	.322	.388
Car.	344	1255	216	338	57	9	28	112	43	111	283	.269	.332	.396

Where He Hits the Ball

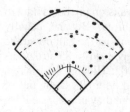
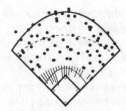

Vs. LHP   **Vs. RHP**

2002 Situational Stats

	AB	H	HR	RBI	Avg		AB	H	HR	RBI	Avg
Home	172	53	6	22	.308	LHP	74	20	3	10	.270
Road	150	31	2	13	.207	RHP	248	64	5	25	.258
First Half	212	55	4	21	.259	Sc Pos	68	22	2	26	.324
Scnd Half	110	29	4	14	.264	Clutch	44	10	0	2	.227

2002 Rankings (National League)

- 7th in lowest on-base percentage for a leadoff hitter (.311)
- Led the Astros in most pitches seen per plate appearance (4.04) and bunts in play (12)

Wade Miller

2002 Season

On many staffs, Wade Miller would be the ace. But on a staff with Roy Oswalt, Miller had to settle for second billing. After a pinched nerve in his neck forced him onto the disabled list for six weeks early in the year, Miller came back to have a superb season, winning 12 straight decisions from July through September. He was the Opening Day starter, but struggled early. His absence, coupled with a slumping Jeff Bagwell, were largely the reasons the Astros got off to such a slow start in April and May.

Pitching

Miller throws a four-seam fastball that has good late movement. His fastball tops out at 95-96 MPH, and his two-seam sinker is equally effective. He has a good slider and curve, both of which team officials hope he will use more in the future. He also shows a decent changeup, and he toyed with a split-finger last season. Miller is a heady pitcher who can fall into trouble with his complicated mechanics when he thinks too much. Fortunately for the Astros, he usually can solve the problem during a game and will overcome poor first innings with strong seven- and eight-inning stints. He is a workhorse who pitched seven innings or more in 14 of his 26 starts, including 10 of his last 13. The Astros love his competitiveness.

Defense & Hitting

Miller is an athletic player who is becoming a better fielder, although he still needs to improve with the glove. Miller's pickoff move is average, though opposing basestealers have been successful against him less than 50 percent of the time over the past two years. His hitting also is slowly improving, but he rarely will help his own cause. He is a reliable bunter, however.

2003 Outlook

Oswalt and Miller became one of the top 1-2 starting-pitching tandems in the majors at the end of last year, and they likely will only get better. Miller seems destined for real stardom, and if he has another big year, the Astros will be hard-pressed to sign him when he becomes eligible for arbitration.

Position: SP
Bats: R **Throws:** R
Ht: 6' 2" **Wt:** 210

Opening Day Age: 26
Born: 9/13/76 in Reading, PA
ML Seasons: 4

Overall Statistics

	W	L	Pct.	ERA	G	GS	Sv	IP	H	BB	SO	HR	Ratio
'02	15	4	.789	3.28	26	26	0	164.2	151	62	144	14	1.29
Car.	37	19	.661	3.86	79	75	0	492.0	455	185	424	63	1.30

How Often He Throws Strikes

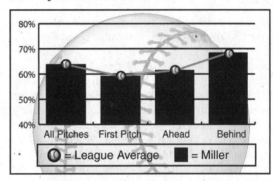

= League Average ■ = Miller

2002 Situational Stats

	W	L	ERA	Sv	IP		AB	H	HR	RBI	Avg
Home	8	2	3.53	0	86.2	LHB	260	66	8	25	.254
Road	7	2	3.00	0	78.0	RHB	347	85	6	33	.245
First Half	4	3	5.43	0	61.1	Sc Pos	153	38	5	48	.248
Scnd Half	11	1	2.00	0	103.1	Clutch	23	6	0	2	.261

2002 Rankings (National League)

- 2nd in winning percentage
- 3rd in most run support per nine innings (6.1)
- 10th in wins and most strikeouts per nine innings (7.9)
- Led the Astros in walks allowed, hit batsmen (6), winning percentage, lowest ERA on the road and most run support per nine innings (6.1)

Roy Oswalt

2002 Season

For much of the 2002 season, Roy Oswalt was one of the league's premier pitchers as he raced to 19 victories and amassed 208 strikeouts. He won a club record nine consecutive starts from July through early September and at times was dominating. He worked at least six innings in 31 of his 34 starts, though manager Jimy Williams' insistence on saving Oswalt's arm for the latter part of the season kept him from getting a single complete game, after he led the Astros with three in 2001. The only chink in the armour was Oswalt's failure to win No. 20 in his final four starts.

Pitching

Oswalt seems to be a pitcher destined for at least one Cy Young Award, if not many. He throws a mesmerizing variety of pitches, all with pinpoint control, and moves those offerings all around the plate. Oswalt's four-seam fastball normally runs 94-95 MPH and tops out at 97. He sets hitters up with it, and then comes back with a devastating curve that goes 73-74 MPH and has a very late break. He occasionally used an effective slider against some teams, and his changeup also is good. Oswalt usually has a strong idea of what he wants to do with a team and needs little direction from behind the plate.

Defense & Hitting

Oswalt is an intense player who doesn't tolerate poor performance in any area of his game. Thus, when he had trouble getting bunts down early in the year, he took extra batting practice for weeks until he worked out the problem. He's the same about defense; he is adept at fielding bunts and throwing runners out.

2003 Outlook

The Astros expect this to be the year Oswalt becomes the toast of the league, if not the majors. Officials say his only drawback is that sometimes he is too competitive and lets it work on his mind when he isn't perfect. Along with Wade Miller, Oswalt gives the Astros a 1-2 tandem that could become the rival of Arizona's devastating Randy Johnson-Curt Schilling combination.

Position: SP
Bats: R **Throws:** R
Ht: 6' 0" **Wt:** 175

Opening Day Age: 25
Born: 8/29/77 in Kosciusko, MS
ML Seasons: 2
Pronunciation: OH-swalt

Overall Statistics

	W	L	Pct.	ERA	G	GS	Sv	IP	H	BB	SO	HR	Ratio
'02	19	9	.679	3.01	35	34	0	233.0	215	62	208	17	1.19
Car.	33	12	.733	2.91	63	54	0	374.2	341	86	352	30	1.14

How Often He Throws Strikes

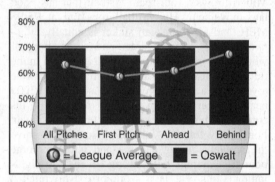

2002 Situational Stats

	W	L	ERA	Sv	IP		AB	H	HR	RBI	Avg
Home	9	4	2.70	0	110.0	LHB	390	98	11	37	.251
Road	10	5	3.29	0	123.0	RHB	480	117	6	42	.244
First Half	9	5	3.35	0	123.2	Sc Pos	214	48	5	61	.224
Scnd Half	10	4	2.63	0	109.1	Clutch	59	16	1	5	.271

2002 Rankings (National League)

- 3rd in wins and innings pitched
- 4th in games started and batters faced (956)
- 5th in ERA, strikeouts, highest strikeout-walk ratio (3.4) and fewest home runs allowed per nine innings (.66)
- 6th in lowest ERA at home
- 8th in lowest on-base percentage allowed (.299) and most strikeouts per nine innings (8.0)
- Led the Astros in wins, games started, innings pitched, hits allowed, batters faced (956), home runs allowed, walks allowed, strikeouts, pitches thrown (3,420), pickoff throws (77), runners caught stealing (7) and GDPs induced (22)

Jose Vizcaino

2002 Season

Jose Vizcaino had perhaps his finest season as a utility infielder and, like Orlando Merced, the team rewarded Vizcaino with a late-season, one-year extension. He appeared in 125 games, starting 90 of those contests at four different infield positions, and his career high-tying .303 batting average was the only .300-plus mark on the team. Vizcaino also tied a career high with five homers, including two game-winners. After he signed the extension, he said it invigorated him, and he hit .351 in August.

Hitting

Vizcaino nearly always gets his bat on the ball, striking out only 40 times in 406 at-bats. He sprays his singles to all fields, but his few extra-base hits go almost exclusively to right. He does not hit many homers, but he hits to the opposite field and behind the runner very well. He's also an adept bunter and an excellent pinch-hitter, going 8-for-23 in that role in 2002. A switch-hitter, Vizcaino was consistent both ways, hitting .337 righthanded and .292 as a lefty. He frequently works the count in his favor and was a clutch hitter all season, batting .333 with runners in scoring position, including a .419 showing with a runner on third.

Baserunning & Defense

Vizcaino has only average speed, but he often makes up for it with his savvy, boyish enthusiasm and hustle. He'll never be a basestealer, however. His defense is not spectacular and he doesn't have great range, but he is steady and makes most of the plays you would expect him to make. Vizcaino committed only four errors while playing all four infield positions last season.

2003 Outlook

Astros officials consider Vizcaino the ultimate utility infielder and team player. He made a bid for everyday play last season with his strong showing at the plate, but he probably never will play on a full-time basis because of his average fielding ability and special value as a sub at all four infield spots.

Position: SS/3B/2B
Bats: B **Throws:** R
Ht: 6' 1" **Wt:** 185

Opening Day Age: 35
Born: 3/26/68 in San Cristobal, DR
ML Seasons: 14
Pronunciation: vis-kie-e-no

Overall Statistics

	G	AB	R	H	D	T	HR	RBI	SB	BB	SO	Avg	OBP	Slg
'02	125	406	53	123	19	2	5	37	3	24	40	.303	.342	.397
Car.	1413	4503	551	1229	160	39	27	390	71	318	614	.273	.321	.344

Where He Hits the Ball

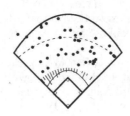

Vs. LHP   **Vs. RHP**

2002 Situational Stats

	AB	H	HR	RBI	Avg		AB	H	HR	RBI	Avg
Home	199	69	4	26	.347	LHP	101	34	1	17	.337
Road	207	54	1	11	.261	RHP	305	89	4	20	.292
First Half	177	54	1	16	.305	Sc Pos	90	30	1	33	.333
Scnd Half	229	69	4	21	.301	Clutch	69	26	2	9	.377

2002 Rankings (National League)

- 1st in batting average on an 0-2 count (.333), batting average on a 3-2 count (.387) and lowest batting average on a 3-1 count (.000)
- 3rd in batting average in the clutch
- 5th in batting average with two strikes (.269)
- 9th in lowest percentage of pitches taken (47.5)
- Led the Astros in batting average, caught stealing (5), lowest percentage of swings that missed (11.5), batting average in the clutch, batting average vs. lefthanded pitchers, batting average on an 0-2 count (.333), on-base percentage for a leadoff hitter (.339), batting average at home, batting average on a 3-2 count (.387) and batting average with two strikes (.269)

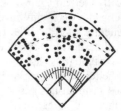

Billy Wagner

Position: RP
Bats: L **Throws:** L
Ht: 5'11" **Wt:** 195

Opening Day Age: 31
Born: 7/25/71 in
Tannersville, VA
ML Seasons: 8

2002 Season

Considering his slow start, Billy Wagner's final saves total of 35 was remarkable. The bad start was caused by a paucity of save opportunities. Wagner had only nine chances in the first two months of the season, and he went into the All-Star break with only 14 saves in 17 opportunities. When the team picked up steam, Wagner was his old reliable self, reaching the 30-save mark for the fourth time in his career. Though his six blown saves were the most he has had in a non-injury season, he still turned in his second straight sterling campaign since his elbow surgery in 2000.

Pitching

Billy the Kid again was a feared closer who challenged hitters with his explosive fastball that frequently hit 100 MPH. He did use his curve more, and he developed a slider that was highly effective, though he still didn't use it often. Wagner did a better job of working both sides of the plate with his fastball, and his 88 strikeouts were his most since his career-high 124 whiffs in 1999. But Wagner was troubled by the six blown saves and a career-high seven home runs allowed.

Defense & Hitting

It's hard to say what Wagner's defense is like, since most of his outs come on either strikeouts or flyballs. In eight seasons, he has 51 total fielding chances and only three errors. The same can be said of his hitting. He's had 13 career at-bats, with a lone hit that came in 1998. Opposing basestealers don't get much of a chance to test Wagner, but the Houston closer did register a career-best two pickoffs last year.

2003 Outlook

Wagner shows no signs of slowing down, and he likely will surpass Dave Smith's club career saves mark of 199 by midseason. The Astros want Wagner to continue to expand the use of his slider, which they believe makes his 100-MPH fastball look like it's 105 MPH. If he gets the chances in 2003, reaching the 40-save mark for the first time in his career should be a given.

Overall Statistics

	W	L	Pct.	ERA	G	GS	Sv	IP	H	BB	SO	HR	Ratio
'02	4	2	.667	2.52	70	0	35	75.0	51	22	88	7	0.97
Car.	25	25	.500	2.69	386	0	181	418.1	281	168	589	40	1.07

How Often He Throws Strikes

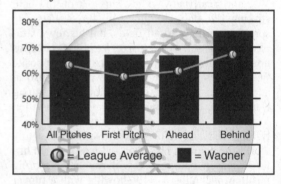

= League Average   = Wagner

2002 Situational Stats

	W	L	ERA	Sv	IP		AB	H	HR	RBI	Avg
Home	3	2	2.91	17	43.1	LHB	61	11	1	4	.180
Road	1	0	1.99	18	31.2	RHB	199	40	6	18	.201
First Half	2	1	2.93	14	40.0	Sc Pos	58	12	2	16	.207
Scnd Half	2	1	2.06	21	35.0	Clutch	168	36	6	18	.214

2002 Rankings (National League)

- 3rd in most strikeouts per nine innings in relief (10.6)
- 5th in fewest baserunners allowed per nine innings in relief (9.0)
- 6th in lowest save percentage (85.4)
- 7th in games finished (61), blown saves (6) and lowest batting average allowed in relief (.196)
- 8th in save opportunities (41)
- 9th in saves
- Led the Astros in saves, games finished (61), wild pitches (6), save opportunities (41), save percentage (85.4) and blown saves (6)

Daryle Ward

2002 Season

Daryle Ward was the Astros' biggest disappointment in 2002, but that was at least in part due to the fact that he was trying to replace perennial All-Star Moises Alou. Ward had shown promise as a power hitter early in his career, so his 12 home runs last season that accompanied a pedestrian 72 RBI were considered a huge bust. After hitting two homers his first six games, including a walkoff game-winner, his power disappeared. He didn't have a single home run between April 7 and June 25.

Hitting

Ward has long been predicted for stardom, so many observers were stunned as he struggled most of the year. He is a student of the game who teammates say has the most close-to-perfect swing on the team. Ward also studies pitchers' tendencies and meticulously works out any hitches in his swing. All that didn't help last season, however. Ward actually hit for average much of the year, but at the No. 5 spot in the lineup, he was needed as a run-producer. And when he finally did start hitting a few homers, his average fell.

Baserunning & Defense

Ward has battled a weight problem most of his adult life, and it severely affects his baserunning and defense. He is the team's worst baserunner and one of the worst in the league. The balls he can get to he handles well, but he doesn't cover much ground in left field. He would be less of a liability of he could play his original position, first base, but that won't happen in Houston as long as the Astros have Jeff Bagwell, as well as another ex-first baseman in Lance Berkman.

2003 Outlook

The Astros say they haven't given up on Ward, and he insists he has his problems worked out. Ward said he was pressing early when he was trying to learn to play every day, and he believes he can turn his fortunes around this season. He'll be given a chance early, but with promising minor leaguer Jason Lane in the wings, Ward better improve quickly.

Position: LF
Bats: L **Throws:** L
Ht: 6' 2" **Wt:** 240

Opening Day Age: 27
Born: 6/27/75 in Lynwood, CA
ML Seasons: 5

Overall Statistics

	G	AB	R	H	D	T	HR	RBI	SB	BB	SO	Avg	OBP	Slg
'02	136	453	41	125	31	0	12	72	1	33	82	.276	.324	.424
Car.	418	1083	110	291	62	2	49	188	1	77	224	.269	.316	.465

Where He Hits the Ball

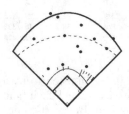 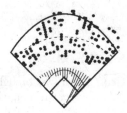

Vs. LHP **Vs. RHP**

2002 Situational Stats

	AB	H	HR	RBI	Avg		AB	H	HR	RBI	Avg
Home	227	62	9	44	.273	LHP	54	11	1	7	.204
Road	226	63	3	28	.279	RHP	399	114	11	65	.286
First Half	270	74	4	34	.274	Sc Pos	128	40	4	58	.313
Scnd Half	183	51	8	38	.279	Clutch	67	16	2	4	.239

2002 Rankings (National League)

- 3rd in assists in left field (9)
- 4th in fielding percentage in left field (.981)
- Led the Astros in batting average with the bases loaded (.467)

Geoff Blum

Position: 3B
Bats: B **Throws:** R
Ht: 6' 3" **Wt:** 200

Opening Day Age: 29
Born: 4/26/73 in
Redwood City, CA
ML Seasons: 4

Overall Statistics

	G	AB	R	H	D	T	HR	RBI	SB	BB	SO	Avg	OBP	Slg
'02	130	368	45	104	20	4	10	52	2	49	70	.283	.367	.440
Car.	447	1297	163	340	72	8	38	165	13	135	249	.262	.336	.418

2002 Situational Stats

	AB	H	HR	RBI	Avg		AB	H	HR	RBI	Avg
Home	163	50	6	28	.307	LHP	65	12	1	6	.185
Road	205	54	4	24	.263	RHP	303	92	9	46	.304
First Half	179	48	3	22	.268	Sc Pos	96	32	5	45	.333
Scnd Half	189	56	7	30	.296	Clutch	60	13	1	5	.217

2002 Season

Geoff Blum was brought in by Houston to be a utility player who could be used around the infield and occasionally in the outfield. But by the middle of the summer, he began to show surprising consistency at the plate and in the field. By season's end, Blum proved to be the best third baseman the team has had in years.

Hitting, Baserunning & Defense

Blum hit .283 and had a career high 52 RBI while also starting 91 games at third. He had his worst season at the plate from the right side, hitting only .185, but he produce a .304 mark from the left. He hit .296 after the All-Star break and impressed team officials with his ability to start the double play. He has average speed makes him nothing more than a modest basestealing threat.

2003 Outlook

The Astros still want Morgan Ensberg, the Opening Day starter at third in 2002, to live up to his considerable potential, and when he does, Blum will be back to a utility role. But officials still liked what they saw from Blum, and were particularly surprised with his glovework. A rough showing in right field notwithstanding, Blum is considered a versatile player who can fill in at a lot of different spots.

Flash Gordon

Position: RP
Bats: R **Throws:** R
Ht: 5'10" **Wt:** 190

Opening Day Age: 35
Born: 11/18/67 in
Sebring, FL
ML Seasons: 14
Nickname: Flash

Overall Statistics

	W	L	Pct.	ERA	G	GS	Sv	IP	H	BB	SO	HR	Ratio
'02	1	3	.250	3.38	34	0	0	42.2	42	16	48	3	1.36
Car.	106	101	.512	4.11	525	203	98	1733.0	1590	839	1546	140	1.40

2002 Situational Stats

	W	L	ERA	Sv	IP		AB	H	HR	RBI	Avg
Home	1	3	2.81	0	25.2	LHB	67	18	2	11	.269
Road	0	0	4.24	0	17.0	RHB	94	24	1	8	.255
First Half	0	0	0.00	0	2.2	Sc Pos	41	12	1	14	.293
Scnd Half	1	3	3.60	0	40.0	Clutch	77	24	1	10	.312

2002 Season

It was largely a lost season for Tom "Flash" Gordon after he tore a muscle in his shoulder in spring training with the Cubs. He was on the disabled list for more than three months. When he returned, he had a respectable 3.42 ERA in 19 appearances with Chicago before being traded to the Astros. His stay with Houston was similar, with a 3.32 ERA in 15 appearances. An effective closer in 2001, he didn't get to close in 2002 and had no saves all season.

Pitching, Defense & Hitting

In his 14th season, Gordon still had a serviceable fastball that topped out at 94 MPH. His best pitch is an overhand curve, and it's still one of the better ones in the league. His downfall is that hitters get plenty of chances to steal on him because he throws that curve so often. With such little time on the mound, he had few chances to show his capable fielding abilities. He has just one career at-bat.

2003 Outlook

Gordon's health continues to be an issue, although he appears fully recovered from the Tommy John surgery he had in 1999. Many still believe he can be an effective closer, the role Gordon relishes, but he won't get any save opportunities in Houston.

Carlos Hernandez

Position: SP
Bats: B **Throws:** L
Ht: 5'10" **Wt:** 185

Opening Day Age: 22
Born: 4/22/80 in
Guacara, VZ
ML Seasons: 2

Overall Statistics

	W	L	Pct.	ERA	G	GS	Sv	IP	H	BB	SO	HR	Ratio
'02	7	5	.583	4.38	23	21	0	111.0	112	61	93	11	1.56
Car.	8	5	.615	3.92	26	24	0	128.2	123	68	110	12	1.48

2002 Situational Stats

	W	L	ERA	Sv	IP		AB	H	HR	RBI	Avg
Home	3	2	4.66	0	56.0	LHB	84	22	2	10	.262
Road	4	3	4.09	0	55.0	RHB	345	90	9	33	.261
First Half	5	4	5.01	0	82.2	Sc Pos	114	25	2	30	.219
Scnd Half	2	1	2.54	0	28.1	Clutch	10	4	0	1	.400

2002 Season

The once-promising future Carlos Hernandez appeared to have became clouded last season, as he never totally shook the left shoulder problems stemming from a 2001 baserunning injury. He spent a month and a half on the DL last season and didn't pitch the final two weeks of the year.

Pitching, Defense & Hitting

Hernandez has put off surgery and repeatedly tried rehab, which hasn't worked so far. His best pitches are a sharp-breaking curve and changeup, and last year he also developed a good slider-cutter. But his velocity dropped from the 91-93 MPH range the year before to 88-90 last year. Shoulder difficulty also made him open up his delivery, leading to control problems. Hernandez can hold his own with the bat and glove, and he is perfect in 32 career chances in the field.

2003 Outlook

Hernandez spent most of the offseason in his home country of Venezuela, rehabbing the shoulder and lifting weights to strengthen it, and rarely throwing at all. Team officials say he's young and has yet to learn to pitch with pain. If he can't, surgery ultimately might be the only answer. The Astros badly need him to fill a spot in the rotation, and he'll be given every chance to do so.

Brian Hunter

Position: CF
Bats: R **Throws:** R
Ht: 6' 3" **Wt:** 180

Opening Day Age: 32
Born: 3/25/71 in
Portland, OR
ML Seasons: 9

Overall Statistics

	G	AB	R	H	D	T	HR	RBI	SB	BB	SO	Avg	OBP	Slg
'02	98	201	32	54	16	3	3	20	5	16	39	.269	.329	.423
Car.	944	3249	487	859	140	27	25	228	260	237	560	.264	.314	.347

2002 Situational Stats

	AB	H	HR	RBI	Avg		AB	H	HR	RBI	Avg
Home	100	26	0	7	.260	LHP	108	26	1	12	.241
Road	101	28	3	13	.277	RHP	93	28	2	8	.301
First Half	94	27	1	7	.287	Sc Pos	53	15	0	15	.283
Scnd Half	107	27	2	13	.252	Clutch	31	8	0	1	.258

2002 Season

Brian Hunter was one of the team's best offseason acquisitions until he had a surprising campaign derailed in mid-July by an appendectomy. He was hitting nearly 25 points above his career .264 average in spot starts and frequent late-inning appearances when he had the surgery, then managed to hit only .252 after he returned five weeks later.

Hitting, Baserunning & Defense

Hunter is a singles hitter who has excellent speed. His performance at the plate the first three months had him playing more before the surgery, though he still struck out too much and didn't walk enough. He can steal bases, but knee problems the last three seasons and difficulties reaching base have limited his playing time and his basestealing totals. The 1999 AL stolen-base champion with 44, he had only five last season. For the Astros, Hunter was used mostly as a late-inning defensive replacement in center field, where he made a number of eye-catching plays last year.

2003 Outlook

Hunter is signed through this season, and the Astros would like to see more of his defensive abilities in late innings. But he's not likely to garner much additional playing time unless he shows more patience at the plate.

Houston

Mark Loretta

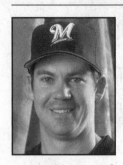

Position: 3B/SS
Bats: R **Throws:** R
Ht: 6' 0" **Wt:** 186

Opening Day Age: 31
Born: 8/14/71 in Santa Monica, CA
ML Seasons: 8

Overall Statistics

	G	AB	R	H	D	T	HR	RBI	SB	BB	SO	Avg	OBP	Slg
'02	107	283	33	86	18	0	4	27	1	32	37	.304	.381	.410
Car.	817	2662	359	779	139	13	31	280	23	256	309	.293	.359	.390

2002 Situational Stats

	AB	H	HR	RBI	Avg		AB	H	HR	RBI	Avg
Home	139	41	2	16	.295	LHP	94	29	2	8	.309
Road	144	45	2	11	.313	RHP	189	57	2	19	.302
First Half	100	27	0	8	.270	Sc Pos	55	21	1	22	.382
Scnd Half	183	59	4	19	.322	Clutch	43	13	0	5	.302

2002 Season

Mark Loretta was brought in late in the season after Julio Lugo broke his arm, and Loretta made an immediate impact. He seemed rejuvenated coming to a team in a division race and hit a whopping .424 in 21 games with Houston. He had hit only .267 with the Brewers. He also looked good in the field for Houston, playing second, short and third, and showing the versatility and consistency the Astros liked.

Hitting, Baserunning & Defense

Loretta is a contact hitter who complemented the Astros lineup of power hitters and free swingers. He hits line drives all over the park, moves runners over and is a good bunter. Defensively he has superb hands and a good arm though only average range at short, but his ability to play any infield position is special. He has moderate speed at best and is no basestealing threat.

2003 Outlook

Though the Astros loved the way he played in his short stint, Loretta is not likely to be back. Team officials still like Lugo's potential, and love his modest price tag. If his hamstring injury heals, Loretta wants to start wherever he is, something he likely wouldn't do with a healthy Lugo around. Besides, Loretta was beyond Houston's budget.

Orlando Merced

Position: RF/LF
Bats: L **Throws:** R
Ht: 6' 1" **Wt:** 195

Opening Day Age: 36
Born: 11/2/66 in San Juan, PR
ML Seasons: 12
Pronunciation: mer-SED

Overall Statistics

	G	AB	R	H	D	T	HR	RBI	SB	BB	SO	Avg	OBP	Slg
'02	123	251	35	72	13	3	6	30	4	26	50	.287	.350	.434
Car.	1268	3786	544	1059	212	26	100	559	54	472	628	.280	.359	.429

2002 Situational Stats

	AB	H	HR	RBI	Avg		AB	H	HR	RBI	Avg
Home	118	36	4	13	.305	LHP	39	9	2	6	.231
Road	133	36	2	17	.271	RHP	212	63	4	24	.297
First Half	91	29	4	16	.319	Sc Pos	77	24	3	27	.312
Scnd Half	160	43	2	14	.269	Clutch	54	16	0	2	.296

2002 Season

Orlando Merced was everything the Astros could have hoped for and more last season, and he earned a one-year contract extension in August as a reward. Merced didn't have the standout year as a pinch-hitter that he had in 2001, but he was even more valuable as a spot starter. He started 53 games at four positions—mostly right field—and appeared at seven different spots in the batting lineup in those games. He hit .293 in his 53 starts.

Hitting, Baserunning & Defense

Merced sprays the ball to all fields and has enough speed and savvy to stretch some singles to doubles. He went past the 1,000-hit plateau for his career in June, and more than 80 percent of those knocks have been against righthanders. That fact earned him the platoon job in right with Richard Hidalgo for much of the second half. Merced played mostly in right, but his versatility in the field makes him valuable in Houston.

2003 Outlook

If he can continue to hit against righties, Merced likely will platoon again with Hidalgo in right. But Merced's fate is tied directly to Hidalgo's performance. If Hidalgo recovers from an offseason shooting incident and rights himself again, Merced would go back to primarily pinch-hitting.

Dave Mlicki

Position: SP
Bats: R **Throws:** R
Ht: 6' 4" **Wt:** 200

Opening Day Age: 34
Born: 6/8/68 in Cleveland, OH
ML Seasons: 10
Pronunciation: muh-LICK-ee

Overall Statistics

	W	L	Pct.	ERA	G	GS	Sv	IP	H	BB	SO	HR	Ratio
'02	4	10	.286	5.34	22	16	0	86.0	101	34	57	11	1.57
Car.	66	80	.452	4.72	262	193	1	1232.2	1337	472	834	171	1.47

2002 Situational Stats

	W	L	ERA	Sv	IP		AB	H	HR	RBI	Avg
Home	2	6	5.30	0	52.2	LHB	148	52	5	23	.351
Road	2	4	5.40	0	33.1	RHB	200	49	6	24	.245
First Half	3	6	3.90	0	55.1	Sc Pos	85	25	2	32	.294
Scnd Half	1	4	7.92	0	30.2	Clutch	5	5	0	3	1.000

2002 Season

Dave Mlicki began 2002 with a strong April, but the season went downhill after that, including a two-month stint on the disabled list with strained rib muscles. He was 3-2 in his first five starts, then didn't win again until early August. Mlicki never regained his mechanics after the injury and eventually was sent to the bullpen.

Pitching, Defense & Hitting

Mlicki's slider has been his best pitch throughout his 10-year career, but it abandoned him most of last season. It once had a short, late break, and he could move it around confidently. Last season, he relied on his sinker and curve, but mostly looked lost much of the year after returning from the injury in late July. Mlicki is an athletic player who comes off the mound well, but he does little to control the running game. His career .125 batting average illustrates his weakness at the plate.

2003 Outlook

Mlicki came to the Astros in the 2000 change-of-scenery trade that gave him and Jose Lima new addresses. He had a decent 2001 while with the Astros, but he dropped off last year and Houston declined to re-sign him after the season. He does not like to relieve, but if his slider returns, that role might fit him better.

Shane Reynolds

Position: SP
Bats: R **Throws:** R
Ht: 6' 3" **Wt:** 215

Opening Day Age: 35
Born: 3/26/68 in Bastrop, LA
ML Seasons: 11

Overall Statistics

	W	L	Pct.	ERA	G	GS	Sv	IP	H	BB	SO	HR	Ratio
'02	3	6	.333	4.86	13	13	0	74.0	80	26	47	13	1.43
Car.	103	86	.545	3.95	274	248	0	1622.1	1738	358	1309	171	1.29

2002 Situational Stats

	W	L	ERA	Sv	IP		AB	H	HR	RBI	Avg
Home	1	2	4.45	0	30.1	LHB	109	28	2	9	.257
Road	2	4	5.15	0	43.2	RHB	183	52	11	29	.284
First Half	3	6	4.86	0	74.0	Sc Pos	73	16	4	27	.219
Scnd Half	0	0	—	0	0.0	Clutch	13	6	2	2	.462

2002 Season

Once the Astros' perennial Opening Day starter, Shane Reynolds finally succumbed to a degenerative disc problem in his back that had bothered him for more than a year. He had back surgery in June and missed the rest of the season. His 13 starts were a testament to his gritty determination, as he pitched in pain most of that time.

Pitching, Defense & Hitting

Reynolds is a cerebral pitcher who usually is effective even when he doesn't have his best stuff. He uses a sinker that runs 87-88 MPH to set up his specialty—a high-70s split-finger. He also has a very good curve. His strengths are that he has a confident plan at all times and moves the ball all over the strike zone with superb control. Reynolds is a competent hitter who can put one over the fence. He comes of the mound well to field bunts but never has been strong at covering first.

2003 Outlook

After the surgery, Reynolds worked obsessively to get back into shape, and doctors pronounced him healthy by November. The Astros didn't pick up an $8 million option for 2003, but he will return for his 12th season in Houston after signing a one-year incentive-laden deal that guarantees $1 million and could approach $7 million.

Houston

Kirk Saarloos

Position: SP
Bats: R **Throws:** R
Ht: 6' 0" **Wt:** 185

Opening Day Age: 23
Born: 5/23/79 in Long Beach, CA
ML Seasons: 1

Overall Statistics

	W	L	Pct.	ERA	G	GS	Sv	IP	H	BB	SO	HR	Ratio
'02	6	7	.462	6.01	17	17	0	85.1	100	27	54	12	1.49
Car.	6	7	.462	6.01	17	17	0	85.1	100	27	54	12	1.49

2002 Situational Stats

	W	L	ERA	Sv	IP		AB	H	HR	RBI	Avg
Home	3	3	5.84	0	37.0	LHB	143	43	8	23	.301
Road	3	4	6.14	0	48.1	RHB	189	57	4	26	.302
First Half	0	2	17.65	0	8.2	Sc Pos	77	26	1	35	.338
Scnd Half	6	5	4.70	0	76.2	Clutch	7	2	2	2	.286

2002 Season

Kirk Saarloos was a surprise to even be in the majors, since it was only his second year of pro ball. But after a dominating 10-game win streak at Double-A, the Astros called him up. He soon began to struggle, however, and was sent down to Triple-A for three weeks. When he returned, Saarloos was much more impressive, winning five straight during his first three weeks back.

Pitching, Defense & Hitting

Saarloos has been compared to one of his role models, Greg Maddux. He has the same approach, with an 86-MPH sinker that he uses to set up a daring changeup. Saarloos has a deceiving arm action with the latter pitch, making it look just like the sinker. But if his sinker doesn't stay down, he gets into trouble fast. When it sinks and he has good command, Saarloos drives hitters bonkers. He's a mediocre hitter who shows little potential. His fielding is better but still needs work.

2003 Outlook

The Astros like Saarloos' poise and makeup, and they think that if he can continue to improve his control and maintain his confidence, he can have long-term success. He'll be given every opportunity to make the rotation again this year, and could become a fixture at the back of it.

Ricky Stone

Position: RP
Bats: R **Throws:** R
Ht: 6' 1" **Wt:** 190

Opening Day Age: 28
Born: 2/28/75 in Hamilton, OH
ML Seasons: 2

Overall Statistics

	W	L	Pct.	ERA	G	GS	Sv	IP	H	BB	SO	HR	Ratio
'02	3	3	.500	3.61	78	0	1	77.1	78	34	63	9	1.45
Car.	3	3	.500	3.49	84	0	1	85.0	86	36	67	10	1.44

2002 Situational Stats

	W	L	ERA	Sv	IP		AB	H	HR	RBI	Avg
Home	3	0	3.23	0	39.0	LHB	80	23	5	14	.288
Road	0	3	3.99	1	38.1	RHB	213	55	4	34	.258
First Half	3	2	1.99	0	45.1	Sc Pos	93	25	3	36	.269
Scnd Half	0	1	5.91	1	32.0	Clutch	79	20	3	11	.253

2002 Season

After eight years in the minors, Ricky Stone came up and pitched effectively in late 2001 before becoming one of the team's biggest surprises last year. Stone started out brilliantly, fashioning a 1.69 ERA over his first 11 appearances, and he seemed to get stronger as he pitched. He had a 1.20 ERA in 14 appearances in June. But he tired, and after making his 62nd appearance on August 18, he gave up eight earned runs in his final 16 outings. He still set the Houston all-time rookie record for appearances with 78.

Pitching, Defense & Hitting

Stone has an ordinary fastball that tops out at 88 MPH that he uses to set up his excellent changeup and slider. His strength is locating the ball around the zone and changing speeds. The Astros love his poise, and they believe he can get out of most jams because of his composure. Stone is not particularly quick off the mound and still is looking for his first major league hit.

2003 Outlook

Stone will not overwhelm anyone with his velocity or stuff, but he's a good bet to be a part of the Astros' bullpen again in middle relief. He probably will be asked to eat up lots of innings in lots of short stints.

Other Houston Astros

Pedro Borbon (**Pos**: LHP, **Age**: 35)

	W	L	Pct.	ERA	G	GS	Sv	IP	H	BB	SO	HR	Ratio
'02	4	4	.500	5.36	72	0	1	50.1	53	25	50	10	1.55
Car.	16	15	.516	4.45	361	0	6	267.0	245	132	224	31	1.41

The Astros acquired Borbon last May in a trade with Toronto. He wound up pitching at least 70 games for the third time in the past four years. He continues to control lefthanded batters well. 2003 Outlook: B

Raul Chavez (**Pos**: C, **Age**: 30, **Bats**: R)

	G	AB	R	H	D	T	HR	RBI	SB	BB	SO	Avg	OBP	Slg
'02	2	4	1	1	1	0	0	0	0	1	0	.250	.500	.500
Car.	34	79	5	20	3	0	1	7	2	5	12	.253	.299	.329

Although Chavez' offense slumped at Triple-A last season, he still saw brief action with Houston in September. If Gregg Zaun's elbow isn't fully healed by spring, Chavez might hang around. 2003 Outlook: C

Nelson Cruz (**Pos**: RHP, **Age**: 30)

	W	L	Pct.	ERA	G	GS	Sv	IP	H	BB	SO	HR	Ratio
'02	2	6	.250	4.48	43	5	0	78.1	90	29	61	12	1.52
Car.	12	18	.400	4.64	184	11	2	294.2	304	98	239	44	1.36

After a rough April, when he battled shoulder fatigue, Cruz pitched fairly well the rest of the way. He even helped out as a starter in midseason. He wasn't as effective at Enron Field as he had been, though. 2003 Outlook: B

Morgan Ensberg (**Pos**: 3B, **Age**: 27, **Bats**: R)

	G	AB	R	H	D	T	HR	RBI	SB	BB	SO	Avg	OBP	Slg
'02	49	132	14	32	7	2	3	19	2	18	25	.242	.346	.394
Car.	53	139	14	34	7	2	3	19	2	18	26	.245	.344	.388

The Astros' third-base job was Ensberg's to lose last spring, and he wound up squandering it by the end of May. While he has decent power, he's now 27 years old, so his star potential would appear limited. 2003 Outlook: C

Adam Everett (**Pos**: SS, **Age**: 26, **Bats**: R)

	G	AB	R	H	D	T	HR	RBI	SB	BB	SO	Avg	OBP	Slg
'02	40	88	11	17	3	0	0	4	3	12	19	.193	.297	.227
Car.	49	91	12	17	3	0	0	4	4	12	20	.187	.288	.220

Everett may have blown the best chance he'll ever have to seize a starting spot when he got off to a slow start last April. He's a good defensive shortstop, but his bat remains suspect. 2003 Outlook: C

Scott Linebrink (**Pos**: RHP, **Age**: 26)

	W	L	Pct.	ERA	G	GS	Sv	IP	H	BB	SO	HR	Ratio
'02	0	0	–	7.03	22	0	0	24.1	31	13	24	2	1.81
Car.	0	0	–	5.79	42	0	0	46.2	55	27	39	6	1.76

Linebrink opened last season with Houston, missed a month with an elbow strain, and was demoted to the minors soon after the All-Star break. A change of scenery may be in order. 2003 Outlook: C

Jim Mann (**Pos**: RHP, **Age**: 28)

	W	L	Pct.	ERA	G	GS	Sv	IP	H	BB	SO	HR	Ratio
'02	0	1	.000	4.09	17	0	0	22.0	19	7	19	3	1.18
Car.	0	1	.000	4.50	23	0	0	30.0	28	12	24	4	1.33

Mann bounced between Houston and the minors last season. He pitched decently for the Astros, especially away from Enron Field. Waived after the campaign, he was claimed by Pittsburgh. 2003 Outlook: C

T.J. Mathews (**Pos**: RHP, **Age**: 33)

	W	L	Pct.	ERA	G	GS	Sv	IP	H	BB	SO	HR	Ratio
'02	0	0	–	3.44	12	0	0	18.1	19	5	13	2	1.31
Car.	32	26	.552	3.82	362	0	16	435.1	406	164	357	49	1.31

Mathews joined the Astros last winter but went on the 60-day disabled list with a strained biceps in May. He was ineffective when he returned in July, was released and later signed with the Cardinals. 2003 Outlook: C

Peter Munro (**Pos**: RHP, **Age**: 27)

	W	L	Pct.	ERA	G	GS	Sv	IP	H	BB	SO	HR	Ratio
'02	5	5	.500	3.57	19	14	0	80.2	89	23	45	5	1.39
Car.	6	8	.429	4.79	59	19	0	161.2	197	62	99	12	1.60

Munro signed with the Astros following the 2001 season and was terrific at Triple-A early last year. He continued to pitch well when called up to Houston in June. He can help as a starter or reliever. 2003 Outlook: B

Hipolito Pichardo (**Pos**: RHP, **Age**: 33)

	W	L	Pct.	ERA	G	GS	Sv	IP	H	BB	SO	HR	Ratio
'02	0	1	.000	81.00	1	0	0	0.1	3	2	0	0	15.00
Car.	50	44	.532	4.44	350	68	20	769.2	838	287	394	54	1.46

Pichardo said he was calling it quits while with the Red Sox in 2001, but signed with the Astros last February. However, tendinitis and a terrible outing apparently convinced him to re-retire by May. 2003 Outlook: D

Brandon Puffer (**Pos**: RHP, **Age**: 27)

	W	L	Pct.	ERA	G	GS	Sv	IP	H	BB	SO	HR	Ratio
'02	3	3	.500	4.43	55	0	0	69.0	67	38	48	3	1.52
Car.	3	3	.500	4.43	55	0	0	69.0	67	38	48	3	1.52

Puffer bounced between the Astros and Triple-A last year, but still got into 55 games for Houston. He was pretty anemic versus lefthanded batters, who reached base more than 50 percent of the time against him. 2003 Outlook: B

Tim Redding (**Pos**: RHP, **Age**: 25)

	W	L	Pct.	ERA	G	GS	Sv	IP	H	BB	SO	HR	Ratio
'02	3	6	.333	5.40	18	14	0	73.1	78	35	63	10	1.54
Car.	6	7	.462	5.44	31	23	0	129.0	140	59	118	21	1.54

After burning a path to the majors in 2001, Redding couldn't sustain his success last season. Considering his power arsenal and good makeup, he might be poised for a breakthrough this year. 2003 Outlook: B

Houston

Barry Wesson (**Pos**: CF, **Age**: 25, **Bats**: R)

	G	AB	R	H	D	T	HR	RBI	SB	BB	SO	Avg	OBP	Slg
'02	15	20	1	4	0	1	0	1	0	1	5	.200	.238	.300
Car.	15	20	1	4	0	1	0	1	0	1	5	.200	.238	.300

Wesson spent a few weeks with Houston after the All-Star break, but was claimed off waivers by Anaheim in September. His on-base percentage is weak, and his middling power doesn't compensate. 2003 Outlook: C

Gregg Zaun (**Pos**: C, **Age**: 31, **Bats**: B)

	G	AB	R	H	D	T	HR	RBI	SB	BB	SO	Avg	OBP	Slg
'02	76	185	18	41	7	1	3	24	1	12	36	.222	.275	.319
Car.	505	1321	159	328	65	7	29	165	18	168	197	.248	.335	.374

After a couple of seasons with Kansas City, Zaun signed a two-year deal with the Astros to serve as Brad Ausmus' backup. Zaun had surgery to repair a torn tendon in his throwing elbow after the season, but he should be ready by Opening Day. 2003 Outlook: B

Alan Zinter (**Pos**: 1B, **Age**: 34, **Bats**: B)

	G	AB	R	H	D	T	HR	RBI	SB	BB	SO	Avg	OBP	Slg
'02	39	44	5	6	2	0	2	3	0	0	19	.136	.136	.318
Car.	39	44	5	6	2	0	2	3	0	0	19	.136	.136	.318

In his 14th season and after 200 minor league homers, Zinter finally made his major league debut last year. A first baseman/catcher, Zinter is a week older than Jeff Bagwell. 2003 Outlook: C

Houston Astros Minor League Prospects

Organization Overview:

Over the past few years, the Astros' farm system has produced a boatload of good pitching prospects. Wade Miller, Roy Oswalt and Tim Redding are all 26 years of age or younger. In addition, Carlos Hernandez and Kirk Saarloos had their moments as rookies last year. And, Houston's best recent product may be outfielder Lance Berkman. Considering its recent spate of top prospect promotions, it's understandable that the Astros' system may suffer a small void in the near term. Although their six affiliates all finished with winning records in 2002, the organization seems to have a lack of depth at the higher levels. But down below, there remain pitching and middle-infield prospects to keep an eye on. Meanwhile, Jason Lane and Brad Lidge figure to have the best shot at contributing as rookies in 2003.

John Buck

Position: C   **Opening Day Age:** 22
Bats: R **Throws:** R   **Born:** 7/7/80 in
Ht: 6' 3" **Wt:** 210   Kemmerer, WY

Recent Statistics

	G	AB	R	H	D	T	HR	RBI	SB	BB	SO	Avg
2001 A Lexington	122	443	72	122	24	1	22	73	4	37	84	.275
2002 AA Round Rock	120	448	48	118	29	3	12	89	2	31	93	.263

After hitting 22 homers in the Class-A South Atlantic League in 2001, Buck moved up to Double-A last year. While his offensive numbers weren't overwhelming at Round Rock, he still delivered a lot of RBI, particularly for a catcher. He's a big, strong guy who's progressed at a steady pace. His power potential has intrigued as he's grown and matured, and his defense also has drawn raves. He's intelligent and calls a nice game behind the plate, with a good arm and quick release. He needs to become more consistent with the bat, and he seemed to tire at times last season. But he looks to be the top receiving prospect in the Astros' system, and Houston's likely catcher of the future. His immediate future appears to be in Triple-A in 2003.

Chris Burke

Position: SS-2B   **Opening Day Age:** 23
Bats: R **Throws:** R   **Born:** 3/11/80 in
Ht: 5' 11" **Wt:** 190   Knoxville, TN

Recent Statistics

	G	AB	R	H	D	T	HR	RBI	SB	BB	SO	Avg
2001 A Michigan	56	233	47	70	11	6	3	17	21	26	31	.300
2002 AA Round Rock	136	481	66	127	19	8	3	37	16	39	61	.264

Burke was an offensive force at the University of Tennessee, leading the Southeastern Conference in batting average (.435), runs (105), home runs (20) and stolen bases (49) in 2001. He played shortstop that sea-

son, and the Astros chose him with the 10th overall pick in June. He flashed five-tool potential in his professional debut that summer. Last year, Burke held his own at Double-A. But he hasn't yet hit with the kind of authority he showed at Tennessee, and his stolen-base rate has declined. He moved to second in 2002, where he played well. His arm is adequate, even for shortstop. He still may be adjusting to hitting with a wood bat.

Jason Lane

Position: OF   **Opening Day Age:** 26
Bats: R **Throws:** L   **Born:** 12/22/76 in Santa
Ht: 6' 2" **Wt:** 220   Rosa, CA

Recent Statistics

	G	AB	R	H	D	T	HR	RBI	SB	BB	SO	Avg
2002 AAA New Orl'ns	111	426	65	116	36	2	15	83	13	31	90	.272
2002 NL Houston	44	69	12	20	3	1	4	10	1	10	12	.290

While Lane always has hit as a pro, he enjoyed a banner season at Double-A in 2001, when he was named the Texas League MVP. Boosted to Triple-A last year, his batting line dipped a bit, though he remained productive. He's one of those rare players, like Rickey Henderson and Cleon Jones, who throw lefthanded yet bat from the right side. But Lane demonstrates good instincts at the plate and in the field. His defense and running ability are better than many people think. He can play either corner-outfield spot and also fill in at first base. He had a chance to show what he could do for the Astros last season, and didn't fail, hitting for power and drawing walks. Having turned 26 years of age, the time is now for Lane to stick in the majors.

Brad Lidge

Position: P   **Opening Day Age:** 26
Bats: R **Throws:** R   **Born:** 12/23/76 in
Ht: 6' 5" **Wt:** 200   Sacramento, CA

Recent Statistics

	W	L	ERA	G	GS	Sv	IP	H	R	BB	SO	HR
2002 AA Round Rock	1	1	2.45	5	0	0	11.0	9	4	3	18	0
2002 NL Houston	1	0	6.23	6	1	0	8.2	12	6	9	12	0
2002 AAA New Orl'ns	5	5	3.39	24	19	0	111.2	83	47	47	110	9

The Astros selected Lidge in the first round of the 1998 draft out of Notre Dame. Since then, he has constantly battled injuries, never finishing a season off the disabled list—until last year. Lidge remained healthy in 2002, which may have helped the most from a mental aspect. He certainly has the physical tools, with a fastball that can reach 96 MPH and a slider in the 84-88 MPH range. His slider has climbed as high as 90 in the past, though he didn't show that kind of velocity during his time with Houston last year. The Astros would like Lidge to reduce his walks and refine his offspeed stuff. He also could use more experience, as he topped 42 innings last year for the first time in five pro seasons.

Tony Pluta

Position: P **Opening Day Age:** 20
Bats: R **Throws:** R **Born:** 10/28/82 in
Ht: 6' 2" **Wt:** 190 Visalia, CA

Recent Statistics

	W	L	ERA	G	GS	Sv	IP	H	R	BB	SO	HR
2001 A Lexington	12	4	3.20	26	26	0	132.1	107	52	86	138	7
2002 A Michigan	11	13	5.92	28	28	0	143.0	155	100	83	120	18

The Astros have shown they aren't afraid to challenge Pluta, a third-round pick in 2000. Although he didn't leave his teens until last October, he already has two full years of Class-A ball under his belt. But after a terrific debut in the South Atlantic League in 2001, his stats weren't quite as impressive in the Midwest League last season. However, the Astros aren't discouraged. Pluta has a gifted arm, with a fastball that's been clocked as high as 99 MPH and the makings of a power curveball. He's a durable youngster who hasn't yet experienced arm problems. And he's a mature kid, which helps explain his success at such a young age. He needs to learn to pitch under control and not overthrow.

Chad Qualls

Position: P **Opening Day Age:** 24
Bats: R **Throws:** R **Born:** 8/17/78 in Harbor
Ht: 6' 5" **Wt:** 205 City, CA

Recent Statistics

	W	L	ERA	G	GS	Sv	IP	H	R	BB	SO	HR
2001 A Michigan	15	6	3.72	26	26	0	162.0	149	77	31	125	8
2002 AA Round Rock	6	13	4.36	29	29	0	163.0	174	92	67	142	9

The Astros selected Qualls and his power arm in the second round of the 2000 draft out of the University of Nevada-Reno. He's a strong hurler with a low-90s fastball and plus movement. He also throws a hard slider, though he could improve his breaking ball. His arm angle has been tough on righthanded batters but sometimes can be a problem for him when he drops down too far. He'll get under his pitches, which results in offerings up in the strike zone and getting hit hard. Qualls is a good competitor who has proven to be durable and has not had arm problems. Signed as a college senior, he's already 24 years of age. While his record was poor at Double-A last season, he'll likely be working at Triple-A in 2003.

Henri Stanley

Position: OF **Opening Day Age:** 25
Bats: L **Throws:** L **Born:** 12/15/77 in
Ht: 5' 10" **Wt:** 190 Columbia, SC

Recent Statistics

	G	AB	R	H	D	T	HR	RBI	SB	BB	SO	Avg
2001 A Michigan	114	400	75	120	24	12	14	76	30	73	84	.300
2002 AA Round Rock	127	456	90	143	36	10	16	72	14	72	85	.314

Although Stanley wasn't drafted when he entered professional baseball, his hitting the past two years has demanded attention. He's an intelligent player who runs well and hits with gap power, as his doubles and triples totals would indicate. He complements his high average with plenty of walks, so he's constantly on base. Really, the only thing Stanley doesn't do well is throw, which probably limits him to left field. Considering his undrafted status, it's not surprising that he plays with a certain level of desire. He's the kind of guy who may not be denied, and soon could be knocking on the door as a fourth or fifth outfielder in Houston.

Tom Whiteman

Position: SS **Opening Day Age:** 23
Bats: R **Throws:** R **Born:** 7/14/79 in
Ht: 6' 3" **Wt:** 175 Oklahoma City, OK

Recent Statistics

	G	AB	R	H	D	T	HR	RBI	SB	BB	SO	Avg
2001 A Lexington	114	389	58	124	26	8	18	57	17	34	106	.319
2001 AA Round Rock	4	16	1	4	0	0	1	1	0	0	5	.250
2002 AA Round Rock	15	56	3	10	2	1	0	5	1	4	17	.179
2002 A Lexington	90	350	50	106	29	2	10	49	6	36	66	.303

Whiteman batted .360 for Oklahoma while leading the Big 12 with 10 triples in 2000. The Astros then picked him in the sixth round of that June's draft. After ranking second in the Class-A South Atlantic League with a .319 average in 2001, Whiteman struggled when promoted to Double-A and spent most of last season back in Lexington. Nevertheless, he possesses loads of potential with the bat. He's built along the lines of Cal Ripken Jr., and an offensive shortstop obviously can be special. Defensively, Whiteman is a fluid fielder with a good arm. He's an average-plus runner with good instincts for the game. The Astros expect him to figure it all out and to move quickly through their system. He could be their shortstop of the future.

Others to Watch

Righthander **Jimmy Barrett** (21) was selected in the third round of the 1999 draft, and he enjoyed his best season in 2002. He has a power arm with a 93-94 MPH fastball and a good breaking pitch. . . **Brooks Conrad** (23) impressed people while playing in Class-A last season. He has pop at the plate and has a chance to be an offensive second baseman. He also makes plays in the field you might not think he would. . . Outfielder **Mike Hill** (26) is a streaky player who has only average tools. But he throws and runs well, is a clutch performer and can't be retired at times. . . Righthander **Jeriome Robertson** (26) resurrected his career with the best ERA in the Triple-A Pacific Coast League last season. He's not overpowering, but has a decent breaking pitch and can keep righthanded hitters off balance. . . Righthander **Rodrigo Rosario** (25) is a couple years older than originally was thought, but he remains a wiry pitcher with a live arm. Though he tired near the end of last season, he pitched well at Double-A. . . After four seasons as a starter, righthander **Tom Shearn** (25) has taken to a relief role. Despite a 93-94 MPH fastball and pretty good breaking ball, he doesn't always pitch with confidence.

Dodger Stadium

Offense

Ballparks come and go, but Dodger Stadium remains one of the toughest places to score runs. The park is just 20 miles from the Pacific Ocean, and the heavy night air keeps flyballs in the yard. Other extra-base hits are reduced, too. And at-bats are cut short by pops that are snagged in the large foul territories in front of both dugouts. Because of the dearth of runs, managers tend to try to play more of an old-school type of game in Chavez Ravine. Try to get an early run or two and hope it holds.

Defense

The outfield wall is concentric with no acute angles, so balls can be expected to take true bounces. However, it gets a little tricky right at the foul poles, and the few triples that are hit in Dodger Stadium often come when a corner guy can't corral one in those areas. A few years back, the club replaced the traditional warning track with a rubberized surface, and it's very dangerous. The transition from infield grass to dirt also can be treacherous, especially later in the season when the hot sun has hardened the surface.

Who It Helps the Most

Pitchers love to take the Dodger Stadium mound, off which the home staff posted a 3.29 ERA (4.11 on the road). Flyball types like Eric Gagne would seem to be helped, as his 1.41 home ERA last year proved.

Who It Hurts the Most

Adrian Beltre and Brian Jordan tend to have an uppercut to their swing, so they aren't necessarily helped by Dodger Stadium. Over the course of his brief career, Beltre has hit almost 50 points higher on the road.

Rookies & Newcomers

Paul Shuey was picked up for the stretch drive last season, and his hard sinking stuff should fit in quite well at Dodger Stadium. With Mark Grudzielanek traded, young Joe Thurston should be in the mix this season, and his slashing hitting style also would seem to fit the park.

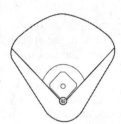

Dimensions: LF-330, LCF-385, CF-395, RCF-385, RF-330

Capacity: 56,000

Elevation: 340 feet

Surface: Grass

Foul Territory: Large

Park Factors

2002 Season

	Home Games Dodgers	Opp	Total	Away Games Dodgers	Opp	Total	Index
G	72	72	144	72	72	144	
Avg	.251	.233	.242	.279	.249	.265	91
AB	2372	2463	4835	2597	2365	4962	97
R	270	265	535	363	300	663	81
H	596	574	1170	725	588	1313	89
2B	103	98	201	154	127	281	73
3B	11	3	14	15	15	30	48
HR	60	75	135	77	66	143	97
BB	202	251	453	187	264	451	103
SO	400	530	930	448	488	936	102
E	45	57	102	32	56	88	116
E-Infield	40	50	90	27	41	68	132
LHB-Avg	.238	.222	.230	.267	.252	.260	88
LHB-HR	16	21	37	28	23	51	78
RHB-Avg	.258	.239	.249	.286	.246	.268	93
RHB-HR	44	54	98	49	43	92	106

2000-2002

	Home Games Dodgers	Opp	Total	Away Games Dodgers	Opp	Total	Index
G	219	219	438	219	219	438	
Avg	.251	.235	.243	.269	.259	.264	92
AB	7170	7490	14660	7753	7245	14998	98
R	909	872	1781	1164	1010	2174	82
H	1797	1761	3558	2084	1879	3963	90
2B	318	315	633	421	396	817	79
3B	31	20	51	47	38	85	61
HR	247	229	476	276	240	516	94
BB	725	780	1505	737	729	1466	105
SO	1379	1653	3032	1411	1513	2924	106
E	166	155	321	144	172	316	102
E-Infield	139	125	264	124	140	264	100
LHB-Avg	.242	.230	.236	.262	.261	.262	90
LHB-HR	83	100	183	98	102	200	94
RHB-Avg	.256	.239	.247	.273	.258	.266	93
RHB-HR	164	129	293	178	138	316	95

2002 Rankings (National League)

- Highest infield-error factor
- Lowest run factor
- Lowest double factor
- Second-lowest batting-average factor
- Second-lowest hit factor
- Second-lowest LHB batting-average factor
- Third-lowest triple factor

Jim Tracy

2002 Season

The Dodgers played as one team last season and that surely was Jim Tracy's doing. In the spring, he preached the value of hustle on the bases and in the field. And the club proved over the course of the season that it had been listening. Though he can get a bit testy at times, Tracy always defends his players, at least in the press, and everyone is made aware of their respective role.

Offense

Though Tracy seems to prefer a set lineup, he platooned Dave Roberts and Marquis Grissom in center field all year and eventually had two guys splitting time at shortstop. As opposed to benching slumping hitters, he tinkered with the batting order, slotting his hot bat behind Shawn Green and letting a cold one slide down a few spots. Tracy tends to play by the book with regard to the bunting game, though he's a bit less predictable when he moves his runners. Dodgers pinch-hitters hit .280 last year, highest in the National League.

Pitching & Defense

Despite entering last season with a bounty of riches in the starting rotation, Tracy and his staff allowed Kevin Brown to dictate his injury rehab, and it cost the club. On the other hand, the decision to give Eric Gagne the ball in the ninth inning turned out well. In fact, Tracy rode his closer pretty hard at times. All of the bullpen roles are well defined, and only Jesse Orosco was used purely as a situational reliever. The lineup tends to be set from an offensive perspective.

2003 Outlook

In Dan Evans, Tracy has a general manager who will fill the roster with better balance. Tracy has been heaped with praise in his young career, but it will get tougher as another year goes by with no playoff games. There were times last season when the skipper seemed to press the panic button. How he holds up under the pressure of a pennant race is a test yet to come.

Born: 12/31/55 in Hamilton, OH

Playing Experience: 1980-1981, ChC

Managerial Experience: 2 seasons

Manager Statistics

Year	Team, Lg	W	L	Pct	GB	Finish
2002	Los Angeles, NL	92	70	.568	6.0	3rd West
2 Seasons		178	146	.549	–	–

2002 Starting Pitchers by Days Rest

	<=3	4	5	6+
Dodgers Starts	1	92	40	20
Dodgers ERA	9.00	3.66	3.77	3.88
NL Avg Starts	1	88	42	21
NL ERA	3.18	4.22	4.14	4.58

2002 Situational Stats

	Jim Tracy	NL Average
Hit & Run Success %	34.3	36.5
Stolen Base Success %	72.2	68.3
Platoon Pct.	52.4	52.7
Defensive Subs	18	19
High-Pitch Outings	3	7
Quick/Slow Hooks	19/6	24/11
Sacrifice Attempts	84	95

2002 Rankings (National League)

- 3rd in stolen-base percentage, squeeze plays (10), starts on three days rest and saves with over 1 inning pitched (9)

Andy Ashby

2002 Season

Andy Ashby pitched about as well as one might expect, considering he turned 35 and had lost almost the entire previous year due to elbow surgery. He looked very good early last season, allowing two earned runs or less in 10 of his first 14 starts. But he wore down as the summer unfolded. After a strong August, Ashby developed a blister on his pitching hand. When it turned into a nasty infection, his season terminated.

Pitching

Everything plays off the hard sinking fastball for Ashby. It topped out in the low 90s last season, down from the 94-95 MPH he could sometimes hit in his prime. Those extra few miles per hour, of course, can make a huge difference. His sinker bores down and in on righthanded hitters, and he complements it with a cutter that breaks in the opposite direction. While he doesn't technically have a changeup, Ashby will take a little off the sinker to keep hitters off balance. Lacking a strikeout pitch, he lives and dies on getting groundball outs. His lifetime ERA on turf (4.94) is a full run higher than on natural grass (3.84).

Defense & Hitting

While he is fundamentally fine with the leather, Ashby's delivery leaves him a bit vulnerable defensively, and he's not the most agile athlete. He telegraphs his move to first, giving opposing basestealers an easy read. He struck out in 23 of 48 at-bats last year, though he did connect for his first major league home run. He's one of the few Dodger pitchers able to get a bunt down when asked.

2003 Outlook

Signed through this season (with an option), Ashby isn't going anywhere. It's not uncommon for pitchers to improve in their second year after elbow surgery. And if it's a matter of mound savvy, the 12-year veteran has plenty to spare. The Dodgers signed him to be their third or fourth starter, so a 12-win season would suit them just fine.

Position: SP
Bats: R **Throws:** R
Ht: 6' 1" **Wt:** 202

Opening Day Age: 35
Born: 7/11/67 in Kansas City, MO
ML Seasons: 12

Overall Statistics

	W	L	Pct.	ERA	G	GS	Sv	IP	H	BB	SO	HR	Ratio
'02	9	13	.409	3.91	30	30	0	181.2	179	65	107	20	1.34
Car.	95	100	.487	4.08	286	273	1	1735.2	1766	523	1130	197	1.32

How Often He Throws Strikes

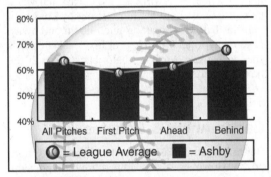

◔ = League Average   ■ = Ashby

2002 Situational Stats

	W	L	ERA	Sv	IP		AB	H	HR	RBI	Avg
Home	5	5	2.99	0	78.1	LHB	372	106	7	33	.285
Road	4	8	4.62	0	103.1	RHB	313	73	13	45	.233
First Half	7	6	3.36	0	109.2	Sc Pos	173	37	7	60	.214
Scnd Half	2	7	4.75	0	72.0	Clutch	27	4	0	0	.148

2002 Rankings (National League)

- 6th in fewest strikeouts per nine innings (5.3)
- 7th in losses, lowest batting average allowed with runners in scoring position and least run support per nine innings (4.2)
- 8th in fewest pitches thrown per batter (3.54)
- 10th in highest stolen-base percentage allowed (77.3)
- Led the Dodgers in losses, hit batsmen (8), highest groundball-flyball ratio allowed (1.5) and lowest batting average allowed with runners in scoring position

Adrian Beltre

2002 Season

Adrian Beltre continued to frustrate Dodgers officials anxious for him to live up to his potential. He hit .304 last April, but then went into the tank over the next two months. Desperate to get more production from their corner infield spots, the club picked up Tyler Houston, and that seemed to get Beltre focused. In the six weeks after the trade, he hit .356 with nine homers and 30 RBI in 37 games. But he ran out of gas down the stretch.

Hitting

Beltre was a very disciplined hitter in the minor leagues, but has gotten into some bad habits in the majors. Though he will take the occasional walk, he's just as likely to get himself out by chasing a high fastball or a breaking pitch down and away. Like many hitters, Beltre is at his best when he's staying back and driving balls back through the box and to the right-center field gap. He has plenty of power, but his home park certainly hasn't helped him.

Baserunning & Defense

Beltre bulked up last winter to try and add more power. However, it also slowed him down a step, though he seldom hurts the club on the basepaths. His lack of progress in the field is another source of consternation. He charges bunts and slow rollers very well and can range far to his glove hand. But Beltre will take a lackadaisical approach on an easy chance or simply toss one away.

2003 Outlook

While many Dodgers fans are ready to give up on Beltre, it's easy to forget he'll turn only 24 this April. That's an age when many players are just making their major league debuts, and Beltre already has a couple of 20-homer seasons under his belt. Still, the young man hasn't made the strides many hoped for by now. Will this be the year when he approaches every at-bat and fielding opportunity with the focus and concentration demanded of a major league professional? Time will tell.

Position: 3B
Bats: R **Throws:** R
Ht: 5'11" **Wt:** 170

Opening Day Age: 23
Born: 4/7/79 in Santo Domingo, DR
ML Seasons: 5
Pronunciation: BELL-tray

Overall Statistics

	G	AB	R	H	D	T	HR	RBI	SB	BB	SO	Avg	OBP	Slg
'02	159	587	70	151	26	5	21	75	7	37	96	.257	.303	.426
Car.	652	2305	302	615	114	16	76	309	53	196	400	.267	.327	.429

Where He Hits the Ball

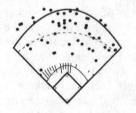
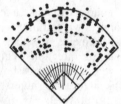

Vs. LHP   **Vs. RHP**

2002 Situational Stats

	AB	H	HR	RBI	Avg		AB	H	HR	RBI	Avg
Home	275	62	7	26	.225	LHP	126	38	6	18	.302
Road	312	89	14	49	.285	RHP	461	113	15	57	.245
First Half	320	76	7	29	.238	Sc Pos	129	33	6	50	.256
Scnd Half	267	75	14	46	.281	Clutch	98	29	3	7	.296

2002 Rankings (National League)

- 2nd in errors at third base (20)
- 3rd in lowest fielding percentage at third base (.954)
- 5th in games played and lowest batting average at home
- 6th in lowest on-base percentage vs. righthanded pitchers (.302)
- Led the Dodgers in at-bats, sacrifice flies (6), games played, most pitches seen per plate appearance (3.75) and batting average on a 3-2 count (.300)

Omar Daal

2002 Season

Omar Daal was happy to return to his original team, until he found himself in the bullpen on Opening Day. Despite his rancor, the little lefty pitched superbly in middle and long relief, something he hadn't done on a regular basis since 1997. When he finally got his opportunity to join the rotation in late May, Daal proved very streaky, and he eventually ran out of steam. He posted a 6.65 ERA in September, when he failed to win any of five starts.

Pitching

Daal barely throws hard enough to break glass, topping out in the mid 80s. He must have pinpoint control in order to get major league hitters out. He has a good curveball that sweeps a long way both horizontally and vertically. Though his changeup differs very little in velocity from the "heater," it keeps batters off balance. The little lefty has a peekaboo delivery that keeps the ball hidden until it comes out of his hand, which adds a few ticks to all of his pitches. Though he wants to start, Daal pitched extremely well out of the bullpen last year.

Defense & Hitting

Daal is a good athlete and handles all phases of the game quite well. His move is so deceptive that baserunners rarely try to steal. He gets off the mound in fine shape and fields his position with aplomb. The 31-year-old is not an automatic out at the plate. He has a .196 lifetime average and was third on the club with eight sacrifices last year.

2003 Outlook

Though he handled himself professionally, Daal felt he was lied to by Dodgers management, and there is little chance the free agent will return. While he doesn't look very impressive on the mound and is by no means a workhorse, he's a solid veteran who will fit quite nicely at the back end of some team's rotation. With decent support, expect Daal to win 10-12 games this season.

Position: SP/RP
Bats: L **Throws:** L
Ht: 6' 3" **Wt:** 204

Opening Day Age: 31
Born: 3/1/72 in Maracaibo, VZ
ML Seasons: 10
Pronunciation: DOLL

Overall Statistics

	W	L	Pct.	ERA	G	GS	Sv	IP	H	BB	SO	HR	Ratio
'02	11	9	.550	3.90	39	23	0	161.1	142	54	105	20	1.21
Car.	64	67	.489	4.40	373	147	1	1105.0	1116	411	753	129	1.38

How Often He Throws Strikes

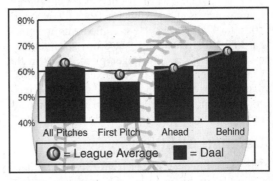

2002 Situational Stats

	W	L	ERA	Sv	IP		AB	H	HR	RBI	Avg
Home	4	4	3.39	0	85.0	LHB	148	36	6	18	.243
Road	7	5	4.48	0	76.1	RHB	447	106	14	51	.237
First Half	7	4	4.15	0	78.0	Sc Pos	119	35	4	47	.294
Scnd Half	4	5	3.67	0	83.1	Clutch	64	11	1	4	.172

2002 Rankings (National League)

- 8th in highest batting average allowed with runners in scoring position
- Led the Dodgers in GDPs induced (18), lowest stolen-base percentage allowed (50.0) and most GDPs induced per nine innings (1.0)

Eric Gagne

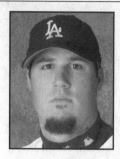

Position: RP
Bats: R **Throws:** R
Ht: 6' 2" **Wt:** 195

Opening Day Age: 27
Born: 1/7/76 in
Montreal, PQ, Canada
ML Seasons: 4
Pronunciation:
gan-YAY

2002 Season

Was there a bigger surprise in baseball last year than Eric Gagne? After scuffling as a highly touted starter, he was moved to the bullpen and anointed the closer once Matt Herges was moved to Montreal. Gagne took to the new role like a duck to water, and he quickly evolved into the dominating late-inning force that every club would love to have. Though his workload eventually took a bit of a toll, he continued to ask for the ball and ended up as one of eight pitchers to ever collect at least 50 saves in a season.

Pitching

Without having to worry about conserving energy, Gagne increased his velocity from 92 MPH in 2001 to 97 last year. He complements it with a hard 87-MPH changeup that drops so much that many think it's a split-finger pitch. Later in the year, he began to mix in the excellent curveball that had served him well as a starter. Gagne's combination of stuff and control is phenomenal, as his strikeout-walk ratio would indicate.

Defense & Hitting

The former hockey player is an excellent athlete. Gagne fields his position like a goalie and gets over to first base in a hurry on grounders to the right side. Though he's got a quick move and uses a compact delivery to the plate, he had so few baserunners last year that he didn't have to worry too much about would-be basestealers. They were 2-for-5 against him in 2002, but have had better success in the past. Gagne is not an automatic out at the slab, though he had just one at-bat last year.

2003 Outlook

Short of curing cancer or solving the world's hunger problems, what could Gagne possibly do for an encore? He's created an aura about him, especially in normally staid Dodger Stadium, where they accompany his entrance with Trevor Hoffmanesque metal rock. If the 27-year-old Canadian can stay healthy, the saves record could be in danger. He's got three solid pitches, impeccable control and that closer's mentality.

Overall Statistics

	W	L	Pct.	ERA	G	GS	Sv	IP	H	BB	SO	HR	Ratio
'02	4	1	.800	1.97	77	0	52	82.1	55	16	114	6	0.86
Car.	15	15	.500	4.02	135	48	52	365.1	323	137	353	53	1.26

How Often He Throws Strikes

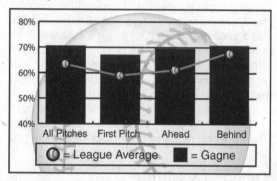

2002 Situational Stats

	W	L	ERA	Sv	IP		AB	H	HR	RBI	Avg
Home	3	0	1.41	26	44.2	LHB	150	32	2	12	.213
Road	1	1	2.63	26	37.2	RHB	141	23	4	7	.163
First Half	0	0	1.39	32	45.1	Sc Pos	75	9	0	9	.120
Scnd Half	4	1	2.68	20	37.0	Clutch	218	39	4	14	.179

2002 Rankings (National League)

- 1st in most strikeouts per nine innings in relief (12.5) and fewest baserunners allowed per nine innings in relief (8.0)
- 2nd in saves, games finished (68), save opportunities (56) and save percentage (92.9)
- 3rd in lowest batting average allowed in relief (.189)
- Led the Dodgers in lowest batting average allowed vs. righthanded batters, save percentage (92.9) and relief ERA (1.97)

Shawn Green

2002 Season

It may seem like ancient history in retrospect, but Shawn Green got off to a terrible start last season. On the morning of May 21, he was hitting .231 with three homers and 21 RBI. Over the next five days, the lanky slugger pounded nine balls out of the park and almost doubled his RBI total (17). Though he eventually returned to planet Earth, Green put up his usual numbers the rest of the campaign. However, he did seem to wear down a bit the last month.

Hitting

Green is first and foremost a pull hitter, and opponents often employ a shift against him. He has second-deck power to right, and it's dangerous to try to sneak anything past him on the inner half. He is quite capable of taking outside pitches back through the box and to left-center. Green can be a selective hitter, especially versus righthanders. He tends to chase more pitches against southpaws, mostly breaking stuff away.

Baserunning & Defense

While his first step may not be the quickest, Green can really pick 'em up and lay 'em down once he gets going. He hits each bag at just the right angle and rarely makes a mistake on the basepaths. After averaging nearly 25 stolen bases between 1998 and 2001, Green went 8-for-13 last year. He seemed a bit slow in the outfield as well, almost as if he wasn't picking up the ball off the bat. His arm isn't a howitzer, but it is accurate.

2003 Outlook

It may have taken awhile for Green to get going last year, but he eventually quieted those who thought his production would suffer without Gary Sheffield behind him in the lineup. Shawn may "look like a college kid carrying his backpack" in the clubhouse, as one teammate admiringly described Green's humble demeanor, but he's taken over a leadership role on the Dodgers' club. The fans love him, and the lineup should be constructed around him over the next few seasons.

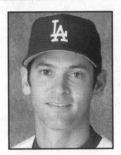

Position: RF
Bats: L **Throws:** L
Ht: 6' 4" **Wt:** 200

Opening Day Age: 30
Born: 11/10/72 in Des Plaines, IL
ML Seasons: 10

Overall Statistics

	G	AB	R	H	D	T	HR	RBI	SB	BB	SO	Avg	OBP	Slg
'02	158	582	110	166	31	1	42	114	8	93	112	.285	.385	.558
Car.	1197	4324	731	1232	270	24	234	714	128	461	850	.285	.358	.521

Where He Hits the Ball

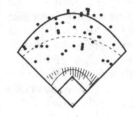

Vs. LHP   **Vs. RHP**

2002 Situational Stats

	AB	H	HR	RBI	Avg		AB	H	HR	RBI	Avg
Home	278	74	18	48	.266	LHP	163	44	11	35	.270
Road	304	92	24	66	.303	RHP	419	122	31	79	.291
First Half	311	87	26	68	.280	Sc Pos	134	37	7	66	.276
Scnd Half	271	79	16	46	.292	Clutch	94	21	3	9	.223

2002 Rankings (National League)

- 2nd in fielding percentage in right field (.994)
- 3rd in home runs and GDPs (26)
- 4th in runs scored and RBI
- 5th in intentional walks (22) and HR frequency (13.9 ABs per HR)
- Led the Dodgers in batting average, hits, RBI, total bases (325), walks, intentional walks (22), times on base (264), strikeouts, pitches seen (2,386), plate appearances (685), slugging percentage, on-base percentage, HR frequency (13.9 ABs per HR), batting average with the bases loaded (.625), batting average vs. righthanded pitchers, cleanup slugging percentage (.556), slugging percentage vs. righthanded pitchers (.561) and on-base percentage vs. righthanded pitchers (.398)

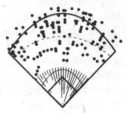

Los Angeles

Mark Grudzielanek

2002 Season

Mark Grudzielanek began last year in a sour mood. Having spent most of his previous seven major league seasons at or near the top of the order, he found himself batting seventh or eighth in Jim Tracy's lineup. A series of nagging injuries to Grudzielanek's back, hand and hamstring didn't help matters. He slumped through most of the first half. The veteran cleared his head at the All-Star break and hit .297 over the second half.

Hitting

Grudzielanek is very aggressive at the plate and loves to smack that first-pitch fastball. He hit .433 last season when putting the first pitch into play. While he occasionally can yank a ball over the left-field wall, he's at his best when he stays back on the pitch and uses the whole field. In fact, many of Grudzielanek's extra-base hits come on line drives down the right-field line. His lack of patience gets him in trouble, as Grudzielanek will chase pitches outside the zone. He is especially vulnerable to high fastballs and struck out a career-high 89 times last year.

Baserunning & Defense

Although Grudzielanek has stolen as many as 33 bases in a season, he isn't a good baserunner. He seems to think he still possesses the speed of his youth and will run himself into many outs. While he doesn't have the softest hands and lacks range, Grudzielanek has made himself into an average second baseman. The converted shortstop has plenty of arm for second, and he worked extremely well with Cesar Izturis around the bag.

2003 Outlook

Grudzielanek never was one of Jim Tracy's favorites, so the club was thrilled to be able to move his contract to the Cubs. If he can stay healthy, he is capable of hitting .290 and producing enough runs to justify his spot in the lineup. However, the 32-year-old's skills appear to be eroding rather quickly, and the Cubs would be better served if Grudzielanek serves as an insurance policy for young Bobby Hill at second base. In that role, Grudzielanek would back up at second and short, and play a bit more at times when Hill struggles.

Position: 2B
Bats: R **Throws:** R
Ht: 6' 1" **Wt:** 185

Opening Day Age: 32
Born: 6/30/70 in Milwaukee, WI
ML Seasons: 8
Pronunciation:
Grud-zi-lawn-ick

Overall Statistics

	G	AB	R	H	D	T	HR	RBI	SB	BB	SO	Avg	OBP	Slg
'02	150	536	56	145	23	0	9	50	4	22	89	.271	.301	.364
Car.	1097	4344	576	1226	223	24	57	382	110	215	597	.282	.324	.384

Where He Hits the Ball

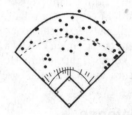
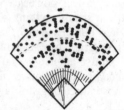

Vs. LHP   **Vs. RHP**

2002 Situational Stats

	AB	H	HR	RBI	Avg		AB	H	HR	RBI	Avg
Home	259	71	5	21	.274	LHP	109	28	3	15	.257
Road	277	74	4	29	.267	RHP	427	117	6	35	.274
First Half	277	68	4	28	.245	Sc Pos	124	33	1	39	.266
Scnd Half	259	77	5	22	.297	Clutch	102	26	4	14	.255

2002 Rankings (National League)

- 2nd in fielding percentage at second base (.989)
- 5th in lowest on-base percentage vs. righthanded pitchers (.297)
- 7th in lowest on-base percentage and lowest percentage of pitches taken (46.8)
- 9th in fewest pitches seen per plate appearance (3.28)

Kazuhisa Ishii

2002 Season

Kazuhisa Ishii got off to a tremendous start with the Dodgers, as he won his first six starts, and 10 of his first 12. However, Ishii lost his command after the All-Star break and all the magic disappeared. His ERA over his last eight starts was 7.56, before his season was ended by a vicious line drive that caused multiple fractures to his cranium and nasal cavity.

Pitching

Ishii has good stuff. His fastball registers in the low 90s with excellent movement, and he mixes in a good changeup. He has a knee-buckling curveball and is able to change speeds with it. However, Ishii often has trouble putting his pitches where he wants them, a problem that tends to haunt him early in starts. Once he settles down, he can get into a groove that lasts innings at a time. In several of his starts, Ishii would pitch from the stretch, just because he couldn't get comfortable with his windup. He showed an uncanny ability to pitch out of trouble.

Defense & Hitting

Ishii isn't a great fielder, as he doesn't get off the mound particularly well and has just fair reactions on comebackers. His move is average for a left-hander and he has a herky-jerky delivery, so opponents attempted 27 steals, 16 successfully. Ishii is pretty much clueless at the plate. He managed to collect just five singles in 50 at-bats and was particularly weak in his sacrifice attempts.

2003 Outlook

It'll be interesting to see if Ishii can make it all the way back from the blow he took to the head, as his psyche seemed rather fragile before that. The command problems apparently date back to his days in Japan, so they're not something that will be fixed easily. The Dodgers have quite a few dollars invested in the 29-year-old, so they'll do everything possible to get him back on the mound and ready to go. When he can find the plate, Ishii is very difficult to hit.

Position: SP
Bats: L **Throws:** L
Ht: 6' 0" **Wt:** 190

Opening Day Age: 29
Born: 9/9/73 in Chiba, Japan
ML Seasons: 1
Pronunciation: kaz-u-heesa ish-ee-e

Overall Statistics

	W	L	Pct.	ERA	G	GS	Sv	IP	H	BB	SO	HR	Ratio
'02	14	10	.583	4.27	28	28	0	154.0	137	106	143	20	1.58
Car.	14	10	.583	4.27	28	28	0	154.0	137	106	143	20	1.58

How Often He Throws Strikes

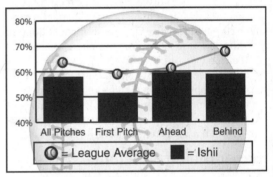

= League Average   = Ishii

2002 Situational Stats

	W	L	ERA	Sv	IP		AB	H	HR	RBI	Avg
Home	6	6	3.86	0	77.0	LHB	130	29	3	12	.223
Road	8	4	4.68	0	77.0	RHB	441	108	17	61	.245
First Half	11	5	3.58	0	100.2	Sc Pos	152	41	5	56	.270
Scnd Half	3	5	5.57	0	53.1	Clutch	18	3	0	1	.167

2002 Rankings (National League)

- 1st in walks allowed
- 2nd in wins among rookies
- 3rd in losses among rookies
- 6th in runners caught stealing (11)
- Led the Dodgers in walks allowed, wild pitches (7), runners caught stealing (11) and most strikeouts per nine innings (8.4)

Brian Jordan

2002 Season

Brian Jordan was shocked by his offseason trade to the Dodgers, but the consummate professional still got off to a fine start. He was hitting almost .300 by the end of May. After struggling through most of the summer, he missed almost the entire month of August with a sore back that troubled him most of the season. Returning September 1, Jordan carried the club down the stretch, as he tied for the major league lead with 30 RBI in September.

Hitting

Jordan is both dangerous and aggressive at the plate, and looks to drive the first fastball he sees. He hit .403 with four homers when he put the first pitch in play last year. Opposing pitchers hope to get him to chase sliders off the outside edge and fastballs up out of the strike zone. Most of his power is to left and left-center, but Jordan can get too pull-happy and ground a lot of outside pitches to shortstop and third base. During his hot streaks—and when he's locked in no one gets hotter—Jordan uses the entire field.

Baserunning & Defense

The former NFL defensive back brings his football mentality to the park every day and carries it to all elements of his game. While a balky knee has pretty much ended his stolen base career, Jordan remains an above-average baserunner who always looks to make the turn. He attacks balls hit into the outfield the same way, and made the adjustment from right to left field with ease. He has a much better arm than most teams are able to send to left.

2003 Outlook

Jordan underwent knee surgery after last season. As a veteran swapped in the middle of a multiyear deal, he has exercised his right to demand a trade. However, he seemed to get more comfortable in Los Angeles as last year progressed, and he could be back. If the club doesn't move him, he can become a free agent, but he probably wouldn't find a better contract than his current one. The Dodgers acquired him for his clubhouse presence. If anything, Jordan exceeded their expectations.

Position: LF
Bats: R **Throws:** R
Ht: 6' 1" **Wt:** 205

Opening Day Age: 36
Born: 3/29/67 in Baltimore, MD
ML Seasons: 11

Overall Statistics

	G	AB	R	H	D	T	HR	RBI	SB	BB	SO	Avg	OBP	Slg
'02	128	471	65	134	27	3	18	80	2	34	86	.285	.338	.469
Car.	1205	4402	664	1262	235	34	167	736	114	293	708	.287	.337	.469

Where He Hits the Ball

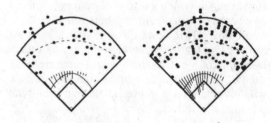

| Vs. LHP | Vs. RHP |

2002 Situational Stats

	AB	H	HR	RBI	Avg		AB	H	HR	RBI	Avg
Home	214	59	7	39	.276	LHP	109	33	6	28	.303
Road	257	75	11	41	.292	RHP	362	101	12	52	.279
First Half	276	76	13	44	.275	Sc Pos	125	34	7	60	.272
Scnd Half	195	58	5	36	.297	Clutch	71	21	2	11	.296

2002 Rankings (National League)

- 2nd in assists in left field (10)
- 3rd in fielding percentage in left field (.982)
- 7th in errors in left field (4)
- 8th in lowest percentage of pitches taken (47.1)
- Led the Dodgers in batting average at home

Eric Karros

2002 Season

Eric Karros went through a rigorous offseason conditioning program and entered the 2002 campaign determined to raise his average, even if it meant a drop in power numbers. He hit .320 through the first two and a half months, but that turned out to be his high-water mark. Not only did he hit only six homers with 38 RBI from June 20th to the end of the season, his average was a paltry .229.

Hitting

Karros stands erect and still at the plate. He is somewhat unusual for a righthanded hitter in that he likes the ball down and in. Though he likes to take balls on the outer half back through the box, the 35-year-old no longer can catch up with better fastballs. Rather, he must try to get ahead in the count and hope for a mistake. And to do that, he must avoid chasing breaking pitches off the outside corner. Karros is a very smart hitter, however, so opposing pitchers must mix up their patterns to keep him off balance.

Baserunning & Defense

Despite being one of the major leagues' slowest baserunners, Karros has managed to steal multiple bases in each of the last nine seasons. Otherwise, he is purely a station-to-station guy. If there is one area in which Karros has made significant improvement over the years, it's on the defensive end. He is much better at scooping up low throws, and he always has been quite deft at making the throw on the front end of double plays.

2003 Outlook

Karros had minor shoulder surgery in early October, correcting a season-long problem that may have been the main reason for his power outage. As a 10-and-5 man, he could have blocked the trade to the Cubs, but Karros honored a verbal agreement he had made with Dodgers owner Bob Daly not to do so. With Dusty Baker at the helm in Chicago, the veteran may get the bulk of the playing time at first over rookie phenom Hee Seop Choi. It is hard to imagine that the club is going to pay $9 million to a part-time player, though a platton situation is not entirely out of the question.

Position: 1B
Bats: R **Throws:** R
Ht: 6' 4" **Wt:** 226

Opening Day Age: 35
Born: 11/4/67 in Hackensack, NJ
ML Seasons: 12
Pronunciation: CARE-ose

Overall Statistics

	G	AB	R	H	D	T	HR	RBI	SB	BB	SO	Avg	OBP	Slg
'02	142	524	52	142	26	1	13	73	4	37	74	.271	.323	.399
Car.	1601	6002	752	1608	302	10	270	976	57	517	1105	.268	.325	.457

Where He Hits the Ball

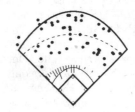

Vs. LHP   **Vs. RHP**

2002 Situational Stats

	AB	H	HR	RBI	Avg		AB	H	HR	RBI	Avg
Home	257	67	9	33	.261	LHP	101	32	3	17	.317
Road	267	75	4	40	.281	RHP	423	110	10	56	.260
First Half	308	90	9	42	.292	Sc Pos	136	41	6	62	.301
Scnd Half	216	52	4	31	.241	Clutch	93	33	2	17	.355

2002 Rankings (National League)

- 1st in fielding percentage at first base (.997)
- 5th in assists at first base (106)
- 7th in batting average in the clutch
- 9th in lowest on-base percentage vs. righthanded pitchers (.304)
- Led the Dodgers in sacrifice flies (6), batting average in the clutch, batting average vs. lefthanded pitchers and on-base percentage vs. lefthanded pitchers (.397)

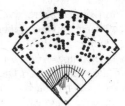

Los Angeles

Paul Lo Duca

2002 Season

Fresh off his breakout season of 2001, Paul Lo Duca picked up where he had left off. Though his power numbers were down, he hit .326 in the season's first half. However, despite his protestations to the contrary, the toll of catching the third most innings in baseball in 2002 clearly wore Lo Duca down. He hit just .233 after the All-Star break and struck out more than he walked, a telltale sign for the active leader in plate appearances per strikeout (minimum 1,000 at-bats).

Hitting

Lo Duca pounds high fastballs and will expand his rather small strike zone to get one he can drive. For a guy who strikes out so seldom, he is surprisingly aggressive. But he adopts a more defensive approach when behind in the count. The 25 homers in 2001 probably were an aberration, as the compact backstop really is a gap hitter. One of the secrets to Lo Duca's hitting success is his ability to handle breaking pitches. He seems to recognize them earlier than most hitters and lays off sliders and curveballs off the plate.

Baserunning & Defense

The constant crouching has robbed Lo Duca of the above-average speed he had when he first arrived in the bigs. He has retained a keen sense for running the bases and seldom will run his club out of an inning. Lo Duca is just an average receiver. His small frame allows him to slide easily to block balls in the dirt, but he often gets lazy and reaches for the ball. Though he has a quick release, he had a lot of trouble with his throwing accuracy last year. Only Mike Piazza allowed more stolen bases.

2003 Outlook

One of the Dodgers' offseason priorities was to acquire a solid backup for Lo Duca, as they simply cannot afford another offensive drop-off. Signed through 2004, he's a huge fan favorite that the Dodgers fully expect to be in the middle of their lineup for years to come.

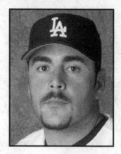

Position: C/1B
Bats: R **Throws:** R
Ht: 5'10" **Wt:** 185

Opening Day Age: 30
Born: 4/12/72 in Brooklyn, NY
ML Seasons: 5

Overall Statistics

	G	AB	R	H	D	T	HR	RBI	SB	BB	SO	Avg	OBP	Slg
'02	149	580	74	163	38	1	10	64	3	34	31	.281	.330	.402
Car.	350	1214	164	352	70	1	40	174	6	89	79	.290	.343	.448

Where He Hits the Ball

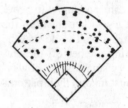 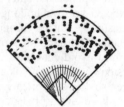

Vs. LHP   **Vs. RHP**

2002 Situational Stats

	AB	H	HR	RBI	Avg		AB	H	HR	RBI	Avg
Home	288	73	5	31	.253	LHP	137	42	2	20	.307
Road	292	90	5	33	.308	RHP	443	121	8	44	.273
First Half	301	98	5	38	.326	Sc Pos	153	47	1	50	.307
Scnd Half	279	65	5	26	.233	Clutch	104	23	1	9	.221

2002 Rankings (National League)

- 1st in lowest percentage of swings that missed (6.8)
- 2nd in lowest percentage of runners caught stealing as a catcher (24.4)
- 6th in highest percentage of swings put into play (54.3) and errors at catcher (8)
- 7th in GDPs (20)
- Led the Dodgers in singles, doubles, hit by pitch (10), lowest percentage of swings that missed (6.8) and batting average with two strikes (.240)

Hideo Nomo

2002 Season

Returning to his original major league team, Hideo Nomo won just three of his first nine starts, largely due to poor run support. He had trouble hitting his spots for a bit in May. But he found his rhythm after making a slight adjustment to his foot placement on the rubber. Over his last 25 starts, the 34-year-old went 13-1. And when the Dodgers were fighting to stay in the pennant race, he went almost a month without allowing more than two earned runs in any start.

Pitching

With his unique delivery, Nomo can get out of kilter and lose his command quite easily. Though he has a decent curve, he relies mostly on two pitches. The four-seamed fastball tops out around 92 MPH and has a little rise to it, while the bottom drops out of his 87-MPH split. When he can get ahead in the count, he makes hitters fish for splits out of the zone, and opponents batted just .198 last season when Nomo got a first-pitch strike.

Defense & Hitting

The tornado-like delivery leaves Nomo in poor fielding position, and he can be a bit clumsy off the mound. He has a weak move to first, and the elongated windup means it's open season for opposing baserunners. In fact, since Nomo came over from Japan in 1995, he's allowed more stolen bases than any other pitcher (258). While he has some power, his approach at the plate is to swing as hard as he can and hope for contact. It is a struggle for Nomo to get the bunt down when asked.

2003 Outlook

Signed as an innings-eating insurance policy due to the many question marks on the Dodgers' staff, Nomo was a godsend for the club. No longer the media sensation he was in the mid-1990s, Nomo is a seasoned veteran whose ability to deliver a solid performance every fifth day makes him a very valuable commodity. He's signed through this year, with an option for 2004.

Position: SP
Bats: R **Throws:** R
Ht: 6' 2" **Wt:** 210

Opening Day Age: 34
Born: 8/31/68 in Osaka, Japan
ML Seasons: 8
Pronunciation: hih-DAY-oh NO-mo

Overall Statistics

	W	L	Pct.	ERA	G	GS	Sv	IP	H	BB	SO	HR	Ratio
'02	16	6	.727	3.39	34	34	0	220.1	189	101	193	26	1.32
Car.	98	77	.560	3.96	250	248	0	1569.0	1351	713	1625	189	1.32

How Often He Throws Strikes

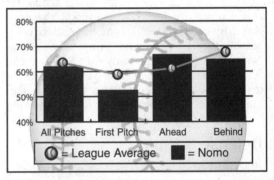

○ = League Average   ■ = Nomo

2002 Situational Stats

	W	L	ERA	Sv	IP		AB	H	HR	RBI	Avg
Home	7	3	3.89	0	108.2	LHB	394	86	8	38	.218
Road	9	3	2.90	0	111.2	RHB	407	103	18	47	.253
First Half	9	5	3.16	0	114.0	Sc Pos	195	49	5	62	.251
Scnd Half	7	1	3.64	0	106.1	Clutch	55	17	0	2	.309

2002 Rankings (National League)

- 1st in lowest fielding percentage at pitcher (.886)
- 2nd in walks allowed, stolen bases allowed (28) and errors at pitcher (4)
- 4th in games started and highest walks per nine innings (4.1)
- 5th in winning percentage
- 7th in wins, innings pitched, batters faced (926) and lowest ERA on the road
- Led the Dodgers in wins, hits allowed, batters faced (926), home runs allowed, strikeouts, pitches thrown (3,453), pickoff throws (123), winning percentage and lowest ERA on the road

Odalis Perez

2002 Season

Originally perceived as a throw-in in the Gary Sheffield deal, Odalis Perez was the Dodgers' best starting pitcher last year. There were questions about his durability, especially when he went through a tough stretch around the All-Star break. However, the young lefthander got his second wind and fashioned a 2.42 ERA over his last 11 starts. He flirted with several no-hitters during the season and basically pitched like a future, if not present, staff ace.

Pitching

Perez has great stuff. His fastball tops out in the low 90s, but with a lot of late tailing action. He complements the heater with a good changeup and sharp curveball. He also has impressive command of the strike zone. Among qualifying National League starters, only Curt Schilling and Randy Johnson had higher strikeout-walk ratios than Perez (4.1). He knows how to pitch, something that shouldn't be so surprising considering he came out of the Atlanta organization.

Defense & Hitting

Perez is very agile and is quite adept at stabbing balls hit back through the box. He also gets off the mound quickly enough to make plays on soft grounders that other pitchers don't even attempt to field. His pickoff move is effective—he nabbed nine opponents last year. He holds his own with the bat. Perez led the staff with 10 sacrifices and made contact in all but 14 plate appearances. When he does hit one into the outfield, he has the speed to take the extra base, as his five doubles tied for the league lead among pitchers.

2003 Outlook

Even Dodgers GM Dan Evans, who reportedly held out for Perez when the Braves were offering Kevin Millwood or Jason Marquis, couldn't have expected the kind of performance he got from his young lefty. If Perez can stay healthy, and it should be remembered that he missed the entire 2000 campaign due to elbow surgery, he should be one of the top young pitchers over the next half-decade. His combination of talent and a diablo-may-care attitude makes Perez look like a long-time winner.

Position: SP
Bats: L **Throws:** L
Ht: 6' 0" **Wt:** 150

Opening Day Age: 25
Born: 6/11/77 in Las Matas de Farfan, DR
ML Seasons: 4
Pronunciation: oh-DALL-iss

Overall Statistics

	W	L	Pct.	ERA	G	GS	Sv	IP	H	BB	SO	HR	Ratio
'02	15	10	.600	3.00	32	32	0	222.1	182	38	155	21	0.99
Car.	26	25	.510	4.12	84	65	0	421.1	400	134	313	41	1.27

How Often He Throws Strikes

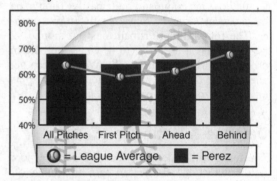

2002 Situational Stats

	W	L	ERA	Sv	IP		AB	H	HR	RBI	Avg
Home	7	6	2.75	0	124.1	LHB	179	40	4	13	.223
Road	8	4	3.31	0	98.0	RHB	628	142	17	61	.226
First Half	10	4	2.81	0	128.0	Sc Pos	146	35	4	50	.240
Scnd Half	5	6	3.24	0	94.1	Clutch	68	17	3	7	.250

2002 Rankings (National League)

- 2nd in balks (3), lowest on-base percentage allowed (.262) and fewest walks per nine innings (1.5)
- 3rd in highest strikeout-walk ratio (4.1) and fewest pitches thrown per batter (3.47)
- 4th in ERA and shutouts (2)
- 5th in complete games (4)
- Led the Dodgers in sacrifice bunts (10), innings pitched, GDPs induced (18), lowest batting average allowed (.226), lowest slugging percentage allowed (.347), lowest ERA at home, most run support per nine innings (4.9) and fewest home runs allowed per nine innings (.85)

Kevin Brown

Position: SP
Bats: R **Throws:** R
Ht: 6' 4" **Wt:** 200

Opening Day Age: 38
Born: 3/14/65 in McIntyre, GA
ML Seasons: 16

Overall Statistics

	W	L	Pct.	ERA	G	GS	Sv	IP	H	BB	SO	HR	Ratio
'02	3	4	.429	4.81	17	10	0	63.2	68	23	58	9	1.43
Car.	183	122	.600	3.22	419	409	0	2840.0	2656	791	2079	178	1.21

2002 Situational Stats

	W	L	ERA	Sv	IP		AB	H	HR	RBI	Avg
Home	1	3	4.38	0	37.0	LHB	106	26	4	16	.245
Road	2	1	5.40	0	26.2	RHB	142	42	5	14	.296
First Half	2	3	4.06	0	44.1	Sc Pos	63	16	2	21	.254
Scnd Half	1	1	6.52	0	19.1	Clutch	8	1	0	1	.125

2002 Season

Despite offseason elbow surgery, Kevin Brown willed his way into an Opening Day start. Recurring pain soon forced him out of the rotation, and a protruding disk sent him back to the operating table in early June. Though he returned as a reliever a few months later, the righthander eventually had to shut it down in early September.

Pitching, Defense & Hitting

The various injuries kept Brown's velocity in the low 90s last season, though he was able to retain the sharp movement of his two-seamed sinking fastball and slider. He never was able to regain his sharp command, so his walks were up and he left too many balls up over the plate. Brown's delivery leaves him falling off the mound, but he fields his position aggressively. Though he hit a career-high .250 and his second career home run last season, he's not very dangerous at the plate.

2003 Outlook

Brown has been on the disabled list six times since joining the Dodgers in 1999. He's pitched fewer than 180 innings over the last two seasons, after averaging almost 220 innings over the previous 12. If any 38-year-old can come all the way back, Brown can, but his whipsaw delivery clearly has taken its toll over the years.

Giovanni Carrara

Position: RP
Bats: R **Throws:** R
Ht: 6' 2" **Wt:** 235

Opening Day Age: 35
Born: 3/4/68 in Anzoategui, VZ
ML Seasons: 6

Overall Statistics

	W	L	Pct.	ERA	G	GS	Sv	IP	H	BB	SO	HR	Ratio
'02	6	3	.667	3.28	63	1	1	90.2	83	32	56	14	1.27
Car.	15	11	.577	5.15	151	18	1	286.1	309	123	196	56	1.51

2002 Situational Stats

	W	L	ERA	Sv	IP		AB	H	HR	RBI	Avg
Home	3	1	2.70	1	46.2	LHB	137	34	6	23	.248
Road	3	2	3.89	0	44.0	RHB	204	49	8	26	.240
First Half	5	2	3.78	1	52.1	Sc Pos	77	18	4	35	.234
Scnd Half	1	1	2.58	0	38.1	Clutch	138	34	9	26	.246

2002 Season

Giovanni Carrara picked up where he left off in 2001, chewing up some important middle innings. A strained right forearm that had been bothering him throughout the summer finally sent him to the disabled list in August. He closed the season strongly, however, and even pitched well in a spot start in late September.

Pitching, Defense & Hitting

Carrara has an easy windup, so his 92-MPH fastball sneaks up a bit on hitters. He has two breaking balls—a slow curve that serves as his offspeed pitch, and a hard one that is somewhere between a slider and cut fastball. None of his pitches are overwhelming, so he must spot them well to succeed. A bit on the chunky side, he's not the smoothest fielder. He has a pretty good move for a righthander, so he's able to keep opponents from running amok. Having spent most of his career in the bullpen, he has just 28 lifetime at-bats.

2003 Outlook

Carrara has established himself as a valuable component in the Dodgers' bullpen. He's eaten up 176 innings over the past two seasons, and his 3.22 ERA over that span is quite respectable. The 35-year-old always is willing to take the ball and can go several innings at a time.

Alex Cora

Position: SS/2B
Bats: L **Throws:** R
Ht: 6' 0" **Wt:** 180

Opening Day Age: 27
Born: 10/18/75 in
Caguas, PR
ML Seasons: 5

Overall Statistics

	G	AB	R	H	D	T	HR	RBI	SB	BB	SO	Avg	OBP	Slg
'02	115	258	37	75	14	4	5	28	7	26	38	.291	.371	.434
Car.	398	1079	117	256	51	14	13	92	11	85	161	.237	.306	.347

2002 Situational Stats

	AB	H	HR	RBI	Avg		AB	H	HR	RBI	Avg
Home	118	40	4	16	.339	LHP	22	7	0	2	.318
Road	140	35	1	12	.250	RHP	236	68	5	26	.288
First Half	94	28	2	11	.298	Sc Pos	55	20	0	20	.364
Scnd Half	164	47	3	17	.287	Clutch	61	17	2	9	.279

2002 Season

Alex Cora used his demotion to a bench role last season as a motivating force to work harder. It paid off. He hit almost 75 points higher than he had in 2001, and he eventually worked his way into a shortstop platoon with Cesar Izturis.

Hitting, Baserunning & Defense

Cora is basically a slap hitter who simply tries to put the ball in play. While he is able to use the entire field, he occasionally can drop the bat head on an inside fastball and coax it over the right-field wall. The hardest throwers still can overpower the diminutive shortstop, but last season Cora seemed to recognize breaking stuff earlier than he had in the past. His biggest deficiency is a lack of speed. He is a fine defensive player, regardless of where he plays. He has soft hands, a gun for an arm, and can turn the double play from either second base or shortstop.

2003 Outlook

Cora's professional approach last year really opened some eyes on the Dodgers' management team, and the trade of Mark Grudzielanek may result in even more playing time for Cora. That said, his skills set is limited, and Cora probably is best suited for a utility role as a spot starter and defensive replacement.

Marquis Grissom

Position: CF/LF
Bats: R **Throws:** R
Ht: 5'11" **Wt:** 188

Opening Day Age: 35
Born: 4/17/67 in Atlanta, GA
ML Seasons: 14
Pronunciation: mar-KEESE

Overall Statistics

	G	AB	R	H	D	T	HR	RBI	SB	BB	SO	Avg	OBP	Slg
'02	111	343	57	95	21	4	17	60	5	22	68	.277	.321	.510
Car.	1827	6989	1019	1889	323	51	183	783	414	489	1057	.270	.318	.410

2002 Situational Stats

	AB	H	HR	RBI	Avg		AB	H	HR	RBI	Avg
Home	170	41	10	26	.241	LHP	133	39	11	29	.293
Road	173	54	7	34	.312	RHP	210	56	6	31	.267
First Half	165	44	10	33	.267	Sc Pos	98	30	4	43	.306
Scnd Half	178	51	7	27	.287	Clutch	76	23	3	20	.303

2002 Season

Though he wasn't particularly happy about it, Marquis Grissom performed well in a center field platoon with Dave Roberts. Grissom hit almost .300 over the first two months and filled in admirably in left when Brian Jordan's back acted up in the second half.

Hitting, Baserunning & Defense

Grissom is a real hacker and makes no bones about it. He will chase fastballs out of the strike zone and can be fooled by breaking stuff away. He's developed more power in his 30s, and can crush mistakes on the inner half. When he hits the ball to the right side, it's by accident. After hitting .229 versus righthanders the previous three seasons, Grissom held his own against them last year. Time has taken a step away, but he still has above-average speed. He gets good jumps on balls in the outfield and his arm is adequate, though he may occasionally airmail a throw.

2003 Outlook

After putting together a fine season in his walkaway year, Grissom has made it clear he wants to play every day. He may get that chance after signing a two-year, $4.25 million contract with the Giants, who have an opening in center field. He should play at least as much as he did in 2002.

Tyler Houston

Position: 3B/1B
Bats: L **Throws:** R
Ht: 6' 1" **Wt:** 218

Opening Day Age: 32
Born: 1/17/71 in Long Beach, CA
ML Seasons: 7

Overall Statistics

	G	AB	R	H	D	T	HR	RBI	SB	BB	SO	Avg	OBP	Slg
'02	111	320	34	90	20	3	7	40	1	16	62	.281	.323	.428
Car.	646	1708	190	452	78	6	61	239	10	113	389	.265	.311	.424

2002 Situational Stats

	AB	H	HR	RBI	Avg		AB	H	HR	RBI	Avg
Home	150	47	6	20	.313	LHP	27	7	0	2	.259
Road	170	43	1	20	.253	RHP	293	83	7	38	.283
First Half	216	68	7	32	.315	Sc Pos	83	25	2	34	.301
Scnd Half	104	22	0	8	.212	Clutch	61	13	1	4	.213

2002 Season

Tyler Houston was traded out of baseball purgatory in Milwaukee last July and into the midst of a pennant race. In his first game with the Dodgers, he collected four hits, scored thrice and knocked in four runs. But that was the last meaningful baseball he played. Houston hit just .148 the rest of the year, serving mostly as a pinch-hitter.

Hitting, Baserunning & Defense

Houston is perceived as a platoon player. In parts of seven major league seasons, he's amassed just 140 at-bats against lefthanded pitching. He tends to be aggressive when he gets the chance to hit. He sits dead red, hoping to yank a fastball on the inner half. Breaking pitches of any sort give him trouble. He never will wow anyone with his defense, but the former catcher can handle either corner infield spot. He's strictly station-to-station on the bases.

2003 Outlook

While he helped the Dodgers by lighting a fire under Adrian Beltre, Houston wasn't happy at his reduced playing time. He was productive with Milwaukee, so there certainly is some talent there. Houston is a free agent who most likely is looking at a part-time role. Maybe he'll find a team where he could fit into a regular platoon.

Cesar Izturis

Position: SS
Bats: B **Throws:** R
Ht: 5' 9" **Wt:** 175

Opening Day Age: 23
Born: 2/10/80 in Barquisimeto, VZ
ML Seasons: 2
Pronunciation: IS-turis

Overall Statistics

	G	AB	R	H	D	T	HR	RBI	SB	BB	SO	Avg	OBP	Slg
'02	135	439	43	102	24	2	1	31	7	14	39	.232	.253	.303
Car.	181	573	62	138	30	4	3	40	15	16	54	.241	.259	.323

2002 Situational Stats

	AB	H	HR	RBI	Avg		AB	H	HR	RBI	Avg
Home	226	52	0	15	.230	LHP	147	45	1	13	.306
Road	213	50	1	16	.235	RHP	292	57	0	18	.195
First Half	313	72	1	24	.230	Sc Pos	110	24	0	29	.218
Scnd Half	126	30	0	7	.238	Clutch	61	10	0	0	.164

2002 Season

Acquired from Toronto last offseason, Cesar Izturis won the starting shortstop job with his sterling play last spring. He got off to a good start in April, but soon looked overmatched. After barely staying above the Mendoza Line over the next three months, Izturis spent the season's second half in a platoon with Alex Cora.

Hitting, Baserunning & Defense

The young switch-hitter has a nice stroke when swinging from his natural right side. Izturis looks to hit the ball on the ground and has a little pop in his bat. He can pull the ball quite a bit at times and is better served by spraying the ball around. He has a lot of work to do from the left side, where his swing is weak, and he struggles to make contact. Izturis is quite fast, but hasn't learned to get a good jump. On defense, he has great range, soft hands and a strong arm. He clearly was the captain of the infield.

2003 Outlook

Izturis lost confidence from the left side last year and wanted to give up switch-hitting, but the Dodgers talked him out of it. He makes the whole infield better with his skill and work ethic. Anything he can add offensively will be a bonus.

Los Angeles

Guillermo Mota

Position: RP
Bats: R **Throws:** R
Ht: 6' 4" **Wt:** 205

Opening Day Age: 29
Born: 7/25/73 in San
Pedro de Macoris, DR
ML Seasons: 4
Pronunciation:
mo-TAH

Overall Statistics

	W	L	Pct.	ERA	G	GS	Sv	IP	H	BB	SO	HR	Ratio
'02	1	3	.250	4.15	43	0	0	60.2	45	27	49	4	1.19
Car.	5	11	.313	4.37	176	0	0	195.2	177	82	131	21	1.32

2002 Situational Stats

	W	L	ERA	Sv	IP		AB	H	HR	RBI	Avg
Home	0	2	3.34	0	29.2	LHB	96	18	1	12	.188
Road	1	1	4.94	0	31.0	RHB	127	27	3	17	.213
First Half	1	0	2.61	0	31.0	Sc Pos	78	19	1	25	.244
Scnd Half	0	3	5.76	0	29.2	Clutch	38	8	0	3	.211

2002 Season

Acquired in a late spring deal for Matt Herges, Guillermo Mota provided solid middle relief last season. Mota compiled almost 100 innings between the majors and minors, and he clearly was gassed by season's end.

Pitching, Defense & Hitting

With the possible exception of Eric Gagne, Mota throws as hard as anyone on the Dodgers. Mota's fastball routinely reaches the upper 90s, though it was down to 92 MPH as he tired near the end of the season. The heater also tends to straighten out when he overthrows it. Mota also has a good hard slider and a decent changeup that he seldom uses in short relief. A converted shortstop, he hasn't been pitching very long and still is learning the nuances of his craft. Opposing basestealers can take advantage of his extended delivery. As might be expected, he fields his position well, and has a .333 lifetime batting average in limited at-bats.

2003 Outlook

Though the deal was assailed as a salary dump, Mota pitched every bit as well as Herges last season. As Mota gains experience, he could develop into a quality setup man. His pitching style is very similar to that of Felix Rodriguez, who started out in the Dodgers' organization as a catcher.

Paul Quantrill

Position: RP
Bats: L **Throws:** R
Ht: 6' 1" **Wt:** 195

Opening Day Age: 34
Born: 11/3/68 in
London, ON, Canada
ML Seasons: 11
Pronunciation:
KWAN-trill

Overall Statistics

	W	L	Pct.	ERA	G	GS	Sv	IP	H	BB	SO	HR	Ratio
'02	5	4	.556	2.70	86	0	1	76.2	80	25	53	1	1.37
Car.	57	68	.456	3.80	616	64	19	1014.0	1164	287	608	97	1.43

2002 Situational Stats

	W	L	ERA	Sv	IP		AB	H	HR	RBI	Avg
Home	3	1	2.31	0	39.0	LHB	122	31	1	11	.254
Road	2	3	3.11	1	37.2	RHB	178	49	0	11	.275
First Half	1	2	3.12	0	43.1	Sc Pos	76	20	1	19	.263
Scnd Half	4	2	2.16	1	33.1	Clutch	173	48	1	17	.277

2002 Season

Paul Quantrill got off to a slow start last season, causing Dodgers officials to wonder if they had made a big mistake acquiring him from Toronto. They kept sending him out there, however, and the veteran reliever eventually turned it around. In fact, he had a 1.57 ERA from June 3 to the end of the season.

Pitching, Defense & Hitting

Quantrill might occasionally hit 90 MPH on the gun with his sinking fastball, and he counters that with a nice little slider. He has a herky-jerky delivery and releases the ball from an odd angle. He must keep everything down to be effective. When Quantrill gets a lot of work, he gets more movement on his sinker. He has nice footwork and relays the ball to first rather quickly for a righthander, and he fields his position just fine. After spending most of his career in American League bullpens, Quantrill hasn't spent much time with a bat in his hands.

2003 Outlook

Quantrill not only wants the ball every day, he needs to pitch on a regular basis in order to be effective. He will be a valuable setup man for the Dodgers again this season, and there is no reason to expect any drop in performance.

Dave Roberts

Position: CF
Bats: L **Throws:** L
Ht: 5'10" **Wt:** 180

Opening Day Age: 30
Born: 5/31/72 in Okinawa, Japan
ML Seasons: 4

Overall Statistics

	G	AB	R	H	D	T	HR	RBI	SB	BB	SO	Avg	OBP	Slg
'02	127	422	63	117	14	7	3	34	45	48	51	.277	.353	.365
Car.	202	587	93	157	19	7	5	48	57	60	71	.267	.336	.349

2002 Situational Stats

	AB	H	HR	RBI	Avg		AB	H	HR	RBI	Avg
Home	191	49	0	14	.257	LHP	25	10	0	4	.400
Road	231	68	3	20	.294	RHP	397	107	3	30	.270
First Half	225	68	2	20	.302	Sc Pos	80	26	1	32	.325
Scnd Half	197	49	1	14	.249	Clutch	52	10	0	6	.192

2002 Season

Dave Roberts was acquired from the Indians for a couple of minor leaguers last offseason. He came in and provided the Dodgers with a much-needed spark at the top of their lineup. Platooning with Marquis Grissom in center field, Roberts proved to be a pest both at the plate and on the basepaths.

Hitting, Baserunning & Defense

The lefty speed merchant looks to slap the ball on the ground and run like hell. Roberts always is looking for an opportunity to lay down a bunt and was fourth in baseball with 17 bunt hits last season. He has a good eye and is perfectly willing to take a free pass. He can be overpowered by the hardest throwers and sometimes will take awkward swings on breaking pitches. Roberts has blazing speed and is a student of the basestealing game. He is an adequate center fielder with a below-average throwing arm.

2003 Outlook

Stuck behind Kenny Lofton in Cleveland, Roberts totaled only 165 major league at-bats over eight seasons in their system. Given the opportunity to play on a regular basis, he was a godsend to the Dodgers. With Grissom off to greener pastures, Roberts may be given every opportunity to play every day this year.

Paul Shuey

Position: RP
Bats: R **Throws:** R
Ht: 6' 3" **Wt:** 215

Opening Day Age: 32
Born: 9/16/70 in Lima, OH
ML Seasons: 9
Pronunciation: SHOE-ee

Overall Statistics

	W	L	Pct.	ERA	G	GS	Sv	IP	H	BB	SO	HR	Ratio
'02	8	2	.800	3.31	67	0	1	68.0	56	31	63	3	1.28
Car.	39	23	.629	3.66	389	0	22	435.1	388	223	474	34	1.40

2002 Situational Stats

	W	L	ERA	Sv	IP		AB	H	HR	RBI	Avg
Home	7	1	3.26	1	38.2	LHB	115	26	1	15	.226
Road	1	1	3.38	0	29.1	RHB	138	30	2	18	.217
First Half	2	0	2.64	0	30.2	Sc Pos	78	19	2	29	.244
Scnd Half	6	2	3.86	1	37.1	Clutch	140	29	1	20	.207

2002 Season

Paul Shuey allowed two earned runs in his first 23 outings with Cleveland last year, before a groin strain sent him to the disabled list. Soon after his return, he was traded to the Dodgers. Clearly trying too hard to impress his new teammates, Shuey allowed 23 of the first 44 batters he faced to reach base, before he settled down and pitched with his usual effectiveness.

Pitching, Defense & Hitting

There never has been any question about Shuey's arm. He's got a 94-MPH fastball, a decent curve and a devastating split that gets most of his strikeouts. When his control deserts him, Shuey tends to make mistakes. His delivery leaves him in an awkward fielding position, and he doesn't react well to balls hit in his direction. Over the last two seasons, opposing basestealers are 19-for-20, which tells a lot about his pickoff move. He collected his first major league hit after coming to the Dodgers.

2003 Outlook

Shuey allowed a .159 average over his final 19 appearances last season, giving the Dodgers a glimpse of what he's capable of. He should provide some excellent setup work this year, at least when healthy. He's been on the DL at least once in each of the past six seasons.

Other Los Angeles Dodgers

Victor Alvarez (Pos: LHP, Age: 26)

	W	L	Pct.	ERA	G	GS	Sv	IP	H	BB	SO	HR	Ratio
'02	0	1	.000	4.35	4	1	0	10.1	9	2	7	1	1.06
Car.	0	1	.000	4.35	4	1	0	10.1	9	2	7	1	1.06

Alvarez started the Dodgers' final game last season, allowing just four hits in seven innings. He isn't a great prospect, but is lefthanded, has some versatility, and can register some strikeouts. 2003 Outlook: C

Kevin Beirne (Pos: RHP, Age: 29)

	W	L	Pct.	ERA	G	GS	Sv	IP	H	BB	SO	HR	Ratio
'02	2	0	1.000	3.41	12	3	0	29.0	26	17	17	4	1.48
Car.	3	3	.500	6.09	46	4	0	85.2	89	43	63	14	1.54

Beirne signed a minor league deal with Los Angeles last year, pitched well at Triple-A, came up to the Dodgers in August and started a few games in September. His contract for 2003 was sold to the Osaka club of the Japanese Pacific League. 2003 Outlook: D

Jolbert Cabrera (Pos: CF/RF, Age: 30, Bats: R)

	G	AB	R	H	D	T	HR	RBI	SB	BB	SO	Avg	OBP	Slg
'02	48	84	8	12	2	0	0	8	1	7	15	.143	.215	.167
Car.	320	585	91	138	22	4	3	61	20	32	80	.236	.285	.303

Cabrera's biggest success last year was surviving a gunshot wound to his buttocks during a carjacking in his native Colombia. He was traded to the Dodgers in July, and can play almost position. 2003 Outlook: C

Bryan Corey (Pos: RHP, Age: 29)

	W	L	Pct.	ERA	G	GS	Sv	IP	H	BB	SO	HR	Ratio
'02	0	0	–	0.00	1	0	0	1.0	0	0	0	0	0.00
Car.	0	0	–	7.20	4	0	0	5.0	6	2	1	1	1.60

Corey has spent the past five summers in five different Triple-A cities. He was with Las Vegas in 2002, though he also had a cup-of-coffee with the Dodgers. He later became a free agent. 2003 Outlook: C

Robert Ellis (Pos: RHP, Age: 32)

	W	L	Pct.	ERA	G	GS	Sv	IP	H	BB	SO	HR	Ratio
'02	0	1	.000	10.13	3	0	0	2.2	6	0	0	1	2.25
Car.	6	6	.500	5.60	25	17	0	99.2	112	38	46	13	1.51

Ellis had a winning record for the world champion Diamondbacks in 2001, but was designated for assignment and spent most of last year in Triple-A. He has signed a minor league contract with the Rangers. 2003 Outlook: C

Dave Hansen (Pos: 1B/3B, Age: 34, Bats: L)

	G	AB	R	H	D	T	HR	RBI	SB	BB	SO	Avg	OBP	Slg
'02	96	120	15	35	6	0	2	17	1	14	22	.292	.363	.392
Car.	974	1477	154	394	70	5	29	184	3	230	267	.267	.365	.380

Hansen may have set a Dodger career record in pinch-hits, but 2002 wasn't his best season in the role. Still, he hit .349 overall after June 1. Hansen moves down the road in southern California after inking a two-year deal with the Padres. 2003 Outlook: B

Mike Kinkade (Pos: 1B, Age: 29, Bats: R)

	G	AB	R	H	D	T	HR	RBI	SB	BB	SO	Avg	OBP	Slg
'02	37	50	7	19	5	0	2	11	1	4	10	.380	.483	.600
Car.	134	267	31	75	13	1	8	34	4	21	51	.281	.360	.427

Kinkade has proven he's a .300 hitter at Triple-A, and he hit really well with the Dodgers last year. He should at least be able to stick in the majors as a solid bat off the bench. 2003 Outlook: C

Chad Kreuter (Pos: C, Age: 38, Bats: B)

	G	AB	R	H	D	T	HR	RBI	SB	BB	SO	Avg	OBP	Slg
'02	41	95	8	25	5	0	2	12	1	10	31	.263	.333	.379
Car.	937	2487	289	591	122	8	54	274	5	358	591	.238	.336	.358

With Paul Lo Duca seizing a greater share of the catching duty, Kreuter saw his playing time decrease in 2002. Kreuter really struggled against righthanders last season, and his walk rate declined. 2003 Outlook: C

Jesse Orosco (Pos: LHP, Age: 45)

	W	L	Pct.	ERA	G	GS	Sv	IP	H	BB	SO	HR	Ratio
'02	1	2	.333	3.00	56	0	1	27.0	24	12	22	4	1.33
Car.	85	78	.521	3.04	1187	4	142	1261.1	1014	560	1150	109	1.25

Although he rarely faces more than two batters at a time, Orosco remains effective. Last year he became the oldest hurler to save a game since Hoyt Wilhelm. Orosco has signed with San Diego for this season. 2003 Outlook: B

Jeff Reboulet (Pos: 2B, Age: 38, Bats: R)

	G	AB	R	H	D	T	HR	RBI	SB	BB	SO	Avg	OBP	Slg
'02	38	48	3	10	3	0	0	2	0	6	13	.208	.291	.271
Car.	925	1968	273	473	90	4	17	177	20	265	354	.240	.333	.316

Reboulet's versatility is a plus, but he suffered a back injury while having one of his least productive seasons. He filed for free agency, though at his age, the suitors may be few. 2003 Outlook: C

Dave Ross (Pos: C, Age: 26, Bats: R)

	G	AB	R	H	D	T	HR	RBI	SB	BB	SO	Avg	OBP	Slg
'02	8	10	2	2	1	0	1	2	0	2	4	.200	.385	.600
Car.	8	10	2	2	1	0	1	2	0	2	4	.200	.385	.600

Ross has nice power for a catcher and will take a walk. Although he strikes out about once per game, he has a chance to push for a spot as Paul Lo Duca's backup. 2003 Outlook: C

Wilkin Ruan (Pos: CF, Age: 24, Bats: R)

	G	AB	R	H	D	T	HR	RBI	SB	BB	SO	Avg	OBP	Slg
'02	12	11	2	3	1	0	0	3	0	0	2	.273	.273	.364
Car.	12	11	2	3	1	0	0	3	0	0	2	.273	.273	.364

Ruan came to the Dodgers' organization via a trade last spring. He has great speed and center field instincts. He did well at Triple-A, though he needs to walk more to help at the top of the order. 2003 Outlook: C

Dennis Springer (**Pos**: RHP, **Age**: 38)

	W	L	Pct.	ERA	G	GS	Sv	IP	H	BB	SO	HR	Ratio
'02	0	1	.000	6.75	1	0	0	1.1	1	2	1	0	2.25
Car.	24	48	.333	5.18	130	98	1	655.1	702	258	296	108	1.46

Knuckleballers sometimes peak relatively late, but Springer probably won't be one of them. He fooled few hitters in Triple-A last year, and has won only 10 of his last 40 major league decisions. 2003 Outlook: C

Jeff Williams (**Pos**: LHP, **Age**: 30)

	W	L	Pct.	ERA	G	GS	Sv	IP	H	BB	SO	HR	Ratio
'02	0	0	–	11.70	10	0	0	10.0	15	7	11	2	2.20
Car.	4	1	.800	7.49	37	4	0	57.2	65	41	30	10	1.84

Williams moved to the bullpen full-time in 2002, and succeeded as the Triple-A closer. But he again failed to establish himself in the majors, and his contract was sold to Hanshin of the Japanese Central League. 2003 Outlook: D

Los Angeles Dodgers Minor League Prospects

Organization Overview:

Slowly but surely, things appear to be looking up for the Dodgers' organization. Though the big club failed to reach the postseason once again last year, they were competitive deep into September. And now they're getting out from under a few of the killer contracts from the Kevin Malone era. Furthermore, as the memory of their five straight Rookies of the Year from 1992 to 1996 becomes a distant one, the club quietly is building their minor league system back up again. Under the enlightened leadership of GM Dan Evans and Director of Player Development Bill Bavasi, they've drafted and/or signed several power arms, and position players with some pop, over the last couple of years. While the Dodgers still lack any top-line prospects in the upper levels, every one of their minor league clubs posted a winning record last year.

Reggie Abercrombie

Position: OF   **Opening Day Age:** 21
Bats: R **Throws:** R   **Born:** 7/15/81 in
Ht: 6' 3" **Wt:** 210   Columbus, GA

Recent Statistics

	G	AB	R	H	D	T	HR	RBI	SB	BB	SO	Avg
2001 A Wilmington	125	486	63	110	17	3	10	41	44	19	154	.226
2002 A Vero Beach	132	526	80	145	23	13	10	56	41	27	158	.276
2002 AA Jacksnville	1	4	1	1	0	0	0	0	1	0	1	.250

While some Dodgers prospects have more speed and others more power, no one in the organization puts the whole package of tools together like Abercrombie. His extra-base totals have jumped from 10 to 30 to 46 in his three professional seasons. He also has stolen 118 bases at a 77-percent clip. When he makes contact, the ball explodes off his bat, but Abercrombie has struck out more than 150 times in each of his two full seasons. He has the speed to play center field and the arm to play right, and he takes good routes to flyballs. Much of his game is still raw, however. It would not surprise anyone in the organization to see the 21-year-old struggle in his first shot at Double-A this year.

Chin-Feng Chen

Position: OF   **Opening Day Age:** 25
Bats: R **Throws:** R   **Born:** 10/28/77 in Tainan
Ht: 6' 1" **Wt:** 189   City, Taiwan

Recent Statistics

	G	AB	R	H	D	T	HR	RBI	SB	BB	SO	Avg
2002 AAA Las Vegas	137	511	90	145	26	4	26	84	1	58	160	.284
2002 NL Los Angeles	3	5	1	0	0	0	0	0	0	1	3	.000

Chen put up such big numbers in his first professional season in 1999 that he's been seen as a bit of a disappointment since. Yet he still socked 26 homers in his first exposure to Triple-A pitching last year. Perhaps more importantly, he stayed healthy all season after losing part of the 2001 campaign due to offseason shoulder surgery. The fact that the corner outfielder held his own at the plate while learning to play first base also impressed the powers that be in the Dodgers' organization. Chen has big-time power from the right side, a rather rare commodity in today's game, and that could earn him a spot on the major league bench before this season is out. In the meantime, he probably will return to Las Vegas to try to make contact a bit more often.

Jonathan Figueroa

Position: P   **Opening Day Age:** 19
Bats: L **Throws:** L   **Born:** 9/15/83 in
Ht: 6' 5" **Wt:** 205   Acarigua, Venezuela

Recent Statistics

	W	L	ERA	G	GS	Sv	IP	H	R	BB	SO	HR
2002 R Great Falls	2	1	1.42	7	7	0	31.2	16	7	19	48	0
2002 A S Georgia	5	2	1.42	8	8	0	44.1	22	10	20	57	1

Though he didn't turn 19 years of age until mid-September, Figueroa overmatched hitters at two levels in his first pro season last year. In fact, he posted the same ERA (1.42) at both Rookie-level Great Falls and South Georgia of the Class-A South Atlantic League. The 6-foot-4 lefty throws a fastball that tops out in the mid 90s. He is able to alter his three-quarters arm slot in order to change the angle of his breaking ball. The former first baseman only started pitching when he was 15, so he still is learning his craft. He needs innings and could use an offspeed pitch, but Figueroa has a chance to be a top-of-the-line starter.

Alfredo Gonzalez

Position: P   **Opening Day Age:** 23
Bats: R **Throws:** R   **Born:** 9/17/79 in Nagua,
Ht: 5' 11" **Wt:** 165   DR

Recent Statistics

	W	L	ERA	G	GS	Sv	IP	H	R	BB	SO	HR
2001 R Great Falls	3	4	3.56	11	8	0	48.0	43	26	12	56	1
2001 A Wilmington	1	0	3.00	2	1	0	9.0	10	4	3	12	0
2002 A Vero Beach	2	1	1.57	17	0	1	34.1	20	6	11	47	3
2002 AA Jacksnville	0	1	1.35	13	0	3	20.0	13	4	2	18	0
2002 AAA Las Vegas	2	3	2.91	14	0	1	21.2	23	10	9	23	1

After spending three years with the Dodgers' affiliate in the Dominican Summer League, Alfredo Gonzalez was deemed ready to pitch in the States in 2001. Last year, he rocketed through three levels and posted a 1.89 ERA, with an impressive strikeout-walk ratio along the way. The 23-year-old has a 94-95 MPH fastball, and his changeup was compared to Pedro Martinez' by one Dodgers official. While Gonzalez is working on a slider, the two pitches probably are enough for a reliever. If he can learn to put the fastball where he wants it more often, he quickly could evolve into one of the key guys that bridge the gap to Eric Gagne.

Joel Hanrahan

Position: P
Bats: R **Throws:** R
Ht: 6' 2" **Wt:** 191

Opening Day Age: 21
Born: 10/6/81 in Des
Moines, IA

Recent Statistics

		W	L	ERA	G	GS	Sv	IP	H	R	BB	SO	HR
2001 A Wilmington		9	11	3.38	27	26	0	144.0	136	71	55	116	13
2002 A Vero Beach		10	6	4.20	25	25	0	143.2	129	74	51	139	11
2002 AA Jacksonville		1	1	10.64	3	3	0	11.0	15	14	7	10	2

Just like his stuff, Hanrahan's minor league numbers are not overly impressive. Then again, he will be just 21 years of age when he joins the rotation for Double-A Jacksonville this season. His fastball tops out in the low 90s, and he mixes it with a sharp slider and a nice changeup. Hanrahan is a gutsy guy who knows how to pitch, so he will throw any of his offerings at any point in the count. Once the Dodgers' 2000 second-round selection is able to hone his mechanics and refine his command, he should settle in as a mid-rotation innings-eater at Dodger Stadium, probably around 2005.

Koyie Hill

Position: C
Bats: B **Throws:** R
Ht: 6' 0" **Wt:** 190

Opening Day Age: 24
Born: 3/9/79 in Tulsa,
OK

Recent Statistics

		G	AB	R	H	D	T	HR	RBI	SB	BB	SO	Avg
2001 A Wilmington		134	498	65	150	20	2	8	79	21	49	82	.301
2002 AA Jacksonville		130	468	67	127	25	1	11	64	5	76	88	.271

Hill has some pop from both sides of the plate, something that can't be said about many catchers now or at any time in baseball history. The former Wichita State third baseman has been a backstop for only a few seasons, so he still is learning the nuances of calling a game. That said, he has a strong and accurate arm along with decent footwork behind the plate. Last year, his first at Double-A Jacksonville, Hill not only hit 11 homers, but also added an eye-opening 25 doubles. Should he continue his progress this season, the 24-year-old could find himself sharing time with Paul Lo Duca and Todd Hundley as soon as 2004.

James Loney

Position: 1B
Bats: L **Throws:** L
Ht: 6' 3" **Wt:** 205

Opening Day Age: 18
Born: 5/7/84 in Missouri
City, TX

Recent Statistics

		G	AB	R	H	D	T	HR	RBI	SB	BB	SO	Avg
2002 R Great Falls		47	170	33	63	22	3	5	30	5	25	18	.371
2002 A Vero Beach		17	67	6	20	6	0	0	5	0	6	10	.299

Though many organizations saw Loney as a pitcher, the Dodgers liked the way he swung the bat and placed their 2002 first-round draft pick at first base. So far at least, they appear to be right. The lanky lefty had no problem handling Rookie-level Pioneer League pitching, hitting .371 with 22 doubles in just 170 at-bats. After only 17 games at high Class-A Vero Beach,

Loney's season ended when a pitch broke his left wrist. He uses the entire field, and the club expects him to fill out and eventually send many of those doubles over the wall. He has good hands and should become an excellent first sacker as his footwork improves. While he probably will return to Vero Beach to start this season, he probably should move up the road to Double-A Jacksonville before the campaign is complete.

Joe Thurston

Position: 2B
Bats: L **Throws:** R
Ht: 5' 11" **Wt:** 175

Opening Day Age: 23
Born: 9/29/79 in
Fairfield, CA

Recent Statistics

		G	AB	R	H	D	T	HR	RBI	SB	BB	SO	Avg
2002 AAA Las Vegas		136	587	106	196	39	13	12	55	22	25	60	.334
2002 NL Los Angeles		8	13	1	6	1	0	0	1	0	0	1	.462

After leading all minor leaguers in both hits and total bases last year, Thurston was named the Dodgers' Minor League Player of the Year for the second time in three seasons. The lefty sprays the ball around the park and looks to take the extra base at every opportunity. Thurston also is adept at bunting, and has averaged 28 stolen bases per year as he's climbed through the system. Though he started out at shortstop, he now plays exclusively at second base, where his range and ability to turn the double play are just average. Thurston is known, however, for coming through at crucial times, both at the plate and in the field. He is a winner who is ready for the majors, and the trade of Mark Grudzielanek opens the door for Thurston to become a regular.

Others to Watch

Luke Allen (24) has hit exactly .300 in six seasons in the Dodgers' system. He could make the big club this season, as he runs pretty well and has a legitimate right-field arm. His inability to hit for big power limits his upside. . . This season is a crucial one in the development of **Willie Aybar** (20). The third baseman has loads of pop in his bat, but he hit .215 at high Class-A Vero Beach last year. He had more walks than strike-outs, so he has at least an understanding of the strike zone. . . In his first 544 pro at-bats, **Victor Diaz** (21) hit .351 with 48 doubles. He finished last season at Double-A, where he may have been in over his head. He has moved from second base to first and back to second again, so defense may be a hindrance. . . Keep an eye on the Dodgers' Minor League Pitcher of the Year, **Edwin Jackson** (19), a converted outfielder who reaches 94 MPH. The righthander posted a 2.06 ERA at two levels over two years by mixing in a solid change-up and a still-in-progress breaker. . . Righthander **Brian Pilkington** (20) recovered from shoulder surgery in 2001 to toss 131.1 innings at two levels of Class-A last year. His fastball hits 91-92 MPH. His curveball is not as knee buckling as that of his uncle, Bert Blyleven, but he brings a professional presence to the mound.

Los Angeles

Offense

Although Miller Park got labeled a hitters' park early on, the results haven't borne that out. It slightly favored the hitter in its inaugural season of 2001, but it favored the pitcher to a comparable extent last year. Miller Park's elements cut both ways. Working for the hitter are its short power alleys and the ability to shut out cold weather. Pitchers are helped by the long foul lines and the glare and shadows that come when the sun is low in the sky.

Defense

There's little foul territory down the first-base line, which eases the burden on first and second basemen who aren't proficient at chasing down foul pops. The deep outfield corners require the left and right fielders to have decent arms, especially the right fielder. On the other hand, the short alleys reduce the amount of ground the center fielder has to cover.

Who It Helps the Most

Richie Sexson has the kind of alley-to-alley power the park figured to help most. He has hit better at Miller Park both years, though it seemed to help his power in 2001 and his average in 2002. Ben Sheets has been somewhat more effective here overall, and Ray King has pitched very well at home for two years in a row. It might have been a fluke that Valerio de los Santos—an extreme flyball pitcher—didn't give up a single homer at Miller Park all year.

Who It Hurts the Most

Ping-hitting Alex Sanchez didn't hit as well at Miller, probably because the center fielder can afford to play a little shallower. Matt Stairs hit for better power and average on the road last year.

Rookies & Newcomers

Keith Ginter has the kind of mid-range power that might get a decent boost from the short power alleys, as long as he doesn't try to pull the ball too much. On the other hand, young shortstop Bill Hall ultimately might suffer if he's too tempted to shoot for the fences.

Dimensions: LF-344, LCF-371, CF-400, RCF-374, RF-345

Capacity: 41,900

Elevation: 635 feet

Surface: Grass

Foul Territory: Small

Park Factors

2002 Season

	Home Games Brewers	Opp	Total	Away Games Brewers	Opp	Total	Index
G	75	75	150	75	75	150	
Avg	.249	.255	.252	.252	.277	.264	96
AB	2417	2579	4996	2580	2473	5053	99
R	277	354	631	305	388	693	91
H	603	658	1261	649	684	1333	95
2B	122	141	263	126	127	253	105
3B	12	14	26	14	13	27	97
HR	58	95	153	71	88	159	97
BB	242	284	526	238	340	578	92
SO	485	519	1004	550	431	981	104
E	46	40	86	53	44	97	89
E-Infield	42	33	75	45	35	80	94
LHB-Avg	.249	.267	.259	.248	.281	.264	98
LHB-HR	20	47	67	21	41	62	104
RHB-Avg	.250	.247	.248	.254	.274	.263	94
RHB-HR	38	48	86	50	47	97	92

2001-2002

	Home Games Brewers	Opp	Total	Away Games Brewers	Opp	Total	Index
G	147	147	294	150	150	300	100
Avg	.253	.261	.257	.247	.270	.258	100
AB	4808	5074	9882	5164	4946	10110	100
R	618	711	1329	639	760	1399	97
H	1218	1324	2542	1277	1336	2613	99
2B	239	273	512	263	265	528	99
3B	25	28	53	30	34	64	85
HR	150	189	339	164	164	328	106
BB	455	591	1046	467	646	1121	95
SO	1099	984	2083	1208	919	2127	100
E	87	82	169	101	77	178	97
E-Infield	78	67	145	83	60	143	103
LHB-Avg	.260	.273	.267	.252	.264	.258	103
LHB-HR	61	91	152	61	71	132	118
RHB-Avg	.250	.253	.251	.245	.274	.259	97
RHB-HR	89	98	187	103	93	196	97

2002 Rankings (National League)
- Third-lowest walk factor

Ned Yost

2002 Season

The Brewers lost 106 games last year, the most in team history. So it's not surprising that Ned Yost will begin this season as Milwaukee's newest manager. Davey Lopes opened 2002 in the role, but was fired in mid-April after the Brewers started 3-12. Jerry Royster inherited a roster of under-achieving veterans, and he didn't stop the slide. Yost has accepted a two-year contract. While his only managing experience consists of three years in the low minors between 1988 and 1990, he since has learned from one of the masters, as a coach on Bobby Cox' staff.

Offense

Yost, a .212 hitter over parts of six major league seasons, must hope the Brewers are better offensively than he was. He served the last four years as the Braves' third-base coach. Cox comes from the Earl Weaver school of managing, which likes to rely on three-run homers. It'll be interesting to see if Yost follows suit. After ranking third in the National League with 209 homers in 2001, the Brewers plummeted to 15th with 139 last year. A return to good health by Richie Sexson and Geoff Jenkins would help, though Jose Hernandez' potential departure would leave a longball void.

Pitching & Defense

Before working as the Braves' third-base coach, Yost was Atlanta's bullpen coach for eight years. Unfortunately, the Brewers don't have any Greg Madduxes or Tom Glavines lying around. But they do have Ben Sheets, who looks like a legitimate building block. Glendon Rusch also can be a respectable starter, while Yost inherits a bullpen with some solid components. Yost was a catcher during his playing career, so obviously he's familiar with pitch-calling and defensive positioning.

2003 Outlook

Yost will face plenty of challenges, including: plugging the hole at shortstop left by the expected defection of Hernandez; determining whether untested Keith Ginter is the answer at third; deciding whether Alex Sanchez is the long-term solution in center field; and sorting out the candidates for the back end of the starting rotation. At least no one will be expecting miracles.

Born: 8/19/54 in Eureka, CA

Playing Experience: 1980-1985, Mil, Tex, Mon

Managerial Experience: No major league managing experience

Manager Statistics (Jerry Royster)

Year	Team, Lg	W	L	Pct	GB	Finish
2002	Milwaukee, NL	53	94	.361	41.0	6th Central
1 Season		53	94	.361	–	–

2002 Starting Pitchers by Days Rest

	<=3	4	5	6+
Brewers Starts	0	80	39	21
Brewers ERA	–	5.70	4.23	4.74
NL Avg Starts	1	88	42	21
NL ERA	3.18	4.22	4.14	4.58

2002 Situational Stats

	Jerry Royster	NL Average
Hit & Run Success %	42.4	36.5
Stolen Base Success %	65.9	68.3
Platoon Pct.	48.9	52.7
Defensive Subs	14	19
High-Pitch Outings	6	7
Quick/Slow Hooks	15/20	24/11
Sacrifice Attempts	96	95

2002 Rankings —Jerry Royster (National League)

- 1st in slow hooks
- 3rd in intentional walks (55)

Paul Bako

Traded To CUBS

2002 Season

After backing up Javy Lopez for Atlanta in 2001, Paul Bako was traded to Milwaukee during spring training of 2002. One of the other players in the deal was Henry Blanco, who had been the Brewers' primary receiver. Bako thus inherited a greater share of the catching chores than he'd handled with the Braves. He had a respectable first half at the plate last year, but completely hit the skids in the second half. He hit just .163 with no homers and six RBI in his final 40 games.

Hitting

Bako is an inside-out hitter who rarely pulls the ball or hits it in the air. He gets most of his base hits by punching balls through the infield, especially to the right side when the first baseman is holding a runner. Lefthanders have overmatched him in the limited chances he's had against them. Bako will take an occasional walk, but he strikes out a bit much for a contact-oriented hitter with little extra-base power. He occasionally was used as a pinch-hitter last year, though he didn't perform well, going 1-for-10. He has struggled with men in scoring position during his major league career, batting .181 in those situations.

Baserunning & Defense

While Bako is a solid all-around receiver with sound fundamentals, he doesn't excel in any one facet of the game. His arm is reasonably strong and accurate, he blocks balls capably, and his pitch-calling never has been questioned. He has little speed, though, and is a non-factor on the basepaths. He has stolen just three bases in 398 games in the big leagues.

2003 Outlook

Bako was traded to the Cubs at the end of November. His role with Chicago will be much more clear-cut than it would have been with the Brewers, as he'll clearly be the understudy to Damian Miller. That probably is a good thing for Bako, as he is the kind of player who contributes best when he isn't overexposed. He is a lefthanded hitter, so the Cubs will find a way to get him some at-bats.

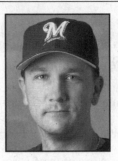

Position: C
Bats: L **Throws:** R
Ht: 6' 2" **Wt:** 205

Opening Day Age: 30
Born: 6/20/72 in Lafayette, LA
ML Seasons: 5
Pronunciation: BACH-oh

Overall Statistics

	G	AB	R	H	D	T	HR	RBI	SB	BB	SO	Avg	OBP	Slg
'02	87	234	24	55	8	1	4	20	0	20	46	.235	.295	.329
Car.	398	1112	100	272	54	5	13	102	3	116	283	.245	.314	.337

Where He Hits the Ball

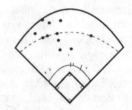 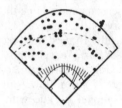

Vs. LHP   **Vs. RHP**

2002 Situational Stats

	AB	H	HR	RBI	Avg		AB	H	HR	RBI	Avg
Home	117	30	2	9	.256	LHP	30	5	0	2	.167
Road	117	25	2	11	.214	RHP	204	50	4	18	.245
First Half	128	35	4	14	.273	Sc Pos	56	11	1	16	.196
Scnd Half	106	20	0	6	.189	Clutch	39	9	0	3	.231

2002 Rankings (National League)

- Led the Brewers in fewest GDPs per GDP situation (7.1%)

Ronnie Belliard

2002 Season

Ronnie Belliard's career has fallen apart with puzzling suddenness. He was in the midst of a fairly good season in 2001 when a sprained ankle virtually ended his year in August. The Brewers then signed Eric Young over the winter and handed him Belliard's second-base job. In 2002, Belliard fought for playing time at second and third, but didn't adjust well to a reserve role and completely stopped hitting. He didn't show nearly the same extra-base prowess he had in 2001, and hit just .168 after July 29.

Hitting

Belliard was a good top-of-the-order hitter when he first came up to the big leagues. But his on-base skills have gone steadily downhill. His batting eye, which used to be a strength, has virtually disappeared. It isn't simply a case of swinging at bad pitches. He often lets good pitches go by and then is forced to swing at bad ones. He is generally a line-drive hitter who uses the whole field, one who once was capable of hitting the ball hard into the gaps. But he rarely hit with any authority last year.

Baserunning & Defense

Though he was an effective basestealer in the minors, Belliard never has developed the technique to be a top thief in the majors. Carrying extra weight probably has been a factor. His defense had steadily gotten better until last year, when he seemed uninspired. Playing third base for the first time (he played one game at third in 1999), his inexperience sometimes showed, but he handled bunts fairly well and showed a strong enough arm to do the job.

2003 Outlook

Belliard now is eligible for arbitration. While there was talk that the Brewers might let him compete for the open third-base job in the spring, it seems more likely they will non-tender him and let him move on. That's especially true after Belliard broke his thumb in December playing winter ball. Trying to re-establish himself as a major league regular may be difficult.

Position: 2B/3B
Bats: R **Throws:** R
Ht: 5' 8" **Wt:** 197

Opening Day Age: 27
Born: 4/7/75 in Bronx, NY
ML Seasons: 5
Pronunciation: BELL-ee-yard

Overall Statistics

	G	AB	R	H	D	T	HR	RBI	SB	BB	SO	Avg	OBP	Slg
'02	104	289	30	61	13	0	3	26	2	18	46	.211	.257	.287
Car.	489	1686	243	443	102	16	30	174	18	199	254	.263	.341	.396

Where He Hits the Ball

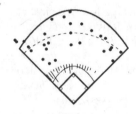

Vs. LHP   **Vs. RHP**

2002 Situational Stats

	AB	H	HR	RBI	Avg		AB	H	HR	RBI	Avg
Home	119	24	0	12	.202	LHP	100	20	3	9	.200
Road	170	37	3	14	.218	RHP	189	41	0	17	.217
First Half	157	37	1	12	.236	Sc Pos	60	10	0	21	.167
Scnd Half	132	24	2	14	.182	Clutch	53	11	0	7	.208

2002 Rankings (National League)

- 1st in lowest batting average on a 3-1 count (.000)
- 10th in lowest batting average on a 3-2 count (.125)

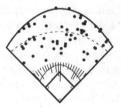

Milwaukee

Mike DeJean

2002 Season

Mike DeJean was thrust into the Brewers' closer's role last year after Curt Leskanic and Chad Fox got hurt. It was DeJean's first chance to be a full-time closer in the majors. He performed well overall, though it wasn't easy. The club's dearth of late-inning leads and manager Jerry Royster's reluctance to use him in non-save situations led to a memorable mound blowup with Royster in July. But DeJean continued to pitch admirably. In fact, he didn't blow a single save chance after June 8, and recorded a 1.46 ERA in September. After saving a total of six games during his first five seasons, he wound up with 27 saves in 2002.

Pitching

DeJean gets groundballs with a low-90s sinker, a hard slider and a splitter. With runners on base, he concentrates even more on keeping the ball down, getting more grounders while giving up more walks and fewer homers. His stuff has good movement, so he's tough to hit, but he gives up his share of bases on balls. He works inside effectively to righthanded hitters, and generally keeps the ball away from lefthanded batters. For the second year in a row, he pitched extremely well when used on a second consecutive day, although he wasn't called upon to do so very often.

Defense & Hitting

Fielding comebackers has become second nature to DeJean, who enjoyed his fifth consecutive errorless season. He did a better job of holding runners last year, permitting only four stolen bases after surrendering 10 the year before. His hitting rarely is a factor, thankfully.

2003 Outlook

Since frequent work keeps DeJean sharp, a better year by the Brewers could help boost his effectiveness while giving him more leads to protect. There's no reason to think he won't be able to continue to be a reliable closer. He is signed through this season, and there's an option for 2004.

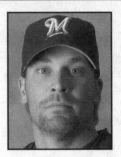

Position: RP
Bats: R **Throws:** R
Ht: 6' 4" **Wt:** 219

Opening Day Age: 32
Born: 9/28/70 in Baton Rouge, LA
ML Seasons: 6
Pronunciation: DAY-zshonn

Overall Statistics

	W	L	Pct.	ERA	G	GS	Sv	IP	H	BB	SO	HR	Ratio
'02	1	5	.167	3.12	68	0	27	75.0	66	39	65	7	1.40
Car.	19	16	.543	4.18	367	1	33	415.2	430	188	263	41	1.49

How Often He Throws Strikes

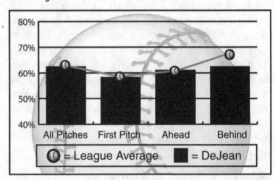

= League Average   = DeJean

2002 Situational Stats

	W	L	ERA	Sv	IP		AB	H	HR	RBI	Avg
Home	1	5	3.77	17	43.0	LHB	143	37	2	14	.259
Road	0	0	2.25	10	32.0	RHB	136	29	5	14	.213
First Half	0	3	3.48	15	44.0	Sc Pos	84	18	1	20	.214
Scnd Half	1	2	2.61	12	31.0	Clutch	181	35	2	15	.193

2002 Rankings (National League)

- 5th in save percentage (90.0)
- 8th in games finished (60)
- Led the Brewers in saves, games finished (60), save opportunities (30), save percentage (90.0), blown saves (3) and relief losses (5)

Jeffrey Hammonds

2002 Season

In 2001, Jeffrey Hammonds' first year after signing a big free-agent contract with Milwaukee, shoulder problems ended his season prematurely. He had surgery that July, from which it was hoped he'd recover fully for 2002. But he apparently never did. The shoulder bothered him all last year, sapping his power and sometimes keeping him out of the lineup entirely. He did play in a career-high 128 games, but attaining that mark was costly, as he hit only .220 without a single homer in 44 games after July 21.

Hitting

Before his shoulder problems, Hammonds hit for a pretty good average and showed respectable power. He could reach the fences from gap to gap, but he hasn't hit the ball to right-center with authority in a while. He's too aggressive to work the count, and fails to take advantage when it's in his favor. He definitely does his best hitting early in the count. He never has come close to the 106 runs he drove in for the Rockies in 2000, his only season with Colorado.

Baserunning & Defense

Hammonds didn't have a good year in the field, either. He saw significant action in center and right field, and in both spots a lot of balls fell in that he might have gotten to a few years ago. Whether he's lost a step due to his repeated injuries or simply was more timid while playing hurt is hard to say. His throwing arm was a liability all year, understandably. He also was less aggressive on the bases and stole only four bags in nine attempts.

2003 Outlook

The Brewers think Hammonds' shoulder will be stronger next season, but there's understandable skepticism. His contract has one year to run, so he'll be out there on the field if he's able to play at all. Given his history, there's little reason to expect him to be healthy and productive for the majority of the campaign.

Position: CF/RF
Bats: R **Throws:** R
Ht: 6' 0" **Wt:** 200

Opening Day Age: 32
Born: 3/5/71 in Scotch Plains, NJ
ML Seasons: 10

Overall Statistics

	G	AB	R	H	D	T	HR	RBI	SB	BB	SO	Avg	OBP	Slg
'02	128	448	47	115	26	5	9	41	4	52	86	.257	.332	.397
Car.	858	2773	436	765	154	17	103	403	65	259	542	.276	.340	.455

Where He Hits the Ball

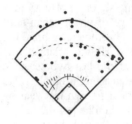

Vs. LHP   **Vs. RHP**

2002 Situational Stats

	AB	H	HR	RBI	Avg		AB	H	HR	RBI	Avg
Home	209	55	2	21	.263	LHP	84	25	3	10	.298
Road	239	60	7	20	.251	RHP	364	90	6	31	.247
First Half	277	78	7	34	.282	Sc Pos	110	25	3	34	.227
Scnd Half	171	37	2	7	.216	Clutch	77	20	4	9	.260

2002 Rankings (National League)

- 5th in sacrifice flies (7)
- Led the Brewers in sacrifice flies (7), batting average vs. lefthanded pitchers, highest percentage of extra bases taken as a runner (57.9) and on-base percentage vs. lefthanded pitchers (.381)

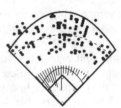

Milwaukee

Jose Hernandez

2002 Season

What a strange season. Jose Hernandez made the All-Star team, hit a career-high .288 and led National League shortstops in home runs. But he was benched the final weekend of the season to prevent him from breaking the major league strikeout record. Even so, it was his best all-around campaign, as he provided strong defense and good offensive production.

Hitting

Hernandez is one of the rare power hitters who has to avoid pulling the ball in order to succeed. His hardest-hit drives come when he stays back and lines the ball to center or right field. It's no secret why he strikes out so often. He swings through a higher percentage of pitches than any-one in the league, and can be fooled by breaking balls and offspeed pitches. He's challenged the strikeout record in each of the last two seasons, and one of these years he just might break it. He managed to keep his average so high last year by batting an incredible .448 when he put the ball in play, something that's sure not to happen again. He's most dangerous when the pitcher has to throw him a strike, such as on a 2-0 or 3-1 count.

Baserunning & Defense

Prone to defensive slumps earlier in his career, Hernandez has become a fine-fielding shortstop. His first-step quickness translates into good range, and his strong arm has become more accurate as his footwork has improved. He has experience playing other positions on the infield and in the outfield. His speed never was more than average, and he's no longer a useful basestealing threat.

2003 Outlook

Hernandez' three-year deal expired at the end of 2002, making him a free agent. He probably will be looking for more money than the Brewers will be willing to offer. Wherever he winds up, he'll bring good pop for a shortstop, even if his average falls back to where it's been in past years.

Position: SS
Bats: R **Throws:** R
Ht: 6' 1" **Wt:** 188

Opening Day Age: 33
Born: 7/14/69 in Vega Alta, PR
ML Seasons: 11
Pronunciation: her-NAN-dezz

Overall Statistics

	G	AB	R	H	D	T	HR	RBI	SB	BB	SO	Avg	OBP	Slg
'02	152	525	72	151	24	2	24	73	3	52	188	.288	.356	.478
Car.	1173	3502	493	894	152	28	133	467	35	286	1053	.255	.314	.429

Where He Hits the Ball

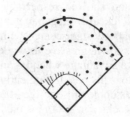 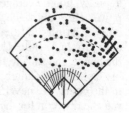

Vs. LHP   **Vs. RHP**

2002 Situational Stats

	AB	H	HR	RBI	Avg		AB	H	HR	RBI	Avg
Home	256	74	13	30	.289	LHP	99	25	8	16	.253
Road	269	77	11	43	.286	RHP	426	126	16	57	.296
First Half	286	82	13	40	.287	Sc Pos	143	40	4	47	.280
Scnd Half	239	69	11	33	.289	Clutch	91	30	7	16	.330

2002 Rankings (National League)

- 1st in strikeouts and highest percentage of swings that missed (35.1)
- 3rd in lowest percentage of swings put into play (31.9)
- 6th in errors at shortstop (19) and fielding percentage at shortstop (.973)
- 10th in highest groundball-flyball ratio (1.7), most pitches seen per plate appearance (4.05) and lowest batting average on an 0-2 count (.085)
- Led the Brewers in GDPs (19), most pitches seen per plate appearance (4.05), batting average in the clutch, slugging percentage vs. left-handed pitchers (.535) and lowest percentage of swings on the first pitch (25.5)
- Led NL shortstops in home runs

Geoff Jenkins

Position: LF
Bats: L **Throws:** R
Ht: 6' 1" **Wt:** 213

Opening Day Age: 28
Born: 7/21/74 in Olympia, WA
ML Seasons: 5

2002 Season

One of the more gruesome injuries of the 2002 season occurred when Geoff Jenkins dislocated his right ankle while sliding into third base on June 17. To those who witnessed it, it seemed astonishing when tests later revealed that he'd suffered no fractures or torn tendons. Still, it was severe enough to end his season, just as he had been coming out of a year-long slump that had seen his average sink as low as .224 on June 5.

Hitting

Jenkins generates good power to all fields by whipping the bat through the strike zone. He isn't afraid to come up empty, and often does. Staying back on offspeed pitches and breaking balls always has been a challenge for him, and he's never been one to resist the urge to offer at anything close. He didn't hit lefties well last year, but that looks like an aberration, as he had learned to hang in quite well against them prior to that point.

Baserunning & Defense

While Jenkins always has been expected to hit, no one ever figured he'd develop into one of the better defensive left fielders in baseball. But that's what he's made himself into, by getting good jumps and going hard for everything that comes anywhere near his territory. His arm remains strong and accurate, despite his history of shoulder problems. He had fairly good speed and ran the bases aggressively before his ankle injury, but he didn't try to steal much over the past two years.

2003 Outlook

Jenkins had been hoping to get back on the field by the end of last season, and new manager Ned Yost reported in November that Jenkins said he was at 95 percent. So it seems safe to say he'll be ready to go this spring. Signed through 2004, Jenkins may be a step or two slower, but his hitting shouldn't be affected, and that's what counts. He never has played in more than 135 games in any major league season, however.

Overall Statistics

	G	AB	R	H	D	T	HR	RBI	SB	BB	SO	Avg	OBP	Slg
'02	67	243	35	59	17	1	10	29	1	22	60	.243	.320	.444
Car.	526	1861	298	519	129	10	94	296	22	146	463	.279	.342	.510

Where He Hits the Ball

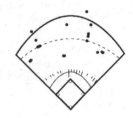

Vs. LHP   **Vs. RHP**

2002 Situational Stats

	AB	H	HR	RBI	Avg		AB	H	HR	RBI	Avg
Home	127	25	4	9	.197	LHP	65	13	2	7	.200
Road	116	34	6	20	.293	RHP	178	46	8	22	.258
First Half	243	59	10	29	.243	Sc Pos	57	11	3	19	.193
Scnd Half	0	0	0	0	–	Clutch	46	11	2	6	.239

2002 Rankings (National League)

- 8th in assists in left field (7)

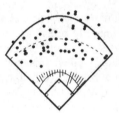

Milwaukee

Nick Neugebauer

Position: SP
Bats: R **Throws:** R
Ht: 6' 3" **Wt:** 235

Opening Day Age: 22
Born: 7/15/80 in Riverside, CA
ML Seasons: 2

2002 Season

In 2001, Nick Neugebauer suddenly developed control of his outstanding stuff and led the Double-A Southern League in strikeouts. Called up that August, he was pulled in his second major league start due to injury. He then underwent arthroscopic surgery in September to repair a partially torn rotator cuff, and his status for 2002 was uncertain. He made the rotation last spring, but his velocity and command had both gone backward. He re-injured his shoulder in May and didn't return until September.

Pitching

Before his surgery, Neugebauer threw in the high 90s. Last year, however, he was topping out in the low 90s. A slurve is his second pitch, and his changeup remains a work in progress. Even last season, righthanded hitters had a tough time with him, while lefthanded hitters continued to give him trouble. Although Neugebauer had problems finding the plate in 2002, it was nothing compared to the extreme control difficulties he had suffered in the minors before turning the corner in 2001. And even when he was pitching well last year, he ran up his pitch count quickly, which often made it difficult for him to go much beyond five innings.

Defense & Hitting

Neugebauer has handled himself well enough in the field, although he hasn't done much at all to slow down his opponents' running game. He has not shown he can hit or bunt, despite having enjoyed some success on both counts while in the minors.

2003 Outlook

It's no exaggeration to say that the development of Nick Neugebauer is one of the most important issues related to the rehabilitation of the Brewers' franchise, for a healthy Neugebauer has a chance to be the team's Kerry Wood. The club can only hope that Neugebauer's shoulder problems have not done permanent damage. The Brewers will be waiting and watching for his velocity and control to return in 2003.

Overall Statistics

	W	L	Pct.	ERA	G	GS	Sv	IP	H	BB	SO	HR	Ratio
'02	1	7	.125	4.72	12	12	0	55.1	56	44	47	10	1.81
Car.	2	8	.200	4.99	14	14	0	61.1	62	50	58	11	1.83

How Often He Throws Strikes

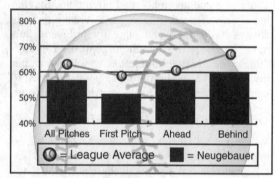

= League Average ■ = Neugebauer

2002 Situational Stats

	W	L	ERA	Sv	IP		AB	H	HR	RBI	Avg
Home	1	4	2.97	0	30.1	LHB	88	28	4	11	.318
Road	0	3	6.84	0	25.0	RHB	124	28	6	18	.226
First Half	1	4	5.09	0	35.1	Sc Pos	61	15	4	21	.246
Scnd Half	0	3	4.05	0	20.0	Clutch	0	0	0	0	–

2002 Rankings (National League)

- 3rd in balks (2)
- Led the Brewers in balks (2)

Glendon Rusch

2002 Season

Lefthander Glendon Rusch was the principal player Milwaukee acquired in the deal that sent Brewers mainstay Jeromy Burnitz to the Mets. Rusch made the deal pay off, eating innings and pitching creditably, if inconsistently, for a team that never made it easy for him to win games.

Pitching

Rusch isn't overpowering and relies on mixing it up and moving the ball around. He throws a high-80s fastball and a good changeup, runs a cutter in on the hands of righthanded hitters and changes speeds on his curve. He sometimes drops down against a lefty. He did a much better job of keeping the ball down and getting groundballs last year, but he still is liable to give up longballs when he leaves the ball up. Hitters can make him pay when he's too eager to get ahead with the first pitch. The Brewers often asked him to pitch deep into games, and he was up to the challenge for the most part.

Defense & Hitting

Rusch made great strides at the plate and in the field last year. He tied for second in the majors in sacrifices. After coming into the season with just six hits in 110 major league at-bats, he batted .288, the best average of any starting pitcher outside Colorado. He also added a slide step that made him one of the toughest pitchers to run against. He allowed only one steal in seven attempts all season. He's an otherwise below-average fielder who sometimes is slow to cover first base.

2003 Outlook

Rusch is signed through this season, with an option for 2004. Though he'll probably never be a big winner, he easily could post a better won-lost record if the Brewers are able to improve at all this year. He seems to have established himself as a lefthanded version of Steve Trachsel, someone who can be counted on to provide 200 innings in the middle of the rotation.

Position: SP
Bats: L **Throws:** L
Ht: 6' 1" **Wt:** 200

Opening Day Age: 28
Born: 11/7/74 in Seattle, WA
ML Seasons: 6
Pronunciation: RUSH

Overall Statistics

	W	L	Pct.	ERA	G	GS	Sv	IP	H	BB	SO	HR	Ratio
'02	10	16	.385	4.70	34	34	0	210.2	227	76	140	30	1.44
Car.	41	64	.390	4.93	161	148	1	910.1	1044	268	667	122	1.44

How Often He Throws Strikes

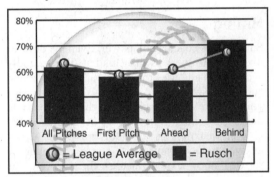

2002 Situational Stats

	W	L	ERA	Sv	IP		AB	H	HR	RBI	Avg
Home	6	5	4.48	0	96.1	LHB	187	44	10	33	.235
Road	4	11	4.88	0	114.1	RHB	626	183	20	75	.292
First Half	5	7	4.92	0	111.2	Sc Pos	186	50	10	78	.269
Scnd Half	5	9	4.45	0	99.0	Clutch	42	9	1	4	.214

2002 Rankings (National League)

- 1st in losses and lowest stolen-base percentage allowed (14.3)
- 2nd in sacrifice bunts (14) and most pitches thrown per batter (3.97)
- 3rd in pitches thrown (3,622)
- 4th in games started, home runs allowed and GDPs induced (27)
- 5th in complete games (4) and most GDPs induced per nine innings (1.2)
- Led the Brewers in sacrifice bunts (14), losses, games started, complete games (4), home runs allowed, walks allowed, pitches thrown (3,622) and GDPs induced (27)

Alex Sanchez

2002 Season

After it became clear last May that Milwaukee's main goal would have to be development for the future rather than immediate contention, manager Jerry Royster installed Alex Sanchez as the Brewers' leadoff man and center fielder against righthanded pitchers. Sanchez was ready for neither role, but then he wasn't expected to be. His rawness manifested itself in a multitude of ways: a poor plate approach, numerous baserunning blunders, mishaps in the outfield and all-around poor fundamentals. On the other hand, he stole bases effectively and batted better than .300 before slumping in August. A broken left ankle ended his season in September.

Hitting

Sanchez has coach's box power. Even his doubles owe more to his legs than his bat. He generally accepts this and tries to hit the ball on the ground and use the whole field. But he also can unleash a go-for-broke swing or chase a high fastball up and out of the zone. His impatience at the plate is his biggest weakness as a leadoff man. He wasn't allowed to face many lefties last year, though he showed no weakness against them during his minor league days.

Baserunning & Defense

Sanchez has great speed and knows how to steal a base, but he has poor baserunning instincts overall and probably ran himself into as many outs as anyone in baseball last year. Sanchez drops more than his share of flyballs in the outfield and takes poor routes, although his legs enable him to outrun many of his mistakes. His weak throwing arm is a liability in center.

2003 Outlook

It could be an uphill fight for Sanchez to establish himself as a major league regular. To do it, he'll have to prove that he can be valuable both as a center fielder and as a leadoff man. He'll get a chance to play every day, but it wouldn't be all that surprising if he were to come up short in one or both areas.

Position: CF/LF
Bats: L **Throws:** L
Ht: 5'10"   **Wt:** 159

Opening Day Age: 26
Born: 8/26/76 in Havana, Cuba
ML Seasons: 2

Overall Statistics

	G	AB	R	H	D	T	HR	RBI	SB	BB	SO	Avg	OBP	Slg
'02	112	394	55	114	10	7	1	33	37	31	62	.289	.343	.358
Car.	142	462	62	128	13	9	1	37	43	36	75	.277	.331	.351

Where He Hits the Ball

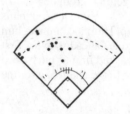 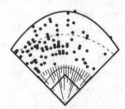

Vs. LHP   **Vs. RHP**

2002 Situational Stats

	AB	H	HR	RBI	Avg		AB	H	HR	RBI	Avg
Home	191	51	0	19	.267	LHP	45	12	0	4	.267
Road	203	63	1	14	.310	RHP	349	102	1	29	.292
First Half	238	73	0	19	.307	Sc Pos	72	23	0	31	.319
Scnd Half	156	41	1	14	.263	Clutch	71	22	0	10	.310

2002 Rankings (National League)

- 2nd in batting average among rookies
- 3rd in errors in center field (5) and batting average on a 3-2 count (.367)
- 4th in caught stealing (14), batting average on a 3-1 count (.667) and RBI among rookies
- 5th in stolen bases
- 6th in triples
- 7th in bunts in play (31)
- 9th in steals of third (4) and on-base percentage for a leadoff hitter (.349)
- Led the Brewers in batting average, triples, stolen bases, caught stealing (14), highest groundball-flyball ratio (2.4), bunts in play (31), steals of third (4), batting average with the bases loaded (.667) and batting average on a 3-1 count (.667)

Richie Sexson

2002 Season

While the rest of the team was succumbing to injuries all around him, first baseman Richie Sexson suffered physical problems of his own. But Sexson managed to stay in the lineup and continue hitting reasonably well. Tendinitis in his left hamstring and behind his left knee severely limited his mobility in the second half. However, the Brewers' cleanup hitter gutted it out without complaint, even as his numbers slipped.

Hitting

It seems Sexson can reach just about any pitch and hit it hard, and that impression isn't far from the truth. Extending his long, strong arms gives him great power and plate coverage, and most pitchers try to counter by tying Sexson up inside. He can get the bat head out often enough to make that pitching tactic a dangerous gamble. He set a career high with 70 walks, but that was due more to being pitched around than to any improvement in his selectivity. A more legitimate positive sign was the drop in Sexson's strikeouts, the result of swinging through fewer pitches and not getting fooled as often.

Baserunning & Defense

A healthy Sexson is a Gold Glove-caliber first baseman, but he didn't have anywhere near his normal range in last season's second half. He still helped out with his ability to dig throws out of the dirt, and with a throwing arm that's one of the best at his position. His speed never is any better than average, but anyone who saw Sexson late last year probably came away thinking he's a huge liability on the basepaths. He scored only 30 runs in the second half, and 10 of them resulted from his own homers.

2003 Outlook

A winter's rest should restore Sexson's leg to full working order. Signed through 2004, he's a good bet to get his offensive numbers back to their 2001 levels. Sexson is a righthanded slugger with legitimate 40-homer ability.

Position: 1B
Bats: R **Throws:** R
Ht: 6' 8" **Wt:** 227

Opening Day Age: 28
Born: 12/29/74 in Portland, OR
ML Seasons: 6
Pronunciation: SECKS-un

Overall Statistics

	G	AB	R	H	D	T	HR	RBI	SB	BB	SO	Avg	OBP	Slg
'02	157	570	86	159	37	2	29	102	0	70	136	.279	.363	.504
Car.	651	2369	370	646	122	14	146	469	8	229	634	.273	.341	.521

Where He Hits the Ball

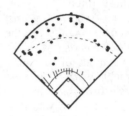 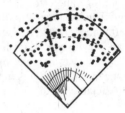

Vs. LHP   **Vs. RHP**

2002 Situational Stats

	AB	H	HR	RBI	Avg		AB	H	HR	RBI	Avg
Home	279	85	13	51	.305	LHP	101	24	3	18	.238
Road	291	74	16	51	.254	RHP	469	135	26	84	.288
First Half	323	91	19	62	.282	Sc Pos	155	45	9	72	.290
Scnd Half	247	68	10	40	.275	Clutch	96	21	3	10	.219

2002 Rankings (National League)

- 2nd in assists at first base (118)
- 5th in highest percentage of swings that missed (29.8)
- 6th in errors at first base (7) and fielding percentage at first base (.995)
- Led the Brewers in home runs, at-bats, runs scored, hits, doubles, total bases (287), RBI, walks, intentional walks (7), hit by pitch (8), times on base (237), pitches seen (2,471), plate appearances (652), games played, slugging percentage, on-base percentage, cleanup slugging percentage (.509), slugging percentage vs. righthanded pitchers (.525), on-base percentage vs. righthanded pitchers (.371) and batting average at home

Ben Sheets

Position: SP
Bats: R **Throws:** R
Ht: 6' 1" **Wt:** 203

Opening Day Age: 24
Born: 7/18/78 in Baton Rouge, LA
ML Seasons: 2

2002 Season

Projected to be the Brewers' ace, young Ben Sheets pitched fairly well before slumping in June and July. That raised concerns, especially after shoulder tendinitis had bothered him in the second half of 2001. This time he bounced back strongly, going 6-2 with a 3.18 ERA over his last 10 starts. His overall numbers were encouraging for a young pitcher with a weak club behind him. His 170 strikeouts were the most by a Brewers hurler since Cal Eldred fanned 180 in 1993.

Pitching

Sheets has two very good pitches—a fastball in the low to mid-90s, and a hard overhand curve. Lacking an effective third pitch, he gives righthanded hitters fits but has problems against lefthanded swingers. He knows how to keep the ball down, but found his best success when he started expanding the upper limits of the strike zone as well. He gets in trouble when he gets too predictable with first-pitch fastballs. He was asked to pitch deeper into games last year, and showed better stamina. He still tended to lose his edge after the 90-pitch mark, however.

Defense & Hitting

Sheets is a good fielder and does a very good job of keeping runners close, showing an above-average pickoff move for a righthander. His ability to control the running game is important because he's able to induce his share of double-play grounders. He struggles at the plate to just make contact and doesn't bunt well, but he will wait out an occasional walk.

2003 Outlook

It was exciting to see the strides Sheets made over the course of last season. There's a good chance his progress will carry through and translate into a big year for him in 2003. It seems the only thing that could stop him is an injury, but his arm has been sound. If he can solve lefthanded hitters, he could make big strides in a hurry.

Overall Statistics

	W	L	Pct.	ERA	G	GS	Sv	IP	H	BB	SO	HR	Ratio
'02	11	16	.407	4.15	34	34	0	216.2	237	70	170	21	1.42
Car.	22	26	.458	4.40	59	59	0	368.0	403	118	264	44	1.42

How Often He Throws Strikes

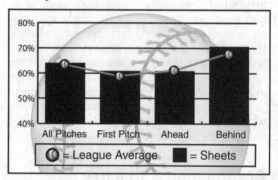

○ = League Average ■ = Sheets

2002 Situational Stats

	W	L	ERA	Sv	IP		AB	H	HR	RBI	Avg
Home	6	7	3.43	0	120.2	LHB	406	129	13	58	.318
Road	5	9	5.06	0	96.0	RHB	438	108	8	37	.247
First Half	4	10	4.19	0	109.2	Sc Pos	207	48	2	64	.232
Scnd Half	7	6	4.12	0	107.0	Clutch	58	12	2	3	.207

2002 Rankings (National League)

- 1st in losses
- 2nd in hits allowed
- 4th in games started and runners caught stealing (12)
- 5th in highest batting average allowed (.281) and highest ERA on the road
- 6th in batters faced (934) and highest on-base percentage allowed (.343)
- 7th in pitches thrown (3,492)
- 8th in hit batsmen (10) and wild pitches (9)
- 9th in innings pitched and least run support per nine innings (4.3)
- Led the Brewers in ERA, wins, innings pitched, batters faced (934), strikeouts, wild pitches (9) and stolen bases allowed (14)

Eric Young

2002 Season

After being signed to a two-year deal in January 2002 to be the Brewers' leadoff hitter, Eric Young flopped miserably. He took a .238 average into July and didn't start hitting until being dropped to the No. 2 spot in the order. Though he finished with a respectable average, he didn't accomplish what he was brought in to do—get on base, score runs and spark the club's offense.

Hitting

Young is the prototypical contact hitter, spraying line drives from foul line to foul line and rarely failing to put the ball in play when he offers at it. Naturally, he's one of the better two-strike hitters in the game. His tendency to put the ball in play holds his walk total down, though, and he isn't terribly patient to begin with. Even more disturbing is the fact that his plate patience has eroded significantly over the last three years. His extra-base power mostly is limited to gap doubles, but he can bunt a runner over when needed.

Baserunning & Defense

Young still is an effective basestealer, though he goes through long stretches where he hardly runs at all, which might be related to a chronic knee problem. He seldom runs against southpaws anymore. His glovework is average at best. He has decent lateral range, but his hands aren't soft, his arm isn't strong and his double-play pivot isn't quick.

2003 Outlook

Young's two most enthusiastic boosters, manager Davey Lopes and GM Dean Taylor, have been fired, so Young might not be feeling all that secure. He still has a year left on his contract, however, and there are no serious challengers to his job. Young may be in the midst of a slow decline, but there's no reason to think he'll take a big step down anytime soon. The Brewers hope his .307 average after last year's All-Star break is a true indication of the skills he retains.

Position: 2B
Bats: R **Throws:** R
Ht: 5' 8" **Wt:** 180

Opening Day Age: 35
Born: 5/18/67 in New Brunswick, NJ
ML Seasons: 11
Nickname: E.Y.

Overall Statistics

	G	AB	R	H	D	T	HR	RBI	SB	BB	SO	Avg	OBP	Slg
'02	138	496	57	139	29	3	3	28	31	39	38	.280	.338	.369
Car.	1375	5020	819	1446	267	42	58	455	408	528	361	.288	.362	.393

Where He Hits the Ball

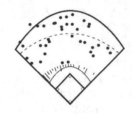

Vs. LHP	**Vs. RHP**

2002 Situational Stats

	AB	H	HR	RBI	Avg		AB	H	HR	RBI	Avg
Home	249	73	2	11	.293	LHP	89	26	1	3	.292
Road	247	66	1	17	.267	RHP	407	113	2	25	.278
First Half	291	76	2	20	.261	Sc Pos	95	18	0	25	.189
Scnd Half	205	63	1	8	.307	Clutch	76	16	0	5	.211

2002 Rankings (National League)

- 1st in highest percentage of swings put into play (57.7)
- 2nd in lowest on-base percentage for a leadoff hitter (.290)
- 3rd in lowest batting average with runners in scoring position
- 4th in lowest fielding percentage at second base (.979)
- 5th in lowest percentage of swings that missed (9.0)
- Led the Brewers in singles, stolen-base percentage (73.8), lowest percentage of swings that missed (9.0), highest percentage of swings put into play (57.7), steals of third (4), batting average on an 0-2 count (.275) and batting average with two strikes (.242)

Jose Cabrera

Position: RP/SP
Bats: R **Throws:** R
Ht: 6' 0" **Wt:** 180

Opening Day Age: 34
Born: 3/24/69 in Santiago, DR
ML Seasons: 6

Overall Statistics

	W	L	Pct.	ERA	G	GS	Sv	IP	H	BB	SO	HR	Ratio
'02	6	10	.375	6.79	50	11	0	103.1	131	36	61	23	1.62
Car.	19	17	.528	4.95	198	11	4	271.0	291	94	192	42	1.42

2002 Situational Stats

	W	L	ERA	Sv	IP		AB	H	HR	RBI	Avg
Home	4	4	7.20	0	55.0	LHB	181	50	13	32	.276
Road	2	6	6.33	0	48.1	RHB	236	81	10	53	.343
First Half	4	5	5.03	0	62.2	Sc Pos	104	33	6	61	.317
Scnd Half	2	5	9.52	0	40.2	Clutch	47	15	4	11	.319

2002 Season

Jose Cabrera always has run hot and cold, but last year it was mostly the latter. Acquired in a late-spring trade, he was used frequently for the season's first two and a half months, with mixed results. After having worked exclusively in relief for the previous five years, he made a couple of emergency starts in May, and joined the rotation in mid-June. As a starter he alternated decent outings with brutal ones. By September, he'd been relegated to the back of the bullpen.

Pitching, Defense & Hitting

Cabrera comes mostly with high fastballs in the low 90s, yielding primarily flyballs. His splitter and change are not effective complementary pitches, and when he falls behind in the count, hitters know they can sit on the fastball. Few pitchers are streakier. His pickoff move remains excellent, although he nailed just one baserunner with it last year. Cabrera is slow to the plate, however, so he can be run on. He's an average fielder, and has no ability to swing the bat.

2003 Outlook

Cabrera was eligible for salary arbitration this past winter. He's better suited to the pen, where he's always capable of getting hot. But he just as easily could pitch his way back to the minors.

Valerio de los Santos

Position: RP
Bats: L **Throws:** L
Ht: 6' 2" **Wt:** 206

Opening Day Age: 30
Born: 10/6/72 in Las Matas, DR
ML Seasons: 5

Overall Statistics

	W	L	Pct.	ERA	G	GS	Sv	IP	H	BB	SO	HR	Ratio
'02	2	3	.400	3.12	51	0	0	57.2	42	26	38	4	1.18
Car.	4	7	.364	4.21	138	2	0	162.1	138	69	132	24	1.28

2002 Situational Stats

	W	L	ERA	Sv	IP		AB	H	HR	RBI	Avg
Home	1	1	1.99	0	31.2	LHB	64	14	1	10	.219
Road	1	2	4.50	0	26.0	RHB	135	28	3	12	.207
First Half	2	2	3.00	0	24.0	Sc Pos	54	9	0	16	.167
Scnd Half	0	1	3.21	0	33.2	Clutch	42	12	0	3	.286

2002 Season

Coming off Tommy John surgery, Valerio de los Santos began 2002 in the minors. He was recalled in mid-May and pitched well, before tiring somewhat toward season's end. He usually was used for an inning at a time rather than as a one-batter specialist. He was one of Milwaukee's most effective relievers, though a lot of his appearances came when the game no longer was close.

Pitching, Defense & Hitting

De los Santos still can tie up hitters upstairs with low-90s heat. That's critical, because his complementary pitches—a slider and splitter—aren't much. Since he comes over the top and doesn't rely on breaking balls, he's effective against hitters from either side of the plate. He gets most of his outs on flyballs. Longballs were a problem in the past, but he made fewer mistakes last year. He's a surehanded fielder but doesn't control the running game very well. He can't hit a lick.

2003 Outlook

Physical problems always have cropped up just when de los Santos seemed on the verge of breaking through. He held up well after returning last year, so perhaps this will be the season he makes it through from beginning to end. If so, he could be a quality setup man or middle reliever.

Jayson Durocher

Position: RP
Bats: R **Throws:** R
Ht: 6' 3" **Wt:** 195

Opening Day Age: 28
Born: 8/18/74 in
Hartford, CT
ML Seasons: 1

Overall Statistics

	W	L	Pct.	ERA	G	GS	Sv	IP	H	BB	SO	HR	Ratio
'02	1	1	.500	1.88	39	0	0	48.0	27	21	44	3	1.00
Car.	1	1	.500	1.88	39	0	0	48.0	27	21	44	3	1.00

2002 Situational Stats

	W	L	ERA	Sv	IP		AB	H	HR	RBI	Avg
Home	0	1	3.28	0	24.2	LHB	75	14	1	2	.187
Road	1	0	0.39	0	23.1	RHB	90	13	2	12	.144
First Half	1	0	1.35	0	13.1	Sc Pos	37	5	2	13	.135
Scnd Half	0	1	2.08	0	34.2	Clutch	35	8	1	6	.229

2002 Season

Short reliever Jayson Durocher came out nowhere last year to be one of the Brewers' biggest surprises. He had signed as a minor league free agent during the offseason and was called up in June. Used in middle relief, he allowed no earned runs in 34 of 39 appearances. He also surrendered a miserly .123 (7-for-57) average with runners on base.

Pitching, Defense & Hitting

Durocher doesn't get cute. He simply rears back and fires his lively 95-MPH fastball. He also throws an occasional splitter or slider, but goes mostly with the high heat. His command always has been inconsistent, but last year he began to throw just enough strikes to keep hitters on the defensive. Durocher generally was given a day off between appearances. He makes good use of the slide step to deter basestealers, and handles himself well enough in the field. He is hitless in six pro at-bats.

2003 Outlook

At age 28, Durocher is no coming star. He'll need to prove he can maintain his command over the course of a full season. If he's able to do that, the Brewers might have themselves a quality setup man.

Nelson Figueroa

Position: RP/SP
Bats: R **Throws:** R
Ht: 6' 1" **Wt:** 155

Opening Day Age: 28
Born: 5/18/74 in
Brooklyn, NY
ML Seasons: 3
Pronunciation:
fig-uh-ROE-uh

Overall Statistics

	W	L	Pct.	ERA	G	GS	Sv	IP	H	BB	SO	HR	Ratio
'02	1	7	.125	5.03	30	11	0	93.0	96	37	51	18	1.43
Car.	5	13	.278	4.74	52	27	0	197.2	208	79	119	30	1.45

2002 Situational Stats

	W	L	ERA	Sv	IP		AB	H	HR	RBI	Avg
Home	1	3	5.29	0	49.1	LHB	154	42	12	27	.273
Road	0	4	4.74	0	43.2	RHB	201	54	6	30	.269
First Half	1	5	4.91	0	66.0	Sc Pos	84	23	4	37	.274
Scnd Half	0	2	5.33	0	27.0	Clutch	22	7	2	4	.318

2002 Season

Though he threw a career-high 93 innings, Nelson Figueroa never got much of a chance to settle into a role last season. He was claimed off waivers in April, joined the Brewers' rotation a couple weeks later as their fifth starter and pitched decently for a few weeks before spraining his ankle. When he returned, he had a few bad starts and was banished to long relief, and later to the minors. He was outrighted off the roster at the end of the year and became a free agent.

Pitching, Defense & Hitting

To make up for his lack of outstanding stuff, Figueroa mixes his pitches and moves the ball around. He throws a high-80s fastball, a sinker, slider and change. It's always a battle for him to get ahead in the count without getting hit, and he can get beat on the first pitch. He's an average fielder in all respects, but is a good hitter.

2003 Outlook

Figueroa is almost 29, so his time is running out. He's pitched consistently well at Triple-A and probably could do a decent job in the majors. Getting enough of a chance to prove it is the key, and Figueroa, a free agent this offseason, needs to go to a team where there's opportunity.

Milwaukee

Keith Ginter

Position: 3B
Bats: R **Throws:** R
Ht: 5'10" **Wt:** 190

Opening Day Age: 26
Born: 5/5/76 in
Norwalk, CA
ML Seasons: 3

Overall Statistics

	G	AB	R	H	D	T	HR	RBI	SB	BB	SO	Avg	OBP	Slg
'02	28	81	7	19	9	0	1	8	0	17	15	.235	.374	.383
Car.	34	90	10	21	9	0	2	11	0	18	18	.233	.364	.400

2002 Situational Stats

	AB	H	HR	RBI	Avg		AB	H	HR	RBI	Avg
Home	39	12	1	5	.308	LHP	13	2	0	0	.154
Road	42	7	0	3	.167	RHP	68	17	1	8	.250
First Half	5	1	0	0	.200	Sc Pos	15	4	0	5	.267
Scnd Half	76	18	1	8	.237	Clutch	15	2	0	3	.133

2002 Season

The Brewers obtained Keith Ginter last September as the player to be named later in the deal that sent Mark Loretta to Houston. Milwaukee immediately installed Ginter as its regular third baseman, and he did a passable job.

Hitting, Baserunning & Defense

Using a short stroke and hitting out of an open stance, Ginter generates decent power. He's a patient hitter who takes walks and gets hit by a lot of pitches. Last year he cut his strikeout rate considerably. He's hit well against lefthanders for several years in a row. He has decent speed but hasn't run much the last two seasons. The biggest question concerns his ability to handle third base. He'd been a second baseman until the beginning of last year, when he was moved to third. He fielded just .929 in 53 games there and was returned to his original position, but he later played third adequately with the Brewers.

2003 Outlook

Ginter is a decent hitter who's capable of putting up respectable numbers. He'll turn 27 this May, however, so his long-term potential is limited. He's expected to win the Brewers' third-base job this spring, though there's a chance he'll come up lacking in the field.

Ray King

Position: RP
Bats: L **Throws:** L
Ht: 6' 1" **Wt:** 242

Opening Day Age: 29
Born: 1/15/74 in
Chicago, IL
ML Seasons: 4

Overall Statistics

	W	L	Pct.	ERA	G	GS	Sv	IP	H	BB	SO	HR	Ratio
'02	3	2	.600	3.05	76	0	0	65.0	61	24	50	5	1.31
Car.	6	8	.429	3.11	204	0	1	159.1	139	69	123	13	1.31

2002 Situational Stats

	W	L	ERA	Sv	IP		AB	H	HR	RBI	Avg
Home	1	0	2.55	0	35.1	LHB	96	21	2	10	.219
Road	2	2	3.64	0	29.2	RHB	143	40	3	16	.280
First Half	2	2	3.27	0	33.0	Sc Pos	61	18	1	20	.295
Scnd Half	1	0	2.81	0	32.0	Clutch	86	22	3	9	.256

2002 Season

Ray King did it again last year—and again, and again and again. He finished with the fourth most relief appearances of any major league lefty, despite missing two weeks in April with a sore elbow. The Brewers' top lefthander out of the pen, King worked as a specialist or setup man as needed. He was very effective, holding lefthanded batters to a .219 average.

Pitching, Defense & Hitting

King's bread and butter is a wide-breaking slider that lefthanded hitters can't help chasing. He complements it with a 90-MPH fastball and will show a splitter to righthanded batters. By keeping everything down, King keeps the ball on the infield and rarely allows it to leave the park. Working several days in a row is second nature to him. He has a big leg kick that makes him fairly easy to run on, and his pickoff move is ordinary. He doesn't move too well in the field, but makes the plays he needs to make. Hitting is irrelevant to his job.

2003 Outlook

King is signed through the end of this season. The Brewers expect him either to continue to play a key role in their bullpen or to bring them something of value in a trade.

Robert Machado

Position: C
Bats: R **Throws:** R
Ht: 6' 1" **Wt:** 210

Opening Day Age: 29
Born: 6/3/73 in Puerto Cabello, VZ
ML Seasons: 7
Pronunciation: muh-CHA-doh

Overall Statistics

	G	AB	R	H	D	T	HR	RBI	SB	BB	SO	Avg	OBP	Slg
'02	73	211	19	55	14	1	3	22	0	17	41	.261	.316	.379
Car.	198	514	53	122	32	2	9	55	0	35	105	.237	.288	.360

2002 Situational Stats

	AB	H	HR	RBI	Avg		AB	H	HR	RBI	Avg
Home	106	24	1	10	.226	LHP	62	14	1	7	.226
Road	105	31	2	12	.295	RHP	149	41	2	15	.275
First Half	109	32	2	15	.294	Sc Pos	52	12	0	17	.231
Scnd Half	102	23	1	7	.225	Clutch	31	5	0	0	.161

2002 Season

Robert Machado was in the right place at the right time last year. He made the Cubs' roster as their third catcher, and in June he was dealt to the Brewers, who had recently lost two of their catchers to injury. Machado split time behind the plate for the Brewers for the rest of the year. He kept his average surprisingly high before slumping in September.

Hitting, Baserunning & Defense

Even when he's hitting well, Machado has little offensive value. He has little power, rarely walks and has trouble catching up to good fastballs. His best tool is a strong throwing arm. He threw out 34.4 percent of attempted basestealers, which would have led the NL if his opponents had had only four more stolen-base attempts. Machado hasn't distinguished himself as a pitch-blocker or game-caller, and he wisely hasn't tried to steal a single base in his 198 major league games.

2003 Outlook

The Brewers purged their catching corps over the winter and announced that Machado would be the leading candidate to start at the beginning of camp. That may have been more out of deference to his experience than his talent, as he never has hit enough to play regularly.

Ruben Quevedo

Position: SP
Bats: R **Throws:** R
Ht: 6' 1" **Wt:** 245

Opening Day Age: 24
Born: 1/5/79 in Valencia Carabobo, VZ
ML Seasons: 3
Pronunciation: keh-VAY-doh

Overall Statistics

	W	L	Pct.	ERA	G	GS	Sv	IP	H	BB	SO	HR	Ratio
'02	6	11	.353	5.76	26	25	0	139.0	159	68	93	28	1.63
Car.	13	26	.333	6.06	57	50	0	283.2	311	152	218	58	1.63

2002 Situational Stats

	W	L	ERA	Sv	IP		AB	H	HR	RBI	Avg
Home	3	4	4.14	0	63.0	LHB	247	67	17	46	.271
Road	3	7	7.11	0	76.0	RHB	305	92	11	48	.302
First Half	4	6	4.33	0	104.0	Sc Pos	127	37	8	67	.291
Scnd Half	2	5	10.03	0	35.0	Clutch	23	3	0	1	.130

2002 Season

Ruben Quevedo gave the Brewers frustration at every turn last year. He experienced a puzzling drop in velocity early in the year, pitched inconsistently in the first half and melted down completely in July and August. He then was sent down to the minors, and soon suffered a strained oblique muscle that ended his season.

Pitching, Defense & Hitting

Quevedo works upstairs even though he lacks the stuff to get away with it. His fastball tops out in the high 80s, and his slider, curve and change are average. The Brewers tried to have him alter styles when his velocity dropped even more in '02, but he was unable or unwilling to do so. He allows a huge number of flyballs, many of which leave the park. He carries a lot of extra weight and does little to help himself in the field or at the plate.

2003 Outlook

New manager Ned Yost reported that Quevedo has dumped some weight this offseason. Unless Quevedo's velocity reappears and he is more willing to make necessary adjustments, it's hard to see him succeeding. The best thing he has going for him is his age, which some have questioned in light of the many false ages identified through new U.S. visa regulations.

Matt Stairs

Position: RF/LF
Bats: L **Throws:** R
Ht: 5' 9" **Wt:** 215

Opening Day Age: 35
Born: 2/27/68 in Saint John, NB, Canada
ML Seasons: 10

Overall Statistics

	G	AB	R	H	D	T	HR	RBI	SB	BB	SO	Avg	OBP	Slg
'02	107	270	41	66	15	0	16	41	2	36	50	.244	.349	.478
Car.	925	2755	439	724	155	6	156	511	23	394	570	.263	.358	.493

2002 Situational Stats

	AB	H	HR	RBI	Avg		AB	H	HR	RBI	Avg
Home	137	30	6	21	.219	LHP	13	2	0	1	.154
Road	133	36	10	20	.271	RHP	257	64	16	40	.249
First Half	84	21	5	16	.250	Sc Pos	78	13	2	19	.167
Scnd Half	186	45	11	25	.242	Clutch	46	11	2	5	.239

2002 Season

Signed by the Brewers last January, Matt Stairs was expected to platoon in right field. But it never quite worked out that way. Hamstring problems and a glut of outfielders kept him on the bench for most of the first half, although Stairs did manage to get semi-regular playing time against righthanders after the break. He performed decently as a pinch-hitter and extra outfielder.

Hitting, Baserunning & Defense

Stairs brings to the table the ability to hit long fly-balls from the left side of the plate. He also contributes his share of walks. But his years of hitting for a good average probably are behind him. It's been a few seasons since he's seen lefthanders more than occasionally. Squat and blocky, he looks slower than he really is, and has adequate range in the outfield corners. He also throws well. His steal attempts have declined each of the past four years.

2003 Outlook

Just like he did last winter, Stairs will try to find a team looking for an outfielder to platoon at one of the corner spots. The free agent probably will keep contributing with the bat, and if he's lucky, Stairs will play more than he has the last couple of years.

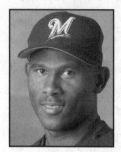

Luis Vizcaino

Position: RP
Bats: R **Throws:** R
Ht: 5'11" **Wt:** 174

Opening Day Age: 28
Born: 8/6/74 in Bani, DR
ML Seasons: 4
Pronunciation: VIS-ky-EE-no

Overall Statistics

	W	L	Pct.	ERA	G	GS	Sv	IP	H	BB	SO	HR	Ratio
'02	5	3	.625	2.99	76	0	5	81.1	55	30	79	6	1.05
Car.	7	5	.583	4.09	125	0	6	140.2	121	56	130	17	1.26

2002 Situational Stats

	W	L	ERA	Sv	IP		AB	H	HR	RBI	Avg
Home	2	1	2.96	4	45.2	LHB	111	25	1	13	.225
Road	3	2	3.03	1	35.2	RHB	176	30	5	14	.170
First Half	5	1	3.26	1	47.0	Sc Pos	87	14	2	22	.161
Scnd Half	0	2	2.62	4	34.1	Clutch	157	26	4	13	.166

2002 Season

The Brewers' best trade last year was the late-spring deal that netted them righthander Luis Vizcaino from Texas for a minor leaguer. Working as the Brewers' primary setup man, Vizcaino was the club's most effective reliever. Opponents hit just .087 (4-for-46) with runners in scoring position and two outs.

Pitching, Defense & Hitting

Vizcaino's mid- to high-90s heat always has impressed, but what made the difference last year was the refinement of his slider to give him a reliable second pitch. He works mostly up in the zone, and when batters do manage to catch up to him, they rarely are able to pull the ball. Though his numbers slipped a bit in September, he never really showed signs of fatigue. While Vizcaino does not pay much attention to baserunners, his catchers can call high fastballs all day and get away with it. His style of pitching doesn't require him to use his fielding skills often, but he makes the plays. At the plate he's an automatic out.

2003 Outlook

Vizcaino has everything one looks for in a future closer. For now he'll keep excelling in the eighth inning until the opportunity to close arises.

Other Milwaukee Brewers

Izzy Alcantara (Pos: RF, Age: 29, Bats: R)

	G	AB	R	H	D	T	HR	RBI	SB	BB	SO	Avg	OBP	Slg
'02	16	32	3	8	1	0	2	5	0	0	6	.250	.250	.469
Car.	51	115	15	31	3	0	6	15	1	6	26	.270	.306	.452

Alcantara has mashed the ball at Triple-A the past three years, but it hasn't earned him more than sporadic time in the majors. His swing might be attractive to a team looking for power off the bench. 2003 Outlook: C

Mike Buddie (Pos: RHP, Age: 32)

	W	L	Pct.	ERA	G	GS	Sv	IP	H	BB	SO	HR	Ratio
'02	1	2	.333	4.54	25	0	0	39.2	46	21	28	5	1.69
Car.	5	4	.556	4.67	87	2	2	131.0	137	52	76	13	1.44

Buddie performed OK for Milwaukee last April, before stumbling in May. After refusing a minor league assignment from the Brewers, he signed with Montreal. But he pitched at Triple-A for the Expos. 2003 Outlook: C

Matt Childers (Pos: RHP, Age: 24)

	W	L	Pct.	ERA	G	GS	Sv	IP	H	BB	SO	HR	Ratio
'02	0	0	—	12.00	8	0	0	9.0	13	8	6	2	2.33
Car.	0	0	—	12.00	8	0	0	9.0	13	8	6	2	2.33

Childers was a ninth-round pick of the Brewers in 1997. He entered last season with fewer than 40 innings above Double-A, but he got into eight games with the Brewers in August, with the expected results. 2003 Outlook: C

Ryan Christenson (Pos: CF, Age: 29, Bats: R)

	G	AB	R	H	D	T	HR	RBI	SB	BB	SO	Avg	OBP	Slg
'02	22	58	5	9	4	0	1	3	0	5	13	.155	.222	.276
Car.	392	833	137	193	41	5	14	86	14	99	212	.232	.313	.343

Selected in the Rule 5 draft last December, Christenson didn't open anyone's eyes at Triple-A or in a September stint with Milwaukee. He later refused a minor league assignment and became a free agent. 2003 Outlook: C

Ben Diggins (Pos: RHP, Age: 23)

	W	L	Pct.	ERA	G	GS	Sv	IP	H	BB	SO	HR	Ratio
'02	0	4	.000	8.63	5	5	0	24.0	28	18	15	4	1.92
Car.	0	4	.000	8.63	5	5	0	24.0	28	18	15	4	1.92

Diggins was a top prospect in the Dodgers' organization before he was traded to the Brewers last July. He's a big guy with a power arm, but he doesn't have a lot of experience above Class-A. 2003 Outlook: C

Jorge Fabregas (Pos: C, Age: 33, Bats: L)

	G	AB	R	H	D	T	HR	RBI	SB	BB	SO	Avg	OBP	Slg
'02	65	155	13	28	4	0	3	22	0	8	13	.181	.216	.265
Car.	646	1827	153	441	56	5	23	211	4	114	217	.241	.284	.315

Fabregas was traded from the eventual World Champion Angels to the Brewers last July. That would seem like a reasonable penance for a player with Fabregas' woeful batting average. He's a free agent. 2003 Outlook: C

Chad Fox (Pos: RHP, Age: 32)

	W	L	Pct.	ERA	G	GS	Sv	IP	H	BB	SO	HR	Ratio
'02	1	0	1.000	5.79	3	0	0	4.2	6	5	3	0	2.36
Car.	7	7	.500	3.33	153	0	2	162.1	141	81	187	15	1.37

After posting a 1.89 ERA over 65 games in 2001, it looked like Fox might deserve a bigger role last season. Instead, Fox encountered more arm problems and lost most of the year. He's a free agent. 2003 Outlook: B

Lenny Harris (Pos: LF/1B/3B, Age: 38, Bats: L)

	G	AB	R	H	D	T	HR	RBI	SB	BB	SO	Avg	OBP	Slg
'02	122	197	23	60	8	2	3	17	4	14	17	.305	.355	.411
Car.	1653	3614	434	985	149	21	34	331	130	253	297	.273	.321	.354

Traded to the Brewers last January, Harris had a solid season coming off the bench for Milwaukee. He then became a free agent, and there's no reason to think he won't find gainful employment. 2003 Outlook: B

Marcus Jensen (Pos: C, Age: 30, Bats: B)

	G	AB	R	H	D	T	HR	RBI	SB	BB	SO	Avg	OBP	Slg
'02	16	35	2	4	0	0	1	4	0	4	11	.114	.200	.200
Car.	145	343	33	63	16	1	6	29	0	50	106	.184	.287	.289

If Jensen couldn't stick with the Brewers, a team with catching problems, it would appear his chances for a big league career have passed him by. He'll test free agency to see if anyone is nibbling. 2003 Outlook: C

Andrew Lorraine (Pos: LHP, Age: 30)

	W	L	Pct.	ERA	G	GS	Sv	IP	H	BB	SO	HR	Ratio
'02	0	1	.000	11.25	5	1	0	12.0	22	6	10	7	2.33
Car.	6	11	.353	6.53	59	26	0	175.0	218	83	113	31	1.72

Lorraine would appear to be the definition of a Triple-A pitcher. He's worked at least 14 games at that level in each of the past nine years. He's a good bet to make it 10 straight this season. 2003 Outlook: C

Brian Mallette (Pos: RHP, Age: 28)

	W	L	Pct.	ERA	G	GS	Sv	IP	H	BB	SO	HR	Ratio
'02	0	0	—	10.80	5	0	0	5.0	7	3	5	3	2.00
Car.	0	0	—	10.80	5	0	0	5.0	7	3	5	3	2.00

Mallette was traded to the Dodgers in October to complete the Tyler Houston deal. Mallette has been effective in the high minors the past couple years, and the Dodgers would like him to add an offspeed pitch to aid his major league chances. 2003 Outlook: C

Mike Matthews (Pos: LHP, Age: 29)

	W	L	Pct.	ERA	G	GS	Sv	IP	H	BB	SO	HR	Ratio
'02	2	1	.667	3.94	47	0	0	45.2	43	29	34	5	1.58
Car.	5	5	.500	4.00	112	10	1	144.0	132	72	114	18	1.42

Matthews was traded from St. Louis to Milwaukee in the Jamey Wright deal late last season. Matthews was used only in a relief role in 2002, but the Brewers reportedly will give him a chance to start this year. 2003 Outlook: B

Milwaukee

Shane Nance (Pos: LHP, Age: 25)

	W	L	Pct.	ERA	G	GS	Sv	IP	H	BB	SO	HR	Ratio
'02	0	0	–	4.26	4	0	0	6.1	4	4	5	1	1.26
Car.	0	0	–	4.26	4	0	0	6.1	4	4	5	1	1.26

Milwaukee acquired Nance last July in the deal involving Ben Diggins and Tyler Houston. Nance's season ended soon after he was called up to the Brewers in August, as the reliever suffered a torn biceps. 2003 Outlook: C

Takahito Nomura (Pos: LHP, Age: 34)

	W	L	Pct.	ERA	G	GS	Sv	IP	H	BB	SO	HR	Ratio
'02	0	0	–	8.56	21	0	0	13.2	11	18	9	2	2.12
Car.	0	0	–	8.56	21	0	0	13.2	11	18	9	2	2.12

The Brewers signed Nomura, a veteran from Japan, last January. But he lasted only a month and a half with Milwaukee, exhibiting an alarming lack of control. And he was only OK at Triple-A. 2003 Outlook: C

Jimmy Osting (Pos: LHP, Age: 25)

	W	L	Pct.	ERA	G	GS	Sv	IP	H	BB	SO	HR	Ratio
'02	0	2	.000	7.50	3	3	0	12.0	18	10	7	3	2.33
Car.	0	2	.000	6.43	6	3	0	14.0	19	12	10	3	2.21

Osting wasn't a bad prospect a few years ago, and he isn't old enough to give up on. But he's bounced around in recent seasons, and he wasn't impressive over three starts with the Brewers last August. 2003 Outlook: C

Dave Pember (Pos: RHP, Age: 24)

	W	L	Pct.	ERA	G	GS	Sv	IP	H	BB	SO	HR	Ratio
'02	0	1	.000	5.19	4	1	0	8.2	7	6	5	1	1.50
Car.	0	1	.000	5.19	4	1	0	8.2	7	6	5	1	1.50

Pember was an eighth-round pick of the Brewers in the 1999 draft, out of Western Carolina. He spent most of 2002 at Double-A, so it's reasonable to assume he'll wind up at Triple-A this spring. 2003 Outlook: C

Everett Stull (Pos: RHP, Age: 31)

	W	L	Pct.	ERA	G	GS	Sv	IP	H	BB	SO	HR	Ratio
'02	0	1	.000	6.30	2	2	0	10.0	15	9	7	0	2.40
Car.	2	5	.286	6.59	26	6	0	57.1	65	45	42	8	1.92

Stull missed much of the 2001 season due to a right shoulder strain. He proved sturdy last season, throwing more than 150 innings at Triple-A, but it did not appear to impress the Brewers. He is now a free agent. 2003 Outlook: C

Ryan Thompson (Pos: LF/RF, Age: 35, Bats: R)

	G	AB	R	H	D	T	HR	RBI	SB	BB	SO	Avg	OBP	Slg
'02	62	137	16	34	9	2	8	24	1	7	38	.248	.295	.518
Car.	416	1257	165	305	71	6	52	176	9	90	347	.243	.301	.433

Thompson was called up last June and proceeded to hit with decent power for the Brewers, though he didn't reach base as often as you'd like. In other words, he was his usual self. 2003 Outlook: C

Milwaukee Brewers Minor League Prospects

Organization Overview:

Never before in franchise history had the Brewers lost 100 games. But they hit rock bottom in 2002 by going an anemic 56-106. Only two other National League teams over the past quarter-century—the 1988 Braves and 1998 Marlins—had endured that many losses. Clearly, the Brewers could use an infusion of talent from within. Unfortunately, Milwaukee's Triple-A affiliate wasn't exactly flushed with prospects last season. Part of the problem has been the Brewers' less than scintillating record with their top draft picks in recent years. Milwaukee does have some decent prospects at lower levels, however, and the system is showing a few signs of flourishing. It'll be interesting to see if the Brewers can resist promoting their best prospects before they're truly ready to contribute.

Cristian Guerrero

Position: OF **Opening Day Age:** 22
Bats: R **Throws:** R **Born:** 7/12/80 in Bani,
Ht: 6' 7" **Wt:** 200 DR

Recent Statistics

	G	AB	R	H	D	T	HR	RBI	SB	BB	SO	Avg
2001 A High Desert	85	327	50	102	18	2	7	41	22	18	79	.312
2002 AA Huntsville	111	394	47	88	17	1	8	48	21	26	101	.223

After a solid season in the high Class-A California League in 2001, Guerrero looked like he might be on a fast track to join his cousin, Vladimir, in the big leagues. But Cristian hit a wall at Double-A last season, when the Southern League seemed to catch up to him. As you might expect from his bloodlines, Guerrero has impressive baseball tools. He's tall and lanky, yet strong. He hasn't hit for extreme power at this point, though that could come as he fills in. He's also stolen at least 20 bases in each of the past four years. But Guerrero's control of the strike zone leaves something to be desired. The native of the Dominican Republic still is fairly young, and he might be asked to repeat Double-A this season.

Bill Hall

Position: SS **Opening Day Age:** 23
Bats: R **Throws:** R **Born:** 12/28/79 in
Ht: 6' 0" **Wt:** 175 Nettleton, MS

Recent Statistics

	G	AB	R	H	D	T	HR	RBI	SB	BB	SO	Avg
2002 AAA Indianapolis	134	465	35	106	20	1	4	31	17	25	105	.228
2002 NL Milwaukee	19	36	3	7	1	1		5	0	3	13	.194

The Brewers selected Hall in the sixth round of the 1998 draft. He seemed to turn a corner in 2001 when he hit better than .300 with impressive power in the high Class-A California League. But he's found the going a bit tougher at higher levels. His performance last year was rather disappointing, even though he saw action with the Brewers in September. Hall is an athletic player with pop in his bat and a nice arm at shortstop. But he's always struck out a lot and hasn't compensated with many walks. He may have been rushed a little in the past, but he's the kind of guy who could come on quickly.

J.J. Hardy

Position: SS **Opening Day Age:** 20
Bats: R **Throws:** R **Born:** 8/19/82 in Tucson,
Ht: 6' 1" **Wt:** 170 AZ

Recent Statistics

	G	AB	R	H	D	T	HR	RBI	SB	BB	SO	Avg
2001 R Brewers	5	20	6	5	2	1	0	1	0	1	2	.250
2001 R Ogden	35	125	20	31	5	0	2	15	1	15	12	.248
2002 A High Desert	84	335	53	98	19	1	6	48	9	19	38	.293
2002 AA Huntsville	38	145	14	33	7	0	1	13	1	9	19	.228

Considering he had been drafted only a year before out of high school, Hardy's rise to Double-A in 2002 really was quite remarkable. The second-round pick is a tremendous defensive player with a great arm and superior instincts. And, it may only be a matter of time before his bat catches up to his talent. Hardy hit for a respectable average and a modicum of power in the high Class-A California League last year. But he struggled a little when jumping up to Huntsville, which was understandable based on his age and experience. It would be nice if he could settle in and enjoy some sustained success, but the Brewers clearly are impressed with what Hardy can do.

Corey Hart

Position: 3B/1B **Opening Day Age:** 21
Bats: R **Throws:** R **Born:** 3/24/82 in
Ht: 6' 0" **Wt:** 180 Lawrenceburg, TN

Recent Statistics

	G	AB	R	H	D	T	HR	RBI	SB	BB	SO	Avg
2001 R Ogden	69	262	53	89	18	1	11	62	14	26	47	.340
2002 A High Desert	100	393	76	113	26	10	22	84	24	37	101	.288
2002 AA Huntsville	28	94	16	25	3	0	2	15	3	7	16	.266

One of the most athletic players in Milwaukee's system, Hart reached Double-A at age 20 last year. He does some good things offensively. He runs well, has decent power and has shown the ability to hit for average. He generated 58 extra-base hits and 24 stolen bases in 100 games at high Class-A High Desert, and looks like he might one day be capable of producing a 30-30 campaign. He's played mostly first base in the past, but he began making the transition to third base in 2002. His defense may not come as easily as his offense, and he could stand to improve his strikeout-walk ratio, but Hart is a nice prospect.

Ben Hendrickson

Position: P   **Opening Day Age:** 22
Bats: R **Throws:** R   **Born:** 2/4/81 in St.
Ht: 6' 3" **Wt:** 195   Cloud, MN

Recent Statistics

	W	L	ERA	G	GS	Sv	IP	H	R	BB	SO	HR
2001 A Beloit	8	9	2.84	25	25	0	133.1	122	58	72	133	3
2002 A High Desert	5	5	2.55	14	14	0	81.1	61	31	41	70	3
2002 AA Huntsville	4	2	2.97	13	13	0	69.2	57	31	35	50	2

Hendrickson has come on strongly the past couple years, posting sub-3.00 ERAs at each of three stops. His 2002 season culminated in Double-A at age 21, and he was named the Brewers' Minor League Pitcher of the Year. Hendrickson has a good arm and presents a nice pitching package. His curveball is effective and his fastball touches the mid-90s. He also throws a change-up. His strikeout rate has deteriorated somewhat as he's climbed the ladder, but he's surrendered very few home runs since 2001. Considering his fairly young age, a return to Huntsville may be in order to begin this season. He projects as a possible future No. 3 starter.

Michael Jones

Position: P   **Opening Day Age:** 19
Bats: R **Throws:** R   **Born:** 4/23/83 in
Ht: 6' 5" **Wt:** 210   Corona, CA

Recent Statistics

	W	L	ERA	G	GS	Sv	IP	H	R	BB	SO	HR
2001 R Ogden	4	1	3.74	9	7	0	33.2	29	17	10	32	1
2002 A Beloit	7	7	3.12	27	27	0	138.2	135	63	62	132	3

The Brewers grabbed Jones with the 12th overall pick in the 2001 draft. He had been a three-sport athlete in high school, and he possesses many of the physical attributes you'd expect from one chosen so high. He's a big guy with enough arm strength to have fired up to 97 MPH at times. He has a tremendous delivery and good arm action. He started slowly at Class-A Benoit in 2002, but was pitching better later in the year. He wound up with numbers that were quite respectable for a 19-year-old competing in the Midwest League. He needs to work on improving his breaking ball, which would figure to make his fastball even more effective.

Dave Krynzel

Position: OF   **Opening Day Age:** 21
Bats: L **Throws:** L   **Born:** 11/7/81 in Dayton,
Ht: 6' 1" **Wt:** 180   OH

Recent Statistics

	G	AB	R	H	D	T	HR	RBI	SB	BB	SO	Avg
2001 A Beloit	35	141	22	43	1	1	1	19	11	9	28	.305
2001 A High Desert	89	383	65	106	19	5	5	33	34	27	122	.277
2002 A High Desert	97	365	76	98	13	12	11	45	29	64	100	.268
2002 AA Huntsville	31	129	13	31	2	3	2	13	13	4	30	.240

Krynzel demonstrated a schizophrenic nature last season. He was terrific in his second crack at the high Class-A California League, reaching double digits in doubles, triples and homers. And his most encouraging statistic may have been his walk rate, which more than doubled from the year before. But all that changed when he faced Double-A pitching. His power deflated and his control of the strike zone absolutely crashed in the Southern League. While there's little question about his speed, he could improve his stolen-base percentage. He's an athletic player who has been compared to Johnny Damon, though Krynzel's arm may be better. A No. 1 pick in 2000, it'll be interesting to see which Dave Krynzel emerges this season.

Brad Nelson

Position: 1B   **Opening Day Age:** 20
Bats: L **Throws:** R   **Born:** 12/23/82 in
Ht: 6' 2" **Wt:** 220   Algona, IA

Recent Statistics

	G	AB	R	H	D	T	HR	RBI	SB	BB	SO	Avg
2001 R Brewers	17	63	10	19	6	1	0	13	0	8	18	.302
2001 R Ogden	13	42	5	11	4	0	0	10	0	3	9	.262
2002 A Beloit	106	417	70	124	38	2	17	99	4	34	86	.297
2002 A High Desert	26	102	24	26	11	0	3	17	0	12	28	.255

A year after getting picked in the fourth round of the 2001 draft, Nelson enjoyed a very productive offensive campaign. He reached 20 homers in his first full season, and he led all minor leaguers with 116 RBI between two levels. He accomplished those feats while still just a teenager. To be able to reach high Class-A before his 20th birthday marks him as someone to keep an eye on. He's very strong and clearly has intriguing power potential. After all, in addition to the homers, he delivered tons of doubles last year, some of which eventually could clear the fence as he matures. Nelson has played first base as a pro, but it's his bat that likely will determine his ultimate success.

Others to Watch

Daryl Clark (23) has nice power and draws his share of walks, which helps compensate for a batting average that has declined as he's moved up the system. He also has shown a knack for the RBI. His position is something of a question, as he played first base, third base and left field last year. . . After working almost exclusively out of the bullpen in previous seasons, lefthander **Wayne Franklin** (29) was a revelation as a starter at Triple-A in 2002. He then was traded from Houston to Milwaukee in the deal for Mark Loretta, and didn't embarrass himself in four September starts with the Brewers. Franklin could compete for a rotation spot this spring. . . Lefthander **Luis Martinez** (23) has a nice arm and has racked up decent strikeout totals, but he's also compiled some high ERAs as a pro. His fastball hits 93 MPH on a good day, and some observers like him quite a bit. . . Outfielder **Jim Rushford** (29) completed quite a story last year, rising from an independent league to the majors in the space of two seasons. He's demonstrated the ability to get on base and hit lots of doubles. But he didn't take advantage of his September trial with the Brewers last year.

Olympic Stadium

Offense

Stade Olympique has played slightly favorable to hitters the last several years. However, run scoring overall is only average due to the fact that it's overly regular shape and poor lighting decreases the number of misplays and walks, respectively. There are speakers that hang high above the field that are in play, allowing otherwise routine high flyballs to deflect off them for extra bases. The effect of 22 regular-season "home" games in Puerto Rico on the offense and pitching staff remains to be seen.

Defense

Even though it is an artificial surface, Olympic Stadium has so many dead spots and seams that it plays with the unpredictability of grass. The field has a sizeable amount of foul territory, and any ball that deflects off a speaker in foul ground still can be caught for an out.

Who It Helps the Most

Lefthanded power hitters generally were the biggest beneficiaries of playing in Montreal in 2002. Troy O'Leary and Wil Cordero posted superior numbers at home. The home turf was especially friendly to Peter Bergeron last year. On the mound, power righthanders like Bartolo Colon, Javier Vazquez and Matt Herges enjoyed significantly better years at home.

Who It Hurts the Most

Righthanded hitters like Fernando Tatis and Michael Barrett struggled to hit in Montreal. T.J. Tucker enjoyed considerably more success away from home; he did not give up a single home run on the road and his ERA was nearly 3.5 runs better. Infielders with exceptional range are more susceptible to the funny hops that are created by the uneven surface.

Rookies & Newcomers

After a strong showing in the Arizona Fall League, Termel Sledge should get a chance to stop the Expos' revolving door in center field. The pitching staff will gain some depth with Seung Song, Sun-Woo Kim and Ron Chiavacci. Josh Karp also could come up late in the season.

Dimensions: LF-325, LCF-375, CF-404, RCF-375, RF-325

Capacity: 46,620

Elevation: 90 feet

Surface: Turf

Foul Territory: Large

Park Factors

2002 Season

	Home Games Expos	Opp	Total	Away Games Expos	Opp	Total	Index
G	72	72	144	72	72	144	
Avg	.271	.260	.265	.252	.273	.262	101
AB	2396	2520	4916	2492	2434	4926	100
R	341	309	650	315	341	656	99
H	649	656	1305	627	664	1291	101
2B	145	150	295	128	123	251	118
3B	15	15	30	16	16	32	94
HR	76	71	147	69	79	148	100
BB	266	201	467	253	256	509	92
SO	458	492	950	545	467	1012	94
E	64	60	124	61	54	115	108
E-Infield	50	52	102	52	46	98	104
LHB-Avg	.287	.266	.276	.245	.272	.258	107
LHB-HR	34	31	65	25	34	59	108
RHB-Avg	.260	.256	.258	.256	.273	.265	97
RHB-HR	42	40	82	44	45	89	94

2000-2002

	Home Games Expos	Opp	Total	Away Games Expos	Opp	Total	Index
G	216	216	432	216	216	432	
Avg	.266	.267	.267	.253	.277	.265	101
AB	7163	7597	14760	7434	7213	14647	101
R	982	1088	2070	919	1072	1991	104
H	1908	2032	3940	1883	1997	3880	102
2B	453	432	885	380	382	762	115
3B	37	41	78	51	50	101	77
HR	206	252	458	206	222	428	106
BB	681	662	1343	681	749	1430	93
SO	1360	1491	2851	1522	1378	2900	98
E	175	155	330	171	152	323	102
E-Infield	141	129	270	139	126	265	102
LHB-Avg	.265	.288	.277	.245	.288	.266	104
LHB-HR	83	112	195	82	102	184	107
RHB-Avg	.267	.253	.260	.260	.269	.264	98
RHB-HR	123	140	263	124	120	244	105

2002 Rankings (National League)

- Third-highest double factor
- Third-highest LHB batting-average factor
- Second-lowest walk factor

Montreal

Frank Robinson

2002 Season

Frank Robinson has a pedigree of jump-starting offenses the first year he takes the helm, and last year was no different. The Expos run production increased significantly over recent seasons. Perhaps the biggest reason for this jump was the improved on-base percentage of his players due to a substantial increase in walks. Under his guidance, Montreal finished above the .500 mark for the first time since 1996.

Offense

Robinson preaches selective aggression at the plate. He wants his hitter to get a good pitch, and then hit it hard. But he also understands what tools his players have, and tailors his team's philosophy to their strengths. If a player has speed, he is not afraid to green-light him. Conversely, Robinson does not tolerate players who are not open to his suggestions, or players who don't play hard every pitch. He is not afraid to play "small ball," and his 2002 Expos were among the National League leaders in stolen-base, sac-bunt and hit-and-run attempts.

Pitching & Defense

Robinson's policy of aggressive play extends to the pitching staff as well—throw strikes, don't nibble and if the guy hits a homer, tip your cap and go after the next guy. One of the results of this strategy has been a slight increase in his pitching staffs to surrender the longball, but, as counterintuitive as it may seem, his team ERAs do go down. One downside is that Robinson tends to leave his starters on the mound; he left his starter out for 120 or more pitches nine times, despite fielding one of the youngest staffs in the league.

2003 Outlook

The Expos are scheduled to be back in Montreal this season for the bulk of their home games. Robinson also returns, though his club will play 22 "home" games in Puerto Rico in 2003. Historically, his teams have kept their turnaround momentum for another year before dropping in the standings. However, Montreal is a very talented, young team that could feed off his experience and change that trend. . . if it isn't gutted to meet financial restraints during the offseason.

Born: 8/31/35 in Beaumont, TX

Playing Experience: 1956-1976, Cin, Bal, LA, Cal, Cle

Managerial Experience: 12 seasons

Manager Statistics

Year	Team, Lg	W	L	Pct	GB	Finish
2002	Montreal, NL	83	79	.512	19.0	2nd East
12 Seasons		763	830	.479	–	–

2002 Starting Pitchers by Days Rest

	<=3	4	5	6+
Expos Starts	0	92	44	17
Expos ERA	–	4.15	3.87	3.94
NL Avg Starts	1	88	42	21
NL ERA	3.18	4.22	4.14	4.58

2002 Situational Stats

	Frank Robinson	NL Average
Hit & Run Success %	30.0	36.5
Stolen Base Success %	64.8	68.3
Platoon Pct.	56.2	52.7
Defensive Subs	29	19
High-Pitch Outings	9	7
Quick/Slow Hooks	25/7	24/11
Sacrifice Attempts	135	95

2002 Rankings (National League)

- 1st in sacrifice bunt attempts, intentional walks (61), defensive substitutions and saves with over 1 inning pitched (11)
- 2nd in stolen base attempts (182), steals of second base (102), steals of third base (16) and mid-inning pitching changes (191)
- 3rd in sacrifice-bunt percentage (83.7%) and squeeze plays (10)

Tony Armas Jr.

2002 Season

It is sometimes hard to remember that Tony Armas Jr. is just 24 years old and still very much in the early stages of the major league learning process. He pitched well during the first half of the 2002 season, especially in June when he held opposing hitters to a .183 average. July and August, on the other hand, were not as kind—0-5, 8.38 ERA and a strained back that landed him on the disabled list. He returned in September to finish his second full big league campaign on a strong note, going 4-0 with a 3.00 ERA over his last five starts.

Pitching

Armas' two best pitches are a moving fastball that runs in the low 90s and a biting curve, but he also has command of a slider, splitter and change. For every step forward he made in 2002, however, he seemed to take one step back. He has become almost unhittable to righthanders, yet he's now like batting practice for lefties. He gave up fewer hits overall per game, but a higher percentage of those were home runs. Still a concern is his inability to go deeper into games; he lasted more than six innings in just 10 of his 29 starts.

Defense & Hitting

Naturally athletic and quick, Armas finally became a good defender this year because he stopped rushing his fielding and throws. He's never been adept at stopping the running game, although he has slowed the track meet somewhat with an improving slide step. His bunting continues to improve, but his hitting skills overall simply are not good.

2003 Outlook

Armas needs to retool his approach to lefties if he's going to move forward in his development. Bartolo Colon's presence from the start of camp will take some of the pressure off, but Armas also must improve his level of focus. If those two things happen, Armas quickly could become a big winner.

Position: SP
Bats: R **Throws:** R
Ht: 6' 4" **Wt:** 215

Opening Day Age: 24
Born: 4/29/78 in Puerto Piritu, VZ
ML Seasons: 4
Pronunciation: ar-MUS

Overall Statistics

	W	L	Pct.	ERA	G	GS	Sv	IP	H	BB	SO	HR	Ratio
'02	12	12	.500	4.44	29	29	0	164.1	149	78	131	22	1.38
Car.	28	36	.438	4.21	81	81	0	462.0	411	221	368	50	1.37

How Often He Throws Strikes

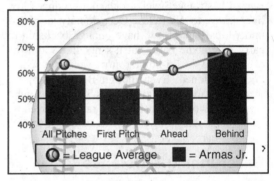

2002 Situational Stats

	W	L	ERA	Sv	IP		AB	H	HR	RBI	Avg
Home	7	6	3.97	0	79.1	LHB	273	84	10	37	.308
Road	5	6	4.87	0	85.0	RHB	339	65	12	40	.192
First Half	8	7	3.92	0	108.0	Sc Pos	148	31	8	56	.209
Scnd Half	4	5	5.43	0	56.1	Clutch	20	6	3	6	.300

2002 Rankings (National League)

- 1st in wild pitches (14) and fielding percentage at pitcher (1.000)
- 3rd in balks (2), lowest batting average allowed vs. righthanded batters and highest walks per nine innings (4.3)
- Led the Expos in walks allowed, hit batsmen (7), stolen bases allowed (18), runners caught stealing (7), lowest batting average allowed (.243), lowest batting average allowed with runners in scoring position and most strikeouts per nine innings (7.2)

Montreal

Michael Barrett

2002 Season

A year after the Expos finally decided on letting Michael Barrett settle in at catcher, he rewarded them with a solid season. He looked like the second coming of Gary Carter for the first two months of the season, hitting .322 with an OPS (on-base + slugging percentage) of .931. Barrett slumped badly in June and July as the bumps and bruises of the position caught up to him. Only a strong August prevented his second-half production from becoming a total disaster. His home-run rate was by far the best of his career.

Hitting

Barrett has a nice level stroke that produces low line drives to all fields. Occasionally he'll get under a ball and it will have enough backspin to carry out of the park, but it's not likely that he ever will be the 25-home run power hitter scouts once envisioned. Even though Barrett is by no means a patient hitter (113 of his 376 at-bats were over after two pitches), his walk rate improved by 89 percent over last year by 46 percent over his previous career average.

Baserunning & Defense

Barrett has decent speed for a catcher and can steal a base or two if the defense isn't vigilant. He rarely takes risks on the basepaths otherwise. Behind the plate, he moves quickly to get in front of balls in the dirt. He doesn't have a strong arm, and he nabbed just 25 percent of opposing basestealers last year. He's a good receiver and generally calls a smart game.

2003 Outlook

Barrett hit a higher percentage of balls into the air in 2002 than in 2001. Should that trend continue, combined with his improving pitch recognition and defense, there's a decent chance he could develop into another All-Star for the Expos. However, Barrett needs to make opposing pitchers work harder when he's at the plate, and he must improve his percentages against the opposition's running game.

Position: C
Bats: R **Throws:** R
Ht: 6' 2" **Wt:** 200

Opening Day Age: 26
Born: 10/22/76 in Atlanta, GA
ML Seasons: 5

Overall Statistics

	G	AB	R	H	D	T	HR	RBI	SB	BB	SO	Avg	OBP	Slg
'02	117	376	41	99	20	1	12	49	6	40	65	.263	.332	.418
Car.	472	1575	167	409	102	7	28	163	8	123	199	.260	.315	.387

Where He Hits the Ball

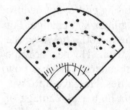   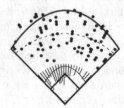

Vs. LHP   **Vs. RHP**

2002 Situational Stats

	AB	H	HR	RBI	Avg		AB	H	HR	RBI	Avg
Home	182	44	4	14	.242	LHP	111	29	1	6	.261
Road	194	55	8	35	.284	RHP	265	70	11	43	.264
First Half	215	61	8	28	.284	Sc Pos	93	25	3	36	.269
Scnd Half	161	38	4	21	.236	Clutch	68	16	1	7	.235

2002 Rankings (National League)

- 3rd in lowest fielding percentage at catcher (.989)
- 4th in errors at catcher (9)
- Led the Expos in sacrifice flies (5) and highest groundball-flyball ratio (1.7)

Orlando Cabrera

2002 Season

Much was expected of Orlando Cabrera after his 96-RBI performance in 2001. Unfortunately, he fell well short of those perhaps-inflated expectations, in large part due to a bulging disc that bothered him all season. His production at the plate suffered, but so too did his defense. In fact, Cabrera led all major league shortstops with 29 errors in 2002, just one season after winning his first Gold Glove.

Hitting

Like many Latin hitters, Cabrera is not driven to take a walk. Nor does he strike out much. Despite a drop in homers and triples last year, his doubles rate actually went up, so the double-digit home-run power still is there. He just wasn't driving the ball as far in 2002. Cabrera makes contact and drives the ball to all fields, although almost all of his home runs are pulled. A good sign for improved production in 2003 is the fact that his walk rate went up nearly 22 percent last season over 2001.

Baserunning & Defense

Cabrera stole 51 bases in a season in the low minors, but he has only been given the green light in the last two years. With his instincts, and as he gains more experience reading pitchers, his stolen-base totals and success rate should continue to go up. Cabrera's range at shortstop is among the best in the game, but his back troubles may be serious and chronic enough to warrant a position change. He has a good enough arm to handle third.

2003 Outlook

Cabrera may not be back with the Expos this season. He had several run-ins with manager Frank Robinson, and it was reported that he and double-play partner Jose Vidro hardly spoke last season. While Cabrera's combination of defense, speed and power should bring a nice return, the Expos may opt to keep him out of necessity. If he's healthy, he should post his best offensive year to date, regardless of where he plays.

Position: SS
Bats: R **Throws:** R
Ht: 5'10" **Wt:** 185

Opening Day Age: 28
Born: 11/2/74 in Cartagena, Colombia
ML Seasons: 6
Pronunciation: kah-bray-RAH

Overall Statistics

	G	AB	R	H	D	T	HR	RBI	SB	BB	SO	Avg	OBP	Slg
'02	153	563	64	148	43	1	7	56	25	48	53	.263	.321	.380
Car.	639	2272	271	595	148	18	45	270	57	153	203	.262	.309	.402

Where He Hits the Ball

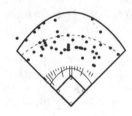 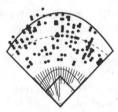

Vs. LHP	Vs. RHP

2002 Situational Stats

	AB	H	HR	RBI	Avg		AB	H	HR	RBI	Avg
Home	286	78	3	34	.273	LHP	125	33	1	14	.264
Road	277	70	4	22	.253	RHP	438	115	6	42	.263
First Half	320	88	4	31	.275	Sc Pos	146	36	1	44	.247
Scnd Half	243	60	3	25	.247	Clutch	98	29	1	11	.296

2002 Rankings (National League)

- 1st in errors at shortstop (29) and lowest fielding percentage at shortstop (.962)
- 3rd in doubles
- 5th in steals of third (5) and batting average on an 0-2 count (.306)
- 10th in stolen-base percentage (78.1) and highest percentage of extra bases taken as a runner (60.5)
- Led the Expos in doubles, stolen-base percentage (78.1), lowest percentage of swings that missed (13.7), highest percentage of swings put into play (50.6) and batting average on an 0-2 count (.306)

Montreal

Bartolo Colon

Position: SP
Bats: R **Throws:** R
Ht: 6' 0" **Wt:** 235

Opening Day Age: 29
Born: 5/24/73 in Altamira, DR
ML Seasons: 6
Pronunciation: bar-TOE-loh ko-LONE

2002 Season

Even though he began the year in Cleveland, it was very likely from the outset that Bartolo Colon would end up somewhere else by the end of the 2002 season. That change came late in June when the Expos offered a package of first baseman Lee Stevens and three very good prospects—infielder Brandon Phillips, pitcher Cliff Lee and outfielder Grady Sizemore—for the Tribe's ace. Between the two clubs, Colon chalked up his first career 20-win season and threw a pair of two-hitters (both with the Expos).

Pitching

Colon challenges hitters with a fastball that he can sink in the low 90s or ride up in the zone at 100 MPH. He also throws a decent change and a hard-breaking curve that's faster than many other pitchers' sliders. What makes Colon special is that he maintains that velocity throughout all nine innings. Most of the time, he keeps a brisk pace. However, when men get on base, he slows down considerably and will get into trouble by over-thinking. In spring training, Cleveland pitching coach Mike Brown suggested he move from the first base side of the pitching rubber to the middle. Although the change hurt his strikeout totals, it helped his control considerably and reduced his home-run rate slightly.

Defense & Hitting

Despite his size, Colon is surprisingly mobile off the mound and has a decent move to first. His slide step is very effective in keeping runners honest. He still is an American League pitcher when it comes to hitting, although he did manage to lay down two sac bunts in his 49 plate appearances.

2003 Outlook

The Expos picked up Colon's $6 million option for 2003, but since then, word from on high has come down, stating that the Expos have to cut salary before the 2003 season kicks off. Teams quickly lined up, looking to pluck Colon and other high-priced players from the Expos. If Colon isn't dealt, the Expos hope to again challenge the Braves for the NL East crown, and he will play a significant part in that effort.

Overall Statistics

	W	L	Pct.	ERA	G	GS	Sv	IP	H	BB	SO	HR	Ratio
'02	20	8	.714	2.93	33	33	0	233.1	219	70	149	20	1.24
Car.	85	49	.634	3.85	179	177	0	1146.2	1099	458	947	118	1.36

How Often He Throws Strikes

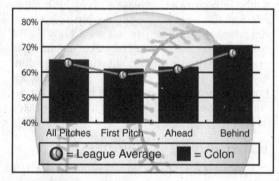

2002 Situational Stats

	W	L	ERA	Sv	IP		AB	H	HR	RBI	Avg
Home	10	3	2.18	0	111.1	LHB	409	99	11	31	.242
Road	10	5	3.61	0	122.0	RHB	460	120	9	45	.261
First Half	11	4	2.74	0	128.1	Sc Pos	184	38	4	54	.207
Scnd Half	9	4	3.17	0	105.0	Clutch	84	17	2	6	.202

2002 Rankings (National League)

- 5th in complete games (4)
- Led the Expos in complete games (4), winning percentage (.714), lowest slugging percentage allowed (.392), highest groundball-flyball ratio allowed (1.6), lowest stolen-base percentage allowed (42.9), lowest ERA at home (2.69), most run support per nine innings (5.5) and fewest home runs allowed per nine innings (.69)

Andres Galarraga

2002 Season

The Expos signed Andres Galarraga to a minor league deal in March 2002 intending him to be a backup at first base. But after starter Lee Stevens failed to produce much of anything in the first half of the season, Galarraga was given a more regular spot in the lineup. While his second-half production wasn't bad, it still was substandard for a first baseman, and a far cry from his halcyon days just four years ago. His .394 slugging percentage was his lowest figure since 1992.

Hitting

Galarraga's age and back troubles have conspired to make him a mistake hitter and not much else. Good fastballs inside tie him up, and he misses breaking pitches away. His bat speed is slowing, and consequently the holes in his strike zone are becoming increasingly large. Galarraga still can drive a mistake out of the park, but most pitchers would rather miss badly and chance that he'll get himself out, instead of risking a mistake that he can clobber.

Baserunning & Defense

Never an especially fast runner, Galarraga's good instincts used to allow him to steal occasionally and take an extra base on a hit. His body just can't do that anymore, limiting his baserunning to station-to-station. While his mobility around first has decreased, he still has a terrific glove for wild throws from the infield. Few in baseball dig out balls in the dirt or odd hops better than Galarraga.

2003 Outlook

Galarraga, who turns 42 next season, probably should retire. After the Expos declined to offer Galarraga salary arbitration, it's less likely that he'll stick around for one more season in Montreal. His charismatic leadership in the clubhouse, especially among Latin players, and assuring glovework at first could be valuable on a team as young as the Expos. But his bat and body have become liabilities.

Position: 1B
Bats: R **Throws:** R
Ht: 6' 3" **Wt:** 250

Opening Day Age: 41
Born: 6/18/61 in Caracas, VZ
ML Seasons: 17
Pronunciation:
ON-dress Gahl-la-RAH-ga
Nickname: Big Cat

Overall Statistics

G	AB	R	H	D	T	HR	RBI	SB	BB	SO	Avg	OBP	Slg
104	292	30	76	12	0	9	40	2	30	81	.260	.344	.394
2140	7814	1158	2248	429	32	386	1381	127	564	1939	.288	.347	.499

Where He Hits the Ball

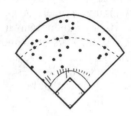
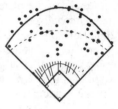

Vs. LHP   **Vs. RHP**

2002 Situational Stats

	AB	H	HR	RBI	Avg		AB	H	HR	RBI	Avg
Home	127	40	7	22	.315	LHP	85	25	0	8	.294
Road	165	36	2	18	.218	RHP	207	51	9	32	.246
First Half	103	28	2	14	.272	Sc Pos	85	22	1	30	.259
Scnd Half	189	48	7	26	.254	Clutch	57	9	0	2	.158

2002 Rankings (National League)

- 2nd in errors at first base (13)
- 6th in lowest batting average in the clutch
- Led the Expos in hit by pitch (9)

Vladimir Guerrero

2002 Season

Guerrero fell one home run shy of becoming the fourth 40-40 player in major league history, but he did manage to hit .300 with 30 homers and 100 RBI for the fifth consecutive season. He recorded his second career 200-hit campaign and tallied his second career hitting streak of at least 20 games. Guerrero's 40 steals were the fourth most in the National League. Even after the Expos fell out of the race in the NL East, he remained focused, hitting .361 over the season's final two months.

Hitting

It's hard to believe that Guerrero, only 26, still is improving. Last year was the first in which he walked more than he struck out. He is very aggressive at the plate, swinging savagely at the first pitch he likes. In fact, 10 of his home runs in 2002 came on the first pitch. While his strike zone is very large, he is increasingly more selective and less prone to flail at pitches outside. He likes to extend his long arms to drive the ball, but he can jerk the inside pitch out as well.

Baserunning & Defense

Guerrero's huge stride allows him to gobble up the basepaths in just a few steps. However, he needs to work on reading pitchers in order to cut down on being thrown out; he was thrown out while trying to steal a major league-leading 20 times. Defensively, he's got very good range but has a tendency to be overly aggressive on balls in front of him. Guerrero's arm is arguably the strongest in the game. Over the past six years, he has more outfield assists (74) than any other National Leaguer.

2003 Outlook

Guerrero will be 27 years old in 2003, an age at which many hitters enjoy their peak season. Offensively, he has the ability to join Alex Rodriguez, Jimmie Foxx, Hack Wilson and Babe Ruth as the only players in history to have 200 hits and 50 homers in a season. If he can rein in his enthusiasm on defense a little to cut down on the mistakes, he could join them in another select fraternity: MVP.

Position: RF
Bats: R **Throws:** R
Ht: 6' 3" **Wt:** 210

Opening Day Age: 27
Born: 2/9/76 in Nizao Bani, DR
ML Seasons: 7
Pronunciation: guh-RAR-oh
Nickname: Miqueas

Overall Statistics

	G	AB	R	H	D	T	HR	RBI	SB	BB	SO	Avg	OBP	Slg
'02	161	614	106	206	37	2	39	111	40	84	70	.336	.417	.593
Car.	892	3369	570	1085	206	31	209	623	114	318	431	.322	.386	.588

Where He Hits the Ball

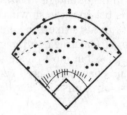 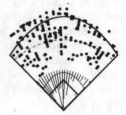

Vs. LHP   **Vs. RHP**

2002 Situational Stats

	AB	H	HR	RBI	Avg		AB	H	HR	RBI	Avg
Home	305	106	20	60	.348	LHP	124	36	6	20	.290
Road	309	100	19	51	.324	RHP	490	170	33	91	.347
First Half	333	108	19	59	.324	Sc Pos	136	45	6	69	.331
Scnd Half	281	98	20	52	.349	Clutch	100	33	8	19	.330

2002 Rankings (National League)

- 1st in hits, total bases (364), caught stealing (20), plate appearances (709), errors in right field (10) and assists in right field (14)
- 2nd in intentional walks (32), times on base (296), batting average vs. righthanded pitchers, cleanup slugging percentage (.612), lowest percentage of pitches taken (43.3), highest percentage of swings on the first pitch (46.1), and lowest fielding percentage in right field (.969)
- 3rd in batting average, games played and batting average with two strikes (.276)
- Led the Expos in home runs, at-bats, runs scored, hits, singles, RBI, sacrifice flies (5), stolen bases, walks, GDPs (20), slugging percentage and on-base percentage

Tomokazu Ohka

2002 Season

Before last season, the knock on Tomo Ohka had been that he was a nice control pitcher, but had no stamina. He laid that misnomer to rest in 2002, pitching at least seven innings in 16 of his 31 starts and throwing a pair of complete games. Slated to be the No. 4 or 5 starter, he finished with the best ERA on the starting staff—seventh best in the National League—and led the Expos in wins. He was named to the major league All-Star team that toured Japan after the season.

Pitching

None of Ohka's pitches are much above average, but he works quickly, has excellent control and possesses very good pitching instincts. His curve probably is his best pitch. His fastball has some late sink, so he gets a good number of groundouts, but his hottest heater rarely comes in at much above 90 MPH. Unlike a lot of pitchers who have comparable stuff, Ohka is unafraid to pitch inside to back hitters off the plate. Oddly enough, righthanders hit him fairly well, but lefties could do almost nothing with him last year.

Defense & Hitting

Ohka is an agile and surehanded fielder off the mound. He is extremely tough to run on. He varies the timing on his delivery very well and has a good pickoff move. He has picked off two opponents in each of the past three seasons. Given that the majority of his experience has come in DH leagues, it's surprising how competent he is with the bat. While he'll never be one of the better hitting pitchers, he is a proficient bunter.

2003 Outlook

Ohka surprised a lot of people with his 2002 performance. However, he had shown glimpses of this kind of ability when he was with the Red Sox. It was just a matter of learning to be consistent. Ohka should continue to thrive off his style, which contrasts with Montreal's trio of power righthanders.

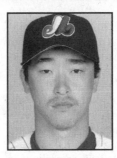

Position: SP
Bats: R **Throws:** R
Ht: 6' 1" **Wt:** 180

Opening Day Age: 27
Born: 3/18/76 in Kyoto, Japan
ML Seasons: 4
Pronunciation: TOE-mo-KAH-zoo OH-kah

Overall Statistics

	W	L	Pct.	ERA	G	GS	Sv	IP	H	BB	SO	HR	Ratio
'02	13	8	.619	3.18	32	31	0	192.2	194	45	118	19	1.24
Car.	20	25	.444	3.91	75	66	0	382.0	419	106	234	43	1.37

How Often He Throws Strikes

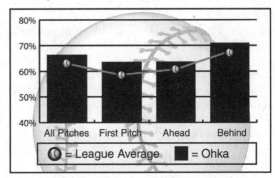

= League Average ■ = Ohka

2002 Situational Stats

	W	L	ERA	Sv	IP		AB	H	HR	RBI	Avg
Home	8	3	3.07	0	99.2	LHB	316	69	6	25	.218
Road	5	5	3.29	0	93.0	RHB	419	125	13	48	.298
First Half	8	4	3.19	0	104.1	Sc Pos	151	35	2	50	.232
Scnd Half	5	4	3.16	0	88.1	Clutch	66	21	2	8	.318

2002 Rankings (National League)

- 1st in fielding percentage at pitcher (1.000)
- 5th in fewest walks per nine innings (2.1) and fewest GDPs induced per nine innings (0.6)
- 6th in fewest pitches thrown per batter (3.52) and highest batting average allowed vs. righthanded batters
- 7th in ERA
- 10th in lowest ERA at home
- Led the Expos in ERA, wins, hit batsmen (7), pickoff throws (89) and lowest ERA on the road

Scott Stewart

2002 Season

Scott Stewart figured to get a few saves as part of a closer-by-committee arrangement last season, but his primary role was to be setup duty. After Scott Strickland was traded and several Expos righthanders were unable to close out games, Stewart was awarded the closer's role all to himself. He pitched well in that capacity, blowing just two of 19 opportunities. But an MRI revealed bone spurs after he developed a sore elbow in September, and though he tried to pitch through the pain, his availability and effectiveness were limited.

Pitching

Stewart does not have a stereotypical closer's fastball. He uses a jerky arm motion to deliver a high-80s sinker that batters have trouble picking up. He will mix in a cutter and a slider, inducing groundballs two-thirds of the time. He has a maximum-effort delivery, lunging off the pitching rubber and using all his weight to propel the ball. He dominated lefthanders last season, limiting them to just two extra-base hits all year.

Defense & Hitting

Because Stewart falls away with his delivery, he only can field grounders to the third-base side of the mound. Anything going the other way will roll to an infielder. As a lefty, he gets a good look at runners on first and does a fine job of holding them. Basestealers have been successful against him just 50 percent of the time for his career. He got his first two at-bats last season and struck out both times.

2003 Outlook

Stewart underwent elbow surgery for bone spurs in late October. The Expos have several closing options at the major league level if he is not ready to go in the spring, and several more power arms in the minors who are just about ready. If Stewart is healthy, he's as good a bet as any to be the Montreal stopper, or at the very least, resume his role as the primary lefty setup man.

Position: RP
Bats: R **Throws:** L
Ht: 6' 2" **Wt:** 225

Opening Day Age: 27
Born: 8/14/75 in Stoughton, MA
ML Seasons: 2

Overall Statistics

	W	L	Pct.	ERA	G	GS	Sv	IP	H	BB	SO	HR	Ratio
'02	4	2	.667	3.09	67	0	17	64.0	49	22	67	4	1.11
Car.	7	3	.700	3.39	129	0	20	111.2	92	35	106	9	1.14

How Often He Throws Strikes

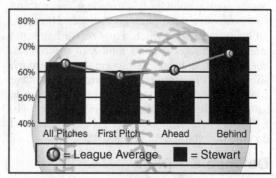

◎ = League Average   ■ = Stewart

2002 Situational Stats

	W	L	ERA	Sv	IP		AB	H	HR	RBI	Avg
Home	1	1	4.55	8	31.2	LHB	88	14	1	5	.159
Road	3	1	1.67	9	32.1	RHB	149	35	3	19	.235
First Half	3	1	1.69	12	42.2	Sc Pos	59	13	2	21	.220
Scnd Half	1	1	5.91	5	21.1	Clutch	140	28	3	18	.200

2002 Rankings (National League)

- 3rd in lowest percentage of inherited runners scored (14.7)
- 8th in first batter efficiency (.161)
- Led the Expos in games pitched, saves, games finished (28), save opportunities (19), lowest batting average allowed vs. lefthanded batters, save percentage (89.5), lowest percentage of inherited runners scored (14.7), lowest batting average allowed in relief (.207), most strikeouts per nine innings in relief (9.4) and fewest baserunners allowed per nine innings in relief (10.1)

Fernando Tatis

2002 Season

Fernando Tatis began the 2002 season on the disabled list recovering from knee surgery. He returned at the end of April and played well for about a month and a half. But conflicts with manager Frank Robinson over his level of intensity and commitment ate away Tatis' production and, eventually, his playing time. After posting 537 at-bats for the Cardinals in his breakout 1999 campaign, Tatis failed to reach 400 at-bats for the third straight year.

Hitting

Tatis showed in 1999 that he has the talent to be one of the best-hitting third baseman in the National League. He flashed good power, a strong ability to make contact and a keen eye for balls and strikes. Injuries have masked that talent the last three years, however, and he has become a little too pull-conscious. This overaggressiveness has opened up some holes in his swing and dug him into unfavorable counts to hit in, costing him production and making him much more strikeout-prone.

Baserunning & Defense

Tatis has decent speed but hasn't used it since he suffered a serious groin injury in 2000. Since then, he has suffered several knee injuries, so his days as a basestealing threat are over. He has good instincts, and he still will take an extra base on hits when it's feasible. Defensively, Tatis has quick feet, soft hands and a strong arm. His range bounced back to pre-injury levels last year, and when he is able to stay healthy, he is one of the better defenders at his position.

2003 Outlook

Tatis still possesses great raw talent, but there always have been questions about his dedication, both to the game and to his fitness, especially on rehab. Unless Tatis shows more passion, manager Frank Robinson may opt for lesser-lights who play hard, like Jamey Carroll. Tatis' production in May of last year was more consistent with his 1999 level, so he does look physically capable of returning to that elite form.

Position: 3B
Bats: R **Throws:** R
Ht: 5'10" **Wt:** 180

Opening Day Age: 28
Born: 1/1/75 in San Pedro de Macoris, DR
ML Seasons: 6
Pronunciation: TAH-tece

Overall Statistics

	G	AB	R	H	D	T	HR	RBI	SB	BB	SO	Avg	OBP	Slg
'02	114	381	43	87	18	1	15	55	2	35	90	.228	.303	.399
Car.	610	2142	324	570	121	8	88	324	41	240	520	.266	.350	.453

Where He Hits the Ball

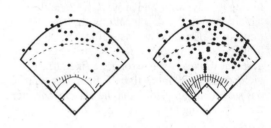

Vs. LHP   **Vs. RHP**

2002 Situational Stats

	AB	H	HR	RBI	Avg		AB	H	HR	RBI	Avg
Home	177	34	5	29	.192	LHP	87	20	5	15	.230
Road	204	53	10	26	.260	RHP	294	67	10	40	.228
First Half	201	56	12	34	.279	Sc Pos	96	21	3	37	.219
Scnd Half	180	31	3	21	.172	Clutch	69	18	4	12	.261

2002 Rankings (National League)

- 2nd in lowest batting average on a 3-2 count (.077)
- 8th in batting average on a 3-1 count (.600), errors at third base (13) and highest percentage of swings that missed (28.2)
- Led the Expos in sacrifice flies (5)

Javier Vazquez

2002 Season

Troubled with a sore elbow out of spring training, Javier Vazquez was not nearly as effective as he had been in 2001. Hitters noticed the slight drop-off in velocity; he gave up more hits, walks and homers while striking out fewer batters. Despite his struggles, he was quite dependable, going into the seventh inning in 25 of his 34 starts. He finished with a career-high 230.1 innings, but had just 10 wins to show for his efforts.

Pitching

Vazquez throws five pitches for strikes: a fastball that he can sink or cut, a slider, curve and above-average change. He walks very few batters, preferring to stay down and around the zone, forcing batters to swing at his locations. Last season he ran into real trouble against lefties, but his final four starts—29 IP, 2.48 ERA, 32 strikeouts—suggest that whatever was wrong, he fixed it. He also yielded nearly 80 more flyballs than in any previous season, an indication that he was uncharacteristically leaving his pitches up.

Defense & Hitting

Vazquez is like a fifth infielder on the mound, making plays on everything in front of him and slow hoppers to either side. He was charged with his third career error in 2002, but that's not bad when you consider he has handled 227 total chances in the big leagues. Vazquez is quick to the plate and his slide step makes him extremely tough to run on. Although 2002 was a down year for him, few pitchers handle the bat as well as Vazquez. He's an excellent bunter and he will draw a walk if his opposite number isn't careful.

2003 Outlook

It remains to be seen if Vazquez' struggles were due to bad luck, lingering tendinitis or something more serious. In any case, the lessons he learned last season, pitching through adversity, should make him a dynamic force behind staff ace Bartolo Colon. With a little better run support, Vazquez could win at least 15 games and reclaim his title as the best unknown starter in baseball.

Position: SP
Bats: R **Throws:** R
Ht: 6' 2" **Wt:** 195

Opening Day Age: 26
Born: 7/25/76 in Ponce, PR
ML Seasons: 5
Pronunciation: VAS-kez

Overall Statistics

	W	L	Pct.	ERA	G	GS	Sv	IP	H	BB	SO	HR	Ratio
'02	10	13	.435	3.91	34	34	0	230.1	243	49	179	28	1.27
Car.	51	56	.477	4.37	158	157	0	998.2	1037	274	835	127	1.31

How Often He Throws Strikes

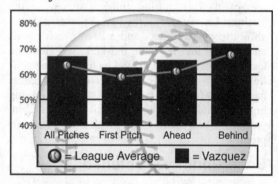

= League Average = Vazquez

2002 Situational Stats

	W	L	ERA	Sv	IP		AB	H	HR	RBI	Avg
Home	5	5	3.07	0	123.0	LHB	417	118	19	49	.283
Road	5	8	4.86	0	107.1	RHB	479	125	9	54	.261
First Half	6	5	3.68	0	134.1	Sc Pos	203	53	6	71	.261
Scnd Half	4	8	4.22	0	96.0	Clutch	86	21	2	9	.244

2002 Rankings (National League)

- 1st in hits allowed
- 3rd in batters faced (971) and fewest walks per nine innings (1.9)
- 4th in games started, innings pitched and highest strikeout-walk ratio (3.7)
- 6th in home runs allowed and pitches thrown (3,544)
- 7th in losses and lowest groundball-flyball ratio allowed (0.9)
- Led the Expos in losses, games started, innings pitched, home runs allowed, strikeouts, pitches thrown (3,544), highest strikeout-walk ratio (3.7) and lowest on-base percentage allowed (.310)

Jose Vidro

2002 Season

Three days before the 2002 regular season began, Jose Vidro was hit by a pitch that cracked his right shoulder blade. Undeterred, he still managed to play in 152 games and post one of his best offensive seasons as a professional. Along with a 21-game hitting streak, he learned the value of a walk, surpassing his previous-best walk total by 20 percent and setting a new personal best for runs scored.

Hitting

Vidro is a headache for opposing managers, especially late in games. He's an excellent contact hitter who smacks line drives to all fields and is one of the National League's more dangerous hitters with two strikes. As a switch-hitter, he doesn't have a significant split. Although he hit righthanders better in 2002, over the last three years combined it has been against lefties that he has enjoyed the most success. Vidro has good power, averaging 18 homers and 43 doubles a season over the last four years, and with his improvement in selectivity, those power numbers are a good bet to increase.

Baserunning & Defense

Vidro has made himself into a good fielder. He doesn't have a quick first step, but he makes the routine plays and will turn in an occasional spectacular play over the middle. He came up through the minors as a third baseman, so his strong arm allows him to play fairly deep. He's not a threat to steal but does run the bases well.

2003 Outlook

Vidro has established himself as one of the top second baseman in the NL, despite being plagued with nagging injuries the last two years. His new-found selectivity at the plate is a good omen for increased production. His inability to stay healthy in recent years has been the only thing obstructing him from becoming one of the elite run producers in baseball.

Position: 2B
Bats: B **Throws:** R
Ht: 5'11" **Wt:** 195

Opening Day Age: 28
Born: 8/27/74 in Mayaguez, PR
ML Seasons: 6
Pronunciation: VEE-droe

Overall Statistics

	G	AB	R	H	D	T	HR	RBI	SB	BB	SO	Avg	OBP	Slg
'02	152	604	103	190	43	3	19	96	2	60	70	.315	.378	.490
Car.	719	2564	396	782	197	9	72	346	14	207	292	.305	.360	.473

Where He Hits the Ball

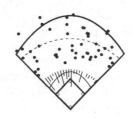

Vs. LHP   **Vs. RHP**

2002 Situational Stats

	AB	H	HR	RBI	Avg		AB	H	HR	RBI	Avg
Home	322	108	11	55	.335	LHP	155	46	3	18	.297
Road	282	82	8	41	.291	RHP	449	144	16	78	.321
First Half	336	108	9	58	.321	Sc Pos	137	51	5	77	.372
Scnd Half	268	82	10	38	.306	Clutch	106	35	3	22	.330

2002 Rankings (National League)

- 1st in batting average with two strikes (.287)
- 2nd in batting average with runners in scoring position
- 3rd in hits and doubles
- 4th in highest percentage of extra bases taken as a runner (66.2)
- 5th in fielding percentage at second base (.986)
- Led the Expos in doubles, sacrifice bunts (11), pitches seen (2,602), batting average with the bases loaded (.714), batting average vs. lefthanded pitchers and batting average on a 3-2 count (.333)

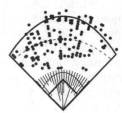

Montreal

Brad Wilkerson

2002 Season

Brad Wilkerson enjoyed a solid all-around season in his first full year in the majors. Shoulder surgery cut out a good chunk out of his 2001 campaign, but he was healthy for all of 2002 and topped 500 at-bats. He finished second on the Expos in homers and third among qualifiers in on-base percentage. He also showed some position flexibility, playing all three outfield positions, as well as some first base. Wilkerson was hitting .277 with 18 home runs before a dreadful September slump cooled his overall numbers.

Hitting

Wilkerson's smooth lefty swing produces line drives to all fields. His strikeout total in 2002 was quite surprising because he's always had a very good eye at the plate. He's a patient hitter who will draw 80-100 walks every season, and he has a history of putting the ball in play when he swings. In the minors, he showed excellent doubles power, which the Expos are hoping will translate into more home runs as he matures.

Baserunning & Defense

Wilkerson, who was one of the best two-way players in NCAA history while at Florida, has a strong, accurate arm that was responsible for 13 outfield assists—the fifth-highest total in the majors last season. He does not have great range, but his reads and routes have been good. Wilkerson has about average speed, but has enjoyed success stealing bases in the minors and could be a 12-15 steals threat once he learns to read major league pitchers better. He's a smart baserunner, taking extra bases on hits when he can.

2003 Outlook

Wilkerson will play every day in left field for Montreal if the Expos can find an adequate first baseman during the offseason. If not, he could be moved to the infield. It may take a year or two to fully develop his power, but Wilkerson should develop into a .300-.400-.500 (average, on-base and slugging) type of hitter.

Position: CF/LF/1B
Bats: L **Throws:** L
Ht: 6' 0" **Wt:** 200

Opening Day Age: 25
Born: 6/1/77 in Daviess, KY
ML Seasons: 2

Overall Statistics

	G	AB	R	H	D	T	HR	RBI	SB	BB	SO	Avg	OBP	Slg
'02	153	507	92	135	27	8	20	59	7	81	161	.266	.370	.469
Car.	200	624	103	159	34	10	21	64	9	98	202	.255	.358	.442

Where He Hits the Ball

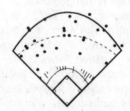
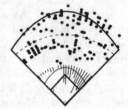

Vs. LHP   **Vs. RHP**

2002 Situational Stats

	AB	H	HR	RBI	Avg		AB	H	HR	RBI	Avg
Home	249	74	12	40	.297	LHP	87	20	5	18	.230
Road	258	61	8	19	.236	RHP	420	115	15	41	.274
First Half	267	77	9	27	.288	Sc Pos	113	28	5	40	.248
Scnd Half	240	58	11	32	.242	Clutch	83	15	2	9	.181

2002 Rankings (National League)

- 1st in home runs among rookies and RBI among rookies
- 2nd in triples
- 3rd in on-base percentage for a leadoff hitter (.373) and errors in center field (5)
- 4th in strikeouts, most pitches seen per plate appearance (4.27) and batting average among rookies
- 5th in assists in left field (8)
- Led the Expos in triples, highest percentage of pitches taken (59.8), fewest GDPs per GDP situation (6.7%) and lowest percentage of swings on the first pitch (17.8)

Peter Bergeron

Position: CF
Bats: L **Throws:** R
Ht: 6' 0" **Wt:** 190

Opening Day Age: 25
Born: 11/9/77 in Greenfield, MA
ML Seasons: 4
Pronunciation: BERR-jer-ron

Overall Statistics

	G	AB	R	H	D	T	HR	RBI	SB	BB	SO	Avg	OBP	Slg
'02	31	123	24	23	3	2	0	7	10	22	44	.187	.310	.244
Car.	297	1061	169	240	41	13	8	55	31	117	236	.226	.305	.312

2002 Situational Stats

	AB	H	HR	RBI	Avg		AB	H	HR	RBI	Avg
Home	72	18	0	4	.250	LHP	20	4	0	1	.200
Road	51	5	0	3	.098	RHP	103	19	0	6	.184
First Half	123	23	0	7	.187	Sc Pos	28	8	0	7	.286
Scnd Half	0	0	0	0	–	Clutch	21	1	0	0	.048

2002 Season

Peter Bergeron's inability to make contact consistently or keep the ball on the ground, something that has plagued him the last three years, once again turned a promising season sour. He was demoted to Triple-A after the first week of May and did not return. Unlike previous years in which he adjusted after each demotion, Bergeron's ineffectiveness continued the rest of the way.

Hitting, Baserunning & Defense

Bergeron should be a pesky leadoff man who draws walks and beats out infield hits. There is no question that he has the eye to draw the walks. The question has been whether he understands his hitting abilities enough to efficiently utilize them. His swing is too long, and he lacks the strength to drive the ball out if he gets it in the air. He bunts well, yet doesn't lay them down very often. In the outfield, he struggles with his reads, but he has good speed and an above-average arm. He's an excellent baserunner and a serious threat to steal.

2003 Outlook

Bergeron probably needs a change of organization if he hopes to stick in the big leagues. But he will need to attune his hitting philosophy to more closely suit his skills and talents if he's to avoid becoming a career Quadruple-A hitter.

Jim Brower

Position: RP
Bats: R **Throws:** R
Ht: 6' 3" **Wt:** 215

Opening Day Age: 30
Born: 12/29/72 in Edina, MN
ML Seasons: 4
Pronunciation: BROW-er

Overall Statistics

	W	L	Pct.	ERA	G	GS	Sv	IP	H	BB	SO	HR	Ratio
'02	3	2	.600	4.37	52	0	0	80.1	77	32	57	7	1.36
Car.	15	16	.484	4.60	124	23	1	297.1	303	133	201	43	1.47

2002 Situational Stats

	W	L	ERA	Sv	IP		AB	H	HR	RBI	Avg
Home	1	0	4.80	0	45.0	LHB	126	32	2	14	.254
Road	2	2	3.82	0	35.1	RHB	179	45	5	24	.251
First Half	3	1	4.56	0	53.1	Sc Pos	86	23	2	31	.267
Scnd Half	0	1	4.00	0	27.0	Clutch	31	13	1	6	.419

2002 Season

Montreal traded Bruce Chen to the Reds for Jim Brower in June. What the Expos gave up in potential they gained in a durable arm that they could use in any number of roles. Brower pitched especially well for them in June, August (except for one horrible outing in Colorado) and September.

Pitching, Defense & Hitting

Brower is not overpowering, generally topping out at 90 MPH, and he throws an average sinker-slider combo while mixing in an occasional cutter. He's durable and deliberate, but his lack of a useable offspeed pitch limits his effectiveness to relief roles. He's generally fairly tough on righthanders, but had trouble last season keeping the ball out of the middle of the plate. He's not a good fielder, and though he has a decent move to first, opposing basestealers have had a lot of success against him throughout his career, because he is quite slow to the plate.

2003 Outlook

Brower likely will be back with the Expos this season. His contract, flexibility and team-first attitude are a plus for any team, but he could be especially valuable on a young Montreal team that is learning how to win and needs his brand of unselfish, soft-spoken leadership.

Wil Cordero

Position: LF/1B
Bats: R **Throws:** R
Ht: 6' 2" **Wt:** 200

Opening Day Age: 31
Born: 10/3/71 in Mayaguez, PR
ML Seasons: 11
Pronunciation: cor-DAIR-oh

Overall Statistics

	G	AB	R	H	D	T	HR	RBI	SB	BB	SO	Avg	OBP	Slg
'02	72	161	22	43	9	0	6	30	2	17	29	.267	.337	.435
Car.	1061	3758	522	1038	229	19	105	487	47	270	652	.276	.331	.431

2002 Situational Stats

	AB	H	HR	RBI	Avg		AB	H	HR	RBI	Avg
Home	73	21	2	17	.288	LHP	93	24	4	15	.258
Road	88	22	4	13	.250	RHP	68	19	2	15	.279
First Half	83	21	2	15	.253	Sc Pos	53	17	4	25	.321
Scnd Half	78	22	4	15	.282	Clutch	32	11	1	8	.344

2002 Season

Wil Cordero, who began the 2002 season spot starting in left field and at first base for Cleveland, was waived by the Indians at the end of April. With the Indians picking up the tab on his salary, the Expos signed him in early May. In July, he earned a semiregular spot in the Montreal lineup as part of a left-field platoon with Troy O'Leary. but a strained back in the first week of September effectively ended Cordero's season.

Hitting, Baserunning & Defense

Cordero is not a patient hitter, but he generally makes contact and puts the ball in play. He has only average power and never has hit as many homers as was predicted of him when he first came to the majors. He fares very well in pinch-hitting situations and doesn't clog the basepaths. His range in the outfield is adequate, but he can play slightly above average due to a decent arm. His soft hands and quick feet are best suited for playing first base.

2003 Outlook

It seemed unlikely that Cordero would return to Montreal, but he agreed to a one-year, $600,000 deal in December. He might be a better fit in the AL, where the designated hitter is used, but he'll bring his pinch-hitting finesse back to Montreal.

Joey Eischen

Position: RP
Bats: L **Throws:** L
Ht: 6' 0" **Wt:** 210

Opening Day Age: 32
Born: 5/25/70 in West Covina, CA
ML Seasons: 6
Pronunciation: EYE-shen

Overall Statistics

	W	L	Pct.	ERA	G	GS	Sv	IP	H	BB	SO	HR	Ratio
'02	6	1	.857	1.34	59	0	2	53.2	43	18	51	1	1.14
Car.	7	4	.636	3.52	154	0	2	174.0	172	80	139	13	1.45

2002 Situational Stats

	W	L	ERA	Sv	IP		AB	H	HR	RBI	Avg
Home	4	0	1.16	1	23.1	LHB	81	14	1	8	.173
Road	2	1	1.48	1	30.1	RHB	111	29	0	12	.261
First Half	2	1	1.78	0	25.1	Sc Pos	65	15	1	20	.231
Scnd Half	4	0	0.95	2	28.1	Clutch	64	15	0	6	.234

2002 Season

After bouncing around the minors for several years, Joey Eischen finally found a home with the team that gave him his first shot in the majors. After a pedestrian 2001 performance in Montreal, he was assigned to Triple-A Ottawa to begin 2002. He pitched lights-out as the Lynx' closer and was promoted to the parent club the first week in May. Eischen continued his newfound dominance, holding the opposition scoreless in 52 of his 59 major league appearances.

Pitching, Defense & Hitting

Eischen is a hard thrower who features a good curve and change. He's unafraid to work inside and will use his fastball in all quadrants of the strike zone. Like many relievers, he doesn't have great range off the mound, but he is surehanded. He committed the first error of his major league career in 2002. He turns out to be a decent hitter for a reliever; he smacked a double and drew a walk in nine trips to the plate.

2003 Outlook

Eischen pitched very effectively on no rest and saved both games he was given to close out last year. While he's a dark horse for the closer's role, there was nothing in his 2002 performance that would suggest he can't handle it.

Matt Herges

Position: RP
Bats: L **Throws:** R
Ht: 6' 0" **Wt:** 200

Opening Day Age: 32
Born: 4/1/70 in Champaign, IL
ML Seasons: 4

Overall Statistics

	W	L	Pct.	ERA	G	GS	Sv	IP	H	BB	SO	HR	Ratio
'02	2	5	.286	4.04	62	0	6	64.2	80	26	50	10	1.64
Car.	22	18	.550	3.52	213	4	8	299.0	301	120	219	30	1.41

2002 Situational Stats

	W	L	ERA	Sv	IP		AB	H	HR	RBI	Avg
Home	1	2	2.66	5	40.2	LHB	92	29	3	13	.315
Road	1	3	6.38	1	24.0	RHB	170	51	7	26	.300
First Half	2	3	3.69	6	39.0	Sc Pos	81	20	5	33	.247
Scnd Half	0	2	4.56	0	25.2	Clutch	136	45	7	24	.331

2002 Season

The Expos traded for Matt Herges right before the start of the season with an eye on making him their closer. He notched six saves in his first eight chances, but he struggled with control and was allowing hits at an alarming rate. The hits finally caught up to him, exploding his ERA in July and August before a strong finish salvaged his season.

Pitching, Defense & Hitting

Herges' fastball normally runs in the low to mid-90s, although last year he had trouble keeping it much above 90 MPH. He throws a hard-breaking curve, but has yet to control it consistently, allowing hitters to sit on his fastball. He is most effective on two days rest and tends to struggle when he is asked to go on less than that. Herges is an average fielder and keeps runners honest with a surprisingly quick move. Though he doesn't get many opportunities, he's a pretty good hitter.

2003 Outlook

The Expos enter the 2003 season with several superior candidates for their closer's job, but even should Frank Robinson opt for a committee, Herges likely won't be a part of it. Herges did well in Los Angeles as a long reliever and spot starter, and his track record since offers considerable evidence that he should return to that dual role.

Jose Macias

Position: CF/3B/2B
Bats: B **Throws:** R
Ht: 5'10" **Wt:** 189

Opening Day Age: 31
Born: 1/25/72 in Panama City, Panama
ML Seasons: 4
Pronunciation: muh-SEE-us

Overall Statistics

	G	AB	R	H	D	T	HR	RBI	SB	BB	SO	Avg	OBP	Slg
'02	123	338	43	84	21	1	7	39	8	21	57	.249	.293	.379
Car.	338	1003	132	260	48	12	18	116	31	71	136	.259	.310	.385

2002 Situational Stats

	AB	H	HR	RBI	Avg		AB	H	HR	RBI	Avg
Home	125	32	4	17	.256	LHP	108	27	0	8	.250
Road	213	52	3	22	.244	RHP	230	57	7	31	.248
First Half	210	51	3	19	.243	Sc Pos	88	26	3	34	.295
Scnd Half	128	33	4	20	.258	Clutch	70	19	2	9	.271

2002 Season

Jose Macias was Detroit's Opening Day center fielder, but the Tigers' need for a third baseman prompted a trade to Montreal on May 16. He quickly became Frank Robinson's super-sub and utilityman, playing center, third, second and short. Macias' hitting picked up in June, and he kept it going until a stray pitch in the first week of September broke the hamate bone in his left hand.

Hitting, Baserunning & Defense

Macias swings at almost everything, but has a knack for making contact with anything remotely near the plate. Despite being a switch-hitter, most of the balls he connects with travel to right field. He doesn't have much power, but any homer he hits likely will come from the left side. He can play multiple positions competently, with second base and center being his best. He has above-average speed, but his inability to read pitchers prevents him from getting the green light.

2003 Outlook

His hand fully healed, Macias will get first crack at starting in center and leading off for the Expos this season. How long Robinson can continue to overlook Macias' inability to get on base consistently remains to be seen, but Macias will be given plenty of opportunities to improve in that area.

Montreal

549

Troy O'Leary

Position: LF
Bats: L **Throws:** L
Ht: 6' 0" **Wt:** 208

Opening Day Age: 33
Born: 8/4/69 in
Compton, CA
ML Seasons: 10
Nickname: Yum-Yum

Overall Statistics

	G	AB	R	H	D	T	HR	RBI	SB	BB	SO	Avg	OBP	Slg
'02	97	273	27	78	12	2	3	37	1	34	47	.286	.371	.377
Car.	1105	3836	529	1062	225	40	122	563	14	320	630	.277	.335	.452

2002 Situational Stats

	AB	H	HR	RBI	Avg		AB	H	HR	RBI	Avg
Home	125	39	1	15	.312	LHP	37	13	0	8	.351
Road	148	39	2	22	.264	RHP	236	65	3	29	.275
First Half	136	42	2	22	.309	Sc Pos	82	25	1	32	.305
Scnd Half	137	36	1	15	.263	Clutch	45	13	1	5	.289

2002 Season

Troy O'Leary signed as a minor league free agent after being released by the Devil Rays in spring training. He hit .337 in Triple-A Ottawa until Peter Bergeron's demotion gave him a chance to play for the parent club in early May. The acquisition of Cliff Floyd at the All-Star break pushed O'Leary to the bench, but three weeks later, Floyd was traded away and O'Leary found himself in a left-field platoon with Wil Cordero.

Hitting, Baserunning & Defense

O'Leary was surprisingly effective against left-handers in a limited role, but his strength still is against righties. He doesn't try to do too much at the plate, going the other way with outside pitches while pulling inside offerings. The significant drop in power is disconcerting, but he makes enough contact and has the discipline to be a solid bat off the bench. O'Leary is not fast and is no threat to steal. He does not have a good arm, and his outfield range is only adequate.

2003 Outlook

O'Leary is a free agent and will get a contract from someone, but probably not the Expos. His effectiveness against lefties in 2002 was encouraging, so he could be given a chance to start somewhere if he can regain his power stroke.

Britt Reames

Position: RP
Bats: R **Throws:** R
Ht: 5'11" **Wt:** 175

Opening Day Age: 29
Born: 8/19/73 in
Seneca, SC
ML Seasons: 3
Pronunciation: REEMS

Overall Statistics

	W	L	Pct.	ERA	G	GS	Sv	IP	H	BB	SO	HR	Ratio
'02	1	4	.200	5.03	42	6	0	68.0	70	38	76	8	1.59
Car.	7	13	.350	4.86	91	26	0	203.2	201	109	193	28	1.52

2002 Situational Stats

	W	L	ERA	Sv	IP		AB	H	HR	RBI	Avg
Home	1	2	3.28	0	35.2	LHB	79	27	3	13	.342
Road	0	2	6.96	0	32.1	RHB	184	43	5	37	.234
First Half	1	2	7.76	0	29.0	Sc Pos	90	27	5	47	.300
Scnd Half	1	2	3.00	0	39.0	Clutch	45	14	1	9	.311

2002 Season

Britt Reames pitched out of the pen primarily, making occasional spot starts. However, inconsistency prevented him from securing a regular role, either as a starter or as a late-inning reliever. His outings ran the gamut in 2002—from the brilliant seven-inning, two-hit effort on August 2 to his dreadful June 2 drubbing at the hands of the Phillies in which he got only one out while surrendering five earned runs.

Pitching, Defense & Hitting

Reames uses a low-90s sinking fastball and a change to set up a hard plus curve. When he's able to locate his curve and his change, he pitches aggressively and can be unhittable. He often pitches tentatively, however, trying to nibble at the corners, and invariably leaves a fat mistake over the heart of the plate. He has a terrific pickoff move and is one of the better fielding pitchers in the National League. He's not much of a hitter, but he swings hard in case he makes contact.

2003 Outlook

Reames certainly has the talent to earn a spot in the rotation, but he needs to establish consistency to secure any significant role. Regardless, he has the stuff to succeed in any role as long as he does not lose faith in that stuff.

Brian Schneider

Position: C
Bats: L **Throws:** R
Ht: 6' 1" **Wt:** 200

Opening Day Age: 26
Born: 11/26/76 in Jacksonville, FL
ML Seasons: 3

Overall Statistics

	G	AB	R	H	D	T	HR	RBI	SB	BB	SO	Avg	OBP	Slg
'02	73	207	21	57	19	2	5	29	1	21	41	.275	.339	.459
Car.	145	363	31	97	28	2	6	46	1	34	68	.267	.327	.405

2002 Situational Stats

	AB	H	HR	RBI	Avg		AB	H	HR	RBI	Avg
Home	99	29	3	13	.293	LHP	25	7	0	2	.280
Road	108	28	2	16	.259	RHP	182	50	5	27	.275
First Half	101	23	1	15	.228	Sc Pos	46	16	0	20	.348
Scnd Half	106	34	4	14	.321	Clutch	44	10	1	5	.227

2002 Season

2002 was Brian Schneider's first full season in the majors after spending much of the previous two years at Triple-A Ottawa. He opened the season on fire, posting an OPS (on-base + slugging percentage) of .915 in April, but he slumped badly in May and June. After the All-Star break, he had one of the hottest bats in the National League, hitting .321 and slugging .538.

Hitting, Baserunning & Defense

Schneider hits for a decent average and has significant value off the bench because he bats from the left side. His splits against lefties are solid, so he has the ability to become an effective starter. While he doesn't have the power potential that Michael Barrett does, he does have decent gap power that might translate into more home runs. Schneider is not particularly patient, but he generally makes contact. His receiving and blocking skills are above average, and his quick release and accurate arm allowed him to throw out runners at a 42-percent clip, good for second best in the NL.

2003 Outlook

Schneider will return as Barrett's backup and catch two to three games a week. Only 26, Schneider could develop into a solid starting backstop if given the opportunity.

T.J. Tucker

Position: RP
Bats: R **Throws:** R
Ht: 6' 3" **Wt:** 245

Opening Day Age: 24
Born: 8/20/78 in Clearwater, FL
ML Seasons: 2

Overall Statistics

	W	L	Pct.	ERA	G	GS	Sv	IP	H	BB	SO	HR	Ratio
'02	6	3	.667	4.11	57	0	4	61.1	69	31	42	5	1.63
Car.	6	4	.600	4.87	59	2	4	68.1	80	34	44	10	1.67

2002 Situational Stats

	W	L	ERA	Sv	IP		AB	H	HR	RBI	Avg
Home	5	3	5.19	1	34.2	LHB	78	21	1	7	.269
Road	1	0	2.70	3	26.2	RHB	160	48	4	24	.300
First Half	4	0	1.75	4	46.1	Sc Pos	81	19	0	23	.235
Scnd Half	2	3	11.40	0	15.0	Clutch	144	40	3	16	.278

2002 Season

Last year was a tale of two seasons for T.J. Tucker. In the first half, he was a dominant righthander with decent control, picking up occasional saves when the matchup warranted. In the second half, he got ripped until a lower back strain sidelined him in August. Opposing hitters resumed their assault once he returned in September.

Pitching, Defense & Hitting

Tucker complements a very good fastball that can touch 95 MPH with a curve and changeup. But he could not establish enough consistency with his breaking pitches in the minors to remain in a rotation. He also doesn't seem to have very good pitching instincts, making ill-advised offerings in unfavorable counts. Tucker quickly gets to balls in the infield, but he sometimes rushes his defensive plays. He has amassed five errors in 19 career chances. Maybe it's due to luck or small sample size, but in five career at-bats, he has four hits.

2003 Outlook

Tucker has closer's stuff, but he struggles with his command and his ability to make smart pitches. He's young, so there is plenty of time to make adjustments. Ideally, pitching one-inning stints in frames 6-8 would allow him to learn the closer's craft, for which his talent seems best suited.

Other Montreal Expos

Jamey Carroll (Pos: 3B, Age: 29, Bats: R)

	G	AB	R	H	D	T	HR	RBI	SB	BB	SO	Avg	OBP	Slg
'02	16	71	16	22	5	3	1	6	1	4	12	.310	.347	.507
Car.	16	71	16	22	5	3	1	6	1	4	12	.310	.347	.507

Carroll played in 16 games with the Expos in 2002, recording a hit in 12 of those appearances. He doesn't possess much power for a third baseman, but could supply a consistent bat off the bench. 2003 Outlook: C

Lou Collier (Pos: LF, Age: 29, Bats: R)

	G	AB	R	H	D	T	HR	RBI	SB	BB	SO	Avg	OBP	Slg
'02	13	11	3	1	1	0	0	0	0	1	3	.091	.231	.182
Car.	279	676	82	162	32	7	7	74	11	70	150	.240	.314	.339

Collier, who was acquired from the Mets, should see time as a utilityman for the Expos in 2003. He spent most of last season with Triple-A Ottawa, batting .316 with six homers in 89 games. 2003 Outlook: C

Tim Drew (Pos: RHP, Age: 24)

	W	L	Pct.	ERA	G	GS	Sv	IP	H	BB	SO	HR	Ratio
'02	1	0	1.000	2.81	7	1	2	16.0	12	2	10	1	0.88
Car.	2	2	.500	6.90	18	10	2	60.0	80	26	30	11	1.77

Acquired from Cleveland in June, Drew went 14-7 with a 3.08 ERA in 28 Triple-A starts. He was called up in September and the Expos experimented with him in a closer's role. Drew notched two saves. 2003 Outlook: B

Wilton Guerrero (Pos: 2B, Age: 28, Bats: B)

	G	AB	R	H	D	T	HR	RBI	SB	BB	SO	Avg	OBP	Slg
'02	103	140	12	31	2	1	0	5	7	7	32	.221	.259	.250
Car.	654	1646	190	466	53	29	11	126	41	64	245	.283	.310	.371

Guerrero started the season with the Reds, but was traded to the Marlins, who then dealt the infielder to Montreal. He hit .221 in 140 at-bats and was released at the end of the season. 2003 Outlook: C

Henry Mateo (Pos: 2B, Age: 26, Bats: B)

	G	AB	R	H	D	T	HR	RBI	SB	BB	SO	Avg	OBP	Slg
'02	22	23	1	4	0	1	0	0	2	2	6	.174	.240	.261
Car.	27	32	2	7	1	1	0	0	2	2	7	.219	.265	.313

Over his career, Mateo's strength has been his speed. However, after averaging 42 steals from 1999-2001, he swiped just 15 bags in Triple-A last season. His OBP was only .306 with Ottawa in 2002. 2003 Outlook: C

Henry Rodriguez (Pos: LF, Age: 35, Bats: L)

	G	AB	R	H	D	T	HR	RBI	SB	BB	SO	Avg	OBP	Slg
'02	20	20	1	1	0	0	0	3	0	4	8	.050	.200	.050
Car.	950	3031	389	784	176	9	160	523	10	276	803	.259	.321	.481

Rodriguez went unsigned after refusing an assignment to the minors in May. Back problems have limited his play over recent years and may prevent the slugger from returning to the major leagues. 2003 Outlook: D

Dan Smith (Pos: RHP, Age: 27)

	W	L	Pct.	ERA	G	GS	Sv	IP	H	BB	SO	HR	Ratio
'02	1	1	.500	3.47	33	0	2	46.2	34	21	34	6	1.18
Car.	5	10	.333	5.22	55	17	2	139.2	140	63	107	18	1.45

Smith was used primarily as a starter over his nine-plus seasons in the minors. However, he was a valuable contributor to the Expos bullpen after being called up in June, appearing in 33 games. 2003 Outlook: C

Ed Vosberg (Pos: LHP, Age: 41)

	W	L	Pct.	ERA	G	GS	Sv	IP	H	BB	SO	HR	Ratio
'02	0	0	–	18.00	4	0	0	1.0	3	1	0	1	4.00
Car.	10	15	.400	4.32	266	3	13	233.1	250	109	179	22	1.54

After posting an 18.00 ERA in four games, Vosberg was assigned to the minors in April. He refused assignment and became a free agent, but failed to sign with another team. At 41, he may be done. 2003 Outlook: D

Masato Yoshii (Pos: RHP, Age: 37)

	W	L	Pct.	ERA	G	GS	Sv	IP	H	BB	SO	HR	Ratio
'02	4	9	.308	4.11	31	20	0	131.1	143	32	74	15	1.33
Car.	32	47	.405	4.62	162	118	0	757.1	805	222	447	112	1.36

Yoshii started and ended the season in the Expos' starting rotation, but spent some time in the bullpen as well. The righthander posted a 3.61 ERA as a starter, compared to a 6.38 ERA in relief. He underwent surgery in September and was released in December. 2003 Outlook: C

Montreal Expos Minor League Prospects

Organization Overview:

The Expos had a deep farm system when the 2002 season began, but GM Omar Minaya plundered most of the top talent in an unsuccessful bid to unseat the Braves atop the National League East. And because of the ownership reorganization that took place in the confusing winter before last season, the Expos were unable to completely assemble their minor league staff before spring training began. This played a role in the decision to send the majority of their true prospects to Double-A, even though several had distinguished themselves at that level in 2001. Because the outgoing ownership took most of the team's resources, scouts did not have any radar guns or computers until mid-April. Despite this handicap, the Expos had a solid draft, signing 23 of their top 26 picks, including potential star Clint Everts, who had the consensus best curve in the draft.

Endy Chavez

Position: OF   **Opening Day Age:** 25
Bats: L **Throws:** L   **Born:** 2/7/78 in Valencia,
Ht: 6' 0" **Wt:** 165   VZ

Recent Statistics

	G	AB	R	H	D	T	HR	RBI	SB	BB	SO	Avg
2002 AAA Ottawa	103	405	67	139	28	5	4	41	21	33	37	.343
2002 NL Montreal	36	125	20	37	8	5	1	9	3	5	16	.296

Chavez not only won the Triple-A International League batting crown last season and was voted the league's 17th-best prospect by opposing managers. He was called up to Montreal, where he hit five triples in the final month. He's an excellent defensive outfielder with plus range and a good arm. He has the speed to be a terrific basestealer, but he doesn't have good instincts, and his ability to read pitchers needs lots of work. He doesn't have home-run power, but he drives balls to the gaps for extra bases, gets on base at an above-average rate and doesn't strike out much—a perfect resume for a No. 1 or No. 2 hitter. Chavez should open this season as the everyday center fielder and leadoff hitter.

Ron Chiavacci

Position: P   **Opening Day Age:** 25
Bats: R **Throws:** R   **Born:** 9/5/77 in
Ht: 6' 2" **Wt:** 220   Scranton, PA

Recent Statistics

	W	L	ERA	G	GS	Sv	IP	H	R	BB	SO	HR
2001 AA Harrisburg	3	11	3.97	25	25	0	147.1	137	77	76	161	12
2002 AA Harrisburg	6	9	4.27	35	10	0	111.2	105	70	65	98	6

After dominating the Double-A Eastern League last season and setting a Harrisburg franchise record for strikeouts, the Expos felt Chiavacci needed to go back to Double-A to sharpen his mechanics. Surprisingly, he struggled in the rotation and was shifted to relief after just nine starts. The move seemed to agree with him to some extent as his ERA improved, but his strikeout rate fell. He throws a very good fastball that runs in on righthanders and touches the mid-90s. He also works with a plus changeup, as well as a curve and slider that grade out as about average. His struggles with command may permanently relegate him to the bullpen. He'll start this season in Triple-A, but it would not be surprising to see him in Montreal by early summer.

Zach Day

Position: P   **Opening Day Age:** 24
Bats: R **Throws:** R   **Born:** 6/15/78 in
Ht: 6' 4" **Wt:** 185   Cincinnati, OH

Recent Statistics

	W	L	ERA	G	GS	Sv	IP	H	R	BB	SO	HR
2002 AAA Ottawa	5	6	3.50	17	16	0	90.0	77	38	32	68	5
2002 NL Montreal	4	1	3.62	19	2	1	37.1	28	18	15	25	3

Montreal acquired Day in July 2001 from the Indians for Milton Bradley. In 2002, Day was the Opening Day starter for Triple-A Ottawa. He had a few rough outings but pitched well enough overall to get called up in June. His major league debut came on his birthday, and he had much to celebrate; he got his first major league win after pitching three hitless innings. Day features a low-90s sinking fastball, a two-plane curve with a hard break, and a pretty good changeup. He tries to get quick groundballs by throwing strikes early in the count. His struggles with control occur when he gets lazy and throws across his body. He pitched well out of the pen in Montreal and may stay there for another season, but he should vie for a spot in the rotation by 2004.

Josh Karp

Position: P   **Opening Day Age:** 23
Bats: R **Throws:** R   **Born:** 9/21/79 in
Ht: 6' 5" **Wt:** 210   Longview, WA

Recent Statistics

	W	L	ERA	G	GS	Sv	IP	H	R	BB	SO	HR
2002 A Brevard Cty	4	1	1.59	7	7	0	45.1	31	9	11	43	1
2002 AA Harrisburg	7	5	3.84	16	16	0	86.2	83	43	34	69	6

Karp made his professional debut this year after holding out all of last summer for a $2.65 million contract. He opened the season in the high Class-A Florida State League, but it quickly was apparent that he would not learn much from a long stay there. He was promoted to the Double-A Eastern League and held his own there in 16 starts. He has a prototypical pitcher's body with a nice easy motion and excellent mechanics. His fastball runs up to 94 MPH with good late movement, which he complements with a tight curve and a major league circle change. If he has a strong spring, the Expos may opt to rush him to the majors, but he would benefit from a year in Triple-A to consolidate what he learned in 2002.

Montreal

Sun-Woo Kim

Position: P   **Opening Day Age:** 25
Bats: R **Throws:** R   **Born:** 9/4/77 in Inchon,
Ht: 6' 2" **Wt:** 188   Korea

Recent Statistics

	W	L	ERA	G	GS	Sv	IP	H	R	BB	SO	HR
2002 AL Boston	2	0	7.45	15	2	0	29.0	34	24	7	18	5
2002 AAA Pawtucket	4	2	3.18	8	8	0	45.1	34	18	16	37	4
2002 AAA Ottawa	3	0	1.24	7	7	0	43.2	29	11	16	28	2
2002 NL Montreal	1	0	0.89	4	3	0	20.1	18	2	7	11	0

Kim logged a lot of miles last season. He was called up to Boston just one week into the campaign after Dustin Hermanson went on the disabled list. After two months of relief work, Kim was sent back to Triple-A Pawtucket in early June. He was recalled later that month and actually got a few starts in before being sent back down at the All-Star break. Three weeks later, he was traded to Montreal as part of the Cliff Floyd deal. Still, his year was quite good overall. He throws a low-90s fastball with good movement and a plus slider. His changeup still needs work and he has periodic struggles with control. He shows some promise as a starter but his control was much better out of the pen.

Luke Lockwood

Position: P   **Opening Day Age:** 21
Bats: L **Throws:** L   **Born:** 7/21/81 in
Ht: 6' 3" **Wt:** 170   Riverside, CA

Recent Statistics

	W	L	ERA	G	GS	Sv	IP	H	R	BB	SO	HR
2001 A Clinton	5	10	2.70	26	26	0	163.1	152	78	49	114	8
2002 A Brevard Cty	10	7	3.37	26	26	0	147.0	155	69	38	86	13

Although he pitched well for being one of the youngest players at his level, Lockwood did not dominate the high Class-A Florida State League last season the way he did the Class-A Midwest League in 2001. Lockwood does not throw hard, although his fastball may gain velocity as he matures. His heater does have a good late sink, however, and he has good command of it on both sides of the plate. He also throws a curve and change that both rate as above-average major league pitches. He is several years away from pitching in the majors, but if the Expos carefully monitor his workloads and give him enough time to mature in the minors, he should develop into a solid member of the rotation.

Terrmel Sledge

Position: OF   **Opening Day Age:** 26
Bats: L **Throws:** L   **Born:** 3/18/77 in
Ht: 6' 0" **Wt:** 185   Fayetteville, NC

Recent Statistics

	G	AB	R	H	D	T	HR	RBI	SB	BB	SO	Avg
2001 AA Harrisburg	129	448	66	124	22	6	9	48	30	51	72	.277
2002 AA Harrisburg	102	396	74	119	18	6	8	43	11	55	70	.301
2002 AAA Ottawa	24	80	12	21	5	2	1	11	1	11	15	.263

Sledge showed some improvement in his second year in Double-A and finally was promoted to Triple-A at the end of the season. After a solid showing in Ottawa, he was sent to the Arizona Fall League, where he finished among the leaders in RBI and maintained his above-average plate discipline. Sledge has decent power, good speed and a discerning eye at the plate. Defensively, he has the range and arm to play just about anywhere in the outfield, but the Expos biggest need right now is in center. His performance against the higher-level competition last season should indicate to the organization that he is ready for a shot at the majors. But the Expos have an abundance of outfield options with tools similar to Sledge already on their major league roster, so unless he has a terrific spring, he'll likely begin 2003 at Triple-A Edmonton.

Seung Song

Position: P   **Opening Day Age:** 22
Bats: R **Throws:** R   **Born:** 6/29/80 in Pusan,
Ht: 6' 1" **Wt:** 192   Korea

Recent Statistics

	W	L	ERA	G	GS	Sv	IP	H	R	BB	SO	HR
2001 A Augusta	3	2	2.04	14	14	0	75.0	56	24	18	79	3
2001 A Sarasota	5	2	1.68	8	8	0	48.1	28	11	18	56	1
2002 AA Trenton	7	7	4.39	21	21	0	108.2	106	61	37	116	11
2002 AA Harrisburg	0	0	0.00	1	1	0	5.0	5	2	0	5	0

Signed out of Korea in 1999 for $800,000, Song was listed by *Baseball America* as the Red Sox' best prospect before last season began. But when an opportunity presented itself to acquire Cliff Floyd, Boston shipped Song, along with Sun-Woo Kim, off to Montreal. Song posted a fairly impressive season in Double-A despite being shut down in mid-August with shoulder soreness. After an examination and an MRI, he was pronounced healthy, suffering only from a bit of arm weariness. Song has a strong, durable body and pitches aggressively with good command of three above-average pitches: a 90-93 MPH fastball, a hard-breaking curve and a changeup. The Expos have no need to rush Song to the majors, but he may force the issue this year if he continues to pitch as well as he has.

Others to Watch

Both **Ron Calloway** (26) and **Matt Cepicky** (25) had solid years for Triple-A Ottawa in 2002, and either could open this season on the major league roster with a strong spring. Both have moderate power, decent speed and play solid defense in the outfield, but they could use some work when it comes to drawing walks. . . . Righthanded hurler **Pat Collins'** (25) shift from the rotation to the bullpen midway through the 2001 campaign has completely transformed him from a mediocre starter to a dominant potential closer. He features a mid-90s moving fastball and is 9-2, 2.08 out of the pen. . . . Righthander **Clint Everts** (18) went fifth overall in last year's draft, but he is such a good athlete that scouts felt he also could have gone in the first several rounds as a shortstop. He did not pitch professionally in 2002, but his superior command and life on his pitches could get him to the majors by late 2004.

Shea Stadium

Offense

Shea Stadium was anything but "home sweet home" for the Mets last year. New York set a National League record by losing 15 straight games at home during August, capping an all-around dismal season for the Flushing faithful. Hitters have to drive the ball to reach the center-field wall, while foul territory, which is larger than most of the space found in newer facilities, can shave a few points off a hitter's batting average. Mets righthanders hit 36 points higher and clubbed 10 more homers on the road than at Shea.

Defense

Shea Stadium is not a demanding place for defenders. The grass surface remains one of the slowest in the league. With the right- and left-field lines both at 338 feet, bloop hits tend more often to fall in front of the corner outfielders.

Who It Helps the Most

Shea is considered a pitchers' park. John Thomson, Jeff D'Amico and the departed Shawn Estes had lower ERAs at home than on the road in '02. Righthanded hitters who drill line drives down the left-field line, such as Montreal's Vladimir Guerrero and Atlanta's Vinny Castilla (who had three homers apiece at Shea last year), have more success than sluggers who hit towering shots.

Who It Hurts the Most

Righthanded power hitters are affected by the steady breeze blowing in from left field. Mike Piazza, known for his majestic homers, hit 21 of his 33 longballs on the road in 2002. Lefthanded power hitters are unaffected due in part to the scoreboard in right, with Jeromy Burnitz hitting 12 of his 19 homers and Mo Vaughn clubbing 16 of his 26 roundtrippers at home.

Rookies & Newcomers

The Mets are counting the days when shortstop Jose Reyes is ready to play. Shea's inconsistent infield shouldn't bother Reyes, who knows the minors' rough diamonds. Tom Glavine and top pitching prospect Aaron Heilman shouldn't feel cramped by Shea's dimensions when they debut with the Mets.

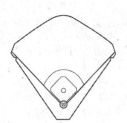

Dimensions: LF-338, LCF-378, CF-410, RCF-378, RF-338

Capacity: 56,749

Elevation: 20 feet

Surface: Grass

Foul Territory: Average

Park Factors

2002 Season

	Home Games Mets	Opp	Total	Away Games Mets	Opp	Total	Index
G	72	72	144	71	71	142	
Avg	.244	.254	.249	.267	.260	.264	94
AB	2392	2555	4947	2496	2352	4848	101
R	290	311	601	326	313	639	93
H	583	648	1231	666	612	1278	95
2B	96	104	200	119	122	241	81
3B	11	13	24	8	17	25	94
HR	72	74	146	67	68	135	106
BB	222	230	452	222	244	466	95
SO	459	515	974	476	460	936	102
E	68	46	114	63	52	115	98
E-Infield	57	42	99	53	44	97	101
LHB-Avg	.254	.261	.257	.257	.246	.252	102
LHB-HR	39	30	69	23	20	43	162
RHB-Avg	.235	.250	.243	.274	.269	.272	89
RHB-HR	33	44	77	44	48	92	80

2000-2002

	Home Games Mets	Opp	Total	Away Games Mets	Opp	Total	Index
G	215	215	430	214	214	428	
Avg	.251	.248	.250	.261	.266	.263	95
AB	7091	7550	14641	7450	7143	14593	100
R	909	909	1818	985	1011	1996	91
H	1783	1871	3654	1945	1898	3843	95
2B	338	339	677	374	387	761	89
3B	23	39	62	27	48	75	82
HR	211	220	431	227	235	462	93
BB	754	652	1406	775	697	1472	95
SO	1367	1638	3005	1441	1410	2851	105
E	175	158	333	153	162	315	105
E-Infield	144	131	275	127	136	263	104
LHB-Avg	.246	.247	.246	.244	.259	.251	98
LHB-HR	70	75	145	60	78	138	109
RHB-Avg	.254	.248	.251	.270	.270	.270	93
RHB-HR	141	145	286	167	157	324	86

2002 Rankings (National League)

- Highest LHB home-run factor
- Lowest RHB batting-average factor
- Second-lowest RHB home-run factor
- Third-lowest double factor

Art Howe

2002 Season

Bobby Valentine was axed as the Mets' skipper after suffering his first sub-.500 season as a Mets manager, despite being owed $2.7 million for the final year of his contract. The Mets then hired Art Howe, who had guided the A's to three straight postseason appearances, including 103 victories and the American League West crown last year. Howe, who didn't see eye-to-eye with A's GM Billy Beane and was criticized for losing in the playoffs to Minnesota, was allowed to depart Oakland despite having one year left on *his* deal.

Offense

In order for Howe to have success in New York, the Mets must hit better than they did in 2002. Howe prefers the Earl Weaver method by playing for three-run homers, and that may be his approach again with Mike Piazza, Mo Vaughn and Jeromy Burnitz comprising the middle of the lineup. Howe has a reputation for playing by the book, running on rare occasions, and taking only calculated chances.

Pitching & Defense

The Mets were brutal defensively last year, with many of the miscues centering on a lack of fundamentals. Howe focuses on fundamentals and will try to upgrade that area, a job that should be easier with a more comfortable Roberto Alomar and a slimmer Vaughn. Howe has handled relievers well in his career. He'll probably need a quicker hook with the likes of Pedro Astacio, John Thomson and a handful of youngsters than he had with Barry Zito, Mark Mulder and Tim Hudson.

2003 Outlook

Howe never experienced security in Oakland, always working on one-year contracts despite keeping the low-budget A's in the hunt. His four-year, $9.4 million deal with the Mets alters his status considerably. His laidback approach will be challenged by the underachieving team of highly paid players found in New York. After the infighting Valentine produced throughout much of his reign, Howe should promote a calmer atmosphere that promises to lead to more victories.

Born: 12/15/46 in Pittsburgh, PA

Playing Experience: 1974-1985, Pit, Hou, StL

Managerial Experience: 12 seasons

Manager Statistics

Year	Team, Lg	W	L	Pct	GB	Finish
2002	Oakland, AL	103	59	.636	–	1st West
12 Seasons		992	951	.511	–	–

2002 Starting Pitchers by Days Rest

	<=3	4	5	6+
Athletics Starts	0	100	32	23
Athletics ERA	–	3.19	3.25	6.55
AL Avg Starts	1	83	44	24
AL ERA	7.15	4.59	4.27	5.03

2002 Situational Stats

	Art Howe	AL Average
Hit & Run Success %	29.4	36.0
Stolen Base Success %	69.7	68.1
Platoon Pct.	56.0	58.9
Defensive Subs	43	23
High-Pitch Outings	2	6
Quick/Slow Hooks	12/7	19/14
Sacrifice Attempts	29	53

2002 Rankings (American League)

- 1st in fewest caught stealings of third base (2), sacrifice-bunt percentage (86.2%), defensive substitutions and 2+ pitching changes in low-scoring games (44)
- 2nd in fewest caught stealings of second base (18), first-batter platoon percentage and one-batter pitcher appearances (46)
- 3rd in intentional walks (32), pinch-hitters used (126) and mid-inning pitching changes (191)

Edgardo Alfonzo

2002 Season

After a disastrous 2001, Edgardo Alfonzo regained his swing while maintaining an exercise program designed to strengthen his back. Able to turn on pitches again, he hit with authority during the second half of last season. He battled a sore left hand during the first two months and spent time on the disabled list in August with a strained left oblique muscle. But Alfonzo moved into third place in hits and fourth place in RBI on the Mets' all-time charts.

Hitting

Alfonzo is a selective and patient hitter with excellent bat control and solid knowledge of the strike zone. His power decreased two years ago in part because he was unable complete his swing due to his ailing back. But he proved during last season's second half that he's still capable of driving fastballs into the gaps. He made adjustments during the year by swinging through most pitches and finishing with the bat held high to give him the necessary whip to drive the ball. The improvement was obvious against lefthanders, against whom Alfonzo increased his batting average by more than 150 points over 2001.

Baserunning & Defense

After not seeing any activity at third base since 1998, Alfonzo moved from second to the hot corner and responded impressively. He always has possessed the soft hands, arm strength and throwing accuracy necessary to play third. He also does an outstanding job of closing the hole with his range to his left, and he has the ability to make the occasional spectacular play. His speed is no better than average, though Alfonzo is an intelligent baserunner who was successful on all six of his stolen-base attempts last season.

2003 Outlook

Alfonzo, who turned down a three-year deal with the Mets last spring, no longer appears to be the 25-homer producer he had been. Still, the free agent can be a consistent .300 hitter who provides 15-20 longballs and steady defense. The health of his back, which could lead to a rapid decline, remains a concern. But for now he remains an above-average option at third base.

Position: 3B
Bats: R **Throws:** R
Ht: 5'11" **Wt:** 187

Opening Day Age: 29
Born: 11/8/73 in St. Teresa, VZ
ML Seasons: 8

Overall Statistics

	G	AB	R	H	D	T	HR	RBI	SB	BB	SO	Avg	OBP	Slg
'02	135	490	78	151	26	0	16	56	6	62	55	.308	.391	.459
Car.	1086	3897	614	1136	212	14	120	538	45	458	498	.292	.367	.445

Where He Hits the Ball

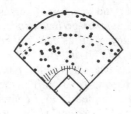

Vs. LHP   **Vs. RHP**

2002 Situational Stats

	AB	H	HR	RBI	Avg		AB	H	HR	RBI	Avg
Home	239	67	8	28	.280	LHP	121	44	4	18	.364
Road	251	84	8	28	.335	RHP	369	107	12	38	.290
First Half	296	90	4	25	.304	Sc Pos	103	34	2	38	.330
Scnd Half	194	61	12	31	.314	Clutch	77	28	2	12	.364

2002 Rankings (National League)

- 1st in lowest batting average on a 3-1 count (.000)
- 3rd in on-base percentage vs. lefthanded pitchers (.477)
- 4th in batting average on the road
- Led the Mets in batting average, runs scored, walks, times on base (220), on-base percentage, batting average in the clutch, batting average vs. lefthanded pitchers, on-base percentage vs. lefthanded pitchers (.477), on-base percentage vs. righthanded pitchers (.361), batting average on the road and batting average on a 3-2 count (.317)
- Led NL third basemen in batting average

Roberto Alomar

2002 Season

The Mets didn't receive the expected increase in offensive production from several newcomers, including Roberto Alomar, who had been obtained from Cleveland in an eight-player deal. While Alomar battled a strained groin in the second half, the ailment played only a small role in the second baseman suffering significant drops across the board. Nevertheless, he stroked the 200th home run of his career and became only the seventh switch-hitter to reach 2,500 hits.

Hitting

Alomar has succeeded as a guess hitter for years. Yet he rarely looked comfortable in 2002 against National League pitching, and was awful versus lefthanders. His .266 batting average matched his rookie year mark as the lowest of his career. One of the game's best bunters and hit-and-run batters, Alomar frustrated the Mets when he tried to bunt for hits with runners in scoring position. For the first time in his career, he seemed to lose confidence before displaying his superior ability to make adjustments in the middle of the season.

Baserunning & Defense

After committing five errors in 2001, Alomar's miscues more than doubled last year (11). Part of that can be attributed to working with a different and more erratic shortstop (Rey Ordonez compared to Omar Vizquel). Still, Alomar remains a Gold Glove-caliber defender with excellent range to both sides. He also has one of the strongest arms among second basemen. While his steals were nearly cut in half, he's an excellent baserunner. He may have lost half a step over the past two years, but he goes from first to third and second to home as well as anyone.

2003 Outlook

Alomar is eligible to become a free agent after 2003. Despite his difficult 2002, the Mets believe he can return to his previous form and become one of the team's standouts. He was adamant that he wanted to remain a Met, even though he had the right to demand a trade. A more competitive situation should rekindle the enthusiasm that the sensitive Alomar appeared to lose last year.

Position: 2B
Bats: B **Throws:** R
Ht: 6' 0" **Wt:** 185

Opening Day Age: 35
Born: 2/5/68 in Ponce, PR
ML Seasons: 15
Pronunciation: AL-uh-mar
Nickname: Robbie

Overall Statistics

	G	AB	R	H	D	T	HR	RBI	SB	BB	SO	Avg	OBP	Slg
'02	149	590	73	157	24	4	11	53	16	57	83	.266	.331	.376
Car.	2183	8386	1414	2546	470	76	201	1071	462	959	1032	.304	.375	.450

Where He Hits the Ball

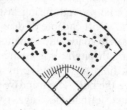 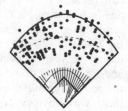

Vs. LHP	Vs. RHP

2002 Situational Stats

	AB	H	HR	RBI	Avg		AB	H	HR	RBI	Avg
Home	282	74	4	21	.262	LHP	162	33	4	14	.204
Road	308	83	7	32	.269	RHP	428	124	7	39	.290
First Half	339	91	7	30	.268	Sc Pos	106	30	2	38	.283
Scnd Half	251	66	4	23	.263	Clutch	105	36	2	11	.343

2002 Rankings (National League)

- 4th in on-base percentage for a leadoff hitter (.371) and lowest on-base percentage vs. left-handed pitchers (.259)
- 6th in stolen-base percentage (80.0), fielding percentage at second base (.983) and lowest batting average vs. lefthanded pitchers
- 7th in errors at second base (11)
- Led the Mets in at-bats, hits, singles, pitches seen (2,626), plate appearances (655), steals of third (3), on-base percentage for a leadoff hitter (.371) and lowest percentage of swings on the first pitch (19.5)

Pedro Astacio

Position: SP
Bats: R **Throws:** R
Ht: 6' 2" **Wt:** 210

Opening Day Age: 33
Born: 11/28/69 in Hato Mayor, DR
ML Seasons: 11
Pronunciation: ah-STAH-see-oh

2002 Season

Pedro Astacio opened last season as the Mets' No. 4 starter. But he wound up sharing the lead role with Al Leiter during the campaign's first few months, before fading in August and September. The righthander enjoyed the best first half of his career, as he won 10 of his first 13 decisions. While he allowed three runs or fewer in 19 of 31 starts, he struggled in seven of his last nine outings, and his ERA rose every month.

Pitching

The Mets weren't concerned about Astacio's frayed labrum during the second half, because his fastball consistently remained in the 90-MPH range. His problem centered on trying to be too fine in the strike zone instead of trusting his stuff. That resulted in poor location of pitches, and he became much easier to hit. At his best, Astacio keeps his pitches low in the zone, resulting in numerous groundball outs. He spots his fastball for strikes and keeps hitters off balance with a big, sharp-breaking curveball and deft changeup. Despite his shoulder problems, Astacio eats innings. He helped save an overworked bullpen during the season's first half by averaging nearly seven innings per start prior to the All-Star break.

Defense & Hitting

Astacio is an athletic pitcher with a live and fluid body. He holds runners well with his quick pick-off move and delivery, resulting in just 10 stolen bases, lowest among Mets starters. His cat-like reflexes also are evident in his ability to defend his position and cover first base. An above-average bunter, Astacio recorded 10 hits last season, but struck out in half of his at-bats.

2003 Outlook

Astacio reached 180 innings last year, which guarantees his $6 million salary in 2003. He returns to a veteran Mets rotation that includes Leiter, Steve Trachsel and newly acquired Tom Glavine. Still, concerns remain about Astacio's lingering shoulder injury. After facing a crossroads in his career a year ago, he could flirt with the 15 wins he averaged in 1998 and 1999 if his shoulder holds up.

Overall Statistics

	W	L	Pct.	ERA	G	GS	Sv	IP	H	BB	SO	HR	Ratio
'02	12	11	.522	4.79	31	31	0	191.2	192	63	152	32	1.33
Car.	115	107	.518	4.53	339	296	0	1934.1	1990	635	1518	250	1.36

How Often He Throws Strikes

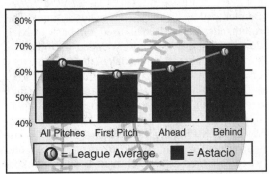

2002 Situational Stats

	W	L	ERA	Sv	IP		AB	H	HR	RBI	Avg
Home	4	6	4.80	0	90.0	LHB	339	81	15	45	.239
Road	8	5	4.78	0	101.2	RHB	395	111	17	52	.281
First Half	8	3	3.17	0	110.2	Sc Pos	156	41	9	67	.263
Scnd Half	4	8	7.00	0	81.0	Clutch	52	14	1	4	.269

2002 Rankings (National League)

- 1st in home runs allowed and hit batsmen (16)
- 2nd in most home runs allowed per nine innings (1.50)
- 3rd in balks (2)
- 5th in highest ERA and highest ERA at home
- 6th in fewest GDPs induced per nine innings (0.6)
- 7th in lowest batting average on an 0-2 count (.053)
- 10th in complete games (3)
- Led the Mets in complete games (3), home runs allowed, hit batsmen (16), balks (2), lowest stolen-base percentage allowed (62.5) and fewest pitches thrown per batter (3.61)

Armando Benitez

2002 Season

Armando Benitez has been one of the game's top closers over the past three years, converting 117 of 129 save opportunities. That success rate of 90.7 percent is the best in the majors since the beginning of 2000 among pitchers with at least 75 save opportunities during that span. Benitez experienced recurring pain in his left ankle after twisting it last July 20, which led to three home runs allowed in his next five appearances. Otherwise, he was effective while becoming the first Met to record three straight seasons with 30 or more saves.

Pitching

Benitez will tie his manager's hands at times. The righthander falters when used on back-to-back days or when he sits for extended periods. His stuff is at its best when he takes the mound every other day, resulting in a 97-MPH fastball. Strictly a fireballer a couple of years ago, Benitez has expanded his repertoire lately to include a split-finger fastball in the low 90s and a hard slider in the 86-88 MPH range. His offerings tend to flatten out and land in the heart of the strike zone when he's tired or too well rested. But when he's at the top of his game, he dominates lefthanded batters and has good command of all his pitches.

Defense & Hitting

Benitez has gained the reputation as a steady fielder over the past few seasons. He continues to get more than his fair share of one-hoppers back to the mound, a sign that his splitter is producing its signature sharp break. He covers first base and holds runners adequately, although he still tends to focus too much on striking out the hitter, which can cause a lapse in concentration. As a closer, Benitez rarely finds himself holding a bat.

2003 Outlook

The 2003 campaign is Benitez' free-agent year, which should give him additional incentive to fill his role with aplomb. He blew only four chances last season and had enough stuff to save considerably more than 33 games if he had been given the opportunity. He should have little difficulty extending his string to four straight years with 30-plus saves.

Position: RP
Bats: R **Throws:** R
Ht: 6' 4" **Wt:** 229

Opening Day Age: 30
Born: 11/3/72 in
Ramon Santana, DR
ML Seasons: 9
Pronunciation:
buh-NEE-tezz

Overall Statistics

	W	L	Pct.	ERA	G	GS	Sv	IP	H	BB	SO	HR	Ratio
'02	1	0	1.000	2.27	62	0	33	67.1	46	25	79	8	1.05
Car.	26	27	.491	3.04	495	0	176	511.1	333	273	689	61	1.19

How Often He Throws Strikes

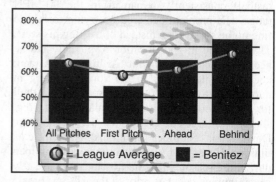

2002 Situational Stats

	W	L	ERA	Sv	IP		AB	H	HR	RBI	Avg
Home	1	0	2.57	17	42.0	LHB	119	19	6	12	.160
Road	0	0	1.78	16	25.1	RHB	123	27	2	10	.220
First Half	0	0	2.34	20	34.2	Sc Pos	62	12	0	14	.194
Scnd Half	1	0	2.20	13	32.2	Clutch	165	32	7	15	.194

2002 Rankings (National League)

- 1st in lowest batting average allowed vs. left-handed batters
- 4th in lowest batting average allowed in relief (.190) and most strikeouts per nine innings in relief (10.6)
- Led the Mets in saves, games finished (52), save opportunities (37), lowest batting average allowed vs. lefthanded batters, save percentage (89.2), relief ERA (2.27), lowest batting average allowed in relief (.190), most strikeouts per nine innings in relief (10.6) and fewest baserunners allowed per nine innings in relief (9.9)

Jeromy Burnitz

2002 Season

Acquired from Milwaukee last January, Jeromy Burnitz may have been the biggest bust of all the Mets in 2002, a feat hard to achieve. He endured a four-month power outage before finally finding his stroke after the team's fate had been determined. Former manager Bobby Valentine tried numerous remedies, including hitting him second in the batting order. But Burnitz had only 12 games with more than one RBI and was brutal with runners in scoring position.

Hitting

After averaging 32 homers and 102 RBI in his last five seasons with the Brewers, Burnitz looked clueless at the plate in 2002. He jumped at pitches and pulled countless offerings into foul territory while pitchers kept him off balance. He finally found his rhythm late in the campaign when he went back to a more pronounced leg kick that allows him to stay back on pitches. Employing one of the more full-effort swings in the game, Burnitz had little chance against southpaws, going two months at midseason without a hit against lefthanded starters.

Baserunning & Defense

There were times when Burnitz appeared to take his offensive struggles onto the field, resulting in nine errors to go along with eight assists. Nevertheless, Burnitz has a strong and accurate arm, a steady glove, and does a better job covering right field than many critics give him credit for. His decent speed also is seen on the basepaths, where Burnitz tied for third on the team with 10 steals, the second highest total of his major league career. He isn't prone to baserunning mistakes, and has a quick first step.

2003 Outlook

Look for Burnitz to do everything possible to get back the level he was at while with Milwaukee. He'll be in his free-agent campaign, and was embarrassed by his showing during his New York debut. With his hefty contract still in tow, Burnitz will be the everyday right fielder and will be counted upon to provide the offensive boost the Mets were hoping to see last year.

Position: RF
Bats: L **Throws:** R
Ht: 6' 0" **Wt:** 213

Opening Day Age: 33
Born: 4/15/69 in Westminster, CA
ML Seasons: 10
Pronunciation: ber-NITS

Overall Statistics

	G	AB	R	H	D	T	HR	RBI	SB	BB	SO	Avg	OBP	Slg
'02	154	479	65	103	15	0	19	54	10	58	135	.215	.311	.365
Car.	1147	3788	641	955	203	23	207	658	58	567	957	.252	.356	.482

Where He Hits the Ball

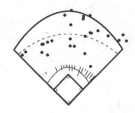

Vs. LHP   **Vs. RHP**

2002 Situational Stats

	AB	H	HR	RBI	Avg		AB	H	HR	RBI	Avg
Home	239	54	12	29	.226	LHP	121	21	3	9	.174
Road	240	49	7	25	.204	RHP	358	82	16	45	.229
First Half	282	58	9	30	.206	Sc Pos	114	21	5	36	.184
Scnd Half	197	45	10	24	.228	Clutch	78	16	5	9	.205

2002 Rankings (National League)

- 1st in lowest batting average, lowest percentage of swings put into play (30.5), lowest batting average vs. lefthanded pitchers and lowest fielding percentage in right field (.966)
- 2nd in errors in right field (9), lowest batting average with runners in scoring position and lowest batting average on the road
- 3rd in lowest batting average with the bases loaded (.083), lowest batting average vs. righthanded pitchers and lowest on-base percentage vs. lefthanded pitchers (.242)
- Led the Mets in caught stealing (7), hit by pitch (10), games played and most pitches seen per plate appearance (4.21)

Roger Cedeno

2002 Season

Roger Cedeno was one of the leading targets of the Shea Stadium boobirds last year. Signed as a free agent to provide some electricity at the top of the Mets' lineup, Cedeno failed to get on base enough to maintain the leadoff job, only to regain it when no one else stepped forward. An increase in muscle and weight negated his speed-oriented game. He also battled dizziness and a rapid heartbeat late in the season.

Hitting

Opposing pitchers took advantage of Cedeno's undisciplined approach at the plate last year. The free swinger chases pitches high in the strike zone and will strike out looking at low offerings. He's not patient enough nor does he walk enough to merit the leadoff spot. Although he's fared better when batting lefthanded in recent years, he actually has more career home runs from the right side in 63 percent fewer at-bats.

Baserunning & Defense

After stealing 55 bases in 2001, Cedeno was not the factor on the basepaths that the Mets hoped he would be last year. He seemed to cherish every time he got on base and didn't run until he had some success at the plate late in the campaign. Cedeno's difficulties with the bat carried over onto the field, which served as a major reason that the Mets had one of baseball's worst defensive outfields. He's an awful glove man who has more errors than assists in his career. He overruns balls to both his left and right, and the accuracy of his throws ranks among the worst in the game.

2003 Outlook

The Mets shopped Cedeno to any team that would listen over the winter, but his outrageous contract limited the interest. So the outfielder likely is stuck in New York. He again will man left field while the Mets hope he regains at least some of the form he showed during his first run with the team in 1999, when he posted career highs with a .313 batting average and 66 stolen bases.

Position: LF
Bats: B **Throws:** R
Ht: 6' 1" **Wt:** 205

Opening Day Age: 28
Born: 8/16/74 in Valencia, VZ
ML Seasons: 8
Pronunciation: sid-AIN-yo

Overall Statistics

	G	AB	R	H	D	T	HR	RBI	SB	BB	SO	Avg	OBP	Slg
'02	149	511	65	133	19	2	7	41	25	42	92	.260	.318	.346
Car.	820	2433	382	674	92	26	30	206	194	260	480	.277	.348	.373

Where He Hits the Ball

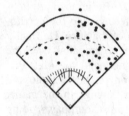
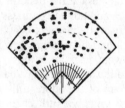

Vs. LHP **Vs. RHP**

2002 Situational Stats

	AB	H	HR	RBI	Avg		AB	H	HR	RBI	Avg
Home	251	58	2	14	.231	LHP	156	36	3	8	.231
Road	260	75	5	27	.288	RHP	355	97	4	33	.273
First Half	291	72	3	23	.247	Sc Pos	98	29	0	32	.296
Scnd Half	220	61	4	18	.277	Clutch	94	24	1	8	.255

2002 Rankings (National League)

- 1st in errors in left field (8)
- 2nd in stolen-base percentage (86.2) and lowest fielding percentage in left field (.966)
- 4th in highest groundball-flyball ratio (2.0)
- 6th in lowest on-base percentage vs. lefthanded pitchers (.275)
- 7th in lowest slugging percentage
- 8th in lowest slugging percentage vs. righthanded pitchers (.349)
- 9th in lowest batting average at home
- Led the Mets in stolen bases, stolen-base percentage (86.2) and highest percentage of extra bases taken as a runner (68.6)

Al Leiter

2002 Season

Unlike the majority of his teammates, Al Leiter got off to a strong start last season and remained one of the most consistent producers for the disappointing Mets. The lefthanded ace worked at least seven innings in 16 outings, and allowed two earned runs or less in 20 of 33 starts. Leiter became the first pitcher in major league history to defeat all 30 teams, when he beat Arizona on April 30.

Pitching

Leiter continues to succeed with his hard, cut fastball that sits in the 90-92 MPH range. The pitch is nothing short of filthy, and overwhelms righthanded hitters who are unable to make contact before it slices the inside corner. Leiter dominates lefties with outside fastballs and sliders, along with changeups he must keep low in the strike zone. He fell out of rhythm last May by failing to follow through on many of his pitches, thereby leaving his offerings up. He returned to normal at midseason, after scaring a few observers in the organization that his maximum effort delivery had finally taken its toll on his pitching elbow.

Defense & Hitting

Leiter still has soft hands and average quickness. He fields his position well, although he did commit three errors last year, tied for tops among Mets pitchers. He also threw over to first base more than any pitcher. But the results had marginal effect, since he surrendered 29 swipes. Once one of the league's worst hitters, Leiter has become a decent bunter. He drove in two runs and posted eight hits for a .151 batting average, after entering the campaign with a career mark of .088.

2003 Outlook

Leiter signed a two-year contract extension last July to avoid entering the free-agent market. While the 37-year-old admits he's nearing the end of his career, Leiter remains one of the tougher lefties in the league, and ranks among the most consistent pitchers at the game's top level. The Mets are counting on him again in 2003.

Position: SP
Bats: L **Throws:** L
Ht: 6' 3" **Wt:** 220

Opening Day Age: 37
Born: 10/23/65 in Toms River, NJ
ML Seasons: 16
Pronunciation: lighter

Overall Statistics

	W	L	Pct.	ERA	G	GS	Sv	IP	H	BB	SO	HR	Ratio
'02	13	13	.500	3.48	33	33	0	204.1	194	69	172	23	1.29
Car.	130	103	.558	3.66	326	296	2	1894.1	1684	874	1621	154	1.35

How Often He Throws Strikes

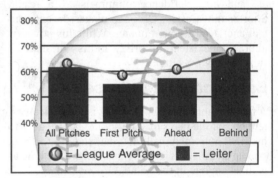

= League Average   = Leiter

2002 Situational Stats

	W	L	ERA	Sv	IP		AB	H	HR	RBI	Avg
Home	4	6	4.26	0	95.0	LHB	154	34	4	14	.221
Road	9	7	2.80	0	109.1	RHB	623	160	19	70	.257
First Half	8	7	2.90	0	111.2	Sc Pos	157	43	2	50	.274
Scnd Half	5	6	4.18	0	92.2	Clutch	61	14	1	2	.230

2002 Rankings (National League)

- 1st in stolen bases allowed (29)
- 3rd in pickoff throws (157) and lowest fielding percentage at pitcher (.914)
- 4th in shutouts (2), runners caught stealing (12), most pitches thrown per batter (3.93) and least run support per nine innings (4.0)
- Led the Mets in wins, losses, games started, shutouts (2), innings pitched, hits allowed, batters faced (868), walks allowed, strikeouts, pitches thrown (3,409), stolen bases allowed (29), runners caught stealing (12), lowest batting average allowed (.250), lowest ERA on the road and most strikeouts per nine innings (7.6)

Rey Ordonez

2002 Season

Rey Ordonez' fielding troubles early last season did little to help a Mets defense that struggled most of the year. He made seven errors in the team's first 11 games before settling down and committing 12 miscues in his last 133 contests. In addition to flashing a steadier glove, Ordonez hit .301 (43-for-143) over his last 49 games.

Hitting

Ordonez continues to frustrate the Mets with his bat. His biggest flaw is swinging at bad pitches, particularly breaking balls on the outside part of the plate. His poor efforts tend to come in bunches, and his confidence plummets as a result. Shortcomings aside, Ordonez makes decent contact and is an efficient bunter. While his power is almost nonexistent, he drives in his fair share of runs for a No. 8 hitter.

Baserunning & Defense

A flamboyant defender, Ordonez is more inconsistent on routine plays than he should be. He goes to his right extremely well and can slide to the ball, pop up and make the strong throw from the hole as well as anyone in the game. Ordonez charged the ball much better last season than he had in recent years, and he does an excellent job of turning the double play. Some scouts believe the 32-year-old has lost half a step in the past two years, which could be forcing him to hurry on some plays. While possessing a quick first step, his speed is average at best on the basepaths, where Ordonez tends to experience lapses of concentration.

2003 Outlook

Ordonez enters the final year of his contract with the Mets shopping his services to anyone who will listen. Top prospect Jose Reyes is making some noise in the minors' upper reaches, which will lead to a change at the shortstop position in the near future. Ordonez remains the starter, but he's on the verge of becoming a backup or a platoon player within the next two years.

Position: SS
Bats: R **Throws:** R
Ht: 5' 9" **Wt:** 159

Opening Day Age: 32
Born: 1/11/71 in Havana, Cuba
ML Seasons: 7
Pronunciation: RAY or-DOAN-yez

Overall Statistics

	G	AB	R	H	D	T	HR	RBI	SB	BB	SO	Avg	OBP	Slg
'02	144	460	53	117	25	2	1	42	2	24	46	.254	.292	.324
Car.	916	2937	275	720	115	17	8	260	28	187	313	.245	.290	.304

Where He Hits the Ball

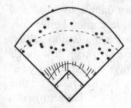 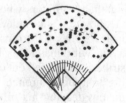

Vs. LHP   **Vs. RHP**

2002 Situational Stats

	AB	H	HR	RBI	Avg		AB	H	HR	RBI	Avg
Home	222	53	0	19	.239	LHP	119	23	0	3	.193
Road	238	64	1	23	.269	RHP	341	94	1	39	.276
First Half	256	61	1	27	.238	Sc Pos	117	30	0	40	.256
Scnd Half	204	56	0	15	.275	Clutch	82	17	1	3	.207

2002 Rankings (National League)

- 1st in lowest slugging percentage and lowest slugging percentage vs. lefthanded pitchers (.227)
- 2nd in lowest on-base percentage vs. lefthanded pitchers (.236)
- 3rd in highest groundball-flyball ratio (2.2) and lowest HR frequency (460.0 ABs per HR)
- 4th in most GDPs per GDP situation (21.3%)
- 5th in lowest on-base percentage, fewest pitches seen per plate appearance (3.20) and lowest batting average vs. lefthanded pitchers
- Led the Mets in sacrifice flies (4), intentional walks (11), highest groundball-flyball ratio (2.2) and highest percentage of swings put into play (52.3)

Mike Piazza

Position: C
Bats: R **Throws:** R
Ht: 6' 3" **Wt:** 215

Opening Day Age: 34
Born: 9/4/68 in Norristown, PA
ML Seasons: 11
Pronunciation: pee-AH-zuh

2002 Season

Even though he failed to bat .300 for the first time in 10 major league seasons, Mike Piazza remained the game's best hitting catcher. He overcame severe tendinitis in his left wrist to earn his 10th All-Star selection. And with 30 or more homers in each of the past eight years, Piazza moved into second place for career home runs as a catcher. He passed Johnny Bench and is only 15 longballs behind Carlton Fisk.

Hitting

Piazza has been forced to display incredible patience over the past two years. Many hitters would try to do too much while their teammates struggle, but Piazza has maintained his composure while simply trying to make solid contact with his classically effortless swing. He murders low and inside pitches, resulting in long, majestic home runs to left field. And he drives pitches on the outside half of the plate to right. Piazza is a feared and productive hitter who has driven in at least 92 runs each of the past 10 seasons.

Baserunning & Defense

Piazza no longer possesses even average speed due to his duties behind the plate. But he remains a knowledgeable if conservative baserunner who doesn't hurt his team with foolish mistakes. It's no secret that Piazza is perhaps the majors' easiest catcher to run on. He retired just 21 of 146 basestealers, an awful 14.4 percent, and didn't nail anyone during a stretch of 44 attempts in the first half. Though more than adequate in calling a game, his mobility behind the plate is below average. Regardless of his shortcomings, Piazza never stops hustling, maintains a warrior mentality and has plenty of heart.

2003 Outlook

For years, the speculation has been that Piazza's ultimate destination is first base. Yet despite turning 34 last September, he will remain behind the plate in 2003, especially with Mo Vaughn around. An additional day off here and there could do wonders for Piazza, who can be expected to return to the .300 level while leading the Mets' power production.

Overall Statistics

	G	AB	R	H	D	T	HR	RBI	SB	BB	SO	Avg	OBP	Slg
'02	135	478	69	134	23	2	33	98	0	57	82	.280	.359	.544
Car.	1393	5116	851	1641	251	6	347	1073	17	563	801	.321	.388	.576

Where He Hits the Ball

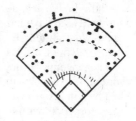 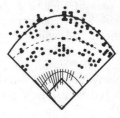

Vs. LHP **Vs. RHP**

2002 Situational Stats

	AB	H	HR	RBI	Avg		AB	H	HR	RBI	Avg
Home	218	60	12	44	.275	LHP	126	36	8	26	.286
Road	260	74	21	54	.285	RHP	352	98	25	72	.278
First Half	267	76	18	56	.285	Sc Pos	125	37	10	66	.296
Scnd Half	211	58	15	42	.275	Clutch	80	18	5	15	.225

2002 Rankings (National League)

- 1st in errors at catcher (12) and lowest percentage of runners caught stealing as a catcher (14.4)
- Led the Mets in home runs, total bases (260), RBI, GDPs (26), slugging percentage, HR frequency (14.5 ABs per HR), cleanup slugging percentage (.555), slugging percentage vs. lefthanded pitchers (.563) and slugging percentage vs. righthanded pitchers (.537)
- Led NL catchers in home runs and RBI

John Thomson

2002 Season

John Thomson arrived from Colorado in a five-player deal at last year's trading deadline and replaced Jeff D'Amico at the end of the Mets' rotation. Thomson enjoyed the healthiest season of his career and opened some eyes in the process. Despite twirling half his games at Coors Field during the season's first four months, Thomson allowed three earned runs or fewer in 22 of 30 starts and didn't surrender four earned runs in 13 of his final 15 outings.

Pitching

Thomson is a control pitcher who eats his fair share of innings. He relies on his above-average, sinking fastball and ranked sixth in the league with 2.18 walks per nine innings. He always has shown the willingness to challenge hitters by throwing strikes. The righthander works off his mid-90s fastball and a solid changeup before going for the kill with his hard sinker, which can be a devastating offering when he's in his groove. Thomson also is one of the more competitive pitchers in the game. If he can package all of his attributes and remain healthy, he could take the next step and become a dominating hurler.

Defense & Hitting

The weakest aspect of Thomson's game centers on his defense. He tends to rush his throws and isn't consistent when catching balls hit back through the box. He also hasn't refined his pick-off move, although he is persistent in trying to hold runners at first base with numerous throws. Thomson has become one of the league's better hitting pitchers of late, producing 11 hits and three RBI last season.

2003 Outlook

At age 29, Thomson is heading into the prime of his career. A series of injuries, including surgery for a torn right labrum, left the righthander considering retirement in August of 2000. But now he's in position to begin living up to some lofty expectations. Matched up against many opponents' fourth and fifth starters, Thomson could experience a breakthrough campaign and help give the Mets one of the deeper yet more unheralded rotations in the National League.

Position: SP
Bats: R **Throws:** R
Ht: 6' 3" **Wt:** 190

Opening Day Age: 29
Born: 10/1/73 in Vicksburg, MS
ML Seasons: 5
Nickname: Red

Overall Statistics

	W	L	Pct.	ERA	G	GS	Sv	IP	H	BB	SO	HR	Ratio
'02	9	14	.391	4.71	30	30	0	181.2	201	44	107	28	1.35
Car.	29	49	.372	4.95	111	110	0	665.1	737	205	421	90	1.42

How Often He Throws Strikes

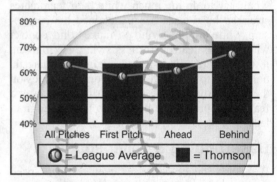

= League Average = Thomson

2002 Situational Stats

	W	L	ERA	Sv	IP		AB	H	HR	RBI	Avg
Home	5	7	4.32	0	93.2	LHB	368	105	13	42	.285
Road	4	7	5.11	0	88.0	RHB	363	96	15	62	.264
First Half	7	7	4.85	0	111.1	Sc Pos	188	47	8	76	.250
Scnd Half	2	7	4.48	0	70.1	Clutch	30	12	3	8	.400

2002 Rankings (National League)

- 1st in fewest GDPs induced per nine innings (0.1)
- 2nd in highest slugging percentage allowed (.471) and fewest GDPs induced per GDP situation (1.7%)
- 4th in highest ERA on the road (5.11)
- 5th in losses (14) and most home runs allowed per nine innings (1.39)
- 6th in home runs allowed (28), fewest walks per nine innings (2.2), highest ERA (4.71), lowest groundball-flyball ratio allowed (0.9) and fewest strikeouts per nine innings (5.3)

Steve Trachsel

2002 Season

After enduring a tale of two seasons in 2001, Steve Trachsel emerged as arguably the Mets' best pitcher from start to finish last year. He threw much better than his won-lost record indicates. For example, after missing three weeks in July due to a strained right trapezius, he went 1-3 with two no-decisions in August despite a 2.25 ERA. Trachsel allowed two or fewer earned runs in 18 of 30 starts, and surrendered just 10 earned runs in 41.0 innings during his final seven outings.

Pitching

When at the top of his game, Trachsel gets ahead of hitters by throwing first-pitch strikes. He keeps opponents off balance by changing speeds and altering the batter's eye level. He works off his two-seam fastball, a pitch that touches 90 MPH, along with an average curveball and decent changeup. His success over the past year and a half has centered on being more aggressive by working faster and challenging hitters to make contact, thereby allowing his fielders to do their jobs. Trachsel is tough on lefthanders, who batted 48 points lower than their righthanded counterparts. He isn't afraid to walk a batter, but has good command and control of his pitches. He rarely makes a mistake, surrendering 16 home runs last year, second lowest among the Mets' primary starters.

Defense & Hitting

One of the better all-around athletes among pitchers, Trachsel fields his position well. He has soft hands, quick feet and covers first base as well as any hurler. That athleticism also is evident at the plate, where last year Trachsel hit the first triple of his career. He posted nine sacrifice hits to pace Mets pitchers.

2003 Outlook

Trachsel agreed to a two-year, $8 million deal in December. The righthander has established himself as a steady, middle-of-the-rotation starter. He has learned how to make adjustments and pitch to his strengths over the past two years, which should lead to another 12-14 wins in 2003.

Position: SP
Bats: R **Throws:** R
Ht: 6' 4" **Wt:** 205

Opening Day Age: 32
Born: 10/31/70 in Oxnard, CA
ML Seasons: 10
Pronunciation: track-s'l

Overall Statistics

	W	L	Pct.	ERA	G	GS	Sv	IP	H	BB	SO	HR	Ratio
'02	11	11	.500	3.37	30	30	0	173.2	170	69	105	16	1.38
Car.	90	108	.455	4.31	279	278	0	1694.1	1729	602	1188	239	1.38

How Often He Throws Strikes

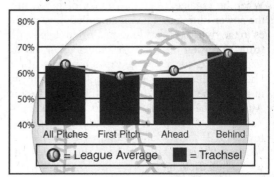

2002 Situational Stats

	W	L	ERA	Sv	IP		AB	H	HR	RBI	Avg
Home	7	6	3.31	0	106.0	LHB	318	74	9	34	.233
Road	4	5	3.46	0	67.2	RHB	342	96	7	33	.281
First Half	6	7	3.87	0	97.2	Sc Pos	146	40	3	49	.274
Scnd Half	5	4	2.72	0	76.0	Clutch	38	15	0	3	.395

2002 Rankings (National League)

- 1st in pickoff throws (193)
- 5th in lowest strikeout-walk ratio (1.5)
- 6th in stolen bases allowed (21) and runners caught stealing (11)
- 9th in fewest strikeouts per nine innings (5.4)
- 10th in most pitches thrown per batter (3.83)
- Led the Mets in ERA, walks allowed, wild pitches (4), pickoff throws (193), lowest slugging percentage allowed (.379), lowest ERA at home and most run support per nine innings (4.8)

Mo Vaughn

2002 Season

The Mets acquired Mo Vaughn from the Angels last winter after he had missed all of 2001 due to a ruptured biceps tendon. But the rotund first baseman looked more like a beer-league softball player than a major leaguer. His miserable first half included a fractured right hand in the season's third game that forced him to miss two weeks. He didn't rediscover his power stroke until late June, but managed to hit .281 with 21 homers in his last 77 games.

Hitting

Vaughn's timing was off throughout the first half. When he regained the consistency of his swing, the power-hitting first baseman pulled most pitches to the right side, resulting in a Bonds-type shift from opposing infields. A career .294 hitter, Vaughn succeeds when he uses the middle of the field, as well as the inside-out stroke he employed in hitting the ball to left field while with Boston. Although he always has piled up strikeouts, Vaughn produced his lowest batting average and fewest RBI since his second season, in part because of his inability to beat out bobbles and would-be infield hits.

Baserunning & Defense

Vaughn's big frame played a role in his lack of range and 18 errors at first base. Though effective with short-hop throws, he had difficulty bending for balls in the dirt and reaching for high tosses. His immobility led to his being replaced on occasion late in games, thereby hurting the offense. He may have been the league's slowest runner on the basepaths. The Mets hope that better conditioning will eliminate the need for a sundial when timing Vaughn's speed.

2003 Outlook

The Mets would love to move Vaughn and his hefty contract, but it's apparent the team is stuck with him. He vowed late last season to report to spring training in better physical condition. If he can achieve that goal while building on his second-half performance, Vaughn has a chance to rekindle memories of the respectable power hitter he was throughout most of the 1990s.

Position: 1B
Bats: L **Throws:** R
Ht: 6' 1" **Wt:** 275

Opening Day Age: 35
Born: 12/15/67 in Norwalk, CT
ML Seasons: 11
Nickname: The Hit Dog

Overall Statistics

G	AB	R	H	D	T	HR	RBI	SB	BB	SO	Avg	OBP	Slg
139	487	67	126	18	0	26	72	0	59	145	.259	.349	.456
1485	5453	851	1605	268	10	325	1049	30	711	1407	.294	.384	.526

Where He Hits the Ball

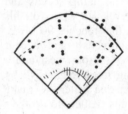

Vs. LHP   **Vs. RHP**

2002 Situational Stats

	AB	H	HR	RBI	Avg		AB	H	HR	RBI	Avg
Home	255	64	16	40	.251	LHP	136	37	7	20	.272
Road	232	62	10	32	.267	RHP	351	89	19	52	.254
First Half	258	64	10	34	.248	Sc Pos	131	36	6	46	.275
Scnd Half	229	62	16	38	.271	Clutch	74	17	2	13	.230

2002 Rankings (National League)

- 1st in errors at first base (18), lowest percentage of extra bases taken as a runner (23.8) and lowest fielding percentage at first base (.984)
- 6th in strikeouts
- 9th in lowest batting average on an 0-2 count (.081)
- 10th in hit by pitch (10)
- Led the Mets in hit by pitch (10) and strikeouts

Jeff D'Amico

Position: SP
Bats: R **Throws:** R
Ht: 6' 7" **Wt:** 250

Opening Day Age: 27
Born: 12/27/75 in St. Petersburg, FL
ML Seasons: 6
Pronunciation: duh-MEEK-oh

Overall Statistics

	W	L	Pct.	ERA	G	GS	Sv	IP	H	BB	SO	HR	Ratio
'02	6	10	.375	4.94	29	22	0	145.2	152	37	101	20	1.30
Car.	35	34	.507	4.41	103	95	0	578.0	583	173	382	91	1.31

2002 Situational Stats

	W	L	ERA	Sv	IP		AB	H	HR	RBI	Avg
Home	4	5	4.21	0	77.0	LHB	269	67	5	30	.249
Road	2	5	5.77	0	68.2	RHB	300	85	15	46	.283
First Half	4	7	4.72	0	103.0	Sc Pos	125	31	6	54	.248
Scnd Half	2	3	5.48	0	42.2	Clutch	34	6	0	3	.176

2002 Season

Obtained from the Brewers last January, Jeff D'Amico began the season in the Mets' rotation. But he went 1-6 in his last 10 starts and was banished to the bullpen in August. D'Amico responded well to the role by posting a 2.16 ERA in 16.2 relief innings.

Pitching, Defense & Hitting

D'Amico struggled with his command as a starter, forcing him to be more perfect with his offerings. His best pitch is a big-breaking curveball that he mixes well with his fastball and changeup to keep hitters off balance. The righthander experiences his greatest trouble when he loses confidence in his 87-89 MPH fastball, which leads to a loss of aggressiveness. He's an excellent fielder with a below-average pickoff move. He and Shawn Estes have replaced Al Leiter as the Mets' worst hitting pitchers.

2003 Outlook

A multitude of injuries hampered D'Amico's efforts when he was with Milwaukee, and he has not experienced consistent success in the majors. After the Mets declined to offer salary arbitration, the free agent will get a look as a No. 4 or 5 starter elsewhere in 2003, and risks becoming a journeyman if he doesn't find some consistency soon.

Mark Guthrie

Position: RP
Bats: R **Throws:** L
Ht: 6' 4" **Wt:** 215

Opening Day Age: 37
Born: 9/22/65 in Buffalo, NY
ML Seasons: 14

Overall Statistics

	W	L	Pct.	ERA	G	GS	Sv	IP	H	BB	SO	HR	Ratio
'02	5	3	.625	2.44	68	0	1	48.0	35	19	44	3	1.13
Car.	49	51	.490	4.11	700	43	14	936.0	949	359	754	95	1.40

2002 Situational Stats

	W	L	ERA	Sv	IP		AB	H	HR	RBI	Avg
Home	4	2	2.93	0	27.2	LHB	75	14	2	6	.187
Road	1	1	1.77	1	20.1	RHB	94	21	1	6	.223
First Half	2	0	1.48	1	24.1	Sc Pos	40	6	3	12	.150
Scnd Half	3	3	3.42	0	23.2	Clutch	92	20	2	7	.217

2002 Season

Obtained from the A's prior to 2002, Mark Guthrie was the Mets' primary lefthander out of the bullpen during the campaign's first two months. He emerged as the team's most consistent reliever. Guthrie set a franchise record by not allowing a run in 33 straight appearances, covering 27.0 innings from May 25 to August 3. The southpaw was unscored upon in 60 of 68 outings overall.

Pitching, Defense & Hitting

Guthrie shuts down lefthanded hitters, and is nearly as tough against righties. He did an excellent job of retiring the first batter faced last season. The lefthander has a heavy fastball in the upper 80s, along with a good curveball and excellent splitter. He's capable of pitching on consecutive days, provided he goes no more than an inning or two. His fielding is average, but his pickoff move is below average for a southpaw. He is 1-for-13 in his career as a hitter, though with just one strikeout.

2003 Outlook

The 37-year-old Guthrie continues to get better with age. He understands his role and has become one of the most effective middlemen in the game. With his ability to strand runners, the free-agent journeyman will maintain a valuable bullpen role with the Mets or another major league club.

Joe McEwing

Position:
RF/SS/1B/2B/3B/LF
Bats: R **Throws:** R
Ht: 5'11" **Wt:** 170

Opening Day Age: 30
Born: 10/19/72 in
Bristol, PA
ML Seasons: 5

Overall Statistics

	G	AB	R	H	D	T	HR	RBI	SB	BB	SO	Avg	OBP	Slg
'02	105	196	22	39	8	1	3	26	4	9	50	.199	.242	.296
Car.	470	1165	153	298	68	9	22	120	22	73	226	.256	.308	.386

2002 Situational Stats

	AB	H	HR	RBI	Avg		AB	H	HR	RBI	Avg
Home	86	12	2	11	.140	LHP	93	19	2	12	.204
Road	110	27	1	15	.245	RHP	103	20	1	14	.194
First Half	112	21	3	15	.188	Sc Pos	48	10	1	20	.208
Scnd Half	84	18	0	11	.214	Clutch	51	10	0	4	.196

2002 Season

Joe McEwing struggled to find his swing last year and had little success at the plate. He missed more than two weeks in July with a strained muscle in his left ribcage and wound up hitting just .140 at Shea Stadium. A favorite of former manager Bobby Valentine, McEwing started games at every position except pitcher and catcher.

Hitting, Baserunning & Defense

McEwing's batting average was the lowest of his pro career. He continued to hit fastballs well and with a little power. But opposing pitchers fed him a steady diet of breaking balls that troubled him, particularly without the luxury of consistent playing time. Possessing average speed, McEwing gets good jumps in the field and on the basepaths and does an excellent job of taking the extra base. While the utilityman's best position is third base, he started only five times there last season.

2003 Outlook

A valuable role player who's been re-signed, McEwing must continually prove himself or risk losing his job to a lower-priced rookie. He brings numerous intangibles to the Mets, with the sum of his game exceeding the value of its individual parts. He'll get another 250 at-bats this year while playing as many as seven different positions.

Timo Perez

Position: CF/LF/RF
Bats: L **Throws:** L
Ht: 5' 9" **Wt:** 167

Opening Day Age: 27
Born: 4/8/75 in Bani,
DR
ML Seasons: 3

Overall Statistics

	G	AB	R	H	D	T	HR	RBI	SB	BB	SO	Avg	OBP	Slg
'02	136	444	52	131	27	6	8	47	10	23	36	.295	.331	.437
Car.	245	732	89	204	40	8	14	72	12	38	66	.279	.317	.413

2002 Situational Stats

	AB	H	HR	RBI	Avg		AB	H	HR	RBI	Avg
Home	210	64	3	17	.305	LHP	64	10	0	3	.156
Road	234	67	5	30	.286	RHP	380	121	8	44	.318
First Half	200	64	5	24	.320	Sc Pos	87	29	2	38	.333
Scnd Half	244	67	3	23	.275	Clutch	68	22	1	8	.324

2002 Season

Timo Perez put together one of the best springs of any Met, only to wind up at Triple-A Norfolk. But he returned to New York early last season and emerged as the team's most consistent hitter. The lone Met to avoid a prolonged slump, he produced solid numbers at the top of the order.

Hitting, Baserunning & Defense

A slap hitter prior to 2002, Perez abandoned his previous approach and showed the ability to drive pitches consistently into the gaps. He struggles versus lefthanders, resulting in a meager .153 lifetime batting average against them. But he more than doubled that mark against righthanders last year and has hit righties for far more power. Perez easily is the Mets' best defensive outfielder. He possesses above-average speed, which allows him to play shallow in center field. Despite his speed, he's only an average baserunner.

2003 Outlook

The Mets are facing a fish-or-cut-bait decision with Perez. Some observers feel he could be the everyday center fielder, but many don't believe he'll hit lefthanded pitching well enough to hold the job. If he fails to take advantage of the situation this spring, Perez will be relegated to fourth-outfielder duties.

Steve Reed

Position: RP
Bats: R **Throws:** R
Ht: 6' 2" **Wt:** 212

Opening Day Age: 37
Born: 3/11/66 in Los Angeles, CA
ML Seasons: 11

Overall Statistics

	W	L	Pct.	ERA	G	GS	Sv	IP	H	BB	SO	HR	Ratio
'02	2	5	.286	2.01	64	0	1	67.0	56	14	50	2	1.04
Car.	40	31	.563	3.52	671	0	18	708.2	639	231	538	86	1.23

2002 Situational Stats

	W	L	ERA	Sv	IP		AB	H	HR	RBI	Avg
Home	1	3	1.62	1	33.1	LHB	83	15	0	5	.181
Road	1	2	2.41	0	33.2	RHB	158	41	2	12	.259
First Half	2	3	1.67	0	37.2	Sc Pos	70	13	0	15	.186
Scnd Half	0	2	2.45	1	29.1	Clutch	121	29	2	7	.240

2002 Season

After signing a minor league contract with the Padres last offseason, Steve Reed earned a bullpen job in spring training. He later joined the Mets at the trading deadline in a five-player deal. He looked more like the consistent setup man he was a few years ago, instead of the aging and ailing reliever who struggled at times in 2001.

Pitching, Defense & Hitting

Reed's success centers on keeping hitters off balance while giving them little to hit. He works the borders of the strike zone with his 87-89 MPH sinking fastball, yet doesn't walk many batters. He also does an excellent job of mixing his decent slider and average changeup. Deception is a strong part of Reed's game when he employs his submarine delivery. He rarely hurts himself with the leather, and does an adequate job of holding runners. He is a non-factor at the plate.

2003 Outlook

A free agent, Reed is a durable and consistent survivor, which has led to his becoming the only righthander to appear in 50 or more games in each of the last 10 seasons. At 37, he'll have to prove himself on an annual basis, but again should rank among the holds leaders as a solid setup man.

Grant Roberts

Position: RP
Bats: R **Throws:** R
Ht: 6' 3" **Wt:** 205

Opening Day Age: 25
Born: 9/13/77 in El Cajon, CA
ML Seasons: 3

Overall Statistics

	W	L	Pct.	ERA	G	GS	Sv	IP	H	BB	SO	HR	Ratio
'02	3	1	.750	2.20	34	0	0	45.0	43	16	31	3	1.31
Car.	4	1	.800	3.58	54	1	0	78.0	78	28	66	5	1.36

2002 Situational Stats

	W	L	ERA	Sv	IP		AB	H	HR	RBI	Avg
Home	1	0	1.89	0	19.0	LHB	69	18	1	7	.261
Road	2	1	2.42	0	26.0	RHB	101	25	2	8	.248
First Half	2	0	1.91	0	37.2	Sc Pos	51	7	1	13	.137
Scnd Half	1	1	3.68	0	7.1	Clutch	33	8	0	2	.242

2002 Season

After compiling a nifty 0.66 ERA in April and May, Grant Roberts landed on the disabled list in June with a right rotator cuff strain. Tendinitis in his right shoulder sent him to the DL again from July 13 to September 10. He also was the center of controversy in September, when pictures were published of him smoking marijuana.

Pitching, Defense & Hitting

When healthy, Roberts' fastball has excellent movement in the 93-94 MPH range. He also throws a hard slider that showed steady improvement last year. But the release point of his curveball remains inconsistent, leading to control problems. Roberts' heater is good enough to retire batters up in the strike zone, though he gets in trouble when he leaves his other offerings up. An above-average defender with good athleticism, Roberts had a single in his lone at-bat last year.

2003 Outlook

If Roberts stays healthy and becomes more serious about his career, he has the natural ability to excel in the major leagues. His maturity has improved over the past 18 months, but he has battled bouts of tendinitis during that time. While he remains a candidate to be the No. 5 starter, Roberts is beginning to establish himself as a setup man.

Scott Strickland

Position: RP
Bats: R **Throws:** R
Ht: 5'11" **Wt:** 180

Opening Day Age: 26
Born: 4/26/76 in
Houston, TX
ML Seasons: 4

Overall Statistics

	W	L	Pct.	ERA	G	GS	Sv	IP	H	BB	SO	HR	Ratio
'02	6	9	.400	3.54	69	0	2	68.2	61	33	69	7	1.37
Car.	12	19	.387	3.38	212	0	20	216.0	181	101	225	22	1.31

2002 Situational Stats

	W	L	ERA	Sv	IP		AB	H	HR	RBI	Avg
Home	5	5	2.82	2	38.1	LHB	96	30	3	14	.313
Road	1	4	4.45	0	30.1	RHB	165	31	4	21	.188
First Half	6	5	3.89	2	39.1	Sc Pos	83	16	3	29	.193
Scnd Half	0	4	3.07	0	29.1	Clutch	135	30	5	20	.222

2002 Season

New York acquired Scott Strickland from Montreal in a seven-player deal on April 5. He impressed Mets officials enough to be considered a possible replacement for Armando Benitez one day. After surrendering a couple of late-game homers during the first half, Strickland posted a 1.99 ERA from August 3 to the end of the season.

Pitching, Defense & Hitting

Strickland has the makeup and talent to be a major league closer. He possesses an outstanding fastball in the 92-94 MPH range, and throws a hard slider and a decent changeup that can dominate righthanded batters. Strickland struggles when his right shoulder opens up during his delivery, causing his fastball to sail through the middle of the zone. His high leg kick allows baserunners to run at will and can leave him out of position on defense. Offensively, he's looking for his first hit.

2003 Outlook

Strickland's occasional difficulties last season have the Mets believing he needs some more experience before he can assume the closer's role. He spent time with John Franco last year discussing the nuances of the game, and Strickland will toil for another season behind Franco and Benitez before a promotion is possible.

John Valentin

Position: SS/1B/3B
Bats: R **Throws:** R
Ht: 6' 0" **Wt:** 185

Opening Day Age: 36
Born: 2/18/67 in
Mineola, NY
ML Seasons: 11
Pronunciation:
VAL-en-tin

Overall Statistics

	G	AB	R	H	D	T	HR	RBI	SB	BB	SO	Avg	OBP	Slg
'02	114	208	18	50	15	0	3	30	0	22	37	.240	.339	.356
Car.	1105	3917	614	1093	281	17	124	558	47	463	524	.279	.360	.454

2002 Situational Stats

	AB	H	HR	RBI	Avg		AB	H	HR	RBI	Avg
Home	108	24	2	15	.222	LHP	73	13	1	5	.178
Road	100	26	1	15	.260	RHP	135	37	2	25	.274
First Half	113	26	3	18	.230	Sc Pos	50	18	1	25	.360
Scnd Half	95	24	0	12	.253	Clutch	53	13	2	12	.245

2002 Season

For the first time since rupturing the patella tendon in his left knee in 2000, John Valentin showed flashes of his previous form. Despite a partial tear in his right rotator cuff that landed him on the DL in May, his improved health enabled the versatile defender to succeed as the Mets' top pinch-hitter.

Hitting, Baserunning & Defense

Valentin continues to stand close to the plate, enabling him to hit the ball to all fields. A consistent bunter, he possesses good bat control, which allows him to hit the ball in the air or on the ground, depending on the situation. In addition to seeing action at first base for the first time in his career, Valentin proved capable of going into the hole and making the throw at shortstop. He also maintains the necessary reflexes to handle either corner infield position, as well as second base.

2003 Outlook

After struggling to find a job prior to last season, Valentin had much more leverage upon entering the free-agent fray this time, though the Mets did not offer him salary arbitration. He believes he can be a full-time player and may receive an opportunity. If not, he can expect to see considerable activity at all four infield positions and to be a frequent pinch-hitter.

Dave Weathers

Position: RP
Bats: R **Throws:** R
Ht: 6' 3" **Wt:** 230

Opening Day Age: 33
Born: 9/25/69 in Lawrenceburg, TN
ML Seasons: 12

Overall Statistics

	W	L	Pct.	ERA	G	GS	Sv	IP	H	BB	SO	HR	Ratio
'02	6	3	.667	2.91	71	0	0	77.1	69	36	61	6	1.36
Car.	44	49	.473	4.64	471	67	7	846.0	932	381	598	76	1.55

2002 Situational Stats

	W	L	ERA	Sv	IP		AB	H	HR	RBI	Avg
Home	2	2	2.06	0	39.1	LHB	105	28	0	16	.267
Road	4	1	3.79	0	38.0	RHB	177	41	6	20	.232
First Half	2	3	2.87	0	47.0	Sc Pos	90	16	1	28	.178
Scnd Half	4	0	2.97	0	30.1	Clutch	163	35	2	22	.215

2002 Season

Dave Weathers emerged as the Mets' top setup man after signing as a free agent last offseason. He led the team with 71 appearances and topped the bullpen with 77.1 innings pitched. The righthander didn't allow a run over 10 outings from April 28 to May 19, or over nine appearances between August 30 and September 22.

Pitching, Defense & Hitting

Weathers thrives by dominating righthanded hitters and inducing grounders with a sinking, low-90s fastball that leads to double plays. His 82-84 MPH slider also has become a tough pitch against hitters from both sides of the plate. Not unlike many relievers, Weathers is most effective when he receives regular work. He doesn't hurt himself with the glove, and he has become much better at holding runners on since developing a slide step a couple years ago. His role as a setup man rarely leads to an at-bat.

2003 Outlook

After toiling for seven teams in 11 years, Weathers found a home prior to last season when he inked a three-year deal worth $9.4 million with the Mets. He earned his keep in their bullpen and will be counted upon for an encore performance in 2003.

Vance Wilson

Position: C
Bats: R **Throws:** R
Ht: 5'11" **Wt:** 190

Opening Day Age: 30
Born: 3/17/73 in Mesa, AZ
ML Seasons: 4

Overall Statistics

	G	AB	R	H	D	T	HR	RBI	SB	BB	SO	Avg	OBP	Slg
'02	74	163	19	40	7	0	5	26	0	5	32	.245	.301	.380
Car.	111	224	22	57	10	0	5	32	0	7	50	.254	.306	.366

2002 Situational Stats

	AB	H	HR	RBI	Avg		AB	H	HR	RBI	Avg
Home	82	18	3	10	.220	LHP	32	4	1	5	.125
Road	81	22	2	16	.272	RHP	131	36	4	21	.275
First Half	89	22	2	14	.247	Sc Pos	42	15	2	22	.357
Scnd Half	74	18	3	12	.243	Clutch	37	7	0	3	.189

2002 Season

Vance Wilson spent his first full season in the major leagues and started a quarter of the Mets' games behind the plate. He hit his first home run on April 13 against Montreal's Javier Vazquez, and responded well to his role by producing at a .357 clip with runners in scoring position.

Hitting, Baserunning & Defense

Wilson earns his keep by upgrading the Mets' defensive efforts at catcher and putting the brakes on opponents' baserunners. While Mike Piazza retired 14.4 percent of basestealers, Wilson nailed 22 of 48 for a rate of 45.8 percent. An excellent defender with quick reactions, Wilson has overcome arm injuries from earlier in his career and possesses good arm strength with excellent accuracy. His bat has some power, and he was a .261 hitter in the minor leagues. Although he stole 11 bases at Triple-A Norfolk in 2000, Wilson's speed is just a hair above average.

2003 Outlook

Wilson believes he can be an everyday catcher. That role is not on the immediate horizon in New York, although it could become a reality if Piazza ever moves to first base. In the meantime, Wilson appears relegated to being one of the game's better backups behind the plate.

Jaime Cerda (**Pos**: LHP, **Age**: 24)

	W	L	Pct.	ERA	G	GS	Sv	IP	H	BB	SO	HR	Ratio
'02	0	0	–	2.45	32	0	0	25.2	22	14	21	0	1.40
Car.	0	0	–	2.45	32	0	0	25.2	22	14	21	0	1.40

After just two-plus seasons in the minors, Cerda made his major league debut last season and did not disappoint, posting a 2.45 ERA in 32 games. He should be a staple in the Mets' bullpen again in 2003. 2003 Outlook: B

McKay Christensen (**Pos**: LF, **Age**: 27, **Bats**: L)

	G	AB	R	H	D	T	HR	RBI	SB	BB	SO	Avg	OBP	Slg
'02	4	3	1	1	0	0	0	0	0	1	1	.333	.500	.333
Car.	99	128	22	32	3	0	2	14	6	10	26	.250	.324	.320

Christensen is a light-hitting outfielder approaching the prime of his career. After being claimed off waivers from the Dodgers in April, he batted .284 at Triple-A Norfolk, stealing 20 bases. 2003 Outlook: C

Brady Clark (**Pos**: LF, **Age**: 29, **Bats**: R)

	G	AB	R	H	D	T	HR	RBI	SB	BB	SO	Avg	OBP	Slg
'02	61	78	9	15	4	0	0	10	1	7	11	.192	.267	.244
Car.	161	218	32	52	8	0	6	30	5	29	29	.239	.332	.358

Clark saw limited playing time after coming over from the Reds in the Shawn Estes deal. However, he hit .307 over six seasons in the minors. If he can find some consistency, the Mets should find a bench spot for him. 2003 Outlook: C

Kane Davis (**Pos**: RHP, **Age**: 27)

	W	L	Pct.	ERA	G	GS	Sv	IP	H	BB	SO	HR	Ratio
'02	1	1	.500	7.07	16	0	0	14.0	15	11	24	2	1.86
Car.	3	8	.273	6.01	81	2	0	97.1	108	56	75	17	1.68

Davis struggled over the first six weeks of the season, posting a 7.07 ERA in 16 games with the Mets. He underwent elbow surgery in July and expects to be fully recovered in time for spring training. 2003 Outlook: C

Pedro Feliciano (**Pos**: LHP, **Age**: 26)

	W	L	Pct.	ERA	G	GS	Sv	IP	H	BB	SO	HR	Ratio
'02	0	0	–	7.50	6	0	0	6.0	9	1	4	0	1.67
Car.	0	0	–	7.50	6	0	0	6.0	9	1	4	0	1.67

Feliciano was claimed by Detroit after being waived by the Mets. The lefthander, who has some minor league experience as a closer, has a good shot at a spot in the Tigers' bullpen next season. 2003 Outlook: C

Raul Gonzalez (**Pos**: CF/LF, **Age**: 29, **Bats**: R)

	G	AB	R	H	D	T	HR	RBI	SB	BB	SO	Avg	OBP	Slg
'02	40	104	13	27	3	0	3	12	4	6	22	.260	.297	.375
Car.	54	120	13	30	3	0	3	12	4	7	27	.250	.289	.350

Acquired from the Reds via trade in August, Gonzalez batted .333 with 13 homers in 114 games at Triple-A, before spending the rest of the season on the Mets' roster. He could make the team in a reserve role. 2003 Outlook: C

Mark P. Johnson (**Pos**: 1B, **Age**: 35, **Bats**: L)

	G	AB	R	H	D	T	HR	RBI	SB	BB	SO	Avg	OBP	Slg
'02	42	51	5	7	4	0	1	4	0	9	18	.137	.267	.275
Car.	428	988	142	229	50	2	38	137	12	154	272	.232	.338	.402

After a successful campaign with the Pirates in 1996, Johnson has had a hard time sticking in the major leagues. His batting against lefties could be to blame. Johnson declared free agency at season's end. 2003 Outlook: C

Satoru Komiyama (**Pos**: RHP, **Age**: 37)

	W	L	Pct.	ERA	G	GS	Sv	IP	H	BB	SO	HR	Ratio
'02	0	3	.000	5.61	25	0	0	43.1	53	12	33	7	1.50
Car.	0	3	.000	5.61	25	0	0	43.1	53	12	33	7	1.50

Komiyama dominated in Triple-A in 2002, going 3-1 with a 1.42 ERA in 17 games, including six starts. He struck out 43 and walked just nine in 44.1 innings. He struggled with the Mets and was released. 2003 Outlook: C

Jason Middlebrook (**Pos**: RHP, **Age**: 27)

	W	L	Pct.	ERA	G	GS	Sv	IP	H	BB	SO	HR	Ratio
'02	2	3	.400	4.73	15	5	0	51.1	44	22	42	2	1.29
Car.	4	4	.500	4.84	19	8	0	70.2	62	32	52	8	1.33

Middlebrook should challenge for a spot in the Mets' starting rotation this season. The righthander, who was acquired from the Padres, has been slowed by arm and groin problems throughout his career. 2003 Outlook: B

Jason Phillips (**Pos**: C, **Age**: 26, **Bats**: R)

	G	AB	R	H	D	T	HR	RBI	SB	BB	SO	Avg	OBP	Slg
'02	11	19	4	7	0	0	1	3	0	1	1	.368	.409	.526
Car.	17	26	6	8	1	0	1	3	0	1	2	.308	.345	.462

Known as a defensive catcher, Phillips has developed some offense as well, batting .289 with 26 homers in his last 200 minor league games. He could challenge Vance Wilson for the backup job in 2003. 2003 Outlook: C

Marco Scutaro (**Pos**: 2B, **Age**: 27, **Bats**: R)

	G	AB	R	H	D	T	HR	RBI	SB	BB	SO	Avg	OBP	Slg
'02	27	36	2	8	0	1	1	6	0	0	11	.222	.216	.361
Car.	27	36	2	8	0	1	1	6	0	0	11	.222	.216	.361

Scutaro is another light-hitting middle infielder in the Mets' system. With Ty Wigginton possessing the same resume, it might be tough for Scutaro to crack the Mets' roster to start the season. 2003 Outlook: C

Esix Snead (**Pos**: CF, **Age**: 26, **Bats**: B)

	G	AB	R	H	D	T	HR	RBI	SB	BB	SO	Avg	OBP	Slg
'02	17	13	3	4	0	0	1	3	4	1	4	.308	.357	.538
Car.	17	13	3	4	0	0	1	3	4	1	4	.308	.357	.538

Snead hit an unimpressive .252 in Double-A, but had four hits in 13 September at-bats with the Mets. The free agent should be ready for spring training after having surgery on his right hand. 2003 Outlook: C

Tony Tarasco (**Pos**: LF/RF, **Age**: 32, **Bats**: L)

	G	AB	R	H	D	T	HR	RBI	SB	BB	SO	Avg	OBP	Slg
'02	60	96	15	24	5	0	6	15	2	8	13	.250	.305	.490
Car.	457	1006	151	241	46	5	34	118	39	106	171	.240	.313	.397

Tarasco has played for six different teams in eight major league seasons, and even spent some time in Japan. He could make it seven, refusing a minor league assignment in October to become a free agent. 2003 Outlook: C

Ty Wigginton (**Pos**: 3B/1B/2B, **Age**: 25, **Bats**: R)

	G	AB	R	H	D	T	HR	RBI	SB	BB	SO	Avg	OBP	Slg
'02	46	116	18	35	8	0	6	18	2	8	19	.302	.354	.526
Car.	46	116	18	35	8	0	6	18	2	8	19	.302	.354	.526

Wigginton hasn't shown quite as much power the last two years in the high minors. Still, his production at Triple-A Norfolk was better the second time around in 2002, and he must be hoping the Mets can't find a third baseman this offseason. 2003 Outlook: C

New York Mets Minor League Prospects

Organization Overview:

Mets GM Steve Phillips never has been shy about using minor league players to acquire veterans for the major league roster. While that approach created a lean farm system before last season, the Mets have accumulated a solid stable of high-ceiling prospects with a combination of deft drafts and key international signings. By selecting pitchers with their first pick in each of the last four drafts, the Mets are stocked with arms, including several that may be called upon in 2003. The lower reaches of the minors feature a bevy of athletic outfielders, while the corner-infield positions have several promising youngsters. With the efforts headed by scouting director Gary LaRocque, the team should see a steady of influx of youth as quickly as this year.

Mike Bacsik

Position: P **Opening Day Age:** 25
Bats: L **Throws:** L **Born:** 11/11/77 in Dallas,
Ht: 6' 3" **Wt:** 190 TX

Recent Statistics

	W	L	ERA	G	GS	Sv	IP	H	R	BB	SO	HR
2002 AAA Norfolk	5	5	3.74	25	14	0	108.1	134	48	25	75	13
2002 NL New York	3	2	4.37	11	9	0	55.2	63	29	19	30	8

The Mets acquired Bacsik from Cleveland in the Roberto Alomar deal prior to last season. Bacsik is capable of starting and working in long relief. Signed by the Indians as an 18th-round draft pick in 1996, the lefthander reached double digits in wins every year from 1998 to 2001, including a dozen victories at Triple-A in 2001. Though not overpowering, Bacsik succeeds with excellent command and by changing speeds. His best pitch is a nasty knuckle-curve. Bacsik's fastball hits 90-91 MPH, and he fools hitters with his straight changeup. He will have an opportunity to compete for a possible opening at the end of New York's rotation.

Craig Brazell

Position: 1B **Opening Day Age:** 22
Bats: L **Throws:** R **Born:** 5/10/80 in
Ht: 6' 3" **Wt:** 211 Montgomery, AL

Recent Statistics

	G	AB	R	H	D	T	HR	RBI	SB	BB	SO	Avg
2001 A Capital City	83	331	51	102	25	5	19	72	0	15	74	.308
2002 A St. Lucie	100	402	38	107	25	3	16	82	2	13	78	.266
2002 AA Binghamton	35	130	14	40	8	0	6	19	0	1	28	.308

The son of Ted Brazell, who played and coached 14 years in the Tigers' system, Craig has emerged as an offensive-oriented first baseman. After leading Class-A Capital City with 19 homers and 72 RBI in 2001, Brazell had a strong first four months at high Class-A St. Lucie last year, before handling a promotion to

Double-A Binghamton with relative ease. The fifth-round draft pick from 1998 is an aggressive hitter who has made major strides by improving his pitch selection and taking pitches to the opposite field. His defense has improved considerably at first base, which could help make him a candidate for the Mets' roster in 2004.

Aaron Heilman

Position: P **Opening Day Age:** 24
Bats: R **Throws:** R **Born:** 11/12/78 in
Ht: 6' 5" **Wt:** 225 Logansport, IN

Recent Statistics

	W	L	ERA	G	GS	Sv	IP	H	R	BB	SO	HR
2001 A St. Lucie	0	1	2.35	7	7	0	38.1	26	11	13	39	0
2002 AA Binghamton	4	4	3.82	17	17	0	96.2	85	43	28	97	7
2002 AAA Norfolk	2	3	3.28	10	7	0	49.1	42	18	16	35	3

The 18th overall pick in the 2001 draft, Heilman signed following his senior season at Notre Dame after failing to come to terms with the Minnesota Twins in 2000. The righthander has made up for lost time by reaching the Triple-A level in his first full professional campaign. After going 4-4 with a 3.82 ERA at Double-A Binghamton to open the 2002 season, Heilman posted a 2-3 record with a 3.28 ERA in 10 outings at Norfolk. His best pitch is a sinking fastball with excellent command. Heilman has made impressive strides with his changeup, and is trying to improve his slider. Scouts believe Heilman could develop into a solid third starter in the major leagues.

Justin Huber

Position: C **Opening Day Age:** 20
Bats: R **Throws:** R **Born:** 7/1/82 in
Ht: 6' 2" **Wt:** 190 Melbourne, Australia

Recent Statistics

	G	AB	R	H	D	T	HR	RBI	SB	BB	SO	Avg
2001 R Kingsport	47	159	24	50	11	1	7	31	4	17	42	.314
2001 A St. Lucie	2	6	0	0	0	0	0	0	0	0	2	.000
2001 A Brooklyn	3	9	0	0	0	0	0	0	0	0	4	.000
2002 A Capital City	95	330	49	96	22	2	11	78	1	45	81	.291
2002 A St. Lucie	28	100	15	27	2	1	3	15	0	11	18	.270

Since signing out of Australia in 2000, Huber has shown he has the potential to be the successor to Mike Piazza behind the plate in New York. After hitting .314 in his professional debut at Rookie-level Kingsport in 2001, Huber was named to the Class-A South Atlantic League year-end All-Star team last season, when he batted .291 with 11 homers and 78 RBI. Huber is a tough and tenacious receiver with quick feet and good mobility. Extremely polished for a 20-year-old, he also works well with pitchers and has made major improvements in calling a game. Huber received a brief promotion to high Class-A St. Lucie last July, and could be on the fast track to the majors with continued success.

Jose Reyes

Position: SS   **Opening Day Age:** 19
Bats: B **Throws:** R   **Born:** 6/11/83 in
Ht: 6' 0" **Wt:** 160   Gonzalez, DR

Recent Statistics

	G	AB	R	H	D	T	HR	RBI	SB	BB	SO	Avg
2001 A Capital City	108	407	71	125	22	15	5	48	30	18	71	.307
2002 A St. Lucie	69	288	58	83	10	11	6	38	31	30	35	.288
2002 AA Binghamton	65	275	46	79	16	8	2	24	27	16	42	.287

Reyes was considered the top prospect in the Double-A Eastern League last year after receiving a midseason promotion from the high Class-A Florida State League. Signed out of the Dominican Republic in 1999, Reyes won't turn 20 until June 11, yet could be starting at Shea Stadium before the end of 2003. He has five-tool talent and has drawn favorable comparisons to major leaguers such as Miguel Tejada and Alfonso Soriano. An outstanding runner with budding power, Reyes led the minors with 19 triples while ranking fifth with 104 runs and sixth with 58 stolen bases last year.

Jae Weong Seo

Position: P   **Opening Day Age:** 25
Bats: R **Throws:** R   **Born:** 5/24/77 in Kwanju,
Ht: 6' 1" **Wt:** 215   South Korea

Recent Statistics

	W	L	ERA	G	GS	Sv	IP	H	R	BB	SO	HR
2002 AAA Norfolk	6	9	3.99	26	24	0	128.2	145	66	22	87	14
2002 AA Binghamton	0	0	5.40	1	0	0	5.0	5	3	1	6	1
2002 NL New York	0	0	0.00	1	0	0	1.0	0	0	0	1	0

Seo continues to battle back from the reconstructive elbow surgery he underwent in 1999. The righthander has struggled to regain the mid-90s velocity on his fastball, which now sits in the 90-91 MPH range. The loss of speed has harmed the effectiveness of his changeup, and he was trying to compensate by developing a hard sinker. The Mets also discovered that Seo wasn't eating prior to games midway through last season, which caused him to lose strength during his starts. If his velocity continues to creep back, and if he maintains his improved physical conditioning, the Korean still could live up to the expectations the Mets held prior to his surgery.

Pat Strange

Position: P   **Opening Day Age:** 22
Bats: R **Throws:** R   **Born:** 8/23/80 in
Ht: 6' 5" **Wt:** 243   Springfield, MA

Recent Statistics

	W	L	ERA	G	GS	Sv	IP	H	R	BB	SO	HR
2002 AAA Norfolk	10	10	3.82	29	25	0	165.0	165	77	59	109	12
2002 NL New York	0	0	1.13	5	0	0	8.0	6	1	1	4	0

Strange possesses great overall stuff, and he also has the body and ability to be a workhorse at the major league level. The Mets' second-round draft pick in 1998, the righthander was named the organization's Minor League Pitcher of the Year in 2000, after going 14-4 during stops at high Class-A St. Lucie and Double-A Binghamton. Strange is a sinkerball pitcher with a 91-93 MPH fastball and a good changeup with excellent command. He allowed six hits and fanned four hitters in eight innings, covering five outings, with the Mets toward the end of the season. He'll be among the many young pitchers vying for a spot on the New York staff this year.

Tyler Walker

Position: P   **Opening Day Age:** 26
Bats: R **Throws:** R   **Born:** 5/15/76 in San
Ht: 6' 3" **Wt:** 255   Francisco, CA

Recent Statistics

	W	L	ERA	G	GS	Sv	IP	H	R	BB	SO	HR
2002 AAA Norfolk	10	5	3.99	28	25	1	142.0	152	65	38	109	13
2002 NL New York	1	0	5.91	5	1	0	10.2	11	7	5	7	3

The Mets have vacillated recently as to whether Walker should be a starter or reliever. He was a closer in college at the University of California and touched 96 MPH with his fastball. After suffering a torn labrum in his right shoulder in late 2000, Walker's heater now resides in the low 90s, and is complemented by his sweeping curveball and solid changeup. He started all but three games at Triple-A Norfolk last season and went 10-5 with a 3.99 ERA and one save. Walker also made his major league debut and tossed 10.2 innings over four relief appearances and one start, picking up his first win at the game's highest level. If he can maintain the consistency of his pitches, Walker will be a serious candidate for the Mets' staff.

Others to Watch

Lefthander **Scott Kazmir** (19) may be the steal of the 2002 draft. He fell to the Mets with the 15th overall pick due to perceived high contract demands. He possesses a mid-90s fastball, a hard slider and a good curveball, and is expected to move quickly. . . Outfielder **Wayne Lydon** (21) made greater strides than any Mets farmhand last year by ranking second in the minors with 87 stolen bases. New York's ninth-round draft pick in 1999, Lydon is an excellent outfielder and a good singles hitter who is trying to perfect the art of switch-hitting. . . Outfielder **Angel Pagan** (21) is a speed-oriented player with good size and the ability to cover center field from gap to gap. Pagan is one of the fastest players in the organization. . . Outfielder **Prentice Redman** (23) continues to emerge as a pleasant surprise. He's been an excellent baserunner since signing as a 10th-round pick in 1999. But he showed the ability to drive the ball in his first taste of Double-A last year by producing a career-best 11 home runs and 35 doubles. . . **David Wright** (20) is a hard-hitting third baseman who was selected as a supplemental pick in the first round of the 2001 draft. He has soft hands and a strong arm on defense, and has the line-drive power that could enable him to hit 25-30 home runs annually in the major leagues.

Veterans Stadium

Offense

In its next-to-last year of existence, the Vet continued to evolve into more of a pitchers' park. The Phillies and their opponents combined to score 130 fewer runs at home than on the road. The Phils' NexTurf surface, in its second year, has had a profoundly negative effect on runs scored. It has dramatically reduced the number of singles through the infield. Doubles are down as well, as the ball doesn't skip through the gaps as quickly as it once did.

Defense

The new surface affords consistent, true hops. It is much easier on the constitutions of home players, who don't require as much rest as before. Just in time for the Vet to close, the Phils have begun to build a pitching staff conducive to their home park, yielding plenty of groundballs to their relatively surehanded infield.

Who It Helps the Most

The park has become extremely friendly to groundball pitchers like Vicente Padilla, Brett Myers, Mike Timlin, Carlos Silva and, if he gets his mechanics back in order, Brandon Duckworth. It helps all of the position players defensively, but especially the starting infielders.

Who It Hurts the Most

The park dramatically hurts groundball hitters like Anderson, Travis Lee and Polanco. Duckworth, an extreme groundball pitcher in his rookie season, couldn't keep the ball down in 2002 and paid dearly.

Rookies & Newcomers

Myers is an especially good fit for the Vet, a groundball pitcher who also should ramp up his strikeout total significantly. Marlon Byrd should be a solid offensive player whose doubles and triples totals might be contained a bit at home, though a 20-homer season could be within reach. David Bell came aboard in November, and Jim Thome signed on in early December. Both are fly-ball hitters who should find the final season of the Vet to their liking.

Dimensions: LF-330, LCF-371, CF-408, RCF-371, RF-330

Capacity: 62,418

Elevation: 20 feet

Surface: Turf

Foul Territory: Large

Park Factors

2002 Season

	Home Games Phillies	Opp	Total	Away Games Phillies	Opp	Total	Index
G	71	71	142	72	72	144	
Avg	.251	.233	.242	.270	.274	.272	89
AB	2338	2402	4740	2571	2452	5023	96
R	295	287	582	347	365	712	83
H	588	560	1148	695	673	1368	85
2B	134	110	244	160	147	307	84
3B	20	13	33	16	19	35	100
HR	73	67	140	77	73	150	99
BB	274	242	516	291	264	555	99
SO	487	524	1011	488	425	913	117
E	33	39	72	45	52	97	75
E-Infield	28	28	56	39	41	80	71
LHB-Avg	.240	.237	.239	.282	.288	.285	84
LHB-HR	32	25	57	33	31	64	94
RHB-Avg	.262	.231	.245	.259	.266	.263	93
RHB-HR	41	42	83	44	42	86	102

2000-2002

	Home Games Phillies	Opp	Total	Away Games Phillies	Opp	Total	Index
G	215	215	430	216	216	432	
Avg	.254	.249	.251	.262	.272	.266	94
AB	7072	7386	14458	7556	7182	14738	99
R	933	972	1905	976	1057	2033	94
H	1796	1840	3636	1977	1950	3927	93
2B	408	449	857	404	406	810	108
3B	56	48	104	44	45	89	119
HR	202	224	426	212	238	450	97
BB	798	780	1578	795	753	1548	104
SO	1492	1608	3100	1473	1321	2794	113
E	103	121	224	144	168	312	72
E-Infield	87	99	186	110	136	246	76
LHB-Avg	.249	.245	.247	.271	.281	.276	90
LHB-HR	87	76	163	76	78	154	104
RHB-Avg	.258	.252	.255	.254	.266	.261	98
RHB-HR	115	148	263	136	160	296	93

2002 Rankings (National League)

- Highest strikeout factor
- Lowest batting-average factor
- Lowest hit factor
- Lowest error factor
- Lowest infield-error factor
- Lowest LHB batting-average factor
- Third-lowest run factor

Larry Bowa

2002 Season

Larry Bowa's second year as the Phillies' manager began with heightened expectations following their season-long run at the Braves in 2001. However, the club was burdened from Day 1 by the inevitable departure of Scott Rolen. It got off to a poor start and never was a factor in the pennant chase. The club did play better down the stretch, and for the second straight year, Bowa tweaked his coaching staff right after the season ended, dismissing pitching coach Vern Ruhle.

Offense

Bowa likes to play a set lineup, and often will sacrifice offense for defense when doling out playing time. Really, the Phils should have produced many more runs last season. They led the league in doubles and triples, and were tied for sixth in homers. However, they barely got a .300 on-base percentage from the top two spots in the order, and their inability to hit with runners in scoring position was almost laughable. The club didn't utilize its team speed nearly as well as in 2001. Bowa is reluctant to give away outs on sacrifice bunts by his position players.

Pitching & Defense

Bowa is more inclined to let a strong starting pitcher go the distance than most major league managers. He prefers clearly defined roles for his relievers, and limits closer Jose Mesa to ninth-inning duty in all but the most extreme circumstances. Bowa is aggressive in all facets of the game, and dislikes issuing intentional walks. He also doesn't like utilizing in-game defensive replacements.

2003 Outlook

With the Rolen matter in the past, the front office added to its payroll in anticipation of the opening of the new stadium in 2004. So Bowa and the Phillies will face rising expectations in 2003. Bowa has excellent support from his front office, and the clubhouse is as unified as it has been in the recent past. In addition, Bowa is immensely popular with the Philadelphia fans, an important issue with a new stadium to fill.

Born: 12/06/45 in Sacramento, CA

Playing Experience: 1970-1985, Phi, ChC, NYM

Managerial Experience: 4 seasons

Manager Statistics

Year	Team, Lg	W	L	Pct	GB	Finish
2002	Philadelphia, NL	80	81	.497	21.5	3rd East
4 Seasons		247	284	.465	–	–

2002 Starting Pitchers by Days Rest

	<=3	4	5	6+
Phillies Starts	1	78	42	30
Phillies ERA	6.75	4.63	3.37	4.98
NL Avg Starts	1	88	42	21
NL ERA	3.18	4.22	4.14	4.58

2002 Situational Stats

	Larry Bowa	NL Average
Hit & Run Success %	27.3	36.5
Stolen Base Success %	70.7	68.3
Platoon Pct.	57.6	52.7
Defensive Subs	16	19
High-Pitch Outings	8	7
Quick/Slow Hooks	17/5	24/11
Sacrifice Attempts	96	95

2002 Rankings (National League)

- 3rd in starts on three days rest

Bobby Abreu

Position: RF/CF
Bats: L **Throws:** R
Ht: 6' 0" **Wt:** 195

Opening Day Age: 29
Born: 3/11/74 in
Aragua, VZ
ML Seasons: 7
Pronunciation:
ah-BRAY-you

2002 Season

Bobby Abreu continued to assert himself as one of the finest all-around offensive players in baseball with another stellar campaign. Although Abreu reached a career high in only one category in 2002 (50 doubles), he came close in other categories. His power numbers were down a bit, but Abreu came on strong down the stretch and played in more than 150 games for the fifth straight year.

Hitting

Abreu has two distinct styles of hitting. Against southpaws, he is content to work the count, keep his hands back and spray line drives. He has only four career homers versus lefties. Against righties, he's a mauler who doesn't swing at bad pitches and consciously tries to drive the ball to all fields. Abreu takes a healthy cut and strikes out quite a bit on high fastballs, but he only expands the strike zone when the situation dictates.

Baserunning & Defense

Abreu is a true power/speed threat. He's an aggressive basestealer whose career success rate of 73 percent is good but not great. After declining in effectiveness with the glove in recent seasons, Abreu worked hard on his defense last season and showed much improved range. While he has a strong throwing arm, he no longer rates among the top assist leaders due to the respect he has gained from opposing baserunners.

2003 Outlook

The Phillies aggressively locked up Abreu with a five-year, $64 million contract extension that begins in 2003. This could have an interesting impact on club efforts to sign Pat Burrell, viewed by most Philadelphians as the superior player. As much as anyone in the game, Abreu's numbers can be penciled in before the beginning of each season. To remain at the elite level in coming years, he will need to maintain his conditioning to retain the speed aspect of his game, and add power against lefthanded pitching.

Overall Statistics

	G	AB	R	H	D	T	HR	RBI	SB	BB	SO	Avg	OBP	Slg
'02	157	572	102	176	50	6	20	85	31	104	117	.308	.413	.521
Car.	850	2989	532	918	215	39	116	468	148	526	667	.307	.409	.522

Where He Hits the Ball

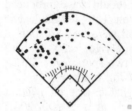 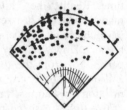

Vs. LHP **Vs. RHP**

2002 Situational Stats

	AB	H	HR	RBI	Avg		AB	H	HR	RBI	Avg
Home	257	73	8	35	.284	LHP	162	49	0	22	.302
Road	315	103	12	50	.327	RHP	410	127	20	63	.310
First Half	288	87	7	43	.302	Sc Pos	144	45	6	67	.313
Scnd Half	284	89	13	42	.313	Clutch	99	30	3	12	.303

2002 Rankings (National League)

- 1st in doubles and pitches seen (2,923)
- 2nd in lowest percentage of swings on the first pitch (12.6)
- 3rd in most pitches seen per plate appearance (4.27)
- Led the Phillies in batting average, runs scored, hits, sacrifice flies (6), stolen bases, walks, times on base (283), games played, on-base percentage, batting average with runners in scoring position, batting average vs. righthanded pitchers, slugging percentage vs. righthanded pitchers (.566), batting average at home, batting average on the road and batting average with two strikes (.253)

Marlon Anderson

Position: 2B
Bats: L **Throws:** R
Ht: 5'11" **Wt:** 200

Opening Day Age: 29
Born: 1/6/74 in
Montgomery, AL
ML Seasons: 5

2002 Season

Marlon Anderson was a major disappointment at the plate and in the field in his third full year as Philadelphia's second baseman. Offensively, his numbers dropped in virtually every category from his solid 2001 campaign, as he fell apart down the stretch. Defensively, he paced National League second basemen with 20 errors.

Hitting

Anderson is a free swinger with an unrefined approach at the plate. Last season's walk total of 42, though a career high, remains unacceptable for a player with limited power potential. He does possess some pop to the gaps, but won't become a good offensive player, even for a middle infielder, until he stops giving away so many at-bats. At his age, his lack of progress leaves little room for hope. After making great strides versus left-handers in 2001, Anderson regressed last season. He has proven to be a poor fit in the on-base and RBI slots in the batting order.

Baserunning & Defense

Anderson is a fast straight-ahead runner, but he hasn't parlayed his speed into basestealing ability or solid baserunning instincts. Now 29, he still doesn't routinely make the right choices when taking the extra base. Defensively, there is nothing fundamentally sound about Anderson's style. His footwork is inconsistent, his arm strength only adequate, and his release unorthodox. His range is above average, however, as he plays extremely deep and hustles consistently.

2003 Outlook

While Anderson isn't as bad defensively as his errors suggest, he still must be productive with the bat to start on a winning ballclub. Anderson's collapse late last season jeopardized his starting job. The Phillies signed David Bell to play third base, and Placido Polanco will move to second unless Anderson can stake a claim to the job in spring training. He may be traded before then to fill other needs. Once he falls out of a starting lineup, Anderson could fade away quickly, as he lacks the versatility and skills set to be a utilityman.

Overall Statistics

	G	AB	R	H	D	T	HR	RBI	SB	BB	SO	Avg	OBP	Slg
'02	145	539	64	139	30	6	8	48	5	42	71	.258	.315	.380
Car.	479	1718	195	457	97	13	26	182	30	114	234	.266	.313	.383

Where He Hits the Ball

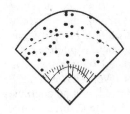 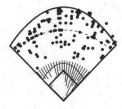

Vs. LHP   **Vs. RHP**

2002 Situational Stats

	AB	H	HR	RBI	Avg		AB	H	HR	RBI	Avg
Home	248	57	4	20	.230	LHP	123	27	0	10	.220
Road	291	82	4	28	.282	RHP	416	112	8	38	.269
First Half	304	84	5	26	.276	Sc Pos	128	27	0	36	.211
Scnd Half	235	55	3	22	.234	Clutch	106	25	1	9	.236

2002 Rankings (National League)

- 1st in errors at second base (20) and lowest fielding percentage at second base (.970)
- 2nd in lowest slugging percentage vs. left-handed pitchers (.252)
- 5th in lowest on-base percentage vs. lefthanded pitchers (.267)
- 7th in lowest batting average at home
- 10th in intentional walks (14) and lowest batting average vs. lefthanded pitchers
- Led the Phillies in intentional walks (14), GDPs (16) and highest groundball-flyball ratio (1.6)

Pat Burrell

2002 Season

Pat Burrell connected the dots of his obvious offensive skills and became a true star in 2002. He was consistently productive, in direct contrast to previous seasons. His worst month arguably was June, when he batted .245 (.469 slugging), though he still managed to drive in 24 runs for the month. He was slowed at times by a minor shoulder injury that ended his season a day early.

Hitting

While Burrell remains a free swinger who strikes out quite often, subtle improvements in his plate discipline have accomplished quite a bit. His strikeout-walk ratio still needs refinement, but he has worked himself into hitters' counts more often, and frequently takes advantage. He worked with Hall of Famer Mike Schmidt in spring training on a variety of issues, such as pitch recognition, keeping his head on and staying inside the ball, and learned his lessons well. Few can hit the ball as hard or as far as Burrell, and he continues to learn to use the entire field. He absolutely annihilates lefthanded pitching.

Baserunning & Defense

These are areas that Burrell could have overlooked, focusing solely on his core power skills. Instead, he spent a chunk of his bonus money on flexibility training a few years back, making himself a complete player. Once a slow, station-to-station baserunner, Burrell now runs quite well, though he'll never be a basestealing threat. Defensively, he has worked extremely hard to become an above-average major league left fielder. He takes direct routes to flyballs, and has slightly above-average range and a plus throwing arm.

2003 Outlook

Burrell now is a star who might take his numbers to a new level in 2003. Expect him to average more than 40 homers per year over the next five seasons, with at least one 50-homer campaign in the mix. The Phillies were expected to attempt to lock him up for the long term in the offseason. Unlike the departed Scott Rolen, Burrell appeared amenable to their advances.

Position: LF
Bats: R **Throws:** R
Ht: 6' 4" **Wt:** 222

Opening Day Age: 26
Born: 10/10/76 in Eureka Springs, AR
ML Seasons: 3
Pronunciation: BURL

Overall Statistics

	G	AB	R	H	D	T	HR	RBI	SB	BB	SO	Avg	OBP	Slg
'02	157	586	96	165	39	2	37	116	1	89	153	.282	.376	.544
Car.	423	1533	223	410	95	5	82	284	3	222	454	.267	.361	.496

Where He Hits the Ball

 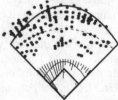

Vs. LHP   **Vs. RHP**

2002 Situational Stats

	AB	H	HR	RBI	Avg		AB	H	HR	RBI	Avg
Home	287	77	18	45	.268	LHP	122	38	12	29	.311
Road	299	88	19	71	.294	RHP	464	127	25	87	.274
First Half	308	86	22	63	.279	Sc Pos	183	54	9	82	.295
Scnd Half	278	79	15	53	.284	Clutch	118	37	9	34	.314

2002 Rankings (National League)

- 3rd in RBI
- 4th in pitches seen (2,800) and on-base percentage vs. lefthanded pitchers (.469)
- 5th in strikeouts, fielding percentage in left field (.979) and assists in left field (8)
- 6th in errors in left field (6)
- Led the Phillies in home runs, total bases (319), RBI, sacrifice flies (6), strikeouts, GDPs (16), games played, slugging percentage, HR frequency (15.8 ABs per HR), cleanup slugging percentage (.526), slugging percentage vs. lefthanded pitchers (.664) and on-base percentage vs. lefthanded pitchers (.469)
- Led NL left fielders in RBI

Brandon Duckworth

2002 Season

It was a mystifying season for Brandon Duckworth. He struck out more than a batter per inning, and at any given moment might appear unhittable. However, his location and focus were quite poor. He didn't react well to adversity. A small mistake often would lead to a big inning and an early exit. He allowed 26 homers in 163 innings, after allowing two in 69 innings in 2001. He also allowed 24 stolen bases, compared to one in 2001. Duckworth didn't mesh well with his catchers or pitching coach. Overall, it was a frustrating year for a talented hurler, who, at 27, isn't as young as you might think.

Pitching

Duckworth throws a low-90s fastball, overhand curve and changeup. He leans on all three when he's on. He has yet to establish a consistent early-game approach. He seems to expend a large amount of mental energy on almost every hitter, often shaking off the catcher and struggling to get into a rhythm. Duckworth actually pitched better versus lefties than righties last year, an indication of how good he can become if he's able to simplify matters. He's far from wild, though his control within the strike zone left much to be desired.

Defense & Hitting

Duckworth is a good athlete who fields his position well, but his sudden indifference toward the running game was astounding. Phillies catchers were quite stingy when it came to allowing stolen bases, except when Duckworth was on the mound. He's a scrappy hitter who generally puts the ball in play and can be counted upon to get a bunt down.

2003 Outlook

Duckworth and Brett Myers likely will be the star pupils of new pitching coach Joe Kerrigan in 2003. There's a lot to work with here, and Kerrigan might be the guy to smooth those rough edges. There aren't a lot of hurlers who can get multiple pitches past hitters, but Duckworth is one of them. He was expected to be a highly sought trade commodity in the offseason—the Yankees expressed early interest—and should be a 12-14 win candidate for someone in 2003.

Position: SP
Bats: R **Throws:** R
Ht: 6' 2" **Wt:** 185

Opening Day Age: 27
Born: 1/23/76 in Salt Lake City, UT
ML Seasons: 2

Overall Statistics

	W	L	Pct.	ERA	G	GS	Sv	IP	H	BB	SO	HR	Ratio
'02	8	9	.471	5.41	30	29	0	163.0	167	69	167	26	1.45
Car.	11	11	.500	4.85	41	40	0	232.0	224	98	207	28	1.39

How Often He Throws Strikes

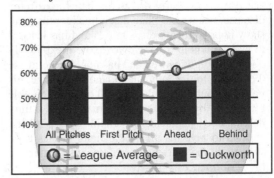

○ = League Average ■ = Duckworth

2002 Situational Stats

	W	L	ERA	Sv	IP		AB	H	HR	RBI	Avg
Home	5	4	4.58	0	94.1	LHB	298	74	10	38	.248
Road	3	5	6.55	0	68.2	RHB	341	93	16	57	.273
First Half	5	6	4.65	0	98.2	Sc Pos	153	43	6	66	.281
Scnd Half	3	3	6.58	0	64.1	Clutch	39	15	3	4	.385

2002 Rankings (National League)

- 1st in fielding percentage at pitcher (1.000) and most pitches thrown per batter (3.97)
- 2nd in highest ERA, highest stolen-base percentage allowed (88.9) and fewest GDPs induced per nine innings (0.2)
- 3rd in stolen bases allowed (24) and most home runs allowed per nine innings (1.44)
- Led the Phillies in home runs allowed, walks allowed, pickoff throws (79), stolen bases allowed (24), most run support per nine innings (5.4) and most strikeouts per nine innings (9.2)

Travis Lee

2002 Season

Travis Lee slid back in most key offensive areas in 2002, his second full year as Philadelphia's regular first baseman. He got off to a poor start, batting only .221 in April, and did not put together a hot streak until his final 33 games, over which he hit .331. While he looks like a power hitter, he simply isn't one. Not a fan favorite, Lee seemed to let home games affect him, as he hit just .223 at Veterans Stadium.

Hitting

Lee boasts impressive raw offensive tools, but never has assembled them into a productive package. He occasionally drives the ball for extreme distance, has decent plate discipline, continues to show improvement versus lefties and has learned to use the whole field. However, he inexplicably doesn't hit righties well and has not learned to use the count to his advantage and maximize his power output. When ahead, he'll often let hittable pitches go by, and is an easy mark after falling behind. Lee is a placid, unexcitable sort. While he appears to give his all on the field, he has been slow to do the extra work necessary to maximize his performance.

Baserunning & Defense

Lee moves well for a big man. Though he is not a significant basestealing threat, he will pick his spots and is an intelligent baserunner who can take the extra base. Defensively, Lee is exceptionally nimble for his size, covers plenty of ground and saves the other infielders plenty of errors with his ability to scoop bad throws.

2003 Outlook

The Phillies used their "Scott Rolen money" to sign Jim Thome to a six-year deal in December. They were willing to spend considerably more than the $3 million they paid Lee in 2002, and the upgrade puts Lee on the trade market. There is room in the majors for a player like Lee. He projects as a J.T. Snow-type who will provide good defense and pedestrian first-base offense for the foreseeable future.

Position: 1B
Bats: L **Throws:** L
Ht: 6' 3" **Wt:** 210

Opening Day Age: 27
Born: 5/26/75 in San Diego, CA
ML Seasons: 5

Overall Statistics

	G	AB	R	H	D	T	HR	RBI	SB	BB	SO	Avg	OBP	Slg
'02	153	536	55	142	26	2	13	70	5	54	104	.265	.331	.394
Car.	704	2432	311	620	120	9	73	336	41	315	465	.255	.340	.402

Where He Hits the Ball

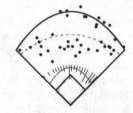 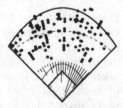

Vs. LHP   **Vs. RHP**

2002 Situational Stats

	AB	H	HR	RBI	Avg		AB	H	HR	RBI	Avg
Home	251	56	8	35	.223	LHP	142	40	6	20	.282
Road	285	86	5	35	.302	RHP	394	102	7	50	.259
First Half	281	70	7	32	.249	Sc Pos	165	45	4	59	.273
Scnd Half	255	72	6	38	.282	Clutch	111	29	3	17	.261

2002 Rankings (National League)
- 3rd in fielding percentage at first base (.996) and lowest batting average at home
- 5th in highest percentage of swings on the first pitch (41.2)
- 8th in lowest percentage of extra bases taken as a runner (39.1)
- 9th in assists at first base (75)
- Led the Phillies in batting average with the bases loaded (.294)

Mike Lieberthal

2002 Season

Mike Lieberthal was a major question mark entering 2002, following season-ending knee surgery in June 2001. He answered the questions positively, reverting to his old durable self behind the plate. He exploded with the bat in late summer to post more than respectable offensive numbers for a catcher, earning a lucrative contract extension. Lieberthal hit eight of his 15 homers in August before hitting the wall in September.

Hitting

Lieberthal is a free-swinging mistake hitter who torches lefthanders. He has made much more consistent contact as his career has progressed. He loves to swing at the first pitch, and had success doing so in 2002 (.303 average, .561 SLG). He is a flyball hitter, but when fed a steady diet of outside pitches, Lieberthal often will hit lazy flies to the opposite field. Offensively, only Mike Piazza is his superior among National League receivers.

Baserunning & Defense

Before his knee injuries, Lieberthal wasn't that slow for a catcher. He now is a painfully slow, though smart baserunner. He is one of the more underrated defensive catchers in baseball. His ability to handle pitchers once was a major issue, but has greatly improved. Basestealers generally don't even bother to test him much anymore—his 0.41 steals allowed per nine innings ranked second in the league among backstops who worked at least 500 innings in 2002. Though his years of working 130 to 140 games probably are over, Lieberthal can be counted on for 110-120 starts.

2003 Outlook

Lieberthal reinjured his knee playing golf shortly after the 2002 season, requiring arthroscopic surgery. He was expected to be 100-percent healthy by spring training. But it remains quite unlikely that he will sustain his productivity until the end of the three-year, $22.25 million contract extension signed during his hot streak last August. He is approaching the age at which virtually all top catchers take a step backward offensively, and his recent injury history doesn't help. Look for him to drop back closer to the pack of NL catchers in 2003.

Position: C
Bats: R **Throws:** R
Ht: 6' 0" **Wt:** 190

Opening Day Age: 31
Born: 1/18/72 in Glendale, CA
ML Seasons: 9
Pronunciation: LEE-ber-thal

Philadelphia

Overall Statistics

	G	AB	R	H	D	T	HR	RBI	SB	BB	SO	Avg	OBP	Slg
'02	130	476	46	133	29	2	15	52	0	38	58	.279	.349	.443
Car.	727	2556	332	689	155	8	99	384	7	213	378	.270	.334	.453

Where He Hits the Ball

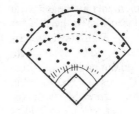

Vs. LHP	Vs. RHP

2002 Situational Stats

	AB	H	HR	RBI	Avg		AB	H	HR	RBI	Avg
Home	214	60	7	27	.280	LHP	107	37	6	12	.346
Road	262	73	8	25	.279	RHP	369	96	9	40	.260
First Half	256	67	6	26	.262	Sc Pos	130	26	4	38	.200
Scnd Half	220	66	9	26	.300	Clutch	84	28	4	15	.333

2002 Rankings (National League)

- 1st in highest percentage of runners caught stealing as a catcher (33.8)
- 5th in hit by pitch (14), lowest batting average with runners in scoring position and lowest batting average with the bases loaded (.095)
- 7th in errors at catcher (6)
- Led the Phillies in hit by pitch (14), GDPs (16), batting average in the clutch and batting average vs. lefthanded pitchers

Jose Mesa

2002 Season

Jose Mesa confounded the experts once again in 2002, breaking the Phillies' single-season saves record with 45, although he did tie for the major league lead with nine blown saves. Except for a horrific July, when he posted a 6.08 ERA, Mesa was quite consistent. While his command wasn't quite up to his 2001 standard (his walk rate nearly doubled), he didn't allow the big blow, yielding only five longballs in 75.2 innings. Even at his advancing age, Mesa remained quite durable.

Pitching

Mesa is still an aggressive hurler as he approaches his 37th birthday. His fastball regularly reaches the low 90s, and he complements his heater with a nasty slider. When he doesn't have the feel for his slider, he struggles to make hitters miss. His July struggles largely were caused by mechanical inconsistencies that flattened out both of his offerings. The key to Mesa's success in Philadelphia has been his ability to retire lefties. Sharp movement on his pitches is imperative—his mistakes will travel a long way once that movement dissipates.

Defense & Hitting

Mesa gets the ball to the plate quickly, and he has effectively controlled the running game since joining the Phillies (two steals in two years). Though he doesn't look particularly athletic, Mesa fields his position well. He's batted exactly once in his 14-year major league career, drawing a walk.

2003 Outlook

The Phillies have rewarded Mesa for a job well done, extending his contract through 2003 (base salary of $4.75 million). The club also holds a $5.5 million option for 2004 that automatically vests if Mesa finishes 55 games this season. In truth, Mesa has been one of the more reliable Phillies the past two years. However, beware that Mesa's decline could be swift and ugly. Don't be shocked by an implosion—20 saves and a 5.00 ERA in 2003 is a possibility.

Position: RP
Bats: R **Throws:** R
Ht: 6' 3" **Wt:** 225

Opening Day Age: 36
Born: 5/22/66 in Azua, DR
ML Seasons: 14
Pronunciation: MAY-sa

Overall Statistics

	W	L	Pct.	ERA	G	GS	Sv	IP	H	BB	SO	HR	Ratio
'02	4	6	.400	2.97	74	0	45	75.2	65	39	64	5	1.37
Car.	65	84	.436	4.22	701	95	225	1241.2	1293	513	851	113	1.45

How Often He Throws Strikes

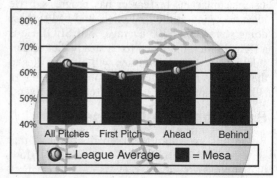

= League Average   = Mesa

2002 Situational Stats

	W	L	ERA	Sv	IP		AB	H	HR	RBI	Avg
Home	3	3	1.98	24	41.0	LHB	142	32	3	11	.225
Road	1	3	4.15	21	34.2	RHB	139	33	2	12	.237
First Half	2	5	2.51	23	43.0	Sc Pos	79	16	1	17	.203
Scnd Half	2	1	3.58	22	32.2	Clutch	215	53	3	20	.247

2002 Rankings (National League)

- 1st in blown saves (9)
- 3rd in save opportunities (54)
- 4th in saves and lowest save percentage (83.3)
- 6th in games finished (64) and relief losses (6)
- 8th in wild pitches (9)
- Led the Phillies in games pitched, saves, games finished (64), save opportunities (54), save percentage (83.3), lowest batting average allowed with runners in scoring position, blown saves (9), relief losses (6), relief ERA (2.97), lowest batting average allowed in relief (.231) and most strikeouts per nine innings in relief (7.6)

Brett Myers

2002 Season

Brett Myers was dominant at Triple-A Scranton-Wilkes Barre last season, except for a brief stretch when he was hampered by blisters on his fingers. Recalled by the Phillies on July 24, he enjoyed his best outing in his debut, pitching an eight-inning two-hitter and prevailing in a showdown with the Cubs' Mark Prior. Myers lost his edge in September, however, posting a 6.08 ERA. He struck out roughly four batters per nine innings in the majors, alarmingly low for someone with such good stuff.

Pitching

Myers combined power and command as well as any minor league hurler in the first half of 2002. He throws a live, mid-90s heater and a powerful overhand curve that is lethal when his release point is locked in and he's setting it up well. His changeup is a viable third offering, and he's also tinkered with a splitter. Myers is a throwback who fully expects to go nine innings each time out. He generally keeps the ball low in the zone, though he struggled to set up hitters. His mechanics got a bit lazy late last season, and many thought he occasionally was tipping his pitches. Despite it all, Myers' ability to consistently retire lefthanded hitters underscored how good he can become.

Defense & Hitting

Myers is a fine all-around athlete who takes pride in all facets of his game. He fields his position well, gets the ball to the plate quickly for a young power pitcher, and does a good job holding runners. Myers takes a healthy cut at the plate, and went deep while in the minors. He's a solid bunter.

2003 Outlook

While Myers isn't guaranteed a rotation spot for 2003, he would have to endure a hideous March to not earn one. New pitching coach Joe Kerrigan seems a perfect mentor for Myers, who needs only minor tweaking to spike his strikeout rate sharply upward. Expect him to earn the No. 3 slot in the Phillies' rotation in 2003. He projects as a solid innings-eater in the near term, and a potential staff ace within two to three seasons.

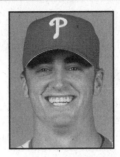

Position: SP
Bats: R **Throws:** R
Ht: 6' 4" **Wt:** 215

Opening Day Age: 22
Born: 8/17/80 in Jacksonville, FL
ML Seasons: 1

Philadelphia

Overall Statistics

	W	L	Pct.	ERA	G	GS	Sv	IP	H	BB	SO	HR	Ratio
'02	4	5	.444	4.25	12	12	0	72.0	73	29	34	11	1.42
Car.	4	5	.444	4.25	12	12	0	72.0	73	29	34	11	1.42

How Often He Throws Strikes

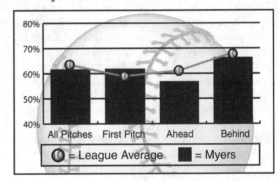

2002 Situational Stats

	W	L	ERA	Sv	IP		AB	H	HR	RBI	Avg
Home	2	4	5.05	0	35.2	LHB	111	25	5	13	.225
Road	2	1	3.47	0	36.1	RHB	153	48	6	18	.314
First Half	0	0	–	0	0.0	Sc Pos	53	11	1	18	.208
Scnd Half	4	5	4.25	0	72.0	Clutch	8	3	1	2	.375

2002 Rankings (National League)

- 5th in most GDPs induced per GDP situation (21.9%)
- Led the Phillies in most GDPs induced per GDP situation (21.9%) and lowest batting average allowed vs. lefthanded batters

Vicente Padilla

2002 Season

Vicente Padilla was one of the breakthrough stars of last season's first half. After an awesome Mexican League campaign, he set the Grapefruit League aflame. He claimed a slot in the Phillies' starting rotation and made the All-Star team. He eventually tired, however, as a full calendar year of pitching caught up to him. His shoulder stiffened, but despite declining power, he avoided a true slump, as he learned to win without his best stuff. He was shut down for good with shoulder soreness on September 24.

Pitching

Padilla is a true power pitcher who mixes a mid-90s fastball with a curve, slider and occasional changeup. He also has introduced a splitter to his repertoire. Early in 2002, he brought his Grade-A stuff to the mound in the first inning, and maintained his velocity deep into games. Later on, he appeared to try to conserve his stuff. He sometimes reached only the upper 80s, reaching back for a little more in tight spots. When he's on, Padilla is a precise power pitcher who consistently keeps the ball low in the strike zone.

Defense & Hitting

Padilla was in much better physical shape last season, and as a result, fielded his position better. He handled the running game well, allowing only five stolen bases. Though Padilla had a poor year at the plate, batting .052 with 31 strikeouts, he takes a healthy cut, has some power potential and is an adequate bunter.

2003 Outlook

Health is the key to Padilla's future. He was expected to limit his winter ball involvement to an Opening Day start, with the hope that rest would be sufficient to get his stuff back to last spring's quality. While it's clear the Phils have a 200-inning horse on their hands, it remains to be seen whether he'll overpower or outsmart hitters for the bulk of those frames. Bet on the former. Padilla did what he had to do to make the Phils' rotation last year, and now will do what he has to do to become a star.

Position: SP
Bats: B **Throws:** R
Ht: 6' 2" **Wt:** 200

Opening Day Age: 25
Born: 9/27/77 in Chinandega, Nicaragua
ML Seasons: 4
Pronunciation: pa-DEE-ya

Overall Statistics

	W	L	Pct.	ERA	G	GS	Sv	IP	H	BB	SO	HR	Ratio
'02	14	11	.560	3.28	32	32	0	206.0	198	53	128	16	1.22
Car.	21	20	.512	3.59	115	32	2	308.0	313	96	208	21	1.33

How Often He Throws Strikes

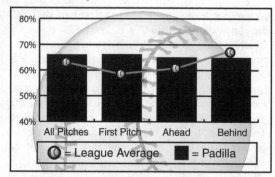

= League Average   = Padilla

2002 Situational Stats

	W	L	ERA	Sv	IP		AB	H	HR	RBI	Avg
Home	6	4	2.27	0	99.0	LHB	379	103	9	37	.272
Road	8	7	4.21	0	107.0	RHB	402	95	7	36	.236
First Half	10	5	3.05	0	121.0	Sc Pos	174	41	5	57	.236
Scnd Half	4	6	3.60	0	85.0	Clutch	74	22	0	8	.297

2002 Rankings (National League)

- 2nd in lowest ERA at home
- 3rd in hit batsmen (15) and balks (2)
- 4th in highest groundball-flyball ratio allowed (2.0)
- 5th in GDPs induced (26)
- 7th in fewest pitches thrown per batter (3.52)
- Led the Phillies in wins, losses, games started, hits allowed, batters faced (862), hit batsmen (15), balks (2), GDPs induced (26), winning percentage, fewest pitches thrown per batter (3.52), lowest ERA at home, most GDPs induced per nine innings (1.1) and fewest walks per nine innings (2.3)

Placido Polanco

2002 Season

Placido Polanco got off to a slow start with the Cardinals last season, due in part to a bruised hand that limited him at the plate. He got back into his typical high-average, low-power groove before being included in the trade-deadline deal that sent Scott Rolen to St. Louis. Polanco performed quite well as a Phillie, hitting .296 while offering steady if un-Rolenlike defense at the hot corner. A reliable spray hitter, Polanco reached career highs in doubles, homers, RBI and walks.

Hitting

Polanco is a free-swinging contact hitter who sprays line drives to all fields, though with limited power for a corner infielder. He has hit left-handers extremely well in recent seasons, batting .350 (2001) and .338 (2002) against them the past two years. Polanco loves to hack, especially on the first pitch, and saw only 3.12 offerings per plate appearance last season. He's a groundball hitter whose 2002 power "surge" likely was an aberration. Don't expect another 30-double season anytime soon.

Baserunning & Defense

Polanco has adequate speed and is an intelligent baserunner, though he'll never be a prolific basestealer. He's a surehanded defender with range that is slightly above average at the hot corner. His arm strength is just adequate, though he compensates by getting rid of the ball quickly. He also has played second base and shortstop at the major league level. His overall set of offensive and defensive skills just might be best suited to the keystone.

2003 Outlook

The Phillies were very impressed with Polanco's reliability and work ethic after acquiring him last season, and he looks like the starting second baseman in 2003. Signing David Bell to play third base will move him to second or to an all-purpose utility role. Polanco has a steadier glove than second-base incumbent Marlon Anderson, and projects as an ideal No. 2 hitter. Expect him to be a vital complementary player in Philadelphia this season.

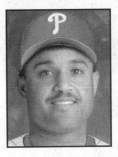

Position: 3B/SS
Bats: R **Throws:** R
Ht: 5'10" **Wt:** 168

Opening Day Age: 27
Born: 10/10/75 in Santo Domingo, DR
ML Seasons: 5
Pronunciation: pluh-SEE-doh poh-LAHNK-oh

Overall Statistics

	G	AB	R	H	D	T	HR	RBI	SB	BB	SO	Avg	OBP	Slg
'02	147	548	75	158	32	2	9	49	5	26	41	.288	.330	.403
Car.	542	1769	246	523	82	14	19	156	24	87	143	.296	.333	.390

Where He Hits the Ball

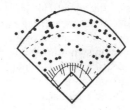 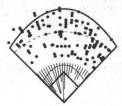

Vs. LHP   **Vs. RHP**

2002 Situational Stats

	AB	H	HR	RBI	Avg		AB	H	HR	RBI	Avg
Home	283	82	8	26	.290	LHP	151	51	3	12	.338
Road	265	76	1	23	.287	RHP	397	107	6	37	.270
First Half	275	79	5	26	.287	Sc Pos	133	35	2	36	.263
Scnd Half	273	79	4	23	.289	Clutch	85	24	0	8	.282

2002 Rankings (National League)

- 2nd in fielding percentage at third base (.978) and fewest pitches seen per plate appearance (3.12)
- 3rd in sacrifice bunts (13)
- 5th in highest groundball-flyball ratio (1.9) and highest percentage of swings put into play (56.5)
- 6th in batting average vs. lefthanded pitchers (.338)
- 9th in lowest percentage of swings that missed (10.3)
- Led the Phillies in batting average on a 3-1 count (.600) and batting average on an 0-2 count (.294)

Jimmy Rollins

2002 Season

Jimmy Rollins took his lumps battling the sophomore jinx last season. He actually got off to a fine start in April, but spiraled downward from there. He hit .227 in June, .160 in July and .194 in September, sprinkling in separate 4-for-41, 0-for-22 and 0-for-21 droughts along the way. The inability of Rollins and Doug Glanville to reach base at the top of the Phillies' order doomed the club's offense. Still, Rollins flashed his diverse offensive skills, and again proved quite durable, missing only a couple of starts in August with a bruised elbow.

Hitting

A switch-hitter, Rollins can hit the ball with authority from either side of the plate. He traditionally is a better lefthanded hitter, but struggled from both sides last season. Rollins' main offensive problem is his insistence on swinging at fastballs in the upper half of the strike zone. He could add 30 points to his average and 50 points to his OBP overnight by laying off the high ones.

Baserunning & Defense

Rollins has established himself as one of the premier basestealers in the game, leading the National League with 46 steals in 2001. But he lost some of his aggressiveness early in 2002 after being thrown out a few times in a brief span. Defensively, Rollins is solid. Other shortstops have modestly better range, but Rollins turns virtually every ball he touches into an out. He is extraordinarily focused and disciplined, and almost all of his throws hit the first baseman squarely in the chest.

2003 Outlook

A young regular's third full season often indicates whether he ultimately will reach his potential. One year ago, teammate Pat Burrell stood at a similar crossroads, and sufficiently addressed his shortcomings to propel himself to stardom. If Rollins can improve his on-base percentage to the eminently reachable .350 level, he'll become one of the best shortstops in the National League. Look for a .280 average, .350 OBP and 40-plus steals from Rollins in 2003, as he seizes the No. 1 or 2 slot in the Phils' lineup for good.

Position: SS
Bats: B **Throws:** R
Ht: 5' 8" **Wt:** 165

Opening Day Age: 24
Born: 11/27/78 in Oakland, CA
ML Seasons: 3

Overall Statistics

	G	AB	R	H	D	T	HR	RBI	SB	BB	SO	Avg	OBP	Slg
'02	154	637	82	156	33	10	11	60	31	54	103	.245	.306	.380
Car.	326	1346	184	353	63	23	25	119	80	104	218	.262	.316	.399

Where He Hits the Ball

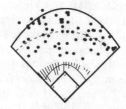 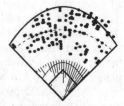

Vs. LHP   **Vs. RHP**

2002 Situational Stats

	AB	H	HR	RBI	Avg		AB	H	HR	RBI	Avg
Home	316	73	3	23	.231	LHP	173	42	3	15	.243
Road	321	83	8	37	.259	RHP	464	114	8	45	.246
First Half	357	93	7	33	.261	Sc Pos	133	34	1	46	.256
Scnd Half	280	63	4	27	.225	Clutch	117	31	1	12	.265

2002 Rankings (National League)

- 1st in at-bats and triples
- 2nd in plate appearances (705), steals of third (7) and fielding percentage at shortstop (.980)
- 5th in caught stealing (13), highest percentage of extra bases taken as a runner (65.2) and lowest on-base percentage for a leadoff hitter (.309)
- 6th in pitches seen (2,716)
- 7th in stolen bases
- Led the Phillies in at-bats, singles, triples, stolen bases, caught stealing (13), plate appearances (705), bunts in play (23), lowest percentage of swings that missed (15.5), steals of third (7) and highest percentage of extra bases taken as a runner (65.2)

Randy Wolf

2002 Season

Randy Wolf's 2002 season started innocently enough. He opened on the disabled list with elbow tendinitis, and followed a miserable April with an ordinary May. Thereafter, however, Wolf was nothing short of one of the best pitchers in baseball, his ordinary 11-9 record notwithstanding. Wolf was untouchable after the All-Star break, posting a 2.10 ERA. This included a stretch in which he allowed a single earned run in 36.2 innings, and followed a similarly excellent finish in 2001.

Pitching

Wolf features three above-average pitches—an 89-91 MPH fastball with sharp movement, a knee-buckling changeup and a curve he often uses as an out pitch against lefthanders. Although he uncharacteristically struggled against lefties last season, Wolf utterly bottled up righties, a clear sign he's capable of much greater things in the near future. When Wolf is throwing strike one—a frequent occurrence last year—he's one tough customer. Batters managed only a .219 average when putting the first pitch in play in 2002, which enabled Wolf to maintain low pitch counts.

Defense & Hitting

Wolf is a solid all-around athlete who helps himself in all facets of the game. He's an active defender who fields his position well, though he has been prone to the occasional throwing error. He has a good pickoff move and keeps runners close. He's also a tough out at the plate for a pitcher and puts the ball in play, usually to the opposite field. He can be counted upon to get a bunt down.

2003 Outlook

Wolf enjoyed a major breakthrough in 2002, even though his record didn't show it. Look for him to put together a full season of excellence in 2003, emerging as the near-term ace of a Philadelphia rotation that looks quite solid at the top. After Tom Glavine and Jamie Moyer spurned the club, the Phillies inked their own lefty, Wolf, to a four-year, $22.5 million deal. Don't rule out a 20-win bonanza this year.

Position: SP
Bats: L **Throws:** L
Ht: 6' 0" **Wt:** 194

Opening Day Age: 26
Born: 8/22/76 in Canoga Park, CA
ML Seasons: 4

Overall Statistics

	W	L	Pct.	ERA	G	GS	Sv	IP	H	BB	SO	HR	Ratio
'02	11	9	.550	3.20	31	31	0	210.2	172	63	172	23	1.12
Car.	38	38	.500	4.07	113	109	0	701.2	658	264	600	83	1.31

How Often He Throws Strikes

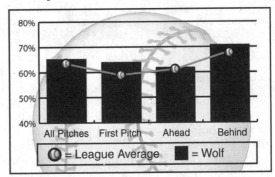

= League Average   = Wolf

2002 Situational Stats

	W	L	ERA	Sv	IP		AB	H	HR	RBI	Avg
Home	4	4	3.05	0	88.2	LHB	120	31	4	12	.258
Road	7	5	3.32	0	122.0	RHB	652	141	19	60	.216
First Half	4	6	4.44	0	99.1	Sc Pos	135	28	5	49	.207
Scnd Half	7	3	2.10	0	111.1	Clutch	74	20	2	7	.270

2002 Rankings (National League)

- 4th in shutouts (2) and lowest on-base percentage allowed (.285)
- 5th in lowest batting average allowed with runners in scoring position and least run support per nine innings (4.0)
- 7th in lowest batting average allowed (.223)
- Led the Phillies in ERA, sacrifice bunts (12), complete games (3), shutouts (2), innings pitched, strikeouts, pitches thrown (3,200), highest strikeout-walk ratio (2.7), lowest batting average allowed (.223), lowest on-base percentage allowed (.285), lowest stolen-base percentage allowed (50.0) and lowest ERA on the road

Terry Adams

Position: RP/SP
Bats: R **Throws:** R
Ht: 6' 3" **Wt:** 215

Opening Day Age: 30
Born: 3/6/73 in Mobile, AL
ML Seasons: 8

Overall Statistics

	W	L	Pct.	ERA	G	GS	Sv	IP	H	BB	SO	HR	Ratio
'02	7	9	.438	4.35	46	19	0	136.2	132	58	96	9	1.39
Car.	44	52	.458	4.10	431	41	39	718.0	713	319	580	49	1.44

2002 Situational Stats

	W	L	ERA	Sv	IP		AB	H	HR	RBI	Avg
Home	2	4	4.35	0	70.1	LHB	232	57	5	30	.246
Road	5	5	4.34	0	66.1	RHB	285	75	4	33	.263
First Half	4	6	4.53	0	95.1	Sc Pos	133	38	3	50	.286
Scnd Half	3	3	3.92	0	41.1	Clutch	102	26	3	12	.255

2002 Season

The Phillies looked to free agent Terry Adams to upgrade their 2002 rotation, and he was an utter disappointment. He lasted only 19 starts, yielding 160 baserunners in just 102.2 innings. Command was a major issue, as his inability to throw a quality first-pitch strike became well documented. Adams cinched his demotion to the bullpen with an 8.57 ERA in July.

Pitching, Defense & Hitting

Adams features a straight, low-90s fastball and a sharp slider, and must keep both offerings low in the strike zone. His 2.70 groundball-flyball ratio last year was in line with career norms. Adams was inconsistent mechanically, and had difficulty early in ballgames. He is a poor defensive player who made four errors in 2002. At the plate, he struggles to make contact or get a bunt down.

2003 Outlook

The Phils declined to exercise their $5.4 million option on Adams for 2003. While they were intrigued by his solid late-season performance in relief, it appeared unlikely that Adams or the club would aggressively pursue a contract, even at a sharply reduced salary. Look for Adams to pitch effectively in middle relief somewhere, though the great starting pitcher experiment has ended.

Marlon Byrd   Top Prospect

Position: CF
Bats: R **Throws:** R
Ht: 6' 0" **Wt:** 225

Opening Day Age: 25
Born: 8/30/77 in Boynton Beach, FL
ML Seasons: 1

Overall Statistics

	G	AB	R	H	D	T	HR	RBI	SB	BB	SO	Avg	OBP	Slg
'02	10	35	2	8	2	0	1	1	0	1	8	.229	.250	.371
Car.	10	35	2	8	2	0	1	1	0	1	8	.229	.250	.371

2002 Situational Stats

	AB	H	HR	RBI	Avg		AB	H	HR	RBI	Avg
Home	26	7	1	1	.269	LHP	9	2	1	1	.222
Road	9	1	0	0	.111	RHP	26	6	0	0	.231
First Half	0	0	0	0	–	Sc Pos	7	0	0	0	.000
Scnd Half	35	8	1	1	.229	Clutch	7	0	0	0	.000

2002 Season

Marlon Byrd was a consistent run producer in Triple-A ball, ranking among minor league leaders in runs scored (103) and doubles (37). But, he disappointed with the Phillies in September, batting .229 with poor plate discipline. He struggled off the field at times, as he was overweight all season and underwent anger management counseling following an altercation with his girlfriend.

Hitting, Baserunning & Defense

Byrd has a quick bat and makes authoritative contact to all fields. He's not a perfect fit in any spot in the lineup. He's not a pure power hitter, and he lacks exceptional plate discipline. That likely will leave him in the No. 6 hole, his primary Triple-A spot in 2002. Though some fancy him a potential power/speed stud, he likely will max out as a 20/20 or 25/15 guy. He runs well for his size. He also has worked hard to develop adequate range and arm strength for center field.

2003 Outlook

Philadelphia's center-field job is Byrd's to lose in 2003, and his late-summer struggles could be a powerful motivational tool. If he's in shape, Byrd should hold the job and be on the short list of Rookie of the Year candidates. However, at 25, he's unlikely to develop into a star.

Dave Coggin

Position: RP
Bats: R **Throws:** R
Ht: 6' 4" **Wt:** 205

Opening Day Age: 26
Born: 10/30/76 in Covina, CA
ML Seasons: 3

Overall Statistics

	W	L	Pct.	ERA	G	GS	Sv	IP	H	BB	SO	HR	Ratio
'02	2	5	.286	4.68	38	7	0	77.0	65	51	64	4	1.51
Car.	10	12	.455	4.52	60	29	0	199.0	199	102	143	13	1.51

2002 Situational Stats

	W	L	ERA	Sv	IP		AB	H	HR	RBI	Avg
Home	0	5	5.36	0	43.2	LHB	122	35	2	21	.287
Road	2	0	3.78	0	33.1	RHB	159	30	2	21	.189
First Half	0	2	5.77	0	48.1	Sc Pos	94	20	1	34	.213
Scnd Half	2	3	2.83	0	28.2	Clutch	39	8	0	6	.205

2002 Season

Dave Coggin lost his spring training battle with Vicente Padilla for a starting slot, but adjusted well to a middle relief role. His overall numbers were ruined by an 8.13 ERA in seven starts. But Coggin had a 2.74 ERA out of the pen and didn't allow a single run in 18 July innings. He underwent surgery for a torn labrum in his throwing shoulder on September 16.

Pitching, Defense & Hitting

Coggin has a diverse four-pitch repertoire, including a low-90s fastball, curve, slider and changeup. But command has been a major issue, especially last season. Coggin lacks a defining out pitch versus lefties, though his effectiveness against righthanders and his ability to last two innings make him an attractive relief option. He fields his position well and does an adequate job of controlling the running game. He is a very poor hitter.

2003 Outlook

Coggin was expected to recover from his shoulder surgery in time for spring training. He will not be guaranteed a spot on the 25-man roster, and his window of opportunity to win a rotation spot in Philadelphia likely has closed. He'll be one of many righthanded arms contending for middle-relief jobs.

Jeremy Giambi

Position: LF/1B/RF/DH
Bats: L **Throws:** L
Ht: 5'11" **Wt:** 216

Opening Day Age: 28
Born: 9/30/74 in San Jose, CA
ML Seasons: 5
Pronunciation: gee-OM-bee

Overall Statistics

	G	AB	R	H	D	T	HR	RBI	SB	BB	SO	Avg	OBP	Slg
'02	124	313	58	81	17	0	20	45	0	79	94	.259	.414	.505
Car.	460	1290	204	347	70	3	47	194	0	225	314	.269	.381	.437

2002 Situational Stats

	AB	H	HR	RBI	Avg		AB	H	HR	RBI	Avg
Home	167	53	12	27	.317	LHP	70	20	1	8	.286
Road	146	28	8	18	.192	RHP	243	61	19	37	.251
First Half	235	65	16	33	.277	Sc Pos	64	12	3	23	.188
Scnd Half	78	16	4	12	.205	Clutch	46	11	1	2	.239

2002 Season

Jeremy Giambi went from being the Opening Day leadoff man for a good Oakland ballclub to a little-used bench player for the Phillies, despite getting on base constantly and contributing exceptional power on an at-bat basis. Although he got off to a hot start in Oakland, he was sent to the Phils for John Mabry on May 22. Giambi was used quite a bit immediately after the deal, but found himself buried on the bench by September.

Hitting, Baserunning & Defense

Giambi is a patient hitter who forces pitchers to throw strikes. He saw an average of 4.52 pitches per plate appearance last season, one of the highest marks in the majors. He handles southpaws well, though he is much less power-conscious against them. He is a slow baserunner who routinely is hampered by nagging injuries. While he played first base and both corner outfield spots in 2002, Giambi basically is a hitter who is best suited for a DH role.

2003 Outlook

The Phils unsuccessfully struggled to find a role for Giambi last season, and went into the offseason dangling him as trade bait. He can be a lethal designated hitter. Look for him to be moved back to the American League and thrive in such a role.

Doug Glanville

Position: CF
Bats: R **Throws:** R
Ht: 6' 2" **Wt:** 174

Opening Day Age: 32
Born: 8/25/70 in Hackensack, NJ
ML Seasons: 7

Overall Statistics

	G	AB	R	H	D	T	HR	RBI	SB	BB	SO	Avg	OBP	Slg
'02	138	422	49	105	16	3	6	29	19	25	57	.249	.292	.344
Car.	948	3556	508	1001	160	31	52	303	156	192	452	.281	.320	.388

2002 Situational Stats

	AB	H	HR	RBI	Avg		AB	H	HR	RBI	Avg
Home	185	43	3	16	.232	LHP	128	32	4	11	.250
Road	237	62	3	13	.262	RHP	294	73	2	18	.248
First Half	226	52	2	16	.230	Sc Pos	98	16	0	20	.163
Scnd Half	196	53	4	13	.270	Clutch	82	25	1	5	.305

2002 Season

The Phillies sealed their offensive fate by re-signing Doug Glanville to a one-year, $4 million contract and entrusting him with a large share of at-bats at the top of their order. He responded with a .292 OBP, which would have been worse if not for a .329 batting average in September. Relegated to part-time duty in June, Glanville reclaimed his starting job down the stretch.

Hitting, Baserunning & Defense

An intelligent man, Glanville doesn't usually take the smartest approach at the plate. He's almost impossible to walk, and is a relatively poor hitter when ahead in the count. As his effectiveness has faded in recent years, he's hit many more lazy fly-balls. Glanville always has been a high-percentage basestealer, but could be more aggressive on the bases. Defensively, he's surehanded, though his range is ordinary for his position.

2003 Outlook

Glanville believed he'd be able to find a job as a starter in the offseason free-agent market. More likely, he'll begin a second career as a fourth outfielder/defensive replacement/speed guy off the bench. He can help in that role. Don't be shocked if he winds up in that capacity with the Phillies.

Ricky Ledee

Position: CF/LF
Bats: L **Throws:** L
Ht: 6' 1" **Wt:** 190

Opening Day Age: 29
Born: 11/22/73 in Ponce, PR
ML Seasons: 5
Pronunciation: la-DAY

Overall Statistics

	G	AB	R	H	D	T	HR	RBI	SB	BB	SO	Avg	OBP	Slg
'02	96	203	33	46	13	1	8	23	1	35	50	.227	.342	.419
Car.	441	1241	183	300	71	14	33	188	24	152	308	.242	.325	.401

2002 Situational Stats

	AB	H	HR	RBI	Avg		AB	H	HR	RBI	Avg
Home	95	16	4	9	.168	LHP	25	2	0	0	.080
Road	108	30	4	14	.278	RHP	178	44	8	23	.247
First Half	105	22	3	11	.210	Sc Pos	56	9	2	16	.161
Scnd Half	98	24	5	12	.245	Clutch	45	8	1	5	.178

2002 Season

Ricky Ledee's odyssey continued when he joined the Phillies, his fourth team in three seasons, in 2002. He didn't respond to intermittent usage early, batting .097 in April. However, he did some damage in July after claiming the lefthanded part of a center-field platoon with Doug Glanville. Despite his low batting average, Ledee's willingness to work the count made him preferable to Glanville or Jimmy Rollins at the top of the order.

Hitting, Baserunning & Defense

Ledee hasn't developed the bat speed to evolve into the power hitter he was expected to become. He is strictly a platoon player. Against righties, he has shown the ability to work the count, isolate the most hittable pitch in an at-bat, and put good wood on it to all fields. Ledee's speed and instincts are average, and his basestealing hasn't emerged. He has adequate range at all three outfield spots, with arm strength slightly below average.

2003 Outlook

The Phillies are expected to entrust rookie Marlon Byrd with the full-time center-field job in 2003. However, there are some questions about his conditioning and ability to hit quality righties. That makes Ledee a logical fit as a lefthanded insurance policy and occasional platoon player.

Joe Roa

Position: SP
Bats: R **Throws:** R
Ht: 6' 1" **Wt:** 194

Opening Day Age: 31
Born: 10/11/71 in
Southfield, MI
ML Seasons: 4

Overall Statistics

	W	L	Pct.	ERA	G	GS	Sv	IP	H	BB	SO	HR	Ratio
'02	4	4	.500	4.04	14	11	0	71.1	78	13	35	11	1.28
Car.	6	10	.375	4.73	44	15	0	144.2	177	38	69	20	1.49

2002 Situational Stats

	W	L	ERA	Sv	IP		AB	H	HR	RBI	Avg
Home	3	1	2.81	0	32.0	LHB	116	38	7	19	.328
Road	1	3	5.03	0	39.1	RHB	164	40	4	16	.244
First Half	0	0	–	0	0.0	Sc Pos	61	16	2	21	.262
Scnd Half	4	4	4.04	0	71.1	Clutch	2	2	1	1	1.000

2002 Season

It was the ultimate Cinderella story—minor league lifer goes 14-0 at Triple-A, and at age 30 gets his first shot in five years at big league hitters. Joe Roa pitched out of the bullpen for a couple weeks after being recalled on July 7, before injuries opened a starting spot. Roa showed impeccable command, but paid for the mistakes he made up in the strike zone.

Pitching, Defense & Hitting

Roa is a finesse hurler with absolutely no margin for error. His fastball only reaches the mid-80s, and his best pitch is a changeup with good command. There are many holes in his game, however—hitters effectively jump on the first pitch, he tends to get off to slow starts, and he has no answer for lefthanded batters. Roa is an adequate defender, and a gritty battler at the plate.

2003 Outlook

Roa is the type of player who must constantly prove himself. Still, the Phils were impressed with him and will give him a chance to break north in 2003. He seems better suited to middle relief—he doesn't issue walks, is tough on righties, and has a bounce-back arm. He'll continue to reside squarely on the major league fringe, though quite likely on the better side of it.

Carlos Silva

Position: RP
Bats: R **Throws:** R
Ht: 6' 4" **Wt:** 225

Opening Day Age: 23
Born: 4/23/79 in Bolivar,
VZ
ML Seasons: 1

Overall Statistics

	W	L	Pct.	ERA	G	GS	Sv	IP	H	BB	SO	HR	Ratio
'02	5	0	1.000	3.21	68	0	1	84.0	88	22	41	4	1.31
Car.	5	0	1.000	3.21	68	0	1	84.0	88	22	41	4	1.31

2002 Situational Stats

	W	L	ERA	Sv	IP		AB	H	HR	RBI	Avg
Home	2	0	3.17	0	48.1	LHB	120	35	0	9	.292
Road	3	0	3.28	1	35.2	RHB	192	53	4	30	.276
First Half	1	0	3.53	0	43.1	Sc Pos	95	24	3	36	.253
Scnd Half	4	0	2.88	1	40.2	Clutch	111	38	4	25	.342

2002 Season

Carlos Silva made the Phillies' roster by pitching well last spring, and quickly asserted himself as one of the more durable middlemen in the National League. He missed some time with a sprained knee, but posted a sub-3.00 ERA in every month except July. For a sizeable chunk of the season, he was the club's most reliable setup man.

Pitching, Defense & Hitting

Silva's best pitch, by far, is his heavy, fairly straight, mid-90s fastball, which he routinely keeps low in the strike zone. He also throws a curveball and changeup, though none of his offerings make hitters miss. Development of a strikeout pitch would greatly enhance his value. He is an adequate fielder who did a decent job of controlling the running game last year. He isn't much of a hitter, though his bunting skills aren't bad.

2003 Outlook

While Silva is a fine reliever, such usage seems a waste of a potential seven-inning starter. He could thrive in that role if he improves one of his breaking pitches. However, the Phillies' most pressing short-term need is in the bullpen. Look for Silva to become Jose Mesa's primary setup man in 2003, and to be ready to step into the breach should the veteran falter.

Bud Smith

Position: SP
Bats: L **Throws:** L
Ht: 6' 0" **Wt:** 170

Opening Day Age: 23
Born: 10/23/79 in
Torrance, CA
ML Seasons: 2

Overall Statistics

	W	L	Pct.	ERA	G	GS	Sv	IP	H	BB	SO	HR	Ratio
'02	1	5	.167	6.94	11	10	0	48.0	67	22	22	4	1.85
Car.	7	8	.467	4.95	27	24	0	132.2	146	46	81	16	1.45

2002 Situational Stats

	W	L	ERA	Sv	IP		AB	H	HR	RBI	Avg
Home	0	1	4.26	0	19.0	LHB	46	15	0	4	.326
Road	1	4	8.69	0	29.0	RHB	152	52	4	30	.342
First Half	0	5	7.18	0	36.1	Sc Pos	58	20	2	32	.345
Scnd Half	1	0	6.17	0	11.2	Clutch	0	0	0	0	–

2002 Season

Bud Smith opened last season in the Cardinals' rotation, but his pitches lacked the snap displayed in his 2001 rookie season. Hit hard early, he went on the disabled list with an inflamed rotator cuff, was demoted to the bullpen, and then sent to Triple-A after his peak velocity dipped to 83 MPH. He went to the Phillies in the Scott Rolen deal, remaining in the minors before being diagnosed with a torn labrum.

Pitching, Defense & Hitting

When on, Smith is a finesse hurler with an exceptional changeup, deceptive curve, and just enough on his fastball to keep hitters honest. Prior to 2002, Smith painted the corners regularly and rarely allowed hitters to find a comfort zone. In '02, he lost his changeup, and his weakened fastball became a predictable batting practice pitch. Smith is a feisty hitter who puts the ball in play, and his quick reflexes make him a solid defender. Basestealers have had their way with him.

2003 Outlook

Health is the key here. Smith is considering off-season surgery to repair his torn labrum, which could wipe out his 2003 season. In any case, he may need to re-establish himself in the minors before the Phillies give him another shot.

Mike Timlin

Position: RP
Bats: R **Throws:** R
Ht: 6' 4" **Wt:** 210

Opening Day Age: 37
Born: 3/10/66 in
Midland, TX
ML Seasons: 12
Pronunciation:
TIM-lin

Overall Statistics

	W	L	Pct.	ERA	G	GS	Sv	IP	H	BB	SO	HR	Ratio
'02	4	6	.400	2.98	72	1	0	96.2	75	14	50	15	0.92
Car.	45	51	.469	3.56	664		4	114	795.1	746	279	599	74	1.29

2002 Situational Stats

	W	L	ERA	Sv	IP		AB	H	HR	RBI	Avg
Home	3	2	2.72	0	49.2	LHB	125	26	4	10	.208
Road	1	4	3.26	0	47.0	RHB	229	49	11	29	.214
First Half	1	3	2.77	0	52.0	Sc Pos	64	15	3	27	.234
Scnd Half	3	3	3.22	0	44.2	Clutch	160	33	7	20	.206

2002 Season

Mike Timlin got off to a good start as a Cardinals setup man in 2002 before being included in the package for Scott Rolen. While Timlin remained stingy with baserunners, his overall numbers would have been even better if not for his uncharacteristically high number of mistakes up in the strike zone.

Pitching, Defense & Hitting

Timlin's stuff remains quite good—his fastball reaches the low 90s and has sharp, downward movement. He combines his heater with a solid slider, and is an extreme groundball pitcher. Timlin's control has improved through the years, reaching career peaks in 2001 and 2002. However, his command within the strike zone was inconsistent last season. He handles righties and lefties equally well, and is a durable type. Timlin controls the running game but is an erratic defender. He's still looking for his first career hit.

2003 Outlook

Timlin made $5.25 million last season, and then became a free agent. While the Phillies wanted to retain him at a lower price, Timlin seemed eager to return to St. Louis. He likely has at least a couple more productive years as an effective middleman, but at a lower price.

Other Philadelphia Phillies

Ricky Bottalico (Pos: RHP, **Age**: 33)

	W	L	Pct.	ERA	G	GS	Sv	IP	H	BB	SO	HR	Ratio
'02	0	3	.000	4.61	30	0	0	27.1	33	13	24	3	1.68
Car.	27	38	.415	4.03	460	0	114	516.0	461	261	483	61	1.40

Bottalico missed the second half of the 2002 season with shoulder problems that required June surgery to repair a tear in his labrum. He should be ready for spring training and likely will re-sign. 2003 Outlook: B

Rheal Cormier (Pos: LHP, **Age**: 35)

	W	L	Pct.	ERA	G	GS	Sv	IP	H	BB	SO	HR	Ratio
'02	5	6	.455	5.25	54	0	0	60.0	61	32	49	6	1.55
Car.	53	54	.495	4.25	407	108	1	957.2	1016	232	593	95	1.30

Cormier struggled away from the Vet last season and saw his overall numbers suffer as a result. He had a 7.53 ERA in 25 games on the road, while posting a 3.16 ERA in 29 home contests. 2003 Outlook: B

Dave Hollins (Pos: 1B, **Age**: 36, **Bats**: B)

	G	AB	R	H	D	T	HR	RBI	SB	BB	SO	Avg	OBP	Slg
'02	14	17	1	2	0	0	0	0	0	0	3	.118	.167	.118
Car.	983	3346	578	870	166	17	112	482	47	464	687	.260	.358	.420

Hollins split last season between Triple-A Scranton and Philadelphia, but was limited to a total of just 28 games. He was sidelined most of the year by an infection in his knee. He likely will not re-sign. 2003 Outlook: C

Hector Mercado (Pos: LHP, **Age**: 28)

	W	L	Pct.	ERA	G	GS	Sv	IP	H	BB	SO	HR	Ratio
'02	2	2	.500	4.62	31	3	0	39.0	32	25	40	2	1.46
Car.	5	4	.556	4.33	99	3	0	106.0	99	63	112	10	1.53

Mercado was acquired from the Reds in March for outfielder Reggie Taylor. The lefthander struck out 43 batters in 33.1 innings at Triple-A, while fanning 40 in 39 innings with the Phillies. 2003 Outlook: C

Jason Michaels (Pos: CF, **Age**: 26, **Bats**: R)

	G	AB	R	H	D	T	HR	RBI	SB	BB	SO	Avg	OBP	Slg
'02	81	105	16	28	10	3	2	11	1	13	33	.267	.347	.476
Car.	87	111	16	29	10	3	2	12	1	13	35	.261	.339	.459

Michaels appeared in 81 games last season, making just 10 starts. However, he prospered in the reserve role, batting .318 from the seventh inning on, compared to .179 in the first six innings. 2003 Outlook: C

Tomas Perez (Pos: 2B/3B/SS, **Age**: 29, **Bats**: B)

	G	AB	R	H	D	T	HR	RBI	SB	BB	SO	Avg	OBP	Slg
'02	92	212	22	53	13	1	5	20	1	21	40	.250	.319	.392
Car.	377	1012	96	248	46	10	11	88	4	83	170	.245	.305	.343

Perez, who played four different positions on the infield in 2002, re-signed with the Phillies, agreeing to a two-year, $1.3 million deal. His role with the team should be similar this season. 2003 Outlook: B

Robert Person (Pos: RHP, **Age**: 33)

	W	L	Pct.	ERA	G	GS	Sv	IP	H	BB	SO	HR	Ratio
'02	4	5	.444	5.44	16	16	0	87.2	79	51	61	13	1.48
Car.	51	42	.548	4.60	199	135	8	885.2	802	430	763	129	1.39

Person struggled with arm problems last season and ended up undergoing shoulder surgery in August. Because of the numbers Person posted the prior three seasons, another team should take a chance on him. 2003 Outlook: C

Dan Plesac (Pos: LHP, **Age**: 41)

	W	L	Pct.	ERA	G	GS	Sv	IP	H	BB	SO	HR	Ratio
'02	3	3	.500	4.21	60	0	1	36.1	27	18	41	6	1.24
Car.	63	70	.474	3.67	1006	14	156	1038.2	948	391	1004	102	1.29

Plesac, who turns 41 in February, is one of seven pitchers in major league history to appear in 1,000 games. He showed no signs of slowing down last year, and postponed retirement with a one-year deal with the Phils. 2003 Outlook: B

Todd Pratt (Pos: C, **Age**: 36, **Bats**: R)

	G	AB	R	H	D	T	HR	RBI	SB	BB	SO	Avg	OBP	Slg
'02	39	106	14	33	11	0	3	16	2	24	28	.311	.449	.500
Car.	452	1049	131	265	59	2	31	146	5	137	285	.253	.347	.401

Pratt spent the entire 2002 season with the Phillies, but only appeared in 39 games. He batted a respectful .311 last year and should re-sign, especially with Mike Lieberthal recovering from knee surgery. 2003 Outlook: B

Nick Punto (Pos: 2B, **Age**: 25, **Bats**: B)

	G	AB	R	H	D	T	HR	RBI	SB	BB	SO	Avg	OBP	Slg
'02	9	6	0	1	0	0	0	0	0	0	3	.167	.167	.167
Car.	13	11	0	3	0	0	0	0	0	0	3	.273	.273	.273

Punto began the 2002 season with the Phillies, but lasted just two weeks, spending the rest of the year in Triple-A. The infielder needs to develop some power and cut down on his strikeouts. 2003 Outlook: C

Jose Santiago (Pos: RHP, **Age**: 28)

	W	L	Pct.	ERA	G	GS	Sv	IP	H	BB	SO	HR	Ratio
'02	1	3	.250	6.70	42	0	0	47.0	56	15	30	7	1.51
Car.	16	19	.457	4.57	200	0	4	261.2	289	79	135	26	1.41

After posting a gaudy 6.70 ERA in three months with the Phillies, Santiago settled down and went 3-2 with an impressive 1.29 ERA in 22 games at Triple-A. He signed with the Indians in November. 2003 Outlook: B

Eric Valent (Pos: RF, **Age**: 25, **Bats**: L)

	G	AB	R	H	D	T	HR	RBI	SB	BB	SO	Avg	OBP	Slg
'02	7	10	1	2	0	0	0	0	0	0	3	.200	.200	.200
Car.	29	51	4	6	2	0	0	1	0	4	14	.118	.196	.157

After belting 20-plus homers the previous three seasons, Valent recorded just nine round-trippers in 140 games in the minors last year. He saw his batting average dip to a career-low .251 as well. 2003 Outlook: C

Philadelphia Phillies Minor League Prospects

Organization Overview:

In the last few years, the Phillies' system has churned out a steady stream of frontline talent, including Scott Rolen, Pat Burrell and Randy Wolf. Still, the common current belief that the Phils possess one of the game's deepest systems is a misconception. While they do have a few high-quality prospects, organizational depth is subpar, especially among position players. There virtually are no proven power hitters in the system. Pitching depth is somewhat better, with at least one significant talent emerging at each level of the system last year. The 2002 draft could turn out to be quite a haul, as first-round lefthander Cole Hamels, second-round righthander Zach Segovia and fifth-round third baseman Jake Blalock all arguably were first-round talents.

Taylor Buchholz

Position: P | **Opening Day Age:** 21
Bats: R **Throws:** R | **Born:** 10/13/81 in Lower
Ht: 6' 4" **Wt:** 225 | Merion, PA

Recent Statistics

		W	L	ERA	G	GS	Sv	IP	H	R	BB	SO	HR
2001 A Lakewood		9	14	3.36	28	26	0	176.2	165	83	57	136	8
2002 A Clearwater		10	6	3.29	23	23	0	158.2	140	66	51	129	11
2002 AA Reading		0	2	7.43	4	4	0	23.0	29	19	6	17	5

Buchholz is a hometown boy, a 2000 sixth-round pick drafted from a suburban Philadelphia high school. After an excellent 2002 season at high Class-A, Buchholz has firmly entrenched himself as a high-level prospect, just shy of Brett Myers-Gavin Floyd status. The righthander possesses the raw stuff, physical stature and command of a long-term No. 2 or 3 major league starter. His fastball consistently reaches the low 90s, and he complements it with a hard curve that ranks among the minors' best, plus a changeup that should eventually become a third plus pitch. Look for Buchholz to fare much better at Reading in 2003, with a midseason move to Triple-A and a September audition in Philly a possibility.

Johnny Estrada

Position: C | **Opening Day Age:** 26
Bats: B **Throws:** R | **Born:** 6/27/76 in
Ht: 5' 11" **Wt:** 209 | Hayward, CA

Recent Statistics

		G	AB	R	H	D	T	HR	RBI	SB	BB	SO	Avg
2002 AAA Scran-WB		118	434	49	121	27	0	11	67	1	26	53	.279
2002 NL Philadelphia		10	17	0	2	1	0	0	2	0	2	2	.118

After spelling the injured Mike Lieberthal at the major league level for much of 2001, it was back to Triple-A for Estrada in 2002. The switch-hitter had an exceptional all-around season there, making authoritative contact at the plate and emerging as a workhorse who effectively controls the running game. Poor plate disci-pline remains a primary weakness. Defensively, his arm strength is well above average, he's overcome an abject lack of quickness to become acceptably agile behind the plate, and he's learned to handle a pitching staff. The signing of Lieberthal to a new long-term deal, along with the Phils' fondness for backup Todd Pratt, made Estrada premium trade bait during the offseason.

Gavin Floyd

Position: P | **Opening Day Age:** 20
Bats: R **Throws:** R | **Born:** 1/27/83 in
Ht: 6' 6" **Wt:** 210 | Annapolis, MD

Recent Statistics

		W	L	ERA	G	GS	Sv	IP	H	R	BB	SO	HR
2002 A Lakewood		11	10	2.77	27	27	0	166.0	119	59	64	140	13

The Phillies drafted Floyd in the first round in 2001. Though he signed too late to play, he has made up for lost time, and is poised to assume the spot vacated by Brett Myers on the Phils' fast track. Floyd showed an exceptional combination of raw stuff, command and mound savvy for his age at Class-A Lakewood last season. He features a live, mid-90s fastball and an improving changeup, but his signature offering is a power curveball that ranks alongside Myers' as the best breaking pitch in the organization. When he's on, Floyd often has no-hitter stuff. As he physically matures, he should evolve into a 200-inning horse who should someday sit next to Myers as a No. 1 or 2 starter in Philly. Look for a bold two-level jump to Double-A in 2003, with a possible major league ETA of mid-2004.

Eric Junge

Position: P | **Opening Day Age:** 26
Bats: R **Throws:** R | **Born:** 1/5/77 in
Ht: 6' 5" **Wt:** 215 | Manhasset, NY

Recent Statistics

		W	L	ERA	G	GS	Sv	IP	H	R	BB	SO	HR
2002 AAA Scran-WB		12	6	3.54	29	29	0	180.2	170	77	67	126	16
2002 NL Philadelphia		2	0	1.42	4	1	0	12.2	14	3	5	11	0

This Dodgers' 1999 11th-round draft pick went to the Phillies following the 2001 season as part of a deal for Omar Daal. Junge surprised with a solid Triple-A season followed by a very credible September major league trial. The righthander has been used almost exclusively as a starter in his pro career, but his narrow repertoire, quirky mechanics and occasionally uneven command cast doubts about whether he'll ever fit in a big league rotation. Junge relies heavily on a low-90s fastball with sharp downward action, but his slider and changeup are not major league-quality pitches at this stage of the game. He experimented with a splitter last season and had some success. With some mechanical tweaking and improved consistency, Junge could evolve into a credible setup man or middle reliever.

Andy Machado

Position: SS | **Opening Day Age:** 22
Bats: B **Throws:** R | **Born:** 1/25/81 in
Ht: 5' 11" **Wt:** 165 | Caracas, VZ

Recent Statistics

	G	AB	R	H	D	T	HR	RBI	SB	BB	SO	Avg
2001 A Clearwater	82	272	49	71	5	8	5	36	23	31	66	.261
2001 AA Reading	31	101	13	15	2	0	1	8	5	12	25	.149
2002 AA Reading	126	450	71	113	24	3	12	77	40	72	118	.251

Savvy talent evaluators have noted that Machado always has ranked among the youngest players at each successive minor league level. It was just a matter of time before the switch-hitter matured physically and began to drive the ball with authority. His swing remains a little long, and he tends to swing through pitches and hit the ball into the air too often. More groundballs would raise his average quite a bit, as Machado has excellent speed. Defensively, he combines well above-average range with a very strong throwing arm, and is becoming more consistent on the routine plays. He's expected to be the everyday Triple-A shortstop in 2003.

Ryan Madson

Position: P | **Opening Day Age:** 22
Bats: L **Throws:** R | **Born:** 8/28/80 in Long
Ht: 6' 6" **Wt:** 180 | Beach, CA

Recent Statistics

	W	L	ERA	G	GS	Sv	IP	H	R	BB	SO	HR
2001 A Clearwater	9	9	3.90	22	21	0	117.2	137	68	49	101	4
2002 AA Reading	16	4	3.20	26	26	0	171.1	150	68	53	132	11

All of the other 29 teams had a chance to snatch Madson in last year's Rule 5 draft, but he slipped through and greatly enhanced his prospect status with a brilliant Double-A campaign. The righthander combines three solid pitches: a live, 90-MPH fastball with sharp downward movement, a hard curve and a changeup. He became much more mechanically consistent last season, and his location within the strike zone greatly improved. Madson's strikeout rate held pretty steady upon his arrival in the upper minors. Still, he doesn't project as a major league power pitcher unless additional physical development adds a tick or two to his fastball. He's about a year away from mounting a charge at a major league rotation spot.

Jorge Padilla

Position: OF | **Opening Day Age:** 23
Bats: R **Throws:** R | **Born:** 8/11/79 in Rio
Ht: 6' 2" **Wt:** 200 | Piedras, PR

Recent Statistics

	G	AB	R	H	D	T	HR	RBI	SB	BB	SO	Avg
2001 A Clearwater	100	358	62	93	13	2	16	66	23	40	73	.260
2002 AA Reading	127	484	71	124	30	2	7	65	32	40	77	.256

This Phillies' 1998 third-round draft pick has been expected to develop into a consistent power source for quite a while now, but that's about the only piece of his game that's lagging behind schedule. He drives the ball with authority to the gaps, but simply doesn't get it into the air enough. Padilla has developed into a polished basestealer and an effective outfielder with solid range and arm strength, and he could play either left or right field. His 2003 Triple-A season looms large. It'll go a long way towards telling whether Padilla is a budding star or a bundle of never-to-be-refined talent.

Chase Utley

Position: 3B | **Opening Day Age:** 24
Bats: L **Throws:** R | **Born:** 12/17/78 in
Ht: 6' 1" **Wt:** 185 | Pasadena, CA

Recent Statistics

	G	AB	R	H	D	T	HR	RBI	SB	BB	SO	Avg
2001 A Clearwater	122	467	65	120	25	2	16	59	19	37	88	.257
2002 AAA Scran-WB	125	464	73	122	39	1	17	70	8	46	89	.263

The Phillies threw down the gauntlet to their 2000 first-round draft pick last season, simultaneously jumping Utley over a level to Triple-A and moving him from second to third base. He accepted the challenge. He has an authoritative line-drive stroke that generates power from gap to gap. He's made some improvements in his areas of weakness, including plate discipline and his handling of lefthanded pitching. He is a smart baserunner and an occasional basestealing threat. Defensively, Utley settled in after a shaky start last season, and has the range, first-step quickness and release to compensate for an ordinary arm. The Phillies signed veteran third baseman David Bell in the offseason, but Utley continued to keep himself in the picture by performing well in the Arizona Fall League.

Others to Watch

Righthanded starter **Brad Baisley** (23) has a high upside, both literally and figuratively, as he stands 6-foot-9 and weighs 205 pounds. Ongoing elbow troubles and mechanical inconsistencies have robbed his pitches of a bit of their life, though he still can push the gun into the low 90s. . . Keep an eye on righthanded starter **Taft Cable** (22), an eighth-round draftee in 2001. The finesse hurler has impeccable command, consistently throwing his upper-80s fastball, curve and changeup for strikes. At best, he could become an innings-gobbling No. 4 starter in the majors. . . It's rare for a Rookie-level performer to be included on this list, but an exception has to be made for righthanded starter **Elizardo Ramirez** (20) on the basis of his scary 73-2 strikeout-walk ratio and 1.10 ERA in the Gulf Coast League. The slight Dominican features a 90-MPH fastball, curveball and changeup. . . Righthanded starter **Robinson Tejeda** (21) pitched for a hideous high Class-A Clearwater club last season, resulting in a 4-8 record. His skills are better assessed by his impressive total of 73 hits allowed in 99.2 innings. Tejeda reaches the low 90s with his fastball, and will need to continue to enhance his curve and changeup to thrive in the upper minors.

PNC Park

Offense

The first impression when PNC Park opened in 2001 was that it would be home to many high-scoring games because of the short dimensions down the lines. However, it has proven to be a fair park, particularly since many flyballs die in the deep left-center gap. Lefthanded hitters have the edge with the 21-foot high right-field wall standing just 320 feet down the line from home plate. Thus, lefthanded pitchers tend to fare better.

Defense

Unlike most venues, it is easier to play right field than left field in PNC Park because there is much less ground to cover. That's why Brian Giles was shifted to left when the Pirates moved from Three Rivers Stadium in 2001. PNC Park's infield had the reputation of being rock hard during the first half of 2001, but it has softened considerably.

Who It Helps the Most

While Giles' power numbers are about equal home and away, he hit .323 in PNC Park last season, as opposed to .272 on the road. Most left-handed pitchers like PNC Park and Scott Sauerbeck and Dave Williams were no exceptions. Sauerbeck had a microscopic 1.21 ERA at PNC Park as opposed to 3.91 on the road, while Williams' home/road split was 3.43/6.45.

Who It Hurts the Most

Righthanded power hitter Craig Wilson watches many of his long drives to left-center be caught just short of the warning track. He hit only .220 at home but .299 on the road last year. Jimmy Anderson bucked the lefty trend as he was raked for a 7.30 ERA at home while posting a respectable 3.64 number elsewhere.

Rookies & Newcomers

The Pirates' top two hitting prospects in the upper levels of their farm system, outfielders Tony Alvarez and J.J. Davis, bat righthanded, which means PNC Park could work against them. However, the Pirates feel Alvarez should be OK because he is a gap hitter, and that Davis' opposite-field power could play well with the short right field.

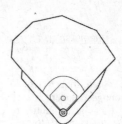

Dimensions: LF-325, LCF-389, CF-399, RCF-375, RF-320

Capacity: 37,898

Elevation: 730 feet

Surface: Grass

Foul Territory: Small

Park Factors

2002 Season

	Home Games			Away Games			
	Pirates	Opp	Total	Pirates	Opp	Total	Index
G	74	74	148	75	75	150	
Avg	.250	.272	.262	.236	.263	.249	105
AB	2389	2576	4965	2523	2430	4953	102
R	317	362	679	286	321	607	113
H	598	701	1299	595	639	1234	107
2B	122	145	267	121	126	247	108
3B	6	16	22	14	12	26	84
HR	57	81	138	78	71	149	92
BB	269	254	523	243	278	521	100
SO	451	445	896	593	423	1016	88
E	59	50	109	51	40	91	121
E-Infield	50	44	94	44	35	79	121
LHB-Avg	.264	.278	.272	.253	.270	.263	103
LHB-HR	25	29	54	31	34	65	82
RHB-Avg	.244	.269	.256	.229	.259	.242	106
RHB-HR	32	52	84	47	37	84	100

2001-2002

	Home Games			Away Games			
	Pirates	Opp	Total	Pirates	Opp	Total	Index
G	149	149	298	147	147	294	
Avg	.254	.269	.261	.235	.272	.253	103
AB	4878	5202	10080	4931	4793	9724	102
R	639	762	1401	549	712	1261	110
H	1237	1398	2635	1157	1302	2459	106
2B	255	294	549	224	265	489	108
3B	16	28	44	26	31	57	74
HR	127	154	281	154	150	304	89
BB	484	519	1003	451	522	973	99
SO	918	877	1795	1143	822	1965	88
E	128	117	245	1059	95	200	121
E-Infield	103	103	206	89	82	171	119
LHB-Avg	.262	.278	.271	.243	.288	.267	102
LHB-HR	54	62	116	56	64	120	90
RHB-Avg	.249	.263	.256	.230	.262	.245	104
RHB-HR	73	92	165	98	86	184	88

2002 Rankings (National League)

- Second-highest error factor
- Second-highest infield-error factor
- Second-lowest strikeout factor

Lloyd McClendon

2002 Season

The Pirates improved by 10 and a half games last year, raising their record to 72-89 after a 62-100 mark in Lloyd McClendon's rookie season of 2001. While he almost always is optimistic in his approach, he also has little tolerance for nonsense and made that known on more than one occasion in 2002. He laid down the law in the second half of the season when he felt his club was losing its focus, including banishing lefthander Jimmy Anderson to the bullpen and benching right fielder Armando Rios for missing a sign.

Offense

Lacking power hitters, McClendon has been forced to manufacture runs during his two seasons on the job. The problem is that the Pirates also don't have exceptional speed, and McClendon has been guilty of running his team into too many outs. As a former bench player, he understands the importance of keeping extra men sharp, and he does a good job of getting most everyone enough at-bats to stay sharp. He too often tries to fit square pegs into round holes, though, such as trying to make Pokey Reese a leadoff hitter and Jason Kendall a middle-of-the-order type.

Pitching & Defense

McClendon has done a good job of handling the Pirates' young pitching staff. He adheres strictly to pitch counts and, unlike some of his predecessors, has resisted the urge to ride some of the organization's promising young arms too hard. McClendon also has well-defined roles for his bullpen and has a knack for getting the right matchups with his relievers in the late innings. He puts a premium on good defensive players, so that a young pitching staff can get as much help as possible.

2003 Outlook

McClendon enters the final year of his contract, so it obviously is a pivotal year. The Pirates played better baseball in almost all facets last season, but they will need to continue to improve for McClendon to stick around past this year. One thing in his favor is that he has the respect of most of his players, who play hard for him.

Born: 1/11/59 in Gary, IN

Playing Experience: 1987-1994, Cin, ChC, Pit

Managerial Experience: 2 seasons

Manager Statistics

Year	Team, Lg	W	L	Pct	GB	Finish
2002	Pittsburgh, NL	72	89	.447	24.5	4th Central
2 Seasons		134	189	.415	–	–

2002 Starting Pitchers by Days Rest

	<=3	4	5	6+
Pirates Starts	1	83	47	19
Pirates ERA	8.44	4.80	3.83	4.42
NL Avg Starts	1	88	42	21
NL ERA	3.18	4.22	4.14	4.58

2002 Situational Stats

	Lloyd McClendon	NL Average
Hit & Run Success %	34.6	36.5
Stolen Base Success %	63.7	68.3
Platoon Pct.	44.4	52.7
Defensive Subs	25	19
High-Pitch Outings	0	7
Quick/Slow Hooks	38/13	24/11
Sacrifice Attempts	98	95

2002 Rankings (National League)

- 1st in double steals (8), pitchouts (70), intentional walks (61) and quick hooks
- 2nd in steals of home plate (1), pitchouts with a runner moving (6), defensive substitutions and first-batter platoon percentage
- 3rd in hit-and-run attempts (104), starts on three days rest and 2+ pitching changes in low-scoring games (40)

Jimmy Anderson

2002 Season

Jimmy Anderson was lifted from Pittsburgh's rotation and banished to long relief on August 13, after going 8-13 with a 5.07 ERA in 25 starts. He was buried in the bullpen, as he pitched just three times after the demotion, and only once in the Pirates' last 31 games. Although PNC Park favors lefthanders, Anderson had a particularly tough time at home, where he went 2-9 with a 7.30 ERA in 15 games.

Pitching

The entire key for Anderson is keeping the ball down in the strike zone. He has an 88-MPH sinker with outstanding movement, and he gets plenty of groundball outs when he keeps the sinker at the knees. However, Anderson gets hit hard on pitches up in the zone, due to subpar velocity and an otherwise ordinary arsenal. He has a decent slider, but his changeup is erratic. He throws an occasional curveball primarily for show. He gets hurt by righthanded hitters because he refuses to throw inside to them.

Defense & Hitting

The pudgy Anderson is a much better athlete than he looks, with the ability to pounce off the mound to field bunts and choppers. However, he struggles to hold runners on base, as he often loses concentration. It is not uncommon to see a runner steal a base while Anderson is standing on the mound holding the ball. Pirates catchers threw out just one in four basestealers with Anderson on the mound last season. He was a decent hitter and bunter when he broke into the major leagues, but is regressing in that part of the game.

2003 Outlook

Anderson's days with the Pirates appear to be numbered. They have waited three seasons for him to become a consistent winner, and it hasn't happened. Many scouts feel Anderson still could be a decent No. 4 or No. 5 starter because of his sinker, but he needs a change of scenery. He also needs to throw more strikes if he wants to find steady work at the back of some team's rotation.

Position: SP
Bats: L **Throws:** L
Ht: 6' 1" **Wt:** 218

Opening Day Age: 27
Born: 1/22/76 in Portsmouth, VA
ML Seasons: 4

Overall Statistics

	W	L	Pct.	ERA	G	GS	Sv	IP	H	BB	SO	HR	Ratio
'02	8	13	.381	5.44	28	25	0	140.2	167	63	47	20	1.64
Car.	24	42	.364	5.17	102	89	0	520.1	593	220	222	50	1.56

How Often He Throws Strikes

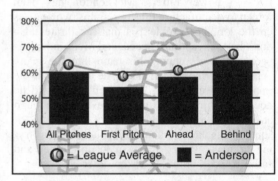

= League Average   = Anderson

2002 Situational Stats

	W	L	ERA	Sv	IP		AB	H	HR	RBI	Avg
Home	2	9	7.30	0	69.0	LHB	128	35	7	15	.273
Road	6	4	3.64	0	71.2	RHB	431	132	13	70	.306
First Half	6	10	5.13	0	100.0	Sc Pos	162	42	4	64	.259
Scnd Half	2	3	6.20	0	40.2	Clutch	11	1	1	1	.091

2002 Rankings (National League)

- 4th in highest batting average allowed vs. righthanded batters
- 5th in pickoff throws (149)
- 6th in stolen bases allowed (21)
- 7th in losses
- Led the Pirates in pickoff throws (149), stolen bases allowed (21), highest groundball-flyball ratio allowed (2.7), fewest pitches thrown per batter (3.51), most run support per nine innings (5.1) and most GDPs induced per nine innings (1.2)

Kris Benson

Position: SP
Bats: R **Throws:** R
Ht: 6' 4" **Wt:** 200

Opening Day Age: 28
Born: 11/7/74 in Superior, WI
ML Seasons: 3

2002 Season

Kris Benson started slowly in 2002 after missing all of the previous year because of reconstructive elbow surgery. He spent the first six weeks of last season on a minor league injury rehabilitation assignment. He then went 0-4 with a 7.79 ERA in his first eight starts with the Pirates. However, Benson finished strong by going 9-2 with a 3.57 ERA in his final 17 starts. He also won his last five decisions.

Pitching

Benson has a four-pitch repertoire with a fastball that reaches 96 MPH and averages 93, a sharp-breaking slider, a curveball and changeup. While he's a power pitcher, he sometimes tries to finesse his way through a lineup by using all of his pitches. That gets him into trouble as he runs up high pitch counts early in games. Benson had problems at times controlling his tailing fastball last season, but it's a major weapon when he gets it in the strike zone. He is a studious pitcher who watches plenty of tape and keeps copious notes on each hitter in the league.

Defense & Hitting

While Benson isn't quick off the mound, he usually makes plays on the balls he gets to. Still, he has committed a pair of errors in each of his three big league seasons. He does a very good job of holding runners on and his pickoff move is hard to read. Benson is improving as a hitter, batting .175 last season. He needs to become more consistent with his bunting.

2003 Outlook

Expectations have been high for Benson ever since the Pirates used the first overall pick in the 1996 draft to select the righthander out of Clemson. And he showed signs of emerging as a No. 1 starter in the latter stages of 2002. With a season under his belt following major surgery, Benson looks poised to have his breakthrough campaign and become a big winner for the Pirates.

Overall Statistics

	W	L	Pct.	ERA	G	GS	Sv	IP	H	BB	SO	HR	Ratio
'02	9	6	.600	4.70	25	25	0	130.1	152	50	79	18	1.55
Car.	30	32	.484	4.13	88	88	0	544.2	542	219	402	58	1.40

How Often He Throws Strikes

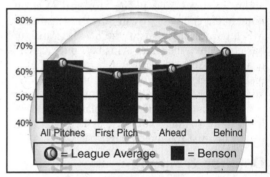

= League Average   ■ = Benson

2002 Situational Stats

	W	L	ERA	Sv	IP		AB	H	HR	RBI	Avg
Home	6	4	5.59	0	66.0	LHB	230	72	10	40	.313
Road	3	2	3.78	0	64.1	RHB	285	80	8	32	.281
First Half	2	4	5.50	0	52.1	Sc Pos	117	36	4	52	.308
Scnd Half	7	2	4.15	0	78.0	Clutch	18	3	0	0	.167

2002 Rankings (National League)

- Led the Pirates in runners caught stealing (8), winning percentage and lowest stolen-base percentage allowed (38.5)

Josh Fogg

2002 Season

The Pirates acquired Josh Fogg, along with Kip Wells and Sean Lowe, in a five-player trade with the Chicago White Sox at the 2001 winter meetings. Fogg was the least heralded of the three pitchers the Pirates received. However, Fogg beat out Lowe for the fifth starter's job in spring training and wound up making 33 starts, the most by a Pirates' rookie since 1899. Fogg was an early Rookie of the Year candidate but then slipped, going 1-5 with a 5.22 ERA in his last nine starts.

Pitching

Fogg has been compared to Greg Maddux for his ability to throw four pitches for strikes at any point in the count. Fogg can throw his fastball 92 MPH, but it usually sits in the 88-MPH area and has good sink. The slider is his best pitch, and his changeup also is good, though he needs to tighten his curveball. While Fogg looks mild-mannered, he is a feisty competitor who will willingly throw inside and knock hitters off the plate. He needs to build more stamina, however, as he faded badly during his first full major league season.

Defense & Hitting

Fogg is a good athlete who has good reactions defensively. He steps off quite frequently to keep runners close to the bag and doesn't allow many stolen bases. He is a poor hitter who strikes out too much. He also needs a lot of work on his bunting, as he laid down only two sacrifice bunts in 62 plate appearances last season.

2003 Outlook

Fogg had a solid rookie season, though his second-half slide gives at least some reason for concern. However, the Pirates believe he'll benefit from a strengthening program this offseason, and he should settle in as the No. 3 starter behind Kris Benson and Kip Wells. Fogg is capable of again winning at least 12 games.

Position: SP
Bats: R **Throws:** R
Ht: 6' 0" **Wt:** 202

Opening Day Age: 26
Born: 12/13/76 in Lynn, MA
ML Seasons: 2

Overall Statistics

	W	L	Pct.	ERA	G	GS	Sv	IP	H	BB	SO	HR	Ratio
'02	12	12	.500	4.35	33	33	0	194.1	199	69	113	28	1.38
Car.	12	12	.500	4.20	44	33	0	207.2	209	72	130	28	1.35

How Often He Throws Strikes

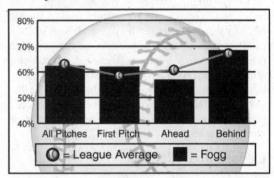

2002 Situational Stats

	W	L	ERA	Sv	IP		AB	H	HR	RBI	Avg
Home	5	6	4.83	0	85.2	LHB	358	105	16	45	.293
Road	7	6	3.98	0	108.2	RHB	388	94	12	48	.242
First Half	9	6	3.56	0	103.2	Sc Pos	166	48	5	65	.289
Scnd Half	3	6	5.26	0	90.2	Clutch	29	7	2	5	.241

2002 Rankings (National League)

- 1st in losses among rookies and least run support per nine innings (3.7)
- 2nd in ERA among rookies
- 4th in wins among rookies and highest ERA at home
- 5th in fewest pitches thrown per batter (3.51) and fewest strikeouts per nine innings (5.2)
- 6th in home runs allowed
- 7th in most home runs allowed per nine innings (1.30)
- Led the Pirates in wins, games started, hits allowed, home runs allowed, hit batsmen (8), GDPs induced (22) and fewest walks per nine innings (3.2)

Brian Giles

2002 Season

Brian Giles had another big year for the Pirates, though he did it in relative anonymity by playing for a club suffering through its 10th straight losing season. He finished second in the National League in both on-base and slugging percentage, despite having little lineup protection. Giles' 135 walks set a Pirates' single-season record for left-handed batters, and came up two short of the club's overall mark that was set by Ralph Kiner in 1951.

Hitting

Giles is one of the most complete hitters in baseball. He hits for power and also is an extremely patient batter who will take a walk. There really is no way to effectively pitch to him. He turns on inside pitches and generates enough power from his compact body to hit outside pitches with authority to the opposite field. Though pitchers routinely try to work around him, Giles rarely gives in by chasing a pitch outside the strike zone. Since arriving in Pittsburgh after the 1998 campaign, he has collected at least 30 doubles and 30 homers every year.

Baserunning & Defense

Giles is deceptively fast, as he takes choppy steps when he runs. He will steal a base if the pitcher quits paying attention to him and also is aggressive on the basepaths. He has played all three outfield spots during his four seasons with the Pirates, but settled into left field in 2002. Giles has above-average range for a left fielder. His arm is better than many runners give him credit for, as he had 13 assists last season.

2003 Outlook

Giles shows no signs of slowing down and again should be a major force in the middle of the Pirates' batting order. He is a bargain in today's market, as he is signed through 2005 with yearly salaries of only $7 million. Many clubs inquire about Giles, but the Pirates would give him up only if they were overwhelmed by a trade offer.

Position: LF
Bats: L **Throws:** L
Ht: 5'10" **Wt:** 202

Opening Day Age: 32
Born: 1/20/71 in El Cajon, CA
ML Seasons: 8
Pronunciation: JYLES

Overall Statistics

	G	AB	R	H	D	T	HR	RBI	SB	BB	SO	Avg	OBP	Slg
'02	153	497	95	148	37	5	38	103	15	135	74	.298	.450	.622
Car.	909	3010	581	909	192	26	188	593	66	589	429	.302	.416	.570

Where He Hits the Ball

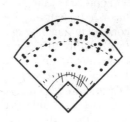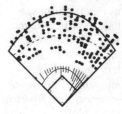

Vs. LHP   **Vs. RHP**

2002 Situational Stats

	AB	H	HR	RBI	Avg		AB	H	HR	RBI	Avg
Home	251	81	15	54	.323	LHP	143	33	8	29	.231
Road	246	67	23	49	.272	RHP	354	115	30	74	.325
First Half	281	84	22	53	.299	Sc Pos	101	29	6	56	.287
Scnd Half	216	64	16	50	.296	Clutch	69	18	3	11	.261

2002 Rankings (National League)

- 1st in assists in left field (13) and lowest groundball-flyball ratio (0.6)
- 2nd in walks, slugging percentage, on-base percentage, highest percentage of pitches taken (65.1), slugging percentage vs. righthanded pitchers (.681) and on-base percentage vs. righthanded pitchers (.485)
- 3rd in intentional walks (24), times on base (290) and HR frequency (13.1 ABs per HR)
- Led the Pirates in batting average, home runs, runs scored, doubles, triples, total bases (309), RBI, stolen bases, walks, times on base (290), plate appearances (644), on-base percentage, HR frequency (13.1 ABs per HR), batting average with the bases loaded (.600) and batting average vs. righthanded pitchers

Jason Kendall

2002 Season

In the first season of a six-year, $60-million contract, Jason Kendall hit below .300 for the second straight year. The dip follows a stretch when he had reached .300 in four of his first five campaigns. Having inherited Kendall's contract when he took over as General Manager midway through the 2001 season, Dave Littlefield tried to trade the three-time All-Star to Colorado last July for Denny Neagle. But the deal fell through. Kendall had a cyst and bone chips removed from his left foot the day after the season ended.

Hitting

Kendall has lost his patient approach at the plate in recent seasons. Some theorize he is trying too hard to justify the richest contract in franchise history. Kendall also has lost the ability to hit with authority the past two years because of an injured left thumb that required reconstructive surgery after the 2001 season. He needs to get back to spraying line drives to all fields, something that made him so successful during the early part of his career. His decline has coincided with the Pirates' move into PNC Park, which doesn't favor righthanded hitters. The park has a deep left-center gap, while the infield swallows up hard groundballs that used to scoot through on the artificial turf at Three Rivers Stadium.

Baserunning & Defense

Kendall once was one of the top basestealing catchers in history. But a severe ankle injury that he suffered in 1999, along with the wear and tear of catching, have slowed him down somewhat. He has had difficulty receiving pitches the past two seasons, symptomatic of the thumb injury. His game calling and throwing always have been weak points and aren't improving with age.

2003 Outlook

Kendall has five years and $50 million left on his contract, making a trade unlikely. With no one ready to take over as the starting catcher, the Pirates will hope—perhaps against hope—that Kendall will be revitalized by being another year removed from thumb surgery.

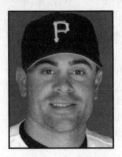

Position: C
Bats: R **Throws:** R
Ht: 6' 0" **Wt:** 195

Opening Day Age: 28
Born: 6/26/74 in San Diego, CA
ML Seasons: 7

Overall Statistics

	G	AB	R	H	D	T	HR	RBI	SB	BB	SO	Avg	OBP	Slg
'02	145	545	59	154	25	3	3	44	15	49	29	.283	.350	.356
Car.	955	3445	536	1035	195	26	58	362	121	345	322	.300	.383	.423

Where He Hits the Ball

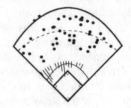 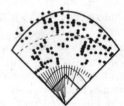

Vs. LHP   **Vs. RHP**

2002 Situational Stats

	AB	H	HR	RBI	Avg		AB	H	HR	RBI	Avg
Home	269	75	1	16	.279	LHP	109	30	1	9	.275
Road	276	79	2	28	.286	RHP	436	124	2	35	.284
First Half	289	83	2	26	.287	Sc Pos	117	28	1	40	.239
Scnd Half	256	71	1	18	.277	Clutch	89	28	2	11	.315

2002 Rankings (National League)

- 2nd in highest percentage of swings put into play (57.6)
- 3rd in lowest percentage of swings that missed (8.1), lowest percentage of swings on the first pitch (13.2) and lowest percentage of runners caught stealing as a catcher (25.0)
- Led the Pirates in at-bats, hits, singles, stolen bases, caught stealing (8), highest groundball-flyball ratio (1.7), lowest percentage of swings that missed (8.1), highest percentage of swings put into play (57.6), on-base percentage vs. lefthanded pitchers (.403), lowest percentage of swings on the first pitch (13.2), batting average on a 3-2 count (.353) and batting average with two strikes (.249)
- Led NL catchers in batting average

Aramis Ramirez

2002 Season

Aramis Ramirez enjoyed a breakthrough season in 2001, when he hit .300 with 34 homers and 112 RBI. But he followed up with a miserable 2002. He was hitting .348 on April 17 when he charged the mound after being hit by a pitch from Milwaukee's Ben Sheets. During the ensuing benches-clearing brawl, Ramirez suffered a sprained right ankle at the bottom of the pile. Though he never went on the disabled list, he wasn't totally healthy again until September.

Hitting

Ramirez's ankle injury greatly affected his ability to hit for power last season. He was forced to stand more erect at the plate to take pressure off the ankle. That caused him to lose the leverage in his swing. Ramirez is at his best when he can extend his arms, showing power to all parts of the park. However, pitchers jammed him more last season and he didn't adjust until later in the year. Though the numbers didn't bear it out in 2002, Ramirez enjoys hitting in the clutch and has a knack for coming through in RBI situations.

Baserunning & Defense

Ramirez always has been a slow runner, but he was reduced to a brisk walk on the bases last season because of his ankle. He is a station-to-station baserunner and rarely attempts to steal. He is erratic in the field, as he tends to get lazy with his footwork, causing his throws to sail off line. He has only adequate range, but still could become at least a decent defender with his good hands and strong arm.

2003 Outlook

Ramirez has much to prove this season after suffering a huge drop-off in 2002. He tends to get down on himself quickly when things are going bad. However, he's still young with plenty of talent, meaning a return to his 2001 levels is possible this year. To increase the likelihood of a rebound, the Pirates have Ramirez working with a nutritionist and strength coach during the offseason. Better conditioning could go a long way for a player with his gifts.

Position: 3B
Bats: R **Throws:** R
Ht: 6' 1" **Wt:** 211

Opening Day Age: 24
Born: 6/25/78 in Santo Domingo, DR
ML Seasons: 5
Pronunciation: ah-RAH-mis

Overall Statistics

	G	AB	R	H	D	T	HR	RBI	SB	BB	SO	Avg	OBP	Slg
'02	142	522	51	122	26	0	18	71	2	29	95	.234	.279	.387
Car.	463	1686	178	437	92	4	64	249	7	103	312	.259	.308	.432

Where He Hits the Ball

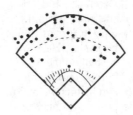
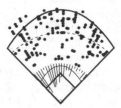

Vs. LHP   **Vs. RHP**

2002 Situational Stats

	AB	H	HR	RBI	Avg		AB	H	HR	RBI	Avg
Home	251	56	7	31	.223	LHP	123	32	9	20	.260
Road	271	66	11	40	.244	RHP	399	90	9	51	.226
First Half	230	50	6	28	.217	Sc Pos	149	34	4	52	.228
Scnd Half	292	72	12	43	.247	Clutch	77	29	8	23	.377

2002 Rankings (National League)

- 1st in sacrifice flies (11)
- 2nd in lowest on-base percentage, lowest batting average vs. righthanded pitchers, lowest on-base percentage vs. righthanded pitchers (.272) and lowest fielding percentage at third base (.946)
- 3rd in lowest batting average, lowest cleanup slugging percentage (.390) and lowest batting average at home
- 4th in batting average in the clutch and errors at third base (19)
- 5th in lowest slugging percentage vs. righthanded pitchers (.346)
- Led the Pirates in sacrifice flies (11), GDPs (17) and batting average in the clutch

Pokey Reese

2002 Season

Following a 2001 campaign in which he batted just .224 for the Reds, Pokey Reese endured a whirlwind offseason. He was traded from Cincinnati to Colorado to Boston, but then wasn't tendered a contract by the Red Sox. He landed in Pittsburgh with a two-year, $6.5-million deal. Reese wound up filling a large hole at second base for the Pirates, and served as the team's primary leadoff hitter for the last month and a half. He finished strong, hitting .333 in his last 15 games and .285 in 64 games after the All-Star break.

Hitting

After a miserable 2001 with Cincinnati and a poor first half of 2002, Reese made great progress in the second half of last season. He turned things around by getting back to the basics. He started taking more pitches, hitting the ball on the ground and using the whole field. He runs into problems when his back leg collapses and he hits the ball in the air, preventing him from utilizing his speed. While the Pirates would like Reese to take over the leadoff role, he shows a knack for coming up with clutch hits, in part because he doesn't try to pull the ball with runners on base.

Baserunning & Defense

Reese has very good speed and outstanding instincts on the bases. He reads pitchers' moves well and has an innate sense of when he can steal a base. Reese is an excellent fielder with good first-step quickness, outstanding range, soft hands and an above-average arm. He also helped the Pirates lead the major leagues in double plays last year.

2003 Outlook

Reese will be back to add energy with his defense at second base and speed on the bases. The Pirates are hopeful he continues his offensive improvement and can prosper in the leadoff spot. Reese underwent an offseason strength and conditioning program after being nagged by injuries to his hamstring, knee, calf, side, finger and elbow in 2002.

Position: 2B
Bats: R **Throws:** R
Ht: 5'11" **Wt:** 188

Opening Day Age: 29
Born: 6/10/73 in Columbia, SC
ML Seasons: 6

Overall Statistics

	G	AB	R	H	D	T	HR	RBI	SB	BB	SO	Avg	OBP	Slg
'02	119	421	46	111	25	0	4	50	12	41	81	.264	.330	.352
Car.	723	2482	325	627	119	15	40	230	132	200	440	.253	.312	.361

Where He Hits the Ball

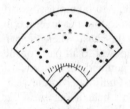 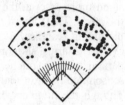

Vs. LHP	**Vs. RHP**

2002 Situational Stats

	AB	H	HR	RBI	Avg		AB	H	HR	RBI	Avg
Home	190	48	3	28	.253	LHP	85	24	1	7	.282
Road	231	63	1	22	.273	RHP	336	87	3	43	.259
First Half	186	44	1	20	.237	Sc Pos	87	29	1	43	.333
Scnd Half	235	67	3	30	.285	Clutch	70	18	1	12	.257

2002 Rankings (National League)

- 3rd in batting average with the bases loaded (.500)
- 4th in fielding percentage at second base (.988) and lowest slugging percentage vs. righthanded pitchers (.342)
- 9th in errors at second base (8)
- Led the Pirates in stolen-base percentage (92.3), batting average with runners in scoring position, batting average on an 0-2 count (.267) and on-base percentage for a leadoff hitter (.349)

Kip Wells

2002 Season

Kip Wells made a successful transition to the National League last year, after being acquired from the Chicago White Sox in a five-player trade at the 2001 winter meetings. He finished with the best ERA of any Pirates' starting pitcher. Still, Wells wound up with a losing record, as Pittsburgh scored three or fewer runs in 16 of his 33 starts. He didn't win after August 24, and went 6-12 in his last 24 starts despite a fine 3.47 ERA.

Pitching

Wells can be overpowering at times, as his fastball was clocked as high as 99 MPH in his first season with the Pirates. His heater usually resides in the 94-MPH range and has decent movement, though it tends to straighten out when he tries to over-throw. In addition to the fastball, Wells has a sinker that produces groundballs, a curveball with a sharp downward break, an adequate slider and a changeup that he sometimes hesitates to use. He also is durable, as he pitched at least six innings in each of his last 10 starts last season.

Defense & Hitting

Wells is a shaky fielder who tends to rush throws on close plays. He pays attentions to runners and has a decent move to first base. He handles the bat well and can put a charge into the ball if opposing pitchers aren't careful. Wells also is an outstanding bunter who helps himself by moving runners.

2003 Outlook

A former No. 1 pick in Chicago, Wells gained the reputation of being soft and an underachiever with the White Sox. He has shattered those myths since joining the Pirates, and is being counted on to be a cornerstone of the starting rotation for many years to come. He should have won more than 12 games last year and figures to improve on that total in 2003.

Position: SP
Bats: R **Throws:** R
Ht: 6' 3" **Wt:** 205

Opening Day Age: 25
Born: 4/21/77 in Houston, TX
ML Seasons: 4

Overall Statistics

	W	L	Pct.	ERA	G	GS	Sv	IP	H	BB	SO	HR	Ratio
'02	12	14	.462	3.58	33	33	0	198.1	197	71	134	21	1.35
Car.	32	35	.478	4.48	100	80	0	466.0	501	205	333	52	1.52

How Often He Throws Strikes

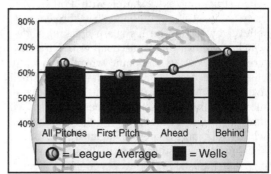

= League Average   = Wells

2002 Situational Stats

	W	L	ERA	Sv	IP		AB	H	HR	RBI	Avg
Home	5	6	3.75	0	98.1	LHB	361	99	11	39	.274
Road	7	8	3.42	0	100.0	RHB	394	98	10	42	.249
First Half	9	6	3.41	0	108.1	Sc Pos	174	43	4	56	.247
Scnd Half	3	8	3.80	0	90.0	Clutch	25	8	0	2	.320

2002 Rankings (National League)

- 3rd in sacrifice bunts (13) and highest groundball-flyball ratio allowed (2.0)
- 5th in losses
- Led the Pirates in ERA, wins, losses, games started, innings pitched, batters faced (845), walks allowed, strikeouts, wild pitches (7), pitches thrown (3,060), highest strikeout-walk ratio (1.9), lowest batting average allowed (.261), lowest slugging percentage allowed (.401), lowest on-base percentage allowed (.328), lowest ERA at home, lowest ERA on the road, fewest home runs allowed per nine innings (.95) and most strikeouts per nine innings (6.1)

Mike Williams

2002 Season

After converting 69 of 82 save opportunities during the previous three seasons, Mike Williams established himself as a premier closer in 2002. He shattered the Pirates' single-season save record of 34, set by Jim Gott in 1988. Williams saved 63.9 percent of the Pirates' wins, the second highest percentage in history behind Bryan Harvey, who saved 70.3 of Florida's victories during the Marlins' expansion season in 1993. Williams' 46 saves were the most ever by a reliever on a team with a losing record.

Pitching

After struggling as a starter with Philadelphia early in his career, Williams has thrived as a reliever by relying on his sharp-breaking slider, which he throws with a curveball grip. He's mastered the slider to the point where he adeptly changes speeds and breaks with it. His fastball averages 88 MPH and tops out at 91. He became more effective last season because he started throwing more fastballs to righthanded hitters, while using more changeups against lefthanders. Williams gives up his share of baserunners and can be painstakingly slow on the mound. However, he doesn't get rattled and has confidence to extricate himself from the toughest of jams. Williams' arm got tired late last season, and his ERA was 5.89 in the final two months.

Defense & Hitting

Like most closers, Williams doesn't do a good job of holding runners. Basestealers were successful on all six attempts last season. He is an adequate fielder who gets off the mound fairly quickly. He made only two plate appearances in 2002, striking out once and getting hit by a pitch. He has just two extra-base hits in 108 career at-bats.

2003 Outlook

Williams will be back as the Pirates' closer for a fifth straight season. While he doesn't overpower hitters like a classic closer, his slider often is unhittable and makes him a success. It may be too much to ask him to reach the 46-save plateau again. But he should get his fair share of opportunities this season, as the Pirates figure to improve on their win total of 72.

Position: RP
Bats: R **Throws:** R
Ht: 6' 2" **Wt:** 200

Opening Day Age: 34
Born: 7/29/68 in Radford, VA
ML Seasons: 11

Overall Statistics

	W	L	Pct.	ERA	G	GS	Sv	IP	H	BB	SO	HR	Ratio
'02	2	6	.250	2.93	59	0	46	61.1	54	21	43	6	1.22
Car.	31	47	.397	4.30	400	55	116	705.1	698	302	545	84	1.42

How Often He Throws Strikes

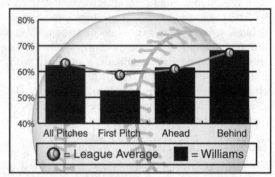

= League Average   = Williams

2002 Situational Stats

	W	L	ERA	Sv	IP		AB	H	HR	RBI	Avg
Home	2	3	3.58	23	32.2	LHB	121	34	1	12	.281
Road	0	3	2.20	23	28.2	RHB	111	20	5	14	.180
First Half	1	2	1.83	25	34.1	Sc Pos	61	14	1	21	.230
Scnd Half	1	4	4.33	21	27.0	Clutch	184	43	5	20	.234

2002 Rankings (National League)

- 3rd in saves
- 4th in save percentage (92.0)
- 5th in save opportunities (50)
- 6th in relief losses (6)
- 9th in games finished (59)
- Led the Pirates in saves, games finished (59), save opportunities (50), save percentage (92.0), relief losses (6) and fewest baserunners allowed per nine innings in relief (11.2)

Craig Wilson

2002 Season

Craig Wilson made 99 starts for the Pirates between two positions last season, starting 65 times in right field and 34 times at first base. It was a streaky year for him. He was the National League Player of the Week from June 10-16, when he hit .500 with four homers and 12 RBI in six games. He also led the club with seven homers in August. However, he posted just one multi-hit game in September, when he hit .222 for the month. He also batted just .180 in July.

Hitting

Wilson is pretty much an all-or-nothing hitter. He has above-average power when he connects, but he also strikes out frequently. He hits the ball hard to all fields, though pitchers exploit his weakness by feeding him high fastballs and breaking pitches off the plate. Wilson also gets into spells when he drops his hands, giving him little chance to catch up with fastballs. As a rookie in 2001, Wilson tied the major league record with seven pinch-hit home runs, but he struggled off the bench last season.

Baserunning & Defense

Wilson is a below-average runner who is not much of a threat to steal or take an extra base. He came up through the minor leagues as a catcher and still is learning the nuances of first base and right field. He made strides in right last season, an easier position to play in PNC Park than in most stadiums. Wilson's range and arm are subpar, though he catches what he gets to and usually hits the cutoff man with his throws. He also got better at first base last season, but he still needs to improve his footwork around the bag.

2003 Outlook

The Pirates needed major offensive upgrades at first base and in right field, and they hope they solved at least part of the equation at first with a late-November trade that brought Randall Simon over from Detroit. That still leaves right field open, and if Wilson is deemed to be the answer there, he should exceed last season's total of 368 at-bats. Wilson's power is intriguing, but he is going to have to cut down on the strikeouts to get the chance to play regularly.

Position: RF/1B
Bats: R **Throws:** R
Ht: 6' 2" **Wt:** 225

Opening Day Age: 26
Born: 11/30/76 in Fountain Valley, CA
ML Seasons: 2

Overall Statistics

	G	AB	R	H	D	T	HR	RBI	SB	BB	SO	Avg	OBP	Slg
'02	131	368	48	97	16	1	16	57	2	32	116	.264	.355	.443
Car.	219	526	75	146	19	2	29	89	5	47	169	.278	.365	.487

Where He Hits the Ball

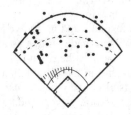 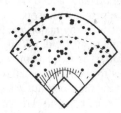

Vs. LHP   **Vs. RHP**

2002 Situational Stats

	AB	H	HR	RBI	Avg		AB	H	HR	RBI	Avg
Home	164	36	3	20	.220	LHP	112	35	5	14	.313
Road	204	61	13	37	.299	RHP	256	62	11	43	.242
First Half	205	57	6	33	.278	Sc Pos	93	23	5	41	.247
Scnd Half	163	40	10	24	.245	Clutch	54	15	1	8	.278

2002 Rankings (National League)

- 1st in hit by pitch (21)
- 3rd in highest percentage of swings that missed (31.2)
- 4th in lowest percentage of swings put into play (32.1)
- Led the Pirates in hit by pitch (21) and batting average on the road

Jack Wilson

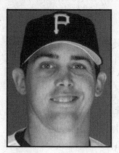

Position: SS
Bats: R **Throws:** R
Ht: 6' 0" **Wt:** 195

Opening Day Age: 25
Born: 12/29/77 in
Westlake Village, CA
ML Seasons: 2
Nickname: Jack Flash

2002 Season

Jack Wilson started 135 games in his second major league season, the most by a Pirates shortstop since Jay Bell made 143 starts in 1996. Although Wilson ranked second on the club behind Brian Giles in runs scored, he faded offensively, as Wilson hit just .219 over the season's final two months. However, his fielding got better as the season wore on and he made only one error in his last 47 games.

Hitting

After often being overpowered as a rookie in 2001, Wilson went on a winter conditioning program and added 15 pounds. The extra weight helped last season, as he no longer was overmatched by major league fastballs and he sprayed hits to all fields. While Wilson made strides as a hitter, he still has much to learn, as he often fishes for breaking balls away and in the dirt. He's a good high-ball hitter and is effective when he can extend his arms. His concentration wavers and he seems to bear down more when batting with runners on base. He also is an excellent bunter who could turn into an outstanding No. 2 man in the batting order if he improves his ability to make contact.

Baserunning & Defense

Wilson is not a burner and doesn't steal many bases. However, he has good instincts on the basepaths and likes to put pressure on the defense. He has outstanding range, a good arm and nice hands, so he has the makings of being a premier defensive shortstop. However, Wilson tends to try to make plays that aren't there and often dives when he has no chance of reaching the ball, which exasperates some teammates.

2003 Outlook

Wilson took a step forward in 2002 and figures to continue to improve in 2003. While his calling card is defense, he has the ability to increase his batting average and extra-base hit totals with another year of weight work and experience.

Overall Statistics

	G	AB	R	H	D	T	HR	RBI	SB	BB	SO	Avg	OBP	Slg
'02	147	527	77	133	22	4	4	47	5	37	74	.252	.306	.332
Car.	255	917	121	220	39	5	7	72	6	53	144	.240	.285	.316

Where He Hits the Ball

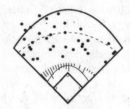 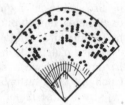

Vs. LHP　　　　**Vs. RHP**

2002 Situational Stats

	AB	H	HR	RBI	Avg		AB	H	HR	RBI	Avg
Home	268	70	2	26	.261	LHP	114	41	2	11	.360
Road	259	63	2	21	.243	RHP	413	92	2	36	.223
First Half	271	75	1	20	.277	Sc Pos	118	34	2	41	.288
Scnd Half	256	58	3	27	.227	Clutch	70	15	0	3	.214

2002 Rankings (National League)

- 1st in sacrifice bunts (17), lowest batting average vs. righthanded pitchers and lowest slugging percentage vs. righthanded pitchers (.278)
- 2nd in lowest slugging percentage
- 3rd in lowest on-base percentage vs. righthanded pitchers (.280)
- 4th in bunts in play (37)
- 5th in fielding percentage at shortstop (.977)
- Led the Pirates in sacrifice bunts (17), bunts in play (37), batting average vs. lefthanded pitchers, highest percentage of extra bases taken as a runner (64.0) and slugging percentage vs. lefthanded pitchers (.526)

Kevin Young

2002 Season

Kevin Young began last season as Pittsburgh's regular first baseman, but he wound up sharing the job with Craig Wilson due to a knee injury and ineffectiveness. Young got off to a dreadful start, hitting a combined .193 in April and May. He also finished poorly, hitting only four home runs in his last 64 games. He had arthroscopic right knee surgery to remove loose tissue the day after the season ended.

Hitting

Young once was a power and RBI threat who fit well in the middle of the Pirates' batting order. Those days are over. He's lost most of his power as he's gotten older. Part of the decline comes from having two arthritic knees, while the rest is due to his slow bat being unable to catch up with good fastballs either inside or up in the strike zone. Young also has become ineffective in clutch situations, as he hit .191 with runners in scoring position last season. He's still effective when he uses the whole field. However, too often he tries to pull the ball, and that doesn't work for a hitter who has little bat speed.

Baserunning & Defense

Young used to be sneaky fast, but his knees prevent him from stealing bases. Still, he sometimes will sneak up an extra 90 feet on the bases if outfielders don't pay attention. He is a very sure-handed first baseman who catches everything he gets to and is adept at corralling poor throws from the other infielders. However, Young's range now is minimal, and more balls get past him down the line than in the past.

2003 Outlook

Young's days as a regular player appear to be over after the Pirates acquired lefthanded-hitting Randall Simon from Detroit in a late-November trade. Young likely will platoon at first base and get far fewer at-bats than in past seasons. Young is owed $6.5 million in the final season of a four-year, $23.5 million contract, making him nearly impossible to trade. He still is highly respected in the clubhouse, but it remains to be seen how he adjusts to a reduced role.

Position: 1B
Bats: R **Throws:** R
Ht: 6' 3" **Wt:** 225

Opening Day Age: 33
Born: 6/16/69 in Alpena, MI
ML Seasons: 11

Overall Statistics

	G	AB	R	H	D	T	HR	RBI	SB	BB	SO	Avg	OBP	Slg
'02	146	468	60	115	26	1	16	51	4	50	101	.246	.322	.408
Car.	1153	3813	528	990	231	17	142	599	82	324	857	.260	.324	.441

Where He Hits the Ball

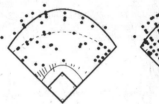
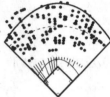

Vs. LHP   **Vs. RHP**

2002 Situational Stats

	AB	H	HR	RBI	Avg		AB	H	HR	RBI	Avg
Home	232	63	7	30	.272	LHP	106	30	7	17	.283
Road	236	52	9	21	.220	RHP	362	85	9	34	.235
First Half	249	58	9	22	.233	Sc Pos	110	21	1	30	.191
Scnd Half	219	57	7	29	.260	Clutch	70	14	1	5	.200

2002 Rankings (National League)

- 2nd in errors at first base (13), lowest groundball-flyball ratio (0.6) and lowest fielding percentage at first base (.991)
- 4th in lowest batting average with runners in scoring position
- 5th in lowest batting average vs. righthanded pitchers and lowest batting average on the road
- 6th in assists at first base (89)
- 9th in most pitches seen per plate appearance (4.08) and lowest batting average
- Led the Pirates in most pitches seen per plate appearance (4.08)

Bronson Arroyo

Position: RP
Bats: R **Throws:** R
Ht: 6' 5" **Wt:** 194

Opening Day Age: 26
Born: 2/24/77 in Key West, FL
ML Seasons: 3
Pronunciation: ah-ROY-yoh

Overall Statistics

	W	L	Pct.	ERA	G	GS	Sv	IP	H	BB	SO	HR	Ratio
'02	2	1	.667	4.00	9	4	0	27.0	30	15	22	1	1.67
Car.	9	14	.391	5.44	53	29	0	187.0	217	85	111	23	1.61

2002 Situational Stats

	W	L	ERA	Sv	IP		AB	H	HR	RBI	Avg
Home	2	0	1.62	0	16.2	LHB	34	10	0	3	.294
Road	0	1	7.84	0	10.1	RHB	72	20	1	10	.278
First Half	0	1	10.80	0	5.0	Sc Pos	32	10	0	11	.313
Scnd Half	2	0	2.45	0	22.0	Clutch	3	0	0	0	.000

2002 Season

Bronson Arroyo bounced between the major leagues and Triple-A three times last season. He spent most of the year with Nashville, the Pirates' top affiliate. He had a fine year in the hitter-friendly Pacific Coast League, going 8-6 with a 2.96 ERA in 22 games. Arroyo made three starts for the Pirates in late August, allowing only four runs in 15 innings. But he then was sent to the bullpen for the remainder of the season.

Pitching, Defense & Hitting

Arroyo pitches backward, in the sense that he often uses his curveball to set up his fastball, which can reach 93 MPH but usually is a tick below average at 88 MPH. His curve is so good that it makes his heater look even faster, and he occasionally can slip the fastball by hitters high in the strike zone. Arroyo has a changeup that is inconsistent. He can be very effective in bursts, but tends to fade in the middle innings. Arroyo may be better suited for relief work.

2003 Outlook

Arroyo will contend for a spot in the Pirates' starting rotation this season. However, he has yet to establish himself as a major league starter. He seems more likely to have a decent career as a reliever.

Brian Boehringer

Position: RP
Bats: B **Throws:** R
Ht: 6' 2" **Wt:** 190

Opening Day Age: 33
Born: 1/8/70 in St. Louis, MO
ML Seasons: 8
Pronunciation: BOH-ring-irr

Overall Statistics

	W	L	Pct.	ERA	G	GS	Sv	IP	H	BB	SO	HR	Ratio
'02	4	4	.500	3.39	70	0	1	79.2	65	33	65	5	1.23
Car.	20	27	.426	4.19	273	21	3	447.0	431	227	365	51	1.47

2002 Situational Stats

	W	L	ERA	Sv	IP		AB	H	HR	RBI	Avg
Home	3	1	3.64	0	42.0	LHB	96	24	1	10	.250
Road	1	3	3.11	1	37.2	RHB	188	41	4	23	.218
First Half	1	2	2.56	0	45.2	Sc Pos	58	22	2	28	.379
Scnd Half	3	2	4.50	1	34.0	Clutch	148	34	2	21	.230

2002 Season

The Pirates signed Brian Boehringer to a minor league contract last January, after he had been non-tendered by San Francisco a month earlier. He proved to be a good pickup. He settled in as the primary righthanded setup man and set a career high with 70 games pitched.

Pitching, Defense & Hitting

Boehringer is a power pitcher who relies on an above-average fastball and a hard slider. He can run his fastball up to 97 MPH, and the heater routinely sits in the 93-MPH range. While Boehringer sticks mainly to hard stuff in his short-relief role, he'll toss an occasional changeup to keep hitters off balance. He's a student of the game and does the little things well, like fielding his position and holding on runners. However, he has a lifetime batting average of .067.

2003 Outlook

Boehringer hit the free-agent market at the end of last season but wound up re-signing with the Pirates for two years and $3.8 million, along with a club option for 2005. He again will serve as the primary righthanded setup man for closer Mike Williams. One thing to be wary about is Boehringer's 4.50 ERA after the All-Star break last year.

Adrian Brown

Position: CF
Bats: B **Throws:** R
Ht: 6' 0" **Wt:** 200

Opening Day Age: 29
Born: 2/7/74 in McComb, MS
ML Seasons: 6

Overall Statistics

	G	AB	R	H	D	T	HR	RBI	SB	BB	SO	Avg	OBP	Slg
'02	91	208	20	45	10	2	1	21	10	19	34	.216	.284	.298
Car.	408	1072	158	280	43	8	11	83	42	106	146	.261	.330	.347

2002 Situational Stats

	AB	H	HR	RBI	Avg		AB	H	HR	RBI	Avg
Home	107	24	0	9	.224	LHP	52	8	0	4	.154
Road	101	21	1	12	.208	RHP	156	37	1	17	.237
First Half	172	33	1	15	.192	Sc Pos	48	11	0	19	.229
Scnd Half	36	12	0	6	.333	Clutch	40	10	0	6	.250

2002 Season

Adrian Brown began 2002 as the starting center fielder and leadoff hitter. He struggled from the outset and lost the everyday job to Chad Hermansen in May. Brown was sent to Triple-A Nashville on July 2 after batting .192 in 70 games. He returned in September after hitting .337 with 22 steals in 51 games in the minors. He hit .333 with the parent club after the recall.

Hitting, Baserunning & Defense

Brown is at his best when he sprays line drives the other way and hits the ball on the ground. He occasionally can turn on hanging breaking balls, especially when batting righthanded. Brown has good speed and instincts on the bases. His once-outstanding range has slipped since a hamstring injury in 2000. His arm strength has dipped to average since shoulder surgery in 2001.

2003 Outlook

Brown's window of opportunity to become the Pirates' regular center fielder closed last October when he was released. He then signed a minor league contract with Tampa Bay. The Pirates felt Brown was suited to be a good fourth or fifth out-fielder when he arrived in the major leagues in 1997, and that seems certain to be his role with the Devil Rays.

Adam Hyzdu

Position: CF/RF/LF
Bats: R **Throws:** R
Ht: 6' 2" **Wt:** 220
Opening Day Age: 31
Born: 12/6/71 in San Jose, CA
ML Seasons: 3
Pronunciation: HIZE-doo

Overall Statistics

	G	AB	R	H	D	T	HR	RBI	SB	BB	SO	Avg	OBP	Slg
'02	59	155	24	36	6	0	11	34	0	21	44	.232	.324	.484
Car.	122	245	33	58	9	0	17	47	0	25	66	.237	.310	.482

2002 Situational Stats

	AB	H	HR	RBI	Avg		AB	H	HR	RBI	Avg
Home	75	25	6	22	.333	LHP	49	10	4	14	.204
Road	80	11	5	12	.138	RHP	106	26	7	20	.245
First Half	12	3	1	2	.250	Sc Pos	43	12	4	25	.279
Scnd Half	143	33	10	32	.231	Clutch	20	6	1	6	.300

2002 Season

Adam Hyzdu has spent at least part of each of his 13 professional seasons in the minor leagues. But he was called up from Triple-A Nashville at the beginning of July and finished the year with the Pirates. Hyzdu hit .413 with 15 RBI in his first 16 games, and was named the National League's Player of the Week for July 15-21. However, he cooled off and hit just .156 in his last 43 games, playing sparingly in September.

Hitting, Baserunning & Defense

Hyzdu has good power and feasts on low fastballs and hanging sliders. However, he gets tied up by slow curveballs and changeups, and becomes overexposed when he plays on a daily basis. Hyzdu has average speed and doesn't run much. He can play all three outfield positions. He is aggressive and has an adequate arm, though his somewhat limited range makes him better suited to the corners.

2003 Outlook

A poor finish last year means Hyzdu once again will find himself on the bubble for a major league job this season, and Japanese teams were showing interest for a second straight year. The Pirates need help in the outfield but have decided Hyzdu is not the answer, except in possibly a limited role.

Pittsburgh

Mike Lincoln

Position: RP
Bats: R **Throws:** R
Ht: 6' 2" **Wt:** 203

Opening Day Age: 27
Born: 4/10/75 in
Carmichael, CA
ML Seasons: 4

Overall Statistics

	W	L	Pct.	ERA	G	GS	Sv	IP	H	BB	SO	HR	Ratio
'02	2	4	.333	3.11	55	0	0	72.1	80	27	50	7	1.48
Car.	7	18	.280	5.15	112	19	0	209.2	252	77	116	31	1.57

2002 Situational Stats

	W	L	ERA	Sv	IP		AB	H	HR	RBI	Avg
Home	1	2	2.59	0	41.2	LHB	87	24	2	9	.276
Road	1	2	3.82	0	30.2	RHB	189	56	5	25	.296
First Half	0	2	2.43	0	33.1	Sc Pos	78	21	2	27	.269
Scnd Half	2	2	3.69	0	39.0	Clutch	60	20	2	11	.333

2002 Season

Mike Lincoln allowed just one run in his first 16.2 innings with the Pirates last season. Still, he was optioned to Triple-A Nashville in the middle of that stretch (May 13) because of a roster crunch. He returned to the minors once more before returning to the Pirates for good in August. He became their primary righthanded middle reliever.

Pitching, Defense & Hitting

Lincoln throws a fastball that reaches 94 MPH and sits in the 91-MPH range. However, he gets hitters out with above-average breaking stuff, throwing both a slider and curveball for strikes on a consistent basis. He tends to tire if used for more than one inning. Lincoln is quick off the mound and has a good pickoff move. He rarely bats, though that's just as well. He struck out in all five plate appearances last season.

2003 Outlook

After going 3-12 with an 8.42 ERA in 19 starts with Minnesota in 1999-2000, Lincoln has found his niche as a middle reliever with the Pirates. His lack of overpowering stuff precludes him from ever closing. But he should carve out a decent career pitching the sixth and seventh innings.

Rob Mackowiak

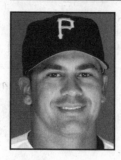

Position: RF/CF/3B
Bats: L **Throws:** R
Ht: 5'10" **Wt:** 190

Opening Day Age: 26
Born: 6/20/76 in Oak
Lawn, IL
ML Seasons: 2
Pronunciation:
mah-KOH-vee-ak

Overall Statistics

	G	AB	R	H	D	T	HR	RBI	SB	BB	SO	Avg	OBP	Slg
'02	136	385	57	94	22	0	16	48	9	42	120	.244	.328	.426
Car.	219	599	87	151	37	2	20	69	13	57	172	.252	.325	.421

2002 Situational Stats

	AB	H	HR	RBI	Avg		AB	H	HR	RBI	Avg
Home	189	49	9	30	.259	LHP	43	13	4	7	.302
Road	196	45	7	18	.230	RHP	342	81	12	41	.237
First Half	222	56	10	27	.252	Sc Pos	98	27	2	29	.276
Scnd Half	163	38	6	21	.233	Clutch	61	13	2	9	.213

2002 Season

Rob Mackowiak proved to be a valuable utility player for the Pirates for a second straight year, as he started 40 games in right field, 37 in center field, 22 at third base and one at second base. Mackowiak also tied for third on the club with 16 homers, after never hitting more than 13 in any of his previous six professional seasons.

Hitting, Baserunning & Defense

Mackowiak has developed good power as he has matured and will murder mediocre fastballs. However, he strikes out far too much and pitchers exploit him by expanding the strike zone. Mackowiak has above-average speed and is particularly adept at taking the extra base. He primarily was an infielder in the minor leagues but quickly has become average at all three outfield spots at the major league level. While he has an outstanding arm and adequate range for the outfield, his infield skills at second and third base are slipping.

2003 Outlook

Mackowiak has power, which is something the Pirates desperately need. Therefore, he figures to get close to 400 at-bats again this season. If he ever could figure out a way to cut down on his swing, he would become a regular.

Abraham Nunez

Position: 2B/SS
Bats: B **Throws:** R
Ht: 5'11" **Wt:** 190

Opening Day Age: 27
Born: 3/16/76 in Santo Domingo, DR
ML Seasons: 6
Pronunciation: NOON-yez

Overall Statistics

	G	AB	R	H	D	T	HR	RBI	SB	BB	SO	Avg	OBP	Slg
'02	112	253	28	59	14	1	2	15	3	27	44	.233	.311	.320
Car.	400	996	102	234	38	7	5	69	25	106	189	.235	.311	.302

2002 Situational Stats

	AB	H	HR	RBI	Avg		AB	H	HR	RBI	Avg
Home	131	30	2	9	.229	LHP	34	6	0	2	.176
Road	122	29	0	6	.238	RHP	219	53	2	13	.242
First Half	158	36	1	10	.228	Sc Pos	43	10	0	12	.233
Scnd Half	95	23	1	5	.242	Clutch	49	14	0	6	.286

2002 Season

Abraham Nunez spent the entire 2002 season, except for a one-week demotion to Triple-A Nashville in May, as one of two Pirates utility infielders (along with Mike Benjamin). Nunez made 37 starts at second base and 15 at shortstop.

Hitting, Baserunning & Defense

Nunez' offensive game is to play small ball by slapping the ball on the ground and bunting. He could stand to gain better plate discipline, however. He has gotten stronger over the years and occasionally can drive the ball into the gap, though his extra-base hits are infrequent. Nunez has good speed and instincts, both of which make him dangerous in basestealing situations and when going from first to third or second to home on a single. He is a solid defensive shortstop with good hands and arm, along with decent range. He isn't quite as comfortable at second base, though he has made strides in turning the double play.

2003 Outlook

Signed for 2003, Nunez will be the Pirates' top utility infielder following the expected departure of Benjamin as a free agent. Nunez once was projected as a starting shortstop, but his talent is a little short to play regularly in the major leagues.

Armando Rios

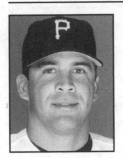

Position: RF/LF
Bats: L **Throws:** L
Ht: 5' 9" **Wt:** 185

Opening Day Age: 31
Born: 9/13/71 in Santurce, PR
ML Seasons: 5

Overall Statistics

	G	AB	R	H	D	T	HR	RBI	SB	BB	SO	Avg	OBP	Slg
'02	76	208	20	55	11	0	1	24	1	16	39	.264	.319	.332
Car.	370	917	131	253	52	8	34	156	14	110	193	.276	.352	.461

2002 Situational Stats

	AB	H	HR	RBI	Avg		AB	H	HR	RBI	Avg
Home	102	25	0	15	.245	LHP	30	9	1	6	.300
Road	106	30	1	9	.283	RHP	178	46	0	18	.258
First Half	109	28	0	9	.257	Sc Pos	63	14	0	22	.222
Scnd Half	99	27	1	15	.273	Clutch	31	8	0	6	.258

2002 Season

Armando Rios began last season as the Pirates' starting left fielder, even though he wasn't fully recovered from the reconstructive left knee surgery he underwent the previous August. He wound up on the disabled list from mid-May through the end of July, and played only semi-regularly the rest of the way. He did hit .404 in his last 26 games.

Hitting, Baserunning & Defense

Rios was able to generate surprising power from his small body in past seasons. But he was rendered a singles hitter in 2002 because of his knee. He tends to get pull-happy and can be jammed. Rios' speed and defense are average. While his ordinary range is more suited to a corner outfield spot, he has played some center field. His arm strength is just average after reconstructive elbow surgery in 2000, though his throws are accurate.

2003 Outlook

The Pirates released Rios in November after deciding they did not want to risk going to a salary arbitration hearing with him. Rios' time with the Pirates was a nightmare, as he blew out his knee in his second game following a July trade in 2001. Rios never has proven he can play regularly and is injury prone.

Scott Sauerbeck

Position: RP
Bats: R **Throws:** L
Ht: 6' 3" **Wt:** 197

Opening Day Age: 31
Born: 11/9/71 in Cincinnati, OH
ML Seasons: 4

Overall Statistics

	W	L	Pct.	ERA	G	GS	Sv	IP	H	BB	SO	HR	Ratio
'02	5	4	.556	2.30	78	0	0	62.2	50	27	70	4	1.23
Car.	16	11	.593	3.48	288	0	5	268.2	240	166	287	18	1.51

2002 Situational Stats

	W	L	ERA	Sv	IP		AB	H	HR	RBI	Avg
Home	5	1	1.21	0	37.1	LHB	95	14	2	9	.147
Road	0	3	3.91	0	25.1	RHB	132	36	2	14	.273
First Half	2	0	2.38	0	34.0	Sc Pos	73	14	0	17	.192
Scnd Half	3	4	2.20	0	28.2	Clutch	126	19	0	8	.151

2002 Season

Scott Sauerbeck was a workhorse as the Pirates' top lefthanded reliever last year. He set the club record for appearances by a lefty with 78, two more than Rod Scurry made in 1982. Sauerbeck also was quite effective, posting a 1.88 ERA in his last 56 games.

Pitching, Defense & Hitting

Sauerbeck is one of the game's premier lefthanded relievers, thanks to a sweeping curveball that ties up lefthanded hitters. He needs to throw his curve for strikes early in the count, because his fastball is only 88 MPH and his slider and change-up are average. However, his curve is so good that he also can be left in the game to face righthanded batters. Although he's a southpaw, Sauerbeck does a poor job holding runners. But he is a good fielder who has committed just one error in four major league seasons. He is 0-for-6 at the plate in his career.

2003 Outlook

Sauerbeck's contract calls for $1.55 million in 2003, and he again will be the Pirates' lefthanded setup man in the bullpen. He also could get an odd save chance on days when closer Mike Williams isn't available. The Pirates like having him and Williams as a late-inning tandem.

Dave Williams

Position: SP
Bats: L **Throws:** L
Ht: 6' 2" **Wt:** 213

Opening Day Age: 24
Born: 3/12/79 in Anchorage, AK
ML Seasons: 2

Overall Statistics

	W	L	Pct.	ERA	G	GS	Sv	IP	H	BB	SO	HR	Ratio
'02	2	5	.286	4.98	9	9	0	43.1	38	24	33	9	1.43
Car.	5	12	.294	4.06	31	27	0	157.1	138	69	90	24	1.32

2002 Situational Stats

	W	L	ERA	Sv	IP		AB	H	HR	RBI	Avg
Home	0	3	3.43	0	21.0	LHB	35	3	0	4	.086
Road	2	2	6.45	0	22.1	RHB	129	35	9	17	.271
First Half	2	5	4.98	0	43.1	Sc Pos	40	8	0	10	.200
Scnd Half	0	0	—	0	0.0	Clutch	2	1	0	0	.500

2002 Season

After going 2-2 with a 3.09 ERA in his first four starts last season, Dave Williams failed to make it through the fifth inning in his next four outings. He was shut down after a May 27 start and underwent season-ending arthroscopic surgery in July to repair a torn labrum.

Pitching, Defense & Hitting

Williams muscled up on his fastball last year, reaching 93 MPH, after usually topping out at 88 MPH as a rookie in 2001. That turned out to be a bad idea. It took movement off the heater and caused his mechanics to get out of whack, which likely led to his shoulder injury. Williams is effective when he mixes his fastball, curveball and changeup. He fields his position well and does a fine job of holding runners on. He can't be taken lightly with the bat, because he can hit for power on occasion.

2003 Outlook

Williams expects to be ready for the start of spring training, though the Pirates will exercise caution. Most likely, he'll begin the season in the minor leagues on an injury rehabilitation assignment. With the Pirates having improved their pitching depth, Williams will have to earn his way back into the rotation once he proves healthy.

Joe Beimel (Pos: LHP, Age: 25)

	W	L	Pct.	ERA	G	GS	Sv	IP	H	BB	SO	HR	Ratio
'02	2	5	.286	4.64	53	8	0	85.1	88	45	53	9	1.56
Car.	9	16	.360	4.98	95	23	0	200.2	219	94	111	21	1.56

Beimel posted a 2.38 ERA in 20 relief appearances in April and May before moving into the rotation and making eight starts in June and July. By year's end, he was being groomed for 2003 setup work. 2003 Outlook: B

Mike Benjamin (Pos: 3B/2B/SS, Age: 37, Bats: R)

	G	AB	R	H	D	T	HR	RBI	SB	BB	SO	Avg	OBP	Slg
'02	108	120	7	18	2	1	0	3	0	7	31	.150	.202	.183
Car.	818	1926	227	442	109	15	24	169	44	106	429	.229	.277	.339

Benjamin missed all of 2001 after Tommy John surgery and barely posted a hitting percentage above .200 in '02, so the Pirates got little out of the two-year extension they gave him in August 2000. 2003 Outlook: C

Mendy Lopez (Pos: 2B, Age: 28, Bats: R)

	G	AB	R	H	D	T	HR	RBI	SB	BB	SO	Avg	OBP	Slg
'02	3	3	0	0	0	0	0	0	0	0	3	.000	.000	.000
Car.	120	290	28	72	13	4	2	25	5	19	69	.248	.299	.341

Lopez got the call when Pokey Reese went on the DL in April. He served as a backup and fanned three times in three at-bats. The Triple-A vet went on to have one of his poorer Triple-A seasons in 2002. He has signed a minor league deal with the Royals, where he has a chance to claim a job. 2003 Outlook: C

Josias Manzanillo (Pos: RHP, Age: 35)

	W	L	Pct.	ERA	G	GS	Sv	IP	H	BB	SO	HR	Ratio
'02	0	0	—	7.62	13	0	0	13.0	20	5	4	5	1.92
Car.	10	10	.500	4.27	232	1	5	299.0	271	134	261	33	1.35

After years of bouncing around, Manzanillo settled into the Pirates' pen in 2000 and had two solid seasons. He had bone chips removed from his elbow in May and was released when he returned and struggled. 2003 Outlook: B

Brian Meadows (Pos: RHP, Age: 27)

	W	L	Pct.	ERA	G	GS	Sv	IP	H	BB	SO	HR	Ratio
'02	1	6	.143	3.88	11	11	0	62.2	62	14	31	7	1.21
Car.	37	50	.425	5.30	116	115	0	662.0	805	193	291	102	1.51

The soft-tossing Meadows frequently has allowed well more than a hit per inning, even in the minors, but his feel for his pitches in 2002 dropped the hit rate at both Triple-A Nashville and Pittsburgh. 2003 Outlook: B

Keith Osik (Pos: C, Age: 34, Bats: R)

	G	AB	R	H	D	T	HR	RBI	SB	BB	SO	Avg	OBP	Slg
'02	55	100	6	16	3	0	2	11	0	6	25	.160	.211	.250
Car.	359	853	74	197	43	4	11	87	6	80	149	.231	.306	.329

Always a part-timer, Osik batted .293 as a rookie in 1996 and then showed three straight years of decline. He batted .293 again in 2000 and has had two years of numeric decline since then. It's your call. 2003 Outlook: C

Al Reyes (Pos: RHP, Age: 31)

	W	L	Pct.	ERA	G	GS	Sv	IP	H	BB	SO	HR	Ratio
'02	0	0	—	2.65	15	0	0	17.0	9	7	21	1	0.94
Car.	15	8	.652	4.12	207	0	3	253.2	216	133	246	32	1.38

Reyes didn't make the Pirates in the spring, but he was lights out at Triple-A Nashville (just 40 hits allowed and 90 K in 66.2 IP) and nearly as good in Pittsburgh. Can he repeat a career year? The Bucs think so, signing him to a one-year deal in December. 2003 Outlook: C

Salomon Torres (Pos: RHP, Age: 31)

	W	L	Pct.	ERA	G	GS	Sv	IP	H	BB	SO	HR	Ratio
'02	2	1	.667	2.70	5	5	0	30.0	28	13	12	2	1.37
Car.	13	26	.333	5.42	73	48	0	313.2	336	161	171	40	1.58

Torres was a top-flight Giants prospect a decade ago, but retired in 1997. He returned in 2002 and showed flashes of his great stuff after a September recall by the Pirates. Torres is a player to watch in the spring. 2003 Outlook: B

Ron Villone (Pos: LHP, Age: 33)

	W	L	Pct.	ERA	G	GS	Sv	IP	H	BB	SO	HR	Ratio
'02	4	6	.400	5.81	45	7	0	93.0	95	34	55	8	1.39
Car.	33	37	.471	5.04	319	64	5	659.0	655	355	498	80	1.53

Despite lots of walks, Villone looked promising after posting a 3.29 ERA in 1996-97 combined. But he has a 5.68 mark from 2000-02. A career 4.40 ERA in relief is OK, but he had a 5.14 ERA as a reliever in '02. 2003 Outlook: C

Pittsburgh

Pittsburgh Pirates Minor League Prospects

Organization Overview:

The Pirates put an emphasis on winning in the minor leagues last season after hiring Brian Graham as their farm director. It is the philosophy of Graham and GM Dave Littlefield that winning and player development go hand in hand. And win the Pirates' six farm clubs did. They went a combined 399-300 (.571), second in baseball to Cleveland's .577. That was a dramatic turn-around for an organization whose farm clubs had combined for one winning season in the previous 33 years. The Pirates also were one of only two organizations, along with the Dodgers, to have each of their six farm teams post winning records. Four of the Pirates' six made the playoffs, with the two full-season Class-A clubs, Lynchburg (Carolina) and Hickory (South Atlantic), capturing league titles.

Tony Alvarez

Position: OF   **Opening Day Age:** 23
Bats: R **Throws:** R   **Born:** 5/10/79 in
Ht: 6' 1" **Wt:** 200   Caracas, VZ

Recent Statistics

	G	AB	R	H	D	T	HR	RBI	SB	BB	SO	Avg
2002 AA Altoona	125	507	79	161	37	1	15	59	29	27	71	.318
2002 NL Pittsburgh	14	26	6	8	2	0	1	2	1	3	5	.308

Alvarez made his first splash in 1999 when he was MVP of the short-season New York-Penn League while with Williamsport. He made a big impression in his first major league camp last spring by going 11-for-23 (.478) in exhibition play. He then had a fine season with Double-A Altoona. Alvarez made the Eastern League postseason All-Star team, as he finished second in the league in batting average and hits, and third in doubles. He received a September callup to the Pirates and performed well, flashing the ability to hit for average while also showing good speed and some power. The Pirates could use a leadoff hitter and center fielder, but prefer Alvarez get some experience at the Triple-A level before he makes a permanent jump to the majors.

Sean Burnett

Position: P   **Opening Day Age:** 20
Bats: L **Throws:** L   **Born:** 9/17/82 in
Ht: 6' 1" **Wt:** 172   Dunedin, FL

Recent Statistics

	W	L	ERA	G	GS	Sv	IP	H	R	BB	SO	HR
2001 A Hickory	11	8	2.62	26	26	0	161.1	164	63	33	134	11
2002 A Lynchburg	13	4	1.80	26	26	0	155.1	118	46	33	96	4

Burnett was the Pirates' first-round pick in 2000, and he's done nothing but mow down hitters since coming into professional baseball. He had his best season yet in 2002, as he was named the high Class-A Carolina League's Pitcher of the Year while helping Lynchburg win the league title. Burnett was second in the league and all of minor league baseball in ERA for a full season, behind Myrtle Beach's Bubba Nelson, and Burnett didn't allow an earned run in five June starts covering 28.1 innings. He primarily has been a finesse pitcher who mixes a Tom Glavine-like changeup with a good curveball. However, Burnett also added a few MPH to his fastball last year and was clocked at 93 in the Futures Game.

Jose Castillo

Position: SS   **Opening Day Age:** 22
Bats: R **Throws:** R   **Born:** 3/19/81 in Las
Ht: 6' 0" **Wt:** 180   Mercedes, VZ

Recent Statistics

	G	AB	R	H	D	T	HR	RBI	SB	BB	SO	Avg
2001 A Lynchburg	125	485	57	119	20	7	7	49	23	21	94	.245
2002 A Lynchburg	134	503	82	151	25	2	16	81	27	49	95	.300

Castillo hopes to follow in a long line of standout Venezuelan shortstops that includes Luis Aparicio, Dave Concepcion, Ozzie Guillen and Omar Vizquel. Castillo has a good blend of offense and defense and was one of the driving forces in high Class-A Lynchburg's run to the Carolina League title last season. He finished third in the league in RBI and flashed good power for a middle infielder, though he needs to continue to refine his strike-zone judgment. While his thick legs cause some scouts to think he eventually will need to move to third base, Castillo has good range at short, along with an outstanding arm. The Pirates presently have no plans of shifting him to another position.

Humberto Cota

Position: C   **Opening Day Age:** 24
Bats: R **Throws:** R   **Born:** 2/7/79 in San Luis
Ht: 6' 0" **Wt:** 205   Rio Colorado, Mexico

Recent Statistics

	G	AB	R	H	D	T	HR	RBI	SB	BB	SO	Avg
2002 AAA Nashville	118	404	51	108	27	1	9	54	5	31	106	.267
2002 NL Pittsburgh	7	17	2	5	1	0	0	0	0	1	4	.294

Cota was the Pirates' Minor League Player of the Year in 2001, when he hit .297 with 14 home runs and 72 RBI for Triple-A Nashville and played in the Futures Game. However, Cota failed to crack the Pirates' major league roster last year with catchers Jason Kendall and Keith Osik entrenched. Cota returned to Nashville and was hitting just .189 on June 12, as he was bothered by a sore right shoulder. However, he heated up once his shoulder healed and wound up having a solid season. Defensively, he blocks balls well and calls a good game, but his throwing is a bit suspect. He likely will be the Pirates' backup catcher in 2003, as Osik became a free agent at the end of last season.

J.J. Davis

Position: OF   **Opening Day Age:** 24
Bats: R **Throws:** R   **Born:** 10/25/78 in
Ht: 6' 5" **Wt:** 250   Glendora, CA

Recent Statistics

	G	AB	R	H	D	T	HR	RBI	SB	BB	SO	Avg
2002 AA Altoona	101	348	51	100	17	3	20	62	7	33	101	.287
2002 NL Pittsburgh	9	10	1	1	0	0	0	0	0	0	4	.100

Davis, the Pirates' first-round draft pick in 1997, looked like a bust in the early part of last season. On May 22, he was hitting only .207 with no homers for Double-A Altoona, while being limited to 10 games because of a sprained ankle. That came after he had hit only .250 with four homers in 67 games for the Curve in 2001, when he continually pestered the Pirates to convert him into a pitcher. He finally became motivated after a talk with Altoona manager Dale Sveum, and Davis finished third in the Eastern League with a .526 slugging percentage. He has outstanding power and athletic ability. He again is considered a top prospect by the Pirates.

Ryan Doumit

Position: C   **Opening Day Age:** 21
Bats: B **Throws:** R   **Born:** 4/3/81 in Moses
Ht: 6' 0" **Wt:** 180   Lake, WA

Recent Statistics

	G	AB	R	H	D	T	HR	RBI	SB	BB	SO	Avg
2001 A Hickory	39	148	14	40	6	0	2	14	2	10	32	.270
2001 R Pirates	7	17	2	4	2	0	0	3	0	2	0	.235
2001 AA Altoona	2	4	0	1	0	0	0	2	0	1	1	.250
2002 A Hickory	68	258	46	83	14	1	6	47	3	18	40	.322

The Pirates have been high on Doumit ever since selecting him in the second round in 1999. He consistently has hit well since entering professional baseball, as his batting average has been better than .281 in three of his four seasons. Doumit's main problem has been injuries. He was limited to 46 games because of a strained back in 2001, then appeared in only 68 contests at Class-A Hickory last season due to a broken pinky. The Pirates believe he can turn into a rarity—a switch-hitting catcher with power. However, he needs to stay on the field to develop his high-ceiling potential.

Duaner Sanchez

Position: P   **Opening Day Age:** 23
Bats: R **Throws:** R   **Born:** 10/14/79 in Cotui,
Ht: 6' 0" **Wt:** 160   DR

Recent Statistics

	W	L	ERA	G	GS	Sv	IP	H	R	BB	SO	HR
2002 AA El Paso	4	3	3.03	31	0	13	35.2	31	16	13	37	1
2002 NL Arizona	0	0	4.91	6	0	0	3.2	3	2	5	4	1
2002 AAA Tucson	1	1	6.75	4	0	1	5.1	6	4	1	9	1
2002 AAA Nashville	0	3	4.76	20	0	6	22.2	23	12	11	20	2
2002 NL Pittsburgh	0	0	15.43	3	0	0	2.1	3	4	2	1	1

Sanchez was one of the biggest revelations in minor league baseball last season. His fastball clocked as high as 103 MPH after Arizona converted him from a start-ing pitcher into a reliever in spring training. He was dominant at times at Double-A El Paso, before the Diamondbacks traded him to the Pirates on July 6 for veteran reliever Mike Fetters. Sanchez struggled some with Triple-A Nashville after the trade and in a September trial with the Pirates. However, the Pirates like how he seems to have no fear and possesses a fast-ball-curveball combination that could make him a dominant closer with more experience. He will contend for a middle relief role with the Pirates in spring training.

John VanBenschoten

Position: P   **Opening Day Age:** 22
Bats: R **Throws:** R   **Born:** 4/14/80 in San
Ht: 6' 4" **Wt:** 215   Diego, CA

Recent Statistics

	W	L	ERA	G	GS	Sv	IP	H	R	BB	SO	HR
2001 A Williamsprt	0	2	3.51	9	9	0	25.2	23	11	10	19	0
2002 A Hickory	11	4	2.80	27	27	0	148.0	119	57	62	145	6

The Pirates raised plenty of eyebrows in 2001 when they used their first-round draft pick to select VanBenschoten as a pitcher, even though he led NCAA Division I with 31 home runs as a first baseman for Kent State that spring. The Pirates are having the last laugh because VanBenschoten, who also served as the Golden Flashes' closer in college, is emerging as a premier starting pitching prospect. He has a 95-MPH fastball with good movement, along with an above-average curveball and developing changeup. The Pirates have slowed down the development path of many of their prospects recently, but VanBenschoten look like he could get to the major leagues in a hurry.

Others to Watch

Righthander **Bobby Bradley** (22) missed all of last season after undergoing reconstructive elbow surgery in October, 2001. Considered the organization's best pitching prospect before the operation, he was impressive in Florida Instructional League play last fall and should be ready to pitch for high Class-A Lynchburg by the start of this season. . . First baseman **Carlos Rivera** (24) hit 22 homers last season for Double-A Altoona, the best mark of his seven-year career. He was placed on the 40-man roster in October. The slick-fielding Rivera also had a .302 batting average and 84 RBI. . . Righthander **Ryan Vogelsong** (25) was acquired from San Francisco in a trade in July 2001. He was on his way to a spot in the major league rotation until needing reconstructive elbow surgery two months later. He struggled in his comeback last year, going a combined 2-6 with a 6.22 ERA in 12 starts with high Class-A Lynchburg and Double-A Altoona. . . First baseman **Walter Young** (23), a 6-foot-5, 296-pounder who signed to play the defensive line at LSU, had a breakthrough year at Class-A Hickory. He was named the South Atlantic League MVP. He needs work on his defense, and the Pirates would like him to lose weight, but his power potential is intriguing.

Busch Stadium

Offense

Busch Stadium has few quirks. It has reachable power alleys, average-height walls, a well-groomed infield surface, and rarely is subject to extreme wind conditions. As a result, it plays as honestly as any ballpark. Power teams aren't penalized by the dimensions. And speed teams can take advantage of the outfield gaps.

Defense

The Cards have good personnel for their fast but true infield. Three of their four infielders won Gold Gloves in 2002. The exception, first baseman Tino Martinez, is one of the best at his position, too. The outfield requires speed and good arms in center and right, something the Cardinals have in Jim Edmonds and J.D. Drew.

Who It Helps the Most

Scott Rolen should blossom in St. Louis, not so much because of the ballpark but because of the supportive atmosphere created by the Cardinals fans. In his first year with St. Louis, Martinez hit .290 at home, but only .236 on the road. Dave Veres compiled a 5-2 record and 1.94 ERA at home last season, compared to 0-6 and a 5.45 ERA away from Busch.

Who It Hurts the Most

Busch Stadium has negative impact on few players, though the knowledgeable fans are quick to turn on players perceived as disappointments. A year after going 15-2 with a 1.62 ERA at home, Matt Morris was more effective on the road last season. The summer heat tends to drain some players, which makes having a deep bench a necessity for the Cardinals.

Rookies & Newcomers

Rolen immediately was embraced by Cards fans, and his personality is made to order for St. Louis. Chuck Finley also fit in well after a long career in the American League. St. Louis and its fans are major selling points for the Cardinals when they seek to acquire players. The homefield advantage figures to only improve when the new ballpark becomes a reality in what is expected to be three years.

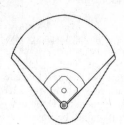

Dimensions: LF-330, LCF-372, CF-402, RCF-372, RF-330

Capacity: 49,814

Elevation: 535 feet

Surface: Grass

Foul Territory: Large

Park Factors

2002 Season

	Home Games			Away Games			
	Cardinals	Opp	Total	Cardinals	Opp	Total	Index
G	75	75	150	75	75	150	
Avg	.265	.242	.253	.268	.263	.266	95
AB	2495	2568	5063	2615	2442	5057	100
R	362	273	635	365	333	698	91
H	661	622	1283	702	643	1345	95
2B	126	134	260	136	117	253	103
3B	8	1	9	17	10	27	33
HR	80	63	143	81	68	149	96
BB	276	259	535	231	260	491	109
SO	439	500	939	440	443	883	106
E	43	53	96	49	52	101	95
E-Infield	34	49	83	38	46	84	99
LHB-Avg	.275	.244	.260	.267	.255	.261	99
LHB-HR	37	22	59	30	29	59	101
RHB-Avg	.258	.241	.249	.270	.268	.269	93
RHB-HR	43	41	84	51	39	90	93

2000-2002

	Home Games			Away Games			
	Cardinals	Opp	Total	Cardinals	Opp	Total	Index
G	223	223	446	221	221	442	
Avg	.274	.247	.260	.265	.265	.265	98
AB	7347	7571	14918	7685	7260	14945	99
R	1173	924	2097	1115	998	2113	98
H	2010	1869	3879	2037	1923	3960	97
2B	362	395	757	398	389	787	96
3B	39	22	61	39	34	73	84
HR	289	248	537	271	244	515	104
BB	859	807	1666	754	744	1498	111
SO	1445	1577	3022	1571	1346	2917	104
E	144	169	313	150	154	304	102
E-Infield	114	131	245	112	135	247	98
LHB-Avg	.284	.251	.268	.280	.262	.271	99
LHB-HR	138	97	235	115	103	218	112
RHB-Avg	.267	.244	.255	.255	.267	.261	98
RHB-HR	151	151	302	156	141	297	99

2002 Rankings (National League)

- Third-highest walk factor
- Lowest triple factor
- Second-lowest RHB batting-average factor

Tony La Russa

2002 Season

Tony La Russa never stood taller as a man and as a manager. He was battered emotionally last year, first by the death of his father and then by the deaths of broadcaster Jack Buck and pitcher Darryl Kile. La Russa also had to cope with a steady stream of injuries. All the while, he refused to publicly bend under the strain and was a source of strength for his players, as he kept them focused all the way to the National League Championship Series. He clearly deserved his fourth Manager of the Year Award.

Offense

Befitting a future Hall of Famer, La Russa adapts his style to his personnel. Without much speed up and down his lineup, the Cardinals were in the middle of the league in stolen base attempts, though La Russa led NL managers in the number of hit-and-run plays used. He is a master at picking spots to keep his bench players sharp and got a lot of mileage out of people like Miguel Cairo, Eduardo Perez and Eli Marrero.

Pitching & Defense

St. Louis always carries at least 12 pitchers because La Russa uses his bullpen for matchups as well as any manager. He and pitching coach Dave Duncan had to use all their wisdom in a season when they were forced to use 14 different starting pitchers. La Russa formed distinct roles in his bullpen with the arrival of proven closer Jason Isringhausen. Defensively, the Cards won four Gold Gloves, a credit to the players' ability and also to the meticulous positioning done by La Russa and his coaches.

2003 Outlook

La Russa hasn't lost anything in terms of intensity or leadership. He now has a clubhouse full of players with excellent rapport and work ethic. Many around baseball quietly rooted for La Russa to get to the World Series last year. He should have another chance to go the distance this season, with a club that is loaded at most positions and a front office always willing to acquire needed reinforcements.

Born: 10/04/44 in Tampa, FL

Playing Experience: 1963-1973, KC, Oak, Atl, ChC

Managerial Experience: 24 seasons

Manager Statistics

Year	Team, Lg	W	L	Pct	GB	Finish
2002	St. Louis, NL	97	65	.599	–	1st Central
24 Seasons		1924	1712	.529	–	–

2002 Starting Pitchers by Days Rest

	<=3	4	5	6+
Cardinals Starts	0	88	34	28
Cardinals ERA	–	4.12	4.14	3.09
NL Avg Starts	1	88	42	21
NL ERA	3.18	4.22	4.14	4.58

2002 Situational Stats

	Tony La Russa	NL Average
Hit & Run Success %	43.5	36.5
Stolen Base Success %	67.2	68.3
Platoon Pct.	49.4	52.7
Defensive Subs	15	19
High-Pitch Outings	5	7
Quick/Slow Hooks	33/9	24/11
Sacrifice Attempts	108	95

2002 Rankings (National League)

- 1st in steals of home plate (2) and hit-and-run attempts (124)
- 2nd in sacrifice-bunt percentage (85.2%), squeeze plays (13), pinch-hitters used (300), quick hooks, relief appearances (472) and 2+ pitching changes in low-scoring games (46)
- 3rd in fewest caught stealings of second base (29), sacrifice bunt attempts, hit-and-run success percentage and one-batter pitcher appearances (43)

St. Louis

J.D. Drew

2002 Season

St. Louis spent another frustrating year waiting for J.D. Drew to emerge. He was slowed all season by a tender right knee, which limited him to only 135 games and at times reduced him to a platoon role. His batting average dropped more than 70 points from 2001, and his power numbers were down significantly. He underwent surgery after the season to remove a tendon from the ailing knee.

Hitting

His weak knee was a factor in the drop-off in Drew's power. However, he also went backward as a hitter. His strikeouts rose at an alarming rate, as he consistently was overpowered by hard stuff and also went out of the strike zone to chase breaking stuff. He was tentative in making adjustments, became impatient and swung at bad pitches too often. At his best, Drew can hit the ball with power to all fields. But he has yet to prove he consistently can stay in a groove for an extended period. For someone so athletic, he also has produced remarkably few doubles.

Baserunning & Defense

Drew clearly was not at his best last year, when he attempted only 10 steals. If healthy, he has excellent speed and excellent baserunning instincts. Also when healthy, he has the ability to play anywhere in the outfield, though he now is set in right, where his arm is outstanding and his range is exceptional.

2003 Outlook

This is a crossroads season for Drew and the Cardinals. Stardom has been predicted for him ever since he was a high-profile draft selection in 1998. However, he has shown only flashes of putting together his exceptional tools. Now eligible for arbitration, Drew is becoming increasingly expensive. The Cardinals have sent signals that they won't wait much longer for him to realize his potential. He's expected to be slowed until May, and possibly longer, as he recovers from his knee surgery. When he does return, it could become a put up or shut up season for Drew.

Position: RF
Bats: L **Throws:** R
Ht: 6' 1" **Wt:** 195

Opening Day Age: 27
Born: 11/20/75 in Valdosta, GA
ML Seasons: 5

Overall Statistics

	G	AB	R	H	D	T	HR	RBI	SB	BB	SO	Avg	OBP	Slg
'02	135	424	61	107	19	1	18	56	8	57	104	.252	.349	.429
Car.	497	1610	295	452	73	15	81	238	57	235	365	.281	.378	.496

Where He Hits the Ball

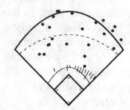 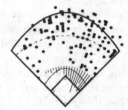

Vs. LHP	Vs. RHP

2002 Situational Stats

	AB	H	HR	RBI	Avg		AB	H	HR	RBI	Avg
Home	209	47	9	28	.225	LHP	84	22	3	13	.262
Road	215	60	9	28	.279	RHP	340	85	15	43	.250
First Half	261	69	11	34	.264	Sc Pos	105	27	5	40	.257
Scnd Half	163	38	7	22	.233	Clutch	62	17	4	7	.274

2002 Rankings (National League)

- 3rd in fielding percentage in right field (.987)
- 6th in fewest GDPs per GDP situation (4.5%) and lowest batting average with the bases loaded (.100)

Jim Edmonds

2002 Season

Though his power and RBI numbers fell, Jim Edmonds had another solid year as St. Louis' center fielder. He was at his best in the first two months of the season, when he largely carried the Cardinals' lineup. A wrist injury slowed him for much of June. But his final batting average of .311 represented a career high. He reached 25 homers for the seventh time and topped a .400 on-base percentage for the third straight season with St. Louis. Edmonds also enjoyed another Gold Glove year in center field.

Hitting

Edmonds will have streaks in which his bat speed seems to slow. He'll pile up strikeouts, often falling victim to the high strikes that can eat up his big swing. However, since coming to St. Louis, Edmonds has become a much more disciplined hitter who has greatly improved his walk totals and become more selective. His opposite-field power is as dangerous as any lefthanded hitter in the league not named Bonds. Edmonds also has proved to be a good big-game hitter in the pennant race and postseason.

Baserunning & Defense

For such a talented player, Edmonds often has baserunning lapses and is a poor percentage basestealer. He occasionally will misjudge his batted balls and not run hard out of the box. But there are few better outfielders. Some observers suspect Edmonds will "style his way" at times to make catches look tougher than they really are. Still, his range is outstanding and nobody makes more diving catches or goes back better on balls. He also has a quick, accurate arm, which helps him rank among the outfield assist leaders every year.

2003 Outlook

Some detractors have surfaced among the Cardinals, who get turned off by Edmonds' cocky attitude. Overall, however, he's settled in as one of the team's core performers. Signed for three more years, he should remain one of the league's best middle-of-the-lineup players.

Position: CF
Bats: L **Throws:** L
Ht: 6' 1" **Wt:** 212

Opening Day Age: 32
Born: 6/27/70 in Fullerton, CA
ML Seasons: 10
Pronunciation: ED-muns

Overall Statistics

	G	AB	R	H	D	T	HR	RBI	SB	BB	SO	Avg	OBP	Slg
'02	144	476	96	148	31	2	28	83	4	86	134	.311	.420	.561
Car.	1155	4145	784	1223	255	15	221	709	45	556	995	.295	.380	.524

Where He Hits the Ball

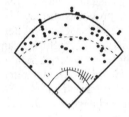
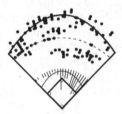

Vs. LHP **Vs. RHP**

2002 Situational Stats

	AB	H	HR	RBI	Avg		AB	H	HR	RBI	Avg
Home	229	70	17	44	.306	LHP	130	34	7	23	.262
Road	247	78	11	39	.316	RHP	346	114	21	60	.329
First Half	229	72	17	44	.314	Sc Pos	122	34	7	52	.279
Scnd Half	247	76	11	39	.308	Clutch	58	11	1	9	.190

2002 Rankings (National League)

- 1st in assists in center field (11)
- 3rd in on-base percentage vs. righthanded pitchers (.443) and errors in center field (5)
- 4th in batting average vs. righthanded pitchers and lowest fielding percentage in center field (.986)
- Led the Cardinals in walks, intentional walks (14), strikeouts, on-base percentage, HR frequency (17.0 ABs per HR), most pitches seen per plate appearance (3.98), cleanup slugging percentage (.583), slugging percentage vs. righthanded pitchers (.592) and batting average at home
- Led NL center fielders in batting average

St. Louis

Chuck Finley

2002 Season

Chuck Finley was everything the Cards could have hoped for after they obtained him in a trade with Cleveland last July 19. Poor run support contributed to his poor record with the Indians, and he had to deal with some distracting off-field issues. But Finley provided needed stability to St. Louis' battered starting rotation, averaging six innings in his 14 starts with the team. The Cardinals won nine of those games, as well as both of his starts in the postseason.

Pitching

He may have turned 40 years of age and logged over 3,000 career innings in the majors, but Finley still can get his fastball consistently into the low 90s. Recovered from neck problems, Finley last year regained the good bite to his great splitter, which always has been his money pitch. He can throw the split at varying speeds, occasionally mixing in a curve as well. He remains a high pitch count and strikeout type of pitcher. But with St. Louis, he started using more changeups and sinking fastballs to induce grounders.

Defense & Hitting

Finley never has been a reliable fielder because of his motion. However, he does a good job of holding runners and usually gives his catchers a reasonable chance to nab thieves. An American Leaguer for 16 years before last season, he isn't a threat at the plate. However, he can bunt if the situation calls for it.

2003 Outlook

St. Louis pursued its free agent and offered salary arbitration, and during the winter meetings in December, Finley and the Cards came close to signing a one-year deal. He would be a key addition to the Cardinals' core of Matt Morris, Woody Williams and Jason Simontacchi. Finley not only pitched well for St. Louis, but also was an outstanding addition to the Redbirds' cohesive and professional clubhouse. But his destination is still up in the air for 2003.

Position: SP
Bats: L **Throws:** L
Ht: 6' 6" **Wt:** 226

Opening Day Age: 40
Born: 11/26/62 in Monroe, LA
ML Seasons: 17
Pronunciation: FIN-lee

Overall Statistics

W	L	Pct.	ERA	G	GS	Sv	IP	H	BB	SO	HR	Ratio
11	15	.423	4.15	32	32	0	190.2	183	78	174	13	1.37
200	173	.536	3.85	524	467	0	3197.1	3069	1332	2610	304	1.38

How Often He Throws Strikes

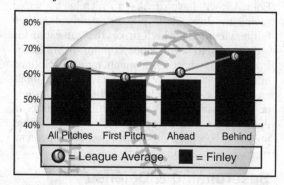

= League Average   = Finley

2002 Situational Stats

	W	L	ERA	Sv	IP		AB	H	HR	RBI	Avg
Home	8	5	4.01	0	92.0	LHB	122	22	1	14	.180
Road	3	10	4.29	0	98.2	RHB	595	161	12	70	.271
First Half	4	11	3.97	0	102.0	Sc Pos	177	45	3	69	.254
Scnd Half	7	4	4.36	0	88.2	Clutch	21	8	1	3	.381

2002 Rankings (National League)

- Did not rank near the top or bottom in any category

Jason Isringhausen

Position: RP
Bats: R **Throws:** R
Ht: 6' 3" **Wt:** 230

Opening Day Age: 30
Born: 9/7/72 in
Brighton, IL
ML Seasons: 7
Pronunciation:
IS-ring-how-zin
Nickname: Izzy

2002 Season

A native of downstate Illinois, Jason Isringhausen had a homecoming of sorts when he signed with the Cardinals as a free agent last December. He then converted 32 of 37 save opportunities in what was a mixed first season with St. Louis. He tied a record with 12 saves in May and didn't allow a home run all year. He also posted an excellent strikeout-walk ratio. However, recurring arm problems caused him to be shut down for extensive periods twice during the season's second half.

Pitching

Isringhausen is tough to beat when he has command of his fastball. He brings it in the 94-97 MPH range, mixing in a late-moving cutter and occasional curve. He is deadly on righthanded batters with his hard stuff. He gets in trouble when he loses the strike zone and occasionally will unravel in such situations, unable to make adjustments. Isringhausen also irritated management by not being forthcoming about his arm troubles, a communications problem that often made his availability uncertain during the last several weeks of 2002.

Defense & Hitting

Isringhausen is a big power pitcher who doesn't worry about getting into fielding position. As a result, he is very awkward when required to make a play, and he committed two errors in only 11 chances last year. He also is very easy to run on for opposing basestealers. Over the past four seasons, they are 36-for-39 when stealing with Isringhausen on the mound. He hasn't had an at-bat since 1999, but exhibited a fairly effective swing when he was with the Mets.

2003 Outlook

The Cardinals ended last year concerned about Isringhausen's durability. They stressed to him the need for better offseason conditioning. Surgery in October may leave him a little behind this spring, but it isn't expected to sideline him for long. Tied up for at least three more years on a multiyear contract, he is firmly entrenched as the St. Louis closer. And with better physical preparation and maturity, he could move into the 40-save echelon.

Overall Statistics

	W	L	Pct.	ERA	G	GS	Sv	IP	H	BB	SO	HR	Ratio
'02	3	2	.600	2.48	60	0	32	65.1	46	18	68	0	0.98
Car.	31	31	.500	3.94	271	52	108	564.2	549	233	444	42	1.38

How Often He Throws Strikes

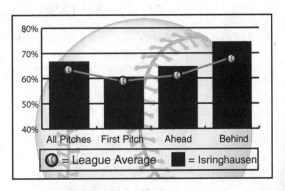

2002 Situational Stats

	W	L	ERA	Sv	IP		AB	H	HR	RBI	Avg
Home	3	2	3.18	15	39.2	LHB	97	24	0	11	.247
Road	0	0	1.40	17	25.2	RHB	134	22	0	7	.164
First Half	2	1	2.57	19	42.0	Sc Pos	55	11	0	17	.200
Scnd Half	1	1	2.31	13	23.1	Clutch	156	31	0	15	.199

2002 Rankings (National League)

- 4th in fewest baserunners allowed per nine innings in relief (9.0)
- 8th in save percentage (86.5)
- Led the Cardinals in saves, games finished (51), save opportunities (37), lowest batting average allowed vs. righthanded batters, save percentage (86.5), blown saves (5), lowest batting average allowed in relief (.199) and most strikeouts per nine innings in relief (9.4)

Eli Marrero

2002 Season

Eli Marrero had a breakout season in 2002. He established career highs in virtually every offensive category, perhaps most impressively driving in 66 runs—nearly twice his previous high. He added to his value by proving his ability to play any outfield position, as well as catch and play first base. He and Craig Biggio (1990) are the only players in the past 15 years to play at least 10 games at catcher and in center field in the same season.

Hitting

It was only two years ago that Marrero's confidence was so low that the Cardinals seriously considered releasing him. However, he has worked to transform himself as a hitter, and the effort has started to pay off. Marrero added a dozen pounds of muscle, while slightly opening his stance and shortening his stroke. Those changes combined to make him a more dangerous hitter, helping him to turn more consistently on inside pitches. The result was that Marrero exploded for 18 home runs in 2002, three times more than his previous high. As his confidence grew, he also improved as a clutch hitter, batting nearly .300 with runners in scoring position.

Baserunning & Defense

One of Marrero's greatest assets always has been speed that is exceptional for a catcher. He is an outstanding baserunner who last year stole 14 bases in 16 attempts. Marrero has fluid catching skills and an above-average arm. However, his immediate future with St. Louis could see him spending more time in the outfield, where he has developed good range and where his arm is an asset. Marrero also can play a serviceable first base.

2003 Outlook

Marrero's stock rose significantly last season. The Cardinals now view him as a real alternative in the outfield should they consider trading J.D. Drew or end up shifting Albert Pujols to first base. Marrero's ability to catch provides St. Louis with outstanding depth, and Tony La Russa considers him the best athlete on the club.

Position: RF/C/LF/CF
Bats: R **Throws:** R
Ht: 6' 1" **Wt:** 180

Opening Day Age: 29
Born: 11/17/73 in Havana, Cuba
ML Seasons: 6
Pronunciation: muh-RARE-oh

Overall Statistics

	G	AB	R	H	D	T	HR	RBI	SB	BB	SO	Avg	OBP	Slg
'02	131	397	63	104	19	1	18	66	14	40	72	.262	.327	.451
Car.	484	1318	185	315	66	7	41	167	46	112	235	.239	.298	.393

Where He Hits the Ball

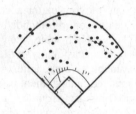 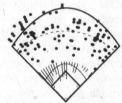

Vs. LHP   **Vs. RHP**

2002 Situational Stats

	AB	H	HR	RBI	Avg		AB	H	HR	RBI	Avg
Home	193	52	9	30	.269	LHP	97	22	1	19	.227
Road	204	52	9	36	.255	RHP	300	82	17	47	.273
First Half	211	56	8	34	.265	Sc Pos	95	28	5	50	.295
Scnd Half	186	48	10	32	.258	Clutch	69	21	5	11	.304

2002 Rankings (National League)

- Led the Cardinals in stolen-base percentage (87.5), batting average in the clutch, batting average on a 3-1 count (.556) and highest percentage of extra bases taken as a runner (69.0)

Tino Martinez

2002 Season

With Mark McGwire retiring after the 2001 season, the Cardinals signed first baseman Tino Martinez to a three-year contract. But Martinez struggled during much of his first year in the National League. He hit only .248 in the first half and needed a late surge over his final 50 games to get himself over 20 home runs and above the .260 mark overall. He finished on a down note with a very quiet playoff performance, in what was his eighth straight postseason appearance.

Hitting

The more aggressive style of pitching in the NL gave Martinez trouble. Always vulnerable to high fastballs, he was handled with hard stuff inside. He fell into the habit of falling off pitches, which made him vulnerable to breaking stuff away. Martinez' performance also deteriorated against lefthanded pitching. By the last two months he often sat against tough southpaws. The Cardinals also were disappointed with his so-so production with men in scoring position.

Baserunning & Defense

Though a very slow runner, Martinez usually uses good judgment on the bases and reads the ball well when trying to take the extra base. He is one of the game's most underrated first basemen, with good range and very good hands. His ability to pick throws out of the dirt was a huge upgrade over McGwire and contributed to making the Cards'.infield defense one of the best in baseball.

2003 Outlook

Privately, Cardinals officials were disappointed with Martinez. However, he's signed for at least two more years to an expensive and largely immovable contract, so he's not going anywhere. St. Louis hopes he'll be more productive now that he's had a year of National League experience under his belt. But Martinez is at an age when bat speed begins to slip, and the Cardinals won't be satisfied with another season of tepid production from what is supposed to be a power position.

Position: 1B
Bats: L **Throws:** R
Ht: 6' 2" **Wt:** 210

Opening Day Age: 35
Born: 12/7/67 in Tampa, FL
ML Seasons: 13

Overall Statistics

	G	AB	R	H	D	T	HR	RBI	SB	BB	SO	Avg	OBP	Slg
'02	150	511	63	134	25	1	21	75	3	58	71	.262	.337	.438
Car.	1616	5874	836	1602	311	18	284	1077	21	623	872	.273	.343	.477

Where He Hits the Ball

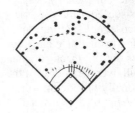 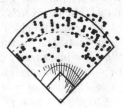

Vs. LHP   **Vs. RHP**

2002 Situational Stats

	AB	H	HR	RBI	Avg		AB	H	HR	RBI	Avg
Home	248	72	12	40	.290	LHP	111	23	4	12	.207
Road	263	62	9	35	.236	RHP	400	111	17	63	.278
First Half	266	66	10	43	.248	Sc Pos	134	33	4	53	.246
Scnd Half	245	68	11	32	.278	Clutch	65	13	1	6	.200

2002 Rankings (National League)

- 2nd in fielding percentage at first base (.996)
- 7th in assists at first base (86) and lowest batting average vs. lefthanded pitchers
- 9th in lowest batting average on the road
- Led the Cardinals in lowest percentage of swings on the first pitch (24.0)

Matt Morris

2002 Season

For Matt Morris, last season was the most difficult of his life. Darryl Kile had served as a role model for Morris, and Matt was as close to Kile as anyone on the Cardinals. Morris struggled to regain his focus after Kile's sudden death. He also had to cope with a late-season hamstring injury that limited his effectiveness in September. The fact that Morris still won 17 games is a credit to his great ability.

Pitching

Morris' stuff is as good as any righthander's in the National League. His velocity sits in the mid-90s and he has improved his changeup to the point where it is another reliable out pitch. Always a flyball pitcher, Morris has started using the assets of his great infield defense and getting more groundouts with his sinking fastball. He has trouble when his delivery gets out of whack or when he starts leaving his fastball over the middle of the plate. He also can occasionally fall victim to trying to use too many different pitches instead of going right at the batter to put him away. Morris' command usually is excellent and he is equally tough on right- and lefthanded hitters.

Defense & Hitting

Morris is slow coming home and his stuff suffers when he tries to use a slide step, which is why he remains vulnerable to the stolen base. He allowed twice as many steals as any other hurler on the Cardinals' staff last season. He fields his position very well and has worked to make himself useful with the bat.

2003 Outlook

Morris obviously was drained by the end of the emotional 2002 season. But one of his greatest assets is his mental toughness. He clearly is one of the game's best pitchers. He is just entering his prime and should flirt with 20 wins per season for the foreseeable future.

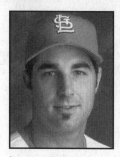

Position: SP
Bats: R **Throws:** R
Ht: 6' 5" **Wt:** 210

Opening Day Age: 28
Born: 8/9/74 in Middletown, NY
ML Seasons: 5

Overall Statistics

	W	L	Pct.	ERA	G	GS	Sv	IP	H	BB	SO	HR	Ratio
'02	17	9	.654	3.42	32	32	0	210.1	210	64	171	16	1.30
Car.	61	34	.642	3.18	147	116	4	810.1	790	246	618	52	1.28

How Often He Throws Strikes

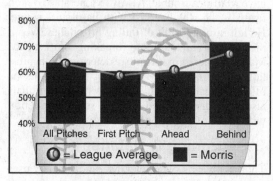

O = League Average   ■ = Morris

2002 Situational Stats

	W	L	ERA	Sv	IP		AB	H	HR	RBI	Avg
Home	8	5	3.82	0	117.2	LHB	374	100	11	49	.267
Road	9	4	2.91	0	92.2	RHB	431	110	5	37	.255
First Half	10	6	3.55	0	126.2	Sc Pos	187	50	2	62	.267
Scnd Half	7	3	3.23	0	83.2	Clutch	43	6	0	2	.140

2002 Rankings (National League)

- 1st in fielding percentage at pitcher (1.000)
- 6th in wins
- Led the Cardinals in wins, losses, games started, innings pitched, hits allowed, batters faced (890), walks allowed, strikeouts, pitches thrown (3,206), stolen bases allowed (18), GDPs induced (22), highest groundball-flyball ratio allowed (1.6), fewest pitches thrown per batter (3.60), most run support per nine innings (5.3), fewest home runs allowed per nine innings (.68), most GDPs induced per nine innings (0.9) and most strikeouts per nine innings (7.3)

Albert Pujols

2002 Season

Albert Pujols shrugged off any hint of a sopho-more jinx. In a league without Barry Bonds, he might have been the National League's Most Valuable Player. Pujols led the Cardinals for a second straight year in most major offensive cate-gories. He made history by being the first player ever to bat at least .300 with 30 homers, 100 RBI and 100 runs scored in each of his first two major league seasons.

Hitting

What's so impressive about Pujols is that after two years, the league hasn't found a way to get him out. He makes adjustments remarkably well. For example, he was hitting around .280 through the first three months last season, when NL pitch-ers seemed to have found a hole with inside fast-balls. But Pujols proceeded to hit .335 with a league-leading 61 RBI after the All-Star break. He waits well on pitches and is strong to all fields. He is selective, reducing his strikeouts and increasing his walks last year. He also is deadly in the clutch, ranking high in 2002 with a .340 average with men in scoring position.

Baserunning & Defense

One weapon not in Pujols' arsenal is running abil-ity. He doesn't have great speed, though he usual-ly is smart about the chances he takes on the bases. With the arrival of third baseman Scott Rolen, Pujols' position for now is left field, where his range is average and his arm is accurate. He also has shown he can play first base adequately.

2003 Outlook

At the ripe age of 23, Pujols has established him-self as one of the game's best players. Not only does he show no weakness as a hitter, he also has impressed with his grounded personality and great work ethic. He is the model of what a fran-chise player should be. One of the Cardinals' next projects will be to sign him to a long-term deal that will keep him in the middle of their lineup for the next decade.

Position: LF/3B/1B
Bats: R **Throws:** R
Ht: 6' 3" **Wt:** 210

Opening Day Age: 23
Born: 1/16/80 in Santo Domingo, DR
ML Seasons: 2
Pronunciation: POO-holes

Overall Statistics

	G	AB	R	H	D	T	HR	RBI	SB	BB	SO	Avg	OBP	Slg
'02	157	590	118	185	40	2	34	127	2	72	69	.314	.394	.561
Car.	318	1180	230	379	87	6	71	257	3	141	162	.321	.399	.586

Where He Hits the Ball

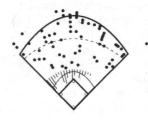
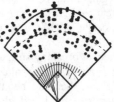

Vs. LHP   **Vs. RHP**

2002 Situational Stats

	AB	H	HR	RBI	Avg		AB	H	HR	RBI	Avg
Home	281	80	14	68	.285	LHP	152	47	8	32	.309
Road	309	105	20	59	.340	RHP	438	138	26	95	.315
First Half	309	91	21	66	.294	Sc Pos	156	53	16	98	.340
Scnd Half	281	94	13	61	.335	Clutch	63	13	1	7	.206

2002 Rankings (National League)

- 2nd in runs scored, RBI, batting average with the bases loaded (.538) and batting average on the road
- 4th in hits, total bases (331) and batting aver-age with two strikes (.272)
- Led the Cardinals in batting average, home runs, runs scored, hits, RBI, doubles, times on base (266), GDPs (20), pitches seen (2,524), games played, slugging percentage, highest percentage of pitches taken (58.3), batting average on an 0-2 count (.273), on-base per-centage vs. lefthanded pitchers (.391) and batting average on a 3-2 count (.343)

St. Louis

Edgar Renteria

2002 Season

No Cardinals player elevated his game more significantly than Edgar Renteria last year. He hit better than .300 for the first time since his rookie year in 1996, tied an 80-year-old club record for RBI by a shortstop, led the Cardinals in stolen bases and was among baseball's best hitters with runners in scoring position. He was terrific in July, hitting better than .400. For good measure, Renteria had an outstanding defensive season and earned the first Gold Glove of his career.

Hitting

Renteria added several pounds of muscle and it showed. He hit consistently all season and regained the extra-base punch that disappeared a year ago. He shortened his stroke and stayed back more on pitches, which allowed him to deal better with hard stuff. He also has improved greatly against breaking stuff while at the same time cutting down on his strikeouts. Renteria is difficult to defense because he hits for extra bases to the opposite field and also pulls pitches for home runs.

Baserunning & Defense

With good speed and even better baserunning instincts, Renteria is a solid basestealer who knows how to pick his spots to run. He shows good judgment in taking the extra base. He has sure hands, a great arm and has learned to position hitters well. He still will have occasional lapses and make careless errors in bunches, but those lapses have become increasingly few and far between.

2003 Outlook

Because he arrived in the majors at such a young age, it's surprising to realize that Renteria is only 27 years old and just reaching his physical prime. If last year is any indication, he is ready to firmly establish himself as one of the best shortstops in the game. He may not be at the Alex Rodriguez or Miguel Tejada level, but Renteria certainly is as good as any shortstop in the National League.

Position: SS
Bats: R **Throws:** R
Ht: 6' 1"   **Wt:** 180

Opening Day Age: 27
Born: 8/7/75 in Barranquilla, Colombia
ML Seasons: 7
Pronunciation: ren-ter-REE-uh

Overall Statistics

	G	AB	R	H	D	T	HR	RBI	SB	BB	SO	Avg	OBP	Slg
'02	152	544	77	166	36	2	11	83	22	49	57	.305	.364	.439
Car.	990	3749	554	1061	180	16	60	393	186	330	543	.283	.341	.388

Where He Hits the Ball

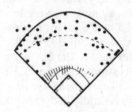 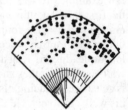

Vs. LHP   **Vs. RHP**

2002 Situational Stats

	AB	H	HR	RBI	Avg		AB	H	HR	RBI	Avg
Home	259	78	4	42	.301	LHP	125	36	3	12	.288
Road	285	88	7	41	.309	RHP	419	130	8	71	.310
First Half	281	80	4	36	.285	Sc Pos	148	55	4	69	.372
Scnd Half	263	86	7	47	.327	Clutch	77	21	2	15	.273

2002 Rankings (National League)

- 3rd in batting average with runners in scoring position
- 6th in errors at shortstop (19)
- 8th in fielding percentage at shortstop (.970)
- Led the Cardinals in stolen bases, steals of third (4) and batting average with runners in scoring position
- Led NL shortstops in batting average and RBI

Scott Rolen

2002 Season

After being traded from Philadelphia to St. Louis in late July, Scott Rolen began his Cardinals career with a 6-for-40 slump. However, he soon heated up and finished strong, driving in 44 runs in his 55 games with St. Louis. For the year, Rolen matched his career highs in homers and runs batted in, while also earning his fourth Gold Glove. His season ended on a down note when a shoulder injury sidelined him for the National League Championship Series.

Hitting

The word around the league was that Rolen could be handled with inside fastballs. Slowed by occasional back troubles, his bat speed had appeared to be waning for much of the last two years. However, after getting settled in St. Louis, he moved slightly off the plate and began driving the ball to all fields, something he does when he's in a good groove. Rolen is a good breaking-ball and offspeed hitter, and he annually wears out left-handed pitching. He also provided the Cardinals with solid work in the clutch, batting .317 with men in scoring position during St. Louis' stretch drive.

Baserunning & Defense

There are few better baserunners in baseball than the hard-driving Rolen. He combines good decisions with extreme aggressiveness to take extra bases and break up double plays. He has stolen as many as 16 bases in a season, so that threat cannot be ignored. Defensively, he now is the standard by which all other third basemen are measured. He routinely makes plays no one else even attempts.

2003 Outlook

Rolen never wanted to stay in Philadelphia, rejecting all Phillies contract offers. However, he's found a home in St. Louis with a new eight-year, $90 million deal that ties him to the Cardinals through 2010. He turns only 28 in April and already is entrenched as his league's best third baseman. It's a title he likely will hold for years to come.

Position: 3B
Bats: R **Throws:** R
Ht: 6' 4" **Wt:** 226

Opening Day Age: 27
Born: 4/4/75 in Jasper, IN
ML Seasons: 7
Pronunciation: ROH-len

Overall Statistics

	G	AB	R	H	D	T	HR	RBI	SB	BB	SO	Avg	OBP	Slg
'02	155	580	89	154	29	8	31	110	8	72	102	.266	.357	.503
Car.	899	3330	570	937	215	23	164	603	74	446	748	.281	.372	.508

Where He Hits the Ball

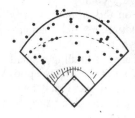

Vs. LHP   **Vs. RHP**

2002 Situational Stats

	AB	H	HR	RBI	Avg		AB	H	HR	RBI	Avg
Home	264	67	14	50	.254	LHP	118	34	6	22	.288
Road	316	87	17	60	.275	RHP	462	120	25	88	.260
First Half	308	78	13	58	.253	Sc Pos	168	48	10	77	.286
Scnd Half	272	76	18	52	.279	Clutch	101	29	7	19	.287

2002 Rankings (National League)

- 2nd in triples (8)
- 4th in lowest cleanup slugging percentage (.464)
- 5th in GDPs (22), errors at third base (16) and lowest fielding percentage at third base (.967)
- 6th in RBI (110)
- Led NL third basemen in home runs (30) and RBI (109)

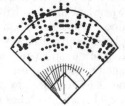

St. Louis

Fernando Vina

2002 Season

Though his production dropped in several areas from his career year of 2001, Fernando Vina put together a solid all-around season for St. Louis. He led National League leadoff men in runs batted in and again played a terrific brand of second base. He won his second straight Gold Glove Award.

Hitting

Vina's batting average and slugging percentage were significantly reduced in 2002. A major reason was his habit of lifting too many balls in the air. He appeared to have taken too seriously the career-high total of nine home runs he had hit in 2001. A good fastball hitter, Vina is at his best when he's slashing balls on the ground or on a line. He puts the ball in play more often than any player in baseball, always ranking among the toughest to strike out, but always totaling a small number of walks, too. He often infuriates opponents by leaning into pitches to steal first base. He's been hit 68 times in the last three years, by far the most in the majors.

Baserunning & Defense

With above-average speed and good quickness, Vina is a decent basestealer. However, his career success rate is only 64 percent, a mediocre mark for a quality leadoff man. But there is no better defensive second baseman. Vina's range is outstanding, his throwing arm is accurate and he has very sure hands. He also turns the double play as well as anyone.

2003 Outlook

The Cardinals may be looking for an alternative to Vina as he approaches the final year of his contract. His name surfaced among trade rumors early in the offseason. Vina has played more than 150 games in each of the last two seasons, but is often less than 100 percent due to frequent leg muscle pulls. St. Louis also would like to see improvement in his chronically low on-base percentage. That said, the Cards still view Vina as one of the best at his position in the National League.

Position: 2B
Bats: L **Throws:** R
Ht: 5' 9" **Wt:** 174

Opening Day Age: 33
Born: 4/16/69 in Sacramento, CA
ML Seasons: 10
Pronunciation: VEEN-yah

Overall Statistics

	G	AB	R	H	D	T	HR	RBI	SB	BB	SO	Avg	OBP	Slg
'02	150	622	75	168	29	5	1	54	17	44	36	.270	.333	.338
Car.	1058	3866	571	1105	175	45	36	313	110	268	259	.286	.352	.382

Where He Hits the Ball

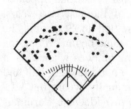

Vs. LHP	Vs. RHP

2002 Situational Stats

	AB	H	HR	RBI	Avg		AB	H	HR	RBI	Avg
Home	291	82	0	25	.282	LHP	143	34	0	13	.238
Road	331	86	1	29	.260	RHP	479	134	1	41	.280
First Half	334	93	1	34	.278	Sc Pos	139	38	1	52	.273
Scnd Half	288	75	0	20	.260	Clutch	84	19	0	8	.226

2002 Rankings (National League)

- 1st in lowest HR frequency (622.0 ABs per HR)
- 2nd in hit by pitch (18), lowest percentage of swings that missed (7.3) and lowest stolen-base percentage (60.7)
- 3rd in singles and highest percentage of swings put into play (57.3)
- Led the Cardinals in at-bats, singles, triples, sacrifice flies (7), caught stealing (11), hit by pitch (18), plate appearances (692), bunts in play (32), lowest percentage of swings that missed (7.3), highest percentage of swings put into play (57.3) and on-base percentage for a leadoff hitter (.333)

Woody Williams

2002 Season

It was a very frustrating season for Woody Williams, who spent nearly half the year on the disabled list due to strained left oblique and strained left ribcage injuries. He was outstanding when he was able to take the ball, allowing more than three runs in only one of 17 starts. The Cardinals went 12-5 in those games, and are 20-8 in Williams' starts since he joined the Redbirds in August of 2001. His ERA has been a sparkling 2.42 as a member of the Cardinals.

Pitching

Over the last two years, Williams has increased the velocity of his good cut fastball into the 90-92 MPH range. Combined with what has become an outstanding changeup, he's as tough as anyone on lefthanded batters. In fact, he's surrendered a lower batting average to lefties than righties in each of the past four seasons. Williams mixes in an occasionally effective curveball and throws all his offerings with solid command. He also is the kind of competitor who rarely falls victim to a big inning. He pitches his way out of jams and usually keeps his pitch counts very manageable.

Defense & Hitting

Because he gathers himself in his delivery, Williams is fairly easy for basestealers to time. However, he does a solid job of trying to hold runners with frequent throws to first. He's a good fielder otherwise and also helps himself with the bat. He's hit over .200 in his major league career and shown occasional power.

2003 Outlook

When Williams has been able to pitch, no Cardinals pitcher has produced more consistent starts. He also is a gamer who has become an important part of the great St. Louis clubhouse mix. At 36 years old, Williams is a classic example of a pitcher blooming late in his career, and the Cardinals recognized his substantial upside by re-signing him to a two-year, $14.9 million contract extension in late November. The deal also includes an $8 million team option for 2005. Williams should be a solid 15-game winner if he can avoid physical troubles.

Position: SP
Bats: R **Throws:** R
Ht: 6' 0" **Wt:** 195

Opening Day Age: 36
Born: 8/19/66 in Houston, TX
ML Seasons: 10

Overall Statistics

	W	L	Pct.	ERA	G	GS	Sv	IP	H	BB	SO	HR	Ratio
'02	9	4	.692	2.53	17	17	0	103.1	84	25	76	10	1.05
Car.	74	67	.525	4.06	273	183	0	1313.0	1262	459	917	189	1.31

How Often He Throws Strikes

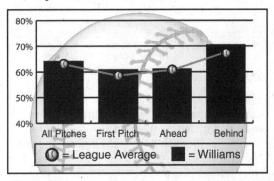

2002 Situational Stats

	W	L	ERA	Sv	IP		AB	H	HR	RBI	Avg
Home	5	1	2.12	0	59.1	LHB	176	32	6	10	.182
Road	4	3	3.07	0	44.0	RHB	203	52	4	17	.256
First Half	6	3	2.35	0	76.2	Sc Pos	60	15	0	14	.250
Scnd Half	3	1	3.04	0	26.2	Clutch	11	4	1	2	.364

2002 Rankings (National League)

- 3rd in lowest batting average allowed vs. left handed batters
- Led the Cardinals in ERA, winning percentage, highest strikeout-walk ratio (3.0), lowest batting average allowed (.222), lowest slugging percentage allowed (.338), lowest on-base percentage allowed (.276), lowest ERA at home, lowest batting average allowed vs. lefthanded batters and fewest walks per nine innings (2.2)

St. Louis

Miguel Cairo

Position: LF/2B
Bats: R **Throws:** R
Ht: 6' 1" **Wt:** 200

Opening Day Age: 28
Born: 5/4/74 in Anaco, VZ
ML Seasons: 7
Pronunciation: KY-roh

Overall Statistics

	G	AB	R	H	D	T	HR	RBI	SB	BB	SO	Avg	OBP	Slg
'02	108	184	28	46	9	2	2	23	1	13	36	.250	.307	.353
Car.	615	1751	224	478	79	15	14	157	72	112	195	.273	.321	.359

2002 Situational Stats

	AB	H	HR	RBI	Avg		AB	H	HR	RBI	Avg
Home	87	24	1	13	.276	LHP	66	18	2	9	.273
Road	97	22	1	10	.227	RHP	118	28	0	14	.237
First Half	97	24	2	12	.247	Sc Pos	58	14	1	20	.241
Scnd Half	87	22	0	11	.253	Clutch	40	11	0	6	.275

2002 Season

Miguel Cairo became a valuable reserve for the Cardinals, making starts at six different positions and ranking among the game's top pinch-hitters. In fact, his 19 pinch-hits placed him second in the National League. Cairo also was pressed into front-line service during the playoffs when Scott Rolen was injured, and went 9-for-17 (.529) in five postseason games.

Hitting, Baserunning & Defense

Cairo rarely lifts the ball with any power. He is an aggressive, first-pitch, fastball hitter who usually puts the ball in play and is a tough out in RBI situations. Cairo is especially effective against left-handed pitching, owning a .317 career average against southpaws. He has above-average speed and quickness and can steal a base. Cairo can play any of the four infield positions, though he is most comfortable at second, where he has good range and can turn the double play.

2003 Outlook

Role players like Cairo with defensive versatility and the ability to pinch-hit are valuable to contenders. He fits in very well on a Cardinals bench that is used so well by Tony La Russa. If Cairo can continue to fit into St. Louis' budget, he should remain one of the club's most important reserves.

Mike Crudale

Position: RP
Bats: R **Throws:** R
Ht: 6' 0" **Wt:** 205

Opening Day Age: 26
Born: 1/3/77 in San Diego, CA
ML Seasons: 1

Overall Statistics

	W	L	Pct.	ERA	G	GS	Sv	IP	H	BB	SO	HR	Ratio
'02	3	0	1.000	1.88	49	1	0	52.2	43	14	47	3	1.08
Car.	3	0	1.000	1.88	49	1	0	52.2	43	14	47	3	1.08

2002 Situational Stats

	W	L	ERA	Sv	IP		AB	H	HR	RBI	Avg
Home	2	0	1.52	0	23.2	LHB	73	18	1	7	.247
Road	1	0	2.17	0	29.0	RHB	116	25	2	18	.216
First Half	1	0	1.80	0	20.0	Sc Pos	63	11	1	21	.175
Scnd Half	2	0	1.93	0	32.2	Clutch	42	9	2	7	.214

2002 Season

Mike Crudale was one of the Cardinals' most pleasant surprises last season. He shuttled between the minors and majors, but established himself as a solid middle-inning reliever with St. Louis. He limited hitters to a .228 batting average, produced an outstanding strikeout-walk ratio and became a regular part of the Cards' bullpen system over the second half.

Pitching, Defense & Hitting

Crudale's velocity is in the low 90s. What makes him tough is a big-breaking slider that he can throw hard and for strikes. The Cardinals love his makeup, as he will challenge hitters and not nibble when he gets ahead in the count. He was particularly tough with runners in scoring position last year, allowing a .175 average in such situations. He handles himself defensively but is fairly easy to run on with his high leg kick. Crudale has little experience as a hitter.

2003 Outlook

Tony La Russa's confidence in Crudale increased as last season wore on. The righthander will come to spring training with a job in the middle of St. Louis' bullpen. He could be a key setup man behind closer Jason Isringhausen.

Luther Hackman

Position: RP
Bats: R **Throws:** R
Ht: 6' 4" **Wt:** 195

Opening Day Age: 28
Born: 10/10/74 in Columbus, MS
ML Seasons: 4

Overall Statistics

	W	L	Pct.	ERA	G	GS	Sv	IP	H	BB	SO	HR	Ratio
'02	5	4	.556	4.11	43	6	0	81.0	90	39	46	7	1.59
Car.	7	8	.467	5.05	84	9	1	135.1	148	69	80	19	1.60

2002 Situational Stats

	W	L	ERA	Sv	IP		AB	H	HR	RBI	Avg
Home	2	2	3.62	0	37.1	LHB	124	37	3	21	.298
Road	3	2	4.53	0	43.2	RHB	190	53	4	24	.279
First Half	1	3	3.96	0	36.1	Sc Pos	95	23	1	36	.242
Scnd Half	4	1	4.23	0	44.2	Clutch	24	9	2	5	.375

2002 Season

With the Cardinals pitching staff riddled by injuries and tragedy, one of its unsung contributors was Luther Hackman. He stepped in to make six starts during some of the more troubled periods in July and August. Although he never lasted more than 5.2 innings in those starts, the Cards won four of the games. Hackman also did serviceable work in middle and long relief.

Pitching, Defense & Hitting

Hackman can be effective with a hard cut fastball and sinker. However, he struggles to maintain a consistent release point and at times is prone to wildness and lack of command in the strike zone. He is slow coming home and can be vulnerable to stolen bases. He had only one hit in 16 at-bats last year, but usually can put the ball into play.

2003 Outlook

While it was thought that Hackman's stint as a starter was purely an emergency role that would not be revisited, the righthander was pitching well as a starter in winter ball in Puerto Rico. He would have to be a long shot for a fifth-starter role—and more openings may exist in the bullpen—but it will be interesting to see how Hackman fits into the 2003 picture.

Steve Kline

Position: RP
Bats: B **Throws:** L
Ht: 6' 1" **Wt:** 215

Opening Day Age: 30
Born: 8/22/72 in Sunbury, PA
ML Seasons: 6

Overall Statistics

	W	L	Pct.	ERA	G	GS	Sv	IP	H	BB	SO	HR	Ratio
'02	2	1	.667	3.39	66	0	6	58.1	54	21	41	3	1.29
Car.	20	23	.465	3.41	444	1	30	409.2	386	174	341	36	1.37

2002 Situational Stats

	W	L	ERA	Sv	IP		AB	H	HR	RBI	Avg
Home	0	1	2.43	3	33.1	LHB	87	20	1	7	.230
Road	2	0	4.68	3	25.0	RHB	128	34	2	13	.266
First Half	0	1	4.29	2	21.0	Sc Pos	67	15	0	15	.224
Scnd Half	2	0	2.89	4	37.1	Clutch	106	23	1	8	.217

2002 Season

Steve Kline missed the entire month of May due to a strained left triceps. It took him until after the All-Star break before he regained his effectiveness. However, he was one of the Cards' best relievers down the stretch. He recorded a hold or save in nine of St. Louis' final 21 wins of the season. He did all that while continuing to don one of the filthiest hats in the major leagues.

Pitching, Defense & Hitting

Kline relies on a heavy sinker and a late-breaking slider. Both offerings produce a lot of groundballs when he has good bite on his pitches, something he had difficulty regaining following his arm troubles. He is a tireless competitor who can be available for three or four outs virtually every day, and is more effective against righthanded hitters. Kline holds runners well and maintains his poise when fielding his position. He is no threat as a hitter.

2003 Outlook

Even with minor arm troubles last year, Kline has appeared in 65 or more games in five straight seasons. He is one of the Cardinals' many real gamers and should remain a key setup man in the St. Louis bullpen.

St. Louis

Mike Matheny

Position: C
Bats: R **Throws:** R
Ht: 6' 3" **Wt:** 205

Opening Day Age: 32
Born: 9/22/70 in
Reynoldsburg, OH
ML Seasons: 9
Pronunciation:
ma-THEEN-ee

Overall Statistics

	G	AB	R	H	D	T	HR	RBI	SB	BB	SO	Avg	OBP	Slg
'02	110	315	31	77	12	1	3	35	1	32	49	.244	.313	.317
Car.	861	2448	230	575	108	6	38	269	7	161	510	.235	.289	.330

2002 Situational Stats

	AB	H	HR	RBI	Avg		AB	H	HR	RBI	Avg
Home	158	37	1	15	.234	LHP	68	18	0	6	.265
Road	157	40	2	20	.255	RHP	247	59	3	29	.239
First Half	163	35	3	17	.215	Sc Pos	72	20	1	31	.278
Scnd Half	152	42	0	18	.276	Clutch	40	9	0	4	.225

2002 Season

Mike Matheny often was benched in the first half of last season. But he regained his regular position with a solid finish in which he hit better than .280 from mid-July on. He then enjoyed a fine postseason, collecting at least one hit in every game he played. In addition, his defense behind the plate remained among the best in the game.

Hitting, Baserunning & Defense

Possessing average bat speed, Matheny can be pounded with average fastballs. However, he opened his stance more over the latter part of last season and was better able to fight off pitches to the opposite field. Matheny is no threat on the bases. His catching mechanics are outstanding and he has a strong arm with a quick release that discourages basestealing attempts. He also is an excellent handler of pitchers.

2003 Outlook

Matheny's sporadic offense sharply reduced his playing time last season. But when it's crunch time, the Cardinals want him behind the plate. They have the offense elsewhere in their lineup to carry his bat. And they have the catching depth to keep Matheny fresh. Despite arthroscopic shoulder surgery last October, he should be in line for around 110 starts again this year.

Jason Simontacchi

Position: SP
Bats: R **Throws:** R
Ht: 6' 2" **Wt:** 185

Opening Day Age: 29
Born: 11/13/73 in
Mountain View, CA
ML Seasons: 1

Overall Statistics

	W	L	Pct.	ERA	G	GS	Sv	IP	H	BB	SO	HR	Ratio
'02	11	5	.688	4.02	24	24	0	143.1	134	54	72	18	1.31
Car.	11	5	.688	4.02	24	24	0	143.1	134	54	72	18	1.31

2002 Situational Stats

	W	L	ERA	Sv	IP		AB	H	HR	RBI	Avg
Home	6	2	3.15	0	71.1	LHB	226	56	9	22	.248
Road	5	3	4.88	0	72.0	RHB	304	78	9	37	.257
First Half	7	1	2.77	0	61.2	Sc Pos	97	24	4	39	.247
Scnd Half	4	4	4.96	0	81.2	Clutch	37	11	2	7	.297

2002 Season

A complete unknown before last year, well-traveled Jason Simontacchi was a savior for the Cardinals' battered pitching staff after arriving as a last-resort option from the minors. Simontacchi became the first Cardinals rookie in 10 years to win his first five decisions in the majors. He finished the season with 11 victories, second most on the club.

Pitching, Defense & Hitting

Simontacchi doesn't knock your eyes out with his velocity. However, his fastball has good movement both as a sinker and a cutter. His out pitch is an excellent changeup, which he will throw at any time in the count. He has a very good pickoff move and holds runners well, with only two runners even trying to run on him last year. He also tied Matt Morris for the lead among Cardinals pitchers with 12 hits in 2002.

2003 Outlook

A pitcher for the Italian Olympic team, a veteran of four organizations, and a hurler with stints both in Venezuela and an independent league, Simontacchi impressed last year with his poise and pitching savvy. He should be expected to win 10-12 games as a No. 4 or 5 starter.

Garrett Stephenson

Position: SP
Bats: R **Throws:** R
Ht: 6' 5" **Wt:** 208

Opening Day Age: 31
Born: 1/2/72 in Takoma
Park, MD
ML Seasons: 6

Overall Statistics

	W	L	Pct.	ERA	G	GS	Sv	IP	H	BB	SO	HR	Ratio
'02	2	5	.286	5.40	12	10	0	45.0	48	25	34	4	1.62
Car.	32	26	.552	4.53	91	77	0	477.0	495	177	317	61	1.41

2002 Situational Stats

	W	L	ERA	Sv	IP		AB	H	HR	RBI	Avg
Home	2	3	4.73	0	32.1	LHB	76	27	2	16	.355
Road	0	2	7.11	0	12.2	RHB	94	21	2	7	.223
First Half	1	4	6.67	0	29.2	Sc Pos	48	15	1	18	.313
Scnd Half	1	1	2.93	0	15.1	Clutch	0	0	0	0	–

2002 Season

Garrett Stephenson has been derailed by injuries the past two seasons. He missed 2001 following elbow surgery. And last year, a series of ailments that included back problems, a diseased tissue in his hamstring and shoulder troubles limited him to just 10 starts. Only three of those starts came after May, with only one lasting as long as six innings.

Pitching, Defense & Hitting

Stephenson is a finesse pitcher who can be effective when he's hitting spots with his sinking fastballs and has the feel for what can be a very good changeup. He must work from ahead in the count because he has no single pitch with which he can challenge a hitter. Stephenson has a good pickoff move and fields his position with decent athleticism. He is no threat with the bat, as he's collected only nine hits in 136 career at-bats.

2003 Outlook

The Cardinals need good memories to recall Stephenson's unlikely 16-win campaign in 2000. Since then, he's been a non-factor due to a series of physical problems. While the Cardinals have grown tired of waiting for him to get healthy, Stephenson may get a rotation spot if he remains healthy in the spring and St. Louis doesn't acquire a fifth starter during the offseason.

Dave Veres

Position: RP
Bats: R **Throws:** R
Ht: 6' 2" **Wt:** 220

Opening Day Age: 36
Born: 10/19/66 in
Montgomery, AL
ML Seasons: 9
Pronunciation:
VEERZ

Overall Statistics

	W	L	Pct.	ERA	G	GS	Sv	IP	H	BB	SO	HR	Ratio
'02	5	8	.385	3.48	71	0	4	82.2	67	39	68	12	1.28
Car.	34	34	.500	3.38	574	0	94	661.1	625	252	591	74	1.33

2002 Situational Stats

	W	L	ERA	Sv	IP		AB	H	HR	RBI	Avg
Home	5	2	1.94	2	46.1	LHB	116	22	4	11	.190
Road	0	6	5.45	2	36.1	RHB	183	45	8	25	.246
First Half	3	3	2.74	2	49.1	Sc Pos	76	20	6	30	.263
Scnd Half	2	5	4.59	2	33.1	Clutch	146	35	6	17	.240

2002 Season

Moved out of the closer's role, Dave Veres was a workhorse in the middle of the Cardinals' bullpen. He was first on the club in appearances and relief innings, but struggled in late-inning work, blowing four of eight save opportunities. He seemed to alternate between good and bad months, and was much more effective at Busch Stadium than he was on the road.

Pitching, Defense & Hitting

Veres' margin for error has become very small with his splitter, which too often flattens or does not sink enough. He now often gets by with a changeup and slider. But neither pitch can consistently put away hitters, which brings Veres back to the splitter. He handles himself well defensively and has allowed just three stolen bases over the past two years. He also handles the bat decently for someone who gets very few chances to hit.

2003 Outlook

St. Louis didn't pick up the option on Veres' contract, nor did they offer him salary arbitration. Veres is a free agent. He no longer is viewed as closer material, though he still can be an asset for a club looking for a veteran competitor to pitch in the seventh or eighth innings.

Rick White

Position: RP
Bats: R **Throws:** R
Ht: 6' 4" **Wt:** 230

Opening Day Age: 34
Born: 12/23/68 in Springfield, OH
ML Seasons: 7

Overall Statistics

	W	L	Pct.	ERA	G	GS	Sv	IP	H	BB	SO	HR	Ratio
'02	5	7	.417	4.31	61	0	0	62.2	62	21	41	4	1.32
Car.	27	38	.415	3.97	341	18	11	539.0	559	172	346	48	1.36

2002 Situational Stats

	W	L	ERA	Sv	IP		AB	H	HR	RBI	Avg
Home	2	3	6.30	0	30.0	LHB	87	26	2	6	.299
Road	3	4	2.48	0	32.2	RHB	148	36	2	21	.243
First Half	2	5	5.29	0	32.1	Sc Pos	68	12	0	21	.176
Scnd Half	3	2	3.26	0	30.1	Clutch	72	17	0	4	.236

2002 Season

Rick White proved to be one of the Cardinals' best stretch-drive acquisitions after they signed him last August. He allowed only two earned runs and 13 hits in his 20 games with St. Louis. He successfully held leads in 17 of those appearances. That effectiveness was a far cry from White's struggles in Colorado, where he was 2-6 with a 6.20 ERA before being released by the Rockies.

Pitching, Defense & Hitting

The Cardinals convinced White to throw more splits and hard sliders, rather than relying too much on his four-seam fastball. By simplifying things, he became more aggressive and regained his good control. He is a workhorse type who can eat up four or five outs on a regular basis. For a big man, White fields his position well. In his relief role, he rarely gets a chance to hit.

2003 Outlook

White might have become another of Cardinals pitching coach Dave Duncan's successful projects. White was the most reliable St. Louis reliever over last season's final six weeks. But the righthander wasn't offered salary arbitration and isn't likely to return to the Cardinals in 2003. He looks like a valuable pick up for a team in need of relief help.

Jamey Wright

Position: SP
Bats: R **Throws:** R
Ht: 6' 5" **Wt:** 234

Opening Day Age: 28
Born: 12/24/74 in Oklahoma City, OK
ML Seasons: 7

Overall Statistics

	W	L	Pct.	ERA	G	GS	Sv	IP	H	BB	SO	HR	Ratio
'02	7	13	.350	5.29	23	22	0	129.1	130	75	77	17	1.59
Car.	50	67	.427	5.17	174	171	0	1030.1	1136	522	541	116	1.61

2002 Situational Stats

	W	L	ERA	Sv	IP		AB	H	HR	RBI	Avg
Home	4	6	5.64	0	67.0	LHB	229	62	9	31	.271
Road	3	7	4.91	0	62.1	RHB	255	68	8	44	.267
First Half	2	7	6.29	0	58.2	Sc Pos	124	34	3	57	.274
Scnd Half	5	6	4.46	0	70.2	Clutch	31	8	1	5	.258

2002 Season

After winning only five of 19 starts with Milwaukee, Jamey Wright was traded to St. Louis as some pitching insurance for the Cardinals' stretch drive. Wright won two of his three starts with the Redbirds and also was used in relief.

Pitching, Defense & Hitting

Wright's stuff has teased people for years. He throws a 90-plus MPH sinking fastball, a power curve, an explosive slider and a decent straight change. However, he has yet to combine his impressive assortment with consistent command, putting far too many batters on with walks and hit batsmen. He is a good athlete who fields his position well and has one of the better righthanded pickoff moves. Wright also can handle the bat.

2003 Outlook

Wright declared his free agency following the 2002 season, and the Cardinals had some interest in having him return. But he wasn't offered salary arbitration in December, all but assuring that Wright will pitch somewhere else in 2003. Many baseball observers expected Wright to emerge once he left Colorado in 2000, and pitching coach Dave Duncan might have been the guy who would help Wright harness his ability. But Wright will move on.

Other St. Louis Cardinals

Andy Benes (Pos: RHP, Age: 35)

	W	L	Pct.	ERA	G	GS	Sv	IP	H	BB	SO	HR	Ratio
'02	5	4	.556	2.78	18	17	0	97.0	80	51	64	10	1.35
Car.	155	139	.527	3.97	403	387	1	2505.1	2377	909	2000	289	1.31

Benes contemplated retirement last spring after getting off to a terrible start. But he was a great success story, posting the NL's best ERA after the All-Star break. Still, he did retire after the season. 2003 Outlook: D

Mike Coolbaugh (Pos: 3B, Age: 30, Bats: R)

	G	AB	R	H	D	T	HR	RBI	SB	BB	SO	Avg	OBP	Slg
'02	5	12	0	1	0	0	0	0	0	1	3	.083	.154	.083
Car.	44	82	10	15	6	0	2	7	0	6	19	.183	.256	.329

Coolbaugh has been stuck in Triple-A for most of the past five years. He has decent power but likely won't hit for a high average. He signed a minor league contract with the Phillies after last season. 2003 Outlook: C

Ivan Cruz (Pos: 1B, Age: 34, Bats: L)

	G	AB	R	H	D	T	HR	RBI	SB	BB	SO	Avg	OBP	Slg
'02	17	14	2	5	0	0	1	3	0	1	3	.357	.400	.571
Car.	41	55	5	15	1	0	2	8	0	3	17	.273	.310	.400

A year after playing in Japan, Cruz knocked the stuffing out of the ball at Triple-A. But it earned him only a modest number of at-bats with St. Louis in September. 2003 Outlook: C

Wilson Delgado (Pos: SS, Age: 30, Bats: B)

	G	AB	R	H	D	T	HR	RBI	SB	BB	SO	Avg	OBP	Slg
'02	12	20	2	4	2	0	2	5	0	0	6	.200	.200	.600
Car.	149	285	36	69	8	1	3	23	4	21	61	.242	.299	.309

Delgado signed a minor league contract with the Cardinals after the 2001 campaign. He spent last season in Triple-A before a September callup. He's a few years older than was once thought. 2003 Outlook: C

Mike DiFelice (Pos: C, Age: 33, Bats: R)

	G	AB	R	H	D	T	HR	RBI	SB	BB	SO	Avg	OBP	Slg
'02	70	174	17	40	11	0	4	19	0	17	42	.230	.297	.362
Car.	422	1242	108	297	63	6	25	130	2	79	272	.239	.289	.360

The Cardinals lost DiFelice in the expansion draft after the 1997 season, but got him back last year. St. Louis has declined a team option and DiFelice again is a free agent. 2003 Outlook: C

Matt Duff (Pos: RHP, Age: 28)

	W	L	Pct.	ERA	G	GS	Sv	IP	H	BB	SO	HR	Ratio
'02	0	0	–	4.76	7	0	0	5.2	3	8	4	0	1.94
Car.	0	0	–	4.76	7	0	0	5.2	3	8	4	0	1.94

Duff was terrific in the minor leagues last season, showing an exceptional strikeout rate. But at age 28, he's pitched a grand total of 10.1 innings above the Double-A level. 2003 Outlook: C

Jeff Fassero (Pos: LHP, Age: 40)

	W	L	Pct.	ERA	G	GS	Sv	IP	H	BB	SO	HR	Ratio
'02	8	6	.571	5.35	73	0	0	69.0	81	27	56	9	1.57
Car.	112	101	.526	3.93	559	217	22	1738.0	1739	607	1461	177	1.35

The Cardinals acquired Fassero in late August for a couple of minor league pitchers. Fassero went 3-0 for the Redbirds down the stretch, and he was effective enough to reach agreement on a one-year, $1.5 million deal to return this season. 2003 Outlook: B

Kevin Joseph (Pos: RHP, Age: 26)

	W	L	Pct.	ERA	G	GS	Sv	IP	H	BB	SO	HR	Ratio
'02	0	1	.000	4.91	11	0	0	11.0	16	6	2	1	2.00
Car.	0	1	.000	4.91	11	0	0	11.0	16	6	2	1	2.00

Joseph came to the Cardinals in the deal for Jason Christiansen in 2001. Joseph's poor strikeout rate didn't hurt him at Triple-A last year, but could sink him against major league hitters. 2003 Outlook: C

In Memorium

Darryl Kile: 1968-2002

	W	L	Pct.	ERA	G	GS	Sv	IP	H	BB	SO	HR	Ratio
'02	5	4	.556	3.72	14	14	0	84.2	82	28	50	9	1.30
Car.	133	119	.528	4.12	359	331	0	2165.1	2135	918	1668	214	1.41

Almost without question, the worst moment of the 2002 season was the report of Kile's death last June. His presence near the top of the Cardinals' rotation will be missed on and off the field.

Gabe Molina (Pos: RHP, Age: 27)

	W	L	Pct.	ERA	G	GS	Sv	IP	H	BB	SO	HR	Ratio
'02	1	0	1.000	1.59	12	0	0	11.1	6	6	4	1	1.06
Car.	2	2	.500	6.20	43	0	0	49.1	56	32	27	8	1.78

Molina signed a minor league deal with the Cardinals prior to last season and pitched well at Triple-A. He also showed enough during his time with St. Louis to merit another shot somewhere. 2003 Outlook: C

Josh Pearce (Pos: RHP, Age: 25)

	W	L	Pct.	ERA	G	GS	Sv	IP	H	BB	SO	HR	Ratio
'02	0	0	–	7.62	3	3	0	13.0	20	8	1	1	2.15
Car.	0	0	–	7.62	3	3	0	13.0	20	8	1	1	2.15

Pearce seemed like a rarity in 2001 when he was one of the few Cardinals pitching prospects who managed to stay healthy. But his luck ran out last year when he underwent shoulder surgery in May. 2003 Outlook: C

Eduardo Perez (**Pos**: RF, **Age**: 33, **Bats**: R)

	G	AB	R	H	D	T	HR	RBI	SB	BB	SO	Avg	OBP	Slg
'02	96	154	22	31	9	0	10	26	0	17	36	.201	.290	.455
Car.	479	1162	144	277	54	3	47	185	14	117	268	.238	.313	.411

After playing in Japan in 2001, Perez returned to the Cardinals last year and delivered some big hits. If he can feast on southpaws as he did last season, he could have a bench job for a while. 2003 Outlook: C

Kerry Robinson (**Pos**: LF/RF, **Age**: 29, **Bats**: L)

	G	AB	R	H	D	T	HR	RBI	SB	BB	SO	Avg	OBP	Slg
'02	124	181	27	47	7	4	1	15	7	11	29	.260	.301	.359
Car.	249	371	65	100	13	5	2	30	18	23	51	.270	.313	.348

Robinson, a native of St. Louis, provides a bit of speed and can play any outfield position. He rarely sees action against lefthanded pitchers. His batting average represents most of his offensive value. 2003 Outlook: C

Nerio Rodriguez (**Pos**: RHP, **Age**: 32)

	W	L	Pct.	ERA	G	GS	Sv	IP	H	BB	SO	HR	Ratio
'02	0	0	–	3.86	3	0	0	4.2	4	1	2	1	1.07
Car.	4	6	.400	6.32	32	7	0	72.2	80	35	38	8	1.58

The Cardinals acquired Rodriguez from the Indians last July. While he's on the wrong side of 30, he pitched well at two Triple-A stops in 2002 and signed a new minor league contract with the Cardinals. 2003 Outlook: C

Travis Smith (**Pos**: RHP, **Age**: 30)

	W	L	Pct.	ERA	G	GS	Sv	IP	H	BB	SO	HR	Ratio
'02	4	2	.667	7.17	12	10	0	54.0	69	20	32	10	1.65
Car.	4	2	.667	6.91	13	10	0	56.0	70	20	33	10	1.61

After stumbling early, Smith provided three pretty good starts following Darryl Kile's death last June. Smith couldn't sustain it, however, and was dispatched back to the minors by the beginning of August. 2003 Outlook: C

Gene Stechschulte (**Pos**: RHP, **Age**: 29)

	W	L	Pct.	ERA	G	GS	Sv	IP	H	BB	SO	HR	Ratio
'02	6	2	.750	4.78	29	0	0	32.0	27	17	21	4	1.38
Car.	8	7	.533	4.58	116	0	6	127.2	122	64	84	20	1.46

Stechschulte didn't pitch quite as well as his record would indicate last season. He struggled at home and with runners on base. The Cardinals demoted him by July, and he then battled injuries. 2003 Outlook: C

So Taguchi (**Pos**: LF, **Age**: 33, **Bats**: R)

	G	AB	R	H	D	T	HR	RBI	SB	BB	SO	Avg	OBP	Slg
'02	19	15	4	6	0	0	0	2	1	2	1	.400	.471	.400
Car.	19	15	4	6	0	0	0	2	1	2	1	.400	.471	.400

Taguchi was a disappointment last spring. Signed out of Japan, he was expected to compete for playing time in the Cardinals' outfield. He instead had a hard time hitting Triple-A pitching, though he impressed enough in a September callup to be in the mix for a reserve role. 2003 Outlook: C

St. Louis Cardinals Minor League Prospects

Organization Overview:

The Cardinals' minor league organization has been questioned in recent years for a perceived lack of depth and talent. But it's hard to argue with the bottom-line record of the major league team. And yes, the farm system has contributed to the big club's success. True, the Cardinals have helped themselves through free agency. But they've also consistently utilized the assets of their farm system, either through callups or trades. When the Cardinals landed Scott Rolen near last year's trading deadline, they had to include a couple of homegrown players in the package. The organization still may be lacking in position players, but the prospects look a bit brighter on the pitching side. That would seem to be advantageous, considering the problems the Cardinals' staff experienced last season, and the age that crept into the rotation. It's possible that pitching reinforcements will be forthcoming in the next year or two.

Shaun Boyd

Position: 2B   **Opening Day Age:** 21
Bats: R **Throws:** R   **Born:** 8/15/81 in Corona,
Ht: 5' 10" **Wt:** 175   CA

Recent Statistics

	G	AB	R	H	D	T	HR	RBI	SB	BB	SO	Avg
2001 A Peoria	81	277	42	78	12	2	5	27	20	33	42	.282
2002 A Peoria	129	520	91	163	36	5	12	60	32	54	78	.313

Boyd was expected to be a decent hitter when the Cardinals used their first No. 1 pick in 2000 to select him. And after last year's performance in the Class-A Midwest League, it looks like he's fulfilling his promise. In fact, Boyd has improved as a hitter each season since turning pro. He has gap power, as evidenced by his high number of doubles in his second year at Peoria. He understands his approach at the plate and knows the strike zone. He also has improved his defense at second base. Although his arm may be a bit below average and he's rushed his throws at times, hurting his accuracy, Boyd has good quickness and has worked on his footwork. He likely will play at high Class-A in 2003.

Danny Haren

Position: P   **Opening Day Age:** 22
Bats: R **Throws:** R   **Born:** 9/17/80 in
Ht: 6' 5" **Wt:** 220   Monterey Park, CA

Recent Statistics

	W	L	ERA	G	GS	Sv	IP	H	R	BB	SO	HR
2001 A New Jersey	3	3	3.10	12	8	1	52.1	47	22	8	57	6
2002 A Peoria	7	3	1.95	14	14	0	101.2	89	32	12	89	6
2002 A Potomac	3	6	3.62	14	14	0	92.0	90	43	19	82	8

Haren formed an impressive tandem with Noah Lowry at Pepperdine in 2001. While Lowry went in the first round that June to San Francisco, Haren was taken by the Cardinals in Round 2. Haren had an outstanding first half in 2002 before tiring in the second. His low-90s fastball isn't overpowering, but he's helped by a delivery that has a little funk and a little deception. He knows how to throw a splitter and should be able to go to it at some point in the future. He needs to work on his slider and changeup as well as his consistency, but Haren is a horse who figures to be an innings type of guy.

Tyler Johnson

Position: P   **Opening Day Age:** 21
Bats: B **Throws:** L   **Born:** 6/7/81 in
Ht: 6' 2" **Wt:** 180   Columbia, MO

Recent Statistics

	W	L	ERA	G	GS	Sv	IP	H	R	BB	SO	HR
2001 R Johnson City	1	1	2.66	9	9	0	40.2	26	17	21	58	1
2001 A Peoria	0	1	3.95	3	3	0	13.2	14	9	10	15	1
2002 A Peoria	15	3	2.00	22	18	0	121.1	96	35	42	132	7

The Cardinals selected Johnson in the 34th round of the 2000 draft out of a California junior college. Signed as a draft-and-follow, he didn't debut until 2001. He then really stepped up last season, ranking second in the Class-A Midwest League with a 2.00 ERA. Johnson is a lefthander with a fastball in the 86-90 MPH range. The fastball has good life, and he's getting a feel for his changeup. But what really separates him is his curveball, the best in the organization. A good competitor who turned 21 last season, Johnson is maturing well and is considered a frontline prospect. He could be at Double-A Tennessee by the end of 2003.

Jimmy Journell

Position: P   **Opening Day Age:** 25
Bats: R **Throws:** R   **Born:** 12/29/77 in
Ht: 6' 4" **Wt:** 205   Springfield, OH

Recent Statistics

	W	L	ERA	G	GS	Sv	IP	H	R	BB	SO	HR
2001 A Potomac	14	6	2.50	26	26	0	151.0	121	54	42	156	8
2001 AA New Haven	1	0	0.00	1	1	0	7.0	0	0	3	6	0
2002 AA New Haven	3	3	2.70	10	10	0	66.2	50	22	18	66	3
2002 AAA Memphis	2	4	3.68	7	7	0	36.2	38	16	18	32	3

Journell looked like he was steamrolling through the minors in 2001, when he reached Double-A in his first full year as a pro. But his progress slowed last season as he fought injuries. Nevertheless, he pitched well at Double-A and didn't embarrass himself in seven Triple-A starts. Perhaps most encouraging, the fourth-round pick in 1999 now has a clean bill of health. Journell features two solid pitches, including a low-90s fastball. Though inconsistent, his slider is a swing-and-miss pitch at times, and can be filthy when he stays on top of it. He also has a changeup, which he might need to throw more often. He could be close to a big league job if he remains injury-free.

St. Louis

Yadier Molina

Position: C **Opening Day Age:** 20
Bats: R **Throws:** R **Born:** 7/13/82 in
Ht: 5' 11" **Wt:** 187 Bayamon, PR

Recent Statistics

	G	AB	R	H	D	T	HR	RBI	SB	BB	SO	Avg
2001 R Johnson City	44	158	18	41	11	0	4	18	1	12	23	.259
2002 A Peoria	112	393	39	110	20	0	7	50	2	21	36	.280

Molina's defense is so impressive that he probably could catch in the majors right now. He has a terrific arm and a good understanding of how to call a game. His manager last year, Danny Sheaffer, a former big league catcher, raved about Molina, as did Cardinals hurlers who were rehabbing at Class-A Peoria. Of course, Molina's brothers Bengie and Jose are catchers for the Angels, so maybe the skills run in the family. Yadier's offense isn't as advanced as his defensive game. He could use more discipline when batting, and could shorten and quicken his swing. The Cardinals will try to keep much of their successful Peoria club intact as it moves up to high Class-A Palm Beach this season, and Molina figures to be a key part.

Chris Narveson

Position: P **Opening Day Age:** 21
Bats: L **Throws:** L **Born:** 12/20/81 in
Ht: 6' 3" **Wt:** 180 Englewood, CO

Recent Statistics

	W	L	ERA	G	GS	Sv	IP	H	R	BB	SO	HR
2001 A Peoria	3	3	1.98	8	8	0	50.0	32	14	11	53	3
2001 A Potomac	4	3	2.57	11	11	0	66.2	52	22	13	53	4
2002 R Johnson City	0	2	5.28	5	0	0	15.1	19	11	6	15	2
2002 A Peoria	2	1	4.46	9	9	0	42.1	49	24	8	36	5

Narveson underwent Tommy John surgery in 2001, and his pitching was limited in his first year back. He averaged around four innings per start between two stops last season, but looks like he's fully recovered from the operation. His fastball resides in the 87-91 MPH range, and it might get a bit better as he goes forward. He also throws an average slider, along with a curveball and changeup. The change has good depth and deception, though it isn't always consistent. He was chosen in the second round in 2000 out of a North Carolina high school, so he's still quite young. He projects as a control type of pitcher, but one who throws lefthanded and figures to have two or three solid-average pitches.

John Nelson

Position: SS/OF **Opening Day Age:** 24
Bats: R **Throws:** R **Born:** 3/3/79 in Denton,
Ht: 6' 1" **Wt:** 193 TX

Recent Statistics

	G	AB	R	H	D	T	HR	RBI	SB	BB	SO	Avg
2001 A New Jersey	66	252	43	60	16	3	8	26	14	35	76	.238
2002 A Peoria	132	481	85	132	28	5	16	63	16	54	123	.274

Nelson played shortstop at the University of Kansas, where he also showed off a 93-94 MPH fastball as a closer. But he didn't really excel in college and waited until the eighth round of the 2001 draft before getting taken by the Cardinals. Last year, however, he began to put his imposing tools to good use and seemed to improve every day. He's a strong guy with a great physique. He played shortstop at Class-A Peoria and has seen action in the outfield as well. His arm obviously rates as a plus, and he's a decent runner. He delivered lots of extra-base hits last year, including a fair number of home runs. The Cardinals might like a higher average, and he wasn't that young for his level, but Nelson is a player to keep an eye on.

Rhett Parrott

Position: P **Opening Day Age:** 23
Bats: R **Throws:** R **Born:** 11/12/79 in
Ht: 6' 2" **Wt:** 185 Dalton, GA

Recent Statistics

	W	L	ERA	G	GS	Sv	IP	H	R	BB	SO	HR
2001 A New Jersey	1	3	4.93	11	11	0	45.2	45	27	28	58	3
2002 A Potomac	8	5	2.71	19	19	0	113.0	91	42	41	82	6
2002 AA New Haven	4	1	2.86	9	9	0	66.0	53	24	13	38	3

The Cardinals plucked Parrott in the ninth round of the 2001 draft. He had been a high-profile pitcher when entering college, but didn't enjoy overwhelming success at Georgia Tech. However, he blossomed at two levels last season, finishing on a high note at Double-A. He has an above-average fastball that reaches the mid-90s, as well as a curveball, slider and changeup. He has command of all his pitches, and worked 179.0 innings in his first full pro season. Parrott's strikeout rate was not as impressive as it was when he debuted in 2001, but he surrendered just over seven hits per nine innings and displayed fine control last year.

Others to Watch

First baseman **Chris Duncan** (21) has found it tough getting out of the Class-A Midwest League. The son of Cardinals pitching coach Dave Duncan, Chris has good raw power and did a better job using the whole field last season. He spent a lot of time working on defense. . . First baseman **John Gall** (24) also has played third and the outfield. He's been a hitting and extra-base machine the past two years, reaching 20 homers at Double-A. . . Outfielder **Dee Haynes** (25) led the Double-A Eastern League with 98 RBI in 2002. He doesn't walk as much as you might like, though his power can be a nice trade-off. He seemed to benefit from a move from right to left field. . . Righthander **Scotty Layfield** (26) works with a low-90s fastball and a good, late, hard slider. He's expected to be the closer at Triple-A this season, but might follow Mike Crudale's example and contribute at some point with the big club. . . Righthander **Justin Pope** (23) missed a lot of time last season with a bone spur in his elbow, but he was almost unhittable at Class-A Peoria. He can run his fastball in on either side of the plate, and his plus slider is a big league pitch. He has good command and is a polished hurler.

Qualcomm Stadium

Offense

Qualcomm Stadium is one of the toughest parks for hitters. There's a large amount of foul ground, and the ball doesn't carry well in night games. The lights are not on standards but instead ring the stadium, adding an extra shadow to contend with between the mound and home plate during day games.

Defense

The Q is no picnic for fielders, either. The lights are set low over the stadium. Their glare interferes with most flyballs and makes looping line drives almost impossible to see. The bullpens, which are in play, abut the outfield corners and turn easy down-the-line singles into extra-base adventures. The stadium plays host to both the NFL Chargers and the San Diego State Aztecs, so the infield can get chewed up, providing for some interesting hops on grounders.

Who It Helps the Most

Qualcomm is not quite a pitchers' paradise, but it comes close. In fact, every Padres pitcher who threw at least 50 innings for San Diego last year posted a better home ERA. Jake Peavy enjoyed an ERA differential of 3.67. Pitching at the Q helps young pitchers gain confidence, since many of their mistakes stay in the yard.

Who It Hurts the Most

Power hitters are the most adversely affected. Over the last three years, Ryan Klesko has hit just 35 of his 85 homers at home. The stadium historically had been tough on batting averages as well, but last year many Padres hitters fared better at home.

Rookies & Newcomers

The Padres will be loaded with rookies and youngsters in 2003. Xavier Nady and Taggert Bozied will bring their power bats to San Diego at some point. The procession of quality arms into San Diego will continue with Brad Baker and Cliff Bartosh getting a taste. Other young starters who debuted in 2002, like Dennis Tankersley, Eric Cyr and Mike Bynum, will get a much longer look.

Dimensions: LF-327, LCF-370, CF-405, RCF-370, RF-330

Capacity: 66,307

Elevation: 20 feet

Surface: Grass

Foul Territory: Large

Park Factors

2002 Season

	Home Games Padres	Opp	Total	Away Games Padres	Opp	Total	Index
G	72	72	144	72	72	144	
Avg	.270	.261	.265	.239	.290	.264	101
AB	2440	2531	4971	2479	2412	4891	102
R	307	312	619	277	419	696	89
H	658	661	1319	592	699	1291	102
2B	102	120	222	113	159	272	80
3B	16	17	33	10	19	29	112
HR	57	73	130	64	91	155	83
BB	249	227	476	227	283	510	92
SO	427	524	951	526	466	992	94
E	53	52	105	59	48	107	98
E-Infield	47	39	86	47	42	89	97
LHB-Avg	.295	.275	.285	.239	.310	.271	105
LHB-HR	31	28	59	33	47	80	73
RHB-Avg	.245	.251	.248	.239	.275	.258	96
RHB-HR	26	45	71	31	44	75	93

2000-2002

	Home Games Padres	Opp	Total	Away Games Padres	Opp	Total	Index
G	219	219	438	219	219	438	
Avg	.250	.252	.251	.258	.283	.270	93
AB	7292	7703	14995	7650	7452	15102	99
R	913	995	1908	1083	1208	2291	83
H	1823	1942	3765	1972	2109	4081	92
2B	327	334	661	399	443	842	79
3B	42	38	80	41	50	91	89
HR	178	254	432	232	282	514	85
BB	811	708	1519	820	826	1646	93
SO	1543	1566	3109	1641	1373	3014	104
E	210	139	349	166	159	325	107
E-Infield	191	110	301	137	133	270	111
LHB-Avg	.269	.257	.263	.266	.292	.279	94
LHB-HR	81	111	192	95	127	222	84
RHB-Avg	.235	.248	.242	.252	.276	.264	92
RHB-HR	97	143	240	137	155	292	85

2002 Rankings (National League)

- Lowest walk factor
- Second-lowest double factor
- Third-lowest home-run factor
- Third-lowest LHB home-run factor

San Diego

Bruce Bochy

2002 Season

Because of injuries and youth, both the 2002 Padres and '02 Indians set a new major league record for most players (59) used in a season. San Diego also set a new big league mark by churning through 37 pitchers. With that kind of turnover, Bruce Bochy was forced to spend much of last year piecing together a jigsaw puzzle rather than forging a cohesive team.

Offense

Bochy preferred to do most of his managing before games, adjusting his lineup almost daily. Once the game began, he preferred to play things straight, which was quite a departure from what he did in his previous years as manager. In fact, the Padres were last in the league in sacrifices and tied for second to last in steals. This might not have been a bad idea had they also not been last in home runs and 10th in walks.

Pitching & Defense

No team in the National League made more mid-inning relief changes than San Diego. While Bochy has the reputation of being careful with his pitchers, perhaps that should be scrutinized further. True, only one starter averaged as many as 100 pitches per game last season. But that one guy was 21-year-old Oliver Perez, who threw at least 105 pitches in six of his 15 starts. Perez might have had more such outings if shoulder stiffness didn't land him on the disabled list in August. Jake Peavy, also 21, threw a similar number of high-pitch games, as did Adam Eaton in 2000 and 2001. While that is a far cry from some of the excessive workloads levied by other managers, one hopes that this will only strengthen and not break those talented young arms.

2003 Outlook

While the Padres will have a deep pitching staff and some very talented offensive players this season, more than half of the team will be 27 years old or younger. Much like Art Howe's experience with Oakland, Bochy's calm, forthright, egoless style is well suited to making this young team a contender. Avoiding injuries and acclimating the youth will be big keys to the Padres' success in 2003.

Born: 4/16/55 in Landes de Boussac, France

Playing Experience: 1978-1987, Hou, NYM, SD

Managerial Experience: 8 seasons

Manager Statistics

Year	Team, Lg	W	L	Pct	GB	Finish
2002	San Diego, NL	66	96	.407	32.0	5th West
8 Seasons		630	648	.493	–	–

2002 Starting Pitchers by Days Rest

	<=3	4	5	6+
Padres Starts	0	88	40	19
Padres ERA	–	4.98	4.68	4.24
NL Avg Starts	1	88	42	21
NL ERA	3.18	4.22	4.14	4.58

2002 Situational Stats

	Bruce Bochy	NL Average
Hit & Run Success %	40.0	36.5
Stolen Base Success %	61.7	68.3
Platoon Pct.	62.5	52.7
Defensive Subs	23	19
High-Pitch Outings	3	7
Quick/Slow Hooks	17/14	24/11
Sacrifice Attempts	63	95

2002 Rankings (National League)

- 1st in mid-inning pitching changes (208), first-batter platoon percentage and one-batter pitcher appearances (49)
- 2nd in steals of home plate (1)
- 3rd in fewest caught stealings of third base (3), double steals (6), defensive substitutions and starting lineups used (123)

Sean Burroughs

2002 Season

Sean Burroughs entered last season as one of the most highly touted prospects in baseball. But he fell substantially short of expectations due to injuries, the most severe of which was a torn right rotator cuff that required offseason surgery. He was placed on the disabled list after a disastrous May in which he hit .111. In June, he was sent to Triple-A to learn second base, a position the Padres felt would be less strenuous on his shoulder. Burroughs returned to San Diego in September and responded by hitting .377 over the final month.

Hitting

Burroughs is mature well beyond his years in his approach to hitting. However, the vicissitude of the major league strike zone is taking some getting used to. He rarely swings at pitches he can't handle, and usually makes solid contact. Although no one expected him to hit for great power last season, it was clear that his shoulder was bothering him, preventing him from following through on his swing.

Baserunning & Defense

Burroughs has average foot speed, but he is a very smart baserunner. While he probably never will steal 20 bases, he's a good bet to steal 10 or more yearly at a decent success rate. He did a pretty good job with his crash course at second base, though it likely would take several years for him to master the nuances of the position. The Padres understand that they're a better defensive team with Burroughs manning third base. At third, he has above-average range, good reflexes and a strong, accurate arm.

2003 Outlook

Burroughs' struggles last season largely were tied to his shoulder injury. His surgery went extremely well, and he's expected to be completely healthy by spring training. It may take a couple of years before he develops 20-plus home-run power, but it will come. In the meantime, he should lurk among the National League's batting average and on-base leaders.

Position: 3B/2B
Bats: L **Throws:** R
Ht: 6' 2" **Wt:** 200

Opening Day Age: 22
Born: 9/12/80 in Atlanta, GA
ML Seasons: 1

Overall Statistics

	G	AB	R	H	D	T	HR	RBI	SB	BB	SO	Avg	OBP	Slg
'02	63	192	18	52	5	1	1	11	2	12	30	.271	.317	.323
Car.	63	192	18	52	5	1	1	11	2	12	30	.271	.317	.323

Where He Hits the Ball

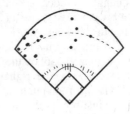 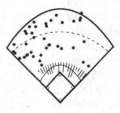

Vs. LHP   **Vs. RHP**

2002 Situational Stats

	AB	H	HR	RBI	Avg		AB	H	HR	RBI	Avg
Home	84	26	0	7	.310	LHP	55	12	0	2	.218
Road	108	26	1	4	.241	RHP	137	40	1	9	.292
First Half	131	29	1	7	.221	Sc Pos	49	9	0	9	.184
Scnd Half	61	23	0	4	.377	Clutch	23	4	0	2	.174

2002 Rankings (National League)

- Did not rank near the top or bottom in any category

San Diego

Adam Eaton

2002 Season

Adam Eaton required Tommy John surgery in 2001, after a strained elbow turned out to be a damaged ligament. A little more than a year later, he was back on the mound in San Diego. While the initial results weren't pretty, his final three outings were very encouraging. Working once against division winner Arizona and twice against playoff contending Los Angeles over the final two weeks, Eaton pitched a total of 21 innings. He allowed just 11 hits, four walks and four earned runs in those games, while striking out 18 batters.

Pitching

Eaton complements a riding fastball that tops out at 94 MPH with a good change, a slider, and a slow curve that looks like it breaks three feet. But what sets him apart from other young "stuff" hurlers are his composure and pitching instincts. Just 25 years of age, Eaton is calm and cool on the mound, and has a knack for making the right pitch. He has good control with all four pitches. The only remaining knock against him is that he surrenders home runs at a fairly high rate.

Defense & Hitting

Eaton is agile coming off the mound and fields his position well. He also hasn't been an easy mark for opposing players to run on. He's comfortable with a bat in his hands. He hit .289 as a rookie in 2000, though he's fallen into the low .100s since then. Eaton has a surprisingly good eye at the plate, drawing 11 walks in just 99 career plate appearances.

2003 Outlook

Eaton will be 18 months removed from his Tommy John surgery at the start of spring training this season. That's the timetable most doctors set for a full recovery from the procedure. Given how Eaton finished last season, 2003 should be a breakthrough year for him. He could establish himself as one of the National League's premier young pitchers.

Position: SP
Bats: R **Throws:** R
Ht: 6' 2" **Wt:** 190

Opening Day Age: 25
Born: 11/23/77 in Seattle, WA
ML Seasons: 3

Overall Statistics

	W	L	Pct.	ERA	G	GS	Sv	IP	H	BB	SO	HR	Ratio
'02	1	1	.500	5.40	6	6	0	33.1	28	17	25	5	1.35
Car.	16	10	.615	4.36	45	45	0	285.0	270	118	224	39	1.36

How Often He Throws Strikes

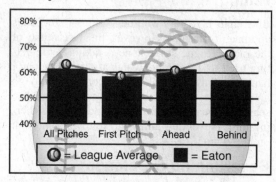

= League Average ■ = Eaton

2002 Situational Stats

	W	L	ERA	Sv	IP		AB	H	HR	RBI	Avg
Home	1	0	4.67	0	17.1	LHB	51	17	4	11	.333
Road	0	1	6.19	0	16.0	RHB	68	11	1	7	.162
First Half	0	0	—	0	0.0	Sc Pos	33	6	1	10	.182
Scnd Half	1	1	5.40	0	33.1	Clutch	11	1	1	1	.091

2002 Rankings (National League)

- Did not rank near the top or bottom in any category

Trevor Hoffman

2002 Season

With 38 saves last year, Trevor Hoffman became the first pitcher in history to record eight straight 30-save seasons. Only Lee Smith, with 10, ever registered more 30-save seasons in his career. Hoffman, the all-time leader in save percentage (89 percent) widened his lead by converting 93 percent of his opportunities in 2002. His two home runs allowed put to rest previous concerns over a rising trend in surrendering the longball.

Pitching

Hoffman pitches off his changeup. It's probably the best change of pace in the big leagues and arguably one of the best ever. His arm motion for the change is exactly the same as it is with his fastball. He'll show a curve and a slider, as well. But the changeup, which he has been known to throw three or four times in a row, is what hitters look for. Savvy veteran that he is, Hoffman occasionally will pour in nothing but his 88-90 MPH fastballs over the heart of the plate, knowing the hitter is waiting only for his famous out pitch.

Defense & Hitting

Despite his high-leg-kick delivery, the former minor league shortstop is quick and agile off the mound. He doesn't hold on runners very well, instead preferring to concentrate on the batter. While he rarely gets to bat, he takes an aggressive swing, which has resulted in two doubles among his four career major league hits.

2003 Outlook

Hoffman's offseason included surgery to clean up some fraying in his right shoulder, very similar to the operation he had after the 1995 season. He should be ready to go this spring. In 2002, he put to rest any notion that he was on the downside of his career, despite the loss of his plus fastball. His changeup and pitching instincts are so well developed, he undoubtedly will be closing for the Padres when they open their new stadium in 2004.

Position: RP
Bats: R **Throws:** R
Ht: 6' 0" **Wt:** 205

Opening Day Age: 35
Born: 10/13/67 in Bellflower, CA
ML Seasons: 10

Overall Statistics

	W	L	Pct.	ERA	G	GS	Sv	IP	H	BB	SO	HR	Ratio
'02	2	5	.286	2.73	61	0	38	59.1	52	18	69	2	1.18
Car.	45	44	.506	2.79	632	0	352	701.0	526	214	797	65	1.06

How Often He Throws Strikes

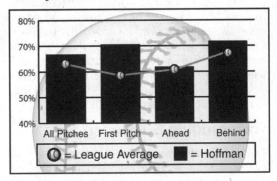

= League Average ■ = Hoffman

2002 Situational Stats

	W	L	ERA	Sv	IP		AB	H	HR	RBI	Avg
Home	2	3	1.72	23	36.2	LHB	102	19	2	7	.186
Road	0	2	4.37	15	22.2	RHB	120	33	0	12	.275
First Half	1	1	2.43	20	33.1	Sc Pos	60	15	0	17	.250
Scnd Half	1	4	3.12	18	26.0	Clutch	168	39	2	19	.232

2002 Rankings (National League)

- 3rd in save percentage (92.7)
- 5th in most strikeouts per nine innings in relief (10.5)
- 7th in saves
- 8th in save opportunities (41)
- Led the Padres in saves, games finished (52), save opportunities (41), lowest batting average allowed vs. lefthanded batters, save percentage (92.7), lowest percentage of inherited runners scored (9.5), relief ERA (2.73), lowest batting average allowed in relief (.234), most strikeouts per nine innings in relief (10.5) and fewest baserunners allowed per nine innings in relief (10.8)

San Diego

Ryan Klesko

2002 Season

For the first time in his career, Ryan Klesko hit .300 while playing full-time. He also set career highs in hits and doubles. He enjoyed the ninth and 10th four-hit games of his career, as well as his fourth career game with six RBI. Injuries to Phil Nevin and Sean Burroughs sidetracked the Padres' plan of having Klesko play right field. By the end of the year, he firmly was entrenched back at first base, his best position.

Hitting

It is just about impossible to get a fastball on the inner half of the strike zone past Klesko. He turns on that pitch about as well as anyone. He improved his coverage of the outside part of the plate last year. He also continued his improvement versus lefthanders, making big strides in both his on-base and slugging percentages against southpaws. While most of Klesko's home-run power still comes from pulling the ball, he has learned to hit with authority to all fields.

Baserunning & Defense

Despite his stolen-base totals dropping significantly, Klesko is a very good and aggressive baserunner. On defense, he's still a bit awkward around the first-base bag and not very polished digging balls on a hop. But he consistently makes some of the nicest flips to the pitcher covering that you'll ever see. In the outfield, he sometimes has trouble reading the ball off the bat and does not always take the best route. But he never gives up on a ball and has a strong, accurate arm.

2003 Outlook

After last year's experiment in right field, Klesko will return to first base in 2003. His continuing improvement versus lefties bodes well for the breakout power season that his minor league numbers indicated he was capable of. He might not ever steal 20 bases again, but that won't prevent him from becoming one of the National League's best all-around offensive threats.

Position: 1B/RF
Bats: L **Throws:** L
Ht: 6' 3" **Wt:** 220

Opening Day Age: 31
Born: 6/12/71 in Westminster, CA
ML Seasons: 11

Overall Statistics

	G	AB	R	H	D	T	HR	RBI	SB	BB	SO	Avg	OBP	Slg
'02	146	540	90	162	39	1	29	95	6	76	86	.300	.388	.537
Car.	1229	4003	657	1140	246	27	224	750	78	556	779	.285	.372	.528

Where He Hits the Ball

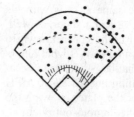 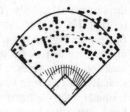

Vs. LHP   **Vs. RHP**

2002 Situational Stats

	AB	H	HR	RBI	Avg		AB	H	HR	RBI	Avg
Home	264	84	11	39	.318	LHP	157	45	8	32	.287
Road	276	78	18	56	.283	RHP	383	117	21	63	.305
First Half	282	85	17	49	.301	Sc Pos	116	38	5	60	.328
Scnd Half	258	77	12	46	.298	Clutch	76	24	3	8	.316

2002 Rankings (National League)

- 4th in lowest fielding percentage at first base (.993)
- 6th in errors at first base (7)
- Led the Padres in batting average, home runs, runs scored, doubles, total bases (290), RBI, walks, intentional walks (11), hit by pitch (4), times on base (242), slugging percentage, on-base percentage, fewest GDPs per GDP situation (4.6%), batting average vs. righthanded pitchers, cleanup slugging percentage (.587), slugging percentage vs. righthanded pitchers (.556), on-base percentage vs. righthanded pitchers (.394) and batting average with two strikes (.226)

Mark Kotsay

2002 Season

Mark Kotsay quietly had a very good year, establishing new career highs in hits, homers, walks and slugging percentage. The 2002 season also marked the third consecutive year that he improved his OPS (on-base + slugging). Not coincidentally, the Padres signed him in July to a contract extension through the 2006 season.

Hitting

Kotsay is a line-drive hitter who likes to go to the opposite field. He took a more aggressive approach last season, as he looked to pull a little more. The tactic helped his home-run numbers, though it increased his strikeout total as well. He has a discerning eye at the plate and the ability to make contact with an extremely high percentage of his swings. Given that, Kotsay should be able to consolidate last year's power gains with fewer strikeouts this season, just as he did in 2000. His groundball-flyball ratio has been decreasing significantly over the last three seasons, which generally is a good omen for a power breakout. A campaign with 70 extra-base hits certainly is possible with his talent.

Baserunning & Defense

Kotsay is a skilled all-around player with great instincts. He's a very good baserunner, although he tied a career worst in 2002 by getting caught stealing nine times. Defensively, he makes great reads, has plus range and possesses a very strong, accurate arm. It's still surprising how often teams try to run on him. After accumulating 57 assists (47 in right field) the previous four years, he tacked on a league-leading 11 from center field in 2002.

2003 Outlook

The Padres would like to move Kotsay back to his more natural position in right field in 2003. However, the Gene Kingsale trade to the Tigers, coupled with San Diego's preponderance of corner outfielders, makes any move to right for Kotsay unlikely. He is slated to remain in center and hit near the top of the order for what portends to be a breakout season.

Position: CF
Bats: L **Throws:** L
Ht: 6' 0" **Wt:** 201

Opening Day Age: 27
Born: 12/2/75 in Whittier, CA
ML Seasons: 6
Pronunciation: COT-say

Overall Statistics

	G	AB	R	H	D	T	HR	RBI	SB	BB	SO	Avg	OBP	Slg
'02	153	578	82	169	27	7	17	61	11	59	89	.292	.359	.452
Car.	740	2639	370	750	136	30	58	298	63	216	311	.284	.337	.424

Where He Hits the Ball

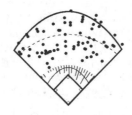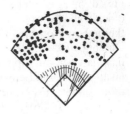

Vs. LHP   **Vs. RHP**

2002 Situational Stats

	AB	H	HR	RBI	Avg		AB	H	HR	RBI	Avg
Home	287	88	11	32	.307	LHP	188	61	5	20	.324
Road	291	81	6	29	.278	RHP	390	108	12	41	.277
First Half	322	100	6	34	.311	Sc Pos	108	31	4	44	.287
Scnd Half	256	69	11	27	.270	Clutch	99	20	1	8	.202

2002 Rankings (National League)

- 1st in on-base percentage for a leadoff hitter (.396), assists in center field (11) and lowest stolen-base percentage (55.0)
- 5th in lowest fielding percentage in center field (.989)
- 6th in triples and errors in center field (4)
- Led the Padres in at-bats, hits, singles, triples, stolen bases, caught stealing (9), strikeouts, pitches seen (2,359), plate appearances (646), games played and on-base percentage for a leadoff hitter (.396)

San Diego

Brian Lawrence

2002 Season

Brian Lawrence was one of the few bright spots on a pitching staff that used a major league record 37 pitchers last year. Lawrence led the Padres in innings pitched, wins and strikeouts, while his 3.69 ERA ranked among the top 25 in the National League. He slowed down in August and September, but that may have been due to fatigue, as he threw 95.1 more innings last season than he had in 2001.

Pitching

Although Lawrence's fastball is average according to the radar gun, he can cut it or sink it with good control. He also has a good changeup, but his out pitch is a hard-breaking slider. He works quickly and keeps his infielders on their toes with the highest groundball-flyball ratio in the league. One big concern is that lefties hit him especially hard last season. Opposing managers may have taken notice, too. Lefthanded batters accumulated more at-bats (413) versus Lawrence than did righthanders (406).

Defense & Hitting

Lawrence progressed in all aspects of his defense last year. He didn't make a single error, and his range off the mound improved. He also did a better job of shutting down the running game with a more refined move to first. Lawrence is not a good hitter, but has learned to coax a walk from pitchers who are struggling. He does a good job of bunting.

2003 Outlook

As well as Lawrence pitched in 2002, and as much as he improved, there still are some things he needs to work on to keep his spot in the rotation secure. He'll need to rein in lefties, or opposing managers will continue to stack their lineups against him. Lawrence also will need to do a better job in the middle and later innings. Batters hit .293 and slugged .427 after his 45th pitch in 2002.

Position: SP
Bats: R **Throws:** R
Ht: 6' 0" **Wt:** 195

Opening Day Age: 26
Born: 5/14/76 in Fort Collins, CO
ML Seasons: 2

Overall Statistics

	W	L	Pct.	ERA	G	GS	Sv	IP	H	BB	SO	HR	Ratio
'02	12	12	.500	3.69	35	31	0	210.0	230	52	149	16	1.34
Car.	17	17	.500	3.60	62	46	0	324.2	337	86	233	26	1.30

How Often He Throws Strikes

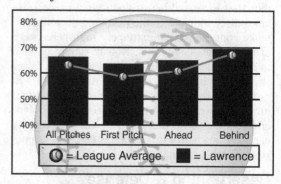

2002 Situational Stats

	W	L	ERA	Sv	IP		AB	H	HR	RBI	Avg
Home	6	5	3.57	0	111.0	LHB	413	134	7	45	.324
Road	6	7	3.82	0	99.0	RHB	406	96	9	38	.236
First Half	7	5	3.65	0	120.2	Sc Pos	196	46	7	70	.235
Scnd Half	5	7	3.73	0	89.1	Clutch	73	22	3	8	.301

2002 Rankings (National League)

- 1st in GDPs induced (29), highest groundball-flyball ratio allowed (2.5) and fielding percentage at pitcher (1.000)
- 2nd in fewest pitches thrown per batter (3.45) and most GDPs induced per nine innings (1.2)
- Led the Padres in ERA, wins, losses, shutouts (2), innings pitched, hits allowed, batters faced (894), hit batsmen (11), strikeouts, pitches thrown (3,086), stolen bases allowed (11), GDPs induced (29), highest strikeout-walk ratio (2.9), lowest slugging percentage allowed (.393), fewest pitches thrown per batter (3.45) and fewest home runs allowed per nine innings (.69)

Phil Nevin

2002 Season

Phil Nevin began last season well enough, hitting .358 with an OPS (on-base + slugging percentage) of .958 in April. But a strained elbow at the start of May, followed by a broken humerus suffered while diving for a ball at the end of the month, ended any notion of Nevin duplicating his tremendous 2001 production. Sidelined until the All-Star break, his shoulder and arm muscles never regained full strength, robbing him of his power in the second half.

Hitting

Nevin's shoulder injury may have been a blessing in disguise. He became more comfortable going to right field on low, outside pitches, a location that previously had given him trouble. The improved plate coverage, along with full health, should pay dividends in the future. Nevin is an emotional player and takes his mistakes very personally. Sometimes he'll try too hard to make amends and will get himself into a hitting funk.

Baserunning & Defense

Although he's not a fast baserunner, Nevin is smart on the basepaths, and no one breaks up a double play with more tenacity. Like his hitting, he can be streaky with his defense. He doesn't have quick feet, which limits his range and causes occasional misplays. But he does have good instincts for the ball and a strong, accurate arm, both of which will serve him well in the outfield.

2003 Outlook

Although he would prefer to play third base, Nevin knows that the Padres are a better team with Sean Burroughs' glove there, and he has volunteered to play left field. Nevin played there with some success in 1996 and 1997 when he was with the Tigers, so the move won't be too much of an adjustment. The health of his shoulder is the biggest concern, but the prognosis is very good that he'll be 100 percent by this spring.

Position: 3B/1B
Bats: R **Throws:** R
Ht: 6' 2" **Wt:** 231

Opening Day Age: 32
Born: 1/19/71 in Fullerton, CA
ML Seasons: 8

Overall Statistics

	G	AB	R	H	D	T	HR	RBI	SB	BB	SO	Avg	OBP	Slg
'02	107	407	53	116	16	0	12	57	4	38	87	.285	.344	.413
Car.	780	2638	376	725	141	4	135	469	13	287	651	.275	.348	.485

Where He Hits the Ball

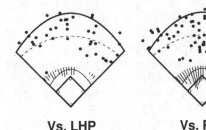

Vs. LHP   **Vs. RHP**

2002 Situational Stats

	AB	H	HR	RBI	Avg		AB	H	HR	RBI	Avg
Home	201	66	5	35	.328	LHP	101	34	5	22	.337
Road	206	50	7	22	.243	RHP	306	82	7	35	.268
First Half	147	43	5	21	.293	Sc Pos	120	31	2	44	.258
Scnd Half	260	73	7	36	.281	Clutch	60	20	4	9	.333

2002 Rankings (National League)

- 1st in lowest cleanup slugging percentage (.355)
- 3rd in batting average with the bases loaded (.500)
- 6th in errors at third base (14)
- Led the Padres in batting average in the clutch, batting average with the bases loaded (.500), batting average vs. lefthanded pitchers, on-base percentage vs. lefthanded pitchers (.407) and batting average at home

Jake Peavy

2002 Season

Injuries ravaged San Diego's pitching staff last season. And like many of the Padres' young starters, Jake Peavy got an opportunity to pitch in the big leagues earlier than originally planned. His first major league start came against the Yankees on June 22 and typified his season in microcosm. Peavy pitched well, holding the Yanks to one run and three hits over six innings. Yet he got tagged with the loss, 1-0. Although he wound up holding the opposition to three earned runs or fewer in 12 of 17 starts, he finished with a 6-7 record. He endured many of the typical rookie struggles with consistency. But by the end of the year, his overall numbers showed considerable promise.

Pitching

Peavy often is compared to Greg Maddux, both in terms of stuff and control. Peavy has a little more length on his fastball, consistently reaching the low 90s. But he hasn't quite honed Maddux' pinpoint control yet. Peavy's slider and changeup are both above average. He has good pitching instincts and enough confidence in his command to throw any of his pitches on any count. His righthanded delivery was much more effective against righthanded batters last year.

Defense & Hitting

Peavy is a good fielder who gets a good number of opportunities to show his prowess with the glove thanks to his groundball-inducing style. Basestealers didn't run wild in his major league debut, though none were caught, either. Peavy looks comfortable with a bat in his hands and takes a full cut at the plate. His stroke yielded three doubles among his seven hits last season. He usually helps himself in sacrifice situations by laying down good bunts.

2003 Outlook

Peavy still is very young to be pitching in the majors. But with his combination of maturity, talent, drive and skill, he will continue to pitch well beyond his years. He'll likely anchor the best young staff in the National League.

Position: SP
Bats: R **Throws:** R
Ht: 6' 1" **Wt:** 180

Opening Day Age: 21
Born: 5/31/81 in Mobile, AL
ML Seasons: 1

Overall Statistics

	W	L	Pct.	ERA	G	GS	Sv	IP	H	BB	SO	HR	Ratio
'02	6	7	.462	4.52	17	17	0	97.2	106	33	90	11	1.42
Car.	6	7	.462	4.52	17	17	0	97.2	106	33	90	11	1.42

How Often He Throws Strikes

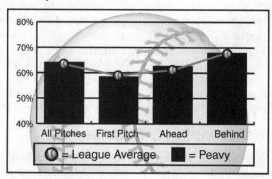

2002 Situational Stats

	W	L	ERA	Sv	IP		AB	H	HR	RBI	Avg
Home	4	1	2.56	0	45.2	LHB	194	63	8	32	.325
Road	2	6	6.23	0	52.0	RHB	193	43	3	17	.223
First Half	0	3	3.60	0	15.0	Sc Pos	96	29	3	39	.302
Scnd Half	6	4	4.68	0	82.2	Clutch	8	1	0	0	.125

2002 Rankings (National League)

- Led the Padres in most run support per nine innings (5.3) and most strikeouts per nine innings (8.3)

Oliver Perez

2002 Season

The Padres were planning to give Oliver Perez another full season in the minor leagues last year. But injuries to the big club's pitching staff and Perez' own excellence—he posted a 1.63 ERA between two minor league stops—forced the Padres to give him a shot. He didn't disappoint, holding the opposition to three runs or fewer in 10 of his 15 starts. He threw several gems, including a 13-strikeout, one-hit effort over six-plus innings at Colorado in early July.

Pitching

Perez has command of a fastball that touches 94 MPH, as well as a sweeping slider, curve and change. He can throw his fastball and slider for strikes from two different arm angles—an almost sidearm delivery, and a three-quarters release. He has a slight hitch in his motion that he can make longer or shorter to further throw off a hitter's timing. Although Perez is lefthanded, opposing righthanded batters combined for a sub-.200 batting average last season. But interestingly, the southpaw was much less susceptible to the longball versus lefthanded swingers. Perez is incredibly poised on the mound and doesn't appear intimidated by any circumstance.

Defense & Hitting

Despite a delivery that takes him to the third-base side of the mound, Perez does a good job fielding the ball. He also limited opposing baserunners to just one stolen base during his 16 appearances with the Padres. He is not a good hitter, striking out in more than a third of his at-bats. His bunting skills need more work as well.

2003 Outlook

Perez experienced some shoulder discomfort that landed him on the disabled list in August. But his last few starts allayed any fears that the condition was anything more than a little stiffness. Still, with such a slight build, injuries are a concern. In fact, an injury could be the only thing that will prevent Perez from becoming an excellent big league starter.

Position: SP
Bats: L **Throws:** L
Ht: 6' 3" **Wt:** 160

Opening Day Age: 21
Born: 8/15/81 in Culiacan, Mexico
ML Seasons: 1

Overall Statistics

	W	L	Pct.	ERA	G	GS	Sv	IP	H	BB	SO	HR	Ratio
'02	4	5	.444	3.50	16	15	0	90.0	71	48	94	13	1.32
Car.	4	5	.444	3.50	16	15	0	90.0	71	48	94	13	1.32

How Often He Throws Strikes

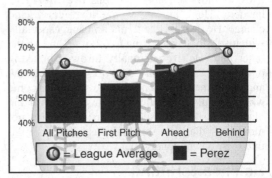

= League Average   = Perez

2002 Situational Stats

	W	L	ERA	Sv	IP		AB	H	HR	RBI	Avg
Home	2	2	3.00	0	42.0	LHB	85	25	1	5	.294
Road	2	3	3.94	0	48.0	RHB	241	46	12	29	.191
First Half	3	1	3.45	0	31.1	Sc Pos	65	14	4	22	.215
Scnd Half	1	4	3.53	0	58.2	Clutch	20	5	0	1	.250

2002 Rankings (National League)

- 4th in lowest batting average allowed vs. righthanded batters
- Led the Padres in lowest batting average allowed vs. righthanded batters

Brett Tomko

2002 Season

Brett Tomko turned out to be the biggest bargain in the deal that also brought Ramon Vazquez and Tom Lampkin from Seattle to San Diego after the 2001 season. Consigned to swingman duties with the Mariners, Tomko was given a shot at the Padres' rotation last spring. He pitched brilliantly for the first month, but lapsed back into old patterns and inconsistency as the season wore on. His 31 homers allowed tied for the second most in the National League.

Pitching

Tomko has good control of four pitches, including a low to mid-90s fastball that runs away from left-handers. He also throws a slider, curve and change. He doesn't like to pitch inside, especially with his fastball, preferring to use it up and on the outer half. He'll occasionally throw a breaking pitch inside, but usually he works that pitch low and out of the strike zone. Tomko's troubles come when he fails to establish the inside part of the plate against righthanded batters. If they're not moved off the plate, his high fastball sails right into their power zone.

Defense & Hitting

Tomko is predominately a flyball pitcher, so he doesn't get much opportunity to flash the leather. However, when a ball does come his way, he'll make the play. Because of his deliberate delivery, he doesn't hold runners very well. Tomko is a good hitter who makes contact and let's opposing pitchers get themselves into trouble if they aren't throwing strikes. He's also an adept bunter.

2003 Outlook

Tomko was a very good addition to San Diego. Whether he becomes the excellent starter someone with his talent should become, or just a good middle-of-the-rotation guy, depends on how quickly he embraces the need to establish himself on the inside half of the plate.

Position: SP
Bats: R **Throws:** R
Ht: 6' 4" **Wt:** 215

Opening Day Age: 29
Born: 4/7/73 in Euclid, OH
ML Seasons: 6

Overall Statistics

	W	L	Pct.	ERA	G	GS	Sv	IP	H	BB	SO	HR	Ratio
'02	10	10	.500	4.49	32	32	0	204.1	212	60	126	31	1.33
Car.	49	42	.538	4.46	164	123	1	840.0	825	286	596	119	1.32

How Often He Throws Strikes

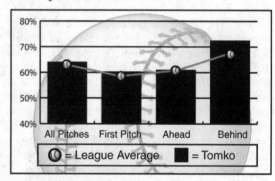

= League Average   = Tomko

2002 Situational Stats

	W	L	ERA	Sv	IP		AB	H	HR	RBI	Avg
Home	6	5	4.13	0	120.0	LHB	374	101	9	35	.270
Road	4	5	5.02	0	84.1	RHB	421	111	22	62	.264
First Half	4	6	3.86	0	116.2	Sc Pos	167	39	3	58	.234
Scnd Half	6	4	5.34	0	87.2	Clutch	52	11	2	4	.212

2002 Rankings (National League)

- 2nd in home runs allowed
- 4th in fewest pitches thrown per batter (3.50)
- 6th in highest slugging percentage allowed (.460), highest ERA on the road and most home runs allowed per nine innings (1.37)
- 9th in fewest GDPs induced per nine innings (0.6)
- Led the Padres in sacrifice bunts (7), games started, complete games (3), home runs allowed, walks allowed, pickoff throws (64), winning percentage, lowest batting average allowed (.267) and lowest on-base percentage allowed (.317)

Bubba Trammell

2002 Season

Despite a strong showing in 2001, Bubba Trammell was consigned to a platoon role when last season began. But when Phil Nevin went down with a broken arm, Ryan Klesko moved back to first base and Trammell became the every-day right fielder. Unfortunately, Trammell was slumping badly at the time, and the extra playing time only served to dig him deeper into the hole. While a strong June brought him back to respectability, July trade rumors coincided with another bad slump. Once the deadline passed, he got hot again, until the September callups cut into his playing time.

Hitting

Trammell likes the ball middle-in and will toma-hawk high, inside fastballs out of the park. He covers the plate pretty well and can drive the ball to all fields, although his home run power is from left to center field. He has a good batting eye for someone with his power, but he can be coaxed into swinging at balls low and outside.

Baserunning & Defense

Trammell is not fleet afoot, so he's pretty much a station-to-station runner and is no threat to steal. Surprisingly, he grounds into very few double plays. Although his reads and route running have improved, his lack of foot speed still limits his outfield range to about average. His arm is aver-age, but he makes accurate throws and never miss-es the cutoff.

2003 Outlook

Although Gene Kingsale was traded, strong Arizona Fall League performances from Xavier Nady and Taggert Bozied, along with Phil Nevin's impending move to the outfield, probably mean Trammell's time in San Diego is nearing an end. The Padres would like to get out from under the $7.5 million and two years left on his contract. Wherever Trammell ends up in 2003, he will pro-vide a solid righthanded power bat, workman-like defense and an unswerving team-first attitude.

Position: RF/LF
Bats: R **Throws:** R
Ht: 6' 2" **Wt:** 220

Opening Day Age: 31
Born: 11/6/71 in Knoxville, TN
ML Seasons: 6
Pronunciation: TRAM-mull

Overall Statistics

	G	AB	R	H	D	T	HR	RBI	SB	BB	SO	Avg	OBP	Slg
'02	133	403	54	98	16	1	17	56	1	53	71	.243	.333	.414
Car.	562	1743	239	458	91	7	82	280	10	204	315	.263	.341	.464

Where He Hits the Ball

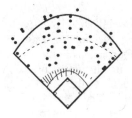 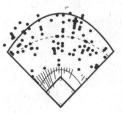

Vs. LHP   **Vs. RHP**

2002 Situational Stats

	AB	H	HR	RBI	Avg		AB	H	HR	RBI	Avg
Home	195	46	5	29	.236	LHP	131	40	7	20	.305
Road	208	52	12	27	.250	RHP	272	58	10	36	.213
First Half	233	52	7	26	.223	Sc Pos	101	23	3	38	.228
Scnd Half	170	46	10	30	.271	Clutch	50	11	1	9	.220

2002 Rankings (National League)

- 3rd in batting average with the bases loaded (.500)
- 4th in lowest batting average on a 3-2 count (.091)
- 6th in errors in right field (4) and lowest bat-ting average with two strikes (.142)
- Led the Padres in batting average with the bases loaded (.500)

San Diego

Ramon Vazquez

2002 Season

Ramon Vazquez was somewhat of a disappointment after being acquired from the Mariners after the 2001 season. He did provide solid defense for the Padres last year in the middle of their infield. But his offense failed to meet expectations in both his ability to reach base and to hit for power. One encouraging sign is that his offensive numbers improved significantly in the second half. An important contributor to Vazquez' slow start was a strained hamstring suffered in spring training that lingered until June. His individual accomplishments included chalking up the first couple four-hit games of his career.

Hitting

Vazquez covers the plate well and has a fairly selective eye while batting. He drew at least 75 walks in a season on three occasions in the minor leagues. He doesn't have much power, but will take the extra base on balls hit to the gap. He's a spray hitter, hitting groundballs and low line drives to all fields. One major concern was his ineffectiveness against lefthanded pitchers, as Vazquez could not handle their inside offerings.

Baserunning & Defense

While Vazquez usually is a smart baserunner, he will let his concentration lapse occasionally, like straying too far from the bag. He doesn't possess great speed, though good instincts make him capable of swiping a dozen bags per season. Defensively, he doesn't show as much range as the Padres were hoping for. But he has sure hands and a strong, accurate arm, making plays on the balls he does reach. He turns the pivot surprisingly well at second base.

2003 Outlook

While the Padres see Vazquez as their starting shortstop this season, he'll get significant competition from college standout and 2002 first-round pick, Khalil Greene. Greene's offensive potential is a substantial improvement over what Vazquez offered last year. Vazquez will have to step up his game at the plate to keep the job.

Position: 2B/SS/3B
Bats: L **Throws:** R
Ht: 5'11" **Wt:** 170

Opening Day Age: 26
Born: 8/21/76 in Aibonito, PR
ML Seasons: 2

Overall Statistics

	G	AB	R	H	D	T	HR	RBI	SB	BB	SO	Avg	OBP	Slg
'02	128	423	50	116	21	5	2	32	7	45	79	.274	.344	.362
Car.	145	458	55	124	21	5	2	36	7	45	82	.271	.335	.352

Where He Hits the Ball

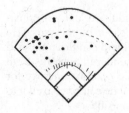 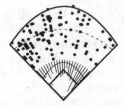

Vs. LHP   **Vs. RHP**

2002 Situational Stats

	AB	H	HR	RBI	Avg		AB	H	HR	RBI	Avg
Home	191	56	0	13	.293	LHP	70	11	0	4	.157
Road	232	60	2	19	.259	RHP	353	105	2	28	.297
First Half	176	44	1	11	.250	Sc Pos	81	21	1	28	.259
Scnd Half	247	72	1	21	.291	Clutch	68	16	0	2	.235

2002 Rankings (National League)

- 3rd in batting average with the bases loaded (.500) and batting average among rookies
- 5th in RBI among rookies
- 7th in on-base percentage for a leadoff hitter (.354)
- Led the Padres in highest groundball-flyball ratio (2.2), steals of third (3) and batting average with the bases loaded (.500)

Deivi Cruz

Position: SS
Bats: R **Throws:** R
Ht: 6' 0" **Wt:** 184

Opening Day Age: 30
Born: 11/6/72 in Nizao de Bani, DR
ML Seasons: 6
Pronunciation: DAY-vee

Overall Statistics

	G	AB	R	H	D	T	HR	RBI	SB	BB	SO	Avg	OBP	Slg
'02	151	514	49	135	28	2	7	47	2	22	58	.263	.294	.366
Car.	854	2919	307	787	185	11	44	324	14	91	314	.270	.294	.386

2002 Situational Stats

	AB	H	HR	RBI	Avg		AB	H	HR	RBI	Avg
Home	260	58	3	26	.223	LHP	161	39	3	11	.242
Road	254	77	4	21	.303	RHP	353	96	4	36	.272
First Half	285	74	4	27	.260	Sc Pos	131	27	2	39	.206
Scnd Half	229	61	3	20	.266	Clutch	82	17	0	11	.207

2002 Season

The Padres signed Deivi Cruz last January as infield insurance, and his contract has turned out to be money well spent. Due to injuries and various shakeups on the roster, Cruz played 147 games at shortstop. Although his offensive numbers showed no improvement over 2001, he provided desperately needed defensive stability at short. Last year's .976 team fielding percentage at the position was a huge improvement over the club's 2001 mark of .941.

Hitting, Baserunning & Defense

Cruz makes contact and has good plate coverage, but he gets himself out on pitches outside the strike zone far too often. He rarely takes a first pitch, even if it's not over the plate. Nearly 44 percent of his plate appearances were over after two pitches. Once on base, he's no threat to steal and doesn't run particularly well. He has a strong arm, good range from side to side and retreats well on popups. But he's slow to charge infield grounders.

2003 Outlook

While the Padres would like to bring back Cruz this season as an insurance policy at short once again, the dollars likely won't be there to make it happen. His defensive reputation and ability to make contact will be attractive to some team.

Jeremy Fikac

Position: RP
Bats: R **Throws:** R
Ht: 6' 2" **Wt:** 185

Opening Day Age: 27
Born: 4/8/75 in Shiner, TX
ML Seasons: 2
Pronunciation: fee-kotch

Overall Statistics

	W	L	Pct.	ERA	G	GS	Sv	IP	H	BB	SO	HR	Ratio
'02	4	7	.364	5.48	65	0	0	69.0	74	34	66	13	1.57
Car.	6	7	.462	4.34	88	0	0	95.1	89	39	85	15	1.34

2002 Situational Stats

	W	L	ERA	Sv	IP		AB	H	HR	RBI	Avg
Home	2	2	4.13	0	32.2	LHB	117	32	3	19	.274
Road	2	5	6.69	0	36.1	RHB	160	42	10	33	.263
First Half	3	5	4.95	0	40.0	Sc Pos	88	20	4	38	.227
Scnd Half	1	2	6.21	0	29.0	Clutch	124	34	9	30	.274

2002 Season

Jeremy Fikac finished 2001 as Trevor Hoffman's primary setup man. Prior to last spring training, Fikac had a fibrous mass removed from his pitching hand. He then was brilliant in April, posting a 1.46 ERA while allowing a .182 average. The good times wouldn't last, however, as he was hit hard the next three months. After rebounding nicely in August, he was pummeled again in September.

Pitching, Defense & Hitting

Fikac has an average fastball which he spots to set up an excellent changeup. He'll also show a decent slider and curve. His problems last season stemmed from an uncharacteristic lack of control. When he wasn't wild outside the strike zone, he was leaving pitches over the middle of the plate. Fikac was a third baseman in college and is a good fielder off the mound. Despite his experience as an everyday player, he's posted just two big league at-bats.

2003 Outlook

Fikac still has a place in the Padres' bullpen and may yet again assert himself as a setup candidate. But he needs to improve his consistency to be considered for any significant role.

Ron Gant

Position: LF
Bats: R **Throws:** R
Ht: 6' 0" **Wt:** 195

Opening Day Age: 38
Born: 3/2/65 in Victoria, TX
ML Seasons: 15

Overall Statistics

G	AB	R	H	D	T	HR	RBI	SB	BB	SO	Avg	OBP	Slg
102	309	58	81	14	1	18	59	4	36	59	.262	.338	.489
1815	6408	1076	1645	302	50	320	1004	243	768	1402	.257	.337	.469

2002 Situational Stats

	AB	H	HR	RBI	Avg		AB	H	HR	RBI	Avg
Home	146	46	9	29	.315	LHP	109	32	7	25	.294
Road	163	35	9	30	.215	RHP	200	49	11	34	.245
First Half	136	34	7	28	.250	Sc Pos	81	25	4	41	.309
Scnd Half	173	47	11	31	.272	Clutch	50	11	3	14	.220

2002 Season

Ron Gant was signed to provide a righthanded complement to Ray Lankford in left field. A broken pinky in late April limited Gant's effectiveness and at-bats in the first half. Fully healed by the All-Star break, he finished strong, hitting .272 and slugging .514 over his final 55 games.

Hitting, Baserunning & Defense

Gant hits lefties as well as ever. He favors balls down in the zone and has the strength to lift those pitches out of the park. He's best suited to starting games, as his numbers off the bench never have been particularly impressive. He still has decent speed on the basepaths, though his days as a true basestealing threat are over. He reads the ball fairly well off the bat and his range is decent, but his arm isn't strong enough to play anywhere but left field. Even then, it's somewhat of a liability.

2003 Outlook

Gant is a free agent this offseason, and he's doubtful to return after the Padres didn't offer him salary arbitration. However, Gant's experience and ability to mash lefthanders will be very attractive to a team that is free-agent shopping.

Wiki Gonzalez

Position: C
Bats: R **Throws:** R
Ht: 5'11" **Wt:** 203

Opening Day Age: 28
Born: 5/17/74 in Aragua, VZ
ML Seasons: 4
Pronunciation: WICK-ee

Overall Statistics

	G	AB	R	H	D	T	HR	RBI	SB	BB	SO	Avg	OBP	Slg
'02	56	164	16	36	8	1	1	20	0	27	24	.220	.330	.299
Car.	245	691	64	167	31	3	17	89	3	69	91	.242	.317	.369

2002 Situational Stats

	AB	H	HR	RBI	Avg		AB	H	HR	RBI	Avg
Home	89	20	1	13	.225	LHP	42	13	1	8	.310
Road	75	16	0	7	.213	RHP	122	23	0	12	.189
First Half	96	23	1	15	.240	Sc Pos	47	12	1	20	.255
Scnd Half	68	13	0	5	.191	Clutch	22	5	0	2	.227

2002 Season

The Padres liked Wiki Gonzalez' potential enough to trade Ben Davis to Seattle after 2001. Rewarded with the starting job and a four-year deal, Gonzalez disappointed by reporting to camp out of shape. His season was a laundry list of injuries, including bone chips in his throwing elbow, which required surgery at the end of the year.

Hitting, Baserunning & Defense

Gonzalez walked more often than he struck out in 2002. That success was due in part to his selectivity, as he took 60 percent of the pitches he faced in 2002. But with his slow foot speed, he'll hit into a lot of double plays. While injuries curtailed his offensive numbers last year, he has the power to hit 12-15 homers. Gonzalez is a very talented defender with quick feet and a strong, accurate arm, though he still needs to refine his technique.

2003 Outlook

Everyone in the organization is hoping Gonzalez will take his starting responsibility a little more seriously next season and come to camp in shape. The Padres traded for Michael Rivera, who will push Gonzalez for playing time if he doesn't. Manager Bruce Bochy, a former catcher himself, plans on working with Gonzalez this offseason to help hone Gonzalez' defensive skills.

Kevin Jarvis

Position: SP
Bats: L **Throws:** R
Ht: 6' 2" **Wt:** 200

Opening Day Age: 33
Born: 8/1/69 in Lexington, KY
ML Seasons: 8

Overall Statistics

	W	L	Pct.	ERA	G	GS	Sv	IP	H	BB	SO	HR	Ratio
'02	2	4	.333	4.37	7	7	0	35.0	36	10	24	5	1.31
Car.	29	38	.433	5.83	148	98	1	642.1	755	207	382	125	1.50

2002 Situational Stats

	W	L	ERA	Sv	IP			AB	H	HR	RBI	Avg
Home	2	1	2.08	0	17.1	LHB		55	12	3	6	.218
Road	0	3	6.62	0	17.2	RHB		79	24	2	11	.304
First Half	2	4	4.37	0	35.0	Sc Pos		31	7	0	10	.226
Scnd Half	0	0	–	0	0.0	Clutch		1	1	1	1	1.000

2002 Season

Kevin Jarvis went from a journeyman in 2001 to the Opening Day starter in 2002. However, a strained elbow sidelined him just two weeks into last season. He came back several times in an effort to pitch through the injury, but to no avail. On July 10, his season ended with surgery to repair a torn flexor tendon.

Pitching, Defense & Hitting

Jarvis' rates were not significantly different from his breakthrough 2001 season. He had good K/BB and H/IP ratios and still gave up homers at a high rate. He pitches aggressively, staying around the plate with his fastball, curve, slider and change, all of which are average. He likes to keep his defense in the game by working quickly and staying down in the zone, so that if a hitter does make good contact, the ball will stay in the park. Jarvis is only an average fielder, but he holds baserunners well. He's a pretty good hitter for a pitcher.

2003 Outlook

Jarvis' rehab probably will prevent him from throwing this offseason, so it will take him longer than spring training to regain all of his strength. The Padres like his tenacity, poise and contract, and would like to see him be a leader on their young staff in 2003.

Gene Kingsale

Traded To TIGERS

Position: RF/LF/CF
Bats: B **Throws:** R
Ht: 6' 3" **Wt:** 190

Opening Day Age: 26
Born: 8/20/76 in Oranjestad, Aruba
ML Seasons: 6
Pronunciation: KING-sale

Overall Statistics

	G	AB	R	H	D	T	HR	RBI	SB	BB	SO	Avg	OBP	Slg
'02	91	219	27	62	10	3	2	28	9	20	47	.283	.350	.384
Car.	172	413	54	109	14	4	2	45	14	29	79	.264	.319	.332

2002 Situational Stats

	AB	H	HR	RBI	Avg		AB	H	HR	RBI	Avg
Home	117	41	0	17	.350	LHP	41	12	1	3	.293
Road	102	21	2	11	.206	RHP	178	50	1	25	.281
First Half	25	6	1	2	.240	Sc Pos	51	20	1	25	.392
Scnd Half	194	56	1	26	.289	Clutch	36	10	0	4	.278

2002 Season

Gene Kingsale began last season with Seattle, but before the Mariners' game in San Diego on June 14, he was released, then promptly claimed by the Padres. With their season largely ruined by injuries, the Pads gave Kingsale an extended look. He made good on his opportunity, finishing third on the team in on-base percentage (minimum 100 at-bats) and tied for second in steals.

Hitting, Baserunning & Defense

Because he didn't start playing baseball until high school, Kingsale still is very much of a prospect, despite his age. He makes fundamental errors on the basepaths and doesn't anticipate pitches very well. He also has a tendency to swing at balls up and out of the strike zone. However, he's an excellent bunter, makes contact with almost every swing and has good speed. He's also very coachable. On defense, he has good instincts for the ball, a strong, very accurate arm, and is versatile enough to play all three outfield positions well.

2003 Outlook

Kingsale showed enough promise to warrant a chance to start in center field this year. That chance comes in Detroit, after the Tigers acquired him in a November trade. With further refinement, he could become a valuable leadoff man.

San Diego

Ray Lankford

Position: LF
Bats: L **Throws:** L
Ht: 5'11" **Wt:** 200

Opening Day Age: 35
Born: 6/5/67 in Los Angeles, CA
ML Seasons: 13

Overall Statistics

G	AB	R	H	D	T	HR	RBI	SB	BB	SO	Avg	OBP	Slg
81	205	20	46	7	1	6	26	2	30	61	.224	.326	.356
1609	5547	932	1510	342	53	232	852	256	799	1495	.272	.364	.478

2002 Situational Stats

	AB	H	HR	RBI	Avg		AB	H	HR	RBI	Avg
Home	95	22	3	13	.232	LHP	31	6	0	2	.194
Road	110	24	3	13	.218	RHP	174	40	6	24	.230
First Half	186	44	6	25	.237	Sc Pos	51	12	1	18	.235
Scnd Half	19	2	0	1	.105	Clutch	31	6	0	3	.194

2002 Season

Ray Lankford began last season with an opportunity to become the Padres' everyday left fielder. But nagging injuries and a slow start conspired to cut into his playing time. A strained hamstring in late June effectively ended his season, as he accumulated only 26 more at-bats.

Hitting, Baserunning & Defense

Injuries can be partially blamed for Lankford's substantial drop-off last season. However, none can be blamed for his continuing ineffectiveness against lefties. He still has a potent bat when motivated to play, but he doesn't appear comfortable with the idea that his role likely will be as a platoon player from now on. Although his bat speed remains good, his swing is long, which gives pitchers several ways to strike him out. With good health, a player with Lankford's speed could be an above-average defender and basestealing threat. His arm is average, though usually accurate.

2003 Outlook

The Padres bought out Lankford's contract this offseason, making him a free agent. Someone will give him a contract and likely will pay for the services of a full-time player. However, given his chronic struggles against lefthanders, Lankford probably should be limited to a platoon role.

Dennis Tankersley

Position: SP
Bats: R **Throws:** R
Ht: 6' 2" **Wt:** 185

Opening Day Age: 24
Born: 2/24/79 in Troy, MO
ML Seasons: 1

Overall Statistics

	W	L	Pct.	ERA	G	GS	Sv	IP	H	BB	SO	HR	Ratio
'02	1	4	.200	8.06	17	9	0	51.1	59	40	39	10	1.93
Car.	1	4	.200	8.06	17	9	0	51.1	59	40	39	10	1.93

2002 Situational Stats

	W	L	ERA	Sv	IP		AB	H	HR	RBI	Avg
Home	0	3	8.06	0	22.1	LHB	80	29	6	21	.363
Road	1	1	8.07	0	29.0	RHB	114	30	4	21	.263
First Half	1	2	7.75	0	33.2	Sc Pos	52	20	4	35	.385
Scnd Half	0	2	8.66	0	17.2	Clutch	4	2	0	1	.500

2002 Season

Dennis Tankersley earned his big league debut in early May. His initial exposure to major league hitters went very well, but beginning with his third start, he struggled with the longball, lost confidence and was back in the minors by mid-June. He used the demotion to regroup and pushed his way back to the majors by the middle of August.

Pitching, Defense & Hitting

While he has a solid fastball that reaches the mid-90s and an improving change, Tankersley's hard-breaking slider is his money pitch, and could become one of the best breaking pitches in the game. His struggles with the longball came from not locating the fastball and change well enough to set up his slider. He plays good fundamental defense—he makes the plays that he can get to. Tankersley is aggressive at the plate and makes surprisingly solid contact; he had two extra-base hits among his four knocks last season.

2003 Outlook

With the signing of Francisco Cordova, Tankersley will have trouble breaking back into the San Diego rotation. However, he could benefit from a year of seasoning in the pen. By the time the Padres open their new ballpark in 2004, he should be ready for duty every fifth day.

Brandon Villafuerte

Position: RP
Bats: R **Throws:** R
Ht: 5'11" **Wt:** 165

Opening Day Age: 27
Born: 12/17/75 in Hilo, HI
ML Seasons: 3
Pronunciation: villa-fwear-tey

Overall Statistics

	W	L	Pct.	ERA	G	GS	Sv	IP	H	BB	SO	HR	Ratio
'02	1	2	.333	1.41	31	0	1	32.0	29	12	25	2	1.28
Car.	1	2	.333	4.07	40	0	1	42.0	45	20	30	5	1.55

2002 Situational Stats

	W	L	ERA	Sv	IP		AB	H	HR	RBI	Avg
Home	0	1	0.63	0	14.1	LHB	56	16	0	5	.286
Road	1	1	2.04	1	17.2	RHB	61	13	2	7	.213
First Half	0	0	—	0	0.0	Sc Pos	41	7	1	11	.171
Scnd Half	1	2	1.41	1	32.0	Clutch	74	20	1	7	.270

2002 Season

Two organizations (Detroit and Texas) in two years had given up on Brandon Villafuerte when the Padres signed him as a minor league free agent following the 2001 season. After Villafuerte had an awful spring training, the Padres assigned him to Triple-A Portland to begin the 2002 campaign. He earned a promotion on July 21, after going 8-4 with one save and a 2.02 ERA over 47 games in the Pacific Coast League. He continued his remarkable year by finishing with a 1.41 ERA for San Diego, holding the opposition scoreless in 27 of 31 appearances.

Pitching, Defense & Hitting

Villafuerte throws a 92-MPH fastball that runs in a little on righthanded batters, and a tight slider that breaks away from them. His delivery doesn't leave him in a good fielding position, especially on balls hit to the third base side. He never has had an at-bat at the big league level.

2003 Outlook

It's somewhat surprising that Texas gave up on Villafuerte, considering he had only one bad outing with them in 2001. But the Padres certainly are grateful. He, along with hard-throwing Tom Davey, will comprise the righthanded component of Trevor Hoffman's setup crew this season.

Kevin Walker

Position: RP
Bats: L **Throws:** L
Ht: 6' 4" **Wt:** 190

Opening Day Age: 26
Born: 9/20/76 in Irving, TX
ML Seasons: 3

Overall Statistics

	W	L	Pct.	ERA	G	GS	Sv	IP	H	BB	SO	HR	Ratio
'02	0	1	.000	5.63	11	0	0	8.0	12	5	11	2	2.13
Car.	7	2	.778	4.15	97	0	0	86.2	66	51	84	7	1.35

2002 Situational Stats

	W	L	ERA	Sv	IP		AB	H	HR	RBI	Avg
Home	0	0	0.00	0	1.2	LHB	21	5	1	2	.238
Road	0	1	7.11	0	6.1	RHB	15	7	1	3	.467
First Half	0	0	—	0	0.0	Sc Pos	11	4	0	3	.364
Scnd Half	0	1	5.63	0	8.0	Clutch	13	4	1	2	.308

2002 Season

Kevin Walker underwent Tommy John surgery in August 2001. Though he was able to return to San Diego almost exactly a year after the procedure, he had not completely recovered. After a couple of outings, he suffered pain in his surgically repaired elbow and went back on the disabled list as a precaution. He returned to the bullpen in September with mixed success.

Pitching, Defense & Hitting

Walker's fastball lacked the same life and velocity it had before the surgery. He topped out around 91 MPH last year, but should eventually regain his 95-MPH form. Control still was an issue, but unlike previous years, when he was wild outside the strike zone, he had trouble keeping the ball away from the middle of the plate last season. Walker moves well for a reliever and does a decent job fielding balls in front of him. He's a pretty good hitter for a reliever.

2003 Outlook

Like most recent Tommy John recipients, Walker's recovery should be complete in his second year after the surgery. Provided he doesn't have any setbacks, he'll be the power lefty that Bruce Bochy and Kevin Towers have desperately craved in the bullpen for the last seven years.

San Diego

Other San Diego Padres

Kevin Barker (**Pos**: 1B, **Age**: 27, **Bats**: L)

	G	AB	R	H	D	T	HR	RBI	SB	BB	SO	Avg	OBP	Slg
'02	7	19	0	3	0	0	0	0	1	1	6	.158	.200	.158
Car.	85	236	27	58	8	0	5	32	3	30	46	.246	.331	.343

After six years in the Brewers organization, Barker signed a minor league contract with the Padres last season. He hasn't hit well at Triple-A and above since 1999, particularly for a first baseman. 2003 Outlook: C

Jason Boyd (**Pos**: RHP, **Age**: 30)

	W	L	Pct.	ERA	G	GS	Sv	IP	H	BB	SO	HR	Ratio
'02	1	0	1.000	7.94	23	0	0	28.1	33	15	18	6	1.69
Car.	1	1	.500	6.88	57	0	0	68.0	77	41	54	8	1.74

Boyd exercised a free-agent option to leave the Padres and then signed with the Red Sox last August. Boyd reached Triple-A in 1998, but never has been able to secure a long-term major league job. He signed a minor league deal with Cleveland in November. 2003 Outlook: C

Brian Buchanan (**Pos**: RF/1B/DH, **Age**: 29, **Bats**: R)

	G	AB	R	H	D	T	HR	RBI	SB	BB	SO	Avg	OBP	Slg
'02	92	227	31	61	10	1	11	28	2	15	59	.269	.322	.467
Car.	191	506	69	134	25	1	22	68	3	42	139	.265	.327	.449

The Padres acquired Buchanan from the Twins last July, and he showed nice power while batting .293 with San Diego. He could be ready to play a larger role this season. 2003 Outlook: B

Javier Cardona (**Pos**: C, **Age**: 27, **Bats**: R)

	G	AB	R	H	D	T	HR	RBI	SB	BB	SO	Avg	OBP	Slg
'02	15	39	2	4	1	0	0	2	0	2	10	.103	.143	.128
Car.	87	175	13	36	10	0	2	14	0	4	31	.206	.228	.297

Cardona was part of the four-player deal with Detroit prior to last season. He blew any chance for more playing time when he hit so badly early, and was outrighted to the minors in May. 2003 Outlook: C

Clay Condrey (**Pos**: RHP, **Age**: 27)

	W	L	Pct.	ERA	G	GS	Sv	IP	H	BB	SO	HR	Ratio
'02	1	2	.333	1.69	9	3	0	26.2	20	8	16	1	1.05
Car.	1	2	.333	1.69	9	3	0	26.2	20	8	16	1	1.05

After four seasons in the minors as a reliever, Condrey became a starter at Triple-A last year and succeeded. He had only one bad appearance when working for the Padres in the final month. 2003 Outlook: C

Francisco Cordova (**Pos**: RHP, **Age**: 30)

	W	L	Pct.	ERA	G	GS	Sv	IP	H	BB	SO	HR	Ratio
'02						Did Not Play							
Car.	42	47	.472	3.96	166	112	12	753.2	755	235	537	75	1.31

Cordova, known for a moving sinker, hard slider and arm angles galore, had elbow surgery for a bone spur in August 2000, then Tommy John surgery in September 2001. An interesting comeback to monitor. 2003 Outlook: B

Cesar Crespo (**Pos**: LF, **Age**: 23, **Bats**: B)

	G	AB	R	H	D	T	HR	RBI	SB	BB	SO	Avg	OBP	Slg
'02	25	29	5	5	2	0	0	0	3	3	6	.172	.250	.241
Car.	80	182	32	37	8	0	4	12	9	28	56	.203	.310	.313

Crespo can play virtually any position around the infield or in the outfield. He's also demonstrated good speed and a good batting eye in the past. At the least, you'd think he'd be a decent bench option. 2003 Outlook: C

Tom Davey (**Pos**: RHP, **Age**: 29)

	W	L	Pct.	ERA	G	GS	Sv	IP	H	BB	SO	HR	Ratio
'02	1	0	1.000	5.57	19	0	0	21.0	23	11	21	2	1.62
Car.	7	6	.538	4.41	114	0	1	136.2	138	70	123	10	1.52

Davey's throwing shoulder, which was strained in 2001, kept him on the disabled list when last season opened. He came back, pitched OK at three levels and signed with Boston in November. 2003 Outlook: C

Kory DeHaan (**Pos**: LF, **Age**: 26, **Bats**: L)

	G	AB	R	H	D	T	HR	RBI	SB	BB	SO	Avg	OBP	Slg
'02	12	11	1	1	0	0	0	0	0	0	6	.091	.091	.091
Car.	102	114	20	22	7	0	2	13	4	5	45	.193	.225	.307

The Padres plucked DeHaan, who had played only 47 games above Class-A, in the Rule 5 draft after the 1999 season. That move doesn't appear to have accelerated his development. He has speed and gap power. 2003 Outlook: C

Matt DeWitt (**Pos**: RHP, **Age**: 25)

	W	L	Pct.	ERA	G	GS	Sv	IP	H	BB	SO	HR	Ratio
'02	0	1	.000	1.23	5	0	0	7.1	6	3	5	1	1.23
Car.	1	3	.250	4.95	29	0	0	40.0	48	22	24	7	1.75

DeWitt was doing nothing wrong early last year, pitching well at Triple-A and then in five games for San Diego. But a sprained throwing shoulder ruined his season, and he was later released. 2003 Outlook: C

Mike Holtz (**Pos**: LHP, **Age**: 30)

	W	L	Pct.	ERA	G	GS	Sv	IP	H	BB	SO	HR	Ratio
'02	2	2	.500	5.40	49	0	0	35.0	42	30	26	5	2.06
Car.	16	20	.444	4.68	350	0	3	238.1	242	127	221	25	1.55

The A's signed Holtz to a two-year deal prior to last season, but had designated him for assignment by the end of May. He didn't really impress after the Padres signed him, and he became a free agent. 2003 Outlook: C

Trenidad Hubbard (**Pos**: OF, **Age**: 36, **Bats**: R)

	G	AB	R	H	D	T	HR	RBI	SB	BB	SO	Avg	OBP	Slg
'02	89	129	16	27	5	0	1	7	9	14	28	.209	.285	.271
Car.	466	746	122	192	32	7	16	70	32	79	163	.257	.331	.383

Although he can play a number of positions, Hubbard hasn't hit well enough with four teams over the past three years to deserve many more chances. The Padres released him last September. 2003 Outlook: C

Jonathan Johnson (Pos: RHP, Age: 28)

	W	L	Pct.	ERA	G	GS	Sv	IP	H	BB	SO	HR	Ratio
'02	1	2	.333	4.11	16	0	0	15.1	15	5	21	2	1.30
Car.	2	3	.400	6.82	38	1	0	62.0	76	38	61	7	1.84

Johnson was the seventh overall pick in 1995, but has not done much to justify the selection. After showing a good strikeout rate with San Diego, the Astros have signed him to a minor league contract. 2003 Outlook: C

Bobby J. Jones (Pos: RHP, Age: 33)

	W	L	Pct.	ERA	G	GS	Sv	IP	H	BB	SO	HR	Ratio
'02	7	8	.467	5.50	19	18	0	108.0	134	21	60	20	1.44
Car.	89	83	.517	4.36	245	241	0	1518.2	1639	412	887	194	1.35

The Padres released Jones last September after he had three stints on the disabled list with a strained oblique muscle, an elbow strain and a back injury. His ERA hasn't been under 5.00 since 1998. 2003 Outlook: C

Bobby M. Jones (Pos: LHP, Age: 30)

	W	L	Pct.	ERA	G	GS	Sv	IP	H	BB	SO	HR	Ratio
'02	0	0	–	5.74	16	2	0	26.2	30	18	18	4	1.80
Car.	14	20	.412	5.77	96	47	0	321.1	363	187	226	44	1.71

Jones was part of five-player trade with the Mets last July, but he couldn't make it past four innings in two starts, got injured, and then was released in September. 2003 Outlook: C

Tom Lampkin (Pos: C, Age: 39, Bats: L)

	G	AB	R	H	D	T	HR	RBI	SB	BB	SO	Avg	OBP	Slg
'02	104	281	32	61	10	1	10	37	4	38	59	.217	.313	.367
Car.	777	1796	224	422	78	8	56	236	23	193	286	.235	.319	.381

At age 38, Lampkin set career highs in at-bats, homers, RBI, walks and strikeouts in 2002, but he may be squeezed out of San Diego by new Padre Mike Rivera, Wiki Gonzalez and other candidates. 2003 Outlook: C

David Lundquist (Pos: RHP, Age: 29)

	W	L	Pct.	ERA	G	GS	Sv	IP	H	BB	SO	HR	Ratio
'02	0	0	–	16.88	3	0	0	2.2	8	5	0	0	4.88
Car.	1	2	.333	7.92	37	0	0	44.1	56	24	37	4	1.80

Lundquist had a hard time retiring anyone when the Padres used him in three games in June. A strained shoulder may have been to blame, but he was released when he came off the disabled list. 2003 Outlook: C

Julius Matos (Pos: 2B/3B, Age: 28, Bats: R)

	G	AB	R	H	D	T	HR	RBI	SB	BB	SO	Avg	OBP	Slg
'02	76	185	19	44	3	0	2	19	1	9	33	.238	.279	.286
Car.	76	185	19	44	3	0	2	19	1	9	33	.238	.279	.286

Matos was with the Padres for the final months of 2002. Sure, he offered defensive flexibility, but it's hard to see what he contributed offensively. He signed with Kansas City in early December. 2003 Outlook: C

Juan Moreno (Pos: LHP, Age: 28)

	W	L	Pct.	ERA	G	GS	Sv	IP	H	BB	SO	HR	Ratio
'02	0	0	–	7.50	4	0	0	6.0	6	10	3	1	2.67
Car.	3	3	.500	4.37	49	0	0	47.1	28	38	39	7	1.39

Moreno was hard to hit in 2001, giving up a .153 average. He was traded twice in the span of a few weeks last spring, going from Texas to San Diego to Boston. The Red Sox later released him. 2003 Outlook: C

Rodney Myers (Pos: RHP, Age: 33)

	W	L	Pct.	ERA	G	GS	Sv	IP	H	BB	SO	HR	Ratio
'02	1	1	.500	5.91	14	0	0	21.1	29	10	11	1	1.83
Car.	7	5	.583	5.08	162	1	1	228.2	254	106	155	27	1.57

Myers worked out of the Padres' bullpen for a couple months in midseason last year, as he continued his recent history of bounching between the majors and minors. 2003 Outlook: C

Doug Nickle (Pos: RHP, Age: 28)

	W	L	Pct.	ERA	G	GS	Sv	IP	H	BB	SO	HR	Ratio
'02	1	0	1.000	7.88	14	0	0	16.0	26	13	9	3	2.44
Car.	1	0	1.000	7.84	20	0	0	20.2	32	15	10	3	2.27

Nickle was the other player the Cardinals received in the deal that netted Scott Rolen. Nickle eventually was waived by St. Louis and then San Diego, getting picked up by the Mets after the season. 2003 Outlook: C

Wil Nieves (Pos: C, Age: 25, Bats: R)

	G	AB	R	H	D	T	HR	RBI	SB	BB	SO	Avg	OBP	Slg
'02	28	72	2	13	3	0	0	3	1	4	15	.181	.224	.250
Car.	28	72	2	13	3	0	0	3	1	4	15	.181	.224	.250

He didn't show it with the Padres, but Nieves can hit for a fairly decent average and chip in some doubles. San Diego's catching situation isn't the strongest, so Nieves might be back. 2003 Outlook: C

Jose Antonio Nunez (Pos: LHP, Age: 24)

	W	L	Pct.	ERA	G	GS	Sv	IP	H	BB	SO	HR	Ratio
'02	0	0	–	0.00	1	0	0	1.0	0	1	0	0	1.00
Car.	4	2	.667	4.50	63	0	0	60.0	62	26	60	7	1.47

Nunez looked like he'd fill an important bullpen role in 2002, but his season ended after one outing on Opening Day. He had surgery for a partially torn rotator cuff and was re-signed in November. 2003 Outlook: C

Jason Pearson (Pos: LHP, Age: 27)

	W	L	Pct.	ERA	G	GS	Sv	IP	H	BB	SO	HR	Ratio
'02	0	0	–	0.00	2	0	0	1.2	1	0	3	0	0.60
Car.	0	0	–	0.00	2	0	0	1.2	1	0	3	0	0.60

Pearson's major league stay consisted of two appearances before he was waived to the Giants. He doesn't appear to be in San Francisco's long-term plans, however. 2003 Outlook: C

Alex Pelaez (Pos: 1B, Age: 26, Bats: R)

	G	AB	R	H	D	T	HR	RBI	SB	BB	SO	Avg	OBP	Slg
'02	3	8	0	2	0	0	0	0	0	0	0	.250	.250	.250
Car.	3	8	0	2	0	0	0	0	0	0	0	.250	.250	.250

Although Pelaez hit better than .300 at Triple-A last year, he doesn't have the kind of power you'd like to see from a corner infielder. He doesn't offer many walks or much speed, either. 2003 Outlook: C

Kevin Pickford (Pos: LHP, Age: 28)

	W	L	Pct.	ERA	G	GS	Sv	IP	H	BB	SO	HR	Ratio
'02	0	2	.000	6.00	16	4	0	30.0	37	20	18	3	1.90
Car.	0	2	.000	6.00	16	4	0	30.0	37	20	18	3	1.90

The Padres tried Pickford as a starter and reliever last season, and he was found lacking in both roles. The southpaw wasn't especially effective at Triple-A, either. He has filed for free agency. 2003 Outlook: C

San Diego

665

Jason Shiell (**Pos**: RHP, **Age**: 26)

	W	L	Pct.	ERA	G	GS	Sv	IP	H	BB	SO	HR	Ratio
'02	0	0	–	27.00	3	0	0	1.1	7	3	1	0	7.50
Car.	0	0	–	27.00	3	0	0	1.1	7	3	1	0	7.50

Shiell was part of the big trade with Atlanta a few years ago involving Ryan Klesko. Shiell has moved to relief the last couple seasons. The Red Sox picked him up on waivers in October. 2003 Outlook: C

Mark Sweeney (**Pos**: 1B, **Age**: 33, **Bats**: L)

	G	AB	R	H	D	T	HR	RBI	SB	BB	SO	Avg	OBP	Slg
'02	48	65	3	11	3	0	1	4	0	4	19	.169	.217	.262
Car.	576	861	97	218	41	4	16	101	9	121	182	.253	.345	.366

Sweeney was traded from Milwaukee to the Mets last offseason, but wound up with the San Diego after New York released him in March. His anemic batting average was jettisoned soon after the All-Star break. 2003 Outlook: C

Brian Tollberg (**Pos**: RHP, **Age**: 30)

	W	L	Pct.	ERA	G	GS	Sv	IP	H	BB	SO	HR	Ratio
'02	1	5	.167	6.13	12	11	0	61.2	88	19	33	11	1.74
Car.	15	14	.517	4.39	50	49	0	297.0	347	80	180	39	1.43

Tollberg ranked second on the Padres with 10 wins in 2001, but he missed most of last season after undergoing Tommy John surgery on his elbow. He may not be fully recovered until 2004. 2003 Outlook: C

J.J. Trujillo (**Pos**: RHP, **Age**: 27)

	W	L	Pct.	ERA	G	GS	Sv	IP	H	BB	SO	HR	Ratio
'02	0	1	.000	10.13	4	0	0	2.2	4	6	3	1	3.75
Car.	0	1	.000	10.13	4	0	0	2.2	4	6	3	1	3.75

Trujillo was highly effective as a closer at Double-A last year, and he wasn't bad at Triple-A, either. But he found the going tougher in his short stint with the Padres in June. 2003 Outlook: C

San Diego Padres Minor League Prospects

Organization Overview:

No organization in baseball has as much quality depth in its farm system as San Diego. Whether it's through the draft or trades, GM Kevin Towers and his scouting staff haven't made many mistakes filling the system with potential. Already laden with pitching talent, the Padres focused on hitters the past two years, signing Jake Gautreau, Taggert Bozied, Marcus Nettles, Josh Barfield and Khalil Greene out of the draft. All of them appear likely to contribute in the majors. Towers also added to his impressive list of trades, acquiring Brad Baker and Bernie Castro last season—both could play significant roles in the near future in San Diego.

Brad Baker

Position: P **Opening Day Age:** 22
Bats: R **Throws:** R **Born:** 11/6/80 in
Ht: 6' 2" **Wt:** 180 Brattleboro, VT

Recent Statistics

	W	L	ERA	G	GS	Sv	IP	H	R	BB	SO	HR
2001 A Sarasota	7	9	4.73	24	23	0	120.0	132	77	64	103	8
2002 A Sarasota	7	1	2.79	12	12	0	61.1	53	22	25	65	4
2002 AA Mobile	4	4	4.48	12	12	0	64.1	47	33	45	57	5

Baker had fallen out of favor in the Red Sox organization after his effort to bulk up cost him a few miles per hour and the movement on his fastball. The Padres saw an opportunity and traded reliever Alan Embree for him last June. Baker immediately was promoted to Double-A. While his control wasn't good, he showed signs that his fastball was returning to form. By the time the Arizona Fall League rolled around, he had regained much of his control. Baker has good pitching instincts, getting ahead of hitters with a lively low-90s fastball, above-average slider and big league change. He occasionally lets his emotions get the best of him, but he can dominate a game once he gets in a rhythm.

Tagg Bozied

Position: 3B **Opening Day Age:** 23
Bats: R **Throws:** R **Born:** 7/24/79 in
Ht: 6' 3" **Wt:** 210 Sioux Falls, SD

Recent Statistics

	G	AB	R	H	D	T	HR	RBI	SB	BB	SO	Avg
2002 A Lk Elsinore	71	282	45	84	23	1	15	60	3	35	60	.298
2002 AA Mobile	60	234	35	50	14	0	9	32	1	16	43	.214

The Padres were able to draft Bozied (pronounced bohz-aid) in the third round of the 2001 draft largely due to signability concerns. Many teams became fascinated with his power after he slugged .936 as a college sophomore in 1999. However, he hadn't been able to reproduce those numbers in his final two years, and with Scott Boras as his agent, all but the Padres shied away. After a holdout that included a stint in an inde-pendent league, he finally signed after the 2001 regular season had ended. He showed a very promising power stroke in his first exposure to minor league pitching. He continued his power surge in the Arizona Fall League. His progress may slow unless he learns to lay off the hard breaking stuff outside. But he has enough talent and drive to make that adjustment.

Mike Bynum

Position: P **Opening Day Age:** 25
Bats: L **Throws:** L **Born:** 3/20/78 in Tampa,
Ht: 6' 4" **Wt:** 200 FL

Recent Statistics

	W	L	ERA	G	GS	Sv	IP	H	R	BB	SO	HR
2002 AA Mobile	4	0	0.82	6	5	0	33.0	17	5	7	29	0
2002 AAA Portland	3	2	3.51	7	7	0	41.0	36	19	7	35	6
2002 NL San Diego	1	0	5.27	14	3	0	27.1	33	16	15	17	3

Bynum's strong performance in Double- and Triple-A earned him a mid-August callup to San Diego last year. While his fastball and change are only average, his slider is exceptional, drawing comparisons to Steve Carlton's. It was voted the best breaking pitch in the Southern League last year. It's so good, he sometimes uses it exclusively, at the expense of his other pitches, which perturbs his managers and pitching coaches to no end. He has a slight hitch in his delivery, which is a nice mechanism to throw off the hitter's timing. But it also can lead to mechanical inconsistencies. The Padres would like to see him use his entire repertoire a little more effectively. Otherwise, a move to the bullpen may be in the offing.

Khalil Greene

Position: SS **Opening Day Age:** 23
Bats: R **Throws:** R **Born:** 10/21/79 in Butler,
Ht: 5' 10" **Wt:** 202 PA

Recent Statistics

	G	AB	R	H	D	T	HR	RBI	SB	BB	SO	Avg
2002 A Eugene	10	37	5	10	1	0	0	6	0	5	6	.270
2002 A Lk Elsinore	46	183	33	58	9	1	9	32	0	12	33	.317

Greene finished his senior season at Clemson impressively, breaking several school and ACC records. He hit .476 with 21 homers and 73 RBI during the regular season. After signing with the Padres, he was sent to the short-season Northwest League, where he showed a discriminating eye at the plate. He was promoted to the high Class-A California League last July and continued to impress observers with his power and ability to hit for average. So impressed was GM Kevin Towers that he suggested Greene has a real chance of opening this season in the majors. There were some initial questions about Greene's defense at short, but he has terrific instincts for the ball. Early indications are that he has adequate range and the arm to stay at the position.

San Diego

Ben Howard

Position: P   **Opening Day Age:** 24
Bats: R **Throws:** R   **Born:** 1/15/79 in
Ht: 6' 2" **Wt:** 190   Danville, IL

Recent Statistics

	W	L	ERA	G	GS	Sv	IP	H	R	BB	SO	HR
2002 AA Mobile	3	1	2.18	6	6	0	33.0	26	10	16	30	2
2002 NL San Diego	0	1	9.28	3	2	0	10.2	13	11	14	10	4
2002 AAA Portland	0	4	6.20	11	7	0	45.0	47	34	15	25	10

During spring training, Howard was the lone survivor of a car accident that claimed the lives of teammates Mike Darr and Duane Johnson. Ten weeks later, Howard was called up to the majors. While his debut showed a lot of promise, it also was clear that, despite having the best fastball in the organization, he still had not mastered control of it. When a move to relief didn't fix things, he was optioned to Double-A in early May. He did earn a promotion to Triple-A at the end of the month, but a strained elbow sidelined him in late June. A return trip to the majors and how long he stays will depend on how quickly he learns to control his fastball. Regardless, he may be better suited to the bullpen.

Xavier Nady

Position: 1B   **Opening Day Age:** 24
Bats: R **Throws:** R   **Born:** 11/14/78 in
Ht: 6' 0" **Wt:** 180   Carmel, CA

Recent Statistics

	G	AB	R	H	D	T	HR	RBI	SB	BB	SO	Avg
2001 A Lk Elsinore	137	524	96	158	38	1	26	100	6	62	109	.302
2002 A Lk Elsinore	45	169	41	47	6	3	13	37	2	28	40	.278
2002 AAA Portland	85	315	46	89	12	1	10	43	0	20	60	.283

It's unusual for a minor league MVP to return to the same level the following year, but Nady had Tommy John surgery last offseason. To allow him to DH full-time until his elbow recovered, the Padres returned Nady to the high Class-A California League. His progress was so encouraging that the Padres promoted him all the way to Triple-A. In his brief stay in the Arizona Fall League, he proved that he was fully recovered. Nady has very good power. If his selectivity improves, he also could hit for a high average. He played several positions in college and was named the California League's best defensive first baseman in 2001. His glove shouldn't prevent him from playing any of the infield or outfield corner positions.

Mark Phillips

Position: P   **Opening Day Age:** 21
Bats: L **Throws:** L   **Born:** 12/30/81 in
Ht: 6' 3" **Wt:** 205   Hanover, PA

Recent Statistics

	W	L	ERA	G	GS	Sv	IP	H	R	BB	SO	HR
2001 A Eugene	3	1	3.74	4	4	0	21.2	16	10	9	19	1
2001 A Ft. Wayne	4	1	2.64	5	5	0	30.2	19	11	14	27	1
2001 A Lk Elsinore	2	1	2.57	5	5	0	28.0	19	8	14	34	0
2002 A Lk Elsinore	10	8	4.19	28	26	0	148.1	123	81	94	156	9

Phillips' ascent through the Padres' system slowed last season. He still showed an excellent strikeout rate, but he lacked the consistency that could have earned him a midseason promotion. He is one of those uncommon lefties who can throw his fastball in the low to mid-90s effortlessly. He also has a plus curve. Unfortunately, he suffers from a lack of control. Some have questioned Phillips' dedication, especially concerning his offseason workout regimen. This apparent nonchalance toward fitness has been singled out as the primary reason he struggles to keep his mechanics in sync. Still, there's no question that Phillips has special talent and would make a terrific major league starter if he ever decides he wants to be as good as his potential.

Michael Rivera

Position: C   **Opening Day Age:** 26
Bats: R **Throws:** R   **Born:** 9/8/76 in Rio
Ht: 6' 0" **Wt:** 210   Piedras, PR

Recent Statistics

	G	AB	R	H	D	T	HR	RBI	SB	BB	SO	Avg
2002 AL Detroit	39	132	11	30	8	1	1	11	0	4	35	.227
2002 AAA Toledo	74	265	43	66	11	1	20	53	0	35	64	.249

Rivera progressed quietly through the Tigers' system, showing some pop with his dead-pull swing. In 2001, working with former catcher and Tigers manager Luis Pujols at Double-A Erie, Rivera blossomed with a breakout year as both a hitter and a catcher. After winning a share of Detroit's starting catching job in spring training last year, he tried to do too much and faltered badly. However, once he was demoted, he salvaged his season with a solid showing in Triple-A Toledo. He may get another shot at a starting job after being traded to San Diego. The Padres were unhappy with incumbent Wiki Gonzalez' effort last year, so if Gonzalez doesn't show more life in 2003, they may turn to Rivera's potentially potent bat. Rivera's defense isn't strong, but he could become serviceable enough behind the plate to get his bat into the lineup.

Others to Watch

The Padres were very pleased they traded for 21-year old **Bernie Castro** (21). The speedy second baseman was voted the league's most exciting player by opposing managers. . . Lefthander **Eric Cyr** (24) earned a callup to the majors after spending the first half of the year at Double-A. Tendinitis in his pitching shoulder sidelined him for a few weeks, but surgery won't be required. . . Righthander **Justin Germano** (20) compiled a combined 14-5 record with an ERA under 3.00 in both the Class-A Midwest and high Class-A California Leagues in 2002. He throws a low-90s fastball, change and a curve he can break two ways. . . Righthander **Mike Nicolas** (21) and lefthander **Rusty Tucker** (22), who both dominated Class-A hitters with 95-plus MPH gas, could move up quickly. Nicolas struck out 121 batters in 77.1 innings in the California League. Tucker struck out 83 in 65.1 innings split between the California and Midwest Leagues.

Pacific Bell Park

Offense

In just its third year, Pacific Bell Park already has become the scorn of hitters throughout the National League. Such accomplished batsmen as Larry Walker and Todd Helton publicly have condemned the park. Even Giants second baseman Jeff Kent blasted the stadium last season, saying it was a miserable place for hitters. Despite its inviting 309-foot distance down the right-field line, it's extremely difficult to hit home runs to right. Rather than try to pull the ball, it's advantageous to try to aim for the sizable alleys.

Defense

The Giants committed just 46 errors at home, eight fewer than the previous season. Opponents made only 65 errors, a testament to Pac Bell's above-average playing surface. The right-field area has plenty of quirks, including a 25-foot fence, but the Giants have been in good hands with Ellis Burks and Reggie Sanders in right field two of the past three years.

Who It Helps the Most

The Giants' 3.03 home ERA was far superior to its 4.09 mark on the road. No Giants starter was helped more by his stadium than Jason Schmidt. He had a 2.37 ERA at Pac Bell, but a 5.02 ERA on the road. Among San Francisco's starting position players, only Rich Aurilia and Reggie Sanders had higher batting averages at home.

Who It Hurts the Most

Lefthanded pull hitters such as Snow are at a disadvantage here. Snow, for example, has hit just four homers at home the past two seasons. He had 10 road homers over the same span. Catcher Benito Santiago also has struggled at Pac Bell. He hit .253 with six homers at home, a contrast to his .302 and 10 figures on the road.

Rookies & Newcomers

Pac Bell invariably will improve every pitcher the Giants sign or promote from the minors. With a potential youth movement in the pitching staff, Kurt Ainsworth, Jerome Williams and Jesse Foppert figure to benefit from the pitcher-friendly confines.

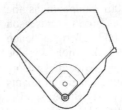

Dimensions: LF-339, LCF-364, CF-399, RCF-421, RF-309

Capacity: 41,467

Elevation: 0 feet

Surface: Grass

Foul Territory: Average

Park Factors

2002 Season

	Home Games Giants	Opp	Total	Away Games Giants	Opp	Total	Index
G	72	72	144	72	72	144	
Avg	.258	.245	.251	.275	.255	.265	95
AB	2329	2443	4772	2545	2346	4891	98
R	320	249	569	388	300	688	83
H	601	599	1200	700	598	1298	92
2B	119	105	224	149	108	257	89
3B	22	17	39	11	10	21	190
HR	62	34	96	116	67	183	54
BB	277	216	493	284	253	537	94
SO	399	440	839	460	411	871	99
E	44	57	101	41	45	86	117
E-Infield	34	44	78	31	41	72	108
LHB-Avg	.260	.248	.253	.297	.265	.278	91
LHB-HR	23	12	35	38	27	65	54
RHB-Avg	.257	.243	.251	.266	.247	.258	97
RHB-HR	39	22	61	78	40	118	54

2001-2002

	Home Games Giants	Opp	Total	Away Games Giants	Opp	Total	Index
G	147	147	294	144	144	288	
Avg	.257	.249	.253	.278	.262	.271	94
AB	4852	5085	9937	5145	4771	9916	98
R	650	585	1235	800	671	1471	82
H	1248	1268	2516	1432	1252	2684	92
2B	261	245	506	290	238	522	97
3B	45	41	86	26	28	54	159
HR	152	82	234	245	153	398	59
BB	578	476	1054	563	529	1092	96
SO	871	964	1835	987	897	1866	98
E	96	94	190	95	92	187	100
E-Infield	76	76	152	69	79	148	101
LHB-Avg	.249	.254	.252	.299	.279	.288	87
LHB-HR	71	24	95	104	61	165	56
RHB-Avg	.261	.246	.254	.269	.250	.261	60
RHB-HR	81	58	139	141	92	233	60

2002 Rankings (National League)

- Second-highest triple factor
- Third-highest error factor
- Lowest home-run factor
- Lowest LHB home-run factor
- Lowest RHB home-run factor
- Second-lowest run factor

San Francisco

Felipe Alou

2002 Season

Felipe Alou was in his 10th campaign as the Expos' manager when he was fired in midseason in 2001. He spent most of 2002 serving as bench coach under Detroit manager Luis Pujols, a job he later admitted he didn't enjoy. After the season, the defending National League-champion Giants opted not to retain manager Dusty Baker, signing Alou to a three-year deal instead. He returns to the city where he spent the first six years of his major league playing career.

Offense

Alou's two biggest strengths are his ability to get the most out of Latin players, and his knack for getting good use out of castoffs and minor league veterans. His nurturing helped the shy Vladimir Guerrero quickly develop into a star, and allowed Javier Vazquez to persevere through his early struggles. Pedro Feliz obviously lacks comparable talent, but if anyone can get the best out of him, Alou can. Alou's preferences for speed and NL-style play seem well suited to pitcher-friendly Pac Bell Park. He never has stressed plate patience and has a strong preference for pure speed over on-base skills at the top of the lineup.

Pitching & Defense

One thing that Alou consistently has shown is an insistence that his players be able to play good defense. Thus, it's likely he'll play outfielders with better range than Marvin Benard, and he'll probably make use of Neifi Perez, even if he doesn't earn an everyday job. With pitchers, he's always been boldly successful in finding a guy's ideal role, converting Jeff Fassero and Dustin Hermanson from the bullpen to the rotation years ago, and shifting Ugueth Urbina from starter to closer.

2003 Outlook

Alou's first priority will be to decide on how to use the new players he has available to him to fill the holes created by the departure of a number of veterans. He'll need to virtually rebuild a batting order that will have lost its leadoff man as well as the run producers who had protected and driven in Barry Bonds.

Born: 5/12/35 in Haina, Dominican Republic

Playing Experience: 1958-1974, SF, Mil, Atl, Oak, NYY, Mon

Managerial Experience: 10 seasons

Manager Statistics

Year	Team, Lg	W	L	Pct	GB	Finish
2001	Mon, NL	21	32	.396	–	–
10 Seasons		691	717	.491	–	–

2002 Starting Pitchers by Days Rest

	<=3	4	5	6+
Giants Starts	0	90	52	14
Giants ERA	–	3.88	3.85	4.30
NL Avg Starts	1	88	42	21
NL ERA	3.18	4.22	4.14	4.58

2002 Situational Stats

	Dusty Baker	NL Average
Hit & Run Success %	35.8	36.5
Stolen Base Success %	77.9	68.3
Platoon Pct.	42.0	52.7
Defensive Subs	16	19
High-Pitch Outings	19	7
Quick/Slow Hooks	22/9	24/11
Sacrifice Attempts	92	95

2002 Rankings —Dusty Baker (National League)

- 1st in stolen-base percentage, fewest caught stealings of second base (20), fewest caught stealings of third base (1) and starts with over 120 pitches (19)

Rich Aurilia

2002 Season

After an All-Star season in 2001, Rich Aurilia plummeted to also-ran status among National League shortstops last year. He was bothered by a right elbow injury, which required surgery in late May, and missed a couple of weeks. But his hitting did not improve much upon his return. After hitting .324 with 37 homers and 97 RBI the year before, Aurilia slipped to .257-15-61 last season. And after hitting in front of Barry Bonds the year before, which led to a steady diet of fastballs, Bonds was moved to cleanup, and Aurilia lost his meal ticket.

Hitting

Forced to adjust his swing to compensate for the pain in his right elbow, Aurilia picked up bad habits the first two months of the season and was a virtual non-factor for the Giants until September, when he hit .293 with seven doubles, three homers and 18 RBI. Known as a high-ball hitter, Aurilia seemed to lose his patience and chased bad pitches throughout the season, trying to duplicate his homer total of a year ago. He is a solid hitter when he shoots balls into the gap rather than trying to yank pitches over the left-field fence.

Baserunning & Defense

Aurilia has improved defensively every season since his 28-error showing in 1999. He cut his errors to a full-season career low of 11 last season. Although he was troubled by the elbow injury, he was accurate in the field. Never considered to have great range, Aurilia makes up for that flaw with a quick release and accurate throws across the diamond. He is not a threat to steal, but he nonetheless makes few baserunning errors.

2003 Outlook

With San Francisco possibly losing four starters from the 2002 season, the team cannot afford another off year from Aurilia at the plate. The Giants cannot expect him to hit better than .300 with 37 homers, as he did two seasons ago, but they would be satisfied with his 20-homer, 80-RBI level in 1999 and 2000.

Position: SS
Bats: R **Throws:** R
Ht: 6' 1" **Wt:** 185

Opening Day Age: 31
Born: 9/2/71 in Brooklyn, NY
ML Seasons: 8
Pronunciation: uh-REEL-yuh
Nickname: Dickie

Overall Statistics

	G	AB	R	H	D	T	HR	RBI	SB	BB	SO	Avg	OBP	Slg
'02	133	538	76	138	35	2	15	61	1	37	90	.257	.305	.413
Car.	864	3093	426	862	164	13	113	415	14	246	465	.279	.332	.450

Where He Hits the Ball

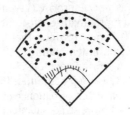 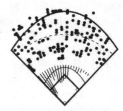

Vs. LHP   **Vs. RHP**

2002 Situational Stats

	AB	H	HR	RBI	Avg		AB	H	HR	RBI	Avg
Home	246	64	4	28	.260	LHP	116	28	2	16	.241
Road	292	74	11	33	.253	RHP	422	110	13	45	.261
First Half	255	66	7	28	.259	Sc Pos	125	35	2	44	.280
Scnd Half	283	72	8	33	.254	Clutch	74	21	3	11	.284

2002 Rankings (National League)

- 1st in fielding percentage at shortstop (.980) and lowest batting average with the bases loaded (.000)
- 5th in sacrifice flies (7) and lowest ground-ball-flyball ratio (0.7)
- 7th in lowest on-base percentage vs. lefthanded pitchers (.276)
- 10th in lowest on-base percentage
- Led the Giants in sacrifice flies (7)

San Francisco

David Bell

2002 Season

The Giants had no idea they'd received such a well-rounded player when they acquired David Bell from Seattle for infielder Desi Relaford. Bell whacked 20 homers, drove in 73 runs and played stellar if not spectacular defense at third base. When Tsuyoshi Shinjo was a bust at leadoff, Bell even took over the No. 1 spot for a while before moving to seventh or eighth in the order. Bell became such a vital component that he was named the Willie McCovey Award winner, which goes annually to the team's most inspirational player.

Hitting

A pronounced flyball hitter who likes to pull the ball, Bell saw a slight improvement in his power totals from 2001. This was not a surprise, given that Pac Bell Park offers a more inviting left-field wall than does Bell's 2001 home, Safeco Field. He was the Giants' top clutch hitter, batting .317 with 50 RBI with runners in scoring position, .385 with the bases loaded and .333 as a pinch-hitter. If there's a knock on Bell, it's his lack of patience at the plate. Once again, he had more strikeouts than walks, making him a perpetual candidate for bottom-of-the-order duties.

Baserunning & Defense

Bell may not be as big as his father, Buddy, but he's inherited his strong arm and soft hands. Bell was among the top third basemen in the National League, making only nine errors at the hot corner. He also played 12 games at second base and three at shortstop. His play in the field was in a manner reminiscent of Bill Mueller during the 1999 and 2000 seasons. Bell may not be blessed with blazing speed, but he's an astute baserunner who scored important runs by using his head.

2003 Outlook

The Giants would love to have re-signed Bell for the 2003 season, but they were outbid by Philadelphia, which signed him to a four-year, $17 million deal in late November. He will fill the third-base slot vacated by Scott Rolen last July. The Giants realize they will be hard pressed to find a replacement for Bell, who is solid offensively and defensively, and who also will bring plenty of intangibles to the Phillies.

Position: 3B/2B
Bats: R **Throws:** R
Ht: 5'10" **Wt:** 195

Opening Day Age: 30
Born: 9/14/72 in Cincinnati, OH
ML Seasons: 8

Overall Statistics

	G	AB	R	H	D	T	HR	RBI	SB	BB	SO	Avg	OBP	Slg
'02	154	552	82	144	29	2	20	73	1	54	80	.261	.333	.429
Car.	880	2935	375	752	162	12	81	351	15	233	435	.256	.313	.402

Where He Hits the Ball

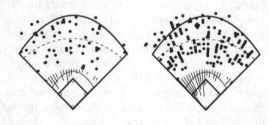

Vs. LHP　　　　**Vs. RHP**

2002 Situational Stats

	AB	H	HR	RBI	Avg		AB	H	HR	RBI	Avg
Home	255	64	7	32	.251	LHP	137	36	5	22	.263
Road	297	80	13	41	.269	RHP	415	108	15	51	.260
First Half	310	77	13	43	.248	Sc Pos	126	40	4	50	.317
Scnd Half	242	67	7	30	.277	Clutch	80	22	3	6	.275

2002 Rankings (National League)

- 3rd in fielding percentage at third base (.973)
- 5th in sacrifice flies (7)
- Led the Giants in sacrifice flies (7), pitches seen (2,425), games played and lowest percentage of swings on the first pitch (26.8)

Barry Bonds

2002 Season

Barry Bonds didn't come close to matching his record-breaking 73 homers of 2001, but in many ways his 2002 season was just as impressive. He became the oldest player, at age 38, to win a National League batting title. He also established major league records for on-base percentage (.582), walks (198) and intentional walks (68). With his 46 homers, he climbed to fourth all time with 613, 47 shy of tying his godfather, Willie Mays.

Hitting

Time has not been a deterrent to Bonds' quick, uppercut swing. While many his age either are retired or slowed by the ravages of time, Bonds has maintained his super-quick bat speed. As the years have progressed he's become an even more disciplined hitter, drawing an astounding 375 walks the past two seasons, breaking his own single-season record he set in 2001. There once was a time when Bonds was susceptible to lefthanders, but those days are over. He hit .384 against lefties last season.

Baserunning & Defense

Once a perennial Gold Glove winner, Bonds has slowed considerably in the field, to the point where he might have to move to first base in the coming years. He has bulked up in recent years, making him stiff and slow in the field. He committed a career-high eight errors in 2002, and he seemed to experience momentary lapses in the field in which he flubbed harmless grounders. Bonds also was slowed by hamstring injuries for most of the first half, preventing him from being much of a factor on the basepaths.

2003 Outlook

Bonds still has yet to show any outward signs of slowing down, at least at the plate. If he continues his pace, he can ascend to third on the home-run chart this season. However, Bonds will have to remain patient at the plate, with managers doing everything they can not to pitch to him. That patience could be tested further if the Giants lose Jeff Kent, who has provided vital protection for Bonds the past six seasons.

Position: LF
Bats: L **Throws:** L
Ht: 6' 2" **Wt:** 228

Opening Day Age: 38
Born: 7/24/64 in Riverside, CA
ML Seasons: 17
Nickname: BB

Overall Statistics

G	AB	R	H	D	T	HR	RBI	SB	BB	SO	Avg	OBP	Slg
143	403	117	149	31	2	46	110	9	198	47	.370	.582	.799
2439	8335	1830	2462	514	73	613	1652	493	1922	1329	.295	.428	.595

Where He Hits the Ball

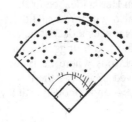 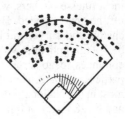

Vs. LHP   **Vs. RHP**

2002 Situational Stats

	AB	H	HR	RBI	Avg		AB	H	HR	RBI	Avg
Home	188	66	19	44	.351	LHP	125	48	21	45	.384
Road	215	83	27	66	.386	RHP	278	101	25	65	.363
First Half	232	80	27	57	.345	Sc Pos	85	32	12	65	.376
Scnd Half	171	69	19	53	.404	Clutch	62	15	5	12	.242

2002 Rankings (National League)

- 1st in batting average, walks, intentional walks (68), times on base (356), slugging percentage, on-base percentage, HR frequency (8.8 ABs per HR), batting average with runners in scoring position, batting average vs. lefthanded pitchers, batting average vs. righthanded pitchers, cleanup slugging percentage (.730), slugging percentage vs. lefthanded pitchers (.976), slugging percentage vs. righthanded pitchers (.719), on-base percentage vs. lefthanded pitchers (.556), on-base percentage vs. righthanded pitchers (.592), batting average on the road and errors in left field (8)
- Led the Giants in batting average, home runs, runs scored, RBI and walks

San Francisco

Livan Hernandez

2002 Season

Livan Hernandez' goal before the 2002 season was to avoid the slow starts that had plagued him throughout his career. He achieved that aim, starting 4-0, but he won just one game in both June and July, and finished with 16 losses. He also was hounded by constant trade talk at and around the trading deadline. The Giants admitted at one point that they had spoken to teams about Hernandez before pulling him off the market.

Pitching

A trimmed-down Hernandez was throwing in the low 90-MPH range to begin the season, but his velocity dropped as the summer progressed. Like most finesse pitchers, when Hernandez' control is off, he gets pounded. He also will throw a slider, change and curve, and he induces a decent number of groundballs with those offerings. But he continues to go through periods where he is hit particularly hard. He allowed 233 hits—the third most in the National League—and opponents hit a gaudy .283 against him.

Defense & Hitting

Hernandez would be a Gold Glove winner in the National League if not for Atlanta's Greg Maddux. For a man of his size, Hernandez is quick and nimble off the mound, fielding his position with grace. He did commit three errors last season, giving him just five in 181 career games. He seemed to forget about baserunners last year, however, allowing 22 of 25 thieves to reach their goal safely on his watch. Hernandez also is considered one of the game's top hitting pitchers, with a .242 career batting average.

2003 Outlook

With a $3.5 million salary, Hernandez is a relative bargain, but the Giants have toyed with the idea of trading him. They have several pitching prospects ready for the major leagues and were hoping they could fetch a hitter for Hernandez. So far, though, they have been unsuccessful in making a deal. If Hernandez pitches 217 innings this season, San Francisco will be forced to pick up a $6 million option for the 2004 season, something the club will try to avoid.

Position: SP
Bats: R **Throws:** R
Ht: 6' 2" **Wt:** 240

Opening Day Age: 28
Born: 2/20/75 in Villa Clara, Cuba
ML Seasons: 7
Pronunciation:
lee-VAHN her-NAN-dezz

Overall Statistics

	W	L	Pct.	ERA	G	GS	Sv	IP	H	BB	SO	HR	Ratio
'02	12	16	.429	4.38	33	33	0	216.0	233	71	134	19	1.41
Car.	69	69	.500	4.42	181	180	0	1216.0	1329	449	817	130	1.46

How Often He Throws Strikes

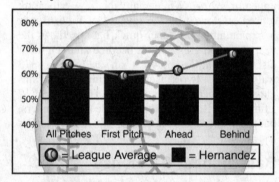

2002 Situational Stats

	W	L	ERA	Sv	IP		AB	H	HR	RBI	Avg
Home	7	9	3.99	0	124.0	LHB	370	110	8	46	.297
Road	5	7	4.89	0	92.0	RHB	454	123	11	55	.271
First Half	6	10	4.94	0	113.0	Sc Pos	194	59	4	79	.304
Scnd Half	6	6	3.76	0	103.0	Clutch	71	17	1	5	.239

2002 Rankings (National League)

- 1st in losses and GDPs induced (29)
- 2nd in pickoff throws (188)
- 3rd in complete games (5), shutouts (3), hits allowed, highest batting average allowed (.283) and highest stolen-base percentage allowed (88.0)
- 4th in most GDPs induced per nine innings (1.2)
- Led the Giants in losses, games started, complete games (5), shutouts (3), innings pitched, hits allowed, batters faced (921), pickoff throws (188), stolen bases allowed (22), GDPs induced (29), highest groundball-fly-ball ratio allowed (1.4) and most GDPs induced per nine innings (1.2)

Jeff Kent

Position: 2B
Bats: R **Throws:** R
Ht: 6' 1" **Wt:** 220

Opening Day Age: 35
Born: 3/7/68 in
Bellflower, CA
ML Seasons: 11

2002 Season

Jeff Kent made more news by what he did away from the diamond than anything he did on it. Early in spring training, he came to camp saying he broke his left wrist when he slipped while washing his truck on March 1. It later was alleged that he was involved in a motorcycle accident while popping wheelies. The injury put Kent on the disabled list to start the season. He also scuffled with Barry Bonds in the dugout during a game in June. Despite the off-field incidents, Kent had arguably his best offensive season.

Hitting

After a slow start, Kent hit .337 with 30 homers and 84 RBI from June 1 on. The big numbers were spurred by a switch in the batting order in late June, when he moved from cleanup to No. 3, ahead of Bonds. Kent has evolved to the point where he can handle almost any type of pitch, but he also can lack patience. He seemed to come alive hitting ahead of Bonds, where he had less pressure to succeed when managers walked Bonds to get to him.

Baserunning & Defense

Although he made 16 errors, Kent has turned himself into a good defensive player. He goes to his right extremely well and makes the off-balance throw as well as anybody in the National League. However, he sometimes makes careless errors due to concentration lapses. Kent never has been blessed with great speed, and he's prone to mistakes on the bases, usually getting caught in rundowns trying to take the extra base on his hits.

2003 Outlook

The six-year relationship between Kent and San Francisco was hanging by a thread. There are those who believe Kent is tired of playing second fiddle to Bonds, whom he does not like. However, that may not be the case and the team was working on a multiyear deal that might keep him a Giant. Still, the Giants singed Ray Durham in December to fill the possible void at second. If Kent leaves, the Giants will miss their most productive second baseman ever, one who might go to the Hall of Fame with a few more above-average seasons.

Overall Statistics

	G	AB	R	H	D	T	HR	RBI	SB	BB	SO	Avg	OBP	Slg
'02	152	623	102	195	42	2	37	108	5	52	101	.313	.368	.565
Car.	1502	5559	866	1604	365	33	253	1007	73	504	1074	.289	.353	.503

Where He Hits the Ball

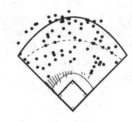
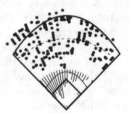

Vs. LHP   **Vs. RHP**

2002 Situational Stats

	AB	H	HR	RBI	Avg
Home	298	90	11	45	.302
Road	325	105	26	63	.323
First Half	334	107	14	55	.320
Scnd Half	289	88	23	53	.304

	AB	H	HR	RBI	Avg
LHP	145	53	11	24	.366
RHP	478	142	26	84	.297
Sc Pos	149	43	6	64	.289
Clutch	96	31	8	19	.323

2002 Rankings (National League)

- 2nd in hits, total bases (352) and errors at second base (16)
- 3rd in at-bats and lowest fielding percentage at second base (.978)
- 4th in batting average vs. lefthanded pitchers
- 5th in doubles and slugging percentage vs. lefthanded pitchers (.669)
- 7th in home runs, GDPs (20), batting average on the road and lowest cleanup slugging percentage (.484)
- Led the Giants in at-bats, hits, singles, doubles, total bases (352), GDPs (20), plate appearances (682) and highest percentage of swings put into play (47.6)
- Led NL second basemen in batting average, home runs and RBI

San Francisco

675

Kenny Lofton

2002 Season

Kenny Lofton split time with two teams—the Chicago White Sox and Giants—in 2002, but it actually was a tale of about *four* seasons for Lofton. He hit .343 the first month of 2002, batted .136 in June, struggled in August with a .190 average and hit .322 the season's final month. Those ups and downs and ebbs and flows apparently were the result of Lofton's health. He was bothered by shoulder and hamstring injuries with the White Sox, and by a hernia problem with the Giants after he was acquired July 28.

Hitting

Lofton always has been tempted by high fastballs, and he accordingly racks up a fair number of strikeouts, especially when he becomes to pull-conscious. He remains an effective bunter, and laid down 14 bunt hits in 2002. The Giants wondered if they had made the right choice by acquiring Lofton when he slumped during his first month with the team. However, he got hot when it counted. He homered in Game 1 of the NLCS and had the game-winning hit in the ninth inning of Game 5, clinching a spot in the World Series.

Baserunning & Defense

Lofton stole 22 bases with the White Sox, but his injuries slowed him considerably with the Giants. At 35, age is beginning to catch up to him. For a player whose game is predicated on speed, that could be a problem the rest of his career. Lofton simply is not the same dazzling center fielder he once was. With the Giants, he seemed to be a step slow on some balls, though he did make a pair of fantastic over-the-shoulder, Willie Mays-type catches.

2003 Outlook

Lofton was a bargain at $1.25 million, and the Giants probably would try to re-sign him at that price. However, Lofton believes he's worth a lot more and was seeking a multiyear contract over the winter. The Giants did not offer him salary arbitration and he will be playing elsewhere this season. After his hot start with the White Sox last year, and his solid finish, he'll likely find some team willing to come up in price.

Position: CF
Bats: L **Throws:** L
Ht: 6' 0" **Wt:** 180

Opening Day Age: 35
Born: 5/31/67 in East Chicago, IN
ML Seasons: 12

Overall Statistics

	G	AB	R	H	D	T	HR	RBI	SB	BB	SO	Avg	OBP	Slg
'02	139	532	98	139	30	9	11	51	29	72	73	.261	.350	.414
Car.	1505	5971	1148	1781	286	78	103	602	508	735	804	.298	.375	.424

Where He Hits the Ball

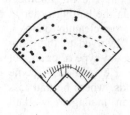 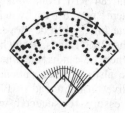

Vs. LHP   Vs. RHP

2002 Situational Stats

	AB	H	HR	RBI	Avg		AB	H	HR	RBI	Avg
Home	254	75	3	22	.295	LHP	109	27	0	8	.248
Road	278	64	8	29	.230	RHP	423	112	11	43	.265
First Half	296	75	4	34	.253	Sc Pos	105	33	0	39	.314
Scnd Half	236	64	7	17	.271	Clutch	69	17	2	9	.246

2002 Rankings (National League)

- 5th in on-base percentage for a leadoff hitter (.364)
- 8th in batting average on a 3-1 count (.600)
- Led the Giants in batting average on a 3-1 count (.600) and on-base percentage for a leadoff hitter (.364)

Robb Nen

2002 Season

Despite his 2.20 ERA and 43 saves, it was not a memorable year for closer Robb Nen. He blew eight saves, many of them resulting in gut-wrenching losses for the Giants. Though he finished strong and had a 1.00 ERA in 10 postseason outings, his right shoulder was shot. Nen underwent arthroscopic surgery after the season to repair a frayed labrum. However, the injury is not seen as significant enough to keep him from missing any time in 2003.

Pitching

When Nen's 90-92 MPH slider is on, he's arguably the nastiest closer in the game. He has one of the more peculiar deliveries, with an odd toe-tap that sometimes can disrupt a hitter's timing. Nen once again was trouble for lefthanded batters, limiting them to a .224 batting average with just one home run last season. However, when he's in one of his funks, he can be predictable and beatable. Nen may have been affected by overuse at various stages of the season, including six appearances over seven days in late August and early September in which his shoulder first began troubling him.

Defense & Hitting

Most closers don't have great moves to first base, but Nen's almost total disregard for runners puts him in binds time after time. If a runner has even average speed, he'll likely steal second off Nen, which is costly in close games. He's not the best fielder, either, and can appear clumsy trying to get his glove on bunts or slow grounders. He finally got his first hit last season—in other words, he's no factor at the plate.

2003 Outlook

Nen exercised the $8.6 million option on his contract for this season. He also holds a $9 million option for 2004. While widely regarded as one of the top closers in the game, he has sent hearts and pulses racing for years in San Francisco, and last season was no exception. Perhaps a healthy right shoulder will lead to easier outings for Nen, and the Giants, this season.

Position: RP
Bats: R **Throws:** R
Ht: 6' 5" **Wt:** 222

Opening Day Age: 33
Born: 11/28/69 in San Pedro, CA
ML Seasons: 10

Overall Statistics

	W	L	Pct.	ERA	G	GS	Sv	IP	H	BB	SO	HR	Ratio
'02	6	2	.750	2.20	68	0	43	73.2	64	20	81	2	1.14
Car.	45	42	.517	2.98	643	4	314	715.0	607	260	793	51	1.21

How Often He Throws Strikes

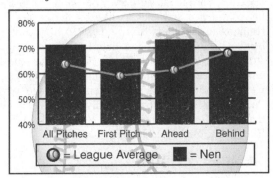

= League Average   ■ = Nen

2002 Situational Stats

	W	L	ERA	Sv	IP		AB	H	HR	RBI	Avg
Home	5	0	1.82	21	39.2	LHB	152	34	1	12	.224
Road	1	2	2.65	22	34.0	RHB	124	30	1	14	.242
First Half	3	0	1.58	24	40.0	Sc Pos	77	20	0	24	.260
Scnd Half	3	2	2.94	19	33.2	Clutch	220	49	1	23	.223

2002 Rankings (National League)

- 3rd in blown saves (8)
- 4th in games finished (66) and save opportunities (51)
- 5th in saves and lowest save percentage (84.3)
- 7th in relief wins (6)
- 8th in most strikeouts per nine innings in relief (9.9)
- 10th in relief ERA (2.20)
- Led the Giants in saves, games finished (66), save opportunities (51), save percentage (84.3), blown saves (8), relief innings (73.2), relief ERA (2.20), most strikeouts per nine innings in relief (9.9) and fewest baserunners allowed per nine innings in relief (10.4)

San Francisco

Russ Ortiz

2002 Season

Once again, Russ Ortiz confounded both fans and critics alike. At times, he can be the Giants' most puzzling starter, nibbling and throwing too many pitches for his own good. At other times, he can be the team's best pitcher, a dominant force. Such was the case last season. He had a so-so first half, but he won his last six starts in the regular season and beat Atlanta twice in the first round of the playoffs.

Pitching

Hitters can look foolish at times against Ortiz. Yet despite owning a low to mid-90s fastball and an effective, hard-breaking curve, he seems to lose his confidence and tries to live on the corners, resulting in too many baserunners. To his credit, he kept his walk total to less than 100 for a second straight season after leading the National League with 125 free passes in 1999. While Ortiz pitches well on the road, he has taken advantage of Pacific Bell Park's pitcher-friendly features better than most Giants hurlers. He is 19-8 with a 2.79 ERA at Pac Bell since July 13, 2000.

Defense & Hitting

Despite his rather large frame, Ortiz fields his position well. He has done a better job of controlling the running game the past two years, but that may speak as much about the presence of Benito Santiago behind the plate as any real improvement by Ortiz. Ortiz has become one of San Francisco's best hitting pitchers, high praise considering Livan Hernandez is his teammate.

2003 Outlook

Just when Ortiz appears on the verge of becoming one of the league's top pitchers, he seems to regress. After winning 18 and 17 games in 1999 and 2001, respectively, he fell to 14 the next year. If history repeats itself, he should rebound to finish in the 17-18 range this season. However, the offseason has been filled with speculation that the Giants would trade Ortiz to acquire a front line hitter. Even though the Giants have promising arms in the minor leagues, it's surprising that they might part with Ortiz. There certainly is enough hitting talent available in the free-agent market.

Position: SP
Bats: R **Throws:** R
Ht: 6' 1" **Wt:** 208

Opening Day Age: 28
Born: 6/5/74 in Encino, CA
ML Seasons: 5
Pronunciation: OR-teez

Overall Statistics

	W	L	Pct.	ERA	G	GS	Sv	IP	H	BB	SO	HR	Ratio
'02	14	10	.583	3.61	33	33	0	214.1	191	94	137	15	1.33
Car.	67	44	.604	4.01	154	144	0	924.2	849	468	712	91	1.42

How Often He Throws Strikes

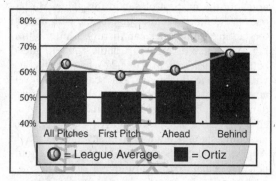

= League Average = Ortiz

2002 Situational Stats

	W	L	ERA	Sv	IP		AB	H	HR	RBI	Avg
Home	5	4	3.41	0	95.0	LHB	397	98	4	39	.247
Road	9	6	3.77	0	119.1	RHB	395	93	11	39	.235
First Half	6	6	3.69	0	112.1	Sc Pos	182	42	2	62	.231
Scnd Half	8	4	3.53	0	102.0	Clutch	49	14	0	5	.286

2002 Rankings (National League)

- 3rd in fewest home runs allowed per nine innings (.63)
- 4th in walks allowed and lowest strikeout-walk ratio (1.5)
- 5th in pitches thrown (3,576) and most pitches thrown per batter (3.93)
- 7th in lowest slugging percentage allowed (.357)
- 8th in lowest stolen-base percentage allowed (50.0) and highest walks per nine innings (3.9)
- Led the Giants in wins, games started, walks allowed, pitches thrown (3,576) and fewest home runs allowed per nine innings (.63)

Kirk Rueter

Position: SP
Bats: L **Throws:** L
Ht: 6' 3" **Wt:** 212

Opening Day Age: 32
Born: 12/1/70 in Centralia, IL
ML Seasons: 10
Pronunciation: REE-ter
Nickname: Woody

2002 Season

The 2002 campaign was just another consistent season for the player who answers to his nickname, "Woody," more than his given name. In each of his his six full seasons with the Giants, Rueter has won between 11-16 games, including 14 the past two years. He also has become the team's top big-game pitcher. After pitching well against Anaheim in Game 4 of the World Series, there were those who believed manager Dusty Baker should have started Rueter on three days rest in Game 7 rather than a well-rested Livan Hernandez. When Hernandez was knocked out early, Rueter pitched four shutout innings.

Pitching

Rueter has been compared most often to Tom Glavine. Both do not have overpowering stuff, forcing them to make a living on the corners. Though Rueter's velocity generally sits in the mid-80s, he will challenge hitters with an effective cutter and changeup. And despite modest strikeout totals, he somehow wins on a consistent basis. He now owns a lifetime 109-68 record, the fifth-highest winning percentage (.616) for a lefty since 1980. His 60-29 career road record (.674) is the second highest among active pitchers with at least 60 road decisions. (Pedro Martinez is first at 77-29, .726.)

Defense & Hitting

An unbelievable competitor, Rueter helps himself both in the field and at the plate. He is hard to run on and turns the double play with ease. He had 11 hits in 2002, marking the fourth time in the last five seasons he's been in double digits in that category. He also tied for third in the National League with 13 sacrifice bunts.

2003 Outlook

Rueter essentially negotiated his last contract to ensure he remains with the Giants. He made just $3.75 million the past two seasons, and he'll earn $4.75 million in the contract's final year in 2003—still a bargain at today's rate. As consistent as Rueter is, Dusty Baker, his former manager, referred to him as "Steady Eddie" last season, and new manager Felipe Alou likely would be satisfied with more of the same in 2003.

Overall Statistics

	W	L	Pct.	ERA	G	GS	Sv	IP	H	BB	SO	HR	Ratio
'02	14	8	.636	3.23	33	33	0	203.2	204	54	76	22	1.27
Car.	109	68	.616	4.07	260	258	0	1473.1	1566	422	696	173	1.35

How Often He Throws Strikes

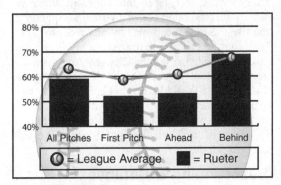

= League Average   = Rueter

2002 Situational Stats

	W	L	ERA	Sv	IP		AB	H	HR	RBI	Avg
Home	5	5	3.02	0	104.1	LHB	176	43	3	14	.244
Road	9	3	3.44	0	99.1	RHB	603	161	19	63	.267
First Half	7	5	3.45	0	114.2	Sc Pos	157	41	4	55	.261
Scnd Half	7	3	2.93	0	89.0	Clutch	37	10	2	2	.270

2002 Rankings (National League)

- 1st in fielding percentage at pitcher (1.000) and fewest strikeouts per nine innings (3.4)
- 2nd in lowest stolen-base percentage allowed (28.6)
- 3rd in sacrifice bunts (13) and lowest strike-out-walk ratio (1.4)
- 5th in GDPs induced (26)
- 6th in most GDPs induced per nine innings (1.1)
- Led the Giants in ERA, sacrifice bunts (13), wins, games started, home runs allowed, lowest stolen-base percentage allowed (28.6), bunts in play (16), lowest ERA on the road and fewest walks per nine innings (2.4)

Reggie Sanders

2002 Season

After leaving the world champion Diamondbacks in a less than amicable split, Reggie Sanders signed a one-year, $1.75 million contract to play for the Giants. Once again, Sanders reached the World Series, though he came up short this time. He also came up short trying to match his career-high power numbers from 2001, finishing with 23 homers and 85 RBI. Sanders played solid defense, but he slumped too often and hit just .244 after the All-Star break.

Hitting

Sanders continued his career-long trend as a streak hitter. He can go on home-run tears that can lead to wins, then lapse into funks in which he strikes outs too often and is a virtual non-factor at the plate. Sanders can hit low and mid-low fastballs, but he can be victimized by high fastballs, one reason why he was benched by Arizona manager Bob Brenly against Roger Clemens in Game 7 of the 2001 World Series. In Game 7 of this past World Series, former Giants manager Dusty Baker removed Sanders for pinch-hitter Tom Goodwin in the sixth inning, an odd move that angered Sanders.

Baserunning & Defense

Sanders has decent speed and stole 18 bases, four more than the previous season. He may have swiped even more had he not been slowed because of right hamstring problems that sidelined him in July. Nonetheless, Sanders logged 140 games, his highest total ever. Sanders continued to play a solid right field, displaying a strong arm and decent range. He matched a career high with 12 outfield assists in 2002.

2003 Outlook

Sanders was not offered salary arbitration by the Giants and was seeking a long-term deal with another team. Because of his age and history of injuries, he may not get what he's looking for. With Sanders' easygoing style and good clubhouse presence, the Giants wouldn't have minded having him back, but probably for only one or two more seasons. That won't be the case, and Sanders will be playing with his sixth team in six seasons.

Position: RF
Bats: R **Throws:** R
Ht: 6' 1" **Wt:** 205

Opening Day Age: 35
Born: 12/1/67 in Florence, SC
ML Seasons: 12

Overall Statistics

G	AB	R	H	D	T	HR	RBI	SB	BB	SO	Avg	OBP	Slg
140	505	75	126	23	6	23	85	18	47	121	.250	.324	.455
1307	4649	793	1238	243	50	218	715	247	536	1210	.266	.347	.481

Where He Hits the Ball

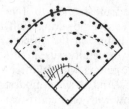

Vs. LHP   **Vs. RHP**

2002 Situational Stats

	AB	H	HR	RBI	Avg		AB	H	HR	RBI	Avg
Home	234	62	12	42	.265	LHP	121	35	8	19	.289
Road	271	64	11	43	.236	RHP	384	91	15	66	.237
First Half	288	73	10	50	.253	Sc Pos	160	38	5	62	.238
Scnd Half	217	53	13	35	.244	Clutch	84	17	4	13	.202

2002 Rankings (National League)

- 3rd in assists in right field (12)
- 4th in errors in right field (5)
- 5th in sacrifice flies (7) and fielding percentage in right field (.984)
- Led the Giants in triples, sacrifice flies (7), stolen bases, caught stealing (6), hit by pitch (12), strikeouts and highest percentage of extra bases taken as a runner (59.5)

Benito Santiago

2002 Season

Benito Santiago was named to the All-Star team for the first time since 1992, becoming one of 10 players ever to appear on an All-Star roster after a 10-year absence. Not bad for a player who just a year prior had been out of work for most of spring training before being signed by the Giants. Santiago has appeared in 259 games the past two seasons, ending a stretch in which he did not play in more than 109 games in any season from 1997 through 2000.

Hitting

Santiago was supposed to be slowing down, or just plain washed up, when he discovered the fountain of youth. He began turning on fastballs again, hitting more homers than he has since 1996. He was considered an early-count hitter, but last season he did a lot of damage deep in counts. In fact, his two-run, game-winning homer in Game 4 of the NLCS off St. Louis' Rick White occurred on a full count. He can be susceptible to up-and-in pitches, and has been known to lay down a bunt to try to get on base.

Baserunning & Defense

Though he still can gun down runners from his knees, Santiago has slowed in this department. He threw out only 27.5 percent (22 of 80) of those runners attempting to steal last season. Santiago also had seven passed balls. However, he continues to call a superior game. Santiago shows remarkable speed for a man of his age, but he sometimes can be foolhardy and occasionally gets caught trying to stretch a double into a triple.

2003 Outlook

Santiago had the perfect demeanor when managers intentionally walked Barry Bonds to get to him last season. Rather than try too hard, Santiago relaxed and more often than not made managers pay for their strategy. It's hard to imagine Santiago having another year like 2002, but he seems full of surprises. The Giants signed Santiago to a two-year, $3.75 million contract before last season, a ridiculously affordable contract for an All-Star.

Position: C
Bats: R **Throws:** R
Ht: 6' 1" **Wt:** 200

Opening Day Age: 38
Born: 3/9/65 in Ponce, PR
ML Seasons: 17
Pronunciation: sahn-tee-AH-go

Overall Statistics

G	AB	R	H	D	T	HR	RBI	SB	BB	SO	Avg	OBP	Slg
126	478	56	133	24	5	16	74	4	27	73	.278	.315	.450
1815	6352	686	1664	291	38	200	841	90	393	1166	.262	.305	.414

Where He Hits the Ball

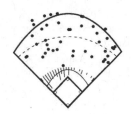 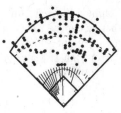

Vs. LHP	**Vs. RHP**

2002 Situational Stats

	AB	H	HR	RBI	Avg		AB	H	HR	RBI	Avg
Home	233	59	6	43	.253	LHP	116	32	4	20	.276
Road	245	74	10	31	.302	RHP	362	101	12	54	.279
First Half	267	73	8	40	.273	Sc Pos	134	35	5	58	.261
Scnd Half	211	60	8	34	.284	Clutch	84	20	5	18	.238

2002 Rankings (National League)

- 3rd in fielding percentage at catcher (.995) and highest percentage of swings on the first pitch (45.4)
- Led the Giants in sacrifice flies (7) and batting average on a 3-2 count (.313)

Jason Schmidt

2002 Season

The Giants awarded Jason Schmidt a four-year, $30 million deal before the season, the largest contract they've given a starting pitcher. But they weren't too happy when he missed so much time with groin, shoulder and elbow injuries, at least some of which were not believed to be serious. Schmidt was also sidetracked by his mother's medical concerns. He was not effective upon his return from the DL in late April, getting rocked in his first two starts and leaving his third start early due to shoulder stiffness. But he was solid the remainder of the season, finishing 13-8 with a 3.45 ERA.

Pitching

Schmidt showed glimpses throughout the season that he can be the Giants' ace, including a dominating eight innings in which he struck out a career-high 13 (later matched) at Yankee Stadium on June 8. He relies on a lively fastball that he can dial up to the low to mid-90s, as well as a hard slider that he can use as a strikeout pitch. Schmidt has proven in his short time with the Giants that he is superior at Pacific Bell Park than he is on the road. He had a 2.37 ERA at home last season, compared to 5.02 on the road.

Defense & Hitting

Schmidt has a reputation for a lack of fielding ability, though he has not made an error the past three seasons. His numbers against the running game have declined over the past couple of years, and he does not have a pickoff move to speak of. He has improved as a hitter, with a .125 batting average last season. He's a career .101 hitter. Sacrifice bunting still challenges Schmidt—he had just four last season.

2003 Outlook

If Schmidt can stay healthy from the outset, he should be able to approach the 17-18 win plateau that many, including the Giants, believe he can attain. He has fallen short of living up to his potential, mostly because he pitched for bad Pittsburgh teams for most of his career, and partly because of a history of injuries. Finally on a winning team, he's gone 20-9 with the Giants.

Position: SP
Bats: R **Throws:** R
Ht: 6' 5" **Wt:** 205

Opening Day Age: 30
Born: 1/29/73 in Lewiston, ID
ML Seasons: 8

Overall Statistics

	W	L	Pct.	ERA	G	GS	Sv	IP	H	BB	SO	HR	Ratio
'02	13	8	.619	3.45	29	29	0	185.1	148	73	196	15	1.19
Car.	69	62	.527	4.33	191	182	0	1135.0	1132	478	924	110	1.42

How Often He Throws Strikes

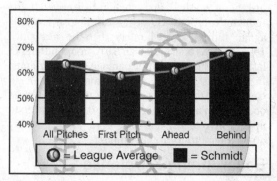

= League Average   = Schmidt

2002 Situational Stats

	W	L	ERA	Sv	IP		AB	H	HR	RBI	Avg
Home	8	5	2.37	0	110.0	LHB	328	85	11	43	.259
Road	5	3	5.02	0	75.1	RHB	350	63	4	30	.180
First Half	4	3	3.75	0	84.0	Sc Pos	138	35	3	53	.254
Scnd Half	9	5	3.20	0	101.1	Clutch	54	10	1	2	.185

2002 Rankings (National League)

- 1st in fielding percentage at pitcher (1.000)
- 2nd in lowest slugging percentage allowed (.329), lowest batting average allowed vs. righthanded batters and lowest groundball-flyball ratio allowed (0.8)
- 3rd in lowest ERA at home, most strikeouts per nine innings (9.5) and most pitches thrown per batter (3.94)
- 4th in shutouts (2), wild pitches (12), lowest batting average allowed (.218) and fewest GDPs induced per nine innings (0.5)
- Led the Giants in strikeouts, wild pitches (12), highest strikeout-walk ratio (2.7), lowest batting average allowed (.218) and lowest on-base percentage allowed (.294)

Marvin Benard

Position: RF/LF
Bats: L **Throws:** L
Ht: 5' 9" **Wt:** 191

Opening Day Age: 33
Born: 1/20/70 in
Bluefields, Nicaragua
ML Seasons: 8
Pronunciation:
buh-NARD

Overall Statistics

	G	AB	R	H	D	T	HR	RBI	SB	BB	SO	Avg	OBP	Slg
'02	65	123	16	34	9	2	1	13	5	7	26	.276	.321	.407
Car.	845	2559	436	700	135	20	54	256	104	261	445	.274	.345	.405

2002 Situational Stats

	AB	H	HR	RBI	Avg		AB	H	HR	RBI	Avg
Home	63	16	0	5	.254	LHP	18	7	0	2	.389
Road	60	18	1	8	.300	RHP	105	27	1	11	.257
First Half	116	34	1	13	.293	Sc Pos	37	9	1	11	.243
Scnd Half	7	0	0	0	.000	Clutch	32	8	0	2	.250

2002 Season

The 2002 season was a complete bust for Marvin Benard, who lost his starting job in spring training and was out for most of the second half with torn cartilage in his left knee that required surgery in early July. Benard hit .293 in the first half, a large chunk of it as a pinch-hitter, before he went on the disabled list.

Hitting, Baserunning & Defense

Since the strike zone was raised two years ago, Benard has been susceptible to high fastballs, and he seems incapable of laying off those pitches, much to his detriment. Benard rarely played center field, where he became a defensive liability. He took poor routes to the ball, and is much more suited to play one of the corner outfield positions. He is a high-percentage basestealer whose opportunities are limited by lack of playing time.

2003 Outlook

With a year remaining on Benard's three-year, $11.1 million contract, the Giants have been unable to trade him and appear to be stuck with him for another season. He can be counted on to be only a fourth or fifth outfielder, and one of the first hitters off the bench. Benard is not bad in that capacity, with a .267 mark for his career as a pinch-hitter.

Shawon Dunston

Position: RF/LF
Bats: R **Throws:** R
Ht: 6' 1" **Wt:** 180

Opening Day Age: 40
Born: 3/21/63 in
Brooklyn, NY
ML Seasons: 18
Pronunciation:
SHAWN

Overall Statistics

	G	AB	R	H	D	T	HR	RBI	SB	BB	SO	Avg	OBP	Slg
'02	72	147	7	34	5	0	1	9	1	3	33	.231	.250	.286
Car.	1814	5927	736	1597	292	62	150	668	212	203	1000	.269	.296	.416

2002 Situational Stats

	AB	H	HR	RBI	Avg		AB	H	HR	RBI	Avg
Home	72	19	0	6	.264	LHP	48	11	0	1	.229
Road	75	15	1	3	.200	RHP	99	23	1	8	.232
First Half	89	19	1	5	.213	Sc Pos	37	9	0	8	.243
Scnd Half	58	15	0	4	.259	Clutch	30	6	0	3	.200

2002 Season

At 39, there were those who wondered if Shawon Dunston had stuck around one year too long. He hit only .213 before the All-Star break. When the Giants needed to create room on the roster for the return of injured players, critics questioned why the team didn't release Dunston. However, he had a big hit in the ninth inning of the clinching Game 5 of the NLCS and homered in Game 6 of the World Series, giving the Giants a temporary lead.

Hitting, Baserunning & Defense

Dunston was virtually useless as a pinch-hitter (.167) and DH (.143) during the regular season. His bat speed was nonexistent, and he rarely got on base because of his propensity to swing at nearly every pitch and avoid walking at all costs, a career-long trend. He was not a liability in the field, however, going errorless in 53 chances in the outfield, shortstop and first base. He continued hustling down the line on every ball he hit.

2003 Outlook

Dunston will be 40 when the season begins, and he's played his final game for the Giants, who did not offer him salary arbitration and showed no inclination to re-sign him. Dunston wants to play another year, but he may be hard pressed to find a team that will give him a job.

San Francisco

Ryan Jensen

Position: SP
Bats: R **Throws:** R
Ht: 6' 0" **Wt:** 205

Opening Day Age: 27
Born: 9/17/75 in Salt
Lake City, UT
ML Seasons: 2

Overall Statistics

	W	L	Pct.	ERA	G	GS	Sv	IP	H	BB	SO	HR	Ratio
'02	13	8	.619	4.51	32	30	0	171.2	183	66	105	21	1.45
Car.	14	10	.583	4.46	42	37	0	214.0	227	91	131	26	1.49

2002 Situational Stats

	W	L	ERA	Sv	IP		AB	H	HR	RBI	Avg
Home	6	4	3.66	0	83.2	LHB	306	88	12	47	.288
Road	7	4	5.32	0	88.0	RHB	352	95	9	41	.270
First Half	9	6	4.45	0	99.0	Scp Pos	174	48	7	69	.276
Scnd Half	4	2	4.58	0	72.2	Clutch	28	8	0	2	.286

2002 Season

Ryan Jensen was not supposed to be in the Giants'
plans in spring training. But a groin injury to
Jason Schmidt put Jensen in the rotation, and he
stayed there all season. Jensen finished with a 13-
8 record, but he registered just four wins after the
All-Star break.

Pitching, Defense & Hitting

Jensen was a major surprise in the first half, winning nine games despite less than stellar stuff. He
reminded people of a younger Mark Gardner, who
relied more on guile and smarts than his ability.
The league seemed to catch on to Jensen in the
second half, however. Jensen was the team's
worst hitting pitcher among its starters, with a
.107 batting average, and he neither distinguished
nor hurt himself defensively. Basestealers take
advantage of him, but he did pick off a pair of runners last year.

2003 Outlook

It's not likely that Jensen will catch the league by
surprise this season as he did in 2002. And with
Kurt Ainsworth, Jerome Williams and Jesse
Foppert ready to pitch in the big leagues, Jensen
may be moved to long relief. Still, he could be a
fine long reliever, or a fourth or fifth starter on a
team searching for rotation help.

Ramon Martinez

Position: SS/2B
Bats: R **Throws:** R
Ht: 6' 1" **Wt:** 183

Opening Day Age: 30
Born: 10/10/72 in
Philadelphia, PA
ML Seasons: 5

Overall Statistics

	G	AB	R	H	D	T	HR	RBI	SB	BB	SO	Avg	OBP	Slg
'02	72	181	26	49	10	2	4	25	2	14	26	.271	.335	.414
Car.	368	924	129	249	48	7	20	106	7	85	119	.269	.335	.402

2002 Situational Stats

	AB	H	HR	RBI	Avg		AB	H	HR	RBI	Avg
Home	103	29	4	15	.282	LHP	59	15	1	8	.254
Road	78	20	0	10	.256	RHP	122	34	3	17	.279
First Half	101	29	2	11	.287	Sc Pos	41	17	3	23	.415
Scnd Half	80	20	2	14	.250	Clutch	31	10	0	3	.323

2002 Season

Back to a reserve role after playing 128 games in
2001, Ramon Martinez turned in a solid season for
the Giants. Realizing his limitations as a full-time
player, San Francisco used him strictly as a role
player in 2002. He saw time at all four infield
positions, though the bulk of his games (40) came
at shortstop when starter Rich Aurilia was hurt.

Hitting, Baserunning & Defense

The Giants have known for years that Martinez'
bat is more valuable off the bench than it is in the
starting lineup. He won't impress anyone with his
bat speed, but he managed to tie a franchise record
with three doubles on August 16 against Florida.
Martinez also has been a slick fielder, particularly
at shortstop. He showed his versatility by starting
four games at first base and making three appearances in left field.

2003 Outlook

The Giants have received plenty of mileage from
Martinez since he first was called up in 1998. He's
now arbitration-eligible, and San Francisco may
balk at paying him more than $1 million for the
role he fills. Then again, maybe he'll still be there
when all the player movement is done and the dust
settles.

Damon Minor

Position: 1B
Bats: L **Throws:** L
Ht: 6' 7" **Wt:** 230

Opening Day Age: 29
Born: 1/5/74 in Canton, OH
ML Seasons: 3

Overall Statistics

	G	AB	R	H	D	T	HR	RBI	SB	BB	SO	Avg	OBP	Slg
'02	83	173	21	41	6	0	10	24	0	24	34	.237	.333	.445
Car.	112	227	27	52	7	0	13	33	0	29	43	.229	.319	.432

2002 Situational Stats

	AB	H	HR	RBI	Avg		AB	H	HR	RBI	Avg
Home	84	17	3	11	.202	LHP	44	11	3	10	.250
Road	89	24	7	13	.270	RHP	129	30	7	14	.233
First Half	108	29	8	18	.269	Sc Pos	54	10	0	10	.185
Scnd Half	65	12	2	6	.185	Clutch	31	4	1	2	.129

2002 Season

Damon Minor became the team's starting first baseman for a while, taking the job from slumping J.T. Snow in early June. Minor had a 37-game stretch entering the All-Star break in which he hit eight homers. However, his offense was nonexistent in the second half, and he became an afterthought when Snow regained the starting job.

Hitting, Baserunning & Defense

Minor showed flashes of the power the Giants expected from the 6-foot-7, 230-pound first baseman. He hit eight homers in the first half, but just two in the second half. Pitchers learned that Minor still has flaws in his long, looping swing. He went to an open stance in the Carlos Baerga mode, but that seemed to hurt his hitting when pitchers adjusted to him. Minor is very slow and no factor on the bases, but he is fairly nimble at first base, committing only one error in 331 chances.

2003 Outlook

With Snow back for at least another season, Minor will be relegated to a backup role again. He'll have to make adjustments and alter his stance if he wants to remain in the big leagues for the long haul. The Giants had hoped Minor would be their first baseman of the future, but they'll have to re-evaluate that theory.

Felix Rodriguez

Position: RP
Bats: R **Throws:** R
Ht: 6' 1" **Wt:** 198

Opening Day Age: 30
Born: 9/9/72 in Montecristi, DR
ML Seasons: 7

Overall Statistics

	W	L	Pct.	ERA	G	GS	Sv	IP	H	BB	SO	HR	Ratio
'02	8	6	.571	4.17	71	0	0	69.0	53	29	58	5	1.19
Car.	24	15	.615	3.48	354	1	8	398.0	341	189	374	30	1.33

2002 Situational Stats

	W	L	ERA	Sv	IP		AB	H	HR	RBI	Avg
Home	4	2	2.80	0	35.1	LHB	107	25	3	18	.234
Road	4	4	5.61	0	33.2	RHB	143	28	2	16	.196
First Half	3	4	5.55	0	35.2	Sc Pos	60	17	2	27	.283
Scnd Half	5	2	2.70	0	33.1	Clutch	157	38	3	24	.242

2002 Season

After two straight dominant seasons as the Giants' primary setup man, the performance of Felix Rodriguez took a precipitous drop in 2002. Part of his problem was a finger injury that he concealed from the training staff for most of the season's first half. He ultimately lost his job to Tim Worrell, then pitched much more like himself, going 5-2 with a 2.70 ERA after the All-Star break.

Pitching, Defense & Hitting

With a repertoire that features fast and faster pitches, when Rodriguez struggles, he can be too predictable. At this stage in his development, he needs an offspeed pitch to complement his hard slider and fastball. A former minor league catcher, Rodriguez can hit. However, he's had one at-bat the past two seasons. He rarely has to field because of the strikeouts and flyballs he coaxes.

2003 Outlook

There was talk the past two seasons that Rodriguez ultimately might replace Robb Nen as the closer in San Francisco. But after Rodriguez' troubling year, those thoughts have been buried, and he will have to fight to regain the setup job he lost. Still, there's little question that he has the ability to again be a dominant pitcher.

San Francisco

Tsuyoshi Shinjo

Position: CF/RF
Bats: R **Throws:** R
Ht: 6' 1" **Wt:** 185
Opening Day Age: 31

Born: 1/28/72 in
Fukuoka, Japan
ML Seasons: 2
Pronunciation:
SU-yo-she Shin-jo

Overall Statistics

	G	AB	R	H	D	T	HR	RBI	SB	BB	SO	Avg	OBP	Slg
'02	118	362	42	86	15	3	9	37	5	24	46	.238	.294	.370
Car.	241	762	88	193	38	4	19	93	9	49	116	.253	.308	.388

2002 Situational Stats

	AB	H	HR	RBI	Avg		AB	H	HR	RBI	Avg
Home	161	39	4	17	.242	LHP	110	32	4	20	.291
Road	201	47	5	20	.234	RHP	252	54	5	17	.214
First Half	265	64	8	29	.242	Sc Pos	85	20	2	27	.235
Scnd Half	97	22	1	8	.227	Clutch	55	7	0	0	.127

2002 Season

The Giants had high hopes that Tsuyoshi Shinjo could be the top-flight center fielder and leadoff hitter they've been lacking for years. No more than a month into the season, the team realized he was just another player passing through. While Shinjo's defense was first-rate, he was a liability at the plate.

Hitting, Baserunning & Defense

Although he hit .268 with 10 homers for the Mets the year before, Shinjo's awkward stance seems to make him incapable of hitting major league pitching on a consistent basis. He batted just .220 in April and lost his job when the Giants acquired Kenny Lofton in late July. Shinjo has a powerful arm and made a number of fantastic catches last season. He also was perfect in five stolen-base attempts.

2003 Outlook

Shinjo became a forgotten man the final two months of the season and did not have his option picked up by the Giants. Another team might be willing to take a chance and sign him as a backup outfielder. For a player with limited hitting skills, he draws an unbelievable amount of attention, mostly from the Japanese media.

J.T. Snow

Position: 1B
Bats: L **Throws:** L
Ht: 6' 2" **Wt:** 209

Opening Day Age: 35
Born: 2/26/68 in Long Beach, CA
ML Seasons: 11
Nickname: Snowball

Overall Statistics

	G	AB	R	H	D	T	HR	RBI	SB	BB	SO	Avg	OBP	Slg
'02	143	422	47	104	26	2	6	53	0	59	90	.246	.344	.360
Car.	1350	4554	643	1196	226	13	165	722	14	607	957	.263	.351	.427

2002 Situational Stats

	AB	H	HR	RBI	Avg		AB	H	HR	RBI	Avg
Home	190	42	1	17	.221	LHP	70	16	2	10	.229
Road	232	62	5	36	.267	RHP	352	88	4	43	.250
First Half	231	53	3	33	.229	Sc Pos	118	32	2	47	.271
Scnd Half	191	51	3	20	.267	Clutch	69	22	0	6	.319

2002 Season

J.T. Snow had only one above-average month, when he hit .326 in July, and batted .246 for a second straight season. It represented another precipitous drop from his 1997-2000 numbers, when he averaged 22 homers and 94 RBI. But last season, Snow could not use injuries as an alibi for his poor numbers, which had been the case in 2001.

Hitting, Baserunning & Defense

Snow has become almost powerless, hitting a career-low six homers last season. His bat speed has slowed markedly in recent years, which could lead to his removal from the lineup on a more regular basis in the near future. Snow committed seven errors, his most since '97, but he remains among the best fielding first baseman in the game. He probably is the slowest of the Giants' starters, and often gets thrown out at the plate.

2003 Outlook

Snow will make $6.85 million this season, which could be his last in San Francisco. He has a $6.5 million option for 2004, which the Giants won't exercise if he continues to struggle at the plate. The Giants can be encouraged by Snow's postseason, when he hit .333, but he has to be more consistent and avoid the dreadful first halves that have haunted him the past two years.

Jay Witasick

Position: RP
Bats: R **Throws:** R
Ht: 6' 4" **Wt:** 235

Opening Day Age: 30
Born: 8/28/72 in Baltimore, MD
ML Seasons: 7
Pronunciation: wi-TASS-ik

Overall Statistics

	W	L	Pct.	ERA	G	GS	Sv	IP	H	BB	SO	HR	Ratio
'02	1	0	1.000	2.37	44	0	0	68.1	58	21	54	3	1.16
Car.	26	28	.481	4.92	199	56	1	506.2	567	236	432	74	1.58

2002 Situational Stats

	W	L	ERA	Sv	IP		AB	H	HR	RBI	Avg
Home	1	0	2.78	0	32.1	LHB	101	23	0	5	.228
Road	0	0	2.00	0	36.0	RHB	147	35	3	11	.238
First Half	1	0	1.98	0	41.0	Sc Pos	54	8	0	11	.148
Scnd Half	0	0	2.96	0	27.1	Clutch	29	4	1	1	.138

2002 Season

By and large, the Giants made a fine move when the acquired Jay Witasick from the Yankees for outfielder John Vander Wal in December 2001. Witasick had a 2.37 ERA in 44 games for San Francisco, most of them in long relief. He was so good in his role that the Giants entertained thoughts of moving him into the rotation. That did not happen, however.

Pitching, Defense & Hitting

Primarily a fastball pitcher, Witasick did a commendable job in long relief and mopup duty. However, he could not shed his label as a pitcher not suited for big-game situations, an issue which came to the forefront when he posted a 7.36 ERA during the postseason for the Giants and allowed three hits and two runs in one-third of an inning in Game 3 against Anaheim. A shaky fielder, Witasick has a career .897 fielding percentage. He went hitless in 2002, and is a career .081 hitter.

2003 Outlook

Witasick is arbitration-eligible, and it's not certain if he'll be returning in 2003. With so many pitchers in their farm system ready for the major leagues, one of them easily could replace him, at a much cheaper rate. It's likely Witasick will be playing for his sixth team in six years.

Tim Worrell

Position: RP
Bats: R **Throws:** R
Ht: 6' 4" **Wt:** 230

Opening Day Age: 35
Born: 7/5/67 in Pasadena, CA
ML Seasons: 10
Pronunciation: wor-RELL

Overall Statistics

	W	L	Pct.	ERA	G	GS	Sv	IP	H	BB	SO	HR	Ratio
'02	8	2	.800	2.25	80	0	0	72.0	55	30	55	3	1.18
Car.	35	45	.438	4.01	451	49	7	748.0	727	298	578	75	1.37

2002 Situational Stats

	W	L	ERA	Sv	IP		AB	H	HR	RBI	Avg
Home	5	1	2.73	0	29.2	LHB	103	21	1	17	.204
Road	3	1	1.91	0	42.1	RHB	156	34	2	9	.218
First Half	5	0	2.06	0	39.1	Sc Pos	82	14	0	23	.171
Scnd Half	3	2	2.48	0	32.2	Clutch	136	23	2	10	.169

2002 Season

In many ways, last season was Tim Worrell's best. He inherited the setup job from struggling Felix Rodriguez early in the season and did not relinquish his role the remainder of the year. Worrell finished with a career-high 80 appearances with a career-low 2.25 ERA. The only real blemish in an otherwise sparkling campaign was a bad outing in Game 6 of the World Series that helped Anaheim overcome a 5-0, seventh-inning deficit.

Pitching, Defense & Hitting

Worrell appeared to gain velocity with both his fastball and slider last season. He also shows a split-finger offering to lefties. He pitched better in the first half for the Giants in 2002. However, he did manage to post a 2.48 ERA after the break. Worrell did not commit an error last season after making two in 2001. He rarely has an opportunity to hit. When he does, there's not much excitement.

2003 Outlook

The Giants picked up Worrell's $2 million option for 2003. Worrell will have a new manager this season, Felipe Alou, who must avoid overusing him, something Dusty Baker often was accused of doing. Worrell will turn 36 in July and cannot be used as often as he was in the past two seasons.

Other San Francisco Giants

Manny Aybar (Pos: RHP, Age: 30)

	W	L	Pct.	ERA	G	GS	Sv	IP	H	BB	SO	HR	Ratio
'02	1	0	1.000	2.51	15	0	0	14.1	16	3	11	1	1.33
Car.	17	18	.486	5.04	183	28	3	362.2	378	162	244	44	1.49

Aybar signed as a free agent with the Giants, but spent most of 2002 at Triple-A Fresno, where he served as the primary closer. The Giants were his seventh organization, though probably not his last. 2003 Outlook: C

Troy Brohawn (Pos: LHP, Age: 30)

	W	L	Pct.	ERA	G	GS	Sv	IP	H	BB	SO	HR	Ratio
'02	0	1	.000	6.35	11	0	0	5.2	5	1	3	1	1.06
Car.	2	4	.333	5.07	70	0	1	55.0	60	24	33	6	1.53

Brohawn pitched in the 2001 World Series for Arizona, and returned to the Giants last season. His biggest Giants contribution likely will be that he was the player dealt for Felix Rodriguez in 1998. 2003 Outlook: C

Jason Christiansen (Pos: LHP, Age: 33)

	W	L	Pct.	ERA	G	GS	Sv	IP	H	BB	SO	HR	Ratio
'02	0	1	.000	5.40	6	0	0	5.0	6	2	1	1	1.60
Car.	17	22	.436	4.09	360	0	13	326.0	295	163	319	27	1.40

Christiansen's season ended early due to elbow woes, and he underwent surgery in May. Injuries have hampered him in the past, too. But the lefthander could be ready for spring training. 2003 Outlook: B

Scott Eyre (Pos: LHP, Age: 30)

	W	L	Pct.	ERA	G	GS	Sv	IP	H	BB	SO	HR	Ratio
'02	2	4	.333	4.46	70	3	0	74.2	80	36	58	4	1.55
Car.	12	20	.375	5.25	165	32	2	302.0	338	165	216	49	1.67

Acquired off waivers from Toronto in August, Eyre performed well for the Giants down the stretch, and then allowed no runs in 10 postseason games. He's been tough on lefties the last two years. 2003 Outlook: B

Pedro Feliz (Pos: 3B, Age: 25, Bats: R)

	G	AB	R	H	D	T	HR	RBI	SB	BB	SO	Avg	OBP	Slg
'02	67	146	14	37	4	1	2	13	0	6	27	.253	.281	.336
Car.	169	373	38	89	13	2	9	35	2	16	78	.239	.271	.357

Feliz has value to a team if he can hit for power, but he demonstrated little last year, and he never has reached base with impressive frequency. He looks like he may never be much more than a bench player. 2003 Outlook: C

Aaron Fultz (Pos: LHP, Age: 29)

	W	L	Pct.	ERA	G	GS	Sv	IP	H	BB	SO	HR	Ratio
'02	2	2	.500	4.79	43	0	0	41.1	47	19	31	4	1.60
Car.	10	5	.667	4.66	167	0	2	181.2	184	68	160	21	1.39

Fultz is the kind of guy who always will have to cling to a spot as a lefty reliever. But that spot is tenuous when he allows lefthanded batters to hit .302, as he did last year. 2003 Outlook: C

Tom Goodwin (Pos: LF/CF, Age: 34, Bats: L)

	G	AB	R	H	D	T	HR	RBI	SB	BB	SO	Avg	OBP	Slg
'02	78	154	23	40	5	2	1	17	16	14	25	.260	.321	.338
Car.	1124	3570	599	959	107	39	23	269	345	346	605	.269	.334	.340

The Dodgers released Goodwin after Dave Roberts seized their center field job. Goodwin wound up with the Giants, where he contributed speed and defense at three positions. 2003 Outlook: C

Trey Lunsford (Pos: C, Age: 23, Bats: R)

	G	AB	R	H	D	T	HR	RBI	SB	BB	SO	Avg	OBP	Slg
'02	3	3	0	2	1	0	0	1	0	0	1	.667	.667	1.000
Car.	3	3	0	2	1	0	0	1	0	0	1	.667	.667	1.000

Lunsford was a 33rd-round draft pick in 2000. He has only 60 at-bats above Double-A, so Lunsford likely will return to the minors this year. 2003 Outlook: C

Bill Mueller (Pos: 3B, Age: 32, Bats: B)

	G	AB	R	H	D	T	HR	RBI	SB	BB	SO	Avg	OBP	Slg
'02	111	366	51	96	19	4	7	38	0	52	42	.262	.350	.393
Car.	778	2674	422	765	152	13	41	274	16	357	355	.286	.370	.399

Mueller broke his kneecap in 2001 and had additional surgery last March. When he returned, his average increased every month after May. Traded to the Giants in September, he's now a free agent. 2003 Outlook: B

Joe Nathan (Pos: RHP, Age: 28)

	W	L	Pct.	ERA	G	GS	Sv	IP	H	BB	SO	HR	Ratio
'02	0	0	–	0.00	4	0	0	3.2	1	0	2	0	0.27
Car.	12	6	.667	4.61	43	29	1	187.1	174	109	117	29	1.51

Nathan has had injuries and hasn't been effective since 2000. The Giants are loaded with intriguing hurlers, so Nathan may need to look elsewhere. 2003 Outlook: C

Cody Ransom (Pos: SS, Age: 27, Bats: R)

	G	AB	R	H	D	T	HR	RBI	SB	BB	SO	Avg	OBP	Slg
'02	7	3	2	2	0	0	0	1	0	1	1	.667	.750	.667
Car.	16	10	3	2	0	0	0	1	0	1	6	.200	.273	.200

Ransom struggled to keep his average above .200 last year. With some speed and good defense at short, he has a chance to contribute somewhere. 2003 Outlook: C

Yorvit Torrealba (Pos: C, Age: 24, Bats: R)

	G	AB	R	H	D	T	HR	RBI	SB	BB	SO	Avg	OBP	Slg
'02	53	136	17	38	10	0	2	14	0	14	20	.279	.355	.397
Car.	56	140	17	40	10	1	2	16	0	14	20	.286	.359	.414

Torrealba showed some skills with the Giants last year. He's still relatively young, and Benito Santiago figures to slow down at some point. 2003 Outlook: B

Chad Zerbe (Pos: LHP, Age: 30)

	W	L	Pct.	ERA	G	GS	Sv	IP	H	BB	SO	HR	Ratio
'02	2	0	1.000	3.04	50	0	0	56.1	52	21	26	3	1.30
Car.	5	0	1.000	3.46	81	1	0	101.1	99	32	53	7	1.29

Zerbe had a nice season for the Giants. He and Matt Ginter are the only two pitchers in history who have worked at least 100 innings and remain undefeated. 2003 Outlook: B

San Francisco Giants Minor League Prospects

Organization Overview:

The Giants' starting lineup in Game 7 of last year's World Series consisted of only two homegrown players (including Rich Aurilia, who originally was drafted by Texas). But that doesn't mean the farm system didn't play a critical role in the team's success. Over the years, prospects were used to land key contributors such as Livan Hernandez, Jason Schmidt and Robb Nen, among others. Don't be surprised if the Giants use more prospects, especially on the pitching side, to find reinforcements in the future. The Giants' minor league strength is on the mound, and a number of their arms figure to reach the big leagues one day. At least two of them, Kurt Ainsworth and Jerome Williams, will be knocking on the door this season. The pickings are a bit slimmer among position players, though Tony Torcato looks like he could be ready for a spot in the bigs.

Kurt Ainsworth

Position: P
Bats: R **Throws:** R
Ht: 6' 3" **Wt:** 185

Opening Day Age: 24
Born: 9/9/78 in Baton Rouge, LA

Recent Statistics

	W	L	ERA	G	GS	Sv	IP	H	R	BB	SO	HR
2002 NL San Fran	1	2	2.10	6	4	0	25.2	22	7	12	15	1
2002 AAA Fresno	8	6	3.41	20	19	0	116.0	101	49	43	119	7

Ainsworth has been a top prospect ever since the Giants grabbed him with their first pick in the 1999 draft. He opened last season in San Francisco's rotation, where he pitched well. But he spent most of the year in Triple-A, where he showed nice progress over 2001. He adjusted to hitters in his second crack at the Pacific Coast League, and did a fine job of maturing his pitches. He throws a 93-95 MPH fastball and is learning how to use it for location. He also has worked with a slider, curveball and changeup. A product of LSU, Ainsworth won twice at the 2000 Olympics and has demonstrated an ability to pitch at the highest level. He probably will compete for a major league job in 2003.

Boof Bonser

Position: P
Bats: R **Throws:** R
Ht: 6' 4" **Wt:** 230

Opening Day Age: 21
Born: 10/14/81 in St. Petersburg, FL

Recent Statistics

	W	L	ERA	G	GS	Sv	IP	H	R	BB	SO	HR
2001 A Hagerstown	16	4	2.49	27	27	0	134.0	91	40	61	178	7
2002 AA Shreveport	1	2	5.55	5	5	0	24.1	30	14	23	3
2002 A San Jose	8	6	2.88	23	23	0	128.1	89	44	70	139	9

Bonser burst on the scene in 2001 with a fabulous season in the Class-A South Atlantic League. The Giants tried to push him to Double-A last year, but that didn't work out as well as hoped. However, it was a different story in high Class-A, where he again struck out more than a batter per inning. Bonser was the Giants' first-round pick out of a Florida high school in 2000, and he's still learning how to pitch. He worked on his slider at San Jose. His fastball reaches the mid-90s, and he can show an excellent boring, sinking action. He boasts a gifted arm and is a good competitor. He will put both features on display in a return trip to Double-A in '03.

Jesse Foppert

Position: P
Bats: R **Throws:** R
Ht: 6' 6" **Wt:** 210

Opening Day Age: 22
Born: 7/10/80 in Reading, PA

Recent Statistics

	W	L	ERA	G	GS	Sv	IP	H	R	BB	SO	HR
2001 A Salem-Keiz	8	1	1.93	14	14	0	70.0	35	18	23	88	7
2002 AA Shreveport	3	3	2.79	11	11	0	61.1	44	22	21	74	3
2002 AAA Fresno	3	6	3.99	14	14	0	79.0	71	37	35	109	12

Foppert resides in nearby San Rafael, Calif. and attended college at the University of San Francisco. So he probably wasn't disappointed when the Giants selected him in the second round of the 2001 draft. And he certainly hasn't disappointed the Giants with his performance since signing. In only his second minor league season, Foppert reached Triple-A and in one good stretch probably could have pitched in the majors. He has size and strength and runs his fastball up to 97 MPH. He also has a hard slider and a splitter than can be a strikeout pitch. He displays a marvelous delivery and looks like he'll be able to make adjustments. Foppert clearly is an outstanding prospect and should be in Triple-A at a minimum this season.

Ryan Hannaman

Position: P
Bats: L **Throws:** L
Ht: 6' 3" **Wt:** 190

Opening Day Age: 21
Born: 8/28/81 in Mobile, AL

Recent Statistics

	W	L	ERA	G	GS	Sv	IP	H	R	BB	SO	HR
2001 R Giants	4	1	2.00	11	11	0	54.0	34	14	31	67	1
2001 A Salem-Keiz	1	1	2.08	3	3	0	13.0	8	5	8	19	1
2002 A Hagerstown	7	6	2.80	24	24	0	131.2	129	54	46	145	9
2002 A San Jose	0	0	3.00	1	1	0	6.0	3	2	3	7	1

The Giants can be proud of their scouting department when it comes to Hannaman. He had played a lot of first base in high school, but the Giants liked his left-handed arm strength and plucked him in the fourth round of the 2000 draft. He really came into his own in the Class-A South Atlantic League last year. He goes after hitters with a low three-quarters delivery, rushing his fastball in the 95-97 MPH range. Hannaman has a pretty good breaking ball, but needs to work on his other pitches besides the fastball. He's also fairly inexperienced on the mound, and could improve the various nuances of pitching, such as holding runners. His next logical step is high Class-A.

San Francisco

Todd Linden

Position: OF   **Opening Day Age:** 22
Bats: B **Throws:** R   **Born:** 6/30/80 in
Ht: 6' 2" **Wt:** 215   Edmonds, WA

Recent Statistics

	G	AB	R	H	D	T	HR	RBI	SB	BB	SO	Avg
2002 AA Shreveport	111	392	64	123	26	2	12	52	9	61	101	.314
2002 AAA Fresno	29	100	18	25	2	1	3	10	2	20	35	.250

Linden was a supplemental first-round draft pick in the 2001 June draft. He signed three months later and made his professional debut last season. Not many players start out at Double-A, but Linden thrived there. He was so impressive that he was bumped up to Triple-A, where he wasn't as imposing but certainly didn't embarrass himself. He's a switch-hitter who shows the ability to combine power with average. Although he struck out quite a bit last season, he compensated with plenty of walks. He is an average runner, but looks like he's better than adequate in the outfield. He still needs to conquer Triple-A, but Linden may not be far away.

Deivis Santos

Position: 1B   **Opening Day Age:** 23
Bats: L **Throws:** L   **Born:** 2/9/80 in Santo
Ht: 6' 1" **Wt:** 170   Domingo, DR

Recent Statistics

	G	AB	R	H	D	T	HR	RBI	SB	BB	SO	Avg
2001 A Hagerstown	131	520	64	151	27	3	12	80	16	25	91	.290
2002 AA Shreveport	109	407	54	127	33	5	3	56	4	18	42	.312
2002 AAA Fresno	23	88	8	25	3	1	3	14	4	2	14	.284

Although the Giants signed Santos out of the Dominican Republic in 1997, he didn't arrive for good in the States until 2001. But he's since roared up the chain in short order, finishing at Triple-A last season. He's a slashing sort of hitter who has demonstrated the ability to drive the ball from gap to gap. Santos has shown occasional signs of power. Lefthanded pitchers don't bother him, but he hasn't drawn a lot of walks overall. He moved to left field to make room for Lance Niekro at Double-A last year, but returned to first base at Fresno. Santos isn't a bad runner and possesses decent skills to play the outfield. He would add versatility to a 25-man roster.

Tony Torcato

Position: OF   **Opening Day Age:** 23
Bats: L **Throws:** R   **Born:** 10/25/79 in
Ht: 6' 1" **Wt:** 195   Woodland, CA

Recent Statistics

	G	AB	R	H	D	T	HR	RBI	SB	BB	SO	Avg
2002 AAA Fresno	130	490	64	142	23	3	13	64	4	29	65	.290
2002 NL San Fran	5	11	0	3	1	0	0	0	0	0	2	.273

The Giants' organization is heavy in pitching prospects, in part because they've used their top pick to select a hurler in seven of the last eight drafts. Torcato was the one exception, getting picked with the 19th overall choice in 1998. He now may be the best pure hitter in San Francisco's minor league system. He's had a nice line-drive swing in the past, and never has hit lower than .290 at any level. The Giants thought his power would come, and sure enough, he established a personal high with 13 home runs last season. Drafted as a third baseman, Torcato has converted to the outfield the past couple years, but still could use some polishing out there. He might be best suited for left.

Jerome Williams

Position: P   **Opening Day Age:** 21
Bats: R **Throws:** R   **Born:** 12/4/81 in
Ht: 6' 3" **Wt:** 190   Honolulu, HI

Recent Statistics

	W	L	ERA	G	GS	Sv	IP	H	R	BB	SO	HR
2001 AA Shreveport	9	7	3.95	23	23	0	130.0	116	69	34	84	14
2002 AAA Fresno	6	11	3.59	28	28	0	160.2	140	76	50	130	16

The Giants used a supplemental first-round pick to take Williams out of a Honolulu high school in 1999. He spent 2002 in Triple-A, and while his won-lost record was near .500, his ERA still ranked eighth in the Pacific Coast League. Williams has the stuff to dominate games and works with a 93-95 MPH fastball. He seems to have a good idea of what he's doing on the mound, and has shown a precocious ability to locate his pitches. After finishing well in the PCL, he was shut down with a tender shoulder in the Arizona Fall League. Williams is on the cusp of the majors.

Others to Watch

Righthander **David Cash** (23) saw time as both a starter and reliever at Double-A in 2002. His role may be undefined, but he's a sinker/slider pitcher who worked in the Arizona Fall League after last season. . . **Francisco Liriano** (19) came a long way in the Class-A South Atlantic League last season. Scouts salivate at his lefthanded stuff. He has a marvelous delivery and throws a 97-MPH fastball, as well as a slider and changeup. . . Lefthander **Noah Lowry** (22) was taken in the first round of the 2001 draft. He may have been abused a bit in college, and minor things prevented him from throwing a lot of innings last year. He's sneaky quick, with a 91-MPH fastball and excellent changeup. . . . **Lance Niekro** (24) has had problems staying healthy. He has hit for a nice average but doesn't walk much. He also possesses doubles power at this point. He played a lot of first base at Double-A last year, but the Giants haven't ruled out third base. . . Lefthander **Erick Threets** (21) reportedly reaches triple digits with his fastball. He's been bothered by injuries, and with his kind of potential, the Giants have been cautious. His arm seems to be fine, and when it is, batters have a hard time hitting the ball fair. . . Injuries limited **Carlos Valderrama** (25) to a DH role last season. He's a center fielder who also can play either corner. He's a plus runner with plus power potential. He's also been a .300 hitter, but stumbled a bit at Double-A last year.

2002 American League Leaders

Batters

Batting Average
minimum 502 PA

Manny Ramirez	.349
Mike Sweeney	.340
Bernie Williams	.333

Home Runs

Alex Rodriguez	57
Jim Thome	52
Rafael Palmeiro	43

Runs Batted In

Alex Rodriguez	142
Magglio Ordonez	135
Miguel Tejada	131

Games Played

4 players tied with	162

At-Bats

Alfonso Soriano	696
Miguel Tejada	662
Ichiro Suzuki	647

Runs Scored

Alfonso Soriano	128
Alex Rodriguez	125
Derek Jeter	124

Hits

Alfonso Soriano	209
Ichiro Suzuki	208
2 players tied with	204

Singles

Ichiro Suzuki	165
Derek Jeter	147
Bernie Williams	146

Doubles

Garret Anderson	56
Nomar Garciaparra	56
Alfonso Soriano	51

Triples

Johnny Damon	11
Randy Winn	9
2 players tied with	8

Stolen Bases

Alfonso Soriano	41
Carlos Beltran	35
Derek Jeter	32

Caught Stealing
minimum

Ichiro Suzuki	15
3 players tied with	13

Walks

Jim Thome	122
Jason Giambi	109
Rafael Palmeiro	104

Intentional Walks

Ichiro Suzuki	27
Carlos Delgado	18
Jim Thome	18

Hit by Pitch

David Eckstein	27
Melvin Mora	20
2 players tied with	15

Strikeouts

Mike Cameron	176
Alfonso Soriano	157
Troy Glaus	144

GDP

Jorge Posada	23
Magglio Ordonez	21
Miguel Tejada	21

Sacrifice Hits

David Eckstein	14
Jeff Cirillo	13
Michael Young	13

Sacrifice Flies

John Olerud	12
Nomar Garciaparra	11
Joe Randa	11

Plate Appearances

Alfonso Soriano	741
Derek Jeter	730
Ichiro Suzuki	728

Times on Base

Jason Giambi	300
Bernie Williams	290
Alex Rodriguez	284

Total Bases

Alex Rodriguez	389
Alfonso Soriano	381
Magglio Ordonez	352

Slugging Percentage
minimum 502 PA

Jim Thome	.677
Manny Ramirez	.647
Alex Rodriguez	.623

Slugging vs. LHP
minimum 125 PA

Magglio Ordonez	.624
Ellis Burks	.581
Alfonso Soriano	.571

Slugging vs. RHP
minimum 377 PA

Jim Thome	.766
Alex Rodriguez	.682
Carlos Delgado	.646

Cleanup Slugging
minimum 150 PA

Jim Thome	.707
Jason Giambi	.640
Magglio Ordonez	.628

On-Base Percentage
minimum 502 PA

Manny Ramirez	.450
Jim Thome	.445
Jason Giambi	.435

OBP vs. LHP
minimum 125 PA

Scott Spiezio	.448
Bernie Williams	.430
Jorge Posada	.420

OBP vs. RHP
minimum 377 PA

Jim Thome	.485
Jason Giambi	.448
Carlos Delgado	.444

Leadoff Hitters OBP
minimum 150 PA

Ichiro Suzuki	.383
Jeremy Giambi	.380
Shannon Stewart	.379

AB per HR
minimum 502 PA

Jim Thome	9.2
Alex Rodriguez	10.9
Rafael Palmeiro	12.7

Ground/Fly Ratio
minimum 502 PA

Ichiro Suzuki	2.48
Derek Jeter	2.23
Ben Grieve	2.08

% Extra Bases Taken
minimum 40 Opp to Advance

Carlos Beltran	76.4
Ray Durham	72.6
Alfonso Soriano	69.5

% Runs/Time on Base
minimum 502 PA

Alfonso Soriano	52.0
Darin Erstad	48.1
Johnny Damon	47.4

SB Success %
minimum 20 SB Attempts

Derek Jeter	91.4
Chris Singleton	90.9
Darin Erstad	88.5

Steals of Third

Alfonso Soriano	9
Ichiro Suzuki	9
Chuck Knoblauch	8

AVG Scoring Position
minimum 100 PA

Manny Ramirez	.435
Mike Sweeney	.402
Miguel Tejada	.375

AVG Late & Close
minimum 50 PA

Scott Spiezio	.420
Bernie Williams	.393
Gary Matthews Jr.	.383

AVG Bases Loaded
minimum 10 PA

Troy Glaus	.600
Jorge Posada	.579
2 players tied with	.571

GDP/GDP Opp
minimum 50 PA

Kenny Lofton	0.00
Mark McLemore	0.03
Johnny Damon	0.04

AVG vs. LHP
minimum 125 PA

Scott Spiezio	.368
Ichiro Suzuki	.356
Bernie Williams	.354

AVG vs. RHP
minimum 377 PA

Mike Sweeney	.334
Jacque Jones	.333
Jim Thome	.333

AVG at Home
minimum 251 PA

Jim Thome	.350
Manny Ramirez	.336
Torii Hunter	.334

AVG on the Road
minimum 251 PA

Manny Ramirez	.360
Bernie Williams	.354
Mike Sweeney	.349

Pitchers

AVG on 3-1 Count
minimum 10 PA

Toby Hall	**.750**
Jared Sandberg	**.750**
Jason Conti	.667

AVG with Two Strikes
minimum 150 PA

Orlando Palmeiro	**.292**
Ichiro Suzuki	.268
Miguel Tejada	.265

AVG on 0-2 Count
minimum 20 PA

Jose Offerman	**.400**
Scott Spiezio	.345
Derek Jeter	.333

AVG on Full Count
minimum 40 PA

Raul Ibanez	**.434**
Chris Singleton	.414
Jim Thome	.362

Pitches Seen

Jason Giambi	**2892**
Carlos Beltran	2854
Alex Rodriguez	2812

Pitches per PA
minimum 502 PA

Frank Thomas	**4.26**
Jason Giambi	4.20
Scott Hatteberg	4.15

% Pitches Taken
minimum 1500 Pitches Seen

John Olerud	**66.4**
Mark McLemore	64.9
Scott Hatteberg	64.5

% Swings that Missed
minimum 1500 Pitches Seen

David Eckstein	**7.5**
Omar Vizquel	8.3
Jerry Hairston Jr.	9.4

% Swings Put in Play
minimum 1500 Pitches Seen

John Olerud	**56.8**
Matt Lawton	54.2
David Eckstein	53.9

Bunts in Play

Neifi Perez	**38**
David Eckstein	35
Kenny Lofton	27

Earned Run Average
minimum 162 IP

Pedro Martinez	**2.26**
Derek Lowe	2.58
Barry Zito	2.75

Wins

Barry Zito	**23**
Derek Lowe	21
Pedro Martinez	20

Losses

Tanyon Sturtze	**18**
Steve W. Sparks	16
Jeff Suppan	16

Won-Lost Percentage
minimum 15 decisions

Pedro Martinez	**.833**
Barry Zito	.821
Jarrod Washburn	.750

Games

Billy Koch	**84**
J.C. Romero	81
Mike Stanton	79

Games Started

Barry Zito	**35**
5 players tied with	34

Complete Games

Paul Byrd	**7**
Mark Buehrle	5
Joe Kennedy	5

Shutouts

Jeff Weaver	**3**
7 players tied with	2

Games Finished

Billy Koch	**79**
Kelvim Escobar	68
Eddie Guardado	62

Innings Pitched

Roy Halladay	**239.1**
Mark Buehrle	239.0
Tim Hudson	238.1

Hits Allowed

Tanyon Sturtze	**271**
Steve W. Sparks	238
Tim Hudson	237

Batters Faced

Tanyon Sturtze	**1008**
Roy Halladay	993
Mark Buehrle	984

Runs Allowed

Tanyon Sturtze	**141**
Steve W. Sparks	134
Jeff Suppan	134

Earned Runs Allowed

Tanyon Sturtze	**129**
Jeff Suppan	123
Steve W. Sparks	116

Home Runs Allowed

Ramon Ortiz	**40**
Paul Byrd	36
Tanyon Sturtze	33

Walks Allowed

Tanyon Sturtze	**89**
C.C. Sabathia	88
Jon Garland	83

Hit Batsmen

Chan Ho Park	**17**
Joe Kennedy	16
Pedro Martinez	15

Strikeouts

Pedro Martinez	**239**
Roger Clemens	192
2 players tied with	182

Wild Pitches

Johan Santana	**15**
Roger Clemens	14
2 players tied with	11

Balks

Steve Kent	**3**
Ramon Ortiz	**3**
C.C. Sabathia	**3**

Run Support per 9 IP
minimum 162 IP

David Wells	**7.46**
Derek Lowe	6.84
Barry Zito	6.79

Baserunners per 9 IP
minimum 162 IP

Pedro Martinez	**9.0**
Derek Lowe	9.3
Tim Wakefield	10.0

Opposition AVG
minimum 162 IP

Pedro Martinez	**.198**
Tim Wakefield	.204
Derek Lowe	.211

Opposition SLG
minimum 162 IP

Derek Lowe	**.302**
Pedro Martinez	.309
Tim Wakefield	.333

Opposition OBP
minimum 162 IP

Pedro Martinez	**.254**
Derek Lowe	.266
Tim Wakefield	.276

Home Runs per 9 IP
minimum 162 IP

Roy Halladay	**0.38**
Derek Lowe	0.49
Pedro Martinez	0.59

Strikeouts per 9 IP
minimum 162 IP

Pedro Martinez	**10.79**
Roger Clemens	9.60
Mike Mussina	7.60

Walks per 9 IP
minimum 162 IP

Rick Reed	**1.2**
Paul Byrd	1.5
Eric Milton	1.6

K/BB Ratio
minimum 162 IP

Pedro Martinez	**5.98**
Rick Reed	4.65
Eric Milton	4.03

Steals Allowed

Frank Castillo	**24**
Roger Clemens	23
2 players tied with	21

Caught Stealing Off

Tanyon Sturtze	**15**
Kevin Appier	13
Danys Baez	11

SB % Allowed
minimum 162 IP

Kenny Rogers	**0.0**
Jeff Weaver	20.0
Mark Buehrle	28.6

GDPs Induced

Tim Hudson	**35**
Jon Garland	32
Derek Lowe	28

GDPs per 9 IP
minimum 162 IP

Jon Garland	**1.5**
Tim Hudson	1.3
Kenny Rogers	1.2

GDP/GDP Opp
minimum 30 BFP

Scot Shields	**0.31**
Doug Davis	0.27
Ben Weber	0.25

Ground/Fly Ratio Off
minimum 162 IP

Derek Lowe	**3.5**
Roy Halladay	2.7
Tim Hudson	2.0

Fielding

AVG Allowed Sc Pos
minimum 125 BFP

Barry Zito	.185
Joel Pineiro	.193
2 players tied with	.196

Pitches Thrown

Barry Zito	3690
Freddy Garcia	3607
Tanyon Sturtze	3576

Pitches per Batter
minimum 162 IP

Paul Byrd	3.45
Mark Mulder	3.49
Tim Hudson	3.49

Pickoff Throws

Roger Clemens	157
Paul Wilson	141
Barry Zito	138

ERA at Home
minimum 81 IP

Derek Lowe	2.10
Joel Pineiro	2.55
Roy Halladay	2.56

ERA on the Road
minimum 81 IP

Pedro Martinez	1.89
Jeff Weaver	2.48
Jarrod Washburn	2.65

AVG vs. LHB
minimum 125 BFP

Arthur Rhodes	.158
Kenny Rogers	.193
Tim Wakefield	.195

AVG vs. RHB
minimum 225 BFP

Pedro Martinez	.191
Barry Zito	.203
Jamie Moyer	.206

Relief ERA
minimum 50 relief IP

Buddy Groom	1.60
J.C. Romero	1.89
Troy Percival	1.92

Relief Wins

Billy Koch	11
Arthur Rhodes	10
2 players tied with	9

Relief Losses

Esteban Yan	8
3 players tied with	7

Saves

Eddie Guardado	45
Billy Koch	44
2 players tied with	40

Blown Saves

Kelvim Escobar	8
Kazuhiro Sasaki	8
Esteban Yan	8

Save Opportunities

Eddie Guardado	51
Billy Koch	50
2 players tied with	46

Save Percentage
minimum 20 SvOp

Troy Percival	90.9
Bob Wickman	90.9
Eddie Guardado	88.2

Holds

J.C. Romero	33
Arthur Rhodes	27
Ricardo Rincon	27

Relief Innings

Billy Koch	93.2
Ramiro Mendoza	91.2
Steve Karsay	88.1

Relief AVG Allowed
minimum 50 relief IP

Cliff Politte	.186
Arthur Rhodes	.187
Troy Percival	.188

Relief Runners/9 IP
minimum 50 relief IP

Arthur Rhodes	7.5
Buddy Groom	8.4
LaTroy Hawkins	8.7

Relief Strikeouts/9 IP
minimum 50 relief IP

David Riske	11.4
Troy Percival	10.9
Kazuhiro Sasaki	10.8

% Inh Runners Scored
minimum 30 Inh Runners

Rich Rodriguez	13.2
Brendan Donnelly	15.6
Jim Mecir	17.9

1st Batter AVG
minimum 40 relief first BFP

Brendan Donnelly	.095
Buddy Groom	.127
Cliff Politte	.128

Errors by Pitcher

Joe Kennedy	10
Mark Redman	6
Ramon Ortiz	4

Errors by Catcher

Jorge Posada	12
Einar Diaz	8
2 players tied with	7

Errors by First Base

Carlos Delgado	12
Jeff Conine	10
Jim Thome	10

Errors by Second Base

Alfonso Soriano	23
Ray Durham	17
Carlos Febles	15

Errors by Third Base

Shea Hillenbrand	23
Robin Ventura	23
2 players tied with	20

Errors by Shortstop

Nomar Garciaparra	25
Neifi Perez	19
Miguel Tejada	19

Errors by Left Field

Bobby Higginson	7
3 players tied with	5

Errors by Center Field

Terrence Long	8
Carlos Beltran	7
3 players tied with	5

Errors by Right Field

Robert Fick	12
Aaron Guiel	6
Matt Lawton	6

% CS by Catchers
minimum 70 SB Attempts

Bengie Molina	42.7
Geronimo Gil	34.4
Einar Diaz	27.4

Batters

Batting Average
minimum 502 PA

Barry Bonds	**.370**
Larry Walker	.338
Vladimir Guerrero	.336

Home Runs

Sammy Sosa	**49**
Barry Bonds	46
2 players tied with	42

Runs Batted In

Lance Berkman	**128**
Albert Pujols	127
Pat Burrell	116

Games Played

Aaron Boone	**162**
Derrek Lee	**162**
Vladimir Guerrero	161

At-Bats

Jimmy Rollins	**637**
Rafael Furcal	636
Jeff Kent	623

Runs Scored

Sammy Sosa	**122**
Albert Pujols	118
Barry Bonds	117

Hits

Vladimir Guerrero	**206**
Jeff Kent	195
Jose Vidro	190

Singles

Luis Castillo	**160**
Juan Pierre	144
Fernando Vina	133

Doubles

Bobby Abreu	**50**
Mike Lowell	44
2 players tied with	43

Triples

Jimmy Rollins	**10**
4 players tied with	8

Stolen Bases

Luis Castillo	**48**
Juan Pierre	47
Dave Roberts	45

Caught Stealing

Vladimir Guerrero	**20**
Luis Castillo	15
Rafael Furcal	15

Walks

Barry Bonds	**198**
Brian Giles	135
Adam Dunn	128

Intentional Walks

Barry Bonds	**68**
Vladimir Guerrero	32
Brian Giles	24

Hit by Pitch

Craig A. Wilson	**21**
Fernando Vina	18
Craig Biggio	17

Strikeouts

Jose Hernandez	**188**
Adam Dunn	170
Derrek Lee	164

GDP

Brad Ausmus	**30**
Todd Zeile	27
2 players tied with	26

Sacrifice Hits

Jack Wilson	**17**
Glendon Rusch	14
5 players tied with	13

Sacrifice Flies

Mike Lowell	**11**
Aramis Ramirez	**11**
Todd Helton	10

Plate Appearances

Vladimir Guerrero	**709**
Jimmy Rollins	705
Rafael Furcal	693

Times on Base

Barry Bonds	**356**
Vladimir Guerrero	296
Brian Giles	290

Total Bases

Vladimir Guerrero	**364**
Jeff Kent	352
Lance Berkman	334

Slugging Percentage
minimum 502 PA

Barry Bonds	**.799**
Brian Giles	.622
Larry Walker	.602

Slugging vs. LHP
minimum 125 PA

Barry Bonds	**.976**
Sammy Sosa	.733
Jeff Bagwell	.685

Slugging vs. RHP
minimum 377 PA

Barry Bonds	**.719**
Brian Giles	.681
Lance Berkman	.639

Cleanup Slugging
minimum 150 PA

Barry Bonds	**.730**
Vladimir Guerrero	.612
Lance Berkman	.596

On-Base Percentage
minimum 502 PA

Barry Bonds	**.582**
Brian Giles	.450
Chipper Jones	.435

OBP vs. LHP
minimum 125 PA

Barry Bonds	**.556**
Sammy Sosa	.526
Edgardo Alfonzo	.477

OBP vs. RHP
minimum 377 PA

Barry Bonds	**.592**
Brian Giles	.485
Jim Edmonds	.443

Leadoff Hitters OBP
minimum 150 PA

Mark Kotsay	**.396**
Mark Bellhorn	.389
Brad Wilkerson	.373

AB per HR
minimum 502 PA

Barry Bonds	**8.8**
Sammy Sosa	11.3
Brian Giles	13.1

Ground/Fly Ratio
minimum 502 PA

Luis Castillo	**3.38**
Juan Pierre	3.15
Rey Ordonez	2.23

% Extra Bases Taken
minimum 40 Opp to Advance

Juan Pierre	**72.5**
Barry Larkin	67.5
Rafael Furcal	67.4

% Runs/Time on Base
minimum 502 PA

Sammy Sosa	**45.9**
Craig Biggio	45.1
Albert Pujols	44.4

SB Success %
minimum 20 SB Attempts

Doug Glanville	**90.5**
Roger Cedeno	86.2
Corey Patterson	85.7

Steals of Third

Andy Fox	**8**
Aaron Boone	7
Jimmy Rollins	7

AVG Scoring Position
minimum 100 PA

Barry Bonds	**.376**
Jose Vidro	.372
Edgar Renteria	.372

AVG Late & Close
minimum 50 PA

Larry Walker	**.468**
Luis Castillo	.379
Jose Vizcaino	.377

AVG Bases Loaded
minimum 10 PA

Timo Perez	**.625**
Albert Pujols	.538
7 players tied with	.500

GDP/GDP Opp
minimum 50 PA

Cliff Floyd	**0.00**
Rob Mackowiak	**0.00**
Erubiel Durazo	0.02

AVG vs. LHP
minimum 125 PA

Barry Bonds	**.384**
Greg Colbrunn	.368
Sammy Sosa	.366

AVG vs. RHP
minimum 377 PA

Barry Bonds	**.363**
Vladimir Guerrero	.347
Todd Helton	.331

AVG at Home
minimum 251 PA

Todd Helton	**.378**
Larry Walker	.362
Barry Bonds	.351

AVG on the Road
minimum 251 PA

Barry Bonds	**.386**
Albert Pujols	.340
Gary Sheffield	.336

Pitchers

AVG on 3-1 Count
minimum 10 PA

Peter Bergeron	1.000
Erubiel Durazo	.750
Dave Roberts	.750

AVG with Two Strikes
minimum 150 PA

Jose Vidro	.287
Barry Bonds	.278
Vladimir Guerrero	.276

AVG on 0-2 Count
minimum 20 PA

Gary Sheffield	.333
Jose Vizcaino	.333
Mark Loretta	.321

AVG on Full Count
minimum 40 PA

Jose Vizcaino	.387
Rafael Furcal	.380
Alex Sanchez	.367

Pitches Seen

Bobby Abreu	2923
Derrek Lee	2896
Adam Dunn	2893

Pitches per PA
minimum 502 PA

Todd Zeile	4.31
Adam Dunn	4.28
Bobby Abreu	4.27

% Pitches Taken
minimum 1500 Pitches Seen

Todd Zeile	65.2
Brian Giles	65.1
Barry Bonds	65.0

% Swings that Missed
minimum 1500 Pitches Seen

Paul Lo Duca	6.8
Fernando Vina	7.3
Jason Kendall	8.1

% Swings Put in Play
minimum 1500 Pitches Seen

Eric Young	57.7
Jason Kendall	57.6
Fernando Vina	57.3

Bunts in Play

Juan Pierre	62
Rafael Furcal	53
Dave Roberts	46

Earned Run Average
minimum 162 IP

Randy Johnson	2.32
Greg Maddux	2.62
Tom Glavine	2.96

Wins

Randy Johnson	24
Curt Schilling	23
Roy Oswalt	19

Losses

Livan Hernandez	16
Glendon Rusch	16
Ben Sheets	16

Won-Lost Percentage
minimum 15 decisions

Randy Johnson	.828
Wade Miller	.789
Curt Schilling	.767

Games

Paul Quantrill	86
Octavio Dotel	83
Tim Worrell	80

Games Started

Tom Glavine	36
Randy Johnson	35
Curt Schilling	35

Complete Games

Randy Johnson	8
A.J. Burnett	7
2 players tied with	5

Shutouts

A.J. Burnett	5
Randy Johnson	4
Livan Hernandez	3

Games Finished

Jose Jimenez	69
Eric Gagne	68
John Smoltz	68

Innings Pitched

Randy Johnson	260.0
Curt Schilling	259.1
Roy Oswalt	233.0

Hits Allowed

Javier Vazquez	243
Ben Sheets	237
Livan Hernandez	233

Batters Faced

Randy Johnson	1035
Curt Schilling	1017
Javier Vazquez	971

Runs Allowed

Mike Hampton	135
Ryan Dempster	127
Glendon Rusch	118

Earned Runs Allowed

Ryan Dempster	125
Mike Hampton	122
Glendon Rusch	110

Home Runs Allowed

Pedro Astacio	32
Rick Helling	31
Brett Tomko	31

Walks Allowed

Kazuhisa Ishii	106
Hideo Nomo	101
Kerry Wood	97

Hit Batsmen

Pedro Astacio	16
Kerry Wood	16
2 players tied with	15

Strikeouts

Randy Johnson	334
Curt Schilling	316
Kerry Wood	217

Wild Pitches

Tony Armas Jr.	14
A.J. Burnett	14
Damian Moss	13

Balks

Brian Anderson	5
Odalis Perez	3
14 players tied with	2

Run Support per 9 IP
minimum 162 IP

Ryan Jensen	6.55
Jason Jennings	6.51
Wade Miller	6.12

Baserunners per 9 IP
minimum 162 IP

Curt Schilling	8.8
Odalis Perez	9.1
Randy Johnson	9.7

Opposition AVG
minimum 162 IP

Randy Johnson	.208
A.J. Burnett	.209
Matt Clement	.215

Opposition SLG
minimum 162 IP

A.J. Burnett	.309
Jason Schmidt	.329
Kevin Millwood	.337

Opposition OBP
minimum 162 IP

Curt Schilling	.251
Odalis Perez	.262
Randy Johnson	.273

Home Runs per 9 IP
minimum 162 IP

A.J. Burnett	0.53
Miguel Batista	0.58
Russ Ortiz	0.63

Strikeouts per 9 IP
minimum 162 IP

Randy Johnson	11.56
Curt Schilling	10.97
Jason Schmidt	9.52

Walks per 9 IP
minimum 162 IP

Curt Schilling	1.1
Odalis Perez	1.5
Javier Vazquez	1.9

K/BB Ratio
minimum 162 IP

Curt Schilling	9.58
Randy Johnson	4.70
Odalis Perez	4.08

Steals Allowed

Al Leiter	29
Hideo Nomo	28
2 players tied with	24

Caught Stealing Off

Tom Glavine	16
Randy Johnson	15
Ryan Dempster	13

SB % Allowed
minimum 162 IP

Glendon Rusch	14.3
Kirk Rueter	28.6
Rick Helling	33.3

GDPs Induced

Livan Hernandez	29
Brian Lawrence	29
Mike Hampton	28

GDPs per 9 IP
minimum 162 IP

Mike Hampton	1.4
Brian Lawrence	1.2
Jason Jennings	1.2

GDP/GDP Opp
minimum 30 BFP

Mark Guthrie	0.25
Aaron Cook	0.22
Scott Sauerbeck	0.22

Ground/Fly Ratio Off
minimum 162 IP

Brian Lawrence	2.5
Greg Maddux	2.2
Vicente Padilla	2.0

Fielding

AVG Allowed Sc Pos
minimum 125 BFP

Randy Johnson	**.146**
Kerry Wood	.182
Tom Glavine	.193

Pitches Thrown

Randy Johnson	**3996**
Curt Schilling	3721
Glendon Rusch	3622

Pitches per Batter
minimum 162 IP

Greg Maddux	**3.23**
Brian Lawrence	3.45
Odalis Perez	3.47

Pickoff Throws

Steve Trachsel	**193**
Livan Hernandez	188
2 players tied with	157

ERA at Home
minimum 81 IP

Randy Johnson	**2.12**
Vicente Padilla	2.27
Jason Schmidt	2.37

ERA on the Road
minimum 81 IP

Matt Clement	**2.55**
Elmer Dessens	2.56
Randy Johnson	2.63

AVG vs. LHB
minimum 125 BFP

Armando Benitez	**.160**
Damian Moss	.165
Woody Williams	.182

AVG vs. RHB
minimum 225 BFP

A.J. Burnett	**.177**
Jason Schmidt	.180
Oliver Perez	.191

Relief ERA
minimum 50 relief IP

Chris Hammond	**0.95**
Joey Eischen	1.34
Darren Holmes	1.81

Relief Wins

4 players tied with	**8**

Relief Losses

Jose Jimenez	**10**
Scott Strickland	9
Dave Veres	8

Saves

John Smoltz	**55**
Eric Gagne	52
Mike Williams	46

Blown Saves

Antonio Alfonseca	**9**
Jose Mesa	**9**
3 players tied with	8

Save Opportunities

John Smoltz	**59**
Eric Gagne	56
Jose Mesa	54

Save Percentage
minimum 20 SvOp

John Smoltz	**93.2**
Eric Gagne	92.9
Trevor Hoffman	92.7

Holds

Paul Quantrill	**33**
Octavio Dotel	31
2 players tied with	30

Relief Innings

Vladimir Nunez	**97.2**
Octavio Dotel	97.1
Joe Borowski	95.2

Relief AVG Allowed
minimum 50 relief IP

Octavio Dotel	**.173**
Scott Williamson	.181
Eric Gagne	.189

Relief Runners/9 IP
minimum 50 relief IP

Eric Gagne	**8.0**
Octavio Dotel	8.2
Mike Timlin	8.5

Relief Strikeouts/9 IP
minimum 50 relief IP

Eric Gagne	**12.5**
Octavio Dotel	10.9
Billy Wagner	10.6

%Inh Runners Scored
minimum 30 Inh Runners

Justin Speier	**5.7**
Jesse Orosco	12.8
Scott Stewart	14.7

1st Batter AVG
minimum 40 relief first BFP

Dan Plesac	**.132**
Brian Boehringer	.143
Kerry Ligtenberg	.143

Errors by Pitcher

T.J. Tucker	**5**
4 players tied with	4

Errors by Catcher

Mike Piazza	**12**
Todd Hundley	11
Javy Lopez	10

Errors by First Base

Mo Vaughn	**18**
Andres Galarraga	13
Kevin Young	13

Errors by Second Base

Marlon Anderson	**20**
Jeff Kent	16
Junior Spivey	15

Errors by Third Base

Todd Zeile	**21**
Adrian Beltre	20
Aaron Boone	20

Errors by Shortstop

Orlando Cabrera	**29**
Rafael Furcal	27
Juan Uribe	27

Errors by Left Field

Barry Bonds	**8**
Roger Cedeno	**8**
Adam Dunn	**8**

Errors by Center Field

Tsuyoshi Shinjo	**6**
Preston Wilson	**6**
3 players tied with	5

Errors by Right Field

Vladimir Guerrero	**10**
Jeromy Burnitz	9
Sammy Sosa	6

% CS by Catchers
minimum 70 SB Attempts

Mike Lieberthal	**33.8**
Brad Ausmus	31.6
Javy Lopez	29.9

About Sporting News & STATS, Inc.

About Sporting News
Sporting News, a division of Vulcan Sports Media, Inc., is a leading U.S. sports media company reaching 18 million people weekly. Sporting News' content is available through many sources, including a weekly magazine, books, a radio network and owned and operated stations, website, wireless devices and iTV. Sporting News' book-publishing division publishes approximately 25 titles annually, including 13 statistical reference titles. Sporting News is the nation's oldest sports publication, having debuted in 1886. Visit SN online at www.sportingnews.com.

About STATS, Inc.
STATS, Inc. is owned by News Corporation (NYSE: NWS). With more than 20 years of experience in sophisticated sports data collection, processing and distribution—STATS is the world's leading sports information and statistical analysis company. STATS provides exclusive information and data from its proprietary databases to fans, professional teams, print and broadcast media, software developers and interactive service providers around the globe while serving as one of the industry's leading fantasy sports game management firms. STATS, Inc.'s business partners include FOX Sports, ESPN, NBC Sports, Univision, OpenTV, AOL Sports, WGN Sports, YES Network, EA Sports, Topps and the Associated Press. (http://biz.stats.com)

Index